The Consumer Credit and Sales Legal Practice Series

FAIR DEBT COLLECTION

VOLUME TWO: APPENDICES

Seventh Edition

See *page ix* for information about the companion website.

Robert J. Hobbs

Contributing Authors: Carolyn L. Carter, O. Randolph Bragg, Joanne S. Faulkner, Richard Rubin

National Consumer Law Center®

7 Winthrop Square, 4th Floor   Boston, MA 02110

www.consumerlaw.org

About NCLC®

The National Consumer Law Center®, a nonprofit corporation founded in 1969, assists consumers, advocates, and public policy makers nationwide who use the powerful and complex tools of consumer law to ensure justice and fair treatment for all, particularly those whose poverty renders them powerless to demand accountability from the economic marketplace. For more information, go to www.nclc.org.

Ordering NCLC Publications

Order securely online at www.nclc.org, or contact Publications Department, National Consumer Law Center, 7 Winthrop Square, 4th Floor, Boston, MA 02110, (617) 542-9595, FAX: (617) 542-8028, e-mail: publications@nclc.org.

Training and Conferences

NCLC participates in numerous national, regional, and local consumer law trainings. Its annual fall conference is a forum for consumer rights attorneys from legal services programs, private practice, government, and nonprofit organizations to share insights into common problems and explore novel and tested approaches that promote consumer justice in the marketplace. Contact NCLC for more information or see our web site.

Case Consulting

Case analysis, consulting and co-counseling for lawyers representing vulnerable consumers are among NCLC's important activities. Administration on Aging funds allow us to provide free consulting to legal services advocates representing elderly consumers on many types of cases. Massachusetts Legal Assistance Corporation funds permit case assistance to advocates representing low-income Massachusetts consumers. Other funding may allow NCLC to provide very brief consultations to other advocates without charge. More comprehensive case analysis and research is available for a reasonable fee. See our web site for more information at www.nclc.org.

Charitable Donations and Cy Pres Awards

NCLC's work depends in part on the support of private donors. Tax-deductible donations should be made payable to National Consumer Law Center, Inc. For more information, contact Gerald Tuckman of NCLC's Development Office at (617) 542-8010 or gtuckman@nclc.org. NCLC has also received generous court-approved *cy pres* awards arising from consumer class actions to advance the interests of class members. For more information, contact Robert Hobbs (rhobbs@nclc.org) or Rich Dubois (rdubois@nclc.org) at (617) 542-8010.

Comments and Corrections

Write to the above address to the attention of the Editorial Department or e-mail consumerlaw@nclc.org.

About This Volume

This is the Seventh Edition of *Fair Debt Collection*. Discard all prior editions and supplements. This book includes a companion website. Continuing developments can be found in periodic supplements to and revised editions of this volume, on the companion website, and in NCLC REPORTS.

Cite This Volume As

National Consumer Law Center, Fair Debt Collection (7th ed. 2011).

Attention

> *This publication is designed to provide authoritative information concerning the subject matter covered. Always use the most current edition and supplement, and use other sources for more recent developments or for special rules for individual jurisdictions. This publication cannot substitute for the independent judgment and skills of an attorney or other professional. Non-attorneys are cautioned against using these materials to conduct a lawsuit without advice from an attorney and are cautioned against engaging in the unauthorized practice of law.*

About the Authors

Robert J. Hobbs is NCLC's deputy director. He has written and consulted since 1972 on debt collection and other consumer credit issues. Prior to that, he was a staff attorney with New Orleans Legal Assistance. He is the author of the 1982, 1987, 1991, 1996, 2000, 2004, 2008, and 2011 editions of this treatise, co-author of *The Practice of Consumer Law* and editor of *Consumer Law Pleadings* (1998-2010), and contributing author to *Collection Actions*. He advises attorneys on their clients' fair debt collection claims, was counsel to amicus curiae in *Heintz v. Jenkins*, 514 U.S. 291 (1995), has served on the FRB's Consumer Advisory Council, is a founder and former board member of the National Association of Consumer Advocates, and coordinates NCLC's annual Fair Debt Collection Practices Conference and the annual Consumer Rights Litigation Conference. He also worked on the enactment of the Fair Debt Collection Practices Act and the FTC Holder and Credit Practices rules.

Carolyn L. Carter is NCLC's deputy director for advocacy and was formerly co-director of Legal Services, Inc., in Gettysburg, Pennsylvania, and director of the Law Reform Office of the Cleveland Legal Aid Society. She is the editor of *Pennsylvania Consumer Law*, editor of the first edition of *Ohio Consumer Law*, co-author of *Collection Actions*, *Consumer Warranty Law*, *Unfair and Deceptive Acts and Practices*, *Repossessions* and *Automobile Fraud*, and a contributing author to other NCLC publications. She is the 1993 recipient of the Vern Countryman Consumer Law Award.

O. Randolph Bragg is an attorney in private practice in Chicago, a former litigation coordinator with the UAW Legal Services Plan in Newark, Delaware, and a former NCLC fellow. He previously was an attorney with Legal Services Corporation funded programs in Pennsylvania and West Virginia. He has litigated FDCPA claims on behalf of consumers in numerous U.S. district and appellate courts and frequently provides training on the FDCPA. He is the 2010 recipient of the Vern Countryman Consumer Law Award.

Joanne S. Faulkner has a private consumer law practice in New Haven, Connecticut, with a major focus on representing consumers under the FDCPA and other consumer protection laws. Previously, she was an attorney at New Haven Legal Assistance for many years. She has served as chair of the Consumer Law Section of the Connecticut Bar Association and as a member of the FRB's Consumer Advisory Council. She has contributed to a number of NCLC publications, including *Fair Credit Reporting* and *Credit Discrimination*. She is the 2002 recipient of the Vern Countryman Award.

Richard Rubin is a private attorney in Santa Fe, New Mexico whose practice is limited to representing consumers in federal appeals and consulting for other consumer rights advocates. He is chair emeritus of the National Association of Consumer Advocates, has taught consumer law at the University of New Mexico School of Law, and presents continuing legal education and attorney training programs throughout the country. He is the 2000 recipient of the Vern Countryman Award and in 2006 was named to Lawdragon 500 Leading Plaintiffs' Lawyers in America.

Acknowledgments

We want to thank everyone who contributed to the prior six editions of this title and its 23 prior supplements—too many people to list here. Special thanks to those who worked on this edition: Mary Kingsley for her extensive contributions to chapters 9 through 11; Nate Player and Kurt Terwilliger for legal research; and the following attorneys who contributed to individual chapters: Jonathan Sheldon, Darlene Wong, Mark Budnitz, Elizabeth De Armond, Chi Chi Wu, Deanne Loonin, Alys Cohen, Arielle Cohen, Margot Saunders, Lauren Saunders, Andrew Pizor, Charles Delbaum, Geoff Walsh, and Tara Twomey. We are also very grateful to Denise Lisio and Eric Secoy for editorial supervision; Kim Calvi for editorial assistance; Shirlron Williams for assistance checking citations; Shannon Halbrook and Microsearch for designing and implementing the companion website; Mary McLean for indexing; and Xylutions for typesetting services.

What Your Library Should Contain

The Consumer Credit and Sales Legal Practice Series contains 18 titles, updated annually, arranged into four libraries, and designed to be an attorney's primary practice guide and legal resource in all 50 states. Titles are available individually, as part of a library, or as part of the complete 18-volume series. Each title includes free access to a companion website containing the treatise's appendices, sample pleadings, primary sources, and other practice aids, allowing pinpoint searches and the pasting of text into a word processor. Access remains free as long as purchasers keep their titles current.

Debtor Rights Library

2009 Ninth Edition (Two Volumes), 2010 Supplement, and Companion Website, Including NCLC's Bankruptcy Forms Software

Consumer Bankruptcy Law and Practice: the definitive personal bankruptcy manual, from the initial interview to final discharge, including consumer rights when a company files for bankruptcy. The ninth edition contains the latest case law interpreting the 2005 Act, and includes such practice aids as the latest Bankruptcy Code, Rules, and fee schedules, a date calculator, over 150 pleadings and forms, software to compute the initial forms, means test data, and a client questionnaire and handout.

2011 Seventh Edition (Two Volumes) and Companion Website

Fair Debt Collection: the basic reference covering the Fair Debt Collection Practices Act and common law, state statutory and other federal debt collection protections. Thousands of unique case summaries cover reported and unreported FDCPA cases by category. The companion website contains sample pleadings and discovery, the FTC Commentary, an index to and the full text of *all* FTC staff opinion letters, and other practice aids.

2010 Third Edition, 2011 Supplement, and Companion Website

Foreclosures: examines RESPA and other federal and state rights to challenge servicer abuses, as well as details on workout options, loan modification, and mediation programs implemented by federal and state governments. The volume also covers standing and substantive and procedural defenses to foreclosure and tactics after the foreclosure sale. Special chapters cover tax liens, land installment sales contracts, manufactured home foreclosures, and other topics.

2010 Seventh Edition and Companion Website

Repossessions: a unique guide to motor vehicle and mobile home repossessions, threatened seizures of household goods, statutory liens, and automobile lease and rent-to-own default remedies. The volume examines UCC Article 9 and hundreds of other federal and state statutes regulating repossessions.

2010 Fourth Edition and Companion Website

Student Loan Law: collection harassment; closed school, disability, and other discharges; tax intercepts, wage garnishment, and offset of social security benefits; and repayment plans, consolidation loans, deferments, and non-payment of loan based on school fraud.

2008 Fourth Edition, 2010 Supplement, and Companion Website

Access to Utility Service: consumer rights as to regulated and unregulated utilities, including telecommunications, terminations, billing errors, low-income payment plans, utility allowances in subsidized housing, LIHEAP, and weatherization.

National Consumer Law Center ■ (617) 542-9595 ■ FAX (617) 542-8028 ■ publications@nclc.org
Order securely online at www.consumerlaw.org

Credit and Banking Library

2010 Seventh Edition (Two Volumes) and Companion Website

Truth in Lending: detailed analysis of *all* aspects of TILA, the Consumer Leasing Act, the Fair Credit Billing Act, the Home Ownership and Equity Protection Act (HOEPA), and the Credit CARD Act, including the major 2010 amendments. Appendices and the website contain the Acts, Reg. Z, Reg. M, and their official staff commentaries, numerous sample pleadings, rescission notices, two programs to compute APRs, TIL legislative history, and a unique compilation of *all Federal Register* notices and supplementary information on Regulation Z since 1969.

2010 Seventh Edition and Companion Website

Fair Credit Reporting: the key resource for handling any type of credit reporting issue, from cleaning up blemished credit records to suing reporting agencies and creditors for inaccurate reports. Covers the new FACTA changes, identity theft, creditor liability for failing to properly reinvestigate disputed information, credit scoring, privacy issues, the Credit Repair Organizations Act, state credit reporting and repair statutes, and common law claims.

2009 Fourth Edition, 2011 Supplement, and Companion Website

Consumer Banking and Payments Law: covers checks, telechecks, electronic fund transfers, electronic check conversions, money orders, and credit, debit, payroll, unemployment, and stored value cards. The title also covers banker's right of setoff, electronic transfers of federal and state benefit payments, and a special chapter on electronic records and signatures.

2009 Fourth Edition, 2011 Supplement, and Companion Website

The Cost of Credit: Regulation, Preemption, and Industry Abuses: a one-of-a-kind resource detailing state and federal regulation of consumer credit in all 50 states. Examines numerous types of predatory lending, federal preemption of state law, credit math calculations, excessive credit charges, credit insurance, and numerous other topics.

2009 Fifth Edition, 2011 Supplement, and Companion Website

Credit Discrimination: analysis of the Equal Credit Opportunity Act, Fair Housing Act, Civil Rights Acts, and state credit discrimination statutes, including reprints of all relevant federal interpretations, government enforcement actions, and numerous sample pleadings.

Consumer Litigation Library

2011 Second Edition and Companion Website

Collection Actions: a complete guide to consumer defenses and counterclaims to collection lawsuits filed in court or in arbitration, with extensive discussion of setting aside default judgments and limitations on a collector's post-judgment remedies. Special chapters include the rights of active duty military, and unique issues involving medical debt, government collections, collector's attorney fees, and bad check laws.

2007 Fifth Edition, 2010 Supplement, and Companion Website

Consumer Arbitration Agreements: successful approaches to challenge arbitration agreements' enforceability and waivers of class arbitration, the interrelation of the Federal Arbitration Act and state law, class actions and punitive damages in arbitration, implications of NAF's withdrawal from consumer arbitrations, the right to discovery, and other topics.

2010 Seventh Edition, 2011 Supplement, and Companion Website

Consumer Class Actions: makes class litigation manageable even for small offices, including numerous sample pleadings, class certification memoranda, discovery, class notices, settlement materials, and much more. Includes a detailed analysis of the Class Action Fairness Act, class arbitration, state class action rules and case law, and other topics.

Website and 2010 Index Guide: ALL pleadings from ALL NCLC treatises, including Consumer Law Pleadings Numbers One through Sixteen

Consumer Law Pleadings: over *2000* notable pleadings from all types of consumer cases, including predatory lending, foreclosures, automobile fraud, lemon laws, debt collection, fair credit reporting, home improvement fraud, student loans, and lender liability. Finding aids pinpoint desired pleading in seconds, ready to paste into a word processor.

Deception and Warranties Library

2008 Seventh Edition, 2010 Supplement, and Companion Website

Unfair and Deceptive Acts and Practices: the only practice manual covering all aspects of a deceptive practices case in every state. Special sections on automobile sales, the federal racketeering (RICO) statute, unfair insurance practices, the FTC Holder Rule, telemarketing fraud, attorney fees, and many other topics.

2007 Third Edition, 2010 Supplement, and Companion Website

Automobile Fraud: examination of title law, "yo-yo" sales, odometer tampering, lemon laundering, sale of salvage and wrecked cars, undisclosed prior use, and prior damage to new cars. The website contains numerous sample pleadings and title search techniques.

2010 Fourth Edition, 2011 Supplement, and Companion Website

Consumer Warranty Law: comprehensive treatment of new and used car lemon laws, the Magnuson-Moss Warranty Act, UCC Articles 2 and 2A, mobile home, new home, and assistive device warranty laws, FTC Used Car Rule, tort theories, car repair and home improvement statutes, service contract and lease laws, with numerous sample pleadings.

NCLC's Companion Websites

Every NCLC manual includes a companion website, allowing rapid access to appendices, pleadings, primary sources, and other practice aids. Search for documents by category or with a table of contents or various keyword search options. All documents can be downloaded, printed, and copy-pasted into a word processing document. Pleadings are also available in Word format. Web access is free with each title ordered and remains free as long as a title is kept current.

Website continually subject to update

Consumer Law on the Web: combines *everything* from the 18 other NCLC companion websites. Using *Consumer Law on the Web,* instead of multiple individual companion websites, is often the fastest and most convenient way to pinpoint and retrieve key documents among the thousands available on our individual companion websites.

Other NCLC Publications for Lawyers

issued 24 times a year

NCLC REPORTS, a four-page newsletter, keeps you up to date 24 times a year with the latest consumer law developments. It is also an essential practice tool, with novel ideas, innovative tactics, and key insights from NCLC's experienced consumer law attorneys. Learn the practice implications of new statutes, regulations, cases and trends.

Second Edition and Companion Website

Foreclosure Prevention Counseling: Preserving the American Dream: explains how to obtain a workout, with advice specifically tailored for Fannie Mae, Freddie Mac, subprime, FHA-insured, VA, and Rural Housing Service loans. The book also details new loan modification initiatives from federal and state governments and industry.

First Edition and Companion Website

Bankruptcy Basics: A Step-by-Step Guide for Pro Bono Attorneys, General Practitioners, and Legal Services Offices: provides everything attorneys new to bankruptcy need to file their first case, with a companion website that contains software, sample pleadings, and other practice aids that greatly simplify handling a bankruptcy case.

Second Edition with CD-Rom

STOP Predatory Lending: A Guide for Legal Advocates: provides a roadmap and practical legal strategy for litigating predatory lending abuses, from small loans to mortgage loans. How to analyze the documents, spot issues, raise legal claims, select defendants, and even craft a community response.

National Consumer Law Center ▪ (617) 542-9595 ▪ FAX (617) 542-8028 ▪ publications@nclc.org

Order securely online at www.consumerlaw.org

First Edition **Instant Evidence: A Quick Guide to Federal Evidence and Objections:** facilitates objection by rule number and includes common objections and motions at every stage of a case—all in under 20 pages! Spiral-bound to lay flat, all pages are laminated, allowing new notations for each trial with a dry-erase pen.

Second Edition with CD-Rom **The Practice of Consumer Law: Seeking Economic Justice:** contains an essential overview to consumer law and explains how to get started in a private or legal services consumer practice. Packed with invaluable sample pleadings and practice pointers for even experienced consumer attorneys.

National Consumer Law Center Guide Series are books designed for consumers, counselors, and attorneys new to consumer law:

2010 Edition **NCLC Guide to Surviving Debt:** a great overview of consumer law. Everything a paralegal, new attorney, or client needs to know about home foreclosures and mortgage modifications, debt collectors, managing credit card debt, whether to refinance, credit card problems, evictions, repossessions, credit reporting, utility terminations, student loans, budgeting, and bankruptcy.

First Edition **NCLC Guide to the Rights of Utility Consumers:** explains consumer rights concerning electric, gas, and other utility services: shut off protections, rights to restore terminated service, bill payment options, weatherization tips, rights to government assistance, and much more.

First Edition **NCLC Guide to Consumer Rights for Domestic Violence Survivors:** provides practical advice to help survivors get back on their feet financially and safely establish their economic independence.

First Edition **NCLC Guide to Mobile Homes:** what consumers and their advocates need to know about mobile home dealer sales practices and an in-depth look at mobile home quality and defects, with 35 photographs and construction details.

First Edition **Return to Sender: Getting a Refund or Replacement for Your Lemon Car:** find how lemon laws work, what consumers and their lawyers should know to evaluate each other, investigative techniques and discovery tips, how to handle both informal dispute resolution and trials, and more.

Visit **www.nclc.org** to order securely online or for more information on all NCLC publications and companion websites, including the full tables of contents, indices, and **web-based searches of the publications' full text**.

National Consumer Law Center ■ **(617) 542-9595** ■ **FAX (617) 542-8028** ■ **publications@nclc.org**
Order securely online at www.consumerlaw.org

About the Companion Website, Other Search Options

The Companion Website

Purchase of any title in NCLC's consumer law practice series includes free access to its companion website. Access remains free with continued subscription to that title. Frequently updated, NCLC companion websites offer the treatises' appendices plus hundreds of additional documents in PDF and Microsoft Word formats—pleadings, forms, statutes, regulations, agency interpretations, legislative and regulatory history, and much more—all easily located with flexible, powerful search tools. Documents can be electronically searched, printed, downloaded, and copy-pasted into a word processor.

Accessing the Companion Website

One-time registration is required to access NCLC companion websites. Once registered, users logging in are granted access to all websites they are authorized to use, with only one username and password required.

Subscribers do *not* need to register more than once.[1] Subscribers purchasing additional NCLC titles are automatically given access to the new websites under their existing username and password. Registering a second time with the same registration number overrides a prior username and password.

To register, go to www.nclc.org/webaccess, and click "New users click here to register." Enter the Companion Website Registration Number found on the packing statement or invoice accompanying this publication.[2] Then enter the requested information and click Enter. An email address may be used for the username or a different username may be chosen.

Once registered, go to **www.nclc.org/webaccess**, enter your username and password, and select the desired companion website from the list of authorized sites.

Libraries and others subscribing to the entire 18-volume set can arrange "IP access" so that a username and password are *not* required. Email publications@nclc.org with a list or range of static IP addresses for which access should be permitted *without* the need to enter a username and password.

We encourage users who find mistakes to notify us using the "Report Errors" button, on the left toolbar. Also on the left toolbar, users can click "My Account" to change personal information.

Use of the companion websites with Internet Explorer requires Adobe Reader 7.0 or later or Adobe Acrobat 7.0 or later. Users of other browsers, or those experiencing problems with the websites, should download the latest version of the free Adobe Reader from Adobe's website at www.adobe.com. A link to Adobe's site is provided on the NCLC companion website login page.

Locating Documents on the Companion Website

The companion website provides three options to locate documents.

1. The search page (the home page) offers keyword searches to find documents—either full-text searches of all documents on the website or of only the documents' titles.

- Narrow the search to documents of a certain type (such as federal statutes or pleadings) by making a selection from the "Document Type" menu, and then perform a full text or document title search.
- If unsure of a keyword's spelling, type the first few letters and click "See choices."
- To locate a specific appendix section, select the appendix section number (e.g., A.2.3) or a partial identifier (e.g., A) in the search page's "Appendix" drop-down fields.
- Click Search Hints for a quick reference to special search operators, wildcards, shortcuts, and complex searches. Read this closely, as syntax and search operators may be slightly different from those of other websites.

---

1 If all your subscriptions to NCLC treatises are allowed to lapse, your account may be deleted; if this happens, you must re-register if you subsequently purchase a book.

2 If you cannot locate this number, contact NCLC Publications at (617) 542-9595 or publications@nclc.org.

2. The contents page (click on the "Contents" tab at the top of the page) is a traditional "branching" table of contents. Click a branch to expand it into a list of sub-branches or documents. Each document appears once on this contents tree.

3. The pleading finder page (click on the "Pleading Finder" tab at the top of the page, *if available*) allows pleadings to be located using one or more menus, such as "Type of Pleading" or "Subject." **Select more than one item from a menu, or deselect items, by holding the Ctrl key while clicking.** For example, make one selection from "Type of Pleading-General," one from "Subject," and three from "Legal Claims" to locate all pleadings of that type and subject that contain one or more of the three legal claims selected. If this search produces insufficient results, simply broaden the search by deselecting "Subject" and/or "Legal Claims" to find pleadings of that type in any subject area or based upon any legal claim. This page also includes optional fields to specify terms to be found in the documents' text or titles, to further narrow search results.

Additional software, related websites, and other information can be located by clicking on links found at the left hand toolbar or on the "Search" page. These links bring you to credit math software, search tips, other websites, tables of contents and indices of all NCLC publications, and other practice aids. Some companion websites have "Software" or "Links" tabs at the top of the page, where this material may also be found.

Finding Word Versions of Website Documents

All documents on the website are in PDF format, and can be copied and pasted into a word processor. Pleadings and certain other documents also are available in Word format, facilitating the opening of entire documents in a word processor. After opening the selected PDF file, click at the top of the page on "Word Version, if available." If a Word version is listed as available, click "DOC Download Document" to save the Word file to your computer.

Documents Found on the Website

The companion website to *Fair Debt Collection* contains the text of the Fair Debt Collection Practices Act, the FTC Official Staff Commentary, *all FTC staff opinion letters* with a subject-matter index, FTC Advisory Opinions, and the new statute regarding federal standards for private tax collectors. The website also includes FDCPA case summaries and the full text of an FDCPA Supreme Court case.

Of special note are numerous sample pleadings, including case preparation checklists, demand letters and sample complaints, sample discovery requests, deposition transcripts of

an FDCPA class representative and collection agency employees, *voir dire* questions, jury instructions and other jury trial documents. The website also includes other pleadings relating to expert testimony, class certification, summary judgment, appeals, and attorney fees and costs.

Locating Topics in This Treatise

Go to www.nclc.org/keyword to electronically search the full text of every chapter and appendix of this title. While the chapters' complete text is not available online, this web-based search engine specifies each page of this title where a word or phrase is found. Select this title, enter a search term or combination of search terms—such as a case name, a regulation cite, or other keywords—and the page numbers containing those terms are listed. Search results are shown with the surrounding text ("hits in context"), facilitating selection of the most relevant pages.

Locating Topics in Other NCLC Manuals or NCLC REPORTS

The full text of all NCLC treatises and supplements, *NCLC REPORTS*, and other publications can be electronically searched to locate relevant topics as described above. Go to www.nclc.org/keyword, and enter a search term or combination of search terms in a similar fashion to performing a keyword search on one title.

Current tables of contents, indices, and other information for all NCLC titles can be found at www.nclc.org/shop. Click *Publications for Lawyers* and scroll down to the book you want. The PDF documents found there can be quickly searched for a word or phrase.

The Quick Reference at the back of Volume 1 lets you pinpoint the correct treatise and treatise sections or appendices that discuss over 1000 different subject areas. These subject areas are listed in alphabetical order and can also be electronically searched at www.nclc.org/qr.

Finding Pleadings

Pleadings relating to this title are found in PDF and Word format on the companion website; search options are discussed above at "Locating Documents on the Website." Over 2000 pleadings are also available at NCLC's *Consumer Law Pleadings* website using the same search techniques discussed above. Pleadings can also be located using *Consumer Law Pleadings*' index guide, which organizes pleadings by type, subject area, legal claim, title, and other categories identical to those on the website.

Summary Contents

Volume 1

Volume 2

Contents

Volume 2

| Appendix K | Fair Debt Collection Practices Act Case Summaries |

Text of the Fair Debt Collection Practices Act

A.1 Cross-Reference Table of Public Law 95-109 Section Numbers with 15 U.S.C. Section Numbers

The Fair Debt Collection Practices Act, as currently codified at 15 U.S.C. §§ 1692–1692p, is reprinted in this appendix. Because many cases, articles, and the Federal Trade Commission refer to the Public Law 95-109 section numbers, the following table is provided. The Public Law 95-109 section numbers are also in brackets following each heading of the Act reprinted in this appendix.

Public Law Section	U.S.C. Section	Manual Section	Codified Heading at 15 U.S.C.
802	1692	Ch. 3	Congressional findings and declaration of purpose
803	1692a	Ch. 4	Definitions
804	1692b	§ 5.3.6	Acquisition of location information
805	1692c	§ 5.3	Communication in connection with debt collection
806	1692d	§ 5.4	Harassment or abuse
807	1692e	§ 5.5	False or misleading representations
808	1692f	§ 5.6	Unfair practices
809	1692g	§ 5.7	Validation of debts
810	1692h	§ 5.8	Multiple debts
811	1692i	§ 5.9	Legal actions by debt collectors
812	1692j	§ 4.2.6	Furnishing certain deceptive forms
813	1692k	Chs. 6, 7	Civil liability
814	1692l	§ 6.13	Administrative enforcement
815	1692m	§ 6.13	Reports to Congress by the Bureau
816	1692n	§ 6.12	Relation to State laws
817	1692o	§ 6.12.2	Exemption for State regulation
818	1692p		Exception for certain bad check enforcement programs operated by private entities.

A.2 Fair Debt Collection Practices Act[1]

15 U.S.C. §§ 1692–1692p; Pub. L. No. 95-109, 91 Stat. 874 (Sept. 20, 1977); Pub. L. No. 95-473, 92 Stat. 1466 (Oct. 17, 1978); Pub. L. No. 95-630, 92 Stat. 3680 (Nov. 10, 1978); Pub. L. No. 98-443, 98 Stat. 1708 (Oct. 4, 1984); Pub. L. No. 99-361, 100 Stat. 768 (July 9, 1986); Pub. L. No. 101-73, 103 Stat. 440 (Aug. 9, 1989); Pub. L. No. 102-242, 105 Stat. 2301 (Dec. 19, 1991); Pub. L. No. 102-550, 106 Stat. 4082 (Oct. 28, 1992); Pub. L. No. 104-88, 109 Stat. 949 (Dec. 29, 1995); Pub. L. No. 104-208, 110 Stat. 3009–425 (Sept. 30, 1996); Pub. L. No. 109-351, tit. VIII, §§ 801(a)(2), 802(a)–(c), 120 Stat. 2006 (Oct. 13, 2006); Pub. L. No. 111-203, tit. X, § 1089(1)–(4), 124 Stat. 2092 (July 21, 2010).

---

1 A note in 15 U.S.C. § 1601 cites section 801 of Pub. L. 95-109, 91 Stat. 874 (Sept. 20, 1977) which provided: "This title [enacting subchapter V of this chapter, section 1692 *et seq.* of this title] may be cited as the 'Fair Debt Collection Practices Act.' " A note in 15 U.S.C. § 1692 cites section 818 of Pub. L. 95-109, which provided: "This title [this subchapter] takes effect upon the expiration of six months after the date of its enactment [Sept. 20, 1977], but section 809 [section 1692g of this title] shall apply only with respect to debts for which the initial attempt to collect occurs after such effective date."

15 U.S.C. § 1692. Congressional findings and declaration of purpose [FDCPA § 802]

(a) There is abundant evidence of the use of abusive, deceptive, and unfair debt collection practices by many debt collectors. Abusive debt collection practices contribute to the number of personal bankruptcies, to marital instability, to the loss of jobs, and to invasions of individual privacy.

(b) Existing laws and procedures for redressing these injuries are inadequate to protect consumers.

(c) Means other than misrepresentation or other abusive debt collection practices are available for the effective collection of debts.

(d) Abusive debt collection practices are carried on to a substantial extent in interstate commerce and through means and instrumentalities of such commerce. Even where abusive debt collection practices are purely intrastate in character, they nevertheless directly affect interstate commerce.

(e) It is the purpose of this subchapter to eliminate abusive debt collection practices by debt collectors, to insure that those debt collectors who refrain from using abusive debt collection practices are not competitively disadvantaged, and to promote consistent State action to protect consumers against debt collection abuses.

15 U.S.C. § 1692a. Definitions [FDCPA § 803]

As used in this subchapter—

(1) The term "Bureau" means the Bureau of Consumer Financial Protection.

(2) The term "communication" means the conveying of information regarding a debt directly or indirectly to any person through any medium.

(3) The term "consumer" means any natural person obligated or allegedly obligated to pay any debt.

(4) The term "creditor" means any person who offers or extends credit creating a debt or to whom a debt is owed, but such term does not include any person to the extent that he receives an assignment or transfer of a debt in default solely for the purpose of facilitating collection of such debt for another.

(5) The term "debt" means any obligation or alleged obligation of a consumer to pay money arising out of a transaction in which the money, property, insurance, or services which are the subject of the transaction are primarily for personal, family, or household purposes, whether or not such obligation has been reduced to judgment.

(6) The term "debt collector" means any person who uses any instrumentality of interstate commerce or the mails in any business the principal purpose of which is the collection of any debts, or who regularly collects or attempts to collect, directly or indirectly, debts owed or due or asserted to be owed or due another. Notwithstanding the exclusion provided by clause (F) of the last sentence of this paragraph, the term includes any creditor who, in the process of collecting his own debts, uses any name other than his own which would indicate that a third person is collecting or attempting to collect such debts. For the purpose of section 1692f(6) of this title, such term also includes any person who uses any instrumentality of interstate commerce or the mails in any business the principal purpose of which is the enforcement of security interests. The term does not include—

(A) any officer or employee of a creditor while, in the name of the creditor, collecting debts for such creditor;

(B) any person while acting as a debt collector for another person, both of whom are related by common ownership or affiliated by corporate control, if the person acting as a debt collector does so only for persons to whom it is so related or affiliated and if the principal business of such person is not the collection of debts;

(C) any officer or employee of the United States or any State to the extent that collecting or attempting to collect any debt is in the performance of his official duties;

(D) any person while serving or attempting to serve legal process on any other person in connection with the judicial enforcement of any debt;

(E) any nonprofit organization which, at the request of consumers, performs bona fide consumer credit counseling and assists consumers in the liquidation of their debts by receiving payments from such consumers and distributing such amounts to creditors; and

(F) any person collecting or attempting to collect any debt owed or due or asserted to be owed or due another to the extent such activity (i) is incidental to a bona fide fiduciary obligation or a bona fide escrow arrangement; (ii) concerns a debt which was originated by such person; (iii) concerns a debt which was not in default at the time it was obtained by such person; or (iv) concerns a debt obtained by such person as a secured party in a commercial credit transaction involving the creditor.

(G) Redesignated (F).[2]

(7) The term "location information" means a consumer's place of abode and his telephone number at such place, or his place of employment.

(8) The term "State" means any State, territory, or possession of the United States, the District of Columbia, the Commonwealth of Puerto Rico, or any political subdivision of any of the foregoing.

[Pub. L. No. 111-203, tit. X, § 1089(2), 124 Stat. 2092 (July 21, 2010)]

15 U.S.C. § 1692b. Acquisition of location information [FDCPA § 804]

Any debt collector communicating with any person other than the consumer for the purpose of acquiring location information about the consumer shall—

(1) identify himself, state that he is confirming or correcting location information concerning the consumer, and, only if expressly requested, identify his employer;

(2) not state that such consumer owes any debt;

(3) not communicate with any such person more than once unless requested to do so by such person or unless the debt collector reasonably believes that the earlier response of such

---

2 15 U.S.C. § 1692a(6)(E), (F), (G) *amended by* Pub. L. No. 99-361, 100 Stat. 768 (July 9, 1986). *See* §§ 3.3.2, 5.5.14, *supra.*

person is erroneous or incomplete and that such person now has correct or complete location information;

(4) not communicate by post card;

(5) not use any language or symbol on any envelope or in the contents of any communication effected by the mails or telegram that indicates that the debt collector is in the debt collection business or that the communication relates to the collection of a debt; and

(6) after the debt collector knows the consumer is represented by an attorney with regard to the subject debt and has knowledge of, or can readily ascertain, such attorney's name and address, not communicate with any person other than that attorney, unless the attorney fails to respond within a reasonable period of time to communication from the debt collector.

15 U.S.C. § 1692c. Communication in connection with debt collection [FDCPA § 805]

(a) Communication with the consumer generally

Without the prior consent of the consumer given directly to the debt collector or the express permission of a court of competent jurisdiction, a debt collector may not communicate with a consumer in connection with the collection of any debt—

(1) at any unusual time or place or a time or place known or which should be known to be inconvenient to the consumer. In the absence of knowledge of circumstances to the contrary, a debt collector shall assume that the convenient time for communicating with a consumer is after 8 o'clock antemeridian and before 9 o'clock postmeridian, local time at the consumer's location;

(2) if the debt collector knows the consumer is represented by an attorney with respect to such debt and has knowledge of, or can readily ascertain, such attorney's name and address, unless the attorney fails to respond within a reasonable period of time to a communication from the debt collector or unless the attorney consents to direct communication with the consumer; or

(3) at the consumer's place of employment if the debt collector knows or has reason to know that the consumer's employer prohibits the consumer from receiving such communication.

(b) Communication with third parties

Except as provided in section 1692b of this title, without the prior consent of the consumer given directly to the debt collector, or the express permission of a court of competent jurisdiction, or as reasonably necessary to effectuate a postjudgment judicial remedy, a debt collector may not communicate, in connection with the collection of any debt, with any person other than the consumer, his attorney, a consumer reporting agency if otherwise permitted by law, the creditor, the attorney of the creditor, or the attorney of the debt collector.

(c) Ceasing communication

If a consumer notifies a debt collector in writing that the consumer refuses to pay a debt or that the consumer wishes the debt collector to cease further communication with the consumer, the debt collector shall not communicate further with the consumer with respect to such debt, except—

(1) to advise the consumer that the debt collector's further efforts are being terminated;

(2) to notify the consumer that the debt collector or creditor may invoke specified remedies which are ordinarily invoked by such debt collector or creditor; or

(3) where applicable, to notify the consumer that the debt collector or creditor intends to invoke a specified remedy.

If such notice from the consumer is made by mail, notification shall be complete upon receipt.

(d) "Consumer" defined

For the purpose of this section, the term "consumer" includes the consumer's spouse, parent (if the consumer is a minor), guardian, executor, or administrator.

15 U.S.C. § 1692d. Harassment or abuse [FDCPA § 806]

A debt collector may not engage in any conduct the natural consequence of which is to harass, oppress, or abuse any person in connection with the collection of a debt. Without limiting the general application of the foregoing, the following conduct is a violation of this section:

(1) The use or threat of use of violence or other criminal means to harm the physical person, reputation, or property of any person.

(2) The use of obscene or profane language or language the natural consequence of which is to abuse the hearer or reader.

(3) The publication of a list of consumers who allegedly refuse to pay debts, except to a consumer reporting agency or to persons meeting the requirements of section 1681a(f) or 1681b(3) of this title.

(4) The advertisement for sale of any debt to coerce payment of the debt.

(5) Causing a telephone to ring or engaging any person in telephone conversation repeatedly or continuously with intent to annoy, abuse, or harass any person at the called number.

(6) Except as provided in section 1692b of this title, the placement of telephone calls without meaningful disclosure of the caller's identity.

15 U.S.C. § 1692e. False or misleading representations [FDCPA § 807]

A debt collector may not use any false, deceptive, or misleading representation or means in connection with the collection of any debt. Without limiting the general application of the foregoing, the following conduct is a violation of this section:

(1) The false representation or implication that the debt collector is vouched for, bonded by, or affiliated with the United States or any State, including the use of any badge, uniform, or facsimile thereof.

(2) The false representation of—

    (A) the character, amount, or legal status of any debt; or

    (B) any services rendered or compensation which may be lawfully received by any debt collector for the collection of a debt.

(3) The false representation or implication that any individual is an attorney or that any communication is from an attorney.

(4) The representation or implication that nonpayment of any debt will result in the arrest or imprisonment of any person or the seizure, garnishment, attachment, or sale of any property or wages of any person unless such action is lawful and the debt collector or creditor intends to take such action.

(5) The threat to take any action that cannot legally be taken or that is not intended to be taken.

(6) The false representation or implication that a sale, referral, or other transfer of any interest in a debt shall cause the consumer to—

    (A) lose any claim or defense to payment of the debt; or

    (B) become subject to any practice prohibited by this subchapter.

(7) The false representation or implication that the consumer committed any crime or other conduct in order to disgrace the consumer.

(8) Communicating or threatening to communicate to any person credit information which is known or which should be known to be false, including the failure to communicate that a disputed debt is disputed.

(9) The use or distribution of any written communication which simulates or is falsely represented to be a document authorized, issued, or approved by any court, official, or agency of the United States or any State, or which creates a false impression as to its source, authorization, or approval.

(10) The use of any false representation or deceptive means to collect or attempt to collect any debt or to obtain information concerning a consumer.

(11) The failure to disclose in the initial written communication with the consumer and, in addition, if the initial communication with the consumer is oral, in that initial oral communication, that the debt collector is attempting to collect a debt and that any information obtained will be used for that purpose, and the failure to disclose in subsequent communications that the communication is from a debt collector, except that this paragraph shall not apply to a formal pleading made in connection with a legal action.[3]

(12) The false representation or implication that accounts have been turned over to innocent purchasers for value.

(13) The false representation or implication that documents are legal process.

(14) The use of any business, company, or organization name other than the true name of the debt collector's business, company, or organization.

(15) The false representation or implication that documents are not legal process forms or do not require action by the consumer.

(16) The false representation or implication that a debt collector operates or is employed by a consumer reporting agency as defined by section 1681a(f) of this title.

15 U.S.C. § 1692f. Unfair practices [FDCPA § 808]

A debt collector may not use unfair or unconscionable means to collect or attempt to collect any debt. Without limiting the general application of the foregoing, the following conduct is a violation of this section:

(1) The collection of any amount (including any interest, fee, charge, or expense incidental to the principal obligation) unless such amount is expressly authorized by the agreement creating the debt or permitted by law.

(2) The acceptance by a debt collector from any person of a check or other payment instrument postdated by more than five days unless such person is notified in writing of the debt collector's intent to deposit such check or instrument not more than ten nor less than three business days prior to such deposit.

(3) The solicitation by a debt collector of any postdated check or other postdated payment instrument for the purpose of threatening or instituting criminal prosecution.

(4) Depositing or threatening to deposit any postdated check or other postdated payment instrument prior to the date on such check or instrument.

(5) Causing charges to be made to any person for communications by concealment of the true purpose of the communication. Such charges include, but are not limited to, collect telephone calls and telegram fees.

(6) Taking or threatening to take any nonjudicial action to effect dispossession or disablement of property if—

    (A) there is no present right to possession of the property claimed as collateral through an enforceable security interest;

    (B) there is no present intention to take possession of the property; or

    (C) the property is exempt by law from such dispossession or disablement.

(7) Communicating with a consumer regarding a debt by post card.

(8) Using any language or symbol, other than the debt collector's address, on any envelope when communicating with a consumer by use of the mails or by telegram, except that a debt collector may use his business name if such name does not indicate that he is in the debt collection business.

15 U.S.C. § 1692g. Validation of debts [FDCPA § 809]

(a) Notice of debt; contents

Within five days after the initial communication with a consumer in connection with the collection of any debt, a debt collector shall, unless the following information is contained in the initial communication or the consumer has paid the debt, send the consumer a written notice containing—

(1) the amount of the debt;

(2) the name of the creditor to whom the debt is owed;

(3) a statement that unless the consumer, within thirty days after receipt of the notice, disputes the validity of the debt, or any portion thereof, the debt will be assumed to be valid by the debt collector;

(4) a statement that if the consumer notifies the debt collector in writing within the thirty-day period that the debt, or any portion thereof, is disputed, the debt collector will obtain verification of the debt or a copy of a judgment against the consumer and a copy of such verification or judgment will be mailed to the consumer by the debt collector; and

---

3   15 U.S.C. § 1692e(11) *amended by* Pub. L. No. 104-208 § 2305, 110 Stat. 3009 (Sept. 30, 1996). *See* §§ 3.3.2, 5.5.14, *supra*.

(5) a statement that, upon the consumer's written request within the thirty-day period, the debt collector will provide the consumer with the name and address of the original creditor, if different from the current creditor.

(b) Disputed debts

If the consumer notifies the debt collector in writing within the thirty-day period described in subsection (a) of this section that the debt, or any portion thereof, is disputed, or that the consumer requests the name and address of the original creditor, the debt collector shall cease collection of the debt, or any disputed portion thereof, until the debt collector obtains verification of the debt or a copy of a judgment, or the name and address of the original creditor, and a copy of such verification or judgment, or name and address of the original creditor, is mailed to the consumer by the debt collector. Collection activities and communications that do not otherwise violate this subchapter may continue during the 30-day period referred to in subsection (a) of this section unless the consumer has notified the debt collector in writing that the debt, or any portion of the debt, is disputed or that the consumer requests the name and address of the original creditor. Any collection activities and communication during the 30-day period may not overshadow or be inconsistent with the disclosure of the consumer's right to dispute the debt or request the name and address of the original creditor.

(c) Admission of liability

The failure of a consumer to dispute the validity of a debt under this section may not be construed by any court as an admission of liability by the consumer.

(d) Legal pleadings

A communication in the form of a formal pleading in a civil action shall not be treated as an initial communication for purposes of subsection (a) of this section.

(e) Notice provisions

The sending or delivery of any form or notice which does not relate to the collection of a debt and is expressly required by the Internal Revenue Code of 1986, title V of Gramm-Leach-Bliley Act [15 U.S.C. § 6801 et seq.], or any provision of Federal or State law relating to notice of data security breach or privacy, or any regulation prescribed under any such provision of law, shall not be treated as an initial communication in connection with debt collection for purposes of this section.

[Pub. L. No. 109-351, tit. VIII, § 802(a)–(c), 120 Stat. 2006 (Oct. 13, 2006)]

15 U.S.C. § 1692h. Multiple debts [FDCPA § 810]

If any consumer owes multiple debts and makes any single payment to any debt collector with respect to such debts, such debt collector may not apply such payment to any debt which is disputed by the consumer and, where applicable, shall apply such payment in accordance with the consumer's directions.

15 U.S.C. § 1692i. Legal actions by debt collectors [FDCPA § 811]

(a) Venue

Any debt collector who brings any legal action on a debt against any consumer shall—

(1) in the case of an action to enforce an interest in real property securing the consumer's obligation, bring such action only in a judicial district or similar legal entity in which such real property is located; or

(2) in the case of an action not described in paragraph (1), bring such action only in the judicial district or similar legal entity—

(A) in which such consumer signed the contract sued upon; or

(B) in which such consumer resides at the commencement of the action.

(b) Authorization of actions

Nothing in this subchapter shall be construed to authorize the bringing of legal actions by debt collectors.

15 U.S.C. § 1692j. Furnishing certain deceptive forms [FDCPA § 812]

(a) It is unlawful to design, compile, and furnish any form knowing that such form would be used to create the false belief in a consumer that a person other than the creditor of such consumer is participating in the collection of or in an attempt to collect a debt such consumer allegedly owes such creditor, when in fact such person is not so participating.

(b) Any person who violates this section shall be liable to the same extent and in the same manner as a debt collector is liable under section 1692k of this title for failure to comply with a provision of this subchapter.

15 U.S.C. § 1692k. Civil liability [FDCPA § 813]

(a) Amount of damages

Except as otherwise provided by this section, any debt collector who fails to comply with any provision of this subchapter with respect to any person is liable to such person in an amount equal to the sum of—

(1) any actual damage sustained by such person as a result of such failure;

(2)

(A) in the case of any action by an individual, such additional damages as the court may allow, but not exceeding $1,000; or

(B) in the case of a class action, (i) such amount for each named plaintiff as could be recovered under subparagraph (A), and (ii) such amount as the court may allow for all other class members, without regard to a minimum individual recovery, not to exceed the lesser of $500,000 or 1 per centum of the net worth of the debt collector; and

(3) in the case of any successful action to enforce the foregoing liability, the costs of the action, together with a reasonable attorney's fee as determined by the court. On a finding by the court that an action under this section was brought in bad faith and for the purpose of harassment, the court may award to the defendant attorney's fees reasonable in relation to the work expended and costs.

(b) Factors considered by court

In determining the amount of liability in any action under subsection (a) of this section, the court shall consider, among other relevant factors—

(1) in any individual action under subsection (a)(2)(A), the frequency and persistence of noncompliance by the debt collector, the nature of such noncompliance, and the extent to which such noncompliance was intentional; or

(2) in any class action under subsection (a)(2)(B) of this section of this section, the frequency and persistence of noncompliance by the debt collector, the nature of such noncompliance, the resources of the debt collector, the number of persons adversely affected, and the extent to which the debt collector's noncompliance was intentional.

(c) Intent

A debt collector may not be held liable in any action brought under this subchapter if the debt collector shows by a preponderance of evidence that the violation was not intentional and resulted from a bona fide error notwithstanding the maintenance of procedures reasonably adapted to avoid any such error.

(d) Jurisdiction

An action to enforce any liability created by this subchapter may be brought in any appropriate United States district court without regard to the amount in controversy, or in any other court of competent jurisdiction, within one year from the date on which the violation occurs.

(e) Advisory opinions of Bureau

No provision of this section imposing any liability shall apply to any act done or omitted in good faith in conformity with any advisory opinion of the Bureau, notwithstanding that after such act or omission has occurred, such opinion is amended, rescinded, or determined by judicial or other authority to be invalid for any reason.

[Pub. L. No. 111-203, tit. X, § 1089(1), 124 Stat. 2092 (July 21, 2010)]

15 U.S.C. § 1692*l*. Administrative enforcement
[FDCPA § 814]

(a) Federal Trade Commission

The Federal Trade Commission shall be authorized to enforce compliance with this title, except to the extent that enforcement of the requirements imposed under this title is specifically committed to another Government agency under any of paragraphs (1) through (5) of subsection (b), subject to subtitle B of the Consumer Financial Protection Act of 2010. For purpose of the exercise by the Federal Trade Commission of its functions and powers under the Federal Trade Commission Act (15 U.S.C. 41 et seq.), a violation of this title shall be deemed an unfair or deceptive act or practice in violation of that Act. All of the functions and powers of the Federal Trade Commission under the Federal Trade Commission Act are available to the Federal Trade Commission to enforce compliance by any person with this title, irrespective of whether that person is engaged in commerce or meets any other jurisdictional tests under the Federal Trade Commission Act, including the power to enforce the provisions of this title, in the same manner as if the violation had been a violation of a Federal Trade Commission trade regulation rule.

(b) Applicable provisions of law[4]

Subject to subtitle B of the Consumer Financial Protection Act of 2010, compliance with any requirements imposed under this subchapter shall be enforced under—

(1) section 8 of the Federal Deposit Insurance Act [12 U.S.C. § 1818], by the appropriate Federal banking agency, as defined in section 3(q) of the Federal Deposit Insurance Act (12 U.S.C. 1813(q)), with respect to—

(A) national banks, Federal savings associations, and Federal branches and Federal agencies of foreign banks;

(B) member banks of the Federal Reserve System (other than national banks), branches and agencies of foreign banks (other than Federal branches, Federal agencies, and insured State branches of foreign banks), commercial lending companies owned or controlled by foreign banks, and organizations operating under section 25 or 25A of the Federal Reserve Act; and

(C) banks and State savings associations insured by the Federal Deposit Insurance Corporation (other than members of the Federal Reserve System), and insured State branches of foreign banks;

(2) the Federal Credit Union Act [12 U.S.C. §§ 1751 et seq.], by the National Credit Union Administration with respect to any Federal credit union;

(3) subtitle IV of Title 49, by the Secretary of Transportation with respect to all carriers subject to the jurisdiction of the Surface Transportation Board;

(4) the Federal Aviation Act of 1958 [part A of subtitle VII of Title 49], by the Secretary of Transportation with respect to any air carrier or any foreign air carrier subject to that Act; and

(5) the Packers and Stockyards Act, 1921 [7 U.S.C. § 181 et seq.] (except as provided in section 406 of that Act [7 U.S.C. §§ 226, 227]), by the Secretary of Agriculture with respect to any activities subject to that Act; and

(6) subtitle E of the Consumer Financial Protection Act of 2010, by the Bureau, with respect to any person subject to this title.

The terms used in paragraph (1) that are not defined in this subchapter or otherwise defined in section 3(s) of the Federal Deposit Insurance Act (12 U.S.C. 1813(s)) shall have the meaning given to them in section 1(b) of the International Banking Act of 1978 (12 U.S.C. 3101).

(c) Agency powers

For the purpose of the exercise by any agency referred to in subsection (b) of this section of its powers under any Act referred to in that subsection, a violation of any requirement imposed under this subchapter shall be deemed to be a violation of a requirement

---

4   15 U.S.C. § 1692*l* *amended by* Pub. L. No. 95-473 § 3(b), 92 Stat. 1466 (Oct. 17, 1978); Pub. L. No. 95-630 Title V § 501, 92 Stat. 3680 (Nov. 10, 1978); Pub. L. No. 98-443 § 9n, 98 Stat. 1708 (Oct. 4, 1984); Pub. L. No. 101-73, Title VII § 744(n), 103 Stat. 440 (Aug. 9, 1989); Pub. L. No. 102-242, Title II § 212(e), 105 Stat. 2301 (Dec. 19, 1991); Pub. L. No. 102-550, Title XVI § 1604(a)(8), 106 Stat. 4082 (Oct. 28, 1992); Pub. L. No. 104-88, Title III § 316, 109 Stat. 949 (Dec. 29, 1995).

imposed under that Act. In addition to its powers under any provision of law specifically referred to in subsection (b) of this section, each of the agencies referred to in that subsection may exercise, for the purpose of enforcing compliance with any requirement imposed under this subchapter any other authority conferred on it by law, except as provided in subsection (d) of this section.

(d) Rules and regulations

Except as provided in section 1029(a) of the Consumer Financial Protection Act of 2010 [12 U.S.C. § 5519(a)], the Bureau may prescribe rules with respect to the collection of debts by debt collectors, as defined in this title.

[Pub. L. No. 111-203, tit. X, § 1089(3), (4), 124 Stat. 2092 (July 21, 2010)]

15 U.S.C. § 1692m. Reports to Congress by the Bureau; views of other Federal agencies [FDCPA § 815]

(a) Not later than one year after the effective date of this subchapter and at one-year intervals thereafter, the Bureau shall make reports to the Congress concerning the administration of its functions under this subchapter, including such recommendations as the Bureau deems necessary or appropriate. In addition, each report of the Bureau shall include its assessment of the extent to which compliance with this subchapter is being achieved and a summary of the enforcement actions taken by the Bureau under section 1692*l* of this title.

(b) In the exercise of its functions under this subchapter, the Bureau may obtain upon request the views of any other Federal agency which exercises enforcement functions under section 1692*l* of this title.

[Pub. L. No. 111-203, tit. X, § 1089(1), 124 Stat. 2092 (July 21, 2010)]

15 U.S.C. § 1692n. Relation to State laws [FDCPA § 816]

This subchapter does not annul, alter, or affect, or exempt any person subject to the provisions of this subchapter from complying with the laws of any State with respect to debt collection practices, except to the extent that those laws are inconsistent with any provision of this subchapter, and then only to the extent of the inconsistency. For purposes of this section, a State law is not inconsistent with this subchapter if the protection such law affords any consumer is greater than the protection provided by this subchapter.

15 U.S.C. § 1692o. Exemption for State regulation [FDCPA § 817]

The Bureau shall by regulation exempt from the requirements of this subchapter any class of debt collection practices within any State if the Bureau determines that under the law of that State that class of debt collection practices is subject to requirements substantially similar to those imposed by this subchapter, and that there is adequate provision for enforcement.

[Pub. L. No. 111-203, tit. X, § 1089(1), 124 Stat. 2092 (July 21, 2010)]

15 U.S.C. § 1692p. Exception for certain bad check enforcement programs operated by private entities [FDCPA § 818]

(a) In general—

(1) Treatment of certain private entities

Subject to paragraph (2), a private entity shall be excluded from the definition of a debt collector, pursuant to the exception provided in section 1692a(6) of this title, with respect to the operation by the entity of a program described in paragraph (2)(A) under a contract described in paragraph (2)(B).

(2) Conditions of applicability

Paragraph (1) shall apply if—

(A) a State or district attorney establishes, within the jurisdiction of such State or district attorney and with respect to alleged bad check violations that do not involve a check described in subsection (b) of this section, a pretrial diversion program for alleged bad check offenders who agree to participate voluntarily in such program to avoid criminal prosecution;

(B) a private entity, that is subject to an administrative support services contract with a State or district attorney and operates under the direction, supervision, and control of such State or district attorney, operates the pretrial diversion program described in subparagraph (A); and

(C) in the course of performing duties delegated to it by a State or district attorney under the contract, the private entity referred to in subparagraph (B)—

(i) complies with the penal laws of the State;

(ii) conforms with the terms of the contract and directives of the State or district attorney;

(iii) does not exercise independent prosecutorial discretion;

(iv) contacts any alleged offender referred to in subparagraph (A) for purposes of participating in a program referred to in such paragraph—

(I) only as a result of any determination by the State or district attorney that probable cause of a bad check violation under State penal law exists, and that contact with the alleged offender for purposes of participation in the program is appropriate; and

(II) the alleged offender has failed to pay the bad check after demand for payment, pursuant to State law, is made for payment of the check amount;

(v) includes as part of an initial written communication with an alleged offender a clear and conspicuous statement that—

(I) the alleged offender may dispute the validity of any alleged bad check violation;

(II) where the alleged offender knows, or has reasonable cause to believe, that the alleged bad check violation is the result of theft or forgery of the check, identity theft, or other fraud that is not the result of the conduct of the alleged offender, the alleged offender may file a crime report with the appropriate law enforcement agency; and **(III)** if the alleged offender notifies the private entity or the district attorney in writing, not later than 30 days after being contacted for the first time pursuant to clause (iv), that there is a dispute pursuant to this subsection, before further restitution efforts are pursued, the district attorney or an employee of the district attorney authorized to make such a determination makes a determination that there is probable cause to believe that a crime has been committed; and

(vi) charges only fees in connection with services under the contract that have been authorized by the contract with the State or district attorney.

(b) Certain checks excluded

A check is described in this subsection if the check involves, or is subsequently found to involve—

(1) a postdated check presented in connection with a payday loan, or other similar transaction, where the payee of the check knew that the issuer had insufficient funds at the time the check was made, drawn, or delivered;

(2) a stop payment order where the issuer acted in good faith and with reasonable cause in stopping payment on the check;

(3) a check dishonored because of an adjustment to the issuer's account by the financial institution holding such account without providing notice to the person at the time the check was made, drawn, or delivered;

(4) a check for partial payment of a debt where the payee had previously accepted partial payment for such debt;

(5) a check issued by a person who was not competent, or was not of legal age, to enter into a legal contractual obligation at the time the check was made, drawn, or delivered; or

(6) a check issued to pay an obligation arising from a transaction that was illegal in the jurisdiction of the State or district attorney at the time the check was made, drawn, or delivered.

(c) Definitions

For purposes of this section, the following definitions shall apply:

(1) State or district attorney

The term "State or district attorney" means the chief elected or appointed prosecuting attorney in a district, county (as defined in section 2 of title 1, United States Code), municipality, or comparable jurisdiction, including State attorneys general who act as chief elected or appointed prosecuting attorneys in a district, county (as so defined), municipality or comparable jurisdiction, who may be referred to by a variety of titles such as district attorneys, prosecuting attorneys, commonwealth's attorneys, solicitors, county attorneys, and state's attorneys, and who are responsible for the prosecution of State crimes and violations of jurisdiction-specific local ordinances.

(2) Check

The term "check" has the same meaning as in section 5002(6) of Title 12.[5]

(3) Bad check violation

The term "bad check violation" means a violation of the applicable State criminal law relating to the writing of dishonored checks.

[Pub. L. No. 109-352, tit. VIII, § 801(a)(2), 120 Stat. 2004 (Oct. 13, 2006)]

A.3 Senate Report No. 95-382 on the Fair Debt Collection Practices Act[6]

Report of the Committee on Banking,
Housing and Urban Affairs
U.S. Senate
Aug. 2, 1977

[*Page 1*]

The Committee on Banking, Housing, and Urban Affairs, to which was referred the bill (H.R. 5294) to amend the Consumer Credit Protection Act to prohibit abuses by debt collectors, having considered same, reports favorably thereon with an amendment and recommends that the bill as amended do pass.

HISTORY OF THE LEGISLATION

On May 12 and 13, 1977, the Consumer Affairs Subcommittee held hearings on four bills to regulate debt collection practices: S. 656, introduced by Senator Biden; S. 918, introduced by Senator Riegle; S. 1130, introduced by Senator Garn for himself and Senators Schmitt and Tower; and H.R. 5294, passed by the House of Representatives on April 4, 1977. After these hearings and before markup by the committee, Senator Riegle offered a composite bill, designated Committee Print No. 1, as a substitute for S. 918.

The Committee met in open markup sessions on June 30 and July 26, 1977, and approved Committee Print No. 1, with amendments, by voice vote. The committee substituted the text of its bill for that of H.R. 5294, which is herewith reported without objection.

NATURE AND PURPOSE OF THE BILL

This legislation would add a new title to the Consumer Credit Protection Act entitled the Fair Debt Collection Practices Act. Its purpose is to protect consumers from a host of unfair, harassing, and deceptive debt collection practices without imposing unnecessary [*Page 2*] restrictions on ethical debt collectors. This bill was strongly supported by consumer groups, labor unions, State and Federal law enforcement officials, and by both national organizations which represent the debt collection profession, the American Collectors Association and Associated Credit Bureaus.

---

5 **(6) Check**

    The term "check"—

        (A) means a draft, payable on demand and drawn on or payable through or at an office of a bank, whether or not negotiable, that is handled for forward collection or return,

        including a substitute check and a travelers check; and

        (B) does not include a noncash item or an item payable in a medium other than United States dollars.

    12 U.S.C. 5002 (6).

6 § 3.3.2, *supra*, describes the legislative history for the Fair Debt Collection Practices Act, and the key place of Senate Report No. 95-382 in that process.

NEED FOR THIS LEGISLATION

The committee has found that debt collection abuse by third party debt collectors is a widespread and serious national problem. Collection abuse takes many forms, including obscene or profane language, threats of violence, telephone calls at unreasonable hours, misrepresentation of a consumer's legal rights, disclosing a consumer's personal affairs to friends, neighbors, or an employer, obtaining information about a consumer through false pretense, impersonating public officials and attorneys, and simulating legal process.

Debt collection by third parties is a substantial business which touches the lives of many Americans. There are more than 5,000 collection agencies across the country, each averaging 8 employees. Last year, more than $5 billion in debts were turned over to collection agencies. One trade association which represents approximately half of the Nation's independent collectors states that in 1976 its members contacted 8 million consumers.

Hearings before the Consumer Affairs Subcommittee revealed that independent debt collectors are the prime source of egregious collection practices. While unscrupulous debt collectors comprise only a small segment of the industry, the suffering and anguish which they regularly inflict is substantial. Unlike creditors, who generally are restrained by the desire to protect their good will when collecting past due accounts, independent collectors are likely to have no future contact with the consumer and often are unconcerned with the consumer's opinion of them. Collection agencies generally operate on a 50-percent commission, and this has too often created the incentive to collect by any means.

The primary reason why debt collection abuse is so widespread is the lack of meaningful legislation on the State level. While debt collection agencies have existed for decades, there are 13 States, with 40 million citizens, that have no debt collection laws. These States are Alabama, Delaware, Georgia, Kansas, Kentucky, Mississippi, Missouri, Montana, Ohio, Oklahoma, Rhode Island, South Carolina, and South Dakota. Another 11 States (Alaska, Arkansas, Indiana, Louisiana, Nebraska, New Jersey, Oregon, Pennsylvania, Utah, Virginia and Wyoming), with another 40 million citizens, have laws which in the committee's opinion provide little or no effective protection. Thus, 80 million Americans, nearly 40 percent of our population, have no meaningful protection from debt collection abuse.

While 37 States and the District of Columbia do have laws regulating debt collectors, only a small number are comprehensive statutes which provide a civil remedy. As an example of ineffective State laws, of the 16 states which regulate by debt collection boards, 12 require by law that a majority of the board be comprised of debt collectors.

The Committee has found that collection abuse has grown from a State problem to a national problem. The use of WATS lines by debt collectors has led to a dramatic increase in interstate collections. State [*Page 3*] law enforcement officials have pointed to this development as a prime reason why federal legislation is necessary, because State officials are unable to act against unscrupulous debt collectors who harass consumers from another State.

One of the most frequent fallacies concerning debt collection legislation is the contention that the primary beneficiaries are "deadbeats." In fact, however, there is universal agreement among scholars, law enforcement officials, and even debt collectors that the number of persons who willfully refuse to pay just debts is miniscule. Prof. David Caplovitz, the foremost authority on debtors in default, testified that after years of research he has found that only 4 percent of all defaulting debtors fit the description of "deadbeat." This conclusion is supported by the National Commission on Consumer Finance which found that creditors list the willful refusal to pay as an extremely infrequent reason for default.

The Commission's findings are echoed in all major studies: the vast majority of consumers who obtain credit fully intend to repay their debts. When default occurs, it is nearly always due to an unforeseen event such as unemployment, overextension, serious illness, or marital difficulties or divorce.

The committee believes that the serious and widespread abuses in this area and the inadequacy of existing State and Federal laws make this legislation necessary and appropriate.

EXPLANATION OF THE LEGISLATION

Scope of the act

This bill applies only to debts contracted by consumers for personal, family, or household purposes; it has no application to the collection of commercial accounts.

The committee intends the term "debt collector," subject to the exclusions discussed below, to cover all third persons who regularly collect debts for others. The primary persons intended to be covered are independent debt collectors. The requirement that debt collection be done "regularly" would exclude a person who collects a debt for another in an isolated instance, but would include those who collect for others in the regular course of business. The definition would include "reciprocal collections" whereby one creditor regularly collects delinquent debts for another pursuant to a reciprocal service agreement, unless otherwise excluded by the act.

The term debt collector is not intended to include the following: "in house" collectors for creditors so long as they use the creditor's true business name when collecting; Government officials, such as marshals and sheriffs, while in the conduct of their official duties; process servers; nonprofit consumer credit counseling services which assist consumers by apportioning the consumer's income among his creditors pursuant to a prior arrangement; and attorneys-at-law while acting in that capacity. One subsidiary or affiliate which collects debts for another subsidiary or affiliate is not a "debt collector" so long as the collecting affiliate collects only for other related entities and its principal business is not debt collection.

Finally, the committee does not intend the definition to cover the activities of trust departments, escrow companies, or other bona fide fiduciaries; the collection of debts, such as mortgages and student loans, by persons who originated such loans; mortgage service com- [*Page 4*] panies and others who service outstanding debts for others, so long as the debts were not in default when taken for servicing; and the collection of debts owed to a creditor when the collector is holding the receivable account as collateral for commercial credit extended to the creditor.

Obtaining location information

While this legislation strongly protects the consumer's right to privacy by prohibiting a debt collector from communicating the consumer's personal affairs to third persons, the committee also recognizes the debt collector's legitimate need to seek the whereabouts of missing debtors. Accordingly, this bill permits debt collectors to contact third persons for the purpose of obtaining the consumer's location. In seeking this information, however, the debt collector must observe certain guidelines: he may not state that the consumer owes a debt nor contact third persons more than once unless necessary to obtain complete information. In addition, a debt collector may not place language or symbols on mail to third persons indicating that the mail relates to debt collection nor continue to contact third parties after learning the name and address of the consumer's attorney, unless the attorney fails to respond to the debt collector's communications.

Prohibited practices

This legislation expressly prohibits a host of harassing, deceptive, and unfair debt collection practices. These include: threats of violence; obscene language; the publishing of "shame lists;" harassing or anonymous telephone calls; impersonating a government official or attorney; misrepresenting the consumer's legal rights; simulating court process; obtaining information under false pretenses; collecting more than is legally owing; and misusing postdated checks. In addition to these specific prohibitions, this bill prohibits in general terms any harassing, unfair, or deceptive collection practice. This will enable the courts, where appropriate, to proscribe other improper conduct which is not specifically addressed.

In addition, this legislation adopts an extremely important protection recommended by the National Commission on Consumer Finance and already the law in 15 States: it prohibits disclosing the consumer's personal affairs to third persons. Other than to obtain location information, a debt collector may not contact third persons such as a consumer's friends, neighbors, relatives, or employer. Such contacts are not legitimate collection practices and result in serious invasions of privacy, as well as the loss of jobs.

Validation of debts

Another significant feature of this legislation is its provision requiring the validation of debts. After initially contacting a consumer, a debt collector must send him or her written notice stating the name of the creditor and the amount owed. If the consumer disputes the validity of the debt within 30 days, the debt collector must cease collection until he sends the consumer verification.

This provision will eliminate the recurring problem of debt collectors dunning the wrong person or attempting to collect debts which the consumer has already paid. Since the current practice of most debt collectors is to send similar information to consumers, this provision will not result in additional expense or paperwork. [*Page 5*]

Legal actions by debt collectors

This legislation also addresses the problem of "forum abuse," an unfair practice in which debt collectors file suit against consumers in courts which are so distant or inconvenient that consumers are unable to appear. As a result, the debt collector obtains a default judgment and the consumer is denied his day in court.

In response to this practice, the bill adopts the "fair venue standards" developed by the Federal Trade Commission. A debt collector who files suit must do so either where the consumer resides or where the underlying contract was signed. When an action is against real property, it must be brought where such property is located.

More than 1,000 collection agencies in all 50 States have already voluntarily agreed to follow these standards. The Com-

mission reports that this standard is effective in curtailing forum abuse without unreasonably restricting debt collectors.

Furnishing deceptive forms

Another common collection abuse is known colloquially as "flat-rating." A "flat-rater" is one who sells to creditors a set of dunning letters bearing the letter-head of the flat-rater's collection agency and exhorting the debtor to pay the creditor at once. The creditor sends these letters to his debtors, giving the impression that a third party debt collector is collecting the debt. In fact, however, the flat-rater is not in the business of debt collection, but merely sells dunning letters.

This bill prohibits the practice of flat-rating because of its inherently deceptive nature. The prohibition on furnishing such forms does not apply, however, to printers and custom stationery sellers who innocently print or sell such forms without knowledge of their intended use.

Civil liability

The committee views this legislation as primarily self-enforcing; consumers who have been subjected to collection abuses will be enforcing compliance.

A debt collector who violates the act is liable for any actual damages he caused as well as any additional damages the court deems appropriate, not exceeding $1,000. In assessing damages, the court must take into account the nature of the violation, the degree of willfullness, and the debt collector's persistence. A debt collector has no liability, however, if he violates the act in any manner, including with regard to the act's coverage, when such violation is unintentional and occurred despite procedures designed to avoid such violations. A debt collector also has no liability if he relied in good faith on an advisory opinion issued by the Federal Trade Commission.

As in all other Federal consumer protection legislation, a consumer who obtains judgment on his behalf is entitled to attorney's fees and costs. In order to protect debt collectors from nuisance lawsuits, if the court finds that an action was brought by a consumer in bad faith and for harassment, the court may award the debt collector reasonable attorney's fees and costs.

Administrative enforcement

This legislation is enforced administratively primarily by the Federal Trade Commission. If a depository institution subject to regulation by another Federal agency engages in debt collection, administrative enforcement authority is lodged with that agency. [*Page 6*]

All enforcement agencies are authorized to utilize all their functions and powers to enforce compliance. The Federal Trade Commission is authorized to treat violations of the act as violations of a trade regulation rule, which empowers the Commission to obtain restraining orders and seek fines in federal district court.

Because the committee regards this as comprehensive legislation which fully addresses the problem of collection abuses, the administrative agencies charged with enforcement are specifically prohibited from issuing additional rules or regulations applicable to persons covered by this legislation.

Relation to State law

The Committee believes that this law ought not to foreclose the States from enacting or enforcing their own laws regarding debt collection. Accordingly, this legislation annuls only "inconsistent" State laws, with stronger State laws not regarded as inconsistent. In addition, States with substantially similar laws may be exempted from the act's requirements (but not its remedies) by applying to the Federal Trade Commission.

COST OF THIS LEGISLATION

Enactment of this legislation will result in no new or additional costs to the Federal Government. The Congressional Budget Office analysis of this bill is contained in the following letter:

CONGRESSIONAL BUDGET OFFICE,
U.S. CONGRESS,
Washington, D.C., July 27, 1977.

HON. WILLIAM PROXMIRE,
Chairman, Committee on Banking, Housing, and Urban Affairs,
U.S. Senate, Washington, D.C.

DEAR MR. CHAIRMAN: Pursuant to section 403 of the Congressional Budget Act of 1974, the Congressional Budget Office has reviewed H.R. 5294, a bill to amend the Consumer Credit Protection Act to prohibit abusive practices by debt collectors, as ordered reported by the Senate Committee on Banking, Housing and Urban Affairs, July 26, 1977.

Based on this review, it appears that no additional cost to the Government would be incurred as a result of enactment of this bill.

Sincerely,

Alice M. Rivlin, *Director.*

CHANGES IN EXISTING LAW

In the opinion of the Committee, it is necessary to dispense with the requirements of subsection 4 of Rule XXIX of the Standing Rules of the Senate in order to expedite the business of the Senate. [*Page 7*]

SECTION-BY-SECTION SUMMARY

Section 801. Short title.—The act may be cited as the "Fair Debt Collection Practices Act."

Section 802. Findings and purpose.—The Congress finds that collection abuses by independent debt collectors are serious and widespread and that existing State laws are inadequate to curb these abuses. The purpose of the title is to eliminate abusive practices, not disadvantage ethical debt collectors, and promote consistent state action.

Section 803. Definitions.—The term "debt collector" is defined to include all third parties who regularly collect consumer debts for others, except for the following persons: "in house" collectors for creditors; affiliates collecting for one another, providing that collection is not the principal business of the affiliate; Government officials collecting in their official capacities; process servers; bona fide consumer credit counseling services; and attorneys-at-law. The term also does not include trust companies and other bona fide fiduciaries; persons collecting loans which they originated; persons who service debts for others; and persons holding receivables as collateral for commercial credit transactions.

Section 804. Acquisition of location information.—When contacting third persons to establish a consumer's whereabouts, a debt collector may not: state that the consumer owes a debt; contact the third person more than once unless reasonably necessary; or use

language symbols on mail indicating that it pertains to debt collection. A debt collector may not contact a third person if the debt collector knows that the consumer is represented by an attorney and has the attorney's name and address.

Section 805. Communication in connection with debt collection.—Without the consumer's consent, a debt collector may not (a) contact a consumer at any unusual or inconvenient time or place (8 a.m. to 9 p.m. is considered convenient); (b) contact a consumer if he is represented by an attorney; or (c) call a consumer at work if the debt collector knows the consumer's employer prohibits such calls.

There is a general prohibition on contacting any third parties (other than to obtain location information) except for: the consumer's attorney; a credit reporting agency; the creditor; the creditor's or debt collector's attorney; or any other person to the extent necessary to effectuate a postjudgment judicial remedy.

If a consumer notifies a debt collector in writing that he refuses to pay a debt or wishes the debt collector to cease further contacts, the debt collector must cease communications except to notify the consumer of the debt collector's or creditor's possible further actions.

Section 806. Harassment or abuse.—A debt collector is prohibited from engaging in any conduct the natural consequence of which is to harass, oppress or abuse any person. The following enumerated practices are violations: threats of violence; use of profane or obscene language; publishing "shame lists"; repeated telephone calls intended [*Page 8*] to annoy or harass; and making telephone calls without disclosing the caller's identity.

Section 807. False or misleading representations.—A debt collector is prohibited from using any false, deceptive or misleading representations to collect debts. The following enumerated practices are violations: misrepresenting that a debt collector is a government official; misrepresenting the amount or nature of a debt; impersonating an attorney; misrepresenting that a consumer will be arrested or his property seized; misrepresenting a consumer's legal rights; deliberately communicating false credit information; utilizing bogus legal documents; and misrepresenting a collection agency as a credit bureau.

Section 808. Unfair practices.—A debt collector is prohibited from using any unfair or unconscionable means to collect debts. The following enumerated practices are violations: collecting amounts in excess of the debt or interest owed; causing charges for communications to be billed to a consumer; repossessing property if there is no valid security interest or if it is exempt by law from repossession; communicating information about a debt by postcard; and using symbols on envelopes indicating that the contents pertain to debt collection.

Section 809. Validation of debts.—Within 5 days after contacting a consumer, the debt collector must in writing notify the consumer of the amount of the debt and the name of the creditor and advise the consumer of the debt collector's duty to verify the debt if it is disputed. If a consumer disputes a debt within 30 days, the debt collector must stop collection until verification is sent to the consumer.

Section 810. Multiple debts.—A debt collector is prohibited from applying payments to disputed debts and, where applicable, must apply payments in accordance with the consumer's directions.

Section 811. Legal actions by debt collectors.—Actions on real property are required to be brought in the judicial district in which the property is located. In personal actions, suits must be brought either where the contract was signed or where the consumer resides.

Section 812. Furnishing certain deceptive forms.—It is made unlawful to compile, design, and furnish forms knowing that they will be used to create the false impression that a third person is collecting a debt.

Section 813. Civil liability.—A debt collector who violates the Act is liable for actual damages plus costs and reasonable attorney's fees. The court may award additional damages of up to $1,000 in individual actions, and in class actions, up to $500,000 or 1 percent of the debt collector's net worth, whichever is less.

Two defenses are provided: good faith reliance on an F.T.C. advisory opinion; and bona fide error notwithstanding procedures to avoid the error. Where a court finds that a suit was brought by a consumer in bad faith and for harassment, the court may award reasonable attorney's fees to the defendant.

Jurisdiction for actions is conferred on U.S. district and state courts; there is a 1 year statute of limitations.

Section 814. Administrative enforcement.—The Act is administratively enforced by the F.T.C. and the Federal bank regulatory agencies. The agencies are empowered to use all their functions and powers to enforce compliance. The agencies are prohibited from promulgating any additional rules or regulations pertaining to debt collectors.

[*Page 9*]

Section 815. Reports to Congress by the Commission.—The F.T.C. shall provide annual reports to Congress on the Act's effectiveness and administrative enforcement.

Section 816. Relation to State laws.—The act annuls state laws only if inconsistent; a state law is not inconsistent if it provides greater protection than this title.

Section 817. Exemption for State regulation.—The F.T.C. may exempt from the Act any collection practices within any State if subject to substantially similar requirements.

Section 818. Effective date.—The act is effective 6 months from enactment.

ADDITIONAL VIEWS OF MESSRS SCHMITT, GARN AND TOWER

It is our view that the Fair Debt Collection Practices Act is an unwarranted Federal intrusion into an area best left to the States. Although we recognize that some debt collectors employ unconscionable practices in collecting debts, we do not feel that the hearings in either the House or Senate subcommittees produced substantial evidence that there is a serious national problem which justifies such detailed Federal regulation of the operation of the business of collecting debts. A far better approach is that contained in S. 1130 which would preserve the States' prerogative of providing a mechanism for the resolution of disputes between debtors and creditors while correcting identified abuses in irresponsible debt collectors operating in interstate commerce. According to an American Bar Association committee, 33 States have already adopted debt collection practices regulation and others are moving in that direction.

Of particular concern to us is the impact that the proliferation of Federal consumer credit regulation is having on small business and on the cost and availability of credit to the consumer. A Federal Fair Debt Collection Practice Act will be one more regulatory burden on small business, the cost of which will be borne by the consumer.

Although we would not take the approach chosen by the majority of the committee, the committee report is a vast improvement over H.R. 5294 passed by the House. We are pleased that the committee included in its final version of the bill many provisions contained in S. 1130. Most important, it dropped the $100 minimum civil penalty provision which courts have construed as requiring the award of the penalty and attorneys fees when a violation of the Act has been established.

This should go a long way in avoiding the type of nuisance suits so prevalent under the Truth in Lending Act.

Harrison Schmitt.
Jake Garn.
John Tower.

Federal Trade Commission Advisory Opinions and Staff Letters Regarding the Fair Debt Collection Practices Act

B.1 Federal Trade Commission Advisory Opinions

B.1.1 Introduction

The Federal Trade Commission has issued four advisory opinions that are set out below.

The earliest advisory opinion, issued Mar. 31, 2000, should be used with caution since it has not been revised in light of 2006 Congressional amendments to the Fair Debt Collection Practices Act on the same subject.[1]

Advisory opinions are approved by the FTC commissioners and have a greater weight of authority than FTC informal staff opinion letters, Appx. B.2, *infra*, and the FTC official staff commentary, Appx. C, *infra*.[2] The substance and effect of the advisory opinions is discussed in § 5.7, *supra*.

B.1.2 Federal Trade Commission FDCPA Advisory Opinion, June 23, 2009

This FTC FDCPA advisory opinion permits a debt collector to respond to a request from a consumer to correct an inaccurate credit report by the debt collector where the consumer had previously requested the debt collector to cease communicating with him or her. *See* § 5.3.8, *supra*.

UNITED STATES OF AMERICA
FEDERAL TRADE COMMISSION
WASHINGTON, D.C. 20580

Office of the Secretary

June 23, 2009

Rozanne M. Anderson, Esq.
ACA International
4040 W. 70th Street
Minneapolis, MN 55345

Andrew M. Beato, Esq.
Stein, Mitchell & Mezines, LLP
1100 Connecticut Avenue, N.W.

---

1 *See* § 5.7.2.5.2, *supra*.
2 *See* §§ 3.3.4, 3.3.6, 7.3, *supra*.

Suite 1100
Washington, DC 20036

Dear Ms. Anderson and Mr. Beato:

This responds to an issue raised in your comment filed on February 11, 2008, on behalf of American Collectors Association International, with the Federal Trade Commission ("Commission") and other agencies charged by Congress in Section 312 of the FACT Act with writing regulations relating to certain duties of furnishers of information to consumer reporting agencies ("CRAs"). On pages 7–8 of your comment, you urged the following action:

> To avoid a statutory conflict between the FDCPA and FACT Act, the regulation should clarify that the act of responding to a consumer dispute is not an attempt to collect a debt under the FDCPA. Further the regulation should clarify that a consumer that sends a written dispute to a furnisher *after* having invoked his or her cease communication rights under the FDCPA has revoked his or [her] cease communication instruction for purposes of communicating with the furnisher to process the dispute. (Emphasis yours)

The Commission is treating this portion of your comment as a request for an advisory opinion interpreting the Fair Debt Collection Practices Act (FDCPA) pursuant to Sections 1.1–1.4 of its Rules of Practice. 16 C.F.R. §§ 1.1–1.4. The subject matter of the request and consequent publication of this Commission advice is in the public interest. 16 C.F.R. § 1.1(a)(2). Specifically, it is in the public interest for the Commission to clarify the intersection of the FDCPA and this new rule implementing the FACT Act, thus encouraging debt collector compliance with both laws.

The applicable provisions of the FDCPA and the furnisher disputes rule (Rule) are:

- Section 805(c) of the FDCPA provides that if a consumer has notified a debt collector in writing that "the consumer wishes the debt collector to cease further communication with the consumer, the debt collector shall not communicate with the consumer with respect to such debt" (with some exceptions not applicable here).
- The Rule requires furnishers of information to CRAs to report the results of a direct dispute to the consumer, 16 CFR § 660.4(e) (3), or notify the consumer if the furnisher determines the dispute is frivolous or irrelevant. 16 CFR § 660.4(f)(2).

The potential conflict arises when a consumer orders a debt collector in writing to cease communication, but at some future time submits a direct dispute about information the debt collector has provided to a CRA. The Rule requires the collector to notify the consumer either of the results of the investigation or of its determination that the dispute is frivolous or irrelevant. Section 805(c) of the FDCPA, however, prohibits the collector from communicating with that consumer with respect to the debt, which could be interpreted to include providing the notice that the Rule requires.

The Commission does not believe that providing the notice the Rule requires undermines the purpose of Section 805(c) of the FDCPA. Section 805(c) empowers consumers to direct collectors to cease contacting them to collect a debt so that consumers can be free of the burden of being subject to unwanted communications. In contrast, communications from debt collectors which do nothing more than respond to disputes consumers themselves have raised do not impose such a burden. Rather, such communications benefit consumers through providing them with information demonstrating that collectors have been responsive to their disputes.

After reviewing the language of the FDCPA and the Rule, and considering the goals of the statute and the regulation, the Commission concludes that a debt collector does not violate Section 805(c) of the FDCPA if the consumer directly disputes information after sending a written "cease communication" to the collector, and the collector complies with the Rule by means of a communication that has no purpose other than complying with the Rule by stating (1) the results of the investigation or (2) the collector's belief that the communication is frivolous or irrelevant.

By direction of the Commission.

Donald S. Clark
Secretary

B.1.3 Federal Trade Commission FDCPA Advisory Opinion, March 19, 2008

This advisory opinion determined that a debt collector enforcing a mortgage could send a homeowner information about settling a mortgage payment delinquency without necessarily overshadowing or being inconsistent with the debt verification notice required by 15 U.S.C. § 1692g(a). The advisory opinion makes clear that the content of a particular communications about settlement rights could overshadow or be inconsistent with a debt verification notice resulting in a violation of the FDCPA. *See* § 5.7.2.7, *supra.*

UNITED STATES OF AMERICA
FEDERAL TRADE COMMISSION
WASHINGTON, D.C. 20580

Office of the Secretary

March 19, 2008

Barbara A. Sinsley
Manuel H. Newburger
Barron, Newburger, Sinsley & Wier, PLLC
2901 West Busch Boulevard
Tampa, Florida 33618

Dear Ms. Sinsley and Mr. Newburger:

This is in response to the request from the USFN, formerly known as the U.S. Foreclosure Network, for a Commission advisory opinion ("Request") regarding whether the Fair Debt Collection Practices Act ("FDCPA")[1] prohibits a debt collector in the foreclosure context from discussing settlement options in the collector's initial or subsequent communications with the consumer. The Request asserts that the receipt of information about settlement options could enable the consumer to save his or her home from foreclosure. As explained more fully below, the Commission concludes that debt collectors do not commit a *per se* violation of the FDCPA when they provide such information to consumers. Moreover, the Commission believes that it is in the public interest for consumers who may be subject to foreclosure to receive truthful, nonmisleading information about settlement options, especially in light of the recent prevalence of mortgage borrowers who are delinquent or in foreclosure.[2]

USFN submitted the Request pursuant to Sections 1.1-1.4 of the Commission's Rules of Practice, 16 C.F.R. §§ 1.1-1.4. The Request focuses on two sections of the FDCPA, Sections

807 and 809, 15 U.S.C. §§ 1692e, 1692g,[3] and presents three specific questions for consideration:

(1) Does a debt collector violate the FDCPA when he, in conjunction with the sending of a "validation notice" pursuant to Section 809(a) of the FDCPA, notifies a consumer of settlement options that may be available to avoid foreclosure?

(2) Does a debt collector violate the FDCPA when he, subsequent to sending the validation notice pursuant to Section 809(a) of the FDCPA, notifies a consumer of settlement options that might be available to avoid foreclosure?

(3) Does a debt collector commit a false, misleading or deceptive act or practice in violation of Section 807 of the FDCPA when he presents to a consumer settlement options that are available to the consumer to avoid foreclosure?

The Request states that there is no case law addressing these specific questions. We address the questions *seriatim.*

USFN's first two questions specifically reference Section 809(a) of the FDCPA, 15 U.S.C. § 1692g(a). Section 809(a) provides, in

---

1   15 U.S.C. §§ 1692–1692p. 1

2   According to press reports, in 2007, there were an estimated 2.2 million foreclosure filings in the United States, a 75% increase from 2006. The number of foreclosure filings increased late in 2007—in December there were 215,749 foreclosure filings, a 97% increase from the number of filings in December 2006. December was the fifth consecutive month in which foreclosure filings topped 200,000. Associated Press, *Home Foreclosure Rate Soars in 2007*, N.Y.TIMES, Jan. 29, 2008, *available at* www.nytimes.com/aponline/us/AP-Foreclosure-Rates.html. Mortgage delinquency is also escalating. The number of borrowers falling behind on first-lien mortgage payments for residences during 2007 was the highest it has been since 1986—2.64 million borrowers fell behind on payments. Michael M. Phillips, Serena Ng & John D. McKinnon, *Battle Lines Form Over Mortgage Plan*, WALL ST. J., Dec. 7, 2007, at A1.

3   The Commission has considered only these sections in rendering this opinion and it should not be construed to pertain to any other section of the FDCPA, to any other law, or to any issue of legal ethics.

pertinent part, that a debt collector must, within the first five days after the initial communication with the debtor, provide a written notice containing specific information including the amount of the debt, the debtor's right to dispute the validity of the debt in writing within 30 days, and the collector's obligation to obtain verification of the debt in response to the consumer's dispute document. Congress enacted Section 809 to "eliminate the recurring problem of debt collectors dunning the wrong person or attempting to collect debts which the consumer has already paid."[4]

Section 809(a) does not expressly prohibit debt collectors from adding language to the written validation notice with the mandatory disclosures. The statute also does not expressly prohibit debt collectors from presenting information to consumers about settlement options in subsequent communications. The Commission therefore concludes that there is no *per se* violation of Section 809(a) of the FDCPA if a debt collector includes information regarding foreclosure settlement options along with a validation notice or in subsequent communications after that notice is delivered.

Nevertheless, collectors must take care that communicating information about settlement options does not undermine the consumer protections in Section 809(a). The touchstones of Section 809(a) are the consumer's rights to dispute his or her debt in writing within 30 days and to obtain verification of that debt from the collector. To protect these rights, in 2006 Congress amended Section 809(b) to expressly state that "[a]ny collection activities and communication during the 30-day period may not overshadow or be inconsistent with the disclosure of the consumer's right to dispute the debt. . . ."[5] This statutory amendment ratified court decisions holding that debt collectors that provide consumers with information in addition to the mandatory disclosures violate Section 809(a) if the additional information effectively obscures the consumer's right to dispute his or her debt and obtain verification from the collector.[6] Specifically, these cases concluded that providing additional information is unlawful if it overshadows or contradicts required disclosures or creates confusion regarding the basic right to dispute the debt and obtain verification from the collector.[7] In making these determinations, courts considered the communication from the perspective of an unsophisticated consumer.[8]

In sum, with respect to USFN's first two questions presented in its Request, the Commission concludes that there is no *per se* violation of Section 809(a) if a debt collector in the foreclosure context discusses settlement options in the collector's initial or subsequent communications with the consumer. This conclusion, however, does not prevent a fact-based finding that a specific communication violates the Act if it overshadows or is inconsistent with the disclosures of the consumer's right to dispute the debt within 30 days.

USFN's third question asks whether a debt collector commits a false, misleading or deceptive act or practice in violation of Section 807 of the FDCPA when he presents to a consumer settlement options that are available to the consumer to avoid foreclosure. Section 807 of the FDCPA establishes a general prohibition against the use of any "false, deceptive or misleading representation or means in connection with the collection of any debt" and provides a list of 16 specific practices that are *per se* false, deceptive or misleading under the Act. In enacting Section 807, Congress noted that this general prohibition on deceptive collection practices would "enable the courts, where appropriate, to proscribe other improper conduct which is not specifically addressed."[9]

As a general matter, the Commission concludes that a debt collector's communication with a consumer regarding his or her options to resolve mortgage debts and to potentially avoid foreclosure would not necessarily violate either the general or specific prohibitions of Section 807. However, we also stress that a particular communication with settlement option information could be deceptive in violation of Section 807 if it contains a false or misleading representation or omission of material fact. Determining whether a specific communication is false or misleading is a fact-based inquiry that considers all the facts and circumstances surrounding the particular communication at issue.[10]

After reviewing the language of the FDCPA, its legislative history, and relevant case law, as well as the information contained in the Request, the Commission concludes that a debt collector in the foreclosure context does not commit a *per se* violation of Sections 807 or 809 of the FDCPA when he or she addresses settlement options in the collector's initial or subsequent communications with the consumer.

By direction of the Commission.
Donald S. Clark
Secretary

B.1.4 Federal Trade Commission FDCPA Advisory Opinion, October 5, 2007

This FTC advisory opinion determines that a debt collector who ceases collection of a debt in response to a section 1692g consumer's dispute or request for verification of the debt may send the consumer one additional communication stating that the debt collector is ceasing its debt collection activities with respect to that debt. *See* § 5:7.3.4, *supra*.

---

4 S. Rep. No. 95-382, at 4 (1977), *reprinted in* 1977 U.S.C.C.A.N. 1695, 1698.

5 15 U.S.C. § 1692g(b).

6 *See, e.g., Swanson v. Oregon Credit Servs.*, 869 F.2d 1222 (9th Cir. 1988).

7 *Id.; See, e.g., Durkin v. Equifax Check Servs.*, 406 F.3d 410 (7th Cir. 2005); *Shapiro v. Riddle & Assocs.*, 351 F.3d 63 (2d Cir. 2003); *Renick v. Dun & Bradstreet Receivable Mgmt. Servs.*, 290 F.3d 1055 (9th Cir. 2002).

8 *See, e.g., Sims v. G.C. Servs.*, 445 F.3d 959 (7th Cir. 2006) ("unsophisticated consumer"); *Smith v. Transworld Sys.*, 953 F.2d 1025 (6th Cir. 1992) ("least sophisticated consumer").

---

9 S. Rep. No. 95-382, at 4 (1977), *reprinted in* 1977 U.S.C.C.A.N. 1695, 1698.

10 *See Jeter v. Credit Bureau, Inc.*, 760 F.2d 1168 (11th Cir. 1985) (noting that FDCPA expands pre-existing FTC deception authority); *see also FTC Policy Statement on Deception*, appended to *In re Cliffdale Associates, Inc.*, 103 F.T.C. 110, 174–84 (1984) (setting forth deception test).

UNITED STATES OF AMERICA
FEDERAL TRADE COMMISSION
WASHINGTON, D.C. 20580

Office of the Secretary

October 5, 2007

Andrew M. Beato, Esq.
Stein, Mitchell & Mezines, L.L.P.
1100 Connecticut Avenue, N.W.
Washington, D.C. 20036

Dear Mr. Beato:

This is in response to ACA International's ("ACA's") request for a Commission advisory opinion ("Request") regarding whether the Fair Debt Collection Practices Act ("FDCPA") prohibits a debt collector from notifying a consumer who disputed a debt that the collector has ceased its collection efforts. ACA submitted the Request pursuant to Sections 1.1-1.4 of the Commission's Rules of Practice, 16 C.F.R. §§ 1.1-1.4. As explained more fully below, the Commission concludes that a debt collector providing such a notice to a consumer would not violate the FDCPA.

The Request focuses primarily on Section 809 of the FDCPA, 15 U.S.C. § 1692g. Section 809(a) provides that, within five days after its initial communication with a consumer about a debt, a debt collector must send the consumer a written notice. Among other things, this notice must state that "if the consumer notifies the debt collector in writing within [thirty days after receipt of the notice] that the debt, or any portion thereof, is disputed, the debt collector will obtain verification of the debt or a copy of a judgment against the consumer and a copy of such verification or judgment will be mailed to the consumer by the debt collector." Section 809(b) provides that if a consumer provides such a notice, the debt collector must cease collection until it has obtained verification of the debt or a copy of the judgment and mailed it to the consumer.

In July 2007, ACA amended its Code of Ethics and Code of Operations ("Ethics Code"). If a debt collector receives a written request for verification and is unable to verify the debt, the Ethics Code now requires "the cessation of all collection efforts, removal of the account from the consumer's credit report or reporting the account as disputed, and prompt notification of the **creditor or legal owner** of the debt that collection activities have been terminated due to the inability to provide verification information." Request at 3 (emphasis added). ACA "also has considered amending the Ethics Code to promote the notification of a **consumer** that collection activity has been terminated if the debt collector is unable to verify the debt following the receipt of a written request for verification." *Id.* (emphasis added). However, ACA has not yet amended its Ethics Code to include such a provision because of "concern that communication with the consumer following a request for verification might be construed as an attempt to collect, even though the intention merely is to inform the consumer that there will no further collections." *Id.* at 2.

We note first that courts have construed Section 809(b) as giving debt collectors two options when they receive a written dispute or a request for verification[1]: (1) provide the requested verification and continue collection activities, or (2) cease all collection ac-

tivities. If the debt collector ceases collection, it is not required to provide verification. *See, e.g., Guerrero v. RJM Acquisitions LLC*, 2007 U.S. App. LEXIS 20072, at *35-36 (9th Cir. Aug. 23, 2007); *Jang v. A.M. Miller & Assocs.*, 122 F.3d 480,483 (7th Cir. 1997); *Wilhelm v. Credico Inc.*, 426 F. Supp. 2d 1030, 1036 (D.N.D. 2006); *Zaborac v. Phillips and Cohen Assocs*, 330 F. Supp. 2d 962, 966 (N.D. Ill. 2004); *Sambor v. Omnia Credit Servs., Inc.*, 183 F. Supp. 2d 1234, 1243 (D. Haw. 2002).

The Request poses the question of whether a debt collector that discontinues debt collection activities after receiving a written request for verification can inform the consumer that it has done so without violating the FDCPA. As noted above, Section 809(b) requires a debt collector to cease collection of a debt until the collector has provided verification of the debt to the consumer if the consumer, in writing within the thirty-day window, has either disputed the debt or requested verification. If a debt collector cannot provide such verification to the consumer, merely informing the consumer that debt collection efforts have been terminated is not an attempt to collect a debt and therefore does not violate the FDCPA.[2]

We note that Congress enacted Section 809 to "eliminate the recurring problem of debt collectors dunning the wrong person or attempting to collect debts which the consumer has already paid."[3] The provision allows a consumer who does not believe that he or she owes a debt to require that the debt collector obtain and provide verification prior to contacting the consumer again. The purpose of Section 809 therefore is to stop further calls and letters from collectors unless the consumer incurred and continues to owe the debt. Interpreting Section 809 as allowing debt collectors to notify consumers that they have ceased collection efforts, without conveying any other message, is consistent with this purpose. A consumer receiving such a notice would benefit both from having the calls and letters from that collector stop and from knowing that the collector will not renew its collection efforts.[4]

1　Courts interpreting Section 809(b) have used the phrases "disputing the debt," "requesting verification," and "requesting validation" interchangeably. *See, e.g., Jang v. A.M. Miller and Assocs.*, 122 F.3d 480, 482 (7th Cir. 1997) (collection agencies

"ceased collection activities immediately upon receiving the requests for validation, in compliance with [Section 809(b)]"); *Wilhelm v. Credico Inc.*, 426 F. Supp. 2d 1030, 1036 (D.N.D. 2006) (debt collector's Section 809(b) obligations triggered "once a debt collector receives a request for verification"); *Sambor v. Omnia Credit Servs., Inc.*, 183 F. Supp. 2d 1234, 1243 (D. Haw. 2002) (debt collector's Section 809(b) obligations triggered "[w]hen timely asked in writing to validate a debt"); *see also Clark's Jewelers v. Humble*, 823 P.2d 818, 821 (Kan. Ct. App. 1991) (a consumer need not use the word "dispute" to trigger the debt collector's obligation to cease collection and provide verification of the debt, as long as the consumer's notice makes clear that the debt is contested).

2　The Request also raises the question whether a notice informing a consumer that collection efforts have ceased "might be construed as a 'communication' in furtherance of collecting the debt." Request at 5. Regardless of whether such a notice is a "communication" under 15 U.S.C. § 1692a(2), a debt collector telling a consumer that debt collection has ceased is not "in furtherance of collecting the debt."

3　S. Rep. No. 95-382, at 4 (1977), *reprinted in* 1977 U.S.C.C.A.N. 1695, 1698.

4　Even if, as the amended Ethics Code now requires, a debt collector that is unable to provide verification of a debt ceases collection efforts, closes the account, and notifies the credit grantor, client, or owner of legal title to the debt that collection activities have been terminated because the collector could not

The only other FDCPA provision that could be implicated by the notification that ACA proposes to require of its members is Section 805(c). That provision provides that, if a consumer notifies a debt collector in writing that he or she "refuses to pay a debt or . . . wishes the debt collector to cease further communication," the debt collector is not permitted to communicate further with the consumer about the debt. However, Section 805(c) includes an express exception to its prohibition on communication that permits a debt collector to "advise the consumer that the debt collector's further efforts are being terminated." Thus, even if a consumer demands in writing that a debt collector cease communicating about a debt, the debt collector would not violate Section 805(c) if it notified the consumer that the collector's collection efforts have ceased.[5]

After reviewing the language of the FDCPA and its legislative history as well as information contained in the Request, the Commission concludes that a debt collector does not violate the FDCPA if, after receiving written notice of a dispute, it informs the consumer that it has ceased collection efforts. By direction of the Commission.

Donald S. Clark
Secretary

B.1.5 *Federal Trade Commission FDCPA Advisory Opinion, March 31, 2000*

This advisory opinion should be used with caution as it has not been revised in light of a 2006 congressional amendment on the same subject.[1] That amendment added 15 U.S.C. § 1692g(d) which provides that a formal legal pleading is not an "initial communication," and thus a formal pleading does not trigger the requirement that a debt validation rights notice be sent to the consumer.[2] The FTC's position in the "First Issue" of the advisory opinion, that collection activities may continue during the thirty-day period the consumer has to dispute the debt, until the consumer disputes the debt in writing, was codified in the same amendments.[3]

UNITED STATES OF AMERICA
FEDERAL TRADE COMMISSION
WASHINGTON, D.C. 20580

Office of the Secretary   March 31, 2000

Basil J. Mezines, Esq.
Stein, Mitchell & Mezines, L.L.P.
1100 Connecticut Avenue, N.W.
Washington, D.C. 20036

---

provide verification of the debt, the credit grantor, client, or debt owner might choose to refer the account to a different debt collector. Thus, although the consumer will no longer be contacted by the first debt collector, he or she might receive collection calls and letters from a different debt collector.

5 We note, however, that any such communication must not violate any other FDCPA provision.

1 Pub. L. No. 109-351 § 802(a), 120 Stat. 2006 (2006).

2 See § 5.7.2.5.2, *supra.*

3 Pub. L. No. 109-351 § 802(c), 120 Stat. 2006 (2006). *See* § 5.7.2.7, *supra.*

Dear Mr. Mezines:

This is in response to the American Collectors Association's ("ACA's") request for two Commission advisory opinions ("Request") regarding the Fair Debt Collection Practices Act ("FDCPA"), which the association submitted pursuant to Sections 1.1–1.4 of the Commission's Rules of Practice, 16 C.F.R. §§ 1.1–1.4. The two issues will be addressed in the order in which they were presented.

FIRST ISSUE:

Does Section 809(b) of the FDCPA permit a collection agency to either demand payment or take legal action during the pendency of the thirty (30) day period for disputing a debt in situations where a debtor has not notified the collection agency that the debt is disputed?

"[The] starting point in every case involving construction of a statute is the language itself." *Southeastern Community College v. Davis*, 442 U.S. 397, 405 (1979) (quoting *Blue Chip Stamps v. Manor Drug Stores*, 421 U.S. 723, 756 (1975) (Powell, J., concurring)). The language of Section 809(b) provides that, "[i]f the consumer notifies the debt collector in writing within the thirty-day period" that the debt is disputed, the debt collector must cease collection of the debt until verification of the debt is obtained and mailed to the consumer.[1] Where Congress intended that debt collectors cease their collection efforts during the thirty-day dispute period, it so specified: if, and only if, a consumer sends the debt collector a notice in writing. Congress did not specify that collectors must cease collection efforts during the dispute period even if consumers send nothing in writing.

The Commission has voiced this opinion in recent annual reports to Congress mandated by the FDCPA. As the Commission stated in the 1999 report, for example, "Nothing within the language of the statute indicates that Congress intended an absolute bar to any appropriate collection activity or legal action within the thirty-day period where the consumer has not disputed the debt." Letter from Chairman Robert Pitofsky to the Honorable Albert Gore, Jr. regarding Twenty-First Annual Report to Congress Pursuant to Section 815(a) of the Fair Debt Collection Practices Act, at 10 (Mar. 19, 1999) ("1999 Annual Report"). Because there appears to be some confusion regarding whether the thirty-day period is a dispute period or a grace period, the Commission has recommended in recent annual reports that Congress clarify the FDCPA by adding a provision expressly permitting appropriate collection activity within the thirty-day period, if the debt collector has not received a letter from the consumer disputing the debt. The Commission emphasized that the clarification should include a

---

1 Section 809(b), 15 U.S.C. § 1692g(b), provides:

If the consumer notifies the debt collector in writing within the thirty-day period described in subsection (a) that the debt, or any portion thereof, is disputed, or that the consumer requests the name and address of the original creditor, the debt collector shall cease collection of the debt, or any disputed portion thereof, until the debt collector obtains verification of the debt or any copy of a judgment, or the name and address of the original creditor, and a copy of such verification or judgment, or name and address of the original creditor, is mailed to the consumer by the debt collector.

caveat that the collection activity should not overshadow or be inconsistent with the disclosure of the consumer's right to dispute the debt specified. 1999 Annual Report at 10-11.[2]

Federal circuit courts that have addressed this issue recently have arrived at the same conclusion. In a 1997 opinion, the Seventh Circuit stated that "[t]he debt collector is perfectly free to sue within the thirty days; he just must cease his efforts at collection during the interval between being asked for verification of the debt and mailing the verification to the debtor." *Bartlett v. Heibl*, 128 F.3d 497, 501 (7th Cir. 1997) (Posner, J.). In the most recent federal appellate court pronouncement on the subject, the Sixth Circuit stated, "A debt collector does not have to stop its collection efforts [during the thirty-day period] to comply with the Act. Instead, it must ensure that its efforts do not threaten a consumer's right to dispute the validity of his debt." *Smith v. Computer Credit*, Inc., 167 F.3d 1052, 1054 (6th Cir. 1999).

The Commission continues to believe that the thirty-day time frame set forth in Section 809 is a *dispute* period within which the consumer may insist that the collector verify the debt, and not a *grace* period within which collection efforts are prohibited. In response to the ACA's question, therefore, the Commission opines that Section 809(b) does permit a collection agency to either demand payment or take legal action during the thirty-day period for disputing a debt when a consumer from whom the collection agency is attempting to collect a debt has not notified the collection agency that the debt is disputed. The collection agency must ensure, however, that its collection activity does not overshadow and is not inconsistent with the disclosure of the consumer's right to dispute the debt specified by Section 809(a).

SECOND ISSUE:

Where an attorney debt collector institutes legal proceedings against a debtor but has no prior communications with the debtor, are the requirements for the validation of debts set forth in Section 809 of the FDCPA supreme to state law or state court rules that otherwise prohibit the inclusion of the validation notice on court documents?

In responding to this issue, the Commission notes first that Section 809(a) of the FDCPA, 15 U.S.C. § 1692g(a), provides:

> (a) Within five days after the initial communication with a consumer in connection with the collection

of any debt, a debt collector shall, unless the following information is contained in the initial communication or the consumer has paid the debt, send the consumer a written notice containing—

> (1) the amount of the debt;
>
> (2) the name of the creditor to whom the debt is owed;
>
> (3) a statement that unless the consumer, within thirty days after receipt of the notice, disputes the validity of the debt, or any portion thereof, the debt will be assumed to be valid by the debt collector;
>
> (4) a statement that if the consumer notifies the debt collector in writing within the thirty-day period that the debt, or any portion thereof, is disputed, the debt collector will obtain verification of the debt or a copy of a judgment against the consumer and a copy of such verification or judgment will be mailed to the consumer by the debt collector; and
>
> (5) a statement that, upon the consumer's written request within the thirty-day period, the debt collector will provide the consumer with the name and address of the original creditor, if different from the current creditor.

Section 803(2) of the FDCPA, 15 U.S.C. § 1692a(2), defines the term "communication" as "the conveying of information regarding a debt directly or indirectly to any person through any medium." In its Staff Commentary, Commission staff stated that the term "communication" "does not include formal legal action (e.g., filing of a lawsuit or other petition/pleadings with a court; service of a complaint or other legal papers in connection with a lawsuit, or activities directly related to such service)." 53 Fed. Reg. at 50101, comment 803(2)-2. Similarly, in the introductory portion of the Staff Commentary, Commission staff opined that "[a]ttorneys or law firms that engage in traditional debt collection activities (sending dunning letters, making collection calls to consumers) are covered by the FDCPA, but those whose practice is limited to legal activities are not covered."[3] *Id.* at 50,100.

Seven years after the Staff Commentary was issued, the United States Supreme Court held that the FDCPA's definition of "debt collector," Section 803(6), 15 U.S.C. § 1692a(6), "applies to attorneys who 'regularly' engage in consumer-debt-collection activity, even when that activity consists of litigation." *Heintz v. Jenkins*, 514 U.S. 291, 299 (1995). In arriving at this conclusion, the Court explicitly considered and rejected Commission staff's introductory remark regarding the coverage of litigation attorneys. *Id.* at 298. In light of *Heintz*, the Commission concludes that, if an attorney debt collector serves on a consumer a court document "conveying information regarding a debt," that court document is a "communication" for purposes of the FDCPA.[4]

---

2   In the Staff Commentary on the Fair Debt Collection Practices Act, 53 Fed. Reg. 50097 (1988) ("Staff Commentary"), and staff opinion letters, Commission staff have consistently read Section 809(b) to permit a debt collector to continue to make demands for payment or take legal action within the thirty-day period. See 53 Fed. Reg. at 50,109, comment 809(b)-1 ("A debt collector need not cease normal collection activities within the consumer's 30-day period to give notice of a dispute until he receives a notice from the consumer."); letter from John F. LeFevre, FDCPA Program Advisor, to S. Joshua Berger (May 29, 1997):

> We interpret the "thirty-day period" as a period within which consumers must dispute their debts in writing in order to avail themselves of their Section 809(b) rights, but not as a "grace" period. Thus, we believe that there is nothing in the Act that prevents you from filing suit during this period, so long as you do not make any representations that contradict Section 809(b).

---

3   The introductory remarks were not part of the Commentary itself. The statement in the Commentary that the quoted remark referred to provided that the term "debt collector" does not include "[a]n attorney whose practice is limited to legal activities (e.g., the filing and prosecution of lawsuits to reduce debts to judgment)." 53 Fed. Reg. at 50,102, comment 803(6)-2.

4   In an opinion letter issued after the *Heintz* decision, Commission staff opined that "all pleadings must be considered 'com-

If an attorney debt collector has had no prior communications with a consumer before serving a summons or other court document on the consumer, that document would constitute the "initial communication" with the consumer if it conveys information regarding a debt. The attorney would therefore have to include the written notice mandated by Section 809(a) (often referred to as the "validation notice") in the court document itself or send it to the consumer "within five days after the initial communication."

According to the ACA's Request, some "state laws or state court rules prohibit the inclusion of additional language such as the validation notice on documents filed with courts." Request at 9. The association asks whether the requirements of Section 809(a) are "supreme to," and thus preempt, these state laws or state court rules. *Id.* Preemption cases generally proceed from "the starting presumption that Congress does not intend to supplant state laws." *New York State Conference of Blue Cross & Blue Shield Plans v. Travelers Ins. Co.*, 514 U.S. 645, 654 (1995).[5] According to the Court in *English v. General Electric Co.*, 496 U.S. 72 (1990):

> [S]tate law is pre-empted under the Supremacy Clause, U.S. Const. Art. VI, cl. 2, in three circumstances. First, Congress can define explicitly the extent to which its enactments pre-empt state law. Pre-emption fundamentally is a question of congressional intent, and when Congress has made its intent known through explicit statutory language, the courts' task is an easy one.
>
> Second, in the absence of explicit statutory language, state law is pre-empted where it regulates conduct in a field that Congress intended the Federal Government to occupy exclusively. Such an intent may be inferred from a "scheme of federal regulation ... so pervasive as to make reasonable the inference that Congress left no room for the States to supplement it," or where an Act of Congress "touch[es] a field in which the federal interest is so dominant that the federal system will be assumed to preclude enforcement of state laws on the same subject." ....
>
> Finally, state law is pre-empted to the extent that it actually conflicts with federal law. Thus, the Court has found pre-emption where it is impossible for a private party to comply with both state and federal requirements, or where state law "stands as an obstacle to the accomplishment and

execution of the full purposes and objectives of Congress."

Id. at 78–79 (omission in internal quotation in original) (citations omitted).

The preemption provision of the FDCPA, Section 816, 15 U.S.C. § 1692n, provides:

> This title does not annul, alter, or affect, or exempt any person subject to the provisions of this title from complying with the laws of any State with respect to debt collection practices, except to the extent that those laws are inconsistent with any provision of this title, and then only to the extent of the inconsistency. For purposes of this section, a State law is not inconsistent with this title if the protection such law affords any consumer is greater than the protection provided by this title.

The Commission does not believe that this section expressly preempts state laws and court rules that prohibit attorney debt collectors from including validation notices in court documents. The quoted provision makes express that Congress did not intend to preempt the field, but allowed only for conflict preemption. However, there is no conflict preemption here.

First, there is no conflict preemption based on impossibility of compliance because it is possible for attorney debt collectors to comply with both the federal provision and the state provisions.[6] Instead of including such notices in court documents, attorney debt collectors in jurisdictions that prohibit validation notices in court documents may deliver the notices to consumers via some other medium—either before serving the court document on the consumer or, if the court document is truly the first communication with the consumer, within five days of serving the court document.[7]

Second, there is no conflict preemption based on state law standing as an obstacle to the full accomplishment and execution of Congressional purposes and objectives. As Congress declared in

---

munications' if they convey 'information regarding a debt directly or indirectly to any person through any medium.' " Letter from John F. LeFevre, FDCPA Program Advisor, to S. Joshua Berger (May 29, 1997). See also Mendus v. Morgan & Associates, 1999 Okla. Civ. App. LEXIS 140, at *19 (Okla. Civ. App. 1999) ("[A] pleading or a summons is a 'communication' under the [FDCPA].").

5 This presumption does not apply to all cases. In particular, the Supreme Court recently held that it does not apply to state laws bearing upon national and international maritime commerce. *United States v. Locke*, 120 S. Ct. 1135, 1148 (2000). *Locke* was apparently based on the relatively large traditional federal role in this area and the relatively small traditional state role, see *id.* at 1147–48, and does not affect the current analysis.

6 *See Codar, Inc. v. Arizona*, No. 94-16902, 1996 U.S. App. LEXIS 21536, at *14–15 (9th Cir. Aug. 19, 1996) (memorandum) (Arizona laws requiring debt collectors to be licensed in the state before they may contact consumers preempted by Section 816 to the extent they prevent unlicenced out-of-state collector from providing Section 809(a) validation notices to Arizona residents who contact such debt collectors to discuss alleged debts; preemption because unlicenced out-of-state collectors that send validation notice would violate state law).

7 The Request refers to a Commission staff opinion letter which advised that, "[u]nder the principles that the Supreme Court set out in *Heintz v. Jenkins*, law firms that are 'debt collectors' presumably must include Section 809 notices in connection with every summons, if the summons is the first communication with the consumer in connection with the collection of a debt." Letter from Thomas E. Kane to Gordon N.J. Kroft (Mar. 8, 1996). While the letter was not binding on the Commission, it does accurately interpret the statute. An attorney debt collector must provide the validation notice "in connection with every summons," if the summons is the first communication with the consumer in connection with the debt. As the Commission notes here, however, the validation notice need not be included in the summons itself. It may be delivered either before or within five days after the summons is served on the consumer.

Section 802(e) of the FDCPA, 15 U.S.C. § 1692(e), the purpose of the panoply of protections under the federal debt collection statute is:

> to eliminate abusive debt collection practices by debt collectors, to insure that those debt collectors who refrain from using abusive debt collection practices are not competitively disadvantaged, and to promote consistent State action to protect consumers against debt collection abuses.

The state provisions about which you inquire do not prevent consumers from receiving the full panoply of protections from abusive debt collection practices afforded by the FDCPA. The only FDCPA provision that could be affected by these state laws and court rules is Section 809(a). As noted above, an attorney debt collector who is prohibited from including the validation notice in court documents may deliver the notice to consumers before serving the consumer with the court document or, if the court document is the first communication with the consumer, within five days after serving the court document. Thus, even in a jurisdiction that prohibits validation notices in court documents, a consumer will receive the validation notice and learn, for example, that the debt collector must provide the consumer with written verification of the debt if the consumer disputes the debt within thirty days. State legislation that prohibits validation notices in court documents also does not stand as an obstacle to the promotion of "consistent State action to protect consumers against debt collection abuses." Consumers will receive their validation notices in jurisdictions that prohibit validation notices in court documents as well as in jurisdictions that permit the practice.

After reviewing state laws and court rules that prohibit validation notices in court documents under a preemption analysis, the Commission concludes that such state legislation is not preempted by the FDCPA.

By direction of the Commission.
Donald S. Clark
Secretary

B.2 FTC Informal Staff Letters

Appendix B.2 contains the text of FTC informal staff letters since 1999 which discuss provisions of the FDCPA. Section 3.3.6, *supra*, discusses and Appendix C, *infra*, reprints the FTC Staff Commentary which the FTC issued December 13, 1988 to supersede many of the prior staff letters contained in this Appendix. Readers should compare the FTC Staff Commentary with any prior letters for conflicts. The text of these FTC informal staff letters and also all letters issued prior to 1999 are included on the companion website to this treatise. The letters are cited in the text of the book where relevant and discussed where appropriate.

The FTC informal staff letters are arranged *chronologically* in this appendix and on the companion website. Letters written on the same date are arranged alphabetically by name of the recipient of the letter. The letters are written in response to inquiries about the FDCPA from creditors, collection agencies and consumers. The volume of FTC informal staff letters declined after the first letters were issued in 1977 and then increased briefly in 1986 and 1987. None have been published since 2002.

Section 3.3.5, *supra* discusses the authority and precedential value of FTC informal staff letters. Some FTC letters reprinted in this appendix are in conflict with court decisions. Some have been overruled by the Supreme Court. Such conflicts are discussed only in the text of this book, not in this Appendix.

An FDCPA sectional index precedes the text of the letters in this Appendix. The index lists the letters under the sections of the FDCPA to which they relate.

Selected FTC Informal Staff Letters are now available on the FTC website: www.ftc.gov/os/statutes/fdcpa/letters.htm.

FDCPA SECTIONAL INDEX TO FTC INFORMAL LETTERS

FDCPA Section	15 U.S.C. Section	Section Topic	Relevant Informal Staff Letter Addressee
802	1692	FINDINGS AND PURPOSE	Marritz (Nov. 6, 1978)
803	1692a	DEFINITIONS	
803(2)	1692a(2)	"Communication"	Gibson (July 13, 1994)
			LaScuola (May 17, 1994)
			Jones (Dec. 30, 1992)
			Novak (Oct. 8, 1992)
			Bennett (July 8, 1991)
			Cranmer (Apr. 25, 1989)

FDCPA Section	15 U.S.C. Section	Section Topic	Relevant Informal Staff Letter Addressee
			Brown (Feb. 14, 1989)
			Kwait (Jan. 24, 1989)
			Weil (Nov. 28, 1988)
			Freeman (Nov. 15, 1988)
			Goldfarb (Nov. 23, 1988)
			Korschun (Oct. 4, 1988)
			Fields (June 28, 1988)
			Nants (Apr. 12, 1988)
			Fentress (July 1, 1987)
			Kinnear (May 19, 1987)
			Corso (Apr. 16, 1987)
			Dunn (Apr. 16, 1987)
			Shuman (Feb. 19, 1987)
			Cantu (Feb. 12, 1987)
			Peters (Feb. 6, 1987)
			Broadway (Jan. 21, 1987)
			Udell (Jan. 20, 1987)
			Goldfarb (Jan. 16, 1987)
			Polito (Jan. 8, 1987)
			Gold (Jan. 5, 1987)
			Anderson (Jan. 5, 1987)
			McPhee (Nov. 17, 1986)
			Pressler (Sept. 12, 1986)
			Nierengarten (Aug. 16, 1986)
			Cope (May 1, 1986)
			Furh (Jan. 9, 1986)
			Cathcart (Feb. 9, 1981)
			Rozga (Sept. 5, 1978)
			Fletcher (Feb. 21, 1978)
			Atteberry (Dec. 30, 1977)
803(3)	1692a(3)	"Consumer"	Goff (Dec. 13, 1993)
			Durham (Aug. 2, 1984)
			Fishman (Dec. 23, 1983)
			Mansfield (Apr. 20, 1978)
			Bachrach (Nov. 16, 1977)
803(4)	1692a(4)	"Creditor"	Fedele (Aug. 30, 1996)
			Pratt (Sept. 16, 1993)
			Zepkin (Sept. 16, 1993)
			Goeringer (Sept. 15, 1993)
			Farmer (Sept. 26, 1989)
			Atteberry (Dec. 30, 1977)
803(5)	1692a(5)	"Debt"	Chesworth (Sept. 16, 1997)
			Cutter (Dec. 13, 1996)
			Green (Sept. 17, 1996)
			Dempsey (Sept. 13, 1996)
			Samuels (June 26, 1995)
			Evans (Aug. 12, 1993)
			Palmer (Aug. 27, 1992)
			Dunn (Aug. 17, 1992)
			Jones (Dec. 9, 1991)
			Philbin (May 24, 1991)
			Paskowitz (July 18, 1990)
			Nants (March 1, 1989)
			Hall (Apr. 11, 1988)

FDCPA Section	15 U.S.C. Section	Section Topic	Relevant Informal Staff Letter Addressee
			Cane (Feb. 12, 1988)
			Levin (Dec. 28, 1987)
			Green (Sept. 21, 1987)
			Wagner (June 29, 1987)
			Hutchinson (June 22, 1987)
			Solomon (June 5, 1987)
			Harwood (June 5, 1987)
			Bath (May 28, 1987)
			Sebok (May 22, 1987)
			Fosbinder (Nov. 16, 1983)
			Marritz (Nov. 6, 1978)
			Bell (May 10, 1978)
			Milhollin (Apr. 19, 1978)
			Stokes (Jan. 30, 1978)
			Baehr (Jan. 3, 1978)
			Cunningham (Jan. 3, 1978)
803(6)	1692a(6)	"Debt Collector"	de Mayo (May 23, 2002) (*Revised*)
			de Mayo (May 1, 2000)
			LeVine (Mar. 20, 1998)
			Stanley (Sept. 13, 1996)
			Fortney (Sept. 13, 1996)
			Bergstrom (Nov. 17, 1995)
			Goodacre (Nov. 6, 1995)
			Arbuckle (Dec. 22, 1993)
			Zepkin (Sept. 16, 1993)
			Goeringer (Sept. 15, 1993)
			Cardonick (May 17, 1993)
			Isgrigg (Dec. 22, 1992)
			Weinberg (Dec. 16, 1992)
			Wytychak (Dec. 16, 1992)
			Zager (Nov. 10, 1992)
			Isgrigg (Nov. 10, 1992)
			Valentine (Nov. 6, 1992)
			Novak (Oct. 8, 1992)
			Masters (Sept. 10, 1992)
			Valentine (Sept. 3, 1992)
			LoPresti (May 4, 1992)
			Jones (Dec. 9, 1991)
			Whitehead (July 19, 1991)
			Bennett (July 8, 1991)
			Fisher (Apr. 30, 1991)
			Cline (Feb. 7, 1991)
			Cline (Feb. 7, 1991)
			Gibson (Feb. 21, 1990)
			Farmer (Sept. 26, 1989)
			Heninburg (July 13, 1989)
			Keever (May 19, 1989)
			Cranmer (Apr. 25, 1989)
			Brown (Feb. 14, 1989)
			Klayman (Nov. 22, 1988)
			Korschun (Oct. 4, 1988)
			Trubek (Sept. 12, 1988)
			Beekman (June 28, 1988)
			Fields (June 28, 1988)

FDCPA Section	15 U.S.C. Section	Section Topic	Relevant Informal Staff Letter Addressee
			Kaufman (June 13, 1988)
			Nants (Apr. 12, 1988)
			Garrison (Apr. 6, 1988)
			Barker (Oct. 22, 1987)
			Knobel (Oct. 5, 1987)
			Nirengarten (Aug. 26, 1987)
			McKneelen (Aug. 4, 1987)
			Fentress (July 1, 1987)
			Hutchinson (June 22, 1987)
			Harwood (June 5, 1987)
			Solomon (June 5, 1987)
			Beal (May 22, 1987)
			Kaplan (May 19, 1987)
			Graham (May 8, 1987)
			Corso (Apr. 16, 1987)
			Garvett (Mar. 10, 1987)
			Shuman (Feb. 19, 1987)
			Cantu (Feb. 12, 1987)
			Broadway (Jan. 21, 1987)
			Dreyfus (Jan. 20, 1987)
			Goldfarb (Jan. 16, 1987)
			Barstow (Jan 9, 1987)
			Jones (Jan. 8, 1987)
			Polito (Jan. 8, 1987)
			Miller (Dec. 10, 1986)
			Sutton (Oct. 23, 1986)
			Raff (Sept. 11, 1986)
			Barker (Aug. 6, 1986)
			Gold (May 7, 1986)
			Jolly (Jan. 17, 1986)
			Rackett (Nov. 15, 1985)
			Butler (Oct. 22, 1984)
			Scalambrino (Oct. 22, 1984)
			Mezines (Nov. 15, 1983)
			Roach (Nov. 8, 1983)
			Fishman (Dec. 23, 1982)
			Cathcart (Aug. 6, 1981)
			Vandenbroek (Apr. 20, 1981)
			Whitlock (Feb. 19, 1981)
			Robinson (Jan. 5, 1981)
			Buchanan (Apr. 21, 1980)
			McDonald (Apr. 10, 1980)
			Skrupa (Apr. 9, 1980)
			Rubin (June 15, 1979)
			Dean (May 30, 1979)
			Smith (May 29, 1979)
			Cotogno (Mar. 8, 1979)
			Gallo (Feb. 15, 1979)
			Markowitz (Nov. 17, 1978)
			Kelley (Oct. 16, 1978)
			Ireland (Sept. 21, 1978)
			Foote (Sept. 11, 1978)
			Kingston (July 5, 1978)
			Richardson (June 14, 1978)

FDCPA Section	15 U.S.C. Section	Section Topic	Relevant Informal Staff Letter Addressee
			Palcanis (June 13, 1978)
			Ward (May 30, 1978)
			Coupel (May 15, 1978)
			Palcanis (May 15, 1978)
			Wickersham (May 15, 1978)
			Cotner (May 11, 1978)
			Aycock (Apr. 13, 1978)
			Palcanis (Apr. 13, 1978)
			Huebner (Mar. 27, 1978)
			Evans (Mar. 7, 1978)
			Master (Feb. 21, 1978)
			Hirsch (Feb. 7, 1978)
			Turner (Jan. 18, 1978)
			Gevigny (Dec. 13, 1977)
			Universal Fin. Co. (Dec. 2, 1977)
			House (Nov. 22, 1977)
			Bachrach (Nov. 16, 1977)
803(6)(A)	1692a(6)(A)	Creditor exemption	Shapiro (Oct. 1, 1997)
			Zepkin (Sept. 16, 1993)
			Goeringer (Sept. 15, 1993)
			Whitehead (July 19, 1991)
			Cardonick (May 17, 1993)
			Loeb (Mar. 12, 1991)
			Cranmer (Apr. 25, 1989)
			Trubek (Sept. 12, 1988)
			Michael (Aug. 15, 1988)
			Beekman (June 28, 1988)
			Knobel (Oct. 5, 1987)
			Green (Sept. 21, 1987)
			Kaplan (May 19, 1987)
			Cantu (Feb. 12, 1987)
			Barker (Aug. 6, 1986)
			Schwam (Oct. 20, 1986)
			Mundell (Mar. 8, 1985)
			Speziali (Sept. 24, 1981)
			Vandenbroek (Apr. 20, 1981)
			LaBran (Oct. 9, 1980)
			Warwood (Oct. 2, 1980)
			Palcanis (Apr. 13, 1978)
			Chromek (Feb. 17, 1978)
803(6)(B)	1962a(6)(B)	Affiliate's exemption	Feldman (Mar. 23, 1994)
			Valentine (Sept. 3, 1992)
			Fisher (Apr. 30, 1991)
			Kaufman (June 18, 1988)
			Kaminski (Sept. 19, 1985)
			Scalambrino (Oct. 22, 1984)
			Roach (Nov. 8, 1983)
			Tanenbaum (Dec. 20, 1980)
			Janes (Dec. 11, 1978)
			Altenberger (Sept. 6, 1978)
			Kingston (July 5, 1978)
803(6)(C)	1692a(6)(C)	Government agency exemption	Mezines (May 17, 1994)
			Williamson (July 15, 1993)
			Silko (Oct. 31, 1985)

FDCPA Section	15 U.S.C. Section	Section Topic	Relevant Informal Staff Letter Addressee
			Silko (Feb. 21, 1985)
			Marritz (Nov. 6, 1978)
			Oleson (Apr. 20, 1978)
			Ridgway (Mar. 27, 1978)
803(6)(D)	1692a(6)(D)	Process server exemption	Simpson (May 30, 1978)
803(6)(E)	1692a(6)(E)	Credit counselor exemption	Hutchinson (June 22, 1987)
			Hirsch (Feb. 7, 1978)
		Repealed attorney exemption[1]	Cathcart (Aug. 6, 1981)
			Kopelson (May 14, 1981)
			Robinson (Jan. 5, 1981)
			Cathcart (Dec. 10, 1980)
			Korn (Sept. 15, 1980)
			Jones (Aug. 14, 1980)
			Fonseca (June 18, 1980)
			Goldberg (Apr. 28, 1980)
			Abelman (Apr. 10, 1980)
			Smith (May 29, 1979)
			Ireland (Sept. 21, 1978)
			Milhollin (Apr. 19, 1978)
			Berins (Jan. 12, 1978)
803(6)(F)	1692a(6)(F)	Collecting for another exemption	Farmer (Aug. 30, 1996)
			Kaufman (June 18, 1988)
			Barker (Oct. 22, 1987)
			Gallo (Feb. 15, 1979)
			Palcanis (June 13, 1978)
803(6)(F)(i)	1692a(6)(F)(i)	Fiduciary and escrow exemption	Bell (Mar. 13, 1987)
803(6)(F)(ii)	1692a(6)(F)(ii)	Debt originator exemption	Janes (Dec. 11, 1978)
			Palcanis (May 15, 1978)
			Wickersham (May 15, 1978)
			Palcanis (Apr. 13, 1978)
803(6)(F)(iii)	1692a(6)(F)(iii)	Debt purchaser exemption	Shapiro (Dec. 20, 1999)
			Shapiro (Oct. 1, 1997)
			Fortney (Sept. 13, 1996)
			Cardonick (May 17, 1993)
			Torkildson (Nov. 9, 1992)
			Sheehan (Aug. 31, 1992)
			Cranmer (Apr. 25, 1989)
			Korschun (Oct. 4, 1988)
			Trubek (Sept. 12, 1988)
			Barker (Oct. 22, 1987)
			Silver (July 13, 1987)
			Hutchinson (June 22, 1987)
			Gold (May 7, 1986)
			Saylor (May 7, 1986)
			Silko (Feb. 21, 1985)
			Butler (Oct. 22, 1984)
			Tanenbaum (July 23, 1980)
			Tanenbaum (May 20, 1980)
			Cotogno (Mar. 8, 1979)
			Cotogno (July 28, 1978)
			Richardson (June 14, 1978)
			Palcanis (June 13, 1978)
			Palcanis (May 15, 1978)

FDCPA Section	15 U.S.C. Section	Section Topic	Relevant Informal Staff Letter Addressee
			Palcanis (Apr. 13, 1978)
			Hackney (Jan. 25, 1978)
803(7)	1692a(7)	"Location information"	Atteberry (Feb. 22, 1990)
			Kwait (Jan. 24, 1989)
			Durham (Aug. 8, 1984)
			Cinalli (Apr. 19, 1978)
			Cinalli (Feb. 17, 1978)
804	1692b	ACQUIRING LOCATION INFORMATION	Charest (Sept. 13, 1996)
			Kwait (Jan. 24, 1989)
			Goldfarb (Nov. 23, 1988)
			Cope (May 1, 1986)
			Durham (Aug. 8, 1984)
			Fierst (Nov. 19, 1979)
			Cathcart (July 27, 1979)
			Shnaider (Sept. 21, 1978)
			Rozga (Sept. 5, 1978)
			Kennedy (July 10, 1978)
			Faulkner (June 15, 1978)
			Dean (May 30, 1978)
			Evenchick (May 30, 1978)
			Mansfield (Apr. 20, 1978)
			Coury (Mar. 7, 1978)
			Atteberry (Dec. 30, 1977)
804(1)	1692b(1)	Revealing locator's identity	Sheldon (Oct. 1, 1980)
			Shnaider (Sept. 21, 1978)
			Kennedy (July 10, 1978)
			Evenchick (May 30, 1978)
			Cinalli (Feb. 17, 1978)
804(2)	1692b(2)	No disclosure of debt	Sitzer (May 21, 1987)
			Sweigart (Apr. 25, 1978)
804(3)	1692b(3)	Repeated contacts	Sweigart (Apr. 25, 1978)
			Atteberry (Dec. 30, 1977)
804(4)	1692b(4)	No postcards	Stockham (May 15, 1986)
			Rozga (Sept. 5, 1978)
804(5)	1692b(5)	Envelope language	Cranston (Jan. 2, 1979)
			Shnaider (Sept. 21, 1978)
			Eskanos (July 19, 1978)
			Kennedy (July 10, 1978)
			Shatsky (June 19, 1978)
			Evenchick (May 30, 1978)
			Fletcher (Feb. 21, 1978)
			Shnaider (Feb. 14, 1978)
804(6)	1692b(6)	Represented consumer	Stockham (May 15, 1986)
			Evenchick (May 30, 1978)
805	1692c	COMMUNICATION IN CONNECTION WITH DEBT COLLECTION	Freeman (Nov. 13, 1988)
			Rozga (Sept. 5, 1978)
			Atteberry (July 18, 1978)
			Taylor (May 3, 1978)
			Mansfield (Apr. 20, 1978)
			Atteberry (Jan. 18, 1978)
			Atteberry (Dec. 30, 1977)
805(a)	1692c(a)	Communication with the consumer generally	Kwait (Jan. 24, 1989)
805(a)(1)	1692c(a)(1)	Times and places of collection	Halliday (Feb. 25, 1986)

FDCPA Section	15 U.S.C. Section	Section Topic	Relevant Informal Staff Letter Addressee
			Mezines (May 22, 1980)
			Rozga (Sept. 5, 1978)
			Atteberry (July 18, 1978)
			Coupel (May 15, 1978)
			Atteberry (Dec. 30, 1977)
			Hamilton (Oct. 18, 1977)
805(a)(2)	1692c(a)(2)	Communication with represented consumer	Edwards (Feb. 7, 1991)
			Hollcraft (May 10, 1988)
			McKneelen (Aug. 4, 1987)
			Stockham (May 15, 1986)
			Zubalsky (Jan. 8, 1980)
			Herold (Aug. 14, 1979)
			Atteberry (July 18, 1978)
805(a)(3)	1692c(a)(3)	Communication at consumer's job	Atteberry (July 18, 1978)
805(b)	1692c(b)	Communications with third parties	Jones (Dec. 30, 1992)
			Borowski (Nov. 6, 1992)
			Zbrzeznj (Sept. 21, 1992)
			Fisher (Aug. 19, 1992)
			Atteberry (Feb. 22, 1990)
			Mezines (Nov. 13, 1989)
			Kwait (Jan. 24, 1989)
			Fields (June 28, 1988)
			Bath (May 28, 1987)
			Graham (May 8, 1987)
			Sitzer (Apr. 21, 1987)
			Bagwell (Mar. 9, 1987)
			Dreyfus (Jan. 20, 1987)
			Goldfarb (Jan. 16, 1987)
			Polito (Jan. 8, 1987)
			Bagwell (Jan 6, 1987)
			Anderson (Jan 5, 1987)
			Gold (Jan. 5, 1987)
			Rosenberg (Jan. 29, 1986)
			Weiss (Apr. 17, 1986)
			Cope (May 1, 1986)
			Clement (Nov. 12, 1985)
			Ogden (May 15, 1981)
			Cathcart (Feb. 9, 1981)
			Cathcart (Dec. 10, 1980)
			Miller (July 7, 1980)
			Cathcart (July 27, 1979)
			McGrath (July 12, 1979)
			Borneman (Apr. 3, 1979)
			Rozga (Sept. 5, 1978)
			Atteberry (July 18, 1978)
			Faulkner (June 15, 1978)
			Evenchick (May 30, 1978)
			Rummel (May 16, 1978)
			Taylor (May 3, 1978)
			Mansfield (Apr. 20, 1978)
			Sweigart (Apr. 15, 1978)
			Coury (Mar. 7, 1978)
			Atteberry (Jan. 18, 1978)
			Atteberry (Jan. 18, 1977)

FDCPA Section	15 U.S.C. Section	Section Topic	Relevant Informal Staff Letter Addressee
			Krieger (undated)
805(c)	1692c(c)	Ceasing communication	Mezines (Apr. 10, 1991)
			Kwait (Jan. 24, 1989)
			Goldfarb (Nov. 23, 1988)
			Clement (Nov. 21, 1985)
			Miller (Mar. 31, 1983)
			Atteberry (Dec. 30, 1977)
805(d)	1692c(d)	"Consumer"	Atteberry (Feb. 12, 1990)
			Atteberry (Dec. 30, 1978)
			Atteberry (July 18, 1978)
806	1692d	HARASSMENT OR ABUSE	Weiss (Apr. 17, 1986)
			Kopelson (May 14, 1981)
			Cathcart (Dec. 10, 1980)
			Osterloh (July 13, 1979)
			Guidry (July 2, 1979)
			Miller (May 22, 1979)
			Cook (Dec. 27, 1978)
			Foote (Sept. 11, 1978)
			Rozga (Sept. 5, 1978)
			Faulkner (June 16, 1978)
			Rummel (May 16, 1978)
			Bell (May 10, 1978)
806(1)	1692d(1)	Threat of violence	Kern (Aug. 4, 1984)
			Bell (May 10, 1978)
806(3)	1692d(3)	Publishing lists of consumers	Mezines (May 17, 1994)
			Ronick (June 5, 1991)
			Farmer (Sept. 26, 1989)
			Graham (May 8, 1987)
			Bagwell (Mar. 9, 1987)
			Clement (Nov. 12, 1985)
			Cathcart (Aug. 24, 1981)
			Kopelson (May 14, 1981)
			Dean (May 30, 1978)
			Woosley (May 30, 1978)
			Rummel (May 16, 1978)
			Bell (May 10, 1978)
			Gilbert (Apr. 28, 1978)
			Mansfield (Apr. 20, 1978)
806(4)	1692d(4)	Advertisement of debt for sale	Graham (May 8, 1987)
806(5)	1692d(5)	Repeated phone calls	Atteberry (July 18, 1978)
			Atteberry (Dec. 30, 1977)
806(6)	1692d(6)	Caller's identification	Knobel (Oct. 5, 1987)
			Cathcart (Dec. 10, 1980)
			Miller (May 22, 1979)
			Berhenke (May 21, 1979)
			Atteberry (Dec. 30, 1978)
			Foote (Sept. 11, 1978)
			Faulkner (June 15, 1978)
			Krieger (undated)
807	1692e	FALSE OR MISLEADING REPRESENTATIONS	Johnson (May 22, 1991)
			Nixon (Feb. 6, 1989)
			Anderson (Nov. 18, 1988)
			Michael (Aug. 15, 1988)

FDCPA Section	15 U.S.C. Section	Section Topic	Relevant Informal Staff Letter Addressee
			VerSteegh (Apr. 4, 1988)
			Lipsett (Dec. 1, 1987)
			Glover (June 25, 1986)
			Weiss (Apr. 17, 1986)
			Clement (Nov. 12, 1985)
			Rackett (Nov. 15, 1985)
			Schorr (July 27, 1981)
			Kopelson (May 14, 1981)
			Vandenbroek (Apr. 20, 1981)
			Dempsey (Jan. 21, 1981)
			Skrupa (Oct. 27, 1980)
			Speziali (Sept. 24, 1980)
			Fardell (Aug. 1, 1980)
			Fonseca (June 18, 1980)
			Neely (Apr. 29, 1980)
			Boyle (Jan. 30, 1980)
			Zubalsky (Jan. 8, 1980)
			Barnfreund (Jan. 2, 1980)
			Cathcart (Jan. 2, 1980)
			Geiger (Sept. 4, 1979)
			McGrath (July 12, 1979)
			Osterloh (July 12, 1979)
			Guidry (July 2, 1979)
			McGrodry (May 24, 1979)
			Miller (May 22, 1979)
			Berhenke (May 21, 1979)
			Feldman (Apr. 30, 1979)
			Garnett (Mar. 16, 1979)
			Kingston (July 5, 1978)
			Evenchick (May 30, 1978)
			Levin (May 30, 1978)
			Woosley (May 30, 1978)
			Davidson (May 18, 1978)
			Rummel (May 16, 1978)
			Gilbert (Apr. 28, 1978)
			Mansfield (Apr. 20, 1978)
			Milhollin (Apr. 19, 1978)
			Cinalli (Feb. 17, 1978)
			Anderson (Feb. 13, 1978)
			Britt (Jan. 20, 1978)
			Turner (Jan. 18, 1978)
			Krieger (undated)
807(1)	1692e(1)	Misrepresenting affiliation with government	Chesworth (Sept. 16, 1997)
			Crouch (Sept. 10, 1996)
			Burwell (Aug. 11, 1992)
807(2)(A)	1692e(2)(A)	Misrepresenting legal status of debt	Mezines (May 17, 1994)
			Knepper (Mar. 31, 1989)
			Nixon (Feb. 6, 1989)
			Michael (Sept. 22, 1988)
			Michael (Aug. 15, 1988)
			Clement (Nov. 12, 1985)
			Abelman (Apr. 10, 1980)
807(2)(B)	1692e(2)(B)	Misrepresenting collector's compensation or services	Nixon (Feb. 6, 1989)

FDCPA Section	15 U.S.C. Section	Section Topic	Relevant Informal Staff Letter Addressee
			Michael (Sept. 22, 1988)
			Michael (Aug. 15, 1988)
			Wehrwein (Aug. 7, 1980)
			Boyle (Jan. 30, 1980)
807(3)	1692e(3)	Impersonating attorney	Challed (May 16, 1994)
			Douglass (Nov. 26, 1993)
			Nixon (Feb. 6, 1989)
			Beekman (June 28, 1988)
			Barker (Aug. 6, 1986)
			Krisor (Oct. 5, 1983)
			Wehrwein (Aug. 7, 1980)
			Smith (May 29, 1979)
			Rozga (Sept. 5, 1978)
807(4)	1692e(4)	False threats of attachment, etc.	Harden (Oct. 28, 1991)
			Klayman (Nov. 22, 1988)
			Weinstein (Apr. 14, 1980)
			Davidson (May 18, 1978)
			Rummel (May 16, 1978)
807(5)	1692e(5)	False threats of legal action	Douglass (Nov. 26, 1993)
			Giloley (Aug. 6, 1992)
			Harden (Oct. 28, 1991)
			Schroeder (Apr. 11, 1991)
			Renner (Apr. 11, 1990)
			Nixon (Feb. 6, 1989)
			Anderson (Nov. 18, 1988)
			Michael (Aug. 15, 1988)
			Lipsett (Dec. 1, 1987)
			Glover (June 25, 1986)
			Weiss (Apr. 17, 1986)
			Clement (Nov. 12, 1985)
			Conboy (Oct. 7, 1983)
			Krisor (Oct. 5, 1983)
			DiPippa (Jan. 5, 1981)
			Skrupa (Oct. 27, 1980)
			Wehrwein (Aug. 7, 1980)
			Goldberg (Apr. 28, 1980)
			Anonymous (Apr. 18, 1980)
			Weinstein (Apr. 14, 1980)
			Skrupa (Apr. 9, 1980)
			Boyle (Jan. 30, 1980)
			Jones (Nov. 20, 1979)
			Fierst (Oct. 19, 1979)
			Gene (Sept. 4, 1979)
			Osterloh (July 13, 1979)
			Guidry (July 2, 1979)
			Jaffe (June 14, 1979)
			Evenchick (May 30, 1978)
			Rummel (May 16, 1978)
			Taylor (May 3, 1978)
			Gilbert (Apr. 28, 1978)
			Aycock (Apr. 13, 1978)
			Cinalli (Feb. 17, 1978)
			Britt (Jan. 20, 1978)
807(7)	1692e(7)	False accusations of crime	Michael (Sept. 22, 1988)

FDCPA Section	15 U.S.C. Section	Section Topic	Relevant Informal Staff Letter Addressee
			Michael (Aug. 15, 1988)
			Guidry (July 2, 1979)
			Rummel (May 16, 1978)
807(8)	1692e(8)	False credit reports	Cass (Dec. 23, 1997)
			Herold (Feb. 28, 1983)
			Eckerle (Nov. 16, 1981)
			Mansfield (Apr. 20, 1978)
807(9)	1692e(9)	Misrepresenting affiliation	Douglass (Nov. 26, 1993)
			Rozga (Sept. 5, 1978)
			Aycock (Apr. 13, 1978)
			Hoivik (Jan. 30, 1978)
807(10)	1692e(10)	Deception	LaScuola (May 17, 1994)
			Challed (May 16, 1994)
			Douglass (Nov. 26, 1993)
			Giloley (Aug. 6, 1992)
			LoPresti (May 4, 1992)
			Schroeder (Apr. 11, 1991)
			Rosenberg (Jan. 16, 1991)
			Spinella (Feb. 21, 1990)
			Knepper (Mar. 31, 1989)
			Nixon (Feb. 6, 1989)
			Michael (Sept. 22, 1988)
			Michael (Aug. 15, 1988)
			Raff (Sept. 11, 1986)
			Clement (Nov. 12, 1985)
			Rackett (Nov. 15, 1985)
			Mezines (Nov. 15, 1983)
			Roach (Nov. 8, 1983)
			Krisor (Oct. 5, 1983)
			Serelson (May 6, 1983)
			Skrupa (Oct. 27, 1980)
			Wehrwein (Aug. 7, 1980)
			Goldberg (Apr. 28, 1980)
			Anonymous (Apr. 18, 1980)
			Weinstein (Apr. 14, 1980)
			Abelman (Apr. 10, 1980)
			McDonald (Apr. 10, 1980)
			Skrupa (Apr. 9, 1980)
			Whitlock (Feb. 19, 1980)
			Jones (Nov. 20, 1979)
			Fierst (Nov. 19, 1979)
			Gene (Sept. 4, 1979)
			McGrath (July 12, 1979)
			Guidry (July 2, 1979)
			Jaffe (June 14, 1979)
			Smith (May 29, 1979)
			Miller (May 22, 1979)
			Garnett (Mar. 16, 1979)
			Evenchick (May 30, 1978)
			Ward (May 30, 1978)
			Rummel (May 16, 1978)
			Gilbert (Apr. 28, 1978)
			Mansfield (Apr. 20, 1978)
			Aycock (Apr. 13, 1978)

FDCPA Section	15 U.S.C. Section	Section Topic	Relevant Informal Staff Letter Addressee
			Huebner (Mar. 27, 1978)
			Mangano (Feb. 22, 1978)
			Cinalli (Feb. 17, 1978)
			Britt (Jan. 20, 1978)
			Krieger (undated)
807(11)	1692e(11)	Disclosing collection purpose	Gamache (July 15, 1997)
			Kramer (Nov. 13, 1996)
			Stewart (Jan. 5, 1993)
			Zager (Nov. 10, 1992)
			Harden (Oct. 28, 1991)
			Nixon (Feb. 6, 1989)
			Shibley (Dec. 14, 1988)
			Goldfarb (Nov. 23, 1988)
			Freeman (Nov. 15, 1988)
			Kinnear (May 19, 1987)
			Anderson (Jan. 5, 1987)
			Raff (Sept. 11, 1986)
			Clement (Nov. 12, 1985)
			Rahe (Aug. 6, 1980)
			Cathcart (July 27, 1979)
			McGrath (July 12, 1979)
			Miller (May 22, 1979)
			Coury (Mar. 7, 1978)
			Atteberry (Dec. 30, 1977)
807(13)	1692e(13)	Simulating legal process	Clement (Nov. 12, 1985)
			Conboy (Oct. 7, 1983
			Schorr (July 27, 1981)
			Horger (Apr. 7, 1981)
			DiPippa (Jan. 5, 1981)
			Wehrwein (Aug. 7, 1980)
			King (Nov. 22, 1978)
			Mansfield (Apr. 20, 1978)
			Aycock (Apr. 13, 1978)
			Britt (Jan. 20, 1978)
807(14)	1692e(14)	True business name	Bergstrom (Nov. 17, 1995)
			LaScuola (May 17, 1994)
			Zager (Nov. 10, 1992)
			Knobel (Oct. 5, 1987)
			Sheldon (Oct. 1, 1980)
			Eskanos (July 19, 1978)
			Evenchick (May 30, 1978)
			Ward (May 30, 1978)
			DeCou (Apr. 12, 1978)
			Huebner (Mar. 27, 1978)
807(16)	1692e(16)	Impersonating a credit bureau	Dankowski (Mar. 6, 2000)
			Isgrigg (Dec. 22, 1992)
			Isgrigg (Nov. 10, 1992)
			Fishman (Jan. 26, 1982)
			Rowley (Apr. 1, 1986)
			Noble (Jan. 18, 1980)
			Shatsky (June 19, 1978)
			Mansfield (Apr. 20, 1978)
			DeCou (Apr. 12, 1978)
			Cole (Mar. 28, 1978)

FDCPA Section	15 U.S.C. Section	Section Topic	Relevant Informal Staff Letter Addressee
			Ambrose (Mar. 27, 1978)
			Krieger (undated)
808	1692f	UNFAIR OR UNCONSCIONABLE COLLECTION MEANS	Powell (Nov. 5, 1997)
			Swerin (June 30, 1986)
			Glover (June 23, 1986)
			Schmidt (Apr. 8, 1986)
			Schorr (July 27, 1981)
			Callison (Feb. 27, 1981)
			Florendo (Jan. 23, 1981)
			Skrupa (Aug. 7, 1980)
			Goldberg (Apr. 28, 1980)
			Osterloh (July 13, 1979)
			Jaffe (June 14, 1979)
			Faulkner (Aug. 8, 1978)
			Rummel (May 16, 1978)
			Zeigler (Apr. 25, 1978)
			Mansfield (Apr. 20, 1978)
			Milhollin (Apr. 19, 1978)
			Ellison (Apr. 12, 1978)
			Towry (Mar. 15, 1978)
808(1)	1692f(1)	Illegal charges	Gibson (July 13, 1994)
			Wilson (May 13, 1994)
			Matthews (May 17, 1993)
			Krisor (Aug. 30, 1989)
			Miller (Dec. 30, 1988)
			Michael (Aug. 15, 1988)
			Swerin (June 30, 1986)
			Glover (June 23, 1986)
			Schmidt (Apr. 8, 1986)
			Conboy (Oct. 7, 1983)
			Carter (June 8, 1982)
			Mastin (May 28, 1982)
			Schorr (July 27, 1981)*
			Callison (Feb. 27, 1981)
			Brier (Jan. 5, 1981)*
			Noble (July 10, 1980)
			Fonseca (June 18, 1980)
			Zubalsky (Jan. 8, 1980)
			Osterloh (July 13, 1979)
			Williams (Sept. 5, 1978)
			Faulkner (Aug. 8, 1978)
			Atteberry (July 18, 1978)
			Evenchick (May 30, 1978)*
			Hawkins (May 30, 1978)*
			Levin (May 30, 1978)*
			Rummel (May 16, 1978)
			Mansfield (Apr. 20, 1978)
			Oleson (Apr. 20, 1978)
			Milhollin (Apr. 19, 1978)*
			Ellison (Apr. 12, 1978)*
			Ritchie (Mar. 15, 1978)*
			Towry (Mar. 15, 1978)*
			Atteberry (Dec. 30, 1977)

FDCPA Section	15 U.S.C. Section	Section Topic	Relevant Informal Staff Letter Addressee
			Oleson (Oct. 19, 1977)
808(2)	1692f(2)	Accepting postdated checks	Entringer (Oct. 15, 1992)
808(3)	1692f(3)	Soliciting postdated checks	Milhollin (Apr. 19, 1978)
808(4)	1692f(4)	Depositing postdated checks	Entringer (Oct. 15, 1992)
808(5)	1692f(5)	Collect phone calls	Mezines (Nov. 15, 1983)
			Atteberry (Dec. 30, 1978)
			Atteberry (July 18, 1978)
			Ellison (Apr. 12, 1978)
			House (Nov. 22, 1977)
808(6)	1692f(6)	False repossession threats	Graham (May 8, 1987)
			Corso (Apr. 16, 1987)
			Gallo (Feb. 15, 1979)
			Richardson (June 14, 1978)
			Wickersham (May 15, 1978)
808(7)	1692f(7)	No postcards	Borneman (Apr. 3, 1979)
			Rozga (Sept. 5, 1978)
808(8)	1692f(8)	Envelope language	Harden (Oct. 28, 1991)
			Kassover (June 19, 1986)
			Clement (Nov. 12, 1985)
			Mezines (Nov. 15, 1983)
			Erickson (Jan. 5, 1981)
			Borneman (Apr. 3, 1979)
			Rozga (Sept. 5, 1978)
			Shatsky (June 19, 1978)
			Gilbert (Apr. 28, 1978) ·
			Zeigler (Apr. 25, 1978)
			Mangano (Feb. 22, 1978)
			Fletcher (Feb. 21, 1978)
			Britt (Jan. 20, 1978)
			Mitten (Jan. 11, 1978)
			Douer (Oct. 25, 1977)
			Krieger (undated)
809	1692g	DEBT VALIDATION	Cass (Dec. 23, 1997)
			Berger (May 29, 1997)
			Castle (June 13, 1995)
			Pavelka (May 18, 1994)
			Isgrigg (Dec. 22, 1992)
			Weinberg (Dec. 16, 1992)
			Novak (Oct. 8, 1992)
			Brown (Feb. 14, 1989)
			Shibley (Dec. 14, 1988)
			Weil (Nov. 28, 1988)
			Goldfarb (Nov. 23, 1988)
			Freeman (Nov. 15, 1988)
			Nants (Apr. 12, 1988)
			Nirengarten (Aug. 26, 1987)
			Wagner (June 29, 1987)
			Kinnear (May 19, 1987)
			Dunn (Apr. 16, 1987)
			Cantu (Feb. 12, 1987)
			Peters (Feb. 6, 1987)
			Barstow (Jan. 9, 1987)
			Polito (Jan. 8, 1987)
			Anderson (Jan. 5, 1987)

FDCPA Section	15 U.S.C. Section	Section Topic	Relevant Informal Staff Letter Addressee
			Luby (Dec. 5, 1986)
			McPhee (Nov. 17, 1986)
			Levin (Nov. 12, 1986)
			Clement (Nov. 12, 1985)
			Serelson (May 6, 1983)
			Herold (Feb. 28, 1983)
			Kodner (Mar. 3, 1979)
			Richardson (June 14, 1978)
			Dean (May 30, 1978)
			Vernick (May 24, 1978)
			Rummel (May 16, 1978)
			Gilbert (Apr. 28, 1978)
			Milhollin (Apr. 19, 1978)
			Cinalli (Feb. 17, 1978)
			Anderson (Feb. 13, 1978)
			Hackney (Jan. 25, 1978)
809(a)	1692g(a)	Validation rights notice	Berger (May 29, 1997)
			Kroft (Mar. 8, 1996)
			Pavelka (May 18, 1994)
			Miller (May 13, 1994)
			Halverson (Nov. 15, 1993)
			Stewart (Jan. 5, 1993)
			Weinberg (Dec. 16, 1992)
			Zager (Nov. 10, 1992)
			Harden (Oct. 28, 1991)
			Rosenberg (Jan. 16, 1991)
			Lynn (July 22, 1988)
			Leiter (March 7, 1988)
			Xiao-Lin (Aug. 3, 1987)
			Beal (May 22, 1987)
			Dunn (Apr. 16, 1987)
			Cantu (Feb. 12, 1987)
			Peters (Feb. 6, 1987)
			Broadway (Jan. 21, 1987)
			Goldfarb (Jan. 16, 1987)
			Barstow (Jan. 9, 1987)
			Fuhr (Jan. 9, 1987)
			Polito (Jan. 8, 1987)
			Anderson (Jan. 5, 1987)
			Gold (Jan. 5, 1987)
			Luby (Dec. 5, 1986)
			McPhee (Nov. 17, 1986)
			Levin (Nov. 12, 1986)
			Sutton (Oct. 23, 1986)
			Raff (Sept. 11, 1986)
			Pressler (Sept. 12, 1986)
			Glover (June 23, 1986)
			Stockham (May 15, 1986)
			Fuhr (Jan. 9, 1986)
			Weiss (Apr. 17, 1986)
			Clement (Nov. 12, 1985)
			Kaminski (Sept. 19, 1985)
			Cathcart (Aug. 6, 1981)
			Dempsey (Jan. 21, 1981)

FDCPA Section	15 U.S.C. Section	Section Topic	Relevant Informal Staff Letter Addressee
			Connelly (Dec. 10, 1980)
			Rahe (Aug. 6, 1980)
			Boyle (Jan. 30, 1980)
			Samuels (Nov. 1, 1979)
			Osterloh (July 13, 1979)
			Brown (May 15, 1979)
			Kodner (Mar. 7, 1979)
			Osborne (Mar. 1, 1979)
			Smoyer (Feb. 6, 1979)
			Cook (Dec. 27, 1978)
			Kelley (Oct. 16, 1978)
			Evenchick (May 30, 1978)
			Woosley (May 30, 1978)
			Brown (May 15, 1978)
			Shnaider (Feb. 21, 1978)
			Miller (Feb. 14, 1978)
			Crawford (Jan. 24, 1978)
			Miller (Jan. 30, 1978)
			Stieger (Jan. 6, 1978)
			Cope (Dec. 23, 1977)
809(b)	1692g(b)	Validating the debt	Cass (Dec. 23, 1997)
			Berger (May 29, 1997)
			Bergstrom (Nov. 7, 1995)
			Wollman (Mar. 10, 1993)
			Krisor (Mar. 3, 1992)
			Xiao-Lin (Aug. 3, 1987)
			Cantu (Feb. 12, 1987)
			Bingham (Jan. 12, 1987)
			Polito (Jan. 8, 1987)
			Kent (Dec. 10, 1986)
			Glover (June 23, 1986)
			Stockham (May 15, 1986)
			Kaminski (Sept. 19, 1985)
			Fardell (Aug. 1, 1980)
			McGrath (July 12, 1979)
			Berhenke (May 21, 1979)
			Brown (May 15, 1979)
			Smoyer (Feb. 6, 1979)
809(c)	1692g(c)	Presumption of validity	Neely (Apr. 29, 1980)
810	1692h	MULTIPLE DEBTS	Goldfarb (Nov. 23, 1988)
			Glover (June 23, 1986)
811	1692i	INCONVENIENT FORUMS	Nursing Homes (June 6, 1995)
			President (Apr. 12, 1995)
			Attorney (Apr. 12, 1995)
			Krisor (Feb. 10, 1994)
			Halverson (Nov. 15, 1993)
			Zepkin (Sept. 16, 1993)
			Masters (Sept. 10, 1992)
			Giloley (Aug. 6, 1992)
			Reffkin (Jan. 29, 1989)
			Kwait (Jan. 24, 1989)
			Shibley (Dec. 14, 1988)
			Brown (Feb. 14, 1989)
			Kwait (Jan. 24, 1989)

FDCPA Section	15 U.S.C. Section	Section Topic	Relevant Informal Staff Letter Addressee
			Freeman (Nov. 15, 1988)
			Schulwst (Sept. 12, 1988)
			Heintz (March 23, 1989)
			Garrison (Apr. 6, 1988)
			Solomon (June 5, 1987)
			Harwood (June 5, 1987)
			Benedict (May 5, 1987)
			Garvett (Mar. 10, 1987)
			Shuman (Feb. 19, 1987)
			Smoyer (Feb. 6, 1979)
			Swaffield (Nov. 17, 1978)
			Eskanos (July 19, 1978)
			Green (Jan. 19, 1978)
811(a)(1)	1692i(a)(1)	Real property forums	Thomasson (July 19, 1978)
			Sweigart (Apr. 25, 1978)
812	1692j	FURNISHING DECEPTIVE FORMS	Beekman (Dec. 13, 1996)
			Lipsett (May 22, 1990)
			Michael (Aug. 15, 1988)
			Beekman (June 28, 1988)
			Knobel (Oct. 5, 1987)
			Peters (Feb. 6, 1987)
			Rackett (Nov. 15, 1985)
			Smith (July 5, 1984)
			Sullivan (Feb. 21, 1983)
			Mezines (Nov. 15, 1983)
			Christy (Jan. 19, 1981)
			Connelly (Dec. 10, 1980)
			Warwood (Oct. 20, 1980)
			Smith (May 29, 1979)
			Berhenke (May 21, 1979)
			Feldman (Apr. 30, 1979)
			Sevigny (Dec. 13, 1978)
			Lisanti (Sept. 29, 1978)
			Ireland (Sept. 21, 1978)
			Lisanti (Aug. 8, 1978)
			Davidson (May 18, 1978)
			Rummel (May 16, 1978)
			Gilbert (Apr. 28, 1978)
			Mansfield (Apr. 20, 1978)
			Huebner (Mar. 27, 1978)
			Anderson (Feb. 13, 1978)
			House (Nov. 22, 1977)
813	1692k	CIVIL LIABILITY	Clement (Nov. 12, 1985)
			Buchanan (Apr. 21, 1980)
			Crawford (Dec. 24, 1979)
			Stokes (Dec. 30, 1978)
			Atteberry (Dec. 30, 1977)
			Oleson (Oct. 19, 1977)
			Atteberry (Dec. 30, 1977)
			Oleson (Oct. 19, 1977)
813(a)(1)	1692k(a)(1)	Actual damages	Schein (Oct. 27, 1980)
813(d)	1692k(d)	Jurisdiction and limitation of action	Oleson (Jan. 20, 1978)
			Oleson (Nov. 29, 1977)
813(e)	1692k(e)	Good faith reliance defense	Faulkner (Sept. 18, 1992)

FDCPA Section	15 U.S.C. Section	Section Topic	Relevant Informal Staff Letter Addressee
			Reffkin (Jan. 29, 1988)
			Erickson (Jan. 5, 1981)
			Cole (Mar. 28, 1978)
			Crawford (Jan. 24, 1978)
			Berins (Jan. 12, 1978)
			Mitten (Jan. 11, 1978)
			Green (Jan. 19, 1978)
814	1692*l*	ADMINISTRATIVE ENFORCEMENT	President (Apr. 12, 1995)
			Attorney (Apr. 12, 1995)
			Mezines (Apr. 10, 1991)
			Miller (Dec. 30, 1988)
			Lipsett (Dec. 1, 1987)
			Goldfarb (Jan. 16, 1987)
			Bingham (Jan. 12, 1987)
			Kern (Aug. 14, 1984)
			Kingston (July 5, 1978)
			Atteberry (Dec. 30, 1977)
814(a)	1692*l*(a)	Federal Trade Commission	Faulkner (Sept. 18, 1992)
			Valentine (Sept. 3, 1992)
			Reffkin (Jan. 29, 1989)
816	1692n	RELATION TO STATE LAWS	Pratt (July 22, 1992)
			Johnson (May 22, 1991)
			Lipsett (Dec. 1, 1987)
			Gene (Sept. 4, 1979)
			Osterloh (July 13, 1979)
			Foote (Sept. 11, 1978)
			Klingensmith (Aug. 9, 1978)
			Eskanos (July 19, 1978)
			Atteberry (July 18, 1978)
817	1692*o*	EXEMPTION FOR STATE REGULATION	Klingensmith (Aug. 9, 1978)
			Atteberry (July 18, 1978)
			Atteberry (Dec. 30, 1977)

---

1   Former FDCPA § 803(6)(F), 15 U.S.C. § 1692a(6)(F), providing a limited attorney exemption, *repealed by* Pub. L. No. 99-361, 100 Stat. 768 (eff. July 9, 1986).

*   Some of these letters were rescinded in part by Carter, F.T.C. Informal Staff Letter (June 8, 1982).

December 20, 1999

Daniel P. Shapiro, Esq.
Goldberg, Kohn, Bell,
Black, Rosenbloom & Moritz, Ltd.
Suite 3700
55 East Monroe Street
Chicago, Illinois 60603-5802

Re: *Section 803(6) of the Fair Debt Collection Practices Act, 15 U.S.C. § 1692a(6)*

Dear Mr. Shapiro:

This is in response to your letter requesting a staff opinion regarding the Fair Debt Collection Practices Act ("FDCPA"). You ask whether your client, Applied Card Systems, Inc. ("ACS"), is a "debt collector," as that term is defined by the FDCPA. The following is your description of ACS's activities that you provided in your letter:

> ACS is a Delaware corporation which has been operating since 1987. It is in the business of servicing the consumer credit card portfolios of lending institutions. Those lenders typically market to potential card holders using direct mail and disclose in those mailings that the credit cards will be serviced by ACS, referencing it by name. Other than marketing, ACS performs all of the servicing tasks and functions regarding the card applicants and, ultimately, the card holders. Specifically:

> - ACS receives the card application/agreement in the mail directly from the applicant;
> - ACS recommends the application for approval or decline based upon criteria established by the lenders and then sends notice of acceptance or rejection to the consumer when a final decision is made;
> - ACS places the order with the card manufacturer to have the credit card sent to the card holder;
> - ACS processes and sends monthly billing statements to the card holder;

- ACS receives payments directly from the card holder and processes those payments;
- ACS receives in-bound customer service inquiries, via telephone and written communication, from card holders such as questions regarding billing statements, reports of lost or stolen cards, and reports of payment disputes with vendors;
- ACS receives written communications from third parties such as notices from bankruptcy courts or other entities, affecting the card holder, and processes such communications;
- In the event of a past-due account ("default"), ACS performs all collection activities; and
- In the event the debt is charged off by the lender, ACS may continue collection efforts, may refer the account to a third-party collector or, at the lender's discretion, may manage the arbitration process as prescribed in the credit card agreement.

Section 803(6)(F)(iii) of the FDCPA, 15 U.S.C. § 1692a(6)(F)(iii), provides that the term "debt collector" does not include

> any person collecting or attempting to collect any debt owed or due or asserted to be owed or due another to the extent such activity . . . (iii) concerns a debt which was not in default at the time it was obtained by such person.

Based on your description of ACS's business activities, it appears that all of the credit card accounts that ACS obtains from lending institutions "are owed or due or asserted to be owed or due another." It also appears that ACS obtains these accounts before they are in default. Based on your description, therefore, it appears that section 803(6)(F)(iii) excludes ACS from the definition of "debt collector" and, thus, most of the FDCPA's provisions. Please note, however, that ACS's activities are still governed by other statutes, such as Section 5(a)(1) of the Federal Trade Commission Act, 15 U.S.C. § 45(a)(1), which prohibits "unfair or deceptive acts or practices in or affecting commerce."

I hope this has been helpful. The views set forth in this informal staff opinion are those of the staff and are not binding on the Commission.

Sincerely,

Thomas E. Kane

March 6, 2000

Lynn M. Dankowski, Esq.
Church, Harris, Johnson & Williams, P.C.
201 West Main Street, Suite 104
Missoula, Montana 59807-7007

Re: *Section 807(16) of the Fair Debt Collection Practices Act*

Dear Ms. Dankowski:

I am responding to your request for an opinion regarding whether your client, a collection agency, would violate the Fair Debt Collection Practices Act ("FDCPA") if it uses the words "Creditor's Bureau" in its name when communicating with consumers. As you point out, section 807(16) of the FDCPA, 15 U.S.C. § 1692e(16), prohibits "debt collectors," such as your client, from falsely representing or implying that they operate or are employed by a "consumer reporting agency," as that term is defined by section 603(f) of the Fair Credit Reporting Act, 15 U.S.C. § 1681a(f).

If a debt collector is also a "consumer reporting agency," the FDCPA does not prohibit the debt collector from using a company name such as "Credit Bureau of __" to indicate that it is a consumer reporting agency. Based on your letter, however, it does not appear that your client's business has a consumer reporting agency component. Thus, the issue is whether your client's use of the proposed company name, "Creditor's Bureau of Missoula," when contacting consumers[1] would be a false representation or implication that the company is, at least in part, a consumer reporting agency. In the Staff Commentary on the FDCPA, Commission staff stated that "[o]nly a bona fide consumer reporting agency may use names such as "Credit Bureau," "Credit Bureau Collection Agency," "General Credit Control," "Credit Bureau Rating, Inc.," or "National Debtors Rating." 53 Fed. Reg. 50097, 50107 (Dec. 13, 1998).[2] All five of these company names imply that the company is in the business of reporting credit information to consumers' prospective creditors. I believe that your client would violate section 807(16) if it used any of these five company names when contacting consumers.

Unlike the five prohibited company names listed above, however, the name "Creditor's Bureau of Missoula" does not, by itself, appear to imply that the company is in the business of reporting credit information to prospective creditors. When most consumers refer to consumer reporting agencies, they use the term "credit bureau," rather than the term "creditor's bureau." Thus, if your client includes nothing else in its collection letters to give consumers the false impression that the company is a consumer reporting agency, it appears that your client would not violate section 807(16) by using the name Creditor's Bureau of Missoula. To strengthen your client's contention that it is not violating section 807(16), however, I recommend that the company's collection communications, both oral and written, make abundantly clear to consumers that they are being contacted by a debt collector and not a credit bureau.

The views expressed in this letter represent an informal staff opinion and are not binding on the Commission. They do, however, reflect the staff's current enforcement position.

Sincerely,

Thomas E. Kane

[Editor's Note: This letter was revised on May 23, 2002; see infra.*]*

May 1, 2000

Richard T. de Mayo, Esq.
President and Chief Executive Officer
TSYS Total Debt Management, Inc.
P.O. Box 6700
Norcross, Georgia 30091-6700

Re: *Section 803(6) of the Fair Debt Collection Practices Act*

Dear Mr. de Mayo:

This responds to your request for a staff opinion regarding the Fair Debt Collection Practices Act ("FDCPA"). You ask whether

---

1 The FDCPA does not address what name a debt collector may use for purposes other than its contacts with consumers.

2 *See also* Letter from Roger J. Fitzpatrick, Attorney, Division of Credit Practices, Federal Trade Commission, to Thomas Isgrigg (*Nov. 10, 1992*) at 3 (attached and available from the Commission's website at *www.ftc.gov/os/statutes/fdcpajump.htm*).

employees of a collection agency are covered by the FDCPA when they attempt to collect debts by contacting consumers under the following circumstances. The collection agency begins to collect the accounts when they are two, three, or four payments past due, but when the creditor has not yet charged the accounts off. The collection agency's employees ("agency employees") use the name of the creditor, rather than the name of the agency, when calling or writing to consumers about the accounts. The agency employees are located at the office of the agency, and the agency controls the practices and procedures that the agency's employees follow in collecting the accounts. You ask whether the FDCPA covers such agency employees (a) when the accounts being collected are "delinquent and not considered in default" by the creditor and (b) when the accounts "are considered in default by the creditor."

Generally, the FDCPA applies only to "debt collectors." The core portion of the FDCPA's Section 803(6), 15 U.S.C. § 1692a(6), defines "debt collector" as "any person who uses any instrumentality of interstate commerce or the mails in any business the principal purpose of which is the collection of any debts, *or* who regularly collects or attempts to collect, directly or indirectly, debts owed or due or asserted to be owed or due another." (Emphasis added.) A person is a "debt collector" if he meets either of these two prongs. The agency employees described in your letter meet both. They have as their principal purpose the collection of debts *and* they "regularly collect[] or attempt[] to collect . . . debts owed . . . or asserted to be owed . . . another." Thus, unless they are exempt from the definition of "debt collector" under a different portion of Section 803(6), they are "debt collectors" and must comply with the entire FDCPA.

The other exemptions from the definition of "debt collector" are assembled in Sections 803(6)(A)–(F). In determining whether the agency employees are exempt, we first look to Section 803(6) (F)(iii), which excludes any person collecting or attempting to collect any debt owed or due or asserted to be owed or due another to the extent such activity . . . (iii) concerns a debt which was not in default at the time it was obtained by such person.

Thus, if the agency employees are collecting debts that were not "in default" when the agency for which they work obtained them, they are not "debt collectors." The FDCPA does not define the term "default." While an account may not go into default on the date the consumer misses the first payment, it is probably in default by the time the consumer falls two months behind in his monthly payments, based on the legislative history of Section 803(6)(F)(iii). The Senate Report on the bill that became the FDCPA makes clear that Congress intended the section to exempt "mortgage service companies and others who service outstanding debts for others, so long as the debts were not in default when taken for servicing." S. Rep. No. 382, 95th Cong., 1st Sess. 7, *reprinted in* 1977 U.S. Code Cong. & Ad. News 1695, 1698. Thus, the exemption was aimed at entities such as mortgage servicers that obtain debts as soon as the debts are incurred and are primarily in the business of accepting timely payments from consumers. While some consumers whose accounts are obtained by these servicers eventually fail to make their regular payments, requiring the servicers to initiate collection procedures, collecting debts in default is not the servicers' primary function.

Whether a creditor "consider[s] a debt in default" has no bearing on whether the debt is truly in default. Similarly, the date that the creditor charges off the debt does not affect the date the debt actually goes into default. Nothing in the FDCPA indicates that Congress intended a creditor's business decisions to determine whether a consumer benefits from the statute's protections. Thus, a collector cannot avoid the FDCPA's coverage by having its creditor/client wait until after accounts have been transferred to the collector before labeling the accounts "in default" or charging the accounts off.

Because the accounts that the collection agency you describe obtains are "in default," the agency employees are not exempt under Section 803(6)(F)(iii). The employees will be "debt collectors" unless they fall within another exemption: Section 803(6)(A). That provision excludes from the definition of "debt collector" "any officer or employee of a creditor while, in the name of the creditor, collecting debts for such creditor." We stated in the Staff Commentary on the FDCPA, 53 Fed. Reg. 50,097 (1988) (available at www.ftc.gov/os/statutes/fdcpajump.htm), that this exemption "includes a collection agency employee who works for a creditor to collect in the creditor's name at the creditor's office under the creditor's supervision because he has become the de facto employee of the creditor." *Id.* at 50,102, comment 803(6)-4(a). Accordingly, agency employees fall within this de facto employee exemption only if they both collect in the creditor's name and are supervised to a large extent by the creditor. Whether the creditor employees supervise agency employees sufficiently for the agency employees to be considered de facto employees will depend on the relevant facts.

The agency employees you describe in your letter do collect in the name of their creditor clients, but they are not covered by the exemption because their collection practices and procedures are controlled entirely by the agency. The fact that the agency employees work on the agency's premises, however, would not have prevented them from meeting the Section 803(6)(A) exemption if they had been supervised sufficiently by creditor employees. Agency employees may work on the agency's premises and still be de facto employees, as long as creditor employees also work on the agency's premises and closely supervise the agency employees' collection efforts. Again, whether that supervision is sufficient to comply with Section 803(6)(A) will depend on the facts.

Finally, we note that, if the agency employees you describe are "debt collectors" under the above analysis, it appears that they and their collection agency would violate Section 807(14) of the FDCPA, 15 U.S.C. § 1692e(14), if they represent to consumers that they are employees of the consumers' creditors. Section 807(14) prohibits "debt collectors" from using "any business, company, or organization name other than the true name of the debt collector's business, company, or organization." If the agency is a "debt collector," it may not use the creditor's name when communicating with consumers from whom it is attempting to collect debts; it must use its own.

I hope you find this information helpful. The views expressed in this letter represent an informal staff opinion and are not binding on the Commission.

Sincerely,

Thomas E. Kane

May 23, 2002

Richard T. de Mayo, Esq.
President and Chief Executive Officer
TSYS Total Debt Management, Inc.
P.O. Box 6700
Norcross, Georgia 30091-6700

Re: *Section 803(6) of the Fair Debt Collection Practices Act*

Dear Mr. de Mayo:

This responds to your request for a staff opinion regarding the Fair Debt Collection Practices Act ("FDCPA"). We first issued an opinion letter in response to the request on May 1, 2000. Following discussions with members of the collection industry since that date and further consideration of the issue, we have decided to withdraw that letter and issue this revised one. The revised letter alters significantly two sections of the May 2000 letter: (1) the discussion concerning when an account goes into default, and (2) the discussion concerning when a collection agency's employees become the creditor's *de facto* employees.

You ask whether employees of a collection agency are covered by the FDCPA when they attempt to collect debts by contacting consumers under the following circumstances. The collection agency begins to collect the accounts when they are two, three, or four payments past due, but when the creditor has not yet charged the accounts off. The collection agency's employees ("agency employees") use the name of the creditor, rather than the name of the agency, when calling or writing to consumers about the accounts. The agency employees are located at the office of the agency, and the agency controls the practices and procedures that the agency's employees follow in collecting the accounts. You ask whether the FDCPA covers such agency employees (a) when the accounts being collected are "delinquent and not considered in default" by the creditor; and (b) when the accounts "are considered in default by the creditor."

Generally, the FDCPA applies only to "debt collectors." The core portion of the FDCPA's Section 803(6), 15 U.S.C. § 1692a(6), defines "debt collector" as "any person who uses any instrumentality of interstate commerce or the mails in any business the principal purpose of which is the collection of any debts, *or who regularly collects or attempts to collect, directly or indirectly, debts owed or due or asserted to be owed or due another.*" (Emphasis added.) A person is a "debt collector" if he meets either of these two prongs. The agency employees described in your letter meet both. They have as their principal purpose the collection of debts and they "regularly collect[] or attempt[] to collect . . . debts owed . . . or asserted to be owed . . . another." Thus, unless they fall under one of the exceptions to the definition of "debt collector" found in a different portion of Section 803(6), they are "debt collectors" and must comply with the entire FDCPA.

The exceptions to the definition of "debt collector" are assembled in Sections 803(6)(A)–(F). In determining whether the agency employees are exempt, we first look to Section 803(6)(F)(iii), which excludes

> any person collecting or attempting to collect any debt owed or due or asserted to be owed or due another to the extent such activity . . . (iii) concerns a debt which was not in default at the time it was obtained by such person.

Thus, if agency employees are collecting debts that were not "in default" when the agency for which they work obtained them, they are not "debt collectors." The FDCPA does not define the term "in default," but whether a debt is in default is generally controlled by the terms of the contract creating the indebtedness and applicable state or federal law. *See, e.g., Skerry v. Mass. Higher Educ. Asst. Corp.*, 73 F. Supp. 2d 47, 53–54 (D. Mass. 1999) (applying definition of "default" in Federal Family Education Loan Program regulations to construe Section 803(6)(F)(iii)); *Jones v. InTuition, Inc.*, 12 F. Supp. 2d 775, 779 (W.D. Tenn. 1998) (same).

We believe that, in the absence of a contractual definition or conclusive state or federal law, a creditor's reasonable, written guidelines may be used to determine when an account is "in default." We note that, in evaluating guidelines to determine reasonableness, we would consider the entirety of the circumstances, including, but not limited to, whether the guidelines are applied consistently and whether they are designed for administering accounts, rather than for circumventing the FDCPA. For example, we would not consider a set of guidelines reasonable if, under those guidelines, the same account were deemed in default for one purpose, such as determining whether the creditor may accelerate the loan, but not in default for purposes of determining whether a third-party collector is a "debt collector" under the FDCPA.

You ask whether the FDCPA covers the agency employees described in your letter (a) when the accounts being collected are "delinquent and not considered in default" by the creditor and (b) when the accounts "are considered in default by the creditor." Implicit in your questions is whether a creditor's classification of a debt is significant for purposes of the FDCPA. As discussed above, our view is that the determination of this issue depends, first, on whether there is a contractual definition of the term "default" or conclusive state or federal law. If so, whether the creditor, through its guidelines, "considers" an account to be in default would not be relevant. If, however, there is neither a contractual definition nor definitive law on which to rely, we believe it would be appropriate to use the creditor's reasonable, written guidelines to determine whether accounts are in default.

If the accounts that the agency employees in your fact situation are attempting to collect were in default when they were obtained by the agency, the agency employees are not exempt from the definition of "debt collector" by virtue of Section 803(6)(F)(iii). They may be exempt, however, under Section 803(6)(A), which exempts from the definition of "debt collector" "any officer or employee of a creditor while, in the name of the creditor, collecting debts for such creditor." The FTC Staff Commentary on the FDCPA, 53 Fed. Reg. 50,097 (1988) (available at www.ftc.gov/os/statutes/fdcpajump.htm), stated that this exemption "includes a collection agency employee who works for a creditor to collect in the creditor's name at the creditor's office under the creditor's supervision because he has become the *de facto* employee of the creditor." Id. at 50,102, comment 803(6)-4(a). In an October 1, 1997 letter to Daniel P. Shapiro, Esq. (available at www.ftc.gov/os/statutes/fdcpa/letters.htm), we concluded that, because of the "extensive degree of control" that the creditor maintained over a collection agency's activities, this "*de facto*" employee exemption applied even to employees of the collection agency who collected in a creditor's name but did not work on the creditor's premises.

Nevertheless, in considering whether this *de facto* employee exemption applies, we must take heed of the plain language of

Section 803(6)(A), which exempts only a creditor's "officers" and "employees." This specific language does not, therefore, encompass broader categories, such as the creditor's representatives or agents. In our view, this statutory distinction limits the *de facto* employee exemption to those collection agency employees who are treated essentially the same as creditor employees. The more that agency employees are treated like creditor employees, the more likely it is that we would deem them *de facto* employees. Whether agency employees—working on the creditor's premises or on the agency's premises—are treated enough like creditor employees to become *de facto* employees of the creditor will depend on the degree of control and supervision exercised by the creditor over the agency employees' collection activity, and how similar that control and supervision is to that exercised by the creditor over its own employees. Relevant facts will include, for example, whether the creditor directly supervises and monitors the collection activities of the agency employees and, if so, how that supervision and monitoring is carried out; whether the creditor trains the agency employees; and whether the agency employees are subject to the same rules, procedures, and disciplinary actions that govern the collection activities of creditor employees. The agency employees you describe in your letter collect in the name of their creditor clients, but, in our view, they are not covered by the Section 803(6)(A) exemption because their collection practices and procedures are controlled by the agency.

One final point: If the agency employees you describe are "debt collectors" under the above analysis, it appears that they and their collection agency would violate Section 807(14) of the FDCPA, 15 U.S.C. § 1692e(14), if they represent to consumers that they are employees of the consumers' creditors. Section 807(14) prohibits "debt collectors" from using "any business, company, or organization name other than the true name of the debt collector's business, company, or organization." If the agency is a "debt collector," it may not use the creditor's name when communicating with consumers from whom it is attempting to collect debts; it must use its own.

I hope you find this information helpful. The views expressed in this letter represent an informal staff opinion and are not binding on the Commission.

Sincerely,

Thomas E. Kane

Federal Trade Commission Staff Commentary on the Fair Debt Collection Practices Act

The FTC staff issued a Fair Debt Collection Practices Act Commentary at 53 Fed. Reg. 50097–50110 (Dec. 13, 1988). On many issues, the Commentary *cannot* be relied upon because the FTC has failed to update and revise the Commentary to reflect contrary court rulings and new interpretations in informal staff letters and the FTC advisory opinion. Moreover, the United States Supreme Court in *Heintz v. Jenkins*, 115 S. Ct. 1489, 131 L. Ed. 2d 395 (1995) recognized that the Commentary is not binding on the Commission or the public and was not entitled to deference when it conflicts with the FDCPA's plain language. In fact, as discussed in § 3.3.6.2, *supra* it was not clear that the FTC had the authority to issue the Commentary. Courts have little difficulty disregarding Commentary provisions when courts view those provisions as incorrect.

Statements of General Policy or Interpretation Staff Commentary On the Fair Debt Collection Practices Act

AGENCY: Federal Trade Commission.

ACTION: Publication of staff commentary.

SUMMARY: The Commission staff is issuing its Commentary on the Fair Debt Collection Practices Act that will supersede all previously issued staff interpretations of the Act. The purpose of the Commentary is to clarify and codify these interpretations.

DATE: December 13, 1988.

ADDRESS: Federal Trade Commission, Washington, DC 20580.

FOR FURTHER INFORMATION CONTACT: Clarke W. Brinckerhoff, Program Advisor, John F. LeFevre, Program Advisor, Division of Credit Practices, Federal Trade Commission, Washington, DC 20580, (202) 326-3208 or (202) 326-3209.

SUPPLEMENTARY INFORMATION: On March 7, 1986, the staff of the Federal Trade Commission ("staff" or "FTC staff") published its proposed Staff Commentary on the Fair Debt Collection Practices Act ("FDCPA") in the Federal Register (51 FR 8019). That notice set forth the text of the proposed Commentary, along with (1) the staff's rationale for issuing the Commentary and (2) a list of the principal areas where it varied in appreciable measure from the informal opinions previously offered by the FTC staff.

That notice also briefly described the FDCPA, the Commission's role in enforcing the statute, and the FTC's staff's interest in improving the present method of providing advice by making informal staff letters available to the public. It explained that the staff viewed the publication of the Commentary as an opportunity to provide a more comprehensive vehicle for providing staff opinions concerning the FDCPA, and to revise previous advice that the staff had come to believe was inconsistent or inaccurate. Both the notice dated March 7, 1986, and the introduction to the proposed Commentary specified that it does not have the force of a trade regulation rule or formal agency action, and that it is not binding on the Commission or the public.

The notice in the Federal Register dated March 7, 1986, stated that the FTC staff would accept public comments on the proposed Commentary to aid in preparation of the final product. Three trade associations, six corporations, the consumer protection division of the offices of three state Attorneys General, one state regulatory agency, one national consumer organization, two local consumer groups, and two law firms responded to this invitation. Although the notice stated the FTC staff was requesting comments until May 6, 1986, all comments were taken into account in preparing the Commentary, even those received after that date.

On July 9, 1986, four months after publication of the proposed Commentary, the President signed into law a bill (Pub. L. 99-3610 repealing former section 803(6)(F), which had exempted "any attorney-at-law collecting a debt as an attorney on behalf of and in the name of a client." The FTC staff has responded to a large number of inquiries from attorneys seeking its views on how the FDCPA applies to their practices. Therefore, the staff has added comments in appropriate locations to reflect the advice it has provided to attorneys on these issues.

This notice (1) summarizes comments received from the public in response to the FTC staff's 1986 publication of the Fair Debt Collection Practices Act Commentary in "proposed" form, (2) highlights the major areas where the staff revised the Commentary based on those comments or refused to do so, and (3) outlines the major issues added to the Commentary, reflecting written advice which the staff has provided to attorneys following repeal of the

[53 Fed. Reg. 50098]

"attorney-at-law collecting a debt" exemption in July 1986.

In this notice, the word "comment" refers to an opinion set forth in the Commentary by the staff, "public commenter" refers to a party that submitted views on the proposed Commentary following its publication in the Federal Register, and "public comments" refers to those views.

Principal Revisions To Commentary Based on Public Comments

Generally, the FTC staff found the public comments helpful in preparing the final version of the Commentary, although not all the proposals were adopted. Most of the public comments were aimed at clarifying the staff's intent. The redraft adopted these suggestions where it appeared that they resulted in an appreciable improvement. The overwhelming majority of the revisions the FTC staff made in the Commentary involved only minor changes (adding a word or parenthetical phrase or making some minor editorial change), and were designed to clarify points or to avoid possible unintended inferences. However, besides the addition of comments relating to attorney debt collectors, there were some changes of a substantive nature that were made based on public comments. This section highlights the most significant of the clarifications and revisions that were made based on public comments.

1. Location information (section 804 (1, 5))

The FTC staff has made adjustments to two comments to acknowledge that a debt collector who is seeking location information by mail may identify his employer when expressly asked to do so. The staff added parenthetical references to comment #4 to section 804, and to comment #4 to section 807(14), which discusses section 804(1) and (5) under the heading "relation to other sections."

One public commenter pointed out that if the person from whom the locaton information is sought replies by expressly requesting the name of the employer of the individual debt collector who sent the letter,[1] sections 804(1) and 804(5) may appear to place conflicting obligations on the debt collection firm. On the one hand, section 804(1) requires a debt collector employee, in communications seeking location information, to "identify his employer" if "expressly requested." Yet section 804(5) generally prohibits a debt collector from using "any language or symbol on any envelope or in the contents of any communication effected in the mails or telegram that indicates that the debt collector is in the debt collection business or that the communication relates to the collection of a debt."

The FTC staff believes a proper interpretation of the FDCPA is to read section 804(1) as controlling this situation, because it specifically addresses the situation in which an individual expressly requests the name of the debt collection firm. In that case, we believe that the debt collection firm must reveal its identity in order to acquire location information. The comments bearing on this issue have therefore been changed to reflect that position.

2. Contact limited to consumer's attorney (section 805(a))

Public commenters argued forcefully that comment #3, stating that a debt collector could not communicate with a consumer who stated that an attorney would represent him with respect to all *future* debts, would place an unreasonable burden on the debt collector. They reported that the standard operating procedure for

---

[1] Such a communication would be signed by the individual debt collector, without indicating that the letter is from a debt collection firm.

many debt collectors is to close the consumer's file once a debt is collected or efforts to collect it cease. Should a second debt from the same consumer be assigned to the debt collector, therefore, the collector might be unaware of the previous file on that debtor and would not know whether the consumer was represented by an attorney with respect to all future debts. These commenters contend that the only way a debt collector could comply with our proposed interpretation would be to check every new debtor file against the closed files to determine whether (1) the collector had ever previously contacted that debtor, (2) the debtor had previously been represented by an attorney, and (2) the debtor had given the collector a blanket notice of legal representation. They suggested instead that, when contacted about a subsequent debt, the consumer should simply inform the debt collector that he is still represented by an attorney and that the debt collector should contact the attorney.

The FTC staff now believes that the portion of comment #3 in the proposed Commentary regarding future representation is simply not supported by the statute, or envisioned by its legislative history. Furthermore, it could easily be the case that the attorney in fact no longer represents the consumer. Accordingly, the staff has modified the second paragraph of comment #3 to section 805(a) to replace the broad reference to "all current and future debts" with the more appropriate "other debts."

3. Consumer consent to third party contacts (section 805(b))

The statement in comment #1 that consumers consent to third party contacts "may be presumed from circumstances" has been deleted. One public commenter expressed concern that this formulation might open the door to overreaching by debt collectors. The deleted phrase was not necessary to the point involved—that consent need not necessarily be in writing—which is better made by providing a clear example of such consent.

4. Lists of debtors (Section 806(3))

One public commenter noted that this section of the proposed Commentary did not completely reflect the FDCPA's reference to sections of the Fair Credit Reporting Act. The description has been amended and a comment has been added to reflect that relationship, in accord with a prior staff opinion on the section and a Commission interpretation on the FCRA.

5. Statement by debt collector of possible action (Section 807(5))

A revision was made to correct the Commentary's inadvertent reference to the *creditor*, rather than to the *debt collector*, in comment #3 to this section. Comment #3 concerns statements by the debt collector about action that is unlikely to be taken in a particular case. Obviously, as several public commenters pointed out, the creditor's knowledge that action is unlikely is not automatically imputed to the debt collector.

6. Documents deceptive as to authorship (Section 807(9))

An appropriate clause has been added to the description and to comment #1, to give a more complete discussion of this section than in the proposed Commentary, which focused only on documents that fraudulently appear to be government documents. One public commenter correctly pointed out that the statute covers a much wider range of deceptive practices as to the source of the document.

7. Letters marked "personal" or "confidential" (Section 808(8))

Comment #3 to this section has been expanded to assert that use of the term "Personal" or "Confidential", as well as

[53 Fed. Reg. 50099]

the word "Telegram" or the like, does not violate this section.

One public commenter stated that debt collectors use designations of this sort to protect the consumer's privacy by attempting to ensure that the envelope is not opened by unauthorized persons, and argued that such terms are essentially part of the letter's address.

The FTC staff agrees that the proposed change is logical. The staff has already recognized that a rigid, literal approach to section 808(8) would lead to absurd results (i.e., taken literally, it would prohibit showing any part of the consumer's address on the envelope). The legislative purpose was to prohibit a debt collector from using symbols or language on envelopes that would reveal that the contents pertain to debt collection—not to totally bar the use of harmless words or symbols on an envelope. Indeed, it was for this reason that comment #3 to this section of the proposed Commentary (in accord with prior informal staff advice) explicitly recognized that the term "Telegram" or similar designation on an envelope does not violate this section.

8. Waiver of venue provision (Section 811)

Numerous public commenters objected to comment #1 to this section, indicating a fear that the staff's interpretation would lead to a flood of waiver provisions hidden in the fine print of consumer credit contracts. Although the FTC staff believes that these parties misread the comment, which clearly stated that any waiver "must be provided to the debt collector," the comment has been expanded to be even more explicit on the point.

Significant Public Comments Not Adopted

There were several areas in which public commenters suggested changes in the Commentary that were not adopted. This section discusses the most significant of those proposals, and sets forth the staff's principal reasons for maintaining its position.

1. Contacts in which the collector does not mention the debt (Sections 803(2), 805(a), 805(c))

Several public commenters contended that the FTC staff's treatment of certain contacts consumers as violations of the FDCPA was incorrect because the contacts did not involve a "communication" under the definition provided in section 803(2), which refers to "conveying of information regarding a debt directly or indirectly to any person." These commenters argued that contacts that do not explicitly refer to the debt are not "communications" and, hence, do not violate any provision where that term is used.

The FTC staff continues to believe that some contacts with consumers can violate section 805(a) or section 805(c) because they at least "indirectly" refer to the debt, even if the obligation isn't specifically mentioned. For example, there is no doubt that a debt collector who has previously contacted a consumer about a debt violates section 805(a) if he calls the consumer at 3 AM and says only "Hi, this is Joe, I haven't forgotten you"—the words may not refer to the debt, but the consumer will know from previous collection efforts by "Joe" what the call is about. The words "or indirectly" in the definition make it clear that Congress intended a common sense approach to this situation. Furthermore, the word "communication" (or variations thereof) is used six times in section 804, which authorizes the seeking of location information from third parties with the general requirement that the debt will *not* be disclosed to such parties, demonstrating that this term was not intended to be limited throughout the statute to acts that specifically refer to the debt, regardless of the definition set forth in section 803(2).

2. Definition of "location information" (section 803(7))

Public commenters made varying suggestions that would effectively amend the section's definition of "location information"—i.e., "a consumer's place of abode and his telephone number at such place, or his place of employment." One public commenter expressed the view that a debt collector was somehow limited by this language to obtaining only one of the three enumerated items (home address or home phone or work address), while others suggested that we interpret the definition to include a fourth item (work phone). Because no public commenter provided a convincing rationale for its position, and because the FTC staff believes that the definition is clear, both suggestions were declined.

3. Use of "copy of a judgment" in notice (section 807(2)(A))

Some public commenters criticized the staff's statement in comment #3 to section 807(2) that the validation notice provided by a debt collector to comply with section 809(a)(4) may use the phrase "copy of a judgment" even where no judgment exists. Staff had previously advised in informal opinion letters that the use of those words violated section 807(2)(A) because they suggested that a judgment existed when it did

not. Because the practical effect of these interpretations was to make verbatim use of the statutory language of section 809(a)(4) of violation of section 807(2)(A), they were rejected by the leading court decision[2] and by the staff in the proposed Commentary. The FTC staff continues to believe its reasons for revising prior staff opinions (discussed in item 5 of the notice in the Federal Register dated March 7, 1986) are well-founded, and thus it has adhered to that position.

One public commenter suggested that we might also permit the phrase "copy of the judgment" as well. Because the phrase used in section 809(a)(4) is "copy of a judgment" (emphasis added) and this language led to the staff's current interpretation, the Commentary has not been revised on this point.

4. False allegations of fraud (section 807(7))

Some public commenters contended that the language of this section, which outlaws the "false representation or implication that the consumer committed any crime or other conduct in order to disgrace the consumer" (emphasis added) demonstrates that specific intent is essential to a violation. The FTC staff agrees that some element of intent is involved, but believes that an intent to disgrace can be inferred from the nature of the acts the consumer is being accused of—fraud (comment 1) or crime (comment 2). Therefore, the comments on this section have not been changed.

5. Disclosure of debt collection purpose (section 807(11))

Several public commenters questioned the staff's refusal to construe section 807(11) as requiring debt collectors to disclose the purpose of each and every written and oral contact, pointing out that court decisions have gone both ways on the issue. The staff's position, reflected in the Commission's Sixth and Seventh Annual Reports to Congress—that such disclosures need not be made where they are obvious or have already been made—has not changed, and the comments provide no new argument for revising that view.

Other public commenters asked the staff to retract the comment stating that a debt collector may not send a note saying only "please call me right away" to a consumer whom the collector has not previously contacted. They argued that such a note could not violate this

[53 Fed. Reg. 50100]

section because it made no reference to the debt and therefore was not a "communication," as defined in section 803(2). Because the staff believes that (1) the intent of section 807(11) was to require that debt collectors' purposes be known to parties they contact, and (2) the use of the term "communication" in other sections of the FDCPA shows that its construction is not always

limited to the definition set forth in section 803(2), this comment was retained.[3]

6. Elements of unfairness (section 808)

Some public commenters criticized comment #2, which concerns general violations of this section of the FDCPA, for construing the term "unfair" in the same way as the Commission has construed it under section 5 of the FTC Act. They argued that the comment would, in effect, repeal some of the subsections of section 808 because the proscribed conduct would not cause the type of injury required, or would not be considered unfair based on a cost/benefit analysis. Because the location of the comment—under section 808 *generally*, as opposed to any of its subsections—makes it clear that the staff did not intend to negate any of the eight types of conduct specified by Congress to be a violation of this provision in subsections (1) through (8), the staff retained this comment.

Other public commenters asked that comment #2 be expanded to state that section 808 does not cover inadvertent acts or any act that was reasonably calculated to collect the debt. Because this comment was meant simply to reflect the FTC staff's view that the Commission's approach to "unfair practices" (as reflected in its treatment of that concept in section 5 of the FTC Act) is applicable in analyzing general violations of section 808, comment #2 has not been substantially revised.

7. Details of validation notices (section 809(a))

Some public commenters objected to the staff's view that section 809(a) imposes no requirements as to form, sequence, location, or type size of the notice (comment 3); to our reasons for reversing prior informal opinions to the contrary (item 10 in the March 7, 1986 notice in the Federal Register); and to our view that the notice may be provided orally (comment 5). However, the public commenters provided no new analysis to change the staff's reading of the section. Therefore, the Commentary has not been changed on this point.

8. Proper forum for suit on an oral contract (section 811(a)(2))

One public commenter suggested deletion of comment 4 to section 811. Section 811(a)(2) clearly states that there are only two districts where suit may be brought by a debt collector on a debt—where the consumer "signed the contract sued upon" and where the consumer "resides at the commencement of the action." The staff decided to retain the comment, which simply notes the obvious fact that if there is only an oral agreement (which by definition can not be "signed"), suit may only be brought where the consumer resides.

9. Miscellaneous requests for added comments

Some public commentors made a number of suggestions that the FTC staff establish new

---

2 Blackwell v. Professional Business Services of Georgia, Inc., 526 F. Supp. 535, 538–39 (N.D. Ga. 1981).

---

3 See discussion of FDCPA section 804 in item 1 of this section of this notice.

principles in the Commentary.[4] Although not all of the proposals were without merit, the staff believes it is unwise to add major new sections to the final version of the Commentary to address issues that have never been the subject of staff correspondence.

New Comments Based on Recent Staff Letters To Attorneys

The staff has added comments to reflect the large volume of written advice it has provided to attorneys following repeal of the "attorney-at-law" exemption in July 1986.[5]

This section synthesizes the conclusions reached in the most significant additions made to the Commentary based on this recent correspondence.

1. Coverage (Sections 803(2, 5, 6), 811)

Attorneys or law firms that engage in traditional debt collection activities (sending dunning letters, making collection calls to consumers) are covered by the FDCPA, but those whose practice is limited to legal activities are not covered.[6]

Similarly, filing or service of a complaint or other legal paper (or transmission of a notice that is a legal prerequisite to enforcement of a debt) is not a "communication" covered by the FDCPA, but traditional collection efforts are covered.[7]

A student loan is a "debt" covered by the FDCPA;[8] however, alimony, tort claims, and non-pecuniary obligations are not covered.[9]

A salaried attorney who collects debts on behalf of, and in the name of, his creditor employer,[10] and a state educational agency that collects student loans,[11] are exempt from coverage by the FDCPA.

Debt collectors (including attorney debt collectors) are subject to the venue limitations of the FDCPA.[12]

2. Communications by debt collectors (sections 805(b), 806(3-4))

An attorney debt collector, who represents either (1) a creditor or (2) a debt collector that previously tried to collect an account, may report his collection efforts to the debt collector.[13]

An attorney may communicate with a witness in a lawsuit that has been filed.[14]

A debt collector may provide a list of consumers, against whom judgments have been entered, to an investigator in order to locate such individuals.[15]

A debt collector may place a public notice required by law as a prerequisite to enforcing the debt.[16]

3. Dispute and verification (section 809)

An attorney debt collector must provide the required validation notice, even if a previous debt collector (or the creditor) has given such notice.[17]

A debt collector does not comply with the obligation to verify the debt simply by including proof with the first communication to the consumer.[18]

[53 Fed. Reg. 50101]

An attorney debt collector may take legal action within 30 days of sending the required validation notice, regardless of whether the consumer disputes the debt; if the consumer disputes the debt, the attorney may still take legal action but must cease other collection efforts (e.g., letters or calls to the consumer) until verification is obtained and mailed to the consumer.[19]

4. Permissible forum to enforce a judgment on a debt (section 811)

If a judgment has been obtained from a forum that satisfies the requirements of this section, a debt collector may bring suit to enforce it in another jurisdiction.[20]

By direction of the Commission. Donald S. Clark, Secretary.

Federal Trade Commission Staff Commentary on the Fair Debt Collection Practices Act

Introduction

This Commentary is the vehicle by which the staff of the Federal Trade Commission publishes its interpretations of the Fair Debt Collection Practices Act (FDCPA). It is a guideline intended to clarify the staff interpretations of the statute, but does not have the force or effect of statutory provisions. It is not a formal trade regulation rule or advisory opinion of the Commission, and thus is not binding on the Commission or the public.

The Commentary is based primarily on issues discussed in informal staff letters responding to public requests for interpretations and on the Commission's enforcement program, subsequent to the FDCPA's enactment. It is intended to synthesize staff views on important issues and to give clear advice where inconsistencies have been discovered among staff letters. In some cases, reflection on the issues posed or relevant court decisions have resulted in a different interpretation from that expressed by the staff in those informal letters. Therefore, the Commentary supersedes the staff views expressed in such correspondence.

In many cases several different sections or subsections of the FDCPA may apply to a given factual situation. This results from the effort by Congress in drafting the FDCPA to be both explicit and comprehensive, in order to limit the opportunities for debt collectors to evade the underlying legislative intention. Although it may be of only technical interest whether a given act violates one, two, or three sections of the FDCPA, the Commentary frequently provides cross references to other applicable sections so that it may serve as a more comprehensive guide for its users. The Commentary attempts to discuss the more common overlapping references, usually under the heading "Relation to other sections," and deals with issues raised by each factual situation under the section or subsection that the staff deems most directly applicable to it.

The Commentary will be revised and updated by the staff as needed, based on the experience of the Commission in responding to public inquiries about, and enforcing, the FDCPA. The Commission welcomes input from interested industry,

---

4   The principal proposals were that the staff add to the Commentary (1) a lengthy new comment in section 803(6) that a party could be a "debt collector" with respect to some accounts but not others, (2) a definition of "default" in connection with section 803(6)(G)(iii) (now section 803(6)(F)(iii)) concerning accounts not in default when received, (3) a statement that section 806(3) does not prohibit a debt collector from responding to a specific credit reference inquiry from a creditor, (4) substantial new material to various comments in section 807(14) to cover a situation where one debt collector provides services as a contractor for another debt collector, (5) a statement that section 808(1) does not prohibit an agreement between a consumer and debt collector, and (6) a statement that the verification required by section 809(b) may be provided by an agent of the debt collector.

5   Although most of the issues raised in those letters related to attorneys as debt collectors, a few of them also asked for interpretations on other issues as well. For the sake of completeness, all significant staff opinions included in this correspondence (which has been widely circulated already) have been included in the Commentary.

6   Section 803(6), comments 1-2.

7   Section 803(2), comment 2; section 809(a), comments 6-7.

8   Section 803(5), comment 1.

9   Section 803(5), comment 2.

10   Section 803(6)(A), comment 4(a).

11   Section 803(6)(C), comment 4(c).

12   Section 811, comment 6.

13   Section 805(b), comment 8.

14   Section 805(b), comment 8.

15   Section 806(3-4), comment 5.

16   Section 806(3-4), comment 6.

17   Section 809(a), comment 7.

18   Section 809(b), comment 1.

19   Section 809(a), comment 8.

---

20   Section 811, comment 5.

consumer, and other public parties on the Commentary and on issues discussed in it.

The staff will continue to respond to requests for informal interpretations. Updates of the Commentary will consider and, where appropriate, incorporate issues raised in correspondence and other public contacts, as well as the Commission's enforcement efforts. Therefore, a party who is interested in raising an issue for inclusion in future editions of the Commentary does not need to make any formal submission or request to that effect.

The Commentary should be used in conjunction with the statute. The abbreviated description of each section or subsection in the Commentary is designed only as a preamble to discussion of issues pertaining to each section and is not intended as a substitute for the statutory text.

The Commentary should not be considered as a reflection of all court rulings under the FDCPA. For example, on some issues judicial interpretations of the statute vary depending on the jurisdiction, with the result that the staff's enforcement position can not be in accord with all decided cases.

Section 801—Short Title

Section 801 names the statute the "Fair Debt Collection Practices Act."

The Fair Debt Collection Practices Act (FDCPA) is Title VIII of the Consumer Credit Protection Act, which also includes other federal statutes relating to consumer credit, such as the Truth in Lending Act (Title I), the Fair Credit Reporting Act (Title VI), and the Equal Credit Opportunity Act (Title VII).

Section 802—Findings and Purpose

Section 802 recites the Congressional findings that serve as the basis for the legislation.

Section 803—Definitions

Section 803(1) defines "Commission" as the Federal Trade Commission.

1. *General.* The definition includes only the Federal Trade Commission, not necessarily the staff acting on its behalf.

Section 803(2) defines "communication" as the "conveying of information regarding a debt directly or indirectly to any person through any medium."

1. *General.* The definition includes oral and written transmission of messages which refer to a debt.

2. *Exclusions.* The term does not include formal legal action (e.g., filing of a lawsuit or other petition/pleadings with a court; service of a complaint or other legal papers in connection with a lawsuit, or activities directly related to such service). Similarly, it does not include a notice that is required by law as a prerequisite to enforcing a contractual obligation between creditor and debtor, by judicial or nonjudicial legal process.

The term does not include situations in which the debt collector does not convey information regarding the debt, such as:

- A request to a third party for a consumer to return a telephone call to the debt collector, if the debt collector does not refer to the debt or the caller's status as (or affiliation with) a debt collector.
- A request to a third party for information about the consumer's assets, if the debt collector does not reveal the existence of a debt.
- A request to a third party in connection with litigation (e.g., requesting a third party to complete a military affidavit that must be filed as a prerequisite to enforcing a default judgment, if the debt collector does not reveal the existence of the debt).

Section 803(3) defines "consumer" as "any natural person obligated or allegedly obligated to pay any debt."

1. *General.* The definition includes only a "natural person" and not an artificial person such as a corporation or other entity created by statute.

Section 803(4) defines "creditor" as "any person who offers or extends credit creating a debt or to whom a debt is owed". However, the definition excludes a party who "receives an assignment or transfer of a debt in default solely for the purpose of facilitating collection of such debt for another."

1. *General.* The definition includes the party that actually extended credit or became the obligee on an account in the normal course of business, and excludes

[53 Fed. Reg. 50102]

a party that was assigned a delinquent debt only for collection purposes.

Section 803(5) defines "debt" as a consumer's "obligation . . . to pay money arising out of a transaction in which the money, arising out of a transportation in which the money, property, insurance, or services (being purchased) are primarily for personal, family, or household purposes. . . ."

1. *Examples.* The term includes:

- Overdue obligations such as medical bills that were originally payable in full within a certain time period (e.g., 30 days).
- A dishonored check that was tendered in payment for goods or services acquired or used primarily for personal, family, or household purposes.
- A student loan, because the consumer is purchasing "services" (education) for personal use.

2. *Exclusions.* The term does not include:

- Unpaid taxes, fines, alimony, or tort claims, because they are not debts incurred from a "transportation (involving purchase of) property * * * or services * * * for personal, family or household purposes."
- A credit card that a cardholder retains after the card issuer has demanded its return. The

cardholder's account balance is the debt.

- A non-pecuniary obligation of the consumer such as the responsibility to maintain adequate insurance on the collateral, because it does not involve an "obligation * * * to pay money."

Section 803(6) defines "debt collector" as a party "who uses any instrumentality of interstate commerce or the mails in * * * collection of * * * debts owed * * * another."

1. *Examples.* The term includes:

- Employees of a debt collection business, including a corporation, partnership, or other entity whose business is the collection of debts owned another.
- A firm that regularly collects overdue rent on behalf of real estate owners, or periodic assessments on behalf of condominium associations, because it "regularly collects * * * debts owned or due another."
- A party based in the United States who collects debts owned by consumers residing outside the United States, because he "uses * * * the mails" in the collection business. The residence of the debtor is irrelevant.
- A firm that collects debts in its own name for a creditor solely by mechanical techniques, such as (1) placing phone calls with pre-recorded messages and recording consumer responses, or (2) making computer-generated mailings.
- An attorney or law firm whose efforts to collect consumer debts on behalf of its clients regularly include activities traditionally associated with debt collection, such as sending demand letters (dunning notices) or making collection telephone calls to the consumer. However, an attorney is not considered to be a debt collector simply because he responds to an inquiry from the consumer following the filing of a lawsuit.

2. *Exclusions.* The term does not include:

- Any person who collects debts (or attempts to do so) only in insolated instances, because the definition includes only those who "regularly" collect debts.
- A credit card issuer that collects its cardholder's account, even when the account is based upon purchases from participating merchants, because the issuer is collecting its own debts, not those "owed or due another."
- An attorney whose practice is limied to legal activities (e.g., the filing and prosecution of lawsuits to reduce debts to judgment).

3. *Application of definition to creditor using another name.* Creditors are generally excluded from the definition of "debt collector" to the extent that they collect their own debts in their own name. However, the term specifically applies to "any creditor who, in the process of collecting his own debts, uses any name other

than his own which would indicate that a third person is" involved in the collection.

A creditor is a debt collector for purposes of this act if:

- He uses a name other than his own to collect his debts, including a fictitious name.
- His salaried attorney employees who collect debts use stationery that indicates that attorneys are employed by someone other than the creditor or are independent or separate from the creditor (e.g., ABC Corp. sends collection letters on stationery of "John Jones, Attorney-at-Law").
- He regularly collects debts for another creditor; however, he is a debt collector only for purposes of collecting these debts, not when he collects his own debt in his own name.
- The creditor's collection division or related corporate collector is not clearly designated as being affiliated with the creditor; however, the creditor is not a debt collector if the creditor's correspondence is clearly labeled as being from the "collection unit of the (creditor's name)," since the creditor is not using a "name other than his own" in that instance.

Relation to other sections.

A creditor who is covered by the FDCPA because he uses a "name other than his own" also may violate section 807(14), which prohibits using a false business name. When he falsely uses an attorney's name, he violates section 807(3).

4. *Specific exemptions from definition of debt collector.*

(a) *Creditor employees.* Section 803(6)(A) provides that "debt collector" does not include "any officer or employee of a creditor while, in the name of the creditor, collecting debts for such creditor".

The exemption includes a collection agency employee, who works for a creditor to collect in the creditor's name at the creditor's office under the creditor's supervision, because he has become the de facto employee of the creditor.

The exemption includes a creditor's salaried attorney (or other) employee who collects debts on behalf of, and in the name of, that creditor.

The exemption does not include a creditor's former employee who continues to collect accounts on the creditor's behalf, if he acts under his own name rather than the creditors's.

(b) *Creditor-controlled collector.* Section 803(6)(B) provides that "debt collector" does not include a party collecting for another, where they are both "related by common ownership or affiliated by corporate control, if the (party collects) only for persons to whom it is so related or affiliated and if the principal business of such person is not the collection of debts".

The exemption applies where the collector and creditor have "common ownership or * * *

corporate control." For example, a company is exempt when it attempts to collect debts of another company after the two entities have merged.

The exemption does not apply to a party related to a creditor if it also collects debts for others in addition to the related creditors.

(c) *State and federal officials.* Section 803(6)(C) provides that "debt collector" does not include any state or federal employee "to the extent that collecting or attempting to collect any debt is in the performance of his official duties".

The exemption applies only to such governmental employees in the performance of their "official duties" and, therefore, does not apply to an attorney employed by a county government who also collected bad checks for local merchants where that activity is outside his official duties.

[53 Fed. Reg. 50103]

The exemption includes a state educational agency that is engaged in the collection of student loans.

(d) *Process servers.* Section 803(6)(D) provides that "debt collector" dos not include "any person while serving or attempting to serve legal process on any other person in connection with the judicial enforcement of any debt".

The exemption covers marshals, sheriffs, and any other process servers while conducting their normal duties relating to serving legal papers.

(e) *Non-profit counselors.* Section 803(6)(E) provides that "debt collector" does not include "any nonprofit organization which, at the request of consumers, performs bona fide consumer credit counseling and assists consumers in the liquidation of their debts by receiving payments from such consumers and distributing such amounts to creditors".

This exemption applies only to non-profit organizations; it does not apply to for-profit credit counseling services that accept fees from debtors and regularly transmit such funds to creditors.

(f) *Miscellaneous.* Section 803(6)(F) provides that "debt collector" does not include collection activity by a party about a debt that "(i) is incidental to a bona fide fiduciary obligation or * * * escrow arrangement; (ii) * * * was originated by such person; (iii) * * * was not in default at the time it was obtained by such person; or (iv) (was) obtained by such person as a secured party in a commercial credit transaction involving the creditor."

The exemption (i) for bona fide fiduciary obligations or escrow arrangements applies to entities such as trust departments of banks, and escrow companies. It does not include a party who is named as a debtor's trustee solely for the purpose of conducting a foreclosure sale (i.e., exercising a power of sale in the event of default on a loan).

The exemption (ii) for a party that originated the debt applies to the original creditor collecting his own debts in his own name. It also applies

when a creditor assigns a debt originally owed to him, but retains the authority to collect the obligation on behalf of the assignee to whom the debt becomes owed. For example, the exemption applies to a creditor who makes a mortgage or school loan and continues to handle the account after assigning it to a third party. However, it does not apply to a party that takes assignment of retail installment contracts from the original creditor and then reassigns them to another creditor but continues to collect the debt arising from the contracts, because the debt was not "originated by" the collector/first assignee.

The exception (iii) for debts not in default when obtained applies to parties such as mortgage service companies whose business is servicing current accounts.

The exemption (iv) for a secured party in a commercial transaction applies to a commercial lender who acquires a consumer account that was used as collateral, following default on a loan from the commercial lender to the original creditor.

(g) *Attorneys.* A provision of the FDCPA, as enacted in 1977 (former section 803(6)(F)), providing that "debt collector" does not include "any attorney-at-law collecting a debt as an attorney on behalf of and in the name of a client," was repealed by Pub. L. 99-361, which became effective in July 1986. Therefore, an attorney who meets the definition set forth in section 803(6) is now covered by the FDCPA.

Section 803(7) defines "location information" as "a consumer's place of abode and his telephone number at such place, or his place of employment."

This definition includes only residence, home phone number, and place of employment. It does not cover work phone numbers, names of supervisors and their telephone numbers, salaries or dates of paydays.

Section 803(8) defines "state" as "any State, territory, or possession of the United States, the District of Columbia, the Commonwealth of Puerto Rico, or any political subdivision of any of the foregoing."

Section 804—Acquisition of Location Information

Section 804 requires a debt collector, when communicating with third parties for the purpose of acquiring information about the consumer's location to "(1) identify himself, state that he is confirming or correcting location information concerning the consumer, and, only if expressly requested, identify his employer;" (2) not refer to the debt, (3) usually make only a single contact with each third party, (4) not communicate by post card, (5) not indicate the collection nature of his business purpose in any written communication, and (6) limit communications to the consumer's attorney, where the collector knows of the attorney, unless the attorney fails to respond to the communication.

1. *General.* Although the FDCPA generally protects the consumer's privacy by limiting debt

collector communications about personal affairs to third parties, it recognizes the need for some third party contact by collectors to seek the whereabouts of the consumer.

2. *Identification of debt collector (section 804(1)).* An individual employed by a debt collector seeking location information must identify himself, but must not identify his employer unless asked. When asked, however, he must give the true and full name of the employer, to comply with this provision and avoid a violation of section 807(14).

An individual debt collector may use an alias if it is used consistently and if it does not interfere with another party's ability to identify him (e.g., the true identity can be ascertained by the employer).

3. *Referral to debt (section 804(2)).* A debt collector may not refer to the consumer's debt in any third party communication seeking location information, including those with other creditors.

4. *Reference to debt collector's business (section 804(5)).* A debt collector may not use his actual name in his letterhead or elsewhere in a written communication seeking location information, if the name indicates collection activity (such as a name containing the word "debt", "collector", or "collection"), except when the person contacted has expressly requested that the debt collector identify himself.

5. *Communication with consumer's attorney (section 804(6)).* Once a debt collector learns a consumer is represented by an attorney in connection with the debt, he must confine his request for location information to the attorney. (See also comments on section 805(a)(2).)

Section 805—Communication in Connection With Debt Collection

Section 805(a)—Communication with the consumer. Unless the consumer has consented or a court order permits, a debt collector may not communicate with a consumer to collect a debt (1) at any time or place which is unusual or known to be inconvenient to the consumer (8AM–9PM is presumed to be convenient), (2) where he knows the consumer is represented by an attorney with respect to the debt, unless the attorney fails to respond to the communication in a reasonable time period, or (3) at work if he knows the consumer's employer prohibits such contacts.

1. *Scope.* For purposes of this section, the term "communicate" is given its commonly accepted meaning. Thus, the section applies to contacts with the consumer related to the collection of the debt, whether or not the debt is specifically mentioned.

[53 Fed. Reg. 50104]

2. *Inconvenient or unusual times or places (section 805(a)(1)).* A debt collector may not call the consumer at any time, or on any particular day, if he has credible information (from the consumer or elsewhere) that it is inconvenient. If the debt collector does not have such informa-

tion, a call on Sunday is not per se illegal.

3. *Consumer represented by attorney (section 805(a)(2)).* If a debt collector learns that a consumer is represented by an attorney in connection with the debt, even if not formally notified of this fact, the debt collector must contact only the attorney and must not contact the consumer.

A debt collector who knows a consumer is represented by counsel with respect to a debt is not required to assume similar representation on other debts; however, if a consumer notifies the debt collector that the attorney has been retained to represent him for other debts placed with the debt collector, the debt collector must deal only with that attorney with respect to such debts.

The creditor's knowledge that the consumer has an attorney is not automatically imputed to the debt collector.

4. *Calls at work (section 805(a)(3)).* A debt collector may not call the consumer at work if he has reason to know the employer forbids such communication (e.g., if the consumer has so informed the debt collector).

Section 805(b)—Communication with third parties. Unless the consumer consents, or a court order or section 804 permits, "or as reasonably necessary to effectuate a postjudgment judicial remedy," a debt collector "may not communicate, in connection with the collection of any debt, with any person other than the consumer, his attorney, a consumer reporting agency if otherwise permitted by law, the creditor, the attorney of the creditor, or the attorney of the debt collector."

1. *Consumer consent to the third party contact.* The consumer's consent need not be in writing. For example, if a third party volunteers that a consumer has authorized him to pay the consumer's account, the debt collector may normally presume the consumer's consent, and may accept the payment and provide a receipt to the party that makes the payment. However, consent may not be inferred only from a consumer's inaction when the debt collector requests such consent.

2. *Location information.* Although a debt collector's search for information concerning the consumer's location (provided in § 804) is expressly excepted from the ban on third party contacts, a debt collector may not call third parties under the pretense of gaining information already in his possession.

3. *Incidental contacts with telephone operator or telegraph clerk.* A debt collector may contact an employee of a telephone or telegraph company in order to contact the consumer, without violating the prohibition on communication to third parties, if the only information given is that necessary to enable the collector to transmit the message to, or make the contact with, the consumer.

4. *Accessibility by third party.* A debt collector may not send a written message that is easily accessible to third parties. For example, he may not use a computerized billing statement that can be seen on the envelope itself.

A debt collector may use an "in care of" letter only if the consumer lives at, or accepts mail at, the other party's address.

A debt collector does not violate this provision when an eavesdropper overhears a conversation with the consumer, unless the debt collector has reason to anticipate the conversation will be overhead.

5. *Non-excepted parties.* A debt collector may discuss the debt only with the parties specified in this section (consumer, creditor, a party's attorney, or credit bureau). For example, unless the consumer has authorized the communication, a collector may not discuss the debt (such as a dishonored check) with a bank, or make a report on a consumer to a non-profit counseling service.

6. *Judicial remedy.* The words "as reasonably necessary to effectuate a postjudgment judicial remedy" mean a communication necessary for execution or enforcement of the remedy. A debt collector may not send a copy of the judgment to an employer, except as part of a formal service of papers to achieve a garnishment or other remedy.

7. *Audits or inquiries.* A debt collector may disclose his files to a government official or an auditor, to respond to an inquiry or conduct an audit, because the disclosure would not be "in connection with the collection of any debt."

8. *Communications by attorney debt collectors.* An attorney who represents either a creditor or debt collector that has previously tried to collect an account may communicate his efforts to collect the account to the debt collector. Because the section permits a debt collector to communicate with "the attorney of the creditor, or the attorney of the debt collector", communications between these parties (even if the attorney is also a debt collector) are not forbidden.

An attorney may communicate with a potential witness in connection with a lawsuit he has filed (e.g., in order to establish the existence of a debt), because the section was not intended to prohibit communications by attorneys that are necessary to conduct lawsuits on behalf of their clients.

Section 805(c)—Ceasing communication. Once a debt collector receives written notice from a consumer that he or she refuses to pay the debt or wants the collector to stop further collection efforts, the debt collector must cease any further communication with the consumer except "(1) to advise the consumer that the debt collector's further efforts are being terminated; (2) to notify the consumer that the debt collector or creditor may invoke specified remedies which are ordinarily invoked by such debt collector or creditor; or (3) where applicable, to notify the consumer that the debt collector or creditor intends to invoke a specified remedy."

1. *Scope.* For purposes of this section, the term "communicate" is given its commonly accepted meaning. Thus, the section applies to any contact with the consumer related to the collection of the debt, whether or not the debt is specifically mentioned.

2. *Request for payment.* A debt collector's response to a "cease communication" notice from the consumer may not include a demand for payment, but is limited to the three statutory exceptions.

Section 805(d)—"consumer" definition. For section 805 purposes, the term "consumer" includes the "consumer's spouse, parent (if the consumer is a minor), guardian, executor, or administrator."

1. *Broad "consumer" definition.* Because of the broad statutory definition of "consumer" for the purposes of this section, many of its protections extend to parties close to the consumer. For example, the debt collector may not call the consumer's spouse at a time or place known to be inconvenient to the spouse. Conversely, he may call the spouse (guardian, executor, etc.) at any time or place that would be in accord with the limitations of section 805(a).

Section 806—Harassment or Abuse

Section 806 prohibits a debt collector from any conduct that would "Harass, oppress, or abuse any person in connection with the collection of a debt." It provides six examples of harassment or abuse.

1. *Scope.* Prohibited actions are not limited to the six subsections listed as examples of activities that violate this provision.

2. *Unnecessary calls to third parties.* A debt collector may not leave telephone messages with neighbors when the debt collector knows the consumer's name and telephone number and could have reached him directly.

3. *Multiple contacts with consumer.* A debt collector may not engage in repeated personal contacts with a consumer with such frequency as to harass him. Subsection (5) deals specifically with harassment by multiple phone calls.

4. *Abusive conduct.* A debt collector may not pose a lengthy series of questions or comments to the consumer without giving the consumer a chance to reply. Subsection (2) deals specifically with harassment involving obscene, profane, or abusive language.

Section 806(1) prohibits the "use or threat of use of violence or other criminal means to harm * * * any person."

1. *Implied threat.* A debt collector may violate this section by an implied threat of violence. For example, a debt collector may not pressure a consumer with statements such as "We're not playing around here—we can play tough" or "We're going to send somebody to collect for us one way or the other."

Section 806(2) prohibits the use of obscene, profane, or abusive language.

1. *Abusive language.* Abusive language includes religious slurs, profanity, obscenity, calling the consumer a liar or a deadbeat, and the use of racial or sexual epithets.

Section 806(3) prohibits the "publication of a list of consumers who allegedly refuse to pay debts," except to report the items to a "consumer reporting agency", as defined in the Fair Credit Reporting Act or to a party otherwise authorized to receive it under that Act.

Section 806(4) prohibits the "advertisement for sale of any debt to coerce payment of the debt."

1. *Shaming prohibited.* These provisions are designed to prohibit debt collectors from "shaming" a customer into payment, by publicizing the debt.

2. *Exchange of lists.* Debt collectors may not exchange lists of consumers who allegedly refuse to pay their debts.

3. *Information to creditor subscribers.* A debt collector may not distribute a list of alleged debtors to its creditor subscribers.

4. *Coded lists.* A debt collector that publishes a list of consumers who have had bad debts, coded to avoid generally disclosing the consumer's identity (e.g., showing only the drivers license number and first three letters of each consumer's name) does not violate this provision, because such publication is permitted under the Fair Credit Reporting Act.

5. *List for use by investigator.* A debtor collector does not violate these provisions by providing a list of consumers against whom judgments have been entered to a private investigator in order to locate such individuals, because section 805(b) specifically permits contacts "reasonably necessary to effectuate a post-judgment judicial remedy."

6. *Public notice required by law.* A debt collector does not violate these provisions by providing public notices that are required by law as a prerequisite to enforcement of a security interest in connection with a debt.

Section 806(5) prohibits contacting the consumer by telephone "repeatedly or continuously with intent to annoy, abuse, or harass any person at the called number."

1. *Multiple phone calls.* "Continuously" means making a series of telephone calls, one right after the other. "Repeatedly" means calling with excessive frequency under the circumstances.

Section 806(6) prohibits, except where section 804 applies, "the placement of telephone calls without meaningful disclosure of the caller's identity."

1. *Aliases.* A debt collector employee's use of an alias that permits identification of the debt collector (i.e., where he uses the alias consistently, and his true identity can be ascertained by the employer) constitutes a "meaningful disclosure of the caller's identity."

2. *Identification of caller.* An individual debt collector must disclose his employer's identity, when discussing the debt on the telephone with consumers or third parties permitted by section 805(b).

3. *Relation to other sections.* A debt collector who uses a false business name in a phone call to conceal his identity violates section 807(14), as well as this section.

Section 807—False or Misleading Representations

Section 807 prohibits a debt collector from using any "false, deceptive, or misleading representation or means in connection with the collection of any debt." It provides sixteen examples of false or misleading representations.

1. *Scope.* Prohibited actions are not limited to the sixteen subsections listed as examples of activities that violate this provision. In addition, section 807(10), which prohibits the "use of any false representation or deceptive means" by a debt collector, is particularly broad and encompasses virtually every violation, including those not covered by the other subsections.

Section 807(1) prohibits "the false representation or implication that the debt collector is vouched for, bonded by, or affiliated with the United States or any State * * * "

1. *Symbol on dunning notice.* A debt collector may not use a symbol in correspondence that makes him appear to be a government official. For example, a collection letter depicting a police badge, a judge, or the scales of justice, normally violates this section.

Section 807(2) prohibits falsely representing either "(A) the character, amount, or legal status of any debt; or (B) any services rendered or compensation which may be lawfully received by" the collector.

1. *Legal Status of debt.* A debt collector may not falsely imply that legal action has begun.

2. *Amount of debt.* A debt collector may not claim an amount more than actually owed, or falsely assert that the debt has matured or that it is immediately due and payable, when it is not.

3. *Judgment.* When a debt collector provides the validation notice required by section 809(a)(4), the notice may include the words "copy of a judgment" whether or not a judgment exists, because section 809(a)(4) provides for a statement including these words. Compliance with section 809(a)(4) in this manner will not be considered a violation of section 807(2)(A).

Section 807(3) prohibits falsely representing or implying that "any individual is an attorney or that any communication is from an attorney."

1. *Form of legal correspondence.* A debt collector may not send a collection letter from a "Pre-Legal Department," where no legal department exists. An attorney may use a computer service to send letters on his own behalf, but a debt collector may not send a computer-generated letter deceptively using an attorney's name.

2. *Named individual.* A debt collector may not falsely represent that a person named in a letter is his attorney.

3. *Relation to other sections.* If a creditor falsely uses an attorney's name rather than his own in his collection communications, he both loses his exemption from the FDCPA's definition of "debt collector" (Section 803(6)) and violates this provision.

Section 807(4) prohibits falsely representing or implying to the consumer that nonpayment "will result in the arrest or imprisonment of any

[53 Fed. Reg. 50106]

person or the seizure, garnishment, attachment, or sale of any property or wages of any person * * *"

Section 807(5) prohibits the "threat to take any action that cannot legally be taken or that is not intended to be taken."

1. *Debt collector's statement of his own definite action.* A debt collector may not state that he will take any action unless he intends to take the action when the statement is made, or ordinarily takes the action in similar circumstances.

2. *Debt collector's statement of definite action by third party.* A debt collector may not state that a third party will take any action unless he has reason to believe, at the time the statement is made, that such action will be taken.

3. *Statement of possible action.* A debt collector may not state or imply that he or any third party may take any action unless such action is legal and there is a reasonable likelihood, at the time the statement is made, that such action will be taken. A debt collector may state that certain action is possible, if it is true that such action is legal and is frequently taken by the collector or creditor with respect to similar debts; however, if the debt collector has reason to know there are facts that make the action unlikely in the particular case, a statement that the action was possible would be misleading.

4. *Threat of criminal action.* A debt collector may not threaten to report a dishonored check or other fact to the police, unless he actually intends to take this action.

5. *Threat of attachment.* A debt collector may not threaten to attach a consumer's tax refund, when he has no authority to do so.

6. *Threat of legal or other action.* Section 807(5) refers not only to a false threat of legal action, but also a false threat by a debt collector that he will report a debt to a credit bureau, assess a collection fee, or undertake any other action if the debt is not paid. A debt collector may also not misrepresent the imminence of such action.

A debt collector's implication, as well as a direct statement, of planned legal action may be an unlawful deception. For example, reference to an attorney or to legal proceedings may mislead the debtor as to the likelihood or imminence of legal action.

A debt collector's statement that legal action has been recommended is a representation that legal action may be taken, since such a recommendation implies that the creditor will act on it at least some of the time.

Lack of intent may be inferred when the amount of the debt is so small as to make the action totally unfeasible or when the debt collector is unable to take the action because the creditor has not authorized him to do so.

7. *Illegality of threatened act.* A debt collector may not threaten that he will illegally contact an employer, or other third party, or take some other

"action that cannot legally be taken" (such as advising the creditor to sue where such advice would violate state rules governing the unauthorized practice of law). If state law forbids a debt collector from suing in his own name (or from doing so without first obtaining a formal assignment and that has not been done), the debt collector may not represent that he will sue in that state.

Section 807(6) prohibits falsely representing or implying that a transfer of the debt will cause the consumer to (A) lose any claim or defense, or (B) become subject to any practice prohibited by the FDCPA.

1. *Referral to creditor.* A debt collector may not falsely state that the consumer's account will be referred back to the original creditor, who would take action the FDCPA prohibits the debt collector to take.

Section 807(7) prohibits falsely representing or implying that the "consumer committed any crime or other conduct in order to disgrace the consumer."

1. *False allegation of fraud.* A debt collector may not falsely allege that the consumer has committed fraud.

2. *Misrepresentation of criminal law.* A debt collector may not make a misleading statement of law, falsely implying that the consumer has committed a crime, or mischaracterize what constitutes an offense by misstating or omitting significant elements of the offense. For example, a debt collector may not tell the consumer that he has committed a crime by issuing a check that is dishonored, when the statute applies only where there is a "scheme to defraud."

Section 807(8) prohibits "Communicating or threatening to communicate to any person (false) credit information * * *, including the failure to communicate that a disputed debt is disputed."

1. *Disputed debt.* If a debt collector knows that a debt is disputed by the consumer, either from receipt of written notice (section 809) or other means, and reports it to a credit bureau, he must report it as disputed.

2. *Post-report dispute.* When a debt collector learns of a dispute after reporting the debt to a credit bureau, the dispute need not also be reported.

Section 807(9) prohibits the use of any document designed to falsely imply that it issued from a state or federal source, or "which creates a false impression as to its source, authorization, or approval."

1. *Relation to other sections.* Most of the violations of this section involve simulated legal process, which is more specifically covered by section 807(13). However, this subsection is broader in that it also covers documents that fraudulently appear to be official government documents, or otherwise mislead the recipient as to their authorship.

Section 807(10) prohibits the "use of any false representation or deceptive means to collect or attempt to collect any debt or to obtain information concerning a consumer."

1. *Relation to other sections.* The prohibition is so comprehensive that violation of any part of section 807 will usually also violate subsection (10). Actions that violate more specific provisions are discussed in those sections.

2. *Communication format.* A debt collector may not communicate by a format or envelope that misrepresents the nature, purpose, or urgency of the message. It is a violation to send any communication that conveys to the consumer a false sense of urgency. However, it is usually permissible to send a letter generated by a machine, such as a computer or other printing device. A bona fide contest entry form, which provides a clearly optional location to enter employment information, enclosed with request for payment, is not deceptive.

3. *False statement or implications.* A debt collector may not falsely state or imply that a consumer is required to assign his wages to his creditor when he is not, that the debt collector has counseled the creditor to sue when he has not, that adverse credit information has been entered on the consumer's credit record when it has not, that the entire amount is due when it is not, or that he cannot accept partial payments when in fact he is authorized to accept them.

4. *Misrepresentation of law.* A debt collector may not mislead the consumer as to the legal consequences of the consumer's actions (e.g., by falsely implying that a failure to respond is an admission of liability).

A debt collector may not state that federal law requires a notice of the debt collector's intent to contact third parties.

5. *Misleading letterhead.* A debt collector's employee who is an attorney may not use "attorney-at-law"

[53 Fed. Reg. 50107]

stationery without referring to his employer, so as to falsely imply to the consumer that the debt collector had retained a private attorney to bring suit on the account.

Section 807(11) requires the debt collector to "disclose clearly in all communications made to collect a debt or to obtain information about a consumer, that the debt collector is attempting to collect a debt and that any information obtained will be used for that purpose", except where section 804 provides otherwise.

1. *Oral communications.* A debt collector must make the required disclosures in both oral and written communications.

2. *Disclosure to consumers.* When a debt collector contacts a consumer and clearly discloses that he is seeking payment of a debt, he need not state that all information will be used to collect a debt, since that should be apparent to the consumer. The debt collector need not repeat the required disclosure in subsequent contacts.

A debt collector may not send the consumer a note saying only "please call me right away" unless there has been prior contact between the parties and the collector is thus known to the consumer.

3. *Disclosures to third parties.* Except when seeking location information, the debt collector must state in the first communication with a third party that he is attempting to collect the debt and that information will be used for that purpose, but need not do so in subsequent communications with that party.

Section 807(12) prohibits falsely representing or implying that "accounts have been turned over to innocent purchasers for value."

1. *Relation to other sections.* Section 807(6)(A) prohibits a false statement or implication that threatening to affect the consumer's rights may be affected by transferring the account; this subsection forbids falsely stating or implying that a transfer to certain parties has occurred.

Section 807(13) prohibits falsely representing or implying that "documents are legal process."

1. *Simulated legal process.* A debt collector may not send written communications that deceptively resemble legal process forms. He may not send a form or a dunning letter that, taken as a whole, appears to simulate legal process. However, one legal phrase (such as "notice of legal action" or "show just cause why") alone will not result in a violation of this section unless it contributes to an erroneous impression that the document is a legal form.

Section 807(14) prohibits the "use of any business, company, or organization name other than the (collector's) true name".

1. *Permissible business name.* A debt collector may use a name that does not misrepresent his identity or deceive the consumer. Thus, a collector may use its full business name, the name under which it usually transacts business, or a commonly-used acronym. When the collector uses multiple names in its various affairs, it does not violate this subsection if it consistently uses the same name when dealing with a particular consumer.

2. *Creditor misrepresentation of identity.* A creditor may not use any name that would falsely imply that a third party is involved in the collection. The in-house collection unit of "ABC Corp." may use the name "ABC Collection Division," but not the name "XYZ Collection Agency" or some other unrelated name.

A creditor violates this section if he uses the name of a collection bureau as a conduit for a collection process that the creditor controls in collecting his own accounts. Similarly, a creditor may not use a fictitious name or letterhead, or a "post office box address" name that implies someone else is collecting his debts.

A creditor does not violate this provision where an affiliated (and differently named) debt collector undertakes collection activity, if the debt collector does business separately from the creditor (e.g., where the debt collector in fact has other clients that he treats similarly to the creditor, has his own employees, deals at arms length with the creditor, and controls the process himself).

3. *All collection activities covered.* A debt collection business must use its real business name, commonly-used name, or acronym in both written and oral communications.

4. *Relation to other sections.* If a creditor uses a false business name, he both loses his exemption from the FDCPA's definition of "debt collector" (section 803(6)) and violates this provision. If a debt collector falsely uses the name of an attorney rather than his true business name, he violates section 807(3) as well as this section. When a debt collector uses a false business name in a phone call, he violates section 806(6) as well as this section.

When using the mails to obtain location information, a debt collector may not (unless expressly requested by the recipient to identify the firm) use a name that indicates he is in the debt collection business, or he will violate section 804(5). When a debt collector's employee who is seeking location information replies to an inquiry about his employer's identity under section 804(1), he must give the true name of his employer.

Section 807(15) prohibits falsely representing or implying that documents are not legal process forms or do not require action by the consumer.

1. *Disguised legal process.* A debt collector may not deceive a consumer into failing to respond to legal process by concealing the import of the papers, thereby subjecting the consumer to a default judgment.

Section 807(16) prohibits falsely representing or implying that a debt collector operates or is employed by a "consumer reporting agency" as defined in the Fair Credit Reporting Act.

1. *Dual agencies.* The FDCPA does not prohibit a debt collector from operating a consumer reporting agency.

2. *Misleading names.* Only a bona fide consumer reporting agency may use names such as "Credit Bureau," "Credit Bureau Collection Agency," "General Credit Control," "Credit Bureau Rating, Inc.," or "National Debtors Rating." A debt collector's disclaimer in the text of a letter that the debt collector is not affiliated with (or employed by) a consumer reporting agency, will not necessarily avoid a violation if the collector uses a name that indicates otherwise.

3. *Factual issue.* Whether a debt collector that has called itself a credit bureau actually qualifies as such is a factual issue, to be decided according to the debt collector's actual operation.

Section 808—Unfair Practices

Section 808 prohibits a debt collector from using "unfair or unconscionable means" in his debt collection activity. It provides eight examples of unfair practices.

1. *Scope.* Prohibited actions are not limited to the eight subsections listed as examples of activities that violate this provision.

2. *Elements of unfairness.* A debt collector's act in collecting a debt may be "unfair" if it causes injury to the consumer that is (1) substantial, (2) not outweighed by countervailing benefits to consumers or competition, and (3) not

reasonably avoidable by the consumer.

Section 808(1) prohibits collecting any amount unless the amount is expressly authorized by the agreement creating the debt or is permitted by law.

1. *Kinds of amounts covered.* For purposes of this section, "amount" includes not only the debt, but also any incidental charges, such as collection

[53 Fed. Reg. 50108]

charges, interest, service charges, late fees, and bad check handling charges.

2. *Legality of charges.* A debt collector may attempt to collect a fee or charge in addition to the debt if either (a) the charge is expressly provided for in the contract creating the debt and the charge is not prohibited by state law, or (B) the contract is silent but the charge is otherwise expressly permitted by state law. Conversely, a debt collector may not collect an additional amount if either (A) state law expressly prohibits collection of the amount or (B) the contract does not provide for collection of the amount and state law is silent.

3. *Legality of fee under state law.* If state law permits collection of reasonable fees, the reasonableness (and consequential legality) of these fees is determined by state law.

4. *Agreement not in writing.* A debt collector may establish an "agreement" without a written contract. For example, he may collect a service charge on a dishonored check based on a posted sign on the merchant's premises allowing such a charge, if he can demonstrate that the consumer knew of the charge.

Section 808(2) prohibits accepting a check postdated by more than five days unless timely written notice is given to the consumer prior to deposit.

Section 808(3) prohibits soliciting any postdated check for purposes of threatening or instituting criminal prosecution.

Section 808(4) prohibits depositing a postdated check prior to its date.

1. *Postdated checks.* These provisions do not totally prohibit debt collectors from accepting postdated checks from consumers, but rather prohibit debt collectors from misusing such instruments.

Section 808(5) prohibits causing any person to incur telephone or telegram charges by concealing the true purpose of the communication.

1. *Long distance calls to the debt collector.* A debt collector may not call the consumer collect or ask a consumer to call him long distance without disclosing the debt collector's identity and the communication's purpose.

2. *Relation to other section.* A debt collector who conceals his purpose in asking consumers to call long distance may also violate section 807(11), which requires the debt collector to disclose his purpose in some communications.

Section 808(6) prohibits taking nonjudicial action to enforce a security interest on property, or threatening to do so, where (A) there is not present right to the collateral, (B) there is no present intent to exercise such rights, or (C) the property is exempt by law.

1. *Security enforcers.* Because the FDCPA's definition of "debt collection" includes parties whose principal business is enforcing security interests only for section 808(6) purposes, such parties (if they do not otherwise fall within the definition) are subject only to this provision and not to the rest of the FDCPA.

Section 808(7) prohibits "Communicating with a consumer regarding a debt by post card."

1. *Debt.* A debt collector does not violate this section if he sends a post card to a consumer that does not communicate the existence of the debt. However, if he had not previously disclosed that he is attempting to collect a debt, he would violate section 807(11), which requires this disclosure.

Section 808(8) prohibits showing anything other than the debt collector's address, on any envelope in any written communication to the consumer, except that a debt collector may use his business name if it does not indicate that he is in the debt collection business.

1. *Business names prohibited on envelopes.* A debt collector may not put on his envelope any business name with "debt" or "collector" in it, or any other name that indicates he is in the debt collection business. A debt collector may not use the American Collectors Association logo on an envelope.

2. *Collector's name.* Whether a debt collector/ consumer reporting agency's use of his own "credit bureau" or other name indicates that he is in the collection business, and thus violates the section, is a factual issue to be determined in each individual case.

3. *Harmless words or symbols.* A debt collector does not violate this section by using an envelope printed with words or notations that do not suggest the purpose of the communication. For example, a collector may communicate via an actual telegram or similar service that uses a Western Union (or other provider) logo and the word "telegram" (or similar word) on the envelope, or a letter with the word "Personal" or "Confidential" on the envelope.

4. *Transparent envelopes.* A debt collector may not use a transparent envelope, which reveals language or symbols indicating his debt collection business, because it is the equivalent of putting information on an envelope.

Section 809—Validation of Debts

Section 809(a) requires a collector, within 5 days of the first communication, to provide the consumer a written notice (if not provided in that communication) containing (1) the amount of the debt and (2) the name of the creditor, along with a statement that he will (3) assume the debt's validity unless the consumer disputes it within 30 days, (4) send a verification or copy of the judgment if the consumer timely disputes the debt, and (5) identify the original creditor upon written request.

1. *Who must provide notice.* If the employer debt collection agency gives the required notice, employee debt collectors need not also provide it. A debt collector's agent may give the notice, as long as it is clear that the information is being provided on behalf of the debt collector.

2. *Single notice required.* The debt collector is not required to provide more than one notice for each debt. A notice need not offer to identify the original creditor unless the name and address of the original creditor are different from the current creditor.

3. *Form of notices.* The FDCPA imposes no requirements as to the form, sequence, location, or typesize of the notice. However, an illegible notice does not comply with this provision.

4. *Alternate terminology.* A debt collector may condense and combine the required disclosures, as long as he provides all required information.

5. *Oral notice.* If a debt collector's first communication with the consumer is oral, he may make the disclosures orally at that time in which case he need not send a written notice.

6. *Legal action.* A debt collector's institution of formal legal action against a consumer (including the filing of a complaint or service of legal papers by an attorney in connection with a lawsuit to collect a debt) or transmission of a notice to a consumer that is required by law as a prerequisite to enforcing a contractual obligation is not a "communication in connection with collection of any debt," and thus does not confer section 809 notice-and-validation rights on the consumer.

7. *Collection activities by attorneys.* An attorney who regularly attempts to collect debts by means other than litigation, such as writing the consumer demand letters (dunning notices) or calling the consumer on the phone about the obligation (except in response to a consumer's call to him after suit has been commenced), must provide the required notice, even if a previous debt collector (or creditor) has given such a notice.

8. *Effect of including proof with first notice.* A debt collector must verify a disputed debt even if he has included proof of the debt with the first communication, because the section is intended to assist the consumer when a debt collector inadvertently contacts the

[53 Fed. Reg. 50109]

wrong consumer at the start of his collection efforts.

Section 809(b) requires that, if the consumer disputes the debt or requests identification of the original creditor in writing, the collector must cease collection efforts until he verifies the debt and mails a response.

Section 809(c) states that a consumer's failure to dispute the validity of a debt under this section may not be interpreted by a court as an admission of liability.

1. *Pre-notice collection.* A debt collector need not cease normal collection activities within the

consumer's 30-day period to give notice of a dispute until he receives a notice from the consumer. An attorney debt collector may take legal action within 30 days of sending the notice, regardless of whether the consumer disputes the debt. If the consumer disputes the debt, the attorney may still take legal action but must cease collection efforts until verification is obtained and mailed to the consumer.

A debt collector may report a debt to a credit bureau within the 30-day notice period, before he receives a request for validation or a dispute notice from the consumer.

Section 810—Multiple Debts

Section 810 provides: "If any consumer owes multiple debts and makes any single payment to any debt collector with respect to such debts, such debt collector my not apply such payment to any debt which is disputed by the consumer and, where applicable, shall apply such payment in accordance with the consumer's directions."

Section 811—Legal Actions by Debt Collectors

Section 811 provides that a debt collector may sue a consumer only in the judicial district where the consumer resides or signed the contract sued upon, except that an action to enforce a security interest in real property which secures the obligation must be brought where the property is located.

1. *Waiver.* Any waiver by the consumer must be provided directly to the debt collector (not to the creditor in the contract establishing the debt), because the forum restriction applies to actions brought by the debt collector.

2. *Multiple defendants.* Since a debt collector may sue only where the consumer (1) lives or (2) signed the contract, the collector may not join an ex-husband as a defendant to a suit against the ex-wife in the district of her residence, unless he also lives there or signed the contract there. The existence of community property at her residence that is available to pay his debts does not alter the forum limitations on individual consumers.

3. *Real estate security.* A debt collector may sue based on the location of a consumer's real property only when he seeks to enforce an interest in such property that secures the debts.

4. *Services without written contract.* Where services were provided pursuant to an oral agreement, the debt collector may sue only where the consumer resides. He may not sue where services were performed (if that is different from the consumer's residence), because that is not included as permissible forum location by this provision.

5. *Enforcement of judgments.* If a judgment is obtained in a forum that satisfies the requirements of this section, it may be enforced in another jurisdiction, because the consumer previously has had the opportunity to defend the original action in a convenient forum.

6. *Scope.* This provision applies to lawsuits brought by a debt collector, including an attorney

debt collector, when the debt collector is acting on his own behalf or on behalf of his client.

Section 812—Furnishing Certain Deceptive Forms

Section 812 prohibits any party from designing and furnishing forms, knowing they are or will be used to deceive a consumer to believe that someone other than his creditor is collecting the debt, and imposes FDCPA civil liability on parties who supply such forms.

1. *Practice prohibited*. This section prohibits the practice of selling to creditors dunning letters that falsely imply that a debt collector is participating in collection of the debt, when in fact only the creditor is collecting.

2. *Coverage*. This section applies to anyone who designs, complies, or furnishes the forms prohibited by this section.

3. *Pre-collection letters*. A form seller may not furnish a creditor with (1) a letter on a collector's letterhead to be used when the collector is not involved in collecting the creditor's debts, or (2) a letter indicating "copy to (the collector)" if the collector is not participating in collecting the creditor's debt. A form seller may not avoid liability by including a statement in the text of a form letter that the sender has not yet been assigned the account for collection, if the communication as a whole, using the collector's letterhead, represents otherwise.

4. *Knowledge required*. A party does not violate this provision unless he knows or should have known that his form letter will be used to mislead consumers into believing that someone other than the creditor is involved in collecting the debt.

5. *Participation by debt collector*. A debt collector that uses letters as his only collection tool does not violate this section, merely because he charges a flat rate per letter, if he is meaningfully "participating in the collection of a debt." The consumer is not misled in such cases, as he would be in the case of a party who supplied the creditor with form letters and provided little or no additional service in the collection process.

The performance of other tasks associated with collection (e.g., handling verification requests, negotiating payment arrangements, keeping individual records) is evidence that such a party is "participating in the collection."

Section 813—Civil Liability

Section 813 (A) imposes civil liability in the form of (1) actual damages, (2) discretionary penalties, and (3) costs and attorney's fees, (B) discusses relevant factors a court should consider in assessing damages, (C) exculpates a collector who maintains reasonable procedures from liability for an unintentional error, (D) permits actions to be brought in federal or state courts within one year from the violation, and (E) shields a defendant who relies on an advisory opinion of the Commission.

1. *Employee liability*. Since the employees of a debt collection agency are "debt collectors," they are liable for violations to the same extent as the agency.

2. *Damages*. The courts have awarded "actual damages" for FDCPA violations that were not just out-of-pocket expenses, but included damages for personal humiliation, embarrassment, mental anguish, or emotional distress.

3. *Application of statute of limitation period*. The section's one year statute of limitations applies only to private lawsuits, not to actions brought by a government agency.

4. *Advisory opinions*. A party may act in reliance on a formal advisory opinion of the Commission pursuant to 16 CFR 1.1–1.4, without risk of civil liability. This protection does not extend to reliance on this Commentary or other informal staff interpretations.

Section 814—Administrative Enforcement

Section 814 provides that the principal

[53 Fed. Reg. 50110]

federal enforcement agency for the FDCPA is the Federal Trade Commission, but assigns enforcement power to other authorities empowered by certain federal statutes to regulate financial, agricultural, and transportation activities, where

FDCPA violations relate to acts subject to those laws.

Section 815—Reports to Congress by Commission

Section 815 requires the Commission to submit an annual report to Congress which discusses its enforcement and other activities administering the FDCPA, assesses the degree of compliance, and makes recommendations.

Section 816—Relations to State Laws

Section 816 provides that the FDCPA preempts state laws only to the extent that those laws are inconsistent with any provision of the FDCPA, and then only to the extent of the inconsistency. A State law is not inconsistent if it gives consumers greater protection than the FDCPA.

1. *Inconsistent laws*. Where a state law provides protection to the consumer equal to, or greater than, the FDCPA, it is not pre-empted by the federal statute.

Section 817—Exemption For State Regulation

Section 817 orders the Commission to exempt any class of debt collection practices from the FDCPA within any State if it determines that State laws regulating those practices are substantially similar to the FDCPA, and contain adequate provision for enforcement.

1. *State exemptions*. A state with a debt collection law may apply to the Commission for an exemption. The Commission must grant the exemption if the state's law is substantially similar to the FDCPA, and there is adequate provision for enforcement. The Commission has published procedures for processing such applications (16 CFR 901).

Section 818—Effective Date

Section 818 provides that the FDCPA took effect six months from the date of its enactment.

1. *Key dates*. The FDCPA was approved September 20, 1977, and became effective March 20, 1978.

[FR Doc. 88-28573 Filed 12-12-88; 8:45 am]

Federal Standards for Private Tax Collectors

While the programs described in this Appendix are no longer active, the statutes governing them have not been repealed. These statutes are reprinted for informational purposes.

TITLE 26—INTERNAL REVENUE CODE
Subtitle F—Procedure and Administration
CHAPTER 64—COLLECTION
Subchapter A—General Provisions

* * *

26 U.S.C. § 6304. Fair tax collection practices

(a) Communication with the taxpayer

Without the prior consent of the taxpayer given directly to the Secretary or the express permission of a court of competent jurisdiction, the Secretary may not communicate with a taxpayer in connection with the collection of any unpaid tax—

(1) at any unusual time or place or a time or place known or which should be known to be inconvenient to the taxpayer;

(2) if the Secretary knows the taxpayer is represented by any person authorized to practice before the Internal Revenue Service with respect to such unpaid tax and has knowledge of, or can readily ascertain, such person's name and address, unless such person fails to respond within a reasonable period of time to a communication from the Secretary or unless such person consents to direct communication with the taxpayer; or

(3) at the taxpayer's place of employment if the Secretary knows or has reason to know that the taxpayer's employer prohibits the taxpayer from receiving such communication.

In the absence of knowledge of circumstances to the contrary, the Secretary shall assume that the convenient time for communicating with a taxpayer is after 8 a.m. and before 9 p.m., local time at the taxpayer's location.

(b) Prohibition of harassment and abuse

The Secretary may not engage in any conduct the natural consequence of which is to harass, oppress, or abuse any person in connection with the collection of any unpaid tax. Without limiting the general application of the foregoing, the following conduct is a violation of this subsection:

(1) The use or threat of use of violence or other criminal means to harm the physical person, reputation, or property of any person.

(2) The use of obscene or profane language or language the natural consequence of which is to abuse the hearer or reader.

(3) Causing a telephone to ring or engaging any person in telephone conversation repeatedly or continuously with intent to annoy, abuse, or harass any person at the called number.

(4) Except as provided under rules similar to the rules in section 804 of the Fair Debt Collection Practices Act (15 U.S.C. 1692b), the placement of telephone calls without meaningful disclosure of the caller's identity.

(c) Civil action for violations of section

For civil action for violations of this section, see section 7433.

[Added Pub. L. No. 105-206, tit. III, § 3466(a), 112 Stat. 768 (July 22, 1998)]

* * *

26 U.S.C. § 6306. Qualified tax collection contracts[1]

(a) In general.—Nothing in any provision of law shall be construed to prevent the Secretary from entering into a qualified tax collection contract.

---

1 The American Jobs Creation Act of 2004, Pub. L. No. 108-357, 118 Stat. 1418 (Oct. 22, 2004) added this note which was not codified:

BIENNIAL REPORT.—The Secretary of the Treasury shall biennially submit (beginning in 2005) to the Committee on Finance of the Senate and the Committee on Ways and Means of the House of Representatives a report with respect to qualified tax collection contracts under section 6306 of the Internal Revenue Code of 1986 (as added by this section) which includes—

(1) a complete cost benefit analysis,

(2) the impact of such contracts on collection enforcement staff levels in the Internal Revenue Service,

(3) the impact of such contracts on the total number and amount of unpaid assessments, and on the number and amount of assessments collected by Internal Revenue Service personnel after initial contact by a contractor,

(4) the amounts collected and the collection costs incurred (directly and indirectly) by the Internal Revenue Service,

(5) an evaluation of contractor performance,

(6) a disclosure safeguard report in a form similar to that required under section 6103(p)(5) of such Code, and

(7) a measurement plan which includes a comparison of the best practices used by the private collectors with the Internal Revenue Service's own collection techniques and mechanisms to identify and capture information on successful collection techniques used by the contractors which could be adopted by the Internal Revenue Service.

The American Jobs Creation Act of 2004, Pub. L. No. 108-357, 118 Stat. 1418 (Oct. 22, 2004) also provides that:

EFFECTIVE DATE.—The amendments made to this section shall take effect on the date of the enactment of this Act.

(b) Qualified tax collection contract.—For purposes of this section, the term "qualified tax collection contract" means any contract which—

(1) is for the services of any person (other than an officer or employee of the Treasury Department)—

(A) to locate and contact any taxpayer specified by the Secretary,

(B) to request full payment from such taxpayer of an amount of Federal tax specified by the Secretary and, if such request cannot be met by the taxpayer, to offer the taxpayer an installment agreement providing for full payment of such amount during a period not to exceed 5 years, and

(C) to obtain financial information specified by the Secretary with respect to such taxpayer,

(2) prohibits each person providing such services under such contract from committing any act or omission which employees of the Internal Revenue Service are prohibited from committing in the performance of similar services,

(3) prohibits subcontractors from—

(A) having contacts with taxpayers,

(B) providing quality assurance services, and

(C) composing debt collection notices, and

(4) permits subcontractors to perform other services only with the approval of the Secretary.

(c) Fees.—The Secretary may retain and use—

(1) an amount not in excess of 25 percent of the amount collected under any qualified tax collection contract for the costs of services performed under such contract, and

(2) an amount not in excess of 25 percent of such amount collected for collection enforcement activities of the Internal Revenue Service.

The Secretary shall keep adequate records regarding amounts so retained and used. The amount credited as paid by any taxpayer shall be determined without regard to this subsection.

(d) No Federal liability.—The United States shall not be liable for any act or omission of any person performing services under a qualified tax collection contract.

(e) Application of fair debt collection practices act.—The provisions of the Fair Debt Collection Practices Act (15 U.S.C. 1692 et seq.) shall apply to any qualified tax collection contract, except to the extent superseded by section 6304, section 7602(c), or by any other provision of this title.

(f) Cross references.—

(1) For damages for certain unauthorized collection actions by persons performing services under a qualified tax collection contract, see section 7433A.

(2) For application of Taxpayer Assistance Orders to persons performing services under a qualified tax collection contract, see section 7811(g).

[Added by Pub. L. No. 108-357, tit. VIII, § 881(a), 118 Stat. 1625 (Oct. 22, 2004)]

* * *

Subtitle F—Procedure and Administration
CHAPTER 76—JUDICIAL PROCEEDINGS
Subchapter B—Proceedings by Taxpayers and Third Parties

* * *

26 U.S.C. § 7433. Civil damages for certain unauthorized collection actions

(a) In general

If, in connection with any collection of Federal tax with respect to a taxpayer, any officer or employee of the Internal Revenue Service recklessly or intentionally, or by reason of negligence, disregards any provision of this title, or any regulation promulgated under this title, such taxpayer may bring a civil action for damages against the United States in a district court of the United States. Except as provided in section 7432, such civil action shall be the exclusive remedy for recovering damages resulting from such actions.

(b) Damages

In any action brought under subsection (a) or petition filed under subsection (e), upon a finding of liability on the part of the defendant, the defendant shall be liable to the plaintiff in an amount equal to the lesser of $1,000,000 ($100,000, in the case of negligence) or the sum of—

(1) actual, direct economic damages sustained by the plaintiff as a proximate result of the reckless or intentional or negligent actions of the officer or employee, and

(2) the costs of the action.

(c) Payment authority

Claims pursuant to this section shall be payable out of funds appropriated under section 1304 of title 31, United States Code.

(d) Limitations

(1) Requirement that administrative remedies be exhausted

A judgment for damages shall not be awarded under subsection (b) unless the court determines that the plaintiff has exhausted the administrative remedies available to such plaintiff within the Internal Revenue Service.

(2) Mitigation of damages

The amount of damages awarded under subsection (b)(1) shall be reduced by the amount of such damages which could have reasonably been mitigated by the plaintiff.

(3) Period for bringing action

Notwithstanding any other provision of law, an action to enforce liability created under this section may be brought without regard to the amount in controversy and may be brought only within 2 years after the date the right of action accrues.

(e) Actions for violations of certain bankruptcy procedures

(1) In general

If, in connection with any collection of Federal tax with respect to a taxpayer, any officer or employee of the Internal Revenue Service willfully violates any provision of section 362 (relating to automatic stay) or 524 (relating to effect of discharge) of title 11, United States Code (or any successor provision), or any regulation promulgated under such provision, such taxpayer may petition the bankruptcy court to recover damages against the United States.

(2) Remedy to be exclusive

(A) In general

Except as provided in subparagraph (B), notwithstanding section 105 of such title 11, such petition shall be the exclusive remedy for recovering damages resulting from such actions.

(B) Certain other actions permitted

Subparagraph (A) shall not apply to an action under section 362(h) of such title 11 for a violation of a stay provided by section 362 of such title; except that—

(i) administrative and litigation costs in connection with such an action may only be awarded under section 7430; and

(ii) administrative costs may be awarded only if incurred on or after the date that the bankruptcy petition is filed.

[Added Pub. L. No. 100-647, tit. VI, § 6241(a), 102 Stat. 3747 (Nov. 10, 1988); amended Pub. L. No. 104-168, tit. VIII, §§ 801(a), 802 (a), 110 Stat. 1465 (July 30, 1996); Pub. L. No. 105-206, tit. III, § 3102(a), (c), 112 Stat. 730 (July 22, 1998)]

26 U.S.C. § 7433A. Civil damages for certain unauthorized collection actions by persons performing services under qualified tax collection contracts

(a) In general.

Subject to the modifications provided by subsection (b), section 7433 shall apply to the acts and omissions of any person performing services under a qualified tax collection contract (as defined in section 6306(b)) to the same extent and in the same manner as if such person were an employee of the Internal Revenue Service.

(b) Modifications.

For purposes of subsection (a):

(1) Any civil action brought under section 7433 by reason of this section shall be brought against the person who entered into the qualified tax collection contract with the Secretary and shall not be brought against the United States.

(2) Such person and not the United States shall be liable for any damages and costs determined in such civil action.

(3) Such civil action shall not be an exclusive remedy with respect to such person.

(4) Subsections (c), (d)(1), and (e) of section 7433 shall not apply.

[Added by Pub. L. No. 108-357, tit. VIII, § 881(b)(1), 118 Stat. 1626 (Oct. 22, 2004)]

* * *

CHAPTER 78—DISCOVERY OF LIABILITY AND ENFORCEMENT OF TITLE
Subchapter A—Examination and Inspection

26 U.S.C. § 7602. Examination of books and witnesses

(a) Authority to summon, etc.

For the purpose of ascertaining the correctness of any return, making a return where none has been made, determining the liability of any person for any internal revenue tax or the liability at law or in equity of any transferee or fiduciary of any person in respect of any internal revenue tax, or collecting any such liability, the Secretary is authorized—

(1) To examine any books, papers, records, or other data which may be relevant or material to such inquiry;

(2) To summon the person liable for tax or required to perform the act, or any officer or employee of such person, or any person having possession, custody, or care of books of account containing entries relating to the business of the person liable for tax or required to perform the act, or any other person the Secretary may deem proper, to appear before the Secretary at a time and place named in the summons and to produce such books, papers, records, or other data, and to give such testimony, under oath, as may be relevant or material to such inquiry; and

(3) To take such testimony of the person concerned, under oath, as may be relevant or material to such inquiry.

(b) Purpose may include inquiry into offense

The purposes for which the Secretary may take any action described in paragraph (1), (2), or (3) of subsection (a) include the purpose of inquiring into any offense connected with the administration or enforcement of the internal revenue laws.

(c) Notice of contact of third parties

(1) General notice

An officer or employee of the Internal Revenue Service may not contact any person other than the taxpayer with respect to the determination or collection of the tax liability of such taxpayer without providing reasonable notice in advance to the taxpayer that contacts with persons other than the taxpayer may be made.

(2) Notice of specific contacts

The Secretary shall periodically provide to a taxpayer a record of persons contacted during such period by the Secretary with respect to the determination or collection of the tax liability of such taxpayer. Such record shall also be provided upon request of the taxpayer.

(3) Exceptions

This subsection shall not apply—

(A) to any contact which the taxpayer has authorized;

(B) if the Secretary determines for good cause shown that such notice would jeopardize collection of any tax or such notice may involve reprisal against any person; or

(C) with respect to any pending criminal investigation.

(d) No administrative summons when there is Justice Department referral

(1) Limitation of authority

No summons may be issued under this title, and the Secretary may not begin any action under section 7604 to enforce any summons, with respect to any person if a Justice Department referral is in effect with respect to such person.

(2) Justice Department referral in effect

For purposes of this subsection—

(A) In general

A Justice Department referral is in effect with respect to any person if—

(i) the Secretary has recommended to the Attorney General a grand jury investigation of, or the criminal prosecution of, such person for any offense connected with the administration or enforcement of the internal revenue laws, or

(ii) any request is made under section 6103 (h)(3)(B) for the disclosure of any return or return information (within the meaning of section 6103 (b)) relating to such person.

(B) Termination

A Justice Department referral shall cease to be in effect with respect to a person when—

(i) the Attorney General notifies the Secretary, in writing, that—

(I) he will not prosecute such person for any offense connected with the administration or enforcement of the internal revenue laws,

(II) he will not authorize a grand jury investigation of such person with respect to such an offense, or

(III) he will discontinue such a grand jury investigation,

(ii) a final disposition has been made of any criminal proceeding pertaining to the enforcement of the internal revenue laws which was instituted by the Attorney General against such person, or

(iii) the Attorney General notifies the Secretary, in writing, that he will not prosecute such person for any offense connected with the administration or enforcement of the internal revenue laws relating to the request described in subparagraph (A)(ii).

(3) Taxable years, etc., treated separately

For purposes of this subsection, each taxable period (or, if there is no taxable period, each taxable event) and each tax imposed by a separate chapter of this title shall be treated separately.

(e) Limitation on examination on unreported income

The Secretary shall not use financial status or economic reality examination techniques to determine the existence of unreported income of any taxpayer unless the Secretary has a reasonable indication that there is a likelihood of such unreported income.

[Aug. 16, 1954, ch. 736, 68A Stat. 901; Pub. L. No. 94-455, tit. XIX, § 1906(b)(13)(A), 90 Stat. 1834 (Oct. 4, 1976); Pub. L. No. 97-248, tit. III, § 333(a), 96 Stat. 622 (Sept. 3, 1982); Pub. L. No. 105-206, tit. III, §§ 3412, 3417 (a), 112 Stat. 751, 757 (July 22, 1998)]

* * *

Chapter 80—General Rules
Subchapter A—Application of Internal Revenue Laws

26 U.S.C. § 7804. Other personnel

Editor's Note: The American Jobs Creation Act of 2004, Pub. L. No. 108-357, 118 Stat. 1418 (Oct. 22, 2004) added subsection (e) to an existing uncodified note:

(e) Individuals performing services under a qualified tax collection contract.—An individual shall cease to be permitted to perform any services under any qualified tax collection contract (as defined in section 6306(b) of the Internal Revenue Code of 1986 [26 U.S.C. § 6306(b)]) if there is a final determination by the Secretary of the Treasury under such contract that such individual

committed any act or omission described under subsection (b) [of this note] in connection with the performance of such services.

[The addition of new subsection (e) by Pub. L. No. 108-357, tit. VIII, § 881 (Oct. 22, 2004) will take effect on Oct. 22, 2004.]

* * *

26 U.S.C. § 7811. Taxpayer Assistance Orders

(a) Authority to issue.

(1) In general.

Upon application filed by a taxpayer with the Office of the National Taxpayer Advocate (in such form, manner, and at such time as the Secretary shall by regulations prescribe), the National Taxpayer Advocate may issue a Taxpayer Assistance Order if—

(A) the National Taxpayer Advocate determines the taxpayer is suffering or about to suffer a significant hardship as a result of the manner in which the internal revenue laws are being administered by the Secretary; or

(B) the taxpayer meets such other requirements as are set forth in regulations prescribed by the Secretary.

(2) Determination of hardship.

For purposes of paragraph (1), a significant hardship shall include—

(A) an immediate threat of adverse action;

(B) a delay of more than 30 days in resolving taxpayer account problems;

(C) the incurring by the taxpayer of significant costs (including fees for professional representation) if relief is not granted; or

(D) irreparable injury to, or a long-term adverse impact on, the taxpayer if relief is not granted.

(3) Standard where administrative guidance not followed.

In cases where any Internal Revenue Service employee is not following applicable published administrative guidance (including the Internal Revenue Manual), the National Taxpayer Advocate shall construe the factors taken into account in determining whether to issue a Taxpayer Assistance Order in the manner most favorable to the taxpayer.

(b) Terms of a Taxpayer Assistance Order.

The terms of a Taxpayer Assistance Order may require the Secretary within a specified time period—

(1) to release property of the taxpayer levied upon, or

(2) to cease any action, take any action as permitted by law, or refrain from taking any action, with respect to the taxpayer under—

(A) chapter 64 (relating to collection),

(B) subchapter B of chapter 70 (relating to bankruptcy and receiverships),

(C) chapter 78 (relating to discovery of liability and enforcement of title), or

(D) any other provision of law which is specifically described by the National Taxpayer Advocate in such order.

(c) Authority to modify or rescind.

Any Taxpayer Assistance Order issued by the National Taxpayer Advocate under this section may be modified or rescinded—

(1) only by the National Taxpayer Advocate, the Commissioner of Internal Revenue, or the Deputy Commissioner of Internal Revenue, and

(2) only if a written explanation of the reasons for the modification or rescission is provided to the National Taxpayer Advocate.

(d) Suspension of running of period of limitation.

The running of any period of limitation with respect to any action described in subsection (b) shall be suspended for—

(1) the period beginning on the date of the taxpayer's application under subsection (a) and ending on the date of the National Taxpayer Advocate's decision with respect to such application, and

(2) any period specified by the National Taxpayer Advocate in a Taxpayer Assistance Order issued pursuant to such application.

(e) Independent action of National Taxpayer Advocate.

Nothing in this section shall prevent the National Taxpayer Advocate from taking any action in the absence of an application under subsection (a).

(f) National Taxpayer Advocate.

For purposes of this section, the term "National Taxpayer Advocate" includes any designee of the National Taxpayer Advocate.

(g) Application to persons performing services under a qualified tax collection contract.

Any order issued or action taken by the National Taxpayer Advocate pursuant to this section shall apply to persons performing services under a qualified tax collection contract (as defined in section 6306(b)) to the same extent and in the same manner as such order or action applies to the Secretary.

[Added by Pub. L. No. 100-647, tit. VI, § 6230(a), 102 Stat. 3733 (Nov. 10, 1988), and amended by Pub. L. No. 104-168, tit. I, §§ 101(b)(1), 102(a), (b), 110 Stat. 1455, 1456 (July 30, 1996); Pub. L. No. 105-206, tit. I, § 1102(c), (d)(1)(C) to (G), (2), (3), 112 Stat. 703, 704 (July 22, 1998); Pub. L. No. 106-554, § 1(a)(7) [tit. III, § 319(28), (29)], 114 Stat. 2763, 2763A-648 (Dec. 21, 2000); Pub. L. No. 108-357, tit. VIII, § 881(c), 118 Stat. 1626 (Oct. 22, 2004)]

Appendix E   Summary of State Debt Collection Statutes

This Appendix summarizes state debt collection practices statutes. It includes debt collection statutes of general applicability, plus statutes relating to collection of child support debts. Selected statutes applicable only to particular industries are noted in the footnotes, especially in states that do not have generally applicable debt collection statutes.

This Appendix is intended as an introduction only and is not all-inclusive. The actual language of the statute and decisions interpreting it should be consulted when filing a case or advising a client.

State debt collection statutes are discussed in Chapter 9, *supra*.

Ala. Code § 40-12-80

Coverage: Debt collectors within the meaning of the FDCPA.
Prohibited Practices: Not specified, but requires licensing.
Private Remedies: No mention of private remedies.

Alaska Stat. §§ 08.24.041 to 08.24.380

Coverage: Collection agencies specifically covered. Repossessors explicitly included. § 08.24.380.
Prohibited Practices: § 08.24.320. Licensing statute primarily to prevent defalcation with creditors' funds. Prohibits use of simulated legal documents.
Private Remedies: No mention of private remedies.

Alaska Stat. §§ 45.50.471 to 45.50.561 (Unfair Trade Practices and Consumer Protection)

Coverage: Collectors' conduct towards debtors is regulated by this statute.[1] Goods and services explicitly include goods or services provided in connection with a consumer credit transaction or with a transaction involving an indebtedness secured by the borrower's residence. § 40.50.561(b)(9).
Prohibited Practices: § 45.50.471(b)(14) makes it an unfair trade practice to represent "that an agreement confers or involves rights, remedies, or obligations which it does not confer or involve, or which are prohibited by law."
Private Remedies: § 45.50.531 provides a private right of action for loss of money or property, for each unlawful act, the greater of three times the actual damages or $500; § 45.50.535 provides for injunctive relief; § 45.50.537 allows for attorney fees and costs.

Ariz. Rev. Stat. Ann. §§ 32-1001 to 32-1057

Coverage: Collection agencies specifically covered. Partial exemption for lawyers and financial institutions; licensure not required, but must conform to certain substantive requirements.
Prohibited Practices: Requires licensing. Designed to prevent oppressive, vindictive or illegal methods of collection. Prohibits

simulated legal process, misrepresentation of debt and costs; use of threats and communications misrepresenting it is a state agency or it is represented by an attorney.
Private Remedies: No mention of private remedies.

Ark. Code Ann. §§ 17-24-101 to 17-24-512 (Fair Debt Collection Practices Act)

Coverage: Collection agencies are specifically covered. Entities that purchase and attempt to collect delinquent accounts or bills are explicitly included. Businesses whose principal purpose is the enforcement of security interests are explicitly included. Child support collectors not operating pursuant to Title IV-D of the Social Security Act are explicitly included. Creditors are not covered. Most financial institutions, real estate professionals, and attorneys who use their own name or the name of their law firm to collect accounts owed to them individually or to their law firm are exempt. Attorneys licensed in Arkansas who are rendering collection services for clients are exempt from provisions regarding licensure, fees, and long-arm jurisdiction.
Prohibited Practices: Licensing statute; limits the amount of collection charges and specifically provides long-arm jurisdiction of non-resident collection agencies. Grounds for revocation of agency license include violence or threats thereof, violation of postal laws, impersonating a law enforcement officer (or possession of badge, uniform, etc., for this purpose), simulated process, publication of a deadbeat list, use of obscene, profane or vulgar language, or contacting a debtor at work (unless efforts to contact the debtor at home have failed). Sections 17-24-501 through 17-24-512 add requirements similar to those of the federal FDCPA for the collection of consumer debts.
Private Remedies: Yes. Private right of action for actual damages plus statutory damages of up to $1000 for individual action, lesser of $500,000 or 1% of collector's net worth for class action, costs, and reasonable attorney fees. Attorney fees for defendant if action is found to be brought in bad faith or for purpose of harassment. Bona fide error defense available. One year statute of limitations.

Cal. Civ. Code §§ 1788 to 1788.33, 1812.700 to 1812.702 (West) (Fair Debt Collection)

Coverage: Collection agencies and creditors covered. Attorneys excluded from definition of "debt collector" in § 1788.2(c), but Bus. & Prof. Code § 6077.5 requires them to comply with the substantive obligations imposed on debt collectors by §§ 1788.10 to 1788.18 and imposes other specific requirements.
Prohibited Practices: Use of physical force, violence, defamation, misrepresentation, threats, obscene, embarrassing, harassing or annoying communications, false representation as an attorney or state agency, use of simulated legal documents. Debt collector must provide, in first written communication with debtor, a notice

---

1   State v. O'Neil Investigations, Inc., 609 P.2d 520 (Alaska 1980).

describing debtors' rights under state and federal debt collection statutes, and the FTC's help line telephone number and Internet address. If a consumer claims to be a victim of identity theft and provides the collector with police report, affidavit, and identifying information, the collector must cease collection efforts while it investigates the claim. If it concludes that identity theft occurred, it must so notify the creditor and any credit bureaus to which it has reported the debt. (Note that the Fair Credit Reporting Act, 15 U.S.C. § 1681t(b)(5)(H), preempts state laws that relate to certain duties of furnishers of identify theft-related information). Civil Code § 1812.700 requires collectors subject to the FDCPA to provide a special notice about rights under state law. Civil Code § 1812.700 requires collectors subject to the FDCPA to provide a special notice about rights under state law.

Private Remedies: Private actions for actual damages, statutory penalties of $100 to $1000, costs and reasonable attorney fees authorized. Although Cal. Civ. Code § 1788.30(a) states that only individual actions may be brought under this Act, courts have held that the legislature intended to permit class actions asserting improper debt collection practices.[2] Creditor not liable if, within 15 days of discovering the violation (or being notified by debtor) it makes the corrections and adjustments necessary to cure the violation. Bona fide error defense available. Remedies under this statute are cumulative, in addition to those provided under other statutes.

Cal. Family Code §§ 5610 to 5616 (West) (Child Support Collectors)

Coverage: Any individual, corporation, attorney, nonprofit organization, or other nongovernmental entity who is engaged by an obligee to collect child support ordered by a court or other tribunal for a fee or other consideration. Does not include attorneys who address child support issues in course of paternity, divorce, separation, etc. proceedings or post-judgment modifications. But does include any private, non-governmental attorney whose business is substantially comprised (i.e., more than 50% of remuneration or time) of the collection or enforcement of child support.

Prohibited Practices: Prohibitions of Civ. Code §§ 1788–1788.16 (see above) apply to child support collectors. May not misstate amount of collection fee, or party obligated to pay it; attempt to collect from anyone other than the obligor unless that person is legally responsible for the obligation or is the legal representative of the obligor. Detailed provisions for protection of obligees, i.e., form and content of contracts, cancellation rights, required notices, etc. May collect only support owed to obligee, not sums assigned to state by applicant for aid.

Private Remedies: A person may bring an action for actual damages incurred as a result of violation of this chapter. Prevailing party attorney fees—but collector may receive fees only if court finds that party bringing the action did not act in good faith. Collector not liable to an obligor under any circumstance in which a debt collector would not have civil liability under § 1788.30 of the Civil Code. Bona fide error defense available. Remedies are cumulative. Waivers are forbidden.

Colo. Rev. Stat. §§ 5-1-101 to 5-12-105 (Consumer Credit Code)

Coverage: Collection agencies and creditors specifically covered.
Prohibited Practices: §§ 5-5-108, 5-5-109. Broad prohibition of unconscionable debt collection, including use of deceptive forms; fraudulent, deceptive or misleading representations; simulated legal process; representing itself as government-approved; unlawful threats; unreasonable communications.
Private Remedies: § 5-5-109(2), (5), and (6). If a person is engaged in, has engaged in or is likely to engage in unconscionable debt collection conduct, the court may grant an injunction and award the consumer actual damages. Reasonable costs and attorney fees available. Attorney fees to prevailing defendant only if consumer knew the action to be groundless. The provisions of this section are in addition to those of law other than the UCCC, but double recovery of actual damages is not permitted.

Colo. Rev. Stat. §§ 12-14-101 to 12-14-136

Coverage: Collection agencies specifically covered. A 1995 amendment deleted the attorney exemption; attorneys who "regularly engage" in debt collection are subject to the statute except for the licensing requirement. Persons engaged in business the principal purpose of which is enforcement of security interests. After January 1, 2008, exemption for gaming or racing licensees who comply with Colo. Rev. Stat. §§ 24-35-601 to 24-35-608, relating to interception of gambling winnings to pay delinquent child support.
Prohibited Practices: 12-14-104 to 12-14-108, and 12-14-112. Licensing statute which prohibits abuse or harassment, misrepresentation, simulated legal process, unlawful threats, venue abuse, or taking or threatening to take any nonjudicial action to effect dispossession or disablement of the property, if there is no present intention to do so, or no present right to possession, or if the property is exempt by law from dispossession or disablement. Section 12-14-113 also prohibits harassment of a debtor's employer or family and makes it an invasion of privacy. Section 12-14-108 requires that if post-dated check is used, consumer must be given three days notice before cashing, check may not be cashed before sale, and check may not be solicited for purposes of threatening criminal prosecution. Requires initial collection notices to refer to state AG website that has information about the statute.
Private Remedies: § 12-14-113. Private right of action for actual damages, plus up to $1000 for an individual, or the lesser of $500,000 or 1% of defendant's net worth for class action. Reasonable costs and attorney fees to prevailing party. Court may award injunctive relief and attorney fees. Bona fide error defense available. Damages not available under the state act if recovered under like provision of FDCPA. Harassment of consumer's family or employer is an invasion of privacy, and a civil action may be brought, which is not subject to the damages limits above. The private remedy provisions of § 12-14-113 do not apply to violations of regulations, which are subject only to administrative enforcement. State agencies and state employees seeking to recover moneys owed to the state pursuant to Colo. Rev. Stat. § 24-30-202.4 are explicitly exempt from § 12-14-113. A criminal statute, § 12-14-129, makes certain violations a Class 1 misdemeanor.

---

2 *See, e.g.,* Palmer v. Stassinos, 233 F.R.D. 546, 547–548 (N.D. Cal. 2006).

Colo. Rev. Stat. §§ 12-14.1-101 to 12-14.1-113 (Colorado Child Support Collection Consumer Protection Act)

Coverage: Person or entity that collects or seeks to collect child support, required to be paid by court or administrative order, if the obligee lives in Colorado at the time of contracting, or the collector has a place of business in Colorado, or the collector contacts more than twenty-five obligors per year in Colorado. Exemptions for attorneys, persons exempt under state debt collection law (Colo. Rev. Stat. § 12-14-103(2)(b)), non-profits that charge no more than a nominal fee, and independent contractors providing services for county government agency that county is required by law to provide.

Prohibited Practices: Incorporates prohibited practices provisions of Colorado Fair Debt Collection statute, *supra*. Also forbids designating a current payment as arrears or interest; intercepting, redirecting, or collecting payments ordered to be made to a central registry, or assigned to the state for public assistance reimbursement; sending an income withholding order without authority; making misleading statements about collector's identity; attempting to collect from an obligor who disputes the debt, without verifying the existence and amount of the obligation, and sending copy of the verification to obligor. Detailed requirements regarding contracts, disclosures, etc. for protection of obligees.

Private Remedies: Provisions of § 12-14-113, except for the statute of limitations in subsection (4), apply to this statute. Statute of limitations is five years after occurrence of violation, except that for willful misrepresentations, statute of limitations runs from obligee's discovery of misrepresentation. Remedies are in addition to and not exclusive of any other provisions of law.

Conn. Gen. Stat. §§ 36a-645 to 36a-647 (Creditors' Collection Practices)

Coverage: Creditors specifically covered, i.e., persons extending credit to consumers residing in Connecticut and those not covered by collection agency statute.[3]

Prohibited Practices: Generally prohibits abusive, harassing, fraudulent, deceptive and misleading practices. The Department of Banking is authorized to adopt regulations specifying acts that violate this provision. Sections 36a-647-2 to 36a-647-7 of the Regulations of Connecticut State Agencies sets strict limits on seeking location information, or other third party contacts. Explicitly forbids threats to repossess or disable property, where there is no present intention or right to do so, or where property is exempt from seizure or disablement; or knowingly filing suit in wrong venue. Regulations[4] parallel the federal Fair Debt Collection Practices Act.

Private Remedies: Section 36a-648 provides that a creditor who uses a prohibited practice to collect a debt is liable to the person harmed for actual damages, up to $1000 additional damages, and attorney fees. The statute creates a bona fide error defense. In addition, the UDAP statute has been construed to provide private remedy.[5]

Conn. Gen. Stat. §§ 36a-800 to 36a-810 (Collection Agencies)

Coverage: Collection agencies specifically covered. Private collectors of municipal property taxes explicitly included. Explicitly includes agencies that take sham assignments or use other subterfuges to evade provisions of this statute. Also specially covers creditors using false names, and non-attorneys who are engaged in the business of collecting child support. Exempts collector's employees, certain escrows, public officers, lawyers, loan servicers. Exempted persons covered by statute on creditor's collection practices.

Prohibited Practices: Section 36a-805 specifies prohibited practices, including instituting suit; adding a fee in excess of 15% of the amount collected; unauthorized practice of law; misrepresentation of attorney involvement; splitting of fees with attorney; receiving or purchasing claims for purpose of suing on them. No creditor may knowingly hire a collector that is not licensed to practice in Connecticut. Regulations found at Regulations Connecticut State Agencies §§ 36a-809-6 to 36a-809-17. A 2002 amendment sets standards for agencies that collect child support, mainly intended to protect recipients: requirement for written contract, a 25% cap on fees, no fee where support collected through efforts of government agency, and requirement that recipients be advised that collection services are available from the state.

Private Remedies: None specified. May be provided by UDAP statute.[6]

Del. Code Ann. tit. 30, § 2301(a)(12) (Occupational Licenses and Fees)

Coverage: Collection agencies. Attorneys are exempt.
Prohibited Practices: None specified. Requires license and annual fee.
Private Remedies: No mention of private remedies.

---

tion of banking regulations, is actionable under UDAP statute); Tillquist v. Ford Motor Credit Co., 714 F. Supp. 607 (D. Conn. 1989). *Cf.* Evanauskas v. Strumpf, 2001 U.S. Dist. LEXIS 14326, 2001 WL 777477 (D. Conn. June 27, 2001) (no private cause of action under Conn. Collection Agency or Creditors Collection Practices Act; UDAP claim fails for other reasons); Cordova v. Larson, 1997 U.S. Dist. LEXIS 23982, 1997 WL 280496 (D. Conn. Apr. 30, 1997) (no private cause of action under § 36a-647 except for Banking Commissioner; plaintiffs did not plead a UDAP claim); Krutchkoff v. Fleet Bank, 960 F. Supp. 541 (D. Conn. 1996) (state Creditor Collection Practices Act does not provide for a private remedy; UDAP claim fails for other reasons).

6 Pabon v. Recko, 122 F. Supp. 2d 311 (D. Conn. 2000) (collection agency misconduct that violates public policy, here violation of banking regulations, is actionable under UDAP statute); Tillquist v. Ford Motor Credit Co., 714 F. Supp. 607 (D. Conn. 1989). *Cf.* Evanauskas v. Strumpf, 2001 U.S. Dist. LEXIS 14326, 2001 WL 777477 (D. Conn. June 27, 2001) (no private cause of action under Conn. Collection Agency or Creditors Collection Practices Act; UDAP claim fails for other reasons); Cordova v. Larson, 1997 U.S. Dist. LEXIS 23982, 1997 WL 280496 (D. Conn. Apr. 30, 1997) (no private cause of action under § 36a-647 except for Banking Commissioner; plaintiffs did not plead a UDAP claim); Krutchkoff v. Fleet Bank, 960 F. Supp. 541 (D. Conn. 1996) (state Creditor Collection Practices Act does not provide for a private remedy; UDAP claim fails for other reasons).

---

3 Conn. Gen. Stat. § 36a-645(3). *See* Wagner v. Am. Nat'l Educ. Corp., Clearinghouse No. 36,132 (D. Conn. 1983).

4 Conn. Agencies Regs. §§ 36a-647-1 to 36a-647-7, *reprinted in* 2 Consumer Cred. Guide (CCH) ¶¶ 6641 to 6648.

5 Pabon v. Recko, 122 F. Supp. 2d 311 (D. Conn. 2000) (collection agency misconduct that violates public policy, here viola-

D.C. Code §§ 22-3401 to 22-3403

Coverage: Any person collecting or aiding in the collection of private debts or obligations; detective agencies.
Prohibited Practices: Use of the term "District of Columbia," "D.C.," etc. to create a false impression of a connection to local government.
Private Remedies: Criminal penalties only; no mention of private remedies.

D.C. Code §§ 28-3814 to 28-3816 (Debt Collection)

Coverage: Collection agencies and creditors specifically covered. Act does not apply to motor vehicle and mortgage loans, which are covered by other sections of D.C. Code.
Prohibited Practices: § 28-3814(c)–(j). Prohibits defamation; unlawful threats; harassment or abusive conduct, including profane language, unreasonable telephone calls, unreasonable publications; fraud including misleading and deceptive representations; any other unreasonable or unconscionable means to collect debt and other enumerated practices. Persons covered must be bonded by the state and pay a fee.
Private Remedies: §§ 28-3813 and 28-3814(j)(1)–(2). Actual, punitive and all proximate damages may be recovered. If willful and repeated violations, debtor may also recover consequential and special damages. Reasonable attorney fees.

D.C. Code §§ 28-3901 to 28-3909 (Consumer Protection Procedures Act)

Coverage: Collection agencies and creditors specifically covered.
Prohibited Practices: § 3904(m). Threatening or harassing a consumer with any act other than legal process, by telephone, cards or letters. Unconscionable terms or provisions (§ 3904(r)). Criteria for unconscionability include knowledge at the time of a credit sale that there is no reasonable possibility of payment in full by the consumer, or taking advantage of age, illiteracy, mental infirmity, language barrier, etc.
Private Remedies: D.C. Code § 28-3905(k)(1) provides for a private cause of action for treble damages, reasonable attorney fees, punitive damages and injunction.

Fla. Stat. §§ 559.55 to 559.785 (Consumer Collection Practices)

Coverage: Collection agencies and creditors specifically covered, but registration requirements do not apply to original creditors, lawyers, financial institutions, real estate and insurance professionals. New § 559.715 specifically allows creditor to assign the right to bill and collect a debt. The assignee is a real party in interest, and may sue in its own name to collect a defaulted debt. The assignee must inform debtor of the assignment as soon as practicable, and at least thirty days before attempting to collect the debt.
Prohibited Practices: For a complete list see § 559.72, but, includes simulating legal process; use of unlawful threats or violence; misrepresentations; harassment; unlawful publications; use of "deadbeat" letters; unreasonable employer or other third-party communications; communicating directly with a consumer known to be represented by counsel; causing charges to be made for collect telephone calls or telegrams by concealing the purpose of the communication. Licensing required only for collection agencies.
Private Remedies: § 559.77. Greater of actual damages or $1000,

plus costs and attorney fees. In class action, up to $1000 per plaintiff, but not more than, in aggregate, $500,000 or 1% of defendant's net worth. Punitive and other equitable relief awarded in judge's discretion. Bona fide error defense available.

Ga. Code Ann. §§ 7-3-1 to 7-3-29 (Industrial Loan Statute)[7]

Coverage: Industrial lenders and their employees or agents, including debt collectors.
Prohibited Practices: § 7-3-25. Prohibits unreasonable collection tactics, including physical harm, trespass, holding the debtor up to public ridicule or degradation; simulated legal process; unreasonable communications (defined); calls or visits between 10 p.m. and 5 a.m.
Private Remedies: § 7-3-29 provides the borrower with a single penalty of the greater of $100 or twice the amount of interest and fees charged the borrower. No class actions. Class actions explicitly forbidden.

Haw. Rev. Stat. §§ 443B-1 to 443B-21 (Collection Agencies)

Coverage: Collection agencies specifically covered. Repossessors included. Excludes attorneys (acting within the scope of their profession), real estate professionals, most financial institutions, employee collecting debts for employer who is not a collection agency, public officials. Debt buyers explicitly included (assignees that regularly accept assignment of debts and sue in their own name).
Prohibited Practices: §§ 443B-15 to 443B-19. Licensing statute prohibiting the use of threats or coercion (defined § 443B-15); harassment and abuse (§ 443B-16); unreasonable publication (§ 443B-17); fraud, deceptive or misleading publication (§ 443B-18); and unfair and unconscionable means (§ 443B-19).[8]
Private Remedies: Private actions are made available by cross-reference to the Hawaii UDAP statute. In § 480-13 it provides for damages the greater of $1000 or treble the actual damages and injunctive relief. If consumer is age 62 or over, court may increase statutory damages to $5000 and impose additional penalties. Court should consider, *inter alia,* whether defendant knew consumer was an elder, and whether consumer was more vulnerable than other consumers. § 480-13.5.

Haw. Rev. Stat. §§ 480D-1 to 480D-5 (Collection Practices)

Coverage: Creditors collecting consumer debts (including debts "asserted to be due"). § 480D-2.
Prohibited Practices: Use or threat of force or other criminal means; use or threat of false accusations; threats of arrest; various other misrepresentations; profane or obscene language; attempts to collect interest, charges or fees not authorized by agreement or by law; seeking or obtaining false acknowledgement that debt was for necessaries. § 480D-3.

---

7 *See also* Ga. Code Ann. §§ 10-1-393.9 to 10-1-393.10 (special provisions of state UDAP statute for private child support collections).

8 Haw. Rev. Stat. § 443B-20 makes certain harassment, abuse, publications, fraud, deceptive, unfair, unconscionable or misleading acts in the collection process violations of the Hawaii UDAP statute, Haw. Rev. Stat. § 480-2. Individual consumers may sue for violations of the Debt Collection Act, using the private right of action provided by the UDAP statute, Fuller v. Pac. Med. Collections, Inc., 78 Haw. 213, 891 P.2d 300 (Haw. Ct. App. 1995).

Private Remedies: Violation of this statute is a UDAP violation. § 480D-4.

Idaho Code Ann. §§ 26-2222 to 26-2251 (Collection Agencies)

Coverage: Collection agencies specifically covered. Includes credit repair, debt pooling and debt counseling, and collection in own name of debts that were delinquent when acquired. § 26-2223. Does not cover attorneys, regulated lenders and mortgage companies (regulated under other statutes), trust companies, governmental agencies, real estate brokers and salespersons in the course of their occupation, abstract and title companies doing escrow business, telephone companies (who make the request as part of their regular billing, before the amount is delinquent), and court-appointed trustees and receivers. § 26-2239.

Prohibited Practices: § 26-2229A. Licensing statute which requires fair, open and honest dealing in the collection of a debt. Prohibits collection of unauthorized interest and fees, simulating legal documents.

Private Remedies: No mention of private remedies, but note that the definition of "trade or commerce" in the UDAP statute includes "collecting debts."

225 Ill. Comp. Stat. §§ 425/1 to 425/9.7 (Collection Agencies)

Coverage: Collection agencies and debt buyers (with and without recourse) specifically covered. §§ 425/2, 425/3. Persons, associations, partnerships, and other legal entities collecting child support debt are specifically made subject to certain restrictions. § 425/2.04. Does not apply to persons whose collection activities are confined to and directly related to the operation of a business other than a collection agency, specifically including lawyers, financial institutions and their affiliates and subsidiaries, real estate brokers acting in the pursuit of their profession, public officers and judicial officers acting under court order, retail stores collecting their own accounts, businesses that contact a creditor's debtors using only the creditor's name, insurance companies, and condominium unit owners' associations and their agents. § 425/2.03.

Prohibited Practices: 225 Ill. Comp. Stat. §§ 425/9.1 to 425/9. Collection agencies must register and post bond, and follow specific requirements for assignment of debts for collection. §§ 425/4 to 425/8c. The statute prohibits debt collectors from engaging in a number of practices, which are defined as unlawful practices and are grounds for denial or revocation of registration. § 425/9. These include unlawful threats, harassment, abusive language, unlawful publication of indebtedness, any conduct that is intended to and does cause debtor or family to suffer mental or physical illness, failure to disclose business name, simulation of legal process, misrepresentation, certain methods of collection of location information, communication by postcard or with language on envelope that reveals debt collection purpose, communication with anyone except debtor's attorney unless attorney fails to respond, calls at unusual times and places (specifically calls between 9:00 p.m. and 8:00 a.m.), calls at workplace if collector knows this is forbidden, contact with consumer known to be represented by attorney. § 425/9. Regulations at Ill. Admin. Code tit. 68, §§ 1210.10 to 1210.240 elaborate on some of these prohibitions.

In addition, the statute includes restrictions on communications with persons other than the debtor to acquire location information (§ 425/9.1); restrictions on communications with the debtor, including the right of the debtor to request in writing that contacts

cease (§ 425/9.2); a requirement of a validation notice (§ 425/9.3); and special provisions for identity theft, including a requirement that collection activity stop upon documentation of identity theft (§ 425/9.4). These requirements are specifically made enforceable by the attorney general under the state UDAP statute. § 425/9.7.

Section 425/2.04 excuses collectors of child support from many of the requirements, including restrictions on frequency of contact, employer contacts, publishing lists of delinquent debtors, publicizing a debt that is disputed, and other conduct "that would not cause a reasonable person mental or physical illness." The statute restricts child support collectors' fees, requires them to apply collections to current support before arrears, prohibits designation of current support as arrears, and requires collectors to give obligee at least all current support collected. 225 Ill. Comp. Stat. § 425/2.04.

Private Remedies: No mention of private actions.[9] A 2008 amendment states that the attorney general may enforce certain provisions under the state UDAP statute.

Ind. Code §§ 25-11-1-1 to 25-11-13

Coverage: Collection agencies specifically covered. Exempts attorneys, real estate brokers, most financial institutions, and public utilities. § 25-11-1-2. Collectors of child support explicitly included.

Prohibited Practices: Licensing statute. None specified.

Private Remedies: No mention of private actions.

Ind. Code § 24-4.5-5-107 (Uniform Consumer Credit Code)

Coverage: Extensions of consumer credit.

Prohibited Acts: "Extortionate" extensions of credit, i.e., those where it is the understanding of the debtor and creditor that, if repayment is delayed, violent or criminal means to harm the person, property or reputation of the debtor may be used.

Private Remedy: Debt is unenforceable by civil judicial process.

Iowa Code §§ 537.7101 to 537.7103 (Consumer Credit Code)

Coverage: Collection agencies and creditors specifically covered.[10] Consumer debts (checks explicitly included).

Prohibited Practices: § 537.7103. Forbids use of threats or coercion (defined); oppression, harassment or abuse (defined); dissemination of information of indebtedness (defined); misrepresentation; publication; simulation of legal process; violation of postal laws; seeking an acknowledgment that a debt is chargeable to the property of husband or wife or both, pursuant to the state necessaries statute, if this is not true; seeking reaffirmation of a debt discharged in bankruptcy without explaining the consequences, and that this is voluntary; charging collection costs unless these are "reasonably related to actions taken by the debt collector" and the collector is legally entitled to collect the fee from the debtor; communicating directly with a debtor known to be represented by counsel, unless counsel has failed to respond. Knowing violation of Iowa Code § 85.27, which forbids debt collection activity by a

---

9   The courts have implied a right of private action under this statute. *See* Blair v. Supportkids, Inc., 222 F. Supp. 2d 1038, 1046 (N.D. Ill. 2002); Trull v. GC Services L.P., 961 F. Supp. 1199, 1206 (N.D. Ill. 1997); Sherman v. Field Clinic, 392 N.E.2d 154 (Ill. App. Ct. 1974).

10 *See* Iowa Code § 537.7102(5). *See also* State *ex. rel.* Miller v. Nat'l Farmer's Org., 278 N.W.2d 905 (Iowa 1979) (the debt collection chapter applies to persons generally).

health care provider (except for the sending of one itemized account) against an injured worker while a contested workers compensation case is pending.

Private Remedies: § 537.5108(2). Provides that actual damages and injunctions are available in private actions for unconscionable conduct in collecting debts. Section 537.5201 authorizes actual and statutory damages for violations of § 537.7103 (unfair debt collection practices).

Kan. Stat. Ann. § 16a-5-107 (Consumer Credit Code)

Coverage: Creditors specifically covered.

Prohibited Practices: Extortionate extensions of credit, i.e., if creditor and consumer understand that delay in repayment may result in the use of violent or criminal means to harm the person, property or reputation of any person.

Private Remedies: Debt arising from extortionate extension of credit is unenforceable by civil judicial process.

Kentucky: None.[11]

La. Rev. Stat. Ann. §§ 9:3552 and 9:3562 (Consumer Credit Code) *See also* § 9:3534.

Coverage: Collection agencies and creditors specifically covered. Rent-to-own transactions explicitly included, § 9:3340.

Prohibited Practices: Requires licensing of collectors, creditors and supervised lenders. Section 9:3562 forbids abusive practices including unreasonable communications (defined); threats of unauthorized action; limits number of personal contacts. Section 9:3534 forbids contract clauses imposing on consumer debtor fees paid to a collection agency to collect the debt but permits attorney fees up to 25% of debt, after default and referral to attorney. Section 9:3534.1 sets requirements for assignment of debts to collectors.

Private Remedies: § 9:3562(5) reserves debtor's right to bring actions under La. Civ. Code Ann. art. 2315 (torts, malicious prosecution and defamation).[12] Statutory damages may be recoverable for violations by an extender of credit. *See* La. Rev. Stat. Ann. § 9:3552(A)(1)(a).

Me. Rev. Stat. tit. 32, §§ 11001 to 11054 (Debt Collection)

Coverage: Collection agencies specifically covered and attorneys whose principal activities include collecting debts. The definition of debt includes child support obligation owed to or owed by Maine resident, and private collectors are covered. (See title 19-A § 2109.) Exclusions: officers, employees, or certain affiliates of creditor; government officials, persons serving legal process, nonprofit consumer credit counselors, collections pursuant to a fiduciary obligation or escrow arrangement, collections of a debt that the collector originated, collections of debt obtained as a secured party in a commercial transaction involving the creditor, persons collecting debt that was not in default when acquired, regulated financial institutions, certain debt collection incidental to a business other than debt collection. The definition of debt also includes

"any obligation or alleged obligation relating to a check returned for insufficient funds if a consumer is subject to an enforcement program operated by a private entity." Pre-trial diversion programs for issuers of worthless checks, operated by private entities, are also excluded. Section 11013-A sets standards for diversion programs, which must operate under the supervision of a prosecutor's office, and register as debt collectors. Certain types of checks are excluded from the program, including payday loans, stop-payments for which the check writer had reasonable cause, and checks that result from identity theft or similar fraud. The forms used by the diversion program, the contract with the prosecutor's office, and the program's quality controls are reviewed by the superintendent of consumer credit protection.

Prohibited Practices: Licensing statute prohibiting unreasonable communication (§ 11012); limits the use of post-dated checks (§ 11013); harassment or abuse (§ 11013(1)); false or misleading representations (§ 11013(2)); unfair practices (defined § 11013(3)); simulated legal process; reporting debt or credit information solely in its own name to a consumer reporting agency (§ 11013); dispossession or disablement, or a false threat thereof, where there is no present right of possession, or the property is exempt (§ 11013(3) (F)); reporting of medical debt for minor child if there is a court order making another person responsible (debt collector must make good faith effort to contact responsible party) (§ 11013(5)). Debt collectors are also forbidden to engage in the business of lending money, or refer consumers to a lender to obtain funds to pay off debt. § 11013(3)(M). Restrictions on repossession: No entry into a dwelling (unless permission has been given after default, and entry is effected without use of force); unsecured property must be inventoried and consumer notified that it will be made available in convenient manner. § 11017. Special requirements if the personal property left in the collateral includes a medical device or equipment needed for health or welfare. § 11017.

Private Remedies: Private actions are authorized with recovery of actual damages plus up to $1000 in "such additional damages as the court may allow," reasonable attorney fees. Class action suits authorized up to $500,000. There is a one-year statutory limitations period. § 11054.

Me. Rev. Stat. tit. 9-A, §§ 5-107, 5-116, 5-117, 5-201 (Consumer Credit Code)

Coverage: Collection agencies and creditors specifically covered.

Prohibited Practices: Force or violence, threat of criminal prosecution, knowing dissemination of false information, more than two employer contacts, disclosure to anyone without legitimate business need, attempt to enforce debt barred by statute or final court decision, simulated process, violation of agency rule. Me. Rev. Stat. tit. 9-A, §§ 5-116 and 5-117.

Private Remedies: tit. 9-A, § 5-201. Private actions are authorized with recovery of actual damages of at least $250 up to $1000, right to refund of excess charges, lost wages and employment reinstatement.

Me. Rev. Stat. tit. 19-A, § 2109 (Limitations on Collection of Child Support)

Coverage: Persons other than employees of the department who enter into an agreement with another to collect child support. The statute also explicitly covers persons regularly engaged in the enforcement of security interests.

Prohibited Practices: Collector is subject to the provisions of tit.

---

11 *See* Ky. Rev. Stat. Ann. § 24A-240 (no entity engaged in business of lending money at interest, nor any collection agency allowed to bring action in small claims court).

12 *See, e.g.*, Robinson v. Goudchaux's, 307 So. 2d 287 (La. 1975) (malicious prosecution by department store which filed suit after bill had been paid); Tuyes v. Chambers, 81 So. 265 (La. 1919) (publicizing debtor's name).

32, ch. 109-A (the Maine Fair Debt Collection Practices Act summarized supra). If either obligor or obligee is a Maine resident. Other requirements for protection of obligees (contract and notice requirements, fee limitations, etc.).

Md. Code Ann., Bus. Reg. §§ 7-101 to 7-502 (West) (Collection Agencies)

Coverage: Licensing statute. Collection agencies covered. Collection agency is defined to include "an entity collecting a claim it owns, if the claim was in default when acquired." Creditors and lawyers exempt, unless lawyer has non-lawyer employee who solicits collection business or contacts debtors, § 7-102. Also exempts financial institutions, mortgage lenders, and real estate professionals.

Prohibited Practices: An agency license may be revoked for violation of the Consumer Debt Collection Act.

Private Remedies: None mentioned in this statute.

Md. Code Ann., Com. Law §§ 14-201 to 14-204 (West) (Debt Collection)

Coverage: Collection agencies and creditors specifically covered.

Prohibited Practices: *See* § 14-202. Force or violence, threats, false threat of criminal prosecution, employer contacts except as permitted by statute, disclosure or threat of disclosure of misinformation, disclosures to persons without legitimate business need, abusive or harassing communications, claim of a right which does not exist, simulated process. *See also* title 15, subtitles 3 and 6 (assignment or attachment of wages), 5 (forbids transfer of debts to out-of-state transferees to evade Maryland collection law), 8 (collection of dishonored checks).

Private Remedies: *See* § 14-203. Actual damages, including damages for emotional distress or mental anguish, with or without accompanying physical injury. A violation of this Act is also a violation of the Consumer Protection Act (Md. Comm. Law Code Ann. § 13-408).

Mass. Gen. Laws ch. 93, §§ 24 to 28 (Collection Agencies)

Coverage: Collection agencies specifically covered, including persons engaged in a business whose principal purpose is enforcement of security interests. Loan servicers are required to register, and are covered by a specific section of the regulations. 209 Mass. Code Regs. 18.21. Excludes lawyers representing clients, certain fiduciaries and escrows, certain process servers, bona fide debt counselors, purchasers who acquired debt that was not in default, and collectors for landlords, regulated utilities, or insurance companies.

Prohibited Practices: Not specified, but requires licensing. The regulations, 209 Mass. Code Regs. 18.01 to 18.24 forbid deadbeat lists, imposition on debtor of costs of locating debtor, envelopes that disclose debt collection purpose, false threats, profane or obscene language, harassing calls (calls limited to two calls per week at home, two per month elsewhere, between hours of 8 a.m. and 9 p.m.), employer contacts if forbidden by employer, more than one household visit per month (must be between 8 a.m. and 9 p.m. and collector must remain outside unless invited in), visits to place of employment (except for repossession purposes), most other public confrontations, unauthorized practice of law or misrepresentation of attorney involvement; splitting fees with lawyer. Regulations 18.14 and 18.15. Limits on contacts with persons in debtor's household, and others. Regulations 18.16 and 18.17. Various misrepresentations, including simulated process, or obtain-

ing bankruptcy reaffirmation without clearly disclosing nature and consequences of reaffirmation. Regulation 18.17. May not solicit postdated check from consumer debtor. Regulation 18.17(3). Regulation 18.21 lists prohibited servicing practices, which include knowingly or recklessly facilitating the illegal repossession of chattel collateral. Servicing is defined at 209 Mass. Code Regs. 18.02.

Private Remedies: No mention of private remedies.[13]

Mass. Gen. Laws ch. 93, § 49 (Unfair, Deceptive Collection Procedures)

Coverage: Creditors, attorneys for creditors, and assignees of creditors specifically covered. The regulations at 940 Mass. Code Regs. 7.03 exclude persons whose activities are solely for purposes of repossession.

Prohibited Practices: Communication to a third party the fact of the debt; communication directly with the debtor if represented by an attorney; harassing or embarrassing communications; simulating judicial process.[14] The regulations, 940 Mass. Code Regs. 7.01 to 7.11, impose substantially the same restrictions as those for collection agencies.

Private Remedies: Mass. Gen. Laws ch. 93, § 49 makes a violation of that section a violation of ch. 93A (unfair or deceptive acts), which provides private remedies.

Mich. Comp. Laws §§ 339.901 to 339.920 (Collection Practices)

Coverage: Collection agencies specifically covered. Repossessors included. Excludes attorneys, financial institutions, real estate professionals, and various other entities whose collection activities are incidental to some other regulated activity.

Prohibited Practices: Licensing statute which prohibits misleading or deceptive communications; misrepresentation as an attorney or credit bureau; simulated legal process; unlawful threats; publication; harassing or oppressive methods; abuse of postal laws (§ 339.915); furnishing legal advice; sharing office space or fee-splitting with attorney; misidentifying agency or employee; accepting checks postdated by more than five days (§ 339.915a).

Private Remedies: Private actions authorized. Allows recovery of the greater of actual damages or $50, or equitable relief. Treble damages or $150 authorized for willful violations. Attorney fees and costs allowed for willful violations. § 339.916.

Mich. Comp. Laws §§ 445.251 to 445.258 (Collections Practices)

Coverage: Banks, attorneys and creditors specifically covered.

Prohibited Practices: Misleading or deceptive communications; misrepresentation; simulated legal process; unlawful threats; publication; harassing or oppressive methods; abuse of postal laws; employing unlicensed collection agent. § 445.252.

Private Remedies: Private actions authorized. Allows recovery of the greater of actual damages or $50 and equitable relief. Treble damages, costs, and reasonable attorney fees allowed for willfulness. § 445.257.

---

13 *But see* Baldassari v. Pub. Fin. Trust, 337 N.E.2d 701 (Mass. 1975) (suggesting in dicta that it would be willing to find a private right of action).

14 940 Mass. Code Regs. §§ 7.01–7.11 (detailed regulation for collectors, including creditors and attorneys).

Minn. Stat. §§ 332.31 to 332.45 (Collection Agencies)

Coverage: Collection agencies specifically covered. Excludes lawyers, financial institutions, real estate professionals and other entities whose collection activities are incidental to another business. (But does include enforcing unsecured claims that have been purchased with recourse to the seller for all or part of the claim not collected.)

Prohibited Practices: Licensing statute prohibits use of simulated legal documents; illegal threats or coercion; misleading or deceptive communications; publication, misrepresenting itself as a government agency; violations of the FDCPA and using fictitious names; enlisting aid of neighbors or third parties to encourage debtor to contact collection agency when debtor has listed phone number; failure to provide full agency name when attempting to collect debt; failure to report monies collected to creditor; use of an automatic dialing and announcing device without a preamble by a live operator; implying or suggesting that health care services will be withheld in an emergency.[15] § 332.37. Regulations at Minn. R. 2870.0100 to 2870.5100 add further substantive prohibitions including the use of constables or other officials authorized to serve process, except when performing their authorized duties; unauthorized practice of law; misrepresenting attorney involvement; authorizing legal action without specific written authorization from creditor; publishing deadbeat list; debt prorating, or holding self out as debt prorater, unless this service is performed without charge to the debtor, or is pursuant to a court order.

Private Remedies: No mention of private remedies.

Mississippi: None.[16]

Missouri: None.[17]

Montana: None.[18]

Neb. Rev. Stat. §§ 45-601 to 45-623 (Collection Agencies)

Coverage: Collection agencies specifically covered. Excludes entities that purchase accounts or claims for valuable consideration and seek to collect in their own name; attorneys handling claims and collections in their own names, and not operating a collection agency under the management of a layperson; financial institutions, real estate professionals, and various other entities whose

collection activities are in connection with another business.

Prohibited Practices: Not specified, but requires licensing. Section 45-622 states that nothing in this act authorizes an agency to engage in the practice of law.

Private Remedies: No mention of private remedies.

Neb. Rev. Stat. §§ 45-1043 to 45-1058 (Installment Loans)

Coverage: Installment loan licensees specifically covered.

Prohibited Practices: Limits lender's communications with consumers and third parties, prohibits specified abusive, deceptive, and unfair practices loosely paralleling certain FDCPA provisions.

Private Remedies: § 45-1048 states that nothing in §§ 45-1043 (regarding contacts with family members) or 45-1046 (regarding requests that collection contacts cease) limits borrower's right to bring action for damages. Section 45-1058 provides for liquidated damages of $500 to $1000, reasonable attorney fees, and costs. Individual actions only. Bona fide error defense available.

Nev. Rev. Stat. §§ 649.005 to 649.435 (Collection Agencies)

Coverage: Collection agencies specifically covered. Excludes lawyers retained to collect claims "in the usual course of . . . their profession"; financial institutions, real estate professionals, and other entities whose collection activities are incidental to another business. Also excludes unit owners' associations and common interest community managers, except managers or employees engaged in foreclosing a lien.

Prohibited Practices: Licensing statute which prohibits the use of false or deceptive means or representations; simulated legal documents; unauthorized collection of interest, fees or charges; harassment; publication of indebtedness. Gives debtor the right to record collection calls after giving notice. Collection agencies are forbidden to operate consumer debt counseling or debt prorating services. § 649.375. The regulations (ch. 649 Nevada Administrative Code) provide that violation of the FDCPA is a ground for license revocation. The regulations also require that "machine derived form letters" must be pre-approved by the administrator.

Private Remedies: No mention of private remedies.

N.H. Rev. Stat. Ann. §§ 358-C:1 to 358-C:4 (Unfair Debt Collection)

Coverage: Collection agencies and creditors specifically covered.

Prohibited Practices: No licensing required but prohibits unfair, deceptive or unreasonable communications (defined); use of unlawful threats (defined); simulated legal process; collection of unlawful fees; any false representations; threats of unlawful garnishment, arrest, seizure or attachment. § 358-C:3.

Private Remedies: Private actions authorized with recovery of the greater of $200, costs and attorney fees or all damages and injunctive relief. For damages, individual actions only; for injunction, class actions permitted. Bona fide error defense available. If court finds action frivolous and brought for harassment, costs and attorney fees to creditor. § 358-C:4. UDAP remedies under N.H. Rev. Stat. Ann. § 358-A:2 also allowed for violations of this Act.

N.J. Stat. Ann. §§ 45:18-1 to 45:18-6.1 (West) (Collection Agencies)

Coverage: Collection agencies specifically covered. Attorneys, banks and trust companies are exempt.

---

15 *See also* Minn. Stat. §§ 325F.91–325F.92 (restricting debt collection activities of rent-to-own companies).

16 Miss. Code Ann. § 97-9-1 makes it a criminal offense to simulate legal process to obtain collection of a debt.

17 A Missouri statute, Mo. Rev. Stat. § 425.300, allows collection agencies to take assignment of claims, in their own names, as real parties in interest for purposes of billing, collection, or bringing suit in their own and the claimant's names. In a lawsuit, agency must be represented by a licensed attorney. Missouri Workers' Compensation law, Mo. Rev. Stat. § 287.140(13) forbids health care providers and debt collectors from dunning the injured worker after receiving actual notice that the treatment is covered by Workers' Compensation. The worker has a private right of action for actual damages, up to $1000 statutory damages, costs and reasonable attorney fees.

18 *See* Mont. Code Ann. § 3-1-602 (justices of peace prohibited from acting as collection agents), §§ 30-19-102 to 30-19-116 (regulating collection practices of rent-to-own companies), §§ 31-1-704, 31-1-723, 31-1-724 (regulating the practices of payday lenders and collectors employed by payday lenders), § 31-1-722 (limiting dishonored check fees for payday loans).

Prohibited Practices:[19] Not specified, but requires bonding.
Private Remedies: No mention of private remedies.

N.M. Stat. Ann. §§ 61-18A-1 to 61-18A-33 (Collection Agencies)

Coverage: Collection agencies specifically covered. Excludes attorneys collecting "as an attorney on behalf of and in the name of a client"; non-profit debt counselors; creditors; collections incident to fiduciary or escrow arrangements; collection of debts that were not delinquent when acquired. Repossessors explicitly included.
Prohibited Practices: Licensing statute allows agencies to take assignment of claims and sue in their own name, but requires that agency appear by a licensed attorney. Effective May 20, 1992, collection agency may collect from debtor amount equal to gross receipts tax and local option tax imposed on collection agencies' receipts resulting from collection of debtor's debt. § 61-18A-28.1.
Private Remedies: No mention of private remedies.

N.Y. Gen. Bus. Law. §§ 600 to 604-b (McKinney)

Coverage: Collection agencies and creditors specifically covered.
Prohibited Practices: *See* § 601. Simulated process, impersonation of a law enforcement officer, various unauthorized disclosures, harassing conduct, claims of rights which do not exist, and threats to take action which is not intended to be taken. New sections 604 through 604-b, which prescribe a procedure for dealing with identity theft, explicitly cover assignees who took assignment of debts that were in default. They require a creditor, upon receipt of a police report and a written statement from an alleged identity theft victim (the contents of which are prescribed by statute) to cease collection efforts and review the information provided. If, after review, the creditor determines not to resume collection efforts, it must notify credit reporting agencies to delete any adverse information it provided as to the debt. In case of violation of this article, the attorney general may apply to the court for an injunction, penalty, and restitution. N.Y. Pen. Law § 190.50 (McKinney) prohibits as an unlawful collection practice simulating legal process and misrepresenting its efforts as judicially sanctioned and makes it a class B misdemeanor. In addition, N.Y.C. Admin. Code § 20-494.1 requires debt collectors providing child support collection services to be licensed, regulates fees and contract terms, and provides other protections.
Private Remedies: No mention of private remedies and New York's highest court has held that this section provides no private remedy.[20]

N.C. Gen. Stat. §§ 58-70-15, 58-70-90 to 58-70-155

Coverage: Collection agencies, including debt buyers, explicitly included. Excludes lawyers (unless operating a collection agency under the management of a layperson); banks and other financial institutions; real estate brokers and agents; certain non-profits; regulated utilities; creditors (and their employees) collecting own debts.
Prohibited Practices: Licensing statute which prohibits the use of threats or coercion; unreasonable publication; deceptive representa-

tions; unconscionable means; unauthorized practice of law. §§ 58-70-90 to 58-70-125. Unfair practices include a debt buyer, or one acting on behalf of a debt buyer, knowingly bringing action on a time-barred claim, or on a claim for which reasonable verification of the debt and documentation of ownership are not available, or failing to give debtor notice 30 days before bringing action. Sections 58-70-150 and 58-70-155 prescribe procedures for suits by debt buyers, specifying what must be included with the complaint and with a motion for default or summary judgment.
Private Remedies: Private actions authorized. Actual damages and a penalty in an amount from $500 to $4000 may be awarded. § 58-70-130.

N.C. Gen. Stat. §§ 75-50 to 75-56 (Prohibited Acts by Debt Collectors)

Coverage: Creditors specifically covered. Section 75-50(3) excludes collection agencies from the coverage of this Act.
Prohibited Practices: Prohibits the use of threats or coercion; unreasonable publication; deceptive representations; unconscionable means; unauthorized practice of law.
Private Remedies: Violation is a UDAP. Treble damages not available, and civil penalty of not less than $500 nor more than $4000, payable to the state Civil Penalty and Forfeiture Fund.

N.D. Cent. Code §§ 13-05-01 to 13-05-10 (Collection Agencies)

Coverage: Collection agencies specifically covered. Private child support collectors explicitly included, if either obligor or obligee is North Dakota resident, or child support order was issued by North Dakota court, or if debt is being maintained on statement automatic data processing system. Exemption for lawyers, financial institutions, creditors (and their employees); real estate brokers; public officials; out-of-state collection agencies, if properly licensed and bonded in state with statute similar to North Dakota's. Mortgage servicers, "individuals who purchase or take accounts receivable for collateral purposes," and persons whose activities are limited to collecting from debtors located in North Dakota by means of interstate communications from facilities in another state, if the person is licensed and bonded in that state and that state has enacted similar legislation, are also exempt. The exemption for lawyers applies only to the licensed attorney, not to "persons either employed by the attorney or acting on behalf of the attorney." The exemption for creditors explicitly excludes "a person who receives an assignment or transfer of a debt in default solely for the purpose of facilitating collection of the debt for another."
Prohibited Practices: Grounds for suspension or removal of collection agency officers or employees include harassment or abuse, false or misleading representations, breach of trust, unfair practices involving collection activity. Child support collectors may not impose fee for support collected primarily by efforts of government agency, nor for collection of current support. May not designate current payment as past due support. If child support debt arises from court order, or if debt is maintained in automated data processing system, collector must forward payments to state within five business days.
Private Remedies: No mention of private remedies. However, child support collector who fails to forward payments to state when required is liable to obligor for the greater of $500 or three times the amount improperly withheld.

---

19 *See also* N.J. Stat. Ann. § 2C:21-19(d) (West) (prohibiting sending or mailing a notice simulating a legal document. Violation is a disorderly person offense.).

20 Varela v. Investors' Ins. Holding Corp., 598 N.Y.S.2d 761, 615 N.E.2d 218 (1993) (no private right of action under Gen. Bus. Law § 602(2)).

Ohio: None.[21]

Okla. Stat. tit. 14A, § 5-107[22]

Coverage: Creditors specifically covered.
Prohibited Practices: Extortionate extensions of credit, i.e., if creditor and consumer understand that delay in repayment may result in the use of violent or criminal means to harm the person, property or reputation of any person. *See also* Okla. Stat. tit. 15, § 755.1. Automatic dialing device may be used by creditor or it assignee, but only between 9 a.m. and 9 p.m. (and not at any hour that would be forbidden by FDCPA).
Private Remedies: Debt arising from extortionate extension of credit is unenforceable by civil judicial process.

Or. Rev. Stat. §§ 646.639 to 646.643 (Unlawful Debt Collection Practices)

Coverage: Collection agencies and creditors specifically covered.
Prohibited Practices: Prohibits use of unlawful threats; obscene language; unreasonable communications (defined); misrepresentation; and simulated legal process. § 646.639(2). Debt collector's compliance with FDCPA deemed compliance with § 646.639. § 646.643.
Private Remedies: Private actions authorized allowing recovery of the greater of actual damages or $200, punitive damages, attorney fees and costs and injunctive relief.

Or. Rev. Stat. §§ 697.005 to 697.105 (Collection Agency Businesses)

Coverage: Debt consolidating[23] and collection agencies and repossessors specifically covered; excludes consumer credit sellers, billing, and factoring. Billing is defined as sending out monthly statements without making personal or phone contact with delinquent debtors. Excludes attorneys and CPAs in the course of their practice, financial institutions, real estate professionals, and landlords' property managers. Also excludes assignees who are not obliged to pay to the assignor any proceeds resulting from collection.
Prohibited Practices: None specified, but requires licensing. State agency has adopted substantive rules regarding acquisition of location information, debt collection communication, harassment or abuse, false or misleading representations, unfair practices, and the effect of compliance with the FDCPA. These rules include specific prohibitions applicable to child support collectors. Or. Admin. R. 441-810-0200 to 441-810-0260.
Private Remedies: Any person injured by certain specified violations may bring action for injunction or for the greater of actual damages or $200. Court also has authority to award punitive damages, attorney fees, and costs.

18 Pa. Cons. Stat. Ann. § 7311 (West) (Unlawful Collection Practices)

Coverage: Collection agencies specifically covered. Attorneys are

---

21 Ohio Rev. Code Ann. § 1319.12, which prescribes the procedure by which collection agencies may accept assignment of claims, permits the agency to sue only where the debtor (or one of the co-debtors) resides, and requires that the agency be represented by an attorney.
22 *See also* Okla. Stat. tit. 12, § 1751 (prohibiting collection agent or agency from bringing an action in small claims court).
23 Registration and regulation of debt consolidators is provided by Or. Rev. Stat. §§ 697.602 to 697.842.

exempt.
Prohibited Practices: Collecting unauthorized fees or charges (i.e., not provided for in agreement or permitted by law), unauthorized practice of law, simulated process, offering debt counseling or debt adjustment services. This is a criminal statute making certain collection practices misdemeanors.
Private Remedies: No mention of private remedies.

73 Pa. Stat. Ann. § 2270.1 to 2270.6 (West) (Fair Credit Extension Uniformity Act)

Coverage: Collection agencies and creditors specifically covered. Also covers private agencies' collection of taxes owed to political subdivisions of the state. Covers attorney collectors except in connection with litigation.
Prohibited Practices: Closely tracks prohibitions of FDCPA. Repeals and replaces debt collection regulation (former 37 Pa. Code ch. 303) adopted under state UDAP statute.
Private Remedies: Violation is a UDAP violation.

R.I. Gen. Laws §§ 19-14.9-1 to 19-14.9-14 (Rhode Island Fair Debt Collection Practices Act)

Coverage: Debt collectors, specifically including "enforcers of security interest." Excludes creditor's employees, public officials, process servers, certain fiduciaries and escrows, owners of debt who acquired it when not in default, attorneys collecting "on behalf of a client," collectors for landlords and certain regulated utilities. Debt collectors must register (exception for financial institutions, mortgage servicers, certain out-of-state collectors).
Prohibited Acts: Restricts the collection of location information: collector must identify self, but identify employer only if asked; not disclose that consumer owes a debt; not communicate by postcard, or use symbols on envelope that indicate debt collection; communicate only with consumer's attorney, once it knows name and contact information for the attorney. Workplace contacts forbidden if collector knows or has reason to know employer forbids such calls. Limits on third-party contacts. Must cease communication if consumer requests in writing. Forbids harassment or abuse (defined); false or misleading representations, including the misrepresentation that papers are, or are not, legal process, false claims of government affiliation, false threats, etc. Forbids numerous unfair practices, including soliciting a post-dated check, or threatening to cash it. Requires debt validation. If there are multiple debts, payment must be applied according to consumer's instruction, and may not be applied to disputed debt. Forbids the furnishing of deceptive forms (i.e., to make it appear debt is being collected by third party).
Private Remedies: Action for actual damages, and statutory damages of up to $1000 for individual or lesser of up to $500,000 or 1% of defendant's net worth in a class action. Costs and reasonable attorney fees for successful plaintiffs. Bona fide error defense if mistake occurred despite reasonable procedures to avoid error, or if error corrected within 15 days error was discovered by creditor, or consumer notified creditor of problem. No double damages. If damages awarded under federal FDCPA, then no damages under this act.

S.C. Code Ann. § 37-5-108 (Consumer Credit Code)

Coverage: Collection agencies and creditors specifically covered. Explicitly includes collection of a rental charge or any other fee or charge in a rent-to-own transaction as defined in § 37-2-701(6).

Prohibited Practices: § 37-5-108(2) through (6). Unconscionable conduct prohibited, including threats, profane or abusive language, excessively frequent contact, or contacts at unusual hours, various misrepresentations, deadbeat lists, simulated process, certain unauthorized disclosures; dispossession or disablement of property, or the threat thereof, where there is no present right, or present intention to do so, or where the property is exempt.

Private Remedies: § 37-5-108(2) and (6). Private actions authorized. Before suit may be initiated, complaint must be filed with Department of Consumer Affairs, which will investigate, evaluate and attempt to resolve it within thirty days; during that period, creditors may act only as "authorized by law" to preserve collateral. Actual damages or statutory damages of $100 to $1000; reasonable and proper attorney fees shall be awarded. Injunctive relief if proper.

South Dakota: None.

Tenn. Code Ann. §§ 62-20-101 to 62-20-127[24] (Collection Agencies)

Coverage: Collection agencies, including debt buyers, explicitly included. Attorneys exempt, § 620-20-103, but note attorney general's opinions stating that this applies only to collection for clients in ordinary course of law practice. Op. Att'y Gen. No. 00-105 (June 8, 2000).

Prohibited Practices: Licensing statute designed to prohibit deceptive use of simulated legal documents and unauthorized practice of law; violation of any state or federal statute regulating the debt collection industry. § 62-20-120. Prohibits attempting to collect from a debtor any fee not provided for by law, except may pass on bank's NSF charge, up to $9 per check. § 62-20-115. Section 62-20-127, which permits collection agencies to take assignment of debts and sue on them in their own name, sets procedural requirements for action on account on assigned debt. Prohibits reporting an unpaid parking ticket to a credit bureau without first notifying the vehicle owner that the debt will be reported if not paid by a specified date.

Private Remedies: No mention of private actions.

Tex. Fin. Code Ann. §§ 392.001 to 392.404, 396.001 to 396.353 (West)

Coverage: Collection agencies, creditors, and private child support collection agencies.

Prohibited Practices: Use of threats; harassment; abuse; unreasonable communications; unfair or unconscionable means; deceptive, fraudulent or misleading representations including the false representation that a private child-support collector is a government agency; deceptive use of credit bureau name; seeking acknowledgment that debt is for necessaries, if this is false; use of any other false representation or deceptive means to collect a debt or obtain information about a consumer. Collecting or attempting to collect for a check, draft, debit or credit card obligation if (1) the check or draft was dishonored or the credit or debit refused, because the check or draft was drawn or the card presented by a person not authorized to use the account, (2) the authorized user has so informed the debt collector and (3) has provided the collector with a copy of the police report filed pursuant to the identity theft statute. (This section does not apply if there is credible evidence,

such as a video recording or witness's statement, that the check, etc. was in fact authorized.) Third party collector must provide notices re debt collection purpose of communications. Creditor may not hire independent debt collector if it has actual knowledge that the collector "repeatedly or continuously" violates this chapter. Tex. Fin. Code Ann. §§ 392.301 to 392.306 (West).[25]

Private Remedies: Private actions authorized for injunctive relief, actual damages, and attorney fees, with minimum statutory damages of $100 for certain violations. Tex. Fin. Code Ann. § 392.403 (West). Violations are also UDAP violations. Tex. Fin. Code Ann. § 392.404 (West). §§ 396.351 and 396.353.

Utah Code Ann. §§ 12-1-1 to 12-1-11 (West) (Collection Agencies)

Coverage: Collection agencies specifically covered. Attorneys, title insurance agencies, title insurance producers, banks, and trust companies excepted.

Prohibited Practices: None specified, but requires bonding.[26] Section 12-1-8, which allows collectors to take assignment of claims and sue, forbids the assignment of time-barred claims, and requires all legal proceedings to be conducted by a licensed attorney. A 2010 amendment allows a creditor to impose on the debtor a collection agency fee charged by a registered collection agency, provided that this is not forbidden by other law, is disclosed a written agreement, and does not exceed the lesser of the agency's actual fee or 40% of the debt.

Private Remedies: No mention of private actions.

Utah Code Ann. §§ 70C-7-105 and 70C-7-106 (West) (UCCC)

Coverage: Creditors.

Prohibited Practices: Unconscionable extension of credit, i.e., one in which debtor and creditor understand that delay or failure to repay may result in the use of violent or criminal means to damage the person, property, or reputation of any person.

Private Remedies: If extension of credit is extortionate, repayment may not be enforced through judicial proceedings and debtor may recover a penalty, as determined by the court, of not less than $100 or more than $5000, plus costs and attorney fees. Class actions prohibited.

Vt. Stat. Ann. tit. 9, §§ 2451a to 2461 (Consumer Fraud)

Coverage: Collection agencies and creditors specifically covered.

Prohibited Practices: § 2453, as interpreted by 06-031 Vt. Code R. § 104, prohibits unfair and deceptive practices, including threats or coercion (defined), harassment (defined), unauthorized disclosures to employers and others, false threats of arrest, garnishment, etc., various false or misleading representations, collection of unauthorized fees, contact with consumer represented by attorney, unauthorized practice of law.

Private Remedies: Private right of action authorized. Allows recovery of actual and statutory damages and exemplary damages up to three times value of consideration given by consumer; equitable relief. Tit. 9, § 2461.

---

24 Tenn. Code Ann. § 62-20-123 is a criminal statute making certain collection activities a class C misdemeanor.

25 Tex. Fin. Code Ann. § 392.202 (West), added in 1993, prescribes a procedure by which debtors may correct inaccurate information in a collector's files, and requires third-party debt collectors to post surety bonds.

26 Utah Code Ann. § 12-1-9 (West). Information about a consumer's creditworthiness is void if a collection agency has not filed a bond.

Va. Code Ann. § 18.2-213

Coverage: Applies to any person "in the collection of a debt."
Prohibited Practices: This is a criminal statute making it a criminal misdemeanor to simulate legal process in the collection of a debt.
Private Remedies: No mention of private remedies.

Wash. Rev. Code §§ 19.16.100 to 19.16.950 (Collection Agencies)

Coverage: Collection agencies specifically covered; definition of out-of-state collector covers only debt collectors as defined by FDCPA. Exempts collection activity directly related to operation of business other than a collection agency, including lawyers, most financial institutions, real estate professionals, property management services that collect assessments, fines, etc., for condo or homeowners' associations, and billing services (if activities limited to sending out periodic statements).
Prohibited Practices: Licensing statute which contains twenty enumerated prohibited practices including unlawful use of postal service; publication of "bad debt" lists; simulation of legal process; threatening credit impairment; harassing communications; intimidation; illegal threats. § 19.16.250. A recent amendment forbids collectors to make more than one contact with an alleged debtor who has reported the theft of checks, or other forms of identity theft, if the debt arises from the stolen checks or misused identity number.
Private Remedies: Private actions are authorized by way of cross-reference to Wash. Rev. Code § 19.86, the Washington UDAP statute. Wash. Rev. Code § 19.16.440.

W. Va. Code §§ 47-16-1 to 47-16-5 (Collection Agencies)

Coverage: Collection agencies specifically covered. Excludes attorneys handling claims and collections in their own names, and not operating a collection agency under the management of a layperson; financial institutions; creditors; real estate professionals; public utilities; person collecting only for businesses under common ownership, or wholly owned corporate control, if main business is not debt collection.
Prohibited Practices: Not specified, but requires licensing.
Private Remedies: No mention of private remedies, except § 47-16-5 which provides that in addition to a civil penalty for operating without a license, a collection agency may "also be civilly liable as otherwise provided by law."

W. Va. Code §§ 46A-2-122 to 46A-2-129a, 48-1-307 (Consumer Credit Protection)

Coverage: Collection agencies and creditors specifically covered. Private collectors of child support also covered.
Prohibited Practices: Licensing statute which prohibits the unauthorized practice of law (§ 46A-2-123); use of threats or coercion (§ 46A-2-124); unreasonable abuse (§ 46A-2-125); unreasonable publication of indebtedness (§ 46A-2-126); fraudulent, deceptive or misleading representations (§ 46A-2-127); unfair or unconscionable means, including soliciting a false statement that a debt was for necessaries, or seeking reaffirmation of discharged debt without explaining consequences of this, and that it is voluntary; making phone calls falsely stating that matter is "urgent" or "an emergency" (§ 46A-2-128); violations of postal laws (§ 46A-2-129). Section 48-1-307 imposes substantially similar prohibitions on private child support collectors.

Private Remedies: Private actions authorized. Allows recovery of: actual damages and penalties of $100 up to $1000; right to refund of excess charges and penalties of $100 up to $1000; and lost wages and reinstatement of employment if employer wrongfully discharged employee. §§ 46A-5-101; 46A-2-131. The debt may also be canceled for a willful debt collection violation by the creditor. § 46A-5-105. Any person who violates the statute governing private child support collectors is liable to the injured party in a civil action. Court may, in its discretion, award costs and attorney fees to injured party. If action brought in bad faith or for purpose of harassment, reasonable attorney fees to defendant.

Wis. Stat. Ann. § 218.04 (West) (Collection Agencies)

Coverage: Collection agencies specifically covered. Exempts lawyers, financial institutions and real estate professionals who are required to have a diploma, license or permit to practice their profession. Also exempts district attorneys or persons contracting with district attorneys collecting pursuant to dishonored check diversion statute. The dishonored check statute, Wis. Stat. Ann. § 971.41 (West), provides its own list of debt collection standards.
Prohibited Practices: Requires licensing. Violations of Wis. Stat. Ann. ch. 421 to 427 or 429 are grounds for suspension or revocation of license.
Private Remedies: No mention of private actions.

Wis. Stat. Ann. §§ 427.101 to 427.105 (West) (Consumer Act)

Coverage: Collection agencies and creditors specifically covered. Consumer transaction includes transaction for agricultural purposes.
Prohibited Practices: Prohibits threats of force, violence or criminal prosecution; falsely disclosing information regarding debtor's reputation for creditworthiness; unreasonable communications (defined). § 427.104.
Private Remedies: Private actions authorized. Allows recovery of actual damages including damages for emotional distress; right to return of collateral; incidental and consequential penalties. § 427.105.

Wyo. Stat. Ann. §§ 33-11-101 to 33-11-116 (Collection Agencies)

Coverage: Collection agencies specifically covered. Excludes lawyers who are in attorney-client relationship with creditor, and collect in creditor's true name; most financial institutions; real estate professionals; mortgage or credit card loan servicers. § 33-11-101.
Prohibited Practices: Furnishing or advertisement of legal services. (A licensed agency may, however, take assignment of a claim and sue as the real party in interest.) § 33-11-114. No other specific prohibitions, but licensing required.
Private Remedies: No mention of private actions.

Wyo. Stat. Ann. § 40-14-507

Coverage: Creditors specifically covered.
Prohibited Practices: Extortionate extensions of credit, i.e., if creditor and consumer understand that delay in repayment may result in the use of violent or criminal means to harm the person, property or reputation of any person.
Private Remedies: Debt arising from extortionate extension of credit is unenforceable by civil judicial process.

Appendix F   Practice Aids

This appendix contains two interview forms and a telephone log form to help clients develop the facts of their fair debt collection claims. These forms are also available on the companion website to this volume, so they can be adapted for your use. The fourth section is a list of abbreviations used by debt collectors that is helpful in deciphering collectors' notes.

F.1 General Interview Checklist for Debt Collection Harassment[1]

F.1.1 General Questions

Client's Name:
Date of Interview:
Name of Interviewer:
Home and work addresses, e-mail addresses, and phone numbers
Name, address, and phone of relative:[2]

First question

- I understand that you have a problem with a debt collector. Please tell me about it.[3]

Background of debt problems

- Is this debt yours?
- When did you first have difficulty paying this debt?
- What caused you to have difficulty paying this debt?
- When did you last make a payment on the debt?

Overview of collection contacts

- When you were first contacted by the debt collector, was it by mail, telephone, or personal visit?
- Name of debt collector?
- How many times did you hear from the debt collector altogether? Give approximate dates, time of day, method of contact (e.g., mail, telephone, personal visit), and name of person and company.
- Did anyone else contact you regarding this debt? Give approximate dates, time of day, method of contact (e.g.,

mail, telephone, personal visit), and name of person and company.

Were other bills involved?

- Do you have any problems with any other bills or debt collectors?[4] Give name, amount, and type of bill.
- For each other bill or debt, how many times have you been contacted? Give approximate dates, time of day, method of contact (e.g., mail, telephone, personal visit), and name of person and company.
- Do any bill collectors ever use false names or not tell you their names when they contact you? Give approximate dates, time of day, and method of contact (e.g., mail, telephone, personal visit) when someone contacted you about a bill but you were not sure whom the person represented. Add any other relevant comments.

F.1.2 Client's General Objectives[5]

Is the client willing to sue?

- What is it you would like me to do for you?
- If necessary, are you willing to have me sue the debt collector to get money damages for you?
- Are you willing to go to court and testify?

Is the client interested in helping other consumers?

- If there is an important principle involved in your law suit, do you want to establish the principle even if it means postponing getting your money damages?
- If the debt collector's behavior has affected other consumers, do you want to represent them in a suit to stop the debt collector's illegal acts even if it means postponing relief for you?
- Are you willing to tell your story to the press to help other consumers deal with a situation like yours?

---

1 This checklist is intended solely for purposes of demonstration. It must be adapted by a competent professional to meet actual needs and local practice.

2 Useful to locate client later.

3 *See* §§ 2.1, 9.11, *supra* (initial interviews of clients with debt collection harassment problems).

---

4 This and the next two questions deal with the issue of causation and potential intervening causes of suffering.

5 *See* § 8.11, *supra.*

F.1.3 Contacts by Letter

NOTE: Complete this section for one collection letter, go to the questions in F.1.5 concerning that letter, and then return to F.1.3 for each additional abusive letter received by the client. Try to go in chronological order.

Locating debt collection letters

- Did you bring the letter(s) with you?
- If not, do you have the letter(s)? If so, will you get the letter(s) to me? If not, what happened to the letter(s)?
- Do you have the envelope(s) in which the letter(s) came? If not, what happened to the envelope(s)?

Content of letters

- If you no longer have the envelope(s), do you remember if anything was written on the envelope(s) other than your name and address and the address of the debt collector?[6]
- If you no longer have the letter(s), do you remember what was said in each letter? Please describe, including the date of each letter.
- Did the letter(s) threaten you? What were the threats?

Did others see the letters?

- Did you receive any of the letter(s) somewhere other than your home? Where?
- Did anyone else read the letter(s)? Who? Give name, address, phone, and relationship to you.

Impact on client

- When you read the first letter that bothered you, how did you feel (e.g., angry, embarrassed, guilty, scared)?[7] What did you do? Were any others with you? What did you say to them? What did they say to you? What did you do next? Did you take any medication?

F.1.4 Contacts by Telephone or Personal Visit

NOTE: After completing this section for each telephone call or personal visit, go to the questions in F.1.5 and then return to the questions in F.1.4 for each subsequent call or visit.

Content of contacts

- Please describe what was said in each telephone call or personal visit and the manner (e.g., calm, angry, mean) in which it was said. Give date, time, name of person calling or visiting, and description of conversation.
- Did anyone overhear your conversation? If yes, please give his/her name, address, phone number, and relationship to you.

---

6 *See, e.g.*, §§ 5.2.1, 5.6.8, *supra*.

7 *See* § 2.1.2, *supra*.

- Did any of the telephone call(s) or personal visit(s) involve threats, insults, or embarrassment to you? What happened? Were any late at night or otherwise inconvenient?

Did others hear the communications?

- Were any of the telephone call(s) or personal visit(s) at a place other than home? If yes, where? Who else was there? Give date, place and address, and others present (name, address, and telephone).

Impact on client

- After the first telephone call or visit that bothered you, how did you feel (e.g., angry, embarrassed, guilty, scared)?[8] What did you do? Were any others with you? What did you say to them? What did they say to you? What did you do next? Did you take any medication?

F.1.5 General Questions on Damages[9]

NOTE: A fuller listing of common types of injuries and losses commonly associated with abusive collection activities is set out in § 2.5.2, *supra*.

Emotional impact

- Did you feel badly after being contacted by the debt collector? On more than one occasion? Describe each occasion: what you felt and what you did.
- Did you ever fear for your own personal safety? Why?
- Did you discuss your feelings with anyone else (e.g., a friend, a doctor, a priest, your social worker, your spouse)? Give the name, address, telephone number, and relationship of each to you, and note when you discussed your feelings with them.
- Would it be okay for me to talk to that person? (Obtain signed release.)

Physical symptoms

- After the debt collector contacted you, did you feel sick? Were you nauseous? Did you vomit? What did you do for this?
- After the debt collector contacted you, did you feel tense? Were you anxious? Did you have headaches? Did you take aspirin or other medication?
- After the debt collector contacted you, did you have trouble with normal day-to-day activities (e.g., sleeping, eating, working, intimate relationships)?
- When did you begin to feel better?
- Did you ever feel like this before? When? Did you see a doctor then? What did the doctor do?

---

8 *See id.*

9 *See* §§ 2.4, 6.3, *supra* (fuller listing and discussion of common types of injuries and losses commonly associated with abusive collection activities).

- Did you see a doctor after the debt collector contacted you? For what did you see the doctor? Did you discuss this debt problem with the doctor? If so, what did the doctor do about it or say? If not, why not?

Impact on job

- Did you take time off from work to see the debt collector, to recuperate from illness, to visit a lawyer, or for any other reason due to this debt? If so, describe the number of days of absence or vacation taken, and how much you would have earned each day if you had worked.
- Were you able to do your job as well after these collection activities as before? If no, please explain.
- If no, did your boss or coworkers notice? What did they say or do?

Out-of-pocket expenses

- Did you go to the collector's office to discuss the bill? When? How did you get there? How much did it cost?
- Did you make any long distance telephone calls or receive any collect calls as a result of this activity? How much did it cost?
- Did you pay for medication, drugs, or doctor's or hospital services because of the collection contacts? How much did it cost?
- Do you have receipts or bills for any of these expenses?

Aggravating factors

- Did you ever tell or write the debt collector that there was a mistake in the bill? If so, what was said?
- Did you ever tell or write the debt collector that you could not afford to pay the debt? When did you tell the debt collector this?
- Did you tell or write the debt collector that his telephone calls or letters were making you feel bad or more ill? When did you tell the debt collector this?
- Did you ask or write the debt collector to stop contacting you? If so, when and how?

F.1.6 Third Party Contacts[10]

NOTE: After completing this subsection for each third party contact, go to the questions in F.1.5 and then return to the questions in F.1.6 for each subsequent third party contact.

Nature of contacts

- Did the debt collector ever leave you a voicemail? Did others hear the voicemail? If so, explain.
- Did the debt collector ever fax or e-mail you? Did anyone else see the fax or e-mail? If so, explain.
- Did the debt collector ever call, write, visit, or talk to others about the debt? Members of your family? Neighbors? Someone at work? A friend? Your social worker? If so, please give the date, name of the person contacted, and the person's relationship to you, and describe the event.
- Were messages ever left for you by the debt collector at a neighbor's, relative's, or friend's house or at work? What did the messages say? Did the debt collector discuss the debt with the person who took the message? What was said?

Impact on consumer

- How did you feel when you learned that the debt collector talked to your friend, neighbor, or other person who knows you (e.g., angry, embarrassed, tense)? What did you do after you found out? What did you do next? Did you discuss your feelings with anyone else?

F.1.7 Miscellaneous Collection Abuses

Deceptive locating activities

- Have you moved since you have had debt problems?[11]
- If yes, after the move did you get a request for information about you and your address from anyone? Please describe.

Legal process

- Have you received any letters, notices, or documents from a lawyer, court, or judge?[12] Do you have them still? What did you do after you received them?

Threats

- Did the debt collector threaten to contact your employer, social worker, or someone else?
- Did the debt collector threaten to sue you, injure your credit rating, repossess your furniture, or garnish your wages?

Correspondence to debt collector

- Have you written any letters to the debt collector?[13] Do you have copies of them? If not, what did they say?
- Have you signed any documents for the debt collector?[14] Do you have copies of them? If not, what did they say?

Post-dated checks

- Were you ever asked to give a check with a date in the future?[15] Did you give one? Why? What happened?

---

10 *See* § 5.3.5, Ch. 9, *supra.*

11 *See* §§ 5.3.6, 5.5.13, 5.5.14, *supra.*
12 *See* §§ 5.5.2, 5.5.7, 5.5.9, 5.5.12, 5.5.16, 5.5.17, 10.2, 10.3, *supra.*
13 *See, e.g.,* § 5.7, *supra.*
14 *See, e.g.,* § 5.3, *supra.*
15 *See, e.g.,* § 5.6.4, *supra.*

F.1.8 General Questions on Underlying Debts[16]

History with the creditor

- Is the debt you just told me about your first debt with this company?
- When did you first owe money to this company?
- Why did you go to them rather than to another company?
- What was the debt for?

Relationships with particular creditor employees

- What is the name of the person who originally assisted you in obtaining this debt?
- Have you spoken with any other people at that office regarding your account?
- If so, what are their names and what did you talk about?

Creditor using false name

- Has this office ever made loans to you or collected from you when it used another name?
- If so, what are all the names it has used?

Refinancing and flipping

- Have you been encouraged to borrow more from them? Have you had difficulty paying before?
- How many times have you had a debt or a debt renewal with this company?
- When did you make them?
- Have you ever paid off a debt in full with this company, without owing any more money?
- If so, when did this happen?

Recent debt history

- Do you have the debt documents with you or at home?

F.1.9 Current Debts

NOTE: Answer the following questions for each current debt.

Nature of the original loan

- Do you have the debt papers? If not, what was the date of the loan or sale?
- What was the debt for?
- How much money did you borrow?
- What was the amount of each payment supposed to be?

---

16 *See* § 2.1.3, *supra.*

- Was there a down payment or deposit?
- How much cash did you receive as a result of the loan?
- Were the payments to be weekly or monthly?

Debt's current status

- Did you pay off the debt or do you still owe money?
- What is the amount you now owe?
- What is the amount of any payments you are making now?
- How often are you making payments?

Disputes relating to the debt

- Was there any insurance sold with the debt? Did you ever file a claim on it?
- Have you ever disagreed with the amount the creditor said you owed?
- If so, did you inform the creditor?
- Did the creditor or a debt collector ever bother you about repaying this debt?

Client's credit reports

- When did you last check your credit reports? Do you have copies we may copy?
- Was this debt listed on them?
- Have you disputed this item on your credit reports? When and how? Was it corrected?
- May we obtain a new copies of your credit reports? (Obtain release.)

Client's income and assets

- I need to find out your income and what property you own to develop a strategy for this case that protects your income and property. What is the amount and source of your income?
- Do you own a house, car, or other valuable property? Please describe it and estimate its current value.

F.2 Chronology of Debt Collection Contacts

Client's Name:
Case Number:
Debt Collector:

Insert below the chronology of debt collection communications:

Date & Time of Contact	Collector's Name and Company	Names of People Contacted	Contacted by Phone? Letter?	What Was Said

F.3 Fair Debt Collection Act Violations Checklist (15 U.S.C. §§ 1692 to 1692p)

F.3.1 Coverage

15 U.S.C. § 1692a(5); see § 4.4, supra.	Does this involve a consumer (not commercial) agreement? _____ Yes _____ No Other: _____
15 U.S.C. § 1692a(6); see §§ 4.2, 4.3, supra.	Does this involve a debt collection agency, debt buyer, or a lawyer that regularly collects debts? _____ Yes _____ No Other: _____
15 U.S.C. § 1692a(6)(A)– (F); see § 4.3, supra.	Does this involve a person not generally covered: a creditor using its own name, corporate affiliate, government officers, process server, nonprofit counselor, servicing company, or repossession company? _____ Yes _____ No Other: _____

F.3.2 Notice Violations

15 U.S.C. § 1692e(11); see § 5.5.14, supra.	Does the first communication, either written and oral, fail to contain the consumer warning: "This is an attempt to collect a debt and any information obtained will be used for that purpose"? _____ Yes _____ No Other: _____
15 U.S.C. § 1692e(11); see § 5.5.14, supra.	Do all communications indicate they are from a debt collector? _____ Yes _____ No Other: _____
15 U.S.C. § 1692g; see § 5.7.2.5, supra.	Did the debt collector fail to send the consumer a validation notice within five days of the initial communication, either written or oral? _____ Yes _____ No Other: _____
15 U.S.C. § 1692g; see § 5.7.2.6, supra.	Does the validation notice fail to contain all the required information, including the current amount of the debt? _____ Yes _____ No Other: _____
15 U.S.C. § 1692g; see § 5.7.2.7, supra.	Does any demand for payment overshadow, or create confusion about, the disclosure of the consumer rights in the validation notice? _____ Yes _____ No Other: _____
15 U.S.C. § 1692g; see § 5.7.2.7, supra.	Does the validation notice and/or debt collection warning appear on the reverse side of the demand letter in small print or in another document without reference thereto? _____ Yes _____ No Other: _____
15 U.S.C. § 1692g; see § 5.7.3.2, supra.	Has the client failed to request validation? *If so, request validation by certified mail.* _____ Yes _____ No Other: _____

15 U.S.C. § 1692g; see
§ 5.7.3.4, supra.

If the consumer made a timely validation request, did the collector continue collection activities?

_____ Yes _____ No

Other: _____

F.3.3 False or Misleading Representations

15 U.S.C. § 1692e(1); see
§ 5.5.3, supra.

Does the communication give the false impression that the debt collector is affiliated with the United States or any state, including the use of any badge, uniform, or facsimile?

_____ Yes _____ No

Other: _____

15 U.S.C. § 1692e(2); see
§ 5.5.4, supra.

Does the communication contain a false impression of the character, amount, or legal status of the alleged debt?

_____ Yes _____ No

Other: _____

15 U.S.C. § 1692e(3); see
§ 5.5.6, supra.

Does the communication give the false impression that any individual is an attorney or that any communication is from an attorney?

_____ Yes _____ No

Other: _____

15 U.S.C. § 1692e(4); see
§ 5.5.7, supra.

Does the communication give the impression that nonpayment of any debt will result in the arrest or imprisonment of any person or the seizure, garnishment, attachment, or sale of any property or wages of any person unless such action is lawful and the debt collector or creditor intends to take such action?

_____ Yes _____ No

Other: _____

15 U.S.C. § 1692e(5); see
§ 5.5.8, supra.

Does the communication threaten to take any action that cannot legally be taken or that is not intended to be taken (e.g., suit, harm to credit reputation)?

_____ Yes _____ No

Other: _____

15 U.S.C. § 1692e(7); see
§ 5.5.10, supra.

Does the communication give the false impression that the consumer committed any crime or other conduct in order to disgrace the consumer?

_____ Yes _____ No

Other: _____

15 U.S.C. § 1692e(8); see
§ 5.5.11, supra.

Does the communication communicate or threaten to communicate to any person credit information which is known or which should be known to be false, including the failure to communicate that a disputed debt is disputed?

_____ Yes _____ No

Other: _____

15 U.S.C. § 1692e(9); see
§ 5.5.12, supra.

Does the communication simulate or falsely represent the document to be authorized, issued or approved by any court, official, or agency of the United States or state?

_____ Yes _____ No

Other: _____

15 U.S.C. § 1692e(13); see
§§ 5.5.12, 5.5.16, supra.

Does the communication give the false impression that documents are legal process?

_____ Yes _____ No

Other: _____

15 U.S.C. § 1692e(14); see § 5.5.17, supra.

Does the communication contain any name other than the true name of the debt collector's business?

_____ Yes _____ No

Other: _____

15 U.S.C. § 1692e(15); see § 5.5.18, supra.

Does the communication give the false impression that documents are not legal process forms or do not require action by the consumer?

_____ Yes _____ No

Other: _____

15 U.S.C. § 1692e(16); see § 5.5.19, supra.

Does the communication give the false impression that a debt collector operates or is employed by a consumer reporting agency?

_____ Yes _____ No

Other: _____

15 U.S.C. § 1692e preface and e(10); see §§ 5.5.2, 5.5.2.3, supra.

Has the debt collector used any other false, deceptive, or misleading representation or means in connection with the debt collection?

_____ Yes _____ No

Other: _____

F.3.4 Unfair Practices

15 U.S.C. § 1692f(1); see § 5.6.3, supra.

Does the debt collector attempt to collect any amount (including interest, attorney fees, collection costs, or expenses) not authorized by the agreement creating the debt or permitted by law?

_____ Yes _____ No

Other: _____

15 U.S.C. § 1692f(2)–(4); see § 5.6.4, supra.

Has the debt collector accepted, solicited, deposited, or threatened to deposit any post-dated check in violation of the Act?

_____ Yes _____ No

Other: _____

15 U.S.C. § 1692f(5); see § 5.6.5, supra.

Has the debt collector caused any charges to be made to the consumer (e.g., collect telephone calls)?

_____ Yes _____ No

Other: _____

15 U.S.C. § 1692f(6); see § 5.6.6, supra.

Has the debt collector taken or threatened to unlawfully repossess or disable the consumer's property?

_____ Yes _____ No

Other: _____

15 U.S.C. § 1692f(7); see § 5.6.7, supra.

Has the debt collector communicated with the consumer by postcard?

_____ Yes _____ No

Other: _____

15 U.S.C. § 1692f(8); see § 5.6.8, supra.

Is there any language or symbol other than the debt collector's address on the envelope that indicates the communication concerns debt collection?

_____ Yes _____ No

Other: _____

15 U.S.C. § 1692f preface;
see § 5.6.1, supra.

Does the debt collector use any other unfair or unconscionable means to collect or attempt to collect the alleged debt (e.g., collecting time barred debts, filing suit without legal authority)?

_____ Yes _____ No

Other: _____

F.3.5 Harassment or Abuse

15 U.S.C. § 1692d(1); see
§ 5.4.2, supra.

Has the debt collector used or threatened the use of violence or other criminal means to harm the consumer or his/her property?

_____ Yes _____ No

Other: _____

15 U.S.C. § 1692d(2); see
§ 5.4.3, supra.

Has the debt collector used profane language or other abusive language?

_____ Yes _____ No

Other: _____

15 U.S.C. § 1692d(4); see
§ 5.4.5, supra.

Has the debt collector advertised for sale any debts?

_____ Yes _____ No

Other: _____

15 U.S.C. § 1692d(5); see
§ 5.4.6, supra.

Has the debt collector caused the phone to ring or engaged any person in telephone conversations repeatedly?

_____ Yes _____ No

Other: _____

15 U.S.C. § 1692d(6); see
§ 5.4.7, supra.

Has the debt collector placed telephone calls without disclosing his/her identity?

_____ Yes _____ No

Other: _____

15 U.S.C. § 1692d preface;
see § 5.4.1, supra.

Has the debt collector engaged in any other conduct the natural consequence of which is to harass, oppress, or abuse any person in connection with the collection of the alleged debt?

_____ Yes _____ No

Other: _____

F.3.6 Communications with the Consumer and Third Parties

15 U.S.C. § 1692c(a)(1); see
§ 5.3.2, supra.

Has the debt collector communicated with the consumer at any unusual time or place or time or place known or which should have been known to be inconvenient to the consumer?

_____ Yes _____ No

Other: _____

15 U.S.C. § 1692c(a)(2); see
§ 5.3.3, supra.

Has the debt collector communicated with the consumer after it knows the consumer to be represented by an attorney?

_____ Yes _____ No

Other: _____

15 U.S.C. § 1692c(a)(3); see
§ 5.3.4, supra.

Has the debt collector contacted the consumer's place of employment when the debt collector knows or has reason to know that the consumer's employer prohibits such communications?

_____ Yes _____ No

Other: _____

15 U.S.C. § 1692c(c); see § 5.3.8, supra.

Has the debt collector contacted the consumer after the consumer has notified the debt collector in writing that the consumer refuses to pay the debt or that the consumer wishes the debt collector to cease further communication?

_____ Yes _____ No

Other: _____

15 U.S.C. § 1692b(1); see § 5.3.6, supra.

In contacting persons other than the consumer, has the debt collector failed to identify him/herself, or failed to state that he/she is confirming or correcting location information concerning the consumer?

_____ Yes _____ No

Other: _____

15 U.S.C. § 1692b(2); see § 5.3.6, supra.

In communications with persons other than the consumer, has the debt collector stated that the consumer owes any debt?

_____ Yes _____ No

Other: _____

15 U.S.C. § 1692b(3); see § 5.3.6, supra.

In communicating with persons other than the consumer, has the debt collector contacted that person more than once (unless requested to do so)?

_____ Yes _____ No

Other: _____

15 U.S.C. § 1692b(4); see § 5.3.6, supra.

In communicating with any person other than the consumer, has the debt collector utilized postcards?

_____ Yes _____ No

Other: _____

15 U.S.C. § 1692b(5); see § 5.3.6, supra.

In communicating with any person other than the consumer, has the debt collector used any language or symbol on any envelope or in the contents of any communication indicating that the sender is in the debt collection business?

_____ Yes _____ No

Other: _____

15 U.S.C. § 1692b(6); see § 5.3.6, supra.

In communicating with any person other than the consumer, has the debt collector done so after knowing the consumer is represented by an attorney?

_____ Yes _____ No

Other: _____

F.3.7 Other Violations

15 U.S.C. § 1692i(a)(2); see § 5.9, supra.

Has the debt collector brought any legal action to collect the debt against the consumer in a location other than (1) where the contract was signed or (2) where the consumer resides?

_____ Yes _____ No

Other: _____

If any of the foregoing questions have been answered "yes," read the cited statutory provision and section in this book to confirm violation.

F.3.8 Damages

15 U.S.C. § 1692k; see § 2.5.2.2.3, supra.

What out-of-pocket damages has your client incurred?

_____ Telephone Calls _____ Mailings _____ Copying
_____ Medication(s) _____ Doctor Bills _____ Lost Work
_____ Travel Expenses Other _____

See § 2.5.2.2.2, *supra*.

Describe any emotional distress. These items may include anxiety, indignation, irritability, nervousness, fear, worry, loss of happiness, headaches, loss of sleep, insomnia, nightmares, nightsweats, crying, loss of appetite, nausea, etc. (Advise the client to note the contacts of the debt collector and the client's reaction and keep a diary if appropriate.)

F.3.9 Documents

List all documents regarding debt collection, damages, and the underlying debt.

F.4 Abbreviations Commonly Used by Collectors[17]

ACR	Address correction requested
ADV	Advise
AM	Morning
AP	Automatic payment or preauthorized payments
Attn:	Attention
ATTY	Attorney
A/U	Address unknown
AUTO	Automobile
BA	Business address
BIF	Balance in full
BIL	Brother-in-law
BK	Bankruptcy
BKRD	Bankruptcy
BP	Broken promise
BPA	Best possible arrangement
BZ	Busy
C/B	Call back
CBR	Credit bureau
CH	Changed
CK	Check
CL	Client
CLT	Client
CO	Call office
COC	Chamber of Commerce
CPC	Cancel per client (creditor took bank account)
CS	Change status
CTA	Classified ad
CTU	Customer turned us down
DB	Debtor
DD	Due date
Disc	Disconnected
DISCO	Disconnect
DK	Doesn't know
DLR	Dialer did not connect
Dor	Debtor

---

17 *See* § 2.4.5, *supra*. These abbreviations or variations of them are commonly used by collectors when recording contacts with debtors. The recording of a contact is usually preceded by a date (e.g. 7/22) and the collector's initials. Thus a common entry would be 7/22 RJH Ph Ho NA Ph NB Lft Msg Urgent. Numbers are often used to refer to particular form collection letters or telephone collection scripts.

EOM	End of month
EOW	Every other week
FC	Field call
FT	Full time
GFD	Gave firm demand
H	Hold (off on collection calls)
HB	Husband
HCI	Hold for client information
HCV	Hold for client verification of debt
HCP	Hold for client payment
HHG	Household goods
HLS	Hard luck story
HO	Home
HOLD	Do not contact
HU	Hung up
JV	Job verification
LA	Legal action
LC	Late charge
LFT	Left
LIB	Library
LM	Left message
LMCO	Left message to call office
LW	Left word
ML	Mail
MO	Money order
MR	Mail returned
MSG	Message
MT	Multiple
NA	No answer
NB	Nearby; neighbor
NI	New information or Not in
NIS	Not in service
N/L	Non-listed
NO EFFORT	Debtor making no effort to pay
NP	No phone
N/P	Non-published
NW	No word
OFC	Office of collector
OOO	Out of order
OOT	Out of town
OOW	Out of work
PDC	Post-dated check
PDN	Payment due notice
PH	Phoned
PHR	Phoned residence
PIF	Payment in full
PM	Afternoon
PMT	Payment
PO	Post office

POB	Place of employment or business
POE	Place of employment or business
PON	Put on notice
PP	Promise to pay
PPA	Payment arrangement accounts
PPM	Evening
PR	Personal information
PTO	Promised to telephone office
R	Residence
RA	Residential address
RE	Real estate
RES	Residence
RC	Request cancellation of collection and send back to creditor
RP	Request paid account status
SEC	Security
SD	Said
SEP	Separated
SOL	Solicited (refinancing)
SOS	Same old story
SP	Spouse
T	Telephone
TC	Town clerk
T/T	Talked to
TX	Tax collector
UE	Unemployed
UPDATE APP	Update (credit) application
VERO	Verification of payment
VOD	Verification of debt provided
W	Wife
WCB	Will call back
WD	Would
WF	Wife
WK	Week
WL	Wrote letter
WN	Wrong number
WOF	Without fail
WT	We telephoned
WV	Won't verify

Appendix G   Sample Complaints

This appendix contains two sample complaints. The first complaint is annotated, and alleges violations of the Fair Debt Collection Practices Act and a state cause of action under federal supplemental jurisdiction. The second complaint is the FDCPA complaint form devised by the UAW Legal Services Plan some years ago, and is not annotated. Two recent Supreme Court decisions have heightened the federal standards for pleading claims in federal court: *Bell Atlantic Corp. v. Twombly*[1] and *Ashcroft v. Iqbal*.[2] The sample complaints in this appendix were written prior to those decisions, but probably meet the standards of those cases.

The complaints in this appendix and dozens of additional FDCPA pleadings from actual cases are on the website accompanying this volume. Hundreds of consumer law pleadings on other topics can be found in National Consumer Law Center, *Consumer Law Pleadings* (Index Guide with Companion Website) and *Consumer Law on the Web*.

G.1 Complaint Including Both Federal and State Causes of Action[3]

UNITED STATES DISTRICT COURT[4]
FOR THE [*name district*] DISTRICT OF [*name state*]

_____)	
[*name of plaintiff*][5])	Civil Action No. _____
Plaintiff,)	COMPLAINT AND
)	DEMAND FOR JURY
v.)	TRIAL[7]
)	
[*name of defendant*][6])	(Unlawful Debt Collection
Defendant.)	Practices)
_____)	

COMPLAINT
I. INTRODUCTION

1. This is an action for damages brought by an individual consumer for Defendant's violations of the Fair Debt Collection Practices Act, 15 U.S.C. § 1692, *et seq.* (hereinafter "FDCPA") and the [*state*] Unlawful Debt Collection Practices Act, __ § __ *et seq.* (hereinafter, "state Act"),[8] which prohibit debt collectors from engaging in abusive, deceptive, and unfair practices.

II. JURISDICTION AND VENUE

2. Jurisdiction of this Court arises under 15 U.S.C. § 1692k(d), 28 U.S.C. § 1337, and supplemental jurisdiction exists for the state law claims pursuant to 28 U.S.C. § 1367. Declaratory relief is available pursuant to 28 U.S.C. §§ 2201 and 2202.[9] Venue in this District is proper in that the defendants transact business here and the conduct complained of occurred here.[10]

III. PARTIES

3. Plaintiff, _____, is a natural person[11] residing in _____.

4. Defendant, _____, is a _____ corporation engaged in the business of collecting debts in this state with its principal place of business located at_____ . The principal purpose of Defendant_____ is the collection of debts using the mails and telephone, and Defendant _____ regularly attempts to collect debts alleged to be due another.[12]

5. Defendant, John Doe,[13] also known as _____ , is a natural person employed by Defendant _____ as a collector at all times relevant to this complaint.

6. Defendants are "debt collectors" as defined by the FDCPA, 15 U.S.C. § 1692a(6).

IV. FACTUAL ALLEGATIONS

7. On or about _____, 19__, Defendant _____ , while employed as a collector by Defendant _____, contacted _____ , Plaintiff's employer, and requested Plaintiff's employer to speak to Plaintiff regarding the importance of paying an alleged debt of $_____ allegedly owed to

---

1 550 U.S. 544 (2007).

2 __ U.S. __, 129 S. Ct. 1937, 173 L. Ed. 2d 868 (2009). *See* § 2.4.7.3, *supra*, and Appx. K.3.8, *infra*.

3 This form is intended solely for purposes of demonstration. It must be adapted by a competent professional to meet actual needs and local practice.

4 *See* §§ 2.4.7, 6.11.1 (choice of forums), *supra*.

5 *See* § 6.2.3 (parties plaintiff), *supra*.

6 *See* §§ 2.4.12, 6.2.5 (juries), *supra*; §§ 2.7, 2.8, 6.2.4 (parties defendant), *supra*.

7 *See* 8 Moore's Federal Practice chs. 38, 40 (2006).

8 *See* §§ 6.11.4 (joinder of supplemental state claims), 10.2 (state debt collection statutes), *supra*. Note that pendent jurisdiction has been codified as supplemental jurisdiction at 28 U.S.C. § 1367.

9 *See* § 6.7 (courts divided on declaratory relief), *supra*.

10 *See* § 6.11.3, *supra*.

11 *See* §§ 4.4, 4.5 (persons and transactions protected by the Act), *supra*.

12 *See* Ch. 4 (persons who must comply with the FDCPA), *supra*.

13 *See* §§ 5.4.7 (use of an alias by debt collection employees), 6.2.4 (joinder of employees as defendants), *supra*.

801

_____ for medical services.[14] Plaintiff's employer informed Plaintiff of this contact the next day.

8. On or about _____, 19__ Plaintiff wrote requesting Defendants not to contact Plaintiff's employer or Plaintiff since the alleged debt was to be paid by Plaintiff's health insurance.[15] A copy is attached as EXHIBIT A.

9. On or about _____, Defendants mailed a letter to Plaintiff which threatened legal action if payment was not received in 5 days and which is attached hereto as Plaintiff's EXHIBIT B and by this reference incorporated herein. No payment was made by Plaintiff and no suit was filed by Defendants against Plaintiff within 5 days of Plaintiff's receipt of EXHIBIT B.

10. As a result of the acts alleged above, Plaintiff suffered headaches, nausea, embarrassment, and lost weight and incurred sick leave and expenses for medication and day care for dependents.[16]

V. FIRST CLAIM FOR RELIEF

11. Plaintiff repeats and realleges and incorporates by reference paragraphs one through nine above.

12. Defendants violated the FDCPA. Defendants' violations include, but are not limited to, the following:

(a) The Defendants violated 15 U.S.C. § 1692c(b) by contacting a third party, the Plaintiff's employer, without the Plaintiff's prior consent.[17]

(b) The Defendants violated 15 U.S.C. § 1692e(2)(A), (5) and (10) by misrepresenting the imminence of legal action by Defendants.[18]

(c) The Defendants violated 15 U.S.C. § 1692c(c) by contacting the Plaintiff after the Plaintiff had requested the Defendants cease communication with the Plaintiff.[19]

(d) The Defendants violated 15 U.S.C. § 1692g by making a threat of suit during the debt validation request period in a manner that overshadowed the notice of validation rights and would create confusion for a least sophisticated consumer about his rights.[20]

(e) The Defendants violated 15 U.S.C. § 1692g(b) by failing to provide verification of the debt and continuing its debt collection efforts after the plaintiff had disputed the debt in writing within thirty days of receiving notice of the 15 U.S.C. § 1692g debt validation rights.[21]

(f) [*Add other allegations of FDCPA violations.*]

13. As a result of the above violations of the FDCPA, the Defendants are liable to the Plaintiff for declaratory judgment that defendants' conduct violated the FDCPA, and Plaintiff's actual damages,[22] statutory damages,[23] and costs and attorney fees.[24]

VI. SECOND CLAIM FOR RELIEF

14. Plaintiff repeats and realleges and incorporates by reference the foregoing paragraphs.

15. Defendants violated the state Act. Defendants' violations of the state Act[25] include, but are not limited to, the following:

(a) The Defendants violated _____ § _____ by contacting a third party, the Plaintiff's employer.

(b) The Defendants violated _____ § _____ by engaging in the business of collecting debts and by attempting to collect an alleged debt from Plaintiff without a valid license.

16. Defendants' acts as described above were done intentionally with the purpose of coercing Plaintiff to pay the alleged debt.

17. As a result of the above violations of the state Act, the Defendants are liable to the Plaintiff for injunctive and declaratory relief and for actual damages, statutory damages,[26] and attorney fees and costs.

WHEREFORE, Plaintiff respectfully prays that judgment be entered against the Defendant for the following:

A. Declaratory judgment that defendants' conduct violated the FDCPA, and declaratory and injunctive relief for the defendants' violations of the state Act.

B. Actual damages.

C. Statutory damages pursuant to 15 U.S.C. § 1692k.

D. Statutory damages pursuant to __ § __.

E. Costs and reasonable attorney fees pursuant to 15 U.S.C. § 1692k and _____ § _____.

F. For such other and further relief as may be just and proper.

Respectfully submitted,

Attorney for Plaintiff
[Address]

DEMAND FOR JURY TRIAL

Please take notice that Plaintiff demands trial by jury in this action.

_____

Attorney for Plaintiff

---

14 *See* § 4.4 (transactions covered by the Act), *supra. See also* § 2.4.7.3 (specificity of pleading), *supra.*

15 A bona fide dispute of the underlying debt is not necessary but may enhance the Plaintiff's position in the eyes of the fact finder. Unless there is an independent jurisdictional basis for doing so, it is unlikely that most federal courts will assume jurisdiction over issues involving the underlying debt. *See* §§ 6.11.4, 7.7.2, 7.7.3, *supra.* If the consumer's legal defense to the underlying claim is not clear, it is to the consumer's advantage for the court not to assume jurisdiction over the underlying debt. *See* §§ 4.3, 6.11.3, *supra.*

16 *See* §§ 2.5, 6.3 (actual damages), *supra.*

17 *See* § 5.3.5 (prohibited third party contacts), *supra.*

18 *See* §§ 5.5.3, 5.5.8, 5.5.13 (false threats of legal action), *supra.*

19 *See* §§ 5.3.8, 6.2 (right to obtain cessation of collection efforts), *supra.*

20 *See* § 5.7.2.7, *supra.*

21 *See* § 5.7.3.4, *supra.*

22 *See* §§ 2.5, 6.3 (actual damages), *supra.*

23 *See* § 6.4 (statutory damages), *supra.*

24 *See* § 6.8 (attorney fees), *supra.*

25 *See* §§ 6.11.4 (supplemental state claims), 10.2 (state debt collection statutes), 10.3 (state consumer protection laws), *supra.*

26 *See* Carrigan v. Central Adjustment Bureau, Inc., 502 F. Supp. 468 (N.D. Ga. 1980) ($100 statutory damages under the FDCPA and $500 statutory damages on pendent state claim were awarded to consumer).

G.2 Complaint Under Fair Debt Collection Practices Act

UNITED STATES DISTRICT COURT
FOR THE [*name district*] DISTRICT OF [*name state*]

```
————————————————  )
                              )
[name of plaintiff]           )
                 Plaintiff,   )
                              )
v.                            )  Civil Action No. ————
                              )
[name of defendant]           )
                 Defendant.   )
————————————————  )
```

COMPLAINT AND DEMAND FOR JURY TRIAL
I. INTRODUCTION

1. This is an action for actual and statutory damages brought by Plaintiff [*name*], an individual consumer, against Defendants [*names*] for violations of the Fair Debt Collection Practices Act, 15 U.S.C. § 1692 *et seq.* (hereinafter "FDCPA"), which prohibits debt collectors from engaging in abusive, deceptive, and unfair practices.

II. JURISDICTION

2. Jurisdiction of this court arises under 15 U.S.C. § 1692k(d) and 28 U.S.C. § 1337. Declaratory relief is available pursuant to 28 U.S.C. §§ 2201 and 2202. Venue in this District is proper in that the defendants transact business here and the conduct complained of occurred here.

III. PARTIES

3. Plaintiff, [*name of plaintiff*], is a natural person residing in [*city*], [*county*], [*state*].

4. Defendant, [*name of defendant*], is a [*state*] corporation engaged in the business of collecting debt in this state with its principal place of business located at [*address*]. The principal purpose of Defendant is the collection of debts in this state and defendant regularly attempts to collect debts alleged to be due another.

5. Defendant [*name*], also known as ————————, is a natural person employed by Defendant [*name*] as a collector at all times relevant to this complaint.

6. Defendants are engaged in the collection of debts from consumers using the mail and telephone. Defendants regularly attempt to collect consumer debts alleged to be due to another. Defendants are "debt collectors" as defined by the FDCPA, 15 U.S.C. § 1692a(6).

IV. FACTUAL ALLEGATIONS

7. By correspondence on the letterhead of [*name*], dated ————————, defendant [*name*] mailed a collection letter over the typewritten name of [*name*] to [*plaintiff name*] demanding payment of a debt in the amount of———————— allegedly due [*creditor*]. A copy is attached hereto as Exhibit A.

8. Exhibit A was received by Mr. or Ms. [*name*] at his/her residence in [*city, state*].

9. The alleged debt of Mr. or Ms. [*name*] claimed in Exhibit A was incurred for personal, family, or household services, i.e. ———————————————— .

10. Exhibit A stated:
   [*Quote the offensive language.*]

11. [*Describe any other relevant facts.*]

12. As a result of the acts alleged above, Plaintiff suffered headaches, nausea, embarrassment, and lost weight and incurred sick leave and expenses for medication and day care for dependents.

V. CLAIM FOR RELIEF

13. Plaintiff repeats and realleges and incorporates by reference to the foregoing paragraphs.

14. Defendants violated the FDCPA. Defendants' violations include, but are not limited to, the following:

(a) [*Set forth the alleged violations of the FDCPA.*]

15. As a result of the foregoing violations of the FDCPA, defendants are liable to the plaintiff [*name*] for declaratory judgment that defendants' conduct violated the FDCPA, actual damages, statutory damages, and costs and attorney fees.

WHEREFORE, plaintiff [*name*] respectfully requests that judgment be entered against defendants [*name*] for the following:

A. Declaratory judgment that defendants' conduct violated the FDCPA;

B. Actual damages;

C. Statutory damages pursuant to 15 U.S.C. § 1692k;

D. Costs and reasonable attorney fees pursuant to 15 U.S.C. §§ 1692k and __, § __; and

E. For such other and further relief as the Court may deem just and proper.

Respectfully submitted,

Attorney for Plaintiff
Address

DEMAND FOR JURY TRIAL

Please take notice that plaintiff [*name*] demands trial by jury in this action.

————————————————

Attorney for Plaintiff

Appendix H　　　Sample Discovery

This appendix contains sample Fair Debt Collection Practices Act interrogatories, requests for production of documents, and requests for admissions. These and more than fifteen other sample FDCPA discovery materials, including transcripts of depositions, are found on the companion website to this treatise. Hundreds of consumer law pleadings on this and other topics also can be found in National Consumer Law Center, *Consumer Law Pleadings* (Index Guide with Companion Website) and *Consumer Law on the Web*.

H.1 Sample Interrogatories

The following interrogatories are to be reviewed and used as applicable to the facts of each case; delete and add as appropriate. These interrogatories are also on the companion website to this treatise. Section 2.4.9, *supra*, discusses discovery issues that have been addressed in fair debt collection opinions. *See also* Appx. K.3.9, *infra*.

Federal Rule Civil Procedure 33(a) limits the number of interrogatories to 25 including subparts. This limitation may be avoided only by leave of court or written stipulation of the parties. For federal litigation, and in state courts which similarly limit discovery, the following sample interrogatories must be reduced to 25 interrogatories.

Many states have adopted standard instructions and/or definitions for discovery requests that can or should be incorporated into appropriate discovery requests. A reference to the local rule, as in the interrogatories below, should be substituted for the long series of definitions and instructions in the sample interrogatories found at Appx. H.1.2, *infra*. Additional sample class interrogatories found at Appx. H.4.1, *infra*, should be considered for addition to the interrogatories if the case is filed as a class action or an amendment to plead a class action is contemplated.

H.1.1 Version One

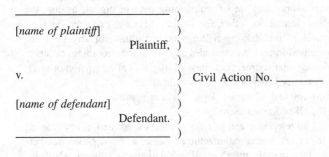

UNITED STATES DISTRICT COURT
FOR THE [*name district*] DISTRICT OF [*name state*]

————————————)	
[*name of plaintiff*])	
Plaintiff,)	
)	
v.)	Civil Action No. ————
)	
[*name of defendant*])	
Defendant.)	
————————————)	

FIRST SET OF INTERROGATORIES

The plaintiff requests defendant to respond to the following interrogatories under oath. Please see Local Rule 26 for definitions. "Documents" includes electronic transmission, and writings and recordings as defined in Fed. R. Evid. 1001. These interrogatories shall be deemed continuing so as to require supplementary answers if you obtain further information between the time answers are served and the time of trial.

1. State the date of each communication from and to [*debt buyer or creditor*] and from and to any servicer, forwarder, or intermediary with regard to plaintiff's account Ref. 0000006 ("plaintiff's account"), and identify all parties to the communication.

2. State the date of each communication from and to [*previous debt buyer*] and from and to any servicer, forwarder, or intermediary with regard to plaintiff's account and identify all parties to the communication.

3. Provide, to the extent known, [*collection employee A's*] full name, present or last known address, the present or last known place and address of employment, and the inclusive dates of her employment by defendant.

4. Provide, to the extent known, [*collection employee B's*] full name, present or last known address, the present or last known place and address of employment, and the inclusive dates of his employment by defendant.

5. State the date of each communication from and to plaintiff with regard to plaintiff's account, and identify all parties to the communication.

6. Please itemize in full the detailed calculation of the amount of interest or other charges added to the plaintiff's account after you received it for collection and the contractual basis therefor.

7. Identify the date and nature of all documents and information defendant received about the plaintiff's account before you began collection efforts regarding the plaintiff's account placed with you for collection.

8. Identify the date and nature of all documents and information defendant received about the plaintiff's account after you began collection efforts regarding the alleged debt you sought to collect.

9. Identify all persons other than plaintiff with whom you communicated about the plaintiff's account, including consumer reporting agencies.

10. On a separate page, please set forth a plain English translation or transcript of the full "contact history," media, collection, or credit records defendant is asked to produce herewith, including the meaning of all codes and abbreviations.

11. Identify each ACA International Compliance Chair who reviewed for compliance with the FDCPA the form letters you sent to plaintiff and the date(s) on which the form letters were reviewed.

12. Provide an interpretation of the codes at the bottom left of

each letter, i.e., 1A03So-1 and 808804.

13. If defendant reported plaintiff's account to any credit bureau, identify the credit bureau and the date(s) of each such report.

Date: [*month*][*day*][*year*]

_____

[*attorney's name*]
Attorney for the Plaintiff

[*street address*]
[*city, state, zip code*]
[*telephone number*]

H.1.2 Version Two

UNITED STATES DISTRICT COURT
FOR THE [*name district*] DISTRICT OF [*name state*]

```
_____  )
[name of plaintiff]       )
                 Plaintiff, )
                          )
v.                        )   Civil Action No. _____
                          )
[name of defendant]       )
                 Defendant. )
_____  )
```

INTERROGATORIES

The Plaintiff requests that the Defendant answer under oath, in accordance with Rule 33 of the Federal Rules of Civil Procedure, the following interrogatories.

INSTRUCTIONS AND DEFINITIONS

A. Answers to the Interrogatories must be furnished within forty-five (45) days of the service of the Summons and Complaint or within thirty (30) days of the service of these Interrogatories, whichever is later.

B. Each Interrogatory should be answered upon your entire knowledge from all sources and all information in your possession or otherwise available to you, including information from your officers, employees, agents, representatives or consultants and information which is known by each of them. An incomplete or evasive answer is a failure to answer.

C. If any answer is qualified, state specifically the terms of each qualification and the reasons for it. If an Interrogatory cannot be answered in full, state the part which can be answered and answer the same in full to the extent possible; state further and specifically the reason(s) why the remainder cannot be answered.

D. Unless otherwise specified in a particular paragraph, provide the information and documents requested for the period of one year prior to the date of filing the complaint to the present. Exhibits A and B refer to Exhibits A and B attached to the Complaint. Each Interrogatory is considered continuing, and if Defendant obtains information which renders its answers or one of them, incomplete or inaccurate, Defendant is obligated to serve amended answers on the undersigned.

E. "Document(s)" shall mean and include any printed, typewritten, handwritten or otherwise recorded matter of whatever character, including specifically, but not exclusively, and without limiting the generality of the foregoing, letters, diaries, desk and other calendars, memoranda, telegrams, posters, cables, reports, charts, statistics, envelopes, studies, newspapers, news reports, business records, book of account(s) or other books, ledgers, balance sheets, journals, personal records, personal notes, any piece of paper, parchment, or other materials similarly used with anything written, typed, printed, stamped, engraved, embossed, or impressed upon it, accountants statements, accounting records of any kind, bank statements, minutes of meetings or other minutes, labels, graphics, notes of meetings or conversations or other notes, catalogues, written agreements, checks, announcements, statements, receipts, returns invoices, bills, warranties, advertisements, guarantees, summaries, pamphlets, prospectuses, bulletins, magazines, publications, photographs, worksheets, computer printouts, telex transmissions or receipts, teletypes, telefaxes, file folders or other folders, tape recordings, and any original or non-identical (whether different from the original by reason of any notation made on such copies or otherwise), carbon, photostatic or photograph copies of such materials. The term "documents" shall also mean and include every other recording of, or means of recording on any tangible form, any form of information, data, communication, or representation, including but not limited to, microfilm, microfiche, any records stored on any form of computer software, audio or video tapes or discs, digitally recorded disks or diskettes, or any other medium whatsoever. For each "document" responsive to any request withheld from production by you on the ground of any privilege, please state:

(a) the nature of the document (e.g., letter, memorandum, contract, etc.);
(b) the author or sender of the document;
(c) the recipient of the document;
(d) the date the document was authored, sent, and/or received; and
(e) the reason such document is allegedly privileged.

"Data" means the physical symbols in the broadest sense, that represent information, regardless of whether the information is oral, written or otherwise recorded.

"Hardware" means the physical components of a computer or any device capable of maintaining recorded data.

"Software" means the entire set of computer programs, procedures, documentation, or other recorded instructions which guide a mechanical device or human in the operation of the computer or mechanical device.

"Computer" means any and all programmable electronic devices or apparatuses, including hardware, software, and other databanks, that can store, retrieve, access, update, combine, rearrange, print, read, process or otherwise alter data whether such data maintained in that device or at some other location. The term "computer" includes any and all magnetic recordings or systems, systems operating on or maintaining data in digital, analog, or hybrid format, or other mechanical devices, or other devices capable of maintaining writings or recordings, of any kind, in condensed format, and includes any disk, tape, recording, or other informational source, regardless of its physical dimension or size.

"Identify" means that you should state:
(a) any and all names, legal, trade or assumed;
(b) all addresses used;
(c) all telephone and tele-fax numbers used; and, if applicable:
(d) brand, make, manufacturer's name, address, phone number and the manufacturer's relationship to any and all defendants in

the above captioned action; and

(e) employer's name, address, phone number and the employer's relationship to any and all defendants in the above captioned action.

"Person(s)" means any human being, sole proprietorship, limited partnership, partnership, association, group of human beings, other legal or de facto entity, or corporation, of whatever kind.

"Explain" means to elucidate, make plain or understandable, to give the reason for or cause of, and to show the logical development or relationships thereof.

"Describe" means to represent or give an account of in words.

"User" means any person or computer which interacts with a different computer.

F. If any Interrogatory may be answered fully by a document, the document may be attached in lieu of an answer if the document is marked to refer to the Interrogatory to which it responds.

INTERROGATORIES

1. State the name(s), business address(es) and job title(s) or capacity(ies) of the officer(s), employee(s) or agent(s) answering or providing any information used to answer each Interrogatory.

2. State the correct legal name of your organization.

3. State any other names which your organization uses to identify itself, whether such names are registered with any official, and the date and place of such registration.

4. State the form of your organization, the date and place the organization was organized and registered and/or licensed to do business.

5. State the name, title, address and job description of each director, partner, shareholder, employee, officer, and manager of Defendant who authorized, approved, or was aware of the collection letters sent to consumers in the form represented by Exhibit A in attempt to collect a debt.

6. State the names, aliases, job title, business and home addresses and telephone numbers, date of initial employment and date of and reason for termination of employment of each of your employees

   a. who contacted Plaintiff or another person regarding this debt; and

   b. who have left your employ within the last two years.

7. State the names, aliases, job title, business and home addresses and telephone numbers, date of initial employment of all current employees who engage in the collection of consumer accounts for Defendant.

8. Does Defendant provide training to new employees involved in the collection of consumer accounts?

   a. if so, describe the training content, timing and duration.

   b. if so, describe all documents and audio or visual materials used in such training.

   c. if so, identify each person involved in providing such training.

9. Identify and describe any documents used to describe, record or establish Defendant's methods and techniques to be used in the collection of consumer accounts.

10. State the number of notices, similar to those sent to the Plaintiff, which were sent out by the Defendant to consumers during the year preceding the date of the notice sent to Plaintiff.

11. State the number of notices, similar to those sent to the Plaintiff, which were sent out by the Defendant since the date of the notice sent to Plaintiff.

12. Identify by title, author, subject, and date any reports, memoranda, e-mails or other correspondence, etc., of the Defendant regarding the use of notices similar to those sent to the Plaintiff.

13. Is Defendant affiliated with any other organization (e.g., common ownership, overlapping offices or managers or common facilities or employees)? If so, describe the affiliation and identify the participants.

14. Describe fully any system(s) Defendant maintains or operates to record contacts of its employees with consumers or third parties in connection with the collection of consumer accounts, and Defendant's policies for operating such a system.

15. Identify and describe each document and record known to Defendant which is related to the account of Plaintiff.

16. State the name(s) and address(es) of Defendant's liability insurer(s) for the last three years and the dates of coverage, type, policy number(s) of each liability insurance policy.

17. Identify and describe each claim made under each liability insurance policy in the last two years, including the date of claim, claim number, the subject of the claim, the status of the claim, the resolution of the claim, and any amounts paid under each policy.

18. Identify any notices that you have given any insurer regarding Plaintiff's claim.

19. Identify the date, time, type (e.g., letter, telephone call), witnesses to or participants in, and the substance of each contact with a person other than Plaintiff made in connection with the collection of Plaintiff's account.

20. Identify each document, record, recording and person furnishing information with regard to your response to the immediately preceding Interrogatory.

21. Identify all present and past contracts or agreements between Defendant and [*name of creditor*] and give the date of the initial contract or agreement with [*name of creditor*].

22. Identify the terms of the agreement between Defendant and [*name of creditor*] pursuant to which Defendant sought to collect this account from the Plaintiff.

23. Describe any other business other than the collection of consumer accounts in which Defendant now engages or in the past has engaged.

24. List and explain all abbreviations and codes, letters, numerals, or symbols regularly used by Defendant in its records and collection activities.

25. How did Defendant locate Plaintiff?

26. Does Defendant file or retain attorney(s) to file law suits to collect consumer accounts?

27. If the answer to the immediately preceding Interrogatory is affirmative:

   a. Identify Defendant's employee(s) who make(s) or approve(s) the decision to file suit or to request an attorney to file suit.

   b. At what point in Defendant's collection process is the decision to sue made?

   c. State what criteria and policies are used in deciding whether to sue (e.g., minimum dollar amount, distance of consumer from Defendant's office, contingency of claim, debtor's assets, defenses to claim) and how those criteria and policies have changed since [*year*] identifying any documents discussing such criteria and policies in use by Defendant since [*year*].

d. Identify the attorney(s) retained by Defendant in [*state*] to file collection suit.

e. Identify the courts in [*name state*] State in which Defendant has initiated law suits in the last year.

f. Identify each document and other method of communication in which [*name of creditor*] authorizes Defendant to initiate law suits against consumers.

28. With regard to the debt allegedly owed by the Plaintiff, identify and itemize the amount of each portion of the debt and the authority therefore.

29. State the date upon which the Defendant began using each type of notice sent to the Plaintiff, and if the Defendant has ceased using such notices, when that happened.

30. Describe the maintenance of all procedures utilized by the Defendant to avoid violation of the Fair Debt Collection Practices Act.

31. Identify all internal and external documents regarding Defendants compliance or noncompliance with the Fair Debt Collection Practices Act.

32. Identify by caption, court, civil action number and result all litigation filed against the Defendant alleging violations of the Fair Debt Collection Practices Act.

33. Identify by name, position, address and phone number all witnesses Defendant proposes to call to trial.

34. List all exhibits Defendant proposes to introduce at trial.

35. Identify each person whom the Defendant expects to call as an expert witness at trial, state the subject matter on which the expert is expected to testify and the substance of the facts and opinions to which the expert is expected to testify, and a summary of the grounds for each opinion.

36. Identify the individual who telephoned Plaintiff on or about [*date*].

a. Where was the individual employed during [*month*] [*year*], what was their position of employment, and responsibilities?

b. How did that individual learn the location and phone number of Plaintiff.

c. Why did that individual telephone Plaintiff?

d. Restate the contents of the telephone conversation between that individual and Plaintiff.

e. Identify all records pertaining to that conversation and their content.

37. Please state in detail the facts upon which you base your denial of Paragraph [*number*] of the Plaintiff's Complaint.

* * * * Repeat each paragraph denied as needed. * * * *

38. Did you receive notice of Plaintiff's bankruptcy from [*name of creditor*] or from any other source prior to the [*date of letter*] written communication to the Plaintiff? If so, please state when and from where you received such information.

39. Do you have any evidence of when the collection account which is the subject of this lawsuit was referred to you and, if so, explain and describe that evidence in detail.

40. Please state in detail the facts upon which you rely for each affirmative defense listed in your Answer.

41. If your response to the Requests for Admissions served simultaneously herewith is anything other than an unqualified admission, then please state as to each denial the specific facts forming the basis for such denial and identify each witness and document upon which you will rely to support your denial.

42. Describe, step-by-step, the process which resulted in Exhibits A and [*any others*] being transmitted to plaintiff, beginning with the date and method of transmission of debtor information to [*name*], e.g., computer tapes or other media delivered (when, by whom, where and to whom); content of computer tape or media; data input (where and by whom); computer entry or other means of directing transmission letters (where and by whom entry made), letter with debtor information printed (from where and by whom); letter with debtor information mailed (from where and by whom); computer tapes or media returned (on what occasion, when, by whom and to whom).

Date: [*month*][*day*][*year*]

_____

[*attorney's name*]
Attorney for Plaintiff

[*street address*]
[*city, state, zip code*]
[*telephone number*]

H.2 Sample Requests for Production

The following request for production of documents should be reviewed before use; delete and add as appropriate to the facts of each case. These requests for production of documents are also on the companion website to this treatise. Section 2.4.9, *supra*, discusses discovery issues that have been addressed in fair debt collection opinions. *See also* Appx. K.3.9, *infra*.

Hundreds of consumer law pleadings on this and other topics can be found in National Consumer law Center, *Consumer Law Pleadings* (Index Guide with Companion Website) and *Consumer Law on the Web*.

H.2.1 Version One

UNITED STATES DISTRICT COURT
FOR THE [*name district*] DISTRICT OF [*name state*]

```
_____  )
                          )
[name of plaintiff]       )
                Plaintiff, )
                          )
v.                        )      Civil Action No. _____
                          )
[name of defendant]       )
                Defendant. )
_____  )
```

FIRST REQUEST FOR PRODUCTION

The plaintiff requests defendant to produce the following documents at the office of plaintiff's attorney within 30 days hereof. Please see the first set of interrogatories for instructions and definitions. If there are no such documents, please so state. If there are such documents, please identify and list appended documents responsive to each request.

1. All documents, or the forms thereof, transmitted *to* plaintiff by or on behalf of defendant with regard to plaintiff's account.

2. All documents transmitted to defendant by or on behalf of [*debt buyer or creditor*] and any intermediary, servicer, or forwarder, with regard to plaintiff's account.

3. All documents reflecting purchase or ownership of the plaintiff's account.

4. All documents transmitted to defendant by or on behalf of plaintiff with regard to plaintiff's account.

5. All documents concerning plaintiff's account and defendant's efforts to investigate and collect thereon, including all internal collection records, collection screens, audit records, credit reports, skip trace reports, and correspondence.

6. Any insurance agreement under which any person carrying on an insurance business may be liable to satisfy all or part of a judgment which may be entered herein or to indemnify or reimburse for payments made to satisfy the judgment.

7. All agreements with [*the debt buyer or creditor*] and any intermediary, servicer, or forwarder concerning collection of debts such as plaintiff's alleged debt.

8. All contracts and retainer agreements with [*previous creditor or debt buyer*] and any intermediary, servicer, or forwarder in effect as of the date you received plaintiff's account for collection and dates thereafter.

9. All documents concerning the amounts listed as owing in your collection letters, including contracts, invoices, formulas, instructions, calculations, canceled checks, logs, and bookkeeping or accounting entries.

10. All manuals, procedures, training materials, and protocols used during [*relevant year(s)*] by defendant to comply with the Fair Debt Collection Practices Act.

11. All documents concerning your procedures reasonably adapted to make sure that your form letters comply with the FDCPA.

12. All documents concerning your procedures reasonably adapted to make sure a debtor is not contacted once defendant receives notice of representation or a cease collection request.

13. All documents which refer or relate to plaintiff, or which are filed, indexed, stored, or retrievable under plaintiff's name, or under any identifying number, symbol, code, or designation assigned to her, including tape recordings of conversations with or about her.

14. Copies of the job applications, resumes, and disciplinary history of [*debt collectors A, B, . . .*].

15. The text of telephone messages left for the consumer as it existed between [*date*] and [*date*].

Date: [*month*][*day*][*year*]

—————————————
[*attorney's name*]
Attorney for the Plaintiff

[*street address*]
[*city, state, zip code*]
[*telephone number*]

H.2.2 *Version Two*

UNITED STATES DISTRICT COURT
FOR THE [*name district*] DISTRICT OF [*name state*]

—————————————)	
[*name of plaintiff*])	
Plaintiff,)	
)	
v.)	Civil Action No. _____
)	
[*name of defendant*])	
Defendant.)	
—————————————)	

REQUEST FOR PRODUCTION OF DOCUMENTS
DIRECTED TO DEFENDANT

Pursuant to Rule 34 of the Federal Rules of Civil Procedure, Plaintiff requests that Defendant produce within (30) days, the documents herein described and permit Plaintiff and his attorneys to inspect them and copy such of them as they may desire. Plaintiff requests that the documents be made available for this inspection at the offices of counsel for the Plaintiff, [*name of plaintiff's attorney*] [*full address*], or at such office of the Defendant's as may be the location of any of the documents requested, in normal business hours, with the least possible disruption to the ordinary course of Defendant's duties and responsibilities.

Plaintiff further requests that this inspection be permitted by Defendant immediately after Defendant's response to this request has been filed, and that his attorneys be permitted to remove from Defendant's custody such of the documents as they desire to copy, on the understanding that Plaintiff's attorneys will be responsible for these documents so long as they are in their possession, that copying will be done at Plaintiff's expense, and that the documents will be promptly returned immediately after copying has been completed.

This request is intended to cover all documents in possession of the Defendant, or subject to his custody and control, regardless of location.

As used in this request, the term "document" means every writing or record of every type and description that is in the possession, control or custody of Defendant, including but without limitation to, correspondence, memoranda, stenographic or handwritten notes, studies, publications, books, pamphlets, pictures, films, voice recordings, reports, surveys; minutes or statistical compilations, data processing cards or computer records, files, disks, or tapes or print-outs; agreements, communications, state and federal governmental hearings, and reports, correspondence, telegrams, memoranda, summaries or records of telephone conversations, summaries or records of personal conversations or interviews, diaries, graphs, reports, notebooks, note charts, plans, drawings, sketches, maps, summaries or records of meetings or conferences, summaries or reports of investigations or negotiations, opinions or reports of consultants, photographs, motion picture film, brochures, pamphlets, advertisements, circulars, press releases, drafts, letters, any marginal comments appearing on any document, and all other writings.

REQUESTS FOR PRODUCTION

Please produce the following:

1. All documents relating to the alleged debt of Plaintiff and the collection thereof.

2. All documents relating to Defendant's activities to collect debts such as Plaintiff's.[1]

3. All form letters, enclosures, envelopes, memoranda, etc. used by the Defendant in its debt collection activity.[2]

4. All material, including video and audio tapes, pertaining to training by or for the Defendant and its employees regarding the Fair Debt Collection Practices Act.[3]

5. An organizational chart for the Defendant.

6. All documents between Defendant and [*creditor's name*] regarding the Plaintiff and collection of his alleged debt.

7. All documents between Defendant and [*name of any other debt collector*] regarding the Plaintiff and collection of his alleged debt.

8. Copies of any litigation filed against the Defendant alleging violations of the Fair Debt Collection Practices Act.[4]

9. A list of all employees engaged in the collection of debts such as the debt Plaintiff allegedly owes, their positions and responsibilities.

10. Any insurance policies covering the Defendant for violation of the Fair Debt Collection Practices Act.

11. All financial reports and statements to investors of the Defendant for the past two years.

12. All income tax returns of the Defendant for the past two years.

13. All documents in the Defendant's possession sent to or received from the [*name creditor*].

14. All documents in the Defendant's possession sent to or received from [*name of any other debt collector*].

15. All internal documents, memoranda, etc., of the Defendant regarding the use of its collection notices and collection efforts.

16. All documents, memoranda, instructions, manuals, etc., of the Defendant surveying the number of notices sent and contacts made by the Defendant in the year preceding the date of the notice sent to Plaintiff.

17. All reports, memoranda, etc., of the Defendant surveying the number of notices and contacts sent by the Defendant since the date of the notice sent to Plaintiff.

18. All operation manuals or similar documents, etc., utilized by the Defendant.[5]

19. All documents relating to the maintenance of procedures by the Defendant adapted to avoid any violation of the Fair Debt Collection Practices Act.

20. All documents relating to the Defendant's procedures to provide verification of the alleged debt.

21. All documents relating to the Defendant's association with a consumer reporting agency, if any.

22. Samples of all postcards and/or envelopes used by the Defendant in its collection practices.

23. Copies of all reports and documents utilized by an expert which Defendant proposes to call at trial.

24. All exhibits which Defendant proposes to introduce at trial.

This Request shall be deemed continuing so as to require further and supplemental production if Plaintiffs obtain additional documents required to be produced herein between the time of the initial production and the time of trial.

Date: _____

_____
[*name of attorney*]
Attorney for Plaintiff
[*street address*]
[*city, state, zip code*]
[*telephone number*]

H.3 Sample Requests for Admissions

The following request for admissions should be reviewed before use; delete and add as appropriate to the facts of each case. These requests for admissions are also on the companion website to this treatise.

Requests for Admission found in this appendix and a number of other FDCPA discovery material are found on the companion website to this treatise. Hundreds of consumer law pleadings on this and other topics can be found in National Consumer Law Center, *Consumer Law Pleadings* (Index Guide with Companion Website) and *Consumer Law on the Web*.

---

1 *See also* Artese v. Academy Collection Service, Inc., 1997 WL 509404 (D. Conn. July 28, 1997) (collector was required to produce documents which focused on the defendant's ability to determine that a debtor had other accounts which the collector was attempting to collect and that the consumer had counsel on some or all of those accounts. In addition, the collector should provide any documents that revealed its ability to obtain from its records the fact that it had earlier collections with the same debtor.).

2 Artese v. Academy Collection Service, Inc., 1997 WL 509404 (D. Conn. July 28, 1997) (consumer requested all form letters used by defendant to collect on this client's accounts. Defendant pointed out that it sent only one letter to the consumer. Plaintiff responded that the letter contained a settlement offer with a deadline. Other letters might give plaintiff a basis for amending the complaint and were discoverable.).

3 *But see* Artese v. Academy Collection Service, Inc., 1997 WL 509404 (D. Conn. July 28, 1997) (a motion to produce the collector's training and operations manuals was overbroad. If any of the manuals contained provisions dealing directly with the alleged violation, i.e., dealing with debtors who had retained counsel, the defendant should produce that portion of the manual.).

4 *But see* Artese v. Academy Collection Service, Inc., 1997 WL 509404 (D. Conn. July 28, 1997) (production requests for "all judgments, court opinions and consent orders relating to this defendant and its acts or practices under the FDCPA" and communications with regulatory authorities concerning its collection practices since 1991 as well as documents relating to its licensing in Connecticut were far too broad. The collector was directed, however, to produce its current Connecticut license and the application).

5 *But see* Artese v. Academy Collection Service, Inc., 1997 WL 509404 (D. Conn. July 28, 1997) (a motion to produce the collector's training and operations manuals was overbroad. If any of the manuals contained provisions dealing directly with the alleged violation, i.e., dealing with debtors who had retained counsel, the defendant should produce that portion of the manual.).

H.3.1 Version One

UNITED STATES DISTRICT COURT
FOR THE [*name district*] DISTRICT OF [*name state*]

```
_____  )
[name of plaintiff]       )
                Plaintiff,  )
                          )
v.                        )  Civil Action No. _____
                          )
[name of defendant]        )
                Defendant.  )
_____  )
```

PLAINTIFF'S REQUEST FOR ADMISSIONS

Pursuant to Fed. R. Civ. P. Rule 36, Plaintiff requests Defendant to admit, for the purposes of this action only, the truth of the following matters and the existence, genuineness and due execution of the referenced documents. "[T]he reasonable inquiry requirement goes beyond parties to the suit, and parties have been required to make inquiry of a person not a party to the action in order to respond to Rule 36 admissions." Moore's Federal Practice (3d ed.) § 36.11[5][d], at 36–33.

1. The account for plaintiff placed with defendant for collection was her personal credit card account.

2. Plaintiff is a natural person who resides in [*state*].

3. Plaintiff is a consumer within the FDCPA.

4. Defendant had and has no information suggesting that the plaintiff's account was a commercial or business account.

5. Defendant intentionally adopted the form of letters sent to plaintiff in connection with its collection efforts.

6. Defendant's agreement with the forwarder [*creditor or debt buyer*] mandated that interest be added to the account.

7. [*Debt buyer or creditor*] was the current creditor on plaintiff's former [*original creditor*] account.

8. Defendant did not advise plaintiff that the amount of the debt might vary from day to day because of, for example, interest, late charges, or other charges.

9. The balance claimed due on defendant's second letter was higher than the balance claimed due on its first letter.

10. Defendant received notice of plaintiff's representation by counsel on [*date*].

11. Defendant received notice of plaintiff's cease request on [*date*].

12. Defendant communicated with plaintiff directly on [*date*].

13. Defendant did not send the notice required by § 1692g within five days of its initial communication with plaintiff.

14. Defendant continued to telephone plaintiff after she requested that all communications be in writing.

15. Defendant's telephone calls and messages did not comply with §§ 1692d(6) or 1692e(11).

Date: [*month*][*day*][*year*]

_____
[*attorney's name*]
Attorney for the Plaintiff

[*street address*]
[*city, state, zip code*]
[*telephone number*]

H.3.2 Version Two

UNITED STATES DISTRICT COURT
FOR THE [*name district*] DISTRICT OF [*name state*]

```
_____  )
[name of plaintiff]       )
                Plaintiff,  )
                          )
v.                        )  Civil Action No. _____
                          )
[name of defendant]        )
                Defendant.  )
_____  )
```

REQUEST FOR ADMISSIONS

Pursuant to Rule 36 of The Federal Rules of Civil Procedure, Plaintiff requests Defendant to admit or deny the truth of the following:

1. Plaintiff [*name plaintiff*] is a "consumer" as defined at 15 U.S.C. § 1692a(3).

2. The obligation allegedly due [*creditor*] is a "debt" as defined at 15 U.S.C. § 1692a(5).

3. Defendant [*name defendant*] is engaged in the business of collecting consumer debts and regularly attempts and collects consumer debts allegedly owed to another and is a "debt collector" as defined at 15 U.S.C. § 1692a(6).

4. Defendant [*name defendant*] mailed or caused to be mailed a letter dated [*date of letter*] to the Plaintiff as exemplified by Exhibit A to Plaintiff's Complaint. [*Repeat for each letter.*]

5. Neither of Defendant's letters, attached to Plaintiff's Complaint as Exhibit A, contains the validation notice required by 15 U.S.C. § 1692g.

6. The notice required by 15 U.S.C. § 1692g was not sent to the Plaintiff by the Defendant within five days after its initial communication to the Plaintiff.

7. Defendant's letter attached to the Plaintiff's Complaint at Exhibit A, does not contain the disclosure required by 15 U.S.C. § 1692e(11): "that the debt collector is attempting to collect a debt and that any information obtained will be used for that purpose." [*Repeat for each letter.*]

8. Defendant has sent [*how many*] notices similar to Exhibit "A" and "B" sent to the Plaintiff during the year preceding the date of the notice sent to Plaintiff.

9. [*Additional request*].

10. [*Additional request*].

11. [*Additional request*].

12. Defendant telephoned the Plaintiff on or about [*date*].

13. Defendant, in his telephone conversation with the Plaintiff on or about [*date*] failed to provide the debt collection warning required by 15 U.S.C. § 1692e(11).

14. Defendant does not maintain procedures reasonably adapted to insure that the debt collection warning required by 15 U.S.C. § 1692e(11) is included in all communications.

15. Defendant does not maintain procedures reasonably adapted to insure that verification of alleged debts are provided upon the request of the consumer.

16. Defendant is not licensed to practice law in the State of [*name state*].

DATE: _____

_____
[*name of attorney*]
Attorney for Plaintiff
[*street address*]
[*city, state, zip code*]
[*telephone number*]

H.4 Sample Class Discovery

Following is sample discovery which may be added where a class action is pled. Again, check the Local Rules of your district court for any other limitations or requirements regarding class actions.

H.4.1 Interrogatories

1. State the number of individuals with addresses within [*state*] to whom collection letters in the form represented by Exhibit A were sent.

2. State the name and address of each individual with an address within [*state*] to whom a collection letter in the form represented by Exhibit A was sent. [*Repeat for each letter.*]

3. State the net worth of defendant [*name*] and how it was computed.

4. State the following information for defendant [*name*]:

(A) Profit before taxes;

(B) Interest expenses;

(C) Depreciation (Amortization);

(D) Controlling Shareholder's compensation (salary and bonuses);

(E) Controlling shareholder's "excess" benefits.

[*Repeat for each defendant.*]

H.4.2 Requests for Admissions

1. Letters in the form of Exhibit A have been sent to more than 30 [*state*] residents.

2. Letters in the form of Exhibit A have been sent to more than 50 [*state*] residents.

3. Letters in the form of Exhibit A have been sent to more than 500 [*state*] residents.

4. Letters in the form of Exhibit A have been sent to more than 1,000 [*state*] residents.

5. Letters in the form of Exhibit A have been sent to more than 5,000 [*state*] residents. [*Repeat for each letter.*]

6. The net worth of defendant [*name*] is equal to or greater than $50,000,000.00.

H.4.3 Requests for Production of Documents

1. All documents showing who has been sent letters in the form of Exhibit A and the number of such letters sent to persons within [*state*]. [*Repeat for each letter.*]

2. All documents demonstrating the calculation of the net worth of [*name*]. [*Repeat for each defendant.*]

Appendix I   Sample Trial Documents

This appendix contains a sample brief in support of a motion for partial summary judgment, sample jury *voir dire* questions, sample jury instructions, a proposed verdict sheet, a pretrial order, a trial brief and two motions in limine—one on plaintiff's personal character and one on attorney fees. All of these documents are also found on the companion website to this treatise.

Consumer law pleadings on this and other topics can be found in National Consumer Law Center, *Consumer Law Pleadings* (Index Guide with Companion Website) and *Consumer Law on the Web*.

I.1 Sample Brief in Support of Motion for Partial Summary Judgment

This sample brief is intended for demonstration, and must be adapted by a legal professional to meet the facts, actual needs, and requirements of each case, as well as local practice. The brief is available as well on the companion website to this treatise.

Consumer law pleadings on this and other topics can be found in National Consumer Law Center, *Consumer Law Pleadings* (Index Guide with Companion Website) and *Consumer Law on the Web*.

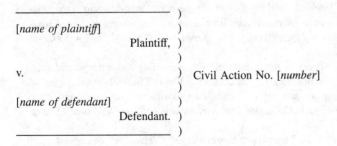

UNITED STATES DISTRICT COURT
FOR THE [*district name*] DISTRICT OF [*state name*]

[*name of plaintiff*]	)
Plaintiff,	)
	)
v.	) Civil Action No. [*number*]
	)
[*name of defendant*]	)
Defendant.	)

PLAINTIFF'S BRIEF IN SUPPORT OF MOTION FORPARTIAL SUMMARY JUDGMENT

970 F.2d 45 (4th Cir. 1992)

Miller v. Payco-General American Credits, Inc.

943 F.2d 482 (4th Cir. 1991)

Pipiles v. Credit Bureau of Lockport, Inc.

886 F.2d 22 (2d Cir. 1989)

Pressley v. Capital Credit & Collection Service, Inc.

760 F.2d 922 (9th Cir. 1985)

Riveria v. MAB Collections, Inc.

682 F. Supp. 174 (W.D.N.Y. 1988)

Russell v. Equifax A.R.S.

74 F.3d 30 (2d Cir. 1996)

Sibley v. Fulton DeKalb Collection Service

677 F.2d 830 (11th Cir. 1982)

Stojanovski v. Strobl and Manoogian, P.C.

783 F. Supp. 319 (E.D. Mich. 1992)

Swanson v. Southern Oregon Credit Service, Inc.

869 F.2d 1222 (9th Cir. 1988)

Taylor v. Perrin Landry, deLaunay & Durand

103 F.3d 1232 (5th Cir. 1997)

Tolentino v. Friedman

46 F.3d 645 (7th Cir. 1995)

United States v. National Financial Services, Inc.

98 F.3d 131 (4th Cir. 1996)

Other Authorities:

15 U.S.C. § 1692 et seq.

Federal Rules of Civil Procedure, Rule 56

I. PROCEDURAL HISTORY

On [*date complaint filed*], Plaintiff [*name*] filed his Complaint and Demand for Jury Trial with this Court, alleging that Defendant [*name*] violated the Fair Debt Collection Practices Act. On or about [*date answer filed*], Defendant filed its Answers and Defenses admitting that it had mailed letter(s) seeking to collect a debt from the Plaintiff, but denying that the Fair Debt Collection Practices Act was violated. The parties have exchanged and answered written discovery.

Plaintiff now files this Motion for Partial Summary Judgment and this brief in support thereof.

II. STATEMENT OF FACTS

By correspondence dated [*date*], Defendant [*name*] mailed letter(s) to Plaintiff [*name*] seeking to collect an alleged debt. (Copies of these letters are attached hereto as Addenda "A" through "___.") These communications state: [*insert language from the collector's correspondence that is attacked by the motion for partial summary judgment*]. The debt collector's demand for payment within [*number*] days is juxtaposed to the 30-day period provided in the validation notice, within which the consumer may make a request in writing to the collector for verification of the debt.

The Defendant's letter suggests that legal action may be taken, stating: [*insert the appropriate language*].

The debt collector's letter(s) fail to contain the debt collection warning: This is an attempt to collect a debt and any information obtained will be used for that purpose.

III. STATEMENT OF QUESTIONS PRESENTED

A. Did the Defendant's Letter Fail to Provide the Debt Collection Warning in Violation of 15 U.S.C. § 1692e(11)?

B. Did the Defendant's Threat to File Suit in a Time Barred Debt Violated the FDCPA?

C. Did Defendant's Telephone Messages Violate the FDCPA?

IV. ARGUMENT
A. Standard for Summary Judgment

Rule 56(c) of the Federal Rules of Civil Procedure provides that summary judgment:

> shall be rendered forthwith if the pleadings, depositions, answers to interrogatories and admissions on file, together with the affidavits, if any, show that there is no genuine issue as to any material fact and that the moving party is entitled to a judgment as a matter of law. A summary judgment, interlocutory in character, may be rendered on the issue of liability alone, although there is a genuine issue as to the amount of damages.

The entry of summary judgment is inappropriate where there exists a genuine and material issue of fact. *Anderson v. Liberty Lobby, Inc.*, 477 U.S. 242, 247–248, 106 S. Ct. 2505, 2509–2510, 91 L. Ed. 2d 202 (1986). Substantive law defines which facts are material and only disputes over facts that might affect the outcome of the case will defeat summary judgment. *Id.* at 248, 106 S. Ct. at 2510. A factual dispute is genuine if a "reasonable jury could return a verdict for the non-moving party." *Id.* Although all inferences to be drawn from the underlying facts must be viewed in the light most favorable to the non-moving party, once the movant has met its burden of demonstrating the absence of a genuine issue of material fact, the party opposing summary judgment "must do more than simply show that there is some metaphysical doubt as to the material facts" to prevent its entry. *Matsushita Electric Industrial Co. v. Zenith Radio Corp.*, 475 U.S. 547, 586–587, 106 S. Ct. 1348, 1355–1356, 89 L. Ed. 2d 538 (1986). It is not sufficient for the party opposing summary judgment to provide a scintilla of evidence supporting its case. *Anderson v. Liberty Lobby, Inc., supra*, 477 U.S. at 252, 106 S. Ct. at 2512.

There is no dispute of facts regarding the letter(s) and their content which Defendant sent to Plaintiff [*name*]. Thus, a grant of partial summary judgment is appropriate for any violations of the Fair Debt Collection Practices Act arising from Defendant's letters.

B. The "Least Sophisticated Consumer" Standard Is Used to Analyze Violations of the Act

The "least sophisticated consumer" standard is used to evaluate whether the debt collector's conduct violated the FDCPA. *LeBlanc v. Unifund CCR Partners*, 601 F.3d 1185, 1193–1194 (11th Cir. 2010); *Miller v. Javitch, Block & Rathbone*, 561 F.3d 588 (6th Cir. 2009). The FDCPA states that its purpose, in part, is "to eliminate abusive debt collection practices by debt collectors." 15 U.S.C. § 1692(e). It is designed to protect consumers from unscrupulous collectors, whether or not there is a valid debt. *Baker v. G.C. Services Corp.*, 677 F.2d 775, 777 (9th Cir. 1982). The FDCPA broadly prohibits unfair or unconscionable collection methods; conduct which harasses, oppresses or abuses any debtor; and any false, deceptive or misleading statements, in connection with the collection of a debt. *Heintz v. Jenkins*, 514 U.S. 291, 115 S. Ct. 1489, 131 L. Ed. 2d 395 (1995). "[I]t limits 'debt' to consumer debt." 15 U.S.C. §§ 1692d, 1692e, and 1692f and requires the debt collector to provide the consumer with his or her rights, 15 U.S.C. § 1692g, under the Act.

The U.S. Court of Appeals for the Fourth Circuit has held that whether a communication or other conduct violates the FDCPA is to be determined by analyzing it from the perspective of the "least sophisticated debtor." *United States v. National Financial Services, Inc.*, 98 F.3d 131 135–136 (4th Cir. 1996). [*Substitute the leading decision from your circuit court, e.g., Brown v. Card Serv. Ctr., 464 F.3d 450, 454 (3d Cir. 2006).*]

"The basic purpose of the least-sophisticated-consumer standard is to ensure that the FDCPA protects all consumers, the gullible as well as the shrewd." *Clomon v. Jackson*, 988 F.2d 1314, 1318 (2d Cir. 1993). *See also Taylor v. Perrin, Landry, deLaunay & Durand*, 103 F.3d 1232, 1236 (5th Cir. 1997); *U.S. v. Nat'l Fin. Serv., Inc.*, 98 F.3d 131, 136 (4th Cir. 1996); *Russell v. Equifax A.R.S.*, 74 F.3d 30 (2d Cir. 1996); *Bentley v. Great Lakes Collection Bureau*, 6 F.3d 60 (2d Cir. 1993); *Graziano v. Harrison*, 950 F.2d 107, 111 (3d Cir. 1991); *Swanson v. S. Oregon Credit Serv., Inc.*, 869 F.2d 1222, 1225–1226 (9th Cir. 1988); *Jeter v. Credit Bureau, Inc.*, 760 F.2d 1168, 1172–1175 (11th Cir. 1985). "While protecting naive consumers, the standard also prevents liability for bizarre or idiosyncratic interpretations of collection notices by preserving a quotient of reasonableness and presuming a basic level of understanding and willingness to read with care." *United States v. National Financial Services, Inc.*, 98 F.3d at 136 (citation omitted). *See also Taylor v. Perrin Landry, deLaunay & Durand*, 103 F.3d 1232, 1236 (5th Cir. 1997); *Russell v. Equifax A.R.S.*, 74 F.3d 30 (2d Cir. 1996); *Avila v. Rubin*, 84 F.3d 222, 226-227 (7th Cir. 1996) ("the standard is low, close to the bottom of the sophistication meter"); *Bentley v. Great Lakes Collection Bureau*, 6 F.3d 60 (2d Cir. 1993); *Clomon v. Jackson*, 988 F.2d 1314 (2d Cir. 1993); *Graziano v. Harrison*, 950 F.2d 107, 111 (3d Cir. 1991); *Jeter v. Credit Bur., Inc.*, 760 F.2d 1168 (11th Cir. 1985).

"The FDCPA is a strict liability statute to the extent it imposes liability without proof of an intentional violation." *Allen ex rel. Martin v. LaSalle Bank, N.A.*, __ F.3d __, 2011 WL 94420, at *3 (3d Cir. Jan. 12, 2011). *See also LeBlanc v. Unifund CCR Partners*, 601 F.3d 1185, 1190 (11th Cir. 2010); *Donohue v. Quick Collect, Inc.*, 592 F.3d 1027, 1030 (9th Cir. 2010); *Ellis v. Solomon and Solomon, P.C.*, 591 F.3d 130, 135(2d Cir. 2010); *Ruth v. Triumph P'ships*, 577 F.3d 790, 805 (7th Cir. 2009). "As the FDCPA is a strict liability statute, proof of one violation is sufficient to support summary judgment for the plaintiff." *Cacace v. Lucas*, 775 F. Supp. 502, 505 (D. Conn. 1990). *See also Stojanovski v. Strobl and Manoogian, P.C.*, 783 F. Supp. 319, 323 (E.D. Mich. 1992); *Riveria v. MAB Collections, Inc.*, 682 F. Supp. 174, 178–179 (W.D.N.Y. 1988). "Because the Act imposes strict liability, a consumer need not show intentional conduct by the debt collector to be entitled to damages." *Guerrero v. RJM Acquisitions L.L.C.*, 499 F.3d 926 (9th Cir. 2007); *Russell v. Equifax A.R.S.*, 74 F.3d at 33. *See also Clark v. Capital Credit & Collection Servs.*, 460 F.3d 1162, 1176 (9th Cir. 2006); *Bentley v. Great Lakes Collection Bureau*, 6 F.3d at 62; *Clomon v. Jackson*, 988 F.2d at 1318. Furthermore, the question of whether the consumer owes the alleged debt has no bearing on a suit brought pursuant to the FDCPA. *McCartney v. First City Bank*, 970 F.2d 45 (5th Cir.

1992); *Baker v. G.C. Services Corp.*, 677 F.2d 775, 777 (9th Cir. 1982).

Whether [*name*] violated the FDCPA must be evaluated from the standpoint of the least sophisticated consumer.

C. Defendant's Failure to Provide the Debt Collection Warning in Its Initial Letter Violates 15 U.S.C. § 1692e(11)

The Act at 15 U.S.C. § 1692e provides, in pertinent part:

> [T]he following conduct is a violation of this section:
>
> (11) The failure to disclose in the initial written communication with the consumer and, in addition, if the initial communication with the consumer is oral, in that initial oral communication, that the debt collector is attempting to collect a debt and that any information obtained will be used for that purpose, and the failure to disclose in subsequent communications that the communication is from a debt collector, except that this paragraph shall not apply to a formal pleading made in connection with a legal action.

The U.S. Courts of Appeals, considering the application of the above provision, have consistently held that in an initial communication the debt collection warning must be provided. *Guerrero v. RJM Acquisitions L.L.C.*, 499 F.3d 926 (9th Cir. 2007); *Tolentino v. Friedman*, 46 F.3d 645 (7th Cir. 1995); *Dutton v. Wolpoff & Abramson*, 5 F.3d 649 (3d Cir. 1993); *Frey v. Gangwish*, 970 F.2d 1516 (6th Cir. 1992); *Carroll v. Wolpoff & Abramson*, 961 F.2d 459 (4th Cir. 1992); *Pipiles v. Credit Bureau of Lockport, Inc.*, 886 F.2d 22, 26 (2d Cir. 1989); *Emanuel v. American Credit Exchange*, 870 F.2d 805, 808 (2d Cir. 1989); *Pressley v. Capital Credit & Collection Services, Inc.*, 760 F.2d 922, 925 (9th Cir. 1985); *Hulshizer v. Global Credit Services, Inc.*, 728 F.2d 1037, 1038 (8th Cir. 1984).

The U.S. Court of Appeals for the Eighth Circuit found the quoted statutory language "unambiguous" and ruled that the failure to include "the clear language of the statute" violated the Act. *Hulshizer v. Global Credit Services, Inc.*, 728 F.2d at 1038. The Court of Appeals for the Ninth Circuit agreed with such an interpretation when the communication involved is an initial communication. *Pressley v. Capital Credit & Collection Services, Inc.*, 760 F.2d at 926.

D. Defendant's Threat to Sue on a Time-Barred Debt Violates the FDCPA

Defendants' practice of sending letters in the form of Exhibits A and/or B to Pennsylvania residents to collect time barred dishonored checks threatening that "[p]ursuant to Pennsylvania law" the consumer "may be subject to a civil penalty, court costs and reasonable attorneys fees after suit has been filed" violates the FDCPA at 15 U.S.C. §§ 1692e(2)(A), e(3), e(5), e(10), 1692f(1), and 1692g(a)(2). The Pennsylvania statute provides that an action to recover "an unaccepted draft to pay the draft must be commenced within three years after dishonor of the draft or ten years after the date of the draft, whichever period expires first." 13 Pa.

C.S. § 3118(c). Here Defendants have attempted to collect Plaintiff's dishonored checks written on March 18 and 20, 1994 with collection letters dated April 24, 2004. PSMF # 14 and 22. Those checks were dishonored shortly after presentment in March, 1994. PSMF # 1. Whether applying the time limitation of three years or 10 years, this time limitation had expired at the time Defendants' letters were sent. Thus, the alleged debts of Plaintiff is time barred.

A debt collector's threat of suit on a time-barred debt violates the FDCPA at 15 U.S.C. §§ 1692e and 1692f. *Kimber v. Federal Financial Corp.*, 668 F. Supp. 1480 (M.D. Ala. 1987). Although a debt collector may request voluntary payment of a time-barred obligation, it may not threaten to file suit. *Freyermuth v. Credit Bureau Servs.*, 248 F.3d 767 (8th Cir. 2001); *Gervais v. Riddle & Assocs., P.C.*, 479 F. Supp. 2d 270 (D. Conn. 2007); *Reese v. Arrow Fin. Serv., L.L.C.*, 202 F.R.D. 83, 92–93 (D. Conn. 2001); *Walker v. Cash Flow Consultants*, 200 F.R.D. 613, 615–616 (N.D. Ill. 2001); *Shorty v. Capital One Bank*, 90 F. Supp. 2d 1330 (D.N.M. 2000) and *Stepney v. Outsourcing Solutions, Inc.*, 1997 WL 722972, 1997 U.S. Dist. LEXIS 18264 (N.D. Ill. Nov. 13, 1997).

The FDCPA prohibits "[t]he threat to take any action that cannot legally be taken or that is not intended to be taken." 15 U.S.C. § 1692e(5). Defendants' statement in Exhibits A and B that "you may be subject to a civil penalty, court costs and reasonable attorneys fees after suit has been filed" was "part and parcel of general representations which a reasonable jury could find to be violative of §§ 1692e(5) and (10), i.e., potentially deceptive or false use of threats to recommend legal action." *Jeter v. Credit Bureau*, 760 F.2d 1168, 1179 (11th Cir. 1985).

In a similar case, the district court found defendant violated the FDCPA by sending misleading letters that threatened suit on a time-barred debt. The court stated:

> As discussed above, the February 17 letter at issue here unambiguously threatened litigation. Defendants respond by arguing only that the statute of limitations did not bar them from pursuing litigation against Goins because the statute of limitations is not a jurisdictional bar, but merely an affirmative defense that can be waived. As the statute of limitations would be a complete defense to any suit, however, the threat to bring suit under such circumstances can at best be described as a "misleading" representation, in violation of § 1692e. As an officer of the court, Boyajian has an obligation to represent to the court to the best of his knowledge, "after an inquiry reasonable under the circumstances," that the claims presented are "warranted by existing law or by a nonfrivolous argument for the extension, modification, or reversal of existing law or the establishment of new law." *See* Fed. R. Civ. P. 11; *see also* State v. Turner, 267 Conn. 414, 430, 838 A.2d 947 (2004) (defining frivolous action as one in which "the lawyer is unable either to make a good faith argument on the merits of the action taken or to support the action taken by a good faith argument for an extension, modification or reversal of existing law."). Sanctions therefore would be appropriate if an attorney knowingly filed suit on an undisputedly time-barred claim. *See* Steinle v.

Warren, 765 F.2d 95 (7th Cir. 1985) (awarding attorney fees to opposing party and imposing Rule 11 sanctions where attorney knew claim was time-barred). That the statute of limitations is an affirmative defense does not relieve defendants of their professional responsibility, when they do not dispute the applicability or viability of the defense. Because defendants were not entitled to sue in such circumstances, the threats to sue in the February 17 letter are improper. *See* Kimber v. Federal Financial Corp., 668 F. Supp. 1480 (M.D. Ala. 1987) (finding FDCPA violation where attorney threatened to sue on a time-barred claim).

Goins v. JBC & Assoc., P.C., 352 F. Supp. 2d 262, 272 (D. Conn. 2005). *See Thinesen v. JBC Legal Group, P.C.*, 2005 WL 2346991, 2005 U.S. Dist. LEXIS 21637, *11 (D. Minn. Sept. 26, 2005).

In *Gervais v. Riddle & Assocs., P.C.*, 363 F. Supp. 2d 345, 352 (D. Conn. 2005) (citation omitted), the district court concluded that statements by the debt collector would indicate to the least sophisticated consumer that " 'the clear import of the language, taken as a whole, is a that [some] type of legal action has already been or is about to be initiated and can be averted from running its course only by payment.' "

Likewise, the district court in *Perretta v. Capital Acquisitions & Mgmt. Co.*, 2003 WL 2183757, at *4, 2003 U.S. Dist. LEXIS 10070, at *14 (N.D. Cal. May 5, 2003), reviewing the debt collector's statements stated: "this court does not hold that as a matter of law, it would be unreasonable for the least sophisticated debtor to interpret defendant's statements as a threat of legal action." The court stated further: "the court concludes that the least sophisticated debtor would be reasonable to interpret the threat of 'further steps' to mean legal action. Indeed, given our rather litigious society, an individual not well versed in the mechanics of debt collection may very well consider legal action to be the next possible—and probable—'step.' Also, the vague nature of defendant's statement lends itself to such an interpretation. . . ." *Id.* at *15 (citation omitted). Also, *see Stepney v. Outsourcing Solutions, Inc.*, 1997 WL 722972, 1997 U.S. Dist LEXIS 18264, at *12–*14 (N.D. Ill. Nov. 4, 1997).

The district court in *Francis v. Snyder*, 389 F. Supp. 2d 1034, 1041 (N.D. Ill. 2005), pondered what the point of saying the consumer is in violation of a state's law would be "other than to indicate to the debtor that she may be sued, particularly when the letter is from an attorney." Similarly, Defendants here invoke "Pennsylvania law" and threaten the consumer with "a civil penalty, costs, and reasonable attorneys fees after suit is filed." This court should find that Defendants have violated 15 U.S.C. § 1692e(5) as did the *Francis v. Snyder* court.

The district court in *Florence v. National Sys.*, 1983 U.S. Dist. LEXIS 20344, at *10–*11 (N.D. Ga. Oct. 14, 1983), stated: "This letter clearly falls within the prohibition of §§ 1692e(5) and e(10) by creating 'the impression that legal action by defendant is a real possibility.' " *Baker v. G.C. Services Corp.*, 677 F.2d 775 (1982), and also misrepresents the legal status of the debt in violation of § 1692e(2). Defendant has unquestionably violated the prohibitions of § 1692e.

Defendants' letters, Exhibits A and B, mislead the least sophisticated consumer to believe that litigation to recover a time-barred debt will be initiated. Exhibits A and B appear on the letterhead of a law firm are purportedly signed by the law firm. Defendants invoke Pennsylvania law stating: "Pursuant to Pennsylvania law, you have thirty (30) days from receipt of this letter to pay the full amount of each check plus a service charge of $30.00 per check for the total payment of $* * *.**. You are cautioned that unless this total amount is paid in full within the thirty (30) day after the date this letter is received, you may be subject to a civil penalty, court costs and reasonable attorneys fees after suit has been filed." The least sophisticated consumer is lead to the conclusion that a suit could and would be filed. This is a false statement. A lawsuit may not be brought because it is barred by the limitations period of either of the three or ten year timeframe in which to bring suit on a dishonored check. Thus, Defendants have threatened the least sophisticated consumer with action that could not legally be taken and misrepresented its ability to do so in violation of 15 U.S.C. §§ 1692e(5) and (10).

E. Defendants' Telephone Messages Violate the FDCPA

The FDCPA prohibits "the placement of telephone calls without meaningful disclosure of the caller's identity." 15 U.S.C. § 1692d(6). Also prohibited is "the failure to disclose . . . that the communication is from a debt collector." 15 U.S.C. § 1692e(11); *Edwards v. Niagara Credit Solutions Inc.*, 586 F. Supp. 2d 1346, 1351–1353 (N.D.Ga. 2008), *aff'd on other grounds,* 584 F.3d 1350 (11th Cir. 2009); Drossin v. National Action Financial Services, Inc., 641 F. Supp. 2d 1314, 1318–1320 (S.D. Fla. 2009).

The district court in *Foti v. NCO Fin. Sys.*, 424 F. Supp. 2d 643, 668–670 (S.D.N.Y. 2006), stated:

> Rather, there is nothing in the context of the January 18 Pre-Recorded Message that would clearly inform a consumer that s/he is speaking to a debt collector, or, for that matter, that the subject of the "business matter" requiring "immediate attention" is a debt. Instead, a consumer would have to, upon hearing the message, recall that it previously received mail from a debt collection agency by the name of "NCO Financial Systems." Such a burden on the consumer is unreasonable. The least sophisticated consumer, who may receive voluminous messages and calls, could easily be confused about the identify of "NCO Financial Systems," particularly given the vague reference in the message to "a personal business matter that requires your immediate attention."

"The Court thus finds that the messages at issue the violated 15 U.S.C. § 1692e(11) because they were communications to a consumer in which the debt collector (Defendant) failed to identify the communication as coming from a debt collector." *Edwards v. Niagara Credit Solutions, Inc., supra,* 1361–1362. *See also Berg v. Merchants Ass'n Collection Div., Inc.*, 586 F. Supp. 2d 1336 (S.D. Fla. 2008).

In *Belin v. Litton Loan Servicing*, 2006 WL 1992410, at *5, 2006 U.S. Dist. LEXIS 47953 (M.D. Fla. July 14, 2006), Judge Bucklew wrote: "the court finds that the messages left on Ms. Belin's answering machine constitute communications that can support a violation of 15 U.S.C. § 1692e(11)." In another case involving telephone messages the court granted summary judgment for the consumer on her claims that the debt collector's telephone messages violated 15 U.S.C. § 1692e(11); *Leyse v. Corporate Collection Servs.*, 2006 WL 2708451, at *4, 6, 2006 U.S. Dist. LEXIS 67719 (S.D.N.Y. Sept. 18, 2006). "Because it appears that defendant's messages are 'communications' subjecting defendant to the provisions of § 1692e(11), it also appears that defendant has violated § 1692e(11) because the messages do not convey the information required by § 1692e(11), in particular, that the messages were from a debt collector." *Hosseinzadeh v. M.R.S. Associates, Inc.*, 387 F. Supp. 2d 1104, 1116 (C.D. Cal. 2005).

Defendants' telephone messages to Plaintiffs failed to meaningfully identify the caller or to state that the call was from a debt collector. Thus, Plaintiffs have demonstrated that Defendants' telephone messages violated 15 U.S.C. § 1692d(6) and § 1692e(11).

F. Plaintiff Reserves the Determination of Damages for the Jury

By this motion, the Plaintiff seeks only an award of partial summary judgment with regard to the Defendant's liability for violations of the Fair Debt Collection Practices Act. The determination of damages, as requested in the Complaint, is reserved for trial by jury. *Kobs v. Arrow Service Bureau, Inc.*, 134 F.3d 893 (7th Cir. 1986); *Sibley v. Fulton DeKalb Collection Services*, 677 F.2d 830 (11th Cir. 1982).

After the determination of liability and damages, Plaintiff will seek an award of attorney fees pursuant to the Fair Debt Collection Practices Act. 15 U.S.C. § 1692k(a)(3). "Because the FDCPA was violated, however, the statute requires the award of costs and reasonable attorney's fee . . ." *Pipiles v. Credit Bureau of Lockport, Inc.*, 886 F.2d at 28. *See also Graziano v. Harrison*, 950 F.2d at 113.

V. CONCLUSION

Defendant [*name*]'s collection letter(s), dated [*date(s)*], violated the Fair Debt Collection Practices Act by failing to provide the debt collection warning in its initial letter in violation of 15 U.S.C. § 1692e(11); (2) threatening to sue on a time-barred debt; and (3) leaving messages without meaningful identification of the caller's identity in violation of 15 U.S.C. § 1692d(6). Applying the least sophisticated consumer standard of analysis, partial summary judgment on the question of liability should be awarded in favor of the Plaintiff on these violations. Plaintiff requests that damages be determined at a trial before jury as requested in his Complaint.

Respectfully submitted,

[*signature*]
[*attorney*]
[*firm*]
[*street address*]
[*city, state zip*]
[*telephone number*]

Attorney for Plaintiff

I.2 Sample Jury *Voir Dire* Questions, Instructions, and Proposed Verdict Sheet

I.2.1 Sample Plaintiff's Request for Voir Dire Questions

This sample request is intended for demonstration, and must be adapted by a legal professional to meet the facts, actual needs, and requirements of each case, as well as local practice. The request is available as well on the companion website to this treatise. Consumer law pleadings on this and other topics can be found in National Consumer Law Center, *Consumer Law Pleadings* (Index Guide with Companion Website) and *Consumer Law on the Web*.

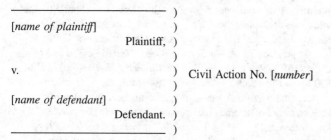

UNITED STATES DISTRICT COURT
FOR THE [*district name*] DISTRICT OF [*state name*]

```
————————————————— )
[name of plaintiff]            )
              Plaintiff,       )
                               )
v.                             )   Civil Action No. [number]
                               )
[name of defendant]            )
              Defendant.       )
————————————————— )
```

PLAINTIFF'S REQUEST FOR *VOIR DIRE* QUESTIONS

Plaintiff [*plaintiff's name*] requests that, at such time as *voir dire* of the jury venire is conducted, the Court ask the jury each of the attached questions number 1 through [*number*].

DATED, this [*date*] day of [*month*], 20_____.
[*attorney's name*]
[*firm*]
[*street address*]
[*city, state zip*]
[*telephone number*]
Attorney for Plaintiff

PLAINTIFF'S REQUESTED *VOIR DIRE*
QUESTION NUMBER [*number*]

Do you know:

• [*plaintiff's name*];
• [*defendant's name*];
• [*plaintiff's attorney's name*];
• [*defendant's attorney's name*];
• [*creditor's name*]; and
• [*witnesses' names*].

PLAINTIFF'S REQUESTED *VOIR DIRE*
QUESTION NUMBER [*number*]

The facts in this case include [*defendant's name*]'s attempt to collect a debt allegedly due to [*creditor's name*] from [*plaintiff*]. Do you have any knowledge of this case?

PLAINTIFF'S REQUESTED *VOIR DIRE*
QUESTION NUMBER [*number*]

Are there any members of the venire who are or have been engaged in or employed by a business or law office which collects debts or who have family members or close friends who are so employed?

PLAINTIFF'S REQUESTED *VOIR DIRE*
QUESTION NUMBER [*number*]

Are there any members of the venire who are or have been engaged in or employed by the business or individual who refers accounts to a debt collector for collection, or who have family members or close friends who are so employed?

PLAINTIFF'S REQUESTED *VOIR DIRE*
QUESTION NUMBER [*number*]

Are there any members of the venire who are or have been engaged in or employed by a business or individual which extends or collects credit, or who have family members or close friends who are so employed?

PLAINTIFF'S REQUESTED *VOIR DIRE*
QUESTION NUMBER [*number*]

Are there any members of the venire who feel for any reason not discussed, that they could not sit and hear this case and thereafter render a verdict which would be fair to both the Plaintiff and the Defendant under the evidence as it may be presented?

PLAINTIFF'S REQUESTED *VOIR DIRE*
QUESTION NUMBER [*number*]

If you determine that the debt collector has violated the Fair Debt Collection Practices Act, would you, for any reason, be unable to award statutory damages as instructed by the Court in addition to actual damages?

I.2.2 Sample Proposed Jury Instructions

These sample jury instructions are intended for demonstration, and must be adapted by a legal professional to meet the facts, actual needs, and requirements of each case, as well as local practice. The jury instructions are available as well on the companion website to this treatise. Consumer law pleadings on this and other topics can be found in National Consumer Law Center, *Consumer Law Pleadings* (Index Guide with Companion Website) and *Consumer Law on the Web*.

UNITED STATES DISTRICT COURT
FOR THE [*district name*] DISTRICT OF [*state name*]

```
_____        )
                           )
[name of plaintiff]        )
                Plaintiff, )
                           )
v.                         )  Civil Action No. [number]
                           )
[name of defendant]        )
               Defendant.  )
_____        )
```

PLAINTIFF'S PROPOSED JURY INSTRUCTIONS

Plaintiff requests that the following proposed Jury Instructions be read to the jury.

[*attorney's name*]
[*firm name*]
[*street address*]
[*city, state zip*]
[*telephone number*]
Attorney for Plaintiff

PLAINTIFF'S PROPOSED JURY INSTRUCTION
NUMBER [*number*]
(Nature of the Action and Legal Definitions)

Plaintiff brings this action against Defendant based on 15 U.S.C. § 1692, et seq., commonly known as the Fair Debt Collection Practices Act, which for convenience, I will refer to as the "Act."

The Act originally enacted by Congress became effective on March 20, 1978, and was again amended and broadened in 1986 and amended several times since. In passing this Act, Congress stated its purpose was "to eliminate abusive debt collection practices by debt collectors, to insure that those debt collectors who refrain from using abusive debt collection practices are not competitively disadvantaged, and to promote consistent State action to protect consumers against debt collection practices." To this end, the Act expressly prohibits debt collectors from engaging in numerous specific acts or practices and also mandatorily requires debt collectors in attempting to collect consumer debts for others to affirmatively perform specific acts.

The Act defines a "debt collector" to include any person who uses any instrumentality of interstate commerce, the mails in any business, the principle purpose of which business is the collection of any debt, directly or indirectly, owed, due, or asserted to be owed or due to another. The Act also defines a "debt collector" to include any person who regularly collects a debt owed to another. Defendant is a "debt collector" within the meaning of the Act.

The Act defines "debt" to mean any obligation or alleged obligation of a consumer to pay money arising out of a transaction in which the money, property, insurance or services which are the subject of the transaction are primarily for personal, family or household purposes, whether or not such obligations have been reduced to judgment. The obligation which Plaintiff is alleged to owe is a "debt" within the meaning of the Act.

The Act defines "consumer" as any person obligated or allegedly obligated to pay any debt. Plaintiff is a "consumer" within the meaning of the Act.

15 U.S.C. § 1692a.

PLAINTIFF'S PROPOSED JURY INSTRUCTION
NUMBER [*number*]
(Obligation to Pay the Debt Does Not Affect Liability Under FDCPA)

Whether or not the Plaintiff owes the debt alleged to be due to [*creditor*] is not a factor in this proceeding. Even if the Plaintiff does owe this obligation, Defendant must comply in all respects with the Fair Debt Collection Practices Act. Therefore, you may not consider whether or not the Plaintiff is indebted to [*creditor*] when determining whether Defendant violated the Fair Debt Collection Practices Act.

Baker v. G.C. Services Corp., 677 F.2d 775, 777 (9th Cir. 1982).

PLAINTIFF'S PROPOSED JURY INSTRUCTION
NUMBER [*number*]
(Plaintiff's Contentions)

Plaintiff contends that the Defendant violated the Act in the following seven particulars:

First, Defendant failed to provide the proper validation notice within five days of its initial communication with the Plaintiff in violation of 15 U.S.C. § 1692g(a);

Second, Defendant failed to include the debt collection warning ("this is an attempt to collect a debt and any information obtained will be used for that purpose") as required by 15 U.S.C. § 1692e(11) in the initial communication to the Plaintiff; and

Third, Defendant communicated with the Plaintiff after the Defendant knew that the Plaintiff was represented by an attorney in violation of 15 U.S.C. § 1692c(a)(2);

Fourth, Defendant threatened to take action that could not legally be taken or that was not intended to be taken in violation of 15 U.S.C. § 1692e(5);

Fifth, Defendant has falsely represented the character, amount or legal status of the debt in its communications to the Plaintiff in violation of 15 U.S.C. § 1692e(2)(A);

Sixth, Defendant has sought to collect an amount that is not authorized by the agreement creating the debt or permitted by law in violation of 15 U.S.C. § 1692f(1); and

Seventh, Defendant has used false representations and deceptive means to collect or attempt to collect the debt allegedly owed by the Plaintiff in violation of 15 U.S.C. § 1692e(10).

[Add or substitute other alleged violations as appropriate to the litigation.]

PLAINTIFF'S PROPOSED JURY INSTRUCTION
NUMBER [*number*]
(Validation of Debt)

The Fair Debt Collection Practices Act requires the debt collector to notify the consumer and provide certain information as follows:

(a) Within five days after the initial communication with a consumer in connection with the collection of any debt, a debt collector shall, unless the following information is contained in the initial communication or the consumer has paid the debt, send the consumer a written notice containing—

(1) the amount of the debt;

(2) the name of the creditor to whom the debt is owed;

(3) a statement that unless the consumer, within thirty days after receipt of the notice, disputes the validity of the debt, or any portion thereof, the debt will be assumed to be valid by the debt collector;

(4) a statement that if the consumer notifies the debt collector in writing within the thirty-day period that the debt, or any portion thereof, is disputed, the debt collector will obtain verification of the debt or a copy of a judgment against the consumer and a copy of such verification or judgment will be mailed to the consumer by the debt collector; and

(5) a statement that, upon the consumer's written request within the thirty-day period, the debt collector will provide the consumer with the name and address of the original creditor, if different from the current creditor.

(b) If the consumer notifies the debt collector in writing within the thirty-day period described in subsection (1) that the debt, or any portion thereof, is disputed, or that the consumer requests the name and address of the original creditor, the debt collector shall cease collection of the debt, or any disputed portion thereof, until the debt collector obtains verification of the debt or a copy of a judgment, or the name and address of the original creditor, and a copy of such verification or judgment, or name and address of the original creditor, is mailed to the consumer by the debt collector.

(c) The failure of a consumer to dispute the validity of a debt under this section may not be construed by any court as an admission of liability by the consumer.

* * *

15 U.S.C. § 1692g.
Baker v. G.C. Services Corp., 677 F.2d 775 (9th Cir. 1982).

PLAINTIFF'S PROPOSED JURY INSTRUCTION
NUMBER [*number*]
(The Validation Notice Must Be Effectively Conveyed)

The Act is not satisfied merely by inclusion of the required notice; the notice Congress required must be conveyed effectively to the debtor. It must be large enough to be easily read and sufficiently prominent to be noticed—even by the least sophisticated debtor.

United States v. National Financial Services, Inc., 98 F.3d 131, 139 (4th Cir. 1996); *Russell v. Equifax A.R.S.*, 74 F.3d 30, 35 (2d Cir. 1996); *Swanson v. Southern Oregon Credit Service, Inc.*, 869 F.2d 1222, 1225 (9th Cir. 1988); *Miller v. Payco-General American Credit, Inc.*, 943 F.2d 482, 484 (4th Cir. 1991).

PLAINTIFF'S PROPOSED JURY INSTRUCTION
NUMBER [*number*]
(Debt Collection Warning)

The failure to disclose in the initial written communication with the consumer and, in addition, if the initial communication with the consumer is oral, in that initial oral communication, that the debt collector is attempting to collect a debt and that any information obtained will be used for that purpose, and the failure to disclose in subsequent communications that the communication is from a debt collector, except that this paragraph shall not apply to a formal pleading made in connection with a legal action.

15 U.S.C. § 1692e(11).
Edwards v. Niagara Credit Solutions, Inc., 584 F.3d 1350 (11th Cir. 2009); *Tolentino v. Friedman*, 46 F.3d 645 (7th Cir. 1995); *Dutton v. Wolpoff & Abramson*, 5 F.3d 649 (3d Cir. 1993); *Frey v. Gangwish*, 970 F.2d 1516 (6th Cir. 1992); *Carroll v. Wolpoff & Abramson*, 961 F.2d 459 (4th Cir. 1992); *Pipiles v. Credit Bureau, Inc.*, 886 F.2d 22 (2d Cir. 1989); *Seabrook v. Onondaga Bureau of Medical Economics, Inc.*, 705 F. Supp. 81 (N.D.N.Y. 1989).

PLAINTIFF'S PROPOSED JURY INSTRUCTION
NUMBER [*number*]
(Communication with Consumer Represented by an Attorney)

The Fair Debt Collection Practices Act states that a debt collector may not communicate with a consumer in connection with the collection of any debt if the debt collector knows the consumer is represented by an attorney with respect to such debt and has knowledge of, or can readily ascertain, such attorney's name and address.

15 U.S.C. § 1692c(a)(2).
Dowling v. Litton Loan Serv., L.P., 2006 WL 3498292 (S.D. Ohio Dec. 1, 2006); *Harvey v. United Adjusters*, 509 F. Supp. 1218 (D. Or. 1981); *Johnson v. Statewide Collections, Inc.*, 778 P.2d 93 (Wyo. 1989).

PLAINTIFF'S PROPOSED JURY INSTRUCTION
NUMBER [*number*]
(Threats to Take Action Which Cannot Legally Be Taken or That Is Not Intended to Be Taken)

The Fair Debt Collection Practices Act states:

A debt collector may not use any false, deceptive, or misleading representation or means in connection with the collection of any debt. Without limiting the general application of the foregoing, the following conduct is a violation of this section:

(5) The threat to take any action that cannot legally be taken or that is not intended to be taken.

15 U.S.C. § 1692e(5). Where the clear import of the collection letter is that the Defendant has already taken action or is about to do so and that such action can only be averted by payment of the debt, the debt collector's failure to take the threatened action violates the Act. Whether the debt collector's threatened action is such a violation, must be determined from the prospective of the least sophisticated consumer or debtor, which I will later explain.

Wilhelm v. Credico, Inc., 519 F.3d 416 (8th Cir. 2008); *Brown v. Card Serv. Ctr.*, 464 F.3d 450 (3d Cir. 2006); *United States v. Nat'l Fin. Servs., Inc.*, 98 F.3d 131 (4th Cir. 1996); *Pipiles v. Credit Bureau, Inc.*, 886 F.2d 22, 25–26 (2d Cir. 1989); *Crossley v. Lieberman*, 868 F.2d 566, 571 (3d Cir. 1989); *Swanson v. Southern Oregon Credit Service*, 869 F.2d 1222, 1227–1228 (9th Cir. 1988).

PLAINTIFF'S PROPOSED JURY INSTRUCTION
NUMBER [*number*]
(The False Representation of the Character, Amount,
or Legal Status of the Debt)

The Fair Debt Collection Practices Act provides:

> A debt collector may not use any false, deceptive, or misleading representation or means in connection with the collection of any debt. Without limiting the general application of the foregoing, the following conduct is a violation of this section:
>
> (2) The false representation of—(A) the character, amount, or legal status of any debt; . . .

15 U.S.C. § 1692e. Falsely stating the amount of the debt violates this section. In determining whether the Act has been violated, you are to analyze the allegation from the viewpoint of the least sophisticated consumer or debtor, which I will explain to you.

Hepsen v. Resurgent Capital Servs., L.P., 2010 WL 2490734 (11th Cir. June 17, 2010); *Reichert v. Nat'l Credit Sys.*, 531 F.3d 1002 (9th Cir. 2008); *Clark v. Capital Credit & Collection Servs., Inc.*, 460 F.3d 1162 (9th Cir. 2006); *Shula v. Lawent*, 359 F.3d 489 (7th Cir. 2004); *Miller v. McCalla, Raymer, Padrick, Cobb, Nichols, & Clark, L.L.C.*, 214 F.3d 872 (7th Cir. 2000), *rehearing en banc denied*, 2000 U.S. App. LEXIS 18232 (7th Cir. July 26, 2000); *Cacace v. Lucas*, 775 F. Supp. 502 (D. Conn. 1990); *West v. Costen*, 558 F. Supp. 564 (W.D. Va. 1983).[1]

PLAINTIFF'S PROPOSED JURY INSTRUCTION
NUMBER [*number*]
(Collection of an Amount Not Authorized by Contract or Law)

The Fair Debt Collection Practices Act states:

> A debt collector may not use unfair or unconscionable means to collect or attempt to collect any debt. Without limiting the general application of the foregoing, the following conduct is a violation of this section:
>
> (1) The collection of any amount (including any interest, fee, charge, or expense incidental to the principal obligation) unless such amount is expressly authorized by the agreement creating the debt or permitted by law.

15 U.S.C. § 1692f. The debt collector's imposition of a service charge which is not authorized by the contract creating the debt or by law violates this section.

Shula v. Lawent, 359 F.3d 489 (7th Cir. 2004); Johnson v. Riddle, 305 F.3d 1107 (10th Cir. 2002); *Duffy v. Landberg*, 215 F.3d 871 (8th Cir.), *rehearing denied*, 2000 U.S. App. LEXIS 16039 (8th Cir. July 10, 2000); *Pollice v. National Tax Funding, L.P.*, 225 F.3d 379 (3d Cir. 2000); *West v. Costen*, 558 F. Supp. 564 (W.D. Va. 1983).

PLAINTIFF'S PROPOSED JURY INSTRUCTION
NUMBER [*number*]
(Using False or Deceptive Means to Collect a Debt)

The Fair Debt Collection Practices Act provides:

> A debt collector may not use any false, deceptive, or misleading representation or means in connection with the collection of any debt. Without limiting the general application of the foregoing, the following conduct is a violation of this section:
>
> (10) The use of any false representation or deceptive means to collect or attempt to collect any debt or to obtain information concerning a consumer.

15 U.S.C. § 1692e. Where the Defendant's letter states that some type of action has already been or is about to be initiated and can be averted only by payment, when such action has not been undertaken, is a violation of this section. In determining whether this section has been violated, you are to apply the least sophisticated consumer standard which I shall explain to you.

Ruth v. Triumph P'ships, 577 F.3d 790 (7th Cir. 2009); *Muha v. Encore Receivable Mgmt., Inc.*, 558 F.3d 623 (7th Cir. 2009); *Brown v. Card Serv. Ctr.*, 464 F.3d 450 (3d Cir. 2006); *Pipiles v. Credit Bureau, Inc.*, 886 F.2d 22, 25–26 (2d Cir. 1989); *Crossley v. Lieberman*, 868 F.2d 566, 571 (3d Cir. 1989); *Jeter v. Credit Bureau, Inc.*, 760 F.2d 1168, 1177–1178 (11th Cir. 1985).

PLAINTIFF'S PROPOSED JURY INSTRUCTION
NUMBER [*number*]
(Violations of the Act Are Measured by the "Least
Sophisticated Debtor" Standard)

In determining whether the Defendant violated the Fair Debt Collection Practices Act you are to apply the "least sophisticated debtor" standard. This law was not made for the protection of experts, but for the public—that vast multitude which includes the ignorant, the unthinking and the credulous, and the fact that a false or misleading statement may be obviously false or misleading to those who are trained and experienced does not change its character, nor take away its power to deceive others less experienced. Thus, in reaching your determination of whether Defendant's communications are false or deceptive you must view them through the eyes of the "least sophisticated debtor."

Rosenau v. Unifund Corp., 539 F.3d 218, 221 (3d Cir. 2008); *Kistner v. Law Offices of Michael P. Margelefsky, L.L.C.*, 518 F.3d 433 (6th Cir. 2008); *Brown v. Card Serv. Ctr.*, 464 F.3d 450 (3d Cir. 2006); *Schweizer v. Trans Union Corp.*, 136 F.3d 233 (2d Cir. 1998); *Swanson v. Southern Oregon Credit Service*, 869 F.2d 1222, 1225–1227 (9th Cir. 1988); *Jeter v. Credit Bureau, Inc.*, 760 F.2d 1168, 1172–1175 (11th Cir. 1985); *Graziano v. Harrison*, 950 F.2d 107, 111 (3d Cir. 1991) (In the Seventh Circuit, the "unsophisticated consumer" standard should be substituted for the "least sophisticated consumer" standard. *See* § 5.2.1, *supra*.)

---

1 *See* § 5.2.1, *supra*.

PLAINTIFF'S PROPOSED JURY INSTRUCTION
NUMBER [*number*]
(Bona Fide Error Defense)

The debt collector is not liable for violation of the Fair Debt Collection Practices Act if it shows a preponderance of the evidence that (1) it did not intend to violate the Act and (2) the violation "resulted from a bona fide error notwithstanding the maintenance of procedures reasonably adapted to avoid any such error."[2]

15 U.S.C. § 1692k(c).
McCollough v. Johnson, Rodenburg & Lauinger, L.L.C., 637 F.3d 939, 948 (9th Cir. 2011); *Owen v. I.C. Sys., Inc.*, 2011 WL 43525 (11th Cir. Jan. 7, 2011); *Hepsen v. Resurgent Capital Servs., L.P.*, 2010 WL 2490734 (11th Cir. June 17, 2010); *Edwards v. Niagara Credit Solutions, Inc.*, 584 F.3d 1350 (11th Cir. 2009); *Ruth v. Triumph P'ships*, 577 F.3d 790 (7th Cir. 2009); *Hartman v. Great Seneca Fin. Corp.*, 569 F.3d 606 (6th Cir. 2009); *Seeger v. AFNI, Inc.*, 548 F.3d 1107 (7th Cir. 2008); *Reichert v. Nat'l Credit Sys, Inc.*, 531 F.3d 1002 (9th Cir. 2008); *Johnson v. Riddle*, 305 F.3d 1107 (10th Cir. 2002); *Smith v. Transworld Systems, Inc.*, 953 F.2d 1025 (6th Cir. 1992); *Pipiles v. Credit Bureau, Inc.*, 886 F.2d 22, 27 (2d Cir. 1989); *Baker v. G.C. Services Corp.*, 677 F.2d 775, 779 (9th Cir. 1982).

PLAINTIFF'S PROPOSED JURY INSTRUCTION
NUMBER [*number*]
(Actual Damages)

I turn now to the law of damages applicable to this case if you reach that phase.

The Act specifically permits damages to be awarded against a debt collector who violates the Act.

First, actual damages may be awarded the Plaintiff as a result of the failure of Defendant to comply with the Act. Actual damages not only include any out-of-pocket expenses but also damages for personal humiliation, embarrassment, mental anguish, and emotional distress.

There is no fixed standard or measure in the case of intangible items such as humiliation, embarrassment, mental anguish and emotional distress. You must determine a fair and adequate award of these items through the exercise of your judgment and experience in the affairs of the world after considering all the facts and circumstances presented during the trial of this case.

McCollough v. Johnson, Rodenburg & Lauinger, L.L.C., 637 F.3d 939, 957 (9th Cir. 2011); *Smith v. Law Office of Mitchell N. Kay*, 124 B.R. 182, 185 (D. Del. 1990); *In re Maxwell*, 281 B.R. 101 (Bankr. D. Ma. 2002); *In re Littles*, 75 B.R. 241, 242 (Bankr. E.D. Pa. 1987).

PLAINTIFF'S PROPOSED JURY INSTRUCTION
NUMBER [*number*]
(Statutory Damages)[3]

In addition to actual damages, and regardless of whether actual damages are awarded, the jury may award statutory damages in an amount not to exceed $1,000.00 for each person affected by the violation of the Act. In determining the amount of statutory damages to be awarded, whether $1.00 or up to and including $1,000.00 for each person, the Act provides that the jury shall consider among other relevant factors, the frequency and persistence of noncompliance by the debt collector, the nature of such noncompliance, and the extent to which noncompliance was intentional.

15 U.S.C. § 1692k(b)(1).
Kobs v. Arrow Service Bureau, Inc., 134 F.3d 893 (7th Cir. 1998); *Robertson v. Horton Bros. Recovery, Inc.*, 2007 WL 2009703 (D. Del. 2007); *Boyce v. Attorney's Dispatch Serv.*, 1999 U.S. Dist. LEXIS 1124 (S.D. Ohio Feb. 2, 1999); *Carn v. Med. Data Sys.*, 2007 Bankr. LEXIS 1334 (Bankr. M.D. Ala. Apr. 5, 2007); *In re Cambron*, 2007 WL 1076685 (Bankr. M.D. Ala. Apr. 5, 2007); *In re Littles*, 75 B.R. 241, 242 (Bankr. E.D. Pa. 1987).

PLAINTIFF'S PROPOSED JURY INSTRUCTION
NUMBER [*number*]
(Unanimous Verdict)

Your verdict must represent the considered judgment of each juror. In order to return a verdict, it is necessary that each juror agree to it. Your verdict must be unanimous.

It is your duty, as jurors, to consult with one another and to deliberate with a view toward reaching an agreement, if you can do so without violence to your individual judgment. Each of you must decide the case for yourself, but do so only after an impartial consideration of the evidence with your fellow jurors. In the course of your deliberation, do not hesitate to re-examine your own views, and change your opinion, if convinced it is erroneous. But do not surrender your honest conviction as to the weight or effect of evidence, solely because of the opinion of your fellow jurors, or for the purpose of returning a verdict.

Remember at all times that you are not partisans. You are judges—judges of the facts. Your sole interest is to seek the truth from the evidence in the case.

PLAINTIFF'S PROPOSED JURY INSTRUCTION
NUMBER [*number*]
(Verdict Return After Deliberations—Verdict Summary Sheets)

In a few moments, the jury will be removed to the jury room for its deliberations, which by custom of this Court shall be presided over by Juror Number One as your foreperson.

A verdict summary sheet has been prepared for your convenience to record your unanimous verdicts. You will take this form to the jury room, and after reaching unanimous agreement on the verdicts to be rendered and the amount, if any, of damages to be awarded with respect to Plaintiff's claim, you will have your foreperson complete the answers to the questions posed on the form in the manner thereon indicated.

After you have completely filled in the answers to the questions in the manner indicated on the verdict sheet, you will return with it to the courtroom for delivery to the Clerk.

---

2 Some courts have indicated that the defense may be used for at least some legal errors. *See* § 7.2, *supra*.

3 Some courts limit the award of statutory damages in an amount up to $1000 *per case*, *per plaintiff*, etc. Check the case law in your jurisdiction. *See* § 6.4.5, *supra*.

I.2.3 *Sample Verdict Sheet*

This sample verdict sheet is intended for demonstration, and must be adapted by a legal professional to meet the facts, actual needs, and requirements of each case, as well as local practice. The verdict sheet is available as well on the companion website to this treatise. Consumer law pleadings on this and other topics can be found in National Consumer Law Center, *Consumer Law Pleadings* (Index Guide with Companion Website) and *Consumer Law on the Web.*

UNITED STATES DISTRICT COURT
FOR THE [*district name*] DISTRICT OF [*state name*]

```
_____  )
                          )
[name of plaintiff]       )
              Plaintiff,  )
                          )
v.                        )   Civil Action No. [number]
                          )
[name of defendant]       )
              Defendant.  )
_____  )
```

PLAINTIFF'S PROPOSED VERDICT SHEET

Pursuant to Rule 49 of the Federal Rules of Civil Procedure, Plaintiff requests that the following Verdict Sheet (Special Interrogatories To The Jury) attached hereto be given to the jury to answer in the course of its deliberations.

[*attorney's name*]
[*firm name*]
[*street address*]
[*city, state zip*]
[*telephone number*]
Attorney for Plaintiff

UNITED STATES DISTRICT COURT
FOR THE [*district name*] DISTRICT OF [*state name*]

```
_____  )
                          )
[name of plaintiff]       )
              Plaintiff,  )
                          )
v.                        )   Civil Action No. [number]
                          )
[name of defendant]       )
              Defendant.  )
_____  )
```

VERDICT SHEET
(Special Interrogatories to the Jury)

(Note: Answer "Yes" or "No" to each question by checking the appropriate space.)

This litigation proceeds pursuant to the Fair Debt Collection Practices Act. Plaintiff is a "consumer" and the obligation allegedly owed is a "debt." Defendant is a "debt collector" within the meaning of the Act. In answering the following questions you are to view the alleged violations of the Fair Debt Collection Practices Act from the perspective of the least sophisticated consumer or debtor.

1. Did Defendant debt collector fail to provide the debt collector warning—"This is an attempt to collect a debt and any information will be used for that purpose"—in its initial communication with the Plaintiff?

YES _____ NO _____

If your answer is "YES," you may award up to $1,000.00 as statutory damages.

Amount of statutory damages: $ _____

2. Did the Defendant debt collector fail to provide the proper thirty-day validation notice in its original communication with the Plaintiff or within five days thereafter?

YES _____ NO _____

If your answer is "YES," you may award up to $1,000.00 as statutory damages.

Amount of statutory damages: $ _____

3. Did the Defendant fail to cease further communications with the Plaintiff once informed that the Plaintiff was represented by an attorney?

YES _____ NO _____

If your answer is "YES," you may award up to $1,000.00 as statutory damages.

Amount of statutory damages: $ _____

4. Did the Defendant debt collector threaten to take any action that cannot legally be taken or that is not intended to be taken?

YES _____ NO _____

If your answer is "YES," you may award up to $1,000.00 as statutory damages.

Amount of statutory damages: $ _____

5. Did the Defendant debt collector make a false representation of the character, amount or legal status of the debt?

YES _____ NO _____

If your answer is "YES," you may award up to $1,000.00 as statutory damages.

Amount of statutory damages: $ _____

6. Did the Defendant debt collector seek to collect any amount that was not expressly authorized by the agreement creating the debt or permitted by law?

YES _____ NO _____

If your answer is "YES," you may award up to $1,000.00 as statutory damages.

Amount of statutory damages: $ _____

7. Did the Defendant debt collector use any false representation or deceptive means to collect or attempt to collect any debt or to obtain information concerning the consumer?

YES _____ NO _____

If your answer is "YES," you may award up to $1,000.00 as statutory damages.

Amount of statutory damages: $ _____

(If you have answered "YES" to any of the questions above, proceed to the next question. If you have answered "NO" to all the questions above, sign and date this document at the bottom.)

8. Did the Plaintiff suffer actual damages, which may include personal humiliation, embarrassment, mental anguish, or emotional distress, e.g. loss of sleep or appetite, nervousness, crying spells, due to the Defendant's conduct?

YES _____ NO _____

If your answer is "YES," set forth the amount of actual damages: $ _____

The above are the jury's unanimous verdict and answers to the special interrogatories.

Dated: _____

_____

Foreperson

[*Add or substitute other alleged violations as appropriate to the litigation.*]

[Note that some courts have limited the award of statutory damages in an amount up to $1,000.00 *per case*, *per plaintiff*, etc. *See* § 6.4.7.1, *supra*. Check the case law in your jurisdiction.]

I.3 Pretrial Order

UNITED STATES DISTRICT COURT
FOR THE CENTRAL DISTRICT OF ILLINOIS
ROCK ISLAND DIVISION

————————————————)	
DEBORAH ASHE and DALE W.)	
ASHE,)	
Plaintiffs,)	
)	
v.)	
)	
GOLIATH TRUST COMPANY,)	
Defendants.)	
————————————————)	

PRETRIAL ORDER

This matter having come before the Court at a pretrial conference held pursuant to Rule 16 of the Federal Rules of Civil Procedure and Local Rule 16.1;

[Attorney for Plaintiff] having appeared as counsel for the plaintiffs Deborah and Dale W. Ashe; and

[Attorney for Defendant] having appeared as counsel for defendant Goliath Trust Company.

(The listing of parties must be complete and appearances must show the individuals who were actually present.)

The following action was taken:

I. NATURE OF ACTION AND JURISDICTION

This is an action for damages brought pursuant to the Fair Debt Collection Practices Act, 15 U.S.C. § 1692 *et seq.*, and the jurisdiction of the Court is invoked under 15 U.S.C. § 1692k(d). The jurisdiction of the Court is not disputed.

II. JOINT STATEMENT

A. JURISDICTION

Jurisdiction lies with this Court pursuant to 15 U.S.C. § 1692k(d).

B. UNCONTESTED ISSUES OF FACT

1. Plaintiff Deborah Ashe is a natural person residing at [Address]. She is a "consumer" as defined by the FDCPA, 15 U.S.C. § 1692a(3).

2. Plaintiff Dale W. Ashe is a natural person residing at [Address]. He is a "consumer" as defined by the FDCPA, 15 U.S.C. § 1692a(3).

3. Defendant Goliath Trust Company is a corporation located at [Address].

4. Defendant is engaged in the collection of debts from consumers using the mail and telephone. Defendant regularly attempts to collect consumer debts alleged to be due another. Defendant was and is a "debt collectors" as defined by the FDCPA, 15 U.S.C. § 1692a(6).

5. Deborah Ashe wrote a personal check in the amount of $22.71 to Health Food Store (HFS) for the purchase of Nutri-Shot EnerGel.

6. Ms. Ashe's purchase of the Nutri-Shot EnerGel was for personal, family, or household purposes, i.e.—a nutritional supplement.

7. Ms. Ashe's check was dishonored.

8. Ms. Ashe was notified by representatives of HFS that her check had been dishonored and was instructed to pay the amount of $47.71.

9. Ms. Ashe paid attorney [Attorney for Health Food Store], who represent HFS, by U.S. Postal Money Order in the amount of $47.71.

10. Ms. Ashe called the Goliath Trust Company in response to its letter and explained that she had already paid attorney [Attorney for Health Food Store].

11. The representative of the Goliath Trust Company told Ms. Ashe that he would check the matter and respond to her.

12. At the beginning of February 2011, Ms. Ashe received another letter from the Goliath Trust Company.

13. In response to that letter Ms. Ashe telephoned the Goliath Trust Company and again informed them that she had previously paid this amount claimed.

14. Ms. Ashe repeated that the debt had been paid, but was informed by the representative of the Goliath Trust Company that she must send the amount and she would receive a refund at a later date if there had been a double payment. She sent in a second payment.

15. Ms. Ashe obtained a copy of the U.S. Postal Money Order from the U.S. Post Office demonstrating her payment of the amount allegedly due to attorney [Attorney for Health Food Store].

16. Ms. Ashe telephoned the Goliath Trust Company and again stated that she had paid this amount twice and had copies of the money orders.

17. Dale W. Ashe immediately again telephoned the Goliath Trust Company attempting to correct the matter.

18. On or about March 11, 2011, the Goliath Trust Company sent Deborah Ashe a check in the amount $47.71 as overpayment on the alleged debt.

C. CONTESTED ISSUES OF FACT

1. At the end of December, 2010, Ms. Ashe was informed by the Goliath Trust Company that if the check remained unpaid and if it was not paid within ten days they would direct the local sheriff to arrest her.

2. The representative of the Goliath Trust Company called Ms. Ashe a "liar" and stated that his records showed that the dishonored check had not been paid and if payment was not received immediately thereafter, Goliath Trust Company would have a warrant for her arrest issued.

3. The representative of the Goliath Trust Company again called her a "liar" and stated further "this is a bunch of bullshit. I don't care what kind of damn paperwork you have in front of you, my records show that you only paid it once, so we don't owe you a damn thing" and the representative of Goliath Trust Company hung up.

4. The representative of the Goliath Trust Company called Mr. Ashe a "son-of-a-bitch" and said further that Ms. Ashe did not double pay and there was no way he was sending a refund.

5. As a result of the conduct of the Goliath Trust Company, Deborah Ashe and Dale W. Ashe suffered actual damages in the form of emotion distress.

D. CONTESTED ISSUES OF LAW

Whether Goliath Trust Company used obscene or profane language or language the natural consequence of which is to abuse the hearer or reader in violation of 15 U.S.C. § 1692d(2);

Whether Goliath Trust Company falsely represented the character, amount, or legal status of any debt in violation of 15 U.S.C. § 1692e(2)(A);

Whether Goliath Trust Company represented or implied that nonpayment of any debt will result in the arrest or imprisonment of any person in violation of 15 U.S.C. § 1692e(4);

Whether Goliath Trust Company used any false representation or deceptive means to collect or attempt to collect any debt in violation of 15 U.S.C. § 1692e(10); and

Whether Goliath Trust Company collected any amount that is not expressly authorized by the agreement creating the debt or prohibited by law in violation of 15 U.S.C. § 1692f(1).

E. JURY DEMAND

A jury trial is demanded.

III. PLAINTIFF'S STATEMENT

A. ITEMIZED STATEMENT OF DAMAGES

Each plaintiff is entitled to an award of actual damages for the emotional distress, embarrassment, anxiety, and humiliation suffered as a result of defendant's conduct. Actual damages for emotional distress are unliquidated and must be determined by the jury. *McCollough v. Johnson, Rodenburg & Lauinger, L.L.C.*, 637 F.3d 939 (9th Cir. 2011); *Sibley v. Fulton Dekalb Collection Service*, 677 F.2d 830 (11th Cir. 1982); *Dewey v. Associated Collectors*, Inc., 927 F. Supp. 1172 (W.D. Wis. 1996).

Each plaintiff is entitled to statutory damages up to $1,000.00 apiece. *Kobs v. Arrow Service Bureau, Inc.*, 134 F.3d 893 (7th Cir. 1998); *Robertson v. Horton Bros. Recovery, Inc.*, 2007 WL 2009703 (D. Del. 2007); Boyce v. Attorney's Dispatch Serv., 1999 U.S. Dist. LEXIS 1124 (S.D. Ohio Feb. 2, 1999); *Beattie v. D.M. Collections, Inc.*, 764 F. Supp. 925, 928 (D. Del. 1991); *Carn v. Med. Data Sys.*, 2007 Bankr. LEXIS 1334 (Bankr. M.D. Ala. Apr. 5, 2007); *In re Cambron*, 2007 WL 1076685 (Bankr. M.D. Ala. Apr. 5, 2007); *In re Littles*, 75 B.R. 241, 242 (Bankr. E.D. Pa. 1987).

IV. WAIVER OF CLAIMS OR DEFENSES
(or JURY DEMAND)

Not applicable.

V. EXHIBITS ATTACHED

The following are attached as exhibits to this order and are made a part hereof [*not reprinted herein*]:

A. Stipulation of Uncontested Facts and Issues of Law (signed by all parties).

B. Plaintiff's Witness List (for each plaintiff).

C. Defendant's Witness List (for each defendant).

D. Plaintiff's Exhibit List (for each plaintiff).

E. Defendant's Exhibit List (for each defendant).

F. Joint Exhibit List.

G. Proposed Jury Instructions (Joint) (or Findings and Conclusions).

H. Plaintiff's Proposed Instructions (only if objections by defendant).

I. Defendant's Proposed Instructions (only if objections by plaintiff).

VI. GENERAL ADDITIONAL

The following additional action was taken:

1. The testimony of the following inmate witnesses is necessary for trial. The Clerk is directed to issue *Writ of Habeas Corpus ad Testificandum* for:

Not applicable.

2. The testimony of the following DOC employees is necessary for trial. The defendants are ordered to produce the following witnesses without subpoena:

Not applicable.

3. The testimony of the following witnesses who are neither inmate nor employees is necessary for trial. The Clerk is directed to issue trial subpoenas for the following. The plaintiff must provide the witness fee ($40) and mileage ($.30 per mile) to the witness, and is responsible for service of the subpoena under Fed. R. Civ. P. 45.

Not applicable.

[Recite amendments to pleadings, additional agreements of the parties on the qualifications of expert witnesses or any other subject, disposition of motions at the conference, etc., if necessary. If no such action was taken, leave this paragraph out of the Order.]

Not applicable.

IT IS UNDERSTOOD BY THE PARTIES THAT:

The plaintiff(s) is (are) limited to [*no*] expert witnesses whose names and qualifications have been disclosed to the defendant(s). The defendant(s) is (are) limited to [*no*] expert witnesses whose names and qualifications have been disclosed to the plaintiff(s).

[This paragraph does not refer to treating or examining physicians or other highly trained witnesses who have *actual* knowledge of the case. It should be left out if no expert witnesses have been listed.]

Any Trial Briefs or Motions in limine shall be submitted no later than fourteen (14) days prior to the commencement of the trial. [Leave out if no trial briefs will be used.]

A party may supplement a list of witnesses or exhibits only upon good cause shown in a motion filed and served upon the other parties prior to trial; except that, upon the development of testimony fairly shown to be unexpected, any party may, with leave of court, call such contrary witnesses or use such exhibits as may be necessary to counter the unexpected evidence, although not previously listed, and without prior notice of any other party.

It is mutually estimated that the length of trial will not exceed *one* full day. The case will be listed on the trial calendar to be tried when reached,

This pre-trial order may be modified at the trial of the action, or prior thereto, to prevent manifest injustice. Such modification may be made either on motion of counsel for any party or on the Court's own motion.

Any additional proposed jury instructions shall be submitted to the Court within five days before the commencement of the trial, but there is reserved to counsel for the respective parties the right to submit supplemental proposals for instructions during the course of the trial or at the conclusion of the evidence on matters that could not reasonably have been anticipated.

IT IS SO ORDERED.

JUDGE

ENTERED:

APPROVED AS TO FORM AND SUBSTANCE:

[Attorneys for the Plaintiffs]

[Attorneys for the Defendant]

I.4 Trial Brief

UNITED STATES DISTRICT COURT
FOR THE CENTRAL DISTRICT OF ILLINOIS

```
_____  )
                       )
DEBORAH ASHE and DALE W.)
ASHE,                  )
            Plaintiffs, )
                       )
v.                     )
                       )
                       )
GOLIATH TRUST COMPANY  )
            Defendant. )
_____  )
```

PLAINTIFFS' TRIAL BRIEF

STATEMENT OF THE CASE

This is an action for damages brought by Deborah Ashe and Dale W. Ashe, individual consumers, for violations by the Goliath Trust Company of the Fair Debt Collection Practices Act, 15 U.S.C. §§ 1692 *et seq.* (hereinafter "FDCPA") which prohibits debt collectors from engaging in abusive, deceptive and unfair practices. Plaintiffs seek an entry of a declaratory judgment that Goliath Trust Company violated the FDCPA and an award actual and statutory damages.

By Minute Entry of August 23, 2011, after telephone hearing, Judge Joe B. Smith granted plaintiffs' motion for default judgment pursuant to Rule 55(a). Magistrate Judge Robert J. Kieth has set this case for a prove-up/evidentiary hearing at [Time, Date] in Peoria.

STATEMENT OF FACTS

Plaintiffs Deborah and Dale W. Ashe are natural persons residing at [address]. Defendant Goliath Trust Company is a corporation located at [address] which is engaged in the collection of debts from consumers using the mail and telephone.

Deborah Ashe wrote a personal check in the amount of $22.71 to Health Food Store (HFS) for the purchase of Nutri-Shot Ener-Gel. Mrs. Ashe's purchase of the Nutri-Shot EnerGel was for personal, family, or household purposes, *i.e.*—a nutritional supplement. Ms. Ashe's check was dishonored.

Ms. Ashe was notified by representatives of HFS that her check had been dishonored and was instructed to pay the amount of $47.71. Ms. Ashe paid attorney [Attorney for Health Food Store], who represent HFS, by U.S. Postal Money Order in the amount of $47.71.

At the end of December, 2010, Ms. Ashe received a letter from the Goliath Trust Company stating that if the check remained unpaid and if it was not paid within ten days they would direct the local sheriff to arrest her. Ms. Ashe called the Goliath Trust Company in response to its letter and explained that she had already paid attorney [Attorney for Health Food Store]. The representative of the Goliath Trust Company told Ms. Ashe that he would check the matter and respond to her.

At the beginning of February 2011, Ms. Ashe received another letter from the Goliath Trust Company. In response to that letter Ms. Ashe telephoned the Goliath Trust Company and again informed them that she had previously paid this amount claimed. The representative of the Goliath Trust Company called her a "liar" and stated that his records showed that the dishonored check had not been paid and if payment was not received immediately thereafter, Goliath Trust Company would have a warrant for her arrest issued. Ms. Ashe repeated that the debt had been paid, but was informed by the representative of the Goliath Trust Company that she must send the amount and she would receive a refund at a later date if there had been a double payment.

Ms. Ashe obtained a copy of the U.S. Postal Money Order from the U.S. Post Office demonstrating her payment of the amount allegedly due to attorney [Attorney for Health Food Store]. Ms. Ashe telephoned the Goliath Trust Company and again stated that she had paid this amount twice and had copies of the money orders. The representative of the Goliath Trust Company again called her a "liar" and stated further "this is a bunch of bullshit. I don't care what kind of damn paperwork you have in front of you, my records show that you only paid it once, so we don't owe you a damn thing" and the representative of Goliath Trust Company hung up.

Dale W. Ashe immediately retelephoned the Goliath Trust Company attempting to correct the matter. The representative of the Goliath Trust Company called Mr. Ashe a "son-of-a-bitch" and said further that Ms. Ashe did not double pay and there was no way he was sending a refund.

On or about March 11, 2011, the Goliath Trust Company sent Deborah Ashe a check in the amount $47.71 as overpayment on the alleged debt.

As a result of the conduct of the Goliath Trust Company, Deborah Ashe and Dale W. Ashe suffered actual damages in the form of emotion distress.

VIOLATIONS OF THE FAIR DEBT COLLECTION PRACTICES ACT

Goliath Trust Company violated the FDCPA by:

a. The use of obscene or profane language or language the natural consequence of which is to abuse the hearer or reader in violation of 15 U.S.C. § 1692d(2);

b. The false representation of the character, amount, or legal status of any debt in violation of 15 U.S.C. § 1692e(2)(A);

c. The representation or implication that nonpayment of any debt will result in the arrest or imprisonment of any person in violation of 15 U.S.C. § 1692e(4);

d. The threat to take any action that cannot legally be taken or that is not intended to be taken in violation of 15 U.S.C. § 1692e(5);

e. The use of any false representation or deceptive means to collect or attempt to collect any debt in violation of 15 U.S.C. § 1692e(10); and

f. The collection of any amount that is not expressly authorized by the agreement creating the debt or prohibited by law in violation of 15 U.S.C. § 1692f(1).

Violations of the Fair Debt Collection Practices Act are analyzed from the viewpoint of the "least sophisticated consumer," *Clomon v. Jackson*, 988 F.2d 1314 (2d Cir. 1993), or "unsophisticated consumer," *Gammon v. GC Services Ltd. Partnership*, 27 F.3d 1254, 1257 (7th Cir. 1994).

> We reiterate that an unsophisticated consumer standard protects the consumer who is uninformed, naive, or trusting, yet it admits an objective element of reasonableness. The reasonableness element in turn shields complying debt collectors from liability for unrealistic or peculiar interpretations of collection letters.

In applying the unsophisticated consumer standard, the Seventh Circuit recently stated: "*Gammon* does not significantly change the *substance* of the 'least sophisticated consumer' standard as it had been routinely *applied* by courts." *Avila v. Van Ru Credit Corp.*, 84 F.3d 222, 227 (7th Cir. 1996). The Circuit observed that "the standard is low, close to the bottom of the sophistication meter." *Id.* at 226.

RELIEF REQUESTED

Deborah Ashe and Dale W. Ashe requests that judgment be entered in their favor against Defendant, Goliath Trust Company, Inc. as follows:

A. Declaratory judgment that Defendant's conduct violated the FDCPA. On remand from the Seventh Circuit, the district court found declaratory relief to a remedy available for violations of the Fair Debt Collection Practices Act. *See Mann v. Acclaim Fin. Servs., Inc.*, 232 F.R.D. 278 (S.D. Ohio 2003);*Woodard v. Online Information Servs.*, 191 F.R.D. 502 (E.D.N.C. 2000); *Gammon v. GC Services Ltd. Partnership* 162 F.R.D. 313 (N.D. Ill. 1995).[1]

B. Actual damages for emotional distress. Deborah and Dale W.

Ashe are entitled to actual damages for emotional distress suffered as a result of defendants' conduct. *McCollough v. Johnson, Rodenburg & Lauinger, L.L.C.*, 637 F.3d 939, 957 (9th Cir. 2011); *Wenrich v. Robert E. Cole, P.C.*, 2000 U.S. Dist. LEXIS 18687 (E.D. Pa. Dec. 22, 2000); *McGrady v. Nissan Motor Acceptance Corp.*, 40 F. Supp. 2d 1323 (M.D. Ala. 1998); *Carrigan v. Central Adjustment Bureau, Inc.*, 502 F. Supp. 468 (N.D. Ga. 1980); *Smith v. Law Offices of Mitchell N. Kay*, 124 B.R. 182, 185 (D. Del. 1991).

In *McCollough v. Johnson, Rodenburg & Lauinger, L.L.C.*, 637 F.3d 939, 957 (9th Cir. 2011), the Ninth Circuit noted:

> At the close of the evidence, the trial judge issued the following jury instructions with respect to damages available under the FDCPA:

> Actual damages include damages for personal humiliation, embarrassment, mental anguish and emotional distress. There is no fixed standard or measure in the case of intangible items such as humiliation, embarrassment, mental anguish or emotional distress. Mental and emotional suffering and distress pass under various names such as mental anguish, nervous shock and the like. It includes all highly unpleasant mental reactions such as fright or grief, shame, humiliation, embarrassment, anger, chagrin, disappointment, worry and nausea. The law does not set a definite standard by which to calculate compensation for mental and emotional suffering and distress. Neither is there any requirement that any witness express an opinion about the amount of compensation that is appropriate for the kind of law.

> The law does require, however, that when making an award for mental and emotional suffering and distress you should exercise calm and reasonable judgment. The compensation must be just and reasonable.

The Ninth Circuit sustained the jury's award of actual damages.

C. Statutory damages of up to $1,000.00 pursuant to 15 U.S.C. § 1692k. "In conclusion, the court holds that when violations of the FDCPA have been proved, 15 U.S.C.A. Section 1692k(a)(2)(A) provides for a single recovery of statutory damages per plaintiff per lawsuit." *Kobs v. Arrow Service Bureau, Inc.*, 134 F.3d 893 (7th Cir. 1998); *Armbruster v. Hecker*, 2010 WL 1643599 (M.D. Pa. Apr. 22, 2010); Robertson v. Horton Bros. Recovery, Inc., 2007 WL 2009703 (D. Del. 2007); Boyce v. Attorney's Dispatch Serv., 1999 U.S. Dist. LEXIS 1124 (S.D. Ohio Feb. 2, 1999); *Beattie v. D.M. Collections, Inc.*, 764 F. Supp. 925, 928 (D. Del. 1991); *Carn v. Med. Data Sys.*, 2007 Bankr. LEXIS 1334 (Bankr. M.D. Ala. Apr. 5, 2007); *In re Cambron*, 2007 WL

---

[1] The Third Circuit and many lower courts do not allow FDCPA declaratory judgment relief. *See* Weiss v. Regal Collections, 385 F.3d 337 (3d Cir. 2004); Vitullo v. Mancini, 684 F. Supp. 2d 760 (E.D. Va. 2010); Campbell v. Watson, 2009 WL 4544395 (E.D. Pa. Nov. 30, 2009); Jancik v. Cavalry Portfolio Servs., L.L.C.,

---

2007 WL 1994026 (D. Minn. July 3, 2007); Sparkman v. Zwicker & Assocs., P.C., 374 F. Supp. 2d 293 (E.D.N.Y. 2005). Jones v. CBE Group, Inc., 215 F.R.D. 558 (D. Minn. 2003); Bishop v. Global Payments Check Recovery Servs., Inc., 2003 WL 21497513 (D. Minn. June 25, 2003). *Cf.* Johnson v. Midland Credit Mgmt. Inc., 2006 WL 2473004 (N.D. Ohio Aug. 24, 2006) (finding declaratory relief unavailable to individual plaintiffs but reserving possibility that it is available on a classwide basis).

1076685 (Bankr. M.D. Ala. Apr. 5, 2007); *In re Littles*, 75 B.R. 241, 242 (Bankr. E.D. Pa. 1987).

The FDCPA, 15 USC § 1692k(a), provides that "any debt collector who fails to comply is liable to such person in an amount equal to . . . such additional damages as the court may allow, but not exceeding $1000." Since this applies to "any debt collector," where multiple debt collectors violate the FDCPA, *each* is liable for a maximum of $1000 statutory damages. *Carrizosa v. Stassinos*, 2010 WL 4393900 (N.D. Cal. Oct. 29, 2010); *Overcash v. United Abstract Group, Inc.*, 549 F. Supp. 2d 193 (N.D.N.Y. 2008); *Ganske v. Checkrite, Ltd.*, 1997 WL 33810208 (W.D. Wis. Jan. 6, 1997).

D. Costs, expenses of litigation, and reasonable attorney's fees pursuant to 15 U.S.C. § 1692k. The circuits have recognized the importance of awarding attorney's fees to successful plaintiff to achieve enforcement of the FDCPA.

> Given the structure of the section, attorney's fees should not be construed as a special or discretionary remedy; rather the Act mandates an award of attorney's fees as a means of fulfilling Congress's intent that the Act should be enforced by debtors as private attorneys general.

Graziano v. Harrison, 950 F.2d 107, 113 (3d Cir. 1991). "Because the FDCPA was violated, however, the statute requires the award of costs and a reasonable attorney's fee . . ." *Pipiles v. Credit Bureau of Lockport, Inc.*, 886 F.2d 22, 28 (2d Cir. 1989). The Seventh Circuit found that attorneys for successful consumers in FDCPA litigation are entitled to an award of attorney's fees at their market rate. *Tolentino v. Friedman*, 46 F.3d 645, 653 (7th Cir. 1995). "Paying counsel in FDCPA cases at rates lower than those they can obtain in the marketplace is inconsistent with the congressional desire to enforce the FDCPA through private actions, and therefore misapplies the law."

Respectfully submitted,
[Attorney for Plaintiff]

I.5 Motion in Limine

I.5.1 *Plaintiff's Character*[2]

I.5.1.1 Motion

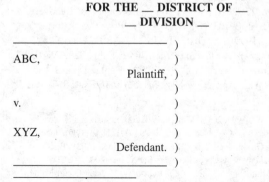

**IN THE UNITED STATES DISTRICT COURT
FOR THE __ DISTRICT OF __
__ DIVISION __**

```
                                    )
ABC,                                )
                     Plaintiff,     )
                                    )
v.                                  )
                                    )
XYZ,                                )
                     Defendant.     )
                                    )
```

2 The text of this motion and supporting memorandum were provided by attorney Joanne S. Faulkner of New Haven, Connecticut.

MOTION IN LIMINE

Because plaintiff's character is not in issue in this case and is not related to any claim or defense, plaintiff moves that defendant be precluded from denigrating plaintiff or plaintiff's status as a private attorney general enforcing public policy; and that defendant's examination of plaintiff and arguments be limited to the issues in this case.

Plaintiff's contemporaneous memorandum suggests typical inflammatory, prejudicial, or otherwise improper tactics which should be precluded.

[Attorney for Plaintiff]

I.5.1.2 Memorandum in Support of Motion in Limine[3]

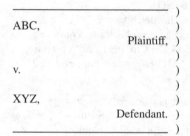

**IN THE UNITED STATES DISTRICT COURT
FOR THE __ DISTRICT OF __
__ DIVISION __**

```
                                    )
ABC,                                )
                     Plaintiff,     )
                                    )
v.                                  )
                                    )
XYZ,                                )
                     Defendant.     )
                                    )
```

**PLAINTIFF'S MEMORANDUM IN SUPPORT OF
MOTION IN LIMINE**

Intimations as to plaintiff's character, and inflammatory or prejudicial arguments are typical in FDCPA cases, even though the only issue is whether defendant violated the Act by its form letters. Direct or implied attacks on the plaintiff are improper. Fed. R. Evid. 401, 403, 404.

Deadbeat argument. "One of the most frequent fallacies concerning debt collection legislation is the contention that the primary beneficiaries are deadbeats." S. Rep. No. 382, 95th Cong., 1st Sess. 3 (1977), *reprinted in* 1977 U.S.C.C.A.N. 1695, 1697. Despite the congressional finding, this defense counsel typically begins his/her memoranda by claiming that, by bringing an FDCPA action, plaintiff seeks to immunize himself from the collection process and the natural, legitimate consequences of nonpayment of debt. Not only is this immaterial and speculative, but the argument is nonsensical. Bringing an FDCPA enforcement action does not immunize anyone from the underlying debt, which is a separate transaction.

"No section of the Act requires an inquiry into the worthiness of the debtor, or purports to protect only 'deserving' debtors. To the contrary, Congress has clearly indicated its belief that no

---

3 *See* Lee v. Robins Preston Beckett Taylor & Gugle Co., L.P.A., 1999 U.S. Dist. LEXIS 12969 (S.D. Ohio July 9, 1999) (motion in limine granted to exclude consumer's prior FDCPA litigation and financial distress.). *But see* Lee v. CBC Co., Inc., 1996 U.S. Dist. LEXIS 21993 (S.D. Ohio Sept. 26, 1996) (motion in limine denied to exclude evidence of consumer's communications with other collectors and of her financial distress.).

consumer deserves to be abused in the collection process." *Bass v. Stolper, Koritzinsky, Brewster & Neider, S.C.*, 111 F.3d 1322, 1330 (7th Cir. 1997). *See also* Federal Trade Comm'n v. Check Investors, Inc., 502 F.3d 159 (3d Cir. 2007).

Defendant should be precluded from making any "deadbeat" claims, which Congress itself recognized as a fallacy.

Plaintiff's motives. The Act relies on and encourages consumers, such as plaintiff, to act as private attorneys general to enforce the public policies expressed therein. 15 U.S.C. § 1692k(a). Indeed, Congress stated its unequivocal intent "that private enforcement actions would be the primary enforcement tool of the Act." *Baker v. G.C. Servs. Corp.*, 677 F.2d 775, 780–781 (9th Cir. 1982). Congress intended that the FDCPA be enforced by private attorneys general. *Wright v. Finance Service of Norwalk, Inc.*, 22 F.3d 647, 650 (6th Cir. 1994).

Defense counsel may attempt to inflame the jury by claiming that plaintiff is in this case for the money. By denigrating the motives of plaintiff, defendant contravenes Congress' express intent that plaintiff properly has such a motive.

Defendant's argument is, of course, meant to reduce the statutory damage recovery. Nothing in the FDCPA allows the jury to consider plaintiff's motives in awarding damages. 15 U.S.C. § 1692k. To determine the amount of statutory damages, the jury considers the nature of the violation, the frequency and persistence of the violation, the extent to which the violation was intentional, and the number of violations. § 1692k(b)(1); *Masuda v. Thomas Richards & Co.*, 759 F. Supp. 1456, 1467 (C.D. Cal. 1991).

Thus, plaintiff's motives are immaterial.

Other FDCPA claims. The only issue is whether this defendant violated the FDCPA, not whether other defendants might have violated the FDCPA. Plaintiff respectfully moves the Court to preclude defendant from alluding to, in any manner, the existence of FDCPA claims other than the one involved in this case. Such reference has no probative value and clearly would be for the sole purpose of unfair prejudice, confusing the issues or misleading the jury. Fed. R. Evid. 403, 404, 608, 802. *McKee v. Erikson*, 37 Conn. App. 146, 152–153, 654 A.2d 1263, 1267 (1995) (appeals to passion or prejudice have no place in the jury system); *DeFelice v. American Inter. Life Assur. Co.*, 112 F.3d 61, 67 (2d Cir. 1997) (evidence excluded when risk of confusing or distracting jury); *Soller v. Moore*, 84 F.3d 964 (7th Cir. 1996) (same); *Haynes v. Coughlin*, 79 F.3d 285, 291–293 (2d Cir. 1996) (evidence of other similar incident inadmissible and prejudicial); *Lanham v. Whitfield*, 805 F.2d 970 (11th Cir. 1986) (evidence of other litigation excluded; confuses the issues, misleading to the jury and causing prejudice to the party); *Bradley v. Soo Line RR. Co.*, 88 F.R.D. 307, 310 (E.D. Wis. 1980) (evidence that more than one claim filed by same plaintiff against same defendant is prejudicial).

Existence of debt. The Defendant is required to comply with the FDCPA whether or not any debt is owed. 15 U.S.C. § 1692a(3), (5),(6). The existence or validity of an underlying debt is not material in an FDCPA action. *McCartney v. First City Bank*, 970 F.2d 45 (5th Cir. 1992); *Baker v. G.C. Services Corp.*, 677 F.2d 775, 777 (9th Cir. 1982). Defendant should not be permitted to examine or refer to any other debt (the discredited "deadbeat" argument) or to whether the plaintiff owes the debt underlying this case. It is simply irrelevant as to whether defendant violated the FDCPA.

Attorney's motives. FDCPA defendants often claim that the plaintiff's attorney's fee recovery is the "engine running this suit." That claim is, again, contrary to the intent of Congress that the FDCPA be enforced by private attorneys rather than overburdened public servants. *Graziano v. Harrison*, 950 F.2d 107, 113–114 (3d Cir. 1991) (FDCPA "mandates an award of attorney's fees as a means of fulfilling Congress' intent that the Act should be enforced by debtors acting as private attorneys general"). *See also Tolentino v. Friedman,* 46 F.3d 645, 651–652 (7th Cir. 1995).

Moreover, the argument is spurious where, as here, it is completely within defendant's power to keep plaintiff's fees to a minimum. Defendants mount a stalwart defense with full awareness that they are exposing their clients to a higher award of fees by doing so. *McGowan v. King, Inc.*, 661 F.2d 48, 51 (5th Cir. 1981). *See also Lipsett v. Blanco*, 975 F.2d 934, 941 (1st Cir. 1992). They cannot be heard to complain when this comes to pass.

CONCLUSION

To avoid improperly prejudicial and inflammatory references, and to restrict the case to the issue at hand (whether defendant violated the FDCPA), plaintiff's motion in limine should be granted.

I.5.2 Attorney Fees[4]

IN THE UNITED STATES DISTRICT COURT FOR THE __ DISTRICT OF __ __ DIVISION __

———————————————)	
ABC,)	
Plaintiff,)	
)	
v.)	
)	
XYZ,)	
Defendant.)	
———————————————)	

MOTION IN LIMINE

Plaintiff ABC moves the Court for an Order that defendant, its witnesses, and attorneys shall not mention within the hearing of the jury the availability of an award of attorney's fees to Mr./Ms. ABC should he/she succeed in this litigation.

"The award of attorney fees is a matter for the judge not the jury." *Brooks v. Cook* , 938 F.2d 1048, 1051 (9th Cir. 1991). The Ninth Circuit went further to state:

> In a case where the Plaintiff is entitled to compensatory damages, informing the jury of the Plaintiff's potential right to receive attorneys' fees might lead the jury to offset the fees by reducing the damage award. Even more troubling, however, is the case where actual damages are small or non-existent. When damages are nominal, there is

---

4 *See* Lee v. Robins Preston Beckett Taylor & Gugle Co., L.P.A., 1999 U.S. Dist. LEXIS 12969 (S.D. Ohio July 9, 1999) (motion in limine granted to exclude evidence of consumer attorney's prior FDCPA litigation and of FDCPA attorney fees awards).

a risk that the jury may believe that the "harm" does not justify the payment of a large fee award. The jury may thus decide to find for Defendant rather than allow the Plaintiffs' attorney to recover fees.

Wherefore, a Motion in Limine should be granted directing defendants' witnesses and attorneys not to mention the availability of attorneys' fees to the successful plaintiff in the presence of the jury.

[Attorney for Plaintiff]

Sample Documents for Award of Attorney Fees

This appendix contains various sample documents related to the award of attorney fees in an FDCPA case—a motion for award of attorney fees, an accompanying affidavit, a proposed order, and a brief. All of these documents are also available on this volume's companion website, as well as five other attorney fee documents. For more detail, consumer law pleadings on this and other topics also can be found in National Consumer Law Center, *Consumer Law Pleadings* (Index Guide with Companion Website) and *Consumer Law on the Web*.

These documents are intended for demonstration and must be adapted to meet the facts, needs, and requirements of each case and local practice. Note that, in federal court, the motion for an award of attorney fees must be filed and served no later than 14 days after the entry of judgment. *See* Fed. R. Civ. P. 54(d)(2)(B). For more discussion of FDCPA attorney fee awards, see § 6.8, *supra*.

J.1 Sample Motion for Award of Attorney Fees

IN THE UNITED STATES DISTRICT COURT
FOR THE [*district name*] DISTRICT OF [*state*]

```
_____  )
                               )
[name of plaintiff(s)]         )
                Plaintiff(s)   )
                               )
v.                             )
                               )
[name of defendant(s)]         )
                Defendant(s).  )
_____  )
```

**PLAINTIFF'S MOTION FOR
AN AWARD OF COSTS AND ATTORNEY FEES**

Plaintiff [*name*] moves this Honorable Court for an Order that defendant [*name*] shall pay to plaintiff an award of costs and attorney fees for defendant's violations of the Fair Debt Collection Practices Act 15 U.S.C. §§ 1692 *et seq.* The following is stated in support thereof.

1. On [*date Complaint filed*], plaintiff [*name*] filed the complaint alleging defendant violated the Fair Debt Collection Practices Act, 15 U.S.C. §§ 1692 *et seq.* ("FDCPA") [*and other federal or state laws. Cite*].

2. Plaintiff herein was represented by [*first plaintiff attorney*] and [*second plaintiff attorney*].

3. Plaintiff's attorney [*first plaintiff attorney*] has expended a total of [*number*] hours on behalf of the plaintiff. An itemized account is contained in the Declaration of [*first plaintiff attorney*] in Support of Plaintiff's Motion for Award of Costs and Attorney Fees, attached hereto as *Exhibit A* to Declaration of [*first plaintiff attorney*].

4. The hourly rate for the services provided by [*first plaintiff attorney*] is $[*number*] per hour. Exhibit __ to Declaration of [*first plaintiff attorney*].

5. The total lodestar calculation for the services of [*first plaintiff attorney*] in this matter is $[*number*] ([*number*] hours x $[*number*]/hr = $[*number*]).

6. [*first plaintiff attorney*]'s law firm incurred costs and litigation expenses of $[*number*] in prosecution of this matter. Attached as *Exhibit B* to Declaration of [*first plaintiff attorney*].

7. Plaintiff's attorney [*second plaintiff attorney*] has expended a total of [*number*] hours on behalf of the plaintiff. An itemized account of the total is contained in Declaration of [*second plaintiff attorney*] in Support of Plaintiff's Motion for Award of Costs and Attorney Fees, attached hereto as *Exhibit A* to Declaration of [*second plaintiff attorney*].

8. The hourly rate for the services provided by [*second plaintiff attorney*] is $[*number*] per hour. Exhibit __ to Declaration of [*second plaintiff attorney*].

9. The total lodestar calculation for the services of [*second plaintiff attorney*] is $[*number*] ([*number*] hours x $[*number*]/hr. = $[*number*]).

10. [*second plaintiff attorney*]'s law firm incurred costs and litigation expenses of $[*number*] in the prosecution of this litigation. Attached to the Motion as *Exhibit B* to Declaration of [*second plaintiff attorney*].

11. Plaintiff's attorneys will submit a Supplemental Declaration after the completion of the briefing of this motion, detailing the additional time and costs expended on this matter.

12. This motion is further supported by the accompanying memorandum of law.

WHEREFORE, plaintiff [*name*] requests that this Honorable Court award reasonable attorney fees for the services of plaintiff's counsel in the amount of $[*number*] and costs of $[*number*], for a total of $[*number*]. Plaintiff further requests costs and attorney fees for the time expended litigating this motion.

[Attorney for Plaintiff]

J.2 Sample Declaration in Support of Motion for Attorney Fees

IN THE UNITED STATES DISTRICT COURT
FOR THE [*district name*] DISTRICT OF [*state*]

```
_____ )
[name of plaintiff(s)]    )
               Plaintiff(s) )
                          )
v.                        )
                          )
[name of defendant(s)]    )
               Defendant(s). )
_____ )
```

DECLARATION OF [*attorney name*]
IN SUPPORT OF PLAINTIFF'S MOTION FOR
AN AWARD OF COSTS AND ATTORNEY FEES

I, [*attorney name*], declare under penalty of perjury, as provided or by the laws of the United States, 28 U.S.C. § 1746, that the following statements are true:

1. I am a member in good standing of the bars of the following courts:

[*list jurisdictions to which admitted and dates of admission*]

2. I am a [*year*] graduate of the [*name of law school*].

[*list all employers and dates where worked as an attorney*].

3. I have authored or contributed to the following publications: [*list publications*]

4. I have lectured to professional groups on consumer law issues including:

[*list groups, subject matter and dates*]

5. I have been involved in consumer cases including:

[*list cases*]

6. I am one of the attorneys for plaintiff [*name*] in the above captioned action. I expended a total of [*number*] hours in this matter. My contemporaneously kept records reflecting our services in this litigation are attached hereto as *Exhibit A*.

7. The reasonable hourly rate for my services is $[*number*] per hour. [*citation of authority supporting hourly rate*]

8. The lodestar calculation of attorney fees for my time expended is ([*number*] hours x $[*number*]/hour) $[*number*].

9. Costs and litigation expenses in the amount of $[*number*] (attached hereto as *Exhibit B*) were incurred by my law firm in this matter.

10. These requested attorney fees and costs were reasonable and necessary to litigation in this matter.

Executed at [*city, state*].
[*date*]

[Attorney for Plaintiff]

J.3 Sample Order for the Award of Attorney Fees

UNITED STATES DISTRICT COURT
FOR THE [*district name*] DISTRICT OF [*state name*]

```
_____ )
[name of plaintiff]       )
               Plaintiff, )
                          )
v.                        )  Civil Action No. [number]
                          )
[name of defendant]       )
               Defendants. )
_____ )
```

ORDER

Upon consideration of Plaintiff's Motion for an Award of Attorney Fees and the parties' briefs thereon,

IT IS HEREBY ORDERED that attorney fees in the amount of $[*amount*] be awarded to Plaintiff's legal counsel.

Dated: [*date*]
[*signature*]
[*name*]
U.S. District Court Judge

J.4 Sample Memorandum in Support of Award of Attorney Fees

IN THE UNITED STATES DISTRICT COURT
FOR THE [*district name*] DISTRICT OF [*state*]

```
_____ )
[name of plaintiff(s)]    )
               Plaintiff(s) )
                          )
v.                        )
                          )
[name of defendant(s)]    )
               Defendant(s). )
_____ )
```

MEMORANDUM IN SUPPORT OF PLAINTIFF'S
MOTION FOR AN AWARD OF COSTS
AND ATTORNEY FEES

I. PROCEDURAL HISTORY

On [*date Complaint filed*], plaintiff [*name*] filed a complaint alleging that defendant [*defendant name*] violated the Fair Debt Collection Practices Act, 15 U.S.C. §§ 1692 *et seq.* ("FDCPA") [*and other federal or state laws. Cite*]. Defendant filed its Answer thereto. [*other pertinent filings*]

II. STATEMENT OF FACTS

In this litigation, plaintiff [*name*] was represented by [*first plaintiff attorney*]. Mr./Ms. [*first plaintiff attorney*] expended [*num-*

ber] hours in representation of plaintiff. (See Paragraph #[*number*], Declaration of [*first plaintiff attorney*] in Support of Plaintiff's Motion for an Award of Costs and Attorney Fees.) The reasonable hourly rate for an attorney of Mr./Ms. [*first plaintiff attorney*]'s experience is $[*number*]. Paragraph #[*number*]. An amount totaling $[*number*] is sought as attorney fees for Mr./Ms. [*first plaintiff attorney*]'s representation of the plaintiff. Paragraph #[*number*]. Mr./Ms. [*first plaintiff attorney*]' firm expended [*number*] in costs and litigation expenses in the prosecution of this action. Paragraph #[*number*]. Exhibit __ of Declaration of [*first plaintiff attorney*].

Plaintiff [*name*] was also represented by [*second plaintiff attorney*] of [*firm name, address*]. Mr./Ms. [*second plaintiff attorney*] expended [*number*] hours in representation of the plaintiff. (See Paragraph #[*number*], Declaration of [*second plaintiff attorney*] in Support of Plaintiff's Motion for an Award of Costs and Attorney Fees.) The reasonable hourly rate for Mr./Ms. [*second plaintiff attorney*] is $[*number*] per hour. Paragraph #[*number*], Declaration of [*second plaintiff attorney*] in Support of Plaintiff's Motion for an Award of Costs and Attorney Fees. An amount totaling $[*number*] is sought as attorney fees for Mr./Ms. [*second plaintiff attorney*]'s representation of the plaintiff. Paragraph #[*number*]. His firm expended $[*number*] in costs and litigation expenses in the prosecution of this action. Paragraph #[*number*].

III. STATEMENT OF QUESTION PRESENTED

Is plaintiff [*name*] entitled to an award of reasonable attorney fees and costs?

Plaintiff respectfully submits that this question should be answered in the affirmative.

IV. ARGUMENT

A. PLAINTIFF [*name*]
WAS SUCCESSFUL IN THIS ACTION

The Fair Debt Collection Practices Act requires the payment of costs and reasonable attorney fees to a successful consumer.

> . . . any debt collector who fails to comply with any provision of this subchapter . . . is liable to such person in an amount equal to the sum of— [actual damages] [statutory damages] and (3) in the case of any successful action to enforce the foregoing liability, the costs of the action, together with a reasonable attorney fee as determined by the court.

15 U.S.C. §1692k(a)(3).

The language of the FDCPA makes an award of attorney fees mandatory. *Mace v. Van Ru Credit Corp.*, 109 F.3d 338, 345 n.3 (7th Cir. 1997), citing *Tolentino v. Friedman*, 46 F.3d 645, 651 (7th Cir. 1995). In litigation pursuant to the Fair Debt Collection Practices Act, the Second Circuit stated "the award of attorney fees to plaintiffs for a debt collector's violation of 'any provision' of the FDCPA is mandatory" *Pipiles v. Credit Bureau of Lockport, Inc.*, 886 F.2d 22, 28 (2d Cir. 1989), citing *Emanuel v. American Credit Exchange*, 870 F.2d 805, 809 (2d Cir. 1989). "The FDCPA's statutory language makes an award of fees mandatory." *Camacho v. Bridgeport Financial, Inc.*, 523 F.3d 973, 978 (9th Cir. 2008) (Camacho II) (citation omitted). *See also Jacobson v. Healthcare*

Fin. Serv., Inc., 516 F.3d 85 (2d Cir. 2008); *Zagorski v. Midwest Billing Servs., Inc.*, 128 F.3d 1164 (7th Cir. 1997); *Tolentino v. Friedman*, 46 F.3d 645 (7th Cir. 1995); *Graziano v. Harrison*, 950 F.2d 107 (3d Cir. 1991).

"Given the structure of the section, attorney's fees should not be construed as a special or discretionary remedy; rather, the Act mandates an award of attorney fees as a means of fulfilling Congress's intent that the Act should be enforced by debtors acting as private attorneys general." *Graziano v. Harrison*, 950 F.2d 107, 113 (3d Cir. 1991). See also *DeJesus v. Banco Popular de Puerto Rico*, 918 F.2d 232, 235 (1st Cir. 1990)(Truth in Lending Act). Plaintiff [*name*] was the prevailing party in this litigation. Statutory damages of $1,000 will be awarded to plaintiff. This is the maximum statutory damages recovery plaintiff can receive. 15 U.S.C. § 1692k(a)(2).

ATTORNEY FEES AVAILABLE BY STATUTE. See also: *Carroll v. Wolpoff & Abramson*, 53 F.3d 626 (4th Cir. 1995); *Lee v. Thomas & Thomas*, 109 F.3d 302 (6th Cir. 1997); *Zagorski v. Midwest Billing Servs.*, 128 F.3d 1164 (7th Cir. 1997); *Hennessy v. Daniels Law Office*, 270 F.3d 551 (8th Cir. 2001); *Hollis v. Roberts*, 984 F.2d 1159 (11th Cir. 1993); *Oslan v. Law Offices of Mitchell N. Kay*, 232 F. Supp. 2d 436 (E.D. Pa. 2002); *Cope v. Duggins*, 203 F. Supp. 2d 650 (E.D. La. 2002); *Irwin v. Mascott*, 112 F. Supp. 2d 937 (N.D. Cal. 2000).

B. PLAINTIFF'S ATTORNEYS ARE TO BE AWARDED FEES PURSUANT TO THE LODESTAR FORMULA

The U.S. Supreme Court has explained the calculation for an award of attorney fees:

> The most useful starting point for determining the amount of a reasonable fee is the number of hours reasonably expended on the litigation multiplied by a reasonable hourly rate. The calculation provides an objective basis on which to make an initial estimate of the value of a lawyer's services.

Hensley v. Eckerhart, 461 U.S. 424, 433; 103 S. Ct. 1933, 1939; 76 L. Ed. 2d 40 (1983). *See Perdue v. Kenny A. ex rel. Winn*, __ U.S. __, 130 S. Ct. 1662, 176 L. Ed. 2d 494 (2010). Although this decision, and others cited hereinafter, arise in the context of the Civil Rights Attorney's Fees Award Act, 42 U.S.C. § 1988, these criteria are equally applicable here. "The standards set forth in this opinion are generally applicable in all cases in which Congress has authorized an award of fees to a 'prevailing party.' " *Hensley v. Eckerhart, supra*, 103 S. Ct. at 1939, n.7. "We have stated in the past that fee-shifting statutes' similar language is a strong indication that they are to be interrupted alike." *Independent Federation of Flight Attendants v. Zipes*, 491 U.S. 754; 109 S. Ct. 2732, 2735 n.2.; 105 L. Ed. 2d 639 (1989) (quoting *Northcross v. Memphis Bd. of Education*, 412 U.S. 427, 428; 93 S. Ct. 2201, 2202; 37 L. Ed. 2d 48 (1973)). The multiplication of the reasonable number of hours expended times the reasonable hourly rate is referred to as the "lodestar." *Tamko Roofing Prods., Inc. v. Ideal Roofing Co., Ltd.*, 282 F.3d 23, 34 (1st Cir. 2002); *I.B. v. N.Y. City Dep't of Educ.*, 336 F.3d 79, 80 (2d Cir. 2003); *Planned Parenthood v. AG*,

297 F.3d 253, 265 (3d Cir. 2002); *Dennis v. Columbia Colleton Med. Ctr.*, 290 F.3d 639, 652 (4th Cir. 2002); *Singer v. City of Waco*, 324 F.3d 813, 829 (5th Cir. 2003); *Paschal v. Flagstar Bank, FSB*, 297 F.3d 431, 434 (6th Cir. 2002); *Divane v. Krull Elec. Co.*, 319 F.3d 307, 317–18 (7th Cir. 2003); *Wheeler v. Missouri Highway & Transp. Comm'n*, 348 F.3d 744, 754 (8th Cir. 2003); *Friend v. Kolodzieczak*, 72 F.3d 1386, 1389 (9th Cir. 1995); *Mallinson-Montague v. Pocrnick*, 224 F.3d 1224, 1234 n12 (10th Cir. 2000); *Loggerhead Turtle v. County Council*, 307 F.3d 1318, 1321 n3 (11th Cir. 2002); *Nat'l Mining Ass'n v. DOL*, 292 F.3d 849, 875 (D.C. Cir. 2002).

In *Johnson v. Georgia Highway Express, Inc.*, 488 F.2d 714, 717–19 (5th Cir.1974), the Fifth Circuit set out twelve factors relevant to the determination of a reasonable attorney fee: (1) the time and labor required; (2) the novelty and difficulty of the questions; (3) the skill required to perform the service properly; (4) the preclusion of other employment by the attorney due to acceptance of the case; (5) the customary fee; (6) whether the fee is fixed or contingent; (7) time limitations imposed by the client or the circumstances; (8) the amount involved and the results obtained; (9) the experience, reputation, and ability of the attorney; (10) the undesirability of the case; (11) the nature and length of the professional relationship with the client; and (12) awards in similar cases. These are often referred to as the *Johnson* factors. However, it is not necessary for the district court to address each of these factors. *Perdue v. Kenny A. ex rel. Winn*, __ U.S. __, 130 S. Ct. 1662, 176 L. Ed. 2d 494 (2010); *Anchondo v. Anderson, Crenshaw & Associates, L.L.C.*, 616 F.3d 1098, 1103–04 (10th Cir. 2010).

Plaintiff's attorney [*first plaintiff attorney*] expended [*number*] hours during the course of this litigation. This amount of time is reasonable. The reasonable hourly rate for an attorney with Mr./Ms. [*first plaintiff attorney*]'s experience in this type of litigation is $[*number*] per hour. Paragraph #[*number*], Declaration of [*first plaintiff attorney*] in Support of Plaintiff's Motion for an Award of Costs and Attorney Fees. This is the prevailing market rate in this type of representation. *Blum v. Stenson*, 465 U.S. 886, 104 S. Ct. 1541, 79 L. Ed. 2d 891 (1984). The lodestar calculation for the efforts of [*first plaintiff attorney*] in this litigation is $[*number*]. Mr./Ms. [*first plaintiff attorney*]'s firm also incurred $[*number*] as costs and expenses of this litigation.

[*Second plaintiff attorney*]'s time in this litigation totaled [*number*] hours. This amount of time is reasonable. The standard hourly rate of $[*number*] charged by Mr./Ms. [*second plaintiff attorney*] is appropriate for an attorney of Mr./Ms. [*second plaintiff attorney*]'s experience in this type of litigation. The lodestar calculation for the efforts of [*second plaintiff attorney*] in this litigation is [*number*]. Mr./Ms. [*second plaintiff attorney*]'s firm also incurred [*number*] as costs and expenses of this litigation.

Retention of two attorneys to represent a party is the norm for federal court litigation. *Randle v. H&P Capital, Inc.*, 2010 WL 2944907, 14–18, 2010 U.S. Dist. LEXIS 74994 (E.D. Va. July 21, 2010). "Counsel may certainly solicit the assistance of other lawyers in working on a case, however, and the time spent by all lawyers on a litigation can be billed so long as the hours claimed are not duplicative." *Davis v. City and County of San Francisco*, 976 F.2d 1536, 1544 (9th Cir.1992). *See also Bouman v. Block*, 940 F.2d 1211, 1236–37 (9th Cir. 1991); *Haak v. Hults Ford-Mercury, Inc.*, 79 F. Supp. 2d 1020, 1023 (W.D. Wis. 1999); *Lenihan v. City of New York*, 640 F. Supp. 822, 825 (S.D.N.Y. 1986); *Pierce v. F.R. Tripler & Co.*, 770 F. Supp. 118, 122 (S.D.N.Y. 1991). Indeed, it

has been held to be an abuse of discretion to limit fees to only one attorney. *A.J. By L.B. v. Kierst*, 56 F.3d 849, 863–64 (8th Cir. 1995); *Ramos v. Lamm*, 713 F.2d 546, 554 (10th Cir. 1983).

Thus, the total lodestar calculation for the award of attorney fees to the plaintiff in this matter totals [*number*] and costs of [*number*].

C. THE LODESTAR MAY NOT BE REDUCED DUE TO THE AMOUNT OF THE JUDGMENT

Plaintiff seeks an award of attorney fees based upon the lodestar formula. The defendants may, however, suggest that a lesser amount is appropriate.

1. Previously Established Rates Are Appropriate ForPlaintiffs' Counsel

The U.S. Supreme Court has stated: "The statute and legislative history establish that 'reasonable fees' under section 1988 are to be calculated according to the prevailing market rates in the relevant community, regardless of whether plaintiff is represented by private or non-profit counsel." *Blum v. Stenson*, *supra*, 465 U.S. at 895, 104 S. Ct. at 1547 (footnote omitted). *See also Perdue v. Kenny A. ex rel. Winn*, __ U.S. __, 130 S. Ct. 1662, 176 L. Ed. 2d 494 (2010).

> In order to encourage able counsel to undertake FDCPA cases, as Congress intended, it is necessary that counsel be awarded fees commensurate with those which they could obtain by taking other types of cases. . . . Paying counsel in FDCPA cases at rates lower than those they can obtain in the marketplace is inconsistent with the congressional desire to enforce the FDCPA through private actions, and therefore misapplies the law.

Tolentino v. Friedman, 46 F.3d 645, 652–653 (7th Cir. 1995).

Generally, the relevant community is the forum in which the court sits. *Camacho II*, *supra*, 523 F.3d at 979 (9th Cir. 2008) (citation omitted). The reasonable hourly rate is that prevailing in the community for similar work performed by lawyers of comparable skill, experience, and reputation. *Id.*

The Seventh Circuit reversed a district court's denial of attorney fees even though the plaintiffs only recovered $100 ($50 each) as FDCPA statutory damages and remanded for determination of an award of attorney fees. *Zagorski v. Midwest Billing Services, Inc.*, 128 F.3d 1164 (7th Cir. 1997). Of course, the amount of reasonable attorneys fees awarded pursuant to the FDCPA is left to the sound discretion of the judge. *Schimmel v. Slaughter*, 975 F. Supp. 1481, 1484 (M.D. Ga. 1997).

2. The Award of Attorney Fees Is Not Limited by the Amount of Damages

As long as the plaintiff is successful, i.e., recovers more than nominal damages, the plaintiff should be awarded attorneys fees pursuant to a lodestar calculation.

"In the absence of any indication that Congress intended to adopt a strict rule that attorney fees under section 1988 be proportionate to damages recovered, we decline to adopt such a rule ourselves." *City of Riverside v. Rivera*, 477 U.S. 561, 581; 106 S. Ct. 2686, 2697; 91 L. Ed. 2d 466 (1986) (footnote omitted). *See also Quaration v. Tiffany & Co.*, 166 F.3d 422 (2d Cir. 1999); *Zagorski v. Midwest Billing Services, Inc., supra.* The benefits to the public as a whole resulting from lawsuits which encourage compliance with statutory provisions are more important than relatively small damage awards. Indeed, when a provision for counsel fees is included in a regulatory act, it is a recognition that enforcement of the statute would be unlikely if an individual had to pay his or her own attorney fees. The Court quoted Senator Tunney's remarks in the Congressional Record:

> If the citizen does not have the resources, his day in court is denied him; the congressional policy which he seeks to assert and vindicate goes unvindicated; and the entire nation, not just the individual citizen, suffers.

City of Riverside v. Rivera, supra at 477 U.S. at 575, 106 S. Ct. at 2694 (citation omitted).

The Third Circuit amplified this thought stating:

> Congress provided fee shifting to enhance enforcement of important civil rights, consumer-protection, and environmental policies. By providing competitive rates we assure that attorneys will take such cases, and hence increase the likelihood that the congressional policy of redressing public interest claims will be vindicated.

Student Public Interest Research Group v. AT&T Bell Laboratories, 842 F.2d 1436, 1449 (3d Cir. 1988). "Congress has relied on such plaintiffs to act as private attorneys general." *Id.*, at 1450 n.13. Also see *Graziano v. Harrison*, 950 F.2d 107, 113 (3d Cir. 1991).

The amount of damages awarded often has borne no relation to the amount of attorney fees granted. "[A]ttorney's fees awarded by district courts have 'frequently outrun the economic benefits ultimately obtained by successful litigants.' " *Evans v. Jeff D.*, 475 U.S. 717, 735; 106 S. Ct. 1531, 1541; 89 L. Ed. 2d 747 (1986) (citation omitted). Upon finding a statutory violation and damages, the attorney fees award should be made in the lodestar amount. *Johnson v. Eaton*, 80 F.3d 148 (5th Cir. 1996).

For example, in *Gradisher v. Check Enforcement Unit*, 2003 WL 187416 (W.D. Mich., Jan. 22, 2003), the district court awarded plaintiff $1,000 statutory damages plus attorneys' fees of $69,872.00 and expenses of $7,808.44. In *Armstrong v. The Rose Law Firm, P.A.*, 2002 WL 31050583 (D. Minn., Sept. 5, 2002), the district court approved the award of $43,180 in attorney fees where the plaintiff recovered $1,000 in statutory damages. The Southern District of Florida affirmed the bankruptcy court's award of attorney fees of $29,037.50 where the plaintiff recovered FDCPA statutory damages of only $1,000. *In re Martinez*, 266 B.R. 523, 544 (Bankr. S.D. Fla. 2001), *aff'd* 271 B.R. 696 (S.D. Fla. 2001). In *Perez v. Perkiss*, 742 F. Supp. 883 (D. Del. 1990), the district court awarded $10,110 in attorney fees plaintiff's recovery was only $1,200. The Seventh Circuit reversed a district court's denial of attorneys' fees even though the plaintiffs only recovered $100 ($50 each) as FDCPA statutory damages and remanded for determination of an award of attorneys' fees. *Zagorski v. Midwest Billing Services, Inc., supra.*

"Unlike most private tort litigants, a plaintiff who brings an FDCPA action seeks to vindicate important rights that cannot be valued solely in monetary terms and congress has determined that the public as a whole has an interest in the vindication of the statutory rights." *Tolentino v. Friedman, supra*, at 652, *citing City of Riverside v. Rivera*, 477 U.S. 561, 106 S. Ct. 2686, 91 L. Ed. 2d 466 (1986).

"When a plaintiff has obtained excellent results, his attorney should recover a full compensatory fee." *Hensley v. Eckerhart, supra*, at 435. Here, [plaintiff's name] will receive compensation for both her actual and statutory damages pursuant to the FDCPA, 15 U.S.C. § 1692k(a).

As the Eastern District of Wisconsin has stated, "[W]hen it comes time for the court to award the fees, it must not penalize [Plaintiff]'s attorneys for responding to [Defendant]'s defense. * * * Law is labor intensive; lawyers are paid for the diligence and the intelligence, commodities that cannot be mass produced on an assembly line." *Diettrich v. Northwest Airlines*, 967 F. Supp. 1132, 1997 U.S. Dist. LEXIS 9071, at *6–7 (E.D. Wis. 1997), *rev'd on other grounds*, 168 F.3d 961 (7th Cir. 1999).

D. PLAINTIFF'S ATTORNEYS ARE ENTITLED TO AN AWARD OF COSTS AND LITIGATION EXPENSES

Plaintiff has requested the award of costs and litigation expenses in addition to an award of attorney fees. The District of Nevada stated that "plaintiffs are also entitled to an award of costs representing out-of-pocket litigation expenses . . . includ[ing] costs incurred in travel (airfare, car rental, hotels and food, gasoline and the like), telephone, postage and photocopying." *Ilick v. Miller*, 68 F. Supp. 2d 1169, 1181 (D. Nev. 1999).

The FDCPA grants the successful plaintiff "the costs of the action." 15 U.S.C. §1692k(a)(3). Long distance telephone and faxing expenses, as well as copying and postage have been awarded as costs. *Sousa v. Miguel* 32 F.3d 1370, 1374 (9th Cir. 1994). Recoverable costs include travel, photocopies, lodging, postage, telephone calls, and computerized research. *Libertad v. Sanchez*, 134 F.Supp.2d 218, 236 (D.P.R. 2001). Costs may be recovered as provided for by statute as well as 28 U.S.C. § 1920. *See Lathem v. Department of Children & Youth Servs.*, 172 F.3d 786, 794 (11th Cir. 1999). Computer research costs are recoverable. *United Nuclear Corp. v. Cannon*, 564 F. Supp. 581, 591–92 (D.R.I. 1983) ("LEXIS is an essential tool of a modern, efficient law office. As such, it saves lawyers' time by increasing the efficacy of legal research. Denial of reimbursement for LEXIS charges in a proper case would be an open invitation to law firms to use high-priced attorney time to perform routine research tasks that can be accomplished quicker and more economically with LEXIS.")

Thus, the plaintiff's litigation expenses and costs are compensable.

E. PLAINTIFF WILL SEEK A SUPPLEMENTAL AWARD OF COSTS, LITIGATION EXPENSES AND ATTORNEY FEES FOR TIME EXPENDED UPON THIS MOTION

The Declarations submitted by plaintiff's attorneys detail the costs and time expended in this litigation prior to the preparation of this brief. The additional cost and time expended preparing this Motion for an Award of Costs and Attorney Fees and briefing will be submitted when work of plaintiff's counsel is completed. An award of fees is appropriate for the time expended in pursuing a Motion For Award Of Attorney Fees. *Camacho v. Bridgeport*

Financial, Inc., 523 F.3d 973, 981–82 (9th Cir. 2008); *Lund v. Affleck*, 587 F.2d 75 (1st Cir. 1978); *Gagne v. Maher*, 594 F.2d 336 (2d Cir. 1979); *David v. City of Scranton*, 633 F.2d 676 (3d Cir. 1980); *Tyler Business Servs., Inc. v. N.L.R.B.*, 695 F.2d 73 (4th Cir. 1982); *Johnson v. State of Miss.*, 606 F.2d 635, 638 (5th Cir. 1979); *Weisenberger v. Huecker*, 593 F.2d 49 (6th Cir. 1979); *In re Burlington N., Employment Practices Litig.*, 832 F.2d 430 (7th Cir. 1987); *Jordan v. Multnomah County*, 815 F.2d 1258, 1264 (9th Cir. 1987). After completion of briefing, plaintiff's counsel will submit Supplemental Declarations for an Award of Attorney Fees.

V. CONCLUSION

Based upon the lodestar calculation, attorney fees should be awarded to plaintiffs' counsel in the amount of [*number*]. An award of [*number*] as costs and litigation expenses should also be awarded. A supplemental Declaration for an award of attorney fees will be submitted after the completion of briefing.

[Attorney for Plaintiff]

Fair Debt Collection Practices Act Case Summaries

This Appendix contains summaries by topic of many thousands of significant FDCPA court opinions that are available on the Westlaw and Lexis databases. An electronic version of each of this treatise's appendices, including this one, is available to current subscribers on the companion website to this treatise. The electronic version facilitates key word and state searches through this extensive collection of cases. For more information about the companion website to this treatise, see page ix, *supra*.

Listing of Topic Categories

K.1 Coverage

K.1.1 "Debt," 15 U.S.C. § 1692a(5)

K.1.1.1 General Principles

Heintz v. Jenkins, 514 U.S. 291, 115 S. Ct. 1489, 131 L. Ed. 2d 395 (1995). "[I]t limits 'debt' to consumer debt."

Brown v. Card Serv. Ctr., 464 F.3d 450 (3d Cir. 2006). The FDCPA is a remedial statute to be broadly construed so as to affect its purpose.

Shula v. Lawent, 359 F.3d 489 (7th Cir. 2004). Court costs relate to the underlying consumer transaction and satisfy the definition of "debt" pursuant to § 1692a(5).

Miller v. McCalla, Raymer, Padrick, Cobb, Nichols & Clark, L.L.C., 214 F.3d 872 (7th Cir.), *rehearing en banc denied*, 2000 U.S. App. LEXIS 18232 (7th Cir. July 26, 2000). The debt for a house purchased as the buyer's residence and then rented when the buyer moved away was consumer debt originally; the subsequent use of the collateral would not alter the applicability of the FDCPA.

Morgovsky v. Creditors' Collection Serv., 19 F.3d 28 (9th Cir. 1994) (table, text at 1994 WL 47153). Collector's report of consumer's debt to a credit reporting agency, without stipulating that the debt was business-related, may violate the FDCPA. The plain language of the FDCPA encompasses both proven and alleged consumer debts. Remanded for determination of whether reporting of business debt to credit reporting agency is "established custom and practice."

McCartney v. First City Bank, 970 F.2d 45 (5th Cir. 1992). FDCPA action was not contingent on the validity of the underlying debt.

Arizona

Caron v. Charles E. Maxwell, P.C., 48 F. Supp. 2d 932 (D. Ariz. 1999). The fact that plaintiff received her house as a gift was not relevant to FDCPA coverage. A collector must comply with the FDCPA whether the house is inherited, donated or purchased.

California

Narog v. Certegy Check Servs., Inc., 2011 WL 70595 (N.D. Cal. Jan. 10, 2011). The court dismissed the *pro se* consumer's complaint that the defendant provided incorrect information to a credit bureau on a paid debt. The complaint failed to state a claim because a "plaintiff cannot allege a claim for violation of the FDCPA based on conduct that occurred after he paid his debt in full, and after the debt collector acknowledged that the debt was paid in full."

Fausto v. Credigy Serv. Corp., 598 F. Supp. 2d 1049 (N.D. Cal. 2009). Debt collector argued there was no debt covered by the FDCPA because the consumer claimed the debt had been paid off. Because an FDCPA "debt" includes an "alleged debt" and the collector had tried to get the consumer to pay the debt, the debt collector's motion for summary judgment was denied.

Georgia

Anderson v. Frederick J. Hanna & Assocs., 361 F. Supp. 2d 1379 (N.D. Ga. 2005). The court held that the debt collector's argument that a lawsuit to collect a debt was not "collection activity" to be patently frivolous.

Illinois

Smith v. Continental Cmty. Bank & Trust Co., 2002 U.S. Dist. LEXIS 11193 (N.D. Ill. June 21, 2002). Consumer failed to state a claim where she failed to allege a consumer transaction was involved.

Clark v. Retrieval Masters Creditors Bureau, Inc., 185 F.R.D. 247 (N.D. Ill. 1999). Whether the consumer had incurred the alleged debt was a separate issue from his FDCPA claim.

Perovich v. Humphrey, 1997 WL 674975 (N.D. Ill. Oct. 28, 1997). The consumers became obligated to pay money to Household based on their purchase of a bed which was used primarily for family and household purposes. The collector argued that this was not a "debt" because it only sought to enforce a security interest against the bed, not to collect money. But this argument only described the characteristic of the defendants' collection activities, not the underlying obligation upon which defendants' acts were based. Further, the consumers alleged that the collector actually sought money because it had no authority to repossess the bed and would only be paid for its services if it collected money. Accepting the truth of the consumers' allegations and making reasonable inferences in their favor, the court found that the complaint described a "debt" sufficient to state a claim under the FDCPA.

Iowa

Fischer v. Unipac Serv. Corp., 519 N.W.2d 793 (Iowa 1994). FDCPA did not apply to loan which was not in default when assigned.

Michigan

Diaz v. G. Reynold Sims & Assocs., P.C., 2011 WL 17620 (E.D. Mich. Jan. 4, 2011). Even where a debt has been legally settled and the judgment dismissed, a subsequent garnishment of a tax refund was an attempt to collect an "alleged" obligation is within the FDCPA.

Burks v. Washington Mut. Bank, 2008 WL 4966656 (E.D. Mich. Nov. 17, 2008). Where the consumer's home had been sold at a sheriff's sale which fully paid off the mortgage, a "debt" no longer existed, and summary judgment was awarded to the debt collector on the FDCPA claims.

Kattula v. Jade, 2008 WL 495298 (E.D. Mich. Feb. 20, 2008). Dismissed complaint, as the debt was a commercial loan to purchase a truck stop.

Minnesota

Wiegand v. JNR Adjustment Co., 2002 U.S. Dist. LEXIS 7292 (D. Minn. Apr. 22, 2002). Attempting to collect the amounts of stolen, forged checks from the checking account owner who reversed payment on them was attempting to collect a "debt" within the FDCPA, notwithstanding the underlying theft and the purported absence of a consensual transaction between the merchant and the putative debtor.

New York

Malone v. City of N.Y., 2006 WL 2524197 (E.D.N.Y. Aug. 30, 2006). *Pro se* plaintiff's complaint alleging various claims of harassment and other misconduct by his supervisors in the course of his employment as a state corrections officer failed to state a claim for harassment and abuse under the FDCPA since the FDCPA only applies to debt collection activities.

Ohio

Adams v. First Fed. Credit Control, Inc., 1992 WL 131121 (N.D. Ohio May 21, 1992). Whether the debt being collected was actually owed was irrelevant to determination of violation of FDCPA.

Oregon

Clark v. Schwabe, Williamson & Wyatt, Clearinghouse No. 44,831 (D. Or. 1990). The FDCPA applies to collection of this debt even though the consumer had filed bankruptcy; whether the consumer actually owes the alleged obligation is irrelevant to FDCPA coverage.

Pennsylvania

Fetters v. Paragon Way, Inc., 2010 WL 5174989 (M.D. Pa. Dec. 15, 2010). A debt, as an "obligation or alleged obligation" of a consumer, includes the situation in which a debt collector mistakenly continues to try to collect a debt that has already been paid. The court distinguished cases that the defendants argued precluded any FDCPA claim once the alleged debt had been paid and therefore no longer existed: "Unlike Posso and Winter, Plaintiff avers that Defendants took coercive action, albeit erroneously, to collect an alleged obligation for payment. In this way, although the debt was already settled, Defendants allegedly represented that the debt was outstanding and engaged in prohibited conduct aimed at collecting on it."

Albanese v. Portnoff Law Assocs., Ltd., 301 F. Supp. 2d 389 (E.D. Pa. 2004). Conflicting inferences can be drawn on the issue of whether a trash collection fee contemplates a transaction that is a covered debt or arises from the fact of ownership. On the one hand, a specific service is rendered. On the other hand, the obligation seems to arise from the fact of ownership and does not depend on the amount of usage or, indeed, the fact of usage. If covered violated §§ 1692e(11) and g.

Piper v. Portnoff Law Assocs., 274 F. Supp. 2d 681 (E.D. Pa. 2003), *aff'd*, 396 F.3d 227 (3d Cir. 2005). A debt collector's decision to proceed *in rem* rather than *in personam* was insignificant when determining whether the underlying obligation fell within the FDCPA's statutory definition of a covered debt.

K.1.1.2 Rent, Condo Fees, and Co-op Fees

K.1.1.2.1 Covered

Romea v. Heiberger & Assocs., 163 F.3d 111 (2d Cir. 1998). Past-due rent is a "debt" as defined, and state mandated three-day demand for payment and eviction notice is a "communication" sent "in connection with the collection of any debt" subject to the FDCPA.

Ladick v. Van Gemert, 146 F.3d 1205 (10th Cir. 1998). Assessment owed to a condominium association was a "debt" as defined. Prior circuit authority establishes that credit was not a component of the definition. The assessment, for maintaining and repairing the common areas, was for a consumer purpose and arose from a transaction, to wit, the consumer's purchase of the condominium with its obligation to abide by the condominium association's rules and levies.

Newman v. Boehm, Pearlstein & Bright, Ltd., 119 F.3d 477 (7th Cir. 1997). Condominium assessments for common expenses for family homes were debts covered by the FDCPA even though the assessment may have been payable in advance of the expenses incurred. There is no credit requirement for debts to be covered by § 1692a(5).

California

Thies v. Law Offices of William A. Wyman, 969 F. Supp. 604 (S.D. Cal. 1997). Homeowner association fees for maintenance and improvement of common areas within a housing development were a debt primarily for personal, family, and household purposes covered by the FDCPA.

Florida

Sanz v. Fernandez, 633 F. Supp. 2d 1356 (S.D. Fla. 2009). Allegations that the defendants operated a landlord collection service and sent the consumer letters demanding past due rent on a residential lease stated facts that established that the defendants were FDCPA debt collectors.

Williams v. Edelman, 408 F. Supp. 2d 1261 (S.D. Fla. 2006). Condominium assessments constituted "debts" under the FDCPA.

Agan v. Katzman & Korr, P.A., 2004 WL 555257 (S.D. Fla. Mar. 16, 2004). Condominium assessments.

Fuller v. Becker & Poliakoff, P.A., 192 F. Supp. 2d 1361 (M.D. Fla. 2002). Delinquent maintenance assessments under a property owners' association contract were debts covered by the FDCPA.

Illinois

Strange v. Wexler, 796 F. Supp. 1117 (N.D. Ill. 1992). Engaging a broker to locate a replacement tenant for the consumer's apartment was a "household purpose" within the meaning of the term "debt" as defined by the Act.

American Mgmt. Consultant, L.L.C. v. Carter, 915 N.E.2d 411 (Ill. App. Ct. 2009). FDCPA applied to forcible entry and detainer action that also sought back rent. Notice posted on door did not comply with § 1692g.

Kansas

Kvassay v. Hasty, 236 F. Supp. 2d 1240 (D. Kan. 2002). Defendant attorneys claimed that their letter to consumers seeking replacement checks, after a medical clinic's deposit bag was lost, was not an attempt to collect a debt because the checks were not dishonored or overdue. Court held that the letter related to an alleged obligation of a consumer to pay money. The lawyers were therefore king to collect a debt, although lawyers were exempt.

Stark v. Hasty, 236 F. Supp. 2d 1214 (D. Kan. 2002). Companion case to *Kvassay*; same result, based on *Kvassay* discussion.

Louisiana

Garner v. Kansas, 1999 WL 262100 (E.D. La. Apr. 30, 1999). A condominium association assessment to repair a common area was a "debt" under the FDCPA.

Maryland

Taylor v. Mount Oak Manor Homeowners Ass'n, Inc., 11 F. Supp. 2d 753 (D. Md. 1998). Obligation to pay homeowners association maintenance fees was a "debt" as defined.

Nevada

Moulton v. Eugene Burger Mgmt. Corp., 2009 WL 205053 (D. Nev. Jan. 26, 2009). Condominium association's attorney was a debt collector.

New Jersey

Hodges v. Sasil Corp., 915 A.2d 1 (N.J. 2007). Even though eviction is an *in rem* action for possession, payment of the rent allows the debtor to avoid eviction. Therefore, an eviction action is an action on a debt. Rent is a debt as defined by the FDCPA.

New York

Garmus v. Borah, Goldstein, Altschuler & Schwartz, 1999 WL 46682 (S.D.N.Y. Feb. 1, 1999). The FDCPA applies to the defendant, since rent is a debt; defendant is a debt collector; and the three-day rent demand notice was a communication (citing *Romea*).

Hairston v. Whitehorn & Delman, 1998 WL 35112 (S.D.N.Y. Jan. 30, 1998). Back rent constituted a debt under the FDCPA.

Finlayson v. Yager, 873 N.Y.S.2d 511 (table), 2008 WL 4571562 (N.Y. Civ. Ct. 2008). "[A]n attorney who regularly engages in consumer debt collection activities and signs a rent demand notice on behalf of a landlord, must comply with the provisions of the

Fair Debt Collection Practices Act (FDCPA) and its thirty-day validation notice provisions."

Pennsylvania

Wenrich v. Robert E. Cole, P.C., 2000 U.S. Dist. LEXIS 18687 (E.D. Pa. Dec. 22, 2000). A claim for rent for a residential apartment was a debt covered by the FDCPA.

Virginia

Dikun v. Streich, 369 F. Supp. 2d 781 (E.D. Va. 2005). Property owners' association assessments for a consumer's residence were held to be debts as defined by the FDCPA.

K.1.1.2.2 Not covered

Colorado

Cook v. Hamrick, 278 F. Supp. 2d 1202 (D. Colo. 2003). A dismissed state action for eviction seeking attorney fees was not covered by the FDCPA because the attorney fee claim was not based on the lease but the proceeding.

Delaware

Route 40 Holdings, Inc. v. Tony's Pizza & Pasta, Inc., 2010 WL 2161819 (Del. Super. Ct. May 27, 2010). The failure to pay rent under a commercial lease is not a debt under the FDCPA.

Florida

Durso v. Summer Brook Preserve Homeowners Ass'n, 641 F. Supp. 2d 1256 (M.D. Fla. 2008). Fines assessed by a homeowner's association do not create a "debt" under the FDCPA.

Azar v. Hayter, 874 F. Supp. 1314 (N.D. Fla. 1995), *aff'd without op.*, 66 F.3d 342 (11th Cir. 1995). *Pro se* complaint did not allege sufficient facts to support a finding that an assessment by the condominium association was a transaction incurred for personal, family, or household purposes to meet the definition of "debt."

Bryan v. Clayton, 698 So. 2d 1236 (Fla. Dist. Ct. App. 1997). Homeowners fee was not a "debt" under FDCPA, refusing to follow *Newman v. Boehm, Pearlstein & Bright, Ltd.*, 119 F.3d 477 (7th Cir. 1997).

Illinois

Gulley v. Pierce & Assocs., 2010 WL 5060257 (N.D. Ill. Dec. 6, 2010). The *pro se* consumer failed to state a claim for alleged FDCPA violations arising from the defendant's filing of an eviction suit; although an "eviction suit or other suit seeking possession or transfer of control of property may constitute collection of a debt in certain circumstances," the eviction in this case "was designed only 'to wrest possession of . . . property,' not collect a debt from [the plaintiff]."

Vosatka v. Wolin-Levin, Inc., 1995 WL 443950 (N.D. Ill. July 21, 1995). Delinquent condominium assessments are not "debts" under the FDCPA.

Galuska v. Blumenthal, 1994 WL 323121 (N.D. Ill. June 26, 1994). Attorney who brought an eviction action against the consumer on behalf of a creditor who had previously foreclosed and obtained legal title to the property, in a settlement agreement was not engaged in collecting a debt covered by the FDCPA. Debt collector's motion for summary judgment was granted and the *pro se* plaintiff was sanctioned $500 under Fed. R. Civ. P. 11(b) after the court concluded the plaintiff's FDCPA claim was not advanced in good faith after being warned by the court.

Indiana

Rael v. Davis, 2006 WL 2346396 (S.D. Ind. Aug. 11, 2006). Collectors' motion to dismiss FDCPA complaint was granted because claims in a state court action for attorney fees and costs of removal of an above ground swimming pool on their property was not a "debt" within the FDCPA as the condominium agreement which provided the prohibition of the pool was silent regarding the condominium association's entitlement to attorney fees and costs of removal. Since the state court's judgment would be based on fee shifting, theories of recovery other that the condominium agreement, there was no transaction and no debt.

Michigan

Bond v. U.S. Bank Nat'l Ass'n, 2010 WL 1265852 (E.D. Mich. Mar. 29, 2010) (*pro se* consumer). Because the bank was not seeking to collect a debt when it initiated the summary eviction proceedings against consumer, its actions could not violate the FDCPA. The eviction complaint confirmed that the bank sought possession rather than monetary damages.

New York

Arrey v. Beaux Arts II, L.L.C., 101 F. Supp. 2d 225 (S.D.N.Y. 2000). Tenant *pro se* removed eviction action to federal court because three-day eviction notice allegedly violated the FDCPA. Remanded "[B]oth the removal and the contention that the alleged violation of the Act constitutes a defense to the nonpayment proceeding are utterly frivolous."

Barry v. Board of Managers of Condo. II, 853 N.Y.S.2d 827 (N.Y. Civ. Ct. 2007). A condominium association was not a "debt collector" within the FDCPA because it was seeking to collect money owed to it.

Missionary Sisters v. Dowling, 703 N.Y.S.2d 362 (N.Y. Civ. Ct. 1999). FDCPA's protections were not triggered by rent demand drafted by counsel as long as rent demand was sent by landlord-creditor and not sent by counsel.

Ohio

Glazer v. Chase Home Fin. L.L.C., 2010 WL 1392156 (N.D. Ohio Jan. 21, 2010). The court rejected the consumer's argument that a property management company's activities (e.g., winterizing the bathroom, damaging the furnace, placing a combination lock on the door) were part of a conspiracy to make him pay the debt. The company was not a debt collector under the Act.

Pennsylvania

Andrews v. Campbell, 1997 WL 148588 (E.D. Pa. Mar. 21, 1997). Judgment for rental of real estate was not a debt primarily for personal, family, or household purposes.

Texas

Thomas v. Ernest Barrientos, P.C., 2006 WL 1096764 (N.D. Tex. Apr. 26, 2006). Defendant was not subject to the FDCPA because, by demanding return of rental furniture, defendant was not attempting to collect money.

K.1.1.3 Dishonored Checks

K.1.1.3.1 Covered

Federal Trade Comm'n v. Check Enforcement, 502 F.3d 159 (3d Cir. 2007). When collecting dishonored checks, defendants were debt collectors collecting a debt subject to the FDCPA.

Volden v. Innovative Fin. Sys., Inc., 440 F.3d 947 (8th Cir. 2006).

Keele v. Wexler, 149 F.3d 589 (7th Cir. 1998). While the FDCPA may apply to consensual transactions, there is no express FDCPA exception for transactions that are not consensual because the consumer entered into them with the intent to defraud the other party. The court would not create a fraud exception where Congress did not create one.

Snow v. Jesse L. Riddle, P.C., 143 F.3d 1350 (10th Cir. 1998). Dishonored check was a "debt" as defined.

Duffy v. Landberg, 133 F.3d 1120 (8th Cir. 1998). A dishonored check was a debt covered by the FDCPA. Since a check written by a consumer in a transaction for household goods or services evidenced the drawer's obligation to pay and this obligation remained even if the check was dishonored, abusive collection practices related to the dishonored check were prohibited by the FDCPA. Since the statutory language was clear, it was not necessary to consult the legislative history, but that history reflected Congress' intent not to limit the FDCPA's protections to debts arising from credit transactions.

Charles v. Lundgren & Assocs., P.C., 119 F.3d 739 (9th Cir. 1997). A dishonored check was a debt covered by the FDCPA. There is no credit requirement for debts to be covered by § 1692a(5).

Radi v. Bennett Law Offices, 117 F.3d 1426 (9th Cir. 1997) (text at 1997 WL 367868). A check was a debt covered by the Act.

Draper v. CRA Sec. Sys., Inc., 117 F.3d 1424 (9th Cir. 1997) (text at 1997 WL 367869). A dishonored check was a debt within the meaning of the FDCPA. FDCPA was not limited to the collection of debt arising out of credit transactions.

Bass v. Stolper, Koritzinsky, Brewster & Neider, S.C., 111 F.3d 1322 (7th Cir. 1997). A check written to purchase consumer goods was a transaction within plain meaning of the definition of "debt" in § 1692a(5) even though the check was later dishonored for insufficient funds.

Zimmerman v. HBO Affiliate Group, 834 F.2d 1163 (3d Cir. 1987) was limited to the theft of services that was before the Third Circuit and was not extended to exclude checks from FDCPA coverage or require a credit transaction before the FDCPA applied.

Ryan v. Wexler & Wexler, 113 F.3d 91 (7th Cir. 1997). Follows *Bass v. Stolper, Koritzinsky, Brewster & Neider, S.C.*, 111 F.3d 1322 (7th Cir. 1997), holding that a dishonored check was a debt covered by the FDCPA.

Broadnax v. Greene Credit Serv., 106 F.3d 400 (6th Cir. 1997) (text at 1997 WL 14777). The payee of a check covering a commercial obligation (the repair of an apartment) altered the check by changing the postdated date to the current date, and cashed it at a supermarket to buy groceries. The collection agency for the supermarket sought to recover the debt against the maker of the check who had stopped payment on the check before the payment date when he realized the repairs for which the check had been given had not been done as promised. The court found that the debt collection activity at issue was subject to the FDCPA. The collector had tried to collect a consumer obligation for the purchase of groceries through the use of arguably abusive, deceptive and unfair debt collection practices.

Arizona

Caron v. Charles E. Maxwell, P.C., 48 F. Supp. 2d 932 (D. Ariz. 1999). The FDCPA was not limited to collection of debts arising out of an offer or extension of credit and applied to collection of dishonored checks.

Price v. Surety Acceptance Corp., 1999 U.S. Dist. LEXIS 22418 (D. Ariz. Aug. 13, 1999). Checks were debts.

California

Ballard v. Equifax Check Servs., 158 F. Supp. 2d 1163 (E.D. Cal. 2001). Personal checks written to retailers created a rebuttable presumption that the debts were for consumer purposes within the FDCPA.

Irwin v. Mascott, 96 F. Supp. 2d 968 (N.D. Cal. 1999). A check written on a personal account was prima facie evidence that the check was written for personal purposes. The court also looked to the predominately consumer customer base of the large retail merchants—K-Mart, Wal-Mart and J.C. Penney—whose debts were being collected.

Johnson v. CRA Sec. Sys., 963 F. Supp. 859 (N.D. Cal. 1997). A dishonored check was a "debt" covered under the FDCPA.

Connecticut

Fulcher v. Wexler, 1997 U.S. Dist. LEXIS 4229 (D. Conn. Feb. 24, 1997). A dishonored check for consumer goods is a debt covered by the FDCPA.

Illinois

Rogers v. Simmons, 2002 U.S. Dist. LEXIS 5457 (N.D. Ill. Mar. 28, 2002). A dishonored check written to a casino was issued for purposes of entertainment and was a "debt" within the FDCPA.

Narwick v. Wexler, 901 F. Supp. 1275 (N.D. Ill. 1995). A check returned for insufficient funds which was written for the purchase of consumer items was a "debt" within the FDCPA; the collector's assertion that the dishonored check was being pursued as fraud claim under the state deceptive practices act was rejected.

Keele v. Wexler, 1995 WL 549048 (N.D. Ill. Sept. 12, 1995). Dishonored checks were "debts" covered by the FDCPA.

Indiana

Hamilton v. Am. Corrective Counseling Serv., 2007 U.S. Dist. LEXIS 11488 (N.D. Ind. Feb. 14, 2007). The court certified the class in this FDCPA case against a bad check diversion company, finding all elements present and specifically holding that the need for some individualized analysis in determining actual damages was not a bar to certification.

Kansas

Kvassay v. Hasty, 236 F. Supp. 2d 1240 (D. Kan. 2002). Defendant attorneys claimed that their letter to consumers asking for replacement checks, after a medical clinic's deposit bag was lost, was not an attempt to collect a debt because the checks were not dishonored or overdue. Court held that the letter related to an alleged obligation of a consumer to pay money. The lawyers were therefore asking to collect a debt, although lawyers were exempt.

Stark v. Hasty, 236 F. Supp. 2d 1214 (D. Kan. 2002). Companion case to *Kvassay*; same result, based on *Kvassay* discussion.

Louisiana

Ernst v. Jesse L. Riddle, P.C., 964 F. Supp. 213 (M.D. La. 1997). A dishonored check was a debt under the FDCPA where it was given to purchase consumer goods.

Byes v. Telecheck Recovery Serv., Inc., 1997 WL 736692 (E.D. La. Nov. 24, 1997). A claim on a dishonored, allegedly forged, check was covered by the FDCPA even though the plaintiff from whom the collector sought payment may not have been a consumer. The collector did not sustain its burden of establishing that the shoes purchased for $450 were not for personal use.

Massachusetts

Rosales v. Nat'l City Corp., 1997 U.S. Dist. LEXIS 23923 (D. Mass. Aug. 31, 1997). Dishonored check was a "debt."

Michigan

Gradisher v. Check Enforcement Unit, Inc., 133 F. Supp. 2d 988 (W.D. Mich. 2001). The collection of the amount owed to another because of a bad check is debt collection under the FDCPA.

Minnesota

Wiegand v. JNR Adjustment Co., 2002 U.S. Dist. LEXIS 7292 (D. Minn. Apr. 22, 2002). Attempting to collect from the checking account owner the amounts of stolen, forged checks that were subsequently dishonored was attempting to collect a "debt" within the FDCPA, notwithstanding the underlying theft and the purported absence of a consensual transaction between the merchant and the putative debtor.

Armstrong v. Rose Law Firm, P.A., 2002 U.S. Dist. LEXIS 4039 (D. Minn. Mar. 7, 2002). The FDCPA contains no fraud or tort exception that would exclude the dishonored check that the defendant was collecting from the definition of a "debt."

Nebraska

Page v. Checkrite, Ltd., Clearinghouse No. 45,759 (D. Neb. 1984). Dishonored checks are debts as defined by § 1692a(5).

Ohio

Kelly v. Montgomery Lynch & Assocs., Inc., 2008 WL 1775251 (N.D. Ohio Apr. 15, 2008). Whether the dishonored check being collected was a debt covered by the FDCPA is viewed not by the nature of the dishonored check itself but by the character of the underlying transaction in which it was tendered as payment. In this case, the "right to receive medical services and to defer payment on those financial obligations" is "a classic transaction out of which debts arise under the FDCPA."

Oregon

Check Cent. Inc. v. Barr, Clearinghouse No. 37,497 (Bankr. D. Or. 1984). Collection activities related to dishonored checks are covered by the FDCPA.

Pennsylvania

Gary v. Goldman & Co., 180 F. Supp. 2d 668 (E.D. Pa. 2002). A dishonored check was a debt under the FDCPA.

Utah

Ditty v. CheckRite, Ltd., 973 F. Supp. 1320 (D. Utah 1997). A dishonored check constituted a "debt" under the FDCPA, and the Act's coverage extended to abusive check collection practices.

Washington

Connor v. Automated Accounts, Inc., 202 F.R.D. 265 (E.D. Wash. 2001). There was no "fraud exception" to the FDCPA; it was irrelevant whether class members might have intended their checks to be dishonored.

Wisconsin

Ganske v. Checkrite, Ltd., 1997 WL 33810208 (W.D. Wis. Jan. 6, 1997). A dishonored check is a "debt" whose collection is subject to the FDCPA.

K.1.1.3.2 Not covered

Connecticut

Tuttle v. Equifax Check Servs., Inc., 11 F. Supp. 2d 225 (D. Conn. 1998), *aff'd*, 190 F.3d 9 (2d Cir. 1999). In view of the split of authority and uncertainty within the Circuit concerning coverage of collection of dishonored checks, including whether check was tendered with the intent to defraud, summary judgment denied.

Illinois

Perez v. Slutsky, 1994 WL 698519 (N.D. Ill. Dec. 12, 1994). A dishonored check was not a "debt" within the FDCPA because there was no offer or extension of credit; "the FDCPA applies only to contractual debts."

Goodman v. S. Credit Recovery, Inc., 1998 WL 240403 (E.D. La. May 12, 1998). Court held that a check was not a "debt," stating: "an initial letter containing validation notice and collector's evidence of computer records showing that the letter was in fact sent lacked sufficient foundation to establish their reliability."

Pennsylvania

Krevsky v. Equifax Check Serv., Inc., 85 F. Supp. 2d 479 (M.D. Pa. 2000). A dishonored check was not a debt under the FDCPA because payment by check was tantamount to paying with cash and did not involve the extension of credit.

Bezpalko v. Gilfillan, Gilpin & Brehman, 1998 WL 321268 (E.D. Pa. June 17, 1998). A check is not a "debt." "[I]t is likely that the Court of Appeals for the Third Circuit will, at some later point, refine its definition of debt under the FDCPA. However, because the decision in *Zimmerman* is the law of this Circuit, I will follow it here."

Sarver v. Capital Recovery Assocs., Inc., 951 F. Supp. 550 (E.D. Pa. 1996). A dishonored check is not a debt under the FDCPA.

K.1.1.3.3 Check diversion exemption

California

del Campo v. Am. Corrective Counseling Serv., Inc., 2010 WL 2473586 (N.D. Cal. June 3, 2010). The § 1692p check diversion amendments did not apply retroactively.

Ohio

Passa v. City of Columbus, 2010 WL 3825387 (S.D. Ohio Sept. 28, 2010). The City of Columbus was not a debt collector under either prong of § 1692a(6) since its check resolution program's primary purpose was to resolve disputes through mediation, and not to attempt to collect debts on behalf of payday lenders.

K.1.1.4 Torts and Insurance Debts

K.1.1.4.1 Covered

Brown v. Budget Rent-A-Car Sys., Inc., 119 F.3d 922 (11th Cir. 1997). Claims arising from a traffic accident to a rental truck involved a "debt" covered by the Act. The collector's argument that only credit transactions were covered by the Act was rejected.

Connecticut

Stewart v. Salzman, 1987 U.S. Dist. LEXIS 16865 (D. Conn. Nov. 2, 1987). An attorney retained by an insurance company is covered by the FDCPA.

Louisiana

Correa v. Rowley, 1997 WL 714858 (E.D. La. Nov. 14, 1997). A loan to pay for insurance for a car for personal use was a debt covered by the FDCPA.

Kahn v. Rowley, 968 F. Supp. 1095 (M.D. La. 1997) (withdrawn from hard cover publication). Defendant's collection of sum owing from consumer's purchase of automobile liability insurance was collection of a "debt," even though such insurance was required by state law and despite the defendant's argument that the insurance did not directly benefit the consumer but only future injured persons, since it nevertheless arose from a consumer "transaction."

Texas

Dickey v. Healthcare Recoveries, Inc., 1998 WL 20728 (Tex. App. Jan. 23, 1998). Healthcare Recoveries investigated tort subrogation claims. HRI was not a debt collector because the obligations arose as a result of torts committed by third persons (auto accidents, for example). HRI was not involved in the consumer transaction whereby plaintiff contracted for health insurance.

K.1.1.4.2 Not covered

Hawthorne v. Mac Adjustments, Inc., 140 F.3d 1367 (11th Cir. 1998). Sum allegedly owing as a result of consumer's negligence was a tort claim that arose from no transaction and therefore was not a "debt" as defined.

Zimmerman v. HBO Affiliate Group, 834 F.2d 1163 (3d Cir. 1987). A tort claim for illegal reception of microwave television signals is not a "debt" covered by the FDCPA.

Illinois

Garner v. Augustine, Kern & Levens, Ltd., 1994 U.S. Dist. LEXIS 1573 (N.D. Ill. Feb. 8, 1994). Case against lawyers who sued for reimbursement of medical expenses dismissed. The FDCPA did not cover the situation where an employee under an employee benefit plan had received benefits that may give rise to a reimbursement obligation but did not respond to the plan's bona fide inquiries as to the existence or nonexistence of the duty of reimbursement, so that the insurer was forced to sue.

Louisiana

Shaw v. Credit Collection Servs., 2008 WL 2941261 (M.D. La. July 28, 2008). Automobile accident claim not covered.

Washington

Leadbetter v. Comcast Cable Communications, Inc., 2005 WL 2030799 (W.D. Wash. Aug. 22, 2005). Collection lawyer's demand for money for copyright infringement arising from alleged illegal music file sharing was not a "debt" as defined by the FDCPA.

K.1.1.5 Other Types of Debts

K.1.1.5.1 Covered

K.1.1.5.1.1 Utility bills

Piper v. Portnoff Law Assocs., Ltd., 396 F.3d 227 (3d Cir. 2005). FDCPA applied to collection of municipal water bill by collection attorneys who also pursued the municipal liens. The court noted that water service was voluntary and involved a *pro tanto* exchange of water for money. The court rejected the argument that there was an *in rem* exemption in the FDCPA.

Pollice v. Nat'l Tax Funding, L.P., 225 F.3d 379 (3d Cir. 2000). Municipal water and sewer bills were debts covered by the FDCPA. The dicta in *Zimmerman* that a debt must involve credit was not controlling.

Connecticut

Clay v. Melchionne, 2000 WL 1838368 (D. Conn. Dec. 7, 2000). Water usage fee owed to a municipality was a "debt."

Florida

Laufman v. Phillips & Burns, Inc., 2008 WL 190604 (M.D. Fla. Jan. 22, 2008). Credit card covered, particularly where collector only purchased consumer accounts.

Hawaii

Keauhou Master Homeowners Ass'n, Inc. v. County of Hawaii, 87 P.3d 883 (Haw. 2004). Sewer debts.

Pennsylvania

Gagliardi v. Clark, 2006 U.S. Dist. LEXIS 70509 (W.D. Pa. Sept. 28, 2006). Dismissed the *pro se* plaintiffs' FDCPA claims complaining that the utility shut off their water service, since the complaint failed to allege that the defendants were collecting a "debt" or that they were "debt collectors" as defined.

Albanese v. Portnoff Law Assocs., Ltd., 301 F. Supp. 2d 389 (E.D. Pa. 2004). FDCPA applies to *in rem* collection proceedings to impose a lien for municipal services on real property. Demand letters were addressed to the persons who owned the property.

Parks v. Portnoff Law Assocs., 243 F. Supp. 2d 244 (E.D. Pa. 2003). A claim that municipal assessments for trash, water, and sewer charges were covered by the FDCPA was settled.

Piper v. Portnoff Law Assocs., 262 F. Supp. 2d 520 (E.D. Pa. 2003). Water and sewer bills, the amount of which were based on the amount of water used, were a "debt" covered by the FDCPA.

K.1.1.5.1.2 Student loans

Georgia

Carrigan v. Cent. Adjustment Bureau, Inc., 494 F. Supp. 824 (N.D. Ga. 1980). A federal student loan is a "debt" covered by the FDCPA.

Nebraska

Beaulieu v. Am. Nat'l Educ. Corp., Clearinghouse No. 30,867 (D. Neb. 1981). A student loan was considered a "debt" under the Act.

K.1.1.5.1.3 Other

Oppenheim v. I.C. Sys., Inc., 627 F.3d 833 (11th Cir. 2010). An individual's obligation under PayPal's contract to pay back PayPal for funds withdrawn from the individual's PayPal account, as a result of a dishonored deposit to the account by a fraudulent purchaser of the individual's laptop over Craigslist, was a transaction and debt to which the FDCPA applied.

McKinney v. Cadleway Properties, Inc., 548 F.3d 496 (7th Cir. 2008). Loan incurred to make home repairs.

Hamilton v. United Healthcare, Inc., 310 F.3d 385 (5th Cir. 2002). The Fifth Circuit reversed the district court and held that a subrogation claim arising from consumer's transaction of purchasing insurance was a "debt" within the coverage of the FDCPA.

California

Bush v. Loanstar Mortgage Serv., L.L.C., 286 F. Supp. 2d 1210 (N.D. Cal. 2003). A loan to purchase one's residence is clearly a debt covered by the FDCPA.

Connecticut

Herbert v. Monterey Fin. Serv., Inc., 863 F. Supp. 76 (D. Conn. 1994). The purchase of a vacation time share was a consumer transaction.

Florida

Oppenheim v. I.C. Sys., Inc., 695 F. Supp. 2d 1303 (M.D. Fla. 2010). Defendant's motion for summary judgment, asserting that the underlying obligation was not an FDCPA "debt," was denied since collection arose from a "transaction" that "create[d] the obligation to pay," to wit, a reversed payment order by PayPal in accordance with the parties' agreement when PayPal determined that buyer of the consumer's used laptop on Craigslist had committed a fraud.

Hawaii

Keauhou Master Homeowners Ass'n, Inc. v. County of Hawaii, 87 P.3d 883 (Haw. 2004). Sewer debts.

Illinois

Peeples v. Blatt, 2001 U.S. Dist. LEXIS 11869 (N.D. Ill. Aug. 14, 2001). An obligation discharged in bankruptcy is a "debt" within the FDCPA.

Maryland

Dorsey v. Morgan, 760 F. Supp. 509 (D. Md. 1991). Obligation to purchase a campground membership is a "debt" within § 1692a(5).

Michigan

DirecTV, Inc. v. Milliman, 2003 WL 23892683 (E.D. Mich. Aug. 26, 2003). Unauthorized signal interception.

New York

Ernst v. Berson Assocs., Ltd., 1994 U.S. Dist. LEXIS 21653 (E.D.N.Y. Aug. 15, 1994). Debt collector's motion to dismiss FDCPA action on the ground that court reporter's bill was not a "debt" within the Act was denied because the obligation was alleged to be a "personal debt" in the complaint.

Jack Mailman & Leonard Flug D.D.S., P.C. v. Whaley, 2002 WL 31988623 (N.Y. Civ. Ct. Nov. 25, 2002). An unpaid medical account is a "debt" as defined by the FDCPA.

Pennsylvania

Albanese v. Portnoff Law Assocs., Ltd., 301 F. Supp. 2d 389 (E.D. Pa. 2004). FDCPA applies to *in rem* collection proceedings to impose a lien for municipal services on real property. Demand

letters were addressed to the persons who owned the property.

Adams v. Law Offices of Stuckert & Yates, 926 F. Supp. 521 (E.D. Pa. 1996). A debt for medical services was a debt under the FDCPA, even though the consumer and physician expected the consumer's insurer to pay the debt, as the consumer was ultimately responsible for paying the debt.

Connelly v. Bosker, 1991 U.S. Dist. LEXIS 21732 (E.D. Pa. Oct. 22, 1991). Assessment for city's paving of driveway was considered a "debt."

Washington

Hansen v. Ticket Track, Inc., 280 F. Supp. 2d 1196 (W.D. Wash. 2003). Delinquent parking fees were debts covered by the FDCPA where the parking lots and their collectors did not treat the obligations as arising from a conversion or a trespass.

K.1.1.5.2 *Not covered*

K.1.1.5.2.1 Tax bills

Pollice v. Nat'l Tax Funding, L.P., 225 F.3d 379 (3d Cir. 2000). Tax bills were not debts covered by the FDCPA.

In re Westberry, 215 F.3d 589 (6th Cir. 2000). Income taxes not consumer debts for purposes of the Bankruptcy Code § 1301 codebtor stay, noting that taxes were not considered consumer debts under the FDCPA.

Beggs v. Rossi, 145 F.3d 511 (2d Cir. 1998) (per curiam). Obligation to pay personal property tax levied on ownership of an automobile was a tax that did not arise from a "transaction" and therefore was not a "debt."

Staub v. Harris, 626 F.2d 275 (3d Cir. 1980). The collection of taxes by a private collection agency is not covered by the Act since there is no "debt" involved as contemplated by the Act.

Colorado

Andrews v. Director, I.R.S., Ogden Utah, 2010 WL 2510578 (D. Colo. Apr. 20, 2010). The court dismissed the *pro se* consumer's FDCPA claim because taxes are not a "debt" within the meaning of the FDCPA.

Florida

United States v. Henry, 2010 WL 299249 (M.D. Fla. Jan. 21, 2010). The *pro se* defendants' FDCPA defense in this IRS tax assessment action was rejected since taxes are not FDCPA debts and the IRS was not a debt collector in accordance with the § 1692a(6)(C) governmental actor exemption.

Illinois

Russell v. United States, 2009 WL 236719 (S.D. Ill. Jan. 30, 2009), *aff'd*, 339 Fed. Appx. 637 (7th Cir. 2009). Federal income taxes.

Iowa

Israel v. Everson, 2005 WL 3277981 (S.D. Iowa Oct. 14, 2005). IRS claim for back taxes was not a "debt."

Kansas

Bandy v. United States, 2008 WL 1867991 (D. Kan. Apr. 24, 2008). Summary judgment entered against the *pro se* taxpayer because under the FDCPA "federal taxes are not a debt, and the IRS is not a debt collector."

South Dakota

Mathis v. United States ex rel. C.I.R., 2003 WL 1950071 (D.S.D. Mar. 19, 2003). Income tax debt was not a consumer debt.

K.1.1.5.2.2 Child support

Okoro v. Garner, 2001 U.S. App. LEXIS 28336 (7th Cir. Oct. 22, 2001). A court ordered child support obligation was not a "debt" under the FDCPA.

Mabe v. G.C. Servs. Ltd. P'ship, 32 F.3d 86 (4th Cir. 1994). Child support obligations did not qualify as "debts" under FDCPA because they were not incurred to receive consumer goods or services.

California

Constable v. Hara, 2009 WL 111726 (E.D. Cal. Jan. 16, 2009), *report and recommendations adopted by* 2009 WL 465780 (E.D. Cal. Feb. 24, 2009). Child support obligations are not "debts" under the FDCPA.

Illinois

Battye v. Child Support Servs., Inc., 873 F. Supp. 103 (N.D. Ill. 1994). Child support obligation was not a "debt" within the FDCPA because it did not arise from a transaction for the extension of credit to pay for personal goods or services.

Massachusetts

Raffaele v. Marrama, 164 F. Supp. 2d 224 (D. Mass. 2001). *Pro se* consumer's claim against ex-wife and her attorney dismissed because child support was not a debt within the FDCPA.

Minnesota

Reno v. SupportKids, Inc., 2004 WL 828150 (D. Minn. Apr. 13, 2004). Collection of child support obligations.

New York

Adymy v. Erie County Child Support Enforcement Unit, 2006 WL 1174322 (W.D.N.Y. May 2, 2006). Child support obligations were not within FDCPA.

Texas

Campbell v. Baldwin, 90 F. Supp. 2d 754 (E.D. Tex. 2000). Consumer's claim against members of the state attorney general's office alleging abusive child support collection efforts dismissed for failure to state a claim because a child support obligation was not a "debt" covered by the FDCPA.

Utah

Jones v. U.S. Child Support Recovery, 961 F. Supp. 1518 (D. Utah 1997). Court earlier decided that a child support obligation was not a "debt" covered by the FDCPA.

Virginia

Vaile v. Willick, 2008 WL 204477 (W.D. Va. Jan. 24, 2008). Claim for attorney fees for representing spouse and children for child support.

K.1.1.5.2.3 Shoplifting, fines, and crimes

United States v. Phillips, 110 Fed. Appx. 431 (5th Cir. 2004). Criminal fines and assessments.

Arizona

Capitol Records, Inc. v. Weed, 2008 WL 1820667 (D. Ariz. Apr. 22, 2008). The plaintiff record company that sued the defendant for damages for unlawfully downloading copyrighted music was not an FDCPA debt collector because any obligation by the defendant to pay did not arise out of a transaction.

California

Yazo v. Law Enforcement Sys., Inc., 2008 WL 4852965 (C.D. Cal. Nov. 7, 2008). To the extent a driver does not have intent or does not have the means to pay for the use of the toll road, yet uses and the toll road anyway, such use constitutes theft and is not a consensual transaction covered by the FDCPA.

Colorado

Rector v. City & County of Denver, 122 P.3d 1010 (Colo. App. Jan. 27, 2005). Rejecting as a matter of law the plaintiff's theory of an implied contract between the government and the individual who parks at a public parking meter, the court held that the penalties assessed for parking meter violations did not arise from a consumer transaction and were not debts covered by the FDCPA, and thus the collection of allegedly unlawful fines and late fees was not subject to the FDCPA.

Connecticut

Coretti v. Lefkowitz, 965 F. Supp. 3 (D. Conn. 1997). Collection of an obligation arising from theft of services did not arise from a "transaction" and therefore was not a "debt" covered by the FDCPA.

Illinois

Reid v. American Traffic Solutions, Inc., 2010 WL 5289108 (S.D. Ill. Dec. 20, 2010). Fines arising from alleged red-light traffic violations are not debts because they are not the product of a negotiation or contract, explicit or implied. The fines are penalties for violating traffic ordinances that were enacted by municipal legislative bodies and, like parking tickets and traffic fines in previous cases, they are not debts under the FDCPA.

Riebe v. Juergensmeyer & Assocs., 979 F. Supp. 1218 (N.D. Ill. 1997). A fine for late return of a public library book was not a "debt" by reason of the absence of an underlying business transaction.

Michigan

DirecTV, Inc. v. Karpinsky, 269 F. Supp. 2d 918 (E.D. Mich. 2003), *vacated in part on other grounds*, 274 F. Supp. 2d 918 (E.D. Mich. 2003). Claim of FDCPA violations against a satellite dish TV provider that was attempting to collect sums owing from the consumer who allegedly pirated the satellite signal dismissed since the underlying obligation did not arise from a contract or other agreement and therefore was not a "debt" as a result of the absence of the "transaction" component.

Minnesota

Shannon v. ACS State & Local Solutions, Inc., 2008 WL 2277814 (D. Minn. May 30, 2008). County-levied motor vehicle fines and restitution do not meet the criteria of an FDCPA "debt."

Missouri

Mills v. City of Springfield, Mo., 2010 WL 3526208 (W.D. Mo. Sept. 3, 2010). A ticket for a traffic violation is not a consensual debt within the meaning of the FDCPA.

North Carolina

DirecTV, Inc. v. Cephas, 294 F. Supp. 2d 760 (M.D.N.C. 2003). The alleged obligation to pay for theft of satellite television signals was not a debt under the FDCPA because of the absence of an underlying transaction.

Ohio

Shorts v. Palmer, 155 F.R.D. 172 (E.D. Ohio 1994). Alleged damages incurred by a drug store when the consumer attempted to steal cigars worth $1.74 did not constitute a "debt" for the purposes of § 1692a(5) and accordingly, the plaintiff's claim—alleging that the defendant attorney's tactics in attempting to collect alleged tort damages violated the FDCPA—was not covered by the FDCPA, and the consumer's complaint was dismissed.

Pennsylvania

Elsom v. Woodward & Lothrop, Inc., 1997 WL 476091, Bankr. L. Rep. ¶ 77,476 (E.D. Pa. Aug. 14, 1997). Alleged obligation arising out of shoplifting incident was not covered by the FDCPA.

South Dakota

Goist v. U.S. Bureau of Prisons, 2002 WL 32079467 (D.S.C. Sep. 25, 2002), *aff'd*, 54 Fed. Appx. 159 (4th Cir. 2003). Criminal restitution debt was not consumer transaction.

Tennessee

Williams v. Redflex Traffic Sys., Inc., 2008 WL 782540 (E.D. Tenn. Mar. 20, 2008), *aff'd on other grounds*, 582 F.3d 617 (6th Cir. 2009). A traffic ticket is not a debt under the FDCPA.

Washington

Betts v. Equifax Credit Info. Servs., Inc., 245 F. Supp. 2d 1130 (W.D. Wash. 2003). Towing and storage charges resulting from impoundment of an abandoned vehicle was not a consumer transaction within the FDCPA.

K.1.1.5.2.4 Other

Arruda v. Sears, Roebuck & Co., 310 F.3d 13 (1st Cir. 2002). Sears' redemption agreements concerning a debt discharged in bankruptcy which did not assert an existing or alleged obligation to pay money, but only to recover secured property, did not state an FDCPA claim.

Barela v. Reed, 2000 U.S. App. LEXIS 517 (9th Cir. Jan. 10, 2000). Dismissal of *pro se* suit against judges affirmed. A contempt sanction was not a "debt" subject to the FDCPA because "it did not arise as a part of a consensual consumer transaction."

Bailey v. Sec. Nat'l Servicing Corp., 154 F.3d 384 (7th Cir. 1998). A forbearance agreement on the consumers' mortgage displaced the defaulted note and was not a "debt" within the FDCPA.

Berman v. G.C. Servs. Ltd. P'ship, 146 F.3d 482 (7th Cir. 1998). Delinquent unemployment insurance contributions were not debts covered under the FDCPA.

Arizona

Gacy v. Gammage & Burnham, 2006 WL 467937 (D. Ariz. Feb. 23, 2006). Letter notifying consumer of the medical service provider's lien on the proceeds of any personal injury recovery was not an effort to collect a debt, in view of lack of admissible documentation that plaintiff owed money or that her obligation was in default.

Connecticut

Chance v. DeFilippo, 361 F. Supp. 2d 21 (D. Conn. 2005). *Pro se* plaintiff's request that the state return his non-driver's identification card or a refund the purchase price of the card was not claim under the FDCPA because plaintiff's complaint did not identify a "debt."

St. Luke's Found. v. Virgil, 1997 WL 435853 (Conn. Super. Ct. July 25, 1997). An alleged breach of an employment contract, i.e., a salary advancement, was not a "debt" covered by the FDCPA.

Illinois

Spiegel v. Judicial Attorney Servs., Inc., 2010 WL 5014116 (N.D. Ill. Dec. 3, 2010). A law suit may be a personal or business debt; the former covered by the FDCPA.

Arnold v. Truemper, 833 F. Supp. 678 (N.D. Ill. 1993). Bank's claim for over-credited deposit did not arise from a transaction and was not a "debt" within FDCPA.

Louisiana

Murungi v. Texas Guaranteed, 693 F. Supp. 2d 597 (E.D. La. 2010), *aff'd*, 2010 WL 3736227 (5th Cir. Sept. 16, 2010). Summary judgment in this student loan collection abuse case was granted to the defendant guarantee agency since it was not an FDCPA "debt collector": "The Court concludes that is not a 'debt collector' subject to the FDCPA because it its actions to collect [plaintiff's] defaulted loan were 'incidental' to its § 1962a(6)(F)(i) 'bona fide fiduciary obligation' to the United States government. [Defendant's] fiduciary relationship to DOE is created by detailed federal regulations governing [defendant's] participation in the Federal Family Education Loan Program (FFELP). Moreover, debt collection is merely incidental to [defendant's] primary function of guaranteeing student loans made by other entities."

Maryland

McCarthy v. Rosenthal, 1996 WL 249991 (D. Md. Jan. 5, 1996). The court construed the term debt narrowly to not apply to a post-judgment satisfaction agreement to pay a judgment on a credit card account because the satisfaction agreement was not a debt incurred as an obligation to receive consumer goods or services.

Massachusetts

Baer v. Harmon Law Offices, P.C., 2009 WL 102698 (D. Mass. Jan. 14, 2009). The "Notice to Quit and Vacate Premises" which did not reference a pre-existing financial obligation and sought to have the tenant vacate the premises was not an attempt to collect a debt and was not covered by the FDCPA.

Minnesota

Hicken v. Arnold, Anderson & Dove, 137 F. Supp. 2d 1141 (D. Minn. 2001). The FDCPA does not apply to a debt arising out of a marital termination agreement because the agreement was not considered to be a consumer transaction.

New York

Beal v. Himmel & Bernstein, L.L.P., 615 F. Supp. 2d 214 (S.D.N.Y. 2009). A judgment to pay legal fees incurred in post-divorce litigation was not a "debt" within the FDCPA.

Orenbuch v. Leopold, Gross & Sommers, P.C., 586 F. Supp. 2d 105 (E.D.N.Y. 2008). The alleged obligation which the defendant attempted to collect—a salary overpayment that resulted from an accounting error made by the plaintiff's former employer—was not a "debt" since it did not arise from a consumer transaction.

Ohio

Renner v. Derin Acquisition Corp., 676 N.E.2d 151 (Ohio Dist. Ct. 1996). The consumer had bought a car using a discount coupon which turned out to be invalid. The car seller requested consumer to pay the discount amount when the coupon was rejected. The consumer filed suit against the car seller and its attorney alleging FDCPA violations. The court found that the debt was not one in which credit was extended and payment deferred, that it did not fall under the FDCPA, and therefore the collection letter from the attorney was not actionable under the FDCPA.

K.1.1.6 Whether Debt Is a Consumer Debt

K.1.1.6.1 Consumer debts covered

Oppenheim v. I.C. Sys., Inc., 627 F.3d 833 (11th Cir. 2010). An individual's obligation under PayPal's contract to pay back PayPal for funds withdrawn from the individual's PayPal account, as a result of a dishonored deposit to the account by a fraudulent purchaser of the individual's laptop over Craigslist, was a transaction and debt to which the FDCPA applied.

Slenk v. Transworld Sys., 236 F.3d 1072 (9th Cir. 2001). Summary judgment was inappropriate and reversed where there was conflicting evidence on whether a backhoe was purchased and used strictly for the building of the buyer's own home or whether it was bought for his construction business.

Miller v. McCalla, Raymer, Padrick, Cobb, Nichols & Clark, L.L.C., 214 F.3d 872 (7th Cir. 2000). The debt for a house purchased as the buyer's residence and then rented when the buyer moved away was consumer debt originally; the subsequent use of the collateral would not alter the applicability of the FDCPA.

Broadnax v. Greene Credit Serv., 106 F.3d 400 (6th Cir. 1997) (table, text at 1997 WL 14777). The payee of a check covering a commercial obligation (the repair of an apartment) altered the check by changing the postdated date to the current date, and cashed it at a supermarket to buy groceries. The collection agency for the supermarket sought to recover the debt against the maker of the check who had stopped payment on the check before the payment date when he realized the repairs for which the check had been given had not been done as promised. The court found that the debt collection activity at issue was subject to the FDCPA. The collector had tried to collect a consumer obligation for the purchase of groceries through the use of arguably abusive, deceptive and unfair debt collection practices.

Arizona

Caron v. Charles E. Maxwell, P.C., 48 F. Supp. 2d 932 (D. Ariz. 1999). Homeowners' association fees were for personal, family, or household purposes.

California

Yee v. Ventus Capital Servs., Inc., 2006 WL 1310463 (N.D. Cal. May 12, 2006). Collection agency's motion for summary judgment was denied where the consumer in his declaration stated the account was primarily for personal, household, and family matters, e.g., entertainment, gasoline, groceries and other such personal expenses, a question to be determined by the trier of fact.

Connecticut

Retained Realty, Inc. v. Spitzer, 643 F. Supp. 2d 228 (D. Conn. 2009). In this non-FDCPA case, where the court cited the FDCPA and other federal consumer protection for guidance, the court held that the phrase "personal, family, or household purposes" in the state statute under scrutiny applied to the debtor's mortgage incurred for the benefit of his cousin to permit her to remain living in her home.

Allen v. BRT Util. Corp., 1996 WL 776583 (D. Conn. Oct. 24, 1996). A water service debt for a residential condominium owned by plaintiffs, who did not live in the condominium but instead rented it to family members, was a debt incurred primarily for household purposes.

Gen. Fin. Servs. v. Chesanek, 1996 WL 22390 (Conn. Super. Ct. Jan. 2, 1996). The party invoking the FDCPA had to provide evidence that the purpose of the debt was personal rather than business-related.

Delaware

Nix v. Welch & White, 2001 U.S. Dist. LEXIS 10364 (D. Del. July 18, 2001), *rev'd on other grounds*, 2003 U.S. App. LEXIS 289 (3d Cir. Jan. 8, 2003). The borrower's intended use of the loan proceeds, not the lender's expectations, determined the purpose of the debt. Consumer's allegations of a "consumer credit transaction" and of defendant's collection efforts that "violate" the FDCPA, without any explanation as to the manner in which that violation occurred, failed to meet the requirements of Rule 8 or state a claim for relief.

Illinois

Spiegel v. Judicial Attorney Servs., Inc., 2011 WL 382809 (N.D. Ill. Feb. 1, 2011). Where the facts of the underlying suits were taken into account, it became clear that the defendants failed to show that the legal fees at issue could not be deemed a "debt" for purposes of the FDCPA. The suits had both a personal and a commercial dimension, and therefore the court was unable to say as a matter of law whether the subject of the transactions at issue was primarily for personal or commercial purposes.

Williams v. Allocated Bus. Mgmt., L.L.C., 2010 WL 2330371 (N.D. Ill. June 8, 2010). The obligation to pay auto accident damages allegedly caused by the consumer was not an FDCPA debt in the absence of the required "consensual transaction" involving "consumer-related goods or services."

Randolph v. Crown Asset Mgmt., L.L.C., 254 F.R.D. 513 (N.D. Ill. 2008). A $60 business-related expense included in a $12,602.69 credit card debt did not establish that the credit card was not primarily used for personal, family, or household purposes.

Rogers v. Simmons, 2002 U.S. Dist. LEXIS 5457 (N.D. Ill. Mar. 28, 2002). A dishonored check written to a casino was issued for purposes of entertainment and was a "debt" within the FDCPA.

Altergott v. Modern Collection Techniques, 1994 WL 319229 (N.D. Ill. June 23, 1994). Even though consumer used a car for business approximately 5% of the time, her use of the car was primarily for personal or household purposes and accordingly the car loan was a debt for purposes of § 1692a(5) and covered by the FDCPA.

Beasley v. Blatt, 1994 WL 362185 (N.D. Ill. July 11, 1994). Where the copy of an automobile lease produced by the consumer conflicted with that produced by the debt collector, the court looked to extrinsic evidence and determined that the automobile in question was used primarily for personal uses, accordingly qualified as a consumer debt under § 1692a(5), and was covered by the FDCPA.

Indiana

Dechert v. Cadle Co., 2003 WL 23008969 (S.D. Ind. Sept. 11, 2003). The defendant's "pure, inadmissible speculation" that the underlying account was not for a consumer purpose was insufficient to rebut the plaintiff's evidence that debt was in fact a consumer account.

Kansas

McDaniel v. South & Assocs., P.C., 325 F. Supp. 2d 1210 (D. Kan. 2004). Person who was had signed a contract for deed with the homeowners was not obligated on note or mortgage and therefore was not a consumer even though he held title to the property subject to the mortgage.

Louisiana

Garner v. Kansas, 1999 WL 262100 (E.D. La. Apr. 30, 1999). The relevant time for determining the intended use of purchased property was at the time of purchase. Accordingly, consumer's purchase of a condominium in which he immediately lived was a consumer use, notwithstanding his subsequent rental of it. In addition, consumer's return to live in the condominium and the fact that the underlying assessment arose during his personal occupancy established a consumer use, since the FDCPA requires that the use be "primarily" for a consumer purpose, not "solely."

Maine

Shapiro v. Haenn, 222 F. Supp. 2d 29 (D. Me. 2002). Loan documents signed by debtor designating its proceeds for business/ investment purposes and debtor's conflicting testimony that he intended loan to buy a lot for a retirement home created a jury question whether the obligation was a consumer debt.

Michigan

Bond v. U.S. Bank Nat'l Ass'n, 2010 WL 1265852 (E.D. Mich. Mar. 29, 2010) (*pro se* consumer). Because consumer lacked any debt with respect to the real property, the bank's summary proceeding action against him could not constitute debt collection and could not violate the FDCPA.

Palazzolo v. Nitzkin, 2005 WL 221431 (Mich. Cir. Ct. Jan. 7, 2005). Defendant's motion for summary disposition on plaintiff's claims for violations of the FDCPA was denied. The defendant argued that the underlying debt was a business loan which had been reduced to judgment. The FDCPA claim was that defendant mistakenly thought plaintiff was the person owing the judgment (they had the same name) and the defendants invaded plaintiffs home and stole some property to pay the other person's judgment.

Mississippi

Moore v. Principal Credit Corp., 1998 WL 378387 (N.D. Miss. Mar. 31, 1998). Where a debt was allegedly owed by their small business, a question of fact arose as to whether the debtors were "consumers" within the FDCPA. The action was not dismissed because they alleged abusive calls were received in their home bringing them within the ambit of protection intended by Congress and would have amended their complaint to allege that the debt involved investment software for their personal use.

Nebraska

Clark v. Brumbaugh & Quandahl, P.C., L.L.O., 2010 WL 3190587 (D. Neb. Aug. 12, 2010). The court denied cross motions for summary judgment in the presence of conflicting evidence that the debt, though opened as a commercial account, was incurred for consumer purposes: "the Court must focus on the nature of the debt that was incurred, and not the purpose for which the Account was opened."

Kawa v. U.S. Bank, 2009 WL 700593 (D. Neb. Mar. 13, 2009). The complaint sufficiently alleged a possible consumer purpose for the underlying debts to require the court to deny the defendants' motion to dismiss the FDCPA claim, since "at this point in the proceedings, the Court cannot definitively say that the extensions of credit were primarily commercial in nature."

New Mexico

Bitah v. Global Collection Servs., Inc., 968 F. Supp. 618 (D.N.M. 1997). Notation on installment contract that transaction was for a consumer purpose established consumer nature of the debt in the absence of any other evidence to the contrary.

New York

Goldstein v. Hutton, Ingram, Yuzek, Gainen, Carroll & Bertolotti, 39 F. Supp. 2d 394 (S.D.N.Y. 1999). A defendant's motion to dismiss suit, which alleged debt was not consumer debt, was denied. Tenant's debt was alleged to be an illegal sublet of a residential apartment for a commercial purpose which presented a question of fact which could not be determined on a motion to dismiss.

Ohio

Graham v. Manley Deas Kochalski L.L.C., 2009 WL 891743 (S.D. Ohio Mar. 31, 2009). Court looked only at refinancing of mortgage on residence and determined it was for consumer purposes, since only 10% of the proceeds were used for investment purposes.

Whittiker v. Deutsche Bank Nat. Trust Co., 605 F. Supp. 2d 914 (N.D. Ohio Mar. 17, 2009). Dismissed because plaintiff made no attempt to show that the foreclosed properties were for personal, family, or household purposes.

Oregon

Clark v. Schwabe, Williamson & Wyatt, Clearinghouse No. 44,831 (D. Or. 1990). Debt for purchase of a duplex home in which the consumer, a relative, and a friend were to live was for personal, family, or household use even though the consumer rented out the other half of the home.

Pennsylvania

Albanese v. Portnoff Law Assocs., Ltd., 301 F. Supp. 2d 389 (E.D. Pa. 2004). Fact question remained as to whether municipal trash services are a consumer debt.

Dolente v. McKenna, 1996 WL 304850 (E.D. Pa. June 6, 1996). A loan to finance a personal investment in a nursing home may have been a debt covered by the FDCPA.

Tennessee

Deplae v. Regional Acceptance Corp., 2010 WL 2270785 (E.D. Tenn. June 3, 2010). The obligation arising from the purchase of a car for consumer purposes is an FDCPA debt.

Texas

Agueros v. Hudson & Keyse, L.L.C., 2010 WL 3418286 (Tex. App. Aug. 31, 2010). Uncontroverted evidence established that that the underlying obligation was a consumer debt.

Garcia v. LVNV Funding L.L.C., 2009 WL 3079962 (W.D. Tex. Sept. 18, 2009). Since plaintiff denied that the debt was his and defendants denied knowledge of whether it was a consumer debt, summary judgment granted to defendants for lack of proof of consumer nature of debt.

Virginia

Sunga v. Broome, 2010 WL 3198925 (E.D. Va. Aug. 12, 2010). The consumer adequately alleged an underlying consumer debt by stating that she purchased the subject condominium for personal and family purposes since the purpose at the time the debt was incurred controls.

Perk v. Worden, 475 F. Supp. 2d 565 (E.D. Va. 2007). The court denied the defendant's motion to dismiss that claimed the absence of a "consumer" debt, where the plaintiff alleged that she used the admittedly business-designated credit card for personal purposes: "The Plaintiff alleges that the 'debt' in the instant case arose out of transactions where the subject was for personal purposes. Plaintiff may well have violated the terms of the corporate credit card agreement by incurring personal debt with it, but that fact, even if true, cannot change the character of the debt and take it out of the FDCPA's jurisdiction."

Washington

Hansen v. Ticket Track, Inc., 280 F. Supp. 2d 1196 (W.D. Wash. 2003). Where parking fees were incurred in consumers' personal endeavors and paid with personal funds, the fees were consumer debts covered by the FDCPA.

Connor v. Automated Accounts, Inc., 202 F.R.D. 265 (E.D. Wash. 2001). There was no "fraud exception" to the FDCPA; it was irrelevant whether class members might have intended their checks to be dishonored.

Campion v. Credit Bureau Servs., Inc., 2000 U.S. Dist. LEXIS 20233 (E.D. Wash. Sept. 19, 2000). Natural person who allegedly owed a debt for medical services was a "consumer" as defined by the FDCPA.

Wisconsin

Stanley v. Stupar, Schuster & Cooper, S.C., 136 F. Supp. 2d 957 (E.D. Wis. 2001). Defendants' argument that attorney fees were not a debt under the FDCPA was denied.

K.1.1.6.2 Business debts not covered

Hobbs v. Duggins, 318 Fed. Appx. 375 (6th Cir. 2009). The legal fees owed as a result of a personal guaranty to pay such fees in business litigation were not subject to the FDCPA because they constituted a "business" debt, rather than a "personal" or consumer debt.

Lingo v. Department of Cmty. & Econ. Dev., 2006 WL 2595095 (11th Cir. Sept. 11, 2006). No FDCPA claim because the loan was made to start a business.

Slenk v. Transworld Sys., 236 F.3d 1072 (9th Cir. 2001). A sole proprietor's purchase would not be for a consumer purpose covered by the FDCPA. If a loan was made for a business purpose, it would not become a consumer loan by virtue of the debt collector's dunning calls to the home of the collector.

Edwards v. Beatty, 2001 U.S. App. LEXIS 20788 (9th Cir. Sept. 20, 2001). The district court was affirmed where the *pro se* plaintiff failed to offer evidence to support his claim that his commercial debt was converted into a consumer debt by defendant's collection activities, i.e., phoning him at home.

Berman v. G.C. Servs. Ltd., P'ship, 146 F.3d 482 (7th Cir. 1998). Obligation to pay unemployment insurance contributions owing from the consumer's hiring of a nanny for his child was an obligation "arising out of a transaction" but was not primarily for consumer purposes, instead being for "general, public benefit," and therefore was not a "debt."

Gowing v. Royal Bank, 100 F.3d 962 (9th Cir. 1996) (table, text at 1996 WL 616665). An investment in a limited partnership was not a consumer debt even though the consumer alleged it was for personal investment.

First Gibraltar Bank v. Smith, 62 F.3d 133 (5th Cir. 1995). A commercial transaction not a "debt" covered by the FDCPA.

Bloom v. I.C. Sys., Inc., 972 F.2d 1067 (9th Cir. 1992). Where the actual purpose of a loan was for a venture capital investment, it was not a debt as defined by the FDCPA and thus not covered by the FDCPA. Attention should be focused on the actual purpose of the loan in determining whether it fits the definition of "debt"; neither the lender's motives (lender was a personal friend of the borrower) nor the manner of documenting the purpose of the loan was dispositive.

Munk v. Fed. Land Bank, 791 F.2d 130 (10th Cir. 1986). FDCPA does not apply to an agricultural loan.

California

Aniel v. T.D. Serv. Co., 2010 WL 3154087 (N.D. Cal. Aug. 9, 2010). The court dismissed the *pro se* complaint since an obligation arising from the refinancing of the consumers' rental property was a business, not a consumer, debt.

Crowe v. Lynch, 2009 WL 250913 (S.D. Cal. Jan. 30, 2009). Commercial debt not protected by FDCPA. A corporate official may not represent a corporation; an attorney is required.

Simmonds & Narita L.L.P. v. Schreiber, 566 F. Supp. 2d 1015 (N.D. Cal. 2008). FDCPA does not apply to debt for legal services arising out of a business transaction, even if the debtor was sued personally.

Cala v. Bush, 2008 WL 4279699 (N.D. Cal. Sept. 12, 2008). Case dismissed since the alleged underlying debt that was being col-

lected was for commercial purposes: "The fact that Defendants were seeking to collect from the wrong individuals does not change the analysis. Nothing in the FDCPA applies to Defendants or their activities because they were seeking to collect a commercial debt."

Manuel v. Shipyard Holdings, 2001 U.S. Dist. LEXIS 18097 (N.D. Cal. Nov. 2, 2001). Evidence of a Small Business Administration guaranty shows loan was made for business purposes and was not covered by the FDCPA.

Connecticut

SNET Information Servs., Inc. v. Vermande, 2005 WL 375182 (Conn. Super. Ct. Jan. 10, 2005). Sole proprietor's business advertising.

Machado v. Southern New England Tel., 2004 WL 3130546 (Conn. Super. Ct. Dec. 22, 2004). Sole proprietor's business advertising.

Franklin Credit Mgmt. Corp. v. Nicholas, 1999 Conn. Super. LEXIS 1123 (Conn. Super. Ct. Apr. 26, 1999). Creditor's motion to strike FDCPA count granted since the debt at issue was related to a commercial venture and was therefore not a "consumer" debt.

Gen. Fin. Servs. v. Chesanek, 1996 WL 22390 (Conn. Super. Ct. Jan. 2, 1996). Consumers' counterclaim under FDCPA was struck by court as it failed to allege that they were consumers or that the proceeds of the mortgage loan being collected on were used for personal, family, or household purposes.

Bank of New Haven v. Liner, 1993 WL 107819 (Conn. Super. Ct. Apr. 1, 1993). FDCPA counterclaim raised against the bank's foreclosure action was dismissed for several reasons including the consumer failed to allege facts that the obligation was a consumer debt per § 1692a(5).

Delaware

Williams v. Howe, 2004 WL 2828058 (Del. Super. Ct. May 3, 2004). An accounting firm fee for services to a union in preparing its tax return.

Florida

Cowley v. Branch Banking & Trust Co., 2010 WL 5209366 (M.D. Fla. Dec. 16, 2010). Where a plain reading of the complaint showed that the debt was incurred as a "business line of credit," the court rejected, with leave to amend, the plaintiffs' contention that the debt arose out of a transaction "for personal or household goods."

Georgia

Lingo v. Albany Dep't of Cmty. & Econ. Dev., 2005 WL 1500504 (M.D. Ga. June 22, 2005). Business debt.

King v. Amoco Oil Co., 357 S.E.2d 291 (Ga. Ct. App. 1987). Claim for commercial fertilizer not a consumer debt.

Idaho

Dun & Bradstreet, Inc. v. McEldowney, 564 F. Supp. 257 (D. Idaho 1983). The FDCPA was not intended to apply to a collection agency collecting only commercial accounts.

Illinois

Williams v. Allocated Bus. Mgmt., L.L.C., 2010 WL 2330371 (N.D. Ill. June 8, 2010). The obligation to pay auto accident damages allegedly caused by the consumer was not an FDCPA debt in the absence of the required "consensual transaction" involving "consumer-related goods or services."

Isaacson v. Saba Commercial Serv. Corp., 636 F. Supp. 2d 722 (N.D. Ill. 2009). Where plaintiff rented the vehicle on behalf of his non-profit business for a cross-country charity run and did not agree to personally guarantee any debts of the business, the debt was squarely outside of the category of transactions that the FDCPA was intended to cover.

Voris v. Creditors Alliance, Inc., 2007 WL 4219198 (N.D. Ill. Nov. 28, 2007).

Goodloe v. National Wholesale Co. Inc., 2004 WL 1631728 (N.D. Ill. July 19, 2004). Lease of business services.

Gammon v. Belzer, 1997 WL 189291 (N.D. Ill. Apr. 11, 1997). Failure to plead that debt was for personal, family, or household purposes resulted in dismissal of complaint with leave to amend within fifteen days.

Torres v. Am. Tel. & Tel. Co., 1988 WL 121547 (N.D. Ill. Nov. 9, 1988). The FDCPA does not apply to collection of commercial debts owed by sole proprietor, a small business.

Indiana

Baird v. ASA Collections, 910 N.E.2d 780 (Ind. Ct. App. 2009). Plaintiff was investor in residential properties, purchasing them for resale, so FDCPA did not apply.

Kansas

Dean v. Gillette, 2005 WL 1631093 (D. Kan. July 11, 2005). "[T]he mere fact that [lawyer] sought to recover the debt from plaintiff personally has no bearing on the [business] nature of the transaction underlying the debt."

Dean v. Gillette, 2005 WL 957043 (D. Kan. Apr. 25, 2005). Provision of legal services regarding various commercial endeavors.

In re Smith, 2008 WL 4148923 (Bankr. D. Kan. Aug. 29, 2008). Checks issued in payment for supplies for dairy farm not within FDCPA.

Kentucky

Winkler v. Germann, 2010 WL 4904992 (Ky. Ct. App. Dec. 3, 2010). Purely business-related debt.

Louisiana

Impressive Printing, Inc. v. Lanier Worldwide, Inc., 2005 WL 3543719 (E.D. La. Nov. 9, 2005). Business transaction.

Am. Bus. Sys., Inc. v. Panasonic Indus. Co., 1988 WL 76220 (E.D. La. July 12, 1988), *aff'd without op.*, 867 F.2d 1426 (5th Cir. 1989). A commercial transaction is not a debt covered by the FDCPA.

Maine

Business Lenders, L.L.C. v. Gazak, 2005 WL 1353378 (D. Me. June 6, 2005). SBA business loan.

Maryland

In re Creditrust Corp., 283 B.R. 826 (Bankr. D. Md. 2002). Court dismissed car dealer's bankruptcy proof of claim that buyer of his released debts violated FDCPA by attempting to collect on them. Debts were business debts. Bona fide error defense would have protected buyer, which did not know debts had been released and returned them to the seller and removed credit reporting promptly upon verification of their release.

Massachusetts

Fleet Nat'l Bank v. Baker, 263 F. Supp. 2d 150 (D. Mass. 2003). A commercial transaction was not a consumer debt covered by the FDCPA.

Minnesota

Holman v. West Valley Collection Serv., 60 F. Supp. 2d 935 (D. Minn. 1999). Commercial debt to purchase a credit card machine was not covered under the FDCPA notwithstanding the fact that the collection agency contacted the debtor at her home.

Oehrlein v. Western Funding, Inc., 1999 U.S. Dist. LEXIS 17919 (D. Minn. Jan. 26, 1999). Vehicle used primarily in the purchaser's lawn care business was not protected by the FDCPA

Missouri

Shafe v. Tek-Collect, Inc., 2007 WL 4365726 (W.D. Mo. Dec. 10, 2007).

Nebraska

Kicken v. Valentine Production Credit Ass'n, 628 F. Supp. 1008 (D. Neb. 1984), *aff'd without op.*, 754 F.2d 378 (8th Cir. 1984). An agricultural loan is excluded.

New Hampshire

Goldsmith v. HSW Fin. Recovery, Inc., 2010 WL 4684031 (D.N.H. Nov. 12, 2010). Commercial debt.

New York

Nat'l Union Fire Ins. Co. v. Hartel, 741 F. Supp. 1139 (S.D.N.Y. 1990). A $93,330 debt incurred to make a tax sheltered investment was not a consumer debt as defined by § 1692a(5).

Nat'l Union Fire Ins. Co. v. Schulman, 1990 WL 116735 (S.D.N.Y. Aug. 8, 1990). An investment of $30,000 cash and a note for $427,800 was for a commercial, and not a personal, purpose; was therefore not a debt within the meaning of § 1692a(5) and was not covered by the FDCPA.

Bank of Boston Int'l v. Arguello Tefel, 644 F. Supp. 1423 (E.D.N.Y. 1986). An FDCPA counterclaim was dismissed as it was based on a purely business related debt.

Am. Credit Card Processing Corp. v. Fairchild, 810 N.Y.S.2d 874 (N.Y. Sup. Ct. 2006). The FDCPA did not apply because the transaction was for business or commercial purposes.

Concord Assets Fin. Corp. v. Radebaugh, 568 N.Y.S.2d 950 (N.Y. App. Div. 1991). Tax shelter investment in commercial real estate business through a limited partnership was not a "debt" within § 1692a(5) because it was not primarily for personal, family or household purposes.

Mendez v. Apple Bank for Sav., 541 N.Y.S.2d 920 (N.Y. Civ. Ct. 1989). Plaintiff who failed to prove that debt was a consumer debt could not recover.

North Carolina

Henderson v. Wells Fargo Bank, 2009 WL 1259355 (W.D.N.C. May 5, 2009). Mortgage loans on commercial property could not be considered consumer debt.

Ohio

Berry v. Sugarman, 2010 WL 1032643 (N.D. Ohio Mar. 17, 2010). Loan stating that it was "for business purposes of the undersigned" was not a consumer debt covered by the FDCPA. Attempts to collect business debts are not covered by the Act even where the collection efforts are directed at an individual.

Thomas v. Central Parking Sys., Inc., 2008 WL 2704291 (S.D. Ohio July 10, 2008). Plaintiff's motion for entry of default judgment denied because the plaintiff failed to make out a prima facie FDCPA case since the underlying unpaid debt was not a consumer debt but was incurred for monthly parking charges for the plaintiff's business; and while the "parking privileges may have had some personal benefit to [the plaintiff], it was a business expense" paid for by the business, and thus "the transaction as a whole" was not "primarily for personal, family, or household purposes."

Oklahoma

Booth v. Mee, Mee & Hoge, P.L.L.C., 2010 WL 988473 (W.D. Okla. Mar. 15, 2010). An equipment lease that expressly stated "You agree that the Equipment will only be used for business purposes and not for personal family or household use" was not a consumer debt covered by the FDCPA. The court rejected the consumers' argument that notwithstanding their representations at the time they incurred the debt, the equipment was ultimately used only at their residence. The court stated that the relevant time for determining the nature of the debt is the time at which the debt was created rather than when collection is attempted.

Beaton v. Reynolds, Ridings, Vogt & Morgan, P.L.L.C., 986 F. Supp. 1360 (W.D. Okla. 1998). Obligation owed by an accountant, a sole proprietor with personal liability, for purchase of professional materials for her profession was for a business purpose and was not a consumer "debt" covered by the FDCPA.

Pennsylvania

Smith v. Zeeky Corp., 2010 WL 1878716 (E.D. Pa. May 7, 2010). Because the transaction was alleged to be for a business purpose and the defendants were creditors, FDCPA claim dismissed.

Andrews v. Wallace, 1997 WL 186322 (E.D. Pa. Apr. 14, 1997). A landlord's debt to a tenant for leasing uninhabitable premises was a business debt not covered by the FDCPA.

Dolente v. McKenna, 1997 WL 117001 (E.D. Pa. Mar. 11, 1997). Receipts of proceeds from the sale of a partnership asset was not a loan and indemnification obligation was not a debt of the type covered by the FDCPA.

Sheehan v. Mellon Bank, 1995 WL 549018 (E.D. Pa. Sept. 13, 1995). Corporate loan not subject to the FDCPA despite the giving of personal items as security for the loan.

Martin v. Berke & Spielfogel, 1995 WL 214453 (E.D. Pa. Apr. 4, 1995). FDCPA was inapplicable to commercial credit card debts.

Ranck v. Fulton Bank, 1994 WL 37744 (E.D. Pa. Feb. 4, 1994), *aff'd without op.,* 40 F.3d 1241 (3d Cir. 1994). FDCPA was inapplicable because debt was a business loan guaranteed by the plaintiff and was therefore not incurred primarily for personal, family or household purposes.

In re Howe, 2009 WL 3747236 (Bankr. E.D. Pa. Nov. 3, 2009). In view of discrepancy between plaintiff's deposition testimony and her affidavit opposing summary judgment, court found that personal credit card account was used for business debt and granted summary judgment to defendant.

In re Lightfoot, 399 B.R. 141 (Bankr. E.D. Pa. 2008). FDCPA did not apply to debtors' purchase of a fleet of trucks.

Puerto Rico

Calo-Rivera v. Banco Popular, 2006 WL 1514377 (D. P.R. May 31, 2006). Debt incurred for business purpose was exempt from the FDCPA, and thus the complaint failed to state an FDCPA claim; the court rejected the argument that a personal guarantor of a business debt may assert an FDCPA claim.

Texas

Garcia v. LVNV Funding L.L.C., 2009 WL 3079962 (W.D. Tex. Sept. 18, 2009). Whether a debt is a consumer debt is determined by the use of loan proceeds by the borrower and not by the motive or intent of the lender.

Hetherington v. Allied Int'l Credit Corp., 2008 WL 2838264 (S.D. Tex. July 21, 2008). Cross-motions for summary judgment in this FDCPA action were denied because the jury must decide whether the debt was consumer or commercial in nature. The debt involved an overdraft of a checking account used for both personal and a small business's expenses.

M. Fabrikant & Sons, Inc. v. Fuller, 1998 WL 892128 (N.D. Tex. Dec. 14, 1998). Obligation incurred for business purposes was not a "debt" under the FDCPA.

Garza v. Bancorp Group, Inc., 955 F. Supp. 68 (S.D. Tex. 1996). The FDCPA does not apply to the debt as it was a commercial debt of a family-owned business which had been incurred for installing security equipment at two family-owned retail stores.

Virginia

Smith v. EVB, 2010 WL 1253986 (E.D. Va. Mar. 23, 2010). The court rejected the *pro se* consumer's FDCPA claim. Where the consumer used 80% of a personal loan to pay off an earlier business loan, the later transaction was "also subsequently business-related," and did not go primarily to "personal, family, or household purposes," as required for the loan to qualify as a "debt" under the FDCPA.

Dunn v. Meridian Mortgage, 2009 WL 1165396 (W.D. Va. May 1, 2009), *aff'd,* 334 Fed. Appx. 566 (4th Cir. 2009). A loan to improve investment business properties was not a debt covered by the FDCPA.

Adkins v. Mathews Nichols & Assocs., L.L.C., 2008 WL 565101 (W.D. Va. Feb. 29, 2008). Purchase of the preparation of a book review as well as promotional services was for a business debt which was not covered by the FDCPA.

K.1.2 "Debt Collector," 15 U.S.C. § 1692a(6)

K.1.2.1 General Definition

Heintz v. Jenkins, 514 U.S. 291, 115 S. Ct. 1489, 131 L. Ed. 2d 395 (1995). "The Act's definition of the term 'debt collector' includes a person 'who regularly collects or attempts to collect, directly or indirectly debts owed [to] . . . another.' "

Mangum v. Action Collection Serv., Inc., 575 F.3d 935 (9th Cir. 2009). No FDCPA claim against employer that received from debt collector wrongfully disclosed information.

Oppong v. First Union Mortgage Corp., 215 Fed. Appx. 114 (3d Cir. 2007). Wells Fargo was a debt collector under the "regularity" prong of the FDCPA, where it obtained 356 defaulted mortgages in the course of its business of acquiring over 550,000 mortgages in a year. The court reasoned that it was the *frequency* with which the mortgage servicer collected defaulted mortgages that was determinative.

McCready v. eBay, Inc., 453 F.3d 882 (7th Cir. 2006). eBay, an Internet sales service company, was not a "debt collector" under the FDCPA since it engaged in no affirmative conduct to collect a debt when it merely suspended a seller's account and otherwise refused to act until the seller resolved pending disputes with his eBay buyers. This *pro se* litigant was ordered to show cause why he should not be sanctioned for engaging in frivolous litigation.

Hamilton v. United Healthcare, Inc., 310 F.3d 385 (5th Cir. 2002). The Fifth Circuit remanded to the district court the issue of whether health insurer seeking to enforce subrogation claim was a "debt collector" pursuant to the FDCPA.

Romine v. Diversified Collection Servs., Inc., 155 F.3d 1142 (9th Cir. 1998). Western Union "indirectly" collected debts by sending a telegram-like letter to a debtor to obtain unlisted telephone numbers for creditors or collection agencies. Western Union "regularly" collected debts because of the volume of its information gathering business for creditors and collectors.

Maguire v. Citicorp Retail Servs., Inc., 147 F.3d 232 (2d Cir. 1998). Where a least sophisticated consumer would have the false impression that a third party was collecting the debt, the creditor was a "debt collector" within the FDCPA.

Taylor v. Perrin, Landry, deLaunay & Durand, 103 F.3d 1232 (5th Cir. 1997). The creditor was a "debt collector" even though it was collecting its own debt because it used a lawyer's letterhead and facsimile signature on its dunning letters, falsely indicating that a third person was collecting the debt, violating §§ 1692e(3) & 1692j. The law firm supplying the letters was also liable.

Brannan v. United Student Aid Funds, Inc., 94 F.3d 1260 (9th Cir. 1996). A student loan guaranty agency which acquired the loan after default in order to pursue collection was a debt collector under § 1692a(6).

Berkery v. Bally's Health & Tennis Corp., 1996 WL 310163 (D.C. Cir. May 28, 1996) (per curiam) (table, text at 1997 WL 358208). On remand, the consumer's complaint under the FDCPA may be dismissed if the health club established either it was not a debt collector because its principal business was not the collection of debts or its employees collected the debt in its own name.

Alabama

Pelfrey v. Educ. Credit Mgmt. Corp., 71 F. Supp. 2d 1161 (N.D. Ala. 1999), *aff'd,* 208 F.3d 945 (11th Cir. 2000). FDCPA complaint against a student loan guarantee agency dismissed based on the "bona fide fiduciary obligation" exception of § 1692a(6)(F)(i) because of the federal requirements for the agency's handling of reserve funds in a fiduciary manner.

Kimber v. Fed. Fin. Corp., 668 F. Supp. 1480 (M.D. Ala. 1987). The first sentence of § 1692a(6) creates a single two-prong test for determination of debt collector status rather than two separate tests.

Arizona

Baker v. Trans Union L.L.C., 2010 WL 2104622 (D. Ariz. May 25, 2010). Because the skip tracer's alleged conduct appeared to be nothing more than "mere information gathering," the court concluded that it was not a "debt collector" for purposes of the FDCPA.

California

del Campo v. Am. Corrective Counseling Serv., Inc., 2010 WL 2473586 (N.D. Cal. June 3, 2010). The court granted summary judgment establishing the FDCPA status and liability of the individual defendant corporate CEO (who was also the primary shareholder) and the CFO, since both were actively involved in the day-to-day operations of the company and thus qualified as debt collectors under the rule that "an individual can be considered a 'debt collector' and be held personally liable without piercing the corporate veil if the individual materially participated in the debt collection activities." Unresolved factual disputes concerning whether a corporate associate of the corporate debt collector participated in collection activities precluded the parties' cross motions for summary judgment on its status and liability as a debt collector.

Allen v. United Fin. Mortgage Corp., 2010 WL 1135787 (N.D. Cal. Mar. 22, 2010). Where amended complaint stated that a defendant acquired its interest in the subject transactions after the consumer defaulted on his obligations, the court inferred that the defendant acquired its interest in the loan or loans in order to foreclose on the consumer's property or to collect upon the consumer's debt. The court stated that the consumer thus "satisfied his low burden at the pleading stage" for establishing that CRC was a "debt collector."

Riley v. Giguiere, 2008 WL 436943 (E.D. Cal. Feb. 14, 2008). Eviction attorney was a debt collector as a claim for rent was included in the evictions.

Roybal v. Equifax, 2006 WL 902276 (E.D. Cal. Apr. 4, 2006). Credit reporting agency's motion to dismiss was granted because the credit reporting agency did not collect debts either directly or indirectly on behalf of themselves or others.

York Gee Au Chan v. North Am. Collectors, Inc., 2006 WL 778642 (N.D. Cal. Mar. 24, 2006). Allegations that each of the defendants was a "debt collector" who set and approved the collection agency's policies, practices, and procedures and directed the unlawful activities alleged in the complaint stated a claim for relief against these individuals.

Aquino v. Credit Control Serv., 4 F. Supp. 2d 927 (N.D. Cal. 1998). Letter sent via Western Union's "Total Collection Solution" message service was not an attempt to collect a debt, and complaint accordingly failed to state a claim for relief as to defendant's status as a debt collector. (*N.B.*: Holding subsequently overruled by the Ninth Circuit in *Romine v. Diversified Collection Servs., Inc.*, 155 F.3d 1142 (9th Cir. 1998).)

Denkers v. United Compucred Collections, Inc., 1996 WL 724784 (N.D. Cal. Nov. 27, 1996). Genuine issue of material fact existed as to whether public utility was a debt collector where it hired a collection agency to only send out dunning letters. The phone number in letters was that of the utility's collection department. The court indicated that a collection agency which served as a mere mailing service might be equivalent to a "flat rater" who provided letters to the creditor with the result the creditor would be considered a debt collector covered by the Act.

Colorado

Alleyne v. Midland Mortgage Co., 2006 U.S. Dist. LEXIS 75851 (D. Colo. Sept. 12, 2006). Dismissed as consumer failed to provide any facts to support the claim that collection lawyers were regularly engaged in debt collection efforts and had waived the ability to offer proof of regularity now being proffered.

Connecticut

Cirkot v. Diversified Sys., 839 F. Supp. 941 (D. Conn. 1993). An entity engaged primarily in the business of providing collection services for companies who have acquired loan portfolios is a "debt collector" covered by the FDCPA.

Little v. World Fin. Network, Inc., 1990 U.S. Dist. LEXIS 20846 (D. Conn. July 15, 1990). Owner of a retailer's accounts is a debt collector since its principal business is the collection of debts. It falls within the first of the two, alternative prongs of § 1692a(6) and not with the exemption of § 1692a(6)(B) since its principal business is debt collection and it collects for companies other than its affiliates (Lane Bryant, The Limited).

Wagner v. Am. Nat'l Educ. Corp., Clearinghouse No. 36,132 (D. Conn. 1983). A debt servicing company servicing a National Direct Student Loan for a vocational school by billing and accounting for nondelinquent payments as well as collecting delinquent payments was not a debt collector under the FDCPA. It was excluded by § 1692a(6)(G)(iii), and was also not a creditor using a false name.

Patrissi Landscaping, Inc. v. Jacunski, 2005 WL 589625 (Conn. Super. Ct. Jan. 21, 2005). The court overruled the fact finder's conclusion that the collection attorney regularly collected debts since the only evidence was a single collection case.

Scappaticci v. G.E. Capital Mortgage Servs., Inc., 2000 Conn. Super. LEXIS 3319 (Conn. Super. Ct. Nov. 27, 2000). Complaint that omitted any allegation that the defendant was acting to collect a debt owed or due to another failed to state a claim under the FDCPA.

Delaware

Games v. Cavazos, 737 F. Supp. 1368 (D. Del. 1990). U.S.A. Funds, a private federal student loan guarantee agency, is a debt collector under § 1692a(6) but exempted by § 1692a(6)(C) since it was merely sending out notices under the control and direction of the U.S. Department of Education. U.S.A. Funds was not exempt under § 1692a(6)(A) or (F).

Florida

Arlozynski v. Rubin & Debski, P.A., 2010 WL 1849081 (M.D. Fla. May 7, 2010). The court denied a motion to dismiss because individuals who control and direct the practices of a collection firm can be personally liable even if they act under the auspices of a corporate entity. In addition, they may be liable as persons who "directly or indirectly" collect or attempt to collect a debt.

Belin v. Litton Loan Serv., L.P., 2006 WL 1992410 (M.D. Fla. July 14, 2006). The employees of a debt collection agency who actually engaged in the allegedly unlawful misconduct and the collection agency itself are jointly and severally liable for the resulting FDCPA violations.

Dowling v. I.C. Sys., Inc., 2005 WL 2675010 (M.D. Fla. Oct. 20, 2005). Collection agency's motion to dismiss its alleged employees was denied as it lacked standing to move on their behalf. The collection agency asserted it had no employees as named by the consumer.

Georgia

Yalanzon v. Citibank N.A., 315 S.E.2d 677 (Ga. Ct. App. 1984). Citibank is entitled to summary judgment where consumer alleged creditor had made harassing telephone calls to collect on VISA charge account in violation of federal laws. Citibank's affidavits alleged it was collecting a debt owed to itself and its principal business is banking and not collecting debts for others.

Idaho

Mangum v. Bonneville Billing & Collections, Inc., 2010 WL 672744 (D. Idaho Feb. 20, 2010). Cross motions for summary judgment on the alleged §§ 1692c(b) and 1692d violations were denied where fact question remained whether the defendant's communication in response to an inquiry from the local police department—the consumer's employer—was done in connection with the collection of the consumer's bad check debts or was instead part of a criminal investigation.

Illinois

Matmanivong v. Unifund CCR Partners, 2009 WL 1181529 (N.D. Ill. Apr. 28, 2009). A debt collector violated the FDCPA where it did not own the debt but nonetheless filed collection suits misrepresenting that it was an assignee of that debt.

Hernandez v. Midland Credit Mgmt., Inc., 2007 WL 2874059 (N.D. Ill. Sept. 25, 2007). The defendant's communication to the consumer concerning the availability of a balance transfer program that would permit the consumer to transfer the current debt to a credit card and create a new debt with the defendant's "credit card partner" was undertaken "in connection with the collection of" the current debt and was thus subject to the substantive provisions of the FDCPA. The debt collector's parent company was also a debt collector since the facts showed that the parent was "thoroughly enmeshed in the debt collection business" and "a significant participant in the debt collection process."

Cole v. Noonan & Lieberman, Ltd., 2005 WL 2848446 (N.D. Ill. Oct. 26, 2005). Without considering the language of the FDCPA the court held collector's employees were not subject to FDCPA claims.

Fisher v. Asset Acceptance, L.L.C., 2005 WL 1799275 (N.D. Ill. July 26, 2005). The FDCPA definition of "debt collector" applies to lawyers who regularly initiate litigation in an attempt to collect consumer debts but the defendant's status as a lawyer/collector "does not mean that it is held to a higher standard than a non-attorney debt collector."

Scally v. Hilco Receivables, L.L.C., 392 F. Supp. 2d 1036 (N.D. Ill. 2005). The defendant debt buyer after default was not indirectly attempting to collect debts where it did not attempt to contact the consumer itself nor was it vicariously liable for the contingent fee collection agency it employed to attempt to its collect debts as it did not direct or control the collection agency. However, the court did note that the debt buyer would qualify as a debt collector had it acted through retained counsel.

Chambers v. Holsten Mgmt. Corp., 2004 WL 723655 (N.D. Ill. Mar. 25, 2004). Neither apartment building owners, the management company, nor their employees, all of whom were alleged to have violated the FDCPA in the collection of rent, were debt collectors.

Kort v. Diversified Collection Servs., Inc., 270 F. Supp. 2d 1017 (N.D. Ill. 2003), *aff'd in part*, 394 F.3d 530 (7th Cir. 2005). Private guaranteed student loan debt collectors are subject to the FDCPA.

Daley v. Provena Hosps., 88 F. Supp. 2d 881 (N.D. Ill. 2000). Consumer's allegations that the defendant health care providers were "debt collectors" were sufficient to state a claim where complaint alleged that the defendants used the name of a non-existent collection agency to collect their own debts or collected their own debts in a name that would indicate that a third party was undertaking the collection efforts.

Lockemy v. Comprehensive Collection Servs., Inc., 1998 WL 832655 (N.D. Ill. Nov. 20, 1998). The plaintiff's motion for

reconsideration of a ruling that Lason Systems was not a debt collector, in view of the Ninth Circuit decision in *Romine*, was denied. Unlike Western Union, Lason does not ask debtors to contact them directly; it updates debtors' addresses through the postal service data base.

Vasquez v. Allstate Ins. Co., 937 F. Supp. 773 (N.D. Ill. 1996). An insurer bringing a claim under its right of subrogation was not a debt collector because its principal purpose was the insurance business not the collection of debts and it was not seeking to collect a debt owed to another.

Fratto v. Citibank, 1996 WL 554549 (N.D. Ill. Sept. 25, 1996). Genuine issue of material fact existed as to whether Citibank was a debt collector where Citibank hired a collection agency for the sole purpose of sending out form letters on an attorney's letterhead and bearing the name of that attorney who never looked at the files and was not licensed to practice in the jurisdictions where the letters were sent. Citibank's phone number was on the attorney letters, and Citibank never forwarded debt to the collection agency or the collection attorney. Because the bank's knowledge of and control over the agency's activities was unclear, the consumer's motion for summary judgment was denied.

Pitts v. D. & S. Tax Assocs., Ltd., 1996 WL 507280 (N.D. Ill. Sept. 14, 1996). Without explanation, the court dismissed consumer's *pro se* complaint under FDCPA finding that the defendant which purchased plaintiff's general real estate tax sale lien on the consumer's home was not a "debt collector."

Villarreal v. Snow, 1996 WL 473386 (N.D. Ill. Aug. 19, 1996). Beneficial Illinois, Inc., a lender, did not become a debt collector by "using" an attorney's name when the attorney spent about one minute on the minimal material sent by the lender on each account.

Cramer v. First of Am. Bank Corp., 1993 WL 742652 (N.D. Ill. Dec. 27, 1993). Consumer pleaded a cause of action sufficient to withstand motion to dismiss where the consumer alleged that the holding company sent a collection letter on behalf of its subsidiary and failed to identify the original creditor.

Gutshall v. Bailey & Assoc., 1991 WL 296730 (N.D. Ill. Aug. 13, 1991). Whether defendant is a "debt collector" as defined at § 1692a(6) involved genuine issue of material fact as to whether defendant used name that would indicate that a third party was collecting the debt and consumer's motion for summary judgment was denied.

Torres v. Am. Tel. & Tel. Co., 1988 WL 121547 (N.D. Ill. Nov. 9, 1988). The telephone company would be a debt collector under § 1692a(6) if it used a false name in some correspondence indicating a third party was involved in collecting a debt.

Challen v. Town & Country Charge, 545 F. Supp. 1014 (N.D. Ill. 1982). An allegation that a bank collects debts owed to VISA, U.S.A., is sufficient to withstand a motion to dismiss the bank as not being a debt collector under the FDCPA. However, the bank would not be a debt collector simply because it used a division name—Town & Country Charge—when collecting its VISA accounts since it used the same name when extending VISA credit and because a division of a bank is not a legal entity.

Indiana

Dechert v. Cadle Co., 2003 WL 23008969 (S.D. Ind. Sept. 11, 2003). The court rejected the defendant's argument that it was not acting as a debt collector and that instead it was only sending "an introductory informational letter" that made no demand for payment following the purchase of the debt by the new assignee, since the letter itself stated that its purpose was to collect a debt.

Kansas

City of Overland Park v. Hilgert, 105 P.3d 742 (Kan. Ct. App. 2005). The state's requirement that lien holders be listed on car titles did not involve debt collection conduct subject to the FDCPA. The court failed to note the FDCPA exemption in § 1692a(6)(C) for state officials.

Kentucky

Stewart v. Barnhart, 2005 WL 3088543 (W.D. Ky. Nov. 14, 2005). *Pro se* plaintiff's failure to allege that the defendant university and its employees, whom he essentially accused of conversion of funds in his student account, acted regularly to collect money on behalf of third parties required dismissal of the complaint for failure to allege that these defendants were debt collectors.

Louisiana

Norris v. Fairbanks Capital Corp., 2004 WL 1638119, *aff'd*, 178 Fed. Appx. 401 (6th Cir. 2006). *Pro se* plaintiff's FDCPA claim dismissed because closing attorney and title company were not debt collectors.

Hamilton v. Trover Solutions, Inc., 2003 WL 21105100 (E.D. La. May 13, 2003), *aff'd*, 104 Fed. Appx. 942 (5th Cir. 2004). On remand, district court found that company that collected subrogation claim for insurer was not a debt collector, because the claim was not delinquent at the time when received.

Maryland

Ransom v. Telecredit Serv. Corp., Clearinghouse No. 46,790 (D. Md. 1991). Although fewer than 1% of the checks it authorized result in collection and fewer than 7% of its employees were involved in such activity, business that purchased dishonored checks and then sought to collect them was a "debt collector" within the definition at § 1692a(6).

Minnesota

Munoz v. Pipestone Fin., L.L.C., 397 F. Supp. 2d 1129 (D. Minn. 2005). The purchaser of defaulted debt portfolios was a debt collector, notwithstanding that it itself did not communicate with the consumer in an attempt to collect debt and where instead the actual collection efforts were performed by another debt collector with whom it contracted.

Thinesen v. JBC Legal Group, P.C., 2005 WL 2346991 (D. Minn. Sept. 26, 2005). Allegations that the defendant collection agency employees were the persons responsible for the agency's illegal collection efforts stated a claim for relief against those employees individually.

Montgomery v. Educ. Credit Mgmt. Corp., 238 B.R. 806 (D. Minn.

1999). Private, nonprofit student loan guarantee agency established pursuant to the Federal Family Education Loan Program in accordance with the Higher Education Act of 1965 fell under the § 1692a(6)(F)(i) fiduciary exemption from FDCPA coverage.

Missouri

Griffin v. Bailey Assocs., 855 F. Supp. 1047 (E.D. Mo. 1994). Where only 10% of the defendant's employees were involved in the collection of debts, the consumer failed to establish that the defendant was a debt collector within § 1692a(6).

Nebraska

Hampton v. Countrywide Home Loans, 2009 WL 1813648 (D. Neb. June 24, 2009). Mortgage companies collecting their own debts were not "debt collectors" within the FDCPA.

Harris v. BWS Credit Servs., Inc., Clearinghouse No. 27,693 (D. Neb. 1980) (order on motions to dismiss). A motion to dismiss based on the assertion that the debt collection agency owned the debts was denied. The term "debt collector" is broad enough to cover persons collecting debts they own, and the record is not clear on whether the collector is covered or not.

Vernon v. BWS Credit Servs., Inc., Pov. L. Rep. ¶ 30,368, Clearinghouse No. 27,693 (D. Neb. 1980). Motion to dismiss by Beneficial Finance—the parent of BWS (a collection agency) and Spiegel's (the creditor)—was denied since Beneficial could be a "debt collector."

Nevada

Long v. National Default Serv. Corp., 2010 WL 3199933 (D. Nev. Aug. 11, 2010). The substitute trustee who was foreclosing on a mortgage, but did not attempt to collect the debt, was not a debt collector obligated to comply with § 1692g; the evidence failed to show that the defendant's principal purpose was the "collection of any debts."

New Hampshire

Silva v. Nat'l Telewire Corp., 2000 U.S. Dist. LEXIS 338 (D.N.H. Jan. 3, 2000). Motion to dismiss denied. Complaint alleged that defendant sent telegrams instructing consumers to call toll free number to receive message, captured the consumers' phone number when they called and provided the numbers to creditors contracting for services. Reviewing the nature of defendant's business activities, court concluded that defendant's promotional materials advertising the use of its service to collect debts provided sufficient evidence to support allegation that defendant was a debt collector.

New Jersey

State v. Long, 630 A.2d 430 (N.J. Super. Ct. 1993). FDCPA did not apply to judgment creditor's efforts to discover judgment debtor's assets where judgment creditor's business was not debt collection.

New York

Kesselman v. The Rawlings Co., L.L.C., 668 F. Supp. 2d 604 (S.D.N.Y. 2009). The defendant insurance subrogation agents who collected money from the insured consumers' personal injury settlements to pay medical bills to reimburse the health insurance plan were not FDCPA "debt collectors" since the defendants obtained the accounts prior to any alleged default in payment.

Larsen v. JBC Legal Group, P.C., 533 F. Supp. 2d 290 (E.D.N.Y. 2008). The president of a collection agency who was actively involved in the debt collection decisions was a debt collector as was the agency. A debt buyer that obtained the debt after default was a debt buyer.

Krapf v. Prof'l Collection Servs., Inc., 525 F. Supp. 2d 324 (E.D.N.Y. 2007). Employees of the debt collector personally involved with the violative conduct are personally liable under the FDCPA.

Ohlson v. Cadle Co., 2006 WL 721505 (E.D.N.Y. Mar. 21, 2006). The court rejected the defendant's contention that only collection agencies, and not individuals, are liable under the FDCPA, holding to the contrary "that officers and employees of the debt collecting agency may be jointly and severally liable with the agency where they have affirmatively acted."

Reade-Alvarez v. Eltman, Eltman & Cooper, P.C., 369 F. Supp. 2d 353 (E.D.N.Y. 2005). The individuals who were personally involved in the collection of the debts at issue were "debt collectors" subject to the FDCPA.

Grammatico v. Sterling, Inc., Clearinghouse No. 47,976 (N.D.N.Y. 1991). Corporation which purchased jewelry company and its accounts was held to be a "debt collector" within § 1692a(6) with regard to its letters to the consumer because it failed to disclose its relationship with the jewelry company thereby leading the consumer to believe a third party was collecting the debt.

Wegmans Food Mkts., Inc. v. Scrimpsher, 17 B.R. 999 (Bankr. N.D.N.Y. 1982). A grocery store which hired an agency to send a series of computer printed letters demanding payment to the store is not a debt collector under § 1692a(6) and is not covered by § 1692j.

Ohio

Alarcon v. Transunion Mktg. Solutions, Inc., 2008 WL 4449387 (N.D. Ohio Sept. 30, 2008). Victim of mixed files whose credit report was adversely effected was not protected by the FDCPA because the alleged false or misleading statements to credit bureaus were not made in connection with collection of a debt. Debt collector's statements to consumer were made in response to her requests to remove incorrect information and not to collect the debt or pressure her to pay the debt. Outside of the context of debt collection efforts, § 1692e is inapplicable and consumer's reliance on it in this situation is misplaced.

Corbett v. Wolfgang, 2006 U.S. Dist. LEXIS 80917 (S.D. Ohio Nov. 6, 2006). The court denied to the consumer's motion for summary judgment and granted the collection attorney's motion for summary judgment finding that the attorney did not regularly collects debts for the purposes of the FDCPA where the evidence showed that he had filed 29 foreclosure cases during the course of the year, that debt collection was less than 1% of his cases, that less than 1% of his revenues was derived from debt collection activity, and that he performed that collection work for only four of his approximately 200 clients.

Powell v. Computer Credit, Inc., 975 F. Supp. 1034 (S.D. Ohio 1997), *aff'd*, 1998 U.S. App. LEXIS 773989 (6th Cir. Oct. 15, 1998). Fact that debt collector printed and mailed letter otherwise sent in the name of the original creditor, which was not a debt collector, did not transform letter into a communication from a debt collector.

Durve v. Oker, 679 N.E.2d 19 (Ohio Ct. App. 1996). Where it was alleged that a physician had sent a collection letter in the name of a collection agency and discovery regarding the relationship between the physician and collection agency was denied, the consumer's FDCPA counterclaim against them was improperly dismissed.

Pennsylvania

Alamo v. ABC Fin. Servs., Inc., 2011 WL 221766 (E.D. Pa. Jan. 20, 2011). Merely identifying oneself as a debt collector does not make one a debt collector under the FDCPA.

Wesley v. Calvary Inv., L.L.C., 2006 WL 1285020 (E.D. Pa. May 9, 2006). If it is both a data furnisher and a debt collector, an entity may be subject to both the FCRA and the FDCPA.

Goslee v. Franklin Mint Corp., 1998 WL 151807 (E.D. Pa. Mar. 31, 1998). A triable issue of fact existed as to whether Franklin Mint acted as a "debt collector" under the FDCPA.

Zhang v. Haven-Scott Assocs., Inc., 1996 WL 355344 (E.D. Pa. June 21, 1996). Sufficient facts were pleaded for the consumer to overcome the employment service and its collector's motions to dismiss on the basis that they were not a debt collector under the FDCPA. Consumer alleged sufficient facts to show that the employment service acted deceptively using the names of an in-house attorney posing as an outside attorney to collect the debt. However, the FDCPA claim was barred by the statute of limitations.

Dolente v. McKenna, 1996 WL 304850 (E.D. Pa. June 6, 1996). The court dismissed the complaint against the creditor which extended credit to the consumer finding that it was not a debt collector under the FDCPA since it was trying to collect its own debt.

Pressman v. Southeastern Fin. Group, Inc., 1995 WL 710480 (E.D. Pa. Nov. 30, 1995). Creditor's motion for summary judgment was denied since there was a question of fact as to whether creditor used name other than its own to collect its debts.

Horne v. Farrell, 560 F. Supp. 219 (M.D. Pa. 1983). A constable wearing a revolver who intimidated a consumer into signing an agreed judgment in a small room adjacent to a court room prior to the consumer's appearance was not a debt collector as defined by § 1692a(6). The constable was not engaged in a business the principal purpose of which was collecting a debt nor was he a creditor. The court did not address whether the constable "regularly collects . . . debts owed . . . another." However, the creditor may be liable under the FDCPA since the constable was collecting the debt in his own name rather than the creditor's name, and this may fall within the provision of § 1692a(6) covering creditors using fictitious collection names.

In re Koresko, 91 B.R. 689 (Bankr. E.D. Pa. 1988). The court indicated in dicta that evidence was lacking of coverage of and violation by the creditor, repossession agency and car auction company.

Virginia

Blagogee v. Equity Trs., L.L.C., 2010 WL 2933963 (E.D. Va. July 26, 2010). Where the plaintiffs never received an express demand for payment, notice of the person to whom their debt should be paid, or a statement indicating that the defendant was attempting to collect a debt, they failed to allege that the defendant was a debt collector as defined by the FDCPA because no reasonable inference could be made that the defendant attempted to collect their personal debt.

Davis v. OneWest Bank, 2010 WL 538760 (E.D. Va. Feb. 12, 2010). Complaint dismissed because the defendant obtained the debt in default when the assets of the consumer's failed creditor were transferred to it by the OTS and thus did not receive the debt "solely for the purpose of facilitating collection of such debt for another" in order to qualify as a "debt collector" under § 1692a(4).

Carter v. Countrywide Home Loans, Inc., 2009 WL 2742560 (E.D. Va. Aug. 25, 2009). Even though the collection of mortgages it acquired after a default was a miniscule portion of its overall business, the court held that defendant "regularly" collected debts because the volume of that part of its business was substantial.

K.1.2.2 Coverage of Specific Types of Collectors

K.1.2.2.1 Attorneys

Jerman v. Carlisle, McNellie, Rini, Kramer & Ulrich L.P.A., 130 S. Ct. 1605 (2010). The defendants, a debt collection law firm and one of its lawyers, did not question the applicability of the FDCPA to them.

Heintz v. Jenkins, 514 U.S. 291, 115 S. Ct. 1489, 131 L. Ed. 2d 395 (1995). Rejects notion that there is an implicit exemption for litigation activities: "The Act does apply to lawyers engaged in litigation . . . In ordinary English, a lawyer who regularly tries to obtain payment of consumer debts through legal proceedings is a lawyer who regularly 'attempts' to 'collect' those consumer debts."

Kistner v. Law Offices of Michael P. Margelefsky, L.L.C., 518 F.3d 433 (6th Cir. 2008). Subjecting the sole member of an L.L.C. to individual liability for violations of the FDCPA will require proof that the individual is a "debt collector," but does not require piercing of the corporate veil. Lawyer is debt collector as a matter of law where he drafted the form dun, was one of only two attorneys at the law firm, was the only member of the L.L.C., was the one who negotiated terms with the mailing service provider used in the debt collection practice, and was involved in the debt collection practice "to oversee compliance with applicable collection laws and when the intervention by a lawyer becomes necessary."

Hester v. Graham, Bright & Smith, P.C., 289 Fed. Appx. 35 (5th Cir. 2008). Whether an attorney is a "debt collector" is a determination to be made on a case-by-case basis applying the following principles: "Attorneys qualify as debt collectors for purposes of the FDCPA when they regularly engage in consumer debt collection, such as litigation on behalf of a creditor client. A person may 'regularly' collect debts even if debt collection is not the principal purpose of his business. If the volume of a person's debt collection services is great enough, it is irrelevant that these services only amount to a small fraction of his total business activity. Whether a party 'regularly' attempts to collect debts is determined, of course, by the volume or frequency of its debt-collection activities." The defendant attorneys were acting regularly and thus were debt collectors as defined when, over the previous two years, they attempted to collect debts on 450 occasions for four clients and filed nearly two hundred collection suits.

Goldstein v. Hutton, Ingram, Yuzek, Gainen, Carroll & Bertolotti, 374 F.3d 56 (2d Cir. 2004). None of the following factors was alone dispositive of the issue of whether a person's debt collection activities met the regularity threshold of the FDCPA. Most important in the analysis is the assessment of facts closely relating to ordinary concepts of regularity, including: (1) the absolute number of debt collection communications issued over the relevant period(s); (2) the frequency of the communications, including whether any patterns of collection activity were discernable; (3) whether the entity had personnel specifically assigned to work on debt collection activity; (4) whether the entity had systems or contractors in place to facilitate such activity; and (5) whether the activity was undertaken in connection with ongoing client relationships with entities that had retained the lawyer or firm to assist in the collection of outstanding consumer debt obligations. "Facts relating to the role debt collection work plays in the practice as a whole should also be considered to the extent they bear on the question of regularity of debt collection activity (debt collection constituting 1% of the overall work or revenues of a very large entity may, for instance, suggest regularity, whereas such work constituting 1% of an individual lawyer's practice might not)." Whether the law practice seeks debt collection business by marketing itself as having debt collection expertise may also be an indicator of the regularity of collection as a part of the practice. Hutton had issued 145 three-day notices within a twelve-month period. Hutton's ongoing relationship with apparently affiliated entities for which it repeatedly sent collection notices within the one-year period under scrutiny further indicates regularity of collection work as part of the firm's business.

Schroyer v. Frankel, 197 F.3d 1170 (6th Cir. 1999). For a court to find that an attorney or law firm "regularly" collects debts, "a plaintiff must show that the attorney or law firm collects debts as a matter of course for its clients or for some clients, or collects debts as a substantial, but not principal, part of his or its general law practice." Plaintiff failed to prove that a law practice "regularly" collected debts where the law firm's debt collection constituted two percent of its overall practice, where no individuals were employed full-time to collect debts, where the debt collection cases of the defendant attorney constituted 7.4% of his annual caseload and where he represented debtors in a majority of his debt collection cases.

Romea v. Heiberger & Assocs., 163 F.3d 111 (2d Cir. 1998). Attorney sending state mandated three-day demand for payment of past-due rent and eviction notice is a "debt collector"; statutory exception of § 1692a(6)(D) is inapplicable as it applies only to process servers.

Garrett v. Derbes, 110 F.3d 317 (5th Cir. 1997). An attorney who collected against 639 different individuals in a nine month period satisfied the requirement that he "regularly" collected debts for another although those 639 cases only represented .5% of his practice. He was regularly collecting consumer debts because that volume was great enough to meet the threshold.

Addison v. Braud, 105 F.3d 223 (5th Cir. 1997). Attorneys who regularly engaged in debt collection litigation were "debt collectors" for the purposes of the FDCPA.

Taylor v. Perrin, Landry, deLaunay & Durand, 103 F.3d 1232 (5th Cir. 1997). The creditor was a "debt collector" even though it was collecting its own debt because it used a lawyer's letterhead and facsimile signature on its dunning letters, falsely indicating that a third person was collecting the debt, violating §§ 1692e(3) & 1692j. The law firm supplying the letters was also liable.

Gowing v. Royal Bank, 100 F.3d 962 (9th Cir. 1996) (table, text at 1996 WL 616665). The bank's attorneys were not debt collectors as they were not regularly engaged in debt collection.

Wadlington v. Credit Acceptance Corp., 76 F.3d 103 (6th Cir. 1996). Attorneys who filed suit on behalf of financer were debt collectors.

Paulemon v. Tobin, 30 F.3d 307 (2d Cir. 1994). Attorney who sent letter to the consumer's counsel prior to the filing of a complaint could not claim to be engaged solely in litigation activities and was not exempt from the operation of the FDCPA. The court did not reach the question (now settled by *Heintz*) of whether a litigation activity exemption may exist under the FDCPA, but indicated its skepticism.

Fox v. Citicorp Credit Servs., Inc., 15 F.3d 1507 (9th Cir. 1994). Rejecting the collection attorney's theory that the FDCPA does not apply to "purely legal activities," the filing of an application for a writ of garnishment in a county other than where the consumers resided or the contract was signed violated § 1692i.

Green v. Hocking, 9 F.3d 18 (6th Cir. 1993). Actions of an attorney while conducting litigation are not covered by the FDCPA. The FDCPA was not designed to inhibit litigation activities. (Overruled by *Heintz*).

Frey v. Gangwish, 970 F.2d 1516 (6th Cir. 1992). The validation notice must be provided within five days of the initial communication even where the first communication was an attorney's post-judgment letter to the consumer.

Scott v. Jones, 964 F.2d 314 (4th Cir. 1992). "We do not accept Jones' argument that he was engaged in the practice of law, not the collection of debts . . . it is clear that the 'principal purpose' of his work was the collection of debt . . . we reach this conclusion both from a common sense construction of the statutory language, and from the simple fact that in the FDCPA itself, Congress chose to regulate the venue of debt-related court actions alongside other, more direct, methods of debt collection." At least 70–80% of the defendant lawyer's legal fees in prior years had been related to high-volume debt collection work.

Carroll v. Wolpoff & Abramson, 961 F.2d 459 (4th Cir. 1992). The 1986 amendment to the FDCPA to eliminate the exclusion of attorneys from the definition of "debt collector" was a repeal, not a reenactment which generally incorporates prior judicial decisions.

Crossley v. Lieberman, 868 F.2d 566 (3d Cir. 1989). An attorney routinely collecting consumer debts is a debt collector under § 1692a(6).

California

Riley v. Giguiere, 631 F. Supp. 2d 1295 (E.D. Cal. 2009). Attorney was debt collector where collections actions constituted 40 to 50% of her total work, including unlawful detainer actions. For a single client she had filed forty debt collection cases over the last three years, comprising approximately 5% of her work and 2% of her income.

Irwin v. Mascott, 94 F. Supp. 2d 1052 (N.D. Cal. 2000). Denial of debt collector's motion to serve third-party malpractice complaint against its legal counsel was appropriate because the FDCPA was a strict liability statute, a plaintiff was not required to establish intentional conduct on the part of the debt collector, there was no affirmative defense of reliance on counsel under the FDCPA, and there was no express right of action for either contribution or indemnity under the FDCPA.

Newman v. CheckRite California, Inc., 912 F. Supp. 1354 (E.D. Cal. 1995). The FDCPA applies to lawyers engaged in litigation.

Colorado

Shapiro & Meinhold v. Zartman, 823 P.2d 120 (Colo. 1992), *aff'g Zartman v. Shapiro & Meinhold*, 811 P.2d 409 (Colo. App. 1990). Attorneys whose collection activities are primarily limited to foreclosures are "debt collectors" if they otherwise fit the definition of § 1692a(6). "Debt collectors include attorneys whose practices are limited to purely legal activities so long as they otherwise meet the definition contained in section 1692a(6)."

First Interstate Bank v. Soucie, 924 P.2d 1200 (Colo. App. 1996). Vicarious liability will be imposed on an attorney's client for the attorney's FDCPA violations if the attorney and client were both debt collectors.

Connecticut

Dichiara v. Pelsinger, 2010 WL 3613798 (D. Conn. Aug. 30, 2010). The court rejected the defendant's contention that he was not a collection attorney based on his contract with a collection agency to act as its attorney "to draft legal papers to enforce unsecured debts owed by the public to certain credit card and other companies who were clients" of the collection agency.

Cashman v. Ricigliano, 2004 WL 1920798 (D. Conn. Aug. 25, 2004). Defendants were debt collectors because they sent ninety letters in five months pursuant to a written agreement with a collection agency, set up a special address and telephone line for the collection efforts; and sued some fifty-three consumers. Focusing on firm revenue as a factor to determine whether the defendant is a debt collector improperly blurs the distinction between "principal purpose" and "regularly" collecting.

Plummer v. Gordon, 193 F. Supp. 2d 460 (D. Conn. 2002). A lawyer who was merely defending a creditor being sued for wrongful repossession was not a debt collector.

Von Schmidt v. Kratter, 9 F. Supp. 2d 100 (D. Conn. 1997). Law firm not regularly engaged in debt collection where it had only one consumer creditor client and handled only twenty-nine matters for that client in two years.

Cacace v. Lucas, 775 F. Supp. 502 (D. Conn. 1990). An attorney who represented four collection agencies, filed over 150 collection suits in a two-year period, and sent one particular collection letter over 125 times in a fourteen-month period was a debt collector even though debt collection was merely incidental to his primary law practice.

Woolfolk v. Rubin, 1990 U.S. Dist. LEXIS 20964 (D. Conn. Feb. 2, 1990). Definition of debt collector includes any attorney who engages in debt collection more than a few times a year.

Stewart v. Salzman, 1987 U.S. Dist. LEXIS 16865 (D. Conn. Nov. 2, 1987). An attorney retained by an insurance company is covered by the FDCPA.

Yale New Haven Hosp. v. Orlins, 1992 WL 110710 (Conn. Super. Ct. May 11, 1992). "Simply stated, if an attorney regularly engages in debt collection activities, that attorney is a 'debt collector under the FDCPA and is subject to its provisions.' . . . This court holds that there is no additional implied exemption for 'attorneys when performing tasks of a legal nature.' "

Delaware

Sutton v. Law Offices of Alexander L. Lawrence, 1992 U.S. Dist. LEXIS 22761 (D. Del. June 17, 1992). Attorney may not avoid notice requirements by relying on client creditor's prior communication. Attorneys who regularly attempt to collect debts by means other than litigation must provide the required validation notice even if previous debt collector or creditor had done so, particularly where communications were from separate parties.

Florida

Agan v. Katzman & Korr, P.A., 2004 WL 555257 (S.D. Fla. Mar. 16, 2004). The court applied *Heintz v. Jenkins* holding that an attorney can be a debt collector under the FDCPA, if he regularly engages in consumer debt collection activity.

Sandlin v. Shapiro & Fishman, 919 F. Supp. 1564 (M.D. Fla. 1996). The law firm was acting as a debt collector by requesting the consumer to pay a mortgage debt.

Azar v. Hayter, 874 F. Supp. 1314 (N.D. Fla. 1995), *aff'd without op.*, 66 F.3d 342 (11th Cir. 1995). A lawyer who only filed suit and did not engage in traditional debt collection activities on behalf of another to enforce a claim was not a "debt collector" within the FDCPA. (Overruled by *Heintz*.)

In re Cooper, 253 B.R. 286 (Bankr. N.D. Fla. 2000). An attorney who merely appears to defend a debt collector from an FDCPA claim does not become a debt collector.

Georgia

State ex rel. Doyle v. Frederick J. Hanna & Assocs., P.C., 695 S.E.2d 612 (Ga. 2010). The debt collection practices of attorneys are subject to investigation by the FTC, which is responsible for enforcing the FDCPA.

Hawaii

Keauhou Master Homeowners Ass'n, Inc. v. County of Hawaii, 87 P.3d 883 (Haw. 2004). 325 recent collection letters were not sufficient to overcome issues of fact about the law firm regularly collecting debt.

Illinois

McKinney v. Cadleway Properties, Inc., 2006 WL 3490433 (N.D. Ill. Dec. 4, 2006), *rev'd on other grounds*, 548 F.3d 496 (7th Cir. 2008). The court held that the collection agency's employee who sent the allegedly offending letter to the consumer was not a "debt collector" because, purporting to follow Seventh Circuit precedent in the *Pettit* case, "The FDCPA does not contemplate personal liability for shareholders or employees of debt collection companies who act on behalf of these companies . . . [T]he debt collection company answers for its employees' violations of the statute."

Donley v. Nordic Properties, Inc., 2003 WL 22282523 (N.D. Ill. Sept. 30, 2003). A creditor seeking to collect its own debt was not a "debt collector"; however, its attorney seeking to collect its debt was a "debt collector."

Chapman v. Fisher, 2001 U.S. Dist. LEXIS 18499 (N.D. Ill. Nov. 8, 2001). Considering objections to the bankruptcy court's findings of fact and conclusions of law, the district court stated that the FDCPA does not apply to attorneys engaged in litigation activity, apparently misunderstanding the decision in *Heintz v. Jenkins*, 514 U.S. 291 (1995).

Gray-Mapp v. Sherman, 100 F. Supp. 2d 810 (N.D. Ill. 1999). Allegations that attorney who prepared and signed the proof of claim was a sole practitioner specializing in debt collection may be sufficient to establish attorney's personal involvement in the alleged inflating of the claim.

Laws v. Cheslock, 1999 U.S. Dist. LEXIS 3416 (N.D. Ill. Mar. 8, 1999). By listing his own name and "attorney at law" in large font at the top of the page, the creditor's in-house collection lawyer gave the misleading impression that he was a solo practitioner. Other factors included the statement that the matter had been "referred to me for collection"; the reference to "my office"; and the use of plural pronouns. The presence of the creditor's name in the letterhead was only one factor in determining whether the attorney employed by the creditor acted in the name of the creditor. Whether a lawyer was a debt collector could be decided as a matter of law, where dunning letter could lead an unsophisticated consumer into believing the lawyer did not work as an employee of the creditor.

Egli v. Bass, 1998 WL 560270 (N.D. Ill. Aug. 26, 1998). Allegations of the attorney's personal involvement in collection activities was sufficient to hold him or her personally liable under the FDCPA.

Mladenovich v. Cannonito, 1998 WL 42281 (N.D. Ill. Jan. 30, 1998). Attorney-defendant was not a debt collector. The evidence of his sending letters under state law to perfect mechanic's liens on real property was not relevant, since such letters did not attempt to collect a debt. Otherwise, the attorney sent twenty-three collection letters on behalf of two clients, and that number was insufficient to establish that he "regularly" collected debts.

Friedman v. Rubinstein, 1997 WL 757875 (N.D. Ill. Dec. 1, 1997). Desert Palace, Inc., d.b.a. Caesars Palace, was a creditor exempt from the FDCPA, as was its in-house counsel. The fact that the initial dealings were in the Caesars Palace name and a suit on NSF checks was in the name, Desert Palace, Inc., d.b.a. Caesars Palace, would not create the impression that a third party collector was involved.

Hartl v. Presbrey & Assocs., 1996 WL 529339 (N.D. Ill. Sept. 16, 1996). A law firm was not a debt collector because it did not regularly collect debts where less than 1% of the firm's business involved debt collection.

Villarreal v. Snow, 1996 WL 473386 (N.D. Ill. Aug. 19, 1996). Creditor was not a "debt collector" but its attorney who reviewed and sent the collection letters was a debt collector.

Galuska v. Blumenthal, 1994 WL 323121 (N.D. Ill. June 26, 1994). Attorneys engaged in debt collection activities (pursuing a foreclosure and negotiating a settlement) are debt collectors within § 1692a(6) and covered by the FDCPA, although their eviction action after settlement was not covered because no debt was involved.

Garner v. Augustine, Kern & Levens, Ltd., 1994 U.S. Dist. LEXIS 1573 (N.D. Ill. Feb. 8, 1994). Case against lawyers who sued for reimbursement of medical expenses dismissed. The FDCPA did not cover the situation where an employee under an employee benefit plan had received benefits that may give rise to a reimbursement obligation but did not respond to the plan's bona fide inquiries as to the existence or nonexistence of the duty of reimbursement, so that the insurer was forced to sue.

Tolentino v. Friedman, 833 F. Supp. 697 (N.D. Ill. 1993). While summons, complaint, and other legal documents filed with the court might not be covered by the FDCPA, a lawyer's dunning notice urging payment of the debt, accompanied by a copy of the summons and complaint, was a communication to which the Act applies.

Indiana

Stefanski v. Kammeyer, 2008 WL 4452346 (N.D. Ind. Sept. 30, 2008). *Pro se* claim dismissed in absence of allegation that lawyer who filed collection suit was a debt collector; because losing state court defendant could not challenge judgment under the *Rooker-Feldman* doctrine.

Kaiser v. Braje & Nelson, L.L.P., 2006 WL 1285143 (N.D. Ind. May 5, 2006). Attorneys were debt collectors since they filed over 100 collection cases in two years and their website indicated a creditor's rights practice.

Kansas

Kvassay v. Hasty, 236 F. Supp. 2d 1240 (D. Kan. 2002). Court did not have enough information to determine whether defendant lawyers acted regularly, where their principal business was insurance defense. However, since defendant lawyers came within the exemption for obtaining debts which were not overdue, it did not matter how "regular" their collection activity was.

Stark v. Hasty, 236 F. Supp. 2d 1214 (D. Kan. 2002). Companion case to *Kvassay*; same result, based on *Kvassay* discussion.

Kentucky

Wade v. George, 2010 WL 2306694 (W.D. Ky. June 7, 2010). The court dismissed the *pro se* complaint because it made the conclusory statement that the defendant attorney was a debtor collector without any factual support. The only debt collecting activity mentioned in the complaint was a single letter from the attorney, and this was not enough to meet the statutory definition.

McCandless v. Rice, 2008 WL 640904 (W.D. Ky. Mar. 4, 2008). The defendant attorney, who represented a real estate agency in a contract dispute in state court against the federal *pro se* plaintiff, was not a "debt collector" under the FDCPA, where the FDCPA plaintiff presented no evidence demonstrating that debt collection is a "substantial part" of the attorney's legal practice and instead argued "that by sending him a 'Validation Notice' which references the FDCPA, [the attorney] placed herself within the provisions of the Act."

Louisiana

Menchel v. Daigrepont, 2003 WL 21220022 (E.D. La. May 19, 2003). Court granted summary judgment to the defendant lawyer and his firm on the basis that they did not "regularly" collect consumer debts where the lawyer's affidavit was not controverted by the plaintiff.

Franco v. Maraldo, 2000 U.S. Dist. LEXIS 3325 (E.D. La. Mar. 15, 2000). Evidence that the defendant attorney handled two isolated incidents of debt collection in his career established that he was not regularly engaged in the collection of debts and was therefore not a "debt collector." Statement that the attorney was a debt collector in conformity with § 1692e(11) in the defendant attorney's letter to the consumer did not establish the attorney's status as a debt collector under the FDCPA, which instead requires proof that the attorney regularly collected debts or that debt collection was its principal business.

Garner v. Kansas, 1999 WL 262100 (E.D. La. Apr. 30, 1999). The lawyer for the condominium association was a "debt collector" and subject to FDCPA.

Reed v. Smith, 1994 U.S. Dist. LEXIS 21463 (M.D. La. July 25, 1994). Where, the attorney defendants were "debt collectors" for the purposes of § 1692a(6), there is no "litigation activity" exemption under the FDCPA for attorneys engaged in "purely legal activities." Louisiana agency law cannot be applied to absolve collection attorneys of liability as mere agents because the FDCPA statutory language evinces a clear intent to hold collection attorneys liable for debt collection activities.

Johnson v. Eaton, Clearinghouse No. 49,970 (M.D. La. 1994). 1986 deletion by Congress of the attorney exemption from the definition of "debt collector" left nothing "to indicate that attorneys in the course of litigation, or engaged in purely legal activities—activities that can only be performed by an attorney—should be excluded from the requirements of the FDCPA."

Maryland

Queen v. Walker, 2010 WL 2696720 (D. Md. July 7, 2010). Allegations that the defendant was a debt collector who failed to provide proper verification when requested stated a claim for violating § 1692g(b) since the FDCPA applies to law firms that are debt collectors.

Taylor v. Mount Oak Manor Homeowners Ass'n, Inc., 11 F. Supp. 2d 753 (D. Md. 1998). Complaint stated a claim for relief against the attorneys as debt collectors as defined, and against the homeowners association for breach of duty of fair dealing and good faith under state law.

Dorsey v. Morgan, 760 F. Supp. 509 (D. Md. 1991). Asserting his status as an employee of the creditor will not shield an attorney from coverage by FDCPA where he sends dunning letters to consumers which appear to be from outside counsel.

Massachusetts

Camara v. Fleury, 285 F. Supp. 2d 90 (D. Mass. 2003). Where consumer failed to submit any evidence to the contrary, law firm's affidavit that only 4.57% of its practice consisted of consumer debt collection sufficiently supported holding that the attorney and his firm were not "debt collectors."

Argentieri v. Fisher Landscapes, Inc., 15 F. Supp. 2d 55 (D. Mass. 1998), *later opinion*, 27 F. Supp. 2d 84 (D. Mass. 1998). Attorney who spent only 0.4% of his time in debt collection matters was not acting regularly and therefore is not a "debt collector" as defined.

Michigan

Russell v. Standard Fed. Bank, 2002 U.S. Dist. LEXIS 12334 (E.D. Mich. June 19, 2002). FDCPA claim dismissed where plaintiff failed to provide the court with sufficient information as to whether defendant law firm collected debts regularly or how it violated the Act.

Williams v. Trott, 822 F. Supp. 1266 (E.D. Mich. 1993). Creditor's attorney who responded to consumer's request for a pay-off figure did not act as a "debt collector" under the FDCPA.

Stojanovski v. Strobl & Manoogian, 783 F. Supp. 319 (E.D. Mich. 1992). Law firm which collected debts only 4% of the time was a "debt collector" because such activity was regular and brought law firm within § 1692a(6).

Jackson v. Flagstar Bank, 2008 WL 7488901 (Mich. Ct. App. Dec. 16, 2008). The trial court's summary dismissal of the defendant attorneys was reversed and remand was ordered to determine their status as debt collectors.

Minnesota

Owens v. Hellmuth & Johnson, P.L.L.C., 550 F. Supp. 2d 1060 (D. Minn. 2008). Law firm collecting for homeowners association was a debt collector where it sought payment of dues that ultimately could be enforced by a lien.

New Jersey

Chulsky v. Hudson Law Offices, P.C., 2011 WL 500202 (D.N.J. Feb. 10, 2011). The court rejected the defendant's motion to dismiss the claim against her individually because the allegations spoke to actions completed in her professional capacity as an attorney for the law firm that owned the plaintiff's debt. Attorneys may be held liable for misleading statements made on behalf of their clients.

Citibank v. Razvi, 2008 WL 2521082 (N.J. Super. Ct. App. Div. June 26, 2008). FDCPA applied to the creditor's attorneys who regularly collected on its behalf, including through litigation.

Hodges v. Feinstein, Raiss, Kelin & Booker, L.L.C., 893 A.2d 21 (N.J. Super. Ct. App. Div. 2006). Law firm that regularly engaged in summary eviction proceedings was subject to the FDCPA. Law firm sought eviction based on nonpayment of costs and attorney fees that did not constitute rent and could not be basis for eviction.

New Mexico

Bitah v. Global Collection Servs., Inc., 968 F. Supp. 618 (D.N.M. 1997). Attorney who authorized collection agency to send his "attorney letters" to debtors in only one state was liable when the agency sent them to debtors in other states "in light of his allowing [the agency] unlimited access to his letterhead and taking absolutely no steps to monitor how it was being used."

Kolker v. Sanchez, 1991 WL 11691589 (D.N.M. Dec. 10, 1991). An attorney who regularly files lawsuits to collect consumer debts was a debt collector.

New York

Goldstein v. Hutton, Ingram, Yuzek, Gainen, Carroll & Bertolotti, 155 F. Supp. 2d 60 (S.D.N.Y. 2001). Where the law firm's income from collections was 0.5% of its total annual income, it was not a debt collector within the FDCPA.

Degrosiellier v. Solomon & Solomon, P.C., 2001 U.S. Dist. LEXIS 15254 (N.D.N.Y. Sept. 27, 2001). A year after a bankruptcy discharge, defendant wrote a letter for Sears seeking return of the secured "personal property." Defendant was a debt collector because the underlying obligation was a personal debt, albeit discharged in bankruptcy, and because his letter said it was from a debt collector and he gave the thirty-day "debt" validation notice.

Sibersky v. Borah, Goldstein, Altschuler & Schwartz, P.C., 2000 U.S. Dist. LEXIS 14043 (S.D.N.Y. Sept. 22, 2000). Allegations that the law firm regularly prepared and sent three-day notices on behalf of the landlord, that the notices were printed on the firm's paper, and that the notices bore abbreviations used internally by the firm could, if proven, show that the firm was a "debt collector."

White v. Simonson & Cohen P.C., 23 F. Supp. 2d 273 (E.D.N.Y. 1998). Defendant law firm, whose only collection effort was to send 35 identical letters on the same day with no ongoing relationship with the creditor and no ensuing lawsuits, is not a debt collector. The decision surveys several cases which discuss the factors courts have used to determine whether a law firm is a debt collector.

Karp v. Siegel, 1998 WL 314769 (S.D.N.Y. June 12, 1998). In-house attorney for the creditor was not subject to the FDCPA.

Firemen's Ins. Co. v. Keating, 753 F. Supp. 1146 (S.D.N.Y. 1990). A law firm engaging in only legal activities, and not in traditional debt collection activities, was not a "debt collector" covered by the FDCPA or its prohibition of filing in distant forums.

Nat'l Union Fire Ins. Co. v. Hartel, 741 F. Supp. 1139 (S.D.N.Y. 1990). A law firm is not a debt collector under the FDCPA where the debt was not incurred for a consumer purpose, and the firm only engaged in legal activities, i.e., filing a suit in a distant forum. (Second holding overruled by *Heintz*).

Nat'l Union Fire Ins. Co. v. Schulman, 1990 WL 116735 (S.D.N.Y. Aug. 8, 1990). A law firm was not covered by the FDCPA since the debt was not covered by the Act, and the firm was engaged in legal activities, not traditional debt collection activities. (Overruled by *Heintz*).

North Carolina

Davis Lake Cmty. Ass'n, Inc. v. Feldmann, 530 S.E.2d 865 (N.C. Ct. App. 2000). Where trial court granted summary judgment in favor of homeowners' association against tenant, and dismissed tenant's FDCPA counterclaims, the trial court did not err in denying tenant's motion to join association's counsel because FDCPA did not apply to homeowners' association trying to collect unpaid assessments and charges due it directly, and attorneys engaged in debt collection on behalf of clients were exempt under state debt collection act.

Ohio

Gauntner v. Doyle, 554 F. Supp. 2d 779 (N.D. Ohio 2008). Attorney was not acting regularly and thus was not a "debt collector" as defined since he only "pursued 4–9 debt collection matters per year, constituting an average of 6.8% of his overall practice during that time period."

Scannell v. Gunnoe & Assocs., 1997 U.S. Dist. LEXIS 23755 (S.D. Ohio Mar. 28, 1997). Whether an attorney was a debt collector was determined by the attorney's volume of debt collection activity, and collection activity constituting one-half of one percent of law firm's cases was insufficient as a matter of law to show that firm regularly collected or attempted to collect debts.

Knight v. Schulman, 102 F. Supp. 2d 867 (S.D. Ohio 1996), *aff'd*, 166 F.3d 1214 (6th Cir. 1998). Private attorney who was not a government official or employee and who sought collection of federally guaranteed student loan was a debt collector under FDCPA.

Sampson v. Banchek, 1991 U.S. Dist. LEXIS 21815 (N.D. Ohio Jan. 8, 1991). An attorney who telephoned the consumer concerning an apartment lease was covered by the FDCPA.

Pennsylvania

Shipp v. Donaher, 2010 WL 1257972 (E.D. Pa. Mar. 25, 2010). Attorneys were not acting to collect a debt when they (1) sent consumer a letter rejecting his check, (2) conversed with the consumer before oral argument in the Superior Court, and (3) filed documents in opposition to the consumer's petition to intervene in the state court proceedings.

Cole v. Charleston, 2009 WL 960337 (E.D. Pa. Apr. 7, 2009). FDCPA claim against attorney dismissed where the consumer could not find evidence that he regularly collected debts.

Flamm v. Sarner & Assocs., P.C., 2006 WL 43770 (E.D. Pa. Jan. 3, 2006). A reasonable jury could find that defendants were debt collectors where they consistently represented one client, where their collection practice was about 3% of revenue, and where the collection practice was an even smaller percent of clientele.

Daniels v. Baritz, 2003 WL 21027238 (E.D. Pa. Apr. 30, 2003). Attorney representing a landlord in collecting on a residential lease was a debt collector.

Dolente v. McKenna, 1996 WL 304850 (E.D. Pa. June 6, 1996). The court denied the motion to dismiss by the law firm representing a creditor as it found the law firm was a debt collector under the FDCPA as it regularly engaged in debt collection for others.

Littles v. Lieberman, 90 B.R. 700 (E.D. Pa. 1988). Attorney in general practice covered by FDCPA where that practice included a minor but regular debt collection practice.

Littles v. Lieberman, 90 B.R. 669 (Bankr. E.D. Pa. 1988), *rev'd*, 90 B.R. 700 (E.D. Pa. 1988). Collection attorney not liable where letter supplied for specific cases was sent by creditor in other cases without attorney's knowledge or authorization.

Crossley v. Lieberman, 90 B.R. 682 (E.D. Pa. 1988), *aff'd*, 868 F.2d 566 (3d Cir. 1989). FDCPA applies to an attorney whose collection work is a minor but regular part of his general practice.

Rhode Island

Egan v. Williams, 709 A.2d 1057 (R.I. 1998). In suit to enjoin foreclosure, plaintiff mortgagor included an FDCPA count against mortgagee's collection attorney. Mortgagee's attorney counter-claimed against plaintiff, citing plaintiff's attorneys as third party defendants, alleging abuse of process in bringing the FDCPA count. Abuse of process against plaintiff allowed to stand, but dismissed without prejudice as to plaintiff's attorneys. (*Contra Kuhn v. Account Control Tech., Inc.*, 865 F. Supp. 1443 (D. Nev. 1994)).

Tennessee

Derenick v. Cohn, 2004 WL 5598428 (E.D. Tenn. Aug. 10, 2004). Attorney's motion for summary judgment on the basis that he was not a debt collector was denied based on evidence that he had filed 277 collection actions in one county court and held himself out as having twenty-five years of experience in creditors' rights.

Texas

McGinnis v. Dodeka, L.L.C., 2010 WL 1856450 (E.D. Tex. May 7, 2010). An attorney is not per se exempt from the FDCPA. A party's general debt collection activities are determinative of whether they meet the statutory definition of a debt collector.

Catherman v. First State Bank, 796 S.W.2d 299 (Tex. App. 1990). A law firm and one of its lawyers were found not to be "debt collectors" under either the FDCPA or the state debt collection statutes. Less than 5 of the firm's 750 active files concerned consumer debts, although there were 10 to 15 consumers loan cases over five years. The lawyer spent less than .5% of his time collecting consumer debts, sending fewer than five letters concerning consumer debts in five years and spent no time on consumer debt collection for months at a time. This evidence did not conclusively establish the firm and the lawyer to be debt collectors, and the jury finding that they were not debt collectors would not be overruled.

Virginia

Nance v. Petty, Livingston, Dawson & Devening, 881 F. Supp. 223 (W.D. Va. 1994). Debt collecting cases made up only .61% of attorney's practice January 1, 1992, to June 1, 1993. He averred that debt collection made up only 1.07% of the firm's cases over the same period.

Washington

Kirk v. Gobel, 622 F. Supp. 2d 1039 (E.D. Wash. 2009). The collection attorney was held to be an FDCPA "debt collector" based on the undisputed evidence that he advertised himself as a collection lawyer and that he "filed supplemental collection proceedings on many creditors' behalf."

Wisconsin

Tomas v. Bass & Moglowski, 1999 U.S. Dist. LEXIS 21533 (W.D. Wis. June 29, 1999). Filing a complaint and other aspects of litigation were actions in connection with the collection of a debt.

Mertes v. Devitt, 734 F. Supp. 872, 874 (W.D. Wis. 1990). Attorney not a debt collector where debt collecting practice made up less than 1% of total practice and he collected less than two times a year over ten years.

K.1.2.2.2 Repossession

Wilson v. Draper & Goldberg, P.L.L.C., 443 F.3d 373 (4th Cir. 2006). Law firm bringing deed of trust foreclosure was a debt collector. The foreclosure was brought based on failure to make mortgage payments entitling Chase to immediate payment of the balance of her loan, as well as fees, penalties, and interest due. The court ruled: "These amounts are all 'debts' under the Act, because they were 'obligation[s] . . . to pay money arising out of a transaction in which the . . . property . . . which [is] the subject of the transaction [is] primarily for personal, family, or household purposes.'" Actions surrounding the foreclosure were attempts to collect money. "Defendants' argument [that foreclosure was not within FDCPA], if accepted, would create an enormous loophole in the Act immunizing any debt from coverage if that debt happened to be secured by a real property interest and foreclosure proceedings were used to collect the debt." By sending a letter seeking payment of an amount to "reinstate the above account," defendants sought to collect an "obligation or alleged obligation of a consumer to pay money arising out of a transaction in which the money, property, insurance, or services which are the subject of the transaction are primarily for personal, family, or household purposes." Defendants were not within the fiduciary exception, since "actions to foreclose on a property pursuant to a deed of trust are not 'incidental' to its fiduciary obligation. Rather, they are central to it." Section 1692f(6) applies to those whose only role in the debt collection process is the enforcement of a security interest. The subsection is not an exception to the definition of debt collector, it is an inclusion to the term debt collector.

Kaltenbach v. Richards, 464 F.3d 524 (5th Cir. 2006). A person whose principal business is the enforcement of security interests is subject only to § 1692f(6), but a person who satisfies § 1692a(6)'s general definition of a "debt collector" is a debt collector for the purposes of the entire FDCPA even when enforcing security interests.

Piper v. Portnoff Law Assocs., Ltd., 396 F.3d 227 (3d Cir. 2005). FDCPA applied to collection of municipal water bill by collection attorneys who also pursued the municipal liens. The court noted that water service was voluntary and involved a *pro tanto* exchange of water for money. The court rejected the argument that there was an *in rem* exemption in the FDCPA.

Thomson v. Professional Foreclosure Corp., 2004 WL 162591 (9th Cir. Jan. 26, 2004). Appeals court summarily affirmed the district court's dismissal on the basis that the defendants were subject only to § 1692f(6) as enforcers of security interests.

Montgomery v. Huntington Bank & Silver Shadow Recovery, Inc., 346 F.3d 693 (6th Cir. 2003). A repossessor who does not attempt to collect money owing and only seeks to recover secured property is not a "debt collector" as defined and therefore is subject only to the provisions of § 1692f(6).

Arruda v. Sears, Roebuck & Co., 310 F.3d 13 (1st Cir. 2002). Sears' redemption agreements concerning a debt discharged in bankruptcy which did not assert an existing or alleged obligation to pay money, but only to recover secured property, did not state an FDCPA claim.

Arizona

Underdog Trucking, L.L.C. v. Arizona Fed. Credit Union, 2010 WL 2179139 (D. Ariz. May 27, 2010). Defendant Western International Recovery Bureau's bald assertion that it was not a debt collector for purposes of the FDCPA because it enforces security interests was insufficient to sustain its motion to dismiss. In alleging that the defendant credit union retained Western to collect on an alleged debt by repossessing the vehicles, the consumers sufficiently pleaded that Western was a debt collector.

California

Pflueger v. Auto Fin. Group, Inc., 1999 U.S. Dist. LEXIS 16701 (C.D. Cal. Apr. 26, 1999). The FDCPA generally does not apply to a repossession company with the exception of § 1692f(6). The repo company did not become a debt collector under the FDCPA when less than two percent of its work consisted of the collection of money for creditors. Summary judgment was denied based on factual issues as to whether there was a breach of the peace sufficient to deprive the repossessor of its present right to possession at the time of the attempted repossession.

Colorado

Ray v. Int'l Bank, Inc., 2005 WL 2305017 (D. Colo. Sept. 21, 2005). Foreclosing attorney covered. "Although foreclosure proceedings do not seek or result in a money judgment, they are an attempt to collect on a debt through realization of the value of property which the debtor has pledged to secure the loan. Through foreclosure, the debt can be partially or fully satisfied."

Connecticut

Clark v. Auto Recovery Bureau, Inc., 889 F. Supp. 543 (D. Conn. 1994). Repossession companies ordinarily subject only to § 1692f(6).

Delaware

Jordan v. Kent Recovery Servs., Inc., 731 F. Supp. 652 (D. Del. 1990). A repossession company was only covered by § 1692f(6) and not other FDCPA provisions. This construction was necessary to give effect to the third sentence of § 1692a(6). The repossession company's repeated conversations with the consumer were not indirect collection of the debt making the company a debt collector covered by the FDCPA.

Florida

Seibel v. Society Lease, Inc., 969 F. Supp. 713 (M.D. Fla. 1997). A repossession company was not a debt collector subject to the FDCPA except for § 1692f(6). The repossession company did not attempt to collect the debt other than repossessing the truck. The repossession of a truck was not "debt collection" within the FDCPA.

Illinois

Purkett v. Key Bank USA, N.A., 45 U.C.C. Rep. Serv. 2d 1201 (N.D. Ill. May 9, 2001). Repossessor could be a debt collector if it regularly demanded fees owed to the bank as a condition of returning the vehicle.

Kansas

McDaniel v. South & Assocs., P.C., 325 F. Supp. 2d 1210 (D. Kan. 2004). Collector violated FDCPA by initiating judicial foreclosure action seeking a money judgment as well as foreclosure after receiving a timely validation request but before responding to it. The court distinguished cases holding that non-judicial foreclosure was not debt collection.

Massachusetts

Pettway v. Harmon Law Offices, P.C., 2005 WL 2365331 (D. Mass. Sept. 27, 2005). "Harmon acted as a debt collector when it solicited borrowers to pay off the underlying mortgages." The fact that it was also pursuing a foreclosure did not insulate it from FDCPA liability.

Michigan

Alexander v. Blackhawk Recovery & Investigation, L.L.C., 731 F. Supp. 2d 674 (E.D. Mich. Aug. 16, 2010). A repossession agency falls outside the ambit of the FDCPA, except for purposes of § 1692f(6).

Burks v. Washington Mut. Bank, 2008 WL 4966656 (E.D. Mich. Nov. 17, 2008). Where the consumer's home had been sold at a sheriff's sale which fully paid off the mortgage, a "debt" no longer existed, and summary judgment was awarded to the debt collector on the FDCPA claims.

Minnesota

Oehrlein v. Western Funding, Inc., 1999 U.S. Dist. LEXIS 17919 (D. Minn. Jan. 26, 1999). Repossessor was only liable under the FDCPA for violating § 1692f(6).

Missouri

Vogler v. Grier Group Mgmt. Co., 309 S.W.3d 328 (Mo. Ct. App. 2010). The collection of condominium association fees did not make a property manager a debt collector because association fees are generally not in default when collected.

New Jersey

Hodges v. Sasil Corp., 915 A.2d 1 (N.J. 2007). Eviction attorneys were debt collectors as an eviction action was an indirect method of collecting rent "summary dispossess litigation is an effective-and at times coercive-mechanism for collecting rent and other fees."

Ohio

Glazer v. Chase Home Fin. L.L.C., 2010 WL 1392156 (N.D. Ohio Jan. 21, 2010). While lawyers in their function as debt collectors are covered by the FDCPA, enforcement of a purported security interest on behalf of a client was not debt collection under the FDCPA (citing non-judicial foreclosure cases).

Colton v. Ford Motor Credit, No. 9190083 (Ohio Ct. App. 1986). Only § 1692f(6) applies to repossession companies.

Oregon

Gonzalez v. Northwest Tr. Servs., Inc., 2005 WL 2297097 (D. Or. Sept. 20, 2005). On an unopposed motion for summary judgment against a *pro se* plaintiff, the court followed the *Hulse* line of cases and held that the defendant who only pursued foreclosure, without seeking payment of money, was not a "debt collector."

Reed v. Am. Honda Fin. Corp., 2005 WL 1175082 (D. Or. Apr. 22, 2005), *superseded*, 2005 WL 1398214 (D. Or. June 10, 2005). The defendant repossession company was subject only to § 1692f(6) of the FDCPA.

Pennsylvania

Kondratick v. Beneficial Consumer Discount Co., 2006 WL 305399 (E.D. Pa. Feb. 8, 2006). Summary judgment was denied in a case including FDCPA claims where determination of whether Beneficial's failure to stop its foreclosure when it entered into an ambiguous mortgage reinstatement agreement with a state homeowner assistance program, was a breach of the reinstatement agreement raised questions for the trier of fact.

South Carolina

Scott v. TitleMax of Columbia, 2010 WL 2867336 (D.S.C. July 19, 2010). The court declined to dismiss the *pro se* complaint related to a delivery action for repossession and the sale of the consumer's automobile, since the question of whether the defendant met the FDCPA definition of "debt collector" involved a factual inquiry that was not well-suited for resolution through a motion to dismiss for pleading deficiency.

Meredith v. Pathfinders Detective & Recovery, Inc., 1983 U.S. Dist. LEXIS 11860 (D.S.C. Nov. 9, 1983). A firm which engages in recovery of goods for lien holders 95% of the time is covered by the third sentence of § 1692a(6).

Tennessee

Johnson v. Americredit Fin. Servs., Inc., 69 U.C.C. Rep. Serv. 861 (M.D. Tenn. 2009). "[T]he only evidence before the Court is that United Auto is a towing company that was acting in its role as a repossession company when it allegedly had dealings with Plaintiff. However, the Sixth Circuit has made clear that a repossession agency does not fall within the definition of a 'debt collector' for purposes of the FDCPA. *Montgomery,* 346 F.3d at 699–701. Thus, summary judgment will be granted to United Auto dismissing the FDCPA claim." The court and the plaintiff both missed the point that since the claim against this towing/repo agency was for a breach of the peace in its attempted repossession, the 6th Circuit's *Montgomery* case actually supports a § 1692f(6) claim, since *Montgomery* holds only that a repo agency was not subject to the FDCPA except for § 1692f(6).

Texas

Thomas v. Ernest Barrientos, P.C., 2006 WL 1096764 (N.D. Tex. Apr. 26, 2006). Defendant was not subject to the FDCPA because, by demanding return of rental furniture, defendant was not attempting to collect money. Furniture rental did not create a security interest under state law, so defendant was not a debt collector because he was not attempting to enforce a security interest.

Virginia

Harris v. Americredit Fin. Servs., Inc., 2005 WL 2180477 (W.D. Va. Sept. 9, 2005). Repossession agencies are subject only to § 1692f(6).

Washington

Barbanti v. Quality Loan Serv. Corp., 2007 U.S. Dist. LEXIS 676 (E.D. Wash. Jan. 3, 2007). Where Ocwen was foreclosing on a deed of trust, the court ruled that the enforcement of a security interest through a non-judicial forfeiture does not constitute the collection of a debt for purposes of the FDCPA.

Fong v. Prof'l Foreclosure Corp., 2005 WL 3134059 (W.D. Wash. Nov. 22, 2005). Foreclosing deed of trust trustee was not a debt collector as defined by the FDCPA as it was enforcing a security interest and not collecting money.

Miller v. Northwest Tr. Servs., Inc., 2005 WL 1711131 (E.D. Wash. July 20, 2005). Mortgage companies and their trustees that engaged in foreclosure are not "debt collectors" under § 1692a(6) because they are not seeking the payment of money.

K.1.2.2.3 Foreclosure companies

Wilson v. Draper & Goldberg, P.L.L.C., 443 F.3d 373 (4th Cir. 2006). Law firm bringing deed of trust foreclosure was a debt collector. The foreclosure was brought based on failure to make mortgage payments entitling Chase to immediate payment of the balance of her loan, as well as fees, penalties, and interest due. The court ruled: "These amounts are all 'debts' under the Act, because

they were 'obligation[s] . . . to pay money arising out of a transaction in which the . . . property . . . which [is] the subject of the transaction [is] primarily for personal, family, or household purposes.'" Actions surrounding the foreclosure were attempts to collect money. "Defendants' argument [that foreclosure was not within FDCPA], if accepted, would create an enormous loophole in the Act immunizing any debt from coverage if that debt happened to be secured by a real property interest and foreclosure proceedings were used to collect the debt." By sending a letter seeking payment of an amount to "reinstate the above account," defendants sought to collect an "obligation or alleged obligation of a consumer to pay money arising out of a transaction in which the money, property, insurance, or services which are the subject of the transaction are primarily for personal, family, or household purposes." Defendants were not within the fiduciary exception, since "actions to foreclose on a property pursuant to a deed of trust are not 'incidental' to its fiduciary obligation. Rather, they are central to it." Section 1692f(6) applies to those whose only role in the debt collection process is the enforcement of a security interest. The subsection is not an exception to the definition of debt collector, it is an inclusion to the term debt collector.

Kaltenbach v. Richards, 464 F.3d 524 (7th Cir. 2006). A person whose principal business is the enforcement of security interests is subject only to § 1692f(6), but a person who satisfies § 1692a(6)'s general definition of a "debt collector" is a debt collector for the purposes of the entire FDCPA even when enforcing security interests.

Piper v. Portnoff Law Assocs., Ltd., 396 F.3d 227 (3d Cir. 2005). FDCPA applied to collection of municipal water bill by collection attorneys who also pursued the municipal liens. The court noted that water service was voluntary and involved a *pro tanto* exchange of water for money. The court rejected the argument that there was an *in rem* exemption in the FDCPA.

Thomson v. Professional Foreclosure Corp., 2004 WL 162591 (9th Cir. Jan. 26, 2004). Appeals court summarily affirmed the district court's dismissal on the basis that the defendants were subject only to § 1692f(6) as enforcers of security interests.

Alabama

Ausar-El v. BAC (Bank of Am.) Home Loan Serv., L.P., 2010 WL 5301033 (M.D. Ala. Nov. 22, 2010). The court dismissed the *pro se* plaintiff's complaint; foreclosure is not debt collection in the Eleventh Circuit.

Arizona

Antlocer v. Bayview Loan Serv., 2010 WL 5297216 (D. Ariz. Dec. 20, 2010). Since a nonjudicial foreclosure proceeding is not the collection of a debt within the FDCPA, the court dismissed the *pro se* plaintiff's complaint.

Narramore v. HSBC Bank USA, N.A., 2010 WL 2732815 (D. Ariz. July 7, 2010). Mortgagees, servicing companies, and trustee fiduciaries are not included in the definition of debt collector.

Earl v. Wachovia Mortgage F.S.B., 2010 WL 2336191 (D. Ariz. June 10, 2010). The *pro se* complaint was dismissed because "a foreclosure trustee is not a debt collector and a non-judicial foreclosure proceeding is not an attempt to collect a debt."

Diessner v. Mortgage Elec. Registration Sys., 618 F. Supp. 2d 1184 (D. Ariz. 2009), *aff'd*, 384 Fed. Appx. 609 (9th Cir. 2010). Non-judicial foreclosure involving property secured by a mortgage is not debt collection.

Mansour v. Cal-Western Reconveyance Corp., 618 F. Supp. 2d 1178 (D. Ariz. 2009). A non-judicial foreclosure proceeding was not the collection of a debt for the purposes of the FDCPA.

Castro v. Executive Trustee Servs., L.L.C., 2009 WL 438683 (D. Ariz. Feb. 23, 2009). Defendants' Rule 12(b)(6) motion to dismiss FDCPA claims was granted with prejudice holding that foreclosure on a deed of trust without seeking recovery of monies was not debt collection covered by the FDCPA.

California

Saldate v. Wilshire Credit Corp., 711 F. Supp. 2d 1126 (E.D. Cal. 2010). "[F]oreclosing on a property pursuant to a deed of trust is not a debt collection within the meaning of the [FDCPA]."

Hedman v. Aurora Loan Servs., 2010 WL 5394007 (E.D. Cal. Dec. 22, 2010). The complaint was dismissed with leave to amend to present sufficient allegations that the defendants, the plaintiffs' mortgage company and its servicer, were FDCPA debt collectors and that they were engaging in debt collection activity rather than simply in foreclosure proceedings.

Anokhin v. BAC Home Loans Serv., L.L.P., 2010 WL 5393972 (E.D. Cal. Dec. 22, 2010). A mortgage servicer is not considered a "debt collector," and foreclosure proceedings are not considered debt collections under the FDCPA.

Tang v. California Reconveyance Co., 2010 WL 5387837 (N.D. Cal. Dec. 22, 2010). To the extent that their FDCPA claims were based on the initiation of a foreclosure proceeding, the *pro se* plaintiffs failed to state a claim, because foreclosing on the property pursuant to a deed of trust is not the collection of a debt within the meaning of the FDCPA.

Reed v. Wells Fargo Home Mortgage Inc., 2010 WL 5136196 (E.D. Cal. Dec. 10, 2010). The court dismissed the *pro se* plaintiff's FDCPA claim since foreclosing on property pursuant to a deed of trust is not the collection of a debt under the Act.

Usher v. Greenpoint Mortgage Funding, Inc., 2010 WL 4983468 (E.D. Cal. Dec. 2, 2010). The FDCPA does not apply to non-judicial foreclosure, as long as the debt was not in default at the time it was assigned.

Geist v. OneWest Bank, 2010 WL 4117504 (N.D. Cal. Oct. 19, 2010). Non-judicial foreclosure was not debt collection.

Hedman v. Aurora Loan Servs., 2010 WL 3784170 (E.D. Cal. Sept. 27, 2010). The complaint failed to state a claim because creditors, mortgage servicing companies, or assignees of a debt are not considered debt collectors as long as the debt was not in default at the time it was assigned, and foreclosure activity is outside the scope of the FDCPA.

Harvey G. Ottovich Revocable Living Trust Dated May 12, 2006 v. Washington Mut., Inc., 2010 WL 3769459 (N.D. Cal. Sept. 22, 2010). The complaint stated an FDCPA claim as it contained allegations that the defendants did not limit their activities to foreclosing on the subject home but also engaged in deceptive conduct in their collection of the underlying debt, namely obfuscating the truth with regard to the loan amounts and payments.

Cruz v. Mortgage Lenders Network, USA, 2010 WL 3745932 (S.D. Cal. Sept. 20, 2010). Mortgage servicing companies attempting to collect a debt in their own name and foreclosing on the property are not covered by the FDCPA, and therefore defendants were not debt collectors.

Green v. Alliance Title, 2010 WL 3505072 (E.D. Cal. Sept. 2, 2010). A mortgage lender or servicer is not a debt collector within the FDCPA.

Hoffman v. Indymac Bank F.S.B., 2010 WL 3463641 (N.D. Cal. Aug. 31, 2010). The court granted the *pro se* homeowner leave to amend to cure the complaint's insufficient and conclusory allegations that the defendant mortgagee was a debt collector.

Miller v. Wells Fargo Home Mortgage, 2010 WL 3431802 (E.D. Cal. Aug. 31, 2010). The court dismissed the *pro se* homeowner's complaint since "a debt collector for purposes of the Act does not include the consumer's creditors, a mortgage servicing company, or an assignee of a debt, as long as the debt was not in default at the time it was assigned . . . Moreover, foreclosing on the subject property pursuant to a deed of trust is not the collection of a debt within the meaning of the FDCPA."

Goodwin v. California Reconveyance Co., 2010 WL 3341831 (E.D. Cal. Aug. 23, 2010). The court dismissed the *pro se* plaintiff's complaint because in California a debt derived from the residential loan transaction does not exist after a non-judicial foreclosure, and therefore the FDCPA does not apply to California foreclosures.

Spurlock v. Carrington Mortgage Servs., Inc., 2010 WL 3069733 (S.D. Cal. Aug. 4, 2010). Foreclosing on a deed of trust is not within FDCPA.

Kozhayev v. America's Wholesale Lender, 2010 WL 3036001 (E.D. Cal. Aug. 2, 2010). Foreclosure pursuant to a deed of trust does not constitute debt collection.

Jelsing v. MIT Lending, 2010 WL 2731470 (S.D. Cal. July 9, 2010). A mortgage servicing company is not a debt collector within the meaning of the FDCPA.

Salazar v. Accredited Home Lenders, Inc., 2010 WL 2674405 (S.D. Cal. July 2, 2010). Complaint failed to state a claim against defendants who foreclosed on a mortgage but did not attempt to collect the debt.

Ultreras v. Recon Trust Co., 2010 WL 2305857 (C.D. Cal. June 7, 2010). "[F]oreclosing on a property under a deed of trust is not the collection of a debt within the meaning of the [FDCPA.]"

Odinma v. Aurora Loan Servs., 2010 WL 2232169 (N.D. Cal. June 3, 2010). Complaint dismissed for failure to state a claim because "foreclosure is not debt collection under the federal Fair Debt Collection Practices Act."

Carter v. Deutsche Bank Nat'l Trust Co., 2010 WL 1875718 (N.D. Cal. May 7, 2010). The court refused to dismiss the claim against a foreclosure trustee. Citing a split of authority on the issue, the court stated: "There is no controlling Ninth Circuit authority on this issue. However, some district courts in this Circuit, and courts in other circuits have held that a foreclosure trustee may be sued under the Act."

Gwin v. Pacific Coast Fin. Servs., 2010 WL 1691567 (S.D. Cal. Apr. 23, 2010). Initiating a non-judicial foreclosure that sought possession but no money did not constitute debt collection activity subject to the FDCPA.

Agbabiaka v. HSBC Bank USA Nat'l Ass'n, 2010 WL 1609974 (N.D. Cal. Apr. 20, 2010). The court dismissed the FDCPA claim since the only facts alleged showed that the defendant was engaged in foreclosure proceedings and not debt collection activities.

Saldate v. Wilshire Credit Corp., 2010 WL 582074 (E.D. Cal. Feb. 12, 2010). "[F]oreclosing on a property pursuant to a deed of trust is not a debt collection within the meaning of the [FDCPA]."

Rogers v. Cal State Mortgage Co. Inc., 2010 WL 144861 (E.D. Cal. Jan. 11, 2010). Consumers failed to state an FDCPA claim arising from the defendants' alleged foreclosure misconduct: "Foreclosing on a trust deed is distinct from the collection of the obligation to pay money."

Gaitan v. Mortgage Elec. Registration Sys., 2009 WL 3244729 (C.D. Cal. Oct. 5, 2009) (unpublished). Foreclosure pursuant to a deed of trust is not within FDCPA.

Crittenden v. HomeQ Servicing, 2009 WL 3162247 (E.D. Cal. Sept. 29, 2009). Foreclosure by deed of trust is not within FDCPA.

Rendon v. Countrywide Home Loans, Inc., 2009 WL 3126400 (E.D. Cal. Sept. 24, 2009). Foreclosing on a deed of trust is not within FDCPA.

Ung v. GMAC Mortgage, L.L.C., 2009 WL 2902434 (C.D. Cal. Sept. 4, 2009) (unpublished). FDCPA claims arising from the defendants' alleged unlawful home foreclosure were dismissed in the absence of allegations that the defendants were debt collectors.

Yulaeva v. Greenpoint Mortgage Funding, Inc., 2009 WL 2880393 (E.D. Cal. Sept. 3, 2009). The court denied the defendants' motion to dismiss based on the argument that the underlying foreclosure activities did not constitute debt collection within the FDCPA, since the consumer's claim was based on defendants' alleged improper "reporting of default to credit reporting agencies, an activity that might have some incidental connection to foreclosure, but that is also squarely connected to debt collection."

Fuentes v. Duetsche Bank, 2009 WL 1971610 (S.D. Cal. July 8, 2009). FDCPA claim dismissed on the pleadings since "the act of foreclosing on a residential loan [is] outside the definition of debt collection."

Duran v. Aurora Loan Servs., 2009 WL 230985 (E.D. Cal. Jan. 30, 2009). The FDCPA does not apply to foreclosure of a deed of trust.

Walker v. Equity 1 Lenders Group, 2009 WL 1364430 (S.D. Cal. May 14, 2009). FDCPA claim dismissed against the defendant mortgage servicer because the complaint did not allege that this defendant was a "debt collector" and failed to allege any debt collection activity on its part, having alleged instead only that it had participated in the non-debt collection activity of foreclosing on the plaintiff's property.

Connors v. Home Loan Corp., 2009 U.S. Dist. LEXIS 48638 (S.D. Cal. May 9, 2009). Motion to dismiss granted: "Although plaintiff makes the legal conclusion that defendants attempted to collect a debt from plaintiff, the facts alleged in the [Second Amended Complaint] unequivocally demonstrate that defendants were foreclosing on the property and were not collecting a debt within the meaning of . . . the FDCPA."

Figueroa v. Citibank, 2009 WL 1024678 (S.D. Cal. Apr. 15, 2009). A trustee pursuant to a deed of trust was not a debt collector under the FDCPA.

Salazar v. Trustee Corps, 2009 WL 690185 (S.D. Cal. Mar. 12, 2009). The defendant was not an FDCPA "debt collector" since it was only "acting as a substituted trustee under a deed of trust to sell the property by power of sale at foreclosure, and was not attempting to collect funds from the debtor plaintiff."

Gamboa v. Trustee Corps, 2009 WL 656285 (N.D. Cal. Mar. 12, 2009). "[F]oreclosing on a property pursuant to a deed of trust is not a debt collection within the meaning of the [FDCPA]."

Izenberg v. ETS Servs., L.L.C., 589 F. Supp. 2d 1193 (C.D. Cal. 2008). Complaint alleging that the defendant home mortgage company engaged in an unlawful foreclosure because it lacked a proper assignment of the mortgage failed to state a claim since the complaint did not aver that the mortgage company was a "debt collector" or that the company was attempting to collect a debt rather than merely engaging in foreclosure.

San Diego Home Solutions, Inc. v. Reconstrust Co., 2008 WL 5209972 (S.D. Cal. Dec. 10, 2008). Foreclosing on property pursuant to a deed of trust was not the collection of a debt within the FDCPA.

Ines v. Countrywide Home Loans, Inc., 2008 WL 2795875 (S.D. Cal. July 18, 2008). *Pro se* consumer's request in this FDCPA action for a TRO staying her home foreclosure denied where the court found insufficient likelihood of success on the merits because "[t]he activity of foreclosing on a property pursuant to a deed of trust is not the collection of a debt within the meaning of the FDCPA."

Colorado

Dillard-Crowe v. CitiBank, 2008 WL 4223271 (D. Colo. Sept. 10, 2008). Defendants' motion to dismiss was granted because the public trustee who conducted foreclosure sales was not a debt collector subject to the FDCPA.

Mayhew v. Cherry Creek Mortgage Co., 2010 WL 935674 (D. Colo. Mar. 10, 2010). Non-judicial foreclosure not subject to FDCPA.

Ray v. Int'l Bank, Inc., 2005 WL 2305017 (D. Colo. Sept. 21, 2005). Foreclosing attorney covered. "Although foreclosure proceedings do not seek or result in a money judgment, they are an attempt to collect on a debt through realization of the value of property which the debtor has pledged to secure the loan. Through foreclosure, the debt can be partially or fully satisfied."

Shapiro & Meinhold v. Zartman, 823 P.2d 120 (Colo. 1992), *aff'g Zartman v. Shapiro & Meinhold*, 811 P.2d 409 (Colo. App. 1990). Attorneys whose collection activities are primarily limited to foreclosures are "debt collectors" if they otherwise fit the definition of § 1692a(6). "Debt collectors include attorneys whose practices are limited to purely legal activities so long as they otherwise meet the definition contained in section 1692a(6)."

District of Columbia

Muldrow v. EMC Mortgage Corp., 657 F. Supp. 2d 171 (D.D.C. 2009). Law firm acting as substitute trustee in judicial foreclosure proceeding is a debt collector where it offered to accept payment arrangements.

Florida

Fuller v. Becker & Poliakoff, P.A., 192 F. Supp. 2d 1361 (M.D. Fla. 2002). Attorney and his firm that regularly did collection and foreclosure work were debt collectors as defined by the FDCPA.

Georgia

Smith v. IndyMac Fed. Bank, F.S.B., 2010 WL 5490728 (N.D. Ga. Sept. 28, 2010). The court dismissed the *pro se* plaintiff's claim, since foreclosure on a security interest is considered "debt collection" activity under the FDCPA only for the purposes of § 1692f(6). Thus, an enforcer of a security interest may be held liable under the FDCPA for its unlawful activities in enforcing security interests if such enforcement is the principal purpose of its business, but in this case, the plaintiff did not allege that MERS was a debt collector, nor did she allege that the principal purpose of its business is the enforcement of security interests.

Illinois

Watkins v. Associated Brokers, Inc., 1998 WL 312124 (N.D. Ill. June 5, 1998). Attorney filing home foreclosure suit to obtain possession of the premises and not the payment of a debt "was obviously outside of the statute."

Blum v. Fisher & Fisher, 961 F. Supp. 1218 (N.D. Ill. 1997). Claim that collection attorney's letter concerning mortgage foreclosure, which stated that the consumer owed attorney fees when none would be due until a foreclosure judgment was obtained, presented questions of fact precluding grant of summary judgment on alleged FDCPA violations of misrepresentation and unfairness.

Galuska v. Blumenthal, 1994 WL 323121 (N.D. Ill. June 26, 1994). Attorney who brought an eviction action against the consumer on behalf of a creditor who had previously foreclosed and obtained legal title to the property, in a settlement agreement was not engaged in collecting a debt covered by the FDCPA. Debt collector's motion for summary judgment was granted and the *pro se* plaintiff was sanctioned $500 under Fed. R. Civ. P. 11(b) after the court concluded the plaintiff's FDCPA claim was not advanced in good faith after being warned by the court.

Indiana

Rosado v. Taylor, 324 F. Supp. 2d 917 (N.D. Ind. 2004). The FDCPA does not apply to a foreclosure action even if the foreclosure attorney seeks attorney fees, but it does apply to a §§ 1692e(11) and 1692g notice sent by the foreclosing attorney.

Kansas

McDaniel v. South & Assocs., P.C., 325 F. Supp. 2d 1210 (D. Kan. 2004). Collector violated FDCPA by initiating judicial foreclosure action seeking a money judgment as well as foreclosure after receiving a timely validation request but before responding to it.

The court distinguished cases holding that non-judicial foreclosure was not debt collection.

Maryland

In re Pultz, 400 B.R. 185 (Bankr. D. Md. 2008). Mortgage servicer was not covered by the FDCPA.

Massachusetts

Pettway v. Harmon Law Offices, P.C., 2005 WL 2365331 (D. Mass. Sept. 27, 2005). "Harmon acted as a debt collector when it solicited borrowers to pay off the underlying mortgages." The fact that it was also pursuing a foreclosure did not insulate it from FDCPA liability.

Michigan

Kevelighan v. Trott & Trott, P.C., 2011 WL 164539 (E.D. Mich. Jan. 18, 2011). Mortgage foreclosure unaccompanied by a demand for payment constitutes enforcement of a security interest that falls outside of the FDCPA, except for § 1692f(6) which was not alleged. The defendant who was engaged solely in mortgage foreclosure was not a debt collector subject to the entirety of the FDCPA when its only debt collection activity was to respond to the consumer's request for information concerning reinstatement: "Responding to a borrower's request for information concerning reinstatement of a loan does not constitute 'debt collection' under the FDCPA."

Claxton v. Orlans Assocs., P.C., 2010 WL 3385530 (E.D. Mich. Aug. 26, 2010). The court dismissed the *pro se* plaintiffs' complaint, since the defendant law firm "who merely represented its client in conducting a mortgage foreclosure by advertisement and did not send Plaintiffs a demand letter" was not a debt collector under the Act.

Gathing v. Mortgage Elec. Registration Sys., Inc., 2010 WL 889945 (W.D. Mich. Mar. 10, 2010). A person enforcing a security interest through non-judicial action cannot be subject to liability under FDCPA unless that person violates § 1692f(6). Here, no liability because mortgage was properly foreclosed.

Mabry v. Ameriquest Mortgage Co., 2010 WL 1052353 (E.D. Mich. Feb. 24, 2010), *report and recommendation adopted*, 2010 WL 1052355 (E.D. Mich. Mar. 19, 2010). Complaint dismissed for failure to state a claim since the defendant was only enforcing a mortgage, was therefore subject solely to § 1692f(6), and, in the absence of any allegation that it was "serv[ing] a dual role as a 'debt collector,'" had no duty to provide § 1692g verification as the complaint alleged.

Pistole v. Mortgage Elec. Registration Sys., Inc., 2008 WL 2566366 (E.D. Mich. June 24, 2008). Mortgagee collecting its own debt was not an FDCPA debt collector.

Herman v. Citimortgage, Inc., 2008 WL 927779 (E.D. Mich. Apr. 4, 2008). *Pro se* consumer's FDCPA claim was dismissed as the consumer's complaint failed to allege that the defendant mortgage company was a debt collector.

Morris v. HomEq Serv. Corp., 2010 WL 537745 (Mich. Ct. App. Feb. 16, 2010). The defendant mortgage servicer was not a "debt collector" since the borrower was not in default when the servicer acquired the loan. "[T]he enforcement of a security interest through a non-judicial foreclosure is not the collection of a debt for purposes of the FDCPA."

Minnesota

Gray v. Four Oak Court Ass'n, Inc., 580 F. Supp. 2d 883 (D. Minn. 2008). The court dismissed the consumer's claims alleging various FDCPA violations, including misrepresenting the amount due and adding unlawful attorney fees, because the collection occurred during a home foreclosure and the court concluded that there was no general FDCPA coverage because "the enforcement of a security interest, including a lien foreclosure, does not constitute the 'collection of any debt.'" The court ignored the defendants' demanding payment of the money due.

Chomilo v. Shapiro, Nordmeyer & Zielke, L.L.P., 2007 WL 2695795 (D. Minn. Sept. 12, 2007). The law firm that was retained to institute non-judicial foreclosure on the consumer's property was not a debt collector subject to the entirety of the FDCPA but was instead an enforcer of a security interest subject only to § 1692f(6).

Mississippi

Frascogna v. Wells Fargo Bank, 2009 WL 2843284 (S.D. Miss. Aug. 31, 2009). Summary judgment granted to the defendant foreclosure attorneys since "where a law firm is hired to conduct a non-judicial foreclosure to enforce a security interest in the property, not to collect any deficiency, the firm's efforts do not constitute debt collection under the FDCPA," and the attorneys thus were not FDCPA-covered debt collectors.

Lumzy v. Mortgage Elec. Registration Sys., Inc., 2008 WL 3992671 (S.D. Miss. Aug. 21, 2008). The court granted the defendant's motion for judgment on the pleadings finding that the complaint did not support an FDCPA claim.

Nebraska

Siegel v. Deutsche Bank Nat'l Trust Co., 2009 WL 3254491 (D. Neb. Oct. 8, 2009). Because foreclosing on a home is not debt collection and defendants were not the debt collectors, the FDCPA complaint was dismissed.

Nevada

Tatro v. Homecomings Fin. Network, Inc., 2011 WL 240255 (D. Nev. Jan. 20, 2011). Nonjudicial foreclosure does not constitute "debt collection" under the FDCPA.

Megino v. Linear Fin., 2011 WL 53086 (D. Nev. Jan. 6, 2011). The court dismissed the *pro se* consumers' complaint "since Defendants are not debt collectors and a nonjudicial foreclosure proceeding is not an action to collect a debt."

Contreras v. Master Fin. Inc., 2011 WL 32513 (D. Nev. Jan. 4, 2011). Nonjudicial foreclosure does not constitute an attempt to collect a debt under the FDCPA.

Rinehold v. Indymac Bank, F.S.B., 2011 WL 13856 (D. Nev. Jan. 4, 2011). Nonjudicial foreclosure does not constitute an attempt to collect a debt under the FDCPA.

Kenneweg v. Indymac Bank, 2011 WL 13853 (D. Nev. Jan. 4, 2011). "[N]on judicial foreclosures are not an attempt to collect a debt under the Fair Debt Collection Practice Act."

Regas v. Freemont Inv. & Loan, 2010 WL 5178029 (D. Nev. Dec. 14, 2010). Nonjudicial foreclosure does not constitute an attempt to collect a debt under the FDCPA and similar state statutes.

Contreras v. Master Fin., Inc., 2010 WL 4608300 (D. Nev. Nov. 4, 2010). "It is well established that non-judicial foreclosures are not an attempt to collect a debt under the Fair Debt Collection Practice Act. . . ."

Long v. Bank of Am. Home Loans Serv., L.P., 2010 WL 3154578 (D. Nev. Aug. 6, 2010). A participant in non-judicial foreclosure is not a "debt collector."

Charov v. Perry, 2010 WL 2673662 (D. Nev. June 30, 2010). The court dismissed the *pro se* plaintiff's complaint since recordation of a notice of default cannot violate the FDCPA: consent to make such a recordation upon default is necessarily given to a trustee in a deed of trust where state law requires such recordation as part of a non-judicial foreclosure.

Bukhari v. Direct Mortgage Corp., 2010 WL 2521750 (D. Nev. June 16, 2010). The *pro se* complaint was dismissed where the defendant mortgage company was a creditor and not a debt collector.

New York

Dolan v. Fairbanks Capital Corp., 2008 WL 4515932 (E.D.N.Y. Sept. 30, 2008). *Pro se* allegation that mortgage servicer acquired loan after default brought servicer within the FDCPA. Plaintiff alleged that his loan defaulted, that he entered into a forbearance agreement with the creditor to prevent foreclosure on his home, and that on November 22, 2000, the servicing of his loan was assigned to defendant. The court rejected defendant's contention that it was not a debt collector because it was unaware of the default status of a loan that it began servicing in November 2000 simply because it "was not a party" to the August 11, 2000 forbearance agreement between the creditor and plaintiff.

North Dakota

Bray v. Bank of Am., 2011 WL 30307 (D.N.D. Jan. 5, 2011). In this case brought by a *pro se* plaintiff, the court found that MERS was not subject to FDCPA as a matter of law. The enforcement of a security interest, including a lien foreclosure, is not debt collection.

Oregon

Stewart v. Mortgage Elec. Registration Sys., Inc., 2010 WL 1054384 (D. Or. Feb. 18, 2010), *report and recommendation adopted,* 2010 WL 1054697 (D. Or. Mar. 19, 2010). *Pro se* mortgagor's FDCPA claims were dismissed because the defendants were exempt creditors and because "foreclosing on property pursuant to a deed of trust is not the collection of a debt within the meaning of the FDCPA."

Caliguri v. Wells Fargo Bank, N.A., 2008 WL 219613 (D. Or. Jan. 24, 2008). A non-judicial foreclosure sale and purchase was not subject to the FDCPA, and there was no support for the *pro se* former homeowner's claims of fraud.

Gonzalez v. Northwest Tr. Servs., Inc., 2005 WL 2297097 (D. Or. Sept. 20, 2005). On an unopposed motion for summary judgment against a *pro se* plaintiff, the court followed the *Hulse* line of cases and held that the defendant who only pursued foreclosure, without seeking payment of money, was not a "debt collector."

Hulse v. Ocwen Fed. Bank, F.S.B., 195 F. Supp. 2d 1188 (D. Or. 2002). Foreclosing on a trust deed was not the collection of a debt because it was not attempt to force debtors to pay money owed.

Pennsylvania

Duraney v. Washington Mut. Bank, 2008 WL 4204821 (W.D. Pa. Sept. 11, 2008), *aff'd*, 2010 WL 2993810 (3d Cir. Aug. 2, 2010). The court dismissed the § 1692d claim arising from the filing of the underlying state court foreclosure action, following the Sixth Circuit in *Harvey* and adopting its reasoning that "employing the court system in the way alleged by the plaintiff cannot be said to be an abusive tactic under the FDCPA."

Kondratick v. Beneficial Consumer Discount Co., 2006 WL 305399 (E.D. Pa. Feb. 8, 2006). Summary judgment was denied in a case including FDCPA claims where determination of whether Beneficial's failure to stop its foreclosure when it entered into an ambiguous mortgage reinstatement agreement with a state homeowner assistance program, was a breach of the reinstatement agreement raised questions for the trier of fact.

South Carolina

Sain v. HSBC Mortgage Servs., Inc., 2010 WL 2902741 (D.S.C. June 10, 2010). The court dismissed the *pro se* complaint since the defendant, who was foreclosing on a mortgage but did not seek a personal judgment against the consumers, was not a debt collector obligated to comply with § 1692g.

Tennessee

Hunter v. Washington Mut. Bank, 2010 WL 2507038 (E.D. Tenn. June 16, 2010). The court denied summary judgment where there were disputed issues of fact concerning whether the defendant law firm, which attempted to collect money owing on the underlying debt while conducting a non-judicial foreclosure, was a debt collector under the Act.

Stamper v. Wilson & Assocs., P.L.L.C., 2010 WL 1408585 (E.D. Tenn. Mar. 31, 2010). A law firm enforcing a security interest through non-judicial foreclosure proceedings does not qualify as a "debt collector" under the FDCPA.

Johnson v. Wilshire Credit Corp., 2009 WL 559950 (E.D. Tenn. Mar. 5, 2009). Although "an entity whose business has the principal purpose of enforcing security interests, without more, is not subject to any of the provisions of the FDCPA except for § 1692f," the defendant substitute-trustees' motion for summary judgment as to their violation of other provisions of the FDCPA was denied, since they failed to establish that they did not also otherwise act as debt collectors while pursuing the underlying home foreclosure.

In re Greer, 2010 WL 4817993 (Bankr. M.D. Tenn. Nov. 22, 2010). The court entered summary judgment for the defendant, a foreclosure substitute trustee who was "not a debt collector under the FDCPA as it clearly was acting to enforce a security interest,"

notwithstanding the conflicting evidence resulting from the "inclusion of the 'boilerplate' FDCPA language" comprised of §§ 1692e(11) and 1692g(a) disclosures in a letter sent to the consumer. The court deemed the inclusion of this language of no consequence since it "was merely precautionary."

White v. Myers, 2001 Tenn. App. LEXIS 814 (Tenn. Ct. App. Oct. 31, 2001). Trial court did not abuse its discretion in imposing Rule 11 sanctions against consumer's attorney for bringing a frivolous FDCPA case against opposing counsel in a prior mortgage foreclosure dispute where the defendant did not engage in debt collection at all and the consumer's attorney failed to investigate the law or facts prior to filing suit.

Texas

Bittinger v. Wells Fargo Bank N.A., 2010 WL 3984626 (S.D. Tex. Oct. 8, 2010). Non-judicial foreclosure is not subject to FDCPA.

Bergs v. Hoover, Bax & Slovacek, L.L.P., 2003 WL 22255679 (N.D. Tex. Sept. 24, 2003). Initiation of foreclosure was not debt collection under the FDCPA, § 1692f(6), when the debt collector sought not payment of the debt but enforcement of the security interest.

Utah

Maynard v. Cannon, 650 F. Supp. 2d 1138 (D. Utah 2008). non-judicial foreclosure of a deed of trust pursuant to Utah law is not subject to the FDCPA.

Virginia

Ruggia v. Washington Mut., 2010 WL 1957218 (E.D. Va. May 13, 2010). An enforcer of a security interest, such as a mortgage company foreclosing on mortgages of real property, falls outside the ambit of the FDCPA.

Areebuddin v. OneWest Bank, F.S.B., 2010 WL 1229233 (E.D. Va. Mar. 24, 2010). Mortgagee and servicer are not debt collectors under the FDCPA.

Carter v. Countrywide Home Loans, Inc., 2009 WL 2742560 (E.D. Va. Aug. 25, 2009). Although Countrywide asserted that only 0.21% of its total business is dedicated to the acquisition and servicing of the loans in default at the time of acquisition, the total dollar value associated with that portion of the business was more than $2 billion and constituted a regular debt collection practice qualifying it as a "debt collector" pursuant to the FDCPA.

Washington

Roman v. Northwest Tr. Servs., Inc., 2010 WL 5146593 (W.D. Wash. Dec. 13, 2010). The court dismissed the *pro se* plaintiffs' claims with prejudice since foreclosing on a trust deed is distinct from the collection of the obligation to pay money and is not covered by the FDCPA.

Barbanti v. Quality Loan Serv. Corp., 2007 U.S. Dist. LEXIS 676 (E.D. Wash. Jan. 3, 2007). Where Ocwen was foreclosing on a deed of trust, the court ruled that the enforcement of a security interest through a non-judicial forfeiture does not constitute the collection of a debt for purposes of the FDCPA.

Fong v. Prof'l Foreclosure Corp., 2005 WL 3134059 (W.D. Wash. Nov. 22, 2005). Foreclosing deed of trust trustee was not a debt collector as defined by the FDCPA as it was enforcing a security interest and not collecting money.

Miller v. Northwest Tr. Servs., Inc., 2005 WL 1711131 (E.D. Wash. July 20, 2005). Mortgage companies and their trustees that engaged in foreclosure are not "debt collectors" under § 1692a(6) because they are not seeking the payment of money.

Wisconsin

Schwoegler v. Am. Family Fin. Servs., 2006 WL 6021148 (W.D. Wis. May 16, 2006). Dismissed FDCPA complaint alleging wrongdoing in state foreclosure action based on *Rooker-Feldman*.

K.1.2.2.4 Printing and mailing services

Illinois

Laubach v. Arrow Serv. Bureau, Inc., 987 F. Supp. 625 (N.D. Ill. 1997). A company that engaged purely in printing and mailing services for debt collection agencies and other businesses and did not collect money from debtors was not a debt collector covered by the FDCPA.

Trull v. Lason Sys., Inc., 982 F. Supp. 600 (N.D. Ill. 1997). A printing and mailing service was not a debt collector. The service did not write, edit (beyond proofreading) or approve dunning communications, or advise the collection agency about their content or use. Furthermore, its Priority-Gram form was not a product used exclusively by debt collectors, nor was it linked in any way to the substantive content of collection letters.

K.1.2.2.5 Check guaranty companies

Arizona

Charles v. Check Rite, Ltd., 1998 U.S. Dist. LEXIS 22512 (D. Ariz. Dec. 14, 1999). Covered.

California

Ballard v. Equifax Check Servs., 27 F. Supp. 2d 1201 (E.D. Cal. 1998). Check guarantee company is a "debt collector" as defined.

Holmes v. Telecredit Serv., 736 F. Supp. 1289 (D. Del. 1990). A check guarantee service is a debt collector covered by the FDCPA. It regularly collects on debts obtained from payees after default. It is not a creditor nor was its "authorization" of a check an origination of the debt.

Hawaii

Alexander v. Moore & Assocs., Inc., 553 F. Supp. 948 (D. Haw. 1982). A check guarantee service for landlords and a credit reporting agency for landlords and other creditors were found not to be debt collectors as defined by § 1692a(6). The check guarantee service did not collect on debts owed to another since it collected on the amount it had paid to the landlord. The credit reporting agency did not collect debts.

Illinois

Winterstein v. CrossCheck, Inc. 149 F. Supp. 2d 466 (N.D. Ill. 2001). The court rejected check guarantee service's arguments that it was not a debt collector. It was not a creditor because the check had been presented to the creditor and forwarded to the guarantee service after default. A purported agreement assigning the check before default exalted form over substance. It was not an originator because it did not participate in the creation of the debt. There was at least an issue of fact as to whether defendant regularly collected debts when it attempted to collect on more than two thousand checks and spent $2 million on debt collection efforts per year.

Nebraska

Page v. Checkrite, Ltd., Clearinghouse No. 45,759 (D. Neb. 1984). Check guarantee agencies and their franchisor are debt collectors as defined by § 1692a(6).

K.1.2.2.6 Debt buyers [See also K.1.2.3.8, Debts assigned before default]

Ruth v. Triumph P'ships, 577 F.3d 790 (7th Cir. 2009). Purchaser of a defaulted debt is a debt collector. Debt buyer's control over the drafting and mailing of the privacy notice by the debt collector plainly constituted affirmative conduct with regard to collecting a debt.

McKinney v. Cadleway Properties, Inc., 548 F.3d 496 (7th Cir. 2008). Debt buyer was a "debt collector" as defined since the debt was in default when the bad debt buyer obtained it.

Neff v. Capital Acquisitions & Mgmt. Co., 352 F.3d 1118 (7th Cir. Dec. 15, 2003). The sale of a paid debt, as if it was not paid by a purchaser of the debt when it was delinquent, was not an attempt to collect a debt and was not covered by the FDCPA.

Pollice v. Nat'l Tax Funding, L.P., 225 F.3d 379 (3d Cir. 2000). The purchaser of sewer and water service debts from a municipality, after default, was a debt collector for the purposes of the FDCPA.

Connecticut

Pacheco v. Joseph McMahon Corp., 698 F. Supp. 2d 291 (D. Conn. 2010). Defendant that acquired debt by assignment that was already in default was a debt collector under the Act. The fact that the defendant used the "alter ego" trade name "Paul Trustee" did not shield him from liability.

Georgia

Long v. G.C. Servs. Corp., Clearinghouse No. 31,345 (S.D. Ga. 1979). Collector's motion to dismiss was denied where collector argued it was not a "debt collector" within § 1692a(6) since it purchased the debt which it sought to collect.

Illinois

Herkert v. MRC Receivables Corp., 655 F. Supp. 2d 870 (N.D. Ill. 2009). Court rejected defendant's argument that it could not be considered a debt collector because it was not directly involved in the collection activities at issue. It held that defendant was a debt collector because its public filings described itself as a "leading consumer debt management company" and a "purchaser and manager of charged-off consumer receivables portfolios," and described what it called "our collection strategies," which included the use of "our own collection workforce."

Miller v. Midland Credit Mgmt., Inc., 621 F. Supp. 2d 621 (N.D. Ill. 2009). Defendant was an FDCPA "debt collector" liable for the § 1692e(5) violation since it was the holding company that purchased the subject bad debts and owned the subject accounts.

Hernandez v. Midland Credit Mgmt., Inc., 2006 WL 695451 (N.D. Ill. Mar. 14, 2006). Allegations showing that the defendant Encore at least "indirectly" engaged in the collection of a debt for a third party were adequate to state a claim that the defendant was a "debt collector" under the FDCPA. Encore is a debt buyer that owns Midland which was collecting the debt by sending out a notice for Encore.

Scally v. Hilco Receivables, L.L.C., 392 F. Supp. 2d 1036 (N.D. Ill. 2005). The defendant debt buyer after default was not indirectly attempting to collect debts where it did not attempt to contact the consumer itself nor was it vicariously liable for the contingent fee collection agency it employed to attempt to its collect debts as it did not direct or control the collection agency. However, the court did note that the debt buyer would qualify as a debt collector had it acted through retained counsel.

Neff v. Capital Acquisitions & Mgmt. Co., 238 F. Supp. 2d 986 (N.D. Ill. 2002). Although the consumer had paid the debt to the first collector, sale of a defaulted credit card account to a second collector was not debt collection in violation of the FDCPA.

Indiana

Dechert v. Cadle Co., 2003 WL 23008969 (S.D. Ind. Sept. 11, 2003). The court rejected the defendant's argument that it was not acting as a debt collector and that instead it was only sending "an introductory informational letter" that made no demand for payment following the purchase of the debt by the new assignee, since the letter itself stated that its purpose was to collect a debt.

Michigan

Asset Acceptance Corp. v. Robinson, 625 N.W.2d 804 (Mich. Ct. App. 2001). An entity that purchases a debt in default is a "debt collector" as defined by the FDCPA.

Minnesota

Munoz v. Pipestone Fin., L.L.C., 397 F. Supp. 2d 1129 (D. Minn. 2005). The purchaser of defaulted debt portfolios was a debt collector, notwithstanding that it itself did not communicate with the consumer in an attempt to collect debt and where instead the actual collection efforts were performed by another debt collector with whom it contracted.

Missouri

Wells v. Southwestern Bell Tel. Co., 626 F. Supp. 2d 1001 (W.D. Mo. 2009). Debt buyer was a debt collector and was not exempt. It could not escape by arguing the debt was not in default.

New York

Sykes v. Mel Harris & Assocs., L.L.C., 2010 WL 5395712 (S.D.N.Y. Dec. 29, 2010). Purchasers of debt in default are debt collectors within the coverage of the FDCPA.

Ohlson v. The Cadle Co., 2008 WL 4516233 (E.D.N.Y. Sept. 30, 2008). Court rejected the claim that employee of debt buyer came within the "employee of creditor" exemption of § 1692a(6)(A), pending determination of whether the debt was in default at the time of purchase and therefore debt buyer was not a creditor.

Pennsylvania

Moses v. The Law Office of Harrison Ross Byck, 2009 WL 2411085 (M.D. Pa. Aug. 4, 2009). An entity acquiring a debt in default is not a "creditor;" thus, L.L.C. fit within the definition of "debt collector" for the purpose of the FDCPA.

Connelly v. Bokser, 1991 U.S. Dist. LEXIS 21732 (E.D. Pa. Oct. 22, 1991). An individual who purchases debts from the city prior to default is a "creditor" under § 1692a(4) and (6).

Tennessee

Johnson v. Americredit Fin., Servs., Inc., 69 U.C.C. Rep. Serv. 2d 861 (M.D. Tenn. 2009). Where the consumer stopped payment on her down payment check because of alleged fraud by the car dealer and tried to cancel her car purchase with the seller shortly after the sale, and where the record was silent as to the precise time when the installment contract was assigned to its pre-arranged assignee, the assignee's motion for summary judgment because it purportedly was an exempt creditor was denied, since "a genuine issue of material fact exists as to whether the Plaintiff was in default when AmeriCredit was assigned the loan."

Johnson v. Wilshire Credit Corp., 2009 WL 559950 (E.D. Tenn. Mar. 5, 2009). The defendant mortgage holder and its servicer qualified as FDCPA debt collectors since the plaintiff alleged that they obtained the mortgage after default and then sought to collect payments.

Virginia

Carter v. Countrywide Home Loans, Inc., 2009 WL 2742560 (E.D. Va. Aug. 25, 2009). Although Countrywide asserted that only 0.21% of its total business is dedicated to the acquisition and servicing of the loans in default at the time of acquisition, the total dollar value associated with that portion of the business was more than \$2 billion and constituted a regular debt collection practice qualifying it as a "debt collector" pursuant to the FDCPA.

K.1.2.2.7 Debt collector's employees

Kistner v. Law Offices of Michael P. Margelefsky, L.L.C., 518 F.3d 433 (6th Cir. 2008). A collection lawyer was responsible under the FDCPA for collection letters sent under his supervision. There in no corporate immunity under the FDCPA for officers of a debt collection agency or law firm who are actively engaged in debt collection.

Pettit v. Retrieval Masters Creditors Bureau, Inc., 211 F.3d 1057 (7th Cir. 2000), *rehearing denied,* 2000 U.S. App. LEXIS 12848

(7th Cir. June 7, 2000). The court held that an owner or any other employee of a collection agency was not liable under the FDCPA except in instances the owner or employee was actively involved in the collection of the debt or where the corporate veil was pierced.

California

Carrizosa v. Stassinos, 2010 WL 4393900 (N.D. Cal. Oct. 29, 2010). An executive who participated in the collection activities can be held personally liable without piercing the corporate veil.

Weakley v. Redline Recovery Servs., L.L.C., 2010 WL 2787656 (S.D. Cal. July 13, 2010). Collection agency employees can be held personally liable under the FDCPA.

Smith v. Levine Leichtman Capital Partners, Inc., 2010 WL 2787549 (N.D. Cal. June 29, 2010). Rejecting the contrary ruling in Petit v. Retrieval Masters Creditor Bureau, Inc., 211 F.3d 1057 (7th Cir.2000), the court adopted the majority rule that a debt collector's "employees may be held liable under the FDCPA without piercing the corporate veil." The complaint stated a claim for FDCPA coverage by alleging that each defendant: "(1) materially participated in collecting the debt at issue; (2) exercised control over the affairs of the business; (3) were personally involved in the collection of the debt at issue; or (4) were regularly engaged, directly or indirectly, in the collection of debts."

del Campo v. Am. Corrective Counseling Serv., Inc., 2010 WL 2473586 (N.D. Cal. June 3, 2010). The court granted summary judgment establishing the FDCPA status and liability of the individual defendant corporate CEO (who was also the primary shareholder) and the CFO, since both were actively involved in the day-to-day operations of the company and thus qualified as debt collectors under the rule that "an individual can be considered a 'debt collector' and be held personally liable without piercing the corporate veil if the individual materially participated in the debt collection activities."

Cruz v. Int'l Collection Corp., 2008 WL 2263800 (N.D. Cal. June 2, 2008). Court refused to dismiss claim against officer of debt collector where complaint alleged that "he sets and approves [defendant's] collection policies, practices and procedures, including the activities alleged in the complaint" and "specifically alleges that each of the letters mailed to her was created or approved by" the officer.

Connecticut

Musso v. Seiders, 194 F.R.D. 43 (D. Conn. 1999). A senior employee, executive, or director of a collection agency may fall within the definition of "debt collector," and allegations that such an individual knew of and approved or ratified the unlawful activities stated a claim under the FDCPA against the defendant in his individual capacity.

Florida

Arlozynski v. Rubin & Debski, P.A., 2010 WL 1849081 (M.D. Fla. May 7, 2010). The court denied a motion to dismiss because individuals who control and direct the practices of a collection firm can be personally liable even if they act under the auspices of a corporate entity. In addition, they may be liable as persons who "directly or indirectly" collect or attempt to collect a debt.

Belin v. Litton Loan Serv., L.P., 2006 WL 1992410 (M.D. Fla. July 14, 2006). The employees of a debt collection agency who actually engaged in the allegedly unlawful misconduct and the collection agency itself are jointly and severally liable for the resulting FDCPA violations.

Dowling v. I.C. Sys., Inc., 2005 WL 2675010 (M.D. Fla. Oct. 20, 2005). Collection agency's motion to dismiss its alleged employees was denied as it lacked standing to move on their behalf. The collection agency asserted it had no employees as named by the consumer.

Illinois

Cole v. Noonan & Lieberman, Ltd., 2005 WL 2848446 (N.D. Ill. Oct. 26, 2005). Without considering the language of the FDCPA the court held collector's employees were not subject to FDCPA claims.

Beasley v. Collectors Training Inst., 1999 U.S. Dist. LEXIS 2575 (N.D. Ill. Feb. 25, 1999). Complaint sufficiently stated a claim against individual officers and employees of a corporation by alleging that the individual defendants collected debts on behalf of a third party. Plaintiff did not need to allege facts to pierce the corporate veil to reach the officers.

Massachusetts

Som v. Daniels Law Offices, P.C., 573 F. Supp. 2d 349 (D. Mass. 2008). Allegation that corporate officer "was personally involved in formulating, implementing, and/or ratifying the [language of the debt-collection letter] and the underlying debt collection practices of defendant law firm" held sufficient to defeat officer's motion to dismiss.

Minnesota

Thinesen v. JBC Legal Group, P.C., 2005 WL 2346991 (D. Minn. Sept. 26, 2005). Allegations that the defendant collection agency employees were the persons responsible for the agency's illegal collection efforts stated a claim for relief against those employees individually.

New York

Ohlson v. Cadle Co., 2006 WL 721505 (E.D.N.Y. Mar. 21, 2006). The court rejected the defendant's contention that only collection agencies, and not employees, are liable under the FDCPA, holding to the contrary "that officers and employees of the debt collecting agency may be jointly and severally liable with the agency where they have affirmatively acted."

Utah

Carvana v. MFG Fin., Inc., 2008 WL 2468539 (D. Utah June 17, 2008). The corporate form does not protect officers, directors, or shareholders from individual liability under the FDCPA; individuals who satisfy the statutory definition can be held personally liable under the FDCPA without piercing the corporate veil.

K.1.2.2.8 Check diversion collectors

California

Schwarm v. Craighead, 552 F. Supp. 2d 1056 (E.D. Cal. 2008). The check diversion amendment, § 1692p, did not apply retroactively to relieve the defendant that administered bad check diversion program from FDCPA liability against claims in class action by recipients of collections letters as it would potentially preclude such recipients from seeking relief under FDCPA.

Pennsylvania

Shouse v. National Corrective Group, Inc., 2010 WL 4942222 (M.D. Pa. Nov. 30, 2010). The court found that the consumer pleaded sufficient facts sufficient to state a claim for violations of the FDCPA and that 15 U.S.C. § 1692p, the explicit exception for district attorney-sanctioned pretrial diversion programs for alleged bad check offenders, did not apply to National Corrective Group.

Washington

Albers v. Nationstar Mortgage L.L.C., 2011 WL 43584 (E.D. Wash. Jan. 3, 2011). The court refused to "create a loophole in the FDCPA immunizing foreclosure proceedings used to collect debt secured by a real property interest." Based upon allegations that the defendant began servicing the plaintiffs' loan after it was allegedly in default, maintained the position that the loan was in default notwithstanding the plaintiffs' continued tender of loan payments, and repeatedly threatened foreclosure, the court found that the plaintiffs alleged sufficient facts to support their FDCPA claim.

K.1.2.3 Scope of Specific Exclusions

K.1.2.3.1 Creditor, 15 U.S.C. § 1692a(6)(A)

K.1.2.3.1.1 Creditor exempt

Madura v. Lakebridge Condo. Ass'n Inc., 2010 WL 2354140 (11th Cir. June 14, 2010). The court dismissed the *pro se* owners' claim because the condominium association collecting its own debt was an exempt creditor.

McCready v. Jacobsen, 2007 WL 1224616 (7th Cir. Apr. 25, 2007). Landlord sending current status of account.

McCready v. eBay, Inc., 453 F.3d 882 (7th Cir. 2006). Defendant was not a debt collector.

Thomas v. Law Firm of Simpson & Cybak, 392 F.3d 914 (7th Cir. 2004). GMAC and its employees.

Gutierrez v. AT&T Broadband, L.L.C., 382 F.3d 725 (7th Cir. 2004). Where South Chicago Cable, Inc., did business as "AT&T Cable" and as "AT&T Broadband" in the formation and collection of cable TV accounts, there was no FDCPA liability of either South Chicago Cable, its collection agency, or AT&T under §§ 1692j or 1692e as the consumer had no reason to believe a third party had entered the picture to collect the debt. A dissenting opinion believed that the consumer was not required under the FDCPA to

guess who was collecting the debt.

Montgomery v. Huntington Bank & Silver Shadow Recovery, Inc., 346 F.3d 693 (6th Cir. 2003). Originating lender.

Schlosser v. Fairbanks Capital Corp., 323 F.3d 534 (7th Cir. 2003). Creditors, who generally are entities that offer or extend credit and who Congress believed are restrained by the desire to protect their good will when collecting past-due accounts, are not covered by the FDCPA; the Act instead covers debt collectors, who may have no future contact with the consumer, and who Congress felt therefore are often unconcerned with the consumer's opinion of them.

Daros v. Chase Manhattan Bank, 2001 U.S. App. LEXIS 21471 (2d Cir. Oct. 1, 2001). Neither bank nor affiliated credit card company was a debt collector.

Sharwell v. Selva, 2001 U.S. App. LEXIS 2252 (6th Cir. Feb. 5, 2001). Movers and insurers in connection with the moving of furniture.

Ioane v. Stein, 162 F.3d 1168 (9th Cir. 1998) (table, text at 1998 WL 757077). Decision against *pro se* plaintiff who sued creditors and their attorneys affirmed. Motion for Rule 11 sanctions against plaintiff denied.

Lewis v. ACB Bus. Servs., Inc., 135 F.3d 389 (6th Cir. 1998). Amex never attempted to collect the debt under an assumed name and was not a debt collector.

Berkery v. Bally's Health & Tennis Corp., 116 F.3d 941 (D.C. Cir. 1997) (text at 1997 WL 358208). Claim that creditor was a debt collector was abandoned.

Benson v. Hafif, 114 F.3d 1193 (9th Cir. 1997) (text at 1997 WL 268337). Conclusory allegations unsupported by averments of fact that the creditor was a debt collector covered by the Act were insufficient.

Gowing v. Royal Bank, 100 F.3d 962 (9th Cir. 1996) (table, text at 1996 WL 616665). The bank was not a debt collector as it was an assignee before default of the original creditor. The bank's attorneys were not debt collectors as they were not regularly engaged in debt collection.

Kinnell v. Convenient Loan Co., 77 F.3d 492 (10th Cir. 1996) (text at 1996 WL 80368) (*pro se*). Loan company not a debt collector.

Wadlington v. Credit Acceptance Corp., 76 F.3d 103 (6th Cir. 1996). A car dealer's financer who serviced the dealer's retail installment sales accounts and appeared on the retail installment contracts as an assignee was exempt as either a creditor or a servicer who took the contract prior to default as provided by § 1692a(4) and (6)(A) or (F).

Houck v. Local Fed. Sav. & Loan, Inc., 996 F.2d 311 (10th Cir. 1993) (text at 1993 WL 191818). Bank was properly dismissed.

Munk v. Fed. Land Bank, 791 F.2d 130 (10th Cir. 1986). An agricultural lender is exempt.

Alabama

Farkas v. Suntrust Mortgage Inc., 2010 WL 5525359 (S.D. Ala. Dec. 15, 2010). The court dismissed the *pro se* plaintiffs' claim since mortgage servicing companies are not debt collectors.

McGrady v. Nissan Motor Acceptance Corp., 40 F. Supp. 2d 1323 (M.D. Ala. 1998). In a wrongful repossession case, court dismissed FDCPA claim against the creditor and found that the creditor did not hold out the repossession company as its agent under the apparent authority doctrine.

In re Lee, 2008 WL 2246917 (Bankr. N.D. Ala. May 29, 2008). Since one creditor was attempting to collect its own debt (and not that of another) and the other creditor took no action to collect the debt, neither defendant was a "debt collector" and subject to FDCPA.

Arizona

Breedlove v. Wells Fargo Bank, N.A., 2010 WL 3000012 (D. Ariz. July 28, 2010). Wells Fargo not a "debt collector."

Caron v. Charles E. Maxwell, P.C., 48 F. Supp. 2d 932 (D. Ariz. 1999). The homeowners' association was a creditor and was not vicariously liable for its collection attorney's FDCPA violation.

United States v. ACB Sales & Serv., Inc., 590 F. Supp. 561 (D. Ariz. 1984). The exclusion of creditors and attorneys from FDCPA coverage is based on a rational relationship to a legitimate government purpose and does not violate the equal protection provisions of the Fifth Amendment.

California

Watts v. Enhanced Recovery Corp., 2011 WL 175922 (N.D. Cal. Jan. 18, 2011). Plaintiff did not allege that the defendant was in the business of collecting debts or had used a name other than its own in collecting its own debts. Complaint did not state a claim.

Edstrom v. Ndex West, L.L.C., 2010 WL 4069482 (E.D. Cal. Oct. 18, 2010). Creditors and servicers exempt.

Quinones v. Chase Bank USA, N.A., 2010 WL 2630017 (S.D. Cal. June 28, 2010). Chase was not a debt collector because it was collecting its own debt.

Starks v. Aqua Fin., Inc., 2010 WL 963787 (C.D. Cal. Mar. 4, 2010). Company that financed a home improvement contract was a creditor.

Hilton v. Washington Mut. Bank, 2010 WL 727247 (N.D. Cal. Mar. 1, 2010). Defendants were exempt creditors.

Matudio v. Countrywide Home Loans, Inc., 2010 WL 114185 (C.D. Cal. Jan. 6, 2010). Defendant not a debt collector.

Garcia v. Wachovia Mortgage Corp., 676 F. Supp. 2d 895 (C.D. Cal. 2009). Foreclosing creditor not subject to FDCPA.

Moya v. Chase Cardmember Serv., 661 F. Supp. 2d 1129 (N.D. Cal. 2009). Credit card company collecting its own debt was not a covered FDCPA "debt collector."

Allen v. United Fin. Mortgage Corp., 660 F. Supp. 2d 1089 (N.D. Cal. 2009). FDCPA did not apply to foreclosing lender or servicer.

Copeland v. Lehman Bros. Bank, 2009 WL 5206435 (S.D. Cal. Dec. 23, 2009). The complaint, which failed to allege sufficient facts to show that defendants were "debt collectors" or engaged in the "collection of a debt" within the meaning of the FDCPA, was dismissed.

Reynoso v. Paul Fin., L.L.C., 2009 WL 3833298 (N.D. Cal. Nov. 16, 2009). The FDCPA's definition of debt collector does not include the consumer's creditors.

Carillo v. Citimortgage, Inc., 2009 WL 3233534 (C.D. Cal. Sept. 30, 2009). Lender is not within FDCPA.

Batiste v. American Gen. Fin., 2009 WL 2590199 (E.D. Cal. Aug. 21, 2009). Creditor does not become debt collector when it sends employees out on field calls to visit clients' houses and collect debts owed.

Olivier v. NDEX West, L.L.C., 2009 WL 2486314 (E.D. Cal. Aug. 12, 2009). Foreclosing creditor not subject to FDCPA.

Nera v. American Home Mortgage Servicing, Inc., 2009 WL 2423109 (N.D. Cal. Aug. 5, 2009). Creditors, mortgagors, and mortgage servicing companies are not "debt collectors" and are exempt from liability under the FDCPA.

Ricon v. Recontrust Co., 2009 WL 2407396 (S.D. Cal. Aug. 4, 2009). A creditor collecting its own debt is not covered by the FDCPA.

Manown v. Cal-Western Reconveyance Corp., 2009 WL 2406335 (S.D. Cal. Aug. 4, 2009). Under the FDCPA, a borrower's home mortgage creditor or servicing company does not qualify as a debt collector.

Aquino v. Capital One Fin. Corp., 2008 WL 1734752 (N.D. Cal. Apr. 14, 2008). FDCPA claim dismissed where the plaintiff did not allege in the complaint and in any event conceded that defendant was not an FDCPA debt collector.

Thomas v. Americredit Fin. Corp., 2007 WL 2694176 (N.D. Cal. Sept. 11, 2007).

Showalter v. Chase Manhattan/Providian, 2005 WL 2000943 (N.D. Cal. Aug. 19, 2005). Chase Manhattan exempt.

Darr v. Sutter Health, 2004 WL 2873068 (N.D. Cal. Nov. 30, 2004). Hospital.

Peterson v. Wells Fargo Bank, N.A., 2000 U.S. Dist. LEXIS 18372 (E.D. Cal. Aug. 17, 2000). Wells Fargo was not subject to the FDCPA.

First N. Am. Nat'l Bank v. Superior Court, 2005 WL 67123 (Cal. Ct. App. Jan. 13, 2005). National retail electronics store's wholly owned credit card subsidiary collecting its own debt arising from purchases at the store was not a third party "debt collector" subject to the FDCPA.

Fuhrman v. California Satellite Sys., Consumer Cred. Guide (CCH) ¶ 96,098 (Cal. App. Dep't Super. Ct. 1986). A cable company excluded.

Colorado

Allen v. Nelnet, Inc., 2007 WL 2786432 (D. Colo. Sept. 24, 2007). Defendant was not a debt collector and instead was exempt as a creditor/servicer of the subject student loan who obtained the account prior to default.

Braun v. Stawiarski, 2006 WL 2793150 (D. Colo. Sept. 28, 2006). Bank excluded.

First Interstate Bank v. Soucie, 924 P.2d 1200 (Colo. App. 1996). The bank was not a debt collector but rather was collecting its own debt as it was suing on a car buyers' promissory note assigned to the bank at the time buyers signed the note. Because the debt was not in default when it was assigned, the assignee of the debt was not a debt collector.

Connecticut

O'Reilly v. Connecticut Light & Power Co., 2009 WL 248428 (D. Conn. Feb. 2, 2009), *aff'd*, 375 Fed. Appx. 44 (2d Cir. 2010). Electric company exempt.

Howard v. Albertus Magnus College, 2004 WL 2009283 (D. Conn. Sept. 7, 2004). Defendant creditor.

In re DeGeorge Fin. Corp., 2002 WL 31096716 (D. Conn. July 15, 2002). Creditor.

Beck v. Alliance Funding Co., 113 F. Supp. 2d 274 (D. Conn. 2000). Creditor and its wholly owned subsidiary, whose principal purpose was not debt collection excluded.

Kloth v. Citibank, N.A., 33 F. Supp. 2d 115 (D. Conn. 1998). Citibank.

Maguire v. Citicorp Retail Servs., Inc., 1997 WL 280540 (D. Conn. May 19, 1997), *vacated in part & remanded*, 147 F.3d 232 (2d Cir. 1998). Creditor which sent collection letter under name of a department of its own corporation was not using a name other than its own which would indicate that a third person was collecting the debt, so the creditor was not a "debt collector" under the FDCPA. Remanded to address whether unsophisticated consumer would think the letter was from a third party.

Cordova v. Larson, 1997 WL 280496 (D. Conn. Apr. 30, 1997). Where there were genuine issues of material fact as to whether an attorney who was an employee of the creditor and sent a dunning letter was principally engaged in the collection of debts or whether the attorney was exempt from the FDCPA as an employee of the creditor, summary judgment for the consumer was denied. The court failed to consider whether the creditor's attorney was covered by the FDCPA because he was using stationery that would create the false impression he was from an independent law office.

Krutchkoff v. Fleet Bank, 960 F. Supp. 541 (D. Conn. 1996). FDCPA did not apply to a bank seeking to collect on its own line of credit.

Wagner v. Am. Nat'l Educ. Corp., Clearinghouse No. 36,132 (D. Conn. 1983). A debt servicing company servicing a National Direct Student Loan for a vocational school by billing and accounting for nondelinquent payments as well as collecting delinquent payments was not a collector. It was excluded by § 1692a(6) (G)(iii) and was not a creditor using a false name.

Scappaticci v. G.E. Capital Mortgage Servs., Inc., 2000 Conn. Super. LEXIS 3319 (Conn. Super. Ct. Nov. 27, 2000). Creditor.

Yale Psychiatric Inst. v. Satta, 1999 Conn. Super. LEXIS 1490 (Conn. Super. Ct. June 11, 1999). The FDCPA did not apply to creditor medical care provider collecting its own debt.

Citibank v. Twerdahl, 1996 WL 157336 (Conn. Super. Ct. Mar. 18, 1996). Citibank.

Cmty. Sav. Bank v. Dovitski, 1994 WL 174754 (Conn. Super. Ct. Apr. 27, 1994). Creditor.

Bank of New Haven v. Liner, 1993 WL 107819 (Conn. Super. Ct. Apr. 1, 1993). Officer or employee of the creditor.

Delaware

Games v. Cavazos, 737 F. Supp. 1368 (D. Del. 1990). U.S.A. Funds, a private federal student loan guarantee agency, is a debt collector under § 1692a(6) but exempted by § 1692a(6)(C) since it was merely sending out notices under the control and direction of the U.S. Department of Education. U.S.A. Funds was not exempt under § 1692a(6)(A) or (F).

Fisher v. Dell Fin. Servs., L.P., 2005 WL 3073669 (Del. Ct. Com. Pl. Sept. 28, 2005). Original creditor excluded.

Williams v. Howe, 2004 WL 2828058 (Del. Super. Ct. May 3, 2004). An accounting firm attempting to collect its own fees for services rendered to a union in preparing its tax return was neither a "debt collector" nor was it collecting a consumer "debt" as those terms are defined by the FDCPA.

District of Columbia

Dubois v. Washington Mut. Bank, 2010 WL 3463368 (D.D.C. Sept. 3, 2010). Chase Home Finance exempt.

Sterling Mirror of Maryland, Inc. v. Gordon, 619 A.2d 64 (D.C. 1993). Creditor and an employee excluded.

Florida

Simon v. National City Mortgage Co., 2010 WL 1539970 (M.D. Fla. Apr. 19, 2010). The original lender was an exempt creditor and the "false name" exception of § 1692a(6) did not apply since the collection entity disclosed that it was "a division of" the named creditor. The court concluded that even the least sophisticated consumer would know from the language on the notices that NCM and NCB were affiliated corporations and that the notices were seeking to collect on consumers' notes and mortgages with NCM.

Reese v. JPMorgan Chase & Co., 686 F. Supp. 2d 1291 (S.D. Fla. 2009). FDCPA claims against defendants were dismissed because they are not debt collectors.

Ross v. Option One Mortgage Serv., Inc., 2008 WL 384440 (M.D. Fla. Feb. 11, 2008). Defendant exempt.

Sabeta v. Baptist Hosp. of Miami, Inc., 410 F. Supp. 2d 1224 (S.D. Fla. 2005). Allowed the plaintiffs to amend their complaint to allege that the hospital was collecting a debt using a name other than its own in violation of the FDCPA where the collection would be alleged to be done by wholly owned subsidiary.

Azar v. Hayter, 874 F. Supp. 1314 (N.D. Fla. 1995), *aff'd without op.*, 66 F.3d 342 (11th Cir. 1995). Management services of condominium association was a creditor.

Georgia

Bradley v. Sovereign Bank, 2010 WL 2731902 (M.D. Ga. July 8, 2010). A bank that is a creditor is not a debt collector for the purposes of the FDCPA.

Bates v. Novastar/Nationstar Mortgage L.L.C., 2008 WL 2622810 (N.D. Ga. June 24, 2008). Dismissed; mortgage lenders collecting their own debts were not "debt collectors."

Johnson v. Ameriquest Mortgage Co., 2007 U.S. Dist. LEXIS 516 (N.D. Ga. Jan. 5, 2007). Mortgage company excluded creditor.

Corely v. John D. Archibold Mem. Hosp., Inc., 2005 WL 4732727 (M.D. Ga. Mar. 31, 2005). Hospital excluded.

Corely v. John D. Archibold Mem. Hosp., Inc., 2005 U.S. Dist. LEXIS 8057 (M.D. Ga. Mar. 31, 2005). Hospital dismissed.

Lingo v. Albany Dep't of Cmty. & Econ. Dev., 2005 WL 1500504 (M.D. Ga. June 22, 2005). City.

Hogland v. Athens Reg'l Health Servs., Inc., 2005 WL 4145738 (M.D. Ga. Jan. 21, 2005). Regional medical center excluded.

Washington v. Med. Ctr. of Cent. Georgia, Inc., 2005 U.S. Dist. LEXIS 2614 (M.D. Ga. Jan. 21, 2005). Medical center.

Washington v. Med. Ctr., Inc., 2005 WL 4157465 (M.D. Ga. Jan. 21, 2005). Medical center excluded.

Meads v. Citicorp Credit Servs., Inc., 686 F. Supp. 330 (S.D. Ga. 1988). Where the credit card servicing agency was a subsidiary of the card issuer, only collected for the parent, and disclosed its subsidiary relationship on its letterhead, the subsidiary is exempt under § 1692a(6)(B), and the creditor could not be said to be using a false name bringing it within the second sentence of § 1692a(6).

NationsBank, N.A. v. Peavy, 488 S.E.2d 699 (Ga. Ct. App. 1997). Creditor and its employees excluded.

Yalanzon v. Citibank N.A., 315 S.E.2d 677 (Ga. Ct. App. 1984). Citibank exempt.

Hawaii

Fitzpatrick v. Association of Apartment Owners of Kai Malu at Wailea, 2011 WL 197222 (D. Haw. Jan. 19, 2011). A homeowners' association and board of directors were not FDCPA debt collectors.

Illinois

Carter v. American Mgmt. Consultants, L.L.C./Riverstone Apartments, 2010 WL 3527600 (N.D. Ill. Sept. 2, 2010). Lessor exempt.

Murray v. JPMorgan Chase N.A., 2010 WL 3283012 (C.D. Ill. Aug. 18, 2010). The court dismissed the *pro se* consumers' FDCPA claim because the creditor and its employees were exempt from coverage.

Gaddy v. Wulf, 2010 WL 1882015 (N.D. Ill. May 11, 2010). An attorney attempting to collect his own debt by sending a letter on his letterhead and signed by himself did not fall within the false name provision of 15 U.S.C. § 1692a(6) and was not a "debt collector."

Perry v. Capital One Bank, 2008 WL 4615462 (C.D. Ill. Oct. 16, 2008). Case dismissed because the FDCPA did not apply to the creditor.

Bilal v. Chase Manhattan Mortgage Corp., 2006 WL 1650008 (N.D. Ill. June 13, 2006). Mortgagee and servicers excluded.

Jeffries v. Dutton & Dutton, P.C., 2006 WL 1343629 (N.D. Ill. May 11, 2006). Mortgage lender excluded.

Murray v. Citibank, N.A., 2004 WL 2367742 (N.D. Ill. Oct. 19, 2004). Creditor seeking to collect its own debt.

Donley v. Nordic Properties, Inc., 2003 WL 22282523 (N.D. Ill. Sept. 30, 2003). A creditor seeking to collect its own debt.

Powell v. Bay View Bank, 2003 WL 22839814 (N.D. Ill. Nov. 25, 2003). Original lender.

Smith v. Continental Cmty. Bank & Trust Co., 2002 U.S. Dist. LEXIS 11193 (N.D. Ill. June 21, 2002). Police and security officers' motion to dismiss was granted because consumer failed to allege that the officers were debt collectors but alleged them to be employees of the bank and therefore exempt.

Broxton-King v. La Salle Bank, N.A., 2001 U.S. Dist. LEXIS 14653 (N.D. Ill. Sept. 19, 2001). Bank not a debt collector.

Williams v. Thomas Pontiac, 1999 U.S. Dist. LEXIS 15045 (N.D. Ill. Sept. 22, 1999). Defendant automobile dealer was not a debt collector and therefore not liable under the FDCPA for the actions of its repossession agent in wrongfully repossessing the consumer's car.

Morency v. Evanston Northwestern Healthcare Corp., 1999 U.S. Dist. LEXIS 14744 (N.D. Ill. Sept. 13, 1999). In a case involving the same defendant creditor as *Larson v. Evanston Northwestern Healthcare* (1999 U.S. Dist. LEXIS 11380 (N.D. Ill. July 19, 1999)), the court adopted the *Larson* rationale to dismiss the consumer's claims against the creditor, ruling that the creditor was not a debt collector under § 1692a(6), although the consumer alleged that the creditor was in effect sending letters in the name of a flat rate collection agency. Factors considered were: the creditor hired the collection agency to continue collection if the collection agency's initial letters did not prompt a payment; the collection agency handled the creditor's validation of debts; the collection agency made recommendations to the creditor for further collection activity the letters had the collection agency's letterhead, address and phone numbers; and the letters directed consumers to call the collection agency, not the creditor, with any questions.

Friedman v. May Dep't Stores Co., 990 F. Supp. 571 (N.D. Ill. 1998). Courts have broadly interpreted the "common ownership" and creditor exceptions.

Watkins v. Associated Brokers, Inc., 1998 WL 312124 (N.D. Ill. June 5, 1998). Originating creditor exempt.

Taylor v. Rollins, Inc., 1998 WL 164890 (N.D. Ill. Mar. 30, 1998). A creditor's alleged approval of debt collection practices did not make it a debt collector subject to the FDCPA.

Kang v. Eisenstein, 962 F. Supp. 112 (N.D. Ill. 1997). Physician who was a partner in clinic was exempt.

Friedman v. Rubinstein, 1997 WL 757875 (N.D. Ill. Dec. 1, 1997). Desert Palace, Inc., d.b.a. Caesars Palace, was creditor exempt, as was its in-house counsel. The fact that the initial dealings were in the Caesars Palace name and a suit on NSF checks was in the name, Desert Palace, Inc., d.b.a. Caesars Palace, would not create the impression that a third party collector was involved.

Villarreal v. Snow, 1996 WL 473386 (N.D. Ill. Aug. 19, 1996). Beneficial Illinois, Inc., a lender, did not become a debt collector by "using" an attorney's name when the attorney spent about one minute on the minimal material sent by the lender on each account and directed his paralegal to send a particular form letter.

Villarreal v. Snow, 1996 WL 28308 (N.D. Ill. Jan. 19, 1996). Creditor was not a "debt collector" but its attorney who reviewed and sent the collection letters was a debt collector.

McClean v. Melville Collections, 1995 WL 646384 (N.D. Ill. Oct. 25, 1995). An in-house collection employee of the creditor was not a "debt collector."

Arnold v. Truemper, 833 F. Supp. 678 (N.D. Ill. 1993). Bank's claim for over-credited deposit did not arise from the extension of credit, and bank was not a creditor. Bank's contact with police department to investigate a possible criminal matter did not qualify either the bank or the police department as a debt collector within FDCPA.

Batchelor v. First Nat'l Bank, 1993 WL 22859 (N.D. Ill. Jan. 20, 1993). Bank seeking to collect its own debt.

Kegley v. Miles Mgmt. Corp., 1992 WL 370251 (N.D. Ill. Dec. 3, 1992). Lessor of real estate which sought to collect its own debts.

Young v. Lehigh Corp., 1989 WL 117960 (N.D. Ill. Sept. 28, 1989). Employees of creditor who use an affiliated entity's similar name when collecting the creditor's debts were not covered since the use of the other name did not indicate that a third party was involved.

Indiana

Purdue Employees, Fed. Credit Union v. Van Houten, 2008 WL 4414712 (N.D. Ind. Sept. 24, 2008). FDCPA claim was dismissed since the credit union was not a covered debt collector but an exempt creditor collecting its own debt.

*E*Trade Consumer Fin. Corp. v. Needles*, 2005 WL 2674930 (N.D. Ind. Oct. 20, 2005). Company collecting its own debt.

Weiss v. Weinberger, 2005 WL 1432190 (N.D. Ind. June 9, 2005). A healthcare provider and receiver excluded.

Iowa

Dau v. Storm Lake Production Credit Ass'n, 626 F. Supp. 862 (N.D. Iowa 1985). Agricultural lender excluded.

Kansas

Mondonedo v. Sallie Mae, Inc., 2008 WL 4491409 (D. Kan. Sept. 29, 2008). Claims against defendant dismissed since it was the creditor not subject to the FDCPA.

Millett v. Ford Motor Credit Co., 2005 U.S. Dist. LEXIS 8806 (D. Kan. Apr. 20, 2005). Creditor.

Lowe v. Surpas Res. Corp., 253 F. Supp. 2d 1209 (D. Kan. 2003). Creditors not generally subject to the FDCPA.

Alvano v. Am. Bank, 1989 WL 156815 (D. Kan. Nov. 3, 1989). Bank's own employees exempt.

McDonnell v. The Music Stand, 886 P.2d 895 (Kan. Ct. App. 1994). Creditor not liable.

Farmers Nat'l Bank v. Hall, 791 P.2d 752 (Kan. Ct. App. 1990). Creditors exempt.

Kentucky

Ward v. Shircliff, 2010 WL 686265 (W.D. Ky. Feb. 23, 2010). *Pro se* tenant complaint failed to state an FDCPA claim for relief since the defendant was the landlord and thus an exempt creditor.

Wintermute v. Discover Card Servs., Inc., 2008 WL 1772758 (W.D. Ky. Apr. 16, 2008). FDCPA claim dismissed since defendant was an exempt creditor and not a debt collector.

Owens v. Cumberland Mortgage, Inc., 2006 U.S. Dist. LEXIS 83667 (W.D. Ky. Nov. 16, 2006). Mortgage company excluded.

Breed v. Nationwide Mut. Ins. Co., 2006 WL 1669876 (W.D. Ky. June 15, 2006). Home equity lender excluded.

Stafford v. Cross Country Bank, 262 F. Supp. 2d 776 (W.D. Ky. 2003). Bank that issued the credit card.

Ray v. Citibank, N.A., 187 F. Supp. 2d 719 (W.D. Ky. 2001). Neither Citibank nor Citicorp Credit Services was a debt collector. Citibank was a creditor; Citicorp was a related entity and collected only for Citicorp.

Winkler v. Germann, 2010 WL 4904992 (Ky. Ct. App. Dec. 3, 2010). Creditors are not subject to the FDCPA when collecting their own accounts.

Louisiana

HSBC Bank Nevada, N.A. v. Murungi, 2010 WL 3170736 (E.D. La. Aug. 11, 2010). Bank exempt.

Thomasson v. Bank One, N.A., 137 F. Supp. 2d 721 (E.D. La. 2001). Where defendant acquired debt before it became in default, it was a creditor.

Decker v. Hibernia Nat'l Bank & Inv. Corp., 1996 WL 696323 (E.D. La. Nov. 26, 1996). The bank was not a debt collector because it was collecting a debt that had been assigned to it before default.

Blalock v. World Pro Travel, Inc., 1996 WL 371800 (E.D. La. July 2, 1996). Creditor using its own name and letterhead.

Maine

Bingaman v. Fleet Fin. Corp., 2000 WL 892011 (D. Me. Mar. 3, 2000). Defendant bank.

Maryland

Flores v. Deutsche Bank Nat'l Trust, Co., 2010 WL 2719849 (D. Md. July 7, 2010). Creditors, mortgagors, and mortgage servicing companies are not debt collectors and are statutorily exempt from liability under the FDCPA.

Akpan v. First Premier Bank, 2010 WL 917886 (D. Md. Mar. 8, 2010). Creditor not within FDCPA.

Sparrow v. SLM Corp., 2009 WL 77462 (D. Md. Jan. 7, 2009). Defendant was an exempt originating creditor.

Boccone v. American Express Co., 2007 WL 2914909 (D. Md. Oct. 4, 2007).

Fries v. Norstar Bank, 1988 WL 75773 (D. Md. Aug. 31, 1988).

Student loan lender, Sallie Mae, state insuring agency and servicing agency are exempt.

Massachusetts

Chiang v. Verizon New England Inc., 2009 WL 102707 (D. Mass. Jan. 13, 2009). Verizon New England's use of the name Verizon Massachusetts to collect its accounts did not fall within the exception to "creditor" for use of a false name and the FDCPA was not violated.

Michigan

South v. Midwestern Audit Servs., Inc., 2010 WL 5089862 (E.D. Mich. Dec. 8, 2010). A creditor uses a false name if it pretends to be someone else or uses a pseudonym or alias, or if it owns and controls the debt collector, thus rendering it the creditor's alter ego. Utility company did not have that relationship with its collection agency.

Mabry v. Ameriquest Mortgage Co., 2010 WL 1052352 (E.D. Mich. Feb. 26, 2010), *report and recommendation adopted*, 2010 WL 1052355 (E.D. Mich. Mar. 19, 2010). Creditor not subject to FDCPA.

Fuller v. Exxon Mobil, M.C., 2009 WL 91707 (E.D. Mich. Jan. 14, 2009). Defendant was a creditor.

Romberger v. Wells Fargo Bank, 2008 WL 3838026 (E.D. Mich. Aug. 14, 2008). *Pro se* plaintiff's FDCPA claims were dismissed for failure to produce evidence that defendants were debt collectors.

Mingo v. City of Detroit, 2008 WL 2566371 (E.D. Mich. June 23, 2008). Utility service provider collecting its own debts is not with the FDCPA.

McCain v. Wells Fargo Home Loans, 2007 WL 4965465 (E.D. Mich. Nov. 26, 2007), *report and recommendation adopted*, 2008 WL 82190 (E.D. Mich. Jan. 8, 2008). Mortgagee exempt.

Doran v. Huntington Nat'l Bank, 2007 U.S. Dist. LEXIS 3917 (E.D. Mich. Jan. 19, 2007). An in-house collector excluded.

Waldo v. Mercedes-Benz Credit Corp., 2006 WL 2460785 (E.D. Mich. Aug. 23, 2006). Auto financer excluded.

Grant v. Trinity Health-Mich., 390 F. Supp. 2d 643 (E.D. Mich. 2005). Hospitals and health care systems.

Turk v. CitiMortgage, 2005 WL 2090888 (E.D. Mich. Aug. 29, 2005). Mortgage lender.

Burton v. William Beaumont Hosp., 347 F. Supp. 2d 486 (E.D. Mich. 2004). Hospital.

Russell v. Standard Fed. Bank, 2000 U.S. Dist. LEXIS 19149 (E.D. Mich. Nov. 27, 2000). Creditor.

Minnesota

Boone v. Wells Fargo Bank, 2009 WL 2086502 (D. Minn. July 13, 2009). The defendant bank is an exempt creditor and not a debt collector.

Mississippi

Smith v. CitiMortgage, Inc., 2009 WL 1976513 (S.D. Miss. July 7, 2009). Summary judgment for defendant mortgage company since it was collecting its own debt in its own name and therefore was an exempt FDCPA creditor.

Robertson v. GE Consumer Fin., Inc., 2008 WL 4868289 (S.D. Miss. Nov. 7, 2008). FDCPA does not apply to creditors.

Robertson v. J.C. Penney Co., 2008 WL 4372760 (S.D. Miss. Sept. 22, 2008). Summary judgment to defendant since it was not a covered FDCPA debt collector, as it "had sold its credit card business, including the plaintiffs' account, more than four years before the events complained of and retained no ownership interest therein."

Hollins v. Heilig-Meyers Furniture Co., 1999 U.S. Dist. LEXIS 15755 (N.D. Miss. Sept. 28, 1999). Creditor collecting its own debt, or its agent, where the creditor did not seek to hide the fact that it was collecting its own debt.

Shamburger v. Grand Casino, Inc., 84 F. Supp. 2d 794 (S.D. Miss. 1998). Creditor.

Keyes v. Sunstar Acceptance Co., 1997 WL 170320 (N.D. Miss. Mar. 25, 1997). Creditors dismissed.

Kizer v. Fin. Am. Credit Corp., 454 F. Supp. 937 (N.D. Miss. 1978). A creditor is not a "debt collector."

Missouri

Wells v. Southwestern Bell Tel. Co., 626 F. Supp. 2d 1001 (W.D. Mo. 2009). Defendant originated the debt and was an exempt creditor.

Leavitt v. Bank of Cairo, 2006 WL 1479502 (E.D. Mo. May 23, 2006). Bank excluded.

Nebraska

Garska v. SLM Corp., 2008 WL 5083886 (D. Neb. Nov. 25, 2008). FDCPA claim dismissed unopposed as no allegation that defendant was a debt collector.

Jonak v. John Hancock Mut. Life Ins. Co., 629 F. Supp. 90 (D. Neb. 1985). Agricultural creditor excluded.

Nevada

Karony v. Dollar Loan Ctr., L.L.C., 2010 WL 5186065 (D. Nev. Dec. 15, 2010). The originating lender was not an FDCPA debt collector.

Wellesley v. Chief Fin. Officer, 2010 WL 2926162 (D. Nev. July 20, 2010). The court dismissed the *pro se* consumer's FDCPA claim since neither the credit card company nor its officers and employees were "debt collectors."

Bukhari v. T.D. Servs. Co., 2010 WL 2762794 (D. Nev. July 13, 2010). The court dismissed the *pro se* consumer's complaint where the defendants were not "debt collectors" because a defendant attempting to collect debts owed to itself, not debts owed to another, is not covered under the Act.

Enriquez v. J.P. Morgan Chase Bank, 2009 WL 160245 (D. Nev. Jan. 22, 2009). Originator of mortgage exempt.

Fleeger v. Bell, 95 F. Supp. 2d 1126 (D. Nev. 2000), *aff'd,* 2001 WL 1491252 (9th Cir. Nov. 26, 2001). Casino trying to collect its own "markers" was not subject to FDCPA.

New Jersey

Alves v. Verizon, 2010 WL 2989988 (D.N.J. July 27, 2010). Verizon exempt as creditor.

Crenshaw v. Computex Info. Servs., Inc., 2010 WL 2951506 (D.N.J. July 21, 2010). FDCPA claims were dismissed against the creditor landlord.

Poltrock v. NJ Auto. Accounts Mgmt. Co., 2008 WL 5416396 (D.N.J. Dec. 22, 2008). The complaint failed to state a claim against the defendant because: (1) as an exempt creditor, it was not vicariously liable for the alleged FDCPA violations of its debt collector, and (2) there was no allegation that it had used a name other than its own so as to lose its creditor exemption pursuant to § 1692a(6).

Bey v. DaimlerChrysler Servs., L.L.C., 2005 WL 1630855 (D.N.J. July 8, 2005). DaimlerChrysler.

Citibank v. Razvi, 2008 WL 2521082 (N.J. Super. Ct. App. Div. June 26, 2008). FDCPA did not apply to the credit card company since it was an exempt creditor collecting its own debt.

State v. Long, 630 A.2d 430 (N.J. Super. Ct. 1993). Judgment creditor exempt where judgment creditor's business was not debt collection.

New York

Fadia v. U-Haul, Inc., 2010 WL 3211075 (W.D.N.Y. Aug. 11, 2010). The court dismissed the *pro se* consumer's complaint since the creditor and its employees were exempt from FDCPA coverage.

Eze v. JP Morgan Chase Bank, N.A., 2010 WL 3189813 (E.D.N.Y. Aug. 11, 2010). The *pro se* consumer failed to state a claim where the defendant was an exempt creditor.

Albano v. Con Edison Co., 2010 WL 2680364 (E.D.N.Y. July 1, 2010). Although Con Edison "regularly" collects debt, it is not a debt collector under the FDCPA but, rather, a creditor.

Owusu v. New York State Ins., 655 F. Supp. 2d 308 (S.D.N.Y. 2009). Creditor who sent a letter regarding the debt in its own name did not qualify as a "debt collector" under the FDCPA.

Williams v. Citibank, 565 F. Supp. 2d 523 (S.D.N.Y. 2008). Where consumer failed to allege that bank was a "debt collector" or came within the "false name exception" his FDCPA claims were dismissed with leave to file an amended complaint.

Burns v. Bank of Am., 655 F. Supp. 2d 240 (S.D.N.Y. 2008), *aff'd,* 360 Fed. Appx. 255 (2d Cir. 2010). Mortgagee was creditor, not debt collector.

Kahaner v. Memorial Sloan-Kettering Cancer Ctr., 2008 WL 4924956 (S.D.N.Y. Nov. 10, 2008). A hospital and its employees are affiliated by corporate control and consequently the FDCPA does not apply to a hospital collecting debts of its own employee-doctors.

Sembler v. Advanta Bank Corp., 2008 WL 2965661 (E.D.N.Y. Aug. 1, 2008). Bank that issued fee-harvesting card not subject to the FDCPA.

Vincent v. Money Store, 402 F. Supp. 2d 501 (S.D.N.Y. 2005). Evidence failed to establish that the creditor/defendant used an alias through its sham employment of outside counsel to collect debts and thus failed to establish the false name exception.

Kolari v. New York-Presbyterian Hosp., 382 F. Supp. 2d 562 (S.D.N.Y. 2005), *vacated on other grounds,* 455 F.3d 118 (2d Cir. 2006). Hospital.

Carlson v. Long Island Jewish Med. Ctr., 378 F. Supp. 2d 128 (E.D.N.Y. 2005). While hospitals were not debt collectors, whether the least sophisticated consumer would have believed that a third party was collecting because of the hospitals' use of a different name could not be decided on a motion to dismiss.

Doherty v. Citibank N.A., 375 F. Supp. 2d 158 (E.D.N.Y. 2005). Original credit card company.

Gorham-Dimaggio v. Countrywide Home Loans, Inc., 2005 WL 2098068 (N.D.N.Y. Aug. 30, 2005). Mortgage company was not using a name indicating a third person was collecting the debt when it transferred the homeowner's call about her last payment to its loan counseling department.

Dolan v. Fairbanks Capital Corp., 2005 WL 1971006 (E.D.N.Y. Aug. 16, 2005). Fairbanks Capital Holding Corp. and PMI Mortgage Insurance Company.

Mazzei v. Money Store, 349 F. Supp. 2d 651 (S.D.N.Y. 2004). A lender, who hired a collection law firm to send out letters on the letterhead of the law firm at fifty dollars a letter declaring mortgages in default and accelerating the balance of the debt but not performing other collection services, did not use a false name and, therefore, did not fall within the coverage of creditors using false names.

Bleich v. Revenue Maximization Group, Inc., 239 F. Supp. 2d 262 (E.D.N.Y. Jan. 10, 2002). Creditor was not a debt collector and could not be held vicariously liable once claims against collector were dismissed.

Shevach v. Am. Fitness Franchise Corp., 2001 U.S. Dist. LEXIS 2899 (S.D.N.Y Mar. 14, 2001). Creditors.

Holder v. Bankers Trust Co., 1998 WL 898323 (S.D.N.Y. Dec. 23, 1998). Creditor and its servicer which had obtained the debt before default.

Harrison v. NBD Inc., 968 F. Supp. 837 (E.D.N.Y. 1997). A vocational school was exempt and did not lose the exemption by using a subsidiary to do its debt collection. The parent corporation would not be liable for the collection subsidiary absent allegations that it dominated the subsidiary to such an extent that they would be considered a single economic enterprise or it controlled all aspects of the subsidiary's collection work.

Griffin v. Key Bank, 1996 WL 191975 (N.D.N.Y. Apr. 15, 1996). Bank which took assignment of a motor vehicle installment contract immediately after the sale was not a debt collector.

Ghartey v. Chrysler Credit Corp., 1992 WL 373479 (E.D.N.Y. Nov. 23, 1992). Creditor and its employee excluded.

Howe v. Reader's Digest Ass'n, Inc., 686 F. Supp. 461 (S.D.N.Y. 1988). Magazine retailer is not a debt collector since it never undertook collection activities; it would not be held responsible on agency grounds without proof of an agency relationship by the consumer.

Orlosky v. Empire Sec. Sys., Inc., 646 N.Y.S.2d 1016 (Sup. Ct. 1996), *aff'd*, 657 N.Y.S.2d 840 (App. 1997). Assignee not debt collector.

Beneficial Homeowner Serv. Corp. v. Butler, 836 N.Y.S.2d 491 (N.Y. App. Div. 2007).

Talk of the Millenium Realty Inc. v. Sierra, 2006 WL 1341014 (N.Y. City Civ. Ct. Jan. 3, 2006). Mortgage broker excluded.

Mendez v. Apple Bank for Sav., 541 N.Y.S.2d 920 (N.Y. Civ. 1989). Bank collecting its own debts excluded.

North Carolina

Henderson v. Wells Fargo Bank, 2009 WL 1259355 (W.D.N.C. May 5, 2009). Defendant, the mortgagee of commercial property, was not a debt collector.

Pierce v. Wells Fargo Bank, 2007 WL 2873594 (M.D.N.C. Feb. 14, 2007), *aff'd*, 229 Fed. Appx. 240 (4th Cir. 2007).

Davis v. Dillard Nat'l Bank, 50 U.C.C. Rep. Serv. 2d 877 (M.D.N.C. 2003). Bank collecting its own debt.

Ohio

Girgis v. Countrywide Home Loans, Inc., 2010 WL 3290985 (N.D. Ohio Aug. 20, 2010). Originating mortgage lender was an exempt creditor.

Berry v. Sugarman, 2010 WL 1032643 (N.D. Ohio Mar. 17, 2010). Creditor's employees are not "debt collectors" covered by the FDCPA.

Glazer v. Chase Home Fin. L.L.C., 2010 WL 1392156 (N.D. Ohio Jan. 21, 2010). The servicer of a loan in good standing does not loses its exempt status as a servicer where an allegedly invalid ownership assignment is made to that same servicer *after* the loan enters the default stage.

Bridge v. Ocwen Fed. Bank, 669 F. Supp. 2d 853 (N.D. Ohio 2009). The defendant banks were an exempt creditor and loan servicer not subject to the FDCPA.

Thomas v. Central Parking Sys., Inc., 2008 WL 2704291 (S.D. Ohio July 10, 2008). Plaintiff's motion for entry of default judgment denied because the plaintiff failed to make out a prima facie FDCPA case since the plaintiff offered no evidence that the defendant was a debt collector, including either that it was collecting a debt in this case for a third party or that it regularly collected debts for third parties.

Frame v. Weltman, Weinberg & Reis, 2006 WL 1348176 (N.D. Ohio May 12, 2006). Discover and its employees or officers, or their affiliates excluded.

Wolfe v. Bank One Corp., 433 F. Supp. 2d 845 (N.D. Ohio 2005).

Bank One could not be held liable for calls made in the name of United Mileage Plus, the name which Bank One had consistently used to do business with the consumer.

Lombardo v. Parkview Fed. Sav. Bank, 2005 WL 1126741 (N.D. Ohio Apr. 20, 2005). Creditor.

Havens-Tobias v. Eagle, 127 F. Supp. 2d 889 (S.D. Ohio 2001). A creditor is not ordinarily vicariously liable for the FDCPA violations of its attorney.

In re Dawson, 2006 WL 2372821 (Bankr. N.D. Ohio Aug. 15, 2006), *aff'd*, 2006 WL 3827459 (N.D. Ohio Dec. 27, 2006). Used car seller excluded.

Capital One Bank (USA) v. Rhoades, 2010 WL 4149255 (Ohio Ct. App. Oct. 21, 2010). Original credit card issuer exempt.

RBS Citizens, N.A. v. Zigdon, 2010 WL 2961534 (Ohio Ct. App. July 29, 2010). A creditor is not debt collector.

Bank of New York Tr. v. Damsel, 2006 WL 2258874 (Ohio Ct. App. Aug. 8, 2006). Holder of the mortgage excluded.

Kondrat v. Morris, 692 N.E.2d 246 (Ohio Ct. App. 1997). The purchaser from the Resolution Trust Corp. of a loan in default which was used to finance a commercial investment in a cable company was held not to be a "debt collector" under FDCPA as it was a creditor enforcing an obligation assigned to it.

Ngaoka v. Society Nat'l Bank, 1990 WL 100416 (Ohio Ct. App. July 19, 1990). Bank exempt.

Colton v. Ford Motor Credit, 1986 WL 8538 (Ohio Ct. App. July 30, 1986). Creditors.

Oklahoma

Warzynski v. Vital Recovery Servs., Inc., 2009 WL 5065687 (N.D. Okla. Dec. 16, 2009). Auto lessor was not a debt collector.

Scoles v. Spellings, 2008 WL 974702 (W.D. Okla. Apr. 8, 2008). Plaintiff conceded and the court agreed that the Secretary of Education was not an FDCPA debt collector in case involving the plaintiff's disputed student loan. The limited discussion invoked the original creditor exemption and that debt collection is not a "principal" part of the secretary's business, and omitted any reference to government exemption.

Spagner v. Latham, Stall, Wagner, Steel & Lehman, P.C., 2005 WL 1950364 (W.D. Okla. Aug. 15, 2005). Originating creditor.

Oregon

Stewart v. Mortgage Elec. Registration Sys., Inc., 2010 WL 1054384 (D. Or. Feb. 18, 2010), *report and recommendation adopted*, 2010 WL 1054697 (D. Or. Mar. 19, 2010). *Pro se* mortgagor's FDCPA claims were dismissed because the defendants were exempt creditors and because "foreclosing on property pursuant to a deed of trust is not the collection of a debt within the meaning of the FDCPA."

Porter v. Wachovia Dealer Servs., Inc., 2007 WL 2693370 (D. Or. Sept. 12, 2007). The consumer's originating creditor, WFS Financial, which in the course of the parties' dealings changed its name to Wachovia Dealer Services, so notified the consumer, and continued to use the new name, remained an exempt creditor when it collected the debt in the latter name since as a matter of law no one would be misled as to its identity.

Reed v. American Honda Fin. Corp., 2005 WL 1398214 (D. Or. June 10, 2005), *superseded*, 2005 WL 1398214 (D. Or. June 10, 2005). American Honda.

Clark v. Capital Credit & Collection Servs., Inc., 2004 WL 1305326 (D. Or. Jan. 23, 2004), *aff'd in part, rev'd in part on other grounds*, 460 F.3d 1162 (9th Cir. 2006). Doctor who bought medical clinic and its accounts receivable was properly disclosed as the creditor and did not come within the debt buyer exception of § 1692a(4).

Pennsylvania

Duraney v. Washington Mut. Bank, 2008 WL 4204821 (W.D. Pa. Sept. 11, 2008), *aff'd*, 2010 WL 2993810 (3d Cir. Aug. 2, 2010). FDCPA claim dismissed against the defendant mortgagee since it was not a debt collector but an exempt creditor who therefore could not be held vicariously liable under the FDCPA for the actions of its debt collector attorney.

Schaffhauser v. Citibank (South Dakota) 2007 WL 2815728 (M.D. Pa. Sept. 25, 2007). Defendant, as the originator and owner of the debt, was an exempt creditor. The creditor's collection of the debt here using name variations and combinations that all included the word "Citibank" would not confuse the least sophisticated consumer into believing that an entity other than the defendant was collecting, and thus defendant did not lose its creditor exemption under the § 1692a(6) false name exception.

Dahlhammer v. Citibank , N.A, 2006 WL 3484352 (M.D. Pa. Nov. 30, 2006). Bank excluded.

Frew v. Van Ru Credit Corp., 2006 WL 2261624 (E.D. Pa. Aug. 7, 2006). U.S. Department of Education excluded.

Sankowski v. Citibank, N.A., 2006 WL 2037463 (E.D. Pa. July 14, 2006). Originating credit card company excluded.

Kaetz v. Chase Manhattan Bank, 2006 WL 1343700 (M.D. Pa. May 17, 2006). Bank excluded.

Oppong v. First Union Mortgage Corp., 407 F. Supp. 2d 658 (E.D. Pa. 2005), *aff'd in part, vacated in part on other grounds*, 215 Fed. Appx. 114 (3d Cir. 2007). *Pro se* plaintiff failed to offer evidence to show that debt collection was a "principal purpose" of Wells Fargo's business or that Wells Fargo "regularly" engaged in debt collection.

Hutt v. Albert Einstein Med. Ctr., 2005 WL 2396313 (E.D. Pa. Sept. 28, 2005). Hospital.

O'Brien v. Valley Forge Specialized Educ. Servs., 2004 WL 2580773 (E.D. Pa. Nov. 10, 2004). School.

Daniels v. Baritz, 2003 WL 21027238 (E.D. Pa. Apr. 30, 2003). Employees or officers of the landlord.

Gary v. Goldman & Co., 180 F. Supp. 2d 668 (E.D. Pa. 2002). A creditor was not vicariously liable for the acts of its collection agency in the absence of allegations that the creditor was a debt collector.

Flamm v. Sarner & Assocs., P.C., 2002 WL 31618443 (E.D. Pa. Nov. 6, 2002). Creditor.

Garland v. Enterprise Leasing Co., 1999 U.S. Dist. LEXIS 18116 (E.D. Pa. Nov. 24, 1999). Car rental company.

Moreiko v. Kurtz, 1998 U.S. Dist. LEXIS 22921 (M.D. Pa. Mar. 31, 1998), *aff'd*, 203 F.3d 817 (3d Cir. 1999). Bank creditor seeking to collect rents from tenants of foreclosed debtor was not a debt collector under the FDCPA because any officer or employee of a creditor collecting a debt in its own name was excluded from the definition of debt collector.

Samero v. Foot & Ankle Specialists, 1997 WL 700805 (E.D. Pa. Oct. 30, 1997). Creditor and its employee.

Castro v. Revere Collection Agency, 1991 WL 147529 (E.D. Pa. July 25, 1991). Creditor exempt under the FDCPA may not be made liable under the FDCPA by state agency principles.

Barch v. Blazer Consumer Discount Co., No. 83-0923 (E.D. Pa. 1984). Creditor and its employees are exempt.

Horne v. Farrell, 560 F. Supp. 219 (M.D. Pa. 1983). Creditor's employee was not subject to the FDCPA. However, the creditor may be subject to the FDCPA where a constable attempts to collect the creditor's debt for the creditor using the constable's name.

In re Koresko, 91 B.R. 689 (Bankr. E.D. Pa. 1988). The court indicated in dicta that evidence was lacking of coverage of and violation by the creditor, repossession agency and car auction company.

Puerto Rico

Melendez-Febus v. Toyota Credit De Puerto Rico Corp., 2009 WL 2950369 (D. P.R. Sept. 9, 2009). Defendant was a creditor and not a debt collector subject to the FDCPA.

South Carolina

Glover v. University Motor Co., 2010 WL 234903 (D.S.C. Jan. 15, 2010). Car dealer was an exempt creditor.

Serfass v. CIT Group/Consumer Fin., Inc., 2008 WL 351116 (D.S.C. Feb. 7, 2008). Defendant, servicing its own mortgage, was not within the FDCPA.

Barnhill v. Bank of Am., N.A., 378 F. Supp. 2d 696 (D.S.C. 2005). Bank of America dismissed.

South Dakota

Baldwin v. First Nat'l Bank, 362 N.W.2d 85 (S.D. 1985). Bank collecting business loan which it extended excluded.

Tennessee

Lufkin v. Capital One Bank (USA), N.A., 2010 WL 2813437 (E.D. Tenn. July 16, 2010). The FDCPA regulates third-party debt collectors who participate in debt collection practices on behalf of creditors rather than the creditor to whom the debt is owed.

Wilson v. GMAC Fin. Servs. Corp., 2009 WL 467583 (E.D. Tenn. Feb. 24, 2009). Consumer's FDCPA claim was dismissed because defendant did not meet the definition of "debt collector."

Fox v. HSBC Mortgage Servs., Inc., 2009 WL 129797 (E.D. Tenn. Jan. 16, 2009). "Debt collector" does not include the consumer's creditor or an assignee of the debt, as long as the debt was not in default at the time of assignment.

Lyons v. Mazda Am. Credit Co., 2005 WL 2174476 (W.D. Tenn. Sept. 6, 2005). Car finance company exempt.

Texas

Patterson v. Sierra Pac. Mortgage Co., 2008 WL 2596904 (N.D. Tex. July 1, 2008). *Pro se* consumer failed to state a claim since the defendant mortgage lender was not an FDCPA debt collector.

Brown v. Crawford, 2008 WL 508390 (N.D. Tex. Feb. 25, 2008). Landlord collecting her own debt was not a "debt collector."

Marketic v. U.S. Bank Nat'l Ass'n, 436 F. Supp. 2d 842 (N.D. Tex. 2006). Home equity lender excluded.

Blanks v. Ford Motor Credit, 2005 WL 991241 (N.D. Tex. Apr. 20, 2005), *aff'd*, 202 Fed. Appx. 664 (5th Cir. 2006). Creditor.

Chatmon v. U.S. Dep't of Educ., 2003 WL 21501919 (N.D. Tex. June 24, 2003). Failing to note the § 1692a(6)(C) exemption for government employees in this *pro se* case, the court held that the Department of Education was not a "debt collector" because the collection of debts was not its principal purpose and because it was a creditor collecting its own debt.

Brincks v. Taylor, 2002 U.S. Dist. LEXIS 606 (N.D. Tex. Jan. 8, 2002). Bank which acquired credit card debt after default was not alleged to regularly collect debts owed to another and therefore was not a "debt collector."

KPMG Peat Marwick v. Texas Commerce Bank, 976 F. Supp. 623 (S.D. Tex. 1997). Bank was exempt as a creditor or as an affiliate under § 1692a(6)(B).

Utah

Maxwell v. Barney, 2008 WL 1981666 (D. Utah May 2, 2008). Ambulance service was a creditor, not a debt collector.

Virginia

Bolouri v. Bank of Am., N.A., 2010 WL 3385177 (E.D. Va. Aug. 24, 2010). Bank of America exempt.

Davis v. OneWest Bank, F.S.B., 2010 WL 538760 (E.D. Va. Feb. 12, 2010). The court dismissed the complaint because the defendant, OneWest Bank, obtained the debt in default when the assets of the consumer's failed creditor, IndyMac, were transferred to it by the OTS and thus did not receive the debt "solely for the purpose of facilitating collection of such debt for another."

Jones v. Baugher, 689 F. Supp. 2d 825 (W.D. Va. 2010). As members of a member-managed L.L.C., defendants were not debt collectors when they collected rent on behalf of their company in the company's name.

Abbott v. SunTrust Mortgage, Inc., 2009 WL 127858 (E.D. Va. Jan. 15, 2009). Defendant was a creditor.

Eley v. Evans, 476 F. Supp. 2d 531 (E.D. Va. 2007).

Kelley v. University of Richmond, 2006 WL 1555933 (E.D. Va. June 2, 2006), *aff'd*, 211 Fed. Appx. 173 (4th Cir. 2006). University excluded.

Scott v. Wells Fargo Home Mortgage, Inc., 326 F. Supp. 2d 709 (E.D. Va. 2003), *aff'd*, 67 Fed. Appx. 238 (4th Cir. 2003). Creditors, mortgagees, and mortgage servicing companies were not debt collectors.

Dickenson v. Townside TV & Appliance, Inc., 770 F. Supp. 1122 (S.D. W. Va. 1990). Creditor which consistently used its creditor business name in dealing with customers, rather than its incorporated name, was not a "debt collector."

Warren v. Bank of Marion, 618 F. Supp. 317 (W.D. Va. 1985). Bank and a retailer excluded.

Washington

Sweatt v. Sunkidd Venture, Inc., 2006 WL 2459081 (W.D. Wash. Aug. 23, 2006). Creditor.

Wisconsin

Wilkinson v. Wells Fargo Bank MN, 2007 WL 1414888 (E.D. Wis. May 9, 2007), *aff'd*, 268 Fed. Appx. 476 (7th Cir. 2008).

Bostwick v. Discover Card Bank, 2005 WL 2076464 (E.D. Wis. Aug. 19, 2005). Discover Card Bank.

Hartman v. Meridian Fin. Servs., Inc., 191 F. Supp. 2d 1031 (W.D. Wis. 2002). A third-party debt collector collecting in the name of the creditor was not subject to the § 1692a(6)(A) exemption since the person so collecting was not an "officer or employee of the creditor."

Univ. of Wis. Med. Found., Inc. v. Turner, 735 N.W.2d 195 (Wis. Ct. App. 2007).

K.1.2.3.1.2 Creditor covered

Nielsen v. Dickerson, 307 F.3d 623 (7th Cir. 2002). Under the "false name" exception to § 1692a(6), the creditor was subject to the FDCPA as a debt collector where it used an attorney to send demand letters but gave him very little information for the letters, paid him per letter, and did not retain him to sue.

Young v. Citicorp Retail Servs., Inc., 159 F.3d 1349 (2d Cir. 1998) (text at 1998 WL 537530). Where Citicorp's attorney allowed a collection letter to create the false impression that she was actually involved as an attorney in collecting the debt for Citicorp, Citicorp became liable as a debt collector under the Act.

Maguire v. Citicorp Retail Servs., Inc., 147 F.3d 232 (2d Cir. 1998). Where a least sophisticated consumer would have the false impression that a third party was collecting the debt, the creditor was a "debt collector" within the FDCPA.

Taylor v. Perrin, Landry, deLaunay & Durand, 103 F.3d 1232 (5th Cir. 1997). The creditor was a "debt collector" even though it was collecting its own debt because it used a lawyer's letterhead and facsimile signature on its dunning letters, falsely indicating that a third person was collecting the debt, violating §§ 1692e(3) & 1692j. The law firm supplying the letters was also liable.

Alabama

Kimber v. Fed. Fin. Corp., 668 F. Supp. 1480 (M.D. Ala. 1987).

The phrase "debt for another" in the definition of creditor means a debt originally owed another.

Arkansas

Webb v. MBNA Am. Bank, 2005 WL 2648019 (E.D. Ark. Oct. 13, 2005). Credit card issuer's motion to dismiss was denied because the consumer's allegation that the defendant was a debt collector must be accepted at this early stage of the proceedings.

California

Denkers v. United Compucred Collections, Inc., 1996 WL 724784 (N.D. Cal. Nov. 27, 1996). Genuine issue of material fact existed as to whether public utility company was a debt collector where it hired a collection agency to only send out dunning letters. The phone number in letters was that of utility's collection department. A collection agency which served as a mere mailing service might be equivalent to a "flat rater" who provided letters to the creditor with the result the creditor would be considered a debt collector covered by the Act.

Pickering v. Coast Ctr. for Orthopedic Arthroscopic Surgery & Treatment, 2009 WL 932629 (Cal. Ct. App. Apr. 8, 2009) (unpublished). FDCPA jury verdict against medical services provider was affirmed over its objections that it is an exempt creditor collecting its own debt; court held that the evidence "permit[ted] a reasonable jury to conclude that used [its collection agent] as a mere surrogate in attempting to collect more than it was entitled to under the Contract for the surgical services and thus that qualified as a 'debt collector' " under the § 1692a(6) false name exception.

Connecticut

Young v. Citicorp Retail Servs., Inc., 1997 WL 280508 (D. Conn. May, 19 1997), *aff'd*, 159 F.3d 1349 (2d Cir. 1998). Creditor that used attorney's name to collect its own debts was a "debt collector" for the purposes of the FDCPA.

Saunders v. Stigers, 1999 Conn. Super. LEXIS 2816 (Conn. Super. Ct. Oct. 20, 1999), *aff'd on other grounds*, 773 A.2d 971 (Conn. App. Ct. 2001). A buyer of nonperforming mortgages may be a covered by the FDCPA but issues of fact required a trial of the issue.

Delaware

Games v. Cavazos, 737 F. Supp. 1368 (D. Del. 1990). U.S.A. Funds, a private federal student loan guarantee agency, is a debt collector under § 1692a(6) but exempted by § 1692a(6)(C) since it was merely sending out notices under the control and direction of the U.S. Department of Education. U.S.A. Funds was not exempt under § 1692a(6)(A) or (F).

Holmes v. Telecredit Serv., 736 F. Supp. 1289 (D. Del. 1990). A check guarantee service is a debt collector covered by the FDCPA. It regularly collects on debts obtained from payees after default. It is not a creditor nor was its "authorization" of a check an origination of the debt.

Florida

Thompson v. CIT Group/Consumer Fin., Inc., 2005 WL 2562606 (M.D. Fla. Oct. 11, 2005). Mortgagor's motion to dismiss was denied because the consumer's allegation that the defendant was a debt collector must be accepted at the early stages of the proceedings.

Sabeta v. Baptist Hosp., Inc., 410 F. Supp. 2d 1224 (S.D. Fla. Feb. 23, 2005). The court permitted the plaintiff to amend the complaint to allege that the defendant hospital, though otherwise a creditor exempt from the FDCPA, lost that exemption by using a name which would indicate that a third person was collecting the debt.

Illinois

Clark v. Pinnacle Credit Servs., L.L.C., 697 F. Supp. 2d 995 (N.D. Ill. 2010). Allegations that bank was "acting in concert" with other defendants and devised a credit card refinancing program for the purpose of collecting delinquent debts, that bank regularly attempted to collect debts, and that bank co-authored and approved a mailing to debtor instructing her to call a number to apply for refinancing program were sufficient to allege that bank was a "debt collector" under the FDCPA.

Daley v. Provena Hosps., 88 F. Supp. 2d 881 (N.D. Ill. 2000). Consumer's allegations that the defendant health care providers were "debt collectors" were sufficient to state a claim where complaint alleged that the defendants used the name of a non-existent collection agency to collect their own debts or collected their own debts in a name that would indicate that a third party was undertaking the collection efforts.

Peters v. AT&T Corp., 43 F. Supp. 2d 926 (N.D. Ill. 1999). A phone company using a collection agency to collect in the collection agency's name was liable under § 1692a(6) as a collection agency for using a name that would indicate that a third party was collecting if that collection agency was no more than a mailing service and did not otherwise engage in traditional collection activity. Disputed facts as to the role of the collection agency precluded summary judgment.

Roe v. Publishers Clearing House, Inc., 39 F. Supp. 2d 1099 (N.D. Ill. 1999). The court denied Publishers Clearing House's motion to dismiss, which claimed that Publishers Clearing House was a creditor and therefore exempt from Act. The court found that Publisher's Clearing House could be liable as a creditor using a name other than its own. G.C. Services sent "pre-collect" letters on its letterhead that said that the matter had not yet been referred for collection, and requested payment directly to Publishers Clearing House. G.C. Services was later assigned to collect only about 20% of the "pre-collect" accounts. When the initial letter was sent, Publishers Clearing House had not yet retained another entity to collect its debts.

Arellano v. Etan Indus., Inc., 1998 WL 911729 (N.D. Ill. Dec. 23, 1998). Conflicting evidence precluded granting cross motions for summary judgment regarding the extent to which either (i) the creditor was collecting its own debts using a false name by misrepresenting the role of the debt collector in the collection process or (ii) the debt collector was misrepresenting its active participation. Consumer's evidence, which was sufficient to create triable fact, was that debt collector only sent series of letters, did not initiate telephone calls to consumers, did not include its telephone number on its duns, and instead directed that payment be made directly to creditor.

Domico v. Etan Indus., Inc., 1998 WL 765058 (N.D. Ill. Oct. 26, 1998). Evidence that creditor retained debt collector to send duns in the debt collector's name but that the debt collector otherwise did not meaningfully participate in the collection process is sufficient to sustain the creditor's status as a debt collector under the exception of § 1692a(6) by using a name other than its own.

Fratto v. Citibank, 1996 WL 554549 (N.D. Ill. Sept. 25, 1996). Citibank could be considered a debt collector where it hired a collection agency to send out form letters on an attorney's letterhead that instructed the debtor to call Citibank's telephone number, where attorney never looked at the files and was not licensed to practice in the jurisdictions where the letters were sent, and Citibank never forwarded debt to the collection agency or the collection attorney.

Torres v. Am. Tel. & Tel. Co., 1988 WL 121547 (N.D. Ill. Nov. 9, 1988). The telephone company would be a debt collector under § 1692a(6) if it used a false name in some correspondence indicating a third party was involved in collecting a debt.

Maryland

Kennedy v. Hankey Group, 2010 WL 1664087 (D. Md. Apr. 22, 2010). The *pro se* consumer adequately stated a claim that the defendant was an FDCPA debt collector and not an exempt creditor by alleging that the defendant was "doing business specializing in the acquisition and servicing of near-prime to sub-prime automotive retail installment contracts and debt collections relating to those contracts" and that the defendant did not provide him with "a copy of the contract proving that [he] owed Westlake a debt and that the alleged debt was unpaid." The court inferred that the defendant acquired the right to pursue debts due under contracts to which it was not a party and that, when consumer asked for a copy of the contract showing that he owed a debt, he was requesting a copy of the assignment from the original creditor.

Ransom v. Telecredit Serv. Corp., 1992 U.S. Dist. LEXIS 22738 (D. Md. Feb. 5, 1992). The exception to the creditor exclusion in § 1692a(4), which applies to "any person to the extent that he receives an assignment or transfer of a debt in default solely for the purpose of facilitating collection of such debt for another," applied to a computerized check authorization service that regularly attempted to collect on dishonored checks purchased from its subscribers because the debts were in default when purchased and debts originally belonged to another.

Massachusetts

In re Maxwell, 281 B.R. 101 (Bankr. D. Mass. 2002). Argument by purchaser of defaulted note that it was not a debt collector was frivolous: it had sent demand letters before becoming the owner of the note; every contact letter claimed that it was a debt collector. Its contact history, the testimony of its witness, and the assignment document also substantiated its status as a debt collector.

Missouri

Kempf v. Famous Barr Co., 676 F. Supp. 937 (E.D. Mo. 1988). Creditor's motion for summary judgment denied on FDCPA coverage of creditor and its employee who allegedly denied working for the creditor while collecting the debt.

Nebraska

Sheldon v. Unum Life Ins. Co., 2006 WL 1288774 (D. Neb. May 9, 2006). Where insurance company directed payment to its Financial Recovery Unit, motion to dismiss denied when least sophisticated consumer might perceive that company is acting under another name for the purpose of debt collector status.

New York

Grammatico v. Sterling, Inc., Clearinghouse No. 47,976 (N.D.N.Y. 1991). Corporation which purchased jewelry company and its accounts was held to be a "debt collector" within § 1692a(6) with regard to its letters to the consumer because it failed to disclose its relationship with the jewelry company thereby leading the consumer to believe a third party was collecting the debt.

Britton v. Weiss, 1989 U.S. Dist. LEXIS 14610 (N.D.N.Y. Dec. 7, 1989). Attorney who was employed by creditor and who included creditor's name as part of his street address in collection letter was still a collector because intent of letter was to deceive debtor into believing that a private attorney had intervened.

Ohio

Kelly v. Montgomery Lynch & Assocs., Inc., 2008 WL 1775251 (N.D. Ohio Apr. 15, 2008). The fact that the subject dishonored check was payable to the defendant debt collector itself and not to the medical provider to whom the debt was incurred did not mean that the collector was collecting its own debt and thus did not convert the defendant debt collector into an exempt creditor.

Canterbury v. Columbia Gas, 2001 WL 1681132 (S.D. Ohio Sept. 25, 2001). Consumer's amended complaint stated a claim under § 1692e against a utility company that used a flat rate collector to routinely send a single collection letter to its customers. The utility company's use of the collection agency was such that the utility was covered under § 1692a(6) by creating the false impression that a third party collector was involved.

Durve v. Oker, 679 N.E.2d 19 (Ohio Ct. App. 1996). Where it was alleged that a physician had sent a collection letter in the name of a collection agency and discovery regarding the relationship between the physician and collection agency was denied, the consumer's FDCPA counterclaim against them was improperly dismissed.

Pennsylvania

Pressman v. Southeastern Fin. Group, Inc., 1995 WL 710480 (E.D. Pa. Nov. 30, 1995). Creditor's motion for summary judgment was denied since there was a question of fact as to whether creditor used name other than its own to collect its debts.

Connelly v. Bokser, 1991 U.S. Dist. LEXIS 21732 (E.D. Pa. Oct. 22, 1991). Whether use of the city's name in collection of debt by an individual, who had purchased the obligation from the city prior to default, is the utilization of "any name other than his own which would indicate that a third person is collecting or attempting to collect such debts" raised material issues of fact requiring denial of summary judgment.

Washington

Lamb v. HSC Real Estate, Inc., 2008 WL 467410 (E.D. Wash. Feb. 19, 2008). Summary judgment was granted for the defendant because it was a creditor when it obtained the right to collect the rents before the rent was past due.

K.1.2.3.2 Affiliated corporations, 15 U.S.C. § 1692a(6)(B)

Daros v. Chase Manhattan Bank, 2001 U.S. App. LEXIS 21471 (2d Cir. Oct. 1, 2001). Neither bank nor affiliated credit card company was a debt collector for the purposes of the FDCPA.

Pollice v. Nat'l Tax Funding, L.P., 225 F.3d 379 (3d Cir. 2000). The § 1692a(6)(c) exemption for government employees did not extend to a collection agency hired by the government to collect water bills.

Pelfrey v. Educ. Credit Mgmt. Corp., 208 F.3d 945, 2000 U.S. App. LEXIS 6272 (11th Cir. Apr. 6, 2000) (per curiam). Affirmed without analysis the holding in *Pelfrey v. Educ. Credit Mgmt. Corp.*, 71 F. Supp. 2d 1161 (N.D. Ala. 1999) that a student loan guarantee agency was exempt from the FDCPA pursuant to § 1692a(6)(F)(i) regarding collection by a fiduciary.

Aubert v. Am. Gen. Fin., Inc., 137 F.3d 976 (7th Cir. 1998). A corporate affiliate is excluded from the FDCPA's coverage if it satisfies two criteria: (1) the affiliate collects debts only for entities with which it is related and (2) the principal business of the affiliate is not debt collection. There is no requirement that the affiliate disclose its relationship to the creditor; therefore, an affiliate could collect debts under an assumed name.

Fox v. Citicorp Credit Servs., Inc., 15 F.3d 1507 (9th Cir. 1994). The existence of material factual dispute as to whether Citicorp Credit Service (CCS) is affiliated with the actual creditor, whether CCS collects debts for non-affiliated entities, or whether debt collection is CCS's principal business precludes the entry of summary judgment on the question of whether CCS is an in-house collector exempt from the coverage of the FDCPA pursuant to § 1692a(6)(B).

California

del Campo v. Am. Corrective Counseling Serv., Inc., 2010 WL 2473586 (N.D. Cal. June 3, 2010). Unresolved factual disputes concerning whether a corporate associate of the corporate debt collector participated in collection activities precluded the parties' cross motions for summary judgment on its status and liability as a debt collector.

Connecticut

Little v. World Fin. Network, Inc., 1990 U.S. Dist. LEXIS 20846 (D. Conn. July 15, 1990). Owner of a retailer's accounts is a debt collector since its principal business is the collection of debts. It falls within the first of the two, alternative prongs of § 1692a(6) and not within the exemption of § 1692a(6)(B) since its principal business is debt collection and it collects for companies other than its affiliates (Lane Bryant, The Limited).

Florida

Brooks v. Suntrust Bank Mortgage, Inc., 2010 WL 3340311 (M.D. Fla. Aug. 25, 2010). The complaint failed to state a claim against the defendant since, as a wholly owned subsidiary of the originating exempt creditor, it was itself exempt under § 1692a(6)(B) as a "person . . . acting as a debt collector for another person, both of whom are related by common ownership or affiliated by corporate control."

Georgia

Meads v. Citicorp Credit Servs., Inc., 686 F. Supp. 330 (S.D. Ga. 1988). Where the credit card servicing agency was a subsidiary of the card issuer, only collected for the parent, and disclosed its subsidiary relationship on its letterhead, the subsidiary was exempt under § 1692a(6)(B), and the creditor could not be said to be using a false name bringing it within the second sentence of § 1692a(6).

Illinois

Hernandez v. Midland Credit Mgmt., Inc., 2006 WL 695451 (N.D. Ill. Mar. 14, 2006). Allegations showing that the defendant Encore at least "indirectly" engaged in the collection of a debt for a third party were adequate to state a claim that the defendant was a "debt collector" under the FDCPA. Encore is a debt buyer that owns Midland which was collecting the debt by sending out a notice for Encore.

Daley v. Provena Hosps., 88 F. Supp. 2d 881 (N.D. Ill. 2000). Corporate affiliation exception of § 1692a(6)(B) was not established where the defendant failed to present any evidence relevant to the relationship between the purported affiliate and the related entity. Corporate affiliation exception of § 1692a(6)(B) to the definition of a "debt collector" applied to violations of § 1692j even though § 1692j itself makes "any person," and not only a "debt collector," liable for any violation, because § 1692j(b) explains that any such person is "liable to the same extent and in the same manner as a debt collector," thus re-incorporating the exception. [*N.B.*: This holding is contrary to the plain language of the FDCPA, conclusory and without any analysis, may be dicta because of other holdings, and makes no sense at all: if the statutory exclusions from the definition of a debt collector apply anyway to § 1692j's "any person" standard, then "any person" will always be a "debt collector," contrary to the statutory language.]

Friedman v. May Dep't Stores Co., 990 F. Supp. 571 (N.D. Ill. 1998). The so-called "common ownership" exception applies only if the subsidiary or affiliate acting as the debt collector does so solely for the entity to which it is related or affiliated and its principal business is not debt collection. Even if Lord & Taylor was construed as the creditor, May was excused from the requirements of the FDCPA under the common ownership exception.

Taylor v. Rollins, Inc., 1998 WL 164890 (N.D. Ill. Mar. 30, 1998). A corporate affiliate was excluded from the FDCPA's coverage so long as it satisfied two conditions: (1) the affiliate collected debts only for entities with which it was affiliated or related, and (2) the principal business of the affiliate was not debt collection. Even if the debt collector used an assumed name, the fact that it was affiliated with the creditor absolves it of liability.

Kegley v. Miles Mgmt. Corp., 1992 WL 370251 (N.D. Ill. Dec. 3, 1992). Entity, which primarily managed the operation and lease of real estate but also collected debts arising from the leasing business and which was owned by the owner of the real estate, was exempt from the definition of "debt collector" pursuant to § 1692a(6)(B).

Young v. Lehigh Corp., 1989 WL 117960 (N.D. Ill. Sept. 28, 1989). A company whose principal business was not debt collection and which only collects debts for affiliated companies was exempt.

Challen v. Town & Country Charge, 545 F. Supp. 1014 (N.D. Ill. 1982). An allegation that a bank collects debts owed to VISA, U.S.A., is sufficient to withstand a motion to dismiss the bank as not being a debt collector under the FDCPA. However, the bank would not be a debt collector simply because it used a division name—Town & Country Charge—when collecting its VISA accounts since it used the same name when extending VISA credit and because a division of a bank is not a legal entity.

Kentucky

Ray v. Citibank, N.A., 187 F. Supp. 2d 719 (W.D. Ky. 2001). Neither Citibank nor Citicorp Credit Services was a debt collector. Citibank was a creditor; Citicorp was a related entity and collected only for Citicorp.

Louisiana

Byes v. Edison Bros. Stores, Inc., 1995 WL 244441 (E.D. La. Apr. 26, 1995). To be excluded from the definition of "debt collector" pursuant to § 1692a(6)(B) it must be shown that (1) the collecting entity must be related by common ownership or affiliated by corporate control, (2) the collecting entity must only collect debts for its corporate relatives or affiliates, and (3) the principal purpose of the creditor must not be the collection of debts. The court found "such person" within the phrase "if the principal business of such person is not the collection of debts" refers to the entity on whose behalf the debt is being collected.

Mississippi

Shamburger v. Grand Casino, Inc., 84 F. Supp. 2d 794 (S.D. Miss. 1998). A corporate affiliate or subsidiary which collected a debt owed to its parent or affiliate was excluded from the definition of "debt collector."

Nebraska

Vernon v. BWS Credit Servs., Inc., Pov. L. Rep. ¶ 30,368, Clearinghouse No. 27,693 (D. Neb. 1980). Motion to dismiss by Beneficial Finance—the parent of BWS (a collection agency) and Spiegel's (the creditor)—was denied since Beneficial could be a "debt collector."

New York

Schuh v. Druckman & Sinel, L.L.P., 602 F. Supp. 2d 454 (S.D.N.Y. 2009). Failure to plead facts to cover mortgagee's creditor.

Burns v. Bank of Am., 655 F. Supp. 2d 240 (S.D.N.Y. 2008), *aff'd*, 360 Fed. Appx. 255 (2d Cir. 2010). Affiliate was not debt collector because affiliation was disclosed and it collected only for the affiliate.

Orenbuch v. N. Shore Health Sys., Inc., 250 F. Supp. 2d 145 (E.D.N.Y. 2003). A debt collector affiliated with the creditor was not a flat-rater pursuant to § 1692j. The FDCPA does not require disclosure of the debt collector's corporate affiliation.

Backuswalcott v. Common Ground Cmty. HDFC, Inc., 104 F. Supp. 2d 363 (S.D.N.Y. 2000). Defendant was the managing agent and nonprofit sole shareholder of a general partnership owning 1% of a homeless hotel. Defendant was exempt under the affiliate exemption. Factors included that debt collection was not defendant's most significant activity; nor its single largest or most important activity; the good will of the tenants was important to defendant which provided many social services. The court recognized that the FDCPA leaves a loophole that should be closed by Congress: a creditor might have debt collection activities conducted by a subsidiary, while evading FDCPA coverage by assigning other activities to that subsidiary so that debt collection was not its principal business. The court refused to pierce the corporate veil to take into account defendant's activities in two other corporations in considering whether debt collection was its principal activity.

Pennsylvania

Jarzyna v. Home Prop., L.P., 2011 WL 382367 (E.D. Pa. Feb. 4, 2011). An entity that qualified for the corporate affiliate exemption from the definition of a debt collector could not be brought back into that definition based on the false name exemption that is by its terms applicable only to an otherwise exempt "creditor."

South Carolina

Phillips v. Periodical Publishers' Serv. Bureau, Inc., Consumer Cred. Guide (CCH) ¶ 95,725 (S.C. 1989). An unincorporated subsidiary of a creditor was exempt under § 1692a(6)(B) where it collected debts only for its parent and its principal business was not the collection of debts.

Texas

KPMG Peat Marwick v. Texas Commerce Bank, 976 F. Supp. 623 (S.D. Tex. 1997). FDCPA cross-claim against bank was dismissed for failure to state a cause of action where bank was exempt as a creditor or as an affiliate under § 1692a(6)(B).

Wisconsin

Hartman v. Meridian Fin. Servs., Inc., 191 F. Supp. 2d 1031 (W.D. Wis. 2002). A collector acting on behalf of a creditor, where both "are related by common ownership or affiliated by corporate control," was not within the § 1692a(6)(B) exemption where the collector's principal business was the collection of debts and where it collected on behalf of unrelated entities as well.

K.1.2.3.3 State and federal officials, 15 U.S.C. § 1692a(6)(C)

Al-Sharif v. United States, 296 Fed. Appx. 740 (11th Cir. 2008). The defendant IRS employees were governmental actors exempt from FDCPA coverage pursuant to § 1692a(6)(C).

Smith v. United States, 2008 WL 5069783 (5th Cir. Dec. 2, 2008). *Pro se* consumer's FDCPA claim against various IRS employees "is entirely without merit, as the statute expressly excludes 'any officer or employee of the United States . . . to the extent that collecting or attempting to collect any debt is in the performance of his official duties' from the definition of 'debt collector.' " 15 U.S.C. § 1692a(6)(C).

Okoro v. Garner, 2001 U.S. App. LEXIS 28336 (7th Cir. Oct. 22, 2001). Federal court lacked subject matter jurisdiction to hear *pro se* prisoner's complaint that state employees collecting past due child support violated the FDCPA since state employees were exempt from coverage and the court ordered child support obligation was not a "debt" under the FDCPA.

Codar Inc. v. Arizona, 1999 U.S. App. LEXIS 949 (9th Cir. Jan. 21, 1999). Congress did not intend to abrogate state immunity when it passed FDCPA, therefore, immunity clause of Eleventh Amendment barred suit against a state and its agencies.

Brannan v. United Student Aid Funds, Inc., 94 F.3d 1260 (9th Cir. 1996). The government exemption under § 1692a(6)(C) only applied to an individual government official or employee who collected debts as part of his job responsibilities and not to a private nonprofit student loan guarantee organization with a government contract.

Heredia v. Green, 667 F.2d 392 (3d Cir. 1981). The defendant "Landlord & Tenant Officer" was exempted from the definition of debt collector by § 1692a(6)(C) since he was a state official and the activities complained about were official duties authorized by the court employing him. The defendant engaged in the pre-eviction activities of sending notices and receiving rent and fees.

Arkansas

Hollowell v. Hosto, 2010 WL 1416519 (E.D. Ark. Apr. 8, 2010). Even if the *pro se* consumer's claim was ripe for adjudication, which it was not, he could not succeed against the defendant state court clerk due to her quasi-judicial immunity in connection with the entry of writs of garnishment.

California

Kenney v. Barnhart, 2006 U.S. Dist. LEXIS 51068, 112 Soc. Sec. Rep. Serv. 401 (C.D. Cal. July 26, 2006). Social Security Administration was not a "debt collector."

Delaware

Games v. Cavazos, 737 F. Supp. 1368 (D. Del. 1990). U.S.A. Funds, a private federal student loan guarantee agency, is a debt collector under § 1692a(6) but exempted by § 1692a(6)(C) since it was merely sending out notices under the control and direction of the U.S. Department of Education.

Florida

United States v. Henry, 2010 WL 299249 (M.D. Fla. Jan. 21, 2010). The *pro se* defendants' FDCPA defense in this IRS tax assessment action was rejected since taxes are not FDCPA debts and the IRS was not a debt collector in accordance with the § 1692a(6)(C) governmental actor exemption.

Dep't of Revenue v. Michaels, 2008 WL 360631 (M.D. Fla. Feb. 8, 2008). Florida Department of Revenue exempt.

Graham v. Rossotti, 2001 U.S. Dist. LEXIS 9499 (M.D. Fla. May 25, 2001). *Pro se* plaintiff's suit for relief from an IRS tax levy was dismissed with prejudice because federal and state collection employees are exempted from the FDCPA.

Illinois

Russell v. United States, 2009 WL 236719 (S.D. Ill. Jan. 30, 2009), *aff'd*, 339 Fed. Appx. 637 (7th Cir. 2009) (unpublished). IRS employees exempt.

Parrish v. City of Highwood, 1998 WL 773994 (N.D. Ill. Oct. 30, 1998). Police officer, who attempted to collect consumer's dishonored check in accordance with police department policy to assist local merchants, is not subject to the FDCPA by reason of the governmental actor exemption of § 1692a(6)(C).

Arnold v. Truemper, 833 F. Supp. 678 (N.D. Ill. 1993). Bank's contact with police department to investigate a possible criminal matter did not qualify either the bank or the police department as a debt collector within FDCPA.

Indiana

Weiss v. Weinberger, 2005 WL 1432190 (N.D. Ind. June 9, 2005). A receiver appointed by the federal court is an officer of the court and excluded from the definition of "debt collector" pursuant to. § 1692a(6)(C).

Iowa

Israel v. Everson, 2005 WL 3277981 (S.D. Iowa Oct. 14, 2005). IRS is exempt from the FDCPA.

Liles v. Am. Corrective Counseling Servs., 131 F. Supp. 2d 1114 (S.D. Iowa 2001). Factual issues prevented a determination of whether a check collection agency was a debt collector. The collector was not a creditor's employee, an officer of the state, and admitted it was collecting debts, not just administering a bad check criminal diversion program.

Kansas

Bandy v. United States, 2008 WL 1867991 (D. Kan. Apr. 24, 2008). Summary judgment entered against the *pro se* taxpayer because under the FDCPA "federal taxes are not a debt, and the IRS is not a debt collector."

Streater v. Cox, 2008 WL 564884 (E.D. Mich. Feb. 28, 2008), *aff'd*, 336 Fed. Appx. 470 (6th Cir. 2009). FDCPA does not apply to state officers or employees.

Michigan

Jackson v. Federal Deposit Ins. Corp., 2010 WL 653151 (E.D. Mich. Feb. 19, 2010). FDCPA claims against the FDIC were dismissed for failure to comply with FIRREA's administrative exhaustion requirement, since the alleged activities "constitute an act or omission of . . . the Corporation as receiver." 12 U.S.C. § 1821(d)(13)(D)(ii).

Burgess v. Lee Acceptance Corp., 2008 WL 5111905 (E.D. Mich. Dec. 4, 2008). Denied deputy sheriff's motion to dismiss; question of fact where the court ordered him to execute the writ to seize property, but plaintiff presented evidence that serving officer was an independent contractor—not an officer of the court within § 1692a(6)(C). No discussion of § 1692a(6)(D).

Hodges v. C.I.R., 2008 WL 2604942 (E.D. Mich. June 30, 2008). The *pro se* consumer's state court complaint against IRS was properly removed to federal court since the complaint alleged an FDCPA claim. Court then dismissed for failure to state a claim based on substantive tax law, without addressing the obvious defects in suing the IRS under the FDCPA.

Gradisher v. Check Enforcement Unit, Inc., 133 F. Supp. 2d 988 (W.D. Mich. 2001). An independent contractor is not entitled to an exception as a government employee to the FDCPA pursuant to § 1692a(6)(C).

Hillman v. Secretary of the Treasury, 2000 U.S. Dist. LEXIS 4544 (W.D. Mich. Mar. 29, 2000), *aff'd on other grounds*, 2003 WL 1194309 (6th Cir. Mar. 11, 2003). *Pro se* complaint was dismissed because the Internal Revenue Service was not subject to the FDCPA.

Montana

Spilman v. Crebo, 561 F. Supp. 652 (D. Mont. 1982). The court could not find any authority by which IRS agents are subject to the FDCPA.

Nevada

Fleeger v. Bell, 95 F. Supp. 2d 1126 (D. Nev. 2000), *aff'd*, 2001 WL 1491252 (9th Cir. Nov. 26, 2001). District attorneys attempting to collect the markers pursuant to state bad check statutes were exempt from the FDCPA as an officer of a state performing official duties.

New Jersey

Huertas v. U.S. Dep't of Educ., 2010 WL 2771767 (D.N.J. July 12, 2010). The *pro se* consumer's FDCPA claims against the U.S. Department of Education were dismissed as invalid since the DOE was not a "debt collector."

New York

Schuh v. Druckman & Sinel, L.L.P., 602 F. Supp. 2d 454 (S.D.N.Y. 2009). Foreclosing attorney covered.

Diaz v. Dep't of Defense, 2008 WL 4671833 (S.D.N.Y. Oct. 23, 2008). Plaintiff's claims against federal government employees who allegedly retained collection agencies to recover money owed by the plaintiff to the government as a result of overpayments and penalties were dismissed since these defendants were exempt government employees.

Ohio

Keefer v. Wiles, Boyle, Burkholder & Bringardner, Co., L.P.A., 2008 WL 4404295 (S.D. Ohio Sept. 23, 2008). The applicability of the § 1692a(6)(C) state actor exemption for these attorney defendants based on their allegations they had been appointed as special counsel to the state attorney general to collect the underlying debt depended on a factual determination—whether they were acting as a "state officer or employee or as an independent contractor"—could not be resolved on a Rule 12 motion.

Al-Amin v. Internal Revenue, 2008 WL 373602 (N.D. Ohio Feb. 8, 2008). IRS exempt.

Georgeadis v. County of Fairfield, 2000 WL 1459418 (S.D. Ohio Sept. 25, 2000). Allegations of misconduct against a state court judge and sheriff's department officials acting to collect a debt against the *pro se* plaintiff failed to state a claim under the FDCPA since each defendant was a state employee exempt from coverage.

Pennsylvania

Frew v. Van Ru Credit Corp., 2006 WL 2261624 (E.D. Pa. Aug. 7, 2006). The U.S. Department of Education collecting a student loan on its own behalf was exempt from the FDCPA under both the governmental official and the creditor exceptions.

Albanese v. Portnoff Law Assocs., Ltd., 301 F. Supp. 2d 389 (E.D. Pa. 2004). Law firm that contracted with municipalities to collect government debt was not within the government officer and employee exemption.

Piper v. Portnoff Law Assocs., 274 F. Supp. 2d 681 (E.D. Pa. 2003), *aff'd*, 396 F.3d 227 (3d Cir. 2005). The exclusion of officers or employees of the government pursuant to § 1692a(6) did not extend to a collection firm hired by the government to collect water and sewer bills.

South Carolina

Gary v. Spires, 473 F. Supp. 878 (D.S.C. 1979), *rev'd on other grounds*, 634 F.2d 722 (S.C. Ct. App. 1980). A county official is not a "debt collector."

South Dakota

Mathis v. United States ex rel. C.I.R., 2003 WL 1950071 (D.S.D. Mar. 19, 2003). IRS agent was not a debt collector.

Tennessee

Little v. Tennessee Student Assistance Corp., 537 F. Supp. 2d 942 (W.D. Tenn. 2008). Case dismissed for lack of subject matter jurisdiction because the defendant is a state entity to which the Eleventh Amendment extends sovereign immunity, Congress did not waive that immunity in the FDCPA, and to the contrary § 1692a(6)(C) exempts state actors from its coverage.

Texas

Flemings v. City of Dallas, 2010 WL 3938377 (N.D. Tex. Aug. 21, 2010). Government officials exempt.

Chatmon v. U.S. Dep't of Educ., 2003 WL 21501919 (N.D. Tex. June 24, 2003). Failing to note the § 1692a(6)(C) exemption for government employees in this *pro se* case, the court held that the Department of Education was not a "debt collector" because the collection of debts was not its principal purpose and because it was a creditor collecting its own debt.

Vermont

Burgess v. U.S. Dep't of Educ., 2006 WL 1047064 (D. Vt. Apr. 17, 2006). Court dismissed *pro se* FDCPA claim, since employee of government agency was exempt from FDCPA.

K.1.2.3.4 *Legal process servers, 15 U.S.C. § 1692a(6)(D)*

Romea v. Heiberger & Assocs., 163 F.3d 111 (2d Cir. 1998). Attorney sending state mandated three-day demand for payment of past-due rent and eviction notice is a "debt collector;" statutory exception of § 1692a(6)(D) is inapplicable as it applies only to process servers.

Illinois

Spiegel v. Judicial Attorney Servs., Inc., 2011 WL 382809 (N.D. Ill. Feb. 1, 2011). Based on the allegations in the complaint, the process server exclusion from the definition of "debt collector" did not apply to the defendant.

Spiegel v. Judicial Attorney Servs., Inc., 2010 WL 5014116 (N.D. Ill. Dec. 3, 2010). While § 1692a(6)(D) generally excludes process servers from FDCPA coverage, the exemption may not apply where a process server was alleged to be "execut[ing] a false Proof of Service Document" and falsely claiming in state court proceedings that they effected personal service on the consumer. . The court found the "defendants' alleged dissembling can nonetheless be viewed as harassment and as a type of conduct that the FDCPA is designed to punish."

Maryland

Mateti v. Activus Fin., L.L.C., 2009 WL 2507423 (D. Md. Aug. 14, 2009). Attorneys cannot rely on the process server exemption to insulate themselves from liability if they either gave the process server incorrect address information or themselves committed a violation in the papers to be served or later improperly relied on affidavits of service that were fraudulent.

Massachusetts

Andrews v. South Coast Legal Servs., Inc., 582 F. Supp. 2d 82 (D. Mass. 2008). The defendants, while acting under court appointment as special process servers in connection with executing on a judgment, were not entitled to invoke the process server exemption of § 1692a(6)(D) since, in addition to merely serving process, they allegedly "prepared false and misleading documents, made demands for costs and fees to which they were not entitled, and engaged in other . . . harassing and coercive" conduct.

Alger v. Ganick, O'Brien & Sarin, 35 F. Supp. 2d 148 (D. Mass. 1999). The exemption of process servers from the definition of debt collector did not exempt a law firm which was collecting a debt and employed the process server, but provided the process server with incorrect and misleading information about the consumer's liability.

Missouri

Worch v. Wolpoff & Abramson, L.L.P., 477 F. Supp. 2d 1015 (E.D. Mo. Feb. 28, 2007). The process server serving notice of a NAF arbitration claim was exempt from FDCPA coverage under the process server exemption of § 1692a(6)(D). The defendant process server, who the plaintiff claimed went beyond mere service of process of the underlying collection papers in this case and made inquiries about the plaintiff's assets and household members in an indirect attempt to collect the debt, was not an FDCPA collector"

since there was no evidence that the defendant "regularly" engaged in such collection activities beyond simply serving process.

Worch v. Wolpoff & Abramson, L.L.P., 2006 WL 1523240 (E.D. Mo. June 1, 2006). The defendant who personally served a notice of arbitration on the consumer and who allegedly then harassed the consumer and otherwise violated the FDCPA was not exempt under § 1692a(6)(D) as a person "serving or attempting to serve legal process . . . in connection with the judicial enforcement of any debt" since arbitration is neither legal process nor judicial enforcement of a debt.

New York

Sykes v. Mel Harris & Assocs., L.L.C., 2010 WL 5395712 (S.D.N.Y. Dec. 29, 2010). The FDCPA protects process servers only "while" they serve process; a process server that allegedly failed to serve consumers with process and provided perjured affidavits of service is removed from the exemption.

Ohio

Byrd v. Law Offices of John D. Clunk Co., 2010 WL 816932 (S.D. Ohio Mar. 8, 2010). Process server was not subject to the FDCPA. Law firm not vicariously liable for acts of independent contractor who served process.

Oregon

McNall v. Credit Bureau, 689 F. Supp. 2d 1265 (D. Or. 2010). Surveys case law on whether process server is debt collector and whether attorney is responsible for process server's actions, granting summary judgment because there was no evidence showing that the process server went beyond the role of messenger in serving the complaint.

Pennsylvania

Duraney v. Washington Mut. Bank, 2008 WL 4204821 (W.D. Pa. Sept. 11, 2008), *aff'd*, 2010 WL 2993810 (3d Cir. Aug. 2, 2010). The court dismissed the § 1692d(3) claim based on the defendant foreclosure attorney's purported responsibility for the sheriff's publication of a foreclosure notice required by state law, since that publication is a form of service of legal process and cannot constitute debt collection activities for purposes of the FDCPA pursuant to the exemption in § 1692a(6)(D).

Flamm v. Sarner & Assocs., P.C., 2006 WL 43770 (E.D. Pa. Jan. 3, 2006). Where court had already found process server was a debt collector because he went beyond merely serving process, whether the lawyers were vicariously liable for the independent contractor's actions was a jury question.

Flamm v. Sarner & Assocs., P.C., 2002 WL 31618443 (E.D. Pa. Nov. 6, 2002). Lawyers who hired process server were not within the process server exemption. Process server who went beyond being merely a messenger in serving legal process and engaged in prohibited abusive or harassing activities to force an individual to repay a debt was no longer exempt under the process server exception and was a covered "debt collector." Attorney debt collector who hired a process server may be liable for the abusive and harassing misconduct of that process server.

Texas

Gardner v. Stewart, 2007 Bankr. LEXIS 555 (Bankr. N.D. Tex. Feb. 16, 2007). The court held that the defendant county sheriff was exempt from FDCPA coverage under § 1692a(6)(D) as "any person while serving or attempting to serve legal process on any person in connection with the judicial enforcement of any debt."

K.1.2.3.5 Nonprofit credit counselors, 15 U.S.C. § 1692a(6)(E)

California

Yang v. DTS Fin. Group, 570 F. Supp. 2d 1257 (S.D. Cal. 2008). The plaintiff stated a claim for relief since the allegation that the defendant debt settlement company was a for-profit organization removed it from the FDCPA exemption in § 1692a(6)(E) for bona fide nonprofit credit counselors.

New York

Limpert v. Cambridge Credit Counseling Corp., 328 F. Supp. 2d 360 (E.D.N.Y. 2004), *amended in part*, 2004 WL 3395347 (E.D.N.Y. Sep 16, 2004). Court dismissed claim that a credit counseling agency was covered by the FDCPA and not exempt under § 1692a(6)(E). It did not consider FDCPA bona fide counseling requirement or its actual nonprofit status. Later decision found the counseling agency was not a nonprofit and reversed its dismissal of a CROA claim but the FDCPA claim was not addressed.

K.1.2.3.6 Fiduciaries and escrows, 15 U.S.C. § 1692a(6) (F)(i)

Rowe v. Educational Credit Mgmt. Corp., 559 F.3d 1028 (9th Cir. 2009). A student loan guarantee agency has a fiduciary obligation within the meaning of § 1692a(6)(F); however, where its sole function was a post-default assignment to collect, the collection function is central, rather than incidental, to its fiduciary duty, and it is thus subject to the FDCPA.

Wilson v. Draper & Goldberg, P.L.L.C., 443 F.3d 373 (4th Cir. 2006). Defendants were not within the fiduciary exception, since "actions to foreclose on a property pursuant to a deed of trust are not 'incidental' to its fiduciary obligation. Rather, they are central to it." Section 1692f(6) applies to those whose only role in the debt collection process is the enforcement of a security interest. The subsection is not an exception to the definition of debt collector, it is an inclusion to the term debt collector.

Alabama

Pelfrey v. Educ. Credit Mgmt. Corp., 71 F. Supp. 2d 1161 (N.D. Ala. 1999), *aff'd*, 208 F.3d 945 (11th Cir. 2000). FDCPA complaint against a student loan guarantee agency dismissed based on the "bona fide fiduciary obligation" exception of § 1692a(6)(F)(i) because of the federal requirements for the agency's handling of reserve funds in a fiduciary manner.

California

Gruen v. EdFund, 2009 WL 2136785 (N.D. Cal. July 15, 2009). Student loan guarantee agency was denied the § 1692a(6)(F) fiduciary exemption on a motion to dismiss: "[A] guarantee agency that does not act as the guarantor of the loan, but instead was assigned the loan in order to act as a collection agent, does not engage in collection activity that is 'incidental to' the original guarantor's fiduciary duty to the Department of Education. . . . Because the complaint alleged that the defendant's only role in the case was to collect the loan assigned to it after the Plaintiff's default, the defendant did not fall within the exception under the FDCPA."

Florida

Reynolds v. Gables Residential Servs., Inc., 428 F. Supp. 2d 1260 (M.D. Fla. 2006). Property manager for residential apartments was a fiduciary and not a debt collector; in addition it had obtained the account before default.

Louisiana

Murungi v. Texas Guaranteed, 693 F. Supp. 2d 597 (E.D. La. 2010), *aff'd*, 2010 WL 3736227 (5th Cir. Sept. 16, 2010). Summary judgment in this student loan collection abuse case granted to the defendant guarantee agency since it is not an FDCPA "debt collector": "The Court concludes that is not a 'debt collector' subject to the FDCPA because it its actions to collect [plaintiff's] defaulted loan were 'incidental' to its § 1962a(6)(F)(i) 'bona fide fiduciary obligation' to the United States government. [Defendant's] fiduciary relationship to DOE is created by detailed federal regulations governing [defendant's] participation in the Federal Family Education Loan Program (FFELP). Moreover, debt collection is merely incidental to [defendant's] primary function of guaranteeing student loans made by other entities."

Reed v. Smith, 1994 U.S. Dist. LEXIS 21463 (M.D. La. July 25, 1994). Where the primary reason for the formation of the attorney-client relationship was the collection of a debt, the attorney's efforts were not exempted from the FDCPA as "incident to a bona fide fiduciary obligation," under § 1692a(F)(i).

Minnesota

Montgomery v. Educ. Credit Mgmt. Corp., 238 B.R. 806 (D. Minn. 1999). Private, nonprofit student loan guarantee agency established pursuant to the Federal Family Education Loan Program in accordance with the Higher Education Act of 1965 fell under the § 1692a(6)(F)(i) fiduciary exemption from FDCPA coverage.

New Jersey

Fisher v. Congress Title, 2007 U.S. Dist. LEXIS 887 (D.N.J. Jan. 8, 2007). The court dismissed the *pro se* plaintiff's claim that the defendant title company which handled the sale of his home and which was supposed to retain certain proceeds in escrow to pay his outstanding creditors misapplied those funds in violation of the FDCPA when it erroneously paid the debts of another individual with a similar name, since the title company's actions occurred incidental to a bona fide escrow arrangement exempt pursuant to § 1692a(6)(F)(i).

New York

Barry v. Board of Managers of Condo. II, 853 N.Y.S.2d 827 (N.Y. Civ. Ct. 2007). Condominium common charges were not a "debt" within the scope of the FDCPA because it was the fiduciary duty of the unit owner to pay such common charges.

Oregon

Rowe v. Educational Credit Mgmt. Corp., 2010 WL 3188026 (D. Or. Aug. 10, 2010). On remand from the published Ninth Circuit opinion that reversed dismissal for failure to state a claim, summary judgment was granted to the defendant student loan guarantee agency since the facts established, contrary to the allegations of the complaint, that it was exempt from the FDCPA under the § 1692a(6)(F)(i) fiduciary exemption.

West Virginia

Seals v. National Student Loan Program, 2004 WL 3314948 (N.D. W. Va. Aug. 16, 2004), *aff'd*, 124 Fed. Appx. 182 (4th Cir. 2005). Student loan guaranty agency was exempt under the fiduciary obligation exception to the FDCPA.

Wisconsin

Berndt v. Fairfield Resorts, Inc., 339 F. Supp. 2d 1064 (W.D. Wis. 2004). Defendant timeshare resort management association was exempt under § 1692a(6)(F)(i).

K.1.2.3.7 Originators, 15 U.S.C. § 1692a(6)(F)(ii)

Buckman v. Am. Bankers Ins. Co., 115 F.3d 892 (11th Cir. 1997). A bail bondsman who arranged a bail bond through an insurance company and later started foreclosure proceeding for the insurance company after the bond was forfeited was exempt from FDCPA coverage under the § 1692a(6)(F)(ii) exemption for a person who originated the debt.

California

Harmon v. GE Money Corp., 2010 WL 2219345 (E.D. Cal. June 1, 2010). The court dismissed the *pro se* complaint where the defendant, an original lender collecting its own debt, was an exempt creditor.

Santos v. U.S. Bank N.A., 2010 WL 2218803 (E.D. Cal. June 1, 2010). Greenpoint exempt.

Robinson v. Managed Accounts Receivables Corp., 654 F. Supp. 2d 1051 (C.D. Cal. 2009). Employees of a debt collection organization may be "debt collectors" under the FDCPA and held personally liable for acts committed during the scope of their employment.

Distor v. U.S. Bank, 2009 WL 3429700 (N.D. Cal. Oct. 22, 2009). Complaint dismissed against the originator of the loan as it does not qualify as a debt collector.

Florida

Centennial Bank v. Noah Group, L.L.C., 2010 WL 5157375 (S.D. Fla. Dec. 2, 2010). Centennial Bank was not a "debt collector," as it either originated the debt as a merged entity with Marine Bank or it obtained the debt upon merging with Marine Bank when the debt was not in default.

Louisiana

Menchel v. Daigrepont, 2003 WL 21220022 (E.D. La. May 19, 2003). Originating creditor collecting its own debt was not a "debt collector."

Pennsylvania

Messett v. Home Consultants, Inc., 2010 WL 1643606 (M.D. Pa. Apr. 22, 2010).

Rubenstein v. Dovenmuehle Mortgage, Inc., 2009 WL 3467769 (E.D. Pa. Oct. 28, 2009). The defendant mortgage company that originated the loan and that was collecting its own debt was exempt under § 1692a(6)(F)(ii).

K.1.2.3.8 Debts assigned before default, 15 U.S.C. § 1692a(6)(F)(iii) [See also K.1.2.2.6, Debt buyers]

McKinney v. Cadleway Properties, Inc., 548 F.3d 496 (7th Cir. 2008). The holder of the loan was a "debt collector" under the FDCPA because it acquired the loan when it was in default.

Brown v. Morris, 243 Fed. Appx. 31 (5th Cir. 2007). The defendant bank collecting a debt that was in default at the time when the bank acquired it was not an FDCPA debt collector notwithstanding § 1692a(6)(F)(iii)'s coverage of collection activities concerning a debt which was "in default at the time it was obtained by such person" since the bank's acquisition of the debt was through merger with the previous holder; in the absence of a definition of "obtained," the court concluded that this usage only covers debts in default that are obtained through transfer or assignment and does not cover the situation here of a merger where the new holder "was not specifically assigned [the debt] for debt-collection purposes."

Oppong v. First Union Mortgage Corp., 215 Fed. Appx. 114 (3d Cir. 2007). Where Wells Fargo acquired servicing rights after default and foreclosed on plaintiff's mortgage, court determined that its collection of debt was regular, even though a small percentage of its activities and therefore Wells Fargo was a debt collector.

Brumberger v. Sallie Mae Servicing Corp., 84 Fed. Appx. 458 (5th Cir. 2004). Appellate court affirmed the district court's dismissal of Sallie Mae because plaintiff did not allege that his debt was in default when Sallie Mae began servicing his loan.

Alibrandi v. Fin. Outsourcing Servs., Inc., 333 F.3d 82 (2d Cir. 2003). A collector could not exclude itself from the definition of debt collector through its contract with the creditor identifying itself as a servicer and the debts it was servicing as delinquent rather than in default when the debt at issue in the case had, in fact, been declared in default before the servicing was transferred. The Second Circuit, however, rejected the consumer's argument that default automatically occurs immediately after payment becomes due and granted the creditor and servicer great leeway in defining what constitutes default.

Schlosser v. Fairbanks Capital Corp., 323 F.3d 534 (7th Cir. 2003). Assignees of a debt are treated as debt collectors covered by the Act if the debt sought to be collected was in default when acquired by the assignee and are treated as creditors who are not covered, if the debt was not in default when acquired. If the parties to the assignment are mistaken about whether a debt is in default when assigned, that mistaken status will not determine whether the assignee is a debt collector or creditor; instead, an assignee that attempts to collect on a debt that it asserts is in default is a debt collector, even if it is mistaken about the default, and an assignee that neither believes nor asserts that a debt is in default when acquired is a creditor.

Whitaker v. Ameritech Corp., 129 F.3d 952 (7th Cir. 1997). Ameritech was not a debt collector because it collected on phone bills which it obtained before default bringing it within the exemption in § 1692a(6)(F)(iii).

Wadlington v. Credit Acceptance Corp., 76 F.3d 103 (6th Cir. 1996). A car dealer's financer who serviced the dealer's retail installment sales accounts and appeared on the retail installment contracts as an assignee was exempt as either a creditor or a servicer who took the contract prior to default as provided by § 1692a(4) and (6)(A) or (F). A financer which was not a debt collector was not vicariously liable for the FDCPA violations of its attorney.

Perry v. Stewart Title Co., 756 F.2d 1197 (5th Cir. 1985). Both mortgage originator servicing company and FNMA, the assignee of the mortgage before default, are excluded from FDCPA coverage.

Alabama

Ausar-El v. BAC (Bank of Am.) Home Loan Serv., L.P., 2010 WL 5301033 (M.D. Ala. Nov. 22, 2010). The court dismissed the *pro se* plaintiff's complaint, since the FDCPA excludes persons collecting a debt when that person either (a) originated the debt, or (b) the collection "concerns a debt which was not in default at the time it was obtained by such persons." Further, according to the Act's legislative history, a mortgagee and its assignee, including mortgage servicing companies, are not debt collectors under the FDCPA when the debt is not in default at the time the mortgage-holder acquires the debt.

Alaska

Barber v. Nat'l Bank, 815 P.2d 857 (Alaska 1991). Mortgage servicing company that obtained a debt before default is exempted from FDCPA coverage by § 1692a(6)(F)(ii).

Arizona

Diessner v. Mortgage Elec. Registration Sys., 618 F. Supp. 2d 1184 (D. Ariz. 2009), *aff'd*, 384 Fed. Appx. 609 (9th Cir. 2010). Mortgage servicers receiving an obligation for servicing which is not in default are not debt collectors within the FDCPA.

Stejic v. Aurora Loan Servs., L.L.C., 75 Fed. R. Serv. 3d 307 (D. Ariz. 2009). Mortgage servicer not a debt collector.

Mitchell v. EMC Mortgage Corp., 2009 WL 3274407 (D. Ariz. Oct. 13, 2009). The FDCPA does not include a mortgage servicing company (which received the obligation before default) within the definition of a debt collector.

Gacy v. Gammage & Burnham, 2006 WL 467937 (D. Ariz. Feb. 23, 2006). Letter notifying consumer of the medical service provider's lien on the proceeds of any personal injury recovery was not an effort to collect a debt, in view of lack of admissible documentation that plaintiff owed money or that her obligation was in default.

Arkansas

Marshall v. Deutsche Bank Nat'l Trust Co., 2011 WL 345988 (E.D. Ark. Feb. 1, 2011). The complaint failed to state any facts to support the conclusion that Wells Fargo Mortgage was a debt collector since there was no evidence to support that the loan was in default when Wells Fargo began servicing the loan.

Dickard v. Oklahoma Mgmt. Servs. for Physicians, L.L.C., Slip Copy, 2007 WL 3025020 (W.D. Ark. Oct. 15, 2007). The defendant, an entity that provided day-to-day management services to physicians, including billing services, was not a debt collector since it obtained the accounts that it was billing prior to default.

Quinn v. Ocwen Fed. Bank, F.S.B., 2006 WL 4495659 (E.D. Ark. Feb. 2, 2006), *aff'd on other grounds*, 470 F.3d 1240 (8th Cir. 2006). Complaint failed to state an FDCPA claim because "the term 'debt collector' does not include creditors, mortgage servicing companies, or an assignee of a debt, as long as the debt was not in default at the time it was assigned."

California

Reyes v. Wells Fargo Bank, N.A., 2011 WL 30759 (N.D. Cal. Jan. 3, 2011). A loan servicer is not a "debt collector" under either the FDCPA or the Rosenthal Act.

Tang v. California Reconveyance Co., 2010 WL 5387837 (N.D. Cal. Dec. 22, 2010). Even if the *pro se* plaintiffs has alleged that the defendants were debt collectors, the defendants would likely have been excluded from the definition, since it appeared that the defendants obtained their interest in the property prior to default.

Reed v. Wells Fargo Home Mortgage Inc., 2010 WL 5136196 (E.D. Cal. Dec. 10, 2010). The court dismissed the *pro se* plaintiff's FDCPA claim since the Act explicitly excludes creditors as well as loan originators or assignees who obtained the right to collect on loan when it was not in default.

London v. Aurora Loan Servs., 2010 WL 3751812 (N.D. Cal. Sept. 24, 2010). Applying the rule that the FDCPA "exempts loan servicing companies, as long as the loan was not in default when it was assigned," the court dismissed the complaint with leave to amend on the factual issue as to when the defendant became the servicer, not on the legal issue of whether a loan servicer is a debt collector.

Anokhin v. BAC Home Loan Serv., L.P., 2010 WL 3294367 (E.D. Cal. Aug. 20, 2010). The complaint was dismissed because a mortgage servicer who obtained the debt prior to default is exempt from FDCPA coverage.

Zhuravlev v. BAC Home Loans Serv., L.P., 2010 WL 2873253 (N.D. Cal. July 20, 2010). Because an entity that foreclosed on property pursuant to a deed of trust is not a "debt collector" where it was clear that the entity obtained its interest prior to default, the FDCPA claim was dismissed and state claims were remanded to state court.

Odinma v. Aurora Loan Servs., 2010 WL 2232169 (N.D. Cal. June 3, 2010). Complaint dismissed for failure to state a claim because "foreclosure is not debt collection under the federal Fair Debt Collection Practices Act."

Gwin v. Pacific Coast Fin. Servs., 2010 WL 1691567 (S.D. Cal. Apr. 23, 2010).

Campiglia v. Saxon Mortgage Servs., Inc., 2010 WL 725560 (N.D. Cal. Mar. 1, 2010). Mortgage servicer not a debt collector.

Saldate v. Wilshire Credit Corp., 2010 WL 582074 (E.D. Cal. Feb. 12, 2010). "[F]oreclosing on a property pursuant to a deed of trust is not a debt collection within the meaning of the [FDCPA.]"

Matudio v. Countrywide Home Loans, Inc., 2010 WL 114185 (C.D. Cal. Jan. 6, 2010). Defendant not a debt collector.

Reynoso v. Paul Fin., L.L.C., 2009 WL 3833298 (N.D. Cal. Nov. 16, 2009). The FDCPA's definition of debt collector does not include any assignee of the debt so long as the debt was not in default at the time of assignment.

Distor v. U.S. Bank, 2009 WL 3429700 (N.D. Cal. Oct. 22, 2009). Complaint dismissed against the loan servicer who obtained the debt prior to default since it is not a debt collector.

Nguyen v. LaSalle Bank, 2009 WL 3297269 (C.D. Cal. Oct. 13, 2009). Defendants were not debt collectors within the FDCPA.

Sanchez v. U.S. Bancorp, 2009 WL 3157486 (S.D. Cal. Sept. 25, 2009). Loan servicer not debt collector.

Santos v. Countrywide Home Loans, 2009 WL 2500710 (E.D. Cal. Aug. 14, 2009). Lender and servicer who acquired mortgage before default not within FDCPA.

Caballero v. Ocwen Loan Servicing, 2009 WL 1528128 (N.D. Cal. May 29, 2009). Creditors, mortgagors, and mortgage servicing companies (who did not receive the mortgage in default) are not "debt collectors" within the coverage of the FDCPA.

Martinez v. Quality Loan Serv. Corp., 2009 WL 586725 (C.D. Cal. Feb. 10, 2009) (unpublished). Where consumer's complaint failed to allege sufficient facts that a loan servicing company was a "debt collector," defendant's motion to dismiss was granted.

Pineda v. Saxon Mortgage Servs., Inc., 2008 WL 5187813 (C.D. Cal. Dec. 10, 2008). Mortgage servicer that did not acquire debt after default not within FDCPA.

Moen v. Merrick Bank Corp., 2007 WL 1381411 (N.D. Cal. May 7, 2007). The FDCPA treats assignees as debt collectors if the debt sought to be collected was in default when acquired by the assignee.

Bouzan v. Diedel, 2005 WL 481323 (Cal. Ct. App. Mar. 2, 2005). Property managers who routinely collected monies on behalf of landlords or homeowners associations were excluded from the FDCPA because of the "debt-not-in-default" exclusion.

Colorado

Sullivan v. Ocwen Loan Servicing L.L.C., 2009 WL 103681 (D. Colo. Jan. 14, 2009). The consumer had sufficiently pleaded that the account was in default when assigned resulting in denial of the motion to dismiss.

Lyons v. WM Specialty Mortgage L.L.C., 2008 WL 2811810 (D. Colo. July 18, 2008). The defendant mortgage company and mortgage servicer were not FDCPA debt collectors since the debt was not in default at the time when each obtained it.

Ricotta v. Owcen Loan Servicing, L.L.C., 2008 WL 516674 (D. Colo. Feb. 22, 2008). When servicing of the loan began at a time when the loan was not in default, defendant was not a "debt collector" within the FDCPA.

Allen v. Nelnet, Inc., 2007 WL 2786432 (D. Colo. Sept. 24, 2007). The court dismissed the *pro se* consumer's complaint because the defendant was not a debt collector and instead was exempt as a creditor/servicer of the subject student loan who obtained the account prior to default.

Smith v. Argent Mortgage Co., L.L.C., 2007 WL 2484296 (D. Colo. June 27, 2007). The court granted the defendant mortgage servicer summary judgment because it obtained the loan prior to default and therefore was not a debt collector subject to the FDCPA.

Smith v. Argent Mortgage Co., L.L.C., 447 F. Supp. 2d 1194 (D. Colo. 2006). Defendant's motion to dismiss *pro se* plaintiffs' complaint was denied because a question of fact existed to whether defendant obtained the debt when it was in default.

Connecticut

Coppola v. Connecticut Student Loan Found., 1989 WL 47419 (D. Conn. Mar. 22, 1989). Student loan servicing agency not a debt collector since it obtained the loan before default and is exempted by § 1692a(6)(F)(iii).

District of Columbia

Edmond v. American Educ. Servs., 2010 WL 4269129 (D.D.C. Oct. 28, 2010). Student loan servicer that acquired before default exempt.

Florida

Centennial Bank v. Noah Group, L.L.C., 2010 WL 5157375 (S.D. Fla. Dec. 2, 2010). Centennial Bank was not a "debt collector," as it either originated the debt as a merged entity with Marine Bank or it obtained the debt upon merging with Marine Bank when the debt was not in default.

Locke v. Wells Fargo Home Mortgage, 2010 WL 4941456 (S.D. Fla. Nov. 30, 2010). "Since Wells Fargo was the mortgage company servicing the Plaintiff's mortgage, it cannot be liable as a 'debt collector' under section 1692."

Reese v. JPMorgan Chase & Co., 686 F. Supp. 2d 1291 (S.D. Fla. 2009). Defendant was servicing a debt which was not in default and thus was not a debt collector within the FDCPA.

North Star Capital Acquisitions, L.L.C. v. Krig, 611 F. Supp. 2d 1324 (M.D. Fla. 2009). Plaintiff, which acquired the debt after it had become delinquent, was a "debt collector" under the FDCPA.

Frazier v. HSBC Mortgage Servs., Inc., 2009 WL 4015574 (M.D. Fla. Nov. 19, 2009), *aff'd on other grounds*, 2010 WL 4204636 (11th Cir. Oct. 26, 2010). Defendant was not a debt collector covered by the FDCPA.

Monroe v. CitiMortgage, Inc., 2007 WL 1560194 (M.D. Fla. May 29, 2007). The court dismissed the complaint for failure to state a claim because "a debt collector does not include the consumer's creditors, a mortgage servicing company, or an assignee of a debt, as long as the debt was not in default at the time it was assigned" and there was "no allegation in Plaintiffs' complaint that the mortgage was in default at the time that CitiMortgage became its assignee."

Williams v. Edelman, 408 F. Supp. 2d 1261 (S.D. Fla. 2006). An entity which serviced the debt before it fell into default was not a "debt collector" as defined by the FDCPA.

Belin v. Litton Loan Serv., L.P., 2006 WL 1992410 (M.D. Fla. July 14, 2006). The complaint stated a claim that the defendant was a "debt collector" since it alleged that the defendant was assigned the debt once it was already in default.

Reynolds v. Gables Residential Servs., Inc., 428 F. Supp. 2d 1260 (M.D. Fla. 2006). Property manager for residential apartments was a fiduciary and not a debt collector; in addition it had obtained the account before default.

Cooper v. Litton Loan Servicing, 253 B.R. 286 (Bankr. N.D. Fla. 2000). One who obtained a loan when it was not in default was not a debt collector.

Osheyack v. Garcia, 814 So. 2d 440 (Fla. 2001). Local telephone company that billed and collected charges for a long-distance carrier was not a debt collector since it acquired the debt and commenced its collection activity prior to default.

Georgia

LaCosta v. McCalla Raymer, L.L.C., 2011 WL 166902 (N.D. Ga. Jan. 18, 2011). A debt collector does not include the consumer's creditors, a mortgage servicing company, or an assignee of a debt, as long as the debt was not in default at the time it was assigned.

Kuria v. Palisades Acquisition XVI, L.L.C., 2010 WL 4780769 (N.D. Ga. Nov. 16, 2010). A company that buys debt already in default may be a "debt collector" despite having "creditor" status.

Hawaii

Pulawa v. Fed. Recovery Servs., Inc., 2006 WL 1153745 (D. Haw. May 1, 2006). Summary judgment was granted to a defendant that acquired plaintiff's health spa account before it was in default, so defendant was not a debt collector as defined in the FDCPA.

Illinois

Simmons v. Med-I-Claims, 2007 U.S. Dist. LEXIS 9403 (C.D. Ill. Feb. 9, 2007). Because there was insufficient evidence regarding at what point the creditor considered the account to be in default,

defendant's motion for summary judgment arguing that it was not a debt collector was denied.

Hutchins v. Fairbanks Capital Corp., 2003 WL 1719997 (N.D. Ill. Mar. 28, 2003). As the mortgage was not in default according to the contract, which required a failure to respond to a notice of missed payment for default, the FDCPA did not apply to the servicer who sent a letter seeking payment of the last two overdue payments. The court distinguished *Schlosser v. Fairbanks Capital Corp.*, 323 F.3d 534 (7th Cir. 2003) where the mortgage servicer had sent notice of default.

Porter v. Fairbanks Capital Corp., 2002 WL 31163702 (N.D. Ill. Sept. 27, 2002). Where the consumer did not allege that the debt was in default at the time it was obtained by the mortgage servicer, the servicer was not properly alleged to be a debt collector.

Winterstein v. CrossCheck, Inc., 149 F. Supp. 2d 466 (N.D. Ill. 2001). The court rejected check guarantee service's arguments that it was not a debt collector. It was not a creditor because the check had been presented to the creditor and forwarded to the guarantee service after default. A purported agreement assigning the check before default exalted form over substance. It was not an originator because it did not participate in the creation of the debt. There was at least an issue of fact as to whether defendant regularly collected debts when it attempted to collect on more than 2000 checks and spent $2 million on debt collection efforts per year.

Indiana

Crawford v. Countrywide Home Loans, Inc., 2010 WL 3273715 (N.D. Ind. Aug. 16, 2010). A defendant who began servicing the subject mortgage prior to default was an exempt creditor.

Magee v. AllianceOne, Ltd., 487 F. Supp. 2d 1024 (S.D. Ind. 2007). The court is not bound by the creditor's determination of when a debt is in default, particularly where the creditor assigns the debt for collection one day and declares it to be in default the next.

Iowa

Fischer v. Unipac Serv. Corp., 519 N.W.2d 793 (Iowa 1994). FDCPA did not apply to loan which was not in default when assigned.

Kansas

Kvassay v. Hasty, 236 F. Supp. 2d 1240 (D. Kan. 2002). Defendant lawyers "obtained" checks which armored car service had lost despite the absence of a consensual relationship with, and indeed over the objection of, the creditor medical clinic, which took affirmative steps to stop the debt collection. The lawyers, on behalf of the insurance carrier were engaged "to assist in the claims process and defend" the armored car service. However, checks, that were overdue because the deposit bag had been lost, were not in default; therefore the lawyers king to collect on behalf of the insurance carrier qualified for the "servicer" exemption under § 1692a(6)(F)(iii)).

Stark v. Hasty, 236 F. Supp. 2d 1214 (D. Kan. 2002). Companion case to *Kvassay*; same result, based on *Kvassay* discussion.

Louisiana

Castrillo v. American Home Mortgage Serv., Inc., 2010 WL 1424398 (E.D. La. Apr. 5, 2010). The court rejected as a "red herring" the mortgage servicer's assertion that it was not a debt collector because it never "obtained" an ownership interest in the *pro se* consumer's loan. The § 1692a(6)(F)(iii) exclusion applies only to debt collectors attempting to collect debts obtained before default, and in this case the debt was assigned after it was already in default.

Dantin v. Rawlings Co., L.L.C., 2005 WL 6075786 (M.D. La. Apr. 13, 2005). Collection of a medical health insurance subrogation claim to funds paid regarding an automobile accident was exempt under § 1692a(6)(F)(iii).

McAdams v. Citifinancial Mortgage Co., 2007 WL 141128 (M.D. La. Jan. 16, 2007). The defendant that obtained the debt through its merger with the original creditor at a time when the debt was in default was a debt collector subject to the FDCPA.

Hamilton v. Trover Solutions, Inc., 2003 WL 21105100 (E.D. La. May 13, 2003), *aff'd per curiam*, 104 Fed. Appx. 942 (5th Cir. 2004). Pursuant to § 1692a(6)(f)(iii) an agency which received subrogation to recover medical expenses prior to default was not subject to the FDCPA.

Brumberger v. Sallie Mae Servicing Corp., 2003 WL 1733548 (E.D. La. Mar. 28, 2003). The FDCPA did not apply to a student loan which was not in default when assigned.

In re Mayer, 199 B.R. 616 (E.D. La. 1996). Local phone company which routinely purchased accounts from long distance carrier and billed customer for both local and long distance service was not a debt collector because the accounts were not delinquent when purchased. Debtor had alleged FDCPA violation by the local carrier which had billed for certain pre-petition long distance charges.

Massachusetts

Pomykala v. PCFS Mortgage Res. Div. of Provident Bank, 2005 WL 2149411 (D. Mass. Sept. 1, 2005). FDCPA did not apply because servicer acquired mortgage loan before default.

Skerry v. Massachusetts Higher Educ. Assistance Corp., 73 F. Supp. 2d 47 (D. Mass. 1999). Student loan guarantor was not "debt collector" where delinquent loan was never defaulted by the guarantor. Finding FTC informal opinions and staff commentaries unpersuasive, the court adopted the Federal Family Education Loan Program definition of "default" because the debt was a student loan.

In re Maxwell, 281 B.R. 101 (Bankr. D. Mass. 2002). Argument by purchaser of defaulted note that it was not a debt collector was frivolous: it had sent demand letters before becoming the owner of the note; every contact letter claimed that it was a debt collector. Its contact history, the testimony of its witness, and the assignment document also substantiated its status as a debt collector.

Michigan

Munson v. Countrywide Home Loans, Inc., 67 U.C.C. Rep. Serv. 2d 692 (E.D. Mich. 2008). Mortgage servicer who obtained the account prior to default was not an FDCPA debt collector.

Givens v. HSBC Mortgage Servs., 2008 WL 4190999 (E.D. Mich. Aug. 26, 2008). *Pro se* plaintiff's amended complaint dismissed with prejudice because it failed to allege the defendants were debt collectors.

Waller v. Life Bank, 2008 WL 495486 (E.D. Mich. Feb. 21, 2008). Where the evidence showed that servicing of the mortgage occurred when the loan was current and not in default, defendants were not "debt collectors" under the FDCPA.

Waller v. Life Bank, 2008 WL 495486 (E.D. Mich. Feb. 21, 2008). Mortgage servicers taking mortgage before default exempt.

Tocco v. Argent Mortgage Co., L.L.C., 2007 U.S. Dist. LEXIS 3533 (E.D. Mich. Jan. 18, 2007). Servicer of the plaintiff's mortgage who obtained the account prior to its default was not a "debt collector."

Orent v. Credit Bureau of Greater Lansing, Inc., 2001 U.S. Dist. LEXIS 17683 (W.D. Mich. Oct. 23, 2001). Where debt was not in default at the time of assignment, assignee was not a debt collector. Where the debt was acquired through merger, the title was transferred to and invested in the surviving corporation which stepped into the shoes of the merged corporation.

Walker v. Michael W. Colton Trust, 33 F. Supp. 2d 585 (E.D. Mich. 1999). The FDCPA claim was dismissed, since one defendant purchased the mortgage debt from Edy's Carpet, Heating & Cooling before it was in default, and its officer was therefore an officer of the creditor.

Morris v. HomEq Serv. Corp., 2010 WL 537745 (Mich. Ct. App. Feb. 16, 2010). Homeowner failed to show debt was acquired after default.

Jackson v. Flagstar Bank, 2008 WL 7488901 (Mich. Ct. App. Dec. 16, 2008). Summary judgment against the consumer was reversed in light of disputed fact whether the defendant loan servicer obtained the account before or after default.

Stafford v. Select Portfolio Servicing Inc., 2008 WL 1733592 (Mich. Ct. App. Apr. 15, 2008). Mortgage servicing company and an assignee of a debt not in default at the time it was assigned were exempt.

Minnesota

Cohen v. Mortgage Elec. Registration Sys., Inc., 2009 WL 4578308 (D. Minn. Dec. 1, 2009). Defendant not a debt collector where consumer did not allege or prove that the mortgage was in default when it became the servicer.

Motley v. Homecomings Fin., L.L.C., 557 F. Supp. 2d 1005 (D. Minn. 2008). Defendant, as servicer of mortgage, not subject to FDCPA.

Thulin v. EMC Mortgage Corp., 2007 WL 3037353 (D. Minn. Oct. 16, 2007). The court held that a debt collector did not include the consumer's creditors, mortgage servicing company, or an assignee of the debt as long as the debt was not in default at the time it was assigned.

Alexander v. Omega Mgmt., Inc., 67 F. Supp. 2d 1052 (D. Minn. 1999). A condominium property management firm sending out monthly bills, even those which attempted to collect an outstanding balance, was not subject to FDCPA because (1) its principal purpose was not the collection of debts (only 3% of defendant's operation was devoted to debt collection); and (2) the defendant was exempt under § 1692a(6)(F)(iii), which exempts from the definition of debt collector those who had responsibility for servicing a debt prior to the time it went into default, since the property management company collected current monthly dues as well.

Missouri

Barnes v. Citigroup Inc., 2010 WL 2557508 (E.D. Mo. June 15, 2010).

Nevada

Karl v. Quality Loan Serv. Corp., 2010 WL 5464812 (D. Nev. Dec. 13, 2010). A mortgagee and its pre-default servicer were not debt collectors.

Croce v. Trinity Mortgage Assurance Corp., 2009 WL 3172119 (D. Nev. Sept. 28, 2009). Mortgage servicer not debt collector.

Johnson v. Wells Fargo Home Mortgage, Inc., 2007 WL 3226153 (D. Nev. Oct. 29, 2007). Wells Fargo acquired the mortgage before default, so was not a creditor.

New Hampshire

Fogle v. Wilmington Fin., 2011 WL 90229 (D.N.H. Jan. 11, 2011). Where the complaint alleged that Countrywide was servicing the loan, not that it acquired the loan outright, and did not allege that the loan was in default when Countrywide began its service, the complaint failed to stated a claim against a "debt collector" under the FDCPA.

New York

Kesselman v. The Rawlings Co., L.L.C., 668 F. Supp. 2d 604 (S.D.N.Y. 2009). Subrogation agents who obtained the debt prior to default were excluded from the definition of debt collector pursuant to § 1692a(6)(F)(ii).

Burchalewski v. Wolpoff & Abramson, L.L.P., 2008 WL 4238933 (W.D.N.Y. Sept. 8, 2008). The motion to dismiss was granted because the complaint was insufficient to categorize purchaser of creditor as a debt collector by alleging it acquired her debt after default.

Cyphers v. Litton Loan Serv., L.L.P., 503 F. Supp. 2d 547 (N.D.N.Y. Aug. 27, 2007). Court granted the defendant mortgage servicer summary judgment holding that it was not a debt collector since the plaintiff presented no evidence that the mortgage was in default at the time the servicer obtained it or that the servicer believed that it was in default at that time.

Healy v. Jzanus Ltd., 2006 WL 898067 (E.D.N.Y. Apr. 4, 2006). The debt collector's motion for summary judgment was granted where the Patient Agreement between the consumer and the hospital showed that the debt was not in default at the time the letter was sent and the FDCPA, therefore, did not apply.

Franceschi v. Mautner-Glick Corp., 22 F. Supp. 2d 250 (S.D.N.Y. 1998). Section 1692a(6)(F)(iii)'s exemption from coverage as a "debt collector" when the debt was "not in default at the time it was obtained by such person" is not limited to a formal assignment or ownership of the debt and includes any person who has responsibility for the account prior to default; therefore, a landlord's management company collecting on past-due rent is not a debt collector in view of its continuing management and rent collection role since the inception of the tenancy.

Barry v. Bd. of Managers of Condo. II, 853 N.Y.S.2d 827 (N.Y. Civ. Ct. 2007). Holding "there is a fiduciary relationship between each unit owner and all other unit owners" and thus "the collection of common charges by the condominium, its managing agent or attorneys acting on its behalf are exempt from the application of the FDCPA."

North Carolina

Jones v. Saxon Mortgage Servs., Inc., 2010 WL 2629782 (W.D.N.C. June 28, 2010). A mortgage servicer that acquired loan before default was not subject to FDCPA.

Fletcher v. Homecomings Fin. L.L.C., 2010 WL 1665265 (M.D.N.C. Apr. 22, 2010). Loan obtained before default not covered.

Ohio

Glazer v. Chase Home Fin. L.L.C., 2010 WL 1391937 (N.D. Ohio Mar. 31, 2010). A party servicing a loan prior to default does not become a debt collector by means of an invalid assignment of a defaulted note and mortgage.

Byrd v. Law Offices of John D. Clunk Co., 2010 WL 816932 (S.D. Ohio Mar. 8, 2010). Since creditor obtained the debt before default, it was not a debt collector subject to liability for the acts of its attorney or process server.

Dowling v. Litton Loan Serv., L.P., 2006 WL 3498292 (S.D. Ohio Dec. 1, 2006). The court held that, notwithstanding the consumer's consistent protest that she was not in default, the servicer of the consumer's mortgage was a "debt collector" because it acquired the debt when the loan was alleged to be in default.

Brown v. Saxon Mortgage Servs., Inc., 2005 WL 3244295 (S.D. Ohio Nov. 30, 2005). Defendant's motion to dismiss was granted where the evidence showed that the defendant began servicing plaintiff's loan three years prior to the loan being declared in default.

Oregon

Kellers v. Ocwen Loan Servicing, L.L.C., 2009 WL 2899813 (D. Or. Sept. 9, 2009). Loan servicer that acquired the debt before default not within FDCPA.

Pennsylvania

Alamo v. ABC Fin. Servs., Inc., 2011 WL 221766 (E.D. Pa. Jan. 20, 2011). Where a loan servicer received a gym membership contract before default, the FDCPA did not apply.

Portley v. Litton Loan Serv. L.P., 2010 WL 1404610 (E.D. Pa. Apr. 5, 2010). Where a mortgage servicer sent the consumer a welcome letter indicating that it received the assignment to collect on the mortgage loan debt "effective June 1, 2007" and where the loan was already in default at the time the servicer obtained the assignment, Defendant was a "debt collector" for the purposes of the FDCPA.

Gruninger v. America's Servicing Co., 2010 WL 653119 (E.D. Pa. Feb. 22, 2010). The defendant servicer of the plaintiff's mortgage was not a covered "debt collector" since it obtained the mortgage prior to default.

Rubenstein v. Dovenmuehle Mortgage, Inc., 2009 WL 3467769 (E.D. Pa. Oct. 28, 2009). Complaint against the consumers' mortgage company and servicer was dismissed for failure to state a claim in the absence of an allegation that the mortgage was in default at the time that the defendants acquired it so as to render the defendants debt collectors subject to the FDCPA.

Ruff v. America's Servicing Co., 2008 WL 1830182 (W.D. Pa. Apr. 23, 2008). Defendant mortgage servicer was not a "debt collector" as defined since the consumer's loan was not in default when the defendant began servicing it.

Jones v. Select Portfolio Servicing, Inc., 2008 WL 1820935 (E.D. Pa. Apr. 22, 2008). FDCPA claim dismissed for failure to state a claim where the conclusory allegation in the complaint that the defendant was an FDCPA debt collector was belied by the specific allegations that the defendant was a servicer who obtained the debt prior to any default.

Conklin v. Purcell, Krug & Haller, 2007 WL 404047 (M.D. Pa. Feb. 1, 2007), *aff'd,* 282 Fed. Appx. 193 (3d Cir. 2008). In a case arising out of foreclosure of the *pro se* plaintiff's property, the company that was servicing a current payment plan or forbearance agreement rather than demanding payment on a defaulted loan is not subject to the FDCPA.

Prince v. NCO Fin. Servs., Inc., 346 F. Supp. 2d 744 (E.D. Pa. 2004). FDCPA exempts a creditor's servicing agent who received the account before it was in default.

Dawson v. Dovenmuehle Mortgage, Inc., 2002 U.S. Dist. LEXIS 5688 (E.D. Pa. Apr. 3, 2002). A loan servicer serviced but did not own the loan. The FDCPA applied to a mortgage servicing company only where the mortgage at issue was in default at the time when servicing began.

Tennessee

Johnson v. AmeriCredit Fin. Servs., Inc., 69 U.C.C. Rep. Serv. 2d 861 (M.D. Tenn. 2009). Where the consumer stopped payment on her down payment check because of alleged fraud by the car dealer and tried to cancel her car purchase with the seller shortly after the sale, and where the record was silent as to the precise time when the installment contract was assigned to its pre-arranged assignee, the assignee's motion for summary judgment because it purportedly was an exempt creditor was denied, since "a genuine issue of material fact exists as to whether the Plaintiff was in default when was assigned the loan."

Johnson v. Wilshire Credit Corp., 2009 WL 559950 (E.D. Tenn. Mar. 5, 2009). The defendant mortgage holder and its servicer qualified as covered FDCPA debt collectors, since the plaintiff alleged that they obtained the mortgage after default and then sought to collect payments.

Jones v. Intuition, Inc., 12 F. Supp. 2d 775 (W.D. Tenn. 1998). Servicing of a student loan before it fell into default was not subject to the FDCPA.

Texas

Cavil v. Trendmaker Homes, Inc., 2010 WL 5464238 (S.D. Tex. Dec. 29, 2010). Where it was unclear from the pleadings whether the debt was in default at the time it was assigned, the court stated it was constrained by the pleadings and denied the defendants' motion to dismiss, even though "the facts in the case might ultimately reveal that the debt was not in default at the time it was transferred, sold or assigned." The legislative history of § 1692a(6) indicates conclusively that a debt collector does not include the consumer's creditors, a mortgage servicing company, or an assignee of a debt, as long as the debt was not in default at the time it was assigned.

Flores v. Millennium Interests, Ltd., 273 F. Supp. 2d 899 (S.D. Tex. 2003), *aff'd on other grounds,* 464 F.3d 521 (5th Cir. 2006). Mortgage servicer that acquired the account before it was in default was not a "debt collector" as defined.

Utah

Pines v. EMC Mortgage Corp., 2008 WL 2901644 (D. Utah July 22, 2008). FDCPA suit was dismissed because it could not be construed that the defendant was a debt collector who allegedly purchased the *pro se* plaintiff's loans in default.

Virginia

Frye v. Bank of Am., N.A., 2010 WL 3244879 (N.D. W. Va. Aug. 16, 2010). The court accepted as true the allegations in the complaint that the defendant obtained the debt after default and therefore did not grant the defendant's motion to dismiss.

Ramirez-Alvarez v. Aurora Loan Servs., L.L.C., 2010 WL 2934473 (E.D. Va. July 21, 2010). Since the defendant was a mortgage loan servicer that received the debt in question while it was not in default, the FDCPA did not apply in this situation.

Horvath v. Bank of New York, 2010 WL 538039 (E.D. Va. Jan. 29, 2010). Mortgagee and servicer that obtained the debt before default were not covered FDCPA debt collectors.

Washington

Thepvongsa v. Regional Tr. Servs. Corp., 2011 WL 307364 (W.D. Wash. Jan. 26, 2011). Where the FDCPA claims arose from nonjudicial foreclosure proceedings and it was unclear from the allegations whether the debt was in default prior to assignment, the court dismissed the *pro se* consumer's complaint without prejudice.

Chapel v. Mortgage Elec. Registration Sys., Inc., 2010 WL 4622526 (W.D. Wash. Nov. 2, 2010). Where there were enough facts to suggest that the defendant may have been assigned the loan after default, even though the *pro se* plaintiff did not expressly allege that the defendant acquired the loan after default, the court did not dismiss the claim.

Lamb v. HSC Real Estate, Inc., 2008 WL 467410 (E.D. Wash. Feb. 19, 2008). Landlord's property management company was exempt as it serviced the rent before default.

West Virginia

Lomax v. Bank of Am., 2010 WL 3271970 (N.D. W. Va. Aug. 18, 2010). Allegations in the complaint that the defendant obtained the debt after default were accepted as true on a motion to dismiss.

Padgett v. OneWest Bank, F.S.B., 2010 WL 1539839 (N.D. W. Va. Apr. 19, 2010). Defendant OneWest Bank, which acquired all of the assets of consumer's defunct mortgagee IndyMac in a sale from the FDIC at a time when consumer's account was in default, qualified as an exempt creditor since the purchase of IndyMac's assets was "without regard to whether a debt was in default" and thus was not an assignment or transfer of a debt "solely for the purpose of facilitating collection of such debt" as required by the exclusion in the § 1692a(4) definition of "creditor."

Seals v. National Student Loan Program, 2004 WL 3314948 (N.D. W. Va. Aug. 16, 2004), *aff'd*, 124 Fed. Appx. 182 (4th Cir. 2005). Sallie Mae acquired the loans before default and was therefore not a debt collector.

Wisconsin

Berndt v. Fairfield Resorts, Inc., 339 F. Supp. 2d 1064 (W.D. Wis. 2004). Defendant timeshare resort management association did was exempt, since it acquired the accounts before default.

Hartman v. Meridian Fin. Servs., Inc., 191 F. Supp. 2d 1031 (W.D. Wis. 2002). A third party who obtained accounts only once a payment was overdue (i.e., beyond the contractual due date) was not exempt from the definition of a debt collector as a pre-collection billing service. Although the creditor claimed that it considered accounts in default only after they were at least thirty days late, the debt collector still was not subject to the § 1692a(6)(F)(iii) exception when it obtained the debts once the payments were overdue but for less than thirty days, since the underlying contracts defined default as not making payment by the due date.

K.1.2.3.9 Certain secured parties, 15 U.S.C. § 1692a(6) (F)(iv)

Connecticut

Deutsche Bank v. Lichtenfels, 48 Conn. L. Rptr. 133 (Super. Ct. 2009). Attorneys enforcing a mortgage were subject to the FDCPA.

Illinois

Friedman v. Textron Fin. Corp., 1997 WL 467175 (N.D. Ill. Aug. 12, 1997). Secured party in a commercial transaction who acquired a consumer account that was used as collateral following default on a loan from the commercial lender to the original creditor was excluded from the definition of "debt collector" pursuant to § 1692a(6)(F)(iv).

Puerto Rico

Melendez-Febus v. Toyota Credit Corp., 2009 WL 2950369 (D. P.R. Sept. 9, 2009). Defendant was an enforcer of a security agreement and not a debt collector.

K.1.2.4 Derivative Liability of Defendants

LeBlanc v. Unifund CCR Partners, 601 F.3d 1185 (11th Cir. 2010). Partners of a debt collector limited partnership may be held jointly and severally liable for the partnership's conduct regardless of whether they violated the FDCPA and whether or not they are debt collectors.

Peter v. G.C. Servs. L.P., 310 F.3d 344 (5th Cir. 2002). General partners are liable for all obligations of the partnership. Thus, G.C. Financial and D.L.S. Enterprises are liable for the FDCPA violations of G.C. Services.

Pollice v. Nat'l Tax Funding, L.P., 225 F.3d 379 (3d Cir. 2000). A collection agency that took assignment of defaulted debts and then hired another collection agency to do the collection work would be vicariously liable for the FDCPA violations of the hired agency. The general partner of the two agencies, both limited partnerships, would also be vicariously liable for their FDCPA violations.

Pettit v. Retrieval Masters Creditors Bureau, Inc., 211 F.3d 1057 (7th Cir. 2000). An owner, officer of corporation, or shareholder may be held personally liable for the corporation's violation of the FDCPA only if he or she personally violated the FDCPA, i.e., the owner cannot be held vicariously liable for statutory violations committed by the corporation's collection agents or other employees. Where the collection agency's owner did not make phone calls in an attempt to collect debts; did not write, review, or directly approve the offending collection letter; did not choose the letterhead; and did not participate in selection of the collection agency's name, the owner was not personally liable for the collection agency's FDCPA violations.

White v. Goodman, 200 F.3d 1016 (7th Cir. 2000). Shareholders of debt collectors were not liable absent piercing of the corporate veil and joining them was frivolous.

Wadlington v. Credit Acceptance Corp., 76 F.3d 103 (6th Cir. 1996). A financer which was not a debt collector was not vicariously liable for the FDCPA violations of its attorney.

Alabama

Bice v. Merchants Adjustment Serv., Clearinghouse No. 41,265 (S.D. Ala. 1985). The motion of collection agency to dismiss alleged FDCPA violations by its lawyer, immune under repealed § 1692a(6)(F) (Supp. II 1978), denied since immunity granted to the attorney did not exonerate the collection agency from liability for its attorney's actions.

Arizona

Caron v. Charles E. Maxwell, P.C., 48 F. Supp. 2d 932 (D. Ariz. 1999). The homeowners' association was a creditor and was not vicariously liable for its collection attorney's FDCPA violation.

Charles v. Check Rite, Ltd., 1998 U.S. Dist. LEXIS 22512 (D. Ariz. Dec. 14, 1999). Whether Check Rite could be vicariously liable for the Lundgren defendants' FDCPA violation as an apparent agent was a question of fact not appropriate for summary judgment.

United States v. ACB Sales & Serv., Inc., 590 F. Supp. 561 (D. Ariz. 1984). The officers of a collection agency are not liable for an

FDCPA violation in which they did not participate absent piercing of corporate veil. Parent corporation which solicited accounts for and supervised the collection activities of local subsidiaries is a debt collector liable for violations of subsidiaries since entire group of corporations are single economic enterprise.

California

Cassady v. Union Adjustment Co., 2008 WL 4773976 (N.D. Cal. Oct. 27, 2008). Where a collection agency turned a collection matter over to its attorney and thereafter relied upon the attorney's judgment and discretion as to how to handle—when and how to proceed with litigation—the collection agency was not vicariously liable for its attorney's violations of the FDCPA.

Schwarm v. Craighead, 552 F. Supp. 2d 1056 (E.D. Cal. 2008). Personal FDCPA liability can be imposed on employees, shareholders, officers and directors without piercing the corporate veil, as long as the individual: (1) materially participated in collecting the debt at issue; (2) exercised control over the affairs of the business; (3) was personally involved in the collection of the debt at issue; or (4) was regularly engaged, directly and indirectly, in the collection of debts. The individual defendant had FDCPA liability where, as a director and president, the individual oversaw collecting debts pursuant to contracts with the district attorneys' offices, was one of only three individuals that had final authority over the company's collection procedures, developed the automated software the company used, and was solely responsible for managing and maintaining the automated computer system that implemented the collection program.

Palmer v. I.C. Sys., Inc., 2005 WL 3001877 (N.D. Cal. Nov. 8, 2005). Debt collectors are not vicariously liable for the wrong committed by the creditor in forwarding an amount not owing.

United States v. Trans Cont'l Affiliates, 1997 WL 26297 (N.D. Cal. Jan. 8, 1997). Where genuine issues of material fact existed as to the degree of knowledge the primary officers of debt collection company had of illegal conduct, as well as how directly they were involved in the activity, summary judgment on the issue of liability was inappropriate for either party.

Newman v. CheckRite California, Inc., 912 F. Supp. 1354 (E.D. Cal. 1995). The managing officer of the check collection agency was personally responsible for the FDCPA violations of his employees under California corporation law and as a debt collector indirectly collecting a debt under the FDCPA. The collection agency was vicariously liable for the FDCPA violations of its attorney.

Colorado

Nelson v. Cavalry Portfolio Servs., L.L.C., 2010 WL 1258045 (D. Colo. Mar. 24, 2010). Where the consumer accepted an offer of judgment from the debt collector, his complaint against the debt buyer was dismissed as moot pursuant to agency principles. Consumer's only claim against Cavalry was based on Cavalry's alleged vicarious liability for the acts of National Action, and he did not contend that Cavalry independently violated the FDCPA.

Allen v. Nelnet, Inc., 2007 WL 2786432 (D. Colo. Sept. 24, 2007). The defendant creditor/servicer was not liable for the alleged FDCPA violations of a corporate affiliate to whom it referred the debt for collection because the affiliate was acting independently using its own name. The activities of the two entities did not form a single economic enterprise and the defendant entity did not control the other entity's debt collection activities.

First Interstate Bank v. Soucie, 924 P.2d 1200 (Colo. App. 1996). Vicarious liability will be imposed on an attorney's client for the attorney's FDCPA violations if the attorney and client were both debt collectors.

Connecticut

Cashman v. Ricigliano, 2004 WL 1920798 (D. Conn. Aug. 25, 2004). Partnership may be sued under the FDCPA since it is responsible for the acts of its partners.

Reese v. Arrow Fin. Servs., Inc., 202 F.R.D. 83 (D. Conn. 2001). Case against individual officers of collection agency dismissed for lack of personal jurisdiction. Any acts were done solely in an official capacity, and the officers did not personally participate in sending the letters, although they allegedly adopted, ratified and approved them.

Moore v. Nat'l Account Sys., Inc., 1991 U.S. Dist. LEXIS 18137 (D. Conn. Nov. 13, 1991) (magistrate's opinion). Parent corporation, Payco Am. Corp., is not legally responsible for the unlicensed activities of its subsidiary corporation without proof of the parent's participation in the collection or dominance of the subsidiary.

Delaware

Shuler v. Dauot, 1989 WL 16974 (Del. Super. Ct. Feb. 2, 1989). A creditor is not a debt collector subject to FDCPA claims for the alleged FDCPA violations of its attorney who may be a debt collector but was not a party to the suit.

Florida

Leblanc v. Unifund CCR Partners, G.P., 552 F. Supp. 2d 1327 (M.D. Fla. May 8, 2008). FDCPA liability was imputed under the FDCPA and state partnership law to the general partners of defendant that only participated indirectly in its actual collection efforts.

Belin v. Litton Loan Serv., L.P., 2006 WL 1992410 (M.D. Fla. July 14, 2006). General partners of a debt collector limited partnership may be held vicariously liable under the FDCPA for the partnership's conduct.

Gottlieb v. Green Oil, Inc., 1998 WL 469849 (S.D. Fla. May 8, 1998). Magistrate judge recommended that complaint not be dismissed against president of Advanced Recovery Associates who signed letter. Officers and employees of the debt collector may be jointly and severally liable with the agency.

Williams v. Collection Team, Inc., 1997 WL 33463668 (S.D. Fla. Oct. 31, 1997). Motion to dismiss the case as to collection agency's officers denied, based on allegation that they were "at all material times, aware of, and/or had ultimate responsibility for, and/or created or approved the various letters, or the basic forms used for the various letters, sent by Collection Team."

In re Cooper, 253 B.R. 286 (Bankr. N.D. Fla. 2000). Creditor was not covered by the FDCPA and collector's liability would not be imputed to the creditor.

Georgia

Johnson v. Ardec Credit Servs., Inc., 1984 U.S. Dist. LEXIS 24889 (N.D. Ga. Mar. 21, 1984) (summary judgment). An attorney sending a collection letter on behalf of a debt collector is excluded from FDCPA liability by § 1692a(6)(F) (now repealed) but debt collector is liable for violations committed by its agents including its attorney.

Illinois

Wisniewski v. Asset Acceptance Capital Corp., 2009 WL 212155 (N.D. Ill. Jan. 29, 2009). The debt buyer that assigned a debt for collection to a subsidiary may be subject to liability for the debt collection violations of its subsidiary where the debt buyer alleged in a memorandum of law to defeat a civil conspiracy count in the same suit that the subsidiary was an agent.

D'Elia v. First Capital, L.L.C., 2008 WL 4344571 (N.D. Ill. Mar. 19, 2008). Motion to dismiss individual defendant denied where plaintiff alleged sufficient facts (sole shareholder, owner, and officer) to justify piercing corporate veil of debt buyer on alter ego theory.

Hernandez v. Midland Credit Mgmt., Inc., 2006 WL 695451 (N.D. Ill. Mar. 14, 2006). Allegations showing that the defendant Encore at least "indirectly" engaged in the collection of a debt for a third party were adequate to state a claim that the defendant was a "debt collector" under the FDCPA. Encore is a debt buyer that owns Midland which was collecting the debt by sending out a notice for Encore.

Scally v. Hilco Receivables, L.L.C., 392 F. Supp. 2d 1036 (N.D. Ill. 2005). The district court held that the defendant debt buyer after default was not indirectly attempting to collect debts where it did not attempt to contact the consumer itself nor was it vicariously liable for the contingent fee collection agency it employed to attempt collect debts as it did not direct or control the collection agency. However, the court did note that the debt buyer would qualify as a debt collector had it acted through retained counsel.

Blair v. Sherman Acquisition, 2004 WL 2870080 (N.D. Ill. Dec. 13, 2004). Collection agencies who sent the Gramm-Leach-Bliley notice on behalf of a debt buyer had enough participation to be liable if the notice was misleading.

Klco v. Elmhurst Dodge, 2002 U.S. Dist. LEXIS 1821 (N.D. Ill. Feb. 4, 2002). Consumer's motion to amend his complaint to add automobile dealership's corporate parent was denied where consumer failed to allege conduct which justified piercing the corporate veil and the motion was untimely.

Miller v. McCalla, Raymer, Padrick, Cobb, Nichols & Clark, L.L.C., 198 F.R.D. 503 (N.D. Ill. 2001). Because the law firm's debt collection activities were in the ordinary course and geographical scope of the partnership business, and the law firm was an agent for the partners, who are bound by its acts and liable for its losses and penalties, the general partners were jointly and severally liable for the partnership's obligations.

Peters v. AT&T Corp., 43 F. Supp. 2d 926 (N.D. Ill. 1999). Applicable state law holding that the general partners of a limited partnership were vicariously liable for the acts of the limited partnership subjected the general partners to FDCPA liability.

Wells v. McDonough, 1999 WL 162796 (N.D. Ill. Mar. 15, 1999). The court held that related corporations were not a single economic enterprise so as to expose the non-debt collector corporation to FDCPA liability for the actions of its sister corporation. Evidence that the two corporations shared a legal department was insufficient to establish the related corporation as a debt collector.

Pikes v. Riddle, 38 F. Supp. 2d 639 (N.D. Ill. 1998). Corporate officer personally involved in the debt collection practices of his company was a "debt collector" within the FDCPA.

Randle v. G.C. Servs., L.P., 25 F. Supp. 2d 849 (N.D. Ill. 1998). General partners of a limited partnership debt collector are vicariously liable under applicable state law for the misconduct of the limited partnership and therefore are themselves debt collectors, liable under the FDCPA for limited partnership's violations.

Jenkins v. Union Corp., 999 F. Supp. 1120 (N.D. Ill. 1998). Collection agency's parent corporation, which itself did not engage in debt collection, was not a debt collector and could not be held liable in the absence of proof that the two corporations acted as a single economic enterprise, that the subsidiary was a mere instrumentality of the parent, or that recognizing the subsidiary's existence would work a fraud or injustice.

Crawford v. Equifax Payment Servs., Inc., 1998 WL 704050 (N.D. Ill. Sept. 30, 1998). When two corporate entities were involved, only one of which directly attempted to collect the alleged debt, the plaintiff must allege facts sufficient, if proved, to pierce the corporate veil in order to prevail against the corporation indirectly involved.

Slater v. Credit Sciences, Inc., 1998 WL 299803 (N.D. Ill. May 29, 1998). Complaint which alleged the direct participation of the president of a corporate debt collector in the collection efforts stated a claim for relief against him.

Pope v. Vogel, 1998 WL 111576 (N.D. Ill. Mar. 5, 1998). Person who was the stockholder of out-of-state collection business as well as its sole officer and who directed the specific operations of the business that collected the debt in the forum state had sufficient contacts with forum state for the court to exercise personal jurisdiction and was a "debt collector" by virtue of his indirect efforts to collect the debt. Also, assignee of debt in default was a "debt collector." Allegations that collector's statements that payment of delinquent credit card balance would "reestablish" the consumer's credit were false and state a claim for relief under § 1692(e).

Stepney v. Outsourcing Solutions, Inc., 1997 WL 722972 (N.D. Ill. Nov. 13, 1997). Complaint against parent corporation was dismissed where it was devoid of allegations to support a finding that the parent so completely dominated the collector's practices as to constitute a single economic enterprise allowing the piercing of the corporate veil. The consumer alleged only its parent's financial interest in the subsidiary's collection activities and approval of the practice of purchasing and attempting to collect old debts.

Perovich v. Humphrey, 1997 WL 674975 (N.D. Ill. Oct. 28, 1997). The complaint suggested that all corporate executive officers were personally liable for all corporate actions, and that was simply not the law. The consumers failed to allege any facts in their complaint indicating that the collector's officers personally violated the FDCPA, requiring dismissal of the claim against the officers.

Friedman v. Anvan Corp., 1997 WL 639046 (N.D. Ill. Oct. 10, 1997). The complaint stated a claim against a corporate signer of a dunning letter even though that corporation was not further identified. The individual signing for that corporation was only a representative, and the claim against him was dismissed for that reason.

Avila v. Van Ru Credit Corp., 1995 WL 55255 (N.D. Ill. Feb. 8, 1995), *aff'd* 84 F.3d 222 (7th Cir. 1996). In order to pierce the corporate veil of a corporate parent, three elements must be shown: (1) control by the parent to such a degree that the subsidiary has become its mere instrumentality, (2) the commission of a fraud or wrong by a parent through its subsidiary, such as violation of a statute, and (3) unjust loss or injury to the claimant, such as insolvency of the subsidiary.

Ellis v. Credit Bureau, 40 Cons. Fin. L. Bull. 49 (N.D. Ill. 1986). A creditor was dismissed as defendant in an FDCPA action as not an indispensable party and not liable under the doctrine of respondent superior.

Kentucky

Etapa v. Asset Acceptance Corp., 373 F. Supp. 2d 687 (E.D. Ky. 2004). Allegedly false statements made by the collection agency in its collection suit could not be attributed to its collection attorneys to establish the attorneys' own FDCPA liability.

Louisiana

Bauer v. Dean Morris, L.L.P., 2010 WL 4103192 (E.D. La. Oct. 18, 2010). A creditor cannot be held vicariously liable for FDCPA violations by a debt collector it retains, but a plaintiff may have a claim against the creditor under principles of common law for negligence based on lack of care in selecting, instructing and supervising third-party debt collectors.

Ernst v. Jesse L. Riddle, P.C., 964 F. Supp. 213 (M.D. La. 1997). An officer of a corporate debt collector may only be held liable if sufficient facts are established to pierce the corporate veil. Long arm jurisdiction could not be exercised over the officer without proof that the officer contacted the state in a capacity other than as a corporate officer.

Byes v. Accelerated Cash Flow, Inc., 1996 WL 291967 (E.D. La. May 29, 1996). Claims against owner and an executive in the collection agency were dismissed for lack of personal jurisdiction, where the consumer failed to allege that either had participated in the FDCPA violation, or that the corporation was an "alter ego" of the owner. There was no evidence that the corporation was undercapitalized or lacked assets to satisfy a possible judgment.

Mississippi

Salem v. J.P. Morgan Chase & Co., 2009 WL 4738182 (S.D. Miss. Dec. 4, 2009). Complaint dismissed since the originating creditor was not subject to the FDCPA and was not vicariously liable under the FDCPA for its third-party debt collector's alleged misconduct.

Frascogna v. Wells Fargo Bank, 2009 WL 2843284 (S.D. Miss. Aug. 31, 2009). "[A] creditor who hires a debt collector is not vicariously liable for the collector's FDCPA violations."

Freeman v. CAC Fin., Inc., 2006 WL 925609 (S.D. Miss. Mar. 31, 2006). Mississippi law requires a plaintiff to prove sufficient control by the creditor over an independent debt collector in order to sustain a claim of vicarious liability for a state claim for negligent supervision.

New Jersey

Bass v. Palisades Collections, L.L.C., 2008 WL 4513812 (D.N.J. Sept. 26, 2008). Plaintiff's claim that debt collector failed to inform creditor and later debt buyer, by proxy, that plaintiff's debt was disputed is beyond the statute of limitations as to debt collector, and meritless as a basis for imputing knowledge on the part of defendant.

Bey v. Daimler Chrysler Servs., L.L.C., 2006 WL 361385 (D.N.J. Feb. 15, 2006). Replevin attorneys were not responsible for the actions of the tow truck driver hired by the creditor.

New Mexico

Martinez v. Albuquerque Collection Servs., 867 F. Supp. 1495 (D.N.M. 1994). "Debt collectors employing attorneys or other agents to carry out debt collection practices that violate the FDCPA are vicariously liable for their agents conduct."

New York

Doherty v. Citibank N.A., 375 F. Supp. 2d 158 (E.D.N.Y. 2005). A creditor, which was not itself a debt collector, was not vicariously liable for the FDCPA violations of the debt collector that it engaged to collect its debts.

Colman v. N. Shore Health Sys., 1998 U.S. Dist. LEXIS 23428 (E.D.N.Y. June 19, 1998). Court declined to pierce corporate veil for affiliated corporations. Affiliates' collection letters were not deceptive if they did not disclose corporate affiliation.

Kohler v. Ford Motor Credit Co., 447 N.Y.S.2d 215 (N.Y. Sup. Ct. 1982), *modified on other grounds*, 462 N.Y.S.2d 297 (N.Y. App. Div. 1983). FMCC was not subject to an FDCPA claim based upon the abusive tactics of the repossessor it hired.

Ohio

Johnson v. Midland Credit Mgmt. Inc., 2006 WL 2473004 (N.D. Ohio Aug. 24, 2006). The court granted summary judgment dismissing the parent corporation of the debt collector subsidiary since the plaintiff presented insufficient evidence of the required showing that the entities were "a single economic enterprise."

Martin v. Select Portfolio Serving Holding Corp., 2006 U.S. Dist. LEXIS 24749 (S.D. Ohio Mar. 17, 2006). The *pro se* plaintiffs' bare allegations of liability against one related corporation for the FDCPA violations of the other corporation failed to state a claim for relief since "[a] mere showing of corporate relatedness, i.e., through ownership, without more, is insufficient to establish liability on the part of one corporation for conduct by another corporation."

Taylor v. Checkrite, Ltd., 627 F. Supp. 415 (S.D. Ohio 1986). Checkrite, a dishonored check collector and reporting agency, is responsible for the FDCPA violations of its franchisee/agent where Checkrite exercises control over the activities of the franchisee which resulted in the violations.

Oregon

McNall v. Credit Bureau, 689 F. Supp. 2d 1265 (D. Or. 2010). Surveys case law on whether process server is debt collector and whether attorney is responsible for process server's actions, granting summary judgment because there was no evidence showing that the process server went beyond the role of messenger in serving the complaint.

Pennsylvania

Martsolf v. JBC Legal Group, P.C., 2008 WL 275719 (M.D. Pa. Jan. 30, 2008). A bad debt buyer was vicariously liable for the FDCPA violations of the attorney-owned collection firm that it retained to collect the debts on its behalf since the two entities "maintained an attorney-client and agent-principal relationship for the purpose of collecting debts."

Flamm v. Sarner & Assocs., P.C., 2006 WL 43770 (E.D. Pa. Jan. 3, 2006). Where court had already found process server was a debt collector because he went beyond merely serving process, whether the lawyers were vicariously liable for the independent contractor's actions was a jury question.

Sankowski v. Citibank, N.A., 2006 WL 2037463 (E.D. Pa. July 14, 2006). A creditor exempt from the FDCPA is not vicariously liable for the FDCPA violations of a debt collector acting on its behalf.

Albanese v. Portnoff Law Assocs., Ltd., 301 F. Supp. 2d 389 (E.D. Pa. 2004). The law firm's president, with duties of supervision and overall responsibility, and the attorney who signed the letters could both be liable under the FDCPA.

Flamm v. Sarner & Assocs., P.C., 2002 WL 31618443 (E.D. Pa. Nov. 6, 2002). Creditor had no vicarious liability for debt collector's actions under federal law, but pendent state creditor practices law claim survived. State claims for defamation for statements made outside the litigation privilege survived motion to dismiss, as did civil conspiracy claims.

Utah

Carvana v. MFG Fin., Inc., 2008 WL 2468539 (D. Utah June 17, 2008). The corporate form does not protect officers, directors, or shareholders from individual liability under the FDCPA; individuals who satisfy the statutory definition can be held personally liable under the FDCPA without piercing the corporate veil.

Brumbelow v. Law Offices of Bennett & Deloney, P.C., 372 F. Supp. 2d 615 (D. Utah 2005). Even if shareholders were not directly involved in the collection efforts, there was a factual question whether they could be liable as indirect debt collectors, since they exercised supervisory authority over the corporation, were intimately involved with the practices and procedures of the corporation, and, in fact, developed and implemented the particular collection practice.

Ditty v. CheckRite, Ltd., 973 F. Supp. 1320 (D. Utah 1997). Holding the check collection agency's attorney liable as its joint venturer would require two predicate findings: (1) that they were engaged in a joint venture, and (2) that the collection agency violated § 1692c(b) by placing consumers' names on its verification system. The summary judgment record did not permit this determination. CheckRite authorized DeLoney & Associates to do

its collection work and then knowingly stood by while the firm utilized the "covenant not to sue" scheme. By its acquiescence, CheckRite impliedly authorized the collection practices of DeLoney & Associates and thus was liable for any violations of law caused by the firm's use of those practices. CheckRite was also liable for its attorney's collection practices under the doctrine of apparent authority. When an officer or director was also a "debt collector" engaged in debt collection activities, he or she may be held personally liable for violations of the FDCPA.

Virginia

West v. Costen, 558 F. Supp. 564 (W.D. Va. 1983). A collection agency and its individual collection employees are all "debt collectors" separately liable for their separate violations of the FDCPA. By piercing the corporate veil, the owner of the collection agency was also found liable for FDCPA violations.

Washington

Semper v. JBC Legal Group, 2005 WL 2172377 (W.D. Wash. Sept. 6, 2005). Lawyer who owned and operated law firm but did not personally participate in the activities at issue was not personally liable.

Campion v. Credit Bureau Servs., Inc., 2000 U.S. Dist. LEXIS 20233 (E.D. Wash. Sept. 19, 2000). Corporate debt collector was liable for the misconduct of its attorney and its employees.

K.1.3 Flat Rate Debt Collection, 15 U.S.C. § 1692j

Gutierrez v. AT&T Broadband, L.L.C., 382 F.3d 725 (7th Cir. 2004). Where South Chicago Cable, Inc., did business as "AT&T Cable" and as "AT&T Broadband" in both the formation and collection of cable TV accounts, there was no FDCPA liability of either South Chicago Cable, its collection agency, or AT&T under §§ 1692j or 1692e as the consumer had no reason to believe a third party had entered the picture to collect the debt. A dissenting opinion believed that the consumer was not required under the FDCPA to guess who was collecting the debt.

Nielsen v. Dickerson, 307 F.3d 623 (7th Cir. 2002). Since the collection was not genuinely from the attorney in the professional sense, he violated the "flat-rating" section of the FDCPA, § 1692j.

White v. Goodman, 200 F.3d 1016 (7th Cir. 2000). Defendant was not a flat-rater. Dunning letters were a collaborative product of creditor and defendant and court presumed that defendant sued consumers from time to time.

Taylor v. Perrin, Landry, deLaunay & Durand, 103 F.3d 1232 (5th Cir. 1997). The creditor was a "debt collector" even though it was collecting its own debt because it used a lawyer's letterhead and facsimile signature on its dunning letters, falsely indicating that a third person was collecting the debt, violating §§ 1692e(3) & 1692j. The law firm supplying the letters was also liable.

California

Denkers v. United Compucred Collections, Inc., 1996 WL 724784 (N.D. Cal. Nov. 27, 1996). Genuine issue of material fact existed as to whether public utility was a debt collector where it hired a collection agency to only send out dunning letters. The phone number in letters was that of the utility's collection department. A collection agency which served as a mere mailing service might be equivalent to a "flat rater" who provided letters to the creditor with the result the creditor would be considered a debt collector covered by the Act.

Connecticut

Wagner v. Am. Nat'l Educ. Corp., Clearinghouse No. 36,132 (D. Conn. 1983). A student loan servicing company does not violate § 1692j by collecting a debt in its own name since it participates in the collection of the debt.

Illinois

Everst v. Credit Prot. Ass'n, L.P., 2003 WL 22048719 (N.D. Ill. Aug. 25, 2003). Where Communications and Cable of Chicago, Inc. consistently installed cable in homes, billed and collected in the names AT&T Broadband or other names licensed to it by its parent corporation, there was no violation of § 1692j as the parent did not design, compile or furnish the collection forms, although it reviewed them.

Daley v. Provena Hosps., 88 F. Supp. 2d 881 (N.D. Ill. 2000). Consumer's allegation that the parent corporation designed, compiled, and furnished collection letters to its subsidiary, a hospital, intending that consumers believe that a collection agency was participating in the collection of the debts stated a claim under § 1692j.

Randle v. G.C. Servs. L.P., 48 F. Supp. 2d 835 (N.D. Ill. 1999). Summary judgment was granted to the consumer suing G.C. Services on its "pre-collect" letter. G.C. Services' involvement was that of a mailing service, not a debt collector. The creditor transmitted the name, address and amount to G.C. Services, but used G.C. Services in only 20% of the cases; all payments were directed to the creditor; and there was no phone number for G.C. Services on the letterhead. G.C. Services was "merely masquerading as the debt collector to convey the impression that the price of poker had gone up and to get the debtor's knees knocking." G.C. Services was found liable under § 1692j but not § 1692e which applies to creditors when they use a third party's name indicating that another collector is involved.

Arellano v. Etan Indus., Inc., 1998 WL 911729 (N.D. Ill. Dec. 23, 1998). Sections 1692e and 1692j(a) are mutually exclusive, since the former applies only to a debt collector and the latter only to those who "falsely pretend to be a debt collector."

Epps v. Etan Indus., Inc., 1998 WL 851488 (N.D. Ill. Dec. 1, 1998). Even though payment was to be made to the creditor (Blockbuster), Credit Protection Association (CPA) was sufficiently involved in sending collection letters and responding to inquiries so that the creditor could not be held liable on the theory that it was using a name other than its own to collect. CPA performed traditional collection activities, charged a percentage of recovery rather than a per-letter rate, and was not merely a mailing service.

Laubach v. Arrow Serv. Bureau, Inc., 987 F. Supp. 625 (N.D. Ill. 1997). Label merging, letter printing, and mass mailing activities

were not violations of § 1692j. There was no evidence that the mailing service contributed to the substance of the letters; there was no evidence that it conceived or suggested the strategy of mailing phony attorney letters; nor did it duplicate a comparable letter from its own files for the collector's use.

Fratto v. Citibank, 1996 WL 554549 (N.D. Ill. Sept. 25, 1996). Genuine issue of material fact existed where Citibank hired a collection agency for the sole purpose of sending out form letters on an attorney's letterhead and bearing the name of that attorney who never looked at the files and was not licensed to practice in the jurisdictions where the letters were sent. Citibank's phone number was on the attorney letters, and Citibank never forwarded a file on the debt to the collection agency or the collection attorney. Because the bank's knowledge of and control over the agency's activities was unclear, the consumer's motion for summary judgment was denied.

Villarreal v. Snow, 1996 WL 473386 (N.D. Ill. Aug. 19, 1996). Beneficial Illinois, Inc., a lender, did not become a debt collector by "using" an attorney's name when the attorney spent about one minute on the minimal material sent by the lender on each account and directed his paralegal to send a particular form letter.

Indiana

Watson v. Auto Advisors, Inc., 822 N.E.2d 1017 (Ind. Ct. App. 2005). There was no misrepresentation of the car dealer's participation in seeking a small claims court judgment.

Michigan

South v. Midwestern Audit Servs., Inc., 2010 WL 5089862 (E.D. Mich. Dec. 8, 2010). In the FDCPA context, the classic "flat rater" is a debt collector who sells his letterhead to a creditor for a fixed per-letter fee (i.e., flat rate), but is not otherwise involved in the collection of the creditor's debts. Matching two utility accounts to roommates for a 10% collection fee took the collection agency outside of flat rating.

New York

Forman v. Academy Collection Serv., Inc., 388 F. Supp. 2d 199 (S.D.N.Y. 2005). The collection agency's letter was not flat-rating within § 1692j because the plaintiffs produced no evidence that the collection agency sold its letterhead or letters to the creditor.

Mazzei v. Money Store, 349 F. Supp. 2d 651 (S.D.N.Y. 2004). A lender, who hired a collection law firm to send out letters on the letterhead of the law firm at fifty dollars a letter declaring mortgages in default and accelerating the balance of the debt but not performing other collection services, did not use a false name and, therefore, did not fall within the coverage of creditors using false names.

Orenbuch v. N. Shore Health Sys., Inc., 250 F. Supp. 2d 145 (E.D.N.Y. 2003). A debt collector affiliated with the creditor was not a flat-rater pursuant to § 1692j. The FDCPA does not require disclosure of the debt collector's corporate affiliation.

Rumpler v. Phillips & Cohen Assocs., Ltd., 219 F. Supp. 2d 251 (E.D.N.Y. 2002). Fact that complaint alleged that debt was referred to third party debt collector for collection and did not allege any other facts to support § 1692j claim was sufficient to undermine claim that defendant was a flat-rater under § 1692j. The court described flat rating as a letter sent by a creditor which appeared to come from a third party collector. The use of the title Esq. did indicate an attorney was collecting the debt where the person's title was given as "Executive Vice President."

Franceschi v. Mautner-Glick Corp., 22 F. Supp. 2d 250 (S.D.N.Y. 1998). Residential management company's collection of past due rent in its own name does not subject the landlord/creditor to debt collector status under § 1692a(6) for collecting in a name "which would indicate that a third person is collecting" a debt or constitute flat rating in violation of § 1692j when the management company in fact itself was collecting the debt and the consumer alleged no confusion as to the relationship between the landlord and the management company.

Wegmans Food Mkts., Inc. v. Scrimpsher, 17 B.R. 999 (Bankr. N.D.N.Y. 1982). A grocery store which hired an agency to send a series of computer printed letters demanding payment to the store is not a debt collector under § 1692a(6) and is not covered by § 1692j.

Ohio

Durve v. Oker, 679 N.E.2d 19 (Ohio Ct. App. 1996). Where it was alleged that a physician had sent a collection letter in the name of a collection agency and discovery regarding the relationship between the physician and collection agency was denied, the consumer's FDCPA counterclaim against them was improperly dismissed.

Pennsylvania

Bezpalko v. Gilfillan, Gilpin & Brehman, 1998 WL 321268 (E.D. Pa. June 17, 1998). No violation of *Avila/Clomon* doctrine where attorney was personally involved in and directed the sending of an attorney dun signed by the attorney's secretary.

Littles v. Lieberman, 90 B.R. 700 (E.D. Pa. 1988). A lawyer who gave his form letter to a creditor for mailing to specific debtors was liable under § 1692j when the creditor sent it to another debtor. The "knowing" requirement of § 1692j was imputed by the lawyer's breach of his duty, as an officer of the court, to control the use of his professional name.

Wyoming

Johnson v. Statewide Collections, Inc., 778 P.2d 93 (Wyo. 1989). Collector's demand for more than the amount of the debt if the debt is not paid by a certain deadline is an unfair practice. The collection letter's recitation of the statutory formula for calculating the correct amount due did not avoid liability for demanding an incorrect amount.

K.1.4 Persons Protected; Standing Issues

Muir v. Navy Fed. Credit Union, 529 F.3d 1100 (D.C. Cir. 2008). A plaintiff joint account holder had standing to bring an FDCPA claim against a debt collector, for the debt collector's alleged action of removing money from the joint account in order to satisfy the debt owed by the other joint account holder in spite of the fact that the debt collector never "directly" communicated with the plaintiff.

Robey v. Shapiro, Marianos & Cejda, L.L.C., 434 F.3d 1208 (10th Cir. 2006). Actual damages are not required for standing under the FDCPA as the attempt to recover unlawful fees was made actionable by Congress.

Sibersky v. Goldstein, 2005 WL 2327235 (2d Cir. Sept. 21, 2005). Husband who was not a consumer (his wife was) did not have standing to pursue an FDCPA claim under §§ 1692e(11) or 1692g and did not plead the exposure to injurious collection activities that would give him a claim under § 1692e(5).

Singer v. Pierce & Assocs., P.C., 383 F.3d 596 (7th Cir. 2004). The court indicated that mortgage servicer's providing a requested mortgage loan payoff letter may not be considered debt collection as to the foreclosing attorney.

Montgomery v. Huntington Bank & Silver Shadow Recovery, Inc., 346 F.3d 693 (6th Cir. 2003). A non-debtor who was subjected to abusive collection tactics may not maintain an action for violations of § 1692c(c), since that section is limited to violations directed at a "consumer" as defined in the Act, but may maintain an action for violation of §§ 1692d and 1692e, which have no such limitation and therefore apply to anyone who is the victim of prescribed misconduct.

Miller v. Wolpoff & Abramson, L.L.P., 321 F.3d 292 (2d Cir. 2003). The consumer need not have been injured by an FDCPA violation arising from an attempt to collect a debt to have standing to assert that violation was targeted at him.

Kropelnicki v. Siegel, 290 F.3d 118 (2d Cir. 2002). Consumer had no standing to claim that the contents of the letter violated the FDCPA because the letter was addressed to her daughter.

Keele v. Wexler, 149 F.3d 589, 594 (7th Cir. 1998). "[T]he FDCPA is designed to protect consumers from the unscrupulous antics of debt collectors, irrespective of whether a valid debt actually exists."

Wright v. Fin. Serv. Inc., 22 F.3d 647 (6th Cir. 1994). Executrix, deceased's daughter, stood in the shoes of the debtor, had authority to open and read letters addressed to the debtor, has standing to bring actions under the FDCPA.

Baker v. G.C. Servs. Corp., 677 F.2d 775, 777 (9th Cir. 1982). "The Act is designed to protect consumers who have been victimized by unscrupulous debt collectors, regardless of whether a valid debt actually exists."

Alabama

Sparks v. Phillips & Cohen Assocs., Ltd., 641 F. Supp. 2d 1234 (S.D. Ala. 2008). "Any person," can be a plaintiff, not just a consumer.

Connecticut

Lemire v. Wolpoff & Abramson, L.L.P., 256 F.R.D. 321 (D. Conn. 2009). In granting class certification, court observed "[t]he legal convention that communications with a represented party's attorney are tantamount to communications with the party herself. . . ."

"[I]n the context of this strict liability statute, the Second Circuit does not require the consumer to demonstrate *damages* in order to have an 'injury' that suffices to establish standing to sue under the FDCPA."

Kimberly v. Great Lakes Collection Bureau, Inc., Clearinghouse No. 50,431B (D. Conn. 1996). Collection agency violated § 1692b(3) by contacting a consumer's mother on numerous occasions without the consumer's permission (which was required after the first contact if that contact was to obtain location information) and stating that consumer owed a debt. Consumer's mother did not have standing to recover under § 1692c(b) which only protects "consumers" as compared to other sections that appear to protect "any person."

Delaware

Dutton v. Wolhar, 809 F. Supp. 1130 (D. Del. 1992), *aff'd*, 5 F.3d 649 (3d Cir. 1993). The protections of the FDCPA are not limited to "consumers"; liability is imposed upon a debt collector who has failed to comply with the Act with respect to "any person" pursuant to § 1692k.

District of Columbia

Muir v. Navy Fed. Credit Union, 366 F. Supp. 2d 1 (D.D.C. 2005). In a bizarre decision, the debt collector's motion to dismiss or for summary judgment was granted because an individual who is not subjected to the practices of a debt collector does not fall within the zone of interests intended to be protected by the statute. The defendant was alleged to have taken $27,000 of the plaintiff's funds for his father's debt from a joint account with his father.

Florida

Drossin v. Nat'l Action Fin. Servs., Inc., 255 F.R.D. 608 (S.D. Fla. 2009). Plaintiff, who received an initial prerecorded telephone message from the debt collector and then a letter from the same entity stating that she owed a debt, had standing to assert FDCPA claims arising from the telephone message that was allegedly intended for another person with the same last name as plaintiff. The FDCPA is broadly written to provide standing to "any person" and should be liberally construed to protect "alleged" debtors.

Belin v. Litton Loan Serv., L.P., 2006 WL 1992410 (M.D. Fla. July 14, 2006). Only the "consumer" has standing to sue for a violation of §§ 1692c & 1692e(11).

Georgia

Whatley v. Universal Collection Bureau, Inc., 525 F. Supp. 1204 (N.D. Ga. 1981). The parties stipulated that statutory damages are limited to one award of $1000 to each plaintiff. Not just a "consumer" (a person allegedly indebted), but "any person" harmed by a violation (the parents of the consumer in this case) has standing under the FDCPA for damages.

Illinois

Greenfield v. Kluever & Platt, L.L.C., 2010 WL 604830 (N.D. Ill. Feb. 16, 2010). A *pro se* consumer who filed a chapter 13 bankruptcy petition on the same day as this FDCPA action without

disclosing the FDCPA case nevertheless had standing since she voluntarily dismissed the bankruptcy promptly.

Fuiten v. Creditor Servs, Bur., Inc., 2006 WL 1582459 (C.D. Ill. June 7, 2006). The court denied the collection agency's motion to dismiss the FDCPA claims finding that plaintiff, a former collection attorney for the collection agency, had sufficiently stated a cause of action by alleging that the collection agency forged his signature to at least 29 legal documents filed in court in connection with the collection agency's efforts to collect debts violating § 1692e(3). The collection attorney withdrew the forged complaints and terminated his relationship with the agency. The court noted that the FDCPA was broadly written to accord a private right of action to "any person."

Harvey v. Nat'l Action Fin. Servs., 79 F. Supp. 2d 896 (N.D. Ill. 1999). Plaintiff filed for bankruptcy after receiving collection letter. Plaintiff had standing to pursue FDCPA suit based on the collection letter where plaintiff amended her personal property schedule to include her FDCPA claim as one hundred percent exempt and the trustee did not object to the listing or assert a right to control the claim.

Flowers v. Accelerated Bureau of Collections, Inc., 1997 WL 136313 (N.D. Ill. Mar. 19, 1997). The spouse of a consumer may bring FDCPA claim if debt collection efforts that would violate the Act were targeted at her. A husband to which a collection call was targeted had standing to sue where the threats to sue and garnish his wages were received by his wife.

Mantell v. Feingold & Levy, 1997 WL 45313 (N.D. Ill. Jan. 30, 1997). Only the consumer (and not the debtor's stepdaughter) might sue for a collection call to the stepdaughter (who was not obligated on the debt) which violated § 1692c(b), limiting communications with third parties. A claim under § 1692e, false and misleading misrepresentation, was available to family members.

Weinberg v. Arcventures, Inc., 1996 WL 385951 (N.D. Ill. July 3, 1996). Genuine issue of material fact existed as to whether the collection agency's letter to the debtor's daughter was an attempt to get the daughter to pay a debt she did not owe or was sent to the daughter, an attorney, as the legal representative of her mother. The letter was sent in response to a request by the daughter, an attorney, for verification of her mother's debt. The collection agency claimed the daughter requested verification as her mother's attorney and lacked standing to bring the FDCPA claim. The daughter claimed the request was made on her mother's behalf. The letter, on its face, would lead an unsophisticated debtor to believe that the recipient personally owed the debt.

Villarreal v. Snow, 1996 WL 28308 (N.D. Ill. Jan. 19, 1996), *dismissed on merits*, 1996 WL 473386 (N.D. Ill. Aug. 19, 1996). An individual who was sent a dunning letter but who was not actually obligated on the debt had standing to recover for a violation of § 1692e and could represent the class of obligated consumers. This individual had signed as owner of the collateral for a loan and was an addressee of the deceptive dunning letter.

Kansas

Jeter v. Alliance One Receivables Mgmt., Inc., 2010 WL 2025213 (D. Kan. May 20, 2010). The court rejected the defendant's argument that it should impose a general rule ("unsupported in the statute") that a consumer who understands that he is not the true target of the defendant's debt collection efforts may not assert a claim under §§ 1692d, 1692e, or 1692f.

Burdett v. Harrah's Kansas Casino Corp., 294 F. Supp. 2d 1215 (D. Kan. 2003). An unobligated spouse, not the target of duns or a representative of the estate, does not have standing to assert an FDCPA violation based on collection efforts aimed at her deceased spouse.

Louisiana

JH Kaspar Oil Co. v. Newton & Assoc., L.L.C., 2008 WL 819094 (E.D. La. Mar. 25, 2008). The FDCPA provides no cause of action to a company that hired a collection agency to collect its debts from its commercial customers to redress the company's claim that the collection agency owed it money that it had collected.

Maryland

Young v. Scott, 2010 WL 2900319 (D. Md. July 22, 2010). A consumer who notified the law firm that her property fraudulently served as collateral for the delinquent mortgage loan had standing as a "consumer" to assert claim for violation of the FDCPA.

Queen v. Walker, 2010 WL 2696720 (D. Md. July 7, 2010). The alleged victim of a forgery and fraud against whom collection efforts were directed had standing to maintain suit for the resulting FDCPA violations.

Whiting v. Deloatch, 2010 WL 2651656 (D. Md. July 1, 2010). The victim of a mortgage rescue scheme was a "consumer" with standing even though title to the property was in the defendant's name and collection actions were aimed at the defendant. "Plaintiff is the true party in interest because what he claims to be his property fraudulently serves as collateral for the delinquent mortgage loan. Because of the alleged fraud, Consumer stands in the shoes of Deloatch and Plaintiff's home may be sold to pay the debt BGW has purportedly attempted to collect, if the Property is foreclosed upon. Moreover, BGW allegedly continued its collection efforts after Plaintiff put the law firm on notice of the alleged fraud."

Dorsey v. Morgan, 760 F. Supp. 509 (D. Md. 1991). Purchaser of a campground membership is a "consumer" within § 1692a(3).

Keane v. Nat'l Bureau of Collections, Clearinghouse No. 35,923 (D. Md. 1983). The pleadings of this case suggest that the plaintiff was not a "consumer" as defined by §§ 1692a(3) or 1692c(d), but rather took advantage of FDCPA provisions protecting "any person."

Massachusetts

Dolan v. Schreiber & Assocs., P.C., 2002 U.S. Dist. LEXIS 6005 (magistrate recommendation), *adopted* 2002 U.S. Dist. LEXIS 5998 (D. Mass. Mar. 29, 2002). An alleged unlawful threat to attach the debtor's property states a claim on behalf of a non-debtor co-owner of the property, since the threat has consequences for the non-debtor whose interest in the property could be harmed.

Michigan

Kaniewski v. Nat'l Action Fin. Servs., 678 F. Supp. 2d 541 (E.D. Mich. 2009). One who knows that he is not alleged to owe the debt is not a "consumer" and does not have standing to bring claims under §§ 1692e and 1692g, but does have standing as any person to bring claims pursuant to § 1692d.

Tworek v. Hudson & Keyse, L.L.C., 2009 WL 4946723 (E.D. Mich. Dec. 14, 2009). Consumer who failed to disclose her FDCPA claim in her bankruptcy papers lacked standing to now assert the claim.

Missouri

Thomas v. Consumer Adjustment Co., 579 F. Supp. 2d 1290 (E.D. Mo. 2008). Third party who answered the call had standing to sue the debt collector: the focus of §§ 1692c(b) and 1692b is not solely on communications with the consumer; it also regulates the content of the communication with third parties and proscribes certain conduct, such as communicating with the third party more than once. Under the unique facts here, where the third party alleges direct harm and actual damages, she has standing.

New York

Schuh v. Druckman & Sinel, L.L.P., 2010 WL 2605340 (S.D.N.Y. June 29, 2010). The consumers could not assert a violation with respect to a letter sent by a foreclosure lawyer to a title and closing company who was not their agent.

Ehrich v. I.C. Sys. Inc., 681 F. Supp. 2d 265 (E.D.N.Y. 2010). Although the consumers themselves did not speak Spanish and thus were not deprived of § 1692g validation notice as a result of the inclusion of a Spanish language sentence that overshadowed the required notice, their mere receipt of the offending collection letter was sufficient to establish FDCPA statutory injury and thus standing.

Schwartz v. Resurgent Capital Servs., L.P., 2009 WL 3756600 (E.D.N.Y. Nov. 9, 2009). The plaintiff was not a "consumer" with standing to sue for the alleged § 1692g(a) disclosure violation where the collector sent the dun to an unknown individual "in care of" the plaintiff at the plaintiff's address.

Barasch v. Estate Info. Servs., L.L.C., 2009 WL 2900261 (E.D.N.Y. Sept. 3, 2009). The widow of the deceased debtor to whose estate the subject dun was addressed lacked standing to sue over the letter's allegedly insufficient § 1692g verification disclosures since she was not the consumer and had not been appointed executrix or personal representative of the estate so as to "stand in the shoes of the consumer."

Bank v. Pentagroup Fin., L.L.C., 2009 WL 1606420 (E.D.N.Y. June 9, 2009). The court erroneously held that one who received recorded calls aimed at a different consumer has no standing under § 1692c. "[Plaintiff] lacks standing to bring a claim under § 1692c because: (1) he was not obligated or allegedly obligated to pay any debt; and (2) he has not alleged that he is a consumer's spouse, parent, guardian, executor or administrator. Accordingly, [defendant's] motion to dismiss [plaintiff's] § 1692c(b) claim is granted."

Conboy v. AT&T Univ. Card Servs. Corp., 84 F. Supp. 2d 492 (S.D.N.Y. 2000), *aff'd*, 241 F.3d 242 (2d Cir. 2001). Because plaintiffs were not obligated to pay their daughter-in-law's debt, they were not "consumers" under the FDCPA. Since § 1692e(11) is limited to communications with consumers, plaintiffs could not state a claim for a violation under that subsection.

Sibersky v. Borah, Goldstein, Altschuler & Schwartz, P.C., 2000 U.S. Dist. LEXIS 14043 (S.D.N.Y. Sept. 22, 2000). Husband who was not a consumer could pursue FDCPA claims under sections not restricted to consumers, such as a § 1692e(5) claim. Since husband did not owe the rent debt or receive the three-day demand letter, his claim for violation of the notice requirements, which applied only to consumers, was dismissed.

Mateer v. Ross, Suchoff, Egert, Hankin, Maidenbaum & Mazel, P.C., 1997 WL 171011 (S.D.N.Y. Apr. 10, 1997). Former tenant had "standing" to file a claim under the FDCPA where that former landlord's collection attorney unlawfully froze bank accounts that were in the name of the tenant's roommate, upon whom he was dependent, and not in his own name, as he suffered from the attorney's action.

Kaschak v. Raritan Valley Collection Agency, 1989 U.S. Dist. LEXIS 19103 (D.N.J. May 22, 1989). An executrix has standing to bring FDCPA claim that deceased could have brought, but she has standing as an individual to sue for her own injuries only where FDCPA's duties run to "any person" rather than to "the consumer."

Riveria v. MAB Collections, Inc., 682 F. Supp. 174 (W.D.N.Y. 1988). The FDCPA private remedy is available to "any person," not just consumers. Therefore, the administrator who had received dunning letters regarding a consumer debt had standing to sue under FDCPA.

North Carolina

Johnson v. Bullhead Invs., L.L.C., 2010 WL 118274 (M.D.N.C. Jan. 11, 2010). The consumer, a person with a name similar to the actual debtor, who was served with the actual debtor's state court collection suit even after she notified the collector of the mistaken identity and who incurred attorney fees in having the collection case against her dismissed and incurred other actual damages as a result of the debt collector's collection efforts, had standing FDCPA violations.

Ohio

Maddox v. Martin Co., L.L.C., 2006 WL 1308211 (S.D. Ohio May 11, 2006). Debtor's aunt protected from violations of § 1692e but not of § 1692c.

Minick v. First Fed. Credit Control, Inc., 1981 U.S. Dist. LEXIS 18622 (N.D. Ohio June 9, 1981). Violations of § 1692c involving the plaintiff's wife who did not join as a party are relevant if they resulted in damages to the plaintiff.

Midland Funding L.L.C. v. Stowe, 2009 WL 5258458 (Ohio Ct. App. Dec. 23, 2009). Reversing the trial court's dismissal of the consumer's FDCPA counterclaim because the consumer lacked standing once he denied the collection complaint allegations that he was the subject debtor, the appellate court held that the FDCPA conveyed standing "for a consumer in [defendant's] position, i.e., one who was wrongfully sued for a debt he did not owe" since "the term 'consumer' meant any natural person obligated or allegedly obligated to pay any debt."

Oregon

Mathis v. Omnium Worldwide, 2006 WL 1582301 (D. Or. June 4, 2006). A daughter of a deceased debtor failed to establish liability under §§ 1692d, 1692e, or 1692f and would not have a claim under § 1692c or § 1692g where the collector was contacting her to locate the executor of the estate.

Mathis v. Omnium Worldwide, 2005 WL 3159663 (D. Or. Nov. 27, 2005). Daughter who was subjected to collection calls for her deceased parent's debt had standing to sue even though she did not owe the debt; FDCPA protections are not limited to consumers, but extend to "any person."

Pennsylvania

Walter v. Palisades Collection, L.L.C., 2010 WL 308978 (E.D. Pa. Jan. 26, 2010). Filing of a collection action against a non-liable spouse can qualify as a violation of the FDCPA.

Cole v. Charleston, 2009 WL 123472 (E.D. Pa. Jan. 15, 2009). Simply because a plaintiff happens to be a lawyer does not mean that he or she should be precluded from protection by the FDCPA.

Wenrich v. Robert E. Cole, P.C., 2000 U.S. Dist. LEXIS 18687 (E.D. Pa. Dec. 22, 2000). Some protections of the FDCPA extended to "any person," including parents alleged to be obligated on the claim, if they were contacted by the collector to pay the debt.

Woodside v. New Jersey Higher Educ. Assistance Auth., 1993 WL 56020 (E.D. Pa. Mar. 2, 1993). Plaintiffs were consumers protected by the FDCPA despite defendant's argument that they are not because plaintiffs have the ability but not the desire to pay the collector's claim.

Texas

Prophet v. Myers, 2009 WL 1437799 (S.D. Tex. May 21, 2009). While acknowledging that "a third-party, non-debtor [has] standing to bring FDCPA claims [where] the alleged debt collection practices were directed towards the third-party," the court granted the defendant summary judgment because the letter at issue was addressed and sent to the plaintiff's son [who has a similar name] at the son's separate address and was in no manner directed to the father, who could not even meet his burden to explain how the letter came into his possession.

Utah

Morgan v. N.A.R., Inc., 2008 WL 639128 (D. Utah Mar. 5, 2008). Summary judgment for the defendants where the consumer alleged that the defendants violated the FDCPA because her wages continued to be garnished after she had satisfied the underlying judgment, since the defendants in fact notified the employer that the judgment had been satisfied prior to the wrongful garnishment, "therefore, any further garnishments were the result of [the employer's] actions, not Defendants.' "

Virginia

Carter v. Countrywide Home Loans, Inc., 2009 WL 2742560 (E.D. Va. Aug. 25, 2009). Even though the plaintiff had not signed the note or the related loan modification agreement, he would be still protected as "consumer" under 15 U.S.C. § 1692c.

Creighton v. Emporia Credit Serv., Inc., 981 F. Supp. 411 (E.D. Va. 1997). Person allegedly obligated on hospital bill was a "consumer" under FDCPA.

West v. Costen, 558 F. Supp. 564 (W.D. Va. 1983). One need not be a consumer (a person alleged to owe the debt) defined by § 1692a(3) to recover under provisions of the FDCPA which apply to any "person," e.g., § 1692e. Other provisions of the FDCPA, e.g., § 1692c, only protect a "consumer."

Washington

Clark v. Bonded Adjustment Co., 204 F.R.D. 662 (E.D. Wash. 2002). In the course of granting class certification based on charging excessive process server fees, the court recognized that the FDCPA applied whether the fee was actually collected or whether the debt collector merely attempted to collect it. Consumers could serve as class representatives even if they had not paid the fee.

K.1.5 Communications Covered

Allen ex rel. Martin v. LaSalle Bank, N.A., 2011 WL 94420 (3d Cir. Jan. 12, 2011). Since § 1692f(1) prohibits "unfair or unconscionable means" regardless of the person to whom the communication was directed, and the FDCPA similarly defines a "communication" expansively, a communication to a consumer's attorney is undoubtedly an indirect communication to the consumer. A communication is "the conveying of information regarding a debt" and is not limited to specific requests for payment.

Gburek v. Litton Loan Serv. L.P., 614 F.3d 380 (7th Cir. 2010). An offer from the mortgage servicer to work out an arrearage in a mortgage debt to avoid foreclosure and a request for financial information from the homeowner from a firm hired to assist the servicer in its loss mitigation process were communications in connection with the collection of a debt covered by the FDCPA, notwithstanding the lack of an explicit demand for a payment of money. The absence of a demand for payment is only one factor in determining whether a communication from a debt collector is made in connection with the collection of any debt. The nature of the parties' relationship, the purpose and context of the communication, and whether there is a debt in default are also relevant. The district court ignored salient facts alleged in the complaint that the consumer's mortgage was in default and that the text of the letters indicated they were sent to induce her to settle her debt in order to avoid foreclosure. The complaint thus sufficiently alleged communications that were "sent in connection with an attempt to collect a debt."

Donohue v. Quick Collect, Inc., 592 F.3d 1027 (9th Cir. 2010). "[A state court] complaint served directly on a consumer to facilitate debt-collection efforts is a communication subject to the requirements of §§ 1692e and 1692f."

Newman v. Ormond, 2010 WL 3623174 (11th Cir. Sept. 20, 2010). Because the trial notice was a document provided by the court rather than the debt collector, the collector could not have made any misrepresentation in violation of the FDCPA in this document.

Edwards v. Niagara Credit Solutions, Inc., 584 F.3d 1350 (11th Cir. 2009). Telephone answering machine messages that asked the consumer to return calls from the defendant debt collector and that did not convey any specific information about a debt were nevertheless "communications" subject to the FDCPA since the reason for the calls was to collect a debt and they thus indirectly conveyed information about the debt.

Muir v. Navy Fed. Credit Union, 529 F.3d 1100 (D.C. Cir. 2008). Court held that a plaintiff joint account holder had standing to bring an FDCPA claim against a debt collector, for the debt collector's alleged action of removing money from the joint account in order to satisfy the debt owed by the other joint account holder in spite of the fact that the debt collector never "directly" communicated with the plaintiff.

McCready v. Jacobsen, 2007 WL 1224616 (7th Cir. Apr. 25, 2007). A landlord's attorney who sent the tenant a single letter informing the tenant pursuant to state law that the landlord was withholding the security deposit and who made no demand for payment of money was accordingly not attempting to collect a debt.

Goldman v. Cohen, 445 F.3d 152 (2d Cir. 2006). A legal pleading was a "communication" within meaning of the FDCPA.

Thomas v. Law Firm of Simpson & Cybak, 392 F.3d 914 (7th Cir. 2004) (2-1 split decision). Law firm's filing of summons and complaint on behalf of creditor in state court after debtor missed payment on installment contract was an "initial communication."

Vega v. McKay, 351 F.3d 1334 (11th Cir. 2003). A summons and complaint was not a communication requiring that § 1692g informal dispute rights be given the consumer. The court did not refer to the contrary FTC Formal Advisory Opinion (Mar. 31, 2000).

Buckley v. Bass & Assoc., 249 F.3d 678 (7th Cir. 2001). Letter seeking information about a consumer's bankruptcy filing was not yet an effort to collect a debt, so the defendant need not comply with "initial communication" requirements under § 1692g.

Santoro v. CTC Foreclosure Serv. Corp., 2001 U.S. App. LEXIS 5024 (9th Cir. Mar. 20, 2001). Ignoring logic and the plain meaning rule, the court held FDCPA did not apply to a letter discussing the creditor's workout policies and a legal notice of foreclosure because they were not duns sent in connection with the collection of a debt.

Alabama

Sparks v. Phillips & Cohen Assocs., Ltd., 641 F. Supp. 2d 1234 (S.D. Ala. 2008). The debt collector's alleged contacts with the deceased debtor's daughter, the daughter's employer, and the employer's daughter in an attempt to determine the proper person to contact to obtain payment from the deceased debtor's estate were all made "in connection with the collection of a debt."

California

Koby v. ARS Nat'l Servs., Inc., 2010 WL 5249834 (S.D. Cal. Dec. 23, 2010). The court denied the plaintiffs' motion to reconsider its ruling that a voicemail merely stating the caller's name and asking for a return call did not convey, directly or indirectly, any information regarding the debt owed and therefore was not a "communication" that required a § 1692e(11) disclosure.

McClenning v. NCO Fin. Sys., Inc., 2010 WL 4795269 (C.D. Cal. Nov. 15, 2010). A question of fact was raised as to whether or not the defendant failed to cease collection of the debt in violation of § 1692g(b) when it made a soft-pull credit inquiry.

Koby v. ARS Nat'l Servs., Inc., 2010 WL 1438763 (S.D. Cal. Mar. 29, 2010). Voicemail messages from debt collectors to debtors are "communications" regardless of whether a debt is mentioned in the message.

Costa v. Nat'l Action Fin. Servs., 634 F. Supp. 2d 1069 (E.D. Cal. 2007). Telephone messages left by a debt collector are "communications" subject to the FDCPA.

Colorado

Ray v. Int'l Bank, Inc., 2005 WL 2305017 (D. Colo. Sept. 21, 2005). On the defendant's motion to dismiss, the court examined the split between the Eleventh Circuit in *Vega* and the Seventh Circuit in *Thomas* on whether a pleading can be an initial FDCPA communication but refused to rule on the issue "at this juncture."

Connecticut

Lemire v. Wolpoff & Abramson, L.L.P., 256 F.R.D. 321 (D. Conn. Mar. 31, 2009). In granting class certification, court observed "[t]he legal convention that communications with a represented party's attorney are tantamount to communications with the party herself...."

Florida

Newman v. Ormond, 2010 WL 680914 (S.D. Fla. Feb. 24, 2010). Summary judgment against *pro se* plaintiff, who relied on state court pleadings which court deemed not subject to FDCPA.

Chalik v. Westport Recovery Corp., 677 F. Supp. 2d 1322 (S.D. Fla. 2009). Where the collector's voicemail message purported to be returning consumer's call, but it was unknown if the caller actually was returning consumer's call or was just claiming to, in order to increase the likelihood that consumer would return her call, a factual issue existed as to whether the call was a "communication" covered by the FDCPA.

Brazier v. Law Offices of Mitchell N. Kay, P.C., 2009 WL 764161 (M.D. Fla. Mar. 19, 2009). Denied defendant's motion for summary judgment since the intended recipient of the letter (sent to consumer c/o attorney) was disputed fact.

Pescatrice v. Orovitz, 539 F. Supp. 2d 1375 (S.D. Fla. 2008). A proposed stipulation sent by the collection attorneys to the consumer as a settlement offer to resolve the underlying state court collection action was a "communication" as defined by the FDCPA.

North Star Capital Acquisitions, L.L.C. v. Krig, 2008 WL 346021 (M.D. Fla. Feb. 7, 2008). By alleging that inclusion of a stipulation of settlement and collection letter with the service of the summons and complaint was improper and misleading, consumers adequately stated an abuse of process claim as well as a claim that fell within the FDCPA.

Illinois

Hutton v. C.B. Accounts, Inc., 2010 WL 3021904 (C.D. Ill. Aug. 3,

2010). Leaving a voicemail message to call back is a "communication" because the purpose was to induce the consumer to call to discuss her outstanding debt.

Matmanivong v. Unifund CCR Partners, 2009 WL 1181529 (N.D. Ill. Apr. 28, 2009). Communications to lawyers and the court are subject to § 1692e of the FDCPA just like communications to consumers.

Ramirez v. Apex Fin. Mgmt., L.L.C., 567 F. Supp. 2d 1035 (N.D. Ill. 2008). The court rejected *Biggs v. Credit Collections, Inc.*, 2007 WL 4034997 (W.D. Okla. Nov. 15, 2007), and followed the overwhelming majority rule of *Foti, et al.*, that the debt collector's voicemail messages were FDCPA "communications."

Lauer v. Mason, Silver, Wenk & Mishkin, L.L.C., 2006 WL 1005090 (N.D. Ill. Apr. 17, 2006). Letter sent to consumer's attorney (not to consumer c/o attorney) was not actionable, where claim was that no validation notice was sent within five days of the communication to the attorney.

Lauer v. Nakon, 2006 WL 418676 (N.D. Ill. Feb. 16, 2006). Defendant's motion to dismiss because there was no direct request for payment was denied. The letter could be construed as either an attempt to induce payment of the judgment previously entered or an attempt to collect payment of the damage done to the property.

Diesi v. Shapiro, 330 F. Supp. 2d 1002 (C.D. Ill. 2004). Where the consumer alleged that the debt collector had misrepresented and inflated the amount of the debt in a mortgage reinstatement letter written to the consumer's attorney, the court dismissed the consumer's complaint for failure to state a claim, holding that communications made to the consumer's attorney are not actionable under the FDCPA.

Porter v. Fairbanks Capital Corp., 2003 WL 21210115 (N.D. Ill. May 21, 2003). A videotape from a mortgage servicer alleged to be a debt collector entitled "Solutions for Today's Homeowners" that demanded no payment and provided no information about the consumer's current loan status and instead merely asked the consumer to contact the servicer about "possible loan workout options" was not a "communication" in connection with the collection of a debt.

Wexler v. Bank of Am. Auto Fin. Corp., 2000 U.S. Dist. LEXIS 12491 (N.D. Ill. Aug. 23, 2000). A letter, in response to Wexler's communication, that did not seek payment but was merely a warning seeking to avert any collection consequences of nonpayment was not a collection activity covered by the FDCPA. Plaintiff Wexler was a defendant in prior FDCPA suits.

Indiana

Captain v. ARS Nat. Servs., Inc., 636 F. Supp. 2d 791 (S.D. Ind. 2009). Section 1692e(5) summary judgment granted to the plaintiff where it was undisputed that the collector misrepresented to the consumer's lawyer that a $15 per day fee would be added to account if it was not paid within two weeks, because that statement was false and deceptive under the "competent attorney" standard established by the Seventh Circuit [*Evory*] applicable to attorney communications.

Gillespie v. Chase Home Fin., L.L.C., 2009 WL 4061428 (N.D. Ind. Nov. 20, 2009). A collection letter requesting that the debtor call its mortgage specialist to resolve a delinquency was not a communication requesting payment covered by the FDCPA under the *Bailey* decision. The mailing of the letter therefore did not violate § 1692c(a)(2).

Maryland

Jackson-Spells v. Francis, 45 F. Supp. 2d 496 (D. Md. 1999). Two settlement letters sent by a lawyer defending a creditor in a replevin action brought *pro se* by a consumer were not communications within the meaning of § 1692a(2).

Michigan

South v. Midwestern Audit Servs., Inc., 2010 WL 5089862 (E.D. Mich. Dec. 8, 2010). Following *Bailey* and *Gburek*, the court found a debt collection agency's sending an obtuse letter to the consumer indicating that the utility bill balance from her boyfriend's prior account was being transferred to her utility account and not demanding payment was not sent "in connection with the collection of a debt" and not subject to the FDCPA.

Gathing v. Mortgage Elec. Registration Sys., Inc., 2010 WL 889945 (W.D. Mich. Mar. 10, 2010). Since FDCPA prohibits actions and unfair practices that may not involve communicating directly with the consumer, *pro se* allegations that co-defendant was debt collector's servicing agent and that co-defendant debt collector is vicariously liable for its servicing agent's acts under the doctrine of respondeat superior, survives motion to dismiss. Summary judgment denied where co-defendant servicing agent offers no support for its contention that statements made in a letter that also includes language required by law or in a response to an inquiry by a plaintiff are exempt from compliance with the FDCPA.

Grden v. Leikin, Ingber & Winters, P.C., 2010 WL 199947 (E.D. Mich. Jan. 19, 2010). "[A]ffidavits attached to state-court complaints are communications governed by the FDCPA." The collector's misstatement of the amount of the debt communicated in response to the consumer's direct inquiry was not made "in connection with the collection of" the consumer's debt and thus did not violate § 1692e(2)(A) where the collector did not demand payment, did not imply that the consumer was in default, and did not "allude to the consequences of default."

Mabbitt v. Midwestern Audit Serv., Inc., 2008 WL 723507 (E.D. Mich. Mar. 17, 2008). Summary judgment for the defendant collector because the collection agency's letter only informed the consumer that her $961.45 balance on an outstanding utility bill owing from a previous residence had been transferred to her sister's current account at their new address. Because it did not contain an explicit request for payment the letter was not "in connection with the collection" of the debt.

Minnesota

Hemmingsen v. Messerli & Kramer, P.A., 2011 WL 494941 (D. Minn. Feb. 7, 2011). Section 1692e did not apply to the collector's allegedly false statements made in its motion for summary judgment and memorandum of law in its unsuccessful state court collection lawsuit since the representations were directed to the court and not the consumer.

Edeh v. Midland Credit Mgmt., Inc., 2010 WL 3893604 (D. Minn. Sept. 29, 2010). "The Court has learned, through its work on countless FDCPA cases, that threatening to report and reporting debts to CRAs is one of the most commonly-used arrows in the debt collector's quiver. Consistent with the views of the FTC-and consistent with the views expressed in Purnell, Quale, and Semper-the Court finds that Midland was engaged in "collection of the debt" in violation of § 1692g(b) when it reported Edeh's disputed debt to the CRAs before sending verification of that debt to Edeh."

Seaworth v. Messerli, 2010 WL 3613821 (D. Minn. Sept. 7, 2010). The court concluded that a pleading sent to the *pro se* consumer's home but never received was not a "communication."

Mark v. J.C. Christensen & Assocs., Inc., 2009 WL 2407700 (D. Minn. Aug. 4, 2009). Messages left by the debt collector on the consumer's answering machine are "communications" under the FDCPA.

Missouri

Settle v. Bank of Am., 2010 WL 682296 (E.D. Mo. Feb. 23, 2010). The mortgagee's alleged failure to properly respond to the *pro se* consumer's request for verification sent prior to any claim of default was not a § 1692g verification violation as it was sent prior to the "initial communication with a consumer in connection with the collection of any debt" that triggers the verification duty.

Thomas v. Consumer Adjustment Co., 579 F. Supp. 2d 1290 (E.D. Mo. 2008). Even though the debt collector did not disclose any information about the account, since the call was made for the purpose of contacting the debtor to obtain collection, it was a "communication" within § 1692a(2).

Anderson v. Gamache & Myers, P.C., 2007 WL 4365745 (E.D. Mo. Dec. 10, 2007). The debt collector's communication to the consumer's agent with power of attorney, a mediation service that did not provide legal advice, was a communication to the consumer, following *Evory*.

Nevada

Charov v. Perry, 2010 WL 2673662 (D. Nev. June 30, 2010). The court dismissed the *pro se* consumer's complaint since recordation of a notice of default cannot violate the FDCPA: consent to make such a recordation upon default is necessarily given to a trustee in a deed of trust where state law requires such recordation as part of a non-judicial foreclosure.

New Jersey

Ogbin v. Fein, Such, Kahn & Shepard, P.C., 2009 WL 1587896 (D.N.J. June 1, 2009). Communications that were directed to the consumers' attorney are not actionable under the FDCPA.

New York

Boyd v. J.E. Robert Co., 2011 WL 477547 (E.D.N.Y. Feb. 2, 2011). The FDCPA is intended to protect consumers from communications initiated by debt collectors, not alleged communications initiated by an escrow agent for all parties to the sale.

Gorham-Dimaggio v. Countrywide Home Loans, Inc., 2005 WL 2098068 (N.D.N.Y. Aug. 30, 2005) (dictum). Unsolicited communication initiated by consumer was not an effort to collect a debt.

Tromba v. M.R.S. Assocs., Inc., 323 F. Supp. 2d 424 (E.D.N.Y. 2004). "[I]n reliance upon *Kropelnicki*, the Court concludes that, under the circumstances alleged in this case, Plaintiff has no cause of action under the FDCPA where a communication was solely directed to her attorney and no threat was made regarding contact with the debtor herself."

North Carolina

Davis v. Trans Union, L.L.C., 526 F. Supp. 2d 577 (W.D.N.C. 2007). Reporting to credit bureaus is a communication within the FDCPA. Allegation that collection agency falsely reported the balance of an account to a credit bureau survived motion to dismiss.

Ohio

Midland Funding L.L.C. v. Brent, 644 F. Supp. 2d 961 (N.D. Ohio 2009). Affidavits attached to complaints for money themselves constitute communications for the purposes of the FDCPA.

Kline v. Mortgage Elec. Registration Sys., Inc., 2009 WL 6093372 (S.D. Ohio Nov. 24, 2009), *report and recommendation adopted*, 2010 WL 1133452 (S.D. Ohio Mar. 22, 2010). Allegations that the defendants misrepresented and inflated various fees and charges owing while pursuing the underlying foreclosure were not actionable since the subject communications were made to the consumer's attorney and thus were outside of the FDCPA per the rule of *Guerrero v. RJM Acquisitions L.L.C.*, 499 F.3d 926 (9th Cir. 2007).

In re Gunter, 334 B.R. 900 (Bankr. S.D. Ohio 2005). Summons and complaint are "communications" within the FDCPA.

Oklahoma

Mendus v. Morgan & Assoc., 994 P.2d 83 (Okla. Ct. App. 1999). A pleading or a summons was a communication under the FDCPA and was the initial communication triggering the validation notice requirements.

Oregon

Avery v. Gordon, 2008 WL 4793686 (D. Or. Oct. 27, 2008). Distinguishing *Guerrero*, held that "a counterclaim for a debt is not a representation made [solely] to an attorney, but rather a demand for money made on the debtor, through a pleading rather than a letter or a phone call. Under *Guerrero* the issue is whether the conduct is aimed at the debtor, regardless of whether the debtor has a lawyer. The *Guerrero* court held that the letter from the debt collector was directed solely at the creditor's lawyer . . ."

Capital Credit & Collection Serv., Inc. v. Armani, 206 P.3d 1114 (Or. Ct. App. 2009). A "false, deceptive, or misleading representation or means in connection with the collection of any debt" under § 1692e includes communications by the debt collector to the debtor's attorney, since the FDCPA applies to direct and indirect collection efforts.

Pennsylvania

Henry v. Shapiro, 2010 WL 996459 (E.D. Pa. Mar. 15, 2010). The FDCPA includes the contents of formal pleadings within its scope except where formal pleadings are explicitly exempted by §§ 1692e(11) and 1692g(d).

Wright v. Phelan, Hallinan & Schmieg, L.L.P., 2010 WL 786536 (E.D. Pa. Mar. 8, 2010). Fax to plaintiff's lawyer who immediately recognized the inconsistent charges did not violate the FDCPA, even when letter was shared with consumer.

Marshall v. Portfolio Recovery Assocs., Inc., 2009 WL 4281488 (E.D. Pa. Nov. 30, 2009). Communications between debt collectors and consumers' attorneys are not subject to the FDCPA.

Inman v. NCO Fin. Sys., Inc. 2009 WL 3415281 (E.D. Pa. Oct. 21, 2009). Followed *Foti*, holding prerecorded messages left on an answering machine were communications.

Duraney v. Washington Mut. Bank, 2008 WL 4204821 (W.D. Pa. Sept. 11, 2008), *aff'd*, 2010 WL 2993810 (3d Cir. Aug. 2, 2010). The court held that allegedly deceptive communications from a debt collector to the consumer's attorney were not subject to the FDCPA, adopting the Ninth Circuit's view in *Guerrero* as opposed to the Fourth Circuit's per the *Sayyed* opinion; but assuming such communications were covered, the court followed the Seventh Circuit's "competent lawyer" standard in *Evory* and still dismissed the § 1692e claims since the consumer "has not even argued, much less demonstrated, that her lawyer was likely to be deceived by the communications he received."

Ahmed v. I.C. Sys., Inc., 2005 WL 3533111 (W.D. Pa. Dec. 20, 2005). Defendant's motion to dismiss was granted because its letter to the consumer's attorney requesting he contact the collection agency was not a communication covered by the FDCPA.

Prince v. NCO Fin. Servs., Inc., 346 F. Supp. 2d 744 (E.D. Pa. 2004). Servicing agent whose dun to the consumer stated that dun was "a communication from a debt collector" did not create an estoppel against the agent that it was a debt collector under the FDCPA because there was no allegation of detrimental reliance.

Sullivan v. Equifax, Inc., 2002 WL 799856 (E.D. Pa. Apr. 19, 2002). The court rejected the argument that sending false information about a delinquent payment to a credit reporting agency was not debt collection conduct.

Texas

Quesenberry v. Alliant Law Group, P.C., 2010 WL 1189457 (E.D. Tex. Mar. 5, 2010), *report and recommendation adopted*, 2010 WL 1189481 (E.D. Tex. Mar. 24, 2010). Under § 1692e, debt collector may violate the Act when it uses "any false, deceptive, or misleading representation or means in connection with the collection of any debt," even when it makes those representations to an attorney. The facsimile was sent "in connection with" collection where it listed the principal amount owed on the debt as well as the allegedly illegal interest charge. Further, it set a deadline to respond to the deferral agreement and threatened: "If we do not receive the signed deferral agreement or hear from you we will proceed with our efforts to resolve this past-due debt."

Blanks v. Ford Motor Credit, 2005 WL 43981 (N.D. Tex. Jan. 7, 2005). The court rejected the argument that sending false information about a delinquent payment to a credit reporting agency was not debt collection conduct.

Wisconsin

Barrows v. Petrie & Stocking, S.C., 2008 WL 3540405 (W.D. Wis. Aug. 13, 2008). The defendant collectors' communications with the consumer's credit union to effectuate a state court garnishment were not exempt from the FDCPA's coverage "simply because the debt collector's communication is directed to a third party and not to the consumer himself" since the FDCPA defines a "communication" broadly as "the conveying of information regarding a debt directly or indirectly to any person through any medium."

K.1.6 Miscellaneous

Walls v. Wells Fargo Bank, N.A., 276 F.3d 502 (9th Cir. 2002). Since plaintiff premised her FDCPA claim on violations of Bankruptcy Code §§ 362 or 524, the claims were barred. Plaintiff's remedies for violations of the Bankruptcy Code were exclusively within the Code itself.

California

Reyes v. Kenosian & Miele, L.L.P., 619 F. Supp. 2d 796 (N.D. Cal. 2008). State court collection complaints are generally subject to the FDCPA.

Colorado

Kelly v. Wolpoff & Abramson, L.L.P., 634 F. Supp. 2d 1202 (D. Colo. 2008). The fact that the bank had "charged off" the credit card debt after 180 days after delinquency was an accounting device required by federal regulations and did not "extinguish" the debt as the plaintiff alleged or alter the right of the defendant to collect it.

Connecticut

Premier Capital, Inc. v. Grossman, 2000 Conn. Super. LEXIS 3137 (Conn. Super. Ct. Nov. 22, 2000), *aff'd in part, rev'd in part on other grounds*, 789 A.2d 565 (Conn. App. Ct. 2002). Notice required by state law making demand for payment was effective even if the notice failed to inform the debtors of their rights under the FDCPA.

Florida

Kaplan v. Assetcare, Inc., 88 F. Supp. 2d 1355 (S.D. Fla. 2000). The court held that plaintiff had stated a cause of action for violation of the FDCPA noting that four of the five letters were within the FDCPA statute of limitations, and that an FDCPA claim arising from a violation of state law need not provide private right of action.

In re Cooper, 253 B.R. 286 (Bankr. N.D. Fla. 2000). A motion to lift the automatic stay to permit collection in another forum was not a collection effort.

Illinois

Cole v. Noonan & Lieberman, Ltd., 2005 WL 2848446 (N.D. Ill. Oct. 26, 2005). When defendants filed an appearance, they were not attempting to collect a debt, so their failure to provide the §§ 1692e and 1692g notices did not violate the FDCPA.

Wagner v. Ocwen Fed. Bank, F.S.B., 2000 U.S. Dist. LEXIS 12463 (N.D. Ill. Aug. 28, 2000). Since Ocwen's activities occurred after the discharge and the bankruptcy court proceedings had concluded, the FDCPA claim was displaced by a bankruptcy claim. "Moreover, Wagner's FDCPA claim, at its foundation, is no different from that of any other debtor who is dunned by a creditor who in fact is not owed any money; the fact that her debt was discharged in bankruptcy does not logically differentiate her case from that of a debtor whose debt was discharged in some other way."

Baldwin v. McCalla, Raymer, Padrick, Cobb, Nichols & Clark, 1999 WL 284788 (N.D. Ill. Apr. 26, 1999). The FDCPA does not apply to misstatements made by creditors in proofs of claim filed in bankruptcy proceedings.

Monitz v. Friedman, 1997 WL 736720 (N.D. Ill. Nov. 18, 1997). Judge *sua sponte* reviewed *pro se* complaint filed by an attorney and required it to be amended to avoid unnecessarily splitting a single count into two and to more clearly allege some wrongful conduct.

Kansas

McDaniel v. South & Assocs., P.C., 325 F. Supp. 2d 1210 (D. Kan. 2004). Collector violated FDCPA by initiating judicial foreclosure action seeking a money judgment as well as foreclosure after receiving a timely validation request but before responding to it. The court distinguished cases holding that non-judicial foreclosure was not debt collection.

Peasley v. Telecheck, Inc., Consumer Cred. Guide (CCH) ¶ 96,996 (Kan. Ct. App. 1981). The FDCPA does not apply to a case where collection efforts occurred before and after the effective date of the Act. [This decision is contrary to the plain language of the Act.]

Louisiana

Louisiana State Bar Ass'n v. Harrington, 571 So. 2d 151 (La. 1990). A private attorney violated the FDCPA by entering a consumer's home without her permission, loudly threatening and embarrassing her. His settlement of FDCPA violations was cited as evidence of misconduct in a bar disciplinary proceeding against him.

New Mexico

Bitah v. Global Collection Servs., Inc., 968 F. Supp. 618 (D.N.M. 1997). Lack of any evidence that collection agency's attorney had any role in the telephone calls that the consumer received from the agency's employees precluded attorney liability for those contacts.

Martinez v. Estate Recoveries, Inc., 1996 U.S. Dist. LEXIS 22667 (D.N.M. Apr. 24, 1996). FDCPA did not apply to the filing of a claim against a decedent's estate. The FDCPA only covered collection practices undertaken as a part of traditional debt collection process and not those activities performed solely to comply with a specific legal requirement.

New York

Mendez v. Apple Bank for Sav., 143 Misc. 2d 915, 541 N.Y.S.2d 920 (N.Y. Civ. 1989). The use of legitimate judicial processes to collect a debt is not covered by FDCPA, as demonstrated by the exemption for process servers.

North Carolina

Brumby v. Trans Union, L.L.C., 2008 WL 3823712 (M.D.N.C. Aug. 13, 2008). The *pro se* consumer's complaint against defendant for reporting an allegedly invalid debt on his credit report was dismissed for failure to state a claim in the absence of any allegation that the defendant was collecting a debt on behalf of a third party and where, to the contrary, "Plaintiff's own allegations indicate that Defendant was not a debt collector, but was instead a consumer reporting agency."

Ohio

Liedtke v. Frank, 2006 WL 625730 (N.D. Ohio Mar. 10, 2006). FDCPA claim alleging passive "credit strangulation" by a collection lawyer's inquiry to credit reporting agency did not state a claim leaving a FCRA claim.

Havens-Tobias v. Eagle, 127 F. Supp. 2d 889 (S.D. Ohio 2001). The factual basis for an FDCPA claim must be clearly stated to avoid dismissal.

K.1.7 General Validity and Interpretation of FDCPA

K.1.7.1 Purposes and General Interpretation

Jerman v. Carlisle, McNellie, Rini, Kramer & Ulrich L.P.A., 130 S. Ct. 1605 (2010). The FDCPA should be interpreted to accomplish its purposes stated in § 1692(e). The court did not address a dissent statement that the court's decision raised free speech issues, as they were not raised below.

Allen ex rel. Martin v. LaSalle Bank, N.A., 2011 WL 94420 (3d Cir. Jan. 12, 2011). The FDCPA is a strict liability statute. "Because this case requires us to construe a congressional statute, principles of statutory construction apply. To discern Congress' intent we begin with the text. *In re Lord Abbett Mut. Funds Fee Litig.*, 553 F.3d 248, 254 (3d Cir.2009). If the statute's plain language is unambiguous and expresses that intent with sufficient precision, we need not look further. *Id.* If the plain language fails to express Congress' intent unequivocally, however, we will examine the surrounding words and provisions in their context. *Tavarez v. Klingensmith*, 372 F.3d 188, 190 (3d Cir.2004). Assuming that every word in a statute has meaning, we avoid interpreting part of a statute so as to render another part superfluous. *Rosenberg v. XM Ventures*, 274 F.3d 137, 141 (3d Cir.2001)."

Ruth v. Triumph P'ships, 577 F.3d 790 (7th Cir. 2009). The FDCPA is a strict liability statute, and debt collectors whose conduct falls short of its requirements are liable here respective of their intentions.

Hartman v. Great Seneca Fin. Corp., 569 F.3d 606 (6th Cir. 2009). Application of the FDCPA did not violate the Commerce Clause, assertedly because the federal government was unconstitutionally interfering with state rules of civil procedure. Neither the Petition Clause of First Amendment or the *Noerr-Pennington* doctrine bars FDCPA suits based on intentional misrepresentations made in state court collection cases. The FDCPA was not unconstitutionally vague as applied to the misconduct in this case, which was an alleged intentional misrepresentation of an exhibit, because such false statements are not immunized by the petition clause.

Jacobson v. Healthcare Fin. Servs., Inc., 516 F.3d 85 (2d Cir. 2008). The "Act is primarily a consumer protection statute, and we have consistently interpreted the statute with that congressional object in mind."

Clark v. Capital Credit & Collection Servs., Inc., 460 F.3d 1162, 1176 (9th Cir. 2006). Court convinced that this reading of the FDCPA is more in harmony with the remedial nature of the statute, which requires the court to interpret it liberally. The collection agency and its lawyer are strictly liable for falsely stating the amount of the debt under § 1692e(2)(A) without regard to knowledge of the mistake. The § 1692k(c) bona fide error defense might shield the collectors but they were not entitled to summary judgment where there was evidence that the mistakes in the medical bills of the particular health care provider had come to their attention and the consumer was entitled to more discovery on the reasonableness of the collectors' procedures to avoid such errors.

Brown v. Card Serv. Ctr., 464 F.3d 450 (3d Cir. 2006). The FDCPA is a remedial statute to be broadly construed so as to effect its purpose.

Kort v. Diversified Collection Servs., Inc., 394 F.3d 530 (7th Cir. 2005). Where the Higher Education Act is silent, the court assumed the FDCPA had full effect because the HEA does not trump or preempt the FDCPA, and the two could be harmonized.

Johnson v. Riddle, 305 F.3d 1107 (10th Cir. 2002). The FDCPA is remedial statute to be liberally construed to accomplish its purposes.

Amond v. Bricefield, Hartnett & Assocs., 175 F.3d 1013 (4th Cir. 1999) (text at 1999 WL 152555). Where collection lawyers had no reason to question the amount of the debt they were attempting to collect, they did not violate the FDCPA. Collection attorneys were not subject to any special, higher duty under the FDCPA solely by virtue of their status as lawyers. The court would not combine Rule 11 with the FDCPA to create a heightened duty of investigation for a lawyer debt collector engaging in ordinary collection activities.

Lewis v. ACB Bus. Servs., Inc., 135 F.3d 389 (6th Cir. 1998). Courts apply the objective test based on the understanding of the "least sophisticated consumer."

Fox v. Citicorp Credit Servs., Inc., 15 F.3d 1507 (9th Cir. 1994). "Reasonableness" of the collector's conduct is not a correct legal standard from which to evaluate violations of §§ 1692d, 1692e and 1692f.

Frey v. Gangwish, 970 F.2d 1516 (6th Cir. 1992). The FDCPA is "an extraordinarily broad statute" and must be enforced "as Congress has written it."

Scott v. Jones, 964 F.2d 314 (4th Cir. 1992). Sparse legislative history has relatively little persuasive weight in comparison to the plain meaning of the statute.

Jeter v. Credit Bureau, Inc., 760 F.2d 1168 (11th Cir. 1985). Since the purposes of the FDCPA stated in § 1692 included the strengthening of federal protections for consumers, courts should interpret the FDCPA to be at least as protective of consumers as was the FTC Act at the time when the FDCPA was enacted. Thus, the

FDCPA's objective standards should be construed to be protective of consumers who are unsophisticated and relatively more susceptible to abuse.

Pressley v. Capital Credit & Collection Servs., Inc., 760 F.2d 922 (9th Cir. 1985). When legislative intent is inconsistent with the plain language of the FDCPA, the court may look to legislative history.

Federal Trade Comm'n v. Shaffner, 626 F.2d 32 (7th Cir. 1980). "Although Congress intended the Act to be enforced primarily by consumers . . . it also authorized the FTC . . . to use all its functions and powers to enforce compliance."

Arizona

Randall v. Nelson & Kennard, 2010 WL 3636258 (D. Ariz. Sept. 20, 2010). The FDCPA is considered a strict liability statute, meaning that a consumer need not show that the debt collector intentionally, fraudulently, or knowingly violated the Act.

Hayden v. Rapid Collection Sys., Inc., 2006 WL 1127180 (D. Ariz. Apr. 27, 2006). Collector's reliance on information from the creditor was immaterial since the FDCPA is a strict liability statute. The court recognized that such reliance might be an aspect of the bona fide error defense.

California

Ramos v. NDEX West, L.L.C., 2009 WL 1675911 (E.D. Cal. June 1, 2009). Court lacked jurisdiction over the complaint, whose general allegations included a claim under the FDCPA arising from purportedly unlawful residential foreclosure activity, because the FDIC had been substituted as the defendant for the originally-named failed bank defendant and the plaintiff did not exhaust administration remedies required by FIRREA: "The exhaustion requirement 'applies to *any* claim or action respecting the assets of a failed institution for which the FDIC is Receiver,' and extends to post-Receivership claims arising out of acts by the Receiver as well as the failed institution."

Reyes v. Kenosian & Miele, L.L.P., 619 F. Supp. 2d 796 (N.D. Cal. 2008). Contents of state court complaint are subject to the FDCPA.

Cassady v. Union Adjustment Co., 2008 WL 4773976 (N.D. Cal. Oct. 27, 2008). The U.S. Supreme Court's decision in *Heinz* strongly suggests that the *Noerr-Pennington* doctrine does not apply to FDCPA actions.

Gorman v. Wolpoff & Abramson, L.L.P., 435 F. Supp. 2d 1004 (N.D. Cal. 2006), *aff'd in part, rev'd in part on other grounds*, 584 F.3d 1147 (9th Cir. 2009). Creditor's knowledge that the consumer did not wish to receive telephone calls could not be imputed to its agent, the defendant attorney debt collector.

Pirouzian v. SLM Corp., 396 F. Supp. 2d 1124 (S.D. Cal. 2005). FDCPA § 1692n does not preempt California's fair debt collection statute since the scope of the state law is merely broader than, and its remedies are not inconsistent with, the federal law.

Bracken v. Harris & Zide, L.L.P., 219 F.R.D. 481 (N.D. Cal. 2004). Because the FDCPA is a remedial rather than penal statute, an FDCPA action survives the death of a debt collector and the trustee of the debt collectors could be substituted as defendants.

Irwin v. Mascott, 94 F. Supp. 2d 1052 (N.D. Cal. 2000). Since the FDCPA is a strict liability statute, no showing of intent was necessary to establish liability.

Colorado

O'Connor v. Check Rite, 973 F. Supp. 1010 (D. Colo. 1997). FDCPA is a strict liability statute and only one violation need be shown to entitle consumer to summary judgment.

Connecticut

Cirkot v. Diversified Fin. Sys., Inc., 839 F. Supp. 941, 944 (D. Conn. 1993). "[T]he FDCPA is remedial in nature and should be liberally construed."

Ayala v. Dial Adjustment Bureau, Inc., 1986 U.S. Dist. LEXIS 30983 (D. Conn. Dec. 4, 1986). The FDCPA should be construed to accomplish the regulatory goals intended by Congress.

Yale New Haven Hosp. v. Orlins, 1992 WL 110710 (Conn. Super. Ct. May 11, 1992). Reliance on legislative history in determining Congress' intent is to be undertaken cautiously. Post-enactment statement by legislator does not have the same convincing weight as those made contemporaneously.

Florida

Chalik v. Westport Recovery Corp., 677 F. Supp. 2d 1322 (S.D. Fla. 2009). The FDCPA establishes a strict liability standard and requires only one violation for a consumer to prevail. A debt collector may still violate the FDCPA while simultaneously following an authorized state procedure.

Pollock v. Bay Area Credit Serv., L.L.C., 2009 WL 2475167 (S.D. Fla. Aug. 13, 2009). FDCPA is a strict liability statute, so the consumer need not show that the violation was intentional.

Berg v. Merchants Ass'n Collection Div., Inc., 586 F. Supp. 2d 1336 (S.D. Fla. 2008). The FDCPA's prohibition barring collector's from leaving pre-recorded voicemail collection messages that are heard by unauthorized third parties does not violate the First Amendment since the prohibition "is narrowly tailored to serve the significant governmental interest of protecting consumers' privacy" and "[d]ebt collectors have several alternative channels of communication available to them, including live conversation via telephone, in person communication, and postal mail."

Kaplan v. Assetcare, Inc., 88 F. Supp. 2d 1355 (S.D. Fla. 2000). The FDCPA was a strict liability statute and knowledge or intent need not be pleaded.

Georgia

Milton v. LTD Fin. Servs., 2011 WL 291363 (S.D. Ga. Jan. 25, 2011). "[T]he FDCPA as a strict liability statute, such that no evidence of intent to mislead or deceive is necessary."

Illinois

Ross v. Commercial Fin. Serv. Inc., 31 F. Supp. 2d 1077, 1079 (N.D. Ill. 1999). "Because it is designed to protect consumers, the FDCPA is generally liberally construed."

Kansas

McDaniel v. South & Assocs., P.C., 325 F. Supp. 2d 1210 (D. Kan. 2004). FDCPA is a remedial statute which should be construed liberally in favor of the consumer.

Louisiana

Sibley v. Firstcollect, Inc., 913 F. Supp. 469 (M.D. La. 1995). To prevail in an FDCPA action, the consumer must prove that: (1) he or she was subject to collection activity arising from consumer debt; (2) the defendant was a debt collector as defined at § 1692a(6); and (3) the defendant was engaged in a prohibited act or omission.

Minnesota

Mark v. J.C. Christensen & Assocs., Inc., 2009 WL 2407700 (D. Minn. Aug. 4, 2009). The FDCPA's requirement that the debt collector identify itself and inform the consumer that the communication is from a debt collector does not violate the First Amendment of the U.S. Constitution.

Bishop v. Global Payments Check Recovery Servs., Inc., 2003 WL 21497513 (D. Minn. June 25, 2003). FDCPA imposes strict liability without regard to whether the consumer was misled by the violation.

Picht v. Hawks, 77 F. Supp. 2d 1041, 1043 (D. Minn. 1999), *aff'd*, 236 F.3d 446 (8th Cir. 2001). The FDCPA is a "remedial, strict liability statute which was intended to be applied in a liberal manner."

Nevada

Pittman v. J.J. Mac Intyre Co., 969 F. Supp. 609 (D. Nev. 1997). There was no requirement under § 1692e that false representations be intentional to be actionable. Because the FDCPA is a strict liability statute, the defendant's culpability was a consideration only in computing damages under § 1692k(b). The consumer had a reasonable expectation of privacy at her work during the working hours that arose from a desire to be left alone to perform the duties for which she was hired. She stated a claim for invasion of seclusion.

New Jersey

Boyko v. Am. Intern. Group, Inc., 2009 WL 5194431 (D.N.J. Dec. 23, 2009). The FDCPA is generally a strict liability statute and does not require proof of actual damages to support a claim.

New York

Arroyo v. Solomon & Solomon, P.C., 2001 U.S. Dist. LEXIS 21908 (E.D.N.Y. Nov. 7, 2001). The FDCPA could provide a remedy for a violation of the FDCPA when the conduct was also a violation of the Higher Education Act which may not have provided a remedy.

Harrison v. NBD, Inc., 968 F. Supp. 837, 844 (E.D.N.Y. 1997). Court declined an expanded construction of the FDCPA while recognizing "the FDCPA is a remedial statute which should be liberally construed."

Cavallaro v. Law Offices of Shapiro & Kriesman, 933 F. Supp. 1148 (E.D.N.Y. 1996). The FDCPA is a strict liability statute.

Quotes *Russell v. Equifax A.R.S.*, 74 F.3d 30, 35 (2d Cir. 1996): "[I]n the general context of consumer protection—of which the Fair Debt Collection Practices Act is a part—'it does not seem unfair to require that one who deliberately goes perilously close to an area of proscribed conduct shall take the risk that he may cross the line.' "

Ohio

Deere v. Javitch, Block & Rathbone L.L.P., 413 F. Supp. 2d 886 (S.D. Ohio 2006). "The Sixth Circuit has described the statute as 'extraordinarily broad' and its terms must be literally enforced."

Kelly v. Great Seneca Fin. Corp., 443 F.3d 954 (S.D. Ohio 2005). The court rejected the collectors' argument that the FDCPA is an unconstitutional exercise of congressional powers in violation of the Tenth Amendment and the Commerce Clause.

Blevins v. Hudson & Keyse, Inc., 395 F. Supp. 2d 655 (S.D. Ohio 2004). The court held that the FDCPA as applied to practicing attorneys did not violate the Tenth Amendment or the Commerce Clause.

Becker v. Montgomery, Lynch, 2003 WL 23335929 (N.D. Ohio Feb. 26, 2003). FDCPA is, for the most part, a strict liability statute.

Oregon

Baker v. G.C. Servs. Corp., Clearinghouse No. 31,230 (D. Or. 1981), *aff'd*, 677 F.2d 775 (9th Cir. 1982). Like TIL, FDCPA is a strict liability statute and no proof of invalidity of debt or injury must be shown by the consumer, who has standing without a proof of injury.

Pennsylvania

Mushinsky v. Nelson, Watson & Assoc., L.L.C., 642 F. Supp. 2d 470 (E.D. Pa. 2009). FDCPA is a remedial statute and should be construed broadly.

Reed v. Pinnacle Credit Servs., L.L.C., 2009 WL 2461852 (E.D. Pa. Aug. 11, 2009). FDCPA is a remedial statute and should be construed broadly.

Texas

Agueros v. Hudson & Keyse, L.L.C., 2010 WL 3418286 (Tex. App. Aug. 31, 2010). "The FDCPA is a strict liability statute, and only one violation of the FDCPA is necessary to establish civil liability."

Utah

Ditty v. Check Rite, Ltd., 182 F.R.D. 639 (D. Utah 1998). Since the FDCPA is a strict liability statute, it does not matter whether plaintiffs read the letter or did not; or whether they paid the unlawful fee or did not. "[I]t is the sending of the illegal letter that creates liability rather than any necessary response on the part of the debtor." "No reliance by the plaintiffs is necessary to make out a violation of the statute." Moreover, the FDCPA protects even dishonest checkwriters: "even if there is some hint of personal dishonesty among the plaintiffs . . . that provides the defendants with impeachment material and no more."

Virginia

Talbott v. G.C. Servs. Ltd. P'ship, 53 F. Supp. 2d 846 (W.D. Va. 1999). To show a violation of the FDCPA, a plaintiff must show: (1) that the plaintiff was a "consumer" within the meaning of the statute; (2) that the defendant collecting the debt was a "debt collector" within the meaning of the statute; and (3) that the defendant violated the FDCPA by act or omission.

Morgan v. Credit Adjustment Bd., Inc., 999 F. Supp. 803 (E.D. Va. 1998). To establish a violation of the FDCPA, three requirements must be satisfied: (1) the plaintiff who has been the target of collection activity must be a "consumer" as defined in § 1692a(3); (2) the defendant collecting the debt must be a "debt collector" as defined in § 1692a(6); and (3) the defendant must have engaged in an act or omission in violation of the FDCPA.

West Virginia

Stover v. Fingerhut Direct Mktg., Inc., 709 F. Supp. 2d 473 (S.D. W. Va. 2009). First Amendment challenge to West Virginia's debt collection laws rejected. Defendants' debt collection practice of calling debtors at home to discuss debts is entitled to only a modicum of First Amendment protection because it: (1) involves commercial speech; (2) pertains to a matter of purely private, rather than public, concern; (3) includes noncommunicative conduct; and (4) implicates plaintiffs' right to privacy in their home. "Defendants' debt collection activities interject commercial speech directly into Plaintiffs' home against their wishes. Defendants' right to engage in this manner of speech is in direct conflict with Plaintiffs' right to privacy in their home. Where these two rights are in the balance, it is the right to privacy that generally carries more weight."

K.1.7.2 Federal Trade Commission Authority and Expertise

Heintz v. Jenkins, 514 U.S. 291, 115 S. Ct. 1489, 131 L. Ed. 2d 395 (1995). The FTC staff's Commentary is not binding on the Commission or the public and is not entitled to deference when it conflicts with the FDCPA's plain language.

Hawthorne v. Mac Adjustments, Inc., 140 F.3d 1367 (11th Cir. 1998). FTC Staff Commentary was "accorded considerable weight."

Fox v. Citicorp Credit Servs., Inc., 15 F.3d 1507 (9th Cir. 1994). Where the FTC Commentary conflicts with the plain language of the FDCPA, the court declined to adopt the FTC position.

Scott v. Jones, 964 F.2d 314 (4th Cir. 1992). Court may not defer to an FTC informal staff letter to the defendant nor to the FTC staff's FDCPA commentary when that would defeat an express congressional requirement in the FDCPA.

Carroll v. Wolpoff & Abramson, 961 F.2d 459 (4th Cir. 1992). The court would not defer to an FTC advisory opinion where it contradicted the statute's unambiguous statement.

Jeter v. Credit Bureau, Inc., 760 F.2d 1168 (11th Cir. 1985). Because Congress found law prior to the FDCPA inadequate to protect consumers, the FDCPA prohibition of deception should be

construed to be at least as protective as FTC law in 1977 when the FDCPA was enacted.

Pressley v. Capital Credit & Collection Servs., Inc., 760 F.2d 922 (9th Cir. 1984). FTC advisory opinions, while not binding on courts, are entitled to some weight.

Hulshizer v. Global Credit Servs., Inc., 728 F.2d 1037 (8th Cir. 1984). A collector was not entitled to rely on an informal FTC Staff letter which contained advice contrary to the plain language of the FDCPA.

Silver v. Woolf, 694 F.2d 8 (2d Cir. 1982). The FDCPA does not preempt consistent state debt collection laws such as Connecticut's statute regulating and requiring licenses of debt collection agencies.

Staub v. Harris, 626 F.2d 275 (3d Cir. 1980). In light of the restriction on the interpretive power given to the FTC and the informal nature of the FTC staff letter, the letter was not binding on courts and was an interpretation of the more likely meaning of the statute. The court declined to follow the letter.

Connecticut

Kizer v. Am. Credit & Collection, Clearinghouse No. 45,928 (D. Conn. 1991). The FTC staff commentary is not binding on the court but was a suggestive factor to be considered.

Yale New Haven Hosp. v. Orlins, 1992 WL 110710 (Conn. Super. Ct. May 11, 1992). Although comment by FTC is entitled to some weight, the court must defer to the clear meaning of the statute.

Delaware

Jordan v. Kent Recovery Servs., Inc., 731 F. Supp. 652 (D. Del. 1990). The precedential value of the FTC Staff Commentary on the FDCPA was limited but may be entitled to some weight.

Georgia

Cravey v. Credit Rating Bureau, Inc., 1991 U.S. Dist. LEXIS 21812 (N.D. Ga. Oct. 24, 1991). Informal FTC staff opinion letter from 1982 was considered useful although its opinion was not binding.

Zoeckler v. Credit Claims & Collection, Inc., 1982 U.S. Dist. LEXIS 18384 (N.D. Ga. Sept. 30, 1982). The advice of a regional FTC staff attorney that the collector's dunning letters complied with the FDCPA was not binding on the court and disregarded as erroneous.

Blackwell v. Prof'l Bus. Servs., 526 F. Supp. 535 (N.D. Ga. 1981). Following *Staub v. Harris*, 626 F.2d 275 (3d Cir. 1980), the court declined to follow FTC informal staff letters.

Illinois

Vosatka v. Wolin-Levin, Inc., 1995 WL 443950 (N.D. Ill. July 21, 1995). "Opinions offered by the FTC in the form of informal staff letters provide courts with 'helpful guidance' in interpreting statutory language, but they are 'by no means binding' on the courts."

Cortright v. Thompson, 812 F. Supp. 772 (N.D. Ill. 1992). FTC informal staff letters do not limit liability and are given less weight than opinions from the U.S. Courts of Appeals and U.S. District Courts.

Indiana

Castell v. Credit Bureau of S. Bend Mishawaka, Inc., Clearinghouse No. 31,794 (N.D. Ind. 1981). Some reliance was placed on an FTC informal staff letter in reaching the decision.

Kentucky

Cox v. Credit Bureau Sys., Inc., Clearinghouse No. 36,392 (W.D. Ky. 1984). Section 1692k(c) and (e) defenses were not available for reliance on informal FTC staff letters which were not binding on FTC and which indicated courts disagreed with FTC.

Nebraska

Page v. Checkrite, Ltd., Clearinghouse No. 45,759 (D. Neb. 1984). Informal FTC staff letters are "merely suggestions" of the "more likely" meaning of the FDCPA and are not binding on courts.

New York

Phillips v. Amana Collection Servs., 1992 WL 227839 (W.D.N.Y. Aug. 25, 1992). Court refused to defer to proposed FTC Staff Commentary.

Britton v. Weiss, 1989 WL 148663 (N.D.N.Y. Dec. 8, 1989). In concluding that an attorney employed by a creditor was covered, court gave weight to FTC's proposed Official Staff Commentary and an opinion letter.

Riveria v. MAB Collections, Inc., 682 F. Supp. 174 (W.D.N.Y. 1988). The proposed FTC Staff Commentary on the FDCPA offers no guidance on the proper placement of validation notices since it only states it must be legible and the statute does not impose particular requirements as to the form of the notice. Additionally, it has not been released and will not be binding when it is.

Ohio

Gasser v. Allen County Claims & Adjustment, Inc., 1983 U.S. Dist. LEXIS 20361 (N.D. Ohio Nov. 3, 1983). FTC informal staff letters were considered relevant interpretations of the FDCPA.

Oregon

Case v. Credit Bureau, Clearinghouse No. 33,577B (D. Or. 1983), *aff'g* Clearinghouse No. 33,577 (D. Or. 1982). In rejecting a motion to reconsider her denial of the collector's motion to dismiss, the court factually distinguished one FTC informal staff letter and found another unpersuasive given the clear meaning of § 1692e(11).

Furth v. United Adjusters, Inc., 1983 U.S. Dist. LEXIS 20368 (D. Or. Nov. 17, 1983). An informal FTC staff letter interpreting the FDCPA was found helpful, though not binding, and was adopted by the court.

Case v. Credit Bureau, Inc., Clearinghouse No. 33,577 (D. Or. 1982). While not binding on courts, FTC informal staff letters are relevant to the analysis of the FDCPA and were followed in this case.

Check Cent., Inc. v. Barr, Clearinghouse No. 37,497 (Bankr. D. Or. 1984). The court disregarded FTC informal staff letters that stated that FDCPA validation notice should not contain the word judgment if there was none, holding the letters were "relevant" but "not binding."

South Carolina

Moore v. Ingram & Assocs., Inc., 805 F. Supp. 7 (D.S.C. 1992). Informal opinion letters from an FTC attorney were not binding on the court.

K.1.7.3 Preemption and Relation to Other Laws [*See also* K.3.7.5, Bankruptcy Court Issues]

Van v. Grant & Weber, 308 Fed. Appx. 46 (9th Cir. 2008). Collection letter containing reminder of a state law requiring debtors to provide new contact information, while warning debtors that the information will be used for purposes of debt collection, did not conflict with §§ 1692e, 1692f, 1692g. The reminder did not conflict with the FDCPA, so it was not preempted by the FDCPA.

Codar v. Arizona, 95 F.3d 1156 (9th Cir. 1996) (table, text at 1996 WL 471335). The court found that the FDCPA preempted Arizona's licensing scheme for debt collectors only to the extent the Arizona law prohibited an out-of-state debt collector from sending the debt validation notice required by § 1692g. Debt collection agency stated a claim in its complaint for a declaration that Arizona regulatory requirements for debt collectors so interfered with interstate commerce as to violate the Commerce Clause.

California

Pirouzian v. SLM Corp., 396 F. Supp. 2d 1124 (S.D. Cal. 2005). A borrower's state fair debt collection practices claims against the servicer of a debt for falsely representing the debt to credit reporting agencies were preempted by the Higher Education Act and the Fair Credit Reporting Act, but not by the FDCPA. The plaintiff's claims were not preempted by the FDCPA, because the state debt collection practices law was broader but consistent with the FDCPA.

Irwin v. Mascott, 94 F. Supp. 2d 1052 (N.D. Cal. 2000). Court must deny on preemption grounds debt collector's motion to add third-party malpractice claim against collector's legal counsel because the FDCPA preempts the state regulation of attorneys where the two conflict, and there was no express or implied right of contribution or indemnity under the FDCPA.

Irwin v. Mascott, 96 F. Supp. 2d 968 (N.D. Cal. 1999). The FDCPA does not preempt state laws that provide consumers with greater protection in the form of injunctive relief covering a period of four years under the state law.

Hood v. Santa Barbara Bank & Trust, 49 Cal. Rptr. 3d 369 (Cal. Ct. App. 2006). Rosenthal Fair Debt Collection Practices Act claims in this RAL (tax refund anticipation loan) litigation were not preempted by regulations of the Office of the Comptroller of the Currency (OCC) because the Rosenthal claim did not impose any substantial limitations upon, or "obstruct, impair, or condition" a bank's actions.

Connecticut

CUDA & Assocs., L.L.C. v. Evon, 2009 WL 5698132 (Conn. Super. Ct. Dec. 16, 2009). The FDCPA does not preempt a state law claim against a consumer and her attorney for allegedly filing a vexatious FDCPA case.

Carocci v. Greenpoint Mortgage Funding, Inc., 2008 WL 4415855 (Conn. Super. Ct. Sept. 9, 2008). Motion to dismiss FDCPA claim on the basis of FCRA preemption denied since "§ 1681t(b)(1)(F) only preempts state law claims . . . [and] the FDCPA is a federal statute" that therefore is not affected.

Gordon v. Faulkner, 2003 WL 22132719 (Conn. Super. Ct. Sept. 4, 2003). Whether the FDCPA preempts a second suit alleging a state law claim for vexatious litigation arising from a previously unsuccessful FDCPA case was not properly raised as a motion to dismiss for lack of subject matter jurisdiction.

Idaho

Shock v. CDI Affiliated Servs., Inc., 2010 WL 672148 (D. Idaho Feb. 20, 2010). Idaho has not been granted an exemption under § 1692o.

Illinois

Gonzalez v. Codilis & Assocs., P.C., 2004 WL 719264 (N.D. Ill. Mar. 31, 2004). Because the state law voluntary payment doctrine provided less protection to consumers than the FDCPA, it was preempted by § 1692n where the debt collector alleged it as a defense to an FDCPA overcharge claim.

Indiana

Miller v. NCO Portfolio Mgmt., Inc., 2010 WL 2671910 (S.D. Ind. June 28, 2010). Failure to make a disclosure required by TILA is not an FDCPA violation.

Louisiana

Burthlong v. Midland Funding, L.L.C., 2010 WL 420554 (E.D. La. Jan. 29, 2010). The consumer's state law negligence claims were not preempted by § 1692n because this section allows for the coexistence of state laws that provide greater consumer protection.

Sibley v. Firstcollect, Inc., 913 F. Supp. 469 (M.D. La. 1995). State collection license requirement offered consumers greater protection and was thus expressly not preempted by § 1692n.

Massachusetts

Som v. Daniels Law Offices, P.C., 573 F. Supp. 2d 349 (D. Mass. 2008). The FDCPA does not preempt state UDAP claims.

Michigan

Large v. LVNV Funding, L.L.C., 2010 WL 3069409 (W.D. Mich. Aug. 2, 2010). The FDCPA is not properly used as an enforcement mechanism for an alleged Truth in Lending Act violation.

Kevelighan v. Trott & Trott, P.C., 2010 WL 2697120 (E.D. Mich. July 7, 2010). Where RESPA has no private cause of action, FDCPA may not be used to assert a violation of RESPA.

Jackson v. Federal Deposit Ins. Corp., 2010 WL 653151 (E.D. Mich. Feb. 19, 2010). The FDCPA claims against the FDIC were dismissed for failure to comply with FIRREA's administrative exhaustion requirement since the alleged activities "constitute an 'act or omission of . . . the Corporation as receiver.' 12 U.S.C. § 1821(d)(13)(D)(ii)."

Mississippi

Thrasher v. Cardholder Servs., 74 F. Supp. 2d 691 (S.D. Miss. 1999). Remand to state court denied. Plaintiff's common law claims of intentional or negligent infliction of emotional distress were preempted by the FDCPA under the doctrine of conflict preemption. Court applied the artful pleading doctrine and ordered plaintiff to recast her cause of action under the FDCPA.

Missouri

Scott v. Suburban Journals of Greater St. Louis, L.L.C., 2009 WL 3514437 (E.D. Mo. Oct. 29, 2009), *aff'd per curiam*, 376 Fed. Appx. 661 (8th Cir. 2010). "[A] violation of the FDCPA is not actionable under 42 U.S.C. § 1981."

New Mexico

Kolker v. Sanchez, Clearinghouse No. 46,774 (D.N.M. 1991). Attorney's preemption defense based on state supreme court's exclusive regulation of lawyer conduct fails because attorney engaged in the unauthorized practice of law by filing suit in name of collection agency rather than true creditor and, thus, violated the state court's standards as well as the New Mexico Unfair Trade Practice Act.

New York

Finlayson v. Yager, 873 N.Y.S.2d 511 (table), 2008 WL 4571562 (N.Y. Civ. Ct. 2008). "[T]he FDCPA notice provisions do not apply where the creditor, rather than a debt collector, directly attempts to collect the debt. As such, if the landlord sends the demand for rent, then the landlord, as a creditor directly trying to collect a debt, would not have to wait the 30-days before commencing his eviction proceedings." Accordingly, "where the petitioner's attorney signs the notice to quit, or where the attorney's name appears with the landlord's name on a notice to quit, then the petitioner must wait the 30-day period to expire before commencing a summary proceeding." Because "the summary proceeding was filed only six (6) days after the notice to quit was served, . . . it was prematurely filed, for the proceeding could not be legally commenced prior to 30-days expiring."

Citibank v. Jones, 706 N.Y.S.2d 301 (N.Y. Dist. Ct. 2000). The FDCPA did not preempt the common law doctrine of account stated—which recognized an agreement between parties to prior transactions as to the account items and the balance due—with respect to a consumer's failure to dispute bills or invoices sent by the creditor, but the Act did preclude a court finding that an account had been stated for failure of a consumer to dispute the validity of a debt in response to a communication from a third party debt collector.

Ohio

Zamos v. Asset Acceptance, L.L.C., 423 F. Supp. 2d 777 (N.D. Ohio 2006). The FCRA does not preempt the FDCPA with regard to a debt collector's furnishing information to a consumer reporting agency.

Oklahoma

Mendus v. Morgan & Assoc., 994 P.2d 83 (Okla. Ct. App. 1999). Where the initial communication was the summons and petition, the FDCPA did not preempt Oklahoma's twenty-day answer period since the provisions could be reconciled and made compatible. Borrowing from *Barlett v. Heibl,* 128 F.3d 497 (7th Cir. 1997), the court recommended safe harbor notification language when the initial contact was by summons and petition. It recommended the collector state that it would defer taking a default in the suit for the thirty-day period. For policy reasons, the court applied its ruling prospectively.

Pennsylvania

Desmond v. Phillips & Cohen Assocs., Ltd., 2010 WL 2710540 (W.D. Pa. July 8, 2010). The FDCPA does not preempt state law tort claims for negligence and invasion of privacy or punitive damages arising therefrom. The state law claims provided greater protection, in the form of punitive damages and other tort relief, than that provided by the FDCPA.

Albanese v. Portnoff Law Assocs., Ltd., 301 F. Supp. 2d 389 (E.D. Pa. 2004). More protective state law did not preempt the applicability of the FDCPA; instead, both laws applied.

Texas

United States v. Sullivan, 1998 WL 223709 (N.D. Tex. Apr. 28, 1998). FDCPA did not preempt state debt collection statute that was more protective of the rights of consumers.

West Virginia

McComas v. Fin. Collection Agencies, 1997 WL 118417 (S.D. W. Va. Mar. 7, 1997). DOE's regulatory scheme for collection of student loans did not preempt the FDCPA.

K.2 Violations

K.2.1 Acquisition of Location Information, 15 U.S.C. § 1692b

Cushman v. GC Servs., L.P., 2010 WL 3926861 (5th Cir. Sept. 30, 2010). The court affirmed a directed verdict for the defendant where the consumer did not offer any evidence that calls to her former employer or tenant were for purposes other than obtaining location information and where the consumer failed to offer affidavits or testimony from those third parties or provide evidence pertaining to the substance of the conversations. "GC's knowledge

of a working phone number for Cushman, unreturned mail, and awareness of a new job does not provide a sufficient evidentiary basis to find that GC sought anything other than "location information" when calling third parties. Such arguments are mere speculation, and thus the evidence is insufficient to survive a Rule 50(a) motion."

United States v. Cent. Adjustment Bureau, Inc., 823 F.2d 880 (5th Cir. 1987). Use of assumed name while seeking to gather information about debtors is not a violation.

California

Estrella v. G L Recovery Group, L.L.C., 2010 WL 679067 (C.D. Cal. Feb. 22, 2010). The consumer's allegation that the defendant violated § 1692b(2) by calling consumer's mother "on more than one occasion" and "communicating with Consumer's mother and stating that Consumer owes a debt" stated a claim for relief under the *Iqbal* standard without alleging any additional details.

Puttner v. Debt Consultants of Am., 2009 WL 1604570 (S.D. Cal. June 4, 2009). The complaint stated a claim for relief by alleging that the defendant's collectors called the consumer's parents without stating that they were confirming or correcting location information, disclosed the existence of the son's debt, and called the parents repeatedly so as to constitute harassment.

Bolton v. Pentagroup Fin. Servs., L.L.C., 2009 WL 734038 (E.D. Cal. Mar. 17, 2009). The defendant's threat to contact the consumer's employer/commanding officer could not have been a lawful attempt to acquire location information since the defendant was speaking to the consumer at the very time when the threat was made.

Connecticut

Kimberly v. Great Lakes Collection Bureau, Inc., Clearinghouse No. 50,431B (D. Conn. 1996). Collection agency violated § 1692b(3) by contacting a consumer's mother on numerous occasions without the consumer's permission (which was required after the first contact if that contact was to obtain location information) and stating that consumer owed a debt. Consumer's mother did not have standing to recover under § 1692c(b) which only protects "consumers" as compared to other sections that appear to protect "any person."

Baker v. I.C. Sys., Inc., 2009 WL 1365002 (Conn. Super. Ct. May 11, 2009). A claim for contacting the consumer's friend despite having the consumer's location information was not well pleaded.

Florida

Magnuson v. NCC Bus. Servs., Inc., 2010 WL 2366535 (M.D. Fla. June 11, 2010). A disputed factual question as to whether the debt collector revealed the debt to a third party precluded summary judgment on the § 1692b claim.

Cooper v. F.A. Mgmt. Solutions, Inc., 2008 WL 299004 (M.D. Fla. Jan. 31, 2008). The court granted summary judgment for the defendants on the consumer's claim that the defendants' attorneys' communication with the state DMV to confirm the consumer's place of residence at a time when the consumer was contesting entry of a default judgment in the state court collection action (the consumer claimed that he did not reside where service occurred) violated the FDCPA's prohibition against third party communications because the attorneys procured his entire driving record and thus went beyond the location information exception. The court explained its ruling as follows:

> [The attorneys'] communications with the DMV cannot be said to have been made "in connection with" the collection of the debt. Rather, the undisputed evidence establishes that Defendant's communication with the DMV was for the purpose of confirming Plaintiff's residential address, essential to its defense against Plaintiff's contention that Defendants had not properly effected service of process on him in the underlying Pinellas County collection case. The plain language of § 1692c(b) requires that a communication be "in connection with the collection of any debt." . . . Since [the attorneys'] communication was not "in connection with the collection" of a debt, they were not prohibited by § 1692c(b). Moreover, obtaining information from a third party for use as evidence under these circumstances cannot be said to constitute an improper "communication" under the FDCPA, as that communication was incident to a legal proceeding. *See Vega v. McKay*, 351 F.3d 1334 (11th Cir. 2003). Defendants were entitled to defend against Plaintiff's challenge to service of process and were collecting the information from the DMV not to collect a debt but to defend against that challenge.

Illinois

Kasalo v. Monco Law Offices, S.C., 2009 WL 4639720 (N.D. Ill. Dec. 7, 2009). The debt collector was entitled as a matter of law to contact the consumer's parents on a second occasion to acquire location information under the exception in § 1692b(3) that allows a subsequent third-party contact where the debt collector "reasonably believes that the earlier response of such person is erroneous or incomplete and that such person now has correct or complete location information" where during the prior six-month period first the consumer and then his purported attorney failed to return the collector's telephone calls.

Shaver v. Trauner, 1998 U.S. Dist. LEXIS 19647 (C.D. Ill. May 29, 1998). Motion to dismiss denied where simultaneously with the initial demand letter, the attorney faxed consumer's employer seeking information about his employment such as his date of hire, his position, whether he was a full or part time employee, whether he was salaried or on commission, and the address of the employer's payroll department. The fax went well beyond location information and thus violated the FDCPA.

Michigan

Mabbitt v. Midwestern Audit Serv., Inc., 2008 WL 723507 (E.D. Mich. Mar. 17, 2008). Summary judgment for the defendant collector on the plaintiff's § 1692b claim where there was no evidence that the defendant had communicated with any person for the purpose of acquiring location information.

Dunaway v. JBC & Assocs., Inc., 2005 WL 1529574 (E.D. Mich. June 20, 2005). The uncontroverted fact that the debt collector called the consumer's employer and falsely informed him that a civil lawsuit had been filed and that criminal charges were pending against the consumer for a dishonored check on which both the civil and criminal statute of limitations had expired established the collector's liability as a matter of law for violating §§ 1692b, 1692c, and 1692e.

Mississippi

Deas v. American Recovery Sys., Inc., 2009 WL 3514560 (N.D. Miss. Oct. 29, 2009). Defendant violated § 1692b(3) by placing dozens of telephone calls to the plaintiff's home, purportedly attempting to locate a third party debtor, after plaintiff informed defendant that the debtor did not live at his residence and requested defendant to cease calling.

Missouri

Terry v. C & D Complete Bus. Solutions, 2011 WL 144920 (W.D. Mo. Jan. 18, 2011). A debt collector's letters to the consumers' employers in connection with the collection of a debt violated § 1692b(2) by disclosing the debt if sent for location purposes or, if not, they violated § 1692c(b) by communicating with a third party in connection with the collection of a debt.

Thomas v. Consumer Adjustment Co., 579 F. Supp. 2d 1290 (E.D. Mo. 2008). Collection call to debtor's home did not meet the "safe harbor" for location information; it did not state that the call was for location information, and did ask for "a better number" where he could reach plaintiff "real quick." The court did not believe this constituted a request regarding plaintiff's "place of abode and his telephone number at such place, or his place of employment."

New York

Fajer v. Kaufman, Burns & Assocs., 2011 WL 334311 (W.D.N.Y. Jan. 28, 2011). In this default action, the court found that the collector's communication to a third party that it would "come after" the plaintiff for payment of the debt violated § 1692b, which limits a debt collector's contact with third parties to acquiring location information.

Krapf v. Collectors Training Inst., Inc., 2010 WL 584020 (W.D.N.Y. Feb. 16, 2010). The complaint stated a claim that the debt collector violated §§ 1692d and 1692e by leaving telephone messages for the consumer falsely stating that her social security number was under investigation. Because defendant's contact with plaintiff's employer "did not involve an inquiry into Plaintiff's location information, but rather, revealed that Plaintiff had a 'business matter,'" and because defendant "later placed another call to Plaintiff's employer in an attempt to use Plaintiff's employer as a means of inducing Plaintiff to return Defendant's call, . . . Defendant contacted a third party in a manner not authorized by § 1692b, [and therefore] Plaintiff sufficiently states claims under §§ 1692b, 1692c(b), and 1692d."

DeGeorge v. LTD Fin. Servs., L.P., 2008 WL 905913 (W.D.N.Y. Mar. 31, 2008). Plaintiff's motion for summary judgment for the collector's alleged impermissible third-party contact denied since a reasonable jury could decide either that the defendant's communication with the plaintiff's brother was an unlawful attempt to collect the debt in violation of § 1692c(b) or was a permissible attempt to locate the plaintiff as allowed by § 1692b.

Oregon

Clark v. Quick Collect, Inc., 2005 WL 1586862 (D. Or. June 30, 2005). The court denied summary judgment to defendant where collector gave agency's name to employer, which would be proper only if collector were seeking location information and not if calling to reach debtor.

Pennsylvania

Romano v. Williams & Fudge, Inc., 644 F. Supp. 2d 653 (W.D. Pa. 2008). Defendant violated § 1692b(2) by discussing a debt with plaintiff's estranged father, § 1692c(b) by asking the father to convey a message, and § 1692e(11) by not providing the required notice in a telephone message. Defendant's bona fide error defense raised factual issues remaining for trial.

Texas

United States v. Cent. Adjustment Bureau, Inc., 667 F. Supp. 370 (N.D. Tex. 1986). Collector violated §§ 1692b & 1692c(b) by contacting third parties.

Gasser v. Allen County Claims & Adjustment, Inc., 1983 U.S. Dist. LEXIS 20361 (N.D. Ohio Nov. 3, 1983). Section 1692b did not provide an excuse for falsely threatening to contact the consumer's employer since the threat implied the debt would be discussed and the defendant already knew where the consumer lived and worked.

Virginia

West v. Costen, 558 F. Supp. 564 (W.D. Va. 1983). Summary judgment was inappropriate where there was a question of fact as to whether third party contacts prohibited by § 1692c(b) were within the exception provided by § 1692b.

K.2.2 Communication in Connection with Debt Collection, 15 U.S.C. § 1692c

K.2.2.1 Time and Place of Communications, 15 U.S.C. § 1692c(a)(1)

California

Gorman v. Wolpoff & Abramson, L.L.P., 435 F. Supp. 2d 1004 (N.D. Cal. 2006), *aff'd in part, rev'd in part on other grounds*, 584 F.3d 1147 (9th Cir. 2009). MBNA's knowledge that the consumer did not wish to receive telephone calls could not be imputed to its agent, the defendant attorney debt collector.

Wan v. Commercial Recovery Sys., Inc., 369 F. Supp. 2d 1158 (N.D. Cal. 2005). The statement in the collector's letter to the consumer that "[i]f you notify us in writing to stop contacting you by telephone at your residence or place of employment, no further contact will be made" did not violate § 1692e or § 1692c(a)(1).

Joseph v. J.J. Mac Intyre Cos., L.L.C., 238 F. Supp. 2d 1158 (N.D. Cal. 2002). Collection agency's uncontroverted evidence of its

long distance carrier's phone records showing all calls to the consumer were made after 8:00 a.m. and before 9:00 p.m. mandates entry of summary judgment against the consumer's claim of receiving phone calls at unreasonable hours.

Pittman v. J.J. Mac Intyre Co., 238 F. Supp. 2d 1158 (N.D. Cal. 2002). The consumer stated a claim for violation of §§ 1692c(a)(1) and 1692d by alleging that notwithstanding warnings on prior occasions that she could not talk at work, the collection agency called the consumer at her place of employment to collect on the debt.

Connecticut

Chiverton v. Fed. Fin. Group, Inc., 399 F. Supp. 2d 96 (D. Conn. 2005). The debt buyer violated § 1692c(a)(1) and (3) by repeatedly calling after the consumer expressly requested the collector not to do so because he was not permitted to receive personal calls at work.

Austin v. Great Lakes Collection Bureau, Inc., 834 F. Supp. 557 (D. Conn. 1993). Continued telephone calls to the consumer at her place of employment, after the collector had been asked to cease such calls because they inconvenienced the consumer, violated § 1692c(a)(1).

Florida

McDermott v. I.C. Sys., Inc., 2010 WL 2331093 (S.D. Fla. June 10, 2010). A disputed issue of fact as to whether the defendant in fact telephoned the consumer after 9:00 p.m. precluded summary judgment on the alleged § 1692c(a)(1) violation.

Brandt v. I.C. Sys., Inc., 2010 WL 582051 (M.D. Fla. Feb. 19, 2010). "Intent may be inferred by evidence that the debt collector continued to call the debtor after the debtor had asked not to be called and had repeatedly refused to pay the alleged debt, or during a time of day which the debtor had informed the debt collector was inconvenient."

Merchant v. Nationwide Collection Serv., Inc., Clearinghouse No. 43,382 (Fla. Cir. Ct. 1988). Two plaintiffs each awarded $2500 actual damages, $1000 statutory damages and $50,000 punitive damages for late night phone calls, threats of arrest, and a third-party contact.

Georgia

Yelvington v. Buckner, Clearinghouse No. 36,581 (N.D. Ga. 1984). The collector telephoning a consumer again, after being told that he was serving customers, violated § 1692c(a)(1).

New York

Krapf v. Collectors Training Inst. of Ill., Inc., 2010 WL 584020 (W.D.N.Y. Feb. 16, 2010). The consumer's allegation that the defendant called her before 8:00 a.m. sufficiently alleged a claim under §§ 1692c(a)(1) and 1692d.

Pennsylvania

Shand-Pistilli v. Professional Account Servs., Inc., 2010 WL 2978029 (E.D. Pa. July 26, 2010). Allegation that debt collector called at 8:58 p.m. did not state a claim for violation of § 1692c(a)(1).

South Carolina

Valentine v. Brock & Scott, P.L.L.C., 2010 WL 1727681 (D.S.C. Apr. 26, 2010). To state a claim under § 1692c(a)(1), a consumer must show that a debt collector communicated at an unusual time or place or at a time or place that it knew or should have known was inconvenient to the consumer. In this case, consumer failed to make out a claim because her complaint failed to mention a single instance that any telephone call was made prior to 8:00 a.m. or after 9:00 p.m. and failed to provide any factual allegation as to what knowledge defendant had, or should have had, or should be presumed to have had, that would have informed defendant that consumer's "convenient times and places" were other than the presumptive times and places contained within the Act.

Texas

Cunningham v. Credit Mgmt., L.P., 2010 WL 3791104 (N.D. Tex. Aug. 30, 2010). Calls to the *pro se* consumer's cell phone did not violate the § 1692c(a) prohibition against communications at a inconvenient time or place, as a "cellular phone is not a time or place."

United States v. Cent. Adjustment Bureau, Inc., 667 F. Supp. 370 (N.D. Tex. 1986). Collector violated the Act by making phone calls before 8:00 a.m. and after 9:00 p.m. Plaintiff was not required to prove those times were inconvenient since § 1692c(a)(1) requires the collector to assume those times are inconvenient.

Wisconsin

Brzezinski v. Vital Recovery Servs., Inc., 2006 WL 1982501 (E.D. Wis. July 12, 2006). The court denied the defendant's motion for summary judgment in which it claimed that its dun was not false or confusing as a matter of law, where the dun stated that the collector would cease communication with the consumer at work or by telephone if the consumer so requested in writing, since § 1692c(a)(1) imposes no such writing requirement, a collector must cease so communicating when so informed orally, and it remained for the trier of fact to determine whether this disclosure therefore was confusing or deceptive.

K.2.2.2 Communicating with Represented Consumer, 15 U.S.C. § 1692c(a)(2)

Tinsley v. Integrity Fin. Partners, Inc., 2011 WL 477486 (7th Cir. Feb. 11, 2011). Since § 1692c as a whole permits debt collectors to communicate freely with a consumer's lawyer, a debt collector's request for payment to the consumer's lawyer did not violate the FDCPA even though the lawyer had sent a refusal to pay and cease communications letter.

Schmitt v. FMA Alliance, 398 F.3d 995 (8th Cir. 2005). The creditor's knowledge of the consumer's representation by an attorney was not imputed to the collection agency.

Randolph v. IMBS, Inc., 368 F.3d 726 (7th Cir. 2004). A collection agency's letter to the debtor who was represented by counsel did not violate the FDCPA where the collector did not know of the representation. The FDCPA does not impute knowledge of the creditor to the debt collector. To the extent that the Ninth Circuit's decision in *Walls v. Wells Fargo* held otherwise, the Seventh Circuit did not follow but instead reaffirmed the approach taken in *Turner v. J.V.D.B. & Assocs., Inc.*, and *Hyman v. Tate*.

Geiger v. Creditors Interchange, Inc., 2003 WL 1465404 (6th Cir. Mar. 19, 2003). Section 1692c(c) prohibits a collector from communicating directly with a consumer if the debt collector knows that the consumer is represented by an attorney but does not require the debt collector to use its attorney to communicate with a consumer.

In re Duke, 79 F.3d 43 (7th Cir. 1996). The creditor, Sears Roebuck, sent a non-coercive and non-threatening letter to debtor's lawyer proposing a reaffirmation agreement and sent a copy to the debtor. Sears offered a $500 line of credit if the debtor reaffirmed and paid back the debt. There was no violation of the automatic stay, but if the sender of the letter was a lawyer, this raised questions under bar rules limiting communications and under the FDCPA if the sender was a collector because of communication with a party who was represented by counsel.

Graziano v. Harrison, 950 F.2d 107 (3d Cir. 1991). A debt collector who knows a consumer is represented by counsel on one debt is not precluded by § 1692c(a)(2) from contacting the consumer on other debts until the collector knows the debtor is represented by counsel with respect to the other debts.

California

Day v. American Home Mortgage Serv., Inc., 2010 WL 2231988 (E.D. Cal. June 3, 2010). Section 1692c(a)(2)'s directive that a collector who knows that the consumer is represented by an attorney communicate only with the consumer's attorney contains no requirement that the collector be informed of the representation in writing.

Escobedo v. Countrywide Home Loans, Inc., 2009 WL 4981618 (S.D. Cal. Dec. 15, 2009). The complaint stated claims for relief under state law that incorporates the FDCPA by sufficiently alleging FDCPA violations resulting from direct communications once informed that the plaintiff was represented by counsel.

Offril v. J.C. Penny Co., 2009 WL 69344 (N.D. Cal. Jan. 9, 2009). Unopposed motion to dismiss granted on this § 1692c(a)(2) claim because: (1) there was no allegation that the creditor or anyone else had informed the debt collector of the attorney's representation of the consumer, and (2) the creditor's knowledge of that representation could not be imputed to the debt collector.

Graff v. Henriques, 2008 WL 3916039 (N.D. Cal. Aug. 25, 2008). Plaintiff's motion for summary judgment that defendant violated the FDCPA by contacting the consumer after knowing she was represented by counsel was denied because questions of fact existed including the failure of plaintiff's counsel to respond to defendant's correspondence.

Yee v. Ventus Capital Servs., Inc., 2006 WL 1310463 (N.D. Cal. May 12, 2006). Collection agency's motion for partial summary judgment was denied because defendants' argument that plaintiff's attorney offered nonlegal services and because it had spoken with a nonlawyer was unpersuasive and its business records were not competent evidence on that point.

Masuda v. Thomas Richards & Co., 759 F. Supp. 1456 (C.D. Cal. 1991). Dunning letters to the consumer, after the collector had been informed of attorney's representation, did not violate the FDCPA where the letter from the collector concerned debts other than those referred to in the attorney's letter.

Connecticut

Silver v. Law Offices of Howard Lee Schiff, P.C., 2010 WL 3000053 (D. Conn. July 28, 2010). The court entered summary judgment for the defendant where the defendant had not yet opened an e-mail notifying it of representation by counsel when a collector called.

Herbert v. Monterey Fin. Servs., Inc., 863 F. Supp. 76 (D. Conn. 1994). Sending a dunning letter to a consumer five days after receiving letter notification of her representation violated § 1692c(a)(2).

Delaware

Langley v. Scanlon, 1993 U.S. Dist. LEXIS 17278 (D. Del. Feb. 5, 1993). To establish a violation of § 1692c(a)(2) two criteria must be established: (1) legal representation of the consumer regarding the alleged debt must exist prior to the communication and (2) prior to the communication the debt collector must have actual knowledge of that representation.

Hubbard v. Nat'l Bond & Collection Assocs., Inc., 126 B.R. 422 (D. Del. 1991), *aff'd without op.*, 947 F.2d 935 (3d Cir. 1991). Consumer failed to establish that the collector knew she was represented by a lawyer when the collector wrote her.

Florida

Kelemen v. Professional Collection Sys., 2011 WL 31396 (M.D. Fla. Jan. 4, 2011). The court denied the defendant's motion for summary judgment on the § 1692c(a)(2) claim since there was "a genuine issue of material fact as to the debt accounts about which [the defendant] contacted Plaintiffs and whether [the defendant] had actual knowledge that Plaintiffs were represented by an attorney with respect to those debt accounts."

Cavanaugh v. HSBC Card Servs. Inc., 2010 WL 3746260 (M.D. Fla. Sept. 22, 2010). A creditor's knowledge that a consumer is represented by counsel cannot be imputed to the debt collector since courts have required that the collector's knowledge must be actual.

Bacelli v. MFP, Inc., 2010 WL 2985699 (M.D. Fla. July 28, 2010). The creditor's knowledge that consumer was represented by counsel was not to be imputed to the debt collector.

Rosario v. Am. Collective Counseling Servs., 2001 U.S. Dist. LEXIS 13455 (M.D. Fla. Aug. 27, 2001). Where collection notices were sent to consumer, albeit at her attorney's address, and the text was plainly addressed to the consumer and not her attorney, the FDCPA was implicated.

Georgia

Florence v. Nat'l Sys., 1983 U.S. Dist. LEXIS 20344 (N.D. Ga. Oct. 14, 1983). The collector violated § 1692c(a)(2) and (c) by sending a threatening letter after being served with the consumer's FDCPA complaint and by sending six letters after the consumer sent the collector a letter stating the account had been paid and the collector should not contact the consumer at work.

Illinois

Salsbury v. Trac A Chec, Inc., 365 F. Supp. 2d 939 (C.D. Ill. 2005). The collector's telephone call to the consumer made after the consumer had filed bankruptcy, in which the collector did not mention the debt at all and which was placed simply to inform the consumer that the collector had verified the attorney's representation and would not be contacting the consumer again, was not a communication "in connection with the collection" of the debt and therefore did not violate § 1692c(a)(2).

Miller v. Allied Interstate, Inc., 2005 WL 1520802 (N.D. Ill. June 27, 2005). The debt collector set forth evidence creating a genuine issue of fact as to whether it knew the consumer was represented by counsel regarding the debt.

Raimondi v. McAllister & Assocs., Inc., 50 F. Supp. 2d 825 (N.D. Ill. 1999). Where the collection agency disputed receiving the attorney's letter of representation, a material factual issue prevented determination of whether the collection agency had actual knowledge that the consumer was represented by an attorney.

Phillips v. N. Am. Capital Corp., 1999 WL 299872 (N.D. Ill. Apr. 30, 1999). Communications with a consumer's attorney cannot give rise to liability for revealing the debt to a third party.

Blum v. Fisher & Fisher, 961 F. Supp. 1218 (N.D. Ill. 1997). Whether the collection attorney could communicate directly with a represented consumer who had not responded to the collection attorney's offer for thirty days presented questions of fact precluding grant of summary judgment.

Cole v. Biehl & Biehl, 1997 WL 733928 (N.D. Ill. Nov. 18, 1997). Where the collector was pursuing Jodi Cole and left a message on the answering machine of Melissa Cole, the plaintiff, the collector did not violate § 1692c(a)(2), prohibiting contacting a represented consumer, because any prior messages to the collector indicated only that Melissa Cole was represented, and the collector did not attempt to collect a debt from Melissa Cole.

Indiana

Gillespie v. Chase Home Fin., L.L.C., 2009 WL 4061428 (N.D. Ind. Nov. 20, 2009). A collection letter requesting that the debtor call its mortgage specialist to resolve a delinquency was not a communication requesting payment covered by the FDCPA under the *Bailey* decision. The mailing of the letter therefore did not violate § 1692c(a)(2).

Thomas v. Boscia, 2009 WL 2778105 (S.D. Ind. Aug. 28, 2009). Summary judgment granted to the plaintiff on the defendants' bona fide error defense to excuse their admitted violation of § 1692c when they communicated directly with her once on notice of her attorney's representation. The defendants' only preventive procedures relied on information provided by the defendants' creditor clients, and thus the procedures were inadequate as a matter of law, since they were incapable of cross-checking for attorney representation when, as here, notification was received independently of their clients.

Keisler v. Encore Receivable Mgmt., Inc., 2008 WL 1774173 (S.D. Ind. Apr. 17, 2008). Summary judgment for the defendant collector on the claim that it violated § 1692c(a)(2) by communicating with the consumer when she was known to be represented by an attorney since the evidence showed that only the creditor actually knew of that representation and the knowledge of the creditor cannot be imputed to the collector under § 1692c(a)(2).

Hill v. Mut. Hosp. Serv., Inc., 454 F. Supp. 2d 779 (S.D. Ind. 2005). Debtor's attorney is not a consumer within prohibition of § 1692c; calling attorney to get bankruptcy information is not an effort to collect a debt.

Zaborac v. Mutual Hosp. Serv., Inc., 2004 WL 2538643 (S.D. Ind. Oct. 7, 2004). The FDCPA prohibits a debt collector from communicating with a consumer once the collector knows the consumer is represented by an attorney.

Kansas

Udell v. Kansas Counselors, Inc., 313 F. Supp. 2d 1135 (D. Kan. 2004). The debt collector did not violate the FDCPA by communicating directly with a consumer regarding newly assigned debts even though the debt collector was aware that the consumer was represented by counsel on prior debts.

Bieber v. Associated Collection Servs., Inc., 631 F. Supp. 1410 (D. Kan. 1986). Asking consumer whether he intended to file for bankruptcy after being informed the consumer was represented by counsel was a legitimate business inquiry and not so extensive as to be prohibited by § 1692c(a)(2).

Clark's Jewelers v. Humble, 823 P.2d 818 (Kan. Ct. App. 1991). Although dunning letters were mailed in care of the consumers' attorney, § 1692c(a)(2), prohibiting communications with represented consumers, was violated by the debt collector's action.

Louisiana

Burthlong v. Midland Funding, L.L.C., 2010 WL 420554 (E.D. La. Jan. 29, 2010). Section 1692c(a)(2), which provides that a debt collector not communicate with a consumer "unless the attorney consents to direct communication with the consumer" does not conflict with the premise that the consumer can consent to direct communication with the debt collector. The FDCPA does not strip a represented consumer of the right to directly contact the debt collector; rather, the statute restrains conduct on the part of the debt collector, not the consumer.

Goodman v. S. Credit Recovery, Inc., 1999 WL 14004 (E.D. La. Jan. 8, 1999). Debt collector who communicated with consumer after it knew that the consumer was represented by counsel regarding another debt, for different amount, owed to a different creditor, did not violate § 1692c(a)(2). Debt collector had no obligation to inquire about other accounts. To establish a violation of § 1692c(a)(2), the plaintiff must show (1) that he was represented by an attorney with regard to that debt, and (2) that the debt collector had actual knowledge of representation regarding that debt prior to the sending of the collection letter.

Massachusetts

In re Webster, 2009 WL 2634576 (Bankr. D. Mass. Aug. 21, 2009). Whether the consumer's attorney refused to confirm his representation when requested by the debt collector was a disputed fact that precluded summary judgment on the plaintiff's claim that the collector's direct consumer contact violated § 1692c(a)(2).

Minnesota

Resler v. Messerli & Kramer, P.A., 2003 WL 193498 (D. Minn. Jan. 23, 2003). The mailing of a writ of execution directly to a represented consumer did not violate § 1692c(a)(2) as the writ was issued directly to the consumer as required by state law and thus within the exception of § 1692c(a) for communications with the express permission of a court.

Mississippi

Hennington v. American Exp. Co., 2010 WL 1329003 (S.D. Miss. Mar. 29, 2010). Section 1692c(a)(2) requires a debt collector must have actual knowledge of the consumer's representation by counsel before contacts are limited to the consumer's counsel.

Missouri

Anderson v. Gamache & Myers, P.C., 2007 WL 4365745 (E.D. Mo. Dec. 10, 2007). Did not reach but indicated that a communication with an agent in fact might violate 15 U.S.C. § 1692c(a)(2).

Simmons v. Miller & Steeno, P.C., 2002 WL 31898324 (E.D. Mo. Dec. 30, 2002). Formal notice of representation not required. Sending the validation rights notice to a represented consumer was a violation.

Nebraska

Randall v. Midland Funding, L.L.C., 2009 WL 2358350 (D. Neb. July 23, 2009). The court found that the plaintiff stated a claim under § 1692c(a)(2), because the pleadings allege defendant contacted the plaintiff by mail after the plaintiff had informed defendant that he was represented by an attorney.

Harris v. BWS Credit Servs., Inc., Clearinghouse No. 27,693 (D. Neb. 1980) (order on motions for summary judgment). The collection agency contacted a third party and contacted a consumer represented by an attorney.

Nevada

Kuhn v. Account Control Tech., Inc., 865 F. Supp. 1443 (D. Nev. 1994). Collector's communication with consumer after being informed of her representation by counsel violated § 1692c(a)(2).

New Jersey

Smith v. Lyons, Doughty & Veldhuius, P.C., 2008 WL 2885887 (D.N.J. July 23, 2008). The consumer failed to state a classwide cause of action for violation of § 1692c(a)(2) and (c) because an individual inquiry of each class member would be required; plaintiff was granted leave to amend the complaint.

New Mexico

Spinarski v. Credit Bureau, Inc., 1996 U.S. Dist. LEXIS 22547 (D.N.M. Sept. 19, 1996). Collector did not violate § 1692c(a)(2) by communicating with a consumer known to be represented by counsel because the collector was informed that the representation concerned the hospital's bill and not the related radiologist's bill which was the subject of the later contact.

New York

Clayson v. Rubin & Rothman, L.L.C., 2010 WL 547476 (W.D.N.Y. Feb. 11, 2010). Rejected defendant's argument that if the consumer had advised it in writing that she had legal representation, defendant would have ceased communication with her and that would have prevented any emotional distress damages. Nothing in the FDCPA requires a debtor to provide *written* notice to a debt collector advising it of her legal representation.

Micare v. Foster & Garbus, 132 F. Supp. 2d 77 (N.D.N.Y. 2001). Where a debt collector had a procedure in place by which it asked creditors whether the debtor was represented by counsel and the creditor suppressed the information, either mistakenly or intentionally, the creditor's knowledge may be imputed to the debt collector and the claim would not be dismissed. The collector's invocation of the bona fide error defense must await a motion for summary judgment.

Buffington v. Schuman & Schuman, P.C., 2001 U.S. Dist. LEXIS 2267 (N.D.N.Y. Feb. 21, 2001). A foreclosing attorney's letter sent directly to the consumer, despite the consumer's representation by an attorney in a bankruptcy in which the collecting attorney obtained a lift of the automatic stay, did not violate the FDCPA because it fell within the exceptions of § 1692c(c)(2) and (3), which the court applied to § 1692c(2) based on loose dicta in a Supreme Court decision.

Powers v. Prof'l Credit Servs., Inc., 107 F. Supp. 2d 166 (N.D.N.Y. 2000). Consumer's attorney notified creditor of representation and settled the debt. The creditor then retained a collector who wrote to consumer seeking balance of the debt. Collector violated prohibition against contacting debtor known to be represented by counsel even though creditor did not tell collector of the representation. "To allow a creditor to hire a debt collector after receiving actual knowledge that the consumer has retained legal representation for that debt and then withhold knowledge of this representation from the debt collector would blatantly circumvent the intent of the FDCPA." The court distinguished other cases because the creditor had not been notified of representation until after the collector started collecting.

Jones v. Weiss, 95 F. Supp. 2d 105 (N.D.N.Y. 2000). Consumer's attorney notified creditor of representation and settled the debt. The creditor then retained a collector who wrote to consumer seeking balance of the debt not knowing of the consumer's representation and payment. Summary judgment for defendant: "[A]n agent cannot be imputed with information that his principal failed to give him."

Burger v. Risk Mgmt. Alternatives, 94 F. Supp. 2d 291 (N.D.N.Y. 2000). Plaintiff alleged that defendant communicated with him knowing of his representation by counsel. Complaint would not be dismissed because of failure to articulate whether he meant actual or constructive knowledge. "It certainly cannot be said, based on the pleading, that the plaintiff could prove no set of facts in support of his claim which would entitle him to relief."

Degonzague v. Weiss, Neuren & Neuren, 89 F. Supp. 2d 282 (N.D.N.Y. 2000). No FDCPA claim had been stated where plaintiff's attorney had sent a letter to the creditor but produced no evidence that the creditor had informed the debt collector.

Filsinger v. Upton, 2000 U.S. Dist. LEXIS 1824 (N.D.N.Y. Feb. 17, 2000). Complaint failed to allege that the collector knew before it communicated with the consumer of the attorney representation, and therefore warranted dismissal of the complaint for failure to state a claim for violation of § 1692c(a)(2).

Countryman v. Solomon & Solomon, 2000 U.S. Dist. LEXIS 1397 (N.D.N.Y. Feb. 7, 2000). Attorney notified creditor of his representation after the account had been sent to the law firm debt collector. The debt collector's communication with the consumer did not violate § 1692c(a)(2) because it had no knowledge of counsel's representation and no amount of review of the file, which had been forwarded, would have disclosed the representation.

Robinson v. Transworld Sys., Inc., 876 F. Supp. 385 (N.D.N.Y. 1995). Collector's knowledge of attorney's representation of consumer regarding earlier debt does not preclude the collector communicating directly with consumer on a later debt.

Phillips v. Amana Collection Servs., 1992 WL 227839 (W.D.N.Y. Aug. 25, 1992). The statute does not define, as two weeks or otherwise, the reasonable time in which the consumer's attorney must respond to the collector's inquiry, and the collector's direct communication to the consumer, knowing of his representation, violated § 1692c(a)(2).

Ohio

Dowling v. Litton Loan Serv., L.P., 2006 WL 3498292 (S.D. Ohio Dec. 1, 2006). Defendant violated the FDCPA because it directed written and telephone communications to the consumer when it knew that she was represented by an attorney.

Minick v. First Fed. Credit Control, Inc., 1981 U.S. Dist. LEXIS 18622 (N.D. Ohio June 9, 1981). Violations of § 1692c involving the plaintiff's wife who did not join as a party are relevant if they resulted in damages to the plaintiff. The collector's communications with the consumer's separated wife after the collector was notified that the consumer was represented by a lawyer violated § 1692c(a)(2). A phone call may violate § 1692c(a)(2) if the debt collector knew the plaintiff was represented by a lawyer.

Oregon

Mathis v. Omnium Worldwide, 2005 WL 3159663 (D. Or. Nov. 27, 2005). Plaintiff may not recover for actions outside the one-year statute, but may use the actions to support claims of abuse, harassment, or knowledge of attorney's representation.

Grassley v. Debt Collectors, Inc., 1992 U.S. Dist. LEXIS 22782 (D. Or. Dec. 14, 1992). Where telephone records failed to demonstrate that the debt collector called debtors after they had retained legal counsel, and it was the collector's policy to cease further communication when informed of the debtor's legal representation, the debtors failed to establish a violation of § 1692c.

Clark v. Schwabe, Williamson & Wyatt, Clearinghouse No. 44,831 (D. Or. 1990). Law firm violated FDCPA by sending consumer a letter demanding payment when it knew he was represented by an attorney. The fact that the consumer's attorney did not object to the firm's starting foreclosure against the consumer does not constitute consent to give preforeclosure notice to the debtor directly.

Furth v. United Adjusters, Inc., 1983 U.S. Dist. LEXIS 20368 (D. Or. Nov. 17, 1983). Sending a dunning letter to a consumer known to be represented by counsel violates § 1692c(a)(2). It was no excuse that the letter informed the consumer of a default judgment.

Harvey v. United Adjusters, 509 F. Supp. 1218 (D. Or. 1981). The debt collector sent two collection notices to the consumer after the consumer, represented by counsel, filed an FDCPA suit and thus violated § 1692c(a)(2) prohibiting communications with a consumer represented by counsel. The collector's state court judgment did not allow it to disregard the § 1692c(a)(2) protections.

Dixon v. United Adjusters, Inc., 1981 U.S. Dist. LEXIS 18392 (D. Or. Feb. 19, 1981). Two letters violated § 1692c(a)(2) since the consumer was represented by a lawyer before it was sent and that representation was implied to continue.

Pennsylvania

Villegas v. Weinstein & Riley, P.S., 2010 WL 2787454 (M.D. Pa. July 14, 2010). Where an attorney is interposed as an intermediary between a debt collector and a consumer, courts assume that the attorney, rather than the FDCPA, will protect the consumer from a debt collector's fraudulent or harassing behavior, and the debt collector's communication directly to the attorney did not state a claim under the FDCPA.

Flores v. Shapiro & Kreisman, 246 F. Supp. 2d 427 (E.D. Pa. 2002). Complaint stated cause of action for communicating with consumer after knowing she was represented by attorney.

In re Klein, 2010 WL 2680334 (Bankr. E.D. Pa. June 29, 2010). A bare allegation that the defendant contacted the consumer after knowledge of attorney representation, without specifics, was insufficient under *Twombly*. "The complaint is vague to the point of being wholly uninformative."

South Dakota

Pearce v. Rapid Check Collection, Inc., 738 F. Supp. 334 (D.S.D. 1990). Letter threatening suit sent to consumer known to be represented by an attorney on that debt was characterized a "technical," *de minimis* violation of § 1692(a)(2) for which no liability would attach.

Texas

Eads v. Wolpoff & Abramson, L.L.P., 538 F. Supp. 2d 981 (W.D. Tex. 2008). The consumer stated a legally cognizable claim against the collection law firm by alleging it violated §§ 1692b(6) and 1692c(a) by serving a state court motion on the consumer when it knew the consumer was represented.

Harding v. Regent, 347 F. Supp. 2d 334 (N.D. Tex. 2004). Collection lawyer's motion to dismiss was denied because factual issues existed as to the alleged violations of §§ 1692c(a)(2), 1692d, 1692e, and 1692f where the collector had repeatedly contacted the consumer after the consumer's lawyer had filed an answer to the collector's suit and faxed it to the collection lawyer.

Virginia

Vitullo v. Mancini, 684 F. Supp. 2d 747 (E.D. Va. 2010). Because defendant was required by West Virginia law to send the notice of acceleration and foreclosure to the grantor's address, and because consumer did not provide the beneficiary or the beneficiary's agent

with an alternate mailing address pursuant to state law, the letter at issue did not violate § 1692c(a)(2).

Dikun v. Streich, 369 F. Supp. 2d 781 (E.D. Va. 2005). The allegation that the collector continued to communicate with the consumer after receiving notification that the consumer was represented by an attorney stated a claim for relief for violating § 1692c(a)(2).

Washington

Clark v. Bonded Adjustment Co., 204 F.R.D. 662 (E.D. Wash. 2002). In the course of granting class certification based on charging excessive process server fees, the court noted that there was no legal distinction between communications to the consumers and to their counsel.

West Virginia

Clements v. HSBC Auto Fin., Inc., 2010 WL 4281697 (S.D. W. Va. Oct. 19, 2010). Where the plaintiffs provided the defendant with their attorney's name and number, there was no genuine issue of material fact as to whether the name of the attorney was easily ascertainable.

In re Carroll, 400 B.R. 497 (Bankr. N.D. W. Va. 2008). A collector's alleged imputed knowledge from its creditor of the consumer's representation by counsel and request to cease communication was insufficient to state a claim for violating §§ 1692c(a)(2) and 1692c(c), which require the collector to have actual knowledge.

Gibson v. Rossman & Co., Civ. Act. No. 81-C-754 (W. Va. Cir. Ct. 1982). Summary judgment was denied as there was an issue of material fact as to whether the collector waited a reasonable period of time for the consumer's attorney to return its phone call pursuant to § 1692c(a)(2) before it contacted the consumer. The collector called the consumer's attorney on May 15, 18, 19 and 21 and called the consumer on May 21.

Wisconsin

Hartman v. Meridian Fin. Servs., Inc., 191 F. Supp. 2d 1031 (W.D. Wis. 2002). Once notified of the consumers' representation by an attorney, the debt collector's direct communications with the consumers violated the FDCPA.

Wyoming

Johnson v. Statewide Collections, Inc., 778 P.2d 93 (Wyo. 1989). Collector violated § 1692c(a)(2) by communicating with a consumer known to be represented by an attorney, even though the collector only sent the consumer a demand for payment of a dishonored check that is required under state law. Collector had duty under § 1692g(b) to cease collection from date it received consumer's attorney's request for validation until it provided written verification of the debt.

K.2.2.3 Communications at Workplace, 15 U.S.C. § 1692c(a)(3)

Horkey v. J.V.D.B. & Assocs., Inc., 333 F.3d 769 (7th Cir. 2003). The consumer's statement that she could not talk at work and that she would return the call from her home was sufficient to place the collector on notice that the employer did not allow such collection calls.

Alabama

Bice v. Merchants Adjustment Serv., Clearinghouse No. 41,265 (S.D. Ala. 1985). A consumer's oral request to cease contacting them at work followed by the collector's subsequent contacts at work did not violate § 1692c(c) since the collector did not know their employer's policy about contacts at work.

Arizona

Nichols v. GC Servs., L.P., 2009 WL 3488365 (D. Ariz. Oct. 27, 2009). Disputed facts precluded summary judgment for either party on the consumer's claims that the defendant violated § 1692c(a)(3) by continuing to telephone him at work after being told not to do so.

California

Robinson v. Managed Accounts Receivables Corp., 654 F. Supp. 2d 1051 (C.D. Cal. 2009). Where the complaint specifically alleged the date and contents of several telephone calls made by defendants with specific alleged facts to show that the defendant knew that plaintiff's employer prohibited her from receiving collection calls at work, a claim was sufficiently stated for violation of § 1692c(a)(3) in order to survive the defendant's motion to dismiss.

Connecticut

Chiverton v. Fed. Fin. Group, Inc., 399 F. Supp. 2d 96 (D. Conn. 2005). The debt collector violated § 1692c(a)(1) and (3) by repeatedly calling after the consumer expressly requested the collector not to do so because he was not permitted to receive personal calls at work.

Illinois

Raimondi v. McAllister & Assocs., Inc., 50 F. Supp. 2d 825 (N.D. Ill. 1999). Because § 1692c(a)(3) explicitly prohibits collection agencies from contacting a consumer's employer, threatening to do so in order to collect a debt amounted to a false representation in violation of § 1692e(10).

Vines v. Sands, 188 F.R.D. 302 (N.D. Ill. 1999). Class action was filed alleging that the inclusion of the notice of Massachusetts residents' rights to stop calls to the consumer's place of employment overshadowed the recitation of the § 1692c(a)(3) right to be free from collector contacts with the consumer at work if prohibited by the employer. The court found that an unsophisticated consumer in Illinois could be left with the impression that he or she did not have the FDCPA right to request communications from the collection agency to cease at the consumer's place of employment.

Herbert v. Wexler & Wexler, 1995 WL 535107 (N.D. Ill. Sept. 5, 1995). The statement "[w]e have advised our client of the fact that you are employed and the location of your employment; we have further advised them that you have the ability to pay this debt but refuse to do so" does not violate § 1692c(b) because the collector has neither contacted or threatened to contact the consumer's employer.

Indiana

Roudebush v. Collecto, Inc., 2004 WL 3316168 (S.D. Ind. Nov. 12, 2004). The court rejected the plaintiff's claim that the following statement unlawfully restricted consumers' rights under § 1692c(a)(3) because a debt collector cannot contact consumers at work whenever the debt collector "knows or has reason to know" that the employer prohibits such contact and the consumer is not required to make any request, oral or written: "You have the right to make a written or oral request that telephone calls regarding your debt not be made to you at your place of employment. Any such oral request will be valid for only ten days unless you provide written confirmation of the request postmarked or delivered within seven days of such request." The court held: "The court finds that Collecto's workplace notice actually goes beyond the requirements of the FDCPA by allowing for any debtor to refuse calls at work for any reason. The FDCPA only protects those employees whose employers do not allow such calls. In this instance, Collecto is extending an additional right to its target debtors, above and beyond those mandated by the FDCPA. Furthermore, Collecto is not required by the FDCPA to inform debtors of their rights under § 1692c(a)(3)." This holding is mistaken: while it is true that this notice expands somewhat the 1692c(a)(3) rights, it also restricts them as well by requiring a writing, yet the court ignored that argument.

Michigan

Dunaway v. JBC & Assocs., Inc., 2005 WL 1529574 (E.D. Mich. June 20, 2005). The uncontroverted fact that the debt collector called the consumer's employer and falsely informed him that a civil lawsuit had been filed and that criminal charges were pending against the consumer for a dishonored check on which both the civil and criminal statute of limitations had expired established the collector's liability as a matter of law for violating §§ 1692b, 1692c, and 1692e.

Missouri

Jenkins v. Eastern Asset Mgmt., L.L.C., 2009 WL 2488029 (E.D. Mo. Aug. 12, 2009). On default, court awarded $1000 statutory damages, $2000 emotional distress damages, and $3250 fees and costs for multiple calls to place of employment threatening suit after being told plaintiff could not accept personal calls at work.

Nevada

Kuhn v. Account Control Tech., Inc., 865 F. Supp. 1443 (D. Nev. 1994). Six calls placed to the consumer's employer within 24 minutes violated § 1692d(5).

New York

Fajer v. Kaufman, Burns & Assocs., 2011 WL 334311 (W.D.N.Y. Jan. 28, 2011). In this default action, the court found that the collector's call to the plaintiff at her workplace after being told by the plaintiff not to do so violated § 1692c(a)(3).

Harrison v. Fed. Pac. Credit Co., L.L.C., 2006 WL 276605 (W.D.N.Y. Feb. 3, 2006). Claim stated under § 1692c(a)(3) based on defendant's weekly telephone calls to plaintiff's place of employment for approximately fifteen months in an attempt to collect a debt which plaintiff disputed.

Ohio

Minick v. First Fed. Credit Control, Inc., 1981 U.S. Dist. LEXIS 18622 (N.D. Ohio June 9, 1981). The question of whether a collection agency's phone call at the plaintiff's business violated § 1692c(a)(3) raised a question of fact regarding knowledge of the plaintiff's employer's policy of prohibiting all but emergency phone calls.

Kleczy v. First Fed. Credit Control, Inc., 486 N.E.2d 204 (Ohio Ct. App. 1984). The collector was liable for a violation of § 1692c(a)(3) where the language "Final Demand For Payment" clearly showed through the envelope mailed to the consumer at work.

Oregon

T Clark v. Quick Collect, Inc., 2005 WL 1586862 (D. Or. June 30, 2005). The court granted summary judgment for defendants where calls at work ceased after oral request. The court denied summary judgment where consumer alleged she was told a request to cease contact at work must be in writing and collector denied saying this.

Pennsylvania

Adams v. Law Offices of Stuckert & Yates, 926 F. Supp. 521 (E.D. Pa. 1996). The collection firm did not violate § 1692c(a)(3) by sending a copy of the collection letter to the consumer's place of work as the firm had no knowledge or reason to know that the consumer's employer prohibited its employees from receiving such communications at the workplace.

Texas

United States v. Cent. Adjustment Bureau, Inc., 667 F. Supp. 370 (N.D. Tex. 1986). Collector violated § 1692c(a)(3) by making phone calls to debtors at work after being requested not to by the debtor or employer.

K.2.2.4 Communications with Third Parties, 15 U.S.C. § 1692c(b)

Edwards v. Niagara Credit Solutions, Inc., 584 F.3d 1350 (11th Cir. 2009). The district court properly denied the bona fide error defense arising from the defendant's failure to identify itself as a debt collector as required by § 1692e(11) when leaving consumers a message on an answering machine; first, the violation was in fact intentional, the result of a deliberate policy decision to not comply with § 1692e(11), purportedly to avoid violating § 1692c(b) in the event that the message was heard by a third party who would then know that a collection agency was calling the consumer; second, to be bona fide "the mistake must be objectively reasonable," and "[i]t was not reasonable for to violate § 1692e(11) of the FDCPA

with every message it left in order to avoid the possibility that some of those messages might lead to a violation of § 1692c(b)."

Ruth v. Triumph P'ships, 577 F.3d 790 (7th Cir. 2009). The lower court erred in granting the defendants summary judgment, as the privacy notice was sent to the consumer in connection with a attempt to collect a debt when it was sent in the same envelope with a dunning letter. The debt collector's privacy statement falsely stated that it would share the consumer's information with others, in violation of § 1692c(b).

Acosta v. Campbell, 309 Fed. Appx. 315 (11th Cir. 2009) (unpublished). A confidential communication issued from foreclosing party or its counsel to counsel for another creditor involved in the foreclosure, regarding the payoff figure, did not violate § 1692c(b), as such a communication was not subject to the FDCPA.

Horkey v. J.V.D.B. & Assocs., 333 F.3d 769 (7th Cir. 2003). Lacing with profanity a request to a co-employee to have the debtor return a call did not violate § 1692c(b) because the debt was not mentioned but did violate § 1692d(2) because it was the second rude call in a short period and the collector expected the profanity to be reconveyed to the debtor.

Arizona

Horvath v. Premium Collection Servs., Inc., 2010 WL 1945717 (D. Ariz. May 13, 2010). Where a debt collector communicates with a consumer reporting agency, the communication, in and of itself, does not support a cause of action under the FDCPA unless that communication is otherwise unlawful.

Nichols v. GC Serv., L.P., 2009 WL 3488365 (D. Ariz. Oct. 27, 2009). Disputed facts precluded summary judgment for either party on the consumer's claims that the defendant violated § 1692c(b) by calling the consumer's mother over a dozen times and revealing the existence of the alleged debt.

California

Escobedo v. Countrywide Home Loans, Inc., 2009 WL 4981618 (S.D. Cal. Dec. 15, 2009). The complaint stated claims for relief under state law that incorporates the FDCPA by sufficiently alleging FDCPA violations resulting from defendant's unlawful calls to the plaintiff's employer.

Puttner v. Debt Consultants of Am., 2009 WL 1604570 (S.D. Cal. June 4, 2009). The complaint stated a claim for relief by alleging that the defendant's collectors called the consumer's parents without stating that they were confirming or correcting location information, disclosed the existence of the son's debt, and called the parents repeatedly so as to constitute harassment.

Owens v. Brachfeld, 2008 WL 3891958 (N.D. Cal. Aug. 20, 2008). Summary judgment was entered for the consumer that the debt collector had violated § 1692c(b), where the debt collector sent an envelope that contained a window through which anyone could see the creditor and account number related to the consumer debt being collected.

Colorado

O'Connor v. Check Rite, 973 F. Supp. 1010 (D. Colo. 1997). Where collector informed consumer's roommate that he was calling regarding the consumer's "bounced check," § 1692c(b) was violated.

Connecticut

Krueger v. Ellis, Crosby & Assocs., Inc., 2006 WL 3791402 (D. Conn. Nov. 9, 2006). Defendant violated the FDCPA by contacting third parties.

Shrestha v. Nadel, 2001 U.S. Dist. LEXIS 12553 (D. Conn. Mar. 21, 2001). Section 1692c(b) permitted a communication concerning a debtor between a debt collector and the attorney for the creditor.

Kimberly v. Great Lakes Collection Bureau, Inc., Clearinghouse No. 50,431B (D. Conn. 1996). Collection agency violated § 1692b(3) by contacting a consumer's mother on numerous occasions without the consumer's permission (which was required after the first contact if that contact was to obtain location information) and stating that consumer owed a debt. Consumer's mother did not have standing to recover under § 1692c(b) which only protects "consumers" as compared to other sections that appear to protect "any person."

Austin v. Great Lakes Collection Bureau, Inc., 834 F. Supp. 557 (D. Conn. 1993). Collector's discussion of the consumer's debt with the consumer's secretary was an improper communication with a third party in violation of § 1692c(b).

Weber v. Payco-Gen. Am. Credits, 1990 U.S. Dist. LEXIS 20978 (D. Conn. Dec. 13, 1990). Threat to conduct an investigation was not a threat to unlawfully communicate with third parties.

Stewart v. Salzman, 1987 U.S. Dist. LEXIS 16865 (D. Conn. Nov. 2, 1987). Discussion of the debt by an attorney with the sister of the debtor violated § 1692c(b) even though the sister telephoned the attorney about the debt. Consent to the conversation could not be implied since § 1692c plainly requires any such consent to be given directly to the debt collector.

Florida

Kelemen v. Professional Collection Sys., 2011 WL 31396 (M.D. Fla. Jan. 4, 2011). The court denied summary judgment to the defendant on the § 1692c(b) claim since the plaintiff asserted that the defendant left a message on the plaintiff's work voicemail that was overheard by her co-worker.

Deuel v. Santander Consumer USA, Inc., 700 F. Supp. 2d 1306 (S.D. Fla. 2010). Court erroneously held that where consumer failed to allege that she was obligated to pay the debt, she was not a "consumer" pursuant to § 1692a(3) and did not have standing to bring a claim against the debt collector for violation of § 1692c(b).

Magnuson v. NCC Bus. Servs., Inc., 2010 WL 2366535 (M.D. Fla. June 11, 2010). A disputed factual question as to whether the debt collector revealed the debt to a third party precluded summary judgment on the issue of violating § 1692b.

Berg v. Merchants Ass'n Collection Div., Inc., 586 F. Supp. 2d 1336 (S.D. Fla. 2008). The complaint stated a claim for violating § 1692c(b) where the plaintiff alleged (1) that relatives and other unauthorized third parties listened to the defendant's pre-recorded voicemail message that disclosed that the plaintiff allegedly owed

the subject debt and (2) that the defendant knew or had reason to know that other persons besides the debtor might hear the defendant's collection message, even though the message stated that it was for the plaintiff and then the following: "If you are not the person requested, disconnect this recording now. By continuing to listen to this recording you acknowledge you are the person requested."

Niven v. Nat'l Action Fin. Servs., Inc., 2008 WL 4190961 (M.D. Fla. Sept. 10, 2008). Consumer's motion for summary judgment for violation of § 1692c(b) was denied because of the debt collector's bona fide error defense raised questions of triable fact.

Belin v. Litton Loan Serv., L.P., 2006 WL 1992410 (M.D. Fla. July 14, 2006). The complaint stated a claim for the defendant's violation of § 1692c(b) prohibiting communicating with a third party in connection with the collection of a debt where the collector left a message with the debtor's mother to return the telephone call, since the purpose of the message was to get the debtor to return the call to discuss the debt and thus indirectly conveyed information about the debt; the court distinguished cases which found no violation where the collector spoke to third parties, asked to speak with the debtor, but did not try to leave a message for the debtor to return the call.

Segal v. Nat'l Action Fin. Servs., Inc., 2006 WL 449176 (M.D. Fla. Feb. 22, 2006). Communication with the consumer's spouse did not constitute an unlawful third party contact in violation of § 1692c(b) since a collector may communicate with the consumer's spouse under the § 1692c(d) definition.

Acosta v. Campbell, 2006 WL 146208 (M.D. Fla. Jan. 18, 2006). The FDCPA does not prohibit a debt collector from communicating to consumer reporting agencies, and "a communication, in and of itself, to a consumer reporting agency, does not support a cause of action under" § 1692c(b). Consumer's claim that the collection attorneys in the underlying state foreclosure action engaged in unlawful third party communication by conveying mortgage balance information to attorneys for other creditors failed to state a claim for violation of § 1692c(b), since "[a]s a practical matter, in a state foreclosure action, the first and second mortgage holders and other creditors must be able to communicate regarding the balance or settlement of the outstanding mortgages."

Arslan v. Florida First Fed. Group, 1995 WL 731175 (M.D. Fla. Oct. 5, 1995). To establish a violation of § 1692c(b), the consumer need not show that defendant specifically stated that it was calling regarding a debt, but merely have demonstrated that the third party listener construed the communication to refer to a debt.

Merchant v. Nationwide Collection Serv., Inc., Clearinghouse No. 43,382 (Fla. Cir. Ct. 1988). Two plaintiffs each awarded $2500 actual damages, $1000 statutory damages and $50,000 punitive damages for late night phone calls, threats of arrest, and a third-party contact.

Idaho

Mangum v. Bonneville Billing & Collections, Inc., 2010 WL 672744 (D. Idaho Feb. 20, 2010). Cross motions for summary judgment on the alleged §§ 1692c(b) and 1692d violations were denied where a fact question remained as to whether the defendant's communication in response to an inquiry from the local police department—the consumer's employer—was made in connection with the collection of the consumer's bad check debts or was instead part of a criminal investigation.

Illinois

Miller v. Midland Credit Mgmt., Inc., 621 F. Supp. 2d 621 (N.D. Ill. 2009). Summary judgment for the defendants on the § 1692c(b) claim (unlawful third party communication) and the § 1692d(3) claim (publication of list of debtors) since the plaintiff failed to submit evidence to support the allegation that the defendants shared information with a third party bank as part of a "balance transfer" joint marketing program. Summary judgment for the plaintiffs on the § 1692e(5) claim where the defendants' privacy notice stated that certain information may be disclosed to third parties unless the consumer opted out, since § 1692c(b) made such disclosure an unlawful third party communication even if the consumer failed to act.

Hernandez v. Midland Credit Mgmt., Inc., 2007 WL 2874059 (N.D. Ill. Sept. 25, 2007). The court granted the consumer summary judgment because the defendant's communication to the consumer that threatened, unless the consumer opted out, to disclose the consumer's personal information to nonaffiliated third parties, i.e., the collector's marketing partners and balance transfer credit card partner, was false and unlawfully threatened to take action prohibited by law since such third-party communications are prohibited by § 1692c(b).

Hernandez v. Midland Credit Mgmt., Inc., 2006 WL 695451 (N.D. Ill. Mar. 14, 2006). The plaintiff stated a claim for defendant's violation of the FDCPA's anti-third party contact rules where the defendant sent the debtor a privacy notice, purportedly in compliance with Gramm-Leach-Bliley, that unlawfully threatened to share the debtor's private information with various third parties unless the debtor opted out, since § 1692c(b) prohibits such third party contact without the need for the debtor to object or otherwise act.

Zanayed v. Gertler & Gertler, Ltd., 2000 U.S. Dist. LEXIS 5827 (N.D. Ill. Mar. 17, 2000). Section 1692c(b) clearly excludes communications which are necessary to "effectuate a post-judgment judicial remedy" in this instance, a wage deduction summons to the employer of a judgment debtor.

Phillips v. N. Am. Capital Corp., 1999 WL 299872 (N.D. Ill. Apr. 30, 1999). Communications with a consumer's attorney cannot give rise to liability for revealing the debt to a third party.

Shaver v. Trauner, 1998 U.S. Dist. LEXIS 19647 (C.D. Ill. May 29, 1998). Motion to dismiss denied where simultaneously with the initial demand letter, the attorney faxed consumer's employer seeking information about his employment such as his date of hire, his position, whether he was a full or part time employee, whether he was salaried or on commission, and the address of the employer's payroll department. The fax went well beyond location information and thus violated the FDCPA.

Perperas v. United Recovery Sys., Inc., 1997 WL 136326 (N.D. Ill. Mar. 19, 1997). Communication with plaintiff's wife did not violate § 1692c(b).

Iowa

In re Hromidko, 302 B.R. 629 (Bankr. N.D. Iowa 2003). The FDCPA prohibits contact with third parties in an attempt to collect debts.

Louisiana

Henderson v. Eaton, 2001 U.S. Dist. LEXIS 13243 (E.D. La. Aug. 23, 2001). Debt collector's motion to dismiss was denied where its letters to the consumer's employer requested confirmation of her employment, her wage scale, type of employment, and the full name of her employer if she had been terminated because the letters were alleged to be communications indirectly conveying information about a debt violating the FDCPA.

Missouri

Terry v. C & D Complete Bus. Solutions, 2011 WL 144920 (W.D. Mo. Jan. 18, 2011). A debt collector's letters to the consumers' employers in connection with the collection of a debt violated § 1692b(2) by disclosing the debt if sent for location purposes or, if not, they violated § 1692c(b) by communicating with a third party in connection with the collection of a debt.

Nebraska

Harris v. BWS Credit Servs., Inc., Clearinghouse No. 27,693 (D. Neb. 1980) (order on motions for summary judgment). The collection agency contacted a third party and contacted a consumer represented by an attorney.

New Jersey

Cohen v. Wolpoff & Abramson, L.L.P., 2008 WL 4513569 (D.N.J. Oct. 2, 2008). Based on *Heintz*, an attorney's communication with a forum in pursuit of arbitration—surely an ordinary remedy—would come within the scope of the § 1692c exception for third-party communications.

Federal Trade Comm'n v. Check Enforcement, 2005 WL 1677480 (D.N.J. July 18, 2005), *aff'd on other grounds*, 502 F.3d 159 (3d Cir. 2007). The collector violated the Act by harassing unobligated family members and by leaving messages on answering machines that children and parents could hear.

Kaschak v. Raritan Valley Collection Agency, 1989 U.S. Dist. LEXIS 19103 (D.N.J. May 22, 1989). The prohibition against communication with a consumer who is represented by an attorney applies only when the collector has actual knowledge of the representation.

New York

Clayson v. Rubin & Rothman, L.L.C., 2010 WL 4628516 (W.D.N.Y. Nov. 16, 2010). The debt collector's act of leaving messages on the adult debtor's mother's answering machine referring to the debt violated the FDCPA as a matter of law. There was no evidence at trial that the plaintiff authorized her mother to submit any of her medical records to the debt collector, and the defendant offered no credible explanation for why the plaintiff's mother would think to give a debt collector whom she did not know some of her daughter's medical records. "Absent some kind of conversation with that debt collector that raised the issue of plaintiff's health as it pertained to plaintiff's ability to pay the debt in question, plaintiff's mother's submission of medical records to defendant would be nonsensical."

Krapf v. Collectors Training Inst., Inc., 2010 WL 584020 (W.D.N.Y. Feb. 16, 2010). Because the defendant's contact with the consumer's employer "did not involve an inquiry into Consumer's location information, but rather, revealed that Consumer had a 'business matter,'" and because the defendant "later placed another call to Consumer's employer in an attempt to use Consumer's employer as a means of inducing Consumer to return Defendant's call," "Defendant contacted a third party in a manner not authorized by § 1692b, [and therefore] Consumer sufficiently states claims under §§ 1692b, 1692c(b), and 1692d."

Mostiller v. Chase Asset Recovery Corp., 2010 WL 335023 (W.D.N.Y. Jan. 22, 2010). The debt collector did not unlawfully disclose the debt to a third party where the consumer's fiancé/roommate happened to overhear a debt collection voicemail message left for her since there was no claim that the collector intended that the third party hear the communication or knew or should have known of the potential risk.

Bank v. Pentagroup Fin., L.L.C., 2009 WL 1606420 (E.D.N.Y. June 9, 2009). The court erroneously held that one who received recorded calls aimed at a different consumer has no standing under § 1692c. "[Plaintiff] lacks standing to bring a claim under § 1692c because: (1) he was not obligated or allegedly obligated to pay any debt; and (2) he has not alleged that he is a consumer's spouse, parent, guardian, executor or administrator. Accordingly, Pentagroup's motion to dismiss [plaintiff's] § 1692c(b) claim is granted."

DeGeorge v. LTD Fin. Servs., L.P., 2008 WL 905913 (W.D.N.Y. Mar. 31, 2008). Plaintiff's motion for summary judgment for the collector's alleged impermissible third-party contact denied since a reasonable jury could decide either that the defendant's communication with the plaintiff's brother was an unlawful attempt to collect the debt in violation of § 1692c(b) or was a permissible attempt to locate the plaintiff as allowed by § 1692b.

Leyse v. Corporate Collection Servs., Inc., 2006 WL 2708451 (S.D.N.Y. Sept. 18, 2006). "CCS has been cornered between a rock and a hard place, not because of any contradictory provisions of the FDCPA, but because the method they have selected to collect debts [prerecorded calls] has put them there."

Harrison v. Fed. Pac. Credit Co., L.L.C., 2006 WL 276605 (W.D.N.Y. Feb. 3, 2006) Claim stated for violation of § 1692c(b) where collector allegedly communicated with plaintiff's supervisor concerning the debt.

Forman v. Academy Collection Serv., Inc., 388 F. Supp. 2d 199 (S.D.N.Y. 2005). Academy's letters claimed that debt was referred to it for "pre-legal" collection and that its special counsel Marvel & Maloney had reviewed the appropriateness of the referral. The collection agency did not violate § 1692c(b), since it could disclose the debt to its own counsel.

Padilla v. Payco Gen. Am. Credits, Inc., 161 F. Supp. 2d 264 (S.D.N.Y. 2001). Inadmissible hearsay alone supporting a claim for unlawful third-party communication could not support motion for summary judgment.

Fava v. RRI, Inc., 1997 WL 205336 (N.D.N.Y. Apr. 24, 1997). Collector's contacts with adult debtor's father violated § 1692c(b) despite collector's claim that father stated that he had daughter's power of attorney, since contacts exceeded location information and daughter's alleged consent, even if true, did not meet statutory requirement that such consent be given directly by the consumer.

Sluys v. Hand, 831 F. Supp. 321 (S.D.N.Y. 1993). Sending collection letters to the consumer's employer violates § 1692c(b).

North Carolina

West v. Nationwide Credit, Inc., 998 F. Supp. 642 (W.D.N.C. 1998). Section 1692c(b) should be broadly interpreted to prohibit a debt collector, in connection with the collection of any debt, from conveying any information relating to a debt to a third party. The consumer's complaint alleging that the debt collector telephoned plaintiff's neighbor leaving collector's name and telephone number and asking the neighbor to have consumer return the call, stated a claim for violation of § 1692c(b).

Ohio

Kleczy v. First Fed. Credit Control, Inc., 486 N.E.2d 204 (Ohio Ct. App. 1984). No violation of FDCPA to attempt to collect part of a medical bill from father of an adult patient since the father had been listed as a responsible party.

Oregon

Clark v. Capital Credit & Collection Servs., Inc., 2004 WL 1305326 (D. Or. Jan. 23, 2004). Pursuit of the husband for his wife's medical expenses was permitted by state family expense law.

Pennsylvania

Shand-Pistilli v. Professional Account Servs., Inc., 2010 WL 2978029 (E.D. Pa. July 26, 2010). The consumer adequately alleged that defendant contacted her employer in violation of § 1692c(b) since the defendant's inquiry into her current employment status went beyond the boundaries of location information and may have implied the existence of a debt to the employer. A debt collector may not seek additional information about a consumer's job including earnings. Once a debt collector has acquired location information, it may not contact third parties for information it already has in its possession or information on salary, or even ask whether an individual is currently employed, because such information is beyond the scope of location information.

Wideman v. Monterey Fin. Servs., Inc., 2009 WL 1292830 (W.D. Pa. May 7, 2009). The complaint stated a claim for an unlawful contact in violation of § 1692c(b), since the collector's telephone message given to the consumer's administrative assistant to return an "urgent" call regarding the disclosed original creditor was a communication that indirectly conveyed information about the debt to a third party.

Romano v. Williams & Fudge, Inc., 644 F. Supp. 2d 653 (W.D. Pa. 2008). Defendant violated § 1692b(2) by discussing a debt with plaintiff's estranged father, § 1692c(b) by asking the father to convey a message, and § 1692e(11) by not providing the required notice in a telephone message. Defendant's bona fide error defense raised factual issues remaining for trial.

South Carolina

Valentine v. Brock & Scott, P.L.L.C., 2010 WL 1727681 (D.S.C. Apr. 26, 2010). Consumer stated a claim for violating § 1692c(b) by alleging that defendant left on her nonexclusive home answering machine collection messages that were overheard by a third party. Note that in reaching this result, the court expressly relied on the consumer's claim that her husband overheard the message, apparently unaware that § 1692c(d) defines each spouse as the consumer for purposes of that section.

Texas

United States v. Cent. Adjustment Bureau, Inc., 667 F. Supp. 370 (N.D. Tex. 1986). Collector violated §§ 1692b & 1692c(b) by contacting third parties.

Utah

Maynard v. Cannon, 650 F. Supp. 2d 1138 (D. Utah 2008). Filing notice of default with the town clerk was not an impermissible third-party contact: the deed gave permission to do so if homeowner defaulted.

Ditty v. CheckRite, Ltd., 973 F. Supp. 1320 (D. Utah 1997). Whether CheckRite, a check collection agency, was liable under § 1692c(b) turned on whether CheckRite itself was a "consumer reporting agency" for purposes of its check verification activities, and that could not be determined on the summary judgment record.

Vermont

Committe v. Dennis Reimer, Co., L.P.A., 150 F.R.D. 495 (D. Vt. 1993). Telephone message was admissible and was not hearsay since it was offered not for the truth of the statement but rather to establish that a third party had been contacted by the collector regarding the debt.

Virginia

Carter v. Countrywide Home Loans, Inc., 2009 WL 2742560 (E.D. Va. Aug. 25, 2009). Even though the plaintiff had not signed the note or the related loan modification agreement, he would be still protected as a "consumer" under 15 U.S.C. § 1692c.

West v. Costen, 558 F. Supp. 564 (W.D. Va. 1983). Communications about debts with consumers' grandparents, uncle, sister, daughter, and mother violate § 1692c(b), but contact with an unobligated spouse is permitted by § 1692c(d). While the mother who was not alleged to owe the debt of a consumer has a cause of action under the FDCPA for other violations, she is not a "consumer" as defined by § 1692a(3) and therefore cannot recover as a victim of a third party contact since § 1692c only protects consumers.

Washington

McLain v. Gordon, 2010 WL 3340528 (W.D. Wash. Aug. 24, 2010). Where a collector obtained leave from a court to contact third parties regarding the consumer's alleged debt, it did not violate § 1692c(b).

K.2.2.5 Ceasing Communications, 15 U.S.C. § 1692c(c)

Heintz v. Jenkins, 514 U.S. 291, 115 S. Ct. 1489, 131 L. Ed. 2d 395 (1995). Section 1692c(c) does not stop a collector from invoking legal process against a nonconsenting consumer.

Tinsley v. Integrity Fin. Partners, Inc., 2011 WL 477486 (7th Cir. Feb. 11, 2011). Since § 1692c as a whole permits debt collectors to communicate freely with a consumer's lawyer, a debt collector's request for payment to the consumer's lawyer did not violate the FDCPA even though the lawyer had sent a refusal to pay and cease communications letter.

Clark v. Capital Credit & Collection Servs., Inc., 460 F.3d 1162 (9th Cir. 2006). Debtor may waive cease communication letter, but only where least sophisticated consumer would understand actions to be waiver. Whether collector's call to debtor violated cease communication letter where it was in response to debtor's call to collection attorney for information about the debt is question of fact. The collector may respond to a request for verification, and initiate suit, even after the consumer requests that letters and phone calls cease.

Montgomery v. Huntington Bank & Silver Shadow Recovery, Inc., 346 F.3d 693 (6th Cir. 2003). A non-debtor who was subjected to abusive collection tactics may not maintain an action for violations of § 1692c(c), since that section is limited to violations directed at a "consumer" as defined in the Act, but may maintain an action for violation of §§ 1692d and 1692e, which have no such limitation and therefore apply to anyone who is the victim of prescribed misconduct.

Lewis v. ACB Bus. Servs., Inc., 135 F.3d 389 (6th Cir. 1998). Where the creditor returned a debt to a collection agency marked as "new" rather than returned, a bona fide error defense existed to the collector's contact of the debtor who had sent a cease communication letter.

Smith v. Transworld Sys., Inc., 953 F.2d 1025 (6th Cir. 1992). Although the debt collector sent from its California headquarters a second letter to the consumer shortly after receiving the consumer's cease and desist letter at its Columbia, Ohio office, the debt collector demonstrated "procedures reasonably adapted to avoid any such error" and thereby established a bona fide error defense. Dissent argued that the debt collector "has intentionally structured and implemented a system that defies compliance with the absolute duty mandated by § 1692c(c)," so bona fide error defense should have been rejected.

Arizona

Nichols v. GC Serv., L.P., 2009 WL 3488365 (D. Ariz. Oct. 27, 2009). Summary judgment granted to the debt collector on the consumer's claim that the collector failed to cease communication after he sent a certified mail § 1692c(c) letter, since the collector denied receiving the letter, the consumer did not receive a return receipt, and "[t]here is no delivery presumption for certified mail when the sender does not receive a requested return receipt."

Grismore v. United Recovery Sys., L.P., 2006 WL 2246359 (D. Ariz. Aug. 3, 2006). The debt collector's cessation of telephone calls upon receipt of the consumer's cease communication letter complied with § 1692c(c).

California

Basinger-Lopez v. Tracy Paul & Assocs., 2009 WL 1948832 (N.D. Cal. July 6, 2009). Default judgment entered on well pleaded facts showing that the defendants engaged in a campaign of unlawful harassment, threats, misrepresentations, and other misconduct in violation of multiple FDCPA provisions. Defendant persisted in contacting plaintiff even after being expressly instructed not to do so, and failed to provide her with any of the notices required by law.

Casas v. Midland Credit Mgmt., Inc., 2009 WL 249992 (S.D. Cal. Jan. 30, 2009). The debt collector violated the FDCPA by continuing to demand payment of the debt which the consumer convincingly stated was not hers.

Reed v. Global Acceptance Credit Co., 2008 WL 3330165 (N.D. Cal. Aug. 12, 2008). Summary judgment denied on the consumer's § 1692c(c) claim because there was "a material issue of fact whether plaintiff actually requested that defendants cease communications regarding the debt." The court reasoned that the consumer's letter, which stated that she both disputed the debt and refused to pay, "makes her intent somewhat unclear;" the defendants in fact sent verification to the consumer before resuming collection activities, and that response supported defendants' claim that they "reasonably understood [the] letter as a request for verification [per § 1692g(b)] and not as a 'cease communications' letter [per § 1692c(c)]."

Colorado

O'Connor v. Check Rite, 973 F. Supp. 1010 (D. Colo. 1997). Where no letter or affidavit was offered to show that the consumer had requested in writing that the debt collector cease communications, the consumer could not demonstrate that § 1692c(c) was violated.

Connecticut

Shrestha v. State Credit Adjustment Bureau, Inc., 117 F. Supp. 2d 142 (D. Conn. 2000). When debtor's letters asked the collection agency to call and also asked the collection agency to stop collection efforts, the collector was not asked to cease contacts and did not violate the FDCPA by calling the debtor.

Herbert v. Monterey Fin. Servs., Inc., 863 F. Supp. 76 (D. Conn. 1994). Contacting a consumer after receiving a letter from the consumer's lawyer saying the consumer does not owe the debt and refuses to pay violated § 1692c(c).

Florida

Bishop v. I.C. Sys., Inc., 2010 WL 1924472 (M.D. Fla. May 12, 2010). Given that the consumers' letter to the debt collector stated "Any further correspondence from your organization or any other collection agency will be discarded or returned to you unopened," the court found that any jury would conclude that the letter demanded that the debt collector stop contacting the consumers. "System's argument rests on the fact that Bishop's letter did not include the actual words of the statute and did not literally say,

'Cease further communication.' But while Bishop did not use those precise words, his words expressed the same message-just with more bite."

Florida Bar v. Committee, 916 So. 2d 741 (Fla. 2005). Among the misconduct which the court held warranted the respondent attorney's suspension from the practice of law was his abuse of § 1692c(c), through which the attorney, a judgment debtor in his own case, repeatedly thwarted the creditor's attempts to conduct post-judgment discovery by invoking this FDCPA cease communication provision to stop the normal course of collection litigation, precisely as the Supreme Court in *Heintz v. Jenkins* held that § 1992c(c) did not permit.

Georgia

Florence v. Nat'l Sys., 1983 U.S. Dist. LEXIS 20344 (N.D. Ga. Oct. 14, 1983). The collector violated § 1692c(a)(2) and (c) by sending a threatening letter after being served with the consumer's FDCPA complaint and by sending six letters after the consumer sent the collector a letter stating the account had been paid and the collector should not contact the consumer at work.

Carrigan v. Cent. Adjustment Bureau, Inc., 494 F. Supp. 824 (N.D. Ga. 1980). The ceasing communication provision was violated.

Illinois

Gulley v. Pierce & Assocs., 2010 WL 5060257 (N.D. Ill. Dec. 6, 2010). The *pro se* complaint alleging that the defendant violated § 1692c(c) by ceasing communication with the consumer without notifying him that it was in fact ceasing such communication failed to state a claim since the statute contains no such requirement.

Medeiros v. Client Servs., Inc., 2010 WL 3283050 (N.D. Ill. Aug. 17, 2010). Section 1692c(c) permits a collector who has received a cease communication notice to continue collection efforts directed at the consumer's attorney.

Startare v. Credit Bureau, L.L.C., 2010 WL 2220583 (N.D. Ill. June 3, 2010). The cease communication directive of § 1692c(c) "applies to communication with a consumer's attorney." Summary judgment granted to the consumer where the collector's communication to the consumer's attorney subsequent to receiving a cease communication notice went beyond the § 1692c(c) exceptions and demanded payment of the debt.

Ramirez v. Apex Fin. Mgmt., L.L.C., 567 F. Supp. 2d 1035 (N.D. Ill. 2008). The collector's § 1692c(c) violations committed over a seven-day period as it continued to contact the consumer while it processed the consumer's cease communication letter were not the result of a bona fide error, since the collector provided an address to which the consumer mailed the letter that required forwarding and built-in internal procedures that delayed activation of the cease communication: "This is not a 'clerical error,' but a loose procedure that resulted in a seven day delay in processing and twenty-one collection calls to Plaintiff."

Vines v. Sands, 188 F.R.D. 302 (N.D. Ill. 1999). Class action was filed alleging that the inclusion of the notice of Massachusetts residents' rights to stop calls to the consumer's place of employment overshadowed the recitation of the § 1692c(a)(3) right to be free from collector contacts with the consumer at work if prohibited by the employer. The court found that an unsophisticated consumer in Illinois could be left with the impression that he or she did not have the FDCPA right to request communications from the collection agency to cease at the consumer's place of employment.

Indiana

Recker v. Cent. Collection Bureau, Inc., 2005 WL 2654222 (S.D. Ind. Oct. 17, 2005). Where the consumer requested verification of the debt and that the collector cease communication, the collector could comply with both §§ 1692c(c) and 1692g by providing the verification with a notice of intent to file suit.

Kansas

Udell v. Kansas Counselors, Inc., 313 F. Supp. 2d 1135 (D. Kan. 2004). The plain language of the FDCPA did not prohibit a collection agency from communicating with a consumer regarding new debts that it was assigned after receiving a cease and desist letter.

Louisiana

Kahn v. Rowley, 968 F. Supp. 1095 (M.D. La. 1997) (withdrawn from hard cover publication). Question of fact precluded summary judgment on issue whether consumer's attorney telephoned collector's office within five days of initial communication to demand that communications cease, and thereby waived debt validation notice requirement.

Minnesota

Cohen v. Beachside Two-I Homeowners' Ass'n, 2006 WL 1795140 (D. Minn. June 29, 2006). Attorneys could continue to communicate despite cease notice because consumer invited a settlement, because the attorney communication was returning a check, and because the attorney was putting consumer on notice of the foreclosure remedy.

Morse v. Dun & Bradstreet, Inc., 87 F. Supp. 2d 901 (D. Minn. 2000). Judgment on the pleadings entered for defendant on the claim that the Colorado notice at issue was misleading to the least sophisticated consumer. The court followed *White v. Goodman*, 200 F.3d 1016 (7th Cir. 2000) which held that an unsophisticated consumer would not falsely infer that the cease collection rights which the notice implied were limited to Colorado consumers were not available to everyone else.

New Jersey

Smith v. Lyons, Doughty & Veldhuius, P.C., 2008 WL 2885887 (D.N.J. July 23, 2008). The consumer failed to state a classwide cause of action for violation of § 1692c(a)(2) and (c) because an individual inquiry of each class member would be required; plaintiff was granted leave to amend the complaint.

Kaschak v. Raritan Valley Collection Agency, 1989 U.S. Dist. LEXIS 19103 (D.N.J. May 22, 1989). The requirement that a collector cease communication under § 1692c(c) is effective upon the collector's actual receipt of the consumer's request that communications cease, even if the collector has not processed the request and has no actual knowledge of the request.

New York

Sembler v. Attention Funding Trust, 2009 WL 2883049 (E.D.N.Y. Sept. 3, 2009), *report and recommendation adopted*, 2009 WL 3055347 (E.D.N.Y. Sept. 24, 2009). Plaintiff's § 1692c(c) claim was dismissed since the complaint failed to allege that the plaintiff made the cease communication request as required in writing.

Johnson v. Equifax Risk Mgmt. Servs., 2004 WL 540459 (S.D.N.Y. Mar. 17, 2004). A consumer's written demand to the collector that it verify the debt pursuant to § 1692g and otherwise cease all other communication effectively invoked the § 1692c(c)'s cease communication remedy and did not improperly attempt to "have it both ways," and the collector's subsequent communications other than to provide verification, comprised of an additional dun and affidavits of forgery for the consumer to sign, violated § 1692c(c).

Micare v. Foster & Garbus, 132 F. Supp. 2d 77 (N.D.N.Y. 2001). In order to prevail on a claim pursuant to § 1692c(c), a consumer must establish that he notified the debt collector in writing that he refused to pay the debt or that communications should cease; notice to the creditor was insufficient.

Brown v. ACB Bus. Servs., 1996 WL 469588 (S.D.N.Y. Aug. 16, 1996). Disclosing the consumer's rights under state laws similar to the § 1692c(c) right to terminate dunning contacts was confusing in that it may have created the erroneous impression that similar rights did not exist under the FDCPA, but this confusing disclosure did not violate the FDCPA.

Ohio

Lamb v. M & M Assoc., 1998 WL 34288694 (S.D. Ohio Sept. 1, 1998). Debt collector's continued collection efforts after receipt of consumer's letter stating that she would not pay until she received the requested breakdown did not violate § 1692c(c) because refusal was conditional.

Oklahoma

Bynum v. Cavalry Portfolio Servs., L.L.C., 2006 WL 850935 (N.D. Okla. Mar. 30, 2006). Where the debt collector disputed receipt of the consumer's cease and desist the letter, a question of material fact existed preventing a determination of the case by summary judgment.

Pennsylvania

Conklin v. Purcell, Krug & Haller, 2007 WL 404047 (M.D. Pa. Feb. 1, 2007), *aff'd*, 282 Fed. Appx. 193 (3d Cir. 2008). Law firm did not violate the FDCPA by sending a notice of sheriff's sale to notify him of attempted judicial remedies, regardless of plaintiff's wishes not to receive communications from debt collectors.

Virginia

Vitullo v. Mancini, 684 F. Supp. 2d 747 (E.D. Va. 2010). A creditor's pursuit of legal remedies, such as non-judicial foreclosure, did not violate the cease communication rule of the FDCPA.

West Virginia

In re Carroll, 400 B.R. 497 (Bankr. N.D. W. Va. 2008). A collector's alleged imputed knowledge (from its creditor) of the consumer's representation by counsel and request to cease communication was insufficient to state a claim for violating §§ 1692c(a)(2) and 1692c(c), which require the collector to have actual knowledge.

K.2.2.6 Other

In re Chapman, 2002 U.S. App. LEXIS 22404 (7th Cir. Oct. 23, 2002). In a *pro se* debtor's adversary proceeding in a chapter 13 bankruptcy, settlement offers made by defendant's attorney during the course of a client-initiated lawsuit did not constitute "communications" as defined by the FDCPA.

Bailey v. Sec. Nat'l Servicing Corp., 154 F.3d 384 (7th Cir. 1998). A letter which did not demand payment but only informed the consumer of the current status of the account was not a "communication" to collect a debt.

Florida

Chalik v. Westport Recovery Corp., 677 F. Supp. 2d 1322 (S.D. Fla. 2009). The FDCPA does not guarantee a debt collector the right to leave answering machine messages; debt collectors have other methods to reach debtors including postal mail, in-person contact, and speaking directly by telephone.

Indiana

Frye v. Bowman, 193 F. Supp. 2d 1070 (S.D. Ind. 2002). The court surveyed split of authority about whether a summons was a communication to collect a debt, but did not decide because a "communication" was not essential to the alleged violations.

Spearman v. Tom Wood Pontiac-GMC, Inc., 2002 WL 31854892 (S.D. Ind. Nov. 4, 2002). Legal pleadings constituted a "communication" as defined by the FDCPA.

Michigan

Mabbitt v. Midwestern Audit Serv., Inc., 2008 WL 723507 (E.D. Mich. Mar. 17, 2008). Summary judgment for the defendant collector because the collection agency's letter only informed the consumer that her $961.45 balance on an outstanding utility bill owing from a previous residence had been transferred to her sister's current account at their new address. Because it did not contain an explicit request for payment the letter was not "in connection with the collection" of the debt.

New Jersey

Kaschak v. Raritan Valley Collection Agency, 1989 U.S. Dist. LEXIS 19103 (D.N.J. May 22, 1989). The collector's duties under § 1692c do not run to the debtor's executrix, but she can bring a claim under § 1692d if the collector abusively causes her harm by continuing to communicate with her.

New York

Missionary Sisters v. Dowling, 703 N.Y.S.2d 362 (N.Y. Civ. Ct. 1999). Petition for rent was not a "communication" subject to the provisions of the FDCPA.

Ohio

Knight v. Schulman, 102 F. Supp. 2d 867 (S.D. Ohio 1996), *aff'd*, 166 F.3d 1214 (6th Cir. 1998). Letter identifying amount of debt, enclosing copy of real estate lien, and notifying debtor of title search in preparation for foreclosure was a communication made to collect a debt, but letter acknowledging receipt of payment and notifying debtor of dismissal of suit and release of judgment was not.

K.2.3 Harassment or Abuse, 15 U.S.C. § 1692d

K.2.3.1 Abusive Language, 15 U.S.C. § 1692d(2)

Horkey v. J.V.D.B. & Assocs., Inc., 333 F.3d 769 (7th Cir. June 20, 2003). The collector's statement to the consumer's co-worker to tell the consumer "to stop being such a [expletive] bitch" violated § 1692d.

Jeter v. Credit Bureau, Inc., 760 F.2d 1168 (11th Cir. 1985). The threat that collector's threatened suit would cause "embarrassment, inconvenience, and further expense" did not violate § 1692d. The statement was not a slur or intimidating to a relatively susceptible consumer and thus was not prohibited by § 1692d(2).

Alabama

Shuler v. Ingram & Assocs., 2010 WL 1838626 (N.D. Ala. May 7, 2010). The court found no FDCPA violation where, as in *Jeter*, *Wright*, and *Thomas*, the debt collector's employees described to consumers the likely consequences of their failure to pay the alleged debt. The statements merely outlined the types of problems a consumer faces if the creditor files a lawsuit to collect on the debt: wage attachment, garnishment, and foreclosure.

California

Basinger-Lopez v. Tracy Paul & Assocs., 2009 WL 1948832 (N.D. Cal. July 6, 2009). Default judgment entered on well pleaded facts showing that the defendants engaged in a campaign of unlawful harassment, threats, misrepresentations, and other misconduct in violation of multiple FDCPA provisions: "Defendant made repeated threats against Plaintiff to sue her, made abusive accusations and threatened to embarrass her by disclosing the debt to her family, neighbors and employer. In addition, Defendant persisted in contacting her even after being expressly instructed not to do so, and failed to provide Plaintiff with any of the notices required by law."

Florida

Kelemen v. Professional Collection Sys., 2011 WL 31396 (M.D. Fla. Jan. 4, 2011). The collector's statement to the consumer to "pay your damn bills" was neither obscene nor profane and "does not rise to the level of offensiveness required by" applicable authority.

Georgia

Hart v. Universal Fid. L.P., 2007 WL 294241 (N.D. Ga. Jan. 26, 2007). Plaintiff's allegations that the defendant's employee, a debt collector collecting a consumer debt, "called plaintiff a 'thief', told plaintiff, among other things, that she had 'stolen,' told plaintiff to 'get a job' to pay the debt, stated a false amount that was being collected, demanded full payment within forty-eight hours, and stated that Universal Fidelity was 'getting ready to file a judgment' " stated a claim for relief for violating the FDCPA stated a claim for abusive, deceptive or unfair debt collection.

Illinois

Nelson-McGourty v. L & P Fin. Adjusters Inc., 2010 WL 3190711 (N.D. Ill. Aug. 12, 2010). Following a bench trial, the court credited the testimony of the collector and discredited the testimony of the consumer with a lengthy analysis of the consumer's choice of words and demeanor to conclude that the collector did not communicate abusively as she testified.

Unterreiner v. Stoneleigh Recovery Assocs., L.L.C., 2010 WL 2523257(N.D. Ill. June 17, 2010). Allegations that the collector "screamed" at the consumer, told her she owed "all kinds of money," and asked, "how could you go and max out a card like that?" did not rise to the level of harassment, oppression and abuse that courts have required to establish a § 1692d violation.

Bassett v. I.C. Sys., Inc., 2010 WL 2179175 (N.D. Ill. June 1, 2010). Allegations that the defendant called the consumer a liar, laughed at him, and accused him of trying to make excuses to get out of paying his debt failed to state a claim under § 1692d(2) since, although "this language is rude," it did not rise to the level of "obscene or profane language or language the natural consequence of which is to abuse the hearer or reader."

Chapman v. Ontra, Inc., 1997 WL 321681, RICO Bus. Disp. Guide 9319 (N.D. Ill. June 6, 1997). Letters were not actionable as abusive or harassing under § 1692d merely for lacking a validation notice or being in violation of other sections of the FDCPA.

Herbert v. Wexler & Wexler, 1995 WL 535107 (N.D. Ill. Sept. 5, 1995). The statement "You cannot even begin to know the trouble and expense that is about to come into your life over this matter as we intend to do whatever is necessary to compel you to pay this obligation" stated a cause of action for violation of § 1692d(2) as the unsophisticated consumer may construe the language as having the natural consequence to harass, oppress or abuse the debtor.

Hoffman v. Partners in Collections, Inc., 1993 WL 358158 (N.D. Ill. Sept. 14, 1993). Plaintiff was not required to identify in the complaint the particular abusive words alleged to violate § 1692d(2) in order to survive defendant's motion to dismiss.

Montana

McCollough v. Johnson, Rodenberg & Lauinger, 610 F. Supp. 2d 1247 (D. Mont. 2009). "The inescapable conclusion is that [the debt collection attorney] asked a *pro se* defendant to admit false information. He either did so knowingly, or neglected to review his minimal file before signing the requests. He served the requests with no ostensible reason to believe that the [consumer] defendant would understand their import. The requests for admission appear to be designed to conclusively establish each element of [the collection law firm's] case against [the consumer] and to use the power of the judicial process against a *pro se* defendant to collect a time-barred debt. This conduct is abusive, unfair and unconscionable."

New Jersey

Federal Trade Comm'n v. Check Enforcement, 2005 WL 1677480 (D.N.J. July 18, 2005), *aff'd on other grounds,* 502 F.3d 159 (3d Cir. 2007). Debt buyer used intimidating, demeaning and insulting language towards consumers in attempting to secure payment.

New Mexico

Spinarski v. Credit Bureau, Inc., Clearinghouse No. 51,963A (D.N.M. May 6, 1996). Collection agency was granted dismissal of consumers' claims that the § 1692e(11) debt collection notice was required on a Post-it note attached to a letter containing that notice and that § 1692d was violated by a description of creditor's remedies including incarceration for failure to appear at a debtor's exam.

New York

Arroyo v. Solomon & Solomon, P.C., 2001 U.S. Dist. LEXIS 21908 (E.D.N.Y. Nov. 7, 2001). Student loan collector's insulting statement, if proven, that consumer who couldn't afford $100 monthly payments should have thought about that when she entered a student loan, would violate § 1692d.

Ohio

Kondrat v. Morris, 692 N.E.2d 246 (Ohio Ct. App. 1997). Threats to take legal action did not in and of themselves constitute harassing or abusive behavior under the FDCPA.

Oregon

McNall v. Credit Bureau, 2008 WL 1881796 (D. Or. Apr. 18, 2008). Consumers stated a claim for relief for defendants' violation of § 1692d when their agents, while attempting to serve process, stood at the entrance of the consumers' home and "in a very loud voice repeatedly yelled plaintiff's name . . . 'come out of your house,' 'I have legal papers for you,' 'you need to come out and get these legal papers now,' 'you need to get your ass out here and open your gate now,' 'I'm not leaving until you come out and open this gate.' "

Clark v. Capital Credit & Collection Servs., Inc., 2004 WL 1305326 (D. Or. Jan. 23, 2004). Informing a consumer that a litigation remedy would be invoked was not a violation of § 1692d, since it included no language that was profane, obscene, or threatened physical harm or violence.

Pennsylvania

Frew v. Van Ru Credit Corp., 2006 WL 2261624 (E.D. Pa. Aug. 7, 2006). The assertion that the "Defendant allegedly likened Plaintiff to a 'scumbag' " stated a claim for using an abusive collection practice prohibited by the FDCPA.

Texas

Iruegas v. Diversified Adjustment Serv., Inc., 2010 WL 1171088 (W.D. Tex. Mar. 22, 2010). A complaint alleging that a debt collector was "extremely rude" and used profane and abusive language during telephone conversations with the consumer sufficiently stated a claim under § 1692d(2).

United States v. Cent. Adjustment Bureau, Inc., 667 F. Supp. 370 (N.D. Tex. 1986). Collector violated § 1692d(2) by using obscene and profane language.

West Virginia

Seals v. Gen. Revenue Corp., 2002 WL 32099632 (N.D. W. Va. Aug. 19, 2002), *aff'd per curiam*, 2002 WL 31856721 (4th Cir. 2002). *Pro se* suit generally alleging rude and insulting language did not state a cause of action for abuse under § 1692d since the words were not racial or ethnic slurs, and were not profane or obscene.

K.2.3.2 Repeated or Continuous Telephone Calls, 15 U.S.C. § 1692d(5)

Meadows v. Franklin Collection Serv., Inc., 2011 WL 479997 (11th Cir. Feb. 11, 2011). The court reversed the lower court's entry of summary judgment for the collector on the § 1692d(5) claim. The collector called the plaintiff's (the parent of a debtor) residence over 300 times in a two and a half year period, sometimes up to three times a day, using mostly robocalls but also personal calls. In addition, the collector sought contact information regarding the plaintiff's adult daughter and another debtor who previously had the same telephone number. The court found that a reasonable jury could conclude that the collector caused the phone to ring with the intent to annoy or harass her in view of the volume and frequency of the calls, the fact that the plaintiff had informed the collector that she did not owe the debts, did not wish to share her daughter's contact information, asked that the calls stop, and stated the calls caused her emotional distress. The court found that the fact that telephone calls were not answered was no defense to the § 1692d(5) claim, since that provision specifically prohibits merely "causing a telephone to ring" with the requisite intent: "The statute itself recognizes that answering the phone is not necessary for there to be harassment. This makes good sense because a ringing telephone, even if screened and unanswered, can be harassing, especially if it rings on a consistent basis over a prolonged period of time and concerns debts that one does not owe."

Clark v. Capital Credit & Collection Servs., Inc., 460 F.3d 1162 (9th Cir. 2006). The repeated requests to pay an allegedly mistaken medical bill stated a claim for harassment and abuse.

Alabama

Shuler v. Ingram & Assocs., 2010 WL 1838626 (N.D. Ala. May 7, 2010). Where the debt collector made telephone calls on five occasions over a seventeen-day period, never called repeatedly at the same location, and only made contact with consumers once (and for less than five minutes), the court found that, collectively, these five telephone call attempts did not violate § 1692d(5), as they were not abusive, annoying, or harassing.

Arizona

Grismore v. United Recovery Sys., L.P., 2006 WL 2246359 (D. Ariz. Aug. 3, 2006). Where the evidence showed that the defendant debt collector telephoned the plaintiff over a several month period nineteen times resulting in only three discussions, the court held that the collector placed the calls only to resolve the debt and not with intent to annoy, abuse, or harass as required to establish a violation of § 1692d(5).

California

Rucker v. Nationwide Credit, Inc., 2011 WL 25300 (E.D. Cal. Jan. 5, 2011). Where the consumer alleged receipt of approximately eighty phone calls from the debt collector in 2009, the evidence was sufficient to create genuine issues of material fact on the issues of whether the defendant's telephone calls violated § 1692d(5).

Clemente v. IC Sys., Inc., 2010 WL 3855522 (E.D. Cal. Sept. 29, 2010). Finding that the plaintiff did no more than plead the elements of the statute, the court dismissed the § 1692d(5) claim due to the plaintiff's failure to plead the time period during which the allegedly repeated, continuous phone calls occurred, the dates of any of the calls, or any approximation of the number of calls.

Arteaga v. Asset Acceptance, L.L.C., 2010 WL 3310259 (E.D. Cal. Aug. 23, 2010). Summary judgment was granted to the collector on the § 1692d claims of telephone harassment since the evidence showed only a series of collection calls that mostly resulted in no answer with no message left and otherwise presented no egregious conduct.

Krapf v. Nationwide Credit Inc., 2010 WL 2025323 (C.D. Cal. May 21, 2010). The fact that the consumer could not specifically remember the dates when the calling alleged to violate the FDCPA started or stopped does not warrant summary judgment for the debt collector, as the consumer presented enough evidence to raise a triable issue of fact.

Robinson v. Managed Accounts Receivables Corp., 654 F. Supp. 2d 1051 (C.D. Cal. 2009). Where the complaint specifically alleged that the defendants threatened to sue the consumer for writing a dishonored check and refusing to provide verification of its claim, the complaint stated a claim for violation of § 1692d.

Hartung v. J.D. Byrider, Inc., 2009 WL 1876690 (E.D. Cal. June 26, 2009). Default judgment recommended for extreme cell phone and text messaging harassment in the amount of $27,000.

Gorman v. Wolpoff & Abramson, L.L.P., 435 F. Supp. 2d 1004 (N.D. Cal. 2006), *aff'd in part, rev'd in part on other grounds*, 584 F.3d 1147 (9th Cir. 2009). Establishing a violation of § 1692d(5)'s prohibition against repeated telephone calls requires evidence of the defendant's intent to annoy, abuse, or harass, and the absence of any such evidence rendered the consumer's mere proof of the collector's numerous telephone calls in support of this violation inadequate.

Hosseinzadeh v. M.R.S. Assocs., Inc., 387 F. Supp. 2d 1104 (C.D. Cal. 2005). The content and context of a series of six telephone messages from the debt collector left on the consumer's answering machine made the issue of whether the messages were harassing, unfair, or deceptive a question of fact for the jury.

Joseph v. J.J. Mac Intyre Cos., L.L.C., 238 F. Supp. 2d 1158 (N.D. Cal. 2002). Collection agency's motion for summary judgment on claim that it made repeated phone calls that were therefore harassing denied where evidence showed over 200 calls during a nineteen month period, including calls following the consumer's express request that all calls cease and calls made immediately after the consumer hung up on the collector. Whether a collector's series of telephone calls constitute illegal harassment depends on both the volume and pattern of the calls. Defendant had no defense to the evidence that its repeated phone calls were harassing based on the fact that it was collecting multiple debts from the consumer.

Connecticut

Chiverton v. Fed. Fin. Group, Inc., 399 F. Supp. 2d 96 (D. Conn. 2005). The debt buyer violated § 1692d(5) by repeatedly calling to collect a paid debt after the consumer had hung up the phone.

Florida

Kelemen v. Professional Collection Sys., 2011 WL 31396 (M.D. Fla. Jan. 4, 2011). The court denied summary judgment to the defendant on the § 1692d(5) claim because the "record contains conflicting information as to the frequency and pattern of calls made."

Waite v. Financial Recovery Servs., Inc., 2010 WL 5209350 (M.D. Fla. Dec. 16, 2010). Although the number of telephone calls (fifty-six) over a period of two months appeared somewhat high, they were unaccompanied by any other egregious conduct to evince an intent to harass, annoy, or abuse, and therefore did not violate § 1692d(5). The number of calls tapered off over the following seven months, the defendant placed no more than four calls to the plaintiff within a single day, and even this conduct occurred only three times spanning a nine-month period.

Clarke v. Weltman, Wienberg & Reis, Co., L.P.A., 2010 WL 2803975 (S.D. Fla. July 15, 2010). A complaint alleging that over a two and a half month period twenty-six messages were left on the consumer's cell phone was sufficient under *Twombly* and *Iqbal* to constitute a violation of § 1692d even if they also constituted a violation of the TCPA. "Each element of the particular statutory claim must be met, regardless of whether the same facts support multiple claims."

Tucker v. CBE Group, Inc., 2010 WL 1849034 (M.D. Fla. May 5, 2010). The court found that as a matter of law, fifty-seven calls with an intent to reach the consumer's daughter, where the defendant left only a total of six messages, made no more than seven calls in a single day, and did not call back the same day after leaving a message, and where no one talked to the defendant or told them to stop calling, did not violate § 1692d(5). Violations of §§ 1692b or 1692c(b) should have been but were not alleged. Consumer and his attorney sanctioned.

Casey v. I.C. Sys., Inc., 2010 WL 415310 (M.D. Fla. Jan. 29, 2010). Genuine issues of fact remained as to the number of times the debt collector caused the consumer's telephone to ring and whether that was done repeatedly or continuously with the intent to annoy, abuse, or harass, or that the caller failed to identify the collector in violation of § 1692d(5).

Brandt v. I.C. Sys., Inc., 2010 WL 582051 (M.D. Fla. Feb. 19,

2010). Defendant's motion for summary judgment denied: "Once Plaintiff allegedly told Defendant to stop calling him, that he had already paid the alleged debt, and that their calls were bothering him, each of the 101 subsequent phone calls to Plaintiff constituted a violation of 15 U.S.C. § 1692d." "Intent may be inferred by evidence that the debt collector continued to call the debtor after the debtor had asked not to be called and had repeatedly refused to pay the alleged debt, or during a time of day which the debtor had informed the debt collector was inconvenient."

Segal v. Nat'l Action Fin. Servs., Inc., 2006 WL 449176 (M.D. Fla. Feb. 22, 2006). The court denied partial summary judgment on the issue of liability for violating § 1692d where there remained outstanding questions of fact as to the frequency and purpose of the multiple, allegedly harassing phone calls made by the debt collector to the consumer. The court granted summary judgment to the defendant debt collector where there was an absence of evidence in support of the claim that this defendant was the source of allegedly abusive and deceptive phone calls to the debtor's spouse.

Illinois

Bassett v. I.C. Sys., Inc., 2010 WL 2179175 (N.D. Ill. June 1, 2010). The defendant's motion for summary judgment was denied since a reasonable jury could find that calling the consumer thirty-one times over twelve days violated the § 1692d(5) prohibition against a debt collector "causing a telephone to ring continuously with the intent to annoy, abuse, or harass." The court found that the defendant's argument that because the consumer turned off his telephone ringer by blocking his incoming calls the telephone did not "ring repeatedly and continuously" was not based on any legal authority and was without merit, especially because Bassett testified that he felt abused by receiving these missed calls.

Majeski v. I.C. Sys., Inc., 2010 WL 145861 (N.D. Ill. Jan. 8, 2010). Summary judgment denied despite "The astonishingly high frequency of calls placed by debt collector during February and May could easily be interpreted as indicative of debt collector's intent to harass by a reasonable juror." However, the court could not decide the issue as a matter of law, given addition facts, such as that consumer screened the calls.

Wisniewski v. Asset Acceptance Capital Corp., 2009 WL 212155 (N.D. Ill. Jan. 29, 2009). Stated a claim under the anti-harassment provisions, § 1692d(5) for repeated rude, threatening phone calls.

Bennett v. Arrow Fin. Servs., L.L.C., 2004 WL 830440 (N.D. Ill. Apr. 14, 2004). Judgment for collector after trial. Telephone calls spaced a couple of weeks apart on a fourteen-year-old debt did not constitute harassment under § 1692d(5).

Kansas

Udell v. Kansas Counselors, Inc., 313 F. Supp. 2d 1135 (D. Kan. 2004). The debt collector's placement of four automated telephone calls to the consumer over a seven-day period without leaving a message did not constitute harassment under § 1692d.

Maryland

Adam v. Wells Fargo Bank, N.A., 2010 WL 3001160 (D. Md. July 28, 2010). The court declined to dismiss the *pro se* consumer's

FDCPA complaint where he specifically alleged facts to show that the defendant engaged in harassment by leaving "dozens of recorded phone calls every week."

Michigan

Pugliese v. Professional Recovery Serv., Inc., 2010 WL 2632562 (E.D. Mich. June 29, 2010). Where over 300 calls were made with only ten contacts because the consumers did not answer the phone or return calls, there was no evidence to demonstrate that the defendants acted intentionally to annoy, harass, or abuse the consumers. "Debt collectors do not necessarily engage in harassment by placing one or two unanswered calls a day in an unsuccessful effort to reach the debtor, if this effort is unaccompanied by any oppressive conduct (threatening messages)."

Minnesota

Venes v. Prof'l Serv. Bureau, Inc., 353 N.W.2d 671 (Minn. Ct. App. 1984). The jury found violations of § 1692d where the collector had called the consumer back immediately after the consumer hung up and had refused to reveal his identity beyond giving the name "Mr. West."

Mississippi

Deas v. American Recovery Sys., Inc., 2009 WL 3514560 (N.D. Miss. Oct. 29, 2009). Defendant violated § 1692d(5) by placing dozens of telephone calls to the plaintiff's home, purportedly attempting to locate a third party debtor, after plaintiff informed defendant that the debtor did not live at his residence and requested defendant to cease calling.

Nevada

Kuhn v. Account Control Tech., Inc., 865 F. Supp. 1443 (D. Nev. 1994). Six calls placed to the consumer's employer within twenty-four minutes violated § 1692d(5).

New Jersey

Bey v. Daimler Chrysler Servs., L.L.C., 2006 WL 361385 (D.N.J. Feb. 15, 2006). Continuous hang-up phone calls did not violate the FDCPA absent allegation of intent to harass.

New York

Fajer v. Kaufman, Burns & Assocs., 2011 WL 334311 (W.D.N.Y. Jan. 28, 2011). In this default action, the court found a violation of § 1692d(5) based on the fact that the plaintiff made a "conclusory allegation" that the defendant called her "constantly and continuously" without alleging the number of calls that she in fact received. "It is clear, however, that Kaufman called her more than once, thereby establishing a violation of this section."

Atchoo v. Redline Recovery Servs., L.L.C., 2010 WL 1416738 (W.D.N.Y. Apr. 5, 2010). The court found that it was not necessary in a claim under § 1692d(5) for the consumer to allege that the defendant made a certain number of phone calls. Also, there is no requirement under this section that the consumer answer the phone. Instead, it is enough that the defendant merely causes the phone to ring continuously with the intent to annoy, abuse, or harass.

Harrison v. Fed. Pac. Credit Co., L.L.C., 2006 WL 276605 (W.D.N.Y. Feb. 3, 2006). Claim stated for violation of § 1692d(5) on the basis that for approximately fifteen months defendant placed weekly telephone calls to plaintiff in an attempt to collect a debt which plaintiff disputed.

North Dakota

Bingham v. Collection Bureau, Inc., 505 F. Supp. 864 (D.N.D. 1981). The court rejected the consumer's claims that the number, pattern and timing of telephone calls were harassing.

Ohio

Gross v. Nationwide Credit, Inc., 2011 WL 379167 (S.D. Ohio Feb. 2, 2011). The plaintiff stated a claim under §§ 1692d and 1692d(5) by alleging that the defendant placed telephone calls to him "multiple times a day over the course of nearly two months" but, when he returned those calls "to determine the nature of the debt he [was] put on hold and not able to speak with a live person." The court stated: "Defendant's argument that being put on hold is a mere inconvenience is an argument better made at summary judgment or trial as greater factual detail will be critical to that determination. Certainly, creating obstacles for the consumer, such as routinely putting consumers on hold for long periods of time and denying them the opportunity to determine the underlying cause of the phone calls demanding payment, is a tactic debt collectors have used in the past, and it is just that type of conduct that the Act was meant to deter."

Oregon

Blue v. Bronson & Migliaccio, 2010 WL 4641666 (D. Or. Nov. 4, 2010). Telephone calls made outside the statute of limitations period were time barred, but they were still relevant in determining whether the calls within the limitations period were part of an abusive or harassing pattern.

Clark v. Quick Collect, Inc., 2005 WL 1586862 (D. Or. June 30, 2005). The court denied summary judgment to defendant where it had called multiple times without leaving messages. "Whether there is actionable harassment or annoyance turns on the volume of calls made and on the pattern of calls" within § 1692d.

Pennsylvania

Shand-Pistilli v. Professional Account Servs., Inc., 2010 WL 2978029 (E.D. Pa. July 26, 2010). Where the consumer's complaint included allegations that she received "continuous calls" to her home from a telephone number owned by defendant and that that the debt collector continued to call her after being asked to cease communication, she stated a plausible claim for violation of § 1692d(5).

Vincent v. E.C.R. Servs., 2007 U.S. Dist. LEXIS 722 (E.D. Pa. Jan. 8, 2007). Plaintiff stated a claim for violating the FDCPA by alleging that the defendant repossession company engaged in repeated phone calls and threats in order to force payment of the debt.

South Carolina

Valentine v. Brock & Scott, P.L.L.C., 2010 WL 1727681 (D.S.C.

Apr. 26, 2010). The court denied the defendant's motion to dismiss: "Consumer alleges that Defendant called Consumer 11 times over a period of 19 days, with two of those calls occurring on the same day."

Tennessee

Brown v. Hosto & Buchan, P.L.L.C., 2010 WL 4352932 (W.D. Tenn. Nov. 2, 2010). The court denied the motion to dismiss where the frequency of the debt collector's calls to the plaintiff's telephone and the manner in which the collector called the plaintiff's cellular telephone using an automatic telephone dialing system could plausibly cause an unsophisticated consumer to feel harassed, oppressed, or abused.

Texas

McVey v. Bay Area Credit Serv., 2010 WL 2927388 (N.D. Tex. July 26, 2010). A complaint alleging that the defendant often called the consumer multiple times per week seeking payment of an alleged debt failed to state a claim for relief that was plausible on its face. "Consumer alleges no facts describing the types of conduct found by other courts to violate the FDCPA, nor does he allege conduct that would appear to have occurred "repeatedly" or "continuously.""

Virginia

Katz v. Capital One, 2010 WL 1039850 (E.D. Va. Mar. 18, 2010). The court found that nothing in the record indicated that phone calls made by the debt collector (no more than two per day) were intended to be annoying, abusive, or harassing. Instead, the record showed that the debt collector, believing consumer's debt to be valid, attempted to take steps to collect that debt, and thus there was no violation of § 1692d.

K.2.3.3 Meaningful Telephone Identification, 15 U.S.C. § 1692d(6)

Edwards v. Niagara Credit Solutions, Inc., 584 F.3d 1350 (11th Cir. 2009). Telephone answering machine messages that asked the consumer to return calls from the defendant debt collector and that did not identify the caller as an employee or agent of a debt collection agency or state that the purpose was an attempt to collect a debt violated § 1692d(6)'s prohibition against placing telephone calls without making any meaningful disclosure of the identity of the caller.

Alabama

Sparks v. Phillips & Cohen Assocs., Ltd., 641 F. Supp. 2d 1234 (S.D. Ala. 2008). "A debt collector's failure to identify herself as such in communications relating to the collection of a debt [is] a per se violation" of § 1692d(6).

Arizona

Garo v. Global Credit & Collection Corp., 2011 WL 251450 (D. Ariz. Jan. 26, 2011). "The fact that a debt collector may leave a message, in which the debt collector is otherwise unidentified, to contact the consumer at a phone number that had previously been contained in the debt collector's correspondence with the consumer is insufficient to identify the subsequent communication as being from a debt collector as is required by § 1692e(11). Further, such a request does not constitute 'meaningful disclosure of the caller's identity' as is required by 15 U.S.C. § 1692d(6)."

California

Rucker v. Nationwide Credit, Inc., 2011 WL 25300 (E.D. Cal. Jan. 5, 2011). The debt collector's failure to leave a message on the consumer's answering machine did not by itself violate § 1692d(6).

Krapf v. Nationwide Credit Inc., 2010 WL 2025323 (C.D. Cal. May 21, 2010). Where the consumer could not recall whether the debt collectors identified themselves in their calls to him, summary judgment was granted to the debt collector on the §§ 1692d(6), 1692e(10), and (11) claims.

Koby v. ARS Nat'l Servs., Inc., 2010 WL 1438763 (S.D. Cal. Mar. 29, 2010). Within the definition of "meaningful disclosure" adopted by the Eastern and Central Districts of California, in each situation where defendant failed to disclose that the caller was a debt collector and that the purpose of the call was to collect a debt, defendant failed to meet the standards prescribed by § 1692d(6) of the FDCPA.

Puttner v. Debt Consultants of Am., 2009 WL 1604570 (S.D. Cal. June 4, 2009). The complaint stated a claim for relief by alleging that the defendant's collectors called the consumer without providing meaningful disclosure of their identity.

Costa v. Nat'l Action Fin. Servs., 634 F. Supp. 2d 1069 (E.D. Cal. 2007). Meaningful disclosure pursuant to § 1692d(6) requires that the caller state his or her name and capacity and disclose enough information so as not to mislead the recipient of the telephone message.

Hosseinzadeh v. M.R.S. Assocs., Inc., 387 F. Supp. 2d 1104 (C.D. Cal. 2005). The collection agency violated § 1692d(6) when its employees failed to disclose defendant's identity and the nature of defendant's business in the messages left on consumer's answering machine.

Joseph v. J.J. Mac Intyre Cos., L.L.C., 238 F. Supp. 2d 1158 (N.D. Cal. 2002). Collection agency's motion for summary judgment denied where the evidence showed that its telephone collector failed to provide meaningful disclosure of the caller's identity by using a desk alias and failing to identify either her employer or the underlying creditor.

Florida

Beeders v. Gulf Coast Collection Bureau, Inc., 2010 WL 2696404 (M.D. Fla. July 6, 2010). The question of whether use of the name "Gulf Coast Collection Bureau" was adequate to inform the least sophisticated consumer that Gulf Coast was a debt collector calling in regard to debt collection activities was a material fact for the jury to determine.

Casey v. I.C. Sys., Inc., 2010 WL 415310 (M.D. Fla. Jan. 29, 2010). Genuine issues of fact remained as to the number of times the debt collector caused the consumer's telephone to ring and whether that was done repeatedly or continuously with the intent to annoy, abuse, or harass, or that the caller failed to identify the collector in violation of § 1692d(6).

Valencia v. Affiliated Group, Inc., 2008 WL 4372895 (S.D. Fla. Sept. 24, 2008). The defendant did not provide meaningful disclosure of the caller's identity as required by § 1692d(6) when its collector left a voicemail with a call back number that only identified the caller's first name and the company that employed her, because "[c]ourts construing Section 1692d(6) have uniformly held that it requires a debt collector to disclose the caller's name, the debt collection company's name, and the nature of the debt collector's business."

Arslan v. Florida First Fed. Group, 1995 WL 731175 (M.D. Fla. Oct. 5, 1995). Using a set of aliases when telephoning violated § 1692d(6) by failing to make meaningful disclosure of the caller's identity.

Georgia

Gilmore v. Account Mgmt., Inc., 2009 WL 2848278 (N.D. Ga. Apr. 27, 2009). Court accepted as true plaintiff's allegations that defendant left a series of prerecorded messages for plaintiff which did not state the name of the company placing calls or that the communications were from a debt collector attempting to collect a debt and concluded that these communications violated § 1692d(6).

Wright v. Credit Bureau, Inc., 548 F. Supp. 591 (N.D. Ga. 1982), *modified on other grounds*, 555 F. Supp. 1005 (N.D. Ga. 1983). The use of an alias or desk name by a collector who accurately disclosed her employer's name and the nature of the business does not violate § 1692d(6) since the natural consequence of such conduct is not to harass, oppress or abuse the consumer.

Illinois

Hutton v. C.B. Accounts, Inc., 2010 WL 3021904 (C.D. Ill. Aug. 3, 2010). Where the caller did not identify her employer or mention that she was calling for debt-collection purposes, leaving a first name and telephone number did not meaningfully identify the debt collector.

Maryland

Sayyed v. Wolpoff & Abramson, L.L.P., 2010 WL 3313888 (D. Md. Aug. 20, 2010). Summary judgment was granted to the collector on the § 1692e(11) claim since the subject subsequent communication clearly identified the defendant as a debt collector.

Minnesota

Mark v. J.C. Christensen & Assocs., Inc., 2009 WL 2407700 (D. Minn. Aug. 4, 2009). A telephone message that merely states the name of the person calling and a telephone number to return the call does not provide meaningful disclosure that the call was from a debt collector. The FDCPA's requirement that the debt collector identify itself and inform that the communication is from a debt collector does not violate the First Amendment of the U.S. Constitution. When a debt collector calls and leaves a message on a consumer's phone, it is not required that the call and message also be considered harassing, oppressing, or abusive in order to be a violation of § 1692d(6).

Baker v. Allstate Fin. Servs, Inc., 554 F. Supp. 2d 945 (D. Minn. 2008). Complaint stated a cause of action by alleging that voicemails violated § 1692d by not disclosing the caller's name, the debt collection company's name, and the nature of the debt collector's business.

Knoll v. Intellirisk Mgmt., 2006 WL 2974190 (D. Minn. Oct. 16, 2006). Denied debt collector's motion to dismiss class action where debt collector used the false name, Jennifer Smith, as the Caller ID finding a claim was stated under §§ 1692d, 1692e, 1692f.

Venes v. Prof'l Serv. Bureau, Inc., 353 N.W.2d 671 (Minn. Ct. App. 1984). The jury found violations of § 1692d where the collector had called the consumer back immediately after the consumer hung up and had refused to reveal his identity beyond giving the name "Mr. West."

New Jersey

Ford v. Consigned Debts & Collections, Inc., 2010 WL 5392643 (D.N.J. Dec. 21, 2010). In this default judgment matter, the court found that a defendant who threatened to sue the plaintiff if the debt was not paid immediately violated § 1692e(5).

Krug v. Focus Receivables Mgmt, L.L.C., 2010 WL 1875533 (D.N.J. May 11, 2010). Consumer's allegations that the debt collector failed to identify itself in telephone messages pursuant to § 1692d(6) or state that the call was from a debt collector pursuant to § 1692e(11) was sufficient to withstand the defendant's motion to dismiss.

New York

Leyse v. Corporate Collection Servs., Inc., 2006 WL 2708451 (S.D.N.Y. Sept. 18, 2006). The identity of the caller was not meaningfully disclosed in prerecorded messages that identified the caller only as CCS (where there had been no previous dealings with CCS) in violation of § 1692d(6).

North Dakota

Bingham v. Collection Bureau, Inc., 505 F. Supp. 864 (D.N.D. 1981). The use of aliases by collection employees was proscribed harassment but was excused as a bona fide error.

Ohio

Pache Mgmt. Co. v. Lusk, 1997 WL 254096 (Ohio Ct. App. May 15, 1997). Use of desk alias did not violate FDCPA.

Kleczy v. First Fed. Credit Control, Inc., 486 N.E.2d 204 (Ohio Ct. App. 1984). Use of a fictitious desk name by a collection employee does not violate the FDCPA.

K.2.3.4 General Standard: Harass, Oppress, or Abuse, 15 U.S.C. § 1692d

K.2.3.4.1 General standard violated

Meadows v. Franklin Collection Serv., Inc., 2011 WL 479997 (11th Cir. Feb. 11, 2011). The court reversed the lower court's entry of summary judgment for the collector on the § 1692d(5) claim. The collector called the plaintiff's (the parent of a debtor) residence over 300 times in a two and a half year period, sometimes up to three times a day, using mostly robocalls but also personal calls. In addition, the collector sought contact information regarding the plaintiff's adult daughter and another debtor who previously had the same telephone number. The court found that a reasonable jury could conclude that the collector caused the phone to ring with the intent to annoy or harass her in view of the volume and frequency of the calls, the fact that the plaintiff had informed the collector that she did not owe the debts, did not wish to share her daughter's contact information, asked that the calls stop, and stated the calls caused her emotional distress.

Evory v. Nat'l Action Fin. Servs., Inc., 505 F.3d 769 (7th Cir. 2007). Although a violation of state law is not in itself a violation of the federal Act, *Beler v. Blatt, Hasenmiller, Leibsker & Moore, L.L.C.*, 480 F.3d 470, 473–474 (7th Cir. 2007), a threat to impose a penalty that the threatener knows is improper because unlawful is a good candidate for a violation of §§ 1692d and 1692e.

Alabama

Winberry v. United Collection Bureau, Inc., 697 F. Supp. 2d 1279 (M.D. Ala. 2010). The court denied the debt collector's motion for summary judgment on the consumers' § 1692d claim. It was undisputed that the collector made at least thirty-three calls during a one-month period; that he said he would call the husband-consumer's employer, neighbors, family, and daughter; that he threatened the husband with garnishment; that he persisted in calling the consumer-wife after being informed that she had health ailments and was not liable for the debt. He sometimes did not identify himself as a debt collector and sometimes threatened legal action not intended to be taken.

Sparks v. Phillips & Cohen Assocs., Ltd., 641 F. Supp. 2d 1234 (S.D. Ala. 2008). Rejecting the defendant's argument that it was entitled to summary judgment because the evidence showed at most "rude and obnoxious" conduct that is legally insufficient to be "harassing, oppressive or abusive," the court concluded that the a jury could find § 1692d violations if it believed the plaintiffs' versions of the disputed facts.

McGrady v. Nissan Motor Acceptance Corp., 40 F. Supp. 2d 1323 (M.D. Ala. 1998). The court denied Nationwide Credit's motion to dismiss, finding that its actions came within the general prohibition of § 1692d (numerous phone calls, including to plaintiff's mother and the financial officer of plaintiff's employer).

Bice v. Merchants Adjustment Serv., Clearinghouse No. 41,265 (S.D. Ala. 1985). The absence of obscenity is no basis to dismiss a claim under § 1692d since it is the province of the jury to determine if letters had the natural consequence of harassing, oppressing or abusing a susceptible consumer.

California

Krapf v. Nationwide Credit Inc., 2010 WL 2025323 (C.D. Cal. May 21, 2010). Where the consumer's testimony, the defendant's records and screen shots of the consumer's phone showed that the defendant called the consumer an average of six times per day for over a month, until the suit was filed, and the screen shots also showed that the defendant would sometimes call twice in a matter of minutes, the court could not say, as a matter of law, that this did not evidence an intent to harass, abuse, or annoy the consumer. Accordingly, the defendant's motion for summary judgment on this point was denied.

Robinson v. Managed Accounts Receivables Corp., 654 F. Supp. 2d 1051 (C.D. Cal. 2009). The defendant's motion to dismiss was defeated, as the complaint stated a plausible claim for violation of § 1692d harassment in connection with the collection of a debt when the plaintiff alleged that she was told by the defendant that she had written a bad check, that she was about to be sued to collect on the debt, and also that she could not be sent a written validation of the debt, which the court inferred from the complaint to be untrue.

Puttner v. Debt Consultants of Am., 2009 WL 1604570 (S.D. Cal. June 4, 2009). The complaint stated a claim for relief by alleging that the defendant's collectors called the consumer's parents without stating that they were confirming or correcting location information, disclosed the existence of the son's debt, and called the parents repeatedly so as to constitute harassment.

Riley v. Giguiere, 2008 WL 436943 (E.D. Cal. Feb. 14, 2008). Former tenant stated a claim under §§ 1692d, 1692e, and 1692f in alleging that the eviction lawyer improperly proceeded to obtain judgment from him despite reason to know he had vacated the apartment many years prior to the eviction.

Hosseinzadeh v. M.R.S. Assocs., Inc., 387 F. Supp. 2d 1104 (C.D. Cal. 2005). The debt collectors, who left messages on the consumer's answering machine, violated § 1692d(6), which requires debt collectors to meaningfully disclose the caller's identity when placing a telephone call, since they failed to identify their employer (they provided their names and a telephone number) and omitted any mention of the purpose or nature of the call or the capacity in which they were calling.

Connecticut

Cirkot v. Diversified Fin. Sys., 839 F. Supp. 941 (D. Conn. 1993). Collector's handwritten note warning: "My special agents will remain in your area to *collect. Believe me*" was a threatening, harassing, and abusive attempt to collect the debt in violation of § 1692d.

Kizer v. Am. Credit & Collection, Clearinghouse No. 45,928 (D. Conn. 1991). The thinly veiled threat that the consumer would not receive prompt medical attention if he did not immediately pay his debt was deceptive violating § 1692e and abusive violating § 1692d.

Florida

Brandt v. I.C. Sys., Inc., 2010 WL 582051 (M.D. Fla. Feb. 19, 2010). The defendant's motion for summary judgment was denied: "Once Consumer allegedly told Defendant to stop calling him, that he had already paid the alleged debt, and that their calls were bothering him, each of the 101 subsequent phone calls to Consumer constituted a violation of § 1692d." "Intent may be inferred by evidence that the debt collector continued to call the debtor after the debtor had asked not to be called and had repeatedly refused to pay the alleged debt, and called during a time of day which the debtor had informed the debt collector was inconvenient."

Belin v. Litton Loan Serv., L.P., 2006 WL 1992410 (M.D. Fla. July 14, 2006). Allegations that a collector telephoned a third party multiple times, was rude, and then abruptly hung up the phone stated a claim for harassment or abuse prohibited by § 1692d.

Merchant v. Nationwide Collection Serv., Inc., Clearinghouse No. 43,382 (Fla. Cir. Ct. 1988). Two plaintiffs each awarded $2500 actual damages, $1000 statutory damages and $50,000 punitive damages for late night phone calls, threats of arrest, and a third-party contact.

Georgia

Florence v. Nat'l Sys., 1983 U.S. Dist. LEXIS 20344 (N.D. Ga. Oct. 14, 1983). The collector violated § 1692d by demanding payment with increasingly harsh threats of harm to consumer's credit and business reputation.

Idaho

Mangum v. Bonneville Billing & Collections, Inc., 2010 WL 672744 (D. Idaho Feb. 20, 2010). Cross motions for summary judgment on the alleged §§ 1692c(b) and 1692d violations were denied where a fact question remained as to whether the defendant's communication in response to an inquiry from the local police department—the consumer's employer—was made in connection with the collection of the consumer's bad check debts or was instead part of a criminal investigation.

Illinois

Washington v. North Star Capital Acquisition, L.L.C., 2008 WL 4280139 (N.D. Ill. Sept. 15, 2008). The consumer's allegation that the defendant filing a collection law suit in a state court despite the availability of a state law defense violated § 1692e of the FDCPA was dismissed for failure to state a claim. Filing a collection suit in itself "does not have the natural consequence of harassing, abusing or oppressing the debtor" and the complaint also did not involve false representations as required by § 1692e.

Rutyna v. Collection Accounts Terminal, Inc., 478 F. Supp. 980 (N.D. Ill. 1979). This opinion finds harassment and deceptive and unfair practices. A letter using an intimidating tone, threatening an investigation and embarrassment clearly violates § 1692d.

Minnesota

Neill v. Bullseye Collection Agency, Inc., 2009 WL 1386155 (D. Minn. May 14, 2009). The consumer's allegations that the collector's printing at the top of its duns the acronym "WWJD," which stands for the phrase "what would Jesus do?", "has the effect of invoking shame or guilt in alleged debtors and portrays the debtor as a sinner who is going to hell" stated a claim for engaging in conduct that is harassing, oppressive, or abusive in violation of § 1692d and unfair or unconscionable in violation of § 1692f.

Montana

McCollough v. Johnson, Rodenberg & Lauinger, 610 F. Supp. 2d 1247 (D. Mont. 2009). A debt collector violated the FDCPA by using the courts to attempt to collect a time-barred debt. While the debt collector's use of discovery in a collection action is not a per se violation of the FDCPA, here the request for admission to admit that a payment was made was served when the debt collector's records showed the payment was not made. The use of the judicial process against a *pro se* defendant, in order to avoid a statute of limitations defense, collecting on a time-barred debt which was an abusive, unfair, and unconscionable practice in violation of the FDCPA. The debt collector's failure to move to set aside the underlying state court default judgment after a summary judgment ruling that the underlying state court action violated the FDCPA because it was time barred constituted an additional FDCPA violation.

Nevada

Karony v. Dollar Loan Ctr., L.L.C., 2010 WL 5186065 (D. Nev. Dec. 15, 2010). Allegations that the collector pursued the plaintiff through litigation and credit reporting to pay a separate debt that was incurred by his wife and for which he was not responsible stated a claim under §§ 1692d and 1692f. The court rejected the defendants' argument that the debt at issue was a "community debt," since that was a factual issue not yet resolved by a trier of fact.

Pittman v. J.J. Mac Intyre Co., 969 F. Supp. 609 (D. Nev. 1997). The consumer stated a claim for violation of §§ 1692c(a)(1) and 1692d by alleging that notwithstanding warnings on prior occasions that she could not talk at work, the collection agency called the consumer at her place of employment to collect on the debt.

New Jersey

Kaschak v. Raritan Valley Collection Agency, 1989 U.S. Dist. LEXIS 19103 (D.N.J. May 22, 1989). Consumer's executrix can sue for abuse or harassment that harms her even though it is directed at consumer, since collector's duties under § 1692d run to "any person."

New York

Henneberger v. Cohen & Slamowitz, L.L.P., 2010 WL 1405578 (W.D.N.Y. Mar. 31, 2010). The court found there was a genuine issue of material fact as to whether defendant's employees threatened to seize Social Security and pension funds that were exempt from collection.

Krapf v. Collectors Training Inst. of Ill., Inc., 2010 WL 584020 (W.D.N.Y. Feb. 16, 2010). The consumer's allegation that the defendant called her before 8:00 a.m. sufficiently alleged claims under §§ 1692c(a)(1) and 1692d. Because the defendant's contact with the consumer's employer "did not involve an inquiry into Consumer's location information, but rather, revealed that Consumer had a 'business matter,' " and because the defendant "later placed another call to Consumer's employer in an attempt to use Consumer's employer as a means of inducing Consumer to return Defendant's call," "Defendant contacted a third party in a manner not authorized by § 1692b, [and therefore] Consumer sufficiently states claims under §§ 1692b, 1692c(b), and 1692d." The complaint stated a claim that the debt collector violated §§ 1692d and 1692e by leaving telephone messages for the consumer falsely stating that her Social Security number was under investigation. The court found that the defendant's suggestion that the consumer's Social Security number was under investigation, or that there was an investigation *against* the consumer's Social Security number, could reasonably be found to constitute harassing, oppressive, or abusive conduct, and the court was not convinced by the defendant's argument that reference to "social" is conclusory or could refer to something other than the consumer's Social Security number.

Bank v. Pentagroup Fin., L.L.C., 2009 WL 1606420 (E.D.N.Y. June 9, 2009). A debt collection program that negligently misplaces numerous calls to a single wrong number can plausibly have the natural consequence of harassment or abuse. Based on the volume of calls alleged, and the fact that some did not identify the debt consumer or contain a return phone number, the court found that the recipient of the calls had sufficiently alleged an "injurious exposure" to offending communication.

Henderson v. Credit Bureau Inc., Clearinghouse No. 45,349 (W.D.N.Y. 1989). Collector who wrote "NO MORE FALSE PROMISES" by hand at bottom of collection letter violated the prohibition against conduct the natural consequence of which is to harass, oppress, or abuse. The only function of that message was to vent the collector's frustrations and compel payment by harassment.

North Dakota

Bingham v. Collection Bureau, Inc., 505 F. Supp. 864 (D.N.D. 1981). The court found that the collector harassed the consumer by telephoning immediately after the consumer hung up the telephone, by inquiring whether she had a wedding ring, and by stating that she should not have children if she could not afford the hospital bill for them.

Ohio

Gross v. Nationwide Credit, Inc., 2011 WL 379167 (S.D. Ohio Feb. 2, 2011). The plaintiff stated a claim under §§ 1692d and 1692d(5) by alleging that the defendant placed telephone calls to him "multiple times a day over the course of nearly two months" but, when he returned those calls "to determine the nature of the debt he [was] put on hold and not able to speak with a live person." The court stated: "Defendant's argument that being put on hold is a mere inconvenience is an argument better made at summary judgment or trial as greater factual detail will be critical to that determination. Certainly, creating obstacles for the consumer, such as routinely putting consumers on hold for long periods of time and denying them the opportunity to determine the underlying cause of the phone calls demanding payment, is a tactic debt collectors have used in the past, and it is just that type of conduct that the Act was meant to deter."

Gasser v. Allen County Claims & Adjustment, Inc., 1983 U.S. Dist. LEXIS 20361 (N.D. Ohio Nov. 3, 1983). A collection letter implying that a collector would contact a variety of third parties violated § 1692d.

United States v. First Fed. Credit Control, Inc., Clearinghouse No. 33,811 (N.D. Ohio 1983). Whether a dunning letter written to servicemen to create the false impression that their commanding officer had been contacted about the indebtedness violated § 1692d by intimidating the recipients must be determined at trial. The letter violated § 1692e.

In re Gunter, 334 B.R. 900 (Bankr. S.D. Ohio 2005). Court refused to dismiss § 1692d claim that continuing to collect, including filing suit and obtaining judgment, after multiple notices of bankruptcy discharge was oppressive, abusive, or harassing.

Oregon

Flores v. Quick Collect, Inc., 2007 WL 433239 (D. Or. Jan. 31, 2007). Court refused to dismiss a claim alleging that setting a debtor examination in a distant venue violated § 1692d.

Grassley v. Debt Collectors, Inc., 1992 U.S. Dist. LEXIS 22782 (D. Or. Dec. 14, 1992). Collector's threat to have the debtor "picked up" violated § 1692d and Or. Rev. Stat. § 646.639(2)(b).

Harvey v. United Adjusters, 509 F. Supp. 1218 (D. Or. 1981). A letter implying, *inter alia,* that the debtor is financially irresponsible and ignores her mail violated § 1692d but the consumer failed to show abusive and obscene phone calls were made by the collector.

Lambert v. Nat'l Credit Bureau, Inc., 1981 U.S. Dist. LEXIS 18623 (D. Or. Apr. 8, 1981). The large bold words "48 Hour Notice—Warning—Pay This Amount" on a dunning letter are designed to instill the belief that dire consequences will follow, and the natural consequence is to harass, oppress or abuse the consumer in violation of § 1692e.

Dixon v. United Adjusters, Inc., 1981 U.S. Dist. LEXIS 18392 (D. Or. Feb. 19, 1981). The collector's letter showing a decapitated man and inquiring "Is this what you do with your head when you get our letters?" violates § 1692d in that it suggests that the consumer is irresponsible and also contained the statement—"if you think what we have been writing is unpleasant, don't challenge us to see what happens if you keep avoiding us"—which is threatening in tone.

Texas

United States v. Cent. Adjustment Bureau, Inc., 667 F. Supp. 370 (N.D. Tex. 1986). The collector violated § 1692d by communicating racial stereotypes, belligerent threats, words like "liar," "deadbeat," "crook," and threats that credit would be ruined.

K.2.3.4.2 General standard not violated

Drennan v. First Resolution Inv. Corp., 2010 WL 3059205 (5th Cir. Aug. 4, 2010) (unpublished). Filing a suit to collect a credit card debt did not constitute either a false or misleading representation or one that was so harassing, oppressive, or unconscionable that it was actionable under the FDCPA, even if, arguendo, the use of a suit on account on a credit card debt did not meet the necessary requirements of Texas's Rule of Civil Procedure 185 or any other such rules or regulations. The circumstances of this case do not constitute a violation of the FDCPA, even if the underlying action was not a proper suit on a sworn account.

Gionis v. Javitch, Block & Rathbone, 238 Fed. Appx. 24 (6th Cir. 2007). Collection attorneys violated § 1692e(5) and (10) because the least sophisticated consumer reading the creditor's affidavit, claiming any attorney fees to which it would be legally entitled and attached to the complaint, would be confused about the creditor's ability to recover attorney fees which were not permitted by Ohio law. This did not violate §§ 1692e(2), 1692f, or 1692d, however.

Harvey v. Great Seneca Fin. Corp., 453 F.3d 324 (6th Cir. 2006). The court held that the consumer's allegation that the defendant debt collector filed a state court collection lawsuit without the means of proving the debt could not be abusive because "filing a lawsuit to attempt to collect a debt is not the kind of conduct that was intended to be covered by section 1692d."

Fox v. Citicorp Credit Servs., Inc., 15 F.3d 1507 (9th Cir. 1994). Consumers' allegations that debt collector improperly threatened to garnish their wages and continued to call them at their place of employment after being requested not to were sufficient to state a claim for harassing behavior under § 1692d.

Alabama

Campbell v. Thompson, 1990 WL 71348 (N.D. Ala. May 23, 1990). Check collector's lawful pursuit of criminal charges against bad check writers was not abuse violating the FDCPA. There was no evidence that a check collection agency's publication to its retailer customers of a list of bad check writer's names and addresses with encoded reasons for dishonor of the check violated the FDCPA.

California

Masuda v. Thomas Richards & Co., 759 F. Supp. 1456 (C.D. Cal. 1991). Mailing of 48 letters to consumer in eight-month period was not considered harassment.

Colorado

Shrestha v. Nadel, 2001 U.S. Dist. LEXIS 12553 (D. Conn. Mar. 21, 2001). The court entered summary judgment in favor of defendant attorney, finding that debtor's funds for which an exemption could have been claimed were not exempt from execution at the time of the attorney's seizure because the debtor had failed to follow the statutory requirements to claim exemptions.

Connecticut

Gaetano v. Payco, Inc., 774 F. Supp. 1404 (D. Conn. 1990). Giving "THIS OPPORTUNITY TO SETTLE THIS MATTER IN A FRIENDLY MANNER" does not oppressively imply that abusive, unfriendly methods are to follow.

Delaware

Beattie v. D.M. Collections, Inc., 754 F. Supp. 383 (D. Del. 1991). Contacting the wrong consumers to collect a debt is not by itself abuse prohibited by § 1692d.

Florida

Chalik v. Westport Recovery Corp., 677 F. Supp. 2d 1322 (S.D. Fla. 2009). Defendants' filing of a sworn statement denying consumer's claim of exemption, without any specific knowledge regarding the exemption, in a garnishment proceeding is not the kind of conduct that was intended to be covered by § 1692d as a matter of law, but could be a violation of § 1692e.

Georgia

Thomas v. LDG Fin. Servs., Inc., 463 F. Supp. 2d 1370 (N.D. Ga. 2006). Complaint failed to state a claim under § 1692d for conversations arising from telephone calls that included some shouting and threats.

Illinois

Unterreiner v. Stoneleigh Recovery Assocs., L.L.C., 2010 WL 2523257(N.D. Ill. June 17, 2010). Allegations that the collector "screamed" at the consumer, told her she owed "all kinds of money," and asked, "how could you go and max out a card like that?" did not rise to the level of harassment, oppression and abuse that courts have required to establish a § 1692d violation.

Majeski v. I.C. Sys., Inc., 2010 WL 145861 (N.D. Ill. Jan. 8, 2010). "Yelling and rude language, while disrespectful, does not by itself violate § 1692d."

Blair v. Sherman Acquisition, 2004 WL 2870080 (N.D. Ill. Dec. 13, 2004). Gramm-Leach-Bliley notice that the debt buyer would share information legally with others did not amount to an abusive threat to publicize consumers' debts.

Taylor v. Fink, 1994 WL 669605 (N.D. Ill. Nov. 25, 1994). Merely threatening to file a lawsuit did not violate § 1692d or § 1692f.

Indiana

Frye v. Bowman, Heintz, Boscia & Vician, P.C., 193 F. Supp. 2d 1070 (S.D. Ind. 2002). Section 1692d did not encompass misrepresentations of the debtor's rights in a summons.

Simmons v. Miller, 970 F. Supp. 661 (S.D. Ind. 1997). There was no intentional violation of §§ 1692d, 1692e, 1692e(2)(A), or 1692f(1) where a claim on an NSF check was filed more than three years but less than six years after the check was written and it was not clear that a six year rather than three year statute of limitations applied.

Kansas

Bieber v. Associated Collection Servs., Inc., 631 F. Supp. 1410 (D. Kan. 1986). Threats to file suit and an inquiry to the consumer about her intention to file bankruptcy after being informed she was represented by a lawyer were not intended to abuse, oppress or harass as a matter of law.

Kentucky

Jones v. Johnson, 2008 WL 4372905 (E.D. Ky. Sept. 22, 2008). The court dismissed the FDCPA claims flowing from underlying state court litigation by stating that "the filing of a single motion in the state court seeking to bring the loans into compliance with Kentucky law and an appeal of the denial of that motion are legitimate actions in a court proceeding" and cannot violate the FDCPA because that conduct "cannot be said to be harassing, oppressive, abusive, unfair or unconscionable."

Maryland

Shah v. Collecto, Inc., 2005 WL 2216242 (D. Md. Sept. 12, 2005). The debt collector's report to the credit bureau that the consumer disputed the debt was not oppressive within § 1692d.

Dorsey v. Morgan, 760 F. Supp. 509 (D. Md. 1991). Attorney's claim that he will seek costs and attorney fees if legal action is filed is neither false nor oppressive where the contract so provides.

Michigan

Wilson v. Merchants & Med. Credit Corp., Inc., 2010 WL 3488617 (E.D. Mich. Sept. 2, 2010). A debt collector's statement that "we know where you work, we know where you live, we know what kind of car you drive, and we will be in further—further contact with you" did not violate §§ 1692d, 1692e or 1692f. "This alleged statement does not suggest that Merchants would refer the case to law enforcement. Rather, it indicates that *Merchants* would be in further contact with Wilson." A debt collector's demand to pay $200 by the end of the day or it would "further the investigation" did not violate §§ 1692d, 1692e, or 1692f.

Saltzman v. I.C. Sys., Inc., 2009 WL 3190359 (E.D. Mich. Sept. 30, 2009). One or two nonthreatening calls per day without leaving a message not oppressive within § 1692d.

Minnesota

Hemmingsen v. Messerli & Kramer, P.A., 2011 WL 494941 (D. Minn. Feb. 7, 2011). Summary judgment was granted on the §§ 1692d and 1692f claims to the defendant collection attorneys who represented the unsuccessful credit card creditor in the underlying state court collection lawsuit. The evidence showed, contrary to the plaintiff's claim that the debt was her ex-husband's alone, that the couple's divorce papers and the monthly statements both indicated that plaintiff was an account debtor and that she signed one $20 payment check: "The fact that the state court denied [the collection attorneys'] summary judgment motion and granted [the consumer's] does not, on its own, indicate that [the collection attorneys] harassed her or used unfair practices to collect the debt."

Gallagher v. Gurstel, Staloch & Chargo, P.A., 645 F. Supp. 2d 795 (D. Minn. 2009). "A single laugh" in a phone call with the debt collector does not violate § 1692d.

Nebraska

Wilson v. Business & Prof'l Credit Mgmt., Inc., Clearinghouse No. 41,672 (D. Neb. 1986). A collection agency's first garnishment of a social security recipient's checking account was not abusive or unfair in violation of §§ 1692d & 1692f where the collector did not know if nonexempt funds were also deposited in the account. The second garnishment of the account, while questionable, was not abusive or unfair where the collector had some reason to believe other funds may have been deposited in the account and the cost of a debtor's exam (about $200) would far exceed the debt ($29.48) or the cost of a garnishment hearing.

Page v. Checkrite, Ltd., Clearinghouse No. 45,759 (D. Neb. 1984). Check guarantee agencies' encoded bulletin of bounced check writers circulated to subscribing retailers did not violate § 1692d, since the retailer was instructed to keep the bulletin out of public view and only part of the consumers' names were listed.

Harris v. BWS Credit Servs., Inc., Clearinghouse No. 27,693 (D. Neb. 1980) (order on motions for summary judgment). The collection agency violated other provisions, but the evidence did not sustain a finding that telephone calls were made with an intent to annoy, abuse, or harass or that § 1692f was violated by a threat to "get" one of the consumers.

New Jersey

State v. Long, 630 A.2d 430 (N.J. Super. Ct. 1993). Judgment creditor's efforts to determine judgment debtor's assets in order to collect judgment did not support harassment conviction under New Jersey law.

New York

Starkey v. Firstsource Advantage, L.L.C., 2010 WL 2541756 (W.D.N.Y. Mar. 11, 2010). The court granted summary judgment for the defendant on the consumer's claim that it violated § 1692d by calling her on her cell phone since the calls were unremarkable collection calls that were not "intended to harass, oppress, or abuse her in any way." With the exception of the consumer's statement that she found the calls to be inconvenient because they interrupted her day and that she found them upsetting, there was insufficient evidence to support such a claim.

Brown v. ACB Bus. Servs., 1996 WL 469588 (S.D.N.Y. Aug. 16, 1996). Two phone calls with a "demeaning and offensive" tone did not constitute harassment within the meaning of the FDCPA.

Wegmans Food Mkts., Inc. v. Scrimpsher, 17 B.R. 999 (Bankr. N.D.N.Y. 1982). Three weekly letters threatening intended criminal prosecution for bad checks did not violate §§ 1692d or 1692e.

Ohio

Deere v. Javitch, Block & Rathbone L.L.P., 413 F. Supp. 2d 886 (S.D. Ohio 2006). "This Court has previously found that filing a civil debt collection lawsuit [without underlying evidence to prove the claim] is not conduct to which FDCPA Section 1692d is addressed."

Davis v. NCO Portfolio Mgmt., Inc., 2006 WL 290491 (S.D. Ohio Feb. 7, 2006). Filing a civil debt collection lawsuit is not conduct to which § 1692d is addressed.

Hartman v. Asset Acceptance Corp., 467 F. Supp. 2d 769 (S.D. Ohio). Affidavit misrepresented that the debt buyer was a holder in due course in a state collection action violating § 1692e(2) and (12) but not §§ 1692e(6)(A) and 1692d.

Boyce v. Attorney's Dispatch Serv., 1999 U.S. Dist. LEXIS 1124 (S.D. Ohio Feb. 2, 1999). Although the debt collection letter improperly threatened criminal prosecution in violation of § 1692e(5), the same threat did not amount to a violation of § 1692d, which prohibits harassment, oppression or abuse.

Smith v. Transworld Sys., 1997 U.S. Dist. LEXIS 23775 (S.D. Ohio July 31, 1997). Debt collector did not violate § 1692d by making non-abusive statements intended to encourage voluntary payment, and fact that creditor mentioned that post-judgment remedies were available if litigation occurred and creditor prevailed did not warrant summary judgment in favor of consumer.

Gasser v. Allen County Claims & Adjustment, Inc., 1983 U.S. Dist. LEXIS 20361 (N.D. Ohio Nov. 3, 1983). A letter implying consumers who do not pay their debts are dishonest does not violate § 1692d.

Kleczy v. First Fed. Credit Control, Inc., 486 N.E.2d 204 (Ohio Ct. App. 1984). Consumer lacked standing to recover for alleged abusive phone calls received by his spouse.

Pennsylvania

Popson v. Galloway, 2010 WL 2985945 (W.D. Pa. July 27, 2010). Follows *Harvey* finding filing suit without providing documentation substantiating the debt does not violate §§ 1692d, 1692e or 1692f.

Whiteside v. Nat'l Credit Sys., Inc., 2000 U.S. Dist. LEXIS 3707 (E.D. Pa. Mar. 27, 2000). Following a bench trial, the court found that the plaintiff failed to meet his burden to prove that any of the collection agency's contacts were abusive or contributed to the consumer's high blood pressure.

Rhode Island

In re Mason, 167 B.R. 327 (Bankr. D.R.I. 1994). Because the consumer's evidence was not adequate to establish that the attorney debt collector was responsible for harassing telephone calls that the consumer received at home and at work, the debt collector was not liable under § 1692d.

Texas

Beeler-Lopez v. Dodeka, L.L.C., 2010 WL 1889428 (E.D. Tex. May 7, 2010). Any violation of the FDCPA's venue provision occurs when the suit is brought. If the consumer does not object to venue, then merely continuing to pursue the action is not a violation of §§ 1692i, 1692d, or 1692e.

Washington

Watkins v. Peterson Enters., 57 F. Supp. 2d 1102 (E.D. Wash. 1999). Since serving multiple writs of garnishment on a consumer over several years did not in itself violate Washington state law, it was not harassment, oppression, or abuse under § 1692d.

K.2.3.5 Other

Montgomery v. Huntington Bank & Silver Shadow Recovery, Inc., 346 F.3d 693 (6th Cir. 2003). A non-debtor who was subjected to abusive collection tactics may not maintain an action for violations of § 1692c(c), since that section is limited to violations directed at a "consumer" as defined in the Act, but may maintain an action for violation of §§ 1692d and 1692e, which have no such limitation and therefore apply to anyone who is the victim of prescribed misconduct.

Alabama

Sparks v. Phillips & Cohen Assocs., Ltd., 641 F. Supp. 2d 1234 (S.D. Ala. 2008). Objective least sophisticated consumer standard applies to determine whether the harassing, oppressive, and abusive criteria of § 1692d are satisfied. Section 1692d liability does not hinge on the falsity of a statement. Even true statements may be harassing or abusive.

California

Riley v. Giguiere, 631 F. Supp. 2d 1295 (E.D. Cal. 2009). For the purposes of determining if defendant's acts violated §§ 1692d and 1692f of the FDCPA, several acts of defendant had to be viewed as a single course of conduct.

Escobedo v. Countrywide Home Loans, Inc., 2009 WL 4981618 (S.D. Cal. Dec. 15, 2009). The complaint stated claims for relief under state law that incorporates the FDCPA by sufficiently alleging FDCPA violations resulting from defendant's harassing phone calls.

Illinois

Miller v. Midland Credit Mgmt., Inc., 621 F. Supp. 2d 621 (N.D. Ill. 2009). Summary judgment for the defendants on § 1692c(b) claim (unlawful third party communication) and § 1692d(3) claim (publication of list of debtors), since the plaintiff failed to submit evidence to support the allegation that the defendants shared information with a third party bank as part of a "balance transfer" joint marketing program.

Feltman v. Blatt, Hasenmiller, Leibsker & Moore, L.L.C., 2008 WL 5211024 (N.D. Ill. Dec. 11, 2008). Filing the plaintiff's Social Security number in the state court proceedings did not violate § 1692d.

Trull v. G.C. Servs. Ltd. P'ship, 961 F. Supp. 1199 (N.D. Ill. 1997). The level of sophistication of the consumer was irrelevant when determining whether unlawful harassment occurred.

Kansas

Jeter v. Alliance One Receivables Mgmt., Inc., 2010 WL 2025213 (D. Kan. May 20, 2010). The court rejected the defendant's argument that it should impose a general rule ("unsupported in the statute") that a consumer who understands that he is not the true target of the defendant's debt collection efforts may not assert a claim under §§ 1692d, 1692e, or 1692f of the FDCPA.

Michigan

Kaniewski v. Nat'l Action Fin. Servs., 678 F. Supp. 2d 541 (E.D. Mich. 2009). One who knows that he is not alleged to owe the debt is not a "consumer" and does not have standing to bring claims under § 1692e or § 1692g, but does have standing as "any person" to bring claims pursuant to § 1692d.

Minnesota

Neill v. Bullseye Collection Agency, Inc., 2009 WL 1386155 (D. Minn. May 14, 2009). The court declined to consider the collector's argument that its use of the acronym "WWJD" was protected by "its constitutional rights to freedom of speech, equal protection of the laws, and free exercise of religion."

Baker v. Allstate Fin. Servs, Inc., 554 F. Supp. 2d 945 (D. Minn. 2008). Voicemail reference to a "matter pending in the State of Minnesota" stated a claim under §§ 1692d and 1692e(2). Voicemail's use of the words "case," "urgent," and "time sensitive" did not falsely suggest that a lawsuit had been filed within §§ 1692d or 1692e(2).

New York

Krapf v. Collectors Training Inst., Inc., 2010 WL 584020 (W.D.N.Y. Feb. 16, 2010). "Plaintiff's allegation that Defendant called her before 8:00 a.m. sufficiently alleges claims under 15 U.S.C. §§ 1692c(a)(1) and 1692d."

Oregon

Mathis v. Omnium Worldwide, 2005 WL 3159663 (D. Or. Nov. 27, 2005). Plaintiff may not recover for actions outside the one-year statute, but may use the actions to support claims of abuse, harassment, or knowledge of attorney's representation.

Pennsylvania

Duraney v. Washington Mut. Bank, 2008 WL 4204821 (W.D. Pa. Sept. 11, 2008), *aff'd*, 2010 WL 2993810 (3d Cir. Aug. 2, 2010). The § 1692d(3) prohibition against publishing a "list of consumers who allegedly refuse to pay debts" applies by its plain language only to disclosing the names of "consumers" in the plural and thus could not apply to the defendant foreclosure attorney's identification in a brief filed in the underlying state court foreclosure action of the plaintiff individually as having not paid her debt. The court dismissed the § 1692d(3) claim based on the defendant foreclosure attorney's purported responsibility for the sheriff's publication of a foreclosure notice required by state law, since that publication is a form of service of legal process and cannot constitute debt collection activities for purposes of the FDCPA pursuant to the exemption in § 1692a(6)(D).

Texas

Eads v. Wolpoff & Abramson, L.L.P., 538 F. Supp. 2d 981 (W.D. Tex. 2008). The consumer stated a legally cognizable claim against the collection law firm by alleging it violated § 1692d by repeated trying to collect a debt that it had been informed was the obligation of a thief of the consumer's identity.

Utah

Maxwell v. Barney, 2008 WL 1981666 (D. Utah May 2, 2008). Collection lawyers did not violate §§ 1692d or 1692f where the ambulance ticket for a rape victim was attached to a debt collection complaint properly filed in the course of litigation proceedings and the information contained on the ambulance ticket provided proof of the debt at issue in the proceedings.

Virginia

Carter v. Countrywide Home Loans, Inc., 2009 WL 2742560 (E.D. Va. Aug. 25, 2009). Even though the plaintiff had not signed the agreement, he would be still covered as "consumer" under 15 U.S.C. § 1692d.

K.2.4 False or Misleading Representations, 15 U.S.C. § 1692e

K.2.4.1 Least Sophisticated Consumer and Other General Standards

Heintz v. Jenkins, 514 U.S. 291, 115 S. Ct. 1489, 131 L. Ed. 2d 395 (1995). "The Fair Debt Collection Practices Act prohibits 'debt collectors' from making false or misleading representations and from engaging in various abusive and unfair practices."

Donohue v. Quick Collect, Inc., 592 F.3d 1027 (9th Cir. 2010).

"[F]alse but non-material representations . . . are not actionable under § 1692e."

Ruth v. Triumph P'ships, 577 F.3d 790 (7th Cir. 2009). Subsections of § 1692e are merely nonexclusive examples of the ways the section can be violated. Where a statement is clearly deceptive, the consumer need not introduce extrinsic evidence to show the statement would be deceptive to the least sophisticated consumer.

Gonzalez v. Kay, 577 F.3d 600 (5th Cir. 2009). "We do not construe the disclaimer in isolation but must analyze whether the letter is misleading as a whole. We caution lawyers who send debt collection letters to state clearly, prominently, and conspicuously that although the letter is from a lawyer, the lawyer is acting solely as a debt collector and not in any legal capacity when sending the letter. The disclaimer must explain to even the least sophisticated consumer that lawyers may also be debt collectors and that the lawyer is operating only as a debt collector at that time. Debt collectors acting solely as debt collectors must not send the message that a lawyer is involved, because this deceptively sends the message that the 'price of poker has gone up.' "

Miller v. Javitch, Block & Rathbone, 561 F.3d 588 (6th Cir. 2009). The defendant state court collection attorney's characterization in the collection complaint of the consumer's credit card debt as a "loan," while perhaps more properly characterized as an "account," nevertheless involved no trickery, would not deceive the least sophisticated consumer as to the nature of the debt, and thus was not the type of false representation that would violate § 1692e. Adopting the position of the Seventh Circuit in *Hahn v. Triumph P'ships L.L.C.*, 557 F.3d 755 (7th Cir. 2009) and *Wahl v. Midland Credit Mgmt., Inc.*, 556 F.3d 643 (7th Cir. 2009) that "materiality [is] required in an action based on § 1692e," the court held that the alleged misrepresentations here were not material and thus could not mislead the least sophisticated consumer.

Muha v. Encore Receivable Mgmt., Inc., 558 F.3d 623 (7th Cir. 2009). If the average unsophisticated consumer would not be influenced by a statement rightly or wrongly claimed to be literally false ("your agreement has been revoked"), the case should end right there. If a technical falsehood is not misleading, it does not violate the FDCPA. False statements that are immaterial in the sense that they would not influence a consumer's decision—in the present context his decision to pay a debt in response to a dunning letter—do not violate the FDCPA. When it is neither clear that a challenged statement is misleading nor clear that it is not, the question whether it is misleading is one of fact. "Confusing language in a dunning letter can have an intimidating effect by making the recipient feel that he is in over his head and had better pay up rather than question the demand for payment. The intimidating effect may have been magnified in this case by the reference to revocation, which might have suggested to an unsophisticated consumer that any right he might have to challenge the demand for payment had been extinguished by the revocation of his contract with the issuer, the original creditor." The defendant should explain why the sentence was included and justify the inclusion, because there is enough indication of confusion to place a burden of production on the defendant.

Hahn v. Triumph P'ships, L.L.C., 557 F.3d 755 (7th Cir. 2009). "[Plaintiff's] only argument is that the letter is false—and, as we have concluded that the statement is true, the case is over. The statement's immateriality is another way to reach the same conclusion." "[T]he difference between principal and interest is no more important to the [FDCPA] than the color of the paper that used." "The statute is designed to provide information that helps consumers to choose intelligently, and by definition immaterial information neither contributes to that objective (if the statement is correct) nor undermines it (if the statement is incorrect)."

Wahl v. Midland Credit Mgmt., Inc., 556 F.3d 643 (7th Cir. 2009). The plaintiff had to show both that the statement was false and that it would mislead the unsophisticated consumer.

Campuzano-Burgos v. Midland Credit Mgmt., Inc., 550 F.3d 294 (3d Cir. 2008). The court summarized the law of deception under the least sophisticated consumer standard:

> A communication is deceptive for purposes of the Act if: "it can be reasonably read to have two or more different meanings, one of which is inaccurate." . . . This standard is less demanding than one that inquires whether a particular debt collection communication would mislead or deceive a reasonable debtor. . . . Nevertheless, the least sophisticated standard safeguards bill collectors from liability for "bizarre or idiosyncratic interpretations of collection notices" by preserving at least a modicum of reasonableness, as well as "presuming a basic level of understanding and willingness to read with care [on the part of the recipient]." Although established to ease the lot of the naive, the standard does not go so far as to provide solace to the willfully blind or non-observant. Even the least sophisticated debtor is bound to read collection notices in their entirety. [Citations omitted.]

Rosenau v. Unifund Corp., 539 F.3d 218, 221 (3d Cir. 2008). "It is a remedial statute that we 'construe . . . broadly, so as to effect its purpose.' " Communications are to be analyzed under the least sophisticated debtor standard. A debt collection letter is deceptive where it can be reasonably read to have two or more different meanings, one of which is inaccurate.

Kistner v. Law Offices of Michael P. Margelefsky, L.L.C., 518 F.3d 433 (6th Cir. 2008). "[A] jury should determine whether the letter is deceptive and misleading-specifically, whether the letter gives the impression that it is from an attorney even though it is not." "[T]he 'more than one reasonable interpretation' standard is applicable to the entirety of § 1692e as a useful tool in analyzing the 'least-sophisticated-consumer' test. *See Clomon*, 988 F.2d at 1319 (discussing the 'more than one reasonable interpretation' test as one of the 'variety of ways' in which courts attempt to protect consumers under the least-sophisticated-consumer standard). Accordingly, the question for the jury becomes whether one can reasonably conclude that the letter sent to Kistner is susceptible to a reading by the least sophisticated consumer that it is from an attorney, even though Margelefsky has admitted that he had no direct role in sending the letter."

Evory v. Nat'l Action Fin. Servs., Inc., 505 F.3d 769 (7th Cir. 2007). Disagreeing with *Guerrerro*, a misrepresentation to a consumer's lawyer by a debt collector may violate the FDCPA if it would deceive a competent lawyer. "All that this argument shows is how unsound it would be to suppose that a communication to a person's lawyer is not a communication to the person. It would make a consumer who had a lawyer worse off than one who did not, because neither he nor his lawyer would have a right to any of the information that the statute requires be disclosed to the consumer." Although a violation of state law is not in itself a violation of the federal Act, *Beler v. Blatt, Hasenmiller, Leibsker & Moore, L.L.C.*, 480 F.3d 470, 473–474 (7th Cir. 2007), a threat to impose a huge monetary penalty that the threatener knows is improper because unlawful is a good candidate for a violation of §§ 1692d and 1692e. "Other circuits, perhaps less kindly disposed to survey evidence than we, treat the deceptive character of a debt collector's communication as a question of law, so that if the communication is not deceptive on its face, the plaintiff is forbidden to try to show that it would be likely to deceive a substantial number of its intended recipients. We disagree with that position." The last question presented by these cases is whether a claim of deception can ever be rejected in this circuit on the pleadings, since we treat issues of deception as ones of fact rather than of law. The answer is yes. A plaintiff might rest on the text of the communication, and have no other evidence to offer, and then if there was nothing deceptive-seeming about the communication the court would have to dismiss the case."

Beler v. Blatt, Hasenmiller, Leibsker & Moore, L.L.C., 480 F.3d 470, 473 (7th Cir. 2007). "Section 1692e does not require clarity in all writings. What it says is that '[a] debt collector may not use any false, deceptive, or misleading representation or means in connection with the collection of any debt.' A rule against trickery differs from a command to use plain English and write at a sixth-grade level. [Plaintiff] does not contend that the complaint was deceptive."

Brown v. Card Serv. Ctr., 464 F.3d 450 (3d Cir. 2006). FDCPA is remedial, strict liability statute to be liberally construed. Communications from collectors to debtors are analyzed from the perspective of the least sophisticated consumer. A debt collection letter is deceptive where it can be reasonably read to have two or more different meanings, one of which is inaccurate.

Greco v. Trauner, Cohen & Thomas, L.L.P., 412 F.3d 360, 363 (2d Cir. 2005). "[O]ur Circuit's 'least sophisticated consumer' standard is an objective analysis that seeks to protect 'the naïve' from abusive practices . . . while simultaneously shielding debt collectors from liability for 'bizarre or idiosyncratic interpretations' of debt collection letters."

Durkin v. Equifax Check Servs., Inc., 406 F.3d 410 (7th Cir. 2005). Because the consumer provided no extrinsic evidence in support of the claims, the court granted summary judgment for the collector on all claims alleging that its series of duns was confusing and misleading; the court's earlier disqualification of the consumer's expert for failing to meet the *Daubert* standards left him with no evidence other than the collector's own expert's testimony that the letters "might" be confusing, testimony which the court found insufficient, stating, "[t]he mere possibility that someone might be confused by the dunning letters does not raise a genuine issue of material fact that the class of unsophisticated consumers receiving Equifax's letters may be confused by them."

Montgomery v. Huntington Bank & Silver Shadow Recovery, Inc., 346 F.3d 693 (6th Cir. 2003). A non-debtor who was subjected to abusive collection tactics may not maintain an action for violations of § 1692c(c), since that section is limited to violations directed at a "consumer" as defined in the Act, but may maintain an action for violation of §§ 1692d and 1692e, which have no such limitation and therefore apply to anyone who is the victim of prescribed misconduct.

Turner v. J.V.D.B. & Assocs., Inc., 330 F.3d 991 (7th Cir. 2003). Section 1692e generally prohibits "false, deceptive or misleading" collection activities without regard to intent. The collector's ignorance of the consumer's bankruptcy did not excuse its post-discharge violation of § 1692e in seeking collection of a discharged debt (reversing summary judgment in the debt collector's favor).

Johnson v. Riddle, 305 F.3d 1107 (10th Cir. 2002). The FDCPA is remedial statute to be liberally construed in favor of the consumer.

Peters v. General Serv. Bureau, Inc., 277 F.3d 1051 (8th Cir. 2002). The court found that a collector's letter requesting the consumer's voluntary appearance in lieu of service of process was not false, deceptive or misleading on its face in the absence of evidence of its deceptiveness. The consumer complained that the letter misstated that service by constable was the only alternative to a voluntary appearance when certified mail service was also available, but the court found that constable service was the only other feasible method. The consumer argued that the statement that the consumer must "appear and defend" was misleading because a consumer would interpret it to require a personal visit to the courthouse, but the court found it was not confusing. The omission of the period for filing an answer did not violate the FDCPA where the collector would provide that information after service. Whether a collection letter was false was a question of law for the court using the unsophisticated consumer test. The court found that, even if the statement about alternative methods of service was literally false, it was not misleading.

White v. Goodman, 200 F.3d 1016 (7th Cir. 2000). Court reasoned that the FDCPA "protects the unsophisticated debtor, but not the irrational one."

Chaudhry v. Gallerizzo, 174 F.3d 394 (4th Cir. 1999). Jury instruction on least sophisticated consumer upheld: "When I refer to a person unsophisticated in matters of law or finance, I am referring to a person of reasonable intelligence who has a basic understanding and has a willingness to listen to what is being said with care. I am not referring to a person who places an unrealistic or irrational interpretation upon what was said."

Transamerica Fin. Servs., Inc. v. Sykes, 171 F.3d 553 (7th Cir. 1999). In dicta, the court stated that a misrepresentation under § 1692e must be knowing and intentional.

Johnson v. Revenue Mgmt. Corp., 169 F.3d 1057 (7th Cir. 1999). "Unsophisticated readers may require more explanation than do federal judges; what seems pellucid to a judge, a legally sophisticated reader, may be opaque to someone whose formal education ended after sixth grade. To learn how an unsophisticated reader reacts to a letter, the judge may need to receive evidence."

Goldberg v. Transworld Sys., Inc., 164 F.3d 617 (2d Cir. 1998) (table, text at 1998 WL 650793). The language "grace period about to expire" does not suggest to the least sophisticated consumer that he has less than thirty days to dispute the debt.

Schweizer v. Trans Union Corp., 136 F.3d 233 (2d Cir. 1998). The "least sophisticated consumer" standard was applied in evaluating FDCPA claims.

Lewis v. ACB Bus. Servs., Inc., 135 F.3d 389 (6th Cir. 1998). Courts apply the objective test based on the understanding of the "least sophisticated consumer."

Jenkins v. Heintz, 124 F.3d 824 (7th Cir. 1997). In a split decision, the Seventh Circuit adopted a narrow interpretation of the FDCPA to prohibit debt collection deception only if the debt collector knew a false statement was false, implying a new requirement that a misrepresentation must be made knowingly for an FDCPA violation to occur. A negligent misrepresentation did not state a claim under the FDCPA.

United States v. Nat'l Fin. Servs., Inc., 98 F.3d 131 (4th Cir. 1996). Fact that collection lawyer had filed a small number of suits and that some of the duns said only that suit would be considered did not lessen the capacity of the letters to deceive an unsophisticated consumer.

Wade v. Regional Credit Ass'n, 87 F.3d 1098 (9th Cir. 1996). While the debt collector violated state law by trying to collect a debt when it was not licensed pursuant to state law, this was not a per se or other violation of the FDCPA. The court used the least sophisticated consumer standard.

Russell v. Equifax A.R.S., 74 F.3d 30 (2d Cir. 1996). The "least sophisticated consumer" lacks the astuteness of an attorney and even the sophistication of the average consumer. The court stated, "in the general context of consumer protection—of which the Fair Debt Collection Practices Act is a part—it does not seem 'unfair to require that one who deliberately goes perilously close to an area of proscribed conduct shall take the risk that he may cross the line.' "

Gammon v. G.C. Servs., 27 F.3d 1254 (7th Cir. 1994). In a case involving § 1692e the court rejected the "least sophisticated consumer" standard but adopted the functionally equivalent "unsophisticated consumer" standard.

Bentley v. Great Lakes Collection Bureau, 6 F.3d 60 (2d Cir. 1993). An objective test based on the understanding of the least sophisticated consumer is applied to the determination of whether a collection letter violates § 1692e.

Clomon v. Jackson, 988 F.2d 1314 (2d Cir. 1993). "The basic purpose of the least-sophisticated-consumer standard is to ensure that the FDCPA protects all consumers, the gullible as well as the shrewd."

Swanson v. S. Oregon Credit Serv., 869 F.2d 1222 (9th Cir. 1988). The least unsophisticated consumer standard was applied.

Jeter v. Credit Bureau, Inc., 760 F.2d 1168 (11th Cir. 1985). An objective standard of deception looking to judicial interpretations of the FTC Act protecting unsophisticated consumer should be applied in interpreting the FDCPA.

Alabama

Sparks v. Phillips & Cohen Assocs., Ltd., 641 F. Supp. 2d 1234 (S.D. Ala. 2008). The least sophisticated consumer standard is applied in an FDCPA action involving an attorney plaintiff.

California

Janti v. Encore Capital Group, Inc., 2010 WL 3058260 (S.D. Cal. Aug. 3, 2010). Where the collection letter stated "if Consumer sent MCM $250 she could stop this account from going to an attorney," it would mislead the hypothetical least sophisticated debtor into believing that legal action was a "real possibility."

Elliott v. Credit Control Servs., Inc., 2010 WL 1495402 (S.D. Cal. Apr. 14, 2010). A letter containing the heading "Warning Notice-Warning Notice" in a dun stating that "This notice and all further steps undertaken by this agency will be in compliance with applicable State and Federal Law(s)" was not false or misleading in violation of § 1692e. The court rejected the consumer's argument that this statement "could lead an unsophisticated debtor to forego obtaining independent legal counsel because the debtor may conclude that Defendants are acting in compliance with state and federal law," finding that "even if the statement was somehow misleading, it would be merely a technical falsehood."

Schwarm v. Craighead, 552 F. Supp. 2d 1056 (E.D. Cal. 2008). The FDCPA imposes strict liability on debt collectors unless there is a bona fide error defense. Whether a communication would "confuse a least sophisticated debtor," thereby violating the FDCPA, is a question of law.

Gonzalez v. Arrow Fin. Servs. L.L.C., 2005 U.S. Dist. LEXIS 19712 (S.D. Cal. July 25, 2005). The debt collector's reference to reporting an FCRA obsolete debt to a credit reporting agency was false and deceptive, notwithstanding the collector's disclaimer "if we are reporting the account," since "the least sophisticated debtor could likely believe his debt is reportable just because the letters indicate the credit bureaus will be notified."

Palmer v. Stassinos, 348 F. Supp. 2d 1070 (N.D. Cal. 2004). The court, not a jury, determines as a matter of law whether a particular collection letter or series of letters violated the FDCPA by confusing a least sophisticated debtor.

Perretta v. Capital Acquisitions & Mgmt. Co., 2003 WL 21383757 (N.D. Cal. May 5, 2003). What the language used in the collection of a debt conveys to the least sophisticated consumer is a question of law for the court in the Ninth Circuit.

Irwin v. Mascott, 96 F. Supp. 2d 968 (N.D. Cal. 1999). The fact that the named plaintiffs had attorneys and may have received advice from their attorneys did not render their claims atypical. The least sophisticated consumer standard is "an objective standard, imposed to further the protective purposes of the FDCPA. The standard applies even to those who have lawyers."

Masuda v. Thomas Richards & Co., 759 F. Supp. 1456 (C.D. Cal. 1991). Least sophisticated debtor standard would be applied to determine whether collector's practice was unfair, deceptive or misleading.

Connecticut

Lemire v. Wolpoff & Abramson, L.L.P., 256 F.R.D. 321 (D. Conn. 2009). In the course of granting class certification, where the defendant cited Second Circuit precedent to suggest that letters sent to attorneys do not give rise a violation of the FDCPA, the court observed that, "The Second Circuit's observation in *Kropelnicki* that attorneys can protect their clients from 'fraudulent or

harassing' behavior does not affect this conclusion, for two reasons. First, the claim that [plaintiff] has raised need not be based on 'fraudulent or harassing' behavior, since the statute also prohibits behavior which is merely 'deceptive' or 'unfair or unconscionable,' and indeed, those were precisely the grounds on which this Court found FDCPA violations in *Gaetano*. Second, the Court of Appeals specifically disclaimed its own observation as dicta, saying it was 'not an issue on which we need to rule today.' "

Bishop v. Nat'l Accounts Sys., Inc., Clearinghouse No. 49,175 (D. Conn. 1993). To determine whether a particular debt collection practice is misleading or deceptive, courts employ the "least sophisticated consumer standard."

Johnson v. NCB Collection Servs., 799 F. Supp. 1298 (D. Conn. 1992) (settled upon collector's payment of $4000 for consumer to withdraw appeal). Challenged collection practices must be evaluated by the likely effect on the least sophisticated consumer.

Latella v. Atl. Advisors, Inc., 1992 U.S. Dist. LEXIS 22849 (D. Conn. May 11, 1992). Whether a collection demand was deceptive or misleading was tested by the "least sophisticated debtor" standard.

Delaware

Dutton v. Wolhar, 809 F. Supp. 1130 (D. Del. 1992), *aff'd*, 5 F.3d 649 (3d Cir. 1993). The least sophisticated debtor standard was more rigorous than an examination of whether a "reasonable consumer" would find a debt collectors' communications false, deceptive, or misleading.

Higgins v. Capitol Credit Servs., Inc., 762 F. Supp. 1128 (D. Del. 1991). A collection notice that would mislead the least sophisticated debtor and cause him to ignore his rights violated the FDCPA.

Florida

Pollock v. Bay Area Credit Serv., L.L.C., 2009 WL 2475167 (S.D. Fla. Aug. 13, 2009). The objective least sophisticated consumer standard applies in evaluating whether the tactic is deceptive.

Brazier v. Law Offices of Mitchell N. Kay, P.C., 2009 WL 764161 (M.D. Fla. Mar. 19, 2009). Whether the letter is self-contradictory and confusing is a question of interpretation and fact, not a pure legal question. Defendant contended that since the language used was identical to the disclaimer in *Greco*, was is appropriately used; however the placement of the disclaimer on the reverse and the use of letterhead are factual question not answered or addressed in *Greco*.

Pescatrice v. Orovitz, 539 F. Supp. 2d 1375 (S.D. Fla. 2008). Although the content of the allegedly deceptive proposed stipulation sent by the collection attorneys to the consumer as a settlement offer to resolve the underlying state court collection action was uncontroverted, the court denied cross motions for summary judgment since it could not determine the issue of deception as a matter of law and as a result whether the material was "deceptive is a material issue of disputed fact for the jury, as fact finder, to resolve."

Fuller v. Becker & Poliakoff, P.A., 192 F. Supp. 2d 1361 (M.D. Fla. 2002). The Eleventh Circuit has adopted the least sophisticated consumer standard for § 1692e(10) claims.

Georgia

Gilmore v. Account, Mgmt., Inc., 2009 WL 2848278 (N.D. Ga. Apr. 27, 2009). The FDCPA imposes strict liability on the debt collector for misstatements of the amount owed as evaluated under the least sophisticated consumer standard.

Schimmel v. Slaughter, 975 F. Supp. 1357 (M.D. Ga. 1997). Attorney letter stating that garnishment was available "after judgment was obtained" could convey to the least sophisticated consumer the impression that a judgment was a virtual certainty and therefore was deceptive.

Schmidt v. Slaughter, Clearinghouse No. 51,961 (M.D. Ga. 1996). A least sophisticated consumer would not understand that the mention of civil process in collection letter meant that criminal bad check process also mentioned would not be pursued.

Phillips v. Stokes, 1992 U.S. Dist. LEXIS 22731 (N.D. Ga. Jan. 8, 1992). Attorney's letter stating that unless the debt was paid in seventy-two hours further action as might be necessary would be taken to satisfy the claims would lead the least sophisticated consumer to believe that legal action would be filed, and thus violated § 1692e(5).

Cravey v. Credit Rating Bureau, Inc., 1991 U.S. Dist. LEXIS 21812 (N.D. Ga. Oct. 24, 1991). Applies least sophisticated standard to collector's use of term "credit bureau."

Wright v. Credit Bureau of Ga., Inc., 548 F. Supp. 591 (N.D. Ga. 1982), *modified on other grounds*, 555 F. Supp. 1005 (N.D. Ga. 1983). The court rejected use of an average reasonable consumer standard under § 1692e and noted that actions in connection with attempts to collect debts are encompassed within the language of § 1692e.

Zoeckler v. Credit Claims & Collections, Inc., 1982 U.S. Dist. LEXIS 18384 (N.D. Ga. Sept. 30, 1982). Using a "reasonable consumer" standard, the court found the collector's first dunning letter not violative of the FDCPA, although the validation notice was in a noticeably smaller print size.

Hawaii

Keli v. Universal Fid. Corp., 1997 U.S. Dist. LEXIS 23940 (D. Haw. Feb. 25, 1997). Collection agency threatened to sue when it had never sued. The threat, among other threats, to *TAKE EVERY STEP* was a threat of legal action to an unsophisticated consumer.

Illinois

Hale v. AFNI, Inc., 2010 WL 380906 (N.D. Ill. Jan. 26, 2010). False statements, by themselves, do not violate the FDCPA; the consumer must also establish that these false statements (1) are confusing or misleading and (2) are material. When FDCPA cases involve statements that are not plainly misleading but might mislead or deceive the unsophisticated consumer, the consumer must present extrinsic evidence—normally consumer surveys—to prove that unsophisticated consumers find the statements at issue confusing or misleading.

Manlapaz v. Unifund CCR Partners, 2009 WL 3015166 (N.D. Ill. Sept. 15, 2009). The falsity of [defendant's employee's] statement that she had personal knowledge of facts that she gleaned from a review of business records was a technicality which would not mislead the unsophisticated consumer and was therefore not material.

Kubert v. Aid Assocs., 2009 WL 1270351 (N.D. Ill. May 7, 2009). The court disapproved and struck the survey evidence offered by the plaintiff as not meeting the *Daubert* standard.

DeKoven v. Plaza Assocs., 2009 WL 901369 (N.D. Ill. Mar. 31, 2009). Expert's survey on the effect of the offer on the least sophisticated consumer was stricken as not complying with *Daubert* standards. "Unfortunately, until debtors challenging dunning letters as misleading or deceptive produce survey evidence that comports with the principles of professional survey research, better-equipped fact finders—i.e., juries—will not have the chance to judge the deceptiveness of these letters." Settlement offer of 65% of the debt valid for a period of thirty-five days was not facially confusing or misleading, because defendant had authority to settle for 60%.

Rodriguez v. Blatt, Hasenmiller, Leibsker & Moore, L.L.C., 2009 WL 631613 (N.D. Ill. Mar. 10, 2009). The court dismissed the § 1692e claim based on two alleged defects in the form of the summons that the attorney defendant employed in the underlying state court collection suit, holding that the defects were "nonmaterial" and thus could not give rise to FDCPA liability.

Longo v. Law Offices of Gerald E. Moore & Assocs., P.C., 2008 WL 4425444 (N.D. Ill. Sept. 26, 2008). A dun addressed to the consumer but mailed to her in care of her attorney at the attorney's address must be read in accordance with the Seventh Circuit's *Evory* opinion through the eyes of a "competent lawyer" and not an unsophisticated consumer. "Even under the 'competent lawyer' standard, a false—as opposed to merely misleading or deceptive—statement made by a debt collector 'would be actionable whether made to the consumer directly or indirectly through his lawyer.' "

Gonzalez v. Lawent, 2005 WL 1130033 (N.D. Ill. Apr. 28, 2005). The collection attorney was strictly liable for violating § 1692e(2) notwithstanding his claimed unintentional misrepresentation of the amount of the alleged debt in a state court collection case.

Turner v. J.V.D.B. & Assocs., Inc., 330 F. Supp. 2d 998 (N.D. Ill. 2004). Following remand from the consumer's successful appeal to the Seventh Circuit, the district court denied the consumer motion for judgment on the pleadings since it construed the appellate opinion's stated rationale that the evidence permitted a reasonable jury to find an FDCPA violation to require a factual, and not a legal determination, of falsity or deception.

Blair v. Sherman Acquisition, 2004 WL 2870080 (N.D. Ill. Dec. 13, 2004). Whether Gramm-Leach-Bliley privacy notice could lead the unsophisticated consumer into thinking that her debt information would be shared with third parties contrary to the FDCPA was a question of fact.

McCabe v. Crawford & Co., 272 F. Supp. 2d 736 (N.D. Ill. 2003). "[I]f a collection letter is confusing on its face, (for example, where the language of the letter is clearly contradictory or inconsistent), the matter may be decided on summary judgment without additional evidence. . . . Where the letter is only potentially misleading or confusing, however, the plaintiff must submit evidence of actual consumer confusion before summary judgment may be granted." The court was unable to determine as a matter of law that the language "Federal Law provides that this debt will be assumed to be valid and owing" violated § 1692e(10) and required additional proof such as a consumer survey.

Kort v. Diversified Collection Servs., Inc., 270 F. Supp. 2d 1017 (N.D. Ill. 2003), *aff'd on other grounds*, 394 F.3d 530 (7th Cir. 2005). In the Seventh Circuit, whether a collection letter would mislead an unsophisticated consumer is a question of fact and not law. However, no Seventh Circuit precedent precludes a court from finding that a collection letter is misleading on its face as distinguished from in its interpretation by an unsophisticated consumer. When the text of a student loan collection letter itself was, on its face, ambiguous enough to mislead an unsophisticated consumer, summary judgment was granted to the consumer.

Clark v. Retrieval Masters Creditors Bureau, Inc., 185 F.R.D. 247 (N.D. Ill. 1999). Applies unsophisticated consumer standard.

Beasley v. Collectors Training Inst., 1999 U.S. Dist. LEXIS 13275 (N.D. Ill. Aug. 17, 1999). Adopting language from *Clomon v. Jackson*, court interpreted "unsophisticated consumer" as a consumer of "below-average sophistication or intelligence but nevertheless possesses 'a rudimentary amount of information about the world and a willingness to read a collection notice with some care.' "

Arango v. G.C. Servs., 1999 U.S. Dist. LEXIS 1143 (N.D. Ill. Feb. 2, 1999). True statement in collection letter that its report might limit consumer's ability to obtain credit from other mail order companies was not misleading. The limitation to direct mail companies was sufficient to prevent an unsophisticated consumer from believing that her access to all credit sources was threatened.

Sledge v. Sands, 182 F.R.D. 255 (N.D. Ill. 1998). A literally true collection letter can still convey a misleading impression in violation of the FDCPA. In plaintiff's motion for summary judgment it was plaintiff's burden to show that the collection letter did not apply to most debtors and, thus, was misleading.

Francisco v. Doctors & Merchants Credit Serv., Inc., 1998 WL 474107 (N.D. Ill. Aug. 3, 1998). Some evidence of actual deception was required before a literally true but potentially misleading statement can be held to violate § 1692e.

Blum v. Fisher & Fisher, 961 F. Supp. 1218 (N.D. Ill. 1997). Summary judgment denied based on unsophisticated consumer standard, which created a jury question that might not have existed using the least sophisticated consumer test. The court rejected the argument that a higher level of sophistication should be assumed where a mortgage was involved.

Drennan v. Van Ru Credit Corp., 950 F. Supp. 858 (N.D. Ill. 1996). Complaint stated a claim where an unsophisticated consumer could interpret defendant's "legal review notification" and "notice of possible wage garnishment," despite frequent use of "may" and "might" as imminent threats when in fact no action was taken for over a year after dunning letters were sent.

Finch v. Silverstein, 1996 WL 467251 (N.D. Ill. Aug. 13, 1996). The consumer stated a claim by alleging that the defendant's correspondence would lead an unsophisticated consumer to believe that a lawsuit was imminent, by including a legal caption and language implying that a lawsuit would be pursued, when suit was not imminent.

Vaughn v. CSC Credit Servs., Inc., 1995 WL 51402 (N.D. Ill. Feb. 3, 1995). "The unsophisticated consumer, while not at the bottom rung of the ladder, is still unsophisticated—uninformed, naive, trusting, possessing below average intelligence."

Tolentino v. Friedman, 833 F. Supp. 697 (N.D. Ill. 1993). A collection attorney's notice urging the consumer to arrange payment of the debt and to avoid bankruptcy put in the same envelope as a copy of a summons and complaint would mislead the least sophisticated debtor about the court's role in the debt collection process.

Friedman v. HHL Fin. Servs., Inc., 1993 WL 367089 (N.D. Ill. Sept. 17, 1993). For violations of § 1692e the court looks at the activity from the prospective of the "least sophisticated consumer."

Cortright v. Thompson, 812 F. Supp. 772 (N.D. Ill. 1992). In determining violations of the FDCPA the court was required to apply the least sophisticated consumer analysis.

Strange v. Wexler, 796 F. Supp. 1117 (N.D. Ill. 1992). The standard of review for FDCPA violations is "whether the conduct would be unfair or deceptive as applied to an unsophisticated consumer."

Indiana

Croteau v. Dearing, 2005 U.S. Dist. LEXIS 1948 (N.D. Ind. Feb. 8, 2005). Because the consumer had not presented an affidavit or other testimony establishing that she was confused by the dunning letter, a genuine issue of material fact existed making summary judgment inappropriate.

Frye v. Bowman, Heintz, Boscia & Vician, P.C., 193 F. Supp. 2d 1070 (S.D. Ind. 2002). Section 1692e prohibits even unintentional misrepresentations in a summons, retracting its own decision in *Simmons v. Miller*, 970 F. Supp. 661, 665 (S.D. Ind. 1997), since overruled. Summary judgment granted to collection attorneys where consumer did not provide facts as to likelihood that the misrepresentations in a summons would mislead consumers.

Payday Today, Inc. v. Hamilton, 911 N.E.2d 26 (Ind. Ct. App. 2009). When the dunning letter is inconsistent, contradictory, and akin to a literally false statement, the court may make a determination that the letter violates the FDCPA as a matter of law.

Louisiana

Johnson v. Eaton, 873 F. Supp. 1019 (M.D. La. 1995). Communications must be viewed from the perspective of the least sophisticated consumer in determining compliance with the FDCPA.

Maryland

Sayyed v. Wolpoff & Abramson, L.L.P., 2010 WL 3313888 (D. Md. Aug. 20, 2010). Summary judgment was granted to the collector on the § 1692e claims occurring in the underlying state court collection case where the consumer was represented by counsel since the alleged misrepresentations were not misleading under the applicable competent attorney standard.

Massachusetts

Pettway v. Harmon Law Offices, P.C., 2005 WL 2365331 (D. Mass. Sept. 27, 2005). "Harmon's payoff and reinstatement letters state an amount owing which includes unearned fees and costs and asks the debtor to '[p]lease make your certified check . . . payable to HARMON LAW OFFICES.' These letters clearly fall within FDCPA's definition of a debt collection communication, whether or not they are prompted by the borrower, and regardless of the fact that a misleading letter was preceded by one that was not."

In re Maxwell, 281 B.R. 101 (Bankr. D. Mass. 2002). Bankruptcy court applied the least sophisticated consumer standard, surveying cases.

Michigan

Kaniewski v. Nat'l Action Fin. Servs., 678 F. Supp. 2d 541 (E.D. Mich. 2009). One who knows that he is not alleged to owe the debt is not a "consumer" and does not have standing to bring claims under § 1692e or § 1692g, but does have standing as "any person" to bring claims pursuant to § 1692d.

Gradisher v. Check Enforcement Unit, Inc., 210 F. Supp. 2d 907 (W.D. Mich. 2002). In determining whether a debt collector violated the FDCPA, courts in the Sixth Circuit apply the "least sophisticated consumer" standard which focuses upon whether the debt collector's actions would mislead or deceive the least sophisticated consumer.

West v. Check Alert Sys., 2001 U.S. Dist. LEXIS 22122 (W.D. Mich. Sept. 7, 2001). Summary judgment granted to collection agency where it represented that interest at 12% was due when this rate exceeded the legal limit of 9% because the consumer failed to show that the misrepresentation was made "knowingly or intentionally," a requirement the court erroneously engrafted onto § 1692e(2).

Diamond v. Corcoran, 1992 U.S. Dist. LEXIS 22793 (W.D. Mich. Aug. 3, 1992). "Language alleged to violate the act is judged under the 'least sophisticated debtor' standard."

Minnesota

Burke v. Messerli & Kramer P.A., 2010 WL 3167403 (D. Minn. Aug. 9, 2010). An unintentional misrepresentation can be actionable under § 1692e; to rule otherwise would render the bona fide error defense superfluous.

Nevada

Edwards v. Nat'l Bus. Factors, Inc., 897 F. Supp. 455 (D. Nev. 1995). Threat of "action" by an attorney "without further notice" is a threat of immediate legal action to the least sophisticated consumer.

New Jersey

Chulsky v. Hudson Law Offices, P.C., 2011 WL 500202 (D.N.J. Feb. 10, 2011). Attorney debt collectors warrant closer scrutiny because their abusive collection practices "are more egregious than those of lay collectors." That the debt was owned and prosecuted by a law firm could have created in a least sophisticated consumer's mind an impression of legal validity not typically imputed to a creditor's actions.

Smith v. Harrison, 2008 WL 2704825 (D.N.J. July 7, 2008). Attorney debt collector's motion to dismiss denied where attorney

argued that his attempted *Greco* disclaimer in a dun sent on attorney stationery and with an attorney signature insulated him from the consumer's claim of a false representation of attorney involvement, with the court providing the following explanation:

> An attorney advising the least sophisticated debtor that he should not imply that an attorney reviewed his account is like asking someone not to think about pink elephants. From the least sophisticated debtor's perspective, a debt collection letter from an attorney would imply that an attorney has reviewed the debtor's account at some level. While Defendant's disclaimer advises the debtor not to imply that an attorney has reviewed his account, the answer to whether an attorney did in fact reviewed [sic] his account is no or yes at some level. A debt collection letter "is deceptive when it can be reasonably read to have two or more different meanings, one of which is inaccurate." *Wilson v. Quadramed Corp.*, 225 F.3d 350, 354 (3d Cir. 2000). Here, there is sufficient ambiguity in Defendant's debt collection letter that the least sophisticated debtor could believe that an attorney has reviewed the debtor's account. Construing § 1692e(3) of the FDCPA liberally and under the standard of the least sophisticated debtor, the Court finds that Plaintiff has stated a claim under the FDCPA.

New Mexico

Spinarski v. Credit Bureau of Lancaster & Palmdale, Inc., 1996 U.S. Dist. LEXIS 22547 (D.N.M. Sept. 19, 1996). Purpose of the "least sophisticated consumer standard" was to protect "the consumer who was uninformed, naive, or trusting, with consideration given to an objective element of reasonableness which shield complying debt collectors from liability for unrealistic or peculiar interpretations of collection letters" (citations omitted).

New York

Nichols v. Frederick J. Hanna & Assocs., P.C., 2011 WL 102665 (N.D.N.Y. Jan. 13, 2011). An unsophisticated consumer is still to be perceived as reasonable and is expected to read a collection notice with care.

Albritton v. Sessoms & Rogers, P.A., 2010 WL 3063639 (E.D.N.C. Aug. 3, 2010). "Based on the absurd results that could come from consumer's interpretation, wherein every *de minimis* error would render a debt collector liable under the FDCPA . . . for the slightest . . . technical falsity, this court applies the materiality standard."

Puglisi v. Debt Recovery Solutions, L.L.C., 2010 WL 376628 (E.D.N.Y. Jan. 26, 2010). To determine whether a practice is deceptive, an objective test based on the understanding of the least sophisticated consumer is applied.

Leone v. Ashwood Fin., Inc., 257 F.R.D. 343 (E.D.N.Y. 2009). The FDCPA is a strict liability statute. Courts use "an objective standard, measured by how the 'least sophisticated consumer' would interpret the notice received from the debt collector."

Tromba v. M.R.S. Assocs., Inc., 323 F. Supp. 2d 424 (E.D.N.Y. 2004). The court erroneously viewed the FDCPA as a harsh statute.

Johnson v. Equifax Risk Mgmt. Servs., 2004 WL 540459 (S.D.N.Y. Mar. 17, 2004). The court held that the "fact that plaintiff is an attorney does not alter the application of the objective 'least sophisticated consumer' standard in this case."

Padilla v. Payco General Am. Credits, Inc., 161 F. Supp. 2d 264 (S.D.N.Y. 2001). An unlawful misrepresentation need not be made willfully or intentionally.

Weber v. Goodman, 9 F. Supp. 2d 163 (E.D.N.Y. 1998). The "least sophisticated consumer" standard was an objective standard intended to protect those most in need of protection.

Berrios v. Sprint Corp., 1998 WL 199842 (E.D.N.Y. Mar. 16, 1998). N.Y. Gen. Bus. Law § 349 requires reliance while the FDCPA did not. The elements of a N.Y. Gen. Bus. Law § 349 claim were (1) that the defendant engaged in a consumer-oriented act or practice which was deceptive or misleading in a material way and (2) that the plaintiff was injured as a result. The standard for whether an act or practice pursuant to N.Y. Gen. Bus. Law. § 349 is misleading is objective, requiring "a showing that a reasonable consumer would have been misled by the defendant's conduct." Because the consumer was not harmed by defendant's actions, plaintiff did not state a claim under N.Y. Gen. Bus. Law § 349. A collection letter that would deceive the least sophisticated consumer but would not deceive a reasonable consumer violated the FDCPA but not N.Y. Gen. Bus. Law § 349.

Rabideau v. Mgmt. Adjustment Bureau, 805 F. Supp. 1086 (W.D.N.Y. 1992). The least sophisticated consumer standard was employed in the analysis of violations of §§ 1692g and 1692e(11).

Henderson v. Credit Bureau Inc., Clearinghouse No. 45,349 (W.D.N.Y. 1989). Writing debtor's employer's name at bottom of a collection notice violated § 1692e(5) because it implies to the least sophisticated consumer that the collector might contact the consumer's employer.

Ohio

Midland Funding L.L.C. v. Brent, 644 F. Supp. 2d 961 (N.D. Ohio 2009). Debt collector communications are evaluated under the FDCPA according to the "least sophisticated consumer" standard. False statements in a debt buyer's affidavit about the affiant's personal knowledge about the debt were material where the consumer disputed the validity of the debt as described by the affiant.

Edwards v. McCormick, 136 F. Supp. 2d 795 (S.D. Ohio 2001). The Sixth Circuit treats the FDCPA as a strict liability statute.

Lee v. Robins Preston Beckett Taylor & Gugle Co., 1999 U.S. Dist. LEXIS 12969 (S.D. Ohio July 9, 1999). Least sophisticated consumer standard applied even if the actual plaintiff might have been more sophisticated as a result of her multiple FDCPA suits.

Smith v. Transworld Sys., 1997 U.S. Dist. LEXIS 23775 (S.D. Ohio July 31, 1997). A debt collection letter violated § 1692e(10) if it was objectively false, or if not objectively false, it would mislead or deceive the least sophisticated consumer.

Knight v. Schulman, 102 F. Supp. 2d 867 (S.D. Ohio 1996), *aff'd*, 166 F.3d 1214 (6th Cir. 1998). "Least sophisticated consumer

standard" was an objective standard under which debt collector was in violation of FDCPA if collection letters or other communications would have deceived least sophisticated consumer.

Adams v. First Fed. Credit Control, Inc., 1992 WL 131121 (N.D. Ohio May 21, 1992). Least sophisticated consumer standard employed to analyze alleged FDCPA violation.

Oregon

Van Westrienen v. Americontinental Collection Corp., 94 F. Supp. 2d 1087 (D. Or. 2000). The debt collector may be held liable for statements made to the consumer's attorney.

Pennsylvania

Mushinsky v. Nelson, Watson & Assoc., L.L.C., 642 F. Supp. 2d 470 (E.D. Pa. 2009). Objective least sophisticated consumer standard applies. Even if the notice was not false, it could be deceptive or misleading to the least sophisticated debtor.

Reed v. Pinnacle Credit Servs., L.L.C., 2009 WL 2461852 (E.D. Pa. Aug. 11, 2009). Objective least sophisticated consumer standard applies. Thus, where there are two possible meanings to a communication, one of which is inaccurate, the least-sophisticated consumer could be misled or deceived by that inconsistency.

Smith v. NCO Fin. Sys., Inc., 2009 WL 1675078 (E.D. Pa. June 12, 2009). Collection letters are analyzed under the least sophisticated debtor standard.

Duraney v. Washington Mut. Bank, 2008 WL 4204821 (W.D. Pa. Sept. 11, 2008), *aff'd*, 2010 WL 2993810 (3d Cir. Aug. 2, 2010). The court held that allegedly deceptive communications from a debt collector to the consumer's attorney were not subject to the FDCPA, adopting the Ninth Circuit's view in *Guerrero* as opposed to the Fourth Circuit's per the *Sayyed* opinion; but assuming such communications were covered, the court followed the Seventh Circuit's "competent lawyer" standard in *Evory* and still dismissed the § 1692e claims since the consumer "has not even argued, much less demonstrated, that her lawyer was likely to be deceived by the communications he received."

Martsolf v. JBC Legal Group, P.C., 2008 WL 275719 (M.D. Pa. Jan. 30, 2008). "Whether a communication is misleading under the FDCPA presents a question of law for the court; disputed facts must be resolved by a jury."

Catherman v. Credit Bureau, 634 F. Supp. 693 (E.D. Pa. 1986). The consumer failed to establish that letters from a collection agency/credit reporting agency threatening the consumer's ability to obtain credit were unconscionable or deceptive. The letters were not likely to convey the impression to an unsophisticated consumer that they would be immediately denied all credit, but only that the there would be a chance of future denials.

South Carolina

Moore v. Ingram & Assocs., Inc., 805 F. Supp. 7 (D.S.C. 1992). A "court must look to whether the letter would mislead a general unsophisticated recipient." Use of the word "judgment" in the § 1692g validation notice was not misleading even though a judgment had not been obtained.

Utah

Ditty v. CheckRite, Ltd., 973 F. Supp. 1320 (D. Utah 1997). A reasonable jury applying the least sophisticated consumer standard could conclude that the letter's warning that "other actions . . . may be considered" threatened suit.

Virginia

Carter v. Countrywide Home Loans, Inc., 2009 WL 2742560 (E.D. Va. Aug. 25, 2009). Where the plaintiff had not signed the note or the related loan modification agreement, he would not be covered as a "consumer" under 15 U.S.C. § 1692e.

Morgan v. Credit Adjustment Bd., Inc., 999 F. Supp. 803 (E.D. Va. 1998). Language demanding "immediate attention" and insisting that the debtor contact the office within seven days from the date of the letter could very likely confuse the least sophisticated debtor, who could reasonably interpret the notice as a demand for immediate payment or immediate action. Actual deception is not necessary to demonstrate that a statement is misleading in violation of the FDCPA.

K.2.4.2 Deceptive Threat of Legal Action

LeBlanc v. Unifund CCR Partners, 601 F.3d 1185 (11th Cir. 2010). The court stated there was a genuine issue of material fact as to whether debt collector's dunning letter, which purported to be from its "Legal Department," was a threat to take legal action under the least sophisticated consumer standard. Where the parties reasonably disagree on the proper inferences that can be drawn from a debt collector's letter, resolution is for the trier of fact, and not for the court on summary judgment.

Ruth v. Triumph P'ships, 577 F.3d 790 (7th Cir. 2009). Privacy notice was threat to take illegal action, since it was claiming a legal right to disclose nonpublic information about the consumer and was threatening to do so unless the consumer affirmatively opted out. To threaten to take some action "to the extent permitted by law" is to imply that, under some set of circumstances, the law actually permits that action to be taken. Here, the defendants have suggested no set of circumstances under which the FDCPA would have permitted disclosure of the plaintiffs' nonpublic information without their consent. If anything, the notice's implication to the contrary makes the statement *more* misleading, not less.

Wilhelm v. Credico, Inc., 519 F.3d 416 (8th Cir. 2008). A categorical threat to sue made in a letter failed to disclose that the debt buyer would not sue any consumer who timely disputed the debt as permitted by § 1692g, as the debt buyer then must cease collection until the debt is verified: "That appears to be a threat to take action 'that cannot legally be taken' within the meaning of § 1692e(5). A reasonable jury might also find that an unequivocal threat to sue in these circumstances constituted use of a 'deceptive means to collect or attempt to collect' a debt that is prohibited by § 1692e(10)."

Brown v. Card Serv. Ctr., 464 F.3d 450 (3d Cir. 2006). The complaint stated a claim for using misleading means in violation of § 1692e where the collector's letter stated that nonpayment "could" result in an attorney referral and suit being filed but the consumer alleged that in fact the collector had no intention of making such a referral.

Owsley v. Coldata, Inc., 2004 WL 1690178 (5th Cir. July 29, 2004). Statement in dunning letter that her account was "scheduled to be returned to [her] creditor who may [*inter alia*] . . . secure advice of counsel regarding appropriate steps to be taken to enforce payment," although suggesting that the collector had counsel on retainer and that the stakes might be raised in the future, would not lead a recipient to believe that legal action was imminent. The letter did not imply that a lawsuit was imminent or that the collector had any say in whether legal action would be taken. Neither did it suggest that the creditor likely would pursue legal action. On the contrary, the letter specifically stated that the creditor might take actions other than pursuing suit.

Peter v. G.C. Servs. L.P., 310 F.3d 344 (5th Cir. 2002). The language, "SHOULD YOU FAIL TO PAY THIS ACCOUNT IN FULL, G.C. SERVICES WILL REVIEW YOUR ACCOUNT AND MAKE RECOMMENDATIONS TO THE DEPARTMENT OF EDUCATION FOR THE MOST EFFECTIVE COLLECTION METHOD ALLOWABLE UNDER FEDERAL LAW" did not violate § 1692e.

Combs v. Direct Mktg. Credit Servs., Inc., 165 F.3d 31 (7th Cir. 1998) (unpublished) (text at 1998 WL 911691). Plaintiff received a letter about a $100 claim of BMG Music Services, which gave her a chance "to resolve this matter amicably" and "advise[d] you to consult with your attorney regarding your liability." The trial court's dismissal for failure to state a claim was affirmed. The statements were simply moderate communications which made neither express nor implied threats of current or imminent litigation under the *Jenkins v. Union Corp.* standards.

United States v. Nat'l Fin. Servs., Inc., 98 F.3d 131 (4th Cir. 1996). Collection agency's mass mailings for American Family Publishers implied that an attorney acting like an attorney had considered the consumers' debts for magazine subscriptions and concluded that the consumer was a candidate for legal action when the attorney had not reviewed the letters or the claims against the debtors. The court found a violation of § 1692e(5) and (10) because collector made false, unintended threats of legal action. The fact that the collection lawyer had filed a small number of suits and that some of the duns said only that suit would be considered did not lessen the capacity of the letters to deceive an unsophisticated consumer.

Bentley v. Great Lakes Collection Bureau, 6 F.3d 60 (2d Cir. 1993). Collection letter's statement that the creditor had authorized whatever legal means necessary to collect the debt implied that legal proceedings were imminent when they were not and would mislead the least sophisticated consumer in violation of § 1692e(5). References to post-judgment proceedings of attachment and garnishment where the collector was not authorized to proceed would mislead the least sophisticated consumer that the collector would take action not intended to be taken.

Graziano v. Harrison, 950 F.2d 107 (3d Cir. 1991). Threat to sue, if payment was not received within ten days, contained on the front of a letter that provided notice of the consumer's right to request verification of the debt, within thirty days, rendered the verification notice ineffective, violating § 1692g, and was confusing, violating § 1692e(10).

Pipiles v. Credit Bureau, Inc., 886 F.2d 22 (2d Cir. 1989). A collector acted deceptively by sending a notice that implied, through vague language, that some type of legal action had already been or was about to be initiated and could only be averted by payment, when the collector actually took no action other than telephone calls to collect debts of less than $150.

Crossley v. Lieberman, 868 F.2d 566 (3d Cir. 1989). An attorney's letter referring to the creditor as "plaintiff" and demanding "damages and costs" was carefully crafted to falsely suggest that the consumer was already sued or in foreclosure. Threatening to proceed with suit within one week was deceptive where the consumer had a thirty-day right to cure her delinquency.

Jeter v. Credit Bureau, Inc., 760 F.2d 1168 (11th Cir. 1985). Whether a collection agency's two statements, one month apart, that it will recommend legal action to a creditor in five days may be deceptive to an unsophisticated consumer, where there was conflicting evidence of the agency's intent and practice, presented a triable issue.

Baker v. G.C. Servs. Corp., 677 F.2d 775 (9th Cir. 1982). It was not clearly erroneous to find that a collector, who did not ever take legal action, falsely implied that it would do so by stating that it would attempt to settle debts out of court before referring them to a lawyer.

Alabama

Sparks v. Phillips & Cohen Assocs., Ltd., 641 F. Supp. 2d 1234 (S.D. Ala. 2008). "Merely advising the debtor of the agency's options with which to pursue the debt is the sort of truism that is legally insufficient to violate § 1692e."

Campbell v. Thompson, 1990 WL 71348 (N.D. Ala. May 23, 1990). Filing affidavits for criminal charges against bad check writers did not involve deception under § 1692e (4) or (5).

Kimber v. Fed. Fin. Corp., 668 F. Supp. 1480 (M.D. Ala. 1987). Filing a time-barred suit when the collector knew of no tolling of the statute of limitations was unconscionable and a deceptive misrepresentation of the legal status of the debt, implying the collector would prevail.

Bice v. Merchants Adjustment Serv., Clearinghouse No. 41,265 (S.D. Ala. 1985). The allegation that a collector's statement that wage garnishment and seizure of personal property would follow suit and judgment was deceptive should not be dismissed since the representation does not distinguish between items exempt from levy and other items.

Arizona

Nichols v. GC Serv., L.P., 2009 WL 3488365 (D. Ariz. Oct. 27, 2009). Disputed facts precluded summary judgment for either party on the consumer's claims that the defendant violated § 1692e(5) by threatening a tax refund seizure that was not intended.

Grismore v. United Recovery Sys., L.P., 2006 WL 2246359 (D. Ariz. Aug. 3, 2006). The court denied summary judgment on the plaintiff's § 1692e(5) claim where the parties submitted conflicting evidence that the debt collector threatened the plaintiff with legal action that it did not intend to take.

Gostony v. Diem Corp., 320 F. Supp. 2d 932 (D. Ariz. 2003).

Threat to file a lawsuit "and /or" garnish wages did not falsely imply present intent to garnish wages before a lawsuit.

United States v. ACB Sales & Serv., Inc., 590 F. Supp. 561 (D. Ariz. 1984). The statement in one letter that collector is "authorized to proceed with any lawful action" and the discussion of creditor remedies in another letter imply a threat of legal action to the average consumer. A disclaimer of present intent to pursue legal action removes implication of threatened legal action from a third letter. The lack of intent to pursue legal action was inferred from the failure of the collector's employee to seek authorization to sue after sending threatening letters.

California

Walsh v. Frederick J. Hanna & Assocs., P.C., 2010 WL 5394624 (E.D. Cal. Dec. 21, 2010). A letter on a law firm's letterhead stating "if you fail to contact this office, our client may consider additional remedies to recover the balance due" did not amount to a false threat of litigation in violation of § 1692e(5).

Lopez v. Rash Curtis & Assocs., 2010 WL 4968064 (E.D. Cal. Dec. 1, 2010). Plaintiff did not provide sufficient facts for the court to determine whether the defendant's alleged garnishment threats were unlawful or not intended.

Arteaga v. Asset Acceptance, L.L.C., 2010 WL 3310259 (E.D. Cal. Aug. 23, 2010). Summary judgment was granted to the collector on § 1692e claims that the collector unlawfully threatened to attach the consumer's bank account where the consumer initiated the phone call, raised the subject regarding the attachment of the bank account, and asked a question about the collector's abilities to attach her account. The response to the customer's direct question on the subject was informational and not a threat.

del Campo v. Am. Corrective Counseling Serv., Inc., 2010 WL 2473586 (N.D. Cal. June 3, 2010). The court granted summary judgment where it was established that the defendants falsely threatened criminal prosecution in their check diversion duns since there was no evidence that "any individual assessment of whether the district attorney would prosecute" or that the district attorney intended to prosecute.

Herrera v. LCS Fin. Servs. Corp., 2009 WL 5062192 (N.D. Cal. Dec. 22, 2009). A plausible claim was stated by the allegation that the least sophisticated debtor would be misled by (1) the debt collector's invocation of foreclosure when foreclosure was an impossibility and (2) a letter that failed to advise the debtor that the debt was due and owing when the debt was subject to California's anti-deficiency law.

Velazquez v. Arrow Fin. Serv., L.L.C., 2009 WL 2780372 (S.D. Cal. Aug. 31, 2009). The court granted the defendant's motion to dismiss the plaintiff's § 1692e(5) claim based on the allegation that the defendant filed its underlying state court collection suit "without adequate investigation and dismiss[ed] that suit because it knew it could not prove its allegations." Plaintiff alleged no facts showing that defendant had no right to institute the action or that defendant did not intend to litigate the action. The California rules of civil procedure allow a plaintiff to voluntarily dismiss an action any time before trial. "That a plaintiff chooses to exercise that right early in the case cannot establish that the action was improperly brought or that the plaintiff never intended to litigate."

Harrington v. Creditors Specialty Serv., Inc., 2009 WL 1992206 (E.D. Cal. July 8, 2009). Default judgment entered as requested for both FDCPA and Rosenthal Act violations for statutory damages in the total amount of $2000, fees in the amount of $3029, and costs of $400, arising from the defendant's false threat of suit and garnishment in violation of § 1692e(5).

Basinger-Lopez v. Tracy Paul & Assocs., 2009 WL 1948832 (N.D. Cal. July 6, 2009). Default judgment entered on well pleaded facts showing that the defendants engaged in a campaign of unlawful harassment, threats, misrepresentations, and other misconduct in violation of multiple FDCPA provisions: "Defendant made repeated threats against Plaintiff to sue her."

Schwarm v. Craighead, 552 F. Supp. 2d 1056 (E.D. Cal. 2008). Under the least sophisticated debtor standard, the court found that the statements in the company's letters constituted threats of legal action or arrest under §§ 1692e(4) and 1692e(5). The threats were false when the company sent letters threatening legal action and arrest to many debtors when it never intended to send the files to the district attorneys' offices because the debtors' files did not meet the minimum requirements for referral.

Canlas v. Eskanos & Adler, P.C., 2005 WL 1630014 (N.D. Cal. July 6, 2005). The court denied a motion to dismiss the claim that a false threat of suit may be implied by a request for "voluntary payment" from a collection attorney so that "further action" would not be taken.

Uyeda v. J.A. Cambece Law Office, P.C., 2005 WL 1168421 (N.D. Cal. May 16, 2005). Court denied motion to dismiss where the letter's use of equivocal language (might or may) could constitute an impermissible threat of unintended legal action or to report adverse information to a credit reporting agency when it did not do so.

Palmer v. Stassinos, 348 F. Supp. 2d 1070 (N.D. Cal. 2004). Stating that the failure to pay "may necessitate using other remedies to collect" implied to the least sophisticated consumer a threat of legal action.

Anderson v. Credit Collection Servs., Inc., 322 F. Supp. 2d 1094 (S.D. Cal. 2004). The collector's unadorned full quotation in its dun of FDCPA § 1692c(b), including its language regarding communications "necessary to effectuate a post-judgment judicial remedy," did not constitute a threat of litigation in the absence of any other reference to or inference of judicial action.

Perretta v. Capital Acquisitions & Mgmt. Co., 2003 WL 21383757 (N.D. Cal. May 5, 2003). Because the least sophisticated consumer would understand threat to "take further steps" on a time-barred debt as threatening litigation, the complaint stated a cause of action under the FDCPA.

Irwin v. Mascott, 96 F. Supp. 2d 968 (N.D. Cal. 1999). Threats to sue, sent to people who did not meet creditor's criteria for suit, violated the FDCPA. When a creditor rarely, if ever, sued, that fact alone may be enough to prove lack of intent to sue.

Baker v. Citibank N.A., 13 F. Supp. 2d 1037 (S.D. Cal. 1998). Because the consumer could have been sued within thirty days, the collection letter was not misleading.

Newman v. CheckRite California, Inc., 912 F. Supp. 1354 (E.D. Cal. 1995). The least sophisticated consumer test applied to determine whether a false threat of legal action was made. Where attorney filed suit only if a check exceeded $50 or if more than three bad checks had been written, the attorney threatened action that was not intended to be taken as to amounts below those thresholds and violated the FDCPA.

Colorado

O'Connor v. Check Rite, 973 F. Supp. 1010 (D. Colo. 1997). The Offer of Settlement letter which conspicuously stated that the decision to institute action had not been made was not a false, deceptive, or misleading representation. Particularly where the collection letter stated "if legal action is taken and a lawsuit is filed, it will be handled by an attorney within your state," the attorney did not falsely represent that he was licensed in a state merely by seeking to collect a debt in that state.

Connecticut

Gervais v. Riddle & Assocs., P.C., 479 F. Supp. 2d 270 (D. Conn. 2007). Vague legal references and law firm letterhead constitute threat of litigation.

Goins v. JBC & Assoc., 2004 WL 2713235 (D. Conn. Nov. 24, 2004). Collector's statement that it reserved the right to use information provided by the plaintiff in further civil proceedings did not violate § 1692e(5) when the collector had not decided whether to sue.

Reese v. Arrow Fin. Servs., Inc., 202 F.R.D. 83 (D. Conn. 2001). Although the issue was not briefed, the court cited several cases holding that mere collection of time-barred debts without threat of litigation does not violate the FDCPA.

Madonna v. Acad. Collection Serv., Inc., 1997 WL 530101 (D. Conn. Aug. 12, 1997). Threat of legal action was not false or deceptive where creditor sues often under similar circumstances and litigation had not been ruled out with regard to the particular consumer, though probability of suit was low.

Herbert v. Monterey Fin. Servs., Inc., 863 F. Supp. 76 (D. Conn. 1994). "Final demand" "to avoid the remedies available under . . . State laws" was a false threat of suit where the collection agency was not authorized to pursue suit.

Bishop v. Nat'l Accounts Sys., Inc., Clearinghouse No. 49,175 (D. Conn. 1993). Debt collector's letter, demanding that if the consumer did not pay the bill immediately or call the collector's office, had the capacity to mislead a consumer to believe that he would be subject to imminent arrest and incarceration.

Young v. Dey, 1994 U.S. Dist. LEXIS 21484 (D. Conn. July 5, 1994). Summary judgment motions denied in part because a genuine issue of fact existed as to whether the debt collector's threat of attachment, without disclosing relevant property exemptions, was misleading pursuant to § 1692e(4).

Woolfolk v. Van Ru Credit Corp., 783 F. Supp. 724 (D. Conn. 1990). A list of creditor's remedies was misleading and "unduly threatening," violating the FDCPA. Whether a threat to take "Action" would be construed by a unsophisticated consumer as a threat of suit is for trial, not summary judgment.

Cacace v. Lucas, 775 F. Supp. 502 (D. Conn. 1990). Attorney's misstatement of intention as to when he would begin litigation violated § 1692e, and his misstatement of the consequences to the debtor of the commencement of a suit violated § 1692e(4).

Gaetano v. Payco, Inc., 774 F. Supp. 1404 (D. Conn. 1990). Stating that it would use "ALL APPROVED MEANS AT OUR COMMAND TO COLLECT DEBTS" and "IMMEDIATE ACTION" did not implicitly threaten suit and the issue of whether it falsely threatened other action was inappropriate for summary judgment. It was not a false representation of intent to sue since there was no evidence of the collector's intent.

Woolfolk v. Rubin, 1989 U.S. Dist. LEXIS 19106 (D. Conn. Nov. 9, 1989). Letters on attorney's letterhead that referred to legal proceeding created the impression that suit was imminent. This was deceptive since the attorney had no authority from the creditor to sue, and was not licensed to sue in the consumer's home state.

Delaware

Sutton v. Law Offices of Alexander L. Lawrence, 1992 U.S. Dist. LEXIS 22761 (D. Del. June 17, 1992). Collection letter sent to debtor in bankruptcy did not violate § 1692e(5) by "threatening to take action that cannot legally be taken or that was not intended to be taken" where debt collector was unaware of the bankruptcy stay.

Beattie v. D.M. Collections, Inc., 754 F. Supp. 383 (D. Del. 1991). Whether the threat to bring suit against the wrong person violated the § 1692e(5) prohibition of threats of illegal action depended upon whether the collector knew or should have known or failed to exercise reasonable care in determining the consumers' liability for the debt.

Florida

Kelemen v. Professional Collection Sys., 2011 WL 31396 (M.D. Fla. Jan. 4, 2011). The court granted summary judgment to the defendant on the § 1692e(4) claim. It found that the statement— "This office urges you to contact us and make arrangements to satisfy your delinquent obligation. Your failure to do so may result in additional collection activity being taken on your account"— was too vague to constitute a threat of litigation, and, in any event, "the inferential leap from a threat of litigation to a threat of seizure, garnishment, attachment or sale of property, is the kind of bizarre or idiosyncratic interpretation not protected under the least sophisticated consumer standard."

Malowney v. Bush/Ross, 2010 WL 3340493 (M.D. Fla. Aug. 25, 2010). Where creditors communicated to their law firm the intent to pursue all legal remedies, including foreclosure, summary judgment was granted to law firm for claims of violation of § 1692e(5), since the creditors fully intended to take the threatened action. In examining alleged violations of § 1692e(5), a court looks only to the debt collector's intent to take the action threatened.

Wise v. CACH, L.L.C., 2010 WL 1257665 (S.D. Fla. Mar. 26, 2010). The court found that the least sophisticated debtor would regard the warning that the defendant's client could "hav[e] the sheriff sell your property in order to pay off the judgment (unless said property is homestead or tenancy by the entireties)," as a reality based reminder, not as a threat to take action that cannot legally be taken.

Sanz v. Fernandez, 633 F. Supp. 2d 1356 (S.D. Fla. 2009). Allegations that the defendants were acting as debt collectors, but failed to register to collect debts as required by state law, stated a claim for violating § 1692e(5), since, "by attempting to collect the debt, [they] threatened to take action that could not legally be taken."

Jelencovich v. Dodge Enter. Inc., 2009 WL 4899405 (S.D. Fla. Dec. 14, 2009). The collector's failure to reference available exemptions when it stated that the judgment creditor had the right to garnish the consumer's wages or bank account did not violate §§ 1692e(5) or 1692e(10) since the statement was in all respects true and, unlike the inapposite cases on which the plaintiff relied, did not suggest that exemptions were unavailable.

Arslan v. Florida First Fed. Group, 1995 WL 731175 (M.D. Fla. Oct. 5, 1995). Falsely representing that a lawsuit to collect the debt was imminent violated § 1692e(2)(A) and (5).

Georgia

Gilmore v. Account, Mgmt., Inc., 2009 WL 2848278 (N.D. Ga. Apr. 27, 2009). Threatening a lawsuit which the debt collector knew or should have known was unavailable by reason of § 1692g(b) was the kind of abusive practice the FDCPA intended to eliminate under §§ 1692e(5) and 1692e(10).

Thomas v. LDG Fin. Servs., Inc., 463 F. Supp. 2d 1370 (N.D. Ga. 2006). Stated a claim for violations of §§ 1692e, 1692e(5), and 1692e(10) where garnishment threatened when consumer said she could not pay.

Schimmel v. Slaughter, 975 F. Supp. 1357 (M.D. Ga. 1997). Attorney letter stating that garnishment was available "after judgment was obtained" could convey to the least sophisticated consumer the impression that a judgment was a virtual certainty and therefore was deceptive.

Phillips v. Stokes, 1992 U.S. Dist. LEXIS 22731 (N.D. Ga. Jan. 8, 1992). Attorney's letter stating that unless the debt was paid in seventy-two hours further action as might be necessary would be taken to satisfy the claims violated § 1692e(5) because no decision had been made as to whether to initiate legal action against the consumer. Attorney's motion to reconsider was denied because attorney's letter would lead the least sophisticated consumer to believe that legal action would be filed.

Johnson v. Ardec Credit Servs., Inc., 1984 U.S. Dist. LEXIS 24889 (N.D. Ga. Mar. 21, 1984). The collection letter headed "Total Equity d/b/a Manchester Apartments v. Jessie Johnson" conveys to a reasonable consumer the false impression that judicial action is pending, violating § 1692e.

Yelvington v. Buckner, Clearinghouse No. 36,581 (N.D. Ga. 1984). Threats of garnishment and suit against the consumer's employer before the collector had filed suit violated § 1692e(5). A letter labeled "FINAL NOTICE" with legal caption, red notary seal and indicating a copy to court clerk violated § 1692e(9) and (13) by simulating legal process and creating a false impression of source or approval.

Florence v. Nat'l Sys., 1983 U.S. Dist. LEXIS 20344 (N.D. Ga. Oct. 14, 1983). Letter threatening suit in federal court in two days violated § 1692e(2),(5) and (10).

Zoeckler v. Credit Claims & Collections, Inc., 1982 U.S. Dist. LEXIS 18384 (N.D. Ga. Sept. 30, 1982). An ambiguous sentence could reasonably give the false impression the suit had been filed although read literally the sentence stated that advice to file a suit was pending.

Blackwell v. Prof'l Bus. Servs., 526 F. Supp. 535 (N.D. Ga. 1981). Allegations were held on motions for summary judgment not to state violations of the FDCPA. The collector's letter stating that it "may" sue and entitled "FINAL NOTICE BEFORE LEGAL REFERRAL" did not create an impression that the collector would file suit and thus did not violate either the general standard of § 1692e or § 1692e(2)(A).

Williams v. Rash, Curtis & Assocs., 1978 U.S. Dist. LEXIS 20395 (N.D. Ga. Dec. 13, 1978). Motion to dismiss was denied. Plaintiff alleged that a letter on a law office's letterhead with the caption "Re: Medical Center of Columbus vs. Defendant Princella Williams" simulated legal process.

Hawaii

Keli v. Universal Fid. Corp., 1997 U.S. Dist. LEXIS 23940 (D. Haw. Feb. 25, 1997). Collection agency threatened to sue when it had never sued. The threat, among other threats, to *TAKE EVERY STEP* was a threat of legal action to an unsophisticated consumer. The misrepresentations violated § 1692e(5).

Illinois

Day v. Check Brokerage Corp., 511 F. Supp. 2d 950 (N.D. Ill. 2007). Where the debt collector failed to offer evidence of a valid assignment, it violated § 1692e and 1692e(5) by threatening legal action in collection agency's name when it could not legally take that step under Illinois law. Where the debt collector admitted that it did not file lawsuits where the consumer resided, both §§ 1692e and 1692e(5) were violated.

Rawson v. Credigy Receivables, Inc., 2006 WL 418665 (N.D. Ill. Feb. 16, 2006). The court held that since the complaint alleged that the defendant threatened to sue on a debt that was time barred under applicable state law, it stated a claim for relief. The consumer argued that the five-year statute of limitations on unwritten or partially unwritten contracts applied to this credit card account.

Francis v. Snyder, 389 F. Supp. 2d 1034 (N.D. Ill. 2005). A collection letter violated § 1692e(5) by indirectly threatening legal action by stating "a bad check can be considered a violation of Illinois Statutes" because it indicates to the debtor that she may be sued particularly since the letter was from an attorney. Legal action was unavailable for a stopped payment check under the Illinois Statute.

Asch v. Teller, Levit & Silvertrust, P.C., 2003 WL 22232801 (N.D. Ill. Sept. 26, 2003). Illinois law requires that payments by check, cash, and garnishment or attachment be credited when made available to the debt collector, i.e., on the day received. Failure by the debt collector to credit payments on the date received and adding interest violates § 1692f(1).

Holt v. Wexler, 2002 U.S. Dist. LEXIS 5244 (N.D. Ill. Mar. 27, 2002). Cross-motions for summary judgment by the parties were denied because statements in a collection letter that payment would

rehabilitate the plaintiff's credit history and that skip tracers may contact employers, relatives, and neighbors did not violate the FDCPA on its face. Determination of any FDCPA violation was left for the trier of fact to decide.

Riddle & Assocs., P.C. v. Kelley, 2001 U.S. Dist. LEXIS 15712 (N.D. Ill. Sept. 28, 2001). A genuine issue of fact remained for trial regarding whether the collection letter communicated to the unsophisticated consumer that legal action was imminent in violation of § 1692e(5).

Walker v. Cash Flow Consultants, Inc., 200 F.R.D. 613 (N.D. Ill. 2001). Attempting to collect a time-barred debt was not an FDCPA violation absent an express or implied threat of litigation where state law barred the remedy but did not extinguish the debt.

Hamid v. Blatt, Hasenmiller, Leibsker, Moore & Pellettieri, 2001 U.S. Dist. LEXIS 13918 (N.D. Ill. Aug. 31, 2001). Consumer's allegations that collection attorney filed suit on a time-barred debt were sufficient to survive debt collector's motion to dismiss FDCPA action.

Peeples v. Blatt, 2001 U.S. Dist. LEXIS 11869 (N.D. Ill. Aug. 14, 2001). Plaintiff's allegations that the defendant misrepresented the legal status and the amount of the alleged debt adequately stated a claim for violation of the FDCPA.

Young v. Manley, 2000 U.S. Dist. LEXIS 13035 (N.D. Ill. Sept. 6, 2000). Defendant law firm brought dischargeability proceedings in about 20% of the cases in which it sent a letter mentioning the possibility. The letter was not a threat to take unintended action. The fact that defendant law firm brings dischargeability proceedings and then settles them did not itself justify any implication that the proceedings were brought for the improper purpose of scaring a debtor into paying.

Clark v. Retrieval Masters Creditors Bureau, Inc., 185 F.R.D. 247 (N.D. Ill. 1999). An unsophisticated consumer, receiving a letter warning of the prospect of a lawsuit, could believe that litigation was imminent and authorized, even though the creditor rarely filed such suits.

Nielsen v. Dickerson, 1999 WL 754566 (N.D. Ill. Sept. 9, 1999). Court granted consumer summary judgment under § 1692e(3) and (5), since the collection law firm had threatened but never filed a collection lawsuit on behalf of creditor. Court also found the collection law firm liable under § 1692j.

Davis v. Commercial Check Control, Inc., 1999 WL 89556 (N.D. Ill. Feb. 16, 1999). References to "criminal prosecution" in a bounced check dunning letter were threats to refer for prosecution as a matter of law. Evidence showed that such referrals were rarely, if ever, made, thus violating § 1692e(4), (5), and (10). Threatening civil prosecution under the applicable bad check statute violated § 1692e(5) where the collection agency had no particularized intention of suing, but was not a violation for threatening legal action that could not legally be taken since the remedy was in fact available.

Veillard v. Mednick, 24 F. Supp. 2d 863 (N.D. Ill. 1998). A dun on an attorney's letterhead is not, by itself, a threat of legal action. Unsigned dun sent on attorney's firm letterhead, where no attorney was actively involved in the consumer's case, is a misrepresentation of attorney participation in the collection process in violation of §§ 1692e and 1692j.

Jenkins v. Union Corp., 999 F. Supp. 1120 (N.D. Ill. 1998). Letter which expressly disavowed any planned legal action but which stated that legal action was an available step did not threaten suit.

Arellano v. Etan Indus., Inc., 1998 WL 911729 (N.D. Ill. Dec. 23, 1998). Collector's statement that it "shall recommend to your creditor that this matter be referred to an attorney, with full authority to take all appropriate action to collect this account" was a threat of litigation; summary judgment was granted for making a false threat since the evidence showed that creditor has never filed suit.

Drennan v. Van Ru Credit Corp., 950 F. Supp. 858 (N.D. Ill. 1996). Complaint stated a claim where an unsophisticated consumer could interpret defendant's "legal review notification" and "notice of possible wage garnishment," despite frequent use of "may" and "might" as imminent threats when in fact no action was taken for over a year after dunning letters were sent. Court also referred to Attorney Albert Rubin as "a discredit to the profession" and noted that he was still "playing chicken" with the FDCPA.

Finch v. Silverstein, 1996 WL 467251 (N.D. Ill. Aug. 13, 1996). The consumer stated a claim by alleging that the defendant's correspondence would lead an unsophisticated consumer to believe that a lawsuit was imminent, by including a legal caption and language implying that a lawsuit would be pursued, when suit was not imminent.

Villarreal v. Snow, 1996 WL 28308 (N.D. Ill. Jan. 19, 1996). A lawyer violated § 1692e by deceptively representing in the debt collection letter that the collector had convinced the creditor not to file suit but rather to give the consumer one more chance to pay the debt when in fact the letter was a standard step in the debt collection process.

Oglesby v. Rotche, 1993 WL 460841 (N.D. Ill. Nov. 5, 1993). Threatening a lawsuit within five days of the date of the correspondence, when no suit was actually filed for over two months, was deceptive from the standpoint of the "least sophisticated consumer" and constituted a threat of action that was not intended to be taken in violation of § 1692e(5) and (10). Letter stating "once judgment has been entered, it is our intent to proceed with the court ordered attachment and garnishment of all wages, property, and other financial assets, all at additional expense to you" violated § 1692e by (1) misrepresenting the breadth of garnishment and attachment and (2) despite the phrase "once judgment has been entered," implying that garnishment of *all* wages and attachment of property is unavoidable once court action had been initiated.

Smith v. Mikell, Clearinghouse No. 34,362C (N.D. Ill. 1982). Denying the collector's motion for summary judgment the court found that a consumer of average intelligence would be misled by the collector's dunning letters which falsely implied that suit would be filed shortly and that the consumer's debt would be increased by $16. Whether the defendant intended to sue within that time and whether the consumers were deceived or relied upon the communication were remaining material factual questions.

Kansas

Bieber v. Associated Collection Servs., Inc., 631 F. Supp. 1410 (D. Kan. 1986). The collector did not misrepresent the availability of wage garnishment under state law in violation of § 1692e(4) since the state prohibition of garnishment after an assignment was inapplicable because the debt was not assigned. Any false representation that 75% of wages would be garnished was a bona fide error excused by § 1692k(c). A collector's letters threatening suit were not deceptive since the creditor eventually sued.

Louisiana

Goodman v. S. Credit Recovery, Inc., 1998 WL 240403 (E.D. La. May 12, 1998). Threat of "further collection procedures" unless the debt was paid did not threaten litigation.

Michigan

Gradisher v. Check Enforcement Unit, Inc., 210 F. Supp. 2d 907 (W.D. Mich. 2002), *aff'd on other grounds*, 502 F.3d 159 (3d Cir. 2007). Notices which stated "Failure to Make Payment Can Result in a Warrant for Your Arrest" would lead even a sophisticated debtor to conclude that the Sheriff's Department had determined that the debtor committed a crime and arrest or criminal prosecution was certain to occur if the debt was not paid violating § 1692e(4) and (5).

Minnesota

Thinesen v. JBC Legal Group, P.C., 2005 WL 2346991 (D. Minn. Sept. 26, 2005). The complaint alleged facts sufficient to show that the defendants violated the FDCPA by threatening suit on time-barred dishonored checks.

Wiegand v. JNR Adjustment Co., 2002 U.S. Dist. LEXIS 7292 (D. Minn. Apr. 22, 2002). Debt collector's duns complied with the requirements of the applicable state dishonored check statute and therefore complied with the FDCPA.

State ex rel. Hatch v. JBC Legal Group, P.C., 2006 WL 1388453 (Minn. Dist. Ct. Apr. 13, 2006). Since Minnesota does not allow recovery on a time-barred debt, defendants' mention of possible suit is a threat to take action that cannot legally be taken, as well as a false representation and deceptive practice. Whether defendants intended to file suit is a question of fact.

Missouri

Terry v. C & D Complete Bus. Solutions, 2011 WL 144920 (W.D. Mo. Jan. 18, 2011). A debt collector's letter threatening to garnish the plaintiffs' wages where no judgment or other authority to do so had been obtained violated § 1692e. The letter did not threaten garnishment at some unknown future date but, rather, after ten days.

Nebraska

Page v. Checkrite, Ltd., Clearinghouse No. 45,759 (D. Neb. 1984). Stating that the creditor will be advised to pursue further action was not deceptive.

Nevada

Edwards v. Nat'l Bus. Factors, Inc., 897 F. Supp. 455 (D. Nev. 1995). Threat of "action" by an attorney "without further notice" is a threat of immediate legal action to the least sophisticated consumer.

New Jersey

Ford v. Consigned Debts & Collections, Inc., 2010 WL 5392643 (D.N.J. Dec. 21, 2010). In this default judgment matter, the court found that a defendant who called the plaintiff and left a recorded message that did not reveal the defendant's identity as a debt collector or its purpose for the phone call violated § 1692d(6).

Federal Trade Comm'n v. Check Enforcement, 2005 WL 1677480 (D.N.J. July 18, 2005). After making threats of arrest and seizure of property or wages in violation of § 1692e(4), the debt buyer neither filed civil or criminal complaints with law enforcement agencies nor levied upon a consumer's wages or property. Defendants violated § 1692e(5) by making false threats to file civil and criminal law suits. For example, regarding civil actions, in some states a foreign corporation not registered to do business in the state is prohibited from bringing suit in the courts of that state. Defendants were not registered in each state where they threatened civil action. As to criminal prosecutions, defendants often made such threats in jurisdictions where such prosecution would already be barred by applicable statutes of limitations. Defendant falsely claimed that a criminal proceeding against a consumer was imminent unless immediate payment was completed, in violation of § 1692e(7).

New Mexico

Spinarski v. Credit Bureau, Inc., 1996 U.S. Dist. LEXIS 22547 (D.N.M. Sept. 19, 1996). Collection agency was granted summary judgment on all the consumer's remaining claims. The collector's statement that it would obtain judgment did not falsely imply that the collector was affiliated with the courts. The consumer failed to show that the collector did not intend to file suit, and the collector stated that no suit was filed because the consumer was agreeable to making payments on the debt. The threat to have the debtor arrested was considered truthful because a debtor could be arrested for failure to appear at a debtor's exam even though the court acknowledged that a least sophisticated consumer could understand the letter to threaten jail for nonpayment of the debt.

New York

Nichols v. Frederick J. Hanna & Assocs., P.C., 2011 WL 102665 (N.D.N.Y. Jan. 13, 2011). A debt collection letter sent by an out-of-state law firm to a debtor on the firm's letterhead, when viewed as a whole, would not reasonably be interpreted by the least sophisticated consumer as a threat of imminent litigation and did not suggest that any threatened legal action could not have been taken even though no firm members were licensed to practice in the state. The letter advised the debtor that the firm was representing the creditor in its collection efforts and that no attorney had yet personally reviewed circumstances of the debtor's account, but noted that if the debtor did not contact the firm the creditor could consider additional remedies to recover the balance due, which could include retaining local counsel.

Ellis v. Cohen & Slamowitz, L.L.P., 701 F. Supp. 2d 215 (N.D.N.Y. 2010). Where the consumer alleged that the debt collector expressed its authority to commence a lawsuit against him without actually being so authorized, the court found that the consumer adequately alleged a claim that was plausible on its face. Alternatively, the consumer sufficiently alleged that the debt collector's

letter may have constituted a threat of suit and that the letter was sent without an intention to commence a lawsuit.

Gutierrez v. GC Servs. Ltd. P'ship, 2010 WL 3417842 (E.D.N.Y. Aug. 27, 2010). The debt collector's statement that it had an obligation to its clients to pursue their accounts "vigorously" was not a false threat and did not amount to deceptive representation in violation of § 1692e(5) and (10): "Even to the least sophisticated consumer, the language in the collection letters used by defendant is innocuous. The letters—read together, as they must—do not threaten litigation by using the word 'vigorously.' To conclude otherwise would require 'bizarre or idiosyncratic interpretations' of the collection letters, which are not countenanced by the FDCPA."

Henneberger v. Cohen & Slamowitz, L.L.P., 2010 WL 1405578 (W.D.N.Y. Mar. 31, 2010). Summary judgment was inappropriate where there was a genuine issue of material fact as to whether defendant's employee threatened to seize resources (Social Security and pension funds) that could not legally be seized.

Leone v. Ashwood Fin., Inc., 257 F.R.D. 343 (E.D.N.Y. 2009). The court denied summary judgment on the factual issue that defendant had no intention to bring suit against any of the recipients of the letter in question merely because the amounts owed were relatively small. The court overlooked *Bentley*. In determining whether a statement constitutes an actual threat of legal action, the court will consider: (1) "whether the threat to bring suit to collect the debt is one made by the debt collector himself, or whether the language merely suggests that the debt collector's client may consider pursuing legal action in the event of nonpayment;" (2) "whether the language in the letters explicitly threatens that legal action will be taken, or whether it simply describes available alternatives which include possible legal action;" and (3) the defendant's ability and intent to carry out the threatened conduct. The defendant's letter implied a present ability by the debt collector itself to move forward with litigation, stating that "*we* may have no alternative than to turn this debt over to an attorney. This action may result in a civil suit being filed against you." (Emphasis added by court.) However, at his deposition, [defendant's president] revealed that, "if we got to the point where we decided the attorney would sue, then we would request an assignment from the particular client. . . ."

Khon v. Paul Michael Mktg. Serv., 2006 U.S. Dist. LEXIS 78455 (E.D.N.Y. Oct. 27, 2006). Denied defendant's motion for judgment on the pleadings where consumer alleged that the collection letter stated that "our client will then have to choose whether or not to take legal action on this claim" was a threat to take action was not intended to be taken in violation of the FDCPA, § 1692e(5) and (10), because defendant's client, had "no intention to bring a legal action."

Spira v. Ashwood Fin., Inc., 371 F. Supp. 2d 232 (E.D.N.Y. 2005). Consumer's motion to reconsider the court's order granting summary judgment for the debt collector, on the basis that additional discovery regarding the meaning of the phrase "it is our intent to pursue collection of this debt through every means available to us" should have been allowed, was denied because extraordinary circumstances required for reconsideration had not been shown. Discovery had been previously allowed.

Failla v. Cohen, 2005 WL 3032560 (E.D.N.Y. Mar. 10, 2005). The court denied the collection firm's motion to dismiss finding that the language "[w]e may proceed with suit against you without waiting thirty days if so requested by our client" stated a claim for violation of § 1692e(5) and (10) where the collectors would allegedly never sue on such a small claim.

Lerner v. Forster, 240 F. Supp. 2d 233 (E.D.N.Y. 2003). The letter as a whole left no doubt that litigation was merely an option, that no decision had been made as to whether to litigate, but that the debtor could avoid the risk of a lawsuit either by paying or arranging to pay.

Degonzague v. Weiss, Neuren & Neuren, 89 F. Supp. 2d 282 (N.D.N.Y. 2000). In order to establish a violation of § 1692e(5), the consumer must show that a lawsuit could not properly be brought or that the defendant did not actually intend to bring a lawsuit.

Unger v. Nat'l Revenue Group, Ltd., 2000 U.S. Dist. LEXIS 18708 (E.D.N.Y. Dec. 8, 2000). The fact that the collector had not filed suit in the last year for a claim of less than $300, where the claim involved $248.81, did not establish a § 1692e(5) violation for a summary judgment motion.

Laster v. Cole, 2000 U.S. Dist. LEXIS 3771 (E.D.N.Y. Mar. 20, 2000). Consumer's argument that collection lawyer misrepresented his intent to recommend suit because he did not make his recommendation immediately at the end of seven days but waited over a month was rejected as the consumer failed to introduce evidence of the collector's intent at the time the threat was made. The delay could have been the result of an unanticipated demand on the collector's time.

Tipping-Lipshie v. Riddle, 2000 U.S. Dist. LEXIS 2477 (E.D.N.Y. Mar. 1, 2000). Whether reference to the collection law firm not having decided whether to pursue suit on a $128 claim was deceptive was not appropriate for summary judgment where the firm introduced some evidence that it had sued for less than $128.

Wiener v. Bloomfield, 901 F. Supp. 771 (S.D.N.Y. 1995). Threat of filing in an improper venue did not violate § 1692i; however, it did violate § 1692e(5) by threatening action that legally could not be taken. Mailing documents which were captioned as "summons and complaint" which were not actually filed with the court violated § 1692e(9) and (13).

Tsenes v. Trans-Continental Credit & Collection Corp., 892 F. Supp. 461 (E.D.N.Y. 1995). Complaint alleged that collector did not have authority to commence legal action which stated claims for violation of §§ 1692e(5), (4), and (10) sufficiently to survive motion to dismiss.

Robinson v. Transworld Sys., Inc., 876 F. Supp. 385 (N.D.N.Y. 1995). § 1692e(5) was not violated where there was no threat of adverse action.

Knowles v. Credit Bureau, 1992 WL 131107 (W.D.N.Y. May 28, 1992). Collector's letter which stated "FAILURE TO PAY WILL LEAVE OUR CLIENT NO CHOICE BUT TO CONSIDER LEGAL ACTION" was not a threat to take unintended action in violation of § 1692e(5).

Riveria v. MAB Collections, Inc., 682 F. Supp. 174 (W.D.N.Y. 1988). Collector's threat to advise creditor of necessity of legal action over a small medical bill was found literally truthful without

consideration of its deceptive implications.

Wegmans Food Mkts., Inc. v. Scrimpsher, 17 B.R. 999 (Bankr. N.D.N.Y. 1982). Three weekly letters threatening intended criminal prosecution for bad checks did not violate §§ 1692d or 1692e.

Ohio

Phipps v. Stellar Recovery, Inc., 2010 WL 1433168 (S.D. Ohio Apr. 5, 2010). The fact that debt collector did not sue the consumer does not settle the questions of whether the debt collector intended to sue the consumer at the time of making the threat to do so or whether it had the legal right to file such a suit.

Kelly v. Montgomery Lynch & Assocs., Inc., 2008 WL 1775251 (N.D. Ohio Apr. 15, 2008). The defendant violated §§ 1692e(5) and 1692e(10) by threatening to take action that was legally unavailable when it informed the consumer that it would bring criminal charges for passing a dishonored check because the criminal statute of limitations had expired when the threat was made and by threatening to take action that was not intended when it threatened that it would bring criminal charges for passing a dishonored check, since in fact it had never prosecuted such charges in the past and had no intention of doing so here.

Dowling v. Litton Loan Serv., L.P., 2006 WL 3498292 (S.D. Ohio Dec. 1, 2006). Because defendant's own records and version of the facts showed that the consumer had only not paid one month's mortgage payment, its duns stating that she was two months behind and threatening foreclosure if payment in the stated amount was not made violated § 1692e(5)'s bar against making unintended or legally unavailable threats.

Edwards v. McCormick, 136 F. Supp. 2d 795 (S.D. Ohio 2001). Ohio Revised Code § 2329.66(A) provides a homestead exemption prohibiting health care creditors from foreclosing on the primary residence of their debtors, and a debt collector's threat to take such action violated § 1692e(5).

Canterbury v. Columbia Gas, 2001 WL 1681132 (S.D. Ohio Sept. 25, 2001). Threatening pursuit of legal means, referral to an attorney, and firm collection action on a time-barred debt was deceptive as an unsophisticated consumer would imply that suit was threatened.

Wright v. Asset Acceptance Corp., 1999 U.S. Dist. LEXIS 20675 (S.D. Ohio Dec. 30, 1999). Genuine issue of material fact existed whether collection agency's letter violated § 1692e(5) since the threat to initiate a suit was made contingent on debt collector learning that plaintiff was working full-time and the consumer failed to show he was working full time. Plaintiff's actual employment status mattered since least sophisticated consumer who was not working full-time would not have construed the letter as threatening a lawsuit but least sophisticated consumer who was employed full-time would.

Boyce v. Attorney's Dispatch Serv., 1999 U.S. Dist. LEXIS 1124 (S.D. Ohio Feb. 2, 1999). Collection agent violated § 1692e(5) where the collection letter stated: "Before a criminal complaint can be initiated and an arrest warrant issued, the criminal procedure requires that you be sent this Notice and given a ten-day opportunity to make full restitution. . . . If this period expires and you have failed to make restitution, you are susceptible to immediate criminal prosecution." The least sophisticated consumer would construe this language as a threat that a criminal prosecution would follow the consumer's failure to immediately pay the debt where the next step was usually referral to a collection attorney and not to criminal authorities.

Lamb v. M & M Assoc., 1998 WL 34288694 (S.D. Ohio Sept. 1, 1998). Collection letter that informed the consumer that she could be sued if the debt remained unpaid and that she could be served with a summons and complaint and that suit could be filed within the thirty-day period to request validation could be interpreted by the least sophisticated consumer as threatening legal action.

Powell v. Computer Credit, Inc., 975 F. Supp. 1034 (S.D. Ohio 1997), *aff'd,* 1998 U.S. App. LEXIS 26797 (6th Cir. Oct. 15, 1998). "FINAL NOTICE" letter did not create a false sense of urgency, did not misrepresent number of previous attempts to collect the debt, and did not falsely threaten legal action.

Smith v. Transworld Sys., 1997 U.S. Dist. LEXIS 23775 (S.D. Ohio July 31, 1997). Use of terms such as "further collection procedures," "legally due," "protracted and unpleasant collection effort," "litigation," "legal action," "court costs," "attorneys fees," "no defense to this claim" in collection letters would be construed by least sophisticated consumer as meaning that legal action could result for failure to pay the debt, and did not constitute misleading threat of legal action.

Gasser v. Allen County Claims & Adjustment, Inc., 1983 U.S. Dist. LEXIS 20361 (N.D. Ohio Nov. 3, 1983). A letter threatening garnishment violated § 1692e(2)(A) since it created the false impression that judgment had been obtained (even though the word "may" was used) and garnishment was impending. Summary judgment was appropriate under § 1692e(4) and (5) on claims that the collector in several letters falsely represented its intent to imminently seek garnishment or file suit where the letters were sent before any decision was made or authority obtained to take legal action, the defendants did not take such action, suit was infrequently pursued (only 2% of debts were referred for suit, though 50–75% of debts uncollected), and the defendant submitted no evidence of intent to pursue suit or garnishment. Another letter stating "legal action may be authorized" was not deceptive since it does not suggest suit was intended at the time. While dunning letters threatening garnishment or legal action in legalese did not violate § 1692e(9) and (10), another form letter with a caption, pink paper, bold lettering, a direction to bring the notice, and make no phone calls suggest officially authorized legal compulsion of some sort violating § 1692e(9) and (13). A letter falsely suggesting that nonpayment alone could result in garnishment violated § 1692e(4).

United States v. First Fed. Credit Control, Inc., Clearinghouse No. 33,811 (N.D. Ohio 1983). Numerous of the collector's letters were found to be deceptive. A letter threatening referral to representatives in the consumer's locale for suit or action which would probably cause embarrassment and expense violated §§ 1692e, 1692e(5) and (10) where the collector had no such representatives and did not file suit out-of-town. Letters threatening referral to an attorney for suit were deceptive violating §§ 1692e and 1692e(10) in the 99% of the cases where the collector did not sue. A threat of garnishment in one of the letters was always false. A letter falsely implying drastic action within twenty-four hours violated §§ 1692e,

1692e(5) and (10). A threat of "more drastic measures" was deceptive violating §§ 1692e, 1692e(5) and (10) where the collector never took legal steps to collect a debt nor reported consumers to a credit reporting agency.

Minick v. First Fed. Credit Control, Inc., 1981 U.S. Dist. LEXIS 18622 (N.D. Ohio June 9, 1981). A letter threatening garnishment presented a triable issue under § 1692e(4) and (5) where no legal action was taken, but the claim was eventually referred to a lawyer. A letter on an attorney's letterhead sent by a collection agency threatening suit and stating an attorney had been retained violated § 1692e where no attorney had been retained and suit was not filed.

Kleczy v. First Fed. Credit Control, Inc., 486 N.E.2d 204 (Ohio Ct. App. 1984). Use of threat, "avoid further action," did not violate § 1692e(5) where the collector sent additional collection letters after that threat.

Oregon

Daley v. A & S Collection Assocs., Inc., 2010 WL 2326256 (D. Or. June 7, 2010). Disputed factual issues precluded summary judgment on the claim that the collector unlawfully threatened to sue on a time-barred debt.

Flores v. Quick Collect, Inc., 2007 WL 433239 (D. Or. Jan. 31, 2007). When the summons for debtor examination threatened contempt or imprisonment for failure to appear, and the debtor appeared but the creditor's lawyer did not, the court refused to dismiss a claim of empty threat under § 1692e(5). If defendants were unable to take immediate action in the court because it was an improper venue, plaintiff's allegations could arguably state a claim for use of false representation or deceptive means to collect on a debt.

Van Westrienen v. Americontinental Collection Corp., 94 F. Supp. 2d 1087 (D. Or. 2000). Where the debt collector threatened seizure or garnishment in five days and it would take some days more than that at best, the consumer established a violation of § 1692e(2)(A) but not §§ 1692e(4) and 1692f(6) where there was evidence that the collector intended to seize the consumer's property. The debt collector's threatened legal action, before it had acquired the right to do so, violated § 1692e(5) and (10).

Lambert v. Nat'l Credit Bureau, Inc., 1981 U.S. Dist. LEXIS 18623 (D. Or. Apr. 8, 1981). An implicit, false threat of legal action was found in the threat to "take such course of action as we judge necessary and appropriate" followed immediately by a listing of supposed court costs in violation of § 1692e(5).

Dixon v. United Adjusters, Inc., 1981 U.S. Dist. LEXIS 18392 (D. Or. Feb. 19, 1981). Two letters did not misrepresent the legal status of the debt nor did threats of imminent, unspecified action (e.g., "time is running out") violate the Act.

Baker v. G.C. Servs. Corp., Clearinghouse No. 31,230 (D. Or. 1981), *aff'd,* 677 F.2d 775 (9th Cir. 1982). A letter threatening "further collection procedures" and mentioning an "out-of-court settlement" violated § 1692e(5) since the collector's policy was not to take legal action for claims of less than $1000. However, a letter referring to "further collection procedures" was not deceptive since it did not imply legal action, and the failure to specify intended action did not violate the Act.

Pennsylvania

Lesher v. Law Office of Mitchell N. Kay, P.C., 2010 WL 2431826 (M.D. Pa. June 14, 2010). The defendant attorney violated § 1692e(3) and (5) by sending a dun containing the *Greco* disclaimer—"no attorney with this firm has personally reviewed the particular circumstances of your account"—since the communication as a whole would still deceptively lead the least sophisticated consumer to believe that an attorney was involved in the collection of the debt and that an attorney could and would take legal action.

Wideman v. Monterey Fin. Servs., Inc., 2009 WL 1292830 (W.D. Pa. May 7, 2009). The allegation that the collector threatened to submit to the IRS a Form 1099C when it had no intent to actually do so stated a claim for violating § 1692e(5).

Martsolf v. JBC Legal Group, P.C., 2008 WL 275719 (M.D. Pa. Jan. 30, 2008). The following statement in the collector's dun constituted a threat to sue under the least sophisticated standard: "You are cautioned that unless this total amount is paid within thirty (30) days after the date this letter is received, you may be subject to a civil penalty, court costs, and reasonable attorney fees after suit has been filed."

Tenuto v. Transworld Sys., Inc., 2002 U.S. Dist. LEXIS 1764 (E.D. Pa. Jan. 31, 2002). In class action where consumers alleged that the collection agency sent a form letter deceptively suggesting that the recipient's wages could be garnished if the debt was not paid and the creditor chose to pursue judicial action, settlement was approved.

Cook v. Gen. Revenue Corp., 2001 U.S. Dist. LEXIS 11181 (E.D. Pa. Aug. 6, 2001). Debt collector's motion to dismiss was denied because the consumer alleged adequate facts to state a claim: that the debt had been paid, suit was time barred, and the collection lawyer wrote unobligated relatives about the alleged debt. The collector failed to demonstrate a bona fide error defense.

Tenuto v. Transworld Sys., Inc., 2000 U.S. Dist. LEXIS 14344 (E.D. Pa. Sept. 29, 2000). Class certification granted as to persons sent letters threatening wage garnishment, normally not available in Pennsylvania.

Bezpalko v. Gilfillan, Gilpin & Brehman, 1998 WL 321268 (E.D. Pa. June 17, 1998). No false threat of suit where attorney had received creditor's authorization of suit prior to sending threatening dun and did in fact file suit.

Crossley v. Lieberman, 90 B.R. 682 (E.D. Pa. 1988), *aff'd*, 868 F.2d 566 (3d Cir. 1989). "The rules of the game have changed. An attorney pursuing a debtor . . . is required to be truthful." District court increased bankruptcy judge's award of $100 to $1000 for a letter falsely threatening imminent foreclosure.

Metz v. HCSC-Credit & Collections, No. 85-3132 (E.D. Pa. 1985) (available on LEXIS). Threat to recommend suit by the creditor is not a threat to engage in the unauthorized practice of law, violating § 1692e(5), since in Pennsylvania such a recommendation is not the practice of law, as it involves no knowledge of the law beyond that possessed by the average person.

In re Belile, 209 B.R. 658 (Bankr. E.D. Pa. 1997). A letter threatening referral to the collection agency's legal department falsely implied imminent legal action because the agency's lawyer was not admitted in the state of the consumer's residence and no action was taken to affiliate with a local lawyer. This violated § 1692e(5) and (10) and the Pa. UDAP statute. The consumer's testimony that the letter created the implication of immediate suit was reasonable.

Littles v. Lieberman, 90 B.R. 669 (Bankr. E.D. Pa. 1988), *rev'd on other grounds*, 90 B.R. 700 (E.D. Pa. 1988). The statement that suit will be filed if no payment is received in a week was a threat of suit, but references to "plaintiff" and "damages and costs" would not reasonably convey impression that suit had already been filed given the threat of future suit.

South Dakota

Pearce v. Rapid Check Collection, Inc., 738 F. Supp. 334 (D.S.D. 1990). Letter threatening suit sent to consumer known to be represented by an attorney on that debt was characterized a "technical," *de minimis* violation of § 1692a(2) for which no liability would attach.

Texas

United States v. Cent. Adjustment Bureau, Inc., 667 F. Supp. 370 (N.D. Tex. 1986). Collector violated § 1692e(4) and (7) by falsely representing the debtor would be arrested or jailed or that property would be seized or garnished. Collector violated § 1692e(5) by threatening suit and other action before it was authorized by the creditor and the threats regarding small accounts where suit was rare. Only one practice of many reviewed was affected by the less sophisticated consumer standard applied, and that involved a statement in a letter that the collector "can" sue on small amounts, which a less sophisticated consumer would understand to be a threat of suit, rather than a statement of capability of suit. The collector's testimony that it only stated during phone calls that it "could" pursue legal remedies was not credible and was contradicted by the evidence. The threat to refer a file to a local representative who will pursue the debtor's case to the fullest extent permitted by law, the statement all action would be dropped upon payment, threatening referral to an attorney and drastic action, and threat of collection action after phone calls discussing possible suit would lead a reasonable consumer to believe suit was threatened. A reference to "collection process" and a statement that the collector may recommend that suit is or is not warranted are not threats to sue. References to "further action," "drastic action," "vigorous prosecution of collection" imply a threat to sue when sent by an attorney.

Utah

Ditty v. CheckRite, Ltd., 973 F. Supp. 1320 (D. Utah 1997). A reasonable jury applying the least sophisticated consumer standard could conclude that the letter's warning that "other actions . . . may be considered" threatened suit. Because the collection agency's attorney's research led him to conclude that the actions listed in the letter could be maintained, he did file a few suits after mailing the letter, and Utah law made the passing of bad checks a criminal offense in some circumstances, there were disputed issues of fact regarding defendants' intent in warning the consumers of their potential liability.

Virginia

Withers v. Eveland, 988 F. Supp. 942 (E.D. Va. 1997). The consumer reasonably interpreted the letter as threatening legal action if the debt was not paid by the payment deadline by the statements that the collector would "institute collection proceedings" and pursue "all legal remedies." As a non-lawyer, the collector could not legally file suit against the consumer and violated § 1692e(5) by threatening suit, an "action that cannot legally be taken or that is not intended to be taken." The collection agency violated § 1692e(10) by falsely representing that unpaid debts would be referred to an attorney for immediate legal action and falsely representing that a debt collection agency had the authority to file suit on behalf of a client.

West v. Costen, 558 F. Supp. 564 (W.D. Va. 1983). Summary judgment was entered for consumers where a collector threatened to seek the arrest of the consumers on bad check charges. The threat was deceptive since the collector never sought criminal complaints. Also deceptive were threats that the creditor would seek the consumers' arrest where the collector did not have any basis to believe the creditor would seek a criminal complaint. Reserved for trial were threats of arrest where the collector asserted that she told consumers that the creditor would have them arrested and there was a basis for the collector to believe the creditor would do so.

Wisconsin

Bystrom v. Burgess Law Office, 2007 WL 5329352 (W.D. Wis. Feb. 20, 2007). Debt collector's uncontested motion for summary judgment was granted where its telephone messages about a "pending legal matter" were found not to be false, misleading, deceptive, unfair or unconscionable even though no collection suit had been filed, although one was contemplated.

Bruesewitz v. Law Offices of Gerald E. Moore & Assocs., P.C., 2006 U.S. Dist. LEXIS 83712 (W.D. Wis. Nov. 15, 2006). The threat to commence arbitration proceedings was intended to be taken at the time of sending letter and was not deceptive: defendants routinely initiated NAF arbitration proceedings in 29,946 cases since 2004 and had 2858 arbitration cases pending.

Klewer v. Cavalry Invs., L.L.C., 2002 U.S. Dist. LEXIS 1778 (W.D. Wis. Jan. 30, 2002). Wisconsin's six-year statute of limitations for contract, Wis. Stat. § 893.43, had run effectively extinguishing the debt according to Wisconsin decisions, not just the judicial remedies available to collect the debt as in most states. Thus, the collection letter misrepresented the legal status of the debt in violation of the FDCPA.

Tomas v. Bass & Moglowski, 1999 U.S. Dist. LEXIS 21533 (W.D. Wis. June 29, 1999). Debt collector's allegations regarding a deficiency claim contained in its state law replevin action for repossession of a dirt bike filed after consumer's monetary debt was discharged in bankruptcy violated § 1692e(5) because debt collector had no right to pursue deficiency.

Sturdevant v. Jolas, P.C., 942 F. Supp. 426 (W.D. Wis. 1996). A demand letter signed by an out-of-state attorney not licensed in the state in which the letter was addressed did not constitute a threat of action that could not legally be taken as local counsel could have been retained. The court also disagreed with the consumer's contention that every collection letter from an attorney carries an implied threat of legal action which may not have been intended to be pursued because then every collection letter from an attorney would be then subject to an FDCPA action to see if the action was intended to be taken. The attorney's letter at issue stated that no decision had been made about further action but that the letter would be the last demand before suit.

Patzka v. Viterbo Coll., 917 F. Supp. 654 (W.D. Wis. 1996). The collection agency violated § 1692e by threatening to take legal action that it could not legally take by threatening to sue on a prohibited collection fee and interest. The college was liable under the Wisconsin Consumer Act for collecting interest which was not disclosed prior to consummation nor authorized by the tuition agreement.

K.2.4.3 Other Deceptive Threats

Heintz v. Jenkins, 514 U.S. 291, 115 S. Ct. 1489, 131 L. Ed. 2d 395 (1995). "The Fair Debt Collection Practices Act prohibits 'debt collectors' from making false or misleading representations and from engaging in various abusive and unfair practices." "[W]e do not see how the fact that a lawsuit turns out ultimately to be unsuccessful could, by itself, make the bringing of it an 'action that cannot legally be taken.' "

Ruth v. Triumph P'ships, 577 F.3d 790 (7th Cir. 2009). Privacy notice was threat to take illegal action, since it was claiming a legal right to disclose nonpublic information about the consumer and was threatening to do so unless the consumer affirmatively opted out. To threaten to take some action "to the extent permitted by law," is to imply that, under some set of circumstances, the law actually permits that action to be taken. Here, the defendants have suggested no set of circumstances under which the FDCPA would have permitted disclosure of the plaintiffs' nonpublic information without their consent. If anything, the notice's implication to the contrary makes the statement *more* misleading, not less.

Muha v. Encore Receivable Mgmt., Inc., 558 F.3d 623 (7th Cir. 2009). "Confusing language in a dunning letter can have an intimidating effect by making the recipient feel that he is in over his head and had better pay up rather than question the demand for payment. The intimidating effect may have been magnified in this case by the reference to revocation, which might have suggested to an unsophisticated consumer that any right he might have to challenge the demand for payment had been extinguished by the revocation of his contract with the issuer, the original creditor."

Kuehn v. Cadle Co., 335 Fed. Appx. 827 (11th Cir. 2009) (unpublished). Defendant's false threat, that plaintiff's failure to supply her tax identification number would subject her to a fifty dollar penalty imposed by the IRS, violated § 1692e(10) as a matter of law.

Evory v. Nat'l Action Fin. Servs., Inc., 505 F.3d 769 (7th Cir. 2007). Although a violation of state law is not in itself a violation of the federal Act, *Beler v. Blatt, Hasenmiller, Leibsker & Moore, L.L.C.*, 480 F.3d 470, 473–474 (7th Cir. 2007), a threat to impose a penalty that the threatener knows is improper because unlawful is a good candidate for a violation of §§ 1692d and 1692e.

Turner v. J.V.D.B. & Assocs., 2006 U.S. App. LEXIS 25835 (7th

Cir. Oct. 16, 2006). "[A] letter that includes a statutory verification notice may still violate § 1692e, if it leads an objectively reasonable, but unsophisticated recipient, to believe the discharged debt is still payable."

Dunlap v. Credit Prot. Ass'n, L.P., 419 F.3d 1011, 1012 (9th Cir. 2005) (per curiam). "We find that CPA's letter would not impermissibly mislead the least sophisticated debtor into believing that his credit would be damaged by a failure to pay a de minimis debt. Any inference regarding credit reporting that can be drawn from CPA's name [Credit Protection Association] is, at best, very weak. Moreover, any such inference is not sustained by the letter's main text, which mentions nothing about credit reporting, complies with FDCPA requirements, and is straightforward and non-threatening. Although CPA does not inform debtors that de minimis debts are rarely reported, the mere omission of this information is not so misleading that it violates the FDCPA. . . . Nor is there any threat of unintended action: CPA's collection letter, at worst, only vaguely and generally implies that the reader should pay his debt in order to protect his credit rating." The complaint was properly dismissed.

Durkin v. Equifax Check Servs., Inc., 406 F.3d 410 (7th Cir. 2005). Letter was not false when it mentioned possible referral to investigator or collection agency, or that steps would be taken even though such steps would be taken only by a computer.

Turner v. J.V.D.B. & Assocs., Inc., 330 F.3d 991 (7th Cir. 2003). Section 1692e generally prohibits "false, deceptive or misleading" collection activities without regard to intent. The collector's ignorance of the consumer's bankruptcy did not excuse its post-discharge violation of § 1692e in seeking collection of a discharged debt (reversing summary judgment in the debt collector's favor).

Picht v. Jon R. Hawks, Ltd., 236 F.3d 446 (8th Cir. 2001). Attorney debt collector's use of state pre-judgment garnishment statute violated state law and therefore § 1692e(5). State law allowed pre-judgment garnishment only if the amount owed was certain and involved no exercise of discretion. Calculation of the amount owed did involve exercise of discretion because included in the claimed amount was a sum for a dishonored check civil penalty of *up to* $100.

White v. Goodman, 200 F.3d 1016 (7th Cir. 2000). Collection letter that demands payment and threatens "further collection activity" does not misrepresent the participation of the collector in the collection process. While "minimal participation is not enough," the evidence shows that the collector routinely is meaningfully involved in sending the initial duns and engages in follow-up collection efforts, defeating consumer's claim.

Ferree v. Marianos, 129 F.3d 130 (10th Cir. 1997) (unpublished) (text at 1997 WL 687693). The foreclosure pleadings did not misrepresent the amount or status of the consumer's debt or threaten to obtain an *in personam* judgment on a debt discharged in bankruptcy.

Gammon v. G.C. Servs., 27 F.3d 1254 (7th Cir. 1994). The debt collector's written statement that: "We provide the systems used by a major branch of the federal government and various state governments. . . . You must surely know the problems you will face later if you do not pay," was sufficient to provide the basis for

a claim upon which relief could be granted under § 1692e.

Swanson v. S. Oregon Credit Serv., 869 F.2d 1222 (9th Cir. 1988). The collector's threat to undertake "a complete investigation [of] your employment and assets" violated § 1692e(5) because the threat suggested the collector would take the illegal action, under § 1692c(b), of contacting the consumer's employer.

Juras v. Aman Collection Serv., Inc., 829 F.2d 739 (9th Cir. 1987). Collector misrepresented its legal right to withhold school transcript after bankruptcy and its legal obligation to withhold transcripts from delinquent graduates.

Alabama

Smith v. Allied Interstate, Inc., 2009 WL 5184313 (M.D. Ala. Dec. 23, 2009). Consumers' complaint, alleging that debt collector's routine practice of sending letters like the one sent to consumer violated the FDCPA by threatening to disclose private information to affiliated and non-affiliated parties as well as other third parties, stated a plausible cause of action.

California

Basinger-Lopez v. Tracy Paul & Assocs., 2009 WL 1948832 (N.D. Cal. July 6, 2009). Default judgment entered on well pleaded facts showing that the defendants engaged in a campaign of unlawful harassment, threats, misrepresentations, and other misconduct in violation of multiple FDCPA provisions: "Defendant made repeated threats against Plaintiff to sue her, made abusive accusations, and threatened to embarrass her by disclosing the debt to her family, neighbors, and employer."

Bolton v. Pentagroup Fin. Servs., L.L.C., 2009 WL 734038 (E.D. Cal. Mar. 17, 2009). The defendant's threat to contact the consumer's employer/commanding officer violated the FDCPA.

Boyle v. Arrow Fin. Servs., L.L.C., 2008 WL 4447727 (N.D. Cal. Oct. 2, 2008). Complying with a state law requiring that the consumer be notified before a negative credit report may be submitted did not violate § 1692e. The notice did not say that a report is required, but merely that it may be submitted. It was not deceptive, abusive, threatening or disruptive.

Uyeda v. J.A. Cambece Law Office, P.C., 2005 WL 1168421 (N.D. Cal. May 16, 2005). Court denied motion to dismiss where the letter's use of equivocal language (might or may) could constitute an impermissible threat of unintended legal action or to report adverse information to a credit reporting agency when it did not do so.

Connecticut

Goins v. JBC & Assocs., 2004 WL 2063562 (D. Conn. Sept. 3, 2004). Claim that debt collector misrepresented that it may have the consumer's driver license number on file was disputed precluding summary judgment.

Herbert v. Monterey Fin. Servs., Inc., 863 F. Supp. 76 (D. Conn. 1994). "Final demand" "to avoid the remedies available under . . . State laws" was a false where the next step was to send another dunning letter.

Kizer v. Am. Credit & Collection, Clearinghouse No. 45,928 (D. Conn. 1991). The thinly veiled threat that the consumer would not receive prompt medical attention if he did not immediately pay his debt was deceptive violating § 1692e and abusive violating § 1692d.

Gaetano v. Payco, Inc., 774 F. Supp. 1404 (D. Conn. 1990). Threats to collect a debt were deceptive violating § 1692e(5) where the collector did not have the required license to collect the debt. Multiple reference to "our investigation" do not threaten unlawful third party contracts.

Thomas v. Nat'l Bus. Assistants, Inc., 1984 U.S. Dist. LEXIS 24876, 1984 WL 585309 (D. Conn. Oct. 5, 1984) (slip copy). A letter implying imminent lawyer referral violated § 1692e(5) and (10) since referral was not intended within time frame threatened.

Florida

Danow v. Borack, 2006 WL 5516577 (S.D. Fla. Jan. 30, 2006), *rev'd in part and remanded on other grounds*, 197 Fed. Appx. 853 (11th Cir. 2006). Letter suggesting plaintiff refinance his home was a recommendation of how to pay the debt not a threat to foreclose contradicting the homestead protection.

Ferguson v. Credit Mgmt. Control, Inc., 140 F. Supp. 2d 1293 (M.D. Fla. 2001). Examples of "threatening" communications include: threats to sue; threats to garnish wages and/or seize assets; threats to contact the debtor's neighbors and/or employer; threats to subject the debtor to additional costs for collecting the debt; threats to investigate the debtor's employment; and threats to transfer the account to an attorney for assessment.

Georgia

Schmidt v. Slaughter, Clearinghouse No. 51,961 (M.D. Ga. 1996). The collection lawyer's letter violated § 1692e(5), prohibiting threats of actions that may not be taken, by falsely threatening criminal prosecution for an NSF check when criminal process was not available and demanding a $20 service charge for which a notice required before the charge could be imposed had not been sent. The check was given for an existing debt which meant it was not covered by the Georgia criminal bad check law. A least sophisticated consumer would not understand that the mention of civil process in the letter meant that the criminal process also mentioned would not be pursued.

Florence v. Nat'l Sys., 1983 U.S. Dist. LEXIS 20344 (N.D. Ga. Oct. 14, 1983). Threats to the consumer's credit rating and reputation if there was no response in five days during the thirty day period for validation were deceptive where the consumer did dispute the debt and violated § 1692e(5) since harm to the consumer's credit rating was not intended and illegal. The letters were also deceptive in they gave the impression that the collector could issue adverse credit ratings and could lawfully communicate with third parties.

Illinois

Miller v. Midland Credit Mgmt., Inc., 621 F. Supp. 2d 621 (N.D. Ill. Mar. 10, 2009). Summary judgment for the plaintiffs on the § 1692e(5) claim where the defendants' privacy notice stated that certain information may be disclosed to third parties unless the consumer opted out, since § 1692c(b) made such disclosure an unlawful third party communication even if the consumer failed to act.

Carroll v. Butterfield Health Care, Inc., 2003 WL 22462604 (N.D. Ill. Oct. 29, 2003). An FDCPA claim was stated against a collection attorney for filing state collection suits based on a relative's illegal guarantee of payment to a nursing home, prohibited by the Medicaid Act, 42 U.S.C. § 1396r(c)(5)(A)(ii). The collector was aware of the illegality from prior guarantors' defenses.

Sherman v. Fin. Credit, L.L.C., 2003 WL 1732601 (N.D. Ill. Apr. 1, 2003). Consumer's allegation, that by mentioning name of her employer in collection letter collector was sending the deceptive or misleading signal that it will somehow use that information to the consumer's detriment in violation of § 1692e, survived motion to dismiss even though argument was "a stretch."

Holt v. Wexler, 2002 U.S. Dist. LEXIS 5244 (N.D. Ill. Mar. 27, 2002). Cross-motions for summary judgment by the parties were denied because statements in a collection letter that payment would rehabilitate the plaintiff's credit history and that skip tracers may contact employers, relatives, and neighbors did not violate the FDCPA on its face. Determination of any FDCPA violation was left for the trier of fact.

Kort v. Diversified Collections Servs., Inc., 2001 U.S. Dist. LEXIS 11701 (N.D. Ill. July 31, 2001). Complaint stated a claim for relief where the student loan collector's letter plausibly suggested to the unsophisticated consumer that garnishment could be initiated with less than the thirty-day notice required by applicable federal regulations. Complaint stated a claim for relief where the student loan collector stated that the borrower must provide written proof of entitlement for an exemption from garnishment, while applicable federal regulations require granting the exemption without such written proof.

Raimondi v. McAllister & Assocs., Inc., 50 F. Supp. 2d 825 (N.D. Ill. 1999). Because § 1692c(a)(3) explicitly prohibits collectors from contacting a consumer's employer, threatening to do so in order to collect a debt amounted to a false representation in violation of § 1692e(10).

Beasley v. Collectors Training Inst., 1999 U.S. Dist. LEXIS 13275 (N.D. Ill. Aug. 17, 1999). Debt collectors violated § 1692e by threatening to contact third party credit grantors and to review plaintiff's past and present employment. Even where threat to review employment history was ambiguous, an unsophisticated consumer could reasonably interpret the letter as a threat to contact employers directly.

Holt v. Wexler, 1999 U.S. Dist. LEXIS 8785 (N.D. Ill. May 28, 1999). Although FDCPA authorizes a debt collector to take reasonably necessary steps to collect a post-judgment remedy including contacting third parties, defendant debt collector's motion to dismiss was denied where dunning letter could mislead unsophisticated consumer to think that debt collector could freely contact any employer, neighbor and relative.

Arango v. G.C. Servs., 1999 U.S. Dist. LEXIS 1143 (N.D. Ill. Feb. 2, 1999). Collection letter which stated "WILDLIFE FACT FILE has already reported your name to a National Delinquent Debtor File. This may adversely affect your ability to obtain credit from other mail order companies" was not misleading even though National Delinquent Debtor File was a consumer reporting agency as defined by the FCRA. The statement was true, and the limitation to direct mail companies was sufficient to prevent an unsophisticated consumer from believing that her access to all credit sources was threatened.

Chapman v. Ontra, Inc., 1997 WL 321681, RICO Bus. Disp. Guide 9319 (N.D. Ill. June 6, 1997). The threat to accelerate the installment payments was not a threat of action that could not have legally been taken or that was not intended to be taken. The collectors were acting as agents for the noteholder which did accelerate the loan and foreclose on the property.

Villarreal v. Snow, 1996 WL 28308 (N.D. Ill. Jan. 19, 1996). Attorney's collection letter stating "Before commencing this action, I have convinced my client to give you one last opportunity to settle this matter" was a false, deceptive, or at the very least, misleading statement.

Herbert v. Wexler & Wexler, 1995 WL 535107 (N.D. Ill. Sept. 5, 1995). The statement "[w]e have advised our client of the fact that you are employed and the location of your employment; we have further advised them that you have the ability to pay this debt but refuse to do so" does not violate § 1692c(b) because the collector has neither contacted or threatened to contact the consumer's employer.

Rutyna v. Collection Accounts Terminal, Inc., 478 F. Supp. 980 (N.D. Ill. 1979). This opinion finds harassment and deceptive and unfair practices. A letter threatening to contact the consumer's employer violated § 1692e(5) since the threatened action was prohibited by § 1692c(b).

Indiana

Captain v. ARS Nat'l Servs., Inc., 636 F. Supp. 2d 791 (S.D. Ind. 2009). Section 1692e(5) summary judgment granted to the plaintiff where it was undisputed that the collector misrepresented to the consumer's lawyer that a $15 per day fee would be added to account if it was not paid within two weeks, because that statement was false and deceptive under the "competent attorney" standard established by the Seventh Circuit [*Evory*] applicable to attorney communications.

Clark v. Pollard, 2000 U.S. Dist. LEXIS 18934 (S.D. Ind. Dec. 28, 2000). There could be no violation of § 1692e or § 1692e(5) where the collection agency engaged what may have been the unauthorized practice of law (by signing court documents), because the collector did not issue any threat or false statements.

Louisiana

Johnson v. Eaton, 873 F. Supp. 1019 (M.D. La. 1995). Repeated reference to the amount of court costs would lead the least sophisticated consumer to think he owed those costs and violated § 1692e(2)(A). Letter questionnaire and unfiled, draft consent judgment created the false impression that they were issued by or approved by a court in violation of § 1692e(9).

Maine

Shapiro v. Haenn, 222 F. Supp. 2d 29 (D. Me. 2002). Threatening conduct in violation of applicable state law may constitute a violation of the FDCPA.

Michigan

Wilson v. Merchants & Med. Credit Corp., Inc., 2010 WL 3488617 (E.D. Mich. Sept. 2, 2010). A debt collector's statement that "we know where you work, we know where you live, we know what kind of car you drive, and we will be in further—further contact with you" did not violate §§ 1692d, 1692e or 1692f. "This alleged statement does not suggest that Merchants would refer the case to law enforcement. Rather, it indicates that *Merchants* would be in further contact with Wilson." A debt collector's demand to pay $200 by the end of the day or it would "further the investigation" did not violate §§ 1692d, 1692e, or 1692f.

Minnesota

Cohen v. Beachside Two-I Homeowners' Ass'n, 2006 WL 1795140 (D. Minn. June 29, 2006), *aff'd*, 272 Fed. Appx. 534 (8th Cir. 2008). Filing a required notice on the land record was not a "threat" to take action; the attorneys intended to foreclose and proceeded accordingly. Even if the notice filed on the land record contained an improper amount for fees, it was not a "threat."

Nebraska

Page v. Checkrite, Ltd., Clearinghouse No. 45,759 (D. Neb. 1984). Threatening to place information about a bounced check in the agencies' bulletins for merchants did not falsely convey the impression that the consumers' full name would appear in the bulletins.

New Jersey

Smith v. Lyons, Doughty & Veldhuius, P.C., 2008 WL 2885887 (D.N.J. July 23, 2008). The consumer stated a cause of action for violation of §§ 1692g and 1692e(10) by alleging that the debt collector's letter failed to total the amount of the debt.

Casterline v. I.C. Sys., Inc., 1991 U.S. Dist. LEXIS 21728 (D.N.J. June 26, 1991). Summary judgment was inappropriate regarding the falsity of the collector's representation of his intent to take further action.

New Mexico

Spinarski v. Credit Bureau, Inc., 1996 U.S. Dist. LEXIS 22547 (D.N.M. Sept. 19, 1996). The threat to have the debtor arrested was considered truthful because a debtor could be arrested for failure to appear at a debtor's exam even though the court acknowledged that a least sophisticated consumer could understand the letter to threaten jail for nonpayment of the debt.

New York

Krapf v. Collectors Training Inst., Inc., 2010 WL 584020 (W.D.N.Y. Feb. 16, 2010). The complaint stated a claim that the debt collector violated §§ 1692d and 1692e by leaving telephone messages for the consumer falsely stating that her Social Security number was under investigation.

Sebrow v. ER Solutions, Inc., 2009 WL 136026 (E.D.N.Y. Jan. 20, 2009). Threat to report to credit bureaus was not false, did not create a false sense of urgency, and did not overshadow the verification right notice. The fact that defendant failed to do so after the fact has no bearing on its intent at the time it sent the letter. Nor is it evidence that the letter threatened unintended reporting to the credit agencies.

Leyse v. Corporate Collection Servs., Inc., 2006 WL 2708451 (S.D.N.Y. Sept. 18, 2006). Dropping the name of an attorney without even a vague threat of legal action does not to a level of false urgency which would violate § 1692e(10). Leaving a vague message that entices a consumer to communicate with the debt collector within a short period of time conveys a false sense of urgency in violation of § 1692e (10).

Arend v. Total Recovery Servs., 2006 U.S. Dist. LEXIS 50479 (E.D.N.Y. July 24, 2006). Section 1692e(10) was not violated by the collection letter's language "WHY HAVE YOU IGNORED OUR NOTICES? THIS MATTER WILL NOT SIMPLY GO AWAY. SEND YOUR PAYMENT IN FULL TODAY AND CLEAR YOUR RECORD WITH OUR OFFICE." The debt collector could harm the consumer's credit rating.

Arroyo v. Solomon & Solomon, P.C., 2001 U.S. Dist. LEXIS 12180 (E.D.N.Y. July 19, 2001). Student loan collector that demanded payment without affording borrower an opportunity to make reasonable and affordable payments as required by federal student loan law violated § 1692e.

Tsenes v. Trans-Continental Credit & Collection Corp., 892 F. Supp. 461 (E.D.N.Y. 1995). In order to state a claim for violation of § 1692e(5), complaint should allege (1) that debt collector threatened action (2) which was "not intended to be taken."

Seabrook v. Onondaga Bureau of Med. Econ., Inc., 705 F. Supp. 81 (N.D.N.Y. 1989). A threat to garnish 10% of a consumer's wages was a *per se* violation of the § 1692e(5) prohibition of illegal actions because of the failure to disclose the exemption of the first $100.50 in weekly disposable earnings and other limitations on garnishment.

Henderson v. Credit Bureau Inc., Clearinghouse No. 45,349 (W.D.N.Y. 1989). Writing debtor's employer's name at bottom of a collection notice violated § 1692e(5) because it implies to the least sophisticated consumer that the collector might contact the consumer's employer.

North Dakota

Bingham v. Collection Bureau, Inc., 505 F. Supp. 864 (D.N.D. 1981). The court rejected the claim that the collector's statement that nonpayment would place the consumer in jeopardy was a misrepresentation and that threats of "action" were false.

Weiss v. Collection Ctr., Inc., 667 N.W.2d 567 (N.D. 2003). The least sophisticated consumer could interpret a letter advising that the debt collector had sought information from the motor vehicle department regarding his vehicle as a threat of its intent to repossess it. Whether a threat to repossess was an idle threat or actually intended was a question of fact precluding summary judgment. State law did not prohibit the seizure of a debtor's property merely because the amount of the debt was small.

Ohio

Maddox v. Martin Co., L.L.C., 2006 WL 1308211 (S.D. Ohio May 11, 2006). Telephone messages left with the debtor's aunt threat-

ening unintended criminal charges were found to violate § 1692e(10). The threat to obtain a "Sheriff's seizure order" did not violate § 1692e(4) as the threat was directed to delinquent car purchaser, not her aunt who received the call on her answering machine. The court awarded the aunt statutory damages of $500.

Hartman v. Asset Acceptance Corp., 467 F. Supp. 2d 769 (S.D. Ohio 2004). FDCPA claims that affidavit misrepresented that the debt buyer was a holder in due course in a state collection action violated § 1692e(2) and (12) but not §§ 1692e(6)(A) and 1692d.

Lamb v. M & M Assoc., 1998 WL 34288694 (S.D. Ohio Sept. 1, 1998). The court concluded as a matter of law that debt collector's statement that consumer's unpaid debt could be reported to a credit bureau was factually accurate and not deceptive.

Gasser v. Allen County Claims & Adjustment, Inc., 1983 U.S. Dist. LEXIS 20361 (N.D. Ohio Nov. 3, 1983). The collector used several deceptive collection letters violating the FDCPA. A letter, the common sense implication of which was a false threat to illegally contact the consumer's employer, violated § 1692e(5) and (10). Reference to "Title XIII in United States Code" in the same letter as authority for making an employer contact was a false representation violating § 1692e(10) since that statute had nothing to do with employer contacts. A letter threatening attorney fees not available to the collector under state law violated § 1692e(10). A letter implying illegal and unintended third party contacts violated § 1692e(5). A letter falsely purporting to be a copy of a cover letter to legal pleadings violates § 1692e(4), (5), and (10).

United States v. First Fed. Credit Control, Inc., Clearinghouse No. 33,811 (N.D. Ohio 1983). A collector's threat to end its leniency and implement other collection methods was false violating §§ 1692e, 1692e(5) and (10) when the collector used no other collection methods.

Oregon

Lambert v. Nat'l Credit Bureau, Inc., 1981 U.S. Dist. LEXIS 18623 (D. Or. Apr. 8, 1981). The threat of imminent collection action was not false since skip tracing was begun shortly after the letter was sent.

Dixon v. United Adjusters, Inc., 1981 U.S. Dist. LEXIS 18392 (D. Or. Feb. 19, 1981). Two letters did not misrepresent the legal status of the debt nor did threats of imminent, unspecified action (e.g., "time is running out") violate the Act.

Pennsylvania

Smith v. NCO Fin. Sys., Inc., 2009 WL 1675078 (E.D. Pa. June 12, 2009). Where the privacy notice could lead the least sophisticated debtor to believe that defendants could and would legally contact employers and other persons to verify nonpublic personal information such as one's Social Security number, credit history, and other financial information, motion to dismiss denied. Violation of § 1692e is not prevented by qualifying language: "We do not disclose the information we collect about you to anyone, except as permitted by law" because the least sophisticated debtor "is not expected to know there is a law that prevents defendants from performing the disclosures they otherwise indicate they will perform."

Wideman v. Monterey Fin. Servs., Inc., 2009 WL 1292830 (W.D. Pa. May 7, 2009). The following statement from the collector's dun would be viewed by the least sophisticated consumer as a threat to file a Form 1009C with the IRS: "Please be advised that we have not filed a 1099C form with the IRS concerning this debt as of yet. It is imperative that you contact this office immediately to make payment arrangements to prevent further action in relation to the recovery of this loan." The consumer adequately alleged the statement was false because the debt collector did not intend to file a 1099C.

Wagner v. Client Servs., Inc., 2009 WL 839073 (E.D. Pa. Mar. 26, 2009). Court refused to dismiss claim that 1099C warning was literally false, where defendant failed to show that plaintiff was not within one of the exceptions to the reporting requirement.

James v. Interstate Credit Collection, Inc., 2005 WL 1017819 (E.D. Pa. Apr. 28, 2005). Contrary to the consumer's claim, the debt collector lawfully accessed the consumer's credit report in accordance with the Fair Credit Reporting Act, and therefore the same conduct did not violate the FDCPA.

Catherman v. Credit Bureau, 634 F. Supp. 693 (E.D. Pa. 1986). The consumer failed to establish that letters from a collection agency/credit reporting agency threatening the consumer's ability to obtain credit were unconscionable or deceptive. The letters were not likely to convey the impression to an unsophisticated consumer that they would be immediately denied all credit, but only that the there would be a chance of future denials.

Texas

Cash v. Allied Interstate, Inc., 2005 WL 1186189 (S.D. Tex. May 18, 2005). Final letter stating, "We are recommending to our client that further actions be taken. These actions may include referring this matter to an attorney or reporting this debt to credit reporting agencies" was not misleading where debt collector returned the account to the creditor with one of three codes recommending actions other than referring or reporting. The next sentence "merely notifies the reader what [the creditor's] 'actions may include' " and such actions were a possibility.

United States v. Cent. Adjustment Bureau, Inc., 667 F. Supp. 370 (N.D. Tex. 1986). The collector violated § 1692e(10) by misrepresenting that a daughter's grades and degree would be cancelled unless a college's claim was paid.

Virginia

Guidry v. Clare, 442 F. Supp. 2d 282 (E.D. Va. 2006). The contention, by the consumer who wrote dishonored checks, that under the FDCPA "debt collectors are categorically forbidden from filing criminal complaints is utterly baseless;" to the contrary, a debt collector may file a criminal complaint in accordance with the express language of § 1692e(4) when such action is lawful and may threaten to do so where doing so is lawful and "the debt collector or creditor intends to take such action."

Washington

Sprinkle v. SB&C Ltd., 472 F. Supp. 2d 1235 (W.D. Wash. 2006). Violation of the Servicemembers Civil Relief Act, by failing to file a military service affidavit, also violated the FDCPA, § 1692e(5)

and (10), particularly since the debtor was deployed in the Middle East at the time. Section 1692e(5) prohibits not only the threat, but also the taking, of illegal action. To rule otherwise "would provide more protection to debt collectors who violate the law than to those who merely threaten or pretend to do so."

Wisconsin

Hartman v. Meridian Fin. Servs., Inc., 191 F. Supp. 2d 1031 (W.D. Wis. 2002). Collector's threat to report to a credit bureau any debt left unpaid more than forty-five days from the "date of placement," without any explanation of when the account was so "placed," was a confusing and misleading misrepresentation in violation of § 1692e.

K.2.4.4 Deceptive Implication of Attorney Involvement, 15 U.S.C. § 1692e(3)

Gonzalez v. Kay, 577 F.3d 600 (5th Cir. 2009). "We caution lawyers who send debt collection letters to state clearly, prominently, and conspicuously that although the letter is from a lawyer, the lawyer is acting solely as a debt collector and not in any legal capacity when sending the letter. The disclaimer must explain to even the least sophisticated consumer that lawyers may also be debt collectors and that the lawyer is operating only as a debt collector at that time. Debt collectors acting solely as debt collectors must not send the message that a lawyer is involved, because this deceptively sends the message that the 'price of poker has gone up.' Although the mere presence of disclaimer language might be dispositive in certain circumstances, the context and placement of that disclaimer is also important." As violations are measured against the least sophisticated or unsophisticated consumer standard, a letter from a debt collector, on a law firm letterhead, implies that a lawyer has become involved in the debt collection process, and the fear of a lawsuit is likely to intimidate most consumers. Disclaimer of attorney involvement on reverse of attorney letterhead "completely contradicted the message on the front of the letter—that the creditor had retained and its lawyers to collect the debt."

Rosenau v. Unifund Corp., 539 F.3d 218 (3d Cir. 2008). The fact that defendant's legal department consisted of non-lawyer "legal liaisons" who coordinated the activities of contract attorneys did not make the use of the title "Legal Department" inaccurate. "It is possible that the phrase 'Legal Department' could imply to the least sophisticated debtor that a lawyer was involved in drafting or sending the letter." That implication was deceptive.

Kistner v. Law Offices of Michael P. Margelefsky, L.L.C., 518 F.3d 433 (6th Cir. 2008). Summary judgment was reversed, since it is a jury that should determine whether the letter is deceptive and misleading—specifically, whether the letter gives the impression that it is from an attorney even though it is not; where the L.L.C.'s letter is printed on law firm letterhead; makes repeated reference to a law firm, and directs remittance to an individually named lawyer but also explicitly states that it is from a debt collector and is "signed" by an unnamed "Account Representative."

Kistner v. Law Offices of Michael P. Margelefsky, L.L.C., 518 F.3d 433 (6th Cir. 2008). "[A] jury should determine whether the letter is deceptive and misleading-specifically, whether the letter gives the impression that it is from an attorney even though it is not." "The L.L.C.'s letter is printed on law firm letterhead, it makes repeated reference to a law firm, and it directs remittance to an individually named lawyer. But it also explicitly states that it is from a debt collector and is 'signed' by an unnamed 'Account Representative.' "

Greco v. Trauner, Cohen & Thomas, L.L.P., 412 F.3d 360, 363, 364 (2d Cir. 2005). A dunning letter on a collection law firm letterhead was not deceptive where it stated: "At this time, no attorney with this firm has personally reviewed the particular circumstances of your account. However, if you fail to contact this office, our client may consider additional remedies to recover the balance due." "Put another way, our prior precedents demonstrate that an attorney can, in fact, send a debt collection letter without being meaningfully involved as an attorney within the collection process, so long as that letter includes disclaimers that should make clear even to the "least sophisticated consumer" that the law firm or attorney sending the letter is not, at the time of the letter's transmission, acting as an attorney."

Shula v. Lawent, 359 F.3d 489 (7th Cir. 2004). Alleged violation of the FDCPA that communication was from an attorney who had not reviewed the file raised issues of material fact which could not be resolved on summary judgment.

Wolf v. Javitch, Block, Eisen & Rathbone, L.L.P., 2004 WL 3964424 (6th Cir. Dec. 16, 2004). The court affirmed the dismissal of the § 1692e(3) claim where the evidence that an attorney with the defendant collection law firm signed the state collection complaint and was assigned to and involved with the underlying state collection case despite the subsequent statement to the consumer's counsel that no attorney had been assigned to the case.

Miller v. Wolpoff & Abramson, L.L.P., 321 F.3d 292 (2d Cir. 2003). Merely being told by a client that a debt was overdue was insufficient to meet the FDCPA standard of meaningful attorney involvement. Summary judgment should not be granted to an attorney collector based on conclusory affidavits in a case involving a claim that the attorney sent collection letters without conducting a meaningful review of the circumstances surrounding each alleged debt, without the consumer having the opportunity to investigate specific facts surrounding the attorney's review. If discovery were to reveal that an attorney mailed over 110,000 letters a month, received very limited information about each file from the creditor, "reviewed the collection files with such speed that no independent judgment could be found to have been exercised, and then issued form collection letters with the push of a button, a reasonable jury could conclude that [the attorney] lacked sufficient professional involvement with plaintiff's file that the letters could be said to be from an attorney."

Nielsen v. Dickerson, 307 F.3d 623 (7th Cir. 2002). Attorney's collection letters misrepresented that an attorney was personally involved, contrary to the standards of *Avila* and *Clomon*. He sent collection letters on behalf of various creditors, but never sued. The creditor did not supply the collection attorney with a copy of a debtor's file, nor did the attorney have access to the creditor's accounts. He specifically relied on the creditor's representations in sending the letters. The attorney did not have any information about the accounts other than demographics: name, address, amount due, etc. His staff conducted a ministerial review of the data provided by the creditor, and he spent a few seconds reviewing the data before the form letters went out in bulk. Thirty days after sending the letter, for which the attorney charged $2.45 each, the account was returned to the creditor.

Boyd v. Wexler, 275 F.3d 642 (7th Cir. 2001). Entry of summary judgment for the defendant collection attorney was reversed when, although the attorney's affidavit stated that he reviewed every file before a dun was sent, the mere volume of that undertaking (tens of thousands in some weeks, hundreds of thousands of duns a year) was sufficient to permit a reasonable jury to conclude that "the defendant violated the Fair Debt Collection Practices Act by rubber stamping his clients' demands for payment, thus misrepresenting to the recipients of his dunning letters that a lawyer had made a minimally responsible determination that there was probable cause to believe that the recipient actually owed the amount claimed by the creditor."

Young v. Citicorp Retail Servs., Inc., 159 F.3d 1349 (2d Cir. 1998) (text at 1998 WL 537530). Oversight of the computer system was not sufficient to establish that a collection letter was issued from an attorney who did not review the consumer's file but signed a high volume of collection letters. A large number of computer generated letters purporting to be from an attorney violated § 1692e(3) and (10).

Taylor v. Perrin, Landry, deLaunay & Durand, 103 F.3d 1232 (5th Cir. 1997). Creditor was a "debt collector" even though it was collecting its own debt because it used a lawyer's letterhead and facsimile signature on its dunning letters falsely indicating that a third person was collecting the debt, violating §§ 1692e(3) & 1692j. The law firm supplying the forms was also responsible.

United States v. Nat'l Fin. Servs., Inc., 98 F.3d 131 (4th Cir. 1996). A collection agency's mass mailings for American Family Publishers implied that an attorney acting like an attorney had considered the consumers' debts for magazine subscriptions and concluded that the consumers were candidates for legal action when the attorney had not reviewed the letters or the claims against the debtors. The court found a violation of § 1692e(5) and (10) because collector made false, unintended threats of legal action. The fact that the collection lawyer had filed a small number of suits and that some of the duns said only that suit would be considered did not lessen the capacity of the letters to deceive an unsophisticated consumer.

Avila v. Rubin, 84 F.3d 222 (7th Cir. 1996). Court found that an attorney signing dunning letters violated the FDCPA by having insufficient involvement because he did not review debtor files, did not decide which letters to send, and did not see particular letters before they were sent.

Clomon v. Jackson, 988 F.2d 1314 (2d Cir. 1993). Mass-produced collection letter bearing name of debt collector's general counsel in the letterhead and facsimile of his signature at its conclusion contained false or misleading communications in violation of §§ 1692c, 1692e(3) and 1692c(10) where the attorney did not review debtor's file or the particular collection letter before the letter was sent.

Arizona

Marchant v. U.S. Collections West, Inc., 12 F. Supp. 2d 1001 (D.

Ariz. 1998). A nonattorney debt collector who signed and filed an application for the writ of garnishment gave the false implication that she was an attorney in violation of the FDCPA.

California

Walsh v. Frederick J. Hanna & Assocs., P.C., 2010 WL 5394624 (E.D. Cal. Dec. 21, 2010). Where an explicit disclaimer in a letter on a law firm's letterhead stated that no attorney had reviewed plaintiff's file, "the least sophisticated debtor would understand that the senders of the letter had not evaluated the plaintiff's file." The letter did not violate § 1692e(3).

Riggs v. Prober & Raphael, 2010 WL 3238969 (N.D. Cal. Aug. 16, 2010). The consumer was granted leave to amend to allege additional facts pursuant to *Iqbal* to support the claim that the defendant attorneys committed a *Clomon/Avila* violation of § 1692e(3).

del Campo v. Am. Corrective Counseling Serv., Inc., 2010 WL 2473586 (N.D. Cal. June 3, 2010). Defendants violated § 1692e(3) and (9) by sending consumers check collection notices on district attorney letterhead that did not identify the corporate collector as its source. "[T]he district attorney's permission does not excuse defendants from adhering to the requirements of the FDCPA. At the very least, the law requires that ACCS identified itself as the true sender of the letter . . . [O]n their face, the Official Notices do not disclose the identity of the actual sender, and create the impression that they were sent directly from the district attorney's office rather than from a private company."

Carrizosa v. Stassinos, 2010 WL 144807 (N.D. Cal. Jan. 10, 2010). Disputed factual issues of the extent of the debt collection attorney's personal knowledge and involvement in sending duns on his professional letterhead precluded summary judgment on the consumers' §§ 1692e(3) and 1692e(14) claims.

Palmer v. Stassinos, 2009 WL 86705 (N.D. Cal. Jan. 9, 2009). Attorneys sending collection letters are required by § 1692e(3) to review the individual debtor's file and have some knowledge of the alleged debt. The practice of sending an initial form letter drafted by an attorney without the attorney's review of the specific debtor's file could be accomplished with meaningful attorney involvement if such a letter was sent under the clear directions and supervision of the attorney. A letter is not "from" an attorney unless the lawyer, consistent with his professional ethical obligations, exercised direct control and supervision over the process by which the letter was sent.

Schwarm v. Craighead, 552 F. Supp. 2d 1056 (E.D. Cal. 2008). The defendant was liable for the company's practice of sending subsequent collection letters with the district attorney's name in the letterhead because a district attorney never reviewed a debtor's file and determined that the company should send a particular letter. Defendant violated § 1692e(3), even though a district attorney did not sign any of the form letters, because the "least sophisticated debtor" could conclude that letters were from an attorney because all of the letters include the name and title of the county's district attorney.

Taylor v. Quall, 471 F. Supp. 2d 1053 (C.D. Cal. 2007). Granted the collection attorney for a debt buyer, Unifund, summary judgment on the consumer's claim that the attorney failed to have in any meaningful involvement in the underlying state court collec-

tion case where the attorney's evidence demonstrated personal involvement in reviewing the plaintiff's file and in making the decisions in that case. The consumer did not contest liability for most of the state court claim.

Gorman v. Wolpoff & Abramson, L.L.P., 435 F. Supp. 2d 1004 (N.D. Cal. 2006). The fact that the collection attorney initiated collection efforts on behalf of a creditor whom the consumer had notified in writing to cease communications did not necessarily establish that the attorney had failed to undertake meaningful involvement to review the file that should or may have contained that notification.

Holsinger v. Wolpoff & Abramson, L.L.P., 2006 U.S. Dist. LEXIS 55406 (N.D. Cal. July 27, 2006). Where consumer acknowledged that one collection attorney had reviewed the consumer's file prior to sending of the collection letter, summary judgment was granted for the debt collector with regard to § 1692e(3). The court denied the collection law firm's motion for summary judgment where it did not present evidence sufficient to show that its third attorney who cosigned the NAF complaint had reviewed the consumer's file and had gained knowledge about his debt.

Newman v. CheckRite California, Inc., 912 F. Supp. 1354 (E.D. Cal. 1995). Inclusion of attorney's name on demand letter without attorney review violated § 1692e(3) by falsely implying attorney involvement.

Masuda v. Thomas Richards & Co., 759 F. Supp. 1456 (C.D. Cal. 1991). Collector's practice of sending form letter signed by an independent attorney who had no knowledge of the debt and who had not consulted with the collector was unfair and deceptive in violation of §§ 1692f and 1692e(3).

Connecticut

Kimberly v. Great Lakes Collection Bureau, Inc., 1993 WL 13651243 (D. Conn. June 2, 1993). The form demand letter was sent from the defendant company, computer generated, and dispatched under the name of a person identified in the letter as "Attorney At Law" and "Corporate Counsel" for defendant. That communication, obviously suggesting that the dunning letter was from an attorney and had received her personal attention, is precisely the misleading mass mailing technique condemned in *Clomon v. Jackson*.

Goins v. Brandon, 367 F. Supp. 2d 240 (D. Conn. 2005). The court granted summary judgment on liability against the attorney collector who signed the dun but who had no personal involvement whatsoever in handling the consumer's debt, since the attorney's defense that another attorney in the office had performed the necessary personal review was insufficient as a matter of law to excuse the defendant attorney's violation of § 1692e(3).

Kimberly v. Great Lakes Collection Bureau, Inc., Clearinghouse No. 50,431B (D. Conn. 1996). The court affirmed its previous ruling that defendant's form demand letter generated by a computer and bearing the name of an attorney falsely suggested that an attorney had personally assessed the file violating § 1692e.

Rosa v. Gaynor, 784 F. Supp. 1 (D. Conn. 1989). Letter was deceptive in conveying impression that attorney, who was not licensed to practice law in the debtor's home state, would sue the debtor there or in an illegal distant forum.

Delaware

Anthes v. Transworld Sys., Inc., 765 F. Supp. 162 (D. Del. 1991). Collection agency was not responsible for alleged violations of FDCPA found in its attorney's correspondence. Letter sent by outside attorney retained by debt collector was neither impersonation of attorney, nor use of a name other than its own, nor "flat-rating" in violation of §§ 1692e(3), 1692e(14) or 1692j(a), respectively. Whether debt collector's routine request for outside attorney to send dunning letters would mislead consumer into believing collection activities had entered a more serious stage raised questions of fact which precluded summary judgment. Debt collector's statement that the debt would be referred to a credit management services office, which it owned, was not deceptive in violation of § 1692e(14) where it operated as a distinct entity.

Florida

Brazier v. Law Offices of Mitchell N. Kay, P.C., 2009 WL 764161 (M.D. Fla. Mar. 19, 2009). Summary judgment denied where plaintiff contends attorney acted in bad faith by placing the disclaimer that the law office was not involved on the back of the letter, out of sight from the law office letterhead and the initial impression of the letter, which created disputed issues of fact.

Leblanc v. Unifund CCR Partners, G.P., 552 F. Supp. 2d 1327 (M.D. Fla. May 8, 2008). Summary judgment to defendant on claim that signature by the "Legal Department" implies attorney involvement with the drafting, review, or sending of the letter.

Dalton v. FMA Enters., Inc., 953 F. Supp. 1525 (M.D. Fla. 1997). Summary judgment was denied as a jury may or may not find meaningful involvement by an attorney before he mailed demand letters. The attorney reviewed a summary from the creditor of the prior and the current balances, the account status, and engaged in more review of 10% of the accounts.

Illinois

Berg v. Blatt, Hasenmiller, Leibsker & Moore L.L.C., 2009 WL 901011 (N.D. Ill. Mar. 31, 2009). Genuine issue of material facts remained on defendant's claim that attorney was meaningfully involved. "The court also finds it difficult to believe that a 'meaningful' review of the complaint against [plaintiff would have failed to detect the gross discrepancy between the debts stated on the face of the complaint and those stated in the affidavit." Nor, apparently, is this the first time that defendant has made such an error.

Zaborac v. Phillips & Cohen Assocs., 330 F. Supp. 2d 962 (N.D. Ill. 2004). The use of the word "Associates" in a business name did not denote a law firm.

Lockett v. Freedman, 2004 WL 856516 (N.D. Ill. Apr. 21, 2004). Attorney collector's motion to dismiss was denied where consumer adequately alleged that attorney lacked knowledge to verify complaint in a state collection action and attempted to collect unauthorized attorney fees.

O'Chaney v. Shapiro & Kreisman, L.L.C., 2004 WL 635060 (N.D. Ill. Mar. 29, 2004). The court granted the defendant's motion to dismiss because the allegation that an attorney's verification attached to a state court foreclosure complaint violated § 1692e failed as a matter of law when the complaint was not based on "personal knowledge" but on "information and belief."

Nance v. Lawrence Friedman P.C., 2000 WL 1230462 (N.D. Ill. Aug. 28, 2000). The court held that "where a collection letter is from the desk of an attorney, the debt collector should be required to demonstrate that an attorney was 'professionally involved in the debtor's file . . . [a]ny other result would sanction the wholesale licencing [sic] of an attorney's name for commercial purposes. . . .' Section 1692e(3) therefore requires an attorney who signs a collection letter to have had direct and personal involvement in the review of the debtor's file and preparation of the letter. An attorney does not have to do the review himself to comply with § 1692e(3); he may approve letters based on the recommendations of those working under him. That said, however, an attorney cannot simply approve a 'form' collection letter and be in compliance. . . . Some form of individual review is required." (Citations omitted). The court held that summary judgment was inappropriate since the attorneys' testimony that they individually reviewed creditors' file materials prior to authorizing the mailing of collection letters and signed log sheets documenting that review was undermined by inconsistencies and an inability to explain what they did or how they were able to accomplish the tasks in the time available. In addition, the court rejected the defendant's contention that the case law in fact requires no more than "cursory, scant or meaningless attorney review of mass-mailed debt collection letters."

Miller v. Knepper & Moga, 1999 U.S. Dist. LEXIS 16362 (N.D. Ill. Oct. 21, 1999). Although state rules of professional conduct did not create an independent cause of action against an attorney for violating them, such a violation was not ruled out as a factor to determine whether the conduct violated the FDCPA. A letter from the hospital's attorney that appeared to suggest that the attorney would be representing the consumer's interests in attempting to have insurance pay the outstanding hospital bill misrepresented the attorney's role as an attorney for the hospital, and not the consumer, and therefore stated a claim for violating § 1692e.

Frey v. Satter, Beyer & Spires, 1999 WL 301650 (N.D. Ill. May 3, 1999). If an attorney's involvement was minimal, sending letters with a facsimile attorney signature could violate *Avila* and *Cloman*, which required that an attorney be directly and personally involved in sending the letter in order to avoid deception.

Laws v. Cheslock, 1999 U.S. Dist. LEXIS 3416 (N.D. Ill. Mar. 8, 1999). The unsophisticated consumer standard was used to evaluate whether a creditor's letter used a name that indicated that a third person was attempting to collect a debt. Creditor's attorney misled the unsophisticated consumer by implying that he was an independent attorney.

Veillard v. Mednick, 24 F. Supp. 2d 863 (N.D. Ill. 1998). A dun on an attorney's letterhead is not, by itself, a threat of legal action. Unsigned dun sent on attorney's firm letterhead, where no attorney was actively involved in the consumer's case, is a misrepresentation of attorney participation in the collection process in violation of §§ 1692e and 1692j.

Egli v. Bass, 1998 WL 560270 (N.D. Ill. Aug. 26, 1998). Allegations that an attorney had not become professionally involved with the collection file, even though the collection letter was signed by a paralegal, stated a claim.

Fratto v. Citibank, 1996 WL 554549 (N.D. Ill. Sept. 25, 1996). Citibank could be considered a debt collector where it hired a collection agency to send out form letters on an attorney's letterhead that instructed the debtor to call Citibank's telephone number, where attorney never looked at the files and was not licensed to practice in the jurisdictions where the letters were sent, and Citibank never forwarded debt to the collection agency or the collection attorney.

Kohlenbrener v. Dickinson, 1996 WL 137656 (N.D. Ill. Mar. 25, 1996). The court denied the consumer's motion for summary judgment on whether a collection letter from an attorney that threatened suit but disclosed she was not licensed to practice in the state where the consumer resided was deceptive. There was a material question of fact whether the letter violated § 1692e.

Massachusetts

Martin v. Sands, 62 F. Supp. 2d 196 (D. Mass. 1999). A dun sent from the collector's "Assignment Division" when no such entity existed violated § 1692e(10). Sending a debtor a copy of a letter purportedly sent to the collector's attorneys when in fact no such original letter was sent violated § 1692e(10).

Michigan

Liang v. Elliott, 2008 WL 4539520 (E.D. Mich. Oct. 8, 2008). The fact that someone other than an attorney may have prepared and sent a collection letter on attorney letterhead does not automatically lead to a "no meaningful involvement" violation of FDCPA. Law firms can comply with FDCPA even when they delegate part of the review process, so long as "the ultimate professional judgment concerning the existence of a valid debt is reserved to the lawyer."

Minnesota

Danielson v. Hicks, 1995 WL 767290 (D. Minn. Oct. 26, 1996). Section 1692e(3) was not violated where paralegal applied the stamped signature of the attorney to the firm's collection letter.

New Jersey

Federal Trade Comm'n v. Check Enforcement, 2005 WL 1677480 (D.N.J. July 18, 2005). Sent out a mass mailing of collection letters that falsely indicated that the correspondence was from an attorney, in violation of § 807(10).

New Mexico

Bitah v. Global Collection Servs., Inc., 968 F. Supp. 618 (D.N.M. 1997). Attorney violated FDCPA where he authorized agency to send duns on his letterhead and where the attorney otherwise had no personal involvement in sending the letters.

Russey v. Rankin, 911 F. Supp. 1449 (D.N.M. 1995). Where collection agency sent a lawyer's dunning letter, both the agency and the lawyer were liable for the false impression that the attorney was involved. Out-of-state collection agencies violated §§ 1692e, 1692e(5), 1692e(10) and 1692f by engaging in collection activities in a state without obtaining required state debt collection licenses.

Martinez v. Albuquerque Collection Servs., 867 F. Supp. 1495 (D.N.M. 1994). Debt collector violated § 1692e(3), prohibiting misrepresentation that a letter was from an attorney, where collector determined to which debtors collection letters were sent using

the letterhead and signature of an attorney who signed 20 to 100 such letters per week after only a review for conflicts with his clients, collector mailed the signed letters, and collector paid the attorney $1 per letter.

New York

Fajer v. Kaufman, Burns & Assocs., 2011 WL 334311 (W.D.N.Y. Jan. 28, 2011). In this default action, the court found that the defendant violated §§ 1692e, 1692e(3), (7), and (10) when its agent falsely represented himself to be an attorney, threatened criminal charges and legal action, and failed to disclose his identity as a debt collector.

Nichols v. Frederick J. Hanna & Assocs., P.C., 2011 WL 102665 (N.D.N.Y. Jan. 13, 2011). A letter on the letterhead of an out-of-state law firm did not violate § 1692e(3) when it was sent to a consumer in New York even though no firm member was licensed to practice in that state.

Miller v. Upton, Cohen & Slamowitz, 687 F. Supp. 2d 86 (E.D.N.Y. 2009). There was no meaningful attorney involvement where, after a perfunctory bankruptcy and decedent review, defendant's computer system would permit, and did permit, a debt-collection letter to be generated upon a bare minimum of data. Indeed, a debt collection letter could be generated on little more than the debtor's identifying information, the client name, and the balance due. An attorney's signature implies that an attorney directly controlled or supervised the process through which the letter was sent and that the signing attorney has personally considered, and formed a specific opinion about, the individual debtor's case. "In evaluating the sufficiency of attorney review, the Court's inquiry focuses not upon general procedure, but upon the sufficiency of the attorney's independent review of a *particular* case prior to the issuance of a debt collection letter. Indeed, as evident in *Nielson*, a law firm may employ a robust set of overarching procedures, but an attorney's failure to conduct an independent review of the particular circumstances of an individual debt collection letter will still doom the process."

Miller v. Wolpoff & Abramson, L.L.P., 471 F. Supp. 2d 243 (E.D.N.Y. 2007). Denied the collection attorneys' motion for summary judgment on the claim that he was not meaningfully involved in making the determination of the consumer's liability where there was unresolved issues of fact whether they conducted a sufficient review of the consumer's case or whether they reasonably relied on the review conducted by the referring attorneys who did a sufficient review.

Forman v. Academy Collection Serv., Inc., 388 F. Supp. 2d 199 (S.D.N.Y. 2005). The collection agency had not acted deceptively under § 1692e since it produced documentation that Marvel & Maloney had indeed reviewed accounts for such obvious impediments to collection as legal representation, and inconsistencies or omissions in data. The letters stated that the decision to sue would be the creditor's, and it was the creditor that had labeled the account "pre-legal."

Sparkman v. Zwicker & Assocs., P.C., 374 F. Supp. 2d 293 (E.D.N.Y. 2005). The court found that the collector's letter with text on the front and back regarding attorney involvement was confusing to the least sophisticated consumer and violated § 1692e.

Reade-Alvarez v. Eltman, Eltman & Cooper, P.C., 369 F. Supp. 2d 353 (E.D.N.Y. 2005). Collector's motion to dismiss was denied as to claims of lack of meaningful attorney review where the letters were computer-generated.

Tromba v. M.R.S. Assocs., Inc., 323 F. Supp. 2d 424 (E.D.N.Y. 2004). The court viewed the FDCPA as a harsh statute and "harbors grave doubts as to whether any reasonable trier of fact, even under the least sophisticated consumer standard, could conclude that 'Senior Legal Associate' was equivalent with 'attorney at law' or 'lawyer.' "

Pujol v. Universal Fid. Corp., 2004 WL 1278163 (E.D.N.Y. June 9, 2004). A dunning letter that was sent in the name of an attorney was found on summary judgment not to deceptively represent the attorney's involvement in the collection of the debt because the letter's express disclaimer that the attorney had not reviewed the details of the account would prevent even a least sophisticated consumer from believing that the attorney had in fact been so involved.

Rumpler v. Phillips & Cohen Assocs., Ltd., 219 F. Supp. 2d 251 (E.D.N.Y. 2002). Collection letter with no indication that it was from a lawyer or law firm (other than the letters "Esq" after the name in the signature line) could not mislead the least sophisticated consumer into believing that the letter came from an attorney.

Grief v. Wilson, Elser, Moskowitz, Edelman & Dicker, L.L.P., 217 F. Supp. 2d 336 (E.D.N.Y. 2002). A dun demanding an additional sum for attorney fees did not falsely represent that the person at the firm whom the dun requested the debtor to contact was an attorney.

Ekinici v. GNOC Corp., 2002 WL 31956011 (E.D.N.Y. Dec. 31, 2002). Where collection lawyer's status as corporate counsel was ambiguous in dunning letter attached to complaint, the court would not dismiss the complaint.

Mizrahi v. Network Recovery Servs., Inc., 1999 U.S. Dist. LEXIS 22145 (E.D.N.Y. Nov. 5, 1999). Despite a facsimile signature, there was no violation of § 1692e(3) where a collection attorney did directly control the process by which collection letters were sent by scanning the initial referral information for any abnormalities and approving the transmittal of information to the mailing house as well as conducting an in depth review herself or through trained and supervised staff.

Kapeluschnik v. Leschack & Grodensky, P.C., 1999 U.S. Dist. LEXIS 22883 (E.D.N.Y. Aug. 25, 1999). The court granted summary judgment for collection attorneys, finding it reasonable to believe that each of three attorneys had reviewed approximately 21,000 letters annually, equaling roughly 400 per week or eighty per day.

Goldberg v. Winston & Morrone, 1997 WL 139526 (S.D.N.Y. Mar. 26, 1997). Where collection letters were mass mailed over an attorney's facsimile signature but attorney reviewed computer printouts and supervised the collection process, the court denied summary judgment deciding that deception was a question for the trier of fact.

Ohio

Minick v. First Fed. Credit Control, Inc., 1981 U.S. Dist. LEXIS

18622 (N.D. Ohio June 9, 1981). A letter on an attorney's letterhead sent by a collection agency threatening suit and stating an attorney had been retained violated § 1692e where no attorney had been retained and suit was not filed.

Oregon

Dunn v. Derrick E. McGavic, P.C., 653 F. Supp. 2d 1109 (D. Or. 2009). The attorney debt collector's verbatim *Greco* disclaimer was inadequate as a matter of law to avoid the false representation of attorney involvement because 1) the disclaimer was "obscured by the relative complexity" of the remainder of the attorney's letter and 2) the letter's references to legal action and its threat of immediate suit implied that the attorney had made a "legal assessment" of the debt when he had not.

Forgey v. Parker Bush & Lane, P.C., 2004 WL 1945737 (D. Or. Sept. 1, 2004). *Pro se* allegation that attorney lacked sufficient independent knowledge to bring lawsuit was dismissed. Based on *Heintz*, an attorney does not have to conduct an independent investigation and is not held to a higher standard than lay debt collectors. It is sufficient if the attorney based the complaint on reasonable knowledge, information and belief, formed after making an inquiry that is reasonable under the circumstances.

Pennsylvania

Lesher v. Law Office of Mitchell N. Kay, P.C., 2010 WL 2431826 (M.D. Pa. June 14, 2010). The defendant attorney violated § 1692e(3) and (5) by sending a dun containing the *Greco* disclaimer—"no attorney with this firm has personally reviewed the particular circumstances of your account"—since the communication as a whole would still deceptively lead the least sophisticated consumer to believe that an attorney was involved in the collection of the debt and that an attorney could and would take legal action.

Lesher v. Law Office of Mitchell N. Kay, P.C., 2009 WL 3487795 (M.D. Pa. Oct. 22, 2009). Defendant's motion to dismiss was denied where the subject letter that was written on attorney letterhead could be read to convey to the least sophisticated consumer the false representation and impression of attorney involvement notwithstanding its *Greco* disclaimer: "at this point in time, no attorney with this firm has personally reviewed the particular circumstances of your account."

Martsolf v. JBC Legal Group, P.C., 2008 WL 275719 (M.D. Pa. Jan. 30, 2008). The subject dun on law firm letterhead with references in the dun that the sender is an attorney would cause the least sophisticated debtor to believe that the letter originated with a lawyer. The required attorney review necessary to comply with § 1692e(3) under the *Clomon/Avila* doctrine "need not be lengthy, but it must permit the attorney to form a professional opinion about whether the debt is potentially viable, barred by the statute of limitations, uncollectible due to the debtor's bankruptcy, and to evaluate similar legal considerations." Summary judgment granted to the plaintiff on the § 1692e(3) claim where the attorney claimed that "when reviewing debts, he uses a variety of software applications, to evaluate large numbers of accounts quickly" so that the "attorneys personally review files in bulk numbers based on the results of computer programs applied to large amounts of data"; the court held "that these rapid, technologically aided review processes do not demonstrate the sort of independent analysis and professional opinion that must occur when a debt collector represents that an attorney has reviewed a debt. An attorney using these processes becomes little more than a computer operator unengaged in a considered legal analysis of the debtor's account."

Littles v. Lieberman, 90 B.R. 700 (E.D. Pa. 1988). A collection lawyer whose letterhead and form collection letter was sent to a consumer by a creditor without the lawyer's authorization violated § 1692j but not § 1692e.

Bezpalko v. Gilfillan, Gilpin & Brehman, 1998 WL 321268 (E.D. Pa. June 17, 1998). No violation of *Avila/Clomon* doctrine where attorney was personally involved in and directed the sending of an attorney dun signed by the attorney's secretary.

Texas

United States v. Cent. Adjustment Bureau, Inc., 667 F. Supp. 370 (N.D. Tex. 1986). The collector violated § 1692e(3) by impersonating an attorney—by referring to himself as a "consumer law expert" and representing that he "knew the law."

Washington

Semper v. JBC Legal Group, 2005 WL 2172377 (W.D. Wash. Sept. 6, 2005). Letter on law office stationery, not signed by an attorney, and the lack of any indication that the communication was administrative or otherwise generated by a non-lawyer employee of the firm, was a false implication of attorney involvement.

K.2.4.5 Unlicensed Collection Agencies

LeBlanc v. Unifund CCR Partners, 601 F.3d 1185 (11th Cir. 2010). A violation of Florida's Consumer Collection Practices Act by a debt collector's failing to register as a consumer collection agency may support a cause of action under § 1692e(5) for threatening to take action it could not legally take.

Kuhne v. Cohen & Slamowitz, L.L.P., 579 F.3d 189 (2d Cir. 2009). The court certified to the state's highest court the question of whether the defendant was required to be licensed pursuant to applicable law to file collection suits in state court and whether defendant was otherwise authorized to so act.

Carlson v. First Revenue Assurance, 359 F.3d 1015 (8th Cir. 2004). A Minnesota statute required debt collection agencies collecting debts in Minnesota be licensed at each location from which it conducted business. This requirement did not apply to the collection agency's Seattle lockbox at which the only activity was the receipt of payments and did not result in a violation of the FDCPA.

Wade v. Regional Credit Ass'n, 87 F.3d 1098 (9th Cir. 1996). While the debt collector violated state law by trying to collect a debt when it was not licensed pursuant to state law, the court rejected other decisions and held that this was not a per se or other violation of the FDCPA. The court used the least sophisticated consumer standard.

Smith v. Transworld Sys., Inc., 953 F.2d 1025 (6th Cir. 1992). Where debt collector is licensed as a collection agency in several states, its statement that it "is a licensed collection agency" did not violate § 1692e(1).

California

Taylor v. Quall, 471 F. Supp. 2d 1053 (C.D. Cal. 2007). Granted the defendant summary judgment on the plaintiff's claim that the defendant debt buyer's failure to properly register its fictitious business name as required by state law violated the FDCPA, since that omission was not a bar under state law to it filing the underlying collection case and thus did not rise to a violation of § 1692e(5)'s prohibition against taking action that could not be legally taken. Applicability of § 1692e(14)'s true name requirement not considered.

Connecticut

Lemire v. Wolpoff & Abramson, L.L.P., 256 F.R.D. 321 (D. Conn. 2009). In the course of granting class certification, court observed, "The common elements that itself admits clearly implicate the precise issue that [plaintiff] raises: whether can legally collect consumer debts in Connecticut without a license, or whether such conduct is prohibited by §§ 1692e or 1692f of the FDCPA."

Krueger v. Ellis, Crosby & Assocs., Inc., 2006 WL 3791402 (D. Conn. Nov. 9, 2006). Defendant violated the FDCPA by not having a state license to collect.

Jomarron v. Nasco Enters., Inc., 2005 WL 2231863 (D. Conn. Aug. 4, 2005). Court awarded after a default judgment hearing the maximum statutory damages of $1000 for the debt collector's FDCPA violation by collecting without having the required state license.

Lindbergh v. Transworld Sys., Inc., 846 F. Supp. 175 (D. Conn. 1994). A debt collector who was authorized to collect debts in Connecticut did not engage in a deceptive debt collection practice by mailing a letter to a Connecticut consumer from a California office which was not registered with Connecticut.

Gaetano v. Payco, Inc., 774 F. Supp. 1404 (D. Conn. 1990). Threats to collect a debt were deceptive violating § 1692e(5) where the collector did not have the required license to collect the debt.

Florida

Leblanc v. Unifund CCR Partners, G.P., 552 F. Supp. 2d 1327 (M.D. Fla. 2008). Plaintiff established a claim under § 1692e(5) for defendant's threat to collect on a debt without being registered in Florida to do so. Defendant's request for summary judgment on the corresponding § 1692f claim was denied.

Thomas v. Commercial Recovery Sys., Inc., 2008 WL 5246296 (M.D. Fla. Dec. 16, 2008). Summary judgment granted for defendant where there was no factual issue that defendant had been properly registered and had give proper notices during its collection efforts.

Thibodeau v. Credit Adjustment Bur., 2006 U.S. Dist. LEXIS 87573 (M.D. Fla. Nov. 4, 2006). Relying on *Ferguson v. Credit Mgmt. Control, Inc.*, 140 F. Supp. 2d 1293 (M.D. Fla. 2001), the court granted summary judgment for the debt collector on the consumer's claims that the debt collector violated the FDCPA and the Florida Consumer Collection Practices Act by failing to be register in the State of Florida.

Thibodeau v. Credit Adjustment Bur., 2006 WL 3498159 (M.D. Fla. Dec. 4, 2006). Relying principally on the Ninth Circuit decision in *Wade*, the court held that the collection agency's sending a collection letter without being licensed as a collection agency in accordance with state law did not violate the FDCPA where the letter contained no false or deceptive statements and did not threaten collection litigation.

Ferguson v. Credit Mgmt. Control, Inc., 140 F. Supp. 2d 1293 (M.D. Fla. 2001). Relying on *Wade v. Regional Credit Ass'n*, 87 F.3d 1098 (9th Cir. 1996), the court held that defendant's letter merely informed the plaintiff that his debt had been referred to the collection agency and, even though collector was not registered with the Florida Department of Banking, this was not a per se violation of § 1692e(5) because no threat of action was contained in the letter. Because nothing in the letter was designed to mislead or deceive the least sophisticated consumer, defendant did not violate § 1692e(10) of the FDCPA by sending the nonthreatening letter without first registering with the Florida Department of Banking.

Hawaii

Keli v. Universal Fid. Corp., 1997 U.S. Dist. LEXIS 23940 (D. Haw. Feb. 25, 1997). Collection agency threatened action it could not legally take as it was not licensed in the state. The misrepresentation violated § 1692e(5).

Sakuma v. First Nat'l Credit Bureau, 1989 U.S. Dist. LEXIS 19120 (D. Haw. Nov. 15, 1989). Collector was not required to make a disclaimer about its lack of license in the consumer's state and its inability to collect there.

Illinois

Berg v. Blatt, Hasenmiller, Leibsker & Moore L.L.C., 2009 WL 901011 (N.D. Ill. Mar. 31, 2009). Summary judgment granted for defendants. Assuming *arguendo* that the statement "authorized *to do business* in Illinois" is literally false as applied to the debt collector, plaintiff has failed to demonstrate how this statement did anything other than further the debt collector's exercise of its right to pursue collection against plaintiff in Illinois state court.

Rice v. Palisades Acquisition XVI, L.L.C., 2008 WL 538921 (N.D. Ill. Feb. 25, 2008). Defendant collecting a purchased debt for itself was not required to be registered under the Illinois Collection Agency Act and therefore not liable under the FDCPA for collecting without a license. Defendant was not "transacting business" within the Illinois Business Corporation Act and was not prohibited from filing suit to recover its debt. Therefore it did not violate the FDCPA.

Schad v. Phoenix Adjusters, Inc., 1995 WL 311440 (N.D. Ill. May 18, 1995). Where collector's letter was forwarded from Maryland to debtor in Illinois, court on its own directed the consumer's counsel to file a memorandum addressing claim of collector's failure to obtain Illinois license.

Indiana

Niemiec v. NCO Fin. Sys., Inc., 2006 WL 1763643 (N.D. Ind. June 27, 2006). Debt buyer need not be licensed under UCCC where a separate corporation handles the collections.

Louisiana

McDaniel v. Asset Retrieval, Inc., 1996 WL 7001 (E.D. La. Jan. 5, 1996). The court entered a default judgment against a collection agency finding it had violated the FDCPA by failing to obtain a license to collect debts in Louisiana where it was collecting or in its home state of Florida and by failing to maintain an agent for service of process.

Sibley v. Firstcollect, Inc., 913 F. Supp. 469 (M.D. La. 1995). A debt collector which was not properly licensed by the state in which it attempted to collect a debt violated § 1692e(5).

Minnesota

Phernetton v. First Revenue Assurance, 2003 WL 21246037 (D. Minn. May 19, 2003). Collector's failure to obtain a license in a state where it maintained a post office box for payment, but where it had no employees, did not violate state law or the FDCPA.

Nevada

Kuhn v. Account Control Tech., Inc., 865 F. Supp. 1443 (D. Nev. 1994). Collector's unlicensed attempts to collect a debt, before the state law was amended, violated § 1692e(5) by threatening action that could not be legally taken, § 1692f because the failure to obtain a license deprived the consumer of her right to have the state review the collector's qualifications, and § 1692e(10) because collector's unlicensed collection activities were deceptive.

New Mexico

Russey v. Rankin, 911 F. Supp. 1449 (D.N.M. 1995). Out-of-state collection agencies violated §§ 1692e, 1692e(5), 1692e(10) and 1692f by engaging in collection activities in a state without obtaining required state debt collection licenses.

New York

Nero v. Law Office of Sam Streeter, P.L.L.C., 655 F. Supp. 2d 200 (E.D.N.Y. 2009). Court rejected claim that mere failure to be licensed, absent an additional threat to litigate, violated the FDCPA.

Wayee v. Recovery's Unlimited, Inc., 2009 WL 3334634 (S.D.N.Y. Oct. 15, 2009). Use of an expired license number by defendant, a licensed debt collector, did not constitute a violation of § 1692e.

Williams v. Goldman & Steinberg, Inc., 2006 U.S. Dist. LEXIS 50222 (E.D.N.Y. July 21, 2006). FDCPA was violated because the debt collector did not have a required city license when it sent its collection letter; consumer awarded $1000 in statutory damages and attorney fees for individual claims in the amount of $995.

Richardson v. Allianceone Receivables Mgmt., 2004 WL 867732 (S.D.N.Y. Apr. 23, 2004). Debt collector's Rule 12(c) motion for judgment on the pleadings was granted for consumer's claim that the FDCPA had been violated by the debt collector's failure to list its New York City license number on its collection letter. While this failure may have violated the city ordinance, it was not false, deceptive, or misleading in violation of the FDCPA. Court distinguished cases in which the debt collector was, in fact, unlicensed.

Carvalho v. Mel S. Harris & Assocs., 2004 WL 1555193 (E.D.N.Y. July 13, 2004). FDCPA complaint alleging that collector was not licensed to do business in New York was dismissed for consumer's failure to overcome the presumption that the collector was actually doing business in Maryland.

Castillo v. Frenkel, 2010 WL 5507904 (N.Y. App. Div. Dec. 23, 2010). The fact that debt collection efforts were initiated in New York City by a debt collector that was not licensed under the city's administrative code did not by itself constitute a violation of the FDCPA.

Oregon

Baker v. G.C. Servs. Corp., Clearinghouse No. 31,230 (D. Or. 1981), *aff'd*, 677 F.2d 775 (9th Cir. 1982). Collecting accounts without the required state license does not violate the Act.

Washington

Semper v. JBC Legal Group, 2005 WL 2172377 (W.D. Wash. Sept. 6, 2005). JBC must comply with state collection licensing laws when there is no exemption for lawyers, even though it is collecting the debt of its affiliated purchasing agency.

Wisconsin

Seeger v. Aid Assocs., Inc., 2007 WL 1029528 (E.D. Wis. Mar. 29, 2007). The debt collector's letter which stated that it was a licensed by the State of Wisconsin when it was not was false and misleading in violation of § 1692e and 1692e(10).

Radaj v. ARS Nat'l Servs., Inc., 2006 WL 2620394 (E.D. Wis. Sept. 12, 2006). FDCPA was violated by affirmative statement that ARS was state licensed when it was not violating § 1692e(1) and (10). Suggestion of state approval enhanced "in the mind of the unsophisticated consumer ARS's legitimacy and power to collect the debt."

Czerwinski v. Risk Mgmt. Alternatives Intern. Corp., 2006 WL 897768 (E.D. Wis. Apr. 4, 2006). The debt collector's motion to dismiss was denied where the complaint alleged that the collector's correspondence stated that it was licensed by the State of Wisconsin when it was not.

K.2.4.6 Use of "Credit Bureau" in Name

Pettit v. Retrieval Masters Creditors Bureau, Inc., 211 F.3d 1057 (7th Cir. 2000). Use of the name "Retrieval Masters Creditors Bureau, Inc." in a letter that stated its debt collection purpose did not create the false impression in the mind of a careful, unsophisticated consumer that the collector was a credit bureau, a common name for a credit reporting agency, instead of a creditors bureau. Survey evidence on the issue might have raised an issue of fact avoiding summary judgment.

McKenzie v. E.A. Uffman & Assocs., Inc., 119 F.3d 358 (5th Cir. 1997). A collection agency which used the name, "Collections Department, Credit Bureau of Baton Rouge," but neither "operated" nor "was employed by" a credit reporting agency violated § 1692e(16). The license to use that name from a credit reporting agency did not legalize the violation.

Georgia

Cater v. Credit Rating Bureau, Inc., 1991 U.S. Dist. LEXIS 21731 (N.D. Ga. Oct. 31, 1991). Use of the name "Credit Rating Bureau" in the yellow pages of a telephone directory and in very large letters in its letterhead, which reads "CRB Service Co., a division of Credit Rating Bureau, Inc., a bonded collection agency," would create the false impression to an unsophisticated consumer, violating § 1692e(16), that the collector operated a credit reporting agency. The decision in *Wright v. Credit Bureau*, 555 F. Supp. 1005 (N.D. Ga. 1983) was distinguishable and no longer good law in light of *Jeter v. Credit Bureau, Inc.*, 760 F.2d 1168 (11th Cir. 1985).

Cravey v. Credit Rating Bureau, Inc., 1991 U.S. Dist. LEXIS 21812 (N.D. Ga. Oct. 24, 1991). Collector's letterhead which contained "CRB Service Co., a division of CREDIT RATING BUREAU, INC.," conveyed the impression from the perspective of the least sophisticated consumer that the collector was in the credit reporting or rating business when the words "Credit Rating Bureau" were more prominent than the others. This violated § 1692e(16), regarding misrepresentation of credit reporting agency affiliation, and § 1692e regarding deception.

Wright v. Credit Bureau, Inc., 555 F. Supp. 1005 (N.D. Ga. 1983), *rev'g* 548 F. Supp. 591 (N.D. Ga. 1982). The use of the collector's name including the words "credit bureau" was not deceptive even though the collector's collection and credit reporting businesses were conducted separately and the credit reporting department did not receive information about delinquent consumers from the collection department. The implication of harm to the consumer's credit rating by the use of the collector's name was either not false because debt delinquency generally results in a diminished credit rating or the use of the additional name "CBI Collections" on the bottom of dunning letters and on return envelopes overcame the deceptive implication of the collector's name.

Hawaii

Sakuma v. First Nat'l Credit Bureau, 1989 U.S. Dist. LEXIS 19120 (D. Haw. Nov. 15, 1989). Use of the term "credit bureau" in the name of a collection agency was not misleading.

Louisiana

Byes v. Credit Bureau Enters., 1996 WL 99360 (E.D. La. Mar. 6, 1996). The use of the name Credit Bureau Enterprises did not violate § 1692e(16) by deceptively suggesting the defendant was a consumer credit reporting company as the collector operated as both a credit reporting agency and collection agency.

Oregon

Case v. Credit Bureau, Inc., Clearinghouse No. 33,577 (D. Or. 1982). The collector's motion to dismiss the consumer's FDCPA claims was denied. In the context of this consumer, the collector's use of its name without an indication that it did not engage in credit reporting activities where the consumer resided created the false impression that the collector might harm the consumer's credit standing in violation of § 1692e(16).

K.2.4.7 Use of Telegrams and Simulated Telegrams

Romine v. Diversified Collection Servs., Inc., 155 F.3d 1142 (9th Cir. 1998). The use of Western Union telegrams conveyed a false sense of urgency in collection of the debt.

Schweizer v. Trans Union Corp., 136 F.3d 233 (2d Cir. 1998). A piece of ordinary first class mail explicitly labeled a telegram would clearly be deceptive under § 1692e. Even the least sophisticated consumer would not mistake an ordinary sheet of paper, even with language like "Priority-Gram" and "Important Notice" printed on it, for a telegram.

California

Anderson v. Credit Collection Servs., Inc., 322 F. Supp. 2d 1094 (S.D. Cal. 2004). A letter containing the Western Union logo but no other indicia of a telegram did not create a false sense of urgency.

Illinois

Trull v. G.C. Servs. Ltd. P'ship, 961 F. Supp. 1199 (N.D. Ill. 1997). Collection letter containing the statements: "This is the last effort I will be making to settle your account"; "Your name will be retained as part of our records along with others who, despite their good name and reputation, have shirked their payment responsibility"; "YOUR ACCOUNT HAS BEEN TRANSFERRED TO [agency's] MASTER DEBTOR FILE"; and "We are anxious to clear our record as well as yours," could mislead the unsophisticated consumer into believing that the collection agency was a credit reporting agency, and that inclusion in the master file would have consequences. Although it may be possible that simulating a telegram in a communication with a debtor would violate the FDCPA by exaggerating its urgency, an unsophisticated consumer could not confuse a collection letter with a telegram, despite similarities in appearance, where the letter came through the mail, did not mention the word "telegram," and stated, "THIS STAR HIGH PRIORITY LETTER IS BEING SENT TO YOU BY [agency]."

New York

Wegmans Food Mkts., Inc. v. Scrimpsher, 17 B.R. 999 (Bankr. N.D.N.Y. 1982). It was deceptive for a collector to title dunning letters "Speed-O-Gram" and "Urgent Message."

Ohio

Gasser v. Allen County Claims & Adjustment, Inc., 1983 U.S. Dist. LEXIS 20361 (N.D. Ohio Nov. 3, 1983). A dunning form letter titled "Tell-A-Gram" violated § 1692e(10).

K.2.4.8 Communicating False Credit Information, 15 U.S.C. § 1692e(8)

Wilhelm v. Credico, Inc., 519 F.3d 416 (8th Cir. 2008). A debt collector may not communicate to a credit bureau or the owner of the account about a debt that is disputed without informing them of the dispute. The court rejected the consumer's argument that the last clause of § 1692e(8) created an affirmative obligation to communicate that a debt is disputed. The court held that clause is only applicable when a new "communication" takes place after the dispute is raised.

Purnell v. Arrow Fin. Servs., L.L.C., 303 Fed. Appx. 297 (6th Cir. 2008). Collector's allegedly false communication which was made to a credit bureau within one year prior to filing suit and which misrepresented that the consumer owed the subject debt stated a timely claim for violations of §§ 1692e(2)(A), 1692e(8), and 1692f(1), notwithstanding that the collector had been making the same alleged misrepresentations to the credit bureau for several years, since that last communication constituted a discrete violation of the Act within the statute of limitations.

Pettit v. Retrieval Masters Creditors Bureau, Inc., 211 F.3d 1057 (7th Cir. 2000). The collection agency's truthful statement that it would refer the consumer's name to a consumer reporting agency did not violate the FDCPA.

Acri v. Nat'l Collection Sys., Inc., 145 F.3d 1336 (9th Cir. 1998) (text at 1998 WL 255271). Summary judgment finding no violation of § 1692e(8) affirmed on basis of uncontroverted evidence that collector immediately advised credit reporting agencies of disputed nature of the debt upon its receipt of the dispute.

Brady v. Credit Recovery Co., 160 F.3d 64 (1st Cir. 1998). Section 1692e(8)'s requirement that a debt collector, when communicating credit information to a third party (here, a credit reporting agency), must communicate that a debt is disputed when the debt is known or should be known to be disputed applies when the disputed nature of the debt is conveyed orally and is not limited to written disputes.

Bloom v. I.C. Sys., Inc., 972 F.2d 1067 (9th Cir. 1992). A debt collector, which reported a debt as "disputed" to a credit reporting agency after being informed by the creditor that the debt was not owed, did not engage in malicious conduct sufficient to support a defamation claim.

Alabama

Quale v. Unifund CCR Partners, 682 F. Supp. 2d 1274 (S.D. Ala. 2010). Consumer's allegations that debt collector, after receiving request for verification, failed to verify the debt and, instead, reported it to consumer reporting agencies without notifying the agencies that the debt was disputed, were sufficient to state a claim.

White v. Global Payments, Inc., 2010 WL 320480 (S.D. Ala. Jan. 21, 2010). Summary judgment granted to the debt collector on the consumer's claim that it violated § 1692e(8) by communicating to consumer reporting agencies false information that the consumer still owed a debt that in fact had been paid, since there was no evidence that the defendant had reported the paid debt as remaining owing and the only evidence showed the defendant's unsuccessful attempts at having the agencies delete the incorrect information.

Arizona

Grismore v. United Recovery Sys., L.P., 2006 WL 2246359 (D. Ariz. Aug. 3, 2006). Since the evidence established that only the underlying creditor, and not the defendant debt collector, reported credit information to a consumer reporting agency, the court granted the defendant summary judgment on the *pro se* plaintiff's claim that the defendant had so reported false information.

Stiff v. Wilshappire Credit Corp., 2006 WL 141610 (D. Ariz. Jan. 17, 2006). Defendant's Rule 12(b)(6) motion to dismiss was denied with the court finding that plaintiff had adequately stated a claim for violations of the FDCPA for misrepresenting the amount of the debt and failing to report the debt was disputed to a credit reporting agency under § 1692e(8).

California

Newman v. OneWest Bank, 2010 WL 797188 (C.D. Cal. Mar. 5, 2010). Allegation that defendants violated the Rosenthal Act and FDCPA by reporting past-due payments when (1) plaintiffs were working in good faith to reasonably modify loan payment terms in accordance with the instructions they received from defendants, and (2) plaintiffs disputed the loan, taken as true, could constitute a violation of the fair debt collection statutes.

Witt v. Experian Info. Solutions, 2008 WL 2682131 (E.D. Cal. June 30, 2008). Leave granted to file an amended complaint to allege §§ 1692e(2) and 1692e(8) violations where the defendant collector allegedly " 're-aged' the debt and reported the note's debt to although the debt was time barred for credit reporting purposes."

Winter v. I.C. Sys. Inc., 543 F. Supp. 2d 1210 (S.D. Cal. 2008). Where the consumer had paid a disputed debt in full and the debt collector thereafter allegedly continued to violate § 1692e(8) by not updating and correcting information previously reported to the credit bureau, the court dismissed the claim because the alleged misconduct could not occur in connection with the collection of a debt that no longer exists.

Palmer v. I.C. Sys., Inc., 2005 WL 3001877 (N.D. Cal. Nov. 8, 2005). Consumer's inquiry about the basis for the additional client charges, was an oral dispute that she owed the amount sought; defendant could not thereafter report to the credit bureaus without also reporting the account as disputed.

Gonzalez v. Arrow Fin. Servs., L.L.C., 2005 U.S. Dist. LEXIS 19712 (S.D. Cal. July 25, 2005). Where the defendant was collecting a debt that was more than seven years old and thus was obsolete in accordance with the FCRA, its dun that stated that upon payment "the appropriate credit bureaus will be notified that this account has been settled" violated § 1692e(5) as a false threat to report the account to a credit reporting agency.

Morgovsky v. Creditors Collection Serv., 1995 WL 316970 (N.D. Cal. May 16, 1995), *aff'd without op.*, 92 F.3d 1193 (9th Cir. 1996). Section 1692e(2)(A) is not violated by reporting a debt of a sole proprietorship on the owner's credit report because the owner is individually responsible.

Florida

Lee v. Security Check, L.L.C., 2010 WL 3075673 (M.D. Fla. Aug. 5, 2010). In a case where the check collector's matched with a erroneous prior address in a consumer's file, there was no FDCPA violation by the check collector because it did not seek payment from that consumer. The court in dicta stated the statute does not

impose liability for furnishing erroneous information to a credit reporting agency or for failing to correct erroneous information provided to a credit reporting agency.

Casey v. I.C. Sys., Inc., 2010 WL 415310 (M.D. Fla. Jan. 29, 2010). Genuine issues of fact remained as to the debt collector threatened to report a debt to credit reporting agencies when it was not owed, violating § 1692e(5).

Acosta v. Campbell, 2006 WL 146208 (M.D. Fla. Jan. 18, 2006). Allegations that the consumer's credit report did not show that the account was disputed stated a claim for the debt collector's violation of § 1692e(8), since whether the collector failed to communicate to the credit reporting agency that the debt was disputed, or did communicate such information but the credit reporting agency did not include the information, is a factual issue.

Georgia

Gilmore v. Account Mgmt., Inc., 2009 WL 2848278 (N.D. Ga. Apr. 27, 2009). The complaint stated a claim for defendant's failure to notify the credit reporting agency that plaintiff disputed the debt thus violating § 1692e(8).

King v. Asset Acceptance, L.L.C., 452 F. Supp. 2d 1272 (N.D. Ga. 2006). Where the debt buyer reported the debt reported to it as fraudulent as disputed to a creditor reporting agency, the FDCPA was not violated as the consumer only later demonstrated the account to be fraudulent.

Vidrine v. Am. Prof'l Credit, Inc., 477 S.E.2d 602 (Ga. Ct. App. 1996). Summary judgment was precluded by the factual issue of whether collection agency violated the FDCPA by failing to tell credit bureaus the debt was disputed. The trial court erred in granting summary judgment. The collection agency did not violate the FDCPA by reporting the claimed debt and the amount of the debt as it verified the amounts, and there was no evidence it knew or should have known that the information was false.

Illinois

Kasalo v. Monco Law Offices, S.C., 2009 WL 4639720 (N.D. Ill. Dec. 7, 2009). Consumer's claim that the collector communicated with a credit reporting agency without disclosing that the debt was known to be disputed, in violation of § 1692e(8), was time barred to the extent that the communication occurred more than one year prior to filing of the complaint and otherwise was timely to extent that the communication occurred within the one-year limitations period.

Kohut v. Trans Union L.L.C., 2004 WL 1882239 (N.D. Ill. Aug. 11, 2004). The court dismissed for failure to state a claim the consumer's allegation that the debt collector violated § 1692e by reporting a debt to a credit reporting agency even though it knew that the same debt had already been reported by the creditor and that the resulting misleading duplicative entry would create undue pressure to pay the debt since the information reported by the debt collector nevertheless was conceded to be accurate. The court failed to consider that the information was only admitted to be partially accurate and the omitted information made it deceptive.

Hogan v. MKM Acquisitions, L.L.C., 241 F. Supp. 2d 896 (N.D. Ill. 2003). Where the consumer failed to provide evidence in support of her claim that the debt collector's statement that paying off its claim would improve her credit rating, summary judgment was awarded to the collector on the basis that it would have removed its claim from the consumer's credit report if she had paid and the court's inference that one less delinquency on a credit report would improve it.

White v. Fin. Credit Corp., 2001 U.S. Dist. LEXIS 21486 (N.D. Ill. Dec. 20, 2001). Court struck plaintiff's expert's testimony as failing to meet the Supreme Court's *Daubert* standard and then granted summary judgment dismissing claim that defendant's dun stating that payment of the debt would "amend your credit report" was untrue and deceptive, holding that the issue was a question of fact and, without the expert testimony, the consumer produced no supporting evidence.

White v. Fin. Credit Corp., 2000 U.S. Dist. LEXIS 8963 (N.D. Ill. June 21, 2000). Certification granted as to a class of Illinois residents who were mailed collection letters asserting that settlement of the debt sought to be collected would improve the consumers' credit rating. If the debt had been reported by the creditor to a credit rating agency, that promise was false because the original delinquency would continue adversely to affect the debtor's credit rating.

Epps v. Etan Indus., Inc., 1998 WL 851488 (N.D. Ill. Dec. 1, 1998). Credit Protection Association (CPA) violated the FDCPA by asserting that it was instructing the creditor to report its experience to the local credit bureau and requesting authorization to report to credit bureaus around the country when (1) the creditor's policy was to not report to credit bureaus; (2) the collection agreement made no reference to CPA's ability to report to credit bureaus; (3) authorization was given to CPA only rarely.

Trull v. G.C. Servs. Ltd. P'ship, 961 F. Supp. 1199 (N.D. Ill. 1997). Collection letter containing the statements: "This is the last effort I will be making to settle your account"; "Your name will be retained as part of our records along with others who, despite their good name and reputation, have shirked their payment responsibility"; "YOUR ACCOUNT HAS BEEN TRANSFERRED TO [agency's] MASTER DEBTOR FILE"; and "We are anxious to clear our record as well as yours," could mislead the unsophisticated consumer into believing that the collection agency was a credit reporting agency, and that inclusion in the master file would have consequences. Although it may be possible that simulating a telegram in a communication with a debtor would violate the FDCPA by exaggerating its urgency, an unsophisticated consumer could not confuse a collection letter with a telegram, despite similarities in appearance, where the letter came through the mail, did not mention the word "telegram," and stated, "THIS STAR HIGH PRIORITY LETTER IS BEING SENT TO YOU BY [agency]."

Hoffman v. Partners In Collections, Inc., 1993 WL 358158 (N.D. Ill. Sept. 14, 1993). Plaintiff's allegation that defendant reported the disputed debt to credit agencies without disclosing that plaintiff disputed the debt adequately pleaded a violation of § 1692e(8); the dispute need not be demonstrated to be "valid" for the protection to apply.

Louisiana

Charles v. Credit Bureau Servs., 1999 U.S. Dist. LEXIS 19665 (E.D. La. Dec. 17, 1999). The least sophisticated consumer would not be deceived or mislead by collection letter where letter did not threaten any action, but merely stated that failure to pay debts that were owed might adversely affect one's credit rating and ability to obtain credit.

Maine

Poulin v. The Thomas Agency, 2011 WL 140477 (D. Me. Jan. 13, 2011). The FDCPA only requires that a debt collector must communicate the disputed nature of the debt. FDCPA does not require a debt collector to independently investigate the merit of the dispute under § 1692g. The consumer believed an unitemized bill for hourly services was inflated. A debt collector can rely on its clients' representations regarding the validity of the debt.

Maryland

Davis v. Delmarva Collection, Inc., 2009 WL 112437 (D. Md. Jan. 15, 2009). Where the consumer's subpoenaed telephone records failed to show a claimed telephone call disputing the debt to the debt collector, the consumer could not meet her burden and summary judgment was awarded to the debt collector.

Massachusetts

Corcoran v. Saxon Mortgage Servs., Inc., 2010 WL 2106179 (D. Mass. May 24, 2010). The court concluded that it would not be futile for the consumer to submit a proposed claim that in reporting the default to credit reporting agencies the defendant failed to disclose that there was a bona fide dispute regarding the underlying validity of the loan and allowed the consumer to file an amended complaint.

Michigan

Shields v. Merchants & Med. Credit Corp., Inc., 2010 WL 2613086 (E.D. Mich. June 28, 2010). Summary judgment was entered for the consumer based on statements made by the debt collector that the account would not come off the consumer's credit report even if it was marked as disputed or paid.

Taylor v. Midland Credit Mgmt., Inc., 2008 WL 544548 (W.D. Mich. Feb. 26, 2008). Where the collector advised the consumer to provide some proof that the debt had been paid or an FTC affidavit of fraud (which the consumer did not do), the reporting of the debt due to the credit reporting agencies as disputed did not violate the FDCPA.

Purnell v. Arrow Fin. Servs., L.L.C., 2007 WL 421828 (E.D. Mich. Feb. 2, 2007). For the purpose of the FDCPA statute of limitations, each monthly credit bureau report presented a separate harm to the plaintiff and an independent opportunity for the defendant to comply with the statute. Even if some of the reports were outside the one-year statute, the plaintiff could proceed based on the reports within the statute of limitations.

Minnesota

Edeh v. Midland Credit Mgmt., Inc., 2010 WL 3893604 (D. Minn. Sept. 29, 2010). "The Court has learned, through its work on countless FDCPA cases, that threatening to report and reporting debts to CRAs is one of the most commonly-used arrows in the debt collector's quiver. Consistent with the views of the FTC—and consistent with the views expressed in *Purnell, Quale,* and *Semper*—the Court finds that Midland was engaged in "collection of the debt" in violation of § 1692g(b) when it reported Edeh's disputed debt to the CRAs before sending verification of that debt to Edeh." Overlooking § 1692e(8), the court rejected the *pro se* plaintiff's argument that a debt collector who, before verifying a disputed debt to a consumer under § 1692g verified that debt to a CRA in response to a dispute notification initiated by the consumer and received from the CRA, engaged in "collection of the debt" in violation of § 1692g(b). "If Midland is liable for verifying Edeh's debt to the CRAs, then Midland is liable under the FCRA, not the FDCPA."

Nebraska

Randall v. Midland Funding, L.L.C., 2009 WL 2358350 (D. Neb. July 23, 2009). "The court finds the plaintiff states a claim under § 1692e(8), since the plaintiff alleges had constructive notice through counsel that the debt was disputed, and reported the debt to a credit reporting service without indicating the dispute."

Nevada

Karony v. Dollar Loan Ctr., L.L.C., 2010 WL 5186065 (D. Nev. Dec. 15, 2010). Allegations that the defendants reported false information to the credit bureaus and failed to inform the credit bureaus that the debt was disputed stated a valid claim for relief under § 1692e.

Perez v. Telecheck Servs., Inc., 208 F. Supp. 2d 1153 (D. Nev. 2002). The collector's communication to Wal-Mart that Perez had an outstanding unpaid check when that was contested by Perez stated a claim under § 1692e(8). The defendant was a debt collector and the alleged conduct was proscribed by the FDCPA.

New Jersey

Casterline v. I.C. Sys., Inc., 1991 U.S. Dist. LEXIS 21728 (D.N.J. June 26, 1991) (unpublished). Summary judgment was inappropriate for a § 1692e(8) claim (making a false credit report) as the collector belatedly reported to the credit reporting agency that the debt was disputed. The violation could be excused as a bona fide error.

New York

Fainbrun v. Southwest Credit Sys., L.P., 246 F.R.D 128 (E.D.N.Y. 2007). The court granted summary judgment to the plaintiff because the following statement in defendant's dun constituted a false threat to report to a credit bureau: "Late payments, missed payments, or other defaults may be reflected on your credit report"; although the collector initially reported the debt to a bureau and continued to update monthly, the court explained that further non-payment could not result in any other or different adverse credit reporting: " 'the least sophisticated consumer' may understand the sentence as implying that additional negative reporting to credit bureaus will result if the consumer continues his or her failure to pay. Because Defendant clearly had no intention or ability to report late or missed payments or any additional defaults

to credit bureaus, regardless of whether [the consumer] paid any or all of the amount demanded, the challenged sentence constitutes a threat and false representation violative of 15 U.S.C. § 1692e(5) and (10)."

In re Risk Mgmt. Alternatives, Inc., 208 F.R.D. 493 (S.D.N.Y. 2002). Where the collection letter did not threaten to report an orally disputed debt to a credit reporting agency as undisputed, the consumer's § 1692e(8) claim was dismissed.

Fasten v. Zager, 49 F. Supp. 2d 144 (E.D.N.Y. 1999). Informing a consumer that adverse credit information could remain on his credit report for five years was a false representation, since the FCRA permits such information to be reported for seven years. The court found this to be a "minor, if not de minimis" violation for which the court in its discretion awarded no statutory damages.

Nielsen v. United Creditors Alliance Corp., 1999 U.S. Dist. LEXIS 13267 (E.D.N.Y. Aug. 19, 1999). The consumer alleged that the statement "take advantage of this opportunity to repair your credit" was false because a settlement of a debt would not "repair" one's credit—instead, an original delinquency would continue to adversely affect the debtor's credit standing. The Court found that, considered through the eyes of an unsophisticated consumer, the consumer sufficiently stated a claim for relief under § 1692(10).

Finnegan v. Univ. of Rochester Med. Ctr., 21 F. Supp. 2d 223 (W.D.N.Y. 1998). Allegations that a debt collector's continued attempts to collect a debt it knew was disputed and failure to communicate to a credit reporting agency that a known disputed debt was disputed (even though dispute was not in writing), state a claim for relief under the FDCPA for misrepresenting the amount and legal status of the debt and for attempting to collect amounts unauthorized by contract or law. Debt collector's misconduct also states a claim for relief under state tort of negligence for its failure to perform its collection contract with the creditor with due care.

North Carolina

Gough v. Bernhardt & Strawser, P.A., 2006 WL 1875327 (M.D.N.C. June 30, 2006). The court held that the *pro se* consumer failed to state a claim against the defendants, who were the collection lawyers in the underlying state court collection suit, for misrepresenting the status of the debt in violation of § 1692e(2)(A) by failing to inform the state court in their collection complaint that the consumer had previously disputed the debt, since the FDCPA contains no such requirement and in any event because the consumer is directed in the summons to so inform the court of any dispute by way of filing an answer. Section 1692e(8) does not require a debt collector filing a state collection complaint to inform the state court that the consumer had previously disputed the debt.

Ohio

Alarcon v. Transunion Mktg. Solutions, Inc., 2008 WL 4449387 (N.D. Ohio Sept. 30, 2008). Victim of mixed files whose credit report was adversely effected was not protected by the FDCPA because the alleged false or misleading statements to credit bureaus were not made in connection with collection of a debt. Debt collector's statements to consumer were made in response to her requests to remove incorrect information and not to collect the debt or pressure her to pay the debt. Outside of the context of debt collection efforts, § 1692e is inapplicable and consumer's reliance on it in this situation is misplaced.

Oklahoma

Hollis v. Stephen Bruce & Assocs., 2008 WL 4570490 (W.D. Okla. Oct. 8, 2008). Summary judgment granted against consumer who asserted that defendants' failure to indicate that the debt was disputed in its state court petition violated § 1692e.

Oregon

McNall v. Credit Bureau, Inc., 2010 WL 3306899 (D. Or. Aug. 19, 2010). The court denied the defendant's bona fide error defense when it reported the debt to credit bureaus without noting the known dispute: "Defendant CBJC made a conscious decision not to report Plaintiffs' debt as disputed when it reported the debt to the credit agencies. Defendant CBJC was required to do so by the specific terms of 15 U.S.C. § 1692e(8). The failure to report was not an unintended factual or clerical mistake."

Daley v. A & S Collection Assocs., Inc., 2010 WL 2326256 (D. Or. June 7, 2010). Summary judgment granted to the consumer on her § 1692e(8) claim where the defendant reported to a credit bureau false information regarding the debt's dates of delinquency and last payment. A "communication need not be directed at the debtor in order to be actionable under the FDCPA."

Clark v. Capital Credit & Collection Servs., Inc., 2004 WL 1305326 (D. Or. Jan. 23, 2004), *aff'd in part, rev'd in part on other grounds*, 460 F.3d 1162 (9th Cir. 2006). After arbitration award in collector's favor for an amount less than claimed due, state court action by collector was dismissed with prejudice. Some months later, collector was reporting the debt without reporting that it had been disputed or that its case had been dismissed. Since the report was not in connection with the collection of a debt, it did not violate the FDCPA. Inexplicably, the court concluded that "the cited statutes are not directed at debt collectors' reports to credit reporting agencies."

Pennsylvania

Wesley v. Cavalry Inv., L.L.C., 2006 WL 2794065 (E.D. Pa. Sept. 27, 2006). Cavalry's motion for summary judgment was denied; question of fact whether four-day delay in updating credit file as disputed violated § 1692e(8).

Semper v. JBC Legal Group, 2005 WL 2172377 (W.D. Wash. Sept. 6, 2005). Collector must communicate that a debt is disputed. The FDCPA does not give debt collectors the authority to determine unilaterally whether a dispute has merit.

Farren v. RJM Acquisition Funding, L.L.C., 2005 WL 1799413 (E.D. Pa. July 26, 2005). The court denied the debt collector summary judgment on its defense that it informed the credit bureau that a disputed debt was disputed and thus met its obligation under § 1692e(8) when it communicated the disputed status seven months after it communicated the substantive credit information; the court held: "Although the statute does not expressly require a reasonably timed notification [of the disputed status], the Court finds that it is reasonable to interpret the statute as impliedly requiring the communication to be made in a reasonable time."

Ahmed v. I.C. Sys., Inc., 2005 WL 3533111 (W.D. Pa. Dec. 20, 2005). Where there was no allegation that the collection agency knew of the consumer's dispute with the creditor, no claim was stated under § 1692e(8).

Thomas v. NCO Fin. Sys., Inc., 2003 WL 22416169 (E.D. Pa. Oct. 21, 2003). Settlement of claim that collector furnished credit reporting agencies with information on obsolete debts.

Sullivan v. Equifax, Inc., 2002 U.S. Dist. LEXIS 7884 (E.D. Pa. Apr. 19, 2002). Allegations, that the debt collector knowingly reported false information about the debt to the credit bureau after it knew that the consumer disputed the debt and failed to inform the credit bureau that the debt was "disputed," stated a claim under the FDCPA. "Because reporting a debt to a credit reporting agency can be seen as a communication in connection with the collection of a debt, the reporting of such a debt in violation of the provisions of § 1692e(8) can subject a debt collector to liability under the FDCPA."

In re Benson, 2010 WL 5689535 (Bankr. E.D. Pa. Oct. 6, 2010). Complaint failed to state a claim because § 1692e(8) does not require a collector to update its credit reporting to list a post-report dispute. The allegations demonstrated that at the time the defendant reported the debt to the credit bureau it had no notice that the consumer disputed the debt, and that it engaged in no subsequent credit reporting after it acquired that notice.

Texas

Iruegas v. Diversified Adjustment Serv., Inc., 2010 WL 1171088 (W.D. Tex. Mar. 22, 2010). A complaint alleging that a debt collector, when speaking with the consumer, threatened to report the disputed account to a credit reporting agency after being informed that the consumer did not owe the account in question sufficiently stated a claim under § 1692e(8).

Virginia

Sunga v. Broome, 2010 WL 3198925 (E.D. Va. Aug. 12, 2010). The consumer's allegation that the defendant's stated that it "may" report the debt to credit bureaus supported a claim for violating § 1692e(8) where the consumer alleged that the underlying information itself was false.

Creighton v. Emporia Credit Serv., Inc., 981 F. Supp. 411 (E.D. Va. 1997). A demand for payment in full upon receipt of dun or else debt would be reported on the consumer's credit report contradicted the validation notice as a matter of law and was a false representation of urgency where collector's policy was not to report a debt to a credit reporting agency for sixty days.

K.2.4.9 Providing 15 U.S.C. § 1692e(11) Notices[1]

Edwards v. Niagara Credit Solutions, Inc., 584 F.3d 1350 (11th Cir. 2009). The district court properly denied the bona fide error defense arising from the defendant's failure to identify itself as a debt collector as required by § 1692e(11) when leaving consumers

---

1 15 U.S.C. § 1692(e)(11) was amended in 1996 changing substantially its requirements and limiting the authority of prior cases interpreting it. *See* § 5.5.14, *supra*.

an answering machine message; first, the violation was, in fact, intentional, the result of a deliberate policy decision to not comply with § 1692e(11), purportedly to avoid violating § 1692c(b) in the event that the message was heard by a third party who would then know that a collection agency was calling the consumer; second, to be bona fide "the mistake must be objectively reasonable," and "[i]t was not reasonable for to violate § 1692e(11) of the FDCPA with every message it left in order to avoid the possibility that some of those messages might lead to a violation of § 1692c(b)." "[Defendant] complains that if it is not permitted to leave out of its answering machine messages the disclosure required by § 1692e(11), the result will be that it cannot leave any messages on answering machines. . . . [T]he answer is that the Act does not guarantee a debt collector the right to leave answering machine messages."

Volden v. Innovative Fin. Sys., Inc., 440 F.3d 947 (8th Cir. 2006). A letter that says it was sent in an attempt to collect a debt was sufficient for even the unsophisticated consumer to understand that such a letter was necessarily from a "debt collector."

Geiger v. Creditors Interchange, Inc., 2003 WL 1465404 (6th Cir. Mar. 19, 2003). Section 1692e(11), as amended, requires a full "mini-Miranda" warning only in the initial communication from a debt collector to a consumer and requires in all subsequent communications disclosure only that the communication is from a debt collector. The letterhead and the body of a subsequent letter clearly disclosed that the sender was a debt collector and thus complied with § 1692e(11). Moreover, the second letter that was sent in response to the consumer's accusation that the collector had violated the FDCPA did not convey information regarding the debt itself, was not a "communication" as defined by § 1692a(2), and therefore did not require the § 1692e(11) disclosure.

Buckley v. Bass & Assocs., P.C., 249 F.3d 678 (7th Cir. 2001). Letter inquiring about bankruptcy status, with no demand for payment, and not giving the §§ 1692e(11) or 1692g notices was not an effort to collect a debt. "[T]he inclusion of the language plaintiff claims was required under the FDCPA was forbidden by the Bankruptcy Code."

Conboy v. AT&T Corp., 241 F.3d 242 (2d Cir. 2001). Parents who were repeatedly contacted to locate their daughter's creditor had no claim under § 1692e(11), which required notices only to consumers. The court could have decided, on the basis that the defendant was an exempt creditor not subject to the FDCPA, without reaching the "consumer" issue.

Chaudhry v. Gallerizzo, 174 F.3d 394 (4th Cir. 1999). A letter from a collector to a settlement attorney giving the payout amount did not require the § 1692e(11) notice.

Odell v. F.A.B., Inc., 132 F.3d 33 (6th Cir. 1997) (text at 1997 WL 778393). Complaint against collection agency for failing to include the § 1692e(11) debt collection warning in a collection complaint was properly dismissed where the consumer failed to rebut collection agency's statement on summary judgment that the agency was not involved in the complaint filed by the creditor hospital.

Dikeman v. Nat'l Educators, Inc., 81 F.3d 949 (10th Cir. 1996). The § 1692e(11) disclosures were not required to avoid deception in a communication to the consumer's attorney verifying the amount of debt in response to the consumer attorney's request for verification because the debt collection purpose of the letter would be apparent to the attorney. The jury had found the debt had not been verified when the verification given was inadequate because it overstated the collector's claim, but the jury excused the violation as a bona fide error.

Russell v. Equifax A.R.S., 74 F.3d 30 (2d Cir. 1996). A second collection notice demanding payment within five days, which was sent only twenty-five days from the first communication, violated §§ 1692g and 1692e(10).

Emanuel v. Am. Credit Exch., 870 F.2d 805 (2d Cir. 1989). Collector violated § 1692e(11) by failing to advise consumer that any information furnished would be used to collect the debt. The violation occurred in the initial letter which did not request information. Disclosure that the dunning letter was to collect a debt was made in the statement that the consumer's account had been turned over to the collector for immediate collection.

Alabama

Winberry v. United Collection Bureau, Inc., 697 F. Supp. 2d 1279 (M.D. Ala. 2010). A debt collector is required by § 1692e(11) to identify in subsequent communications that it is a debt collector.

Arizona

Garo v. Global Credit & Collection Corp., 2011 WL 251450 (D. Ariz. Jan. 26, 2011). "The fact that a debt collector may leave a message, in which the debt collector is otherwise unidentified, to contact the consumer at a phone number that had previously been contained in the debt collector's correspondence with the consumer is insufficient to identify the subsequent communication as being from a debt collector as is required by § 1692e(11). Further, such a request does not constitute 'meaningful disclosure of the caller's identity' as is required by 15 U.S.C. § 1692d(6)."

California

Koby v. ARS Nat'l Servs., Inc., 2010 WL 5249834 (S.D. Cal. Dec. 23, 2010). The court denied the plaintiffs' motion to reconsider its ruling that a voicemail merely stating the caller's name and asking for a return call did not convey, directly or indirectly, any information regarding the debt owed and therefore was not a "communication" that required a § 1692e(11) disclosure.

del Campo v. Am. Corrective Counseling Serv., Inc., 2010 WL 2473586 (N.D. Cal. June 3, 2010). The court granted summary judgment to the consumers on their §§ 1692e(11) and 1692g claims since the defendant's duns entirely omitted the FDCPA-mandated disclosures.

Krapf v. Nationwide Credit Inc., 2010 WL 2025323 (C.D. Cal. May 21, 2010). Where the consumer could not recall whether the debt collectors identified themselves in their calls to him, summary judgment was granted to the debt collector on the §§ 1692d(6), 1692e(10) and (11) issues.

Koby v. ARS Nat'l Servs., Inc., 2010 WL 1438763 (S.D. Cal. Mar. 29, 2010). Where defendant failed to disclose that it was attempting to collect a debt and any information obtained will be used for that purpose, judgment on the pleadings was not appropriate with respect to claims under § 1692e(11) based upon the voicemail messages left with the consumers.

Schwarm v. Craighead, 552 F. Supp. 2d 1056 (E.D. Cal. 2008). The defendant was liable under § 1692e(11) for failure to include the requisite disclosure in most of the letters. Indeed, one letter negated the requisite disclosure: "This is not a Civil issue under 15 U.S.C. 1692e requiring the following statement; 'This is an attempt to collect a debt and any information obtained will be used for that purpose.' This is a Criminal issue under Penal Code 476a."

Reed v. Global Acceptance Credit Co., 2008 WL 3330165 (N.D. Cal. Aug. 12, 2008). Whether the defendant's voicemail messages sufficiently identified the caller as a debt collector for § 1692e(11) was a question of fact that precluded summary judgment because the consumer may have recognized the collection company's name, which was disclosed in the voicemail, as a debt collector as she had previously communicated with it. The court assumed that the failure to disclose the caller is debt collector in subsequent calls did not violate § 1692e(11) unless the failure to disclose was deceptive.

Costa v. Nat'l Action Fin. Servs., 634 F. Supp. 2d 1069 (E.D. Cal. 2007). Telephone messages left by a debt collector violated the FDCPA when they failed to convey the information required by § 1692e(11). Subsequent telephone calls by the consumer to the debt collector after the collector had informed plaintiff that the calls were to collect her account do not violate § 1692e(11).

Hosseinzadeh v. M.R.S. Assocs., Inc., 387 F. Supp. 2d 1104 (C.D. Cal. 2005). Messages left by the debt collector on the consumer's telephone answering machine which did not ask for payment of the debt or mention the debt but which instructed that there was an important matter regarding which the consumer should contact the named person were each a "communication" as defined by the FDCPA; accordingly, the failure of the collector to disclose that the messages were from a debt collector violated § 1692e(11).

Colorado

O'Connor v. Check Rite, 973 F. Supp. 1010 (D. Colo. 1997). Where the front of the collection letter clearly and conspicuously referred the reader to important information on the reverse side, the § 1692e(11) warning was properly given to the consumer.

Connecticut

Krueger v. Ellis, Crosby & Assocs., Inc., 2006 WL 3791402 (D. Conn. Nov. 9, 2006). Defendant violated the FDCPA by not sending required notices.

Ignatowski v. G.C. Servs., 3 F. Supp. 2d 187 (D. Conn. 1998). Failure to include the debt collection warning of § 1692e(11) in a facsimile transmission to the debtor's lawyer did not violate the FDCPA when the nature of the collection effort was clear from the content of the transmission.

Woolfolk v. Van Ru Credit Corp., 783 F. Supp. 724 (D. Conn. 1990). Student loan collection agency violated the FDCPA by failing to provide § 1692e(11) notices.

Cacace v. Lucas, 775 F. Supp. 502 (D. Conn. 1990). An attorney's failure to include in his collection letters the notice required by § 1692e(11) violated the Act.

Gaetano v. Payco, Inc., 774 F. Supp. 1404 (D. Conn. 1990). The collector's notice complied with § 1692e(11) when it stated on the back of a dunning letter: WE ARE A PROFESSIONAL COLLECTION AGENCY ATTEMPTING TO COLLECT A DEBT, WE ARE ENTITLED TO USE, AND WE INTEND TO USE, ALL APPROVED MEANS AT OUR COMMAND TO COLLECT DEBTS WHICH HAVE BEEN REFERRED TO US AND ANY INFORMATION WE OBTAIN WILL BE USED AS A BASIS TO ENFORCE COLLECTION OF THE DEBT.

Gonsalves v. Nat'l Credit Sys., Inc., 1990 U.S. Dist. LEXIS 20944 (D. Conn. Aug. 13, 1990). Failure to include the § 1692e(11) notice in three of five collection letters violated the Act.

Traverso v. Sharinn, 1989 U.S. Dist. LEXIS 19100 (D. Conn. Sept. 15, 1989). The disclosures required by § 1692e(11) are mandatory, even if the consumer could ascertain from the contents of the letter that its purpose was to collect a debt, and even if the letter sought no information.

Butler v. Int'l Collection Serv., Inc., 1989 U.S. Dist. LEXIS 19102 (D. Conn. June 6, 1989). Printing the notices required by §§ 1692e(11) & 1692g(a) on the back of a dunning letter in small, lighter type following two dunning paragraphs violated the Act's requirement of adequate notices suitable for unsophisticated consumers because the only reference on the front was the small, obscurely placed word "over."

Delaware

Sutton v. Law Offices of Alexander L. Lawrence, 1992 U.S. Dist. LEXIS 22761 (D. Del. June 17, 1992). Section 1692e(11) required a debt collector to disclose that it was attempting to collect a debt and that any information obtained from the debtor will be used for that purpose. Even though a debt collector's initial communication contained the required disclosures, a subsequent letter sent by a separate party must also contain the § 1692e(11) disclosures.

Smith v. Fin. Collection Agencies, 770 F. Supp. 232 (D. Del. 1991). Debt collector's demand for immediate payment did not grossly overshadow the debt collection warning required by § 1692e(11).

Beattie v. D.M. Collections, Inc., 754 F. Supp. 383 (D. Del. 1991). The failure to provide the debt collection warning required by § 1692e(11), if required in a follow-up phone call, was excused as a bona fide error since it was the collector's policy, repetitiously supported, to provide the warning in all phone calls.

Florida

Beeders v. Gulf Coast Collection Bureau, Inc., 2010 WL 2696404 (M.D. Fla. July 6, 2010). The question of whether use of the name "Gulf Coast Collection Bureau" was adequate to inform the least sophisticated consumer that Gulf Coast was a debt collector calling in regard to debt collection activities was a material fact for the jury to determine.

Chalik v. Westport Recovery Corp., 677 F. Supp. 2d 1322 (S.D. Fla. 2009). The FDCPA does not guarantee a debt collector the right to use voicemail or leave answering machine messages. Debt collectors have other methods to reach debtors including postal mail, in-person contact, and speaking directly by telephone.

Sanz v. Fernandez, 633 F. Supp. 2d 1356 (S.D. Fla. 2009). Allegations that the defendants were debt collectors who failed to make the §§ 1692e(11) and 1692g(a) disclosures stated a claim for relief.

Belin v. Litton Loan Serv., L.P., 2006 WL 1992410 (M.D. Fla. July 14, 2006). The complaint stated a claim for the defendant's violation of § 1692e(11) since the messages left on the consumer's answering machine did not contain the required disclosure and each message was a "communication," notwithstanding that it did not directly convey information about the debt, since the purpose of the messages was to get the debtor to return the calls to discuss the debt and thus indirectly conveyed information about the debt.

Danow v. Borack, 2006 WL 5516577 (S.D. Fla. Jan. 30, 2006), *rev'd in part and remanded on other grounds,* 197 Fed. Appx. 853 (11th Cir. 2006). There is no statutory requirement that the letter quote verbatim the language of § 1692e(11).

Acosta v. Campbell, 2006 WL 146208 (M.D. Fla. Jan. 18, 2006). Allegations that the collection attorney in the underlying state foreclosure action unlawfully failed to disclose in motions and discovery documents in that case were from a debt collector did not state a claim for relief since § 1692e(11) exempts that disclosure from such pleadings.

Sandlin v. Shapiro & Fishman, 919 F. Supp. 1564 (M.D. Fla. 1996). The court found that the failure of the defendant to include the second part of the § 1692e(11) warning in its collection letter was a violation of the FDCPA so denied defendant's motion to dismiss.

Hawaii

Sakuma v. First Nat'l Credit Bureau, 1989 U.S. Dist. LEXIS 19120 (D. Haw. Nov. 15, 1989). Collector failed to disclose in its initial letter as required by § 1692e(11) that information would only be used for the purpose of collection.

Illinois

Hutton v. C.B. Accounts, Inc., 2010 WL 5463108 (C.D. Ill. Dec. 29, 2010). The court denied the plaintiff's motion to reconsider its earlier denial of class certification. The earlier denial was based upon the court's finding that individual issues of proof would predominate over class issues because some of the class members may already have known who the collector was and why it was calling. "[S]ome of the approximately 62,093 putative class members may have received debt collection calls and letters from CBA prior to getting any offending voicemails. Individuals who received calls and letters which satisfied § 1692e(11)'s disclosure requirements prior to receiving offending calls and letters may not have actionable FDCPA claims."

Smith v. Greystone Alliance L.L.C., 2010 WL 2680147 (N.D. Ill. June 30, 2010). The court certified a class comprised of consumers for whom the defendant left voicemail messages without identifying itself as a debt collector as required by § 1692e(11).

Hutton v. C.B. Accounts, Inc., 2010 WL 5070882 (C.D. Ill. Dec. 3, 2010). The court denied class certification for this § 1692e(11) violation since individual issues of proof would predominate over class issues: "some of the approximately 62,093 putative class members may have received debt collection calls and letters from CBA prior to getting any offending voicemails. Individuals who received calls and letters which satisfied § 1692e(11)'s disclosure requirements prior to receiving offending calls and letters may not have actionable FDCPA claims."

Porter v. Fairbanks Capital Corp., 2003 WL 21210115 (N.D. Ill. May 21, 2003). The failure to place the § 1692e(11) notice on each monthly statement sent by a debt collector to a consumer in default on her loan stated a claim for relief where the statements demanded payment by including a recitation of "late charges due" and therefore constituted a "communication."

James v. Olympus Servicing, L.P., 2002 WL 31307540 (N.D. Ill. Oct. 9, 2002). The court denied a motion to dismiss plaintiff's claim that no § 1692e(11) notice appeared on a mortgage servicer's overdue statements. It distinguished *Bailey v. Security Nat'l Servicing Corp.,* 154 F.3d 384, 387 (7th Cir. 1998), where the servicer did not claim that amounts were past due.

Young v. Manley, 2000 U.S. Dist. LEXIS 13035 (N.D. Ill. Sept. 6, 2000). Defendant law firm sent a letter to plaintiff's bankruptcy attorney threatening a dischargeability proceeding based on the amount of credit card charges just before bankruptcy. The letter contained neither of the required FDCPA notices. The consumer's attorney was not a "consumer" within the FDCPA and did not need its protections; a collector was, indeed, required to communicate with the attorney who represented the debtor. The letter was not an indirect collection effort. The §§ 1692(e)(11) and 1692(g) count was dismissed.

Ross v. Commercial Fin. Servs., Inc., 31 F. Supp. 2d 1077 (N.D. Ill. 1999). Subsequent collection letter which stated "Commercial Financial Services is a different kind of debt collection company" met the requirements of § 1692e(11).

Laws v. Cheslock, 1999 U.S. Dist. LEXIS 3416 (N.D. Ill. Mar. 8, 1999). Defendant attorney did not violate § 1692e(11) because he made it clear he was collecting a debt even though he did not use the statutory language.

Epps v. Etan Indus., Inc., 1998 WL 851488 (N.D. Ill. Dec. 1, 1998). Credit Protection Association did not violate § 1692e(11) by failing to state that it was a debt collector, since the least sophisticated consumer could tell it was attempting to collect a debt.

Taylor v. Fink, 1994 WL 669605 (N.D. Ill. Nov. 25, 1994). Debt collection warning pursuant to § 1692e(11) was required in collection notice.

Altergott v. Modern Collection Techniques, 1994 WL 319229 (N.D. Ill. June 23, 1994). Debt collector's letter which merely listed the debt collector's name, loan number and amount due was insufficient to apprise the consumer that any information obtained would be used for the purpose of collecting the debt and thereby violated § 1692e(11) notice requirements.

Friedman v. HHL Fin. Servs., Inc., 1993 WL 367089 (N.D. Ill. Sept. 17, 1993). The debt collection warning pursuant to § 1692e(11) is sufficient when stated on the front of the collection letter and need not be restated on the back.

Indiana

Stefansson v. Source One Mortgage, 2004 WL 540921 (S.D. Ind. Jan. 29, 2004). *Pro se*'s allegation that attorney did not include the § 1692e(11) notice in pleadings rejected because of the exemption for pleadings in that section.

In re Revere, 2007 WL 4879279 (Bankr. N.D. Ind. Oct. 22, 2007). Court criticized the annoying habit of placing § 1692e(11) language, in bolded capital letters, on all of its filings.

Louisiana

Johnson v. Eaton, 873 F. Supp. 1019 (M.D. La. 1995). Letter questionnaire and unfiled, draft consent judgment failed to contain the debt collection warning in violation of § 1692e(11).

Maryland

Davis v. R & R Prof'l Recovery, Inc., 2009 WL 400627 (D. Md. Feb. 17, 2009). The § 1692e(11) disclosure that the communication was from a debt collector was satisfied by virtue of the debt collector's call to the consumer's attorney starting with referral to the consumer's attorney's faxed demand for FDCPA damages the day before.

Senftle v. Landau, 390 F. Supp. 2d 463 (D. Md. 2005). Attorney debt collector had no obligation to disclose in its collection pleadings that he was a debt collector since § 1692e(11) unambiguously exempts formal pleadings from its purview.

Dorsey v. Morgan, 760 F. Supp. 509 (D. Md. 1991). If an attorney is a debt collector, failure of his correspondence to contain the validation notice and debt collection warning violates §§ 1692g and 1692e(11).

Michigan

South v. Midwestern Audit Servs., Inc., 2010 WL 5089862 (E.D. Mich. Dec. 8, 2010. Following *Bailey* and *Gburek*, the court found a debt collection agency's sending an obtuse letter to the consumer indicating that the utility bill balance from her boyfriend's prior account was being transferred to her utility account and not demanding payment was not sent "in connection with the collection of a debt" and not subject to the FDCPA.

Carrier v. LJ Ross & Assoc., 2008 WL 544550 (E.D. Mich. Feb. 26, 2008). Where the plaintiff consumer contended that the defendant collector's phone calls made to the plaintiff were violative of § 1692e(11) the court denied the plaintiff's motion to exclude the recordings of any conversations between the plaintiff and the defendant and held that "(2) the probative value of the taped recordings outweighs any prejudicial effects that they may have under Fed. R. Evid. 403; and (3) the projected statements in the recordings are not hearsay, as defined by Fed. R. Evid. 801(c) because they are not being proffered to prove the "truth of the matter asserted."

Gradisher v. Check Enforcement Unit, Inc., 210 F. Supp. 2d 907 (W.D. Mich. 2002). The collector must provide the debt collection warning to the consumer pursuant to § 1692e(11).

Latimer v. Transworld Sys., Inc., 842 F. Supp. 274 (E.D. Mich. 1993). Although the validation notice and debt collection warning were in smaller print than other portions of the letter, §§ 1692g and 1692e(11) were not violated.

Stojanovski v. Strobl & Manoogian, 783 F. Supp. 319 (E.D. Mich. 1992). Failure to include the debt collection warning of § 1692e(11) is a clear violation of the Act.

Minnesota

Grambart v. Global Payments Check Recovery Servs., Inc., 2011 WL 124230 (D. Minn. Jan. 14, 2011). The *pro se* consumer failed to state a claim for a § 1692e(11) violation since the defendant's two written communications that allegedly failed to state they were from a debt collector stated clearly that they were in response "to your request for a statement of your account" and thus, "[s]uch communication, initiated by the debtor," was not sent for "the collection of any debt." [*N.B.* The court relied solely on *Bailey v. Sec. Nat'l Servicing Corp.*, 154 F.3d 384, 388–389 (7th Cir. 1998), apparently not aware that that reliance, particularly here where the letters actually demanded payment, was limited and undermined by the Seventh Circuit's recent decision in *Gburek v. Litton Loan Servicing L.P.*, 614 F.3d 380 (7th Cir. 2010).]

Burke v. Messerli & Kramer P.A., 2010 WL 3167403 (D. Minn. Aug. 9, 2010). By including the § 1692e(11), disclosure, Messerli expressly conveyed that the letter was "an attempt to collect a debt." The argument that the letter was not a communication in connection with the collection of a debt when the language of the letter is directly to the contrary was unconvincing.

Cohen v. Beachside Two-I Homeowners' Ass'n, 2006 WL 1795140 (D. Minn. June 29, 2006), *aff'd as modified on other grounds*, 272 Fed. Appx. 534 (8th Cir. 2008). Filing a required notice on the land record was not a communication with the consumer for the purposes of the § 1692e(11) notice requirement.

Missouri

Lewis v. Hanks, 1991 U.S. Dist. LEXIS 21807 (E.D. Mo. Feb. 26, 1991). Debt collector's letter did not provide the debt collection warning required by § 1692e(11).

Nebraska

Page v. CheckRite, Ltd., Clearinghouse No. 45,759 (D. Neb. 1984). Check guarantee agencies violated FDCPA by failing to provide any explicit § 1692e(11) notices.

Beaulieu v. Am. Nat'l Educ. Corp., Clearinghouse No. 30,892 (D. Neb. 1981). Summary judgment was granted to the consumer for the collector's failure to disclose that information obtained would be used for collecting the debt.

Harris v. BWS Credit Servs., Inc., Clearinghouse No. 27,693 (D. Neb. 1980) (order on motions for summary judgment). The collection agency failed to disclose the collection purpose of its communication as required by § 1692e(11).

New Jersey

Krug v. Focus Receivables Mgmt, L.L.C., 2010 WL 1875533 (D.N.J. May 11, 2010). Consumer's allegations that the debt collector failed to identify itself in telephone messages pursuant to § 1692d(6) or state that the call was from a debt collector pursuant to § 1692e(11) was sufficient to withstand the defendant's motion to dismiss.

Nicholls v. Portfolio Recovery Assocs., L.L.C., 2010 WL 1257738 (D.N.J. Mar. 29, 2010). Consumer's claim that the collection letters would cause the consumer to stop reading after reaching the amount due was held to be a bizarre and idiosyncratic legal conclusion and her claims for violation of § 1692e were dismissed. "[T]he least sophisticated debtor is presumed to have, at the very least, read with care."

Nicholas v. CMRE Fin. Servs., Inc., 2010 WL 1049935 (D.N.J. Mar. 16, 2010). Regardless of whether the prerecorded telephone message was an effort to initiate communication or subsequent to an initial communication, the message is subject to the provisions of 15 U.S.C. § 1692e(11).

Shanker v. Fair Collection & Outsourcing, L.L.C., 2009 WL 1767580 (D.N.J. June 19, 2009). Debt collector need not use the "magic words" as long as the communication conveys the information that it is from a debt collector. Here, the communication sufficiently conveyed that information in that it was entitled "Verification of Debt" and suggested that consumer "call your collector."

Smith v. Lyons, Doughty & Veldhuius, P.C., 2008 WL 2885887 (D.N.J. July 23, 2008). Section 1692e(11) does not require a debt collector to repeat the initial communication disclosures in subsequent communications.

Robinson v. Credit Serv. Co., 1991 WL 186665 (D.N.J. Sept. 16, 1991). Collector violated § 1692e(11) by failing to include a statement in its dunning letter that any information provided by the consumer would be used for the purpose of collecting the debt.

Workman v. Scheer, 1990 U.S. Dist. LEXIS 20982 (D.N.J. Mar. 8, 1990). Although attorney's letter could be construed as an attempt to collect a debt, the least sophisticated consumer would not perceive "that any information obtained will be used for that purpose," thus violating § 1692e(11).

New Mexico

Anchondo v. Anderson, Crenshaw & Assocs., L.L.C., 583 F. Supp. 2d 1278 (D.N.M. 2008). The collector's motion to dismiss was denied where the collector left a voicemail call-back message in which it did not identify itself or disclose that the communication was an attempt to collect a debt since, if the call, as alleged, "pertained to a debt, then the voicemail message was a 'communication' subject to the disclosure requirements of the FDCPA."

Spinarski v. Credit Bureau, Inc., Clearinghouse No. 51,963A (D.N.M. May 6, 1996). Collection agency was granted dismissal of consumers' claims that the § 1692e(11) debt collection notice was required on a post-it note attached to a letter containing that notice and that § 1692d was violated by a description of creditor's remedies including incarceration for failure to appear at a debtor's exam.

New York

Pifko v. CCB Credit Servs., Inc., 2010 WL 2771832 (E.D.N.Y. July 7, 2010). Allegations that the defendant left the consumer voicemail messages without identifying itself as a debt collector stated a claim for violating § 1692e(11).

Krapf v. Collectors Training Inst. of Ill., Inc., 2010 WL 584020 (W.D.N.Y. Feb. 16, 2010). The obligation of a collector to identify itself as a debt collector under § 1692(11) is not limited to the initial communication with the consumer but also applies to subsequent communications.

Leyse v. Corporate Collection Servs., Inc., 2006 WL 2708451 (S.D.N.Y. Sept. 18, 2006). Failure to provide the debt collection notice in prerecorded messages to the consumer violated § 1692e(11). "CCS has been cornered between a rock and a hard place, not because of any contradictory provisions of the FDCPA, but because the method they have selected to collect debts has put them there."

Foti v. NCO Fin. Sys., Inc., 424 F. Supp. 2d 643 (S.D.N.Y. 2006). Collector's prerecorded phone message left on the consumer's voicemail only requesting the debtor to return the call regarding an important personal "business matter" was a "communication" as defined by the FDCPA, and thus the allegation that the collector failed to provide the § 1692e(11) disclosure in that message stated a claim for relief. Collector's disclosure in a subsequent telephone conversation that he was collecting two specified accounts in stated amounts that had been "sent for collection" adequately gave the § 1692e(11) subsequent communication disclosure.

Lawrence v. Borah, Goldstein, Altschuler, Schwartz & Nahins, P.C., 2005 WL 2875383 (S.D.N.Y. Nov. 1, 2005). Three day rent demand was the initial communication but did not provide the notice required by § 1692e(11).

Dowling v. Kucker Kraus & Bruh, L.L.P., 2005 WL 1337442 (S.D.N.Y. June 6, 2005). Debt collectors could not evade the notice requirements of the FDCPA merely by having a creditor sign a demand for rent that the collector prepared and mailed.

Degonzague v. Weiss, Neuren & Neuren, 89 F. Supp. 2d 282 (N.D.N.Y. 2000). The collector's letter, which clearly stated that the "above-captioned matter" had been referred to this office for immediate attention by People's Bank in an attempt to collect a debt and any information obtained will be used for that purpose, satisfied § 1692e(11).

Fava v. RRI, Inc., 1997 WL 205336 (N.D.N.Y. Apr. 24, 1997). One of collector's letters to consumer's father did not need the § 1692e(11) notice since the letter did not convey any information regarding the debt and therefore was not a "communication" as defined in § 1692a(2).

Cavallaro v. Law Offices of Shapiro & Kriesman, 933 F. Supp. 1148 (E.D.N.Y. 1996). It was a factual question as to whether defendants disclosed they were attempting to collect a debt in the collection letter and had sent validation notice to plaintiff. A UCC notice of sale of collateral to the consumer was not required to contain a § 1692e(11) debt collection notice because it was not an attempt to collect a debt but was designed to comply with the UCC.

Rabideau v. Mgmt. Adjustment Bureau, 805 F. Supp. 1086 (W.D.N.Y. 1992). Although the reader was directed to information on the back, placement of the FDCPA notices on the reverse side of the collector's letter in dot matrix print smaller than the explanation of payment by credit card which appeared in larger print did not effectively convey the information required by §§ 1692g and 1692e(11) to the least sophisticated consumer.

Phillips v. Amana Collection Servs., 1992 WL 227839 (W.D.N.Y. Aug. 25, 1992). Notices on the reverse of the collection letter without reference to it on the front were insufficient to place a consumer on notice of his legal rights and violated §§ 1692g and 1692e(11).

Siler v. Mgmt. Adjustment Bureau, 1992 WL 32333 (W.D.N.Y. Feb. 18, 1992). Debt collector's initial communication to the consumer which contained the validation notice required by § 1692g(a) and the debt collection warning required by § 1692e(11) on the reverse side, with reference to them on the front, "in a smaller, lighter typeface than any on the front," with larger print below soliciting credit card information if the consumer chose to pay the debt in this method, was not in compliance with FDCPA.

Grammatico v. Sterling, Inc., Clearinghouse No. 47,976 (N.D.N.Y. 1991). Failure to include the language of § 1692e(11) in communication to consumer violated FDCPA.

Read v. Amana Collection Servs., 1991 U.S. Dist. LEXIS 21773 (W.D.N.Y. Jan. 15, 1991). Placing the notices required by §§ 1692e(11) and 1692g on the back of a dunning letter, in smaller type size, and with no reference to the notices on the front of the letter was a strategic placement violating those provisions.

Ohio

Boyce v. Attorney's Dispatch Serv., 1999 U.S. Dist. LEXIS 1124 (S.D. Ohio Feb. 2, 1999). Collection agent violated the §§ 1692g and 1692e(11) notice requirements where the collection letter did not contain the requisite notices.

Knight v. Schulman, 102 F. Supp. 2d 867 (S.D. Ohio 1996), *aff'd*, 166 F.3d 1214 (6th Cir. 1998). Letter identifying amount of debt, enclosing copy of real estate lien, and notifying debtor of title search in preparation for foreclosure was a communication made to collect a debt, but letter acknowledging receipt of payment and notifying debtor of dismissal of suit and release of judgment was not.

Sylvester v. Laks, 1991 U.S. Dist. LEXIS 21777 (N.D. Ohio Aug. 1, 1991). A follow-up letter violated the § 1692e(11) notice requirement because the § 1692e(11) notice on a separate paper should have been referred to in the dunning letter. Summary judgment was denied the consumer partly because of a factual dispute and partly because of a bona fide error defense where the violation involved the failure of a dunning letter to refer to an alleged separate § 1692e(11) notice.

Silverman v. Roetzel & Andress, L.P.A., 861 N.E.2d 834 (Ohio Ct. App. 2006). The cover letters which were sent by collection attorneys serving a state collection suit on the debtor in accordance with state court service rules and which demanded no money, asked for no information, and otherwise were no more than ordinary transmittal sheets were not communications that required the § 1692e(11) disclosure.

Oregon

Peters v. Collection Tech. Inc., 1991 U.S. Dist. LEXIS 21810 (D. Or. Dec. 5, 1991). Debt collector's letter failed to inform the consumer that any information obtained would be used for the purpose of collection in violation of § 1692e(11).

Clark v. Schwabe, Williamson & Wyatt, Clearinghouse No. 44,831 (D. Or. 1990). Even debt collection notices that do not seek information must include the statement required by § 1692e(11) that any information furnished would be used to collect the debt.

Zurcher v. Credit Bureau, Inc., 1983 U.S. Dist. LEXIS 20366 (D.

Or. Nov. 8, 1983). The failure to include the § 1692e(11) notice in a dunning letter violates the FDCPA; $200 statutory damages were awarded.

Case v. Credit Bureau, Inc., Clearinghouse No. 33,577 (D. Or. 1982). The failure of the collector to clearly disclose that it is collecting a debt and any information obtained will be used for that purpose violates § 1692e(11).

Check Cent., Inc. v. Barr, Clearinghouse No. 37,497 (Bankr. D. Or. 1984). The failure to include the § 1692e(11) notice in a dunning collection letter violates the FDCPA.

Pennsylvania

Gryzbowski v. I.C. Sys., Inc., 691 F. Supp. 2d 618 (M.D. Pa. 2010). Collector's failure to identify itself as a debt collector when leaving messages violated § 1692e(11).

Vlachos v. Douglas M. Marinos & Assocs., 2010 WL 3749280 (M.D. Pa. Sept. 21, 2010). A complaint for a violation of § 1692e(11) must plead facts suggesting three elements: that the defendants are debt collectors; that they failed to disclose in an initial oral communication that they were attempting to collect a debt and that the information obtained would be used for that purpose; and that the plaintiff is a consumer. *In forma pauperis* petition dismissed without prejudice to refiling.

Wideman v. Monterey Fin. Servs., Inc., 2009 WL 1292830 (W.D. Pa. May 7, 2009). The collector conceded that the allegation that it sent the consumer emails that did not identify itself as a debt collector stated a claim for violating § 1692e(11).

Romano v. Williams & Fudge, Inc., 644 F. Supp. 2d 653 (W.D. Pa. 2008). Defendant violated § 1692b(2) by discussing a debt with plaintiff's estranged father, § 1692c(b) by asking the father to convey a message, and § 1692e(11) by not providing the required notice in a telephone message. Defendant's bona fide error defense raised factual issues remaining for trial.

Farren v. RJM Acquisition Funding, L.L.C., 2005 WL 1799413 (E.D. Pa. July 26, 2005). While the statement by the debt collector, a purchaser of bad debt, that it was not a "collection agency" (as opposed to a debt collector) might by itself mislead the least sophisticated consumer to believe that the defendant was not attempting to collect a debt, the specific contrary language in the dun eliminated any such possibility, and thus the statement did not violate § 1692e.

Albanese v. Portnoff Law Assocs., Ltd., 301 F. Supp. 2d 389 (E.D. Pa. 2004). The § 1692e(11) notice requirement does not apply to formal pleadings made in connection with a legal action, and a Praecipe for Writ of Execution is such a pleading.

Adams v. Law Offices of Stuckert & Yates, 926 F. Supp. 521 (E.D. Pa. 1996). The bona fide error defense was not available to a collection firm for its failure to include the § 1692e(11) warning as the defendant offered no evidence of specific procedures followed to ensure compliance with the FDCPA. Posting a reminder to include the required language in correspondence next to a word processor, as opposed to a system of proofreading letters, was insufficient to qualify for adequate procedure to guard against such errors.

Pilewski v. Capital Credit Bureau, 1996 WL 221757 (E.D. Pa. Apr. 24, 1996). Plaintiff stated a claim upon which relief may be granted when he alleged that dunning letter did not include the warning that information obtained would be used for purpose of collecting a debt.

Rhode Island

In re Mason, 167 B.R. 327 (Bankr. D.R.I. 1994). Consumer who failed to establish that debt collector did not give the required § 1692e(11) notice in phone conversations relating to the collection of a debt was not entitled to relief.

South Carolina

Valentine v. Brock & Scott, P.L.L.C., 2010 WL 1727681 (D.S.C. Apr. 26, 2010). Consumer failed to state a "subsequent communications" violation under § 1692e(11) since the complaint specifically alleged that the collector's employees stated in each voicemail that they were calling in order to collect a debt.

Texas

Youngblood v. G.C. Servs. Ltd. P'ship, 186 F. Supp. 2d 695 (W.D. Tex. 2002). § 1692e(11) and § 1692g notices in gray type on gray background were sufficiently legible. § 1692e(11) and § 1692g notices on reverse were proper where face of dun prominently referenced the notice on reverse.

United States v. Cent. Adjustment Bureau, Inc., 667 F. Supp. 370 (N.D. Tex. 1986). Postcard stating "URGENT CALL WITHIN 48 HOURS" without identifying the collector violated § 1692e(11).

Virginia

Zevgolis v. Greenberg Law Firm, P.C., 2011 WL 251024 (E.D. Va. Jan. 26, 2011). A postjudgment debtor's summons served was not an "initial communication" triggering the obligation to make disclosures required by § 1692e(11). The summons was not a communication from the debt collector, but rather a summons issued at the request of the debt collector by an authorized clerk of court performing official duties.

Sears v. Federal Credit Corp., 2009 WL 2601378 (W.D. Va. Aug. 18, 2009). Where the caller stated that he was calling because defendant had tried to "settle a case" and may have "initiated legal action," or was calling regarding a legal action which could affect plaintiff's federal income tax liability, calls did not indicate that they were regarding an alleged debt as required by FDCPA, but the calls could have been with regard to a host of issues, thus confusing the least sophisticated consumer and violating § 1692e(11) disclosure requirements as well.

Hill v. Select Group, Inc., 2009 WL 2225509 (E.D. Va. July 23, 2009). The court permitted the filing of an amended complaint to allege a class action to remedy the defendant's failure to provide compliant §§ 1692e(11) and 1692g notices; the defendant's opposition to the amendment based on futility, because the defendant purportedly was not a covered debt collector, was an issue that went to the merits of the claim and would not be considered in the case's current posture.

Washington

Motherway v. Gordon, 2010 WL 2803052 (W.D. Wash. July 15, 2010). The court found that it did not make sense to require a debt collection law firm to restate it is a debt collector state court discovery requests and motions, and that the § 1692e(11) exception for pleadings applied to post-pleading litigation documents.

K.2.4.10 Disclosing the Amount of the Debt, 15 U.S.C. §§ 1692e(2)(A), 1692g(a)(1) [*See also* K.2.2.6, Other]

Heintz v. Jenkins, 514 U.S. 291, 115 S. Ct. 1489, 131 L. Ed. 2d 395 (1995). Involved claim that creditor misrepresented amount due on a car loan because the amount included charges for unauthorized forced placed insurance premiums.

Donohue v. Quick Collect, Inc., 592 F.3d 1027 (9th Cir. 2010). The debt collector did not charge a rate of interest in excess of that allowed by state law and thus did not violate §§ 1692f or 1692e. The collector did not violate § 1692e since its mislabeling in a collection complaint of a $32 charge as "interest," when in fact the charge was comprised of both interest and pre-assignment finance charges, would not mislead the least sophisticated consumer and therefore was not materially false.

Newman v. Ormond, 2010 WL 3623174 (11th Cir. Sept. 20, 2010). Rejecting the *pro se* plaintiff's claim that the debt collector misrepresented the character, amount, or legal status of the debt, the court found that the documentation the collector sent to the plaintiff expressly stated that the amount of the debt might vary daily based on additional interest, late charges, and collection costs, and was not a misrepresentation simply because the amount listed in it differed from the amount ultimately sought in settlement and judgment. Also, because the trial notice was a document provided by the court rather than the debt collector, the collector could not have made any misrepresentation in violation of the FDCPA in this document.

Hepsen v. Resurgent Capital Servs., L.P., 2010 WL 2490734 (11th Cir. June 17, 2010). The difference between the amount demanded by the collector and the lower amount later demanded by Resurgent, on behalf of the creditor LVNV, supported a reasonable inference that the collector's demand was inaccurate. Because § 1692g(b) does not modify § 1692e, which prohibits a debt collector from attempting to collect an inaccurate debt, the collector could still be liable for sending an inaccurate demand letter to the consumer even if the FDCPA does not explicitly require that a collector verify the debt before sending a demand.

Hahn v. Triumph P'ships, L.L.C., 557 F.3d 755 (7th Cir. 2009). Debt buyer claimed an "amount due" to which it added its own interest. Even though the "amount due" included the underlying creditor's interest, the statement was not false. "An 'amount' that is due can include principal, interest, penalties, attorneys' fees, and other components. Interest then can be added to that total." "When interest is compounded, today's interest becomes tomorrow's principal, so all past-due amounts accurately may be described as 'principal due.'"

Wahl v. Midland Credit Mgmt., Inc., 556 F.3d 643 (7th Cir. 2009). Because of interest and late fees, a debt of less than $70 ballooned to over $1000 by the time a bad debt buyer purchased it. The buyer stated that the balance it bought was "principal" and added its own interest thereafter. The plaintiff had to show both that the statement was false, and that it would mislead the unsophisticated consumer. From the perspective of the debt buyer, the interest charged by the original creditor was very much part of the principal. Defendant obtained the entire debt, including interest, presumably for pennies on the dollar; so the starting or original amount owed, as far as it was concerned, was full amount of the debt. The amount of the debt from the collector's perspective was what *it* was seeking. This would not be technically false or deceptive to the consumer.

Barany-Snyder v. Weiner, 539 F.3d 327 (6th Cir. 2008). The defendant collection attorneys did not violate §§ 1692e or 1692f(1) when they attached to their complaint in the underlying state court collection suit the parties' contract which contained an illegal provision that purported to permit the recovery of reasonable attorney fees but that they never sought to enforce.

Reichert v. Nat'l Credit Sys., 531 F.3d 1002 (9th Cir. 2008). Where no judicial proceedings had been held and no determination regarding attorney fees had been made, the debt collector's attempt to collect $225 in attorney fees violated the FDCPA by attempting to collect an amount not expressly authorized by the agreement or by law. Debt collector's argument that it was attempting to collect precisely the amount they were instructed to collect by the creditor was rejected because the additional attorney fees were not authorized by contract or law.

Barnes v. Advanced Call Ctr. Techs., L.L.C., 493 F.3d 838 (7th Cir. 2007). Summary judgment was granted in favor of the debt collector on the consumer's claim for violation of § 1692g(a)(1) where the collector's letter reflected the amount past due, not the total amount owed.

Evory v. Nat'l Action Fin. Servs., Inc., 505 F.3d 769 (7th Cir. 2007). Although a violation of state law is not in itself a violation of the federal Act, *Beler v. Blatt, Hasenmiller, Leibsker & Moore, L.L.C.*, 480 F.3d 470, 473–474 (7th Cir. 2007), a threat to impose a penalty that the threatener knows is improper because unlawful is a good candidate for a violation of §§ 1692d and 1692e.

Clark v. Capital Credit & Collection Servs., Inc., 460 F.3d 1162 (9th Cir. 2006). The collection agency and its lawyer are strictly liable for falsely stating the amount of the debt under § 1692e(2)(A) without regard to knowledge of the mistake. The § 1692k(c) bona fide error defense might shield the collectors but they were not entitled to summary judgment where there was evidence that the mistakes in the medical bills of the particular health care provider had come to their attention and the consumer was entitled to more discovery on the reasonableness of the collectors' procedures to avoid such errors.

McMillan v. Collection Prof'ls Inc., 455 F.3d 754 (7th Cir. 2006). The Seventh Circuit reversed and remanded the district court's dismissal holding that the FDCPA complaint stated a claim for violation of §§ 1692e and 1692f arising from the debt collector's statement "YOU ARE EITHER HONEST OR DISHONEST YOU CANNOT BE BOTH." By calling into question a debtor's honesty and good intentions, when there are reasons for dishonored checks, simply because a check was dishonored, a collection letter maybe making a statement that is false or misleading to the unsophisticated consumer.

Richmond v. Higgins, 435 F.3d 825 (8th Cir. 2006). In an inexplicable decision the court held that the alleged demand for illegal charges for health care services should be dismissed because it was not alleged to have been disputed promptly after the collector initially communicated with the consumer.

Olvera v. Blitt & Gaines, P.C., 431 F.3d 285 (7th Cir. 2005). The court rejected the consumer's argument that the debt buyer charged interest exceeding state limitations violating § 1692(A)(2). The court found that the state law allowed a higher rate to licensees and banks but had never been construed to prevent their assignees from charging that rate.

Fields v. Wilber Law Firm, P.C., 383 F.3d 562 (7th Cir. 2004). Including collection attorney fees in the amount of the debt before obtaining a judgment did not violate § 1692g(a) where the contract authorized reasonable attorney fees. The failure to disclose that the $388.54 veterinary claim included a claim for a $250 attorney collection fee stated a claim for misrepresenting the character of the debt under §§ 1692e and 1692f.

Schletz v. Acad. Collection Serv., Inc., 365 F.3d 572 (7th Cir. 2004). Letter which disclosed amount of interest owed as zero, but also says "[i]f applicable, your account may have or will accrue interest at a rate specified in your contractual agreement with the original creditor" properly stated the amount due as of the date of the letter.

Shula v. Lawent, 359 F.3d 489 (7th Cir. 2004). Where no judgment for costs had been entered against the consumer, the collecting attorney's letter demanding payment of such costs was false and misleading in violation of § 1692e, as well as § 1692f(1).

Singer v. Pierce & Assocs., P.C., 383 F.3d 596 (7th Cir. 2004). The mortgage servicer's seeking $2574 in attorney fees as a part of the loan payoff when the mortgaged home was sold by the consumer while a foreclosure action was pending did not violate § 1692g where the mortgage authorized the collection of "reasonable" fees. The fee was not made unreasonable by the state foreclosure court's interlocutory decision that $1100 was a reasonable fee for the foreclosing attorney, who was not a party to the payoff letter.

Taylor v. Cavalry Inv., L.L.C., 365 F.3d 572 (7th Cir. 2004). A statement of the amount due as of the date of the initial dun together with notice that the amount owing would increase with additional interest over time met the requirements of § 1692g.

Shapiro v. Riddle & Assocs., P.C., 351 F.3d 63 (2d Cir. 2003). A $98 collection fee authorized by contract was found reasonable where the collector had reviewed the file and mailed a dunning letter.

Miller v. Wolpoff & Abramson, L.L.P., 321 F.3d 292 (2d Cir. 2003). Where an attorney fee of $323 was sought in a collection suit on a $1618 credit card balance, it was not an excessive fee and seeking it did not violate the FDCPA. The fact that part of the fee would be paid to a referral agency and that payment could be unethical did not state a claim for unfair practices under the FDCPA. The claim that fee violated state law prohibiting collection fees was not timely raised.

Veach v. Sheeks, 316 F.3d 690 (7th Cir. 2003). Since the consumer could not be held liable for treble damages, court costs, or attorney fees until judgment, those charges could not be part of the "remaining principal balance" of a claimed debt. Therefore, Sheeks' notice including those charges in the amount of the debt misrepresented the actual debt that the collector was owed, a misrepresentation that violated § 1692e.

Freyermuth v. Credit Bureau Servs., Inc., 248 F.3d 767 (8th Cir. 2001). Service charge on checks was permitted by Article 2 of the UCC as incidental damages.

Gearing v. Check Brokerage Corp., 233 F.3d 469 (7th Cir. 2000). A false, unintentional representation that the collector was a subrogee entitled to dishonored check penalties from the consumer violated § 1692e(2) and (10).

Duffy v. Landberg, 215 F.3d 871 (8th Cir.), *rehearing denied*, 2000 U.S. App. LEXIS 16039 (8th Cir. July 10, 2000). Demanding a $100 civil penalty for small bounced checks was deceptive and unfair violating §§ 1692e, 1692e(5) and 1692f where the state law allowed a penalty **up to** $100 and provided that it was available if the consumer settled the claim before it reached the court. Referring to the imposition of attorney fees when state law did not authorize them for small checks violated § 1692e(5). Attempts to collect very small interest overcharges violated the plain language of § 1692f(1).

Miller v. McCalla, Raymer, Padrick, Cobb, Nichols & Clark, L.L.C., 214 F.3d 872 (7th Cir. 2000), *rehearing en banc denied*, 2000 U.S. App. LEXIS 18232 (7th Cir. July 26, 2000). A law firm's statement of a part of the balance of the debt violated the requirement of § 1692g that the collector state the amount of the debt. The letter stated the unpaid balance of the debt without accrued late charges, interest, etc. with an 800-number to call for the daily balance.

Kojetin v. CU Recovery, Inc., 212 F.3d 1318 (8th Cir. 2000). Imposition of a percentage-based collection fee resulted in a violation of the requirement for the collector to state the amount of the debt when state law prohibited such a percentage-based fee and required that any such fee must be based on the actual costs of collection.

Ballinger v. Fu, 2000 U.S. App. LEXIS 10783 (6th Cir. May 9, 2000). *Pro se* complaint was properly dismissed where it alleged that collectors violated FDCPA, the Fair Credit Reporting Act, and state law by collecting accounts after the consumer had written "paid in full" on the memo line and the back of the check. Two elements of accord and satisfaction not alleged were the existence of a bona fide dispute of the debts and evidence of acceptance of the accord.

Chaudhry v. Gallerizzo, 174 F.3d 394 (4th Cir. 1999). The amount of the debt did not need to contain the amount of collection attorney fees as the fees could be waived by the collector and the fees were still accruing. The collector later demanded $8600 in fees, less than the accrued amount.

Amond v. Bricefield, Hartnett & Assocs., 175 F.3d 1013 (4th Cir. 1999) (text at 1999 WL 152555). Where collection lawyers had no reason to question the amount of the debt they were attempting to collect, they did not violate the FDCPA. Collection attorneys were not subject to any special, higher duty under the FDCPA solely by virtue of their status as lawyers. The court would not combine Rule 11 with the FDCPA to create a heightened duty of investigation for a lawyer debt collector engaging in ordinary collection activities.

Ferree v. Marianos, 129 F.3d 130 (10th Cir. 1997) (unpublished) (text at 1997 WL 687693). Foreclosure pleadings did not misrepresent the amount or status of the consumer's debt or threaten to obtain an *in personam* judgment of a debt discharged in bankruptcy.

Lee v. Main Accounts, Inc., 125 F.3d 855 (6th Cir. 1997) (unpublished) (text at 1997 WL 618803). Collector's statement that payment by credit card required a 5% additional charge to pay for the collector's merchant charge imposed by the Visa credit card issuer was not an attempt to collect an illegal, unconscionable or deceptive charge.

Jenkins v. Heintz, 124 F.3d 824 (7th Cir. 1997). In a split decision, the Seventh Circuit adopted a narrow interpretation of the FDCPA to prohibit debt collection deception only if the debt collector knew a false statement was false, implying a new requirement that a misrepresentation must be made knowingly for an FDCPA violation to occur. A negligent misrepresentation did not state a claim under the FDCPA.

Smith v. Transworld Sys., Inc., 953 F.2d 1025 (6th Cir. 1992). Misstatement of the amount of the debt due to the creditor's erroneous referral was excused as a bona fide error pursuant to § 1692k(c). An independent investigation by the debt collector of the accuracy of the debt was not required by FDCPA.

Alabama

Bice v. Merchants Adjustment Serv., Clearinghouse No. 41,265 (S.D. Ala. 1985). The misrepresentation that the collector did not accept partial payments was actionable.

Arizona

Maldonado v. CACV, L.L.C., 2007 U.S. Dist. LEXIS 4461 (D. Ariz. Jan. 18, 2007). Demand for post-judgment interest in the underlying state court collection suit did not violate the FDCPA since the rate sought was lawful and not, as the consumer contended, prohibited by applicable state law.

Stiff v. Wilshappire Credit Corp., 2006 WL 141610 (D. Ariz. Jan. 17, 2006) Defendant's Rule 12(b)(6) motion to dismiss was denied with the court finding that plaintiff had adequately stated a claim for violations of the FDCPA for misrepresenting the amount of the debt and failing to report the debt was disputed to a credit reporting agency under § 1692e(8).

Axtell v. Collections U.S.A. Inc., 2002 WL 32595276 (D. Ariz. Oct. 22, 2002). Where the entitlement to fees in the underlying agreement only permitted fees to the "prevailing party" in any "legal action to enforce compliance," the collector's demand for payment of a sum for attorney fees incurred prior to and outside of litigation was unlawful.

Charles v. Check Rite, Ltd., 1998 U.S. Dist. LEXIS 22512 (D. Ariz. Dec. 14, 1999). Court found that imposition of a $25 check fee was authorized by UCC § 2-709 as "incidental damages" and a $110 collection fee was also authorized by another state law and that seeking such charges was not an FDCPA violation. Check Rite was the assignee of the check and stood in the position of the seller.

California

Reyes v. Kenosian & Miele, L.L.P., 619 F. Supp. 2d 796 (N.D. Cal. 2008). Collection attorney's request for fees under an inapplicable statute in a state collection complaint did not violate §§ 1692e or 1692f where the underlying agreement authorized reasonable collection fees.

Schwarm v. Craighead, 552 F. Supp. 2d 1056 (E.D. Cal. 2008). The collection of unauthorized fees violated § 1692f(1) as well as § 1692e(2)(A)–(B), which prohibits "[t]he false representation of—(A) the character, amount, or legal status of any debt; or (B) any services rendered or compensation which may be lawfully received by any debt collector for the collection of a debt."

Shubin v. Midland Credit Mgmt., Inc., 2008 WL 5042849 (C.D. Cal. Nov. 24, 2008). Where the creditor simply told the debt collector the wrong amount to collect, after it was asked to provide only the amount that is legally due and owing, the debt collector was not liable.

Abels v. JBC Legal Group, Inc., 434 F. Supp. 2d 763 (N.D. Cal. 2006). Debt collector's motion to dismiss an FDCPA suit alleging it was seeking fees on a dishonored check was denied. The complaint did not allege that assignment of the check to the debt collector included the same rights enjoyed by the original creditor raising an issue of fact. Even if the debt collector had received an assignment of all rights of the original creditor, the assessment of incidental and proximate damages would be based on those damages that the original creditor suffered and not the debt collector's costs.

Holsinger v. Wolpoff & Abramson, L.L.P., 2006 U.S. Dist. LEXIS 55406 (N.D. Cal. July 27, 2006). The court denied the collection law firm's motion for summary judgment because a trier of fact could find that the debt collector's failure to identify the attorneys fees in its collection letter could be misleading to the least sophisticated consumer and that $2466.87 collection fee claimed for filing an NAF arbitration was unreasonable. Seeking post-judgment interest at a lower rate than the contract rate was not deceptive.

Ramsire v. Collectcorp, Inc., 2005 WL 3095948 (N.D. Cal. Nov. 17, 2005). A debt collector's alleged willingness to later settle debts for less than the full amount owed did not render false, deceptive, or misleading the statement in its initial collection letter that collection efforts would continue if payment in full were not then made.

Palmer v. I.C. Sys., Inc., 2005 WL 3001877 (N.D. Cal. Nov. 8, 2005). Defendant attempted to collect the amount forwarded by its client, without knowing that the amount included unrecoverable bad check charges. Absent a dispute from the consumer, the collector was not liable for collecting a debt not owing. Defendant did not falsely represent the amount of the debt when it merely tried to collect the amount forwarded by the creditor.

Joseph v. J.J. Mac Intyre Cos., L.L.C., 238 F. Supp. 2d 1158 (N.D. Cal. 2002). Defendant did not violate the FDCPA when it attempted to collect interest in conformity with state law.

Valdez v. Hunt & Henriques, 2002 U.S. Dist. LEXIS 4575 (N.D. Cal. Mar. 19, 2002). A collection letter reciting the amount owed in its caption as the dollar amount "plus interest" but stating in its first sentence merely the dollar amount would not unlawfully confuse the least sophisticated consumer to believe that any amount other than the dollar amount recited was owed.

Ballard v. Equifax Check Servs., 158 F. Supp. 2d 1163 (E.D. Cal. 2001). Service charge added by collector to dishonored check, which was not authorized by state law or the contract creating the debt, violated §§ 1692e and 1692f and the California Unfair Business Practices Act.

Ballard v. Equifax Check Servs., Inc., 186 F.R.D. 589 (E.D. Cal. 1999). Court found there was no authorization to charge the $20 service charge for NSF checks where Equifax did no more than post a notice of the charge in its offices and collecting the charge was deceptive.

Ballard v. Equifax Check Servs., 27 F. Supp. 2d 1201 (E.D. Cal. 1998). A dishonored check charge is not permitted by state law as incidental damages under Article 2 of the Uniform Commercial Code, and the holder of the check is limited to recovering the face amount of the check under Article 3 of the Uniform Commercial Code; therefore, the check guarantee company's demand for payment of a dishonored check fee misrepresents the character and legal status of the debt.

Newman v. CheckRite California, Inc., 912 F. Supp. 1354 (E.D. Cal. 1995). Lawyers collecting debts for a check collection agency violated §§ 1692e and 1692f by adding on an $85 charge that was not authorized by the contract or state law and labeling it a "legal notice" fee misrepresenting that the fee was legally due. Lawyers collecting debts for a check collection agency violated §§ 1692e(5) and 1692f(1) by seeking attorney fees in a state action to collect a dishonored check when no attorney fees were authorized. The collection agency violated §§ 1692e and 1692f(1) by asserting that the consumers were liable for treble the amount of their dishonored checks when they were not because the agency failed to use the statutorily required certified mail to make that demand and demanded payment in ten days rather than the statutory thirty days permitted to avoid treble charges. The collection agency violated §§ 1692e(1) and 1692f(1) by asserting that a consumer owed an amount which only the merchant and not the agency was entitled to recover under state law. The collection agency was entitled to a trial to show that it was entitled to a $25 to $30 service fee by showing that the consumers assented to the charge when they read posted signs on merchants' cash registers and understood them to provide for the charge as a condition of the sale.

Imperial Merchant Servs., Inc. v. Hunt, 212 P.3d 736 (Cal. 2009). Upon certification of the question from the Ninth Circuit, the California Supreme Court held that the statutory damages for a dishonored check pursuant to Cal. Civil Code § 1719 (West) are exclusive in the sense that a debt collector who recovers a service charge pursuant to § 1719 may not also recover prejudgment interest under § 3287.

Colorado

Kelly v. Wolpoff & Abramson, L.L.P., 634 F. Supp. 2d 1202 (D. Colo. 2008). The failure of the bank's collector to disclose the putative tax benefits accruing to the bank from charging off the delinquent credit card debt in accordance with federal regulations did not misrepresent the amount of the debt in violation of § 1692e(2)(A).

Connecticut

Pacheco v. Joseph McMahon Corp., 698 F. Supp. 2d 291 (D. Conn. 2010). The transmission of an e-mail asserting that it would cost the consumer "a fortune in legal fees" and that her balance would be "in excess of $2000 before legal fees" constituted a violation of § 1692e(2)(A) where under state law the consumer's legal fees could not have exceeded $300.

Ballou v. Law Offices Howard Lee Schiff, P.C., 2010 WL 2070266 (D. Conn. May 21, 2010). In order to determine whether the debt collector's attempt to have interest added to an execution on a judgment violated the FDCPA, the district court certified to the Connecticut Supreme Court the question of whether post-judgment interest automatically applies to any unpaid balance under a judgment where the court entered an installment payment order.

Chiverton v. Fed. Fin. Group, Inc., 399 F. Supp. 2d 96 (D. Conn. 2005). After one consumer had sent the debt collector paperwork that the debt was satisfied, the debt buyer's representation that the debt was still outstanding was false and in violation of § 1692e(2). The false threat of arrest to an elderly consumer was deceptive.

Goins v. JBC & Assocs., 2004 WL 2063562 (D. Conn. Sept. 3, 2004). Check collector's pre-suit demand for the maximum civil penalty that a court might award in a future collection suit violated the FDCPA, since the that was not the current amount of the debt required by § 1692g; the consumer would be not liable for the additional sum unless it was awarded by a court. Dun was deceptive as it greatly misrepresented the amount owed to an identified creditor; the debt collector argued but failed to prove a legal basis for the discrepancy.

Madonna v. Acad. Collection Serv., Inc., 1997 WL 530101 (D. Conn. Aug. 12, 1997). Statement that the judgment would be added to the current balance was false and deceptive since it suggested to the least sophisticated consumer that the final amount owing will be duplicative.

Cacace v. Lucas, 775 F. Supp. 502 (D. Conn. 1990). The attorney's mistaken demand in a collection letter for an amount more than twice the amount owed was a violation of § 1692e(2)(A).

Butler v. Int'l Collection Serv., Inc., 1989 U.S. Dist. LEXIS 19102 (D. Conn. June 6, 1989). A debt collector's claiming a $15 illegal charge added by the creditor violated § 1692e(2)(A) even though the illegal charge was unknown to the collector.

Piscatelli v. Universal Adjustment Servs., Inc., Consumer Cred. Guide (CCH) ¶ 96,337 (D. Conn. 1985). Adding a 25% collection fee to agency's claim violated § 1692e(2)(A) where state statute limited such fees to 15%.

District of Columbia

Debt Buyers' Ass'n v. Snow, 481 F. Supp. 2d 1 (D.D.C. 2006). Court lacked jurisdiction under the Anti-Injunction Act to grant the relief requested by the plaintiff debt buyers to enjoin the IRS from enforcing its requirement that the debt buyers file a form 1099-C, where the debt buyers claim that they are incapable of distinguishing between interest and principal when they receive assignment of a gross amount of a debt and that compliance with the IRS rules would effectively force them to violate the FDCPA by necessarily misrepresenting those components; debt buyers' mere claim that they normally do not receive such component information would not prevent them from requiring as a condition of buying bad debts that such information be provided.

Florida

Bacelli v. MFP, Inc., 2010 WL 2985699 (M.D. Fla. July 28, 2010). The creditor's failure to show reasonable procedures to discover that an account had been discharged in bankruptcy, precluded defendant's bona fide error defense.

Hepsen v. J.C. Christensen & Assocs., Inc., 2009 WL 3064865 (M.D. Fla. Sept. 22, 2009). When a debt collector demands an incorrect amount of money in a dunning letter, it makes a false and misleading representation in violation of § 1692e(2)(A).

Pack v. Unifund CCR Partners, G.P., 2008 WL 686800 (M.D. Fla. Mar. 13, 2008). Summary judgment awarded for the defendant debt buyer where the consumer alleged that the defendant had violated §§ 1692d, 1692e, and 1692f in prosecuting the underlying state court collection case but the consumer failed to produce any evidence to support its case that the amount of the state claim was erroneous, instead claiming that the defendant's testimony that the amount was correct was insufficient.

Williams v. Edelman, 408 F. Supp. 2d 1261 (S.D. Fla. 2006). The court held that the complaint could fairly be read that defendant, being fully aware that plaintiff had paid her fees, nonetheless attempted to collect additional fees or interest not authorized by the declaration of condominium.

Agan v. Katzman & Korr, P.A., 328 F. Supp. 2d 1363 (S.D. Fla. 2004). The court denied collector's motion to strike pre-billing worksheets attached to the complaint, since they showed that law firm sought excessive fees in a state court action. The worksheets were in the nature of settlement documents in the state condominium assessment action, but contained otherwise discoverable evidence as to the federal FDCPA claim. Court rejected argument that defendant's business would be adversely affected if they could not provide attorney fee substantiation to a debtor without fear that the debtor will turn around and sue: "[A]ny collection agency or collection lawyer must comply with the requirements of federal law in collecting on a debt. If that means the agency or attorney must scrutinize her attorney time records more carefully, that is a price that federal law requires."

Fuller v. Becker & Poliakoff, P.A., 192 F. Supp. 2d 1361 (M.D. Fla. 2002). Collection letter stating that failure to pay will result in the consumer incurring substantial amounts in attorney fees and costs unlawfully conveyed to the least sophisticated consumer that the creditor would automatically prevail in subsequent litigation.

Sandlin v. Shapiro & Fishman, 919 F. Supp. 1564 (M.D. Fla. 1996). The court denied defendant's motion to dismiss as plaintiff may be able to prove a violation of § 1692e(2)(A) as defendant imposed a $60 payoff disclosure fee and the note prohibited such a fee.

Sandlin v. Shapiro & Fishman, 168 F.R.D. 662 (M.D. Fla. 1996). Court denied class certification for FDCPA suit finding that while there was a common question of whether unauthorized mortgage payoff fees were charged other requirements for class certification were not met.

In re Cooper, 253 B.R. 286 (Bankr. N.D. Fla. 2000). A lawyer who filed a proof of claim in a bankruptcy of the consumer in good faith without any knowledge of an error by the creditor in calculating the claim was not in violation of the FDCPA and the consumer was limited to bankruptcy remedies. Attorneys may reasonably rely in good faith on information provided by the creditor, and are not liable for filing a claim which is ultimately unsuccessful without a statement of any basis that an increased installment payment was excessive, no FDCPA claim was stated.

Georgia

Milton v. LTD Fin. Servs., 2011 WL 291363 (S.D. Ga. Jan. 25, 2011). A consumer wishing to sue a collector for misrepresenting the amount of the debt must first utilize § 1692g's dispute procedure, but summary judgment was denied on the plaintiff's purported failure since a genuine issue of material fact remained as to whether the plaintiff properly utilized the debt validation procedure prior to filing suit.

Sanchez v. United Collection Bureau, Inc., 649 F. Supp. 2d 1374 (N.D. Ga. 2009). Summary judgment for the defendant where the plaintiff failed to meet her burden to produce any evidence to support her alleged § 1692e(2)(A) violation that the collector misrepresented the amount of the debt: "Although Plaintiff has presented evidence showing that two other debt collection agencies sent collection letters to Plaintiff alleging an amount due on the debt that was *different* than the amount stated in [defendant's] Apr. 20, 2007 collection letter, she has presented no evidence that the amount showing as due from was a *false* representation of the total amount then due on the debt. Nor has she presented evidence showing what she contends was the 'correct' amount. . . ."

Gilmore v. Acc. Mgmt., Inc., 2009 WL 2848278 (N.D. Ga. Apr. 27, 2009). Accepting plaintiff's alleged facts as true, court concluded that plaintiff owed no debt to defendant and therefore defendant's representations to both plaintiff and the credit reporting agencies that the debt was $1010, or double the amount owed that it previously asserted, would have violated § 1692e(2)(A).

Teemogonwuno v. Todd, Bremer & Larsen, Inc., Clearinghouse No. 45,946A & B (N.D. Ga. 1991). Debt collector's attempt to collect an amount which included, but did not itemize, $4000 as collection fees on a student loan would deceive the "least sophisticated consumer" concerning the character and amount of the debt in violation of § 1692e(2)(A) and (10). Under Georgia law non-legal expenses were not recoverable as collection costs.

Johnson v. Ardec Credit Servs., Inc., 1984 U.S. Dist. LEXIS 24889 (N.D. Ga. Mar. 21, 1984). Collection letter which misstated amount of debt violated Act.

Hawaii

Sambor v. Omnia Credit Servs., 183 F. Supp. 2d 1234 (D. Haw. 2002). The recitation on different dates of differing amounts owing in a telephone dun and a letter did not violate § 1692e or § 1692g as the discrepancy correctly resulted from the accrual of interest and fees.

King v. Int'l Data Servs., 2002 WL 32345923 (D. Haw. Aug. 5, 2002). Including a statement of the total amount of charges by and

payments to the creditor for over ten years was confusing and deceptive.

Illinois

Acik v. I.C. Sys., Inc., 640 F. Supp. 2d 1019 (N.D. Ill. 2009). The debt collector violated § 1692e by failing to disclose what the "Additional Client Charges" of $78.50 included.

Kasalo v. Monco Law Offices, S.C., 2009 WL 4639720 (N.D. Ill. Dec. 7, 2009). An Internet gambling debt was not void under state law; the defendant's attempt to collect that debt did not misrepresent the amount owed.

Berg v. Blatt, Hasenmiller, Leibsker & Moore L.L.C., 2009 WL 901011 (N.D. Ill. Mar. 31, 2009). Inaccurate and confusing statement of the amount of interest violates the FDCPA, subject to a bona fide error defense.

Longo v. Law Offices of Gerald E. Moore & Assocs., P.C., 2008 WL 4425444 (N.D. Ill. Sept. 26, 2008). FDCPA claim asserting that a dun that was sent to the consumer in care of her attorney and that stated that any payment made by telephone would be subject to a $7.50 "convenience fee" was dismissed since (1) the consumer failed to show that the statement was a false representation, and (2) the statement "would not deceive a competent lawyer," the standard imposed by the Circuit in its *Evory* opinion in this situation for a non-false representation.

Day v. Check Brokerage Corp., 511 F. Supp. 2d 950 (N.D. Ill. 2007). The debt collector falsely represented the amount of the debt (but not the legal status) by adding both a $25 "Returned Check Charge" and a $20 "Bank Charge to Merchant" in violation of § 1692e and 1692e(2)(A). Where the debt collector falsely stated that the consumer "could be liable" for treble damages, attorneys fee, and court costs, it violated § 1692e and 1692e(2)(A). Where the debt collector incorrectly (under) stated the amount of "Filing Fee," "Sheriff Service," and "Filing of Citation," it violated § 1692e and 1692e(10).

Smith v. First Nat'l Collection Bureau, Inc., 2007 WL 4365335 (N.D. Ill. Dec. 10, 2007). Summary judgment was entered for the debt collector for a high fee credit card on the consumer's FDCPA claim that the collector's statement of "$0 interest" was false because the card balance included $560.19 interest. The statement was not false because the amount of post-charged-off interest was zero.

Ruth v. M.R.S. Assocs., Inc., 2006 WL 1207926 (N.D. Ill. Apr. 4, 2006). Disclosure that interest may accrue on unpaid balances was a truism and not deceptive or misleading.

In re Ocwen Fed. Bank F.S.B. Mortgage Serv. Litig., 2005 WL 1027118 (N.D. Ill. Apr. 25, 2005). The default and attorney fees imposed by the bank foreclosing on the consumers' mortgages were permitted in accordance with the underlying contracts, and the imposition of those fees by the bank's collection attorneys therefore did not violate the FDCPA.

Zaborac v. Phillips & Cohen Assocs., 330 F. Supp. 2d 962 (N.D. Ill. 2004). Section 1692g(a)(1) requires statement of the amount the consumer allegedly owes, not the unpaid principle balance.

Gonzalez v. Lawent, 2004 WL 2036409 (N.D. Ill. Sept. 10, 2004). An attorney who verified a collection complaint on behalf of the creditor "on information and belief" and who had no personal knowledge of that the debt had been paid did not violate the FDCPA since the verification did not purport to be made on personal knowledge. The attorney debt collector's verification of the collection complaint complied with applicable state law that allowed verification of a complaint on information and belief and therefore did not violate the FDCPA. The allegation that an attorney who verified a collection complaint "on information and belief" in fact had been presented evidence prior to verifying the complaint that the debt in question had been paid in full stated a claim for violating the FDCPA.

Olvera v. Blitt & Gaines, P.C., 2004 WL 887372 (N.D. Ill. Apr. 26, 2004). The complaint alleged that the assignee of a credit card debt violated the FDCPA by falsely representing the legal status of the debt and trying to collect interest at a rate which violated the Illinois Interest Act. While the court concluded that an assignee could charge the contract rate, the collection attorneys' Rule 12(b)(6) motion to dismiss was denied because neither party had produced evidence of the interest rate agreed to be paid.

Lockett v. Freedman, 2004 WL 856516 (N.D. Ill. Apr. 21, 2004). Attorney collector's motion to dismiss was denied where consumer adequately alleged that attorney lacked knowledge to verify complaint in a state collection action and attempted to collect unauthorized attorney fees.

Bennett v. Arrow Fin. Servs., L.L.C., 2004 WL 830440 (N.D. Ill. Apr. 14, 2004). Because plaintiff submitted no evidence that the interest charged was unauthorized, that claim failed.

Gonzalez v. Codilis & Assocs., P.C., 2004 WL 719264 (N.D. Ill. Mar. 31, 2004). Seventh Circuit's holding in *Veach v. Sheets* that a debt collector may not dun for attorney fees that have not been yet awarded by a court was limited to cases under Indiana law, where that rule applied; Illinois law, applicable here, permitted such a demand, but only for fees that are "reasonable." The holding in *Shula v. Lawent* that dunning for court costs that have not been awarded in pending litigation did not apply in this case where, in contrast to *Shula*, the agreement between the parties provided for the debtor's payment of costs incurred.

Collins v. Sparacio, 2004 WL 555957 (N.D. Ill. Mar. 19, 2004). Consumer's claim that the liquidated damages expressly provided in the parties' underlying contract were an inequitable or illegal penalty clause, although cognizable as a defense under state law in the collection action, could not as a matter of law establish a § 1692e violation against the collection attorney, who was not a party to the contract and who sued on behalf of a client to recover those damages in the collection suit. A prayer in a collection suit for an unspecified amount for court costs was not a confusing presentation of the amount of the debt since the amount of the court costs that might be awarded was not knowable as a practical matter when suit was filed.

Asch v. Teller, Levit & Silvertrust, P.C., 2003 WL 22232801 (N.D. Ill. Sept. 26, 2003). Illinois law requires that payments by check, cash, and garnishment or attachment be credited when made available to the debt collector, i.e., on the day received. Failure by the debt collector to credit payments on the date received violates § 1692e(2) and (10).

Whaley v. Shapiro & Kreisman, L.L.C., 2003 WL 22232911 (N.D. Ill. Sept. 16, 2003). An argument that contracted for collection attorney fees could be collected in Illinois only by court action was rejected.

Smith v. G.C. Servs., L.P., 2003 WL 22012229 (N.D. Ill. Aug. 25, 2003), *vacated and reconsideration granted by* 2003 WL 22208027 (N.D. Ill. Sept. 23, 2003). The unpaid balance amount of a student loan was sufficiently disclosed despite a footnote in the letter that there may be accrued but unposted interest, in the absence of evidence that the disclosed balance was not correct.

Collins v. Sparacio, 2003 WL 21254256 (N.D. Ill. May 30, 2003). Consumer's unadorned allegations that the attorney debt collector from the underlying state court collection suit misrepresented in that suit the amount of the debt and attempted to collect sums not authorized by the contract or law sufficiently met the federal notice pleading requirements to state a claim for relief.

Porter v. Fairbanks Capital Corp., 2003 WL 21210115 (N.D. Ill. May 21, 2003). Complaint stated a claim for relief under § 1692e for demanding payment for attorney fees to reinstate the loan under the heading "recoverable corporate advances" when the same document contained a heading "legal fees" and read zero. However, complaint failed to state a claim for relief for demanding, in order to reinstate the loan, payment of attorney fees that were not challenged as unreasonable but had not yet been approved by a court, since the loan agreement authorized such fees and neither the agreement nor applicable law required that such fees be first established by court order to be considered due and owing.

Jolly v. Shapiro, 237 F. Supp. 2d 888 (N.D. Ill. 2002). Disclosure of the amount of the debt mandated by § 1692g does not require calculating the amount owing as of the precise date of the dun and may be disclosed as of a stated date certain together with the "safe harbor" language devised by the Seventh Circuit in *Miller* as to the appropriate adjustments for the continuing accrual of interest and fees.

Wilkerson v. Bowman, 200 F.R.D. 605 (N.D. Ill. 2001). Collection letter did not state the amount of the debt as required by the § 1692g when it stated: "Balance: $3484.02, less applicable rebate, if any, $.00 accrued interest and/or late charges, up to $350.00 attorney fees, exact amount to be determined by agreement between you and us or by a court, and 20.00 % interest per annum from February 4, 2000."

Hamid v. Blatt, Hasenmiller, Leibsker, Moore & Pellettieri, 2001 U.S. Dist. LEXIS 13918 (N.D. Ill. Aug. 31, 2001). Consumer's allegations that collection attorney filed suit on a time-barred debt were sufficient to survive debt collector's motion to dismiss FDCPA action.

Peeples v. Blatt, 2001 U.S. Dist. LEXIS 11869 (N.D. Ill. Aug. 14, 2001). Plaintiff's allegations that the defendant misrepresented the legal status and the amount of the alleged debt adequately stated a claim for violation of the FDCPA.

Patterson v. N. Shore Agency, 126 F. Supp. 2d 1138 (N.D. Ill. 2000). Requiring video and book club purchasers who became delinquent to pay for three future items was not unreasonable or unconscionable and no FDCPA claim was stated by the practice.

Wagner v. Ocwen Fed. Bank, F.S.B., 2000 U.S. Dist. LEXIS 12463 (N.D. Ill. Aug. 28, 2000). Ocwen purchased Wagner's mortgage after her bankruptcy discharge, and tried to collect on it, even after plaintiff expressly told Ocwen of the discharge. "Wagner has stated a claim for violation of the FDCPA; a creditor who seeks to collect on a debt that no longer exists violates the statute. *See* 15 U.S.C. § 1692e(2)(A)."

Jones v. Kunin, 2000 U.S. Dist. LEXIS 6380 (S.D. Ill. May 1, 2000). The court denied the motion to dismiss a complaint which alleged that collection letter asserting the consumers liable under a fraudulent check statute was deceptive as the statute did not apply to the postdated payday loan checks the consumers wrote; a postdated check implies there are insufficient funds in the account.

Shea v. Codilis, 2000 U.S. Dist. LEXIS 4202 (N.D. Ill. Mar. 27, 2000). Stating the principal balance when there was also interest due violated the § 1692g(a)(1) requirement that the collector state the amount of the debt.

Harvey v. Nat'l Action Fin. Servs., 79 F. Supp. 2d 896 (N.D. Ill. 1999). Validation notice sufficiently stated the amount of the debt by disclosing a set amount plus referring to small additional charges which could be determined by a free telephone call. Relying on the "unsophisticated consumer" standard, the court reasoned that "the provision of a telephone number to get the current balance will lead to less head-scratching than providing various per diem formulae from which our unsophisticated consumer can attempt to calculate a current balance."

Blum v. Fisher & Fisher, 961 F. Supp. 1218 (N.D. Ill. 1997). Claim that collection attorney's letter concerning mortgage foreclosure, which stated that the consumer owed attorney fees when none would be due until a foreclosure judgment was obtained, presented questions of fact precluding grant of summary judgment on alleged FDCPA violations of misrepresentation and unfairness.

Keele v. Wexler, 1996 WL 124452 (N.D. Ill. Mar. 19, 1996), *aff'd,* 149 F.3d 589 (7th Cir. 1998). Motion for class certification of a Colorado class was granted. Lawyers sent letters attempting to collect for NSF checks written to Wal-Mart. The letters demanded a $12.50 fee not permitted by the contract or a statute in addition to a $20 service charge.

Holloway v. Pekay, 1996 WL 19580 (N.D. Ill. Jan. 18, 1996). Information regarding lender's attorney fees and costs charged to class members in collection actions was discoverable pursuant to Fed. R. Civ. P. 26(b)(2) in FDCPA action because it was "reasonably calculated to lead to the discovery of admissible evidence."

Brunn v. Gaines, 1995 WL 88799 (N.D. Ill. Mar. 1, 1995). Plaintiff's vague claims that unauthorized insurance had been added to his loan by the creditor failed to state a claim pursuant to the FDCPA against the assignee which sought only to collect the amount assigned.

Friedman v. HHL Fin. Servs., Inc., 1993 WL 367089 (N.D. Ill. Sept. 17, 1993). Difference in the amount due stated in a later collection letter because of an additional medical treatment which had not been previously included; thus the letter was not incorrect or confusing in violation of the FDCPA.

Strange v. Wexler, 796 F. Supp. 1117 (N.D. Ill. 1992). Filing of a verified complaint by the attorney collector claiming attorney fees to which he was not entitle violated § 1692e(2)(B).

PRA III, L.L.C. v. Hund, 846 N.E.2d 965 (Ill. App. Ct. Mar. 3,

2006). Assignee did not violate FDCPA by seeking interest at the rate permitted to original creditor, since Illinois law permitted an assigned to collect interest at the original rate.

Indiana

Bull v. Asset Acceptance, L.L.C., 444 F. Supp. 2d 946 (N.D. Ind. Aug. 15, 2006). Debt collector did not violate the FDCPA merely by seeking an "outlandish" amount of attorney fees where the consumer had agreed to pay only "reasonable" attorney fees in the event of default. Once a consumer has agreed to pay attorney fees in the event of default, he cannot use the FDCPA to contest the reasonableness of the fees.

Kaiser v. Braje & Nelson, L.L.P., 2006 WL 1285143 (N.D. Ind. May 5, 2006). Overstatement of amount of attorney fees in court application did not violate FDCPA where court modified the amount upon consumers' objection.

Miller v. Javitch, Block & Rathbone, L.L.P., 397 F. Supp. 2d 991 (N.D. Ind. 2005). *Pro se* could not successfully dispute amount of debt on the basis of his credit report showing that the original creditor had reported a zero balance after the debt was sold to another.

Stines v. M.R.S. Assocs., Inc., 2005 WL 2428200 (S.D. Ind. Sept. 30, 2005). Summary judgment was granted for the debt collector whose letter stated that the balance may be periodically increased due to the addition of interest or other charges.

Smith v. American Revenue Corp., 2005 WL 1162906 (N.D. Ind. May 16, 2005). Follow-up letter demanding payment of a lump sum for "various accounts" was confusing on its face and misrepresented the character of the debt. There were actually 14 accounts in varying amounts; debtor was not required to look elsewhere to figure out what debts might be included, and letter made proof of payment of any particular account difficult.

Pickard v. Lerch, 2005 WL 1259629 (S.D. Ind. May 26, 2005). Attorney violated FDCPA by stating an amount owed several hundred dollars less than was asserted to be owed by the collection agency that purchased the debt.

Nance v. Ulferts, 282 F. Supp. 2d 912 (N.D. Ind. 2003). Attempting to collect usurious interest violated §§ 1692e and 1692f notwithstanding that the loan agreement purported to authorize collection of the illegal amounts. Defendants' assertion that they had no reason to know that the amounts that they attempted to collect were usurious until the issuance of an intervening state appellate court decision was no defense to their liability. Since the state dishonored check law provision allowing for treble damages excluded post-dated checks, the consumer was entitled to summary judgment for the collector's illegal attempt to collect treble damages on a post-dated payday loan check.

Bernstein v. Howe, 2003 WL 1702254 (S.D. Ind. Mar. 31, 2003). A collection letter demanding payment of a specific amount "plus interest and attorneys fees" violated § 1692e(2)(a) because no attorney fees were actually owed at the time of the letter. At most, attorney fees may be awarded in the future.

Spearman v. Tom Wood Pontiac-GMC, Inc., 2002 WL 31854892 (S.D. Ind. Nov. 4, 2002). Including in the amount of the debt in the § 1692g notice accompanying a lawsuit unspecified reasonable attorney fees and costs did not violate the standard enunciated by the Seventh Circuit in *Miller* decision. *But see Veach v. Sheeks*, 316 F.3d 690, 2003 WL 102992 (7th Cir. Jan. 13, 2003).

Wehrheim v. Secrest, P.C., 2002 WL 31427515 (S.D. Ind. Oct. 9, 2002). Seeking in a motion for summary a greater rate of interest than provided by the note was considered a dubious FDCPA claim as the consumer's lawyer would not pass on the deception to the consumer.

Wehrheim v. Secrest, 2002 WL 31242783 (S.D. Ind. Aug. 16, 2002). It was not deceptive under the FDCPA to specify an excessive claim in a state court complaint, so long as there was a reasonable basis in law for the claim.

Jackson v. Aman Collection Serv., Inc., 2001 U.S. Dist. LEXIS 22238 (S.D. Ind. Dec. 14, 2001). Court noted that its decisions not precedential and not to be published. Collection agency's motion to dismiss denied where consumer alleged that collection letter violated § 1692g(a)(1) by failing to state the entire amount due, but rather, seeking an amount due plus an unspecified amount of "accruing interest."

Hill v. Priority Fin. Servs., Inc., 2001 U.S. Dist. LEXIS 16900 (S.D. Ind. Sept. 28, 2001). The admitted fact that the debt collector requested treble damages and attorney fees with regard to an NSF check violated § 1692e.

Brooks v. Auto Sales & Servs. Inc., 2001 U.S. Dist. LEXIS 8059 (S.D. Ind. June 15, 2001). Plaintiff's claim that the attorney sought excessive fees in litigation stated a cause of action under §§ 1692e(2)(B) and 1692f(1).

Bawa v. Bowman, Heintz, Boscia & Vician, 2001 U.S. Dist. LEXIS 7842 (S.D. Ind. May 30, 2001). Summary judgment was granted for consumers where collection letter did not state the amount of the debt but demanded a sum "plus accrued interest and/or late charges, and attorney fees, exact amount to be determined by agreement between you and us or by a court."

Payday Today, Inc. v. Hamilton, 911 N.E.2d 26 (Ind. Ct. App. 2009). An attorney's collection letter violated the FDCPA by stating that a lawsuit may be filed "if you fail to pay in full the amount due," which nowhere provided the amount that constitutes "the full amount due," stating further that resolution of the matter without litigation would require the consumer to "pay the following amounts . . . [including] attorney fees of $300.00," and directing the consumer to send payment to the offices of the attorney, as it would cause a reasonable person (let alone an unsophisticated debtor) to reasonably believe that the "full amount due" are those amounts the consumer had been advised "must be paid" to avoid litigation and resolve the matter.

Kansas

McCammon v. Bibler, Newman & Reynolds, P.A., 515 F. Supp. 2d 1220 (D. Kan. 2008). The defendant's attempt to collect court costs and interest awarded as part of the underlying default judgment in state court did not violate the FDCPA. Various disputed facts flowing from the parties inconsistent views of their oral negotiations over the payment of the underlying debt and the amounts and components demanded precluded entry of summary judgment.

Louisiana

Ducrest v. Alco Collections, Inc., 931 F. Supp. 459 (M.D. La. 1996). A collection agency was not liable for misrepresenting the amount of the debt under § 1692c(2)(a) or collecting an amount not owed under § 1692f(1) where it relied on the landlord's information and passed that information on to the consumer who asked for verification. The agency was not required to make an independent investigation.

Maryland

Hawkins v. Citicorp Credit Servs., Inc., 665 F. Supp. 2d 518 (D. Md. 2009). The complaint alleging that defendants collected an unlawful rate of interest and thus violated § 1692e(2)(A) was dismissed since applicable law authorized the rate charged.

Ransom v. Telecredit Serv. Corp., 1992 U.S. Dist. LEXIS 22738 (D. Md. Feb. 5, 1992). Demand for payment of $15 service charge for dishonored check violated § 1692e(2)(A) where consumer asserted that she did not see notice of such service charge and debt collector did not produce evidence to the contrary.

Massachusetts

Gathuru v. Credit Control Serv., Inc., 623 F. Supp. 2d 113 (D. Mass. 2009). The addition and inclusion of the debt collector's contingency fee to the amount due in its first letter was a misrepresentation in violation of § 1692e(2)(A) because the collection fee was not yet due.

Som v. Daniels Law Offices, P.C., 573 F. Supp. 2d 349 (D. Mass. 2008). Denied motion to dismiss since whether a demand for a percentage-based legal fee violated the FDCPA depended on facts not before the court.

Pettway v. Harmon Law Offices, P.C., 2005 WL 2365331 (D. Mass. Sept. 27, 2005). Law firm's motion for summary judgment was denied because the FDCPA claims, that foreclosing attorney fees were overstated by including unaccrued fees that would later be rebated and whether the collection letter was false or misleading, presented quintessential jury questions.

Alger v. Ganick, O'Brien & Sarin, 35 F. Supp. 2d 148 (D. Mass. 1999). Allegation that lawyer falsely inflated the balance due in a statement to a process server seeking an arrest warrant stated a claim under §§ 1692e(2) and 1692f(2).

In re Maxwell, 281 B.R. 101 (Bankr. D. Mass. 2002). Purchaser of defaulted mortgage violated § 1692e(2)(A) by demanding varying amounts which the purchaser could not substantiate.

Michigan

Grden v. Leikin, Ingber & Winters, P.C., 2010 WL 199947 (E.D. Mich. Jan. 19, 2010). The collector's misstatement of the amount of the debt communicated in response to the consumer's direct inquiry was not made "in connection with the collection of" the consumer's debt and thus did not violate § 1692e(2)(B) where the collector did not demand payment, did not imply that the consumer was in default, and did not "allude to the consequences of default."

Richard v. Oak Tree Group, Inc., 614 F. Supp. 2d 814 (W.D. Mich. 2008). The inclusion of unaccrued collection agency fees hidden within the stated amount of the debt did not violate § 1692g(a)(1) but did violate § 1692e(2)(A), (B), and § 1692f(1).

Pistole v. Mortgage Elec. Registration Sys., Inc., 2008 WL 2566366 (E.D. Mich. June 24, 2008). Summary judgment granted to mortgage company on *pro se* mortgagor's FDCPA claims that the defendant misrepresented the amount and status of the debt, failed to give default notice required by the mortgage, and foreclosed without a current right to do so when in fact the consumer was in default, the status and amount of the debt were accurately stated, and notice was properly given.

Stolicker v. Muller, Muller, Richmond, Harms, Myers & Sgroi, P.C., 2005 WL 2180481 (W.D. Mich. Sept. 9, 2005). Where the contract allowed for reasonable attorney fees, defendant's claim to a percentage fee (25%) violated §§ 1692e (2), (10), and 1692f(1). A reasonable attorney fee requires a court determination. Court distinguished *Spears*, which focused on whether the chosen percentage was reasonable, rather than the procedural aspect of claiming that a percentage fee was due despite the contract language that was otherwise.

West v. Check Alert Sys., 2001 U.S. Dist. LEXIS 22122 (W.D. Mich. Sept. 7, 2001). Summary judgment granted to collection agency where it represented that interest at 12% was due (when this exceeded the legal limit of 9%) because the consumer failed to show that the misrepresentation was made "knowingly or intentionally," a requirement the court erroneously engrafted onto § 1692e(2).

McCallum v. Cape Condo. Assoc., 2006 WL 171511 (Mich. Ct. App. Jan. 24, 2006). Since window assessment was valid, plaintiff had no claim under the FDCPA.

Minnesota

Munoz v. Pipestone Fin., L.L.C., 2006 WL 2786911 (D. Minn. Sept. 26, 2006). Debt buyer's motion for summary judgment was denied because it did not refute that the assignment of the debt described as "receivables" did not include interest not yet accrued or future attorney fees which the debt buyer had nevertheless sought to collect.

Erickson v. Johnson, 2006 WL 453201 (D. Minn. Feb. 22, 2006). Since plaintiff was not a party to the credit card account, defendants' demand for attorney fees based on the credit card agreement violated §§ 1692f(1) and 1692e.

Munoz v. Pipestone Fin., L.L.C., 397 F. Supp. 2d 1129 (D. Minn. 2005). The sale to a debt collector of defaulted debt portfolios described in the sales documents as the creditor's "receivables" did not include the rights to post-purchase interest and attorney fees. Following contract law, the plain meaning of the word "receivables" in *Black's Law Dictionary* is "amount owed." The collector's attempts to collect those additional amounts which were not owed to it violated the FDCPA.

Cohen v. Beachside Two-I Homeowners' Ass'n, 2005 WL 3088361 (D. Minn. Nov. 17, 2005). *Pro se* plaintiff's motion for partial summary judgment was denied with the court holding that (1) while the attorneys potentially charged fees in excess of the statutory amount for the lien foreclosure, fact issues remained concerning the portion of the fees attributable to the foreclosure and the applicability of the bona fide error defense under the

FDCPA, and (2) late fees were not authorized by the association's governing documents, but it remained to be determined whether late fees were voluntarily paid, and whether the documents authorized the collection of attorney fees.

Thinesen v. JBC Legal Group, P.C., 2005 WL 2346991 (D. Minn. Sept. 26, 2005). The complaint alleged facts sufficient to show that the defendants demanded dishonored check fees in excess of that allowed by state law and thus violated the FDCPA.

Wiegand v. JNR Adjustment Co., 2002 U.S. Dist. LEXIS 7292 (D. Minn. Apr. 22, 2002). Dun that recited the aggregate amount allegedly owing and that further explained that this amount was comprised of "the check amount plus the posted worthless check charge" met the requirement of the FDCPA to "be explicit regarding the amount owed."

Armstrong v. Rose Law Firm, P.A., 2002 U.S. Dist. LEXIS 4039 (D. Minn. Mar. 7, 2002). Debt collector's recitation of availability of a civil dishonored check penalty failed to comply with applicable state law and therefore violated the FDCPA.

Maneval v. Jon R. Hawks, Ltd., 1999 U.S. Dist. LEXIS 22899 (D. Minn. Oct. 12, 1999). The court accepted collector's argument that Minnesota law allowed him to send a letter demanding $100 over the amount of a bounced check, even though that amount could not be assessed at the inception of litigation. This decision may be peculiar to Minnesota.

Kojetin v. C.U. Recovery, Inc., 1999 U.S. Dist. LEXIS 1745 (D. Minn. Feb. 17, 1999) (magistrate's ruling adopted by the district court at 1999 U.S. Dist. LEXIS 10930 (D. Minn. Mar. 29, 1999), *aff'd* 212 F.3d 1318 (8th Cir. 2000). The agreement between the debt collector and the creditor allowed the debt collector to charge the consumer a 15% collection fee. The agreement between the consumer and the creditor, however, only allowed "reasonable attorney's fees and costs incident to collection." The court found that seeking the 15% fee, which was not expressly authorized by the consumer, violated § 1692f, and constituted the type of false and misleading representation of the type that the FDCPA was designed to foreclose.

State ex rel. Hatch v. JBC Legal Group, P.C., 2006 WL 1388453 (Minn. Dist. Ct. Apr. 13, 2006). Defendants' misstatement of the statutory penalty cannot be excused on the basis that it was merely an effort to collect incidental damages under UCC Article 2, which applies only to the sale of goods, not to dishonored checks. The misstatement was false or misleading. Defendants' statement that you "may" be liable for attorney fees was false in that recovery of attorney fees for a dishonored check was limited by a precondition that defendants did not meet. Defendants claimed that the $30 fee they imposed was a cost of collection. "However, the burden of proving a cost of collection, as with any award, is upon the person claiming the award. JBC made the claim, and has not produced any evidence that it was entitled to recover $30 in costs on all claims." The practice of assessing such a fee without determining the actual cost of collection was deceptive and misleading generally and misrepresented the status of the debt.

Missouri

Eckert v. LVNV Funding L.L.C., 647 F. Supp. 2d 1096 (E.D. Mo. 2009). Defendant's motion to dismiss plaintiff's § 1692e(2) claim that defendant failed to apply the credit of $1297.03 to the amount of $5881.73 and therefore made a false representation as to the amount due on the credit card account in violation of FDCPA was denied, as plaintiff had alleged sufficient facts.

Nevada

Prince v. U.S. Bancorp, 2010 WL 3385396 (D. Nev. Aug. 25, 2010). The consumer's complaint alleging that the defendant purchased the "loan" from America Servicing Company, that ASC was the servicer of a loan, and that ASC misrepresented the amount of the debt by charging the plaintiff unauthorized fees, interest, and other charges was sufficient to state a claim under § 1692e.

New Jersey

Nicholls v. Portfolio Recovery Assocs., L.L.C., 2010 WL 1257738 (D.N.J. Mar. 29, 2010). Consumer's claim that the collection letters would cause the consumer to stop reading after reaching the amount due was held to be a bizarre and idiosyncratic legal conclusion and her claims for violation of § 1692e were dismissed. "[T]he least sophisticated debtor is presumed to have, at the very least, read with care."

Scioli v. Goldman & Warshaw P.C., 651 F. Supp. 2d 273 (D.N.J. 2009). Notwithstanding the plaintiff's argument that statutory attorney fees are only due and owing after judgment is entered for the debt collector and its status as the prevailing party is established, the court dismissed the complaint for failure to state claims under § 1692e(2)(A) because the least sophisticated consumer would not be deceived by a debt collector listing a specific sum of statutory fees in the space provided in the court-approved form summons; not only did the form summons contain a blank space to insert the amount of fees requested, but it also disclosed that all amounts listed are only the amounts being requested: "[Plaintiff] essentially asks this Court to hold that the form summons created by the State of New Jersey, and used by countless lawyers and nonlawyers throughout the State, violates the FDCPA. But such a holding would defy common sense and would not further the goals of the FDCPA."

Federal Trade Comm'n v. Check Enforcement, 2005 WL 1677480 (D.N.J. July 18, 2005). Misrepresented to consumers that their alleged debts were greater than the debt owed, adding $125 or $130 over the value of a consumer's alleged NSF check.

Still v. JBC Assocs., P.C., 2005 WL 1334715 (D.N.J. June 3, 2005). A factual issue existed on whether the collector violated the FDCPA by representing that a $25 service charge for a returned check was authorized by state law, when a notice of the charge was posted in the store.

United States v. Consumer Fin. Corp., Clearinghouse No. 36,036 (D.N.J. 1982) (consent decree). Collector agreed to an injunction against engaging in a number of deceptive practices, including misrepresenting the amount of the debt.

New Mexico

Martinez v. Albuquerque Collection Servs., 867 F. Supp. 1495 (D.N.M. 1994). Collection agency violated §§ 1692e(2) and 1692f(1) by collecting inflated charges for a gross receipts tax and

attorney fees and by compounding interest. Where state law authorized collector to charge interest on definite sums due by contract, FDCPA was not violated.

Jacober v. Nemeco, Inc., Clearinghouse No. 46,760 (D.N.M. 1991) (consent order). Check guarantee and collection agency agreed to notify the consumers that they may be responsible for the agency's $19.04 service charge on dishonored checks only if the merchant accepting the check posted a sign allowing the charge and the consumer knew of the charge.

New York

Shami v. National Enter. Sys., 2010 WL 3824151 (E.D.N.Y. Sept. 23, 2010). The court concluded that a complaint involving a collection letter including the language "You can now pay by automated phone system . . . or on the internet. Transaction fees will be charged if you use the automated phone system or the internet to make payment on this account. You are not required to use the automated phone system or the internet to make payment on this account" sufficiently pleaded a cause of action for violation of §§ 1692f(1) and 1692e(2).

Pifko v. CCB Credit Servs., Inc., 2010 WL 2771832 (E.D.N.Y. July 7, 2010). The defendants complied with §§ 1692g(a)(1) and 1692e by disclosing the current amount of the debt without any additional or qualifying language that would explain that the amount increases over time with the addition of interest: "Here . . . the debt collection letters contain no additional language that could mislead or confuse Consumers about the amount due. . . ."

Adlam v. FMS, Inc., 2010 WL 1328958 (S.D.N.Y. Apr. 5, 2010). The FDCPA does not require that a debt collection letter warn a consumer that the debt may increase. Section 1692g(a)(1) requires only that a notice state "the amount of the debt." Under this section, debt collectors must disclose the amount past due as of the date the letter is sent, not the consumer's overall balance with the creditor.

Weiss v. Zwicker & Assocs., P.C., 664 F. Supp. 2d 214 (E.D.N.Y. 2009). A debt collector has no obligation to explain why a consumer's debt has increased from the time that the initial dun was sent: "The Court finds that there is nothing confusing or misleading about the increased amount of debt stated [in the second dun] as even the most unsophisticated consumer would understand that credit card debt accrues interest."

Leone v. Ashwood Fin., Inc., 257 F.R.D. 343 (E.D.N.Y. 2009). The defendant's letter was misleading when it represented that the debts were "assigned to" defendant when, apparently, no written assignments had been made.

Overcash v. United Abstract Group, Inc., 549 F. Supp. 2d 193 (N.D.N.Y. 2008). The debt buyer sent a letter to the consumer demanding repayment not in the amount of $1353.15 that the debt was originally sold for, but for $41,701.58. A prior purchaser of the debt had mailed the consumer that the debt was paid in full.

Stark v. Hudson & Keyse L.L.C., 2008 WL 4866046 (E.D.N.Y. Nov. 7, 2008). Debt collector's lawsuit in a permissible, but higher trial court than required to recover an alleged debt and seeking costs in connection with the state collection suit cannot provide a basis for an FDCPA violation of §§ 1692e or 1692f.

Russell v. Hartweg, 2008 WL 2157122 (W.D.N.Y. May 20, 2008). Motion to dismiss denied; stated amount of debt was confusing because of language "If this account is already a judgment, interest at 9% will be added."

McDowall v. Leschack & Grodensky, P.C., 279 F. Supp. 2d 197 (S.D.N.Y. 2003). Where the letter demanded a specific dollar amount "plus interest and attorney's fees," it failed to state the amount of the debt violating § 1692g(a)(1).

Grief v. Wilson, Elser, Moskowitz, Edelman & Dicker, L.L.P., 217 F. Supp. 2d 336 (E.D.N.Y. 2002). Failure of the collector's initial notice to state that any request for verification of the debt or the identity of the original creditor must be in writing violated the verification disclosure requirements. The statement in the initial dun that the amount of the debt was the underlying balance plus a sum for "attorneys' fees up to" a stated dollar amount presented the least sophisticated consumer with "a variety of amounts of the debt" and therefore failed to disclose the specific amount of the debt owing, in violation of § 1692g(a)(1).

Padilla v. Payco General Am. Credits, Inc., 161 F. Supp. 2d 264 (S.D.N.Y. 2001). Since applicable federal student loan regulations required that payments be applied first to interest and then to the principal, evidence that student loan debt collector told the consumer that her payment would be applied to principal first, if true, would establish an unlawful misrepresentation.

Micare v. Foster & Garbus, 132 F. Supp. 2d 77 (N.D.N.Y. 2001). The FDCPA is a strict liability statute and a claim need not allege that the misrepresentation that a paid debt was owed was intentional.

Stonehart v. Rosenthal, 2001 U.S. Dist. LEXIS 11566 (S.D.N.Y. Aug. 13, 2001). The collection lawyer's statement of the full amount of a dental bill that was disputed, relying on the dentist, did not violate § 1692e.

Harrison v. NBD Inc., 968 F. Supp. 837 (E.D.N.Y. 1997). The statement that the "balance due" was $1979 and the consumer's "liability" was $247 was open to two interpretations, one of which was false, and therefore it was deceptive.

Wegmans Food Mkts., Inc. v. Scrimpsher, 17 B.R. 999 (Bankr. N.D.N.Y. 1982). It was deceptive for a collector to seek a $5 service charge for a dishonored check without showing more of a contractual basis than a posted notice in the store warning of the charge.

North Carolina

Johnson v. Bullhead Inv., L.L.C., 2010 WL 118274 (M.D.N.C. Jan. 11, 2010). The consumer stated a claim for relief for violations of § 1692e as a result of the debt collector's persistent collection efforts that she pay a debt that she did not owe and that were directed at her as a result of mistaken identity.

North Dakota

Eaton v. Credit Bureau, Inc., 2007 WL 2781844 (D.N.D. Sept. 21, 2007). The defendant violated the FDCPA by attempting to collect statutory dishonored check civil penalties that could only be assessed by a court prior to any litigation.

Ohio

Foster v. D.B.S. Collection Agency, 463 F. Supp. 2d 783 (S.D. Ohio 2006). Defendants' standard request for attorney fees in Ohio debt collection action complaints violated of § 1692e(2)(B), since Ohio law did not allow attorney fees in cases against consumers. Defendants' suits against spouses on the presumption that spouses would be liable for non-medical debts violated § 1692e(2).

Dowling v. Litton Loan Serv., L.P., 2006 WL 3498292 (S.D. Ohio Dec. 1, 2006). Because defendant's own records and version of the facts showed that the consumer had only not paid one month's mortgage payment, its duns stating that she was two months behind and threatening foreclosure if payment in the stated amount was not made violated § 1692e(2)(A)'s prohibition against misrepresenting the status or amount of the debt.

Gionis v. Javitch, Block & Rathbone, 405 F. Supp. 2d 856 (S.D. Ohio 2005). Collection attorneys violated § 1692e(5) and (10) because the least sophisticated consumer reading the creditor's affidavit, claiming any attorney fees to which it would be legally entitled and attached to the complaint, would be confused about the creditor's ability to recover attorney fees which were not permitted by Ohio law. This did not violate §§ 1692e(2),1692f, or 1692d, however.

Kelly v. Great Seneca Fin. Corp., 443 F. Supp. 954 (S.D. Ohio 2005). The allegations that the defendant debt collection agency and its collection attorneys filed a state court collection action in which they allegedly misrepresented the amount and legal status of the debt stated a claim for violating §§ 1692e(2), (5), and (10) and 1692f(1).

Davidson v. Weltman, Weinberg & Reis, 285 F. Supp. 2d 1093 (S.D. Ohio 2003). Requirement of the payment of attorney fees as a condition to reinstatement of the mortgage did not violate Ohio public policy, and plaintiff's complaint including the FDCPA claims was dismissed.

Hodrosky v. Polo Club Apartments, 1997 WL 156712 (Ohio Ct. App. Apr. 3, 1997). It was not deceptive either to threaten suit when the collector had the authority to sue or to request the price of a new carpet for the consumer's former apartment without an allowance for the carpet's depreciation.

Durve v. Oker, 679 N.E.2d 19 (Ohio Ct. App. 1996). Claim that the amounts of the physician's bills for services was deceptive was improperly dismissed where the physician and his collectors claimed that the amount due was four different amounts ranging from $137.80 to $302.80 and failed to verify the bills.

Oregon

Lane v. Gordon, 2011 WL 488901 (D. Or. Feb. 7, 2011). Summary judgment was granted to the defendant despite the fact that a collection letter demanded $1370.54 but the complaint filed by the defendant months later alleged that the consumer owed "the principal sum of $848.63, with accrued interest of $516.52, resulting in a total of $1,365.15, plus interest on the principal at the rate of 9% per annum from February 16, 2009." The court stated: "Defendant simply sought less in the complaint than the full amount due and owing; since the amounts stated in the February 10 demand letter and in the July 2009 complaint were both correct, defendant did not make a false statement."

Van Westrienen v. Americontinental Collection Corp., 94 F. Supp. 2d 1087 (D. Or. 2000). Where the debt collector threatened the consumer with attorneys fees without explaining the process to recover such fees, it violated § 1692e(10).

Pennsylvania

Fetters v. Paragon Way, Inc., WL 5174989. (M.D. Pa. Dec. 15, 2010). A debt, as an "obligation or alleged obligation" of a consumer, includes the situation in which a debt collector mistakenly continues to try to collect a debt that has already been paid. The court distinguished cases that the defendants argued precluded any FDCPA claim once the alleged debt had been paid and therefore no longer existed: "Unlike Posso and Winter, Plaintiff avers that Defendants took coercive action, albeit erroneously, to collect an alleged obligation for payment. In this way, although the debt was already settled, Defendants allegedly represented that the debt was outstanding and engaged in prohibited conduct aimed at collecting on it."

Wright v. Phelan, Hallinan & Schmieg, L.L.P., 2010 WL 786536 (E.D. Pa. Mar. 8, 2010). Fax to plaintiff's lawyer who immediately recognized the inconsistent charges did not violate the FDCPA, even when letter was shared with consumer.

Duraney v. Washington Mut. Bank, 2008 WL 4204821 (W.D. Pa. Sept. 11, 2008), *aff'd*, 2010 WL 2993810 (3d Cir. Aug. 2, 2010). A demand letter that requested two amounts of money—one to reinstate the mortgage and the other for attorney fees currently owing—was not deceptive in violation of § 1692e since the letter was unambiguous and the charges were clearly itemized and explained so as not to mislead or confuse the least sophisticated consumer.

Mushinsky v. Nelson, Watson & Assoc., L.L.C., 642 F. Supp. 2d 470 (E.D. Pa. 2009). Where the "principal" included pre-existing interest and charges, two standard dictionaries support the contention that "principal" does not include interest, and this interpretation is certainly not "bizarre or idiosyncratic."

Martsolf v. JBC Legal Group, P.C., 2008 WL 275719 (M.D. Pa. Jan. 30, 2008). The defendants' demand for $30 as a returned check fee did not violate § 1692f(1) or § 1692e(2)(A) since the amount was an authorized charge under state law as UCC incidental damages.

Dougherty v. Wells Fargo Home Loans, Inc., 425 F. Supp. 2d 599 (E.D. Pa. 2006). Plaintiff stated a claim for violation of § 1692e because describing collection attorney fees only as "recoverable corporate advances" in the mortgage servicer's statement of the payout amount could be confusing and deceptive statement of the debt to the least sophisticated consumer.

Farren v. RJM Acquisition Funding, L.L.C., 2005 WL 1799413 (E.D. Pa. July 26, 2005). A debt collector who disclosed the debt in the amount that it was referred to it by the creditor and who was unaware at the time that the consumer had been the victim of identity theft was not liable for any violation of § 1692e(2)(A) arising from the fact that the consumer did not owe the debt.

In re Crippen, 346 B.R. 115 (Bankr. E.D. Pa. 2006). The complaint that alleged that the defendant was a consumer debt collector who attempted to collect an amount in excess of that allowed by the underlying contract and applicable state law stated a claim for violating §§ 1692e(2) and 1692f(1).

Tennessee

Spangler v. Conrad, 2010 WL 2389481 (E.D. Tenn. June 9, 2010). An alleged discrepancy in the amount of interest allegedly owing that the attorney defendant disclosed in reliance on the referring client did not violate § 1692e(2)(a).

Dowdy v. Solutia Healthcare TAS, Inc., 2006 WL 3545047 (M.D. Tenn. Dec. 8, 2006). Since collection agency knew dentist doubled the amount due before sending account to the collection agency, it violated §§ 1692e and 1692f by representing the amount forwarded by the dentist, $10,781.06, as the amount of the debt without itemization or explanation.

Texas

Eads v. Wolpoff & Abramson, L.L.P., 538 F. Supp. 2d 981 (W.D. Tex. 2008). Allegation that collection suit claimed $225 more than the arbitration award, by including the state filing fee, stated a claim under §§ 1692f(1) and 1692e(5).

Agueros v. Hudson & Keyse, L.L.C., 2010 WL 3418286 (Tex. App. Aug. 31, 2010). The debt collector's attempt to collect an amount double what its own records showed to be owing violated §§ 1692e and 1692f.

Utah

Reed v. AFNI, Inc., 2011 WL 112430 (D. Utah Jan. 13, 2011). An allegation that the debt sought to be collected was not owed, standing alone, cannot form a basis for a "false and misleading practices" claim under the FDCPA.

Brumbelow v. Law Offices of Bennett & Deloney, P.C., 2005 WL 1566689 (D. Utah June 21, 2005). Defendants' request for a "settlement fee" instead of a "covenant not to sue fee" is a distinction without a difference. The statute did not allow collection of such a fee; alternative theories for collecting a fee not permitted by statute were rejected.

Scott v. Riddle, 2000 WL 33980013 (D. Utah Dec. 4, 2000). Seeking penalties under a shoplifting statute inapplicable to bad checks misrepresents the character, amount, and legal status of a debt, and is an attempt to collect an amount not legally owing.

Ditty v. CheckRite, Ltd., 973 F. Supp. 1320 (D. Utah 1997). Each letter purported to make a settlement offer comprised of the face amount of the check, a $15 service charge, and a figure listed as "Legal Consideration for Covenant Not to Sue." The letters failed to advise debtors that the state dishonored instruments statute prohibited the collection of any amount greater than the face amount of the check, plus a $15 service fee, unless a lawsuit was filed. Given this omission and defendants' efforts to collect excessive fees under the guise of a covenant not to sue, the court found that no reasonable juror could conclude that defendants' mailings did not falsely represent the amounts defendants could lawfully collect, in violation of § 1692e(2)(A) and (10).

Virginia

Sunga v. Broome, 2010 WL 3198925 (E.D. Va. Aug. 12, 2010).

The collector's alleged multiple misrepresentations of the amount of the debt, including by as little as $1.41 in unlawful interest and by $16.00 in prohibited fees (with an additional penny in unlawful interest as a result of the overstated $16.00) and as much as $1100 in unlawful attorney fees, stated a claim for violating §§ 1692e(2)(A) and 1692f(1).

Neild v. Wolpoff & Abramson, L.L.P., 453 F. Supp. 2d 918 (E.D. Va. 2006). The consumer's averments that the defendant falsely represented the amount of the debt stated a cause of action for violation of § 1692e(2)(A).

Dikun v. Streich, 369 F. Supp. 2d 781 (E.D. Va. 2005). Consumer's allegation that the attorney debt collector falsely represented in state court proceedings the compensation to which the attorney could be entitled under state law stated a claim for relief for violation of § 1692e(2)(b).

West v. Costen, 558 F. Supp. 564 (W.D. Va. 1983). The collector and its employees violated § 1692e(2)(A) and (B) by attempting to collect an illegal $15 service charge on bad checks without disclosing that the charge had been added to the amount demanded and by implying the charge was lawful.

Washington

Kirk v. Gobel, 622 F. Supp. 2d 1039 (E.D. Wash. 2009). The defendant collection lawyer violated § 1692e when he sought and received a default judgment in state court that included attorney fees that were prohibited under applicable state law. The defendant collection lawyer violated §§ 1692e(2)(B) and 1692f(1) by requesting in the state collection court service of process fees that were prohibited by applicable state law since the process server was unregistered.

Hylkema v. Rentcollect Corp., 2006 U.S. Dist. LEXIS 70224 (W.D. Wash. Sept. 28, 2006). The court granted the defendant summary judgment on the consumer's claim that the defendant was collecting a debt in an amount greater than what he lawfully owed since the contested addition of interest was authorized by state law.

Semper v. JBC Legal Group, 2005 WL 2172377 (W.D. Wash. Sept. 6, 2005). Returned check fee was not UCC incidental damages since defendant was not a seller. Demanding a returned check fee that was not allowed by contract or statute was a false representation under § 1692e (2), (10).

Clark v. Bonded Adjustment Co., 204 F.R.D. 662 (E.D. Wash. 2002). In the course of granting class certification based on charging excessive process server fees, the court recognized that the FDCPA applied whether the fee was actually collected or whether the debt collector merely attempted to collect it.

Watkins v. Peterson Enters., 57 F. Supp. 2d 1102 (E.D. Wash. 1999). Collection agency violated § 1692e(2)(A) when it included costs and fees associated with prior unsuccessful writs of garnishment in the balance it sought to collect.

West Virginia

McComas v. Fin. Collection Agencies, 1997 WL 118417 (S.D. W. Va. Mar. 7, 1997). Motion to dismiss was denied where FDCPA complaint raised allegations of telephone harassment, threat of unintended action, charging an unauthorized amount, and debt

collector represented it was affiliated with the U.S. government.

Health Plan, Inc. v. DeGarmo, 1996 WL 780508 (N.D. W. Va. Oct. 28, 1996). Class action was certified in a counterclaim against HMO for improperly requesting more than its costs in its subrogation and reimbursement claims against its patients. The class consisted of all group enrollees in the HMO. RICO and FDCPA violations were alleged.

Wisconsin

Barrows v. Petrie & Stocking, S.C., 2008 WL 3540405 (W.D. Wis. Aug. 13, 2008). The defendant collectors violated the FDCPA by serving on the consumer's credit union a garnishment summons and complaint that claimed statutory disbursement charges in excess of the $40 allowed by applicable state law, in violation of §§ 1692e(2)(B), 1692e(10), and 1692f(1).

Bruesewitz v. Law Offices of Gerald E. Moore & Assocs., P.C., 2006 U.S. Dist. LEXIS 83712 (W.D. Wis. Nov. 15, 2006). Debt collector's letter did not deceptively state the amount of the debt where it offered to settle for 80% of the debt under § 1692e(5).

Czerwinski v. Risk Mgmt. Alternatives Intern. Corp., 2006 WL 897768 (E.D. Wis. Apr. 4, 2006). The debt collector's motion to dismiss was denied where the complaint alleged that the collector's correspondence claimed an "amount delinquent: $30.00" possibly creating confusion about the amount due.

Stanley v. Stupar, Schuster & Cooper, S.C., 136 F. Supp. 2d 957 (E.D. Wis. 2001). Plaintiff's complaint based on defendants' statement of the debt as "$987.71, plus attorneys fees," stated claims for violations of §§ 1692g(a)(1), 1692e, and 1692f(1).

Patzka v. Viterbo Coll., 917 F. Supp. 654 (W.D. Wis. 1996). Collection agency violated § 1692e by threatening to take legal action that it could not legally take by threatening to sue on a prohibited collection fee and interest; college was also liable under the Wisconsin Consumer Act for collecting interest which was not disclosed prior to consummation nor authorized by the tuition agreement.

K.2.4.11 False Representation of Character or Legal Status of the Debt, 15 U.S.C. § 1692e(2)(A)

Miller v. Javitch, Block & Rathbone, 561 F.3d 588 (6th Cir. 2009). The defendant state court collection attorney's characterization in the collection complaint of the consumer's credit card debt as a "loan," while perhaps more properly characterized as an "account," nevertheless involved no trickery, would not deceive the least sophisticated consumer as to the nature of the debt, and thus was not the type of false representation that would violate § 1692e.

Purnell v. Arrow Fin. Servs., L.L.C., 303 Fed. Appx. 297 (6th Cir. 2008). Collector's allegedly false communication which was made to a credit bureau within one year prior to filing suit and which misrepresented that the consumer owed the subject debt stated a timely claim for violations of §§ 1692e(2)(A), 1692e(8), and 1692f(1), notwithstanding that the collector had been making the same alleged misrepresentations to the credit bureau for several years, since that last communication constituted a discrete violation of the Act within the statute of limitations.

Magrin v. Unifund CCR Partners, Inc., 2002 WL 31804268 (9th Cir. Dec. 10, 2002). The consumer stated a valid claim for relief under the FDCPA when he alleged that a debt collector had made false representations as to the legal status of the debt in connection with the sale, transfer, or assignment of the debt to another debt collector, with the knowledge that purchaser, transferee, or assignee intended to initiate or continue attempts to collect the debt.

Arkansas

Bagwell v. Portfolio Recovery Assocs., L.L.C., 2009 WL 1708227 (E.D. Ark. June 5, 2009). Motion to dismiss based on consumer's fifteen-year-old bankruptcy denied; the defendant debt buyer was not a party to the bankruptcy, was not listed as a creditor, and was not specifically enjoined by the Bankruptcy Court from collecting the debt. "Plaintiff is not attempting to hold Defendants in contempt for a violation of the bankruptcy discharge order but, rather, Plaintiff is attempting to establish FDCPA liability based on Defendants' pursuit of a debt which Plaintiff claims is not owed."

California

Bush v. Loanstar Mortgage Servs., L.L.C., 286 F. Supp. 2d 1210 (N.D. Cal. 2003). The failure to disclose the California Civil Code § 2924(c) deed of trust reinstatement rights in the FDCPA debt validation notice did not violate § 1692e(2)(A).

Colorado

Kelly v. Wolpoff & Abramson, L.L.P., 634 F. Supp. 2d 1202 (D. Colo. 2008). The court rejected the plaintiff's argument that charging off a debt extinguishes it. Even though according to generally accepted accounting principles codified into federal regulations and made applicable to the creditor, retail loans that become past due for 180 days "should be classified a Loss and charged off." [Uniform Retail Credit Classification and Account Management Policy, 65 Fed. Reg. 36903 (June 12, 2000).] And such "charging off" essentially amounts to a ledger book reclassification and is an accounting practice which defendant freely admits it follows. The court also stated the plaintiff's argument amounts to the absurd proposition that credit card holders who are unable to pay their debt need merely stop payment for 180 days, at which point—through the inexorable interplay of accounting and tax reporting requirements—such debts will automatically become taxable income and be extinguished. The court held this theory as ridiculous and as a case that could invite imposition of Rule 11 sanctions on the plaintiff.

Maresh v. Borenstein, 2008 WL 2797037 (D. Colo. July 18, 2008). Adopting the reasoning in *Kelly v. Wolpoff & Abramson, L.L.P.*, 634 F. Supp. 2d 1202 (D. Colo. 2008), denied FDCPA claim that creditor's " 'charging off' of Plaintiff's debt under Generally Accepted Accounting Principles ('GAAP') somehow 'extinguished' a credit card debt and judgment as a matter of law."

Illinois

Weathers v. Gem City Account Serv., Inc., 2010 WL 3210985 (C.D. Ill. Aug. 13, 2010). A complaint alleging that the defendant attempted to collect a medical debt in violation of applicable federal and state Medicaid law stated a claim for violating § 1692e(2)(A).

Nelson-McGourty v. L & P Fin. Adjusters Inc., 2010 WL 3190711 (N.D. Ill. Aug. 12, 2010). Following a bench trial, the court credited the testimony of the collector and discredited the testimony of the consumer to conclude that the collector did not engage in prohibited conduct with respect to falsely representing the legal status of the debt.

Manlapaz v. Unifund CCR Partners, 2009 WL 3015166 (N.D. Ill. Sept. 15, 2009). The falsity of a debt collector's statement in her affidavit filed in state court that she had personal knowledge of facts that she gleaned from a review of business records was a technicality which would not mislead the unsophisticated consumer and was therefore not material. She could have had sufficient information to establish the admissibility of the business records to establish the debt. The consumer stated a claim by alleging that the bill attached to the state court pleading was actually a document constructed by the debt buyer to simulate a bill. The consumer stated a claim by alleging the debt buyer falsely represented that it owned the debt it claimed she owed.

Matmanivong v. Unifund CCR Partners, 2009 WL 1181529 (N.D. Ill. Apr. 28, 2009). A debt collector violated the FDCPA where it did not own the debt but nonetheless filed collection suits misrepresenting that it was an assignee of that debt.

Gros v. Midland Credit Mgmt., Inc., 2008 WL 4671717 (N.D. Ill. Oct. 20, 2008). Where the consumer presented "no" extrinsic evidence regarding the communications alleged to be in violation of §§ 1692e and 1692f (other than dunning letters seeking payment of a debt held to be paid in a prior lawsuit and the prior judgment), summary judgment was granted for the debt collector on the FDCPA claims.

Kolowski v. Blatt, Hasenmiller, Leibsker & Moore, L.L.C., 2008 WL 4372711 (N.D. Ill. Mar. 20, 2008). Dismissal granted on claim that filing a motion to confirm an arbitration award more than one year after it was entered violated the FDCPA, since court believed the one-year restriction was permissive. Thus, filing the motion to confirm was not a false representation of the legal status of the debt (§ 1692e) nor an attempt to collect a debt that was not permitted by law (§ 1692f).

Bianchi v. The Bureaus, Inc., 2008 WL 597587 (N.D. Ill. Feb. 27, 2008). The collector violated §§ 1692e(2)(A) and 1692c(a)(2) when it telephoned the consumer more than two months after she had filed for bankruptcy.

Indiana

Keisler v. Encore Receivable Mgmt., Inc., 2008 WL 1774173 (S.D. Ind. Apr. 17, 2008). Cross motions for summary judgment denied on § 1692e(2)(A) claim where the collector stated in its initial dun that the debtor "owed" money to its client/creditor, when in fact and to the contrary, but unbeknownst to the collector, the consumer had already filed bankruptcy: "The measure of whether a statement is false is measured by an objective standard, which turns not on the question of what the debt collector knew but on whether the debt collector's communication would deceive or mislead an unsophisticated, but reasonable, consumer," and the resulting liability is tempered only by the bona fide error defense, which in this case the court held raised triable issues of intent and adequacy of the collector's procedures.

Massa v. I.C. Sys., Inc., 2008 WL 504329 (S.D. Ind. Feb. 21, 2008). Misrepresentation of client charges due and owing was actionable under the FDCPA.

Louisiana

Wagner v. BellSouth Telecomms. Inc., 2008 WL 348784 (M.D. La. Feb. 7, 2008). *Pro se* stated a cause of action under § 1692e(2)(A) where he alleged the collection agency reported inaccurately the date of delinquency.

Maryland

Ransom v. Telecredit Serv. Corp., 1992 U.S. Dist. LEXIS 22738 (D. Md. Feb. 5, 1992). Representation that consumer committed a felony for passing two small dishonored checks, when the maximum penalty would be a fine of not more than $100 (a misdemeanor), violated § 1692e(10).

Minnesota

Hollis v. Northland Group, Inc., 2009 WL 250075 (D. Minn. Feb. 2, 2009). The plaintiff failed to state claim for deception regarding the debt collector filing a report with a credit reporting agency on a debt that was obsolete under the Fair Credit Reporting Act.

Baker v. Allstate Fin. Servs, Inc., 554 F. Supp. 2d 945 (D. Minn. 2008). Voicemail reference to a "matter pending in the State of Minnesota" stated a claim under §§ 1692d and 1692e(2). Voicemail's use of the words "case," "urgent," and "time sensitive" did not falsely suggest that a lawsuit had been filed within §§ 1692d or 1692e(2).

Erickson v. Johnson, 2006 WL 453201 (D. Minn. Feb. 22, 2006). Defendants misrepresented the character, amount, or legal status of the debt by claiming plaintiff owed a credit card debt that was opened in his name by his ex-wife without his authorization and owed only by his ex-wife. Defendants' verification letter was deceptive as it did not explain why Citibank was entitled to collect a credit card account Citibank had issued in AT&T's name and that was confusing to the least sophisticated consumer. Since the consumer was not liable on the credit card account, defendants' demand for attorney fees based on the credit card agreement violated §§ 1692f(1) and 1692e.

Nebraska

Jenkins v. General Collection Co., 538 F. Supp. 2d 1165 (D. Neb. 2008). "If the Defendants had presented their state-court actions as ones based on written contract, after having first determined after a reasonable inquiry that their claims were not barred by the five-year statute of limitations, the ambiguity in Nebraska law on the subject of which statute of limitations applies to credit card collection actions would shield the Defendants from liability under the FDCPA."

New Jersey

Robinson v. Credit Serv. Co., 1991 WL 186665 (D.N.J. Sept. 16, 1991). Dunning a parent of a twenty-year-old child for the child's

medical bill may misrepresent the parent's liability, violating §§ 1692e(2)(A) and 1692e(10), depending upon the factual question of whether the child was emancipated.

New Mexico

Billsie v. Brooksbank, 525 F. Supp. 2d 1290 (D.N.M. 2007). Denied summary judgment due to issues of fact regarding whether defendant garnished the wrong person.

Ohio

Midland Funding L.L.C. v. Brent, 644 F. Supp. 2d 961 (N.D. Ohio 2009). "The contents of the affidavit itself, and in particular the fact that the affiant allegedly had personal knowledge that the debt was valid, would effectively serve to validate the debt to the reader, whether that was [the consumer] or a court." Therefore, the affidavit was false, deceptive, and misleading in its use in conjunction with an attempt to collect a debt, and the debt collectors have violated FDCPA § 1692e.

Kline v. Mortgage Elec. Registration Sys., Inc., 2009 WL 6093372 (S.D. Ohio Nov. 24, 2009). Defendants' motion to dismiss granted because "[t]he filing of a foreclosure action by a plaintiff in the process of obtaining an assignment not yet fully documented is not a deceptive, misleading, or abusive tactic and does not violate the FDCPA."

Rice v. Great Seneca Fin. Corp., 556 F. Supp. 2d 792 (S.D. Ohio 2008). Billing statement generated by debt buyer was a true reflection of its own account and was not misleading, so did not violate the FDCPA, even though it was very similar in form to a credit card billing statement. Defendant set forth in great detail the process for obtaining the debts and electronic systems utilized to acquire, store, and transmit the financial information for each account.

Kelly v. Montgomery Lynch & Assocs., Inc., 2008 WL 1775251 (N.D. Ohio Apr. 15, 2008). The defendant's assessment of a dishonored check fee that was less than the maximum amount authorized by state statute accordingly did not falsely represent the character, amount, or legal status of the debt in violation of §§ 1692e(2)(A) or 1692e(10).

Oregon

Avery v. Gordon, 2008 WL 4793686 (D. Or. Oct. 27, 2008). Suit on a version of a credit card agreement which never applied to the consumer's account misrepresented the character or legal status of the account. The "agreement" did not apply because the consumer did not use her credit card until a later "agreement" had been mailed.

Grassley v. Debt Collectors, Inc., 1992 U.S. Dist. LEXIS 22782 (D. Or. Dec. 14, 1992). Unrebutted testimony that collector told debtor's wife that she was obligated for her husband's debt, when she was not, violated § 1692e(2)(A).

Pennsylvania

Reed v. Pinnacle Credit Servs., L.L.C., 2009 WL 2461852 (E.D. Pa. Aug. 11, 2009). The letter arguably made a false representation as to the character or legal status of the debt, in violation of

§ 1692e(2) by stating: "If your present debt is outside the applicable statute of limitations period, then a lawsuit cannot be filed to collect this debt. [Defendant debt collector] will not bring legal action to collect this debt even when the debt is within the reporting period." However, binding language of the condensed agreement in no way precludes defendant from initiating legal action on transferred balances.

Texas

Tostado v. Citibank (South Dakota), 2010 WL 55976 (W.D. Tex. Jan. 4, 2010). Consumer's argument that defendant did not own the debt or the right to sue was dismissed, as defendant demonstrated that it owned the account despite securitization and thus was not subject to FDCPA.

Meroney v. Pharia, L.L.C., 688 F. Supp. 2d 550 (N.D. Tex. 2009). FDCPA complaint was dismissed for failure to state a claim where the court found that the least sophisticated consumer would not be misled by the state court collection complaint and affidavit.

Virginia

Cappetta v. GC Servs., Ltd. P'ship, 654 F. Supp. 2d 453 (E.D. Va. 2009). Defendant debt collector's motion for judgment on the pleadings denied, since the complaint alleged that the defendant misrepresented that the plaintiff was an obligor on the credit card account, that it was in possession of the credit card account application, and that the credit card company had provided it with her Social Security number and had named her an obligor on the account. "These misrepresentations, if true, clearly violate § 1692e."

In re Jones, 2009 WL 2068387 (Bankr. E.D. Va. July 16, 2009). The court held on summary judgment that the defendant had violated § 1692e(2)(A): "[T]he dunning letter sent by Defendant to Plaintiff falsely represented the status of the debt as valid, due, and owing because it was sent after the Plaintiff commenced this bankruptcy case and the filing of the Plaintiff's bankruptcy petition changed the legal status of the debt by operation of the automatic stay of 11 U.S.C. § 362 and the discharge injunction of 11 U.S.C. § 524."

Washington

Buckalew v. Suttell & Hammer, P.S., 2010 WL 3944477 (E.D. Wash. Oct. 7, 2010). The use of the case caption on the "Affidavit of Creditor" that did not bear a court name or a case number, in conjunction with a letter specifically stating that "at this time, suit has not been initiated," would not lead a "least sophisticated consumer" to believe that suit had already been initiated against him or her, and does not misrepresent the legal status of the debt or its source or approval.

Wisconsin

Eichman v. Mann Bracken, L.L.C., 689 F. Supp. 2d 1094 (W.D. Wis. 2010). *Pro se* survives dismissal of allegation that defendants knew or should have known that she did not owe a debt to bank because *after* the arbitration award in 2008, bank issued her a 1099-C form canceling her debt.

K.2.4.12 Deceptive Practices in Debt Collection Suits

Drennan v. First Resolution Inv. Corp., 2010 WL 3059205 (5th Cir. Aug. 4, 2010). Filing a suit to collect a credit card debt did not constitute either a false or misleading representation or one that was so harassing, oppressive, or unconscionable that it was actionable under the FDCPA, even if, arguendo, the use of a suit on account on a credit card debt did not meet the necessary requirements of Texas's Rule of Civil Procedure 185 or any other such rules or regulations. The circumstances of this case do not constitute a violation of the FDCPA, even if the underlying action was not a proper suit on a sworn account.

Hartman v. Great Seneca Fin. Corp., 569 F.3d 606 (6th Cir. 2009). Summary judgment for the defendant debt buyer and its attorneys reversed where question of material fact existed whether the defendants' representations made in state collection court were false or deceptive in violation of § 1692e. The defendants attached to the collection complaints documents which they represented were copies of the consumers' credit card account statements, when in fact the documents were actually created by the defendants based on general information they received electronically about the debts, lacked any detail as to purchases or payments made, and were printed to appear to be recent credit card bills.

Miller v. Javitch, Block & Rathbone, 561 F.3d 588 (6th Cir. 2009). The defendant state court collection attorney's allegation in the collection complaint that the plaintiff/assignee of the debt "acquired, for valuable consideration, all right, title and interest in and to the claim set forth below originally owed by Defendant(s) to [original creditor]" did not violate § 1692(e)(12) "by falsely or misleadingly implying that [the original creditor] assigned her debt to an innocent purchaser for value who enjoyed protection under the holder-in-due-course rule," since the "statement says nothing about holders in due course[, and] no reason exists to think that the least-sophisticated consumer gives any thought to holders in due course—by definition, the least-sophisticated consumer lacks any knowledge of the *concept*." (Emphasis in original.)

Miller v. Wolpoff & Abramson, L.L.P., 309 Fed. Appx. 40 (7th Cir. 2009). *Pro se* consumer failed to rebut one debt buyer's evidence that it owned the consumer's credit card account despite another debt buyer's dunning the consumer on the same account at the time the first claimed ownership.

Beler v. Blatt, Hasenmiller, Leibsker, Moore, L.L.C., 480 F.3d 470 (7th Cir. 2007). The court granted the law firm's motion for summary judgment ruling that state court collection complaint was not confusing as to the relationship of the J.C. Penney charge account to GE Capital and Monogram Bank as it would not plainly be confusing to a significant fraction of the population and no evidence to the contrary was introduced.

Gionis v. Javitch, Block, Rathbone, L.L.P., 238 Fed. Appx. 24 (6th Cir. 2007). Affidavit seeking collection attorney fees attached to a debt collection complaint would falsely created the deceptive impression that Ohio law would permit the recovery of collection attorney fees in a suit against consumer when that recovery was prohibited by Ohio law. Fearing an increase in the collection attorney fees, an unsophisticated consumer would be more likely to settle the claim than if the affidavit not been filed. The analysis was further complicated by the fact that the underlying credit card agreement's selection of federal and Arizona law as governing the agreement could have resulted in the affidavit being literally true if the Arizona law rather than Ohio law applied. That did not mitigate the deceptiveness of the statement to an unsophisticated consumer, however.

Harvey v. Great Seneca Fin. Corp., 453 F.3d 324 (6th Cir. 2006). Consumer's allegation that the defendant debt collector filed a state court collection lawsuit without the means of proving the debt was insufficient to state a claim for violating § 1692e where the plaintiff failed to allege any specific instance of misrepresentation or deception, such as filing a false supporting affidavit.

Peters v. General Serv. Bureau, Inc., 277 F.3d 1051 (8th Cir. 2002). The court found that a collector's letter requesting the consumer's voluntary appearance in lieu of service of process was not false, deceptive or misleading on its face in the absence of evidence of its deceptiveness. The consumer complained that the letter misstated that service by constable was the only alternative to a voluntary appearance when certified mail service was also available, but the court found that constable service was the only other feasible method. The consumer argued that the statement that the consumer must "appear and defend" was misleading because a consumer would interpret it to require a personal visit to the courthouse, but the court found that it was not confusing. The omission of the period for filing an answer did not violate the FDCPA where the collector would provide that information after service. Whether a collection letter was false was a question of law for the court using the unsophisticated consumer test. The court found that, even if the statement about alternative methods of service was literally false, it was not misleading.

Poirier v. Alco Collections, Inc., 107 F.3d 347 (5th Cir. 1997). Collection agency's act of filing suit to collect debt owed by tenant to landlord, where assignment between the landlord and the collection agency did not transfer ownership of the debt, constituted the unauthorized practice of law under Louisiana law (since amended), and violated § 1692e(5).

Fox v. Citicorp Credit Servs., Inc., 15 F.3d 1507 (9th Cir. 1994). Consumers' allegations that debt collector agreed to a payment schedule and then demanded increased payments and filed a wage garnishment without contacting the consumer's attorney as promised were sufficient to state a claim for false, deceptive or misleading representations under § 1692e(5).

Arkansas

Morrison v. Hosto, Buchan, Prater & Lawrence, P.L.L.C., 2009 WL 3010917 (E.D. Ark. Sept. 17, 2009). Note attached to the complaint was factually true, included statutorily mandated language, and invited settlement. Merely attaching a notice to the complaint did not violate the FDCPA.

Born v. Hosto & Buchan, P.L.L.C., 2010 WL 2431063 (Ark. June 17, 2010). While bringing or threatening to bring litigation outside the applicable statute of limitations can give rise to a cause of action under the FDCPA, there was no viable claim in this case. Because the statute of limitations had not run on the debt collection complaint, the FDCPA claim was properly dismissed.

California

Owings v. Hunt & Henriques, 2010 WL 3489342 (S.D. Cal. Sept. 3, 2010). A consumer on duty with the National Guard was entitled to the benefits of the Servicemembers Civil Relief Act so as to render false and misleading and unfair under the FDCPA the defendant's declaration that plaintiff was not in active military service.

Riley v. Giguiere, 631 F. Supp. 2d 1295 (E.D. Cal. 2009). Whether defendant used improper means in pursuing an unlawful detainer action by serving process at the wrong address in violation of §§ 1692d, 1692e, and 1692f of the FDCPA involved issues of fact that precluded summary judgment.

Johnson v. JP Morgan Chase Bank, 2008 WL 5100177 (E.D. Cal. Dec. 1, 2008). Case dismissed as to one defendant since state court action against plaintiff in defendant's name was without its knowledge and defendant had no interest in any claim against plaintiff.

Riley v. Giguiere, 2008 WL 436943 (E.D. Cal. Feb. 14, 2008). Former tenant stated a claim under §§ 1692d, 1692e, and 1692f in alleging that the eviction lawyer improperly proceeded to obtain judgment from him despite reason to know he had vacated the apartment many years prior to the eviction.

Reyes v. Kenosian & Miele, L.L.P., 619 F. Supp. 2d 796 (N.D. Cal. 2008). Unifund failed to submit credible evidence that it was assigned the debt or that it was the proper party in its state collection case. However, its collection attorneys defeated the FDCPA claim that they misrepresented Unifund's ownership when they submitted evidence of ownership in the FDCPA suit.

Mello v. Great Seneca Fin. Corp., 526 F. Supp. 2d 1020 (C.D. Cal. 2007). The consumer alleged that defendant filed its lawsuit without intention or ability to obtain evidence of plaintiffs alleged debt according to defendant's pattern and practice of filing lawsuits without intention or ability to obtain evidence of alleged debts making it "deceptive" under FDCPA. But since defendant did not address this claim when seeking its dismissal the court held it improper to dismiss.

Connecticut

Pacheco v. Joseph McMahon Corp., 698 F. Supp. 2d 291 (D. Conn. 2010). The transmission of an e-mail misrepresenting the debt buyer as part of the debt collection agency constituted a violation of § 1692e(10).

Egletes v. Law Offices Howard Lee Schiff, P.C., 2010 WL 3025236 (D. Conn. July 30, 2010). Where the defendant attempted to garnish wages with interest on the judgment when the judgment struck a provision for interest, it was "inexcusable" for the collection lawyers to seek interest.

Shrestha v. Nadel, 2001 U.S. Dist. LEXIS 12553 (D. Conn. Mar. 21, 2001). The court entered summary judgment in favor of defendant attorney, finding that debtor's funds for which an exemption could have been claimed were not exempt from execution at the time of the attorney's seizure because the debtor had failed to follow the statutory requirements to claim exemptions.

Shrestha v. State Credit Adjustment Bureau, Inc., 117 F. Supp. 2d 142 (D. Conn. 2000). Collection agency that waited until after a state court hearing to release bank account funds, regarding which the consumer asserted a state "wild card" exemption, did not violate the FDCPA prohibition against deception because the wild card exemption was not self-executing.

Florida

Knighten v. Palisades Collections, L.L.C., 2010 WL 2696768 (S.D. Fla. July 6, 2010). The claim that a debt collector filed suit on a time barred debt failed where Palisades never owned the debt and its law firm sued in the collector's name without its knowledge or consent.

Chalik v. Westport Recovery Corp., 677 F. Supp. 2d 1322 (S.D. Fla. 2009). Defendants' filing of a sworn statement denying consumer's claim of exemption, without any specific knowledge regarding the exemption, in a garnishment proceeding is not the kind of conduct that was intended to be covered by § 1692d as a matter of law, but could be a violation of § 1692e.

Sanz v. Fernandez, 633 F. Supp. 2d 1356 (S.D. Fla. 2009). Allegations that the defendants, who were not lawyers, filed an eviction complaint seeking attorney fees as agent for the landlord, when state law prohibits such fees to nonlawyers, stated a claim for violating §§ 1692d, 1692e, 1692e(2)(A), 1692e(2)(B), 1692e(5), 1692e(10), and 1692f.

Ugarte v. Sunset Constr., Inc., 2008 WL 4723600 (M.D. Fla. Oct. 21, 2008). The consumer adequately stated an FDCPA claim where her complaint alleged that the debt collector sought to collect unauthorized attorney fees in its state court collection action.

Gonzalez v. Erskine, 2008 WL 6822207 (S.D. Fla. Aug. 7, 2008). Filing a verified complaint to collect a debt in state court allegedly against the wrong person did not violate the FDCPA

Acosta v. Campbell, 2006 WL 146208 (M.D. Fla. Jan. 18, 2006). Collection attorney in the underlying state foreclosure action did not make false representations in that case since the entity named as the plaintiff in that case had standing to foreclose in light of the assignment of the mortgage to it.

Georgia

Kuria v. Palisades Acquisition XVI, L.L.C., 2010 WL 4780769 (N.D. Ga. Nov. 16, 2010). A consumer who was wrongly sued in state court stated a claim for §§ 1692e and 1692f violations based on allegations that the defendant's collection suit was part "of a pattern and practice of abusive, scattershot litigation to collect debts" where the debt buyer "knew when filing the suit not only that it lacked knowledge of the validity of the underlying debt, but also that it never intended to investigate or verify the debt's validity." The court found that the defendant's intent was not to take its claims against the plaintiff to trial, at which it would have to prove that its claim had merit, but rather to obtain a default judgment against the plaintiff or to enter into a voluntary settlement with him. Since the defendant's actions were allegedly "rooted in bad faith, reckless disregard toward debtors, and abuse of process," the court found that the consumer alleged "more than mere lack of knowledge or lack of a 'paper trail' asserted in" distinguishable cases.

Illinois

Jenkins v. Centurion Capital Corp., 2009 WL 3414248 (N.D. Ill. Oct. 20, 2009). The court held that FDCPA was not violated where the defendants filed a state court lawsuit against plaintiff with only an affidavit attesting to its record keeping methods as documentation and the plaintiff alleged that defendants violated § 1692e by filing a lawsuit, the allegations of which they knew they could not prove at that time.

Berg v. Blatt, Hasenmiller, Leibsker & Moore L.L.C., 2009 WL 901011 (N.D. Ill. Mar. 31, 2009). Summary judgment for defendant on claim that affiant misrepresented that she was "the employee/agent of: " when in fact she was employed by defendant's "debt servicer." Since the debt servicer acts as defendant's agent in pursuing collection on its accounts and is part of the same corporate family as defendant, the court found plaintiff's claim without merit. Summary judgment for defendant on claim that affidavit falsely purports to be based on "the original books and records" of defendant where defendant obtains computer records of accounts when purchased and then transfers that information to the debt servicer. "That the records [affiant] used in reviewing the affidavit were electronic copies stored in [the debt servicer's] computer records do not make them any less authentic or accurate."

Rodriguez v. Blatt, Hasenmiller, Leibsker & Moore, L.L.C., 2009 WL 631613 (N.D. Ill. Mar. 10, 2009). The court dismissed the § 1692e claim based on two alleged defects in the form of the summons that the attorney defendant employed in the underlying state court collection suit, holding that the defects were "nonmaterial" and thus could not give rise to FDCPA liability.

Krawczyk v. Centurion Capital Corp., 2009 WL 395458 (N.D. Ill. Feb. 18, 2009). The affidavits of two debt buyers stating the balance and date of last payment on a credit card were not hearsay as they were not introduced to establish the truth of those facts but to show the effect of the data on the debt buyers. The data were also business records admissible to prove the balance and date of last payment. The debt buyers were entitled to rely on creditor's statement that a payment had been made within the statute limitations restarting the five-year period of limitations. Their violation, if any, was a bona fide error.

Wisniewski v. Asset Acceptance Capital Corp., 2009 WL 212155 (N.D. Ill. Jan. 29, 2009). No claim stated for filing a second debt collection suit as first suit was dismissed without prejudice.

Davis v. World Credit Fund I, L.L.C., 543 F. Supp. 2d 953 (N.D. Ill. 2008). Summary judgment for the defendant on plaintiff's claim that it violated §§ 1692e(2)(A) and 1692f(1) by suing plaintiff in state court on a debt that was not owed where the defendant produced unrebutted contrary evidence from the original creditor and its assignee.

Randolph v. Crown Asset Mgmt., L.L.C., 254 F.R.D. 513 (N.D. Ill. 2008). FDCPA class certified on the basis of state court collection complaints that allegedly failed to attach a copy of an assignment that complied with state law as required for licensed debt collectors and where business records affidavits were filed in state collection suits allegedly falsely verifying that the collector was a holder in due course.

Rosales v. Unifund CCR Partners, 2008 WL 5156681 (N.D. Ill. Dec. 5, 2008). Case dismissed because allegedly false allegations of personal knowledge in the affidavits submitted by defendant's employee can be dealt with in the state court proceedings, not as violations of the FDCPA. FDCPA is not applicable to state court pleading requirements.

Washington v. North Star Capital Acquisition, L.L.C., 2008 WL 4280139 (N.D. Ill. Sept. 15, 2008). The court dismissed the consumer's allegation that the defendant's pleading in the state court action was insufficient as the alleged assignment was not attached to that complaint. The court held that the FDCPA does not address state court litigation nor does it provide any requirements for what must be attached to a state court complaint and thus as the consumer's claim is premised on an alleged violation of a state pleading requirements, the FDCPA would not be used as a vehicle to litigate claims arising under the state civil procedure rules. The court also stated the FDCPA was designed to provide basic, overarching rules for debt collection activities; it was not meant to convert every violation of a state debt collection law into a federal violation and the FDCPA should not be used as a way to piggyback one's state claims into federal court.

Guevara v. Midland Funding NCC-2 Corp., 2008 WL 4865550 (N.D. Ill. June 20, 2008). A consumer may state a claim for violations of the FDCPA based on misrepresentation and unfair collection practices which are contained in a state court complaint.

Fisher v. Asset Acceptance, L.L.C., 2005 WL 1799275 (N.D. Ill. July 26, 2005). Collection attorney's sworn verification of the state collection complaint "on information and belief," when there was in fact insufficient documentation to prove the nature and extent of the indebtedness by the plaintiff/bad-debt-purchaser, did not violate either §§ 1692e or 1692f since the attorney did not claim to provide the verification on personal knowledge.

Gonzalez v. Lawent, 2004 WL 2036409 (N.D. Ill. Sept. 10, 2004). An attorney who verified a collection complaint on behalf of the creditor "on information and belief" and who had no personal knowledge of that the debt had been paid did not violate the FDCPA since the verification did not purport to be made on personal knowledge. The attorney debt collector's verification of the collection complaint complied with applicable state law that allowed verification of a complaint on information and belief and therefore did not violate the FDCPA. The allegation that an attorney who verified a collection complaint "on information and belief" in fact had been presented evidence prior to verifying the complaint that the debt in question had been paid in full stated a claim for violating the FDCPA.

Donley v. Nordic Props., Inc., 2003 WL 22282523 (N.D. Ill. Sept. 30, 2003). A second lawsuit seeking to collect rent which had previously been sought in the first lawsuit dismissed on the merits violated § 1692e(5).

Strange v. Wexler, 796 F. Supp. 1117 (N.D. Ill. 1992). Filing of a verified complaint by the attorney collector claiming attorney fees to which he was not entitle violated § 1692e(2)(B).

Indiana

Fausset v. Mortgage First, L.L.C., 2010 WL 987169 (N.D. Ind. Mar. 12, 2010). The mere filing of a lawsuit by a party without the required debt collection licensed in the state was not a misrepresentation under § 1692e.

Ketchem v. American Acceptance, Co., L.L.C., 641 F. Supp. 2d 782 (N.D. Ind. 2008). The complaint stated a claim under §§ 1692e(2)(b) and 1692f(1) by alleging that the defendant debt buyer L.L.C. and its attorneys attempted to collect attorney fees to which they were not entitled in the underlying collection litigation. This was based on the allegation that the credit card contract sued upon, only allowed fees when "the account was referred to an independent attorney" and the attorneys were not independent because the law firm and its principals were the sole owners of the L.L.C.

Hall v. Leone Halpin & Konopinski, L.L.P., 2008 WL 608609 (N.D. Ind. Feb. 28, 2008). State court complaint requesting $1900 collection attorney fees based upon the fee schedule from a different county (the county where the action was pending did not have a fee schedule) did not violate §§ 1692e or 1692f.

Miller v. Javitch, Block & Rathbone, L.L.P., 397 F. Supp. 2d 991 (N.D. Ind. 2005). Court dismissed *pro se*'s complaint that state court collection suit was time barred because the statute of limitations is procedural and the applicable statute of limitations had not run in the state where the consumer currently resided and was sued. Court rejected *pro se*'s claim that debt buyer's records were hearsay and did not show it owned the debt, because *pro se* had the burden to show lack of ownership on his summary judgment motion.

Clark v. Pollard, 2000 U.S. Dist. LEXIS 18934 (S.D. Ind. Dec. 28, 2000). Allegation that collection agency practiced law in state small claims court without a license in violation of § 1692e(5) was dismissed because the alleged actions were taken rather than threatened and the actions had not been attacked in the state court where they were approved. The court's dismissal avoided *Rooker-Feldman* issues.

Kansas

Kujawa v. Palisades Collection, L.L.C., 614 F. Supp. 2d 788 (D. Kan. 2008). Summary judgment entered against consumer on the basis of bona fide error, where consumer knew the collection efforts were aimed at someone with the same name but a different address and Social Security number, and the mistaken lien on his property was promptly released.

Dillon v. Riffel-Kuhlmann, 574 F. Supp. 2d 1221 (D. Kan. 2008). Summary judgment against non-responding *pro se* plaintiff granted to defendant since failure to serve process in a state court action did not violate the FDCPA, and service was actually made. Summary judgment against non-responding *pro se* plaintiff granted on claim that defendant misrepresented his debt to state court, where plaintiff presents no evidence that he did not owe the debt or that the default judgment was obtained improperly.

Bieber v. Associated Collection Servs., Inc., 631 F. Supp. 1410 (D. Kan. 1986). The representation that a hospital had "assigned" a debt to a collector when it had placed the account on a contingent fee basis was not misleading. The collector's denial during suit that it was an assignee was not deceptive since it had ceased collecting the debt.

Maryland

Sayyed v. Wolpoff & Abramson, L.L.P., 2010 WL 3313888 (D. Md. Aug. 20, 2010). Summary judgment was granted to the collector on the §§ 1692e(2) and 1692f(1) claims since the prayer in the underlying collection suit for an award of attorney fees in a specific amount was not prohibited by applicable law and involved no misrepresentation and since the consumer was represented by counsel, the alleged misrepresentations were not misleading under the applicable competent attorney standard.

Michigan

Grden v. Leikin, Ingber & Winters, P.C., 2010 WL 199947 (E.D. Mich. Jan. 19, 2010). Service of the "Combined Affidavit of Open Account and Motion for Default Judgment" attached to the state court collection complaint would not mislead least sophisticated consumers to believe that they were already in default and thus did not violate § 1692e. The collector's misstatement of the amount of the debt communicated in response to the consumer's direct inquiry was not made "in connection with the collection of" the consumer's debt and thus did not violate § 1692e(2)(B) where the collector did not demand payment, did not imply that the consumer was in default, and did not "allude to the consequences of default."

Minnesota

Hemmingsen v. Messerli & Kramer, P.A., 2011 WL 494941 (D. Minn. Feb. 7, 2011). Section 1692e did not apply to the collector's allegedly false statements made in its motion for summary judgment and memorandum of law in its unsuccessful state court collection lawsuit since the representations were directed to the court and not the consumer.

Riermersma v. Messerli & Kramer, P.A., 2008 WL 2390729 (D. Minn. June 9, 2008). Defendant's request for a specific amount of attorney fees as "due and owing" in a state court prayer for relief did not violate the FDCPA.

Frisch v. Messerli & Kramer, P.A., 2008 WL 906183 (D. Minn. Mar. 31, 2008). Summary judgment for the defendant collection attorneys on the claim that they filed a false affidavit in violation of § 1692e(10) in the underlying state collection case when they swore in support of a default judgment that "no answer or other pleading has been received by or served upon Plaintiff or its attorney" and that the "Defendant has not otherwise defended in the action," even though the consumer had sent the attorneys a letter disputing the debt, because under state law the letter was insufficient to defend or answer and thus the statements in the affidavit were not false.

Pierce v. Steven T. Rosso, P.A., 2001 WL 34624006 (D. Minn. Dec. 21, 2001). The defendant collection attorney's failure to strictly comply with the requirements of applicable state rules of civil procedure when he served process on the consumer in the underlying collection suit did not constitute a violation of the FDCPA since the noncompliance, though rendering the underlying service ineffective, was not a deceptive or false representation.

Missouri

Copeland v. Kramer & Frank, P.C., 2010 WL 2232712 (E.D. Mo. June 1, 2010). Disputed facts precluded summary judgment to the attorney collectors who allegedly enticed the consumer, acting *pro se* in the underlying state collection case, to sign a consent judgment under false and deceptive pretenses.

Eckert v. LVNV Funding L.L.C., 647 F. Supp. 2d 1096 (E.D. Mo. 2009). Plaintiff stated a claim for misrepresenting the amount due and the claim was not barred by witness nor litigation immunity. Another claim was dismissed as insufficient facts were alleged to support the claim that defendant violated § 1692e(10) by filing the state court petition outside of the statute of limitations period.

Anderson v. Gamache & Myers, P.C., 2007 WL 4365745 (E.D. Mo. Dec. 10, 2007). There was no deception by the debt collector accepting payments from the consumer with an understanding with the consumer's agent with a power of attorney that the debt collector would take a default judgment at the same time.

Montana

McCollough v. Johnson, Rodenberg & Lauinger, 587 F. Supp. 2d 1170 (D. Mont. 2008). The defendant collection attorneys violated § 1692e(2)(B) by requesting in the state court collection complaint attorney fees to which it was not entitled under applicable state law.

New Jersey

Chulsky v. Hudson Law Offices, P.C., 2011 WL 500202 (D.N.J. Feb. 10, 2011). The plaintiff sufficiently alleged that Hudson Law's operation of the debt buying and collection business would render its attempt to collect the debt unenforceable under New Jersey professional organizations and professional responsibility law and violated § 1692e by misrepresenting the viability of its state collection suit. Thus the plaintiff sufficiently alleged that the defendant misrepresented the legal status of her debt by attempting to a collect on a debt that was unenforceable. Attorneys may be held liable for misleading statements made on behalf of their law firm clients.

New York

Sykes v. Mel Harris & Assocs., L.L.C., 2010 WL 5395712 (S.D.N.Y. Dec. 29, 2010). Consumers alleging that a debt buyer, a law firm, and a process server entered into joint ventures to purchase debt portfolios, pursued debt collection litigation en masse against the alleged debtors, used "sewer service" (the practice of failing to serve a summons and complaint and then filing a fraudulent affidavit attesting to service), and sought to collect millions of dollars in fraudulently obtained default judgments stated causes of action for violations of the FDCPA, RICO, and New York's General Business Law § 349.

Hasbrouck v. Arrow Fin. Servs. L.L.C., 2010 WL 1257885 (N.D.N.Y. Mar. 26, 2010). The court denied the debt collector's motion on the pleadings where the consumer's complaint that the defendant filed a false or "phony" affidavit in seeking a default judgment against her gave rise to at least a "plausible inference of falsity" and alleged a potentially viable claim under the FDCPA.

Gargiulo v. Forster & Garbus Esqs., 651 F. Supp. 2d 188 (S.D.N.Y. 2009). Admittedly truthful affidavit submitted in the underlying collection suit stating that the consumer was in default on the subject account could not be the basis for the asserted claim of a § 1692e violation.

Moore v. Diversified Collection Servs., Inc., 2009 WL 1873654 (E.D.N.Y. June 29, 2009). The consumer's FDCPA complaint alleging a violation of 15 U.S.C. § 1692e for the collector's wage garnishment stated a cause of action, but did not state claims for violation of §§ 1692d, 1692f, and 1692g.

Mateer v. Ross, Suchoff, Egert, Hankin, Maidenbaum & Mazel, P.C., 1997 WL 171011 (S.D.N.Y. Apr. 10, 1997). Collection attorney's act of freezing consumer's bank account on the basis of a judgment that had been vacated, and the misrepresentation to the consumer's bank when the bank investigated the existence of a judgment, clearly brought debtor's claim within the FDCPA. Collector's motion to dismiss was denied.

North Carolina

Albritton v. Sessoms & Rogers, P.A., 2010 WL 3063639 (E.D.N.C. Aug. 3, 2010). Where the amount, character, and legal status of the debt in question was not questioned, the consumer's claims dealing only with an inconsistency in the debt collector's affidavit filed in state court failed to state a claim under § 1692e(2).

North Dakota

Gough v. Bernhardt & Strawser, P.A., 2006 WL 1875327 (M.D.N.C. June 30, 2006). The court held that the *pro se* consumer failed to state a claim against the defendants, who were the collection lawyers in the underlying state court collection suit, for misrepresenting the status of the debt in violation of § 1692e(2)(A) by failing to inform the state court in their collection complaint that the consumer had previously disputed the debt, since the FDCPA contains no such requirement and in any event because the consumer is directed in the summons to so inform the court of any dispute by way of filing an answer. Section 1692e(8) does not require a debt collector filing a state collection complaint to inform the state court that the consumer had previously disputed the debt.

Ohio

Myers v. Asset Acceptance L.L.C., 2010 WL 3522470 (S.D. Ohio Sept. 7, 2010). An affidavit submitted with a complaint against a debtor, in which an employee swore that the debt information was accurate and that he was competent to express an opinion on its correctness, would not have misled the least sophisticated consumer into believing that the employee's representations were based on any personal knowledge he had regarding the underlying debt. A statement of account included as an attachment to a complaint was not deceptive or misleading, because while it included the debtor's account number and balance owed, it would not have misled the least sophisticated consumer into believing that it was a monthly statement.

Nelson v. American Power & Light, 2010 WL 3219498 (S.D. Ohio Aug. 12, 2010). The complaint stated a claim for violating § 1692e where the defendant filed a state court eviction complaint containing inadequate grounds to support an eviction. The allegation that the defendant imposed unlawful excessive charges in its underlying state court complaint stated a claim for violating § 1692e.

Jordan v. John Soliday Fin. Group, L.L.C., 2010 WL 1462345

(N.D. Ohio Apr. 12, 2010). An outstanding question of fact as to the chain of title and ownership of the debt precluded summary judgment on the consumer's claim that the defendants violated the FDCPA when they attempted to collect a delinquent loan without the authority to do so. The court reserved for the trier of fact whether the defendants' attachment of documents to the state court collection complaint that revealed the consumer's Social Security number violated the FDCPA.

Kline v. Mortgqage Elec. Sec. Sys., 2010 WL 1133452 (S.D. Ohio Mar. 22, 2010). Initiating a foreclosure action before the note and mortgage have been assigned to the financial institution, on behalf of which that action was initiated, does not violate the FDCPA as long as the assignment occurs before final judgment is entered.

Midland Funding L.L.C. v. Brent, 644 F. Supp. 2d 961 (N.D. Ohio 2009). Deposition testimony showed there were two patently false claims in the affidavit: first, that the affiant had any personal knowledge regarding consumer's debt, and second, that the affiant was involved with the decision or act of hiring the law firm to pursue legal action. The employee did not learn anything about the accounts, which the affidavit stated were owed based on his personal knowledge, when the employee merely signed the affidavits en mass, about 400 each day, without any personal knowledge about the amount claimed, owed, or the ownership the claim. Another paragraph described how defendant acquired the debt and, if it is read alone, it only states a fact that is very likely true. However, when read in conjunction with paragraph one: "I make the statements herein based upon my personal knowledge," it is apparently false.

Whittiker v. Deutsche Bank Nat'l Trust Co., 605 F. Supp. 2d 914 (N.D. Ohio 2009). The filing of a foreclosure action by a plaintiff in the process of obtaining an assignment not yet fully documented was not a deceptive, misleading, or abusive tactic and did not violate the FDCPA.

Kline v. Mortgage Elec. Registration Sys., 2009 WL 6093372 (S.D. Ohio Nov. 24, 2009). Defendants' motion to dismiss granted because "[t]he filing of a foreclosure action by a plaintiff in the process of obtaining an assignment not yet fully documented is not a deceptive, misleading, or abusive tactic and does not violate the FDCPA."

Hill v. Javitch, Block & Rathbone, L.L.P., 574 F. Supp. 2d 819 (S.D. Ohio 2008). Defendant did not violate the FDCPA by not having documentation in hand supporting its claim when it filed suit where it did not make false statements or file false documents. Defendant's mailing of the summons and complaint to the wrong address was not an unfair, unconscionable, false, or misleading debt collection practice as a matter of law; defendant withdrew the complaint upon dispute.

Evans v. Midland Funding L.L.C., 574 F. Supp. 2d 808 (S.D. Ohio 2008). Citing *Miller v. Javitch,* "[T]he filing of an action for 'money loaned' by a credit card issuer or its successor to recover funds owed from a credit card holder" did not violate §§ 1692e(2)(A) or 1692e(10) as it was not a false statement to characterize a credit card obligation as a loan. Whether the characterization of a credit card debt is deceptive or misleading, and whether defendant has a bona fide error defense cannot be decided as a matter of law without discovery. Denied judgment on the pleadings pending discovery on whether defendant falsely or misleadingly implied that their respective debt buyer creditors had acquired all rights, title, and interest in their alleged debts. Denied judgment on the pleadings on plaintiff's claim that defendants sued on a non-existent debt where plaintiff was merely an authorized user.

Todd v. Weltman Weinberg & Reis Co., L.P.A., 2008 WL 419943 (S.D. Ohio Feb. 14, 2008). Factual issues precluded summary judgment on whether the collection lawyer's affidavit for garnishment misrepresented that the affiant had a reasonable basis to believe there to be nonexempt funds in the accounts of judgment debtors.

Ison v. Javitch, Block & Rathbone, 2007 WL 2769674 (S.D. Ohio Sept. 18, 2007). Denied the motion to dismiss. Plaintiff stated a claim by alleging that the collection attorneys attached to the underlying state court collection complaint an affidavit that they knew falsely claimed that the affiant had "personal knowledge" of the facts attested to, to wit, "the amount owed, the annual percentage rate, whether late fees can be added, whether over-limit charges can be added and whether attorney fees and/or costs of collection can be added to the debt," in violation of § 1692e, including § 1692e(10), and § 1692f.

Foster v. D.B.S. Collection Agency, 463 F. Supp. 2d 783 (S.D. Ohio 2006). Because purchaser of the collection agency had not filed a trade name certificate after acquiring the collection agency, she could not legally file lawsuits in the collection agency's name. Collection agency and its attorney violated § 1692e when they commenced and maintained debt collection lawsuits in state court against the class members, even though they did not have the legal capacity to do so. The collection agency engaged in the unauthorized practice of law by bringing suits in its own name without becoming the legal and equitable owner of the account, and thereby violated § 1692e(5).

Deere v. Javitch, Block & Rathbone, L.L.P., 413 F. Supp. 2d 886 (S.D. Ohio 2006). "[F]iling a lawsuit supported by the client's affidavit attesting to the existence and amount of a debt, is not a false representation about the character or legal status of a debt, nor is it unfair or unconscionable. . . . [The] 'theory' . . . [is] that Melville buys old, defaulted debt for pennies on the dollar. In these transactions, the seller of the debt provides only minimal summary information about the original debt. Melville, represented by JB&R, then routinely files state court collection actions supported only by the summary information. The default rate on these lawsuits 'is at least ninety percent' according to Deere. Obtaining a default permits Melville/JB&R to garnish the judgment debtor, even though the debt was never 'proved up' in a contested court action. But when a debtor appears in the action and asks for documentation on the debt, the Defendants routinely dismiss the collection action, based on the economics of pursuing a judgment in those circumstances. This no different from filing a lawsuit on a time-barred claim, and thus violates Sections 1692e, 1692e(10) or 1692f. The Court disagrees. Deere does not allege that anything in the state court complaint was false, or that the complaint was baseless. She essentially alleges that more of a paper trail should have been in the lawyers' hands. The FDCPA imposes no such obligation. Ohio law permits a plaintiff an absolute right to one dismissal without prejudice for any reason or for no reason, any time before trial."

Davis v. NCO Portfolio Mgmt., Inc., 2006 WL 290491 (S.D. Ohio Feb. 7, 2006). Filing a lawsuit supported by debt buyers affidavit attesting to the existence and amount of a debt, is not a false representation about the debt, nor is it unfair or unconscionable. The consumer did not allege that anything in the state court complaint was false or that the complaint itself was baseless. She essentially alleged that more of a paper trail should have been in the lawyers' hands or attached to the complaint. The FDCPA imposes no such obligation.

Montgomery v. Donnett, 2006 WL 293727 (S.D. Ohio Feb. 7, 2006). The filing of landlord's action barred by res judicata, like a time-barred claim, violated the FDCPA. Even if the prior state court judgment had been amended to not bar the subsequent claim, it did not alter the FDCPA violation that already had occurred.

Lamb v. Javitch, Block & Rathbone, L.L.P., 2005 WL 4137786 (S.D. Ohio Jan. 24, 2005). The consumer stated a cause of action for violation of the FDCPA for the law firm's failure to set an oral hearing on its motion to confirm the arbitration award, and the court denied the law firm's motion to dismiss that was based in part on res judicata and *Rooker Feldman*.

Pache Mgmt. Co. v. Lusk, 1997 WL 254096 (Ohio Ct. App. May 15, 1997). Mispleading an action to enforce a rental agreement as an action on an account bears no relation to the validity or amount of the alleged debt and therefore did not violate the FDCPA.

Oklahoma

Bynum v. Cavalry Portfolio Servs., L.L.C., 2005 WL 2789199 (N.D. Okla. Sept. 29, 2005). An action for violation of the FDCPA did not arise from filing a lawsuit that was not served.

Oregon

Flores v. Quick Collect, Inc., 2007 WL 2769003 (D. Or. Sept. 18, 2007). The court granted the defendants summary judgment on the consumer's claim that the warning included in the order, requiring her to appear for a post-judgment debtor's examination that she may be charged with contempt of court and arrested if she failed to appear, was false, oppressive, or unfair because the defendants never intended to arrest her and could not have legally arrested her for failure to appear because the debtor examination was sought in an venue that was allegedly unlawful pursuant to § 1692i, since the "threat" was issued by the court and not by the defendants and in any event she could have been held in contempt if she did not appear regardless of the FDCPA venue provision.

Capital Credit & Collection Serv., Inc. v. Armani, 206 P.3d 1114 (Or. Ct. App. 2009). Jury could properly conclude that litigation after reaching a settlement agreement violated § 1692e.

Pennsylvania

Popson v. Galloway, 2010 WL 2985945 (W.D. Pa. July 27, 2010). Follows *Harvey* finding filing suit without providing documentation substantiating the debt does not violate §§ 1692d, 1692e or 1692f.

Whiteman v. Burton Neil & Assocs., P.C., 2008 WL 4372842 (M.D. Pa. Sept. 19, 2008). "[A]ctions [taken] during the state court lawsuit can lead to FDCPA liability."

Gigli v. Palisades Collection, L.L.C., 2008 WL 3853295 (M.D. Pa. Aug. 14, 2008). The mere filing of a lawsuit without immediate means of proof that the debt was due is not a misrepresentation or deceptive under § 1692e(10).

Phath v. J. Scott Watson, P.C., 2008 WL 623837 (E.D. Pa. Mar. 7, 2008). The consumer's claim that the collection attorney's verification attached to the underlying state court collection complaint was false and deceptive in violation of § 1692e(10) was dismissed for failure to state a claim because the allegedly false facts were only averred, as permitted by state law, on "knowledge, information and belief." Also, there could be no deception because the verification was true in that the "statement can be read only to have one meaning, that he was verifying that the facts contained in the complaint were true based on knowledge, information and belief. The statement is not open to any other reasonable interpretation." The consumer's claim that the collection attorney's verification attached to the underlying state court collection complaint violated § 1692e(9) in that it "creates a false impression as to its source, authorization, or approval" was dismissed for failure to state a claim because, "[w]hile [the consumer] may be able to establish that the verification does not strictly comport with the language of Pa. R. Civ. P. 102(c) [dealing with the contents of verifications], this procedural error does not create a false impression as to its source, authorization, or approval. Moreover, this error is one that courts in Pennsylvania hold to be de minimis."

Dixon v. Law Offices of Peter E. Meltzer & Assocs., P.C., 2007 WL 275877 (E.D. Pa. Jan. 26, 2007). The defendant collection attorneys' error in mislabeling the notice of the consumer's deposition in the underlying state court collection litigation as being "in aid of execution of judgment" did not violate § 1692e(10) because sending the notices was not a "means to collect" the debt since "the sole action the notices prompted from [the consumer] was his appearance at the scheduled deposition. The state court had already issued an order compelling [the consumer's] presence at the deposition, and the mislabeled notice simply provided the date upon which [the consumer] was required to appear."

Tennessee

Spangler v. Conrad, 2010 WL 2389481 (E.D. Tenn. June 9, 2010). The defendant's attempt to collect a sum certain in reasonable attorney fees authorized by the loan agreement did not violate the FDCPA. The attorney defendant did not violate §§ 1692e and 1692f merely by attaching to the state court collection complaint the client's sworn statement of account allegedly misstating the amount of the debt. "A debt collection attorney should be allowed to confidently rely upon an affidavit of Sworn Account executed by his client that sets forth the total amount owed."

Texas

Beeler-Lopez v. Dodeka, L.L.C., 2010 WL 1889428 (E.D. Tex. May 7, 2010). Any violation of the FDCPA's venue provision occurs when the suit is brought. If the consumer does not object to venue, then merely continuing to pursue the action is not a violation of §§ 1692i, 1692d, or 1692e.

Walker v. Pharia, L.L.C., 2010 WL 565654 (N.D. Tex. Feb. 18, 2010). The court dismissed the consumer's § 1692e claims that the defendant's state court collection petition and attached affidavit contained conflicting and false information. "The Court concludes it wholly implausible that any consumer would have been mislead

after reading the entirety of Pharia's state-court petition."

Gibson v. Grupo de Ariel, L.L.C., 2006 WL 42369 (N.D. Tex. Jan. 9, 2006). An FDCPA claim can be premised on flawed legal proceedings because the FDCPA prohibits fraudulent, deceptive, or misleading representations, including those made in judicial or governmental proceedings.

Washington

McLain v. Gordon, 2010 WL 3340528 (W.D. Wash. Aug. 24, 2010). Naming the debt buyer as the creditor in the collection complaint, while false, was not material, would not likely confuse the least sophisticated consumer, and did not violate section § 1692e(10). Service of an unfiled Washington state complaint as permitted by Washington procedure does not violate the FDCPA. "[T]he Court is unwilling to hold that service of an unfiled complaint violates the FDCPA, because the ramifications of this rule would require debt collectors to always file first and then serve. This is simply too sweeping of a proposition for the Court to countenance and is not required by either legislative act or court rule. There are legitimate reasons to serve unfiled complaints. For instance, a debt collector may wish to portray to a consumer honestly that it may file the summons and complaint if the debtor refuses to respond through less formal means."

Kirk v. Gobel, 622 F. Supp. 2d 1039 (E.D. Wash. 2009). The defendant collection lawyer violated § 1692e when he sought and received a default judgment in state court that included attorney fees that were prohibited under applicable state law and §§ 1692e(2)(B) and 1692f(1) by requesting service of process fees that were prohibited by applicable state law since the process server was unregistered.

Sprinkle v. SB&C Ltd., 2006 WL 2671364 (W.D. Wash. Sept. 18, 2006). Violation of the state garnishment statute by failing to file a military service affidavit also violated the FDCPA, § 1692e(5) and (10), particularly since the debtor was deployed in the Middle East at the time. Section 1692e(5) prohibits not only the threat, but also the taking, of illegal action. To rule otherwise "would provide more protection to debt collectors who violate the law than to those who merely threaten or pretend to do so."

Campion v. Credit Bureau Servs., Inc., 2000 U.S. Dist. LEXIS 20233 (E.D. Wash. Sept. 19, 2000). Attorney debt collector's inclusion in writ of garnishment of an estimate of the costs and attorney fees that would be incurred complied with applicable state law that required such an estimate and therefore did not violate § 1692f; however, stating that such estimate was part of the existing unsatisfied judgment was false and therefore violated § 1692e. Absent a threat to take any action, there can be no violation of § 1692e(5).

K.2.4.13 False Impression of Communication's Source, Authorization, or Approval, 15 U.S.C. § 1692e(9)

Campuzano-Burgos v. Midland Credit Mgmt., Inc., 550 F.3d 294 (3d Cir. 2008). A settlement letter that was sent in the name of a corporate senior officer who had no personal involvement in the collection of the debt would not deceive the least sophisticated consumer into believing that he received a personal communication from the named officer and, in contrast to a dunning letter or a communication from an attorney, would be understood as only "a notice from a company" because of the letter's specific content and format.

California

del Campo v. Am. Corrective Counseling Serv., Inc., 2010 WL 2473586 (N.D. Cal. June 3, 2010). Defendants violated § 1692e(3) and (9) by sending consumers check collection notices on district attorney letterhead that did not identify the corporate collector as its source. "[T]he district attorney's permission does not excuse defendants from adhering to the requirements of the FDCPA. At the very least, the law requires that ACCS identified itself as the true sender of the letter . . . [O]n their face, the Official Notices do not disclose the identity of the actual sender, and create the impression that they were sent directly from the district attorney's office rather than from a private company."

Schwarm v. Craighead, 552 F. Supp. 2d 1056 (E.D. Cal. 2008). The form letters likewise violated §§ 1692e(9) and 1692e(14).

Dorner v. Commercial Trade Bureau, 2008 WL 1704137 (E.D. Cal. Apr. 10, 2008). Consumer stated a claim that could not be resolved as a matter of law under Rule 12(b)(6) by alleging that the defendant's use of the name "Commercial Trade Bureau of California" gave "the false impression that the debt collection company was in some way associated with the State of California" in violation of §§ 1692e(1), 1692e(9), and 1692e(10).

Connecticut

Bishop v. Nat'l Accounts Sys., Inc., Clearinghouse No. 49,175 (D. Conn. 1993). Debt collector's communication was deceptive and misleading in that it created the false impression of a partnership between the defendant and the state government.

Johnson v. NCB Collection Servs., 799 F. Supp. 1298 (D. Conn. 1992) (settled upon collector's payment of $4000 for consumer to withdraw appeal). Use of the words "Revenue Department" in the return address on the collector's envelope did not violate §§ 1692e(9), 1692e(14), or 1692f(8) by suggesting the correspondence was from a governmental agency, using a name other than the collector's "true" name, or disclosing the purpose of the correspondence.

Thomas v. Nat'l Bus. Assistants, Inc., 1984 U.S. Dist. LEXIS 24876, 1984 WL 585309 (D. Conn. Oct. 5, 1984) (slip copy). Forms violated § 1692e(9) since they appear to be federal government forms. The word "National" in collector's name was prominent and at least one form contained a prominent box stating "Pursuant to the Federal Fair Debt Collection Practices Act, Section 809, Validation of Debts."

Georgia

Faust v. Texaco Ref. & Mktg., Inc., 270 B.R. 310 (Bankr. M.D. Ga. 1998). G.C. Services violated § 1692e(1) by implying it was vouched for by the government.

Illinois

Arango v. G.C. Servs., 1999 U.S. Dist. LEXIS 1143 (N.D. Ill. Feb. 2, 1999). Use of the word "national" in National Delinquent Debtor File, without more, does not suggest government affiliation rendering the title misleading.

Philipps v. G.C. Servs., 1994 WL 127283 (N.D. Ill. Apr. 7, 1994). Debt collector's statement—"You should know that we are an experienced collection agency. We provided the systems used by a major branch of the federal government and various state governments to collect delinquent taxes,"—did not deceptively imply that the government was involved in the debt collector's collection efforts or that the debt collector had access to federal government records and accordingly, was not in violation of § 1692e(1). The Seventh Circuit subsequently reached the opposite conclusion in *Gammon v. G.C. Servs., supra.*

Tolentino v. Friedman, 833 F. Supp. 697 (N.D. Ill. 1993). A collection attorney's notice urging the consumer to arrange payment of the debt and to avoid bankruptcy put in the same envelope as a copy of a summons and complaint would mislead the least sophisticated debtor about the court's role in the debt collection process in violation of § 1692e(9) which prohibits the false representation that a document is authorized, issued, or approved by any court, official, or agency and § 1692e(13) which prohibits the false implication that a document constitutes legal process.

Indiana

Beeson v. Med-1 Solutions, L.L.C., 2008 WL 4443224 (S.D. Ind. Sept. 25, 2008), *vacated in part on other grounds*, 2008 WL 4545333 (S.D. Ind. Oct. 8, 2008). Despite the fact that defendant sent collection letters in the name of the hospital and in its own name, and sued in its own name, the unsophisticated consumer would be aware that defendant was acting as agent for the hospital and would not be deceived.

Michigan

Gradisher v. Check Enforcement Unit, Inc., 210 F. Supp. 2d 907 (W.D. Mich. 2002). Although the debt collector was an independent contractor with the county, its notices purporting to be from the sheriff's department gave the false impression that they were from the sheriff in violation of § 1692e(9) and 1692e(14).

Minnesota

Wald v. Morris, Carlson, & Hoelscher, P.A., 2010 WL 4736829 (D. Minn. Nov. 16, 2010). There remained a genuine issue of material fact as to whether the defendants violated the Act by falsely implying that the documents enclosed with a collection letter, the summons and complaint, were legal process, when sending them without the acknowledgement of service as required by state rules.

Missouri

Thomas v. Consumer Adjustment Co., 579 F. Supp. 2d 1290 (E.D. Mo. 2008). Where debt collector, using the first name of the consumer's brother, asked for the debtor indicating it was urgent for the consumer to return the call, the jury was to decide if the false sense of urgency was deceptive.

New York

DeSantis v. Roz-Ber, Inc., 51 F. Supp. 2d 244 (E.D.N.Y. 1999). Consumer was denied permission to amend to assert that the name New Jersey Creditor Collection Agency could give the least sophisticated consumer the impression that the collector was affiliated with the state.

Ohio

Adams v. First Fed. Credit Control, Inc., 1992 WL 131121 (N.D. Ohio May 21, 1992). Use of the word "federal" in collector's letterhead which was surrounded on both sides with icons resembling the great seal of the United States would lead a consumer to believe that the sender was related to the federal government. Criminal penalty pursuant to 18 U.S.C. § 712 for use of words "national," "Federal," or "United States," the initials "U.S.," or any emblem, insignia, or name which falsely conveys a relation to the United States government in the collection of private debts lends persuasive authority that § 1692e was violated.

Pache Mgmt. Co. v. Lusk, 1997 WL 254096 (Ohio Ct. App. May 15, 1997). Use of the word "federal" in a debt collector's name, together with prominent statement that the collector was a private corporation, did not unlawfully imply affiliation with government.

Washington

Buckalew v. Suttell & Hammer, P.S., 2010 WL 3944477 (E.D. Wash. Oct. 7, 2010). The use of the case caption on the "Affidavit of Creditor" that did not bear a court name or a case number, in conjunction with a letter specifically stating that "at this time, suit has not been initiated," would not lead a "least sophisticated consumer" to believe that suit had already been initiated against him or her, and does not violate simulate or falsely represent to be a document authorized, issued, or approved by a court or official of the United States or any state.

LeClair v. Suttell & Assocs., P.S., 2010 WL 417418 (W.D. Wash. Jan. 29, 2010). The court declined to hold under state law that service of an unfiled summons and complaint violated § 1692e(9).

K.2.4.14 Use of True Business Name, 15 U.S.C. § 1692e(14)

Lester E. Cox Med. Ctr. v. Huntsman, 408 F.3d 989 (8th Cir. 2005). The hospital violated § 1692e(14) by using a fictitious name to collect its debts.

Peter v. G.C. Servs. L.P., 310 F.3d 344 (5th Cir. 2002). Use of the United States Department of Education's name and address as the return address on the envelope, as well as a statement that the envelope is not be used for private communication, violated §§ 1692e(14) and 1692f(8).

Arizona

Grismore v. United Recovery Sys., L.P., 2006 WL 2246359 (D. Ariz. Aug. 3, 2006). Since the evidence established that the defendant debt collector employed no name other than its own, the court granted the defendant summary judgment on the *pro se* plaintiff's claim that the defendant had used a business, company, or organization name other than the defendant's true name in violation of § 1692e(14).

Gostony v. Diem Corp., 320 F. Supp. 2d 932 (D. Ariz. 2003). Identifying the creditor by the name of the apartment complex rather than the name of the individuals who owned the complex was not a false representation. Use of pseudonym by a debt collector was not a deceptive practice.

California

Carrizosa v. Stassinos, 2010 WL 4393900 (N.D. Cal. Oct. 29, 2010). A debt collector who sometimes sent duns in the name of the creditor was liable under § 1692e(14).

Palmer v. Stassinos, 2009 WL 86705 (N.D. Cal. Jan. 9, 2009). Debt collectors sending letters on the letterhead of the creditor violated 15 U.S.C. § 1692e(14).

Owens v. Brachfeld, 2008 WL 3891958 (N.D. Cal. Aug. 20, 2008). Summary judgment was entered for the consumer that the debt collector had violated § 1692e(14) where the debt collector used the name of a corporate entity which could not be found on the California Secretary of State website and awarded the consumer damages of $2100 plus attorney fees and costs.

Connecticut

Johnson v. NCB Collection Servs., 799 F. Supp. 1298 (D. Conn. 1992) (settled upon collector's payment of $4000 for consumer to withdraw appeal). The collectors' use of an office name or alias assigned to an individual was not false, deceptive, or misleading to the least sophisticated consumer, in violation of § 1692e, although telephone calls to that name might be forwarded to any of several collectors. Use of the words "Revenue Department" in the return address on the collector's envelope did not violate §§ 1692e(9), 1692e(14), or 1692f(8) by suggesting the correspondence was from a governmental agency, using a name other than the collector's "true" name, or disclosing the purpose of the correspondence.

Latella v. Atl. Advisors, Inc., 1992 U.S. Dist. LEXIS 22849 (D. Conn. May 11, 1992). Collection letters signed in the name of a nonexistent person were sufficient to establish a violation of § 1692e.

Kizer v. Am. Credit & Collection, Clearinghouse No. 45,928 (D. Conn. 1991). A licensed trade name, required to be used by Connecticut statute, was the collector's "true" name required by § 1692e(14).

Moore v. Nat'l Account Sys., Inc., 1991 U.S. Dist. LEXIS 18137 (D. Conn. Nov. 13, 1991) (magistrate's opinion). Collector's use of the name "National Business Division" when its Connecticut collector's license permitted it to collect only in the name of "National Account Systems, Inc." violated §§ 1692e and 1692e(10), prohibiting deception generally and requiring the use of a true name.

Supan v. Med. Bureau of Econ., Inc., 1991 U.S. Dist. LEXIS 20352 (D. Conn. Oct. 3, 1991), *adopted by* 785 F. Supp. 304 (D. Conn. 1991) (magistrate's opinion). Collector violated FDCPA by misrepresenting that the names on its letters were those of its employees when they were actually of nonexistent persons.

Florida

Danow v. Borack, 2006 WL 5516577 (S.D. Fla. Jan. 30, 2006), *rev'd in part and remanded on other grounds,* 197 Fed. Appx. 853 (11th Cir. 2006). Claim that defendant did not use a registered legal name was dismissed discussing the cases that allowed the use of debt collection aliases under the FDCPA. "The name is not a fabrication, but rather is the name held out to the public and the name under which it conducts business."

Arslan v. Florida First Fed. Group, 1995 WL 731175 (M.D. Fla. Oct. 5, 1995). Collector's use of an unregistered fictitious name violated § 1692e(10) and (14).

Illinois

Cole v. Noonan & Lieberman, Ltd., 2005 WL 2848446 (N.D. Ill. Oct. 26, 2005). *Pro se* stated a claim for deception based on letter claiming Ocwen was the creditor when Ocwen was not the entity to whom the debt was owed.

Blum v. Lawent, 2003 WL 22078306 (N.D. Ill. Sept. 8, 2003). Because a jury could reasonably determine that a consumer would not be mislead by a collection lawyer misnaming a dentist, rather than the dentist's corporate employer, as the plaintiff in a collection action, the court found there was an issue of fact for which summary judgment was inappropriate.

Everst v. Credit Prot. Ass'n, L.P., 2003 WL 22048719 (N.D. Ill. Aug. 25, 2003). Where Communications and Cable of Chicago, Inc. consistently acted in the names AT&T Broadband or other names licensed to it by its parent corporation, there was no misrepresentation of the involvement of a third party collector or use of a name that was not the collector's true name as required by § 1692e(14).

Weinstein v. Fink, 2001 U.S. Dist. LEXIS 2075 (N.D. Ill. Feb. 21, 2001). The FDCPA does not require a collection agency which retained the attorney who brought the collection suit in the creditor's name to be named as a plaintiff in a collection action where the agency neither owned the debt nor prosecuted the lawsuit.

Scott v. Universal Fid. Corp., 1999 U.S. Dist. LEXIS 13425 (N.D. Ill. Aug. 30, 1999). Consumer alleged that collection agency used a false and misleading assumed name, Fidelity Financial Services, registered in Texas but not in Illinois, and was therefore liable under FDCPA.

Philipps v. G.C. Servs., 1994 WL 127283 (N.D. Ill. Apr. 7, 1994). Consumer's complaint alleging that debt collector's collection letter indicated it was sent by J. Moran, when in fact no such person existed, was sufficient to state a claim under § 1692e(10) and the debt collector's motion to dismiss was denied.

Minnesota

Cohen v. Beachside Two-I Homeowners' Ass'n, 2005 WL 3088361 (D. Minn. Nov. 17, 2005). *Pro se* plaintiff's motion for partial summary judgment was denied with the court holding that no evidence was presented regarding the defendant mortgagee's true name, and the court could not determine whether the defendant mortgagee used an assumed name.

Montana

McCollough v. Johnson, Rodenberg & Lauinger, 610 F. Supp. 2d 1247 (D. Mont 2009). A debt collector violated the FDCPA by using the courts to attempt to collect a time-barred debt. While the debt collector's use of discovery in a collection action is not a per se violation of the FDCPA, here the request for admission to admit that a payment was made was served when the debt collector's records showed the payment was not made. The use of the judicial process against a *pro se* defendant, in order to avoid a statute of limitations defense, collecting on a time-barred debt was an abusive, unfair, and unconscionable practice in violation of the FDCPA. The debt collector's failure to move to set aside the underlying state court default judgment, after a summary judgment ruling that the underlying state court action violated the FDCPA because it was time barred, constituted an additional FDCPA violation.

New Mexico

Martinez v. Albuquerque Collection Servs., 867 F. Supp. 1495 (D.N.M. 1994). Debt collection agency violated § 1692e(5) by filing suit in its own name pursuant to a nominal assignment, which was the unauthorized practice of law under New Mexico decisions. It violated §§ 1692e(2) and 1692f(1).

Kolker v. Sanchez, Clearinghouse No. 46,774 (D.N.M. 1991). Attorney, who filed suit in name of collection agency rather than in name of true creditor, engaged in the unauthorized practice of law in violation of § 1692e.

New Jersey

Boyko v. Am. Intern. Group, Inc., 2009 WL 5194431 (D.N.J. Dec. 23, 2009). Section 1692e(14) at its core clearly prohibits the use of a name that is neither the collector's actual corporate name nor its official trade name, licensed or otherwise.

New York

Ohlson v. The Cadle Co., 2008 WL 4516233 (E.D.N.Y. Sept. 30, 2008). Court rejected plaintiff's "true name" (§ 1692e(14)) claim that defendant was the true owner of the alleged debt but the collection documents falsely represent another creditor as the owner. That defendant supplies office space, telephone lines, computers, or even personnel to the creditor does not indicate that defendant is the owner of the debt. At best, it shows administrative overlap in their operations.

Burchalewski v. Wolpoff & Abramson, L.L.P., 2008 WL 4238933 (W.D.N.Y. Sept. 8, 2008). A claim for deception was stated where plaintiff was sued by creditor when it was defunct after it had been sold to another company.

Orenbuch v. N. Shore Health Sys., Inc., 250 F. Supp. 2d 145 (E.D.N.Y. 2003). A debt collector who utilized the name by which it was known to the public and was registered with the Department of State used its "true name" and did not violate § 1692e(14). The FDCPA does not require disclosure of the debt collector's corporate affiliation.

Weber v. Goodman, 9 F. Supp. 2d 163 (E.D.N.Y. 1998). Creditor violated § 1692e by creating misleading impression that a third party was collecting debt when the third party was not meaningfully involved in collection process.

Texas

Youngblood v. G.C. Servs. Ltd. P'ship, 186 F. Supp. 2d 695 (W.D. Tex. 2002). The given name of the employee from whose desk the letter was sent was immaterial, and the use of a professional name or desk name was not a violation of § 1692e.

Wisconsin

Hartman v. Meridian Fin. Servs., Inc., 191 F. Supp. 2d 1031 (W.D. Wis. 2002). The third party debt collector's communication with consumers in the name of the creditor was a false representation in violation of § 1692e.

Wyoming

Johnson v. Statewide Collections, Inc., 778 P.2d 93 (Wyo. 1989). The use of the name "Checkrite" when the collector is registered as "Statewide Collections, Inc., d/b/a Checkrite" does not violate § 1692e(14). Even use of a correct name can be deceptive, however, if it tends to deceive debtors about the collector's true identity.

K.2.4.15 Misrepresenting Collector As Credit Reporting Agency, 15 U.S.C. § 1692e(16)

Connecticut

Shrestha v. State Credit Adjustment Bureau, Inc., 117 F. Supp. 2d 142 (D. Conn. 2000). The collector's name was not misleading about it being a credit bureau, particularly in view of its written disclaimer stating that it was a debt collector and not a credit reporting agency.

Illinois

Trull v. G.C. Servs. Ltd. P'ship, 961 F. Supp. 1199 (N.D. Ill. 1997). Collection letter containing the statements: "This is the last effort I will be making to settle your account"; "Your name will be retained as part of our records along with others who, despite their good name and reputation, have shirked their payment responsibility"; "YOUR ACCOUNT HAS BEEN TRANSFERRED TO [agency's] MASTER DEBTOR FILE"; and "We are anxious to clear our record as well as yours," could mislead the unsophisticated consumer into believing that the collection agency was a credit reporting agency, and that inclusion in the master file would have consequences.

Louisiana

Charles v. Credit Bureau Servs., 1999 U.S. Dist. LEXIS 19665 (E.D. La. Dec. 17, 1999). Company that operated as both a credit reporting agency and collection agency did not deceive or mislead when it used the name "credit bureau." Employee statement that company was not a credit bureau was not a misrepresentation when employee was responding to an inquiry related to a collection letter.

Byes v. Credit Bureau Enters., Inc., 1995 WL 540235 (E.D. La. Sept. 11, 1995). Discovery regarding collector's credit reporting activities was relevant to the claim that collector used a deceptive name.

K.2.4.16 Debt Settlement Offers

DeKoven v. Plaza Assocs., 599 F.3d 578 (7th Cir. 2010). The absence of safe harbor language in a dunning letter falsely communicating that the creditor's initial settlement offer would be final does not lead to per se liability on the part of the debt collector. The evidence required to determine liability is a consumer survey, but in this case the survey was properly deemed inadmissible.

Goswami v. American Collections Enter., Inc., 377 F.3d 488 (5th Cir. 2004). The letter stated, falsely, that "only during the next thirty days, will our client agree to settle your outstanding balance due with a thirty (30%) percent discount off your above balance owed." In actual fact, the creditor had authorized the collector to give debtors a 30% discount at any time, not just for a period of thirty days. In fact, the collector was authorized to offer a 50% discount at the time the consumer received the collection letter. The statement in the collection letter was untrue. An "amnesty" reference clearly referred to the debt forgiveness offer made in the body of the letter, and even unsophisticated consumers would not believe it implied a criminal charge would be sought.

California

Hancock v. Receivables Mgmt. Solutions, Inc., 2006 WL 1525723 (N.D. Cal. May 30, 2006). "*Goswami* is distinguishable. Here, none of the letters stated that the settlement offer was "only" valid for the next thirty days; none of the letters gave the false impression that the offer would irrevocably lapse."

Callanta v. GC Servs., 2006 WL 1072028 (N.D. Cal. Apr. 21, 2006). Settlement offer of limited duration was not deceptive or misleading since it did not state that the offer was effective "only" in that time frame. Request to pay by money order or certified check did not create false sense of urgency where no negative consequences were threatened.

Johnson v. AMO Recoveries, 427 F. Supp. 2d 953 (N.D. Cal. 2005). The court held that only false offers that "expressly state that an opportunity to settle the debt at a discount will be lost after a given date" constitute a violation; the offer here stated, "This settlement offer shall be null and void if not received by," yet the court found no falsehood, stating "Not only would 'the least sophisticated debtor' understand that the expiration of a mere 'offer' does not necessarily foreclose the possibility of the parties later agreeing to its terms, but the practical consequence of holding offer letters unlawful would be to prohibit settlement offers that are anything but the debt collector's best and final offer." The court held that the defendant's 60% settlement offer that stated that it would be "null and void" after a date certain did not misrepresent the settlement authority that the defendant collector had from its creditor-client. "Whether [the creditor] would have been willing to settle for 60% of the debt after [the collector's] offer became "null and void" on [the date certain] is irrelevant. Because [the collector] did not purport to convey a firm offer from [the creditor], [the consumer] cannot state a claim for misrepresentation of settlement authority." The defendant's series of settlement offers did not create a false sense of urgency.

Minick v. Tate & Kirlin Assocs., 2005 WL 1566548 (N.D. Cal. July 5, 2005). The court granted the debt collector's motion to dismiss where repeated settlement offers of 50% were made because the letters did not purport to be one-time offers or state that the entire balance would become due after the expiration dates.

Illinois

DeKoven v. Plaza Assocs., 2009 WL 901369 (N.D. Ill. Mar. 31, 2009). Expert's survey on the effect of the offer on the least sophisticated consumer was stricken as not complying with *Daubert* standards. "Unfortunately, until debtors challenging dunning letters as misleading or deceptive produce survey evidence that comports with the principles of professional survey research, better-equipped fact finders—i.e., juries—will not have the chance to judge the deceptiveness of these letters." Settlement offer of 65% of the debt valid for a period of thirty-five days was not facially confusing or misleading just because defendant had authority to settle for 60%.

Gully v. Arrow Fin. Servs., L.L.C., 2006 WL 3486815 (N.D. Ill. Dec. 1, 2006). The court granted the defendant summary judgment and rejected the plaintiff's *Goswami* claim that the defendant had falsely represented its settlement authority in offering a reduced, single-payment settlement opportunity that was supposedly available until a date certain because the letters did not represent that no future settlement offers would be available.

Jackson v. Midland Credit Mgmt., Inc., 445 F. Supp. 2d 1015 (N.D. Ill. 2006). The collector's offer of a thirty-day 50% "settlement opportunity" was not false or deceptive since "the letter in this case does not have the explicit language of a one time only offer" that would be unlawful pursuant to the *Goswami* precedent.

Jackson v. National Action Fin. Servs., Inc., 441 F. Supp. 2d 877 (N.D. Ill. 2006), *aff'd sub nom. Evory v. RJM Acquisitions Funding, Inc.*, 505 F.3d 769 (7th Cir. 2007). The court granted the defendant summary judgment, holding that its offer to settle a debt for a percentage and that stated that "in order to take advantage of this offer, your payment must be received in our office" by a specific date, was not false or deceptive, even though the defendant was always willing to settle debts for the percentage cited in the letters even if payment was made after the specified date and even would later accept smaller offers, since the purported deadline did not exclude such later compromises and the dun did not state a false, explicit "one-time-only offer" of the type that violates the FDCPA.

Nichols v. Northland Groups, Inc., 2006 WL 897867 (N.D. Ill. Mar. 31, 2006). The court found that Northland's settlement offer would mislead and confuse the unsophisticated consumer.

Kubert v. Aid Assocs., 2006 WL 328239 (N.D. Ill. Feb. 9, 2006). Defendant's motion for judgment on the pleadings was granted where its settlement offer stated the offer would be valid for thirty-five days. Without evidence to the contrary, the offer could not be reasonably interpreted to indicate that the offer did not extended beyond the thirty-five days.

Hernandez v. AFNI, Inc., 428 F. Supp. 2d 776 (N.D. Ill. 2006). The collector's letter stating that it would accept a payment of about 50% of the debt to settle the debt if it was received by a specified date was not deceptive even if the collector regularly accepted such payments after the specified date as full settlement of the debt. The court reached that result in part by viewing the collection letter as making an offer that expired by its literal terms after the deadline

and the consumer's payment after the deadline as a counteroffer. It also distinguished other collection letters in which the offer was cast as a one time only offer. The court did not consider that the letter was a misrepresentation of the debt collector's settlement policy.

Gully v. Van Ru Credit Corp., 381 F. Supp. 2d 766 (N.D. Ill. 2005). The debt collector's discounted settlement offer, which stated that it would be revoked if payment was not received by a date certain but which the consumer alleged would still be available after that date, was not a misrepresentation since the offer was not falsely couched as a "one-time offer" or otherwise presented as a settlement that would not be available at some other time in the future.

Jackson v. National Action Fin. Servs., Inc., 227 F.D.R. 184 (N.D. Ill. 2005). An FDCPA class was certified claiming that the debt collector confused and misled the unsophisticated consumer by offering to settle for approximately 75% of the debt and shortly after the time in which to accept the offer expired sent the consumer another offer to settle at approximately 50% of the balance.

Jones v. Risk Mgmt. Alternatives, Inc., 2003 WL 21654365 (N.D. Ill. July 11, 2003). In an FDCPA challenge to a collector's limited time offer letter alleging that repeated identical letters to consumer offering alleged "one time" settlement offer for limited time violated § 1692(e), the court certified a class action pursuant to Rule 23(a) and (b)(3).

Pleasant v. Risk Mgmt. Alternatives, Inc., 2003 WL 164227 (N.D. Ill. Jan. 23, 2003). Plaintiff's complaint alleges that the collection agency's "one time" settlement offer of 1/2 the debt if paid in a few weeks, was not, in fact, a "one time" offer at all stating a claim under § 1692e.

Indiana

Headen v. Asset Acceptance, L.L.C., 2006 WL 839482 (S.D. Ind. Mar. 28, 2006). The court rejected the plaintiff's contention that a limited-time settlement offer would mislead a debtor where the collector would in fact be willing to extend the deadline or even thereafter settle for less than the initial offer. Following its dismissal with leave to amend in *Headen v. Asset Acceptance, L.L.C.*, 383 F. Supp. 2d 1097 (S.D. Ind. 2005), the court now dismissed with prejudice plaintiffs' amended complaint that alleged survey evidence to support the claim that the collector's limited-time offer was understood by survey respondents to actually offer a false "one time only" offer as prohibited by *Goswami*. The court held that the survey questions were defective and in any event "Congress did not intend to regulate settlement negotiations by requiring a debt collector to make its first offer its best and final offer."

Headen v. Asset Acceptance, L.L.C., 383 F. Supp. 2d 1097 (S.D. Ind. 2005). Judgment on the pleadings was granted for the debt collector because its collection letter was not false or deceptive when it offered an opportunity to settle the debt by payment of a reduced amount by a date certain but did not indicate that it was a one time only offer. "A debt collector is free to make offers of limited duration, to terminate them at the given date, and then to make a new offer of similar or even identical terms effective immediately."

New York

Reade-Alvarez v. Eltman, Eltman & Cooper, P.C., 369 F. Supp. 2d 353 (E.D.N.Y. 2005). Debt collector's later renewal of an expired offer of a reduced payment plan did not, by itself, constitute a violation of the FDCPA. Collector's motion to dismiss was granted as to FDCPA claims that letters were false, deceptive or misleading, the unauthorized practice of law, and that the offer to settle would expire in ten days.

Kahen-Kashani v. National Action Fin. Servs., Inc., 2004 WL 2126707 (W.D.N.Y. Sept. 21, 2004). "Unlike the letter in *Goswami*, the letters sent by the defendant did not communicate that this was a one-time, take-it-or-leave-it offer. In fact, they explicitly communicated that it may be possible to extend the offer under certain circumstances."

Pujol v. Universal Fid. Corp., 2004 WL 1278163 (E.D.N.Y. June 9, 2004). Because the plaintiff failed to controvert the collector's affidavit confirming that the offer in its dun that a single payment by a date certain of 80% of the amount owing would extinguish the debt, the court rejected the plaintiff's unexplained contention that the offer was deceptive.

Pennsylvania

Kiliszek v. Nelson, Watson & Assocs., L.L.C., 2006 WL 335788 (M.D. Pa. Feb. 14, 2006). A deadline in the collection letter containing a settlement offer did not imply that the offer was a one time only offer, and this FDCPA claim was dismissed.

Buzoiu v. Risk Mgmt. Alternatives, Inc., 2003 WL 22938052 (E.D. Pa. Sept. 15, 2003). A settlement offer with a stated deadline by which the consumer must accept could be construed by the least sophisticated consumer as one-time offer that would then expire, and therefore the allegation that the collector in fact would accept the same terms at a later date stated a claim for engaging in deceptive or false collection representations.

King v. Arrow Fin. Servs., L.L.C., 2003 WL 21780973 (E.D. Pa. July 31, 2003). An offer of settlement for 40% of its claim if full payment was received by a specific date was not deceptive because the collection agency offered to accept the same settlement later as an unsophisticated consumer would understand the first offer as a settlement position that could be renewed.

Texas

Prophet v. Myers, 645 F. Supp. 2d 614 (S.D. Tex. 2008). Settlement offers must accurately reflect the terms a debt collector is authorized by the creditor to make.

Goswami v. Am. Collections Enter., Inc., 280 F. Supp. 2d 624 (S.D. Tex. 2003). It was not deceptive to offer to accept 70% of the debt for a limited thirty-day period, when that was a negotiating position and the creditor allowed the collector to accept as little as 50% for more than the thirty-day period. A letter titled, "Settlement Offer & Amnesty Period," did not imply that nonpayment would result in criminal or other government prosecution.

Washington

McLain v. Gordon, 2010 WL 3340528 (W.D. Wash. Aug. 24, 2010). A collector may negotiate a settlement for less than the amount owed.

K.2.4.17 Time-Barred Debts

Avery v. First Resolution Mgmt., Corp., 568 F.3d 1018 (9th Cir. 2009). The debt collector did not file a time-barred debt, since it was filed within the Oregon statute of limitations. The shorter New Hampshire period of limitations prescribed by the contract was applicable under Oregon choice of law rules until the N.H. law was determined to be tolled as to an Oregon consumer, in which case Oregon law reverted to its own, longer statute of limitations.

Freyermuth v. Credit Bureau Servs., Inc., 248 F.3d 767 (8th Cir. 2001). Effort to collect time-barred checks did not violate the FDCPA when it was not accompanied by a threat of suit.

Alabama

Kimber v. Fed. Fin. Corp., 668 F. Supp. 1480 (M.D. Ala. 1987). Filing a time-barred suit when the collector knew of no tolling of the statute of limitations was unconscionable and a deceptive misrepresentation of the legal status of the debt, implying the collector would prevail.

Arkansas

Born v. Hosto & Buchan, P.L.L.C., 2010 WL 2431063 (Ark. June 17, 2010). While bringing or threatening to bring litigation outside the applicable statute of limitations can give rise to a cause of action under the FDCPA, there was no viable claim in this case because the statute of limitations had not run.

California

Janti v. Encore Capital Group, Inc., 2010 WL 3058260 (S.D. Cal. Aug. 3, 2010). The complaint adequately alleged that the legal status of the consumer's debt was falsely represented by threatening suit on a debt that was time barred. Moreover, the complaint alleged that one of the defendants sent the consumer a letter indicating that it "was reporting the time-barred debt to credit reporting companies."

Abels v. JBC Legal Group, P.C., 428 F. Supp. 2d 1023 (N.D. Cal. 2005). Court dismissed claim that attorney letterhead implicitly threatened suit on a time-barred debt. Instead, court viewed letter "as informational in providing a prudential reminder that the debtor may be in violation of a particular civil code provision and that the penalties for such a violation could be serious."

Mello v. Great Seneca Fin. Corp., 526 F. Supp. 2d 1020 (C.D. Cal. 2007). Denied defendant collection lawyer's motion to dismiss finding although anti-SLAPP law could apply, plaintiff showed a reasonable prospect of success on his claim that suit was filed beyond the statute of limitations.

Connecticut

Lindbergh v. Transworld Sys., Inc., 846 F. Supp. 175 (D. Conn. 1994). When consumer failed to respond to the debt collector's proper validation notice within thirty days and the consumer could not show that the debt collector was otherwise aware that the collection of the debt was barred by a state statute of limitations, the debt collector was not liable for false representations or unfair collection practices under §§ 1692e(2)(A) or 1692f for its attempt to collect a debt which was barred by the statute of limitations.

Florida

Knighten v. Palisades Collections, L.L.C., 2010 WL 2696768 (S.D. Fla. July 6, 2010). A lawyer who files a lawsuit beyond the statute of limitations violates the FDCPA. The claim that Palisades filed suit on a time-barred debt failed where Palisades never owned the debt and its law firm sued in the collector's name without its knowledge or consent. A lawyer violated numerous provisions of the FDCPA by filing a time-barred lawsuit for a party that lacked standing.

Pincus v. Law Offices of Erskine & Fleisher, 617 F. Supp. 2d 1265 (S.D. Fla. 2009). The collection attorney defendants whose underlying state court collection suit was dismissed as barred by the statute of limitations were now collaterally estopped in this FDCPA affirmative suit from re-litigating that issue and from now arguing that the collection suit was not time barred.

Gaisser v. Portfolio Recovery Assocs., L.L.C., 571 F. Supp. 2d 1273 (S.D. Fla. 2008). The consumer stated a claim for the defendants' unlawful filing of suit on a time-barred debt because New Hampshire's shortened statute of limitations applied as a result of the underlying contract's choice of law provision; the court's rejected *Avery v. First Resolution Mgmt. Corp.*, 2007 WL 1560653 (D. Or. May 25, 2007), that had held that N.H. law tolled the statute of limitations because of the consumer's absence from the state.

McCorriston v. L.W.T., Inc., 536 F. Supp. 2d 1268 (M.D. Fla. 2008). Credit card agreement that specified that Delaware law applied to substantive matters, including the statute of limitations, controlled the time frame within which the debt collector may initiate the collection action. Although the debt collector was wrong in its choice of the applicable statute of limitations within which to bring its collection action, the debt collector's procedures were "reasonably adapted" to prevent a legal error and established a bona fide error defense pursuant to § 1692k(c).

Pack v. Unifund CCR Partners, G.P., 2008 WL 686800 (M.D. Fla. Mar. 13, 2008). The consumer presented no evidence to rebut the debt buyer's testimony that the collection case was filed within the applicable statute of limitations by it as the lawful owner of the debt to collect the accurate and actual amount owed.

Illinois

Herkert v. MRC Receivables Corp., 655 F. Supp. 2d 870 (N.D. Ill. 2009). Filing or threatening to file suits to collect a credit card debt, time-barred under the Illinois statute of limitations for unwritten contracts, violates the FDCPA.

Davis v. World Credit Fund I, L.L.C., 543 F. Supp. 2d 953 (N.D. Ill. 2008). Summary judgment for the defendant on plaintiff's claim that it violated §§ 1692e(2)(A) and 1692f(1) by suing plaintiff on a time-barred debt, since plaintiff had made a partial payment that tolled the statute under state law and rendered the collection suit timely.

Ramirez v. Palisades Collection L.L.C., 2008 WL 2512679 (N.D. Ill. June 23, 2008). The court certified the class based on the collector's alleged FDCPA violation of suing consumers in state court more than five years after last payment or charge-off in cases where the collector subjected itself to the state's shortened five-year statute of limitations as a consequence of failing to attach a copy of the underlying contract to its collection complaints. Five-year statute of limitations for unwritten contracts, rather than ten-year statute for written contracts, applied to credit card account. Because defendant filed plainly time-barred suits against unwitting consumers, it is subject to liability under §§ 1692e and 1692f.

Murray v. CCB Credit Servs., Inc., 2004 WL 2943656 (N.D. Ill. Dec. 15, 2004). Debt collector's mere dunning of the consumer in an attempt to collect a time-barred debt did not violate the FDCPA since the running of the statute of limitations would only bar defendant from collecting through the courts, but it does not extinguish plaintiff's debt or the right to seek payment without the use or threat to use litigation.

Weniger v. Arrow Fin. Servs. L.L.C., 2004 WL 2609192 (N.D. Ill. Nov. 17, 2004). Since defendants did not produce a written contract (which would be subject to a ten-year statute of limitations), the five-year statute for oral contracts precluded dismissal of the FDCPA claim that the debt was time barred.

Griffith v. Capital One Bank, 2001 U.S. Dist. LEXIS 21953 (S.D. Ill. July 23, 2001). Relying on *Freyermuth v. Credit Bureau Servs., Inc.*, 248 F.3d 767 (8th Cir. 2001), the court held that there must be a threat of suit before collection of a time-barred debt violates the FDCPA. The reporting of the time-barred claim to a credit reporting agency was not deceptive, as the debt was still owed, although the consumer had a defense to its collection in court.

Stepney v. Outsourcing Solutions, Inc., 1997 WL 722972 (N.D. Ill. Nov. 13, 1997). Collector's knowing attempts to collect time-barred debts violated the FDCPA.

Indiana

Miller v. Javitch, Block & Rathbone, L.L.P., 397 F. Supp. 2d 991 (N.D. Ind. 2005). Court dismissed *pro se*'s complaint that state court collection suit was time barred because the statute of limitations is procedural and the applicable statute of limitations had not run in the state where the consumer currently resided and was sued. Court rejected *pro se*'s claim that debt buyer's records were hearsay and did not show it owned the debt, because *pro se* had the burden to show lack of ownership on his summary judgment motion.

Simmons v. Miller, 970 F. Supp. 661 (S.D. Ind. 1997). There was no intentional violation of §§ 1692d, 1692e, 1692e(2)(A), or 1692f(1) where a claim on an NSF check was filed more than three years but less than six years after the check was written and it was not clear that a six year rather than three year statute of limitations applied.

Maryland

Wallace v. Capital One Bank, 168 F. Supp. 2d 526 (D. Md. 2001). A debt collector's contact with a debtor about a time-barred bad debt was not necessarily an affirmative deceptive representation that the debt collector could sue on the debt. Unless it is alleged that a debt collector has engaged in a course of conduct that tricks a debtor into waiving his legal right to assert a statute of limitations defense, no violation of the FDCPA occurred merely because a debt validation notice silent on the time-bar issue was sent to the debtor.

Spencer v. Hendersen-Webb, 81 F. Supp. 2d 582 (D. Md. 1999). Representing that the debt could be collected for twelve years when it was not under seal and subject to a three-year statute of limitations violated §§ 1692e(2)(A) and 1692f(1).

Michigan

Dunaway v. JBC & Assocs., Inc., 2005 WL 1529574 (E.D. Mich. June 20, 2005). The uncontroverted fact that the debt collector called the consumer's employer and falsely informed him that a civil lawsuit had been filed and that criminal charges were pending against the consumer for a dishonored check on which both the civil and criminal statute of limitations had expired established the collector's liability as a matter of law for violating §§ 1692b, 1692c, and 1692e.

Minnesota

Wald v. Morris, Carlson, & Hoelscher, P.A., 2010 WL 4736829 (D. Minn. Nov. 16, 2010). A debt collector who threatened to sue the consumer on time-barred debt violated §§ 1692e(2)(A), (5), and (10), and 1692f.

Montana

McCollough v. Johnson, Rodenberg & Lauinger, 610 F. Supp. 2d 1247 (D. Mont. 2009). A debt collector violated the FDCPA by using the courts to attempt to collect a time-barred debt. While the debt collector's use of discovery in a collection action is not a per se violation of the FDCPA, here the request for admission to admit that a payment was made was served when the debt collector's records showed the payment was not made. The use of the judicial process against a *pro se* defendant, in order to avoid a statute of limitations defense, collecting on a time-barred debt was an abusive, unfair, and unconscionable practice in violation of the FDCPA. The debt collector's failure to move to set aside the underlying state court default judgment, after a summary judgment ruling that the underlying state court action violated the FDCPA because it was time barred, constituted an additional FDCPA violation.

New Jersey

Bodine v. First Nat'l Collection Bureau, Inc., 2010 WL 5149847 (D.N.J. Dec. 13, 2010). An effort to collect a time-barred debt with no threat of suit does not violate the FDCPA. Where nothing in the pleadings suggested that the defendant attempted or threatened to commence an action to recover the debt, the issue of the statute of limitations was irrelevant.

Jackson v. Midland Funding, L.L.C., 2010 WL 5036486 (D.N.J. Dec. 10, 2010). Granted summary judgment for the consumer on a *Kimber* violation, filing a collection suit in state court that was barred by the applicable statute of limitations.

New Mexico

Shorty v. Capital One Bank, 90 F. Supp. 2d 1330 (D.N.M. 2000). Sending a legally sufficient debt validation notice to a debtor without notifying the debtor that the debt was time-barred by the statute of limitations did not violate § 1692e(2)(A), misrepresenting the status of the debt. It would be a violation to threaten suit on a time-barred debt.

Martinez v. Albuquerque Collection Servs., 867 F. Supp. 1495 (D.N.M. 1994). Attempts to collect time-barred accounts also violated the FDCPA.

New York

James v. Merchants & Prof'ls, Inc., 2010 WL 785803 (E.D.N.Y. Mar. 8, 2010). Despite its default, judgment entered for defendant since sending a collection letter without being licensed by the city as a debt collector does not violate the FDCPA.

Larsen v. JBC Legal Group, P.C., 533 F. Supp. 2d 290 (E.D.N.Y. 2008). Threats to sue on a time-barred check violated were deceptive.

North Dakota

Jackson v. Financial Recovery Servs., Inc., 2006 WL 1234891 (D.N.D. May 3, 2006). Since debt was not stale, collection letters were not an effort to deceive consumer into renewing time-barred debt.

Ohio

Dudek v. Thomas & Thomas Attys. & Counselors at Law, L.L.C., 702 F. Supp. 2d 826 (N.D. Ohio 2010). Whether a debt is time barred is directly related to the status of the debt within § 1692e(2)(A). Since statute of limitations borrowing statute did not apply retroactively, and statute of limitations is procedural, state court case was timely within Ohio's six or fifteen year statutes.

Wright v. Asset Acceptance Corp., 1999 U.S. Dist. LEXIS 20675 (S.D. Ohio Dec. 30, 1999). Where consumer did not show that his debt was time barred or that the limitations period would be extended, complaint did not state a § 1692e violation by alleging that collector's letter asked debtor to acknowledge debt. The least sophisticated consumer standing in the shoes of plaintiff could not have inadvertently revived a time-barred debt that was not time barred.

Oregon

Daley v. A & S Collection Assocs., Inc., 2010 WL 2326256 (D. Or. June 7, 2010). Disputed factual issues precluded summary judgment on the claim that the collector unlawfully threatened to sue on a time-barred debt.

Pennsylvania

Martsolf v. JBC Legal Group, P.C., 2008 WL 275719 (M.D. Pa. Jan. 30, 2008). Summary judgment granted to the consumer on the *Kimber* violation: "JBC's letter threatens litigation, and sending it to [the consumer] after expiration of the limitations period violated the FDCPA."

Tennessee

Spangler v. Conrad, 2010 WL 2389481 (E.D. Tenn. June 9, 2010). The defendant did not file a time-barred collection suit since under applicable state law the consumer's intervening partial payment restarted the statute of limitations.

Utah

Reed v. AFNI, Inc., 2011 WL 112430 (D. Utah Jan. 13, 2011). A debt collector is permitted to collect on a debt after the statute of limitations has expired provided that those efforts do not include the threat or actual filing of a lawsuit.

K.2.4.18 Deceptive Statements About Urgency

Romine v. Diversified Collection Servs., Inc., 155 F.3d 1142 (9th Cir. 1998). The use of Western Union telegrams conveyed a false sense of urgency in collection of the debt.

Connecticut

Shrestha v. State Credit Adjustment Bureau, Inc., 117 F. Supp. 2d 142 (D. Conn. 2000). Collection agency's unopposed assertion that it did not decide on, manage, direct or control litigation against the debtor warranted summary judgment in favor of the collector on an unauthorized practice of law claim.

Illinois

Nelson-McGourty v. L & P Fin. Adjusters Inc., 2010 WL 3190711 (N.D. Ill. Aug. 12, 2010). Following a bench trial, the court credited the testimony of the collector and discredited the testimony of the consumer to conclude that the collector did not create a false sense of urgency during the single telephone collection call at issue.

New Hampshire

Silva v. Nat'l Telewire Corp., 2000 U.S. Dist. LEXIS 13986 (D.N.H. Sept. 22, 2000). Class of upwards of 300 certified on letter which allegedly created false sense of urgency.

New York

Ohlson v. The Cadle Co., 2008 WL 4516233 (E.D.N.Y. Sept. 30, 2008). Court rejected claim of false sense of urgency/false deadline. The letter did not set a deadline for payment; rather it set a date to contact the defendant. Indeed, it even stated a willingness to discuss a reasonable payment arrangement. The language suggested, even to the least sophisticated consumer that there is "potential for negotiation."

Ohio

Powell v. Computer Credit, Inc., 975 F. Supp. 1034 (S.D. Ohio 1997), *aff'd*, 1998 U.S. App. LEXIS 26797 (6th Cir. Oct. 15, 1998). Letter stating that creditor required "immediate payment" did not create a false sense of urgency. "FINAL NOTICE" letter did not create a false sense of urgency, did not misrepresent number of previous attempts to collect the debt, and did not falsely threaten legal action.

Lewis v. ABC Bus. Servs., Inc., 911 F. Supp. 290 (S.D. Ohio 1996), *aff'd*, 135 F.3d 389 (6th Cir. 1998). Statements that the account was undergoing "final review" and "It is important that arrangements be made as soon as possible" did not convey a false sense of urgency. The false statement that the account was "in the office of M. Hall" for final review did not violate § 1692e(10), as it was the permissible use of a pseudonym.

Virginia

Creighton v. Emporia Credit Serv., Inc., 981 F. Supp. 411 (E.D. Va. 1997). A demand for payment in full upon receipt of dun or else debt would be reported on the consumer's credit report contradicted the validation notice as a matter of law and was a false representation of urgency where collector's policy was not to report a debt to a credit reporting agency for sixty days.

K.2.4.19 State Required Notices

White v. Goodman, 200 F.3d 1016 (7th Cir. 2000). A dunning letter that contained the "Colorado" notice did not imply that nonresidents of Colorado did not have similar rights and was, therefore, not deceptive.

California

Luna v. Alliance One Receivables Mgmt., Inc., 2006 WL 357823 (N.D. Cal. Feb. 16, 2006). Defendant's motion to dismiss was granted because the FDCPA does not require debt collectors to send the notice required by the California statute. The letter without the statement was not false or abusive.

Illinois

Withers v. Equifax Risk Mgmt. Servs., 40 F. Supp. 2d 978 (N.D. Ill. 1999). The use of specific "Massachusetts" and "Colorado" notices in a letter to an Illinois consumer was misleading and unfair because it incorrectly implied that those rights were not available to the Illinois consumer.

Farley v. Diversified Collection Servs., 1999 U.S. Dist. LEXIS 16174 (N.D. Ill. Sept. 28, 1999). Language that suggested that only Colorado residents had the right to require a collector to cease communications was a misrepresentation in violation of § 1692e.

Jenkins v. Union Corp., 999 F. Supp. 1120 (N.D. Ill. 1998). Presenting the disclosures required by Colorado law similar to § 1692c(c)'s cease communication provision under the heading "Colorado" was misleading and therefore violated the FDCPA by suggesting that the cease communication rights were available only to Colorado residents.

Wisconsin

Borcherding-Dittloff v. Transworld Sys., Inc., 58 F. Supp. 2d 1006 (W.D. Wis. 1999). The "Colorado" notice violated § 1692e absent an explanatory phrase, such as: "We are required under state law to notify consumers of the following rights. This list does not contain a complete list of the rights consumers have under state and federal law." Transworld's argument that no harm was done was unavailing because the FDCPA is a strict liability statute. Transworld had no bona fide error defense.

K.2.4.20 Other Deceptive Acts

Ruth v. Triumph P'ships, 577 F.3d 790 (7th Cir. 2009). A privacy notice that stated "to the extent permitted by law, we may collect and/or share all of the information we obtained in servicing your account" violated § 1692e(5) and (10) when it was sent in the envelope containing a collection letter as it was sent "in connection with" the collection of a debt.

Thomasson v. GC Servs. Ltd. P'ship, 321 Fed. Appx. 557 (9th Cir. 2008). Summary judgment for the defendant reversed where the evidence showed that the collection company's monitoring—but not recording—the consumers' telephone calls without notification was a deceptive practice in violation of § 1692e(10):

> [Plaintiffs] presented evidence that knew that consumers were more likely to discontinue their telephone calls with before revealing information about themselves and their debts if they were notified that their calls were being, or could be, monitored. From their evidence, the [plaintiffs] argue that purposefully failed to notify debtors that their calls were being, or could be, monitored in order to "obtain information concerning a consumer." Taking the evidence in the light most favorable to the [plaintiffs], we conclude that they have raised a factual dispute as to whether violated § 1692e.

Van v. Grant & Weber, 308 Fed. Appx. 46 (9th Cir. 2008). Collection letter containing reminder of a state law requiring debtors to provide new contact information, while warning debtors that the information will be used for purposes of debt collection, did not conflict with §§ 1692e, 1692f, 1692g.

Barnes v. Advanced Call Ctr. Techs., L.L.C., 493 F.3d 838 (7th Cir. 2007). Debt collector's statement that upon payment of the "Current Amount Due" all collection activity will be stopped was not a false statement in violation of § 1692e.

McMillan v. Collection Prof'ls Inc., 455 F.3d 754 (7th Cir. 2006). Consumer stated a claim for violating § 1692e where the dun to collect a dishonored check stated, "YOU ARE EITHER HONEST OR DISHONEST YOU CANNOT BE BOTH," thus falsely implying that the consumer was dishonest in not paying the debt, when there was no evidence that the alleged nonpayment resulted from dishonesty and to the contrary were many conceivable honest explanations for the failure of the check to clear and the consumer not to pay the returned check. Though the statement, "YOU ARE EITHER HONEST OR DISHONEST YOU CANNOT BE BOTH," may be literally true, it also may be understood by an unsophisticated consumer to falsely imply that the debtor committed a crime or other conduct in order to disgrace him or her, and thus the complaint stated a claim for violating § 1692e(7).

Volden v. Innovative Fin. Sys., Inc., 440 F.3d 947 (8th Cir. 2006). Though IFS, by the terms of the contract, made a false representation, that representation was made to a third party, not to the consumer. The consumer argues that the "in connection with" language in § 1692e includes false representation made to others while in the process of collecting a debt. But breaching the contract with the third party would not violate any legislative enactment and therefore does not violate the FDCPA.

Carlson v. First Revenue Assurance, 359 F.3d 1015 (8th Cir. 2004). The FDCPA was not meant to convert every violation of state debt collection law into a federal violation. "Only those collection activities that use 'any false, deceptive, or misleading representation or means,' including 'the threat to take any action that cannot

illegally be taken' under state law, will also constituted FDCPA violations."

Neff v. Capital Acquisitions & Mgmt. Co., 352 F.3d 1118 (7th Cir. 2003). While purchasers of defaulted credit card accounts were "debt collectors," the FDCPA claim based on a nonexistent TILA violation was dismissed. Purchasers of defaulted credit card accounts who charged interest to the card holder but extended no credit privileges were not "creditors" subject to TILA and were not required to send periodic credit card statements.

Heard v. Bonneville Billing & Collections, 216 F.3d 1087 (10th Cir. June 26, 2000) (unpublished) (text at 2000 U.S. App. LEXIS 14625). A check collector violated the FDCPA and UDAP by persisting to collect on bad checks against the check writer's mother after the collector was informed that she was not the signer nor any longer on the joint account. The consumer's mother failed to show harm to herself and therefore lacked standing to assert the collector's receiving part of its attorney fee as FDCPA or UDAP claim based on ethical rules prohibiting a lawyer from splitting a fee with a nonlawyer.

Goldberg v. Transworld Sys., Inc., 164 F.3d 617 (2d Cir. 1998) (text at 1998 WL 650793). The language "grace period about to expire" does not suggest to the least sophisticated consumer that he has less than thirty days to dispute the debt. In addition, stating that the consumer "may eliminate the possibility of additional costs" is "no threat whatsoever, false or otherwise."

Schnitzspahn v. F.A.B., Inc., 156 F.3d 1232 (6th Cir. 1998) (unpublished) (text at 1998 WL 466109). The court summarily found no FDCPA violations. The collector did not misrepresent the character or amount of the debt, it did not threaten to take any action prohibited by law or that it did not intend to take, nor did it file a lawsuit that did not contain proper disclosures.

Lewis v. ACB Bus. Servs., Inc., 135 F.3d 389 (6th Cir. 1998). The collection agency's use of the unassigned alias or office name "M. Hall" would not mislead the least sophisticated debtor regarding the amount of the debt, the consequences of nonpayment, or the rights of the debtor and does not violate the FDCPA.

Bentley v. Great Lakes Collection Bureau, 6 F.3d 60 (2d Cir. 1993). Collection letter's false statement that the collector had attempted to contact the consumer and that the debt had been referred to someone's desk where a decision would be made violated the Act by implying that personal attention was being given to the debt when in fact it was not.

Dutton v. Wolpoff & Abramson, 5 F.3d 649 (3d Cir. 1993). Law firm's letter which states "we will release all liens if you pay this" creates a question for the jury as to whether such a statement is misleading in violation of § 1692e(10) when no liens existed.

Alabama

Sparks v. Phillips & Cohen Assocs., Ltd., 641 F. Supp. 2d 1234 (S.D. Ala. 2008). A statement that the decedent debtor's estate was subject to liquidation to pay her debts did not violate §§ 1692e(2) or 1692e(10): "[The debt collector] never told [decedent's daughter] that defendant would force a sale of the house, that it intended to do so, or the like. Instead, [the debt collector] merely stated that *could* force a sale of the house. That innocuous statement is not violative of § 1692e(2) or § 1692e(10) because it is not false but is a statement of defendant's legal rights under Alabama law. Entry of summary judgment in defendant's favor is therefore warranted as to those claims."

Arizona

Grismore v. United Recovery Sys., L.P., 2006 WL 2246359 (D. Ariz. Aug. 3, 2006). Since the evidence established that the defendant debt collector pulled the consumer's credit report for only the permissible and stated purpose of collecting the subject debt, the court granted the defendant summary judgment on the *pro se* plaintiff's claim that the debt collector had violated § 1692e(10) by using false pretenses to procure the credit report. The court granted the defendant summary judgment since the *pro se* plaintiff failed to present any evidence to support the allegation that defendant debt collector misrepresented itself as a "holder" or "holder in due course."

California

Durham v. Continental Cent. Credit, 2009 WL 3416114 (S.D. Cal. Oct. 20, 2009). Where the consumer had agreed to the payment of a collection fee, the collector's addition of a 40% collection fee to the principal did not violate § 1692e. A second collection letter which did not reiterate the consumer's right to dispute the debt sent within the thirty-day validation period demanding immediate payment violated § 1692g.

Perez v. EMC Mortgage Corp., 2009 WL 702825 (N.D. Cal. Mar. 17, 2009). Dismissed the consumer's FDCPA claims alleging that the defendant was not legally entitled to initiate foreclosure and had falsely represented its right to do so, since the public record (of which the court took judicial notice) showed that a different entity from the defendant initiated the foreclosure and "was a proper party to take such action."

Hernandez v. California Reconveyance Co., 2009 WL 464462 (E.D. Cal. Feb. 24, 2009). Where the complaint about a foreclosure on plaintiff's home lacked allegations of false or misleading representations to violate § 1692e, defendant's Rule 12(b)(6) motion to dismiss was granted without prejudice.

Sicairos v. NDEX West, L.L.C., 2009 WL 385855 (S.D. Cal. Feb. 13, 2009). Since California deed of trust foreclosure process did not require the filing of the original note, that failure did not violate the FDCPA.

Cruz v. MRC Receivables Corp., 563 F. Supp. 2d 1092 (N.D. Cal. 2008). Use of name and title of senior vice president on form collection letters (which he had read and approved) was not misleading or deceptive nor unfair or unconscionable in violation of §§ 1692e or 1692f.

Voris v. Resurgent Capital Servs., L.P., 494 F. Supp. 2d 1156 (S.D. Cal. 2007). Whether the collection letter which began with a "preapproved" credit card solicitation would induce the least sophisticated consumer to discard it as junk mail and whether this constitutes a false, deceptive, or misleading means to collect a debt in violation of § 1692e and 1692e(10) was a question of fact to be determined by the jury.

Khosroabadi v. North Shore Agency, 439 F. Supp. 2d 1118 (S.D. Cal. 2006). The debt collector's failure to include in its letter the notice required by the California debt collection statute was not an unfair or deceptive method of debt collection.

Hapin v. Arrow Fin. Servs., 428 F. Supp. 2d 1057 (N.D. Cal. 2006). Court dismissed claim that use of words "customer" and "account representative" could deceive the least sophisticated consumer about the collection nature of the letter. Court dismissed claim that defendant's use of the terminology "regain your financial future" was misleading or abusive.

Johnson v. Phillips & Cohen Assocs., Ltd., 2006 WL 2355340 (N.D. Cal. Aug. 15, 2006). The court dismissed the FDCPA claim based on the collector's failure to provide a notice required by state law since such a violation of state law "does not automatically trigger a violation of the federal FDCPA" and the resulting omission was not unfair, deceptive, or misleading.

Hosseinzadeh v. M.R.S. Assocs., Inc., 387 F. Supp. 2d 1104 (C.D. Cal. 2005). The content and context of a series of six telephone messages from the debt collector left on the consumer's answering machine made the issue of whether the messages were harassing, unfair, or deceptive a question of fact for the jury. Whether the debt collector's use of aliases constituted a false representation or deceptive means to collect or attempt to collect a debt was a question of fact for the fact finder.

Wan v. Commercial Recovery Sys., Inc., 369 F. Supp. 2d 1158 (N.D. Cal. 2005). The communication language in the collector's letter to the consumer that "[i]f you notify us in writing to stop contacting you by telephone at your residence or place of employment, no further contact will be made" did not violate § 1692e or § 1692c(a)(1).

Hipolito v. Alliance Receivables Mgmt., Inc., 2005 WL 1662137 (N.D. Cal. July 15, 2005). The statement in the initial dun to "pay in full to [stop] all collection activity" did not unlawfully suggest to the least sophisticated consumer that payment was the only method to stop subsequent collection. The court dismissed for failure to state a claim the allegation that the statement that the "debt may remain open on your credit report for up to seven years" unlawfully misrepresented the law or was an illegal threat to report to a credit bureau, holding instead that the statement was an accurate representation of both law and fact that, without more, constituted no threat at all.

Forsberg v. Fidelity Nat'l Credit Servs., 2004 U.S. Dist. LEXIS 7622 (S.D. Cal. Feb. 25, 2004). Claim stated for misrepresenting that numerous other communications had occurred between the collection agency and the consumer; misrepresentation would create a false sense of urgency. FDCPA claim stated against collection agency for representing a debt was owed that had been discharged in bankruptcy.

Baker v. Citibank N.A., 13 F. Supp. 2d 1037 (S.D. Cal. 1998). Collection letter's statement that "We have tried repeatedly to talk to you but no avail" was false and misleading even though the collector had called the wrong telephone number. Material issues of disputed fact existed about the content of telephone calls, and summary judgment could not be granted.

Connecticut

Chiverton v. Fed. Fin. Group, Inc., 399 F. Supp. 2d 96 (D. Conn.

2005). The false threat of arrest to an elderly consumer was deceptive.

Madonna v. Acad. Collection Serv., Inc., 1997 WL 530101 (D. Conn. Aug. 12, 1997). A threat to report an unpaid account to the creditor as the consumer's refusal to cooperate was not false or deceptive since the failure to pay was in fact a refusal to cooperate. Recital of lawful remedies that might be pursued after a judgment was not false or deceptive.

Gaetano v. Payco, Inc., 774 F. Supp. 1404 (D. Conn. 1990). It was not deceptive for a collector to state "an investigation has disclosed that you are employed" when only information from the creditor indicated the consumer was employed and the collector determined only that the employer's phone was disconnected. The collector did not misrepresent its authority to collect when only its parent was authorized by the creditor to collect since no consumer would be misled.

Woolfolk v. Rubin, 1989 U.S. Dist. LEXIS 19106 (D. Conn. Nov. 9, 1989). Collector is liable for sending deceptive letters, even though they were sent to the consumer's attorney rather than directly to the consumer.

Ocwen Fed. Bank, F.S.B. v. Waller, 2005 WL 648049 (Conn. Super. Ct. Feb. 14, 2005). The court held that an earlier forbearance agreement between the consumer and the mortgagee contained no obligation that the mortgagee continue to accept late payments, and thus the *pro se* consumer's FDCPA counterclaim asserting otherwise in this foreclosure action was rejected.

Delaware

Dutton v. Wolhar, 809 F. Supp. 1130 (D. Del. 1992), *aff'd,* 5 F.3d 649 (3d Cir. 1993). Mere reallegation of violations of other sections of the FDCPA was not sufficient to constitute a violation of § 1692e(10).

Beattie v. D.M. Collections, Inc., 754 F. Supp. 383 (D. Del. 1991). Alleged violations of the more general provisions of § 1692e(10) should be tried under the more specific subsections of § 1692e which specifically address the alleged violations. A debt collector violates § 1692e(2)(A) by mistakenly dunning the wrong person when the collector fails to exercise reasonable care in ascertaining the facts, such as relying on information from the creditor or from another person on which a reasonable person would not have relied.

Florida

Hepsen v. J.C. Christensen & Assocs., Inc., 2009 WL 3064865 (M.D. Fla. Sept. 22, 2009). Defendant misrepresented the current creditor to be its client instead of disclosing the actual current creditor.

Shorr v. Am. Collection Sys., Inc., Clearinghouse No. 29,301 (S.D. Fla. 1980) (default judgment). The collector concealed toll call purposes.

Georgia

Milton v. LTD Fin. Servs., 2011 WL 291363 (S.D. Ga. Jan. 25, 2011). The court found that by ceasing all collection activity upon receiving the plaintiff's validation request, the defendant merely followed a course of action explicitly permitted by the FDCPA. Thus the plaintiff's claim that the defendant made a false representation by stating that it would validate debts upon request without having any intention to do so failed, and summary judgment was granted to the defendant.

Florence v. Nat'l Sys., 1983 U.S. Dist. LEXIS 20344 (N.D. Ga. Oct. 14, 1983). The collector violated § 1692e(7) by accusing the consumer who had already paid the debt to the collector of disregarding all good business practices.

Illinois

Bassett v. I.C. Sys., Inc., 2010 WL 2179175 (N.D. Ill. June 1, 2010). The court granted summary judgment to the defendant on the § 1692e(10) claim since the fact that the defendant called the consumer a liar, laughed at him, and accused him of trying to make excuses to get out of paying his debt when it knew that he was suffering from post-traumatic stress and bipolar disorders did not constitute a false or deceptive representation.

Miller v. Allied Interstate, Inc., 2005 WL 1520802 (N.D. Ill. June 27, 2005). A demand to collect a debt discharged in bankruptcy is considered a false collection activity pursuant to § 1692e(2)(A).

Blair v. Sherman Acquisition, 2004 WL 2870080 (N.D. Ill. Dec. 13, 2004). If a Gramm-Leach-Bliley notice was a communication in an effort to collect a debt, requiring consumers to affirmatively notify Sherman that they do not want their information shared is a misstatement of consumers' Gramm-Leach-Bliley privacy rights that violated the FDCPA.

Kort v. Diversified Collection Servs., Inc., 270 F. Supp. 2d 1017 (N.D. Ill. 2003), *aff'd on other grounds,* 394 F.3d 530 (7th Cir. 2005). Student loan collection letter which imposed a deadline for action to avoid a wage garnishment of less than thirty days, when such a deadline was not required by the Higher Education Act, violated the FDCPA. If a collector chooses to establish a deadline in its letter when not required to do so, it must not be misleading to the unsophisticated consumer.

Zanayed v. Gertler & Gertler, Ltd., 2000 U.S. Dist. LEXIS 5827 (N.D. Ill. Mar. 17, 2000). Disclosure of a false creditor may state a claim for violation of the FDCPA.

Davis v. Commercial Check Control, Inc., 1999 WL 89556 (N.D. Ill. Feb. 16, 1999). Whether the collection agency's statement in a bounced check dunning letter that "A SEARCH OF ALL YOUR ASSETS IS BEING INSTIGATED" was a deceptive statement and a false threat in violation of § 1692e raised a question for the jury to determine whether in fact "all" assets were indeed investigated. Statement that account balances were reported to Trans Union could not be read as a matter of law as incorrectly implying that either Trans Union operated, or was employed by, the debt collector.

Randle v. G.C. Servs., L.P., 25 F. Supp. 2d 849 (N.D. Ill. 1998). Collection agency's duns that allegedly misrepresents its active participation in collecting the debt states a claim for relief for violating §§ 1692e(10) and 1692j.

Arellano v. Etan Indus., Inc., 1998 WL 911729 (N.D. Ill. Dec. 23, 1998). Sections 1692e and 1692j(a) are mutually exclusive, since the former applies only to a debt collector and the latter only to those who "falsely pretend to be a debt collector."

Blum v. Fisher & Fisher, 961 F. Supp. 1218 (N.D. Ill. 1997). Claim that collection attorney's letter, which lulled the homeowner into inaction when a response or independent legal advice was needed, presented questions of fact precluding grant of summary judgment on alleged FDCPA violations of misrepresentation.

Lawson v. Mgmt. Adjustment Bureau, Inc., 1997 WL 283027 (N.D. Ill. May 15, 1997). A student loan administrative garnishment notice which included broadly stated reasons why a debtor could not request a wage-garnishment hearing (e.g., the school was unsatisfactory) could deter a debtor from pursuing a hearing in which she might be able to provide a valid reason why her wages should not be garnished, and therefore debtor's complaint stated a claim for which relief could be granted under §§ 1692e(2)(A), (6), and (10).

Johnson v. Midland Career Inst., 1996 WL 54187 (N.D. Ill. Feb. 8, 1996). Where a loan servicing center sent demands for payment of student loan before effective date of federal rules regarding a closed school discharge of the loan and did not make any other demands at the time forbidden by those rules, the FDCPA claim that it had misrepresented the student's rights was dismissed.

Smith v. Mikell, Clearinghouse No. 34,362C (N.D. Ill. 1982). It is immaterial whether violations of § 1692e are harassing, abusive or sharp.

Indiana

Keisler v. Encore Receivable Mgmt., Inc., 2008 WL 1774173 (S.D. Ind. Apr. 17, 2008). Cross motions for summary judgment denied where the collector stated in its initial dun that the debtor had "ignored" the "previous attempts . . . made by our client to resolve this debt voluntarily," when in fact the consumer had responded to the client/creditor's repeated telephone contacts and had explained her circumstances, including that she was ill, could not pay the debt, might seek credit counseling, and might file bankruptcy; thus a jury could find the statement that she had "ignored" the creditor's attempts to resolve the debt false or deceptive in violation of § 1692e.

Lucas v. M.R.S. Assocs., Inc., 2005 WL 1926570 (N.D. Ind. Aug. 11, 2005). The alleged confusion in the debt collector's dun was not so apparent on its face, which offered to accept a portion of the debt as full payment, that it could be established without resort to extrinsic evidence, and, since the consumer offered no such extrinsic evidence, under Seventh Circuit precedent summary judgment was entered for the defendant.

Spearman v. Tom Wood Pontiac-GMC, Inc., 2002 WL 31854892 (S.D. Ind. Nov. 4, 2002). Collector's incorrect § 1692g validation disclosure that any dispute must be in writing was a false representation in violation of § 1692e.

Wehrheim v. Secrest, 2002 WL 31242783 (S.D. Ind. Aug. 16, 2002). "Taking an illegal action may violate some provision of the FDCPA, but it does not violate § 1692e(5)."

Maryland

Shah v. Collecto, Inc., 2005 WL 2216242 (D. Md. Sept. 12, 2005).

The reporting of a paid debt as still owing was not a per se violation of § 1692e(5) where collector had no reason to know it had been paid.

Keane v. Nat'l Bureau of Collections, Clearinghouse No. 35,923 (D. Md. 1983). A jury returned a verdict of $1000 statutory and $5000 actual damages on two counts of a complaint alleging violation of § 1692e by falsely accusing the plaintiff of knowing and hiding her ex-husband's whereabouts from the collector.

Massachusetts

Dolan v. Schreiber & Assocs., P.C., 2002 U.S. Dist. LEXIS 6005 (D. Mass. Mar. 19, 2002) (magistrate recommendation), *adopted* 2002 U.S. Dist. LEXIS 5998 (D. Mass. Mar. 29, 2002). The complaint's allegations of a consumer debt being collected by a debt collector who made a false representation of the identity of the original creditor stated a claim for relief.

In re Hart, 246 B.R. 709 (Bankr. D. Mass. 2000). Loan servicer's unilateral adjustment of the consumer's mortgage payments and misrepresentation that the adjustment was required by the creditor violated §§ 1692e(5) and 1692f(1).

Michigan

Velderman v. Midland Credit Mgmt., Inc., 2005 WL 2405959 (W.D. Mich. Sept. 29, 2005). The court relied upon a transcript of the telephone conversation in finding that the debt collector violated §§ 1692e(2)(A) and (10) by representing to the consumer that his failure to dispute the debt within thirty days of receipt of the validation letter made him legally responsible for the debt and thereafter only by proving fraudulent activity on the part of the bank could the consumer show his dispute was valid.

Minnesota

Neill v. Bullseye Collection Agency, Inc., 2009 WL 1386155 (D. Minn. May 14, 2009). The allegation that the collector sent a letter entitled "SECOND NOTICE" that was in fact its third letter to the consumer failed to state a claim for violating § 1692e since the purported "misrepresentation was immaterial and therefore not actionable," citing, *inter alia*, the recent cases of *Miller v. Javitch, Block & Rathbone*, 561 F.3d 588 (6th Cir. 2009) and *Hahn v. Triumph P'ships, L.L.C.*, 557 F.3d 755 (7th Cir. 2009).

Knoll v. Intellirisk Mgmt., 2006 WL 2974190 (D. Minn. Oct. 16, 2006). Denied debt collector's motion to dismiss class action where debt collector used the false name, Jennifer Smith, as the Caller ID finding a claim was stated under §§ 1692d, 1692e, 1692f.

Mississippi

Moody v. Kramer & Frank, P.C., 2010 WL 883660 (E.D. Mo. Mar. 5, 2010). The fact that creditor is being represented by two different firms in two different underlying cases does not violate the FDCPA.

Nebraska

Randall v. Midland Funding, L.L.C., 2009 WL 2358350 (D. Neb. July 23, 2009). Where the consumer telephoned the collection attorneys after receiving his first dun and stated that he disputed the debt because he was a theft of identity victim, the allegation that the attorneys then stated that they did not have to provide any information about the account stated a claim under § 1692e for making a false, misleading, or deceptive representation.

New Jersey

Hurwitz v. Hecker, 2009 WL 4282194 (D.N.J. Nov. 30, 2009). "Debtor's allegations do not rise above a speculative level because it is implausible to allege that a consumer, sophisticated or otherwise, would read a notice addressed to residents of another state and believe that such notice applied to him or herself. In fact, such allegations are insufficient to raise a reasonable expectation that discovery will reveal any evidence to substantiate Debtor's claim in this regard."

Cohen v. Wolpoff & Abramson, L.L.P., 2008 WL 4513569 (D.N.J. Oct. 2, 2008). Claims for the unauthorized practice of law (by pursuing an arbitration proceeding) do not give rise to a misrepresentation cause of action under the FDCPA. Plaintiff points to nothing within the FDCPA that would allow this court to find that an attorney licensed in one jurisdiction who engaged in debt collection in another jurisdiction is not an attorney within the meaning of the FDCPA. Nothing in the FDCPA, its purposes, or its legislative history, suggests that Congress included within the scope of abusive practices multi-jurisdictional collection efforts by attorneys.

New Mexico

Kolker v. Sanchez, 1991 WL 11691589 (D.N.M. Dec. 10, 1991). A lawyer/collector who, in violation of applicable state law, assisted the unauthorized practice of law by filing collection suits in the name of a collection agency on a contingency assignment from the creditor violated § 1692e(5) by undertaking unlawful collection activity.

Spinarski v. Credit Bureau, Inc., 1996 U.S. Dist. LEXIS 22547 (D.N.M. Sept. 19, 1996). Collection agency was granted summary judgment on all the consumer's remaining claims. The collector's statement that it would obtain judgment did not falsely imply that the collector was affiliated with the courts.

New York

Ellis v. Cohen & Slamowitz, L.L.P., 701 F. Supp. 2d 215 (N.D.N.Y. 2010). Where the debt collector's letter offered to resolve the debt by including forgiveness that may be taxable under 26 U.S.C. § 61(a)(12), and the taxes levied specific to that additional taxable income would in essence diminish the actual net value of the discount offered by the debt collector, the consumer's complaint stated a claim for violation of the FDCPA for deceptive or misleading collection practices by failing to warn the consumer that the amount forgiven could affect his tax status, and the debt collector's motion to dismiss was denied.

Krapf v. Collectors Training Inst. of Ill., Inc., 2010 WL 584020 (W.D.N.Y. Feb. 16, 2010). The complaint stated a claim that the debt collector violated §§ 1692d and 1692e by leaving telephone messages for the consumer falsely stating that her Social Security number was under investigation. The court found that the defendant's suggestion that the consumer's Social Security number was

under investigation, or that there was an investigation *against* the consumer's Social Security number, could reasonably be found to constitute harassing, oppressive, or abusive conduct, and the court was not convinced by the defendant's argument that reference to "social" is conclusory or could refer to something other than the consumer's Social Security number.

Arend v. Total Recovery Servs., 2006 U.S. Dist. LEXIS 50479 (E.D.N.Y. July 24, 2006). It was not false or deceptive for the debt collector to offer the consumer additional time to exercise his right to obtain verification of the debt.

Jackson v. Immediate Credit Recovery, Inc., 2006 WL 3453180 (E.D.N.Y. Nov. 28, 2006). Providing the state required "Colorado" language did not violate § 1692e. Sending a second collection letter after the expiration of the time in which the consumer could request verification would not contradict or overshadow the validation notice in violation of § 1692e(5) and (10).

Jackson v. Immediate Credit Recovery, Inc., 2006 U.S. Dist. LEXIS 85928 (E.D.N.Y. Nov. 28, 2006). Court followed the weight of authority in ruling that the Colorado notice was not confusing or misleading. Whether the defendant's mention of "bad debt" and "good credit" violated the FDCPA depended on facts not before the court on cross motions for judgment on the pleadings, such as defendant's authority to make credit reports.

Scott v. Enhanced Recovery Corp., 2006 WL 1517755 (E.D.N.Y. May 31, 2006). Without analysis other than to state that the issue was fact-based, the court summarily denied the motion to dismiss the claim that the collector's recitation of state disclosures, entitled simply "Massachusetts Residents" and "California Residents," was misleading because the recited state mandated information also applied under the FDCPA to all consumers.

Wyler v. Computer Credit, Inc., 2006 WL 2299413 (E.D.N.Y. Mar. 3, 2006). The collection agency's letter was not deceptive because it advised the consumer that he could phone the creditor hospital to discuss the debt when the hospital failed advise the collection agency that he had called informing the hospital that his insurance had paid the hospital.

Arroyo v. Solomon & Solomon, P.C., 2001 U.S. Dist. LEXIS 21908 (E.D.N.Y. Nov. 7, 2001). Student loan collector's representation, if proven, that the consumer must pay $100, or $75, per month when she could only afford $5 violated the § 1692e because she was entitled to a fair and reasonable payment plan under the Higher Education Act.

Finnegan v. Univ. of Rochester Med. Ctr., 21 F. Supp. 2d 223 (W.D.N.Y. 1998). Allegation that a debt collector was informed orally by the consumer that he has disputed the debt with the creditor and nevertheless continues to attempt to collect the debt states a claim for relief under § 1692e(2)(A) ("false representation of the character, amount, or legal status of any debt") and § 1692f(1) (collection of amounts unauthorized by contract or law).

Wiener v. Bloomfield, 901 F. Supp. 771 (S.D.N.Y. 1995). Conflicting deadlines alone were not a violation of the FDCPA.

Read v. Amana Collection Servs., 1991 U.S. Dist. LEXIS 21773 (W.D.N.Y. Jan. 15, 1991). The claim that the collectors' instruction to the consumer to telephone violated the FDCPA because it would mislead consumers about the need to write the collector to preserve certain FDCPA rights was not appropriate for summary judgment.

Young v. Credit Bureau Inc., 729 F. Supp. 1421 (W.D.N.Y. 1989). Same holding as *Spencer v. Credit Bureau Inc., supra.*

Spencer v. Credit Bureau Inc., Clearinghouse No. 45,350 (W.D.N.Y. 1989). Sending successive "48-hour" "final" notices was not deceptive.

North Carolina

Beasley v. Sessoms & Rogers, P.A., 2010 WL 1980083 (E.D.N.C. Mar. 1, 2010). Defendants did not unlawfully limit the consumer's right to dispute the debt at any time in violation of § 1692e since their statement that "you must advise us within thirty days" of a dispute was limited to the § 1692g validation disclosure and "Defendants did not state (expressly or implicitly) that consumer would not, thereafter, be able to dispute her debt."

Johnson v. Bullhead Inv., L.L.C., 2010 WL 118274 (M.D.N.C. Jan. 11, 2010). The consumer stated a claim for relief for violations of § 1692e as a result of the debt collector's persistent collection efforts that she pay a debt that she did not owe and that were directed at her as a result of mistaken identity.

North Dakota

Jackson v. Financial Recovery Servs., Inc., 2006 WL 1234891 (D.N.D. May 3, 2006). Two letters on same account sent to different addresses (because consumer had moved) did not deceive the consumer into thinking there were two debts. Where letters contained proper validation notices, detachable payment slip was not false, misleading, or deceptive.

Bingham v. Collection Bureau, Inc., 505 F. Supp. 864 (D.N.D. 1981). The collector misrepresented that the creditor was a "member" of the collector's organization.

Ohio

Jordan v. John Soliday Fin. Group, L.L.C., 2010 WL 1462345 (N.D. Ohio Apr. 12, 2010). An outstanding question of fact as to the chain of title and ownership of the debt precluded summary judgment on the consumer's claim that the defendants violated the FDCPA when they attempted to collect a delinquent loan without the authority to do so. The court reserved for the trier of fact whether the defendants' attachment to the underlying state court collection complaint of documents that revealed the consumer's Social Security number violated the FDCPA.

Midland Funding L.L.C. v. Brent, 644 F. Supp. 2d 961 (N.D. Ohio 2009). With regard to the Sixth Circuit's materiality standard, "The contents of the affidavit itself, and in particular the fact that the affiant allegedly had personal knowledge that the debt was valid, would effectively serve to validate the debt to the reader, whether that was [the consumer] or a court." Therefore, the affidavit was false, deceptive, and misleading in its use in conjunction with an attempt to collect a debt, and the debt collectors have violated FDCPA § 1692e.

Richeson v. Javitch, Block & Rathbone, L.L.P., 576 F. Supp. 2d 861 (N.D. Ohio 2008). Collector did not violate § 1692e(10) by sending a dun to an identity theft victim. Collector was not required to, and in fact expressly informed consumer that it did not, investigate the factual underpinnings of the alleged debt. Instead, as it was entitled to do, the collector relied upon the representations of its client.

Kelly v. Montgomery Lynch & Assocs., Inc., 2008 WL 1775251 (N.D. Ohio Apr. 15, 2008). The defendant violated § 1692e(7) by falsely representing that the consumer committed a crime when it informed the consumer that it would bring criminal charges for passing a dishonored check, because the consumer had in fact met the requirements of the state dishonored check statute by satisfying the debt within ten days of receiving notice that his check had been dishonored.

Hartman v. Asset Acceptance Corp., 467 F. Supp. 2d 769 (S.D. Ohio 2004). A literally false statement (that the creditor was a holder in due course) violated the FDCPA as a matter of law, §§ 1692e(2), 1692e(12).

Todd v. Weltman, Weinberg & Reis, Co., L.P.A., 348 F. Supp. 2d 903 (S.D. Ohio 2004), *aff'd*, 434 F.3d 432 (6th Cir. 2006). Even if § 1692e is limited to misrepresentations made to the debtor, the state law requirement that pleadings be served on the debtor meant that the collection attorney's misrepresentation to the court met this standard.

Wright v. Asset Acceptance Corp., 1999 U.S. Dist. LEXIS 20675 (S.D. Ohio Dec. 30, 1999). Material issue of fact prevented summary judgment on claims that collection agency misrepresented its ownership of the debt and its authority to sue.

Gasser v. Allen County Claims & Adjustment, Inc., 1983 U.S. Dist. LEXIS 20361 (N.D. Ohio Nov. 3, 1983). A dunning form letter titled "Tell-A-Gram" violated § 1692e(10). A letter's false implication that the consumer's employers had been contacted violated § 1692e(5). The use of an ineffective confession of judgment note violated § 1692e(10) and (2)(A).

United States v. First Fed. Credit Control, Inc., Clearinghouse No. 33,811 (N.D. Ohio 1983). A letter written to create the false impression that the collector was trying to contact a serviceman's commanding officer violated § 1692e(5) and (10). The false statement that the collector has representatives or associate offices everywhere violated § 1692e(10). A letter falsely stating that the collector had verified the consumer's employment was false violating FDCPA § 1692e.

Pache Mgmt. Co. v. Lusk, 1997 WL 254096 (Ohio Ct. App. May 15, 1997). Letter to collect for physical damage to apartment under rental agreement stating possibility that consumer committed "criminal mischief" did not violate § 1692e(7) in absence of evidence that statement was made to "disgrace" the consumer and because statement did not falsely represent that the consumer committed a crime.

Durve v. Oker, 679 N.E.2d 19 (Ohio Ct. App. 1996). Where it was alleged that a physician had sent a collection letter in the name of a collection agency and discovery regarding the relationship between the physician and collection agency was denied, the consumer's FDCPA counterclaim against them was improperly dismissed. The claim that the physician had failed to inform his collectors that the claim was disputed should not have been dismissed.

Oregon

Van Westrienen v. Americontinental Collection Corp., 94 F. Supp. 2d 1087 (D. Or. 2000). Where the collector, which employed only one investigator or detective, stated that it had multiple detectives and an investigating division violated § 1692e(10). The debt collector's false statement that he was a multi-millionaire also violated § 1692e(10). Statements on the debt collector's website about foreign offices, number of staff, and a physician on its board were misrepresentations and violated § 1692e(10).

Van Westrienen v. Americontinental Collection Corp., 1999 U.S. Dist. LEXIS 16069 (D. Or. Sept. 2, 1999). A misrepresentation made by a debt collector to the consumer's attorney (that "he was a multimillionaire, that he always collects his debts, and that if the consumers contested the alleged debt they would have to pay his attorney's fees") was actionable by the consumer under §§ 1692e and 1692f.

Harvey v. United Adjusters, 509 F. Supp. 1218 (D. Or. 1981). A letter stating the collector had "Representation Everywhere" and stating the importance of a good credit rating was not deceptive where the collector's trade association had 2800 correspondent members.

Pennsylvania

Mushinsky v. Nelson, Watson & Assoc., L.L.C., 642 F. Supp. 2d 470 (E.D. Pa. 2009). A collection letter is deceptive if it can reasonably have two meanings, one of which is inaccurate. The decision in *Hahn* was distinguished, as the plaintiff in *Hahn* did not contend that the notice at issue there was misleading or deceptive—she only argued that it was *false*.

Reed v. Pinnacle Credit Servs., L.L.C., 2009 WL 2461852 (E.D. Pa. Aug. 11, 2009). The letter was subject to at least two interpretations, one of which was inaccurate, because it stated that "will not bring legal action to collect this debt even when the debt is within the reporting period." However, the condensed agreement provided that "[a]ny claim, dispute or controversy (whether in contract, tort, or otherwise) at any time arising from or relating to your Account, any transferred balances or this Condensed Agreement . . . will be resolved by binding arbitration. . . ."

Pearson v. LaSalle Bank, 2009 WL 1636037 (E.D. Pa. June 9, 2009). Several misrepresentations in foreclosure complaint were de minimis and did not "materially affect" the collection of the debt. Note that the plain language of the FDCPA mandates that the nature of the violation is to be considered only in determining damages.

Nelson v. Select Fin. Servs., Inc., 430 F. Supp. 2d 455 (E.D. Pa. 2006). The collector's second letter falsely represented to plaintiff that her inaction "verified the validity" of the debt, in violation of §§ 1692e and 1692e(10). The court based its decision on the different meanings of "assumed to be valid" and dictionary definitions of the term "verification" repeatedly used in § 1692g: "The OED [*Oxford English Dictionary* (2d ed. 1989)] defines verify as (1) "To prove by good evidence or valid testimony; to testify or affirm formally or upon oath;" and (2) "To show to be true by demonstration or evidence; to confirm the truth or authenticity of; to substantiate." XIX OED 540. *Webster's* defines it as (1) "to confirm or substantiate in law by oath or proof: add the legal

verification to (a pleading or petition)" and "to swear to or affirm the truth of;" (2) "to prove to be true: establish the truth of: conclusively demonstrate by presentation of facts or by sound reasoning or argument;" and (3) "to serve as conclusive evidence, argument, proof, or demonstration of." *Webster's* 2543. The new theory that defendants charged compound interest was untimely.

South Carolina

Moore v. Ingram & Assocs., Inc., 805 F. Supp. 7 (D.S.C. 1992). Use of the word "judgment" in the § 1692g validation notice was not misleading even though a judgment had not been obtained.

Duncan v. Nichols, 451 S.E.2d 24 (S.C. Ct. App. 1994). Attorney's letter to consumer which repeats the language of § 1692g(a)(4), even though a judgment does not exist, is not misleading in violation of § 1692e.

Texas

Cash v. Allied Interstate, Inc., 2005 WL 1693941 (S.D. Tex. July 19, 2005). Letter entitled "final notice" and giving a "final opportunity" to pay within ten days created a false sense of urgency stated a claim under § 1692e(10). Nothing happened after ten days, and the letter did not represent a "final" opportunity.

Virginia

In re Accelerated Recovery Sys., Inc., 431 B.R. 138 (W.D. Va. 2010). Collector violated § 1692e(7) by handwriting on the dun for dishonored checks, "if we file warrants, it will be a felony."

Sunga v. Broome, 2010 WL 3198925 (E.D. Va. Aug. 12, 2010). The consumer's allegation that the defendant falsely stated that an applicable state law exemption was not available stated a claim for violation of § 1692e.

Morgan v. Credit Adjustment Bd., Inc., 999 F. Supp. 803 (E.D. Va. 1998). Language demanding "immediate attention" and insisting that the debtor contact the office within seven days from the date of the letter could very likely confuse the least sophisticated debtor, who could reasonably interpret the notice as a demand for immediate payment or immediate action. Actual deception is not necessary to demonstrate that a statement is misleading in violation of the FDCPA. The same statements that form the basis of liability under §§ 1692g and 1692e(5) also create liability under § 1692e(10).

K.2.5 Unfair Practices, 15 U.S.C. § 1692f

K.2.5.1 General Unfairness Standards

Allen ex rel. Martin v. LaSalle Bank, N.A., 2011 WL 94420 (3d Cir. Jan. 12, 2011). Section 1692f broadly prohibits improper means "to collect or attempt to collect" any debt, and its list of violative conduct in § 1692f is not exhaustive. Thus, "collection" in § 1692f(1) includes attempted collection as well as actual collection.

Donohue v. Quick Collect, Inc., 592 F.3d 1027 (9th Cir. 2010). "[F]alse but non-material representations . . . are not actionable under § 1692f." The collector did not violate § 1692f since its mislabeling in a collection complaint of a $32 charge as "interest," when in fact the charge was comprised of both interest and pre-assignment finance charges, would not mislead the least sophisticated consumer and therefore was not materially false.

LeBlanc v. Unifund CCR Partners, 601 F.3d 1185 (11th Cir. 2010). The court adopted the least sophisticated consumer standard for § 1692f analysis.

Beler v. Blatt, Hasenmiller, Leibsker & Moore, L.L.C., 480 F.3d 470 (7th Cir. 2007). The collection law firm had the consumer's bank freeze her Social Security disability funds in her bank account for twenty-three days, and the consumer alleged that violated her right to those funds exempt from seizure. "Her theory is that it is 'unfair' or 'unconscionable' for a debt collector to violate any other rule of positive law . . . First, § 1692f creates its own rules (or authorizes courts and the FTC to do so); it does not so much as hint at being an enforcement mechanism for other rules of state and federal law. This is not a piggyback jurisdiction clause. If the Law Firm violated the Social Security Act, that statute's rules should be applied. Second, the Law Firm did not violate any anti-attachment rule. No exempt property reached [the creditor]. The citation used the precise language required by state law, see 735 ILCS 5/2-1402(b), telling the Bank not to turn over any exempt asset. . . . [Plaintiff] could prevail under § 1692f only if we were to declare, as a matter of federal common law, that a pre-citation hearing is essential to 'fair' debt collection, lest exempt assets be immobilized for even a brief period, even though a freeze plus a post-citation hearing complies with state law. Whatever may be said for or against pre-citation hearings as a matter of wise public policy, such a rule should be adopted (if at all) through the administrative process or a statutory amendment rather than judicial definition of the phrase 'unfair or unconscionable.' None of these illustrations implies that federal courts should make new rules that change how state-court judgments are collected. Subsection (6) is especially interesting. It says that creditors may not take 'nonjudicial' actions that seize property exempt by law. The implication is that state judicial proceedings are outside the scope of § 1692f."

Turner v. J.V.D.B. & Assocs., Inc., 330 F.3d 991 (7th Cir. 2003). Section 1692f does not contain the element of knowledge or intent.

Johnson v. Riddle, 305 F.3d 1107 (10th Cir. 2002). The FDCPA is remedial statute to be liberally construed in favor of the consumer.

Picht v. Hawks, 236 F.3d 446 (8th Cir. 2001). The collection agents filed a collection lawsuit against the consumers on a dishonored check for the check amount and a statutory penalty, obtained a default judgment, and attached the consumer's bank account. The defendants violated FDCPA because they had no authority under Minnesota law to obtain the default judgment since there were more than contractual damages sought.

California

Masuda v. Thomas Richards & Co., 759 F. Supp. 1456 (C.D. Cal. 1991). Least sophisticated debtor standard would be applied to determine whether collector's practice is unfair, deceptive or misleading.

Florida

Chalik v. Westport Recovery Corp., 677 F. Supp. 2d 1322 (S.D. Fla. 2009). A claim of a violation of § 1692f is deficient if it does not identify any misconduct beyond that which the consumer asserts violate other provisions of the FDCPA.

Maryland

Sayyed v. Wolpoff & Abramson, L.L.P., 2010 WL 3313888 (D. Md. Aug. 20, 2010). "[A] debtor cannot maintain a cause of action under the FDCPA based on a claim that a debt collection attorney violated a state rule of ethical conduct."

Michigan

Lovelace v. Stephens & Michaels Assocs., Inc., 2007 WL 3333019 (E.D. Mich. Nov. 9, 2007). Denied the collector summary judgment where the collector drew a check on the consumer's bank account on the basis of an alleged oral authorization but the parties' evidence was in conflict whether such authorization was in fact given. Claimed to violate § 1692f and (1).

Minnesota

Baker v. Allstate Fin. Servs, Inc., 554 F. Supp. 2d 945 (D. Minn. 2008). Congress enacted § 1692f to catch conduct not otherwise covered by the FDCPA. Multiple specific FDCPA provisions address the types of conduct alleged. Section 1692f is, therefore, inapplicable.

Nebraska

Randall v. Midland Funding, L.L.C., 2009 WL 2358350 (D. Neb. July 23, 2009). The complaint failed to state a claim for relief under § 1692f by providing no allegations other than those that supported other violations that the court had already sustained: "[T]he plaintiff fails to provide any facts showing a § 1692f violation beyond those facts alleged to violate other sections of the Act. A claim under § 1692f is deficient when the facts fail to show any improper debt collection activity other than the misconduct that the plaintiff claims is a violation of other provisions of the FDCPA."

Hage v. Gen. Serv. Bureau, 306 F. Supp. 2d 883 (D. Neb. 2003). "Use of unfair or unconscionable means" under the FDCPA can be established with a showing that a debt collector's act in collecting a debt "causes injury to the consumer that is (1) substantial, (2) not outweighed by countervailing benefits to consumers or competition, and (3) not reasonably avoidable by the consumer."

Nevada

Karony v. Dollar Loan Ctr., L.L.C., 2010 WL 5186065 (D. Nev. Dec. 15, 2010). Allegations that the collector pursued the plaintiff through litigation and credit reporting to pay a separate debt that was incurred by his wife and for which he was not responsible stated a claim under §§ 1692d and 1692f. The court rejected the defendants' argument that the debt at issue was a "community debt," since that was a factual issue not yet resolved by a trier of fact.

New York

Fajer v. Kaufman, Burns & Assocs., 2011 WL 334311 (W.D.N.Y. Jan. 28, 2011). The unfair or unconscionable conduct alleged must be in addition to the acts that a plaintiff alleges violate other sections of the FDCPA.

Krapf v. Collectors Training Inst. of Ill., Inc., 2010 WL 584020 (W.D.N.Y. Feb. 16, 2010). To state a claim under § 1692f, "the unfair or unconscionable conduct alleged must be in addition to the acts that a consumer alleges violate other sections of the FDCPA."

Tsenes v. Trans-Continental Credit & Collection Corp., 892 F. Supp. 461 (E.D.N.Y. 1995). List of violations found in the § 1692f subsections are nonexhaustive, and a cause of action was provided in the prefatory language.

North Carolina

Johnson v. Bullhead Inv., L.L.C., 2010 WL 118274 (M.D.N.C. Jan. 11, 2010). The consumer stated a claim for relief for violations of § 1692f as a result of the debt collector's persistent collection efforts that she pay a debt that she did not owe and that were directed at her as a result of mistaken identity.

Ohio

Kline v. Mortgage Elec. Sec. Sys., 2009 WL 6093372 (S.D. Ohio Nov. 24, 2009). The defendants' motion to dismiss was granted because "[t]he filing of a foreclosure action by a plaintiff in the process of obtaining an assignment not yet fully documented is not a deceptive, misleading, or abusive tactic and does not violate the FDCPA."

Lamb v. Javitch, Block & Rathbone, L.L.P., 2005 WL 4137786 (S.D. Ohio Jan. 24, 2005). The consumer stated a cause of action for violation of the FDCPA for the law firm's failure to set an oral hearing on its motion to confirm the arbitration award, and the court denied the law firm's motion to dismiss that was based in part on res judicata and *Rooker Feldman*. The contractual term requiring the consumer to affirmatively request MBNA to advance the arbitration fees was not unfair and the law firm did not violate the FDCPA by seeking arbitration. The claim that it was confusing violating the FDCPA to issue summons rather than the appropriate state process to confirm an arbitration in state court was dismissed because the summons was the court clerk's error, not the collection attorney's error, and because it was barred by *Rooker Feldman*.

Edwards v. McCormick, 136 F. Supp. 2d 795 (S.D. Ohio 2001). Section 1692f serves as a backstop function catching those unfair practices which somehow managed to slip by § 1692d and § 1692e.

Oregon

Daley v. A & S Collection Assocs., Inc., 2010 WL 2326256 (D. Or. June 7, 2010). The court rejected the consumer's theory that a violation of the FCRA constitutes an unfair or unconscionable debt collection activity under the FDCPA. In contrast to the FDCPA violation for a collector reporting false information to a credit bureau, the court found no FDCPA remedy for a collector who reports information that is defined as obsolete under the FCRA.

Pennsylvania

Shand-Pistilli v. Professional Account Servs., Inc., 2010 WL 2978029 (E.D. Pa. July 26, 2010). The consumer failed to allege a plausible claim for violation of § 1692e by claiming a collection letter misstated the last day for her to request verification of the debt because she did not plead the date she received the verification notice, triggering the thirty-day time period to request verification.

Texas

McGinnis v. Dodeka, L.L.C., 2010 WL 1856450 (E.D. Tex. May 7, 2010). The court found that the facts alleged by the consumer, including the lack of clarity in the assignment history in the state court petition and the issue regarding repeated demand letters, were sufficient to state a claim under § 1692f and § 1692f(1).

Virginia

Carter v. Countrywide Home Loans, Inc., 2009 WL 2742560 (E.D. Va. Aug. 25, 2009). The court erroneously held that where the plaintiff husband had not signed the mortgage agreement and was not alleged to be obligated he would not be protected as a "consumer" under § 1692f. The court failed to note only subsections 1692f(7) and (8) were limited to consumers with the rest of § 1692 more broadly applicable.

K.2.5.2 Collection of Unauthorized Amounts

Allen ex rel. Martin v. LaSalle Bank, N.A., 2011 WL 94420 (3d Cir. Jan. 12, 2011). "Collection" in § 1692f(1) includes attempted collection as well as actual collection.

Donohue v. Quick Collect, Inc., 592 F.3d 1027 (9th Cir. 2010). The debt collector did not charge a rate of interest in excess of that allowed by state law and thus did not violate § 1692f.

Newman v. Ormond, 2010 WL 3623174 (11th Cir. Sept. 20, 2010). Rejecting the *pro se* plaintiff's § 1692f(1) claim, the court found that by signing her promissory notes, the plaintiff expressly agreed to pay the reasonable costs of collection should she default on her payments, including reasonable attorney fees, that the collector's request for attorney fees complied with Florida law, and that the request did not amount to a violation of the FDCPA simply because the amount ultimately awarded may have differed from the amount requested.

Seeger v. AFNI, Inc., 548 F.3d 1107 (7th Cir. 2008). Debt buyer's demand for an additional 15% collection fee violated § 1692f(1) since the charge was not authorized by law or the underlying contract; applicable state law only permitted such a recovery if the amount was actually incurred as an out-of-pocket cost of collection and not, as attempted here, to unlawfully "permit[ ] a third-party purchaser of an account to recover its internal costs."

Barany-Snyder v. Weiner, 539 F.3d 327 (6th Cir. 2008). The defendant collection attorneys did not violate §§ 1692e or 1692f(1) when they attached to their complaint in the underlying state court collection suit the parties' contract which contained an illegal provision that purported to permit the recovery of reasonable attorney fees but that they never sought to enforce.

Purnell v. Arrow Fin. Servs., L.L.C., 303 Fed. Appx. 297 (6th Cir. 2008). Collector's allegedly false communication, which was made to a credit bureau within one year prior to filing suit and which misrepresented that the consumer owed the subject debt, stated a timely claim for violations of §§ 1692e(2)(A), 1692e(8), and 1692f(1), notwithstanding that the collector had been making the same alleged misrepresentations to the credit bureau for several years, since that last communication constituted a discrete violation of the Act within the statute of limitations.

Beler v. Blatt, Hasenmiller, Leibsker & Moore, L.L.C., 480 F.3d 470 (7th Cir. 2007). The collection law firm had the consumer's bank freeze her Social Security disability funds in her bank account for twenty-three days, and the consumer alleged that violated her right to those funds exempt from seizure. The court held that the freeze was not the transfer of the funds to the debt collector and did not violate the FDCPA in the absence of an FTC advisory opinion.

Robey v. Shapiro, Marianos & Cejda, L.L.C., 434 F.3d 1208 (10th Cir. 2006). Collection law firm's mere demand for "reasonable attorney fees" in its foreclosure actions as permitted by state law without disclosing that it was operating under a flat fee arrangement with its client did not violate FDCPA by attempting to collect an unlawful or unauthorized amount.

Olivera v. Blitt & Gaines, P.C., 431 F.3d 285 (7th Cir. 2005). Buyer of Chase credit card account could continue to charge the Chase rate rather than the lower state rate, and thus did not violate §§ 1692e or 1692f(1).

Shula v. Lawent, 359 F.3d 489 (7th Cir. 2004). Where no judgment for costs had been entered against the consumer, the collecting attorney's letter demanding payment of such costs violated § 1692e and was an attempt to collect an amount not authorized by contract or law in violation of § 1692f(1).

Rizzo v. Pierce & Assoc., 351 F.3d 791 (7th Cir. 2003). No § 1692f(1) violation because the late fee complained about was lawfully charged under state law.

Shapiro v. Riddle & Assocs., P.C., 351 F.3d 63 (2d Cir. 2003). A collection attorney fee of $98 was not unreasonable where the collection attorney reviewed the claim before it sent its first dunning letter.

Miller v. Wolpoff & Abramson, L.L.P., 321 F.3d 292 (2d Cir. 2003). Where an attorney fee of $323 was sought in a collection suit on a $1618 credit card balance, it was not an excessive fee and seeking it did not violate the FDCPA. The fact that part of the fee would be paid to a referral agency and that payment could be unethical did not state a claim for unfair practices under the FDCPA. The claim that fee violated state law prohibiting collection fees was not timely raised.

Johnson v. Riddle, 305 F.3d 1107 (10th Cir. 2002). Imposition of a $250 shoplifting fee on a dishonored check was not permitted by law under § 1692f(1) where the state supreme court would hold that the $15 maximum fee in the dishonored check law would apply.

Freyermuth v. Credit Bureau Servs., Inc., 248 F.3d 767 (8th Cir. 2001). Service charge on checks was permitted by Article 2 of the UCC as incidental damages.

Pollice v. Nat'l Tax Funding, L.P., 225 F.3d 379 (3d Cir. 2000). Interest and late charges imposed by the collection agency exceeded a state limitation of 10% and violated § 1692f(1). That ordinances preempted by state law allowed higher charges did not make the charges permissible or expressly authorized.

Duffy v. Landberg, 215 F.3d 871 (8th Cir.), *rehearing denied*, 2000 U.S. App. LEXIS 16039 (8th Cir. July 10, 2000). Demanding a $100 civil penalty for small bounced checks was deceptive and unfair violating § 1692e, 1692e(5), and 1692f where the state law allowed a penalty **up to $100** and provided that it was available if the consumer settled the claim before it reached the court. Referring to the imposition of attorney fees when state law did not authorize them for small checks violated § 1692e(5). Attempts to collect very small interest overcharges violated the plain language of § 1692f(1).

Tuttle v. Equifax Check, 190 F.3d 9 (2d Cir. 1999). A consumer consented to the imposition of a returned check fee under § 1692f(1) if the consumer tendered a check with knowledge of a posted sign stating the fee would be imposed. Service charges and fees may be added to a debt under § 1692f(1) where state law expressly permitted them or the underlying contract provided them and state law allowed them. UCC Art. 2 allowed a check guarantee agency/collector to collect its actual costs of collection as commercially reasonable incidental damages.

Transamerica Fin. Servs., Inc. v. Sykes, 171 F.3d 553 (7th Cir. 1999). Collecting a forged note may violate other law but was not a violation of 1692f(1), which is limited to attempting to collect fees not authorized by the contract or law.

Lee v. Main Accounts, Inc., 125 F.3d 855 (6th Cir. 1997) (unpublished) (text at 1997 WL 618803). Collector's statement that payment by credit card required a 5% additional charge to pay for the collector's merchant charge imposed by the Visa credit card issuer was not an attempt to collect an illegal, unconscionable or deceptive charge.

Alabama

White v. Global Payments, Inc., 2010 WL 320480 (S.D. Ala. Jan. 21, 2010). Summary judgment granted to the debt collector on the consumer's claim that it violated § 1692f(1) by communicating to consumer reporting agencies false information that the consumer still owed a debt that in fact had been paid, since there was no evidence that the defendant had reported the paid debt as remaining owing and the only evidence showed the defendant's unsuccessful attempts at having the agencies delete the incorrect information.

Arizona

Maldonado v. CACV, L.L.C., 2007 U.S. Dist. LEXIS 4461 (D. Ariz. Jan. 18, 2007). Demand for post-judgment interest in the underlying state court collection suit did not violate the FDCPA since the rate sought was lawful and not, as the consumer contended, prohibited by applicable state law.

Hayden v. Rapid Collection Sys., Inc., 2006 WL 1127180 (D. Ariz. Apr. 27, 2006). Court denied motion to dismiss, since the debt collector was attempting to collect an amount neither "expressly authorized" by the apartment rental lease, nor "expressly permitted" by any state law.

Gostony v. Diem Corp., 320 F. Supp. 2d 932 (D. Ariz. 2003). Forty percent collection fee, added before litigation, was not authorized by the apartment rental agreement which referred only to a "prevailing party's" entitlement to reasonable fees.

Axtell v. Collections U.S.A., Inc., 2002 WL 32595276 (D. Ariz. Oct. 22, 2002). Where the entitlement to fees in the underlying agreement only permitted fees to the "prevailing party" in any "legal action to enforce compliance," the collector's demand for payment of a sum for attorney fees incurred prior to and outside of litigation was unlawful.

Charles v. Check Rite, Ltd., 1998 U.S. Dist. LEXIS 22512 (D. Ariz. Dec. 14, 1999). Court found that imposition of a $25 check fee was authorized by UCC 2-709 as "incidental damages" and a $110 collection fee was also authorized by another state law and that seeking such charges was not an FDCPA violation. Check Rite was the assignee of the check and stood in the position of the seller.

Duran v. Credit Bureau, 1981 U.S. Dist. LEXIS 15811 (D. Ariz. Nov. 17, 1981), *modified*, 93 F.R.D. 607 (D. Ariz. 1982). In its initial decision the court noted that since § 1692f(1) is not violated by an *attempt* to collect an illegal fee, plaintiff's description of the class of consumers was overly broad and should have included only those who *paid* an illegal collection fee. In the later decision, without discussion of its earlier contrary reasoning, the court defined the class to include consumers from whom the collector attempted to collect allegedly illegal fees.

Grant Road Lumber Co. v. Wystrach, 682 P.2d 1146 (Ariz. Ct. App. 1984). Since suit by a collection agency was permitted in Arizona, it was not unauthorized practice of law and not unfair under § 1692f. Since contract provided for collection fees, seeking collection and attorney fees did not violate § 1692f(1).

California

Lopez v. Rash Curtis & Assocs., 2010 WL 4968064 (E.D. Cal. Dec. 1, 2010). The plaintiff's complaint did not contain adequate to state a claim for violation of § 1692(f) for threatening to add attorney fees.

McClenning v. NCO Fin. Sys., Inc., 2010 WL 4795269 (C.D. Cal. Nov. 15, 2010). The defendant's proffer of a promissory note providing for reasonable attorney fees supported the legality of its fee demand, creating a disputed fact regarding a violation of § 1692f(1).

Carrizosa v. Stassinos, 2010 WL 4393900 (N.D. Cal. Oct. 29, 2010). The court granted summary judgment of liability against the debt collector for violating § 1692f(1) by seeking to collect both prejudgment interest on unpaid checks and treble damages, measures prohibited by state law. A debt collector violated § 1692f(1) by attempting to collect from an individual listed on the check header but who had not signed or delivered the check in question.

del Campo v. Am. Corrective Counseling Serv., Inc., 2010 WL 2473586 (N.D. Cal. June 3, 2010). Defendants violated § 1692f(1) by collecting a check diversion "program fee" that was not permitted by applicable law but was pre-approved by the local district attorneys with whom they worked, since "a fee is not permitted by law simply because a district attorney says it is."

Carrizosa v. Stassinos, 2010 WL 144807 (N.D. Cal. Jan. 10, 2010).

Summary judgment granted on the consumers' § 1692f(1) claim where the debt collector attempted to collect both prejudgment interest and treble damages when state law prohibited the collection of both amounts.

Durham v. Continental Cent. Credit, 2009 WL 3416114 (S.D. Cal. Oct. 20, 2009). Where the consumer had agreed to the payment of a collection fee, the collector's addition of a 40% collection fee to the principal did not violate 15 U.S.C. § 1692f(1).

Palmer v. Stassinos, 2009 WL 86705 (N.D. Cal. Jan. 9, 2009). California law does not expressly authorize the collection of prejudgment interest on a debt resulting from a bad check, if the collection of interest is sought in addition to treble damages or a service fee, it would violate § 1692f(1).

Reyes v. Kenosian & Miele, L.L.P., 619 F. Supp. 2d 796 (N.D. Cal. 2008). Collection attorney's request for fees under an inapplicable statute in a state collection complaint did not violate §§ 1692e or 1692f where the underlying agreement authorized reasonable collection fees.

Schwarm v. Craighead, 552 F. Supp. 2d 1056 (E.D. Cal. 2008). The collection of unauthorized fees violated § 1692f(1) as well as § 1692e(2)(A)–(B), which prohibits "[t]he false representation of—(A) the character, amount, or legal status of any debt; or (B) any services rendered or compensation which may be lawfully received by any debt collector for the collection of a debt."

Palmer v. Stassinos, 419 F. Supp. 2d 1151 (N.D. Cal. 2005). Remedies under the state's comprehensive check recovery statute providing for fees and treble damages were the exclusive remedies allowed for writing a dishonored check and therefore did not allow the collector to also assess interest under generally applicable law; therefore, consumer's allegation that the collector attempted to collect interest in violation of state law stated a claim under the FDCPA.

Joseph v. J.J. Mac Intyre Cos., L.L.C., 238 F. Supp. 2d 1158 (N.D. Cal. 2002). Defendant did not violate the FDCPA when it attempted to collect interest in conformity with state law.

Ballard v. Equifax Check Servs., 158 F. Supp. 2d 1163 (E.D. Cal. 2001). Service charge added by collector to dishonored check, which was not authorized by state law or the contract creating the debt, violated §§ 1692e and 1692f and the California Unfair Business Practices Act.

Irwin v. Mascott, 96 F. Supp. 2d 968 (N.D. Cal. 1999). The burden of proving the statutory exception found in § 1692f(1) [unless the charge is expressly authorized by agreement or permitted by law] was on the person claiming the exception. A posted notice was not enough to show an express agreement. There must be proof that the check writer saw and intended to agree to the terms.

Ballard v. Equifax Check Servs., Inc., 186 F.R.D. 589 (E.D. Cal. 1999). Letters from a check authorization business demanding a $20 service charge were subject to § 1692f.

Ballard v. Equifax Check Servs., 27 F. Supp. 2d 1201 (E.D. Cal. 1998). Check guarantee company's evidence that the merchant agreed to post a notice stating its policy of collecting a $20 dishonored check fee, in the absence of any evidence that the sign was in fact posted or that the consumer read it, is inadequate to establish the mutual assent between the merchant and the consumer that the consumer would be bound by that agreement.

Newman v. CheckRite California, Inc., 912 F. Supp. 1354 (E.D. Cal. 1995). In absence of state law provision so permitting, attorneys' action requesting attorney fees for collecting a dishonored check violated §§ 1692f(1) and 1692e(5).

Connecticut

Egletes v. Law Offices Howard Lee Schiff, P.C., 2010 WL 3025236 (D. Conn. July 30, 2010). Where the defendant attempted to garnish wages with interest on the judgment when the judgment struck a provision for interest, it was "inexcusable" for the collection lawyers to seek interest.

Piscatelli v. Universal Adjustment Servs., Inc., Consumer Cred. Guide (CCH) ¶ 96,377 (D. Conn. 1985). Adding a 25% collection fee to agency's claim violated § 1692f(1) where a state statute limited such fees to 15%.

Porter v. Somers, 1993 WL 280118 (Conn. Super. Ct. July 12, 1993). The prohibition in § 1692f(1) on collecting an amount not permitted by law supported the claim under a state consumer protection act (UDAP) that such conduct was unfair.

Delaware

Dutton v. Wolhar, 809 F. Supp. 1130 (D. Del. 1992), *aff'd*, 5 F.3d 649 (3d Cir. 1993). Seeking costs violated § 1692f, where an attorney collector brought an action in a county other than where the consumer resided, because recovery of costs of suit filed in an inconvenient forum was prohibited by Delaware statute.

Florida

Sandlin v. Shapiro & Fishman, 919 F. Supp. 1564 (M.D. Fla. 1996). Plaintiff claimed that the imposition of a $60 payoff disclosure fee for the mortgage loan violated § 1692f and the Florida debt collection statute as an unauthorized fee. The court found the plaintiff had sufficiently stated a cause of action and denied defendant's motion to dismiss.

Georgia

Schmidt v. Slaughter, Clearinghouse No. 51,961 (M.D. Ga. 1996). The collection lawyer violated § 1692f(1), prohibiting collecting an amount not permitted by law, by demanding a $20 service charge for an NSF check when a notice required before the charge could be imposed had not been sent.

Illinois

Acik v. I.C. Sys., Inc., 640 F. Supp. 2d 1019 (N.D. Ill. 2009). The hospital form which provided that the patient was responsible for "all costs and fees, including attorneys fees, and interest" did not expressly authorize collection fees; therefore, the attempted recovery of collection fees and attempted collection of interest prior to the start date violated § 1692f.

Day v. Check Brokerage Corp., 511 F. Supp. 2d 950 (N.D. Ill. 2007). Where the debt collector failed to send notice by certified mail as required by Illinois law, it was permitted to charge only $25 in fees, not the $45 in fees demanded thereby violating §§ 1692f and 1692f(1).

Olvera v. Blitt & Gaines, P.C., 2004 WL 887372 (N.D. Ill. Apr. 26, 2004). The complaint alleged that the assignee of a credit card debt violated the FDCPA by falsely representing the legal status of the debt and trying to collect interest at a rate which violated the Illinois Interest Act. While the court concluded that an assignee could charge the contract rate, the collection attorneys' Rule 12(b)(6) motion to dismiss was denied because neither party had produced evidence of the interest rate agreed to be paid.

Lockett v. Freedman, 2004 WL 856516 (N.D. Ill. Apr. 21, 2004). Attorney collector's motion to dismiss was denied where consumer adequately alleged that attorney lacked knowledge to verify complaint in a state collection action and attempted to collect unauthorized attorney fees.

Bennett v. Arrow Fin. Servs., L.L.C., 2004 WL 830440 (N.D. Ill. Apr. 15, 2004). Judgment for collector after trial. Plaintiff did not prove that the addition of interest was unauthorized under § 1692f(1).

Gonzalez v. Codilis & Assocs., P.C., 2004 WL 719264 (N.D. Ill. Mar. 31, 2004). Complaint stated a claim for relief based on the debt collector dunning for attorney fees which had been requested in pending collection litigation but had not been awarded where, although state law permitted a party to recover "reasonable attorney's fees" before they are awarded by a court, the complaint alleged that the amount claimed was in fact not reasonable.

Collins v. Sparacio, 2004 WL 555957 (N.D. Ill. Mar. 19, 2004). Collection attorney who sued in state court to recover the liquidated damages expressly provided in the parties' underlying contract did not violate § 1692f(1).

Collins v. Sparacio, 2003 WL 21254256 (N.D. Ill. May 30, 2003). Consumer's unadorned allegations that the attorney debt collector from the underlying state court collection suit misrepresented in that suit the amount of the debt and attempted to collect sums not authorized by the contract or law sufficiently met the federal notice pleading requirements to state a claim for relief.

Porter v. Fairbanks Capital Corp., 2003 WL 21210115 (N.D. Ill. May 21, 2003). Complaint failed to state a claim for unlawfully attempting to collect unauthorized charges where the underlying contract permitted assessment of the challenged accumulated late charges and other fees to reinstate the loan. Complaint also failed to state a claim for relief for demanding, in order to reinstate the loan, payment of attorney fees that were not challenged as unreasonable but had not yet been approved by a court, since the loan agreement authorized such fees and neither the agreement nor applicable law required that such fees be first established by court order to be considered due and owing.

Shula v. Lawent, 2002 WL 31870157 (N.D. Ill. Dec. 23, 2002). Illinois statutes make court costs "recoverable," but where the debt collector failed to request a court order imposing such costs, demand for payment of those amounts was not "permitted by law" and violated §§ 1692f(1) and e.

James v. Olympus Servicing, L.P., 2002 WL 31307540 (N.D. Ill. Oct. 9, 2002). The court dismissed, with leave to amend, § 1692f(1) claims based on unlawful late charges because plaintiff had not pleaded exactly when those charges were assessed in relation to the acceleration and reinstatement of the loan. The court dismissed § 1692f(1) claims that Illinois law prohibited the imposition of attorney fees pursuant to a contract, without a court order.

Vickey v. Asset Acceptance, L.L.C., 2004 WL 1510026, U.S. Dist. LEXIS 12426 (N.D. Ill. July 2, 2002). The Illinois Interest Act does not prevent an unlicensed entity from obtaining the rights to an account from a licensed creditor and charging interest in excess of the statutory maximum where the consumer had agreed to pay that amount to the original creditor.

Rogers v. Simmons, 2002 U.S. Dist. LEXIS 5457 (N.D. Ill. Mar. 28, 2002). The collection of attorney fees above $350 in an action to collect a dishonored check, without documentation, even when the state court routinely sets a default cap in such actions of $350, was permitted by Illinois law and therefore did not constitute an automatic violation of the FDCPA but did strongly suggest that $350 was the maximum bona fide and reasonable fee for bad check default cases.

Ozkaya v. Telecheck Servs., Inc., 982 F. Supp. 578 (N.D. Ill. 1997). A check collector's $25 service fee on a stopped payment check violated state law permitting only those fees expressly permitted and state law only permitted a service charge with respect to NSF and no account checks, not stopped checks. Therefore. the consumer's claim for violation of § 1692f(1) would not be dismissed.

Blum v. Fisher & Fisher, 961 F. Supp. 1218 (N.D. Ill. 1997). Claim that collection attorney's letter concerning mortgage foreclosure, which stated that the consumer owed attorney fees when none would be due until a foreclosure judgment was obtained, presented questions of fact precluding grant of summary judgment on alleged FDCPA violations of misrepresentation and unfairness.

Indiana

Fausset v. Mortgage First, L.L.C., 2010 WL 987169 (N.D. Ind. Mar. 12, 2010). Federal courts may look to state law to determine if a fee is "permitted by law" under § 1692f(1).

Ketchem v. American Acceptance, Co., L.L.C., 641 F. Supp. 2d 782 (N.D. Ind. 2008). The plaintiff stated a claim for defendants' unlawful attempt to collect attorney fees to which they were not entitled based on the state rule that barred a fee recovery where there is a substantial identity of interest between the client and attorney; the complaint alleged that the attorneys here were principals in both the debt buyer and the law firm and that "[defendant L.L.C.] was created as a vehicle for [the law firm] to buy debt for its own account rather than collect debts for others."

Hall v. Leone Halpin & Konopinski, L.L.P., 2008 WL 608609 (N.D. Ind. Feb. 28, 2008). State court complaint requesting $1900 collection attorney fees based upon the fee schedule from a different county (the county where the action was pending did not have a fee schedule) did not violate §§ 1692e or 1692f.

Niemiec v. NCO Fin. Sys., Inc., 2006 WL 1763643 (N.D. Ind. June 27, 2006). Defendant's purchase of a regulated Beneficial small loan without being licensed to make such loans, and collecting thereon at the regulated rate, did not violate the FDCPA.

Conner v. Howe, 344 F. Supp. 2d 1164 (S.D. Ind. 2004). An attorney, who attempted to collect a payday loan which was void due to the excessive interest charged, violated § 1692f(1) by attempting to collect an amount of interest which was not permitted by law.

Nance v. Ulferts, 282 F. Supp. 2d 912 (N.D. Ind. 2003). Attempting to collect usurious interest violated §§ 1692e and 1692f notwithstanding that the loan agreement purported to authorize collection of the illegal amounts. Defendants' assertion that they had no reason to know that the amounts that they attempted to collect were usurious until the issuance of an intervening state appellate court decision was no defense to their liability. Since the state dishonored check law provision allowing for treble damages excluded post-dated checks, the consumer was entitled to summary judgment for the collector's illegal attempt to collect treble damages on a post-dated payday loan check.

Brooks v. Auto Sales & Servs. Inc., 2001 U.S. Dist. LEXIS 8059 (S.D. Ind. June 15, 2001). Plaintiff's claim that the attorney sought excessive fees in litigation stated a cause of action under §§ 1692e(2)(B) and 1692f(1).

Kansas

Settle v. Franklin Collection Servs., Inc., 2010 WL 3488827 (Kan. Ct. App. Aug. 27, 2010). The court affirmed the dismissal of the *pro se* consumer's complaint, since the plaintiff did not allege the basis for the claim that the charge was fraudulent or that the debt collector ever actually collected, i.e., received actual payment from the plaintiff, but only that it attempted to collect the debt.

Louisiana

Ducrest v. Alco Collections, Inc., 931 F. Supp. 459 (M.D. La. 1996). A collection agency was not liable for misrepresenting the amount of the debt under § 1692c(2)(a) or collecting an amount not owed under § 1692f(1) where it relied on the landlord's information and passed that information on to the consumer who asked for verification. The agency was not required to make an independent investigation.

Byes v. Credit Bureau Enters., 1996 WL 99360 (E.D. La. Mar. 6, 1996). Consumer stated a claim against the check collection agency for violating § 1692f as the collector has not submitted any evidence to show that it had authority to collect a fee for a bounced check allegedly forged in the consumer's name.

Maryland

Sayyed v. Wolpoff & Abramson, L.L.P., 2010 WL 3313888 (D. Md. Aug. 20, 2010). Summary judgment was granted to the collector on the §§ 1692e(2) and 1692f(1) claims since the prayer in the underlying collection suit for an award of attorney fees in a specific certain was not prohibited by applicable law.

Spencer v. Hendersen-Webb, 81 F. Supp. 2d 582 (D. Md. 1999). Debt collector's fax violated § 1692f(1) by attempting to collect attorney fees before suit when that was not authorized by the lease.

Massachusetts

Gathuru v. Credit Control Serv., Inc., 623 F. Supp. 2d 113 (D. Mass. 2009). A percentage-based fee need not be specifically mentioned in an agreement in order to satisfy the FDCPA's "expressly authorized" requirement of § 1692f(1).

Andrews v. South Coast Legal Servs., Inc., 582 F. Supp. 2d 82 (D. Mass. 2008). The consumer's allegation that the defendants, while executing on a judgment for a consumer debt, collected unauthorized additional incidental fees in violation of applicable state law stated a claim for violating § 1692f(1).

In re Maxwell, 281 B.R. 101 (Bankr. D. Mass. 2002). Purchaser of defaulted note violated the § 1692f(1) by demanding interest even though it had no documents on which it could determine how much interest it was entitled to demand.

In re Hart, 246 B.R. 709 (Bankr. D. Mass. 2000). Loan servicer's unilateral adjustment of the consumer's mortgage payments and misrepresentation that the adjustment was required by the creditor violated §§ 1692e(5) and 1692f(1).

Michigan

Kevelighan v. Trott & Trott, P.C., 2010 WL 2697120 (E.D. Mich. July 7, 2010). To the extent that the defendants attempted to collect immediate repayment of advances for property taxes and insurance, applied consumers' principal payments to repayment of advances not yet due, and used consumers' failures to make repayment of the advances as grounds for declaring default, defendants may have engaged in unfair debt collection practices. The consumers sufficiently alleged unfair debt collection practices in violation of § 1692f(1) when they asserted that the defendants attempted to collect attorney fees in excess of the amounts allowed under Michigan law.

Grden v. Leikin, Ingber & Winters, P.C., 2010 WL 199947 (E.D. Mich. Jan. 19, 2010). The collector's misstatement of the amount of the debt communicated in response to the consumer's direct inquiry was not made "in connection with the collection of" the consumer's debt and thus did not violate § 1692f where the collector did not demand payment, did not imply that the consumer was in default, and did not "allude to the consequences of default."

Richard v. Oak Tree Group, Inc., 614 F. Supp. 2d 814 (W.D. Mich. 2008). The consumer's agreement to pay "collection costs and expenses incurred" is not an agreement to pay a collection agency's maximum potential commission based upon percentage of the unpaid balance and violated § 1692f(1).

Lovelace v. Stephens & Michaels Assocs., Inc., 2007 WL 3333019 (E.D. Mich. Nov. 9, 2007). Denied the collector summary judgment where the collector drew a check on the consumer's bank account on the basis of an alleged oral authorization but the parties' evidence was in conflict whether such authorization was in fact given. Claimed to violate §§ 1692f and 1692f(1).

Gradisher v. Check Enforcement Unit, Inc., 210 F. Supp. 2d 907 (W.D. Mich. 2002). Collection of a fee pursuant to a county ordinance, even if the fee was invalid, did not violate § 1692f(1) but may violate due process rights where no hearing was provided.

Minnesota

Cohen v. Beachside Two-I Homeowners' Ass'n, 2006 WL 1795140 (D. Minn. June 29, 2006), *aff'd, as modified on other grounds*, 272 Fed. Appx. 534 (8th Cir. 2008). Even if the notice filed on the land record contained an amount in excess of that permitted by statute for fees, it was not an effort to collect an amount not owing because the agreement provided for the collection of reasonable fees.

Erickson v. Johnson, 2006 WL 453201 (D. Minn. Feb. 22, 2006). Since plaintiff was not a party to the credit card account, defendants' demand for attorneys fees based on the credit card agreement violated §§ 1692f(1) and 1692e.

Armstrong v. Rose Law Firm, P.A., 2002 U.S. Dist. LEXIS 4039 (D. Minn. Mar. 7, 2002). Debt collector's recitation of availability of a civil dishonored check penalty failed to comply with applicable state law and therefore violated the FDCPA.

Maneval v. Jon R. Hawks, Ltd., 1999 U.S. Dist. LEXIS 22899 (D. Minn. Oct. 12, 1999). The court accepted collector's argument that Minnesota law allowed him to send a letter demanding $100 over the amount of a bounced check, even though that amount could not be assessed at the inception of litigation. This decision may be peculiar to Minnesota.

Kojetin v. C.U. Recovery, Inc., 1999 U.S. Dist. LEXIS 1745 (D. Minn. Mar. 29, 1999) (magistrate's ruling), *adopted*, 1999 U.S. Dist. LEXIS 10930 (D. Minn. Mar. 29, 1999), *aff'd*, 212 F.3d 1318 (8th Cir. 2000). The agreement between the debt collector and the creditor allowed the debt collector to charge the consumer a fifteen percent collection fee. The agreement between the consumer and the creditor, however, only allowed "reasonable attorney's fees and costs incident to collection." The court found that seeking the fifteen percent fee, which was not expressly authorized by the consumer, violated § 1692f, and constituted the type of false and misleading representation that the FDCPA was designed to foreclose.

Venes v. Prof'l Serv. Bureau, Inc., 353 N.W.2d 671 (Minn. Ct. App. 1984). The collector/assignee violated § 1692f by charging interest on a debt to the Mayo Clinic which had a policy of not charging its patients interest.

Missouri

Eckert v. LVNV Funding L.L.C., 647 F. Supp. 2d 1096 (E.D. Mo. 2009). The court dismissed plaintiff's claim that defendant violated the FDCPA by seeking to collect interest accrued on the credit card account since November 22, 2005, as plaintiff's complaint contained no assertions as to when plaintiff received demand for payment or even that defendant sought prejudgment interest on the credit card account in the state court action. Held that the complaint failed to allege facts sufficient to state a claim for violation of § 1692f(1).

Montana

McCollough v. Johnson, Rodenberg & Lauinger, 587 F. Supp. 2d 1170 (D. Mont. 2008). Summary judgment awarded consumer on § 1692f(1) claim that the collection law firm filed a state debt collection suit seeking collection attorney fees without any authorization of the fees in law or an authenticated contract applicable to the transaction. A form credit card agreement postdating the default was not authenticated nor could it be applicable as it was dated after the account was in default.

Nebraska

Hage v. Gen. Serv. Bureau, 306 F. Supp. 2d 883 (D. Neb. 2003). Defendants violated § 1692f(1) by collecting attorney fees before obtaining judgment contrary to a state statute. State law determines whether collection of an amount is "permitted by law" under § 1692f(1). Under § 1692f(1), an additional amount may be collected if state law expressly permitted it, even if the contract was silent on the matter; but, if state law neither affirmatively permitted nor expressly prohibited collection of an additional amount, the amount can be collected only if the customer expressly agreed to it in the contract.

Page v. CheckRite, Ltd., Clearinghouse No. 45,759 (D. Neb. 1984). An $8 service charge for a bounced check was commercially reasonable and lawfully recoverable by a check guarantee service which had provided retailers with a decal for each cash register advising customers of the charge.

New Jersey

Kennedy v. United Collection Bureau, Inc., 2010 WL 445735 (D.N.J. Feb. 3, 2010). Dismissed claim that exact amount of collection cost must be included in the creditor agreement to be permissible within § 1692f(1).

New Mexico

Martinez v. Albuquerque Collection Servs., 867 F. Supp. 1495 (D.N.M. 1994). A collection agency violated §§ 1692e(2) and 1692f(1) by collecting inflated charges on a gross receipts tax, attorneys fees and compound interest. Charging prejudgment legal interest did not violate the FDCPA because it was authorized by state law. A collection agency's attempts to collect time-barred accounts violated the FDCPA. The consumer's summary judgment motion was denied, however, where there was unclear evidence of which of several debts had been involved, and some debts were not time barred.

New York

Fajer v. Kaufman, Burns & Assocs., 2011 WL 334311 (W.D.N.Y. Jan. 28, 2011). In this default action, the collector also violated § 1692f(1) by seeking payment from the plaintiff of an amount greater than her actual debt.

Shami v. National Enter. Sys., 2010 WL 3824151 (E.D.N.Y. Sept. 23, 2010). The court concluded that the complaint sufficiently pleaded a cause of action for violation of §§ 1692f(1) and 1692e(2). The complaint involved a collection letter including the language "You can now pay by automated phone system . . . or on the internet. Transaction fees will be charged if you use the automated phone system or the internet to make payment on this account. You are not required to use the automated phone system or the internet to make payment on this account."

Hunt v. Cornicello & Tendler, L.L.P., 2009 WL 3335935 (S.D.N.Y. Oct. 13, 2009). The request by collection attorneys in an eviction complaint for $3000 in attorney fees, when the lease only authorized reasonable attorney fees, did not violate the FDCPA, citing *Winn v. Unifund CCR Partners*, 2007 WL 974099 at *3 (D. Ariz. Mar. 30, 2007).

Larsen v. JBC Legal Group, P.C., 533 F. Supp. 2d 290 (E.D.N.Y. 2008). By stating that they would attempt to collect from plaintiff an amount of damages for a dishonored check that is not permitted by state law the collection agency and debt buyer violated § 1692f(1).

Padilla v. Payco Gen. Am. Credits, Inc., 161 F. Supp. 2d 264 (S.D.N.Y. 2001). Regardless of whether the amount sought was reasonable, student loan debt collector violated § 1692f by assessing collection fees in excess of the 18.5% of outstanding balance permitted by federal regulations.

Finnegan v. Univ. of Rochester Med. Ctr., 21 F. Supp. 2d 223 (W.D.N.Y. 1998). Allegations that a debt collector's continued attempts to collect a debt it knew was disputed and failure to communicate to a credit reporting agency that a known disputed debt was disputed (even though dispute was not in writing), state a claim for relief under the FDCPA for misrepresenting the amount and legal status of the debt and for attempting to collect amounts unauthorized by contract or law. Debt collector's misconduct also states a claim for relief under state tort of negligence for its failure to perform its collection contract with the creditor with due care.

Read v. Amana Collection Servs., 1991 U.S. Dist. LEXIS 21773 (W.D.N.Y. Jan. 15, 1991). The claim that § 1692f(1) was violated by a statement that prompt payment would avoid collection fees was not appropriate for summary judgment.

North Dakota

Bingham v. Collection Bureau, Inc., 505 F. Supp. 864 (D.N.D. 1981). The court found a number of violations. The court rejected a claim that the collector imposed excessive interest charges.

Ohio

Midland Funding L.L.C. v. Brent, 644 F. Supp. 2d 961 (N.D. Ohio 2009). There was a question of material fact as to whether the debt collectors violated the FDCPA by attempting to collect interest at a higher rate than allowed by law.

Kelly v. Montgomery Lynch & Associates, Inc., 2008 WL 1775251 (N.D. Ohio Apr. 15, 2008). Cross motions for summary judgment denied on the § 1692f(1) claim that the collector had assessed an unauthorized $5 telephone check processing fee where the evidence was disputed whether the consumer had in fact orally approved the fee.

Foster v. D.B.S. Collection Agency, 463 F. Supp. 2d 783 (S.D. Ohio 2006). Because defendants did not have the legal capacity to bring suit, they violated § 1692f(1) by seeking court costs, fees, and interest.

Kelly v. Great Seneca Fin. Corp., 443 F. Supp. 954 (S.D. Ohio 2005). The allegations that the defendant debt collection agency and its collection attorneys filed a state court collection action in which they allegedly misrepresented the amount and legal status of the debt stated a claim for violating §§ 1692e(2), (5), and (10), and 1692f(1).

Lamb v. Javitch, Block & Rathbone, L.L.P., 2005 WL 4137778 (S.D. Ohio Jan. 24, 2005). Because the agreement provided for reasonable attorney fees that was valid under Delaware law selected by the choice of law provision , the court dismissed the consumer's claim that unauthorized fees were sought in violation of § 1692f(1).

Todd v. Weltman, Weinberg & Reis Co., L.P.A., 348 F. Supp. 2d 903 (S.D. Ohio 2004), *aff'd on immunity issue*, 434 F.3d 432 (6th Cir. 2006). District court decision holds that allegation that the defendant collection attorneys falsely misrepresented in their affidavits in support of state court garnishments the state of the debtors' non-exempt assets, when in fact the attorneys had no information or knowledge whatsoever concerning the matter, stated a claim for violating §§ 1692e and 1692f. Court of appeals decision holds that the attorneys could not claim absolute immunity.

Foster v. D.B.S. Collection Agency, 2002 WL 32993859 (S.D. Ohio Mar. 8, 2002). The consumer stated a claim for the defendant collector's violation of § 1692f(1) by receiving and retaining payment for court costs which were not awarded or owing in an underlying state collection case that was actually dismissed.

Taylor v. Luper, Sheriff & Niedenthal, 74 F. Supp. 2d 761 (S.D. Ohio 1999). A one-third contingent fee was not excessive or unreasonable where collection attorney and creditor had an oral contingent fee agreement and where the collector's lodestar recovery would exceed the one-third contingent fee.

Lewis v. ACB Bus. Servs., Inc., 911 F. Supp. 290 (S.D. Ohio 1996), *aff'd,* 135 F.3d 389 (6th Cir. 1998). The processing fee for an "American Express Moneygram" was not an illegal charge in violation of § 1692f(1) where that service was voluntarily chosen by the debtor and where the fee was standard and was not paid to the collector or to an entity it controlled.

Damsel v. Shapiro, 2001 Ohio App. LEXIS 4052 (Ohio Ct. App. Sept. 13, 2001). All fees recited in the mortgage reinstatement figure were authorized by the mortgage agreement and therefore in conformity with § 1692f.

Durve v. Oker, 679 N.E.2d 19 (Ohio. Ct. App. 1996). There was no evidence of an agreement allowing the physician to recover legal expenses and fees so the physician should not have been granted summary judgment on the consumer's FDCPA claim that the claim for those expenses and fees violated § 1692f.

Pennsylvania

Martsolf v. JBC Legal Group, P.C., 2008 WL 275719 (M.D. Pa. Jan. 30, 2008). The defendants' demand for $30 as a returned check fee did not violate § 1692f(1) or § 1692e(2)(A) since the amount was an authorized charge under state law as UCC incidental damages.

Dougherty v. Wells Fargo Home Loans, Inc., 425 F. Supp. 2d 599 (E.D. Pa. 2006). Charging attorney collection fees incurred during plaintiff's bankruptcy without the bankruptcy court's approval to release the mortgage on sale of the home did not violate § 1692f(1) as the fees were authorized by the mortgage.

Kiliszek v. Nelson, Watson & Assocs., L.L.C., 2006 WL 335788 (M.D. Pa. Feb. 14, 2006). The debt collector's showing of authorization of collection fees and post default interest in the credit card agreement defeated the *pro se* consumer's § 1692f(1) claim.

Piper v. Portnoff Law Assocs., 262 F. Supp. 2d 520 (E.D. Pa. 2003). It was likely to be found unreasonable for the law firm to charge $150 in attorney fees to prepare and mail a form letter regardless of the time spent in its preparation.

Adams v. Law Offices of Stuckert & Yates, 926 F. Supp. 521 (E.D. Pa. 1996). As the court had found defendant liable under § 1692g for a dunning letter that overshadowed the validation notice, it

declined to find the defendant liable for the same acts under § 1692f as it found the violations not to reflect an abuse of a superior economic position.

In re Crippen, 346 B.R. 115 (Bankr. E.D. Pa. 2006). The complaint that alleged that the defendant was a consumer debt collector who attempted to collect an amount in excess of that allowed by the underlying contract and applicable state law stated a claim for violating §§ 1692e(2) and 1692f(1).

Tennessee

Spangler v. Conrad, 2010 WL 2389481 (E.D. Tenn. June 9, 2010). The defendant's attempt to collect a sum certain in reasonable attorney fees authorized by the loan agreement did not violate the FDCPA.

Texas

Eads v. Wolpoff & Abramson, L.L.P., 538 F. Supp. 2d 981 (W.D. Tex. 2008). Allegation that collection suit claimed $225 more than the arbitration award, by including the state filing fee, stated a claim under §§ 1692f(1) and 1692e(5).

Agueros v. Hudson & Keyse, L.L.C., 2010 WL 3418286 (Tex. App. Aug. 31, 2010). The debt collector's attempt to collect an amount double what its own records showed to be owing violated §§ 1692e and 1692f.

Utah

Maynard v. Cannon, 2006 WL 2403591 (D. Utah Aug. 21, 2006). A debt collector who had filed in the public record a mortgage default notice containing an incorrect amount owed and who thereafter did not verify the amount of the debt as the consumer requested did not comply with § 1692f by failing to withdraw or correct the public notice attempting to collect the debt.

Scott v. Riddle, 2000 WL 33980013 (D. Utah Dec. 4, 2000). Seeking penalties under a shoplifting statute inapplicable to bad checks misrepresents the character, amount, and legal status of a debt, and is an attempt to collect an amount not legally owing.

Ditty v. CheckRite, Ltd., 973 F. Supp. 1320 (D. Utah 1997). Collecting a $73 to $83 charge, listed as "Legal Consideration for Covenant not to Sue," that was not permitted by law violated § 1692f(1).

Virginia

Sunga v. Broome, 2010 WL 3198925 (E.D. Va. Aug. 12, 2010). The collector's alleged multiple misrepresentations of the amount of the debt, including by as little as $1.41 in unlawful interest and by $16.00 in prohibited fees (with an additional penny in unlawful interest as a result of the overstated $16.00) and as much as $1100.00 in unlawful attorney fees, stated a claim for violating §§ 1692e(2)(A) and 1692f(1).

Neild v. Wolpoff & Abramson, L.L.P., 453 F. Supp. 2d 918 (E.D. Va. 2006). The consumer's claims that she was charged by the defendant for items not specifically contained in the underlying agreement stated a cause of action for violation of § 1692f and 1692f(1).

Talbott v. G.C. Servs. Ltd. P'ship, 53 F. Supp. 2d 846 (W.D. Va.

1999). The imposition of a 35% collection fee was reasonable and authorized by MCI's tariff and was not in violation of the FDCPA.

West v. Costen, 558 F. Supp. 564 (W.D. Va. 1983). Imposition of a $15 service charge on each bad check it collected violated § 1692f(1) since there was no evidence of a contract providing for the charge and the charge was not expressly permitted by state or federal law. It made no difference that state law did not prohibit such charges or permitted them in other contexts. The attempt to collect such charges violated § 1692e(2).

Washington

McLain v. Gordon, 2010 WL 3340528 (W.D. Wash. Aug. 24, 2010). It is not unfair for a collector to offer a settlement for less than the amount owed and later make a higher offer when the first offer was accepted but was not met.

Kirk v. Gobel, 622 F. Supp. 2d 1039 (E.D. Wash. 2009). The defendant collection lawyer violated §§ 1692e(2)(B) and 1692f(1) by requesting in the state collection court service of process fees that were prohibited by applicable state law since the process server was unregistered.

Russo v. Puckett & Redford, P.L.L.C., 2009 WL 3837529 (W.D. Wash. Nov. 17, 2009). Partial summary judgment was entered on behalf of the consumer for the debt collector's attempt to collect a service fee for an unregistered process server.

Hansen v. Ticket Track, Inc., 280 F. Supp. 2d 1196 (W.D. Wash. 2003). A collector's motion for summary judgment was denied where the consumer showed it was attempting to collect a fee illegal under state law.

Campion v. Credit Bureau Servs., Inc., 2000 U.S. Dist. LEXIS 20233 (E.D. Wash. Sept. 19, 2000). Attorney debt collector's inclusion in writ of garnishment of an estimate of the costs and attorney fees that would be incurred complied with applicable state law that required such an estimate and therefore did not violate § 1692f; however, stating that such estimate was part of the existing unsatisfied judgment was false and therefore violated § 1692e. Absent a threat to take any action, there can be no violation of § 1692e(5).

In re Hodges, 342 B.R. 616 (Bankr. E.D. Wash. 2006). Debt collector violated § 1692f(1) by attempting to collect charges which were not authorized by the underlying fee agreement between the consumer and the attorney/creditor. Debt collector, acting on behalf of the debtor's former bankruptcy attorney, violated § 1692f(1) by attempting to collect the bankruptcy filing fee advance that was discharged by the debtors' bankruptcy, misconduct which also was a violation of the bankruptcy discharge injunction.

Wisconsin

Barrows v. Petrie & Stocking, S.C., 2008 WL 3540405 (W.D. Wis. Aug. 13, 2008). The defendant collectors violated the FDCPA by serving on the consumer's credit union a garnishment summons and complaint that claimed statutory disbursement charges in excess of the $40 allowed by applicable state law, in violation of §§ 1692e(2)(B), 1692e(10), and 1692f(1).

Stanley v. Stupar, Schuster & Cooper, S.C., 136 F. Supp. 2d 957

(E.D. Wis. 2001). Plaintiff's complaint based on defendants' statement of the debt as "$987.71, plus attorneys fees," stated claims for violations of §§ 1692g(a)(1), 1692e, and 1692f(1).

Patzka v. Viterbo Coll., 917 F. Supp. 654 (W.D. Wis. 1996). The collection agency violated § 1692f by charging a collection fee and interest not allowed by the contract or state law because it was not disclosed and was prohibited by state law.

Citicorp Credit Servs., Inc. v. Justmann, 570 N.W.2d 61 (Wis. Ct. App. 1997) (unpublished) (text at 1997 WL 370205). No violation of § 1692f(1) by seeking and receiving attorney fees in a collection suit where contract permitted such an award.

Wyoming

Johnson v. Statewide Collections, Inc., 778 P.2d 93 (Wyo. 1989). Collector's demand for more than the amount of the debt if the debt was not paid by a certain deadline was an unfair practice. The collection letter's recitation of the statutory formula for calculating the correct amount due did not avoid liability for demanding an incorrect amount.

K.2.5.3 Postdated Checks

Alabama

McGrady v. Nissan Motor Acceptance Corp., 40 F. Supp. 2d 1323 (M.D. Ala. 1998). The court denied Nationwide Credit's motion to dismiss the claim that demanding a post-dated check when Nationwide knew that plaintiff did not have sufficient funds could establish a § 1692f violation (unfair or unconscionable).

Oregon

Grassley v. Debt Collectors, Inc., 1992 U.S. Dist. LEXIS 22782 (D. Or. Dec. 14, 1992). Absent proof that collector's request for postdated checks was for the purpose of threatening criminal prosecution, a violation to § 1692f(3) was not proven.

Texas

United States v. Cent. Adjustment Bureau, Inc., 667 F. Supp. 370 (N.D. Tex. 1986). The collector violated § 1692f(3) by soliciting postdated checks with the purpose of threatening criminal prosecution.

K.2.5.4 Repossession Practices

Arruda v. Sears, Roebuck & Co., 310 F.3d 13 (1st Cir. 2002). Defendant attorneys who sought only to replevy secured property post-bankruptcy were not attempting to collect a "debt," i.e., an obligation to pay money, and therefore were not subject to the FDCPA, since to rule otherwise would be contrary to the plain language of the definition. The plaintiffs alleged that the replevin remedy was merely a pressure tactic to extract a cash settlement.

Arkansas

Peace v. Mortgage Elec. Registration Sys., Inc., 2010 WL 2384263 (E.D. Ark. June 11, 2010). The court dismissed the *pro se* complaint filed "in an attempt to stop a non-judicial foreclosure sale" for failure "to state a plausible claim for relief under § 1692f(6) (A)."

California

Pflueger v. Auto Fin. Group, Inc., 1999 U.S. Dist. LEXIS 16701 (C.D. Cal. Apr. 26, 1999). Summary judgment was denied based on factual issues as to whether the breach of the peace was sufficient to deprive the repossessor of its present right to possession at the time of the attempted repossession violating § 1692f(6) (A).

Connecticut

Plummer v. Gordon, 193 F. Supp. 2d 460 (D. Conn. 2002). Despite repossessor's agreement to hold the car for the consumer, it did not violate the FDCPA by turning it over to the creditor, since the creditor's lien was valid.

Clark v. Auto Recovery Bureau, Inc., 889 F. Supp. 543 (D. Conn. 1994). A breach of the peace in the course of a repossession may violate this provision because a repossessor loses its right to possessions under the Uniform Commercial Code if obtaining possession would result in a breach of the peace. No violation as repair company had obtained possession of the car before the consumer objected.

Delaware

Jordan v. Kent Recovery Servs., Inc., 731 F. Supp. 652 (D. Del. 1990). A repossession company was only covered by § 1692f(6) and not other FDCPA provisions. This construction was necessary to give effect to the third sentence of § 1692a(6).

Georgia

Fulton v. Anchor Sav. Bank, 452 S.E.2d 208 (Ga. Ct. App. 1994). Dismissal of FDCPA count arising from automobile repossession was reversed because genuine issues of material fact existed as to bank's present right of possession.

Illinois

Williams v. Republic Recovery Servs., Inc., 2010 WL 2195519 (N.D. Ill. May 27, 2010). Actual repossession is not a prerequisite for liability under § 1692f(6).

Purkett v. Key Bank USA, N.A., 45 U.C.C. Rep. Serv. 2d 1201 (N.D. Ill. 2001). When repossession company broke into locked garage to repossess, it breached the peace and became a debt collector because it had no present right to repossess by breach of peace.

Leguillou v. Lynch Ford, Inc., 2000 U.S. Dist. LEXIS 1668 (N.D. Ill. Feb. 10, 2000). The defendant was not liable under § 1692f(6) (A) for a wrongful repossession where it was not claiming to act under a security agreement.

Johnson v. Grossinger Motorcorp, Inc., 753 N.E.2d 431 (Ill. App. Ct. 2001). Claim of violating § 1692f(6) based on wrongful repossession properly dismissed where defendant peacefully repossessed the collateral in a manner that did not violate state law.

Michigan

Alexander v. Blackhawk Recovery & Investigation, L.L.C., 731 F. Supp. 2d 674 (E.D. Mich. Aug. 16, 2010). The consumer's allegations that the defendant's breach of peace self-help car repossession deprived it of a present right of possession stated a claim for violating § 1692f(6). To determine whether a repossession agency has violated § 1692f(6), courts look to the applicable state self-help repossession statute that identifies the circumstances under which an enforcer of a security interest does not have a present right to the collateral at issue. The court denied the defendant's motion for summary judgment because a question of fact remained as to whether the repossession agency breached the peace and thereby lost its right to possession of the vehicle. Where on several occasions, an agency employee Blackhawk went to the plaintiff's residence at unreasonable hours, pounded loudly on the door while yelling, used offensive language, and tried to break into the garage, these incidents were likely to lead to an immediate public disturbance or provoke violence, and further, this type of conduct, if true, is the type of abusive practice Congress sought to prevent in enacting FDCPA and specifically § 1692f(6).

Minnesota

Gallagher v. Gurstel, Staloch & Chargo, P.A., 645 F. Supp. 2d 795 (D. Minn. 2009). Section 1692f(6) does not apply to a garnishment summons which is not a "non-judicial action."

Osborne v. Minn. Recovery Bureau, Inc., 59 U.C.C. Rep. Serv. 2d 879 (D. Minn. 2006). The FDCPA claim was dismissed because the repossessor's breach of the peace in connection with an unsuccessful repossession did not deprive them of their present right of possession and plaintiffs failed to state a claim for violation of the FDCPA. Consumer entitled to trial for the repossessor's UCC violation.

Akerlund v. TCF Nat'l Bank, 2001 U.S. Dist. LEXIS 22816 (D. Minn. June 11, 2001). Repossession company did not violate FDCPA because the creditor still had the present right of repossession, even though company breached the peace by criminal trespass in the course of repossession.

Revering v. Norwest Bank, 1999 U.S. Dist. LEXIS 20726 (D. Minn. Nov. 30, 1999). Repossession company was not liable for a violation of § 1692f(6)(A) where the creditor represented to the repossession company that it had the right to possess the vehicle even though creditor may not have mailed demand for timely payments. The FDCPA did not require the repossession company to conduct an independent investigation.

Saice v. MidAmerica Bank, 1999 WL 33911356 (D. Minn. Sept. 30, 1999). Since the issue of whether the current right of possession to collateral under § 1692f(6) is determined by applicable state law, the defendant repossessor's motion for summary judgment was denied where material facts remained unresolved, i.e., whether the repossession occurred without a breach of the peace.

Oehrlein v. Western Funding, Inc., 1999 U.S. Dist. LEXIS 17919 (D. Minn. Jan. 26, 1999). An attempted repossession once the consumer was late in payment gave the repossessor a present right of possession under state law and § 1692f(6) where the purchase contract provided for such a right "immediately" upon default.

James v. Ford Motor Credit Co., 842 F. Supp. 1202 (D. Minn. 1994), *aff'd*, 47 F.3d 961 (8th Cir. 1995). Because Credit Co. had present possessory right to car at the time of repossession under Minnesota law, the repossession company was not subject to liability for repossession activities under § 1692f(6).

New Mexico

Larranaga v. Mile High Collection & Recovery Bureau, Inc., 807 F. Supp. 111 (D.N.M. 1992), *rev'g in part*, 780 F. Supp. 780 (D.N.M. 1992). Section 1692f(6)(A) protected only property claimed as collateral (a car), not to the incidental taking of personal property inside the secured vehicle.

New York

Durandisse v. U.S. Auto Task Force, 2009 WL 2337133 (S.D.N.Y. July 30, 2009). Where the consumer failed to present evidence that the repossession companies did not have a "present right" to her automobile "via a valid security interest," § 1692f(6) did not apply. The consumer showed that the debt was paid prior to the repo, but the creditor had mishandled the payment.

Ghartey v. Chrysler Credit Corp., 1992 WL 373479 (E.D.N.Y. Nov. 23, 1992). Section 1692f(6) applied to repossession agencies, those businesses which were employed by the owner of collateral to dispossess the debtor of the collateral and return it to the owner.

North Dakota

Weiss v. Collection Ctr., Inc., 667 N.W.2d 567 (N.D. 2003). The least sophisticated consumer could interpret a letter advising that the debt collector had sought information from the motor vehicle department regarding his vehicle as a threat of its intent to repossess it. Whether a threat to repossess was an idle threat or actually intended was a question of fact precluding summary judgment. State law did not prohibit the seizure of a debtor's property merely because the amount of the debt was small.

Pennsylvania

Krajewski v. Am. Honda Fin. Corp., 557 F. Supp. 2d 596 (E.D. Pa. 2008). Repossession agent did not dispute it was a debt collector; its motion for summary judgment denied because whether it had a present right to possess the car depends on whether plaintiff had, in fact, defaulted under the contract.

South Carolina

Meredith v. Pathfinders Detective & Recovery, Inc., 1983 U.S. Dist. LEXIS 11860, 20367 (D.S.C. Nov. 9, 1983). A repossession company violated § 1692f(6) by repossessing the consumer's car prior to the expiration of the consumer's right under state law to cure his default.

Foster v. Ford Motor Credit Co., 382 S.E.2d 254 (S.C. Ct. App. 1989), *rev'd*, 395 S.E.2d 440 (S.C. 1990). A legal repossession that did not result in a breach of the peace did not give the consumers a claim under the FDCPA.

Utah

Burnett v. Mortgage Elec. Registration Sys., Inc., 2009 WL 3582294

(D. Utah Oct. 27, 2009). Complaint dismissed for failure to state a claim for violating § 1692f(6) since "the Deed of Trust expressly gives both the authority to foreclose and the authority to appoint a successor trustee" and thus the defendant, who was the trustee in the plaintiff's non-judicial home foreclosure, had the necessary "present right to the possession of the property" when he foreclosed.

Wisconsin

Barber v. Galindo, 2006 U.S. Dist. LEXIS 3356 (E.D. Wis. Jan. 18, 2006). Repossession did not violate the FDCPA when creditor had present right to possession.

Tomas v. Bass & Moglowski, 1999 U.S. Dist. LEXIS 21533 (W.D. Wis. June 29, 1999). Allegations in debt collector's state law replevin action for repossession of a dirt bike after consumer's monetary debt was discharged in bankruptcy were not false, deceptive or misleading because debt collector was not seeking amount that was owed and discharged.

K.2.5.5 Postcards and Envelopes

Strand v. Diversified Collection Serv., Inc., 380 F.3d 316 (8th Cir. 2004). Avoiding what it perceived as an absurd result by applying the plain language of the FDCPA, the court held that § 1692f(8) permitted such benign language on the envelope as the collection agency's initials, "DCS," corporate logo, and the statements, "PERSONAL AND CONFIDENTIAL" and "IMMEDIATE REPLY REQUESTED" as these words did not indicate the letter was to collect a debt.

Goswami v. American Collections Enter., Inc., 377 F.3d 488 (5th Cir. 2004). FDCPA does not bar the innocuous "priority letter" markings on a collection envelope. Nothing about the marking "priority letter" intimated that the contents of the envelope related to collection of delinquent debts, and thus the language was neither threatening nor embarrassing. The court purported to find ambiguity in § 1692f only by completely ignoring the clear and plain language of the second sentence of that section: "the following conduct is a violation of this section."

Peter v. G.C. Servs. L.P., 310 F.3d 344 (5th Cir. 2002). Use of the United States Department of Education's name and address as the return address on the envelope, as well as a marker that the envelope is not to be used for private communication, violated §§ 1692e(14) and 1692f(8).

Connecticut

Lindbergh v. Transworld Sys., Inc., 846 F. Supp. 175 (D. Conn. 1994). Debt collector's use of a symbol that contained the word "transmittal" on the envelope, but did not indicate or imply that the letter was an attempt to collect a debt, was not a prohibited debt collection practice under § 1692f(8).

Johnson v. NCB Collection Servs., 799 F. Supp. 1298 (D. Conn. 1992) (settled upon collector's payment of $4000 for consumer to withdraw appeal). Encoding the consumer's account number and amount on the payment envelope did not violate the FDCPA. Use of the words "Revenue Department" in the return address on the collector's envelope did not violate §§ 1692e(9), 1692e(14), or

1692f(8) by suggesting the correspondence was from a governmental agency, using a name other than the collector's "true" name, or disclosing the purpose of the correspondence.

Illinois

Davis v. Baron's Creditors Serv. Corp., 2001 U.S. Dist. LEXIS 19008 (N.D. Ill. Nov. 19, 2001). Although recognizing that the unsophisticated consumer could view the envelope's return address of "Baron's Creditor's Service Corporation" as indicating defendant was in the debt collection business in violation of § 1692f(8), the court denied cross-motions for summary judgment, holding that it was a question of fact for the jury.

Rutyna v. Collection Accounts Terminal, Inc., 478 F. Supp. 980 (N.D. Ill. 1979). This opinion finds harassment and deceptive and unfair practices. The use of the name "Collection Accounts Terminal, Inc." on a collection envelope violated § 1692f(8).

Indiana

Castell v. Credit Bureau, Inc., 15 Clearinghouse Rev. 956 (No. 31,794) (N.D. Ind. 1981). Summary judgment was entered for the consumers who received letters from defendant in which defendant's name clearly projected through the window of the envelope in violation of § 1692f(8). The collector did not carry its burden of showing that its name did not indicate it was a collector. The collector was listed in the yellow pages under debt collectors and attempted to collect $1.4 million of debts in the last two years.

Ohio

Gasser v. Allen County Claims & Adjustment, Inc., 1983 U.S. Dist. LEXIS 20361 (N.D. Ohio Nov. 3, 1983). A collection postcard violates § 1692f(7).

Oregon

Mathis v. Omnium Worldwide, 2006 WL 1582301 (D. Or. June 4, 2006). The court held that an envelope containing the name "Estate Recoveries, Inc.," along with the phrase "Over 15 Years of Service to the Financial Industry" did not violate § 1692f(8) as it did not indicate it was from a debt collector.

Baker v. G.C. Servs. Corp., Clearinghouse No. 31,230 (D. Or. 1981), *aff'd on other grounds*, 677 F.2d 775 (9th Cir. 1982). A logo which does not indicate the collection purpose of an envelope violates § 1692f(8) in a technical way but not the underlying purpose. Summary judgment on that claim was denied. Collecting accounts without the required state license does not violate the Act.

K.2.5.6 Garnishment, Execution, Exempt Property

Lee v. Javitch, Block & Rathbone L.L.P., 601 F.3d 654 (6th Cir. 2010). The court reversed a jury verdict finding that the defendant collection attorneys violated the FDCPA by submitting a false affidavit in the underlying state collection action stating that they had a reasonable basis to believe that the subject bank account contained nonexempt funds, as required by state law to initiate garnishment. The court found the evidence showed that the attorneys had in fact conducted a reasonable investigation supporting the truth of the affidavit, that no other reasonable steps could have been taken that would have revealed that the funds were exempt, and that the suggested alternative of subpoenaing the consumer's bank records prior to garnishment was an extraordinary measure that was not required under the applicable reasonableness standard.

Todd v. Weltman, Weinberg & Reis, Co., L.P.A., 434 F.3d 432 (6th Cir. 2006). Collection attorneys who falsely misrepresented state of debtors' non-exempt assets in affidavits in support of state court garnishments, when they had no knowledge or information whatever concerning the matter, could not claim absolute immunity.

Fox v. Citicorp Credit Servs., Inc., 15 F.3d 1507 (9th Cir. 1994). Consumers' allegations that the debt collector filed a garnishment action when the consumers were current in their payments was sufficient to state a claim for unfair or unconscionable collection practices under § 1692f.

Alabama

Bice v. Merchants Adjustment Serv., Clearinghouse No. 41,265 (S.D. Ala. 1985). Claim that the creditor misrepresented its willingness to accept partial payments and its legal right to claim exempt property, while actionable deception under § 1692e, did not state a claim under § 1692f.

Arizona

Riordan v. Jaburg & Wilk, P.C., 2010 WL 3023292 (D. Ariz. July 30, 2010). Although the fact that the defendant subpoenaed the consumer's bank records after quashing three such subpoenas invites speculation that the defendant did not have the statutorily requisite reasonable belief that only nonexempt funds were in the account, the court could not conclude that such a theory was plausible without more facts.

Arkansas

Hollowell v. Hosto, 2010 WL 1416519 (E.D. Ark. Apr. 8, 2010). Where no exempt funds had yet been taken from the *pro se* consumer's account when he filed the case, and the hold on the account had not been in place for an unreasonably long period of time, the court found that there was no unlawful garnishment and the FDCPA claim was not ripe for adjudication. Even if the *pro se* consumer's claim was ripe for adjudication, which it was not, he could not succeed against the defendant state court clerk due to her quasi-judicial immunity in connection with the entry of writs of garnishment.

Connecticut

Egletes v. Law Offices Howard Lee Schiff, P.C., 2010 WL 3025236 (D. Conn. July 30, 2010). Where the defendant attempted to garnish wages with interest on the judgment when the judgment struck a provision for interest, it was "inexcusable" for the collection lawyers to seek interest.

Silver v. Law Offices of Howard Lee Schiff, P.C., 2010 WL 3000053 (D. Conn. July 28, 2010). The court found no violation to take exempt bank funds where the consumer did not use the statutory procedure to claim the "wildcard" exemption. Where no funds were actually garnished, the threat to garnish 25% of wages was not actionable.

Shrestha v. Nadel, 2001 U.S. Dist. LEXIS 12553 (D. Conn. Mar. 21, 2001). The court entered summary judgment in favor of defendant attorney, finding that debtor's funds for which an exemption could have been claimed were not exempt from execution at the time of the attorney's seizure because the debtor had failed to follow the statutory requirements to claim exemptions.

Illinois

Beler v. Blatt, Hasenmiller, Leibsker, Moore, L.L.C., 2006 WL 1423118 (C.D. Ill. May 18, 2006). The court granted the law firm's motion for summary judgment and held that Illinois debt collector's freezing the debtor's exempt Social Security funds in a bank account was not unfair or unconscionable. The court pointed out that one part of the state attachment notice instructed that only nonexempt funds should be frozen.

Montana

Wetherelt v. Larsen Law Firm, P.L.L.C., 577 F. Supp. 2d 1128 (D. Mont. 2008). A debt collector who availed itself of lawful garnishment procedure despite prior unsworn claims of the consumer that her only funds were exempt social security, did not act unfairly or unconscionably by garnishing her checking account.

Nebraska

Wilson v. Bus. & Prof'l Credit Mgmt., Inc., Clearinghouse No. 41,672 (D. Neb. 1986). The collection agency's first garnishment of a social security recipient's checking account was not abusive or unfair in violation of §§ 1692d & 1692f where the collector did not know if nonexempt funds were also deposited in the account. The second garnishment of the account, while questionable, was not abusive or unfair where the collector had some reason to believe other funds may have been deposited in the account and the cost of a debtor's exam (about $200) would far exceed the debt ($29.48) or the cost of a garnishment hearing.

New York

McCarthy v. Wachovia Bank, N.A., 2011 WL 79854 (E.D.N.Y. Jan. 11, 2011). Summary judgment was granted to the defendant law firm on the FDCPA claim that it engaged in unlawful garnishment since the garnishment complied in all respects with applicable law.

Henneberger v. Cohen & Slamowitz, L.L.P., 2010 WL 1405578 (W.D.N.Y. Mar. 31, 2010). Summary judgment was inappropriate where there was a genuine issue of material fact as to whether defendant's employee threatened to seize resources (Social Security and pension funds) that could not legally be seized.

Ohio

Todd v. Weltman Weinberg, Reis & Co., L.P.A., 2008 WL 419943 (S.D. Ohio Feb. 14, 2008). The FDCPA prohibits false garnishment affidavits filed in state court.

Texas

Bray v. Cadle Co., 2010 WL 4053794 (S.D. Tex. Oct. 14, 2010). The court found the plaintiff stated a claim that the defendants engaged in "unfair or unconscionable means to collect" the debt by alleging that: 1) his bank account was exempt by law from garnishment by the Social Security Act; and 2) the defendants garnished the bank account, despite knowing or having reason to know that it contained Social Security funds and despite having failed to conduct pre-garnishment discovery.

Washington

George v. Atlantis Credit Corp., Clearinghouse No. 33,645 (Wash. Super. Ct. 1982). A collector violated § 1692f by applying for writs of garnishment without a statement, as required by state law, that the collector had reason to believe and believed the garnishee held nonexempt property owned by the debtor.

Wisconsin

Barrows v. Petrie & Stocking, S.C., 2008 WL 3540405 (W.D. Wis. Aug. 13, 2008). The defendant collectors violated the FDCPA by serving on the consumer's credit union a garnishment summons and complaint that claimed statutory disbursement charges in excess of the $40 allowed by applicable state law, in violation of §§ 1692e(2)(B), 1692e(10), and 1692f(1).

K.2.5.7 Unlicensed Collection

Connecticut

Lemire v. Wolpoff & Abramson, L.L.P., 256 F.R.D. 321 (D. Conn. 2009). In the course of granting class certification, court observed, "The common elements that itself admits clearly implicate the precise issue that [plaintiff] raises: whether can legally collect consumer debts in Connecticut without a license, or whether such conduct is prohibited by §§ 1692e or 1692f of the FDCPA."

St. Denis v. New Horizon Credit, Inc., 2006 WL 1965779 (D. Conn. July 12, 2006). The court entered default judgment for the maximum statutory damages, even in the absence of evidence of the defendant's intent or of the frequency or persistence of its unlawful debt collection activity of attempting to collect a debt in the state without being licensed to do so, because the nature of the violation "carries the potential for much wider spread illegality and concomitant injury than a violation related solely to one individual debtor" and "evince[s] either intentional disregard of or reckless indifference to" applicable state law by "a member of a regulated industry."

Florida

Leblanc v. Unifund CCR Partners, G.P., 552 F. Supp. 2d 1327 (M.D. Fla. 2008). Plaintiff established a claim under § 1692e(5) for defendant's threat to collect on a debt without being registered in Florida to do so. Defendant's request for summary judgment on the corresponding § 1692f claim was denied.

Illinois

Schad v. Phoenix Adjusters, Inc., 1995 WL 311440 (N.D. Ill. May 18, 1995). Where collector's letter was forwarded from Maryland to debtor in Illinois, court on its own directed the consumer's counsel to file a memorandum addressing claim of collector's failure to obtain Illinois license.

Minnesota

State ex rel. Hatch v. JBC Legal Group, P.C., 2006 WL 1388453 (Minn. Dist. Ct. Apr. 13, 2006). Lawyers are excluded from Minnesota licensing provisions but whether lawyer defendants were engaged in the practice of law is a question of fact.

Nevada

Kuhn v. Account Control Tech., Inc., 865 F. Supp. 1443 (D. Nev. 1994). Collector's unlicensed attempts to collect a debt, before the state law was amended, violated § 1692f because the failure to obtain a license deprived the consumer of her right to have the state review the collector's qualifications, and § 1692e(5) and (10).

New Mexico

Russey v. Rankin, 911 F. Supp. 1449 (D.N.M. 1995). Out-of-state collection agencies violated §§ 1692e, 1692e(5), 1692e(10) and 1692f by engaging in collection activities in a state without obtaining required state debt collection licenses.

New York

Castillo v. Frenkel, 2010 WL 5507904 (N.Y. App. Div. Dec. 23, 2010). The fact that debt collection efforts were initiated in New York City by a debt collector that was not licensed under the city's administrative code did not by itself constitute a violation of the FDCPA.

Scott v. J. Anthony Cambece Law Office, P.C., 600 F. Supp. 2d 479 (E.D.N.Y. 2009). The complaint stated an FDCPA claim against the defendant law firm for collecting debts without a debt collection license as required by the applicable New York City municipal code, since the code does not contain a per se exemption for attorneys as the defendant argued.

McDowell v. Vengroff, Williams & Assocs., Inc., 2006 WL 1720435 (E.D.N.Y. June 21, 2006). The case was dismissed for failure to state a claim, where the claim was that defendant did not have a local New York City collection license.

K.2.5.8 Time-Barred Debts

Alabama

Kimber v. Federal Fin. Corp., 668 F. Supp. 1480 (M.D. Ala. 1987). Filing a time-barred claim without reason to believe the statute of limitations had been tolled was unfair, violating § 1692f.

Connecticut

Lindbergh v. Transworld Sys., Inc., 846 F. Supp. 175 (D. Conn. 1994). When the consumer failed to respond to the debt collector's proper validation notice within thirty days and the consumer could not show that the debt collector was otherwise aware that the collection of the debt was barred by a state statute of limitations, the debt collector was not liable for false representations or unfair collection practices under §§ 1692e(2)(A) or 1692f for its attempt to collect a debt which was barred by the statute of limitations.

Florida

Knighten v. Palisades Collections, L.L.C., 2010 WL 2696768 (S.D. Fla. July 6, 2010). A lawyer violated numerous provisions of the FDCPA by filing a time-barred lawsuit for a party that lacked standing.

Illinois

Ramirez v. Palisades Collection L.L.C., 2008 WL 2512679 (N.D. Ill. June 23, 2008). Five-year statute of limitations for unwritten contracts, rather than ten-year statute for written contracts, applied to credit card account. Because defendant filed a plainly time-barred suit against an unwitting consumer, it is subject to liability under §§ 1692e and 1692f.

Hamid v. Blatt, Hasenmiller, Leibsker, Moore & Pellettieri, 2001 U.S. Dist. LEXIS 13918 (N.D. Ill. Aug. 31, 2001). Consumer's allegations that collection attorney filed suit on a time-barred debt were sufficient to survive debt collector's motion to dismiss FDCPA action.

Stepney v. Outsourcing Solutions, Inc., 1997 WL 722972 (N.D. Ill. Nov. 13, 1997). Collector's knowing attempts to collect time-barred debts violated the FDCPA.

Indiana

Simmons v. Miller, 970 F. Supp. 661 (S.D. Ind. 1997). There was no intentional violation of §§ 1692d, 1692e, 1692e(2)(A), or 1692f(1) where a claim on an NSF check was filed more than three years but less than six years after the check was written and it was not clear that a six year rather than three year statute of limitations applied.

Maryland

Spencer v. Hendersen-Webb, 81 F. Supp. 2d 582 (D. Md. 1999). Representing that the debt could be collected for twelve years when it was not under seal and subject to a three-year statute of limitations violated §§ 1692e(2)(A) and 1692f(1).

Minnesota

Wald v. Morris, Carlson, & Hoelscher, P.A., 2010 WL 4736829 (D. Minn. Nov. 16, 2010). A debt collector who threatened to sue the consumer on time barred debt violated §§ 1692e(2)(A), (5), (10), and 1692f.

Montana

McCollough v. Johnson, Rodenberg & Lauinger, 610 F. Supp. 2d 1247 (D. Mont. 2009). A debt collector violated the FDCPA by using the courts to attempt to collect a time-barred debt. While the debt collector's use of discovery in a collection action is not a per se violation of the FDCPA, here the request for admission to admit that a payment was made was served when the debt collector's records showed the payment was not made. The use of the judicial process against a *pro se* defendant, in order to avoid a statute of limitations defense, collecting on a time-barred debt was an abusive, unfair, and unconscionable practice in violation of the FDCPA. The debt collector's failure to move to set aside the underlying state court default judgment, after a summary judgment ruling that the underlying state court action violated the FDCPA because it was time barred, constituted an additional FDCPA violation.

New Jersey

Bodine v. First Nat'l Collection Bureau, Inc., 2010 WL 5149847 (D.N.J. Dec. 13, 2010). An effort to collect a time-barred debt with no threat of suit does not violate the FDCPA. Where nothing in the pleadings suggested that the defendant attempted or threatened to commence an action to recover the debt, the issue of the statute of limitations was irrelevant.

K.2.5.9 Unfair Practices in Debt Collection Suits

Drennan v. First Resolution Inv. Corp., 2010 WL 3059205 (5th Cir. Aug. 4, 2010). Filing a suit to collect a credit card debt did not constitute either a false or misleading representation or one that was so harassing, oppressive, or unconscionable that it was actionable under the FDCPA, even if, arguendo, the use of a suit on account on a credit card debt did not meet the necessary requirements of Texas's Rule of Civil Procedure 185 or any other such rules or regulations. The circumstances of this case do not constitute a violation of the FDCPA, even if the underlying action was not a proper suit on a sworn account.

Hartman v. Great Seneca Fin., Corp., 569 F.3d 606 (6th Cir. 2009). Summary judgment for the defendant debt buyer and its attorneys reversed where a question of material fact existed as to whether the debt buyer's representations made in state collection court were an unfair means of collecting a debt in violation of § 1692f. The debt buyers attached to the collection complaints documents which they represented were copies of the consumers' credit card account statements, when in fact the documents were actually created by the defendants based on general information they received electronically about the debts, lacked any detail as to purchases or payments made, and were printed to appear to be recent credit card bills.

Piche v. Clark County Collection Serv., Inc., 2004 WL 2943686 (9th Cir. Dec. 21, 2004). Use by the debt collector of a confession of judgment remedy that is generally permissible under state law was not an unfair practice that violated the FDCPA merely because FTC and banking rules prohibit its use in other contexts.

Arizona

Walker v. Gallegos, 167 F. Supp. 2d 1105 (D. Ariz. 2001). Plaintiff's allegation that attorney sued plaintiff claiming plaintiff was liable to pay even though he was not the debtor and had signed no contract survived motion to dismiss. The court cited *Kimber* for the proposition that filing a lawsuit without first inquiring whether there was an absolute defense violated § 1692f.

Arkansas

Born v. Hosto & Buchan, P.L.L.C., 2010 WL 2431063 (Ark. June 17, 2010). Because the statute of limitations had not run on the state debt collection complaint, the FDCPA claim for suing on a time barred claim was properly dismissed.

California

Owings v. Hunt & Henriques, 2010 WL 3489342 (S.D. Cal. Sept. 3, 2010). A consumer on duty with the National Guard was entitled to the benefits of the Servicemembers Civil Relief Act so as to render false and misleading and unfair under the FDCPA the defendant's declaration that plaintiff was not in active military service.

Mulinix v. Unifund CCR Partners, 2008 WL 2001747 (S.D. Cal. May 5, 2008). Plaintiff's allegations under §§ 1692d and 1692e(4), 1692e(5), and 1692f survive a motion to dismiss, because they were not limited to the mere filing of an ultimately unsuccessful lawsuit. Instead, plaintiff appears to allege that defendant filed the lawsuit despite plaintiff's repeated attempts to communicate that he did not owe the debt, failed to comply with discovery requests, and then continued the lawsuit in the face of "repeated demands that the lawsuit be dismissed" well past the discovery deadline, and even until the trial date, all without ever producing evidence of ownership of the debt in response to a written request. According to plaintiff, defendant finally dismissed the lawsuit "mere hours before the case was scheduled for trial."

Riley v. Giguiere, 2008 WL 436943 (E.D. Cal. Feb. 14, 2008). Former tenant stated a claim under §§ 1692d, 1692e, and 1692f in alleging that the eviction lawyer improperly proceeded to obtain judgment from him despite reason to know he had vacated the apartment many years prior to the eviction.

Georgia

Kuria v. Palisades Acquisition XVI, L.L.C., 2010 WL 4780769 (N.D. Ga. Nov. 16, 2010). A consumer who was wrongly sued in state court stated a claim for §§ 1692e and 1692f violations based on allegations that the defendant's collection suit was part "of a pattern and practice of abusive, scattershot litigation to collect debts" where the debt buyer "knew when filing the suit not only that it lacked knowledge of the validity of the underlying debt, but also that it never intended to investigate or verify the debt's validity." The court found that the defendant's intent was not to take its claims against the plaintiff to trial, at which it would have to prove that its claim had merit, but rather to obtain a default judgment against the plaintiff or to enter into a voluntary settlement with him. Since the defendant's actions were allegedly "rooted in bad faith, reckless disregard toward debtors, and abuse of process," the court found that the consumer alleged "more than mere lack of knowledge or lack of a 'paper trail' asserted in" distinguishable cases.

Illinois

Jenkins v. Centurion Capital Corp., 2009 WL 3414248 (N.D. Ill. Oct. 20, 2009). The court held that FDCPA was not violated where the defendants filed a state court lawsuit against plaintiff with only an affidavit attesting to its record keeping methods and documentation, and the plaintiff alleged that defendants violated § 1692f by filing a lawsuit when they knew they could not prove the allegation of the suit at the time of filing.

Guevara v. Midland Funding NCC-2 Corp., 2008 WL 4865550 (N.D. Ill. June 20, 2008). A consumer may state a claim for violations of the FDCPA based on misrepresentation and unfair collection practices which are contained in a state court complaint.

Lockett v. Freedman, 2004 WL 856516 (N.D. Ill. Apr. 21, 2004). Attorney collector's motion to dismiss was denied where consumer adequately alleged that attorney lacked knowledge to verify complaint in a state collection action and attempted to collect unauthorized attorney fees.

Blum v. Lawent, 2003 WL 22078306 (N.D. Ill. Sept. 8, 2003). A collection lawyer misnaming a dentist, rather than the dentist's corporate employer, as the plaintiff in a collection action was not unfair.

Bradley v. Fairbanks Capital Corp., 2003 WL 21011801 (N.D. Ill. May 5, 2003). Allegation that it violated the FDCPA for an attorney to verify a complaint based upon information supplied by the plaintiff (which was permitted by state law), failed to state a claim.

Young v. Meyer & Njus, P.A., 1997 WL 452685 (N.D. Ill. Aug. 6, 1997). Court refused to dismiss allegation that § 1692f was violated by attorney who verified complaint based on the review of a computer print-out from the creditor which provided insufficient information to prove the debt at trial. Possibility of creditor's attorney being a witness in collection suit was not an unconscionable means of collection in violation of § 1692f.

Indiana

Frye v. Bowman, Heintz, Boscia & Vician, P.C., 193 F. Supp. 2d 1070 (S.D. Ind. 2002). Section 1692f did not apply to misrepresentations of the debtor's rights in a summons.

Minnesota

Hemmingsen v. Messerli & Kramer, P.A., 2011 WL 494941 (D. Minn. Feb. 7, 2011). Summary judgment was granted on the §§ 1692d and 1692f claims to the defendant collection attorneys who represented the unsuccessful credit card creditor in the underlying state court collection lawsuit. The evidence showed, contrary to the plaintiff's claim that the debt was her ex-husband's alone, that the couple's divorce papers and the monthly statements both indicated that plaintiff was an account debtor and that she signed one $20 payment check: "The fact that the state court denied [the collection attorneys'] summary judgment motion and granted [the consumer's] does not, on its own, indicate that [the collection attorneys] harassed her or used unfair practices to collect the debt."

Montana

McCollough v. Johnson, Rodenberg & Lauinger, 2009 WL 176867 (D. Mont. Jan. 8, 2009). A debt collector violated the FDCPA by using the courts to attempt to collect a time-barred debt. While the debt collector's use of discovery in a collection action is not a per se violation of the FDCPA, here the request for admission to admit that a payment was made was served when the debt collector's records showed the payment was not made. The use of the judicial process against a *pro se* defendant, in order to avoid a statute of limitations defense, collecting on a time-barred debt was an abusive, unfair, and unconscionable practice in violation of the FDCPA. The state Rule 11 requires that "an attorney may not file a request for admission unless that attorney, after reasonable inquiry, be-

lieves that it is well grounded in fact." Noting the collection law firm's defense that the state rules of professional conduct state could not be the basis for civil liability the court noted that the preamble to those rules provided that "truthfulness must be the hallmark of the legal profession, and the stock-in-trade of all lawyers." The debt collector's failure to move to set aside the underlying state court default judgment, after a summary judgment ruling that the underlying state court action violated the FDCPA because it was time barred, constituted an additional FDCPA violation.

New Jersey

Scioli v. Goldman & Warshaw P.C., 651 F. Supp. 2d 273 (D.N.J. 2009). Notwithstanding the plaintiff's argument that statutory attorney fees are only due and owing after judgment is entered for the debt collector and its status as the prevailing party is established, the court dismissed the complaint for failure to state claims under § 1692f(1) because the least sophisticated consumer would not be deceived by a debt collector listing a specific sum of statutory fees in the space provided in the court-approved form summons. Not only did the form summons contain a blank space to insert the amount of fees requested but it also disclosed that all amounts listed are only the amounts being requested: "Scioli essentially asks this Court to hold that the form summons created by the State of New Jersey, and used by countless lawyers and nonlawyers throughout the State, violates the FDCPA. But such a holding would defy common sense and would not further the goals of the FDCPA."

Hodges v. Feinstein, Raiss, Kelin & Booker, L.L.C., 893 A.2d 21 (N.J. Super. Ct. App. Div. Mar. 8, 2006), *aff'd sub nom. Hodges v. Sasil Corp.*, 915 A.2d 1 (N.J. 2007). The court commented on "the fundamental unfairness of a complaint that characterizes as 'rent' the additional late charges and legal fees for which the tenant may be contractually liable under the lease but not required to pay to avoid eviction." The complaint gave the appearance of a due process violation.

New York

Sykes v. Mel Harris & Assocs., L.L.C., 2010 WL 5395712 (S.D.N.Y. Dec. 29, 2010). Consumers alleging that a debt buyer, a law firm, and a process server entered into joint ventures to purchase debt portfolios, pursued debt collection litigation en masse against the alleged debtors, used "sewer service" (the practice of failing to serve a summons and complaint and then filing a fraudulent affidavit attesting to service), and sought to collect millions of dollars in fraudulently obtained default judgments stated causes of action for violations of the FDCPA, RICO, and New York's General Business Law § 349.

Stark v. Hudson & Keyse L.L.C., 2008 WL 4866046 (E.D.N.Y. Nov. 7, 2008). Debt collector's lawsuit in a permissible, but higher trial court than required to recover an alleged debt and seeking costs in connection with the state collection suit cannot provide a basis for an FDCPA violation of §§ 1692e or 1692f.

Ohio

Myers v. Asset Acceptance L.L.C., 2010 WL 3522470 (S.D. Ohio Sept. 7, 2010). An affidavit submitted with a complaint against a debtor, in which an employee swore that the debt information was accurate and that he was competent to express an opinion on its correctness, would not have misled the least sophisticated consumer into believing that the employee's representations were based on any personal knowledge he had regarding the underlying debt. A statement of account included as an attachment to a complaint was not deceptive or misleading, because while it included the debtor's account number and balance owed, it would not have misled the least sophisticated consumer into believing that it was a monthly statement. The representations were not unfair practices.

Montgomery v. Donnett, 2006 WL 293727 (S.D. Ohio Feb. 7, 2006). The filing of landlord's action barred by res judicata, like a time-barred claim, violated the FDCPA. Even if the prior state court judgment had been amended to not bar the subsequent claim, it did not alter the FDCPA violation that already had occurred.

Hartman v. Asset Acceptance Corp., 467 F. Supp. 769 (S.D. Ohio 2004). FDCPA claims that affidavit misrepresented that the debt buyer was a holder in due course of a credit card account in a state collection action violated § 1692e(2) and (12) but not §§ 1692e(6)(A) and 1692d.

Oregon

Flores v. Quick Collect, Inc., 2007 WL 2769003 (D. Or. Sept. 18, 2007). The court granted the defendant's summary judgment on the consumer's claim that the warning included in the order requiring her to appear for a post-judgment debtor's examination, warning that she may be charged with contempt of court and arrested if she failed to appear, was false, oppressive, or unfair, because the defendants never intended to arrest her and could not have legally arrested her for failure to appear because the debtor examination was sought in an venue that was allegedly unlawful pursuant to § 1692i, since the "threat" was issued by the court and not by the defendants and in any event she could have been held in contempt if she did not appear regardless of the FDCPA venue provision.

Flores v. Quick Collect, Inc., 2007 WL 433239 (D. Or. Jan. 31, 2007). Use of an illegal or improper summons may constitute an unfair or unconscionable means to collect a debt under § 1692f.

Pennsylvania

Popson v. Galloway, 2010 WL 2985945 (W.D. Pa. July 27, 2010). Follows *Harvey* finding filing suit without providing documentation substantiating the debt does not violate §§ 1692d, 1692e or 1692f.

Tennessee

Spangler v. Conrad, 2010 WL 2389481 (E.D. Tenn. June 9, 2010). The collection attorney defendant did not violate §§ 1692e and 1692f merely by attaching to the state court collection complaint his client's sworn statement of account allegedly misstating the amount of the debt. "A debt collection attorney should be allowed to confidently rely upon an affidavit of Sworn Account executed by his client that sets forth the total amount owed."

Utah

Maxwell v. Barney, 2008 WL 1981666 (D. Utah May 2, 2008). Collection lawyers did not violate the §§ 1692d or 1692f where the ambulance ticket for a rape victim was attached to a debt collection complaint properly filed in the course of litigation proceedings and the information contained on the ambulance ticket provided proof of the debt at issue in the proceedings.

Wisconsin

Tomas v. Bass & Moglowski, 1999 U.S. Dist. LEXIS 21533 (W.D. Wis. June 29, 1999). A deficiency claim contained in debt collector's state law replevin action for repossession of a dirt bike filed after consumer's monetary debt was discharged may violate § 1692f because the allegation may be an unfair effort to induce redemption.

K.2.5.10 Other Unfair Practices

LeBlanc v. Unifund CCR Partners, 601 F.3d 1185 (11th Cir. 2010). The court remanded the issue of whether a dunning letter that purported to be from a debt collector's "Legal Department" and possibly constituted a threat to take action that could not legally have been taken was "unfair and unconscionable" under § 1692f. The issue presented a question for the jury.

Van v. Grant & Weber, 308 Fed. Appx. 46 (9th Cir. 2008). Collection letter containing reminder of a state law requiring debtors to provide new contact information, while warning debtors that the information will be used for purposes of debt collection, did not conflict with §§ 1692e, 1692f, 1692g.

McMillan v. Collection Prof'ls Inc., 455 F.3d 754 (7th Cir. 2006). Consumer stated a claim for violating § 1692f where the collection letter called into question the debtor's honesty and good intentions and that could constitute an unfair or unconscionable practice.

Goswami v. Am. Collections Enter., Inc., 377 F.3d 488 (5th Cir. 2004). The court refused to give a literal interpretation to § 1692f(8) as it would impinge on the collector's free speech right to put the words "Priority Letter" on the envelope containing a dunning letter. The court did not consider whether those words might confuse a consumer about the urgency of the letter or its importance, given that the U.S. Postal Service expedites "Priority Mail" for an additional postage fee.

Shapiro v. Riddle & Assocs., P.C., 351 F.3d 63 (2d Cir. 2003). The agreement between the consumer and Riddle's client explicitly permitted the creditor to collect a reasonable fee if it were required to employ a collection agency or attorney, as it obviously was. The consumer's contention that a $98 collection fee for sending a demand letter and preparing suit was unreasonable was viewed as an uphill battle.

Turner v. J.V.D.B. & Assocs., Inc., 330 F.3d 991 (7th Cir. 2003). A letter which simply provides the § 1692g(a) language does not violate § 1692f even when another FDCPA section has been violated by sending the letter (in this case because the debt had been discharged).

Juras v. Aman Collection Serv., Inc., 829 F.2d 739 (9th Cir. 1987). Court dismissed an FDCPA claim that it was unfair to withhold the student's transcript. The *pro se* debtor asserted that withholding a transcript was tantamount to taking security for a student loan, which is prohibited by law, and was consequently an unfair debt collection practice.

Alabama

Sparks v. Phillips & Cohen Assocs., Ltd., 641 F. Supp. 2d 1234 (S.D. Ala. 2008). Summary judgment for the defendant on plaintiff's § 1692f claims because they merely "rehash" and duplicate "their claims under other FDCPA sections."

California

Riley v. Giguiere, 631 F. Supp. 2d 1295 (E.D. Cal. 2009). Plaintiff alleged that collection attorney for his former lessor used improper means in pursuing an unlawful detainer action against him by obtaining service against him at the wrong address in violation of §§ 1692d, 1692e, and 1692f. Court held that issues of fact required a trial of the claims.

Cruz v. MRC Receivables Corp., 563 F. Supp. 2d 1092 (N.D. Cal. 2008). Use of name and title of senior vice president on form collection letters (which he had read and approved) was not misleading or deceptive nor unfair or unconscionable in violation of §§ 1692e or 1692f.

Voris v. Resurgent Capital Servs., L.P., 494 F. Supp. 2d 1156 (S.D. Cal. 2007). The court denied the debt collector's motion for judgment on the pleadings that collection letters which appear to be a credit card solicitation was not an unfair or unconscionable practice in violation of §§ 1692f or 1692f(8).

Khosroabadi v. North Shore Agency, 439 F. Supp. 2d 1118 (S.D. Cal. 2006). The debt collector's failure to include in its letter the notice required by the California debt collection statute was not an unfair or deceptive method of debt collection.

Johnson v. Phillips & Cohen Assocs., Ltd., 2006 WL 2355340 (N.D. Cal. Aug. 15, 2006). The court dismissed the FDCPA claim based on the collector's failure to provide a notice required by state law since such a violation of state law "does not automatically trigger a violation of the federal FDCPA" and the resulting omission was not unfair, deceptive, or misleading.

Masuda v. Thomas Richards & Co., 759 F. Supp. 1456 (C.D. Cal. 1991). Collector's practice of sending form letter signed by an independent attorney who had no knowledge of the debt and who had not consulted with the collector was unfair and deceptive in violation of §§ 1692f and 1692e(3).

Delaware

Beattie v. D.M. Collections, Inc., 754 F. Supp. 383 (D. Del. 1991). The *attempt* to collect from one not obligated was not a violation of § 1692f(1). A debt collector violated § 1692e(2)(A) by mistakenly dunning the wrong person when the collector fails to exercise reasonable care.

Georgia

Williams v. Rash, Curtis & Assocs., 1978 U.S. Dist. LEXIS 20395 (N.D. Ga. Dec. 13, 1978). Motion to dismiss was denied. Plaintiff alleged that threats of action during the thirty-day period for requesting validation violated the validation provisions or were unfair.

Illinois

Lee v. Northland Group, 2003 WL 25765398 (N.D. Ill. Apr. 24, 2003). The court may not rewrite the plain language of TILA, and neither defendant meets the TILA definition of a creditor. Since plaintiff's FDCPA claims are entirely predicated on her nonexistent TILA violation, those claims must also be dismissed.

Turner v. J.V.D.B. & Assocs., Inc., 211 F. Supp. 2d 1108 (N.D. Ill. 2002), *rev'd in part,* 330 F.3d 991 (7th Cir. 2003). Creditor's knowledge that the consumer had filed bankruptcy was not imputed under the FDCPA to the debt collector, which therefore was not liable for the resulting improper communication with the debtor.

Taylor v. Fink, 1994 WL 669605 (N.D. Ill. Nov. 25, 1994). "Merely threatening to file a lawsuit did not violate [15 U.S.C.] § 1692d" or § 1692f.

Smith v. Mikell, Clearinghouse No. 34,362C (N.D. Ill. 1982). Unfair practices are prohibited by § 1692f without regard to whether conduct is harassing, abusive or sharp. A collector may communicate the collector's right to sue but may not misrepresent a suit was intended or collect litigation related costs that were not yet incurred.

Massachusetts

Cacares v. Jackson, 2011 WL 99003 (D. Mass. Jan. 11, 2011). The court rejected the *pro se* plaintiff's claim that Unifund, as a buyer and seller of debt, owed a duty of good faith and fair dealing that arises out of the FDCPA.

Michigan

Wilson v. Merchants & Med. Credit Corp., Inc., 2010 WL 3488617 (E.D. Mich. Sept. 2, 2010). A debt collector's statement that "we know where you work, we know where you live, we know what kind of car you drive, and we will be in further—further contact with you" did not violate §§ 1692d, 1692e or 1692f. "This alleged statement does not suggest that Merchants would refer the case to law enforcement. Rather, it indicates that *Merchants* would be in further contact with Wilson." A debt collector's demand to pay $200 by the end of the day or it would "further the investigation" did not violate §§ 1692d, 1692e, or 1692f.

Minnesota

Neill v. Bullseye Collection Agency, Inc., 2009 WL 1386155 (D. Minn. May 14, 2009). The consumer's allegations that the collector's printing at the top of its duns the acronym "WWJD," which stands for the phrase "what would Jesus do?", "has the effect of invoking shame or guilt in alleged debtors and portrays the debtor as a sinner who is going to hell" stated a claim for engaging in conduct that is harassing, oppressive, or abusive in violation of § 1692d and unfair or unconscionable in violation of § 1692f.

Knoll v. Intellirisk Mgmt., 2006 WL 2974190 (D. Minn. Oct. 16, 2006). Denied debt collector's motion to dismiss class action where debt collector used the false name, Jennifer Smith, as the Caller ID finding a claim was stated under §§ 1692d, 1692e, 1692f.

Nebraska

Hulshizer v. Global Credit Servs., Inc., Clearinghouse No. 36,146 (D. Neb. 1983), *aff'd on other grounds*, 728 F.2d 1037 (8th Cir. 1984). A notification of a consumer's right to cure a default was not unfair or unconscionable.

Harris v. BWS Credit Servs., Inc., Clearinghouse No. 27,693 (D. Neb. 1980) (order on motions for summary judgment). The evidence did not sustain a finding that § 1692f was violated by a threat to "get" one of the consumers.

New York

Wegmans Food Mkts., Inc. v. Scrimpsher, 17 B.R. 999 (Bankr. N.D.N.Y. 1982). The failure to include the collector's address in the dunning letters (the address appeared on the envelope) was unfair since it nullified the consumer's rights under § 1692g(b).

Ohio

Jordan v. John Soliday Fin. Group, L.L.C., 2010 WL 1462345 (N.D. Ohio Apr. 12, 2010). The court reserved for the trier of fact whether the defendants' attachment to the underlying state court collection complaint of documents that revealed the consumer's Social Security number violated the FDCPA.

Kleczy v. First Fed. Credit Control, Inc., 21 Ohio App. 3d 56, 486 N.E.2d 204 (1984). No violation of FDCPA to attempt to collect part of a medical bill from father of an adult patient since father had been listed as a responsible party.

Oregon

Skelley v. Ray Klein, Inc., 2010 WL 438148 (D. Or. Feb. 3, 2010). *Pro se* plaintiff's allegation that defendant engaged in unfair or unconscionable means by refusing to take less than payment in full does not violate § 1692f.

Pennsylvania

Catherman v. Credit Bureau, 634 F. Supp. 693 (E.D. Pa. 1986). The consumer failed to establish that letters from a collection and credit reporting agency threatening the consumer's ability to obtain credit were unconscionable or deceptive. The letters were not likely to convey the impression to an unsophisticated consumer that they would be immediately denied all credit, but only that there would be a chance of future denials.

South Carolina

Foster v. Ford Motor Credit Co., 382 S.E.2d 254 (S.C. Ct. App. 1989), *rev'd*, 395 S.E.2d 440 (S.C. 1990). The consumer's allegation that they never received a required notice of default and right to cure did not establish an FDCPA violation since the creditor complied with the state requirement that it mail the notice.

Virginia

Neild v. Wolpoff & Abramson, L.L.P., 453 F. Supp. 2d 918 (E.D. Va. 2006). The consumer's allegation that defendant violated the FDCPA merely by attempting to collect a disputed debt did not state a cause of action upon which relief could be granted.

In re Stacy, 21 B.R. 49 (Bankr. W.D. Va. 1982). A collector's continuing dunning of a consumer after the consumer filed bankruptcy and an automatic stay of collection efforts was issued by the bankruptcy court may have constituted a violation of the FDCPA.

Washington

In re Hodges, 342 B.R. 616 (Bankr. E.D. Wash. 2006). Sending a collection letter which showed the demand for payment through the address window violated § 1692f(8).

K.2.6 Validation of Debts, 15 U.S.C. § 1692g

K.2.6.1 Least Sophisticated Consumer and Other General Standards

Ellis v. Solomon & Solomon, P.C., 591 F.3d 130 (2d Cir. 2010). "To recover damages under the FDCPA, a consumer does not need to show intentional conduct on the part of the debt collector." Described and applied the least sophisticated consumer analysis.

Sims v. GC Servs. L.P., 445 F.3d 959 (7th Cir. 2006). The unsophisticated consumer standard applied. A letter cannot be confusing as a matter of law unless a significant fraction of unsophisticated consumers would be confused. Since the FDCPA is a strict liability law, the good or bad intent of the debt collector is immaterial.

Thomas v. Law Firm of Simpson & Cybak, 354 F.3d 696, 2004 WL 51733 (7th Cir. Jan. 13, 2004), *vacated*, 2004 WL 242950 (7th Cir. Feb. 10, 2004). Courts should give effect to the plain meaning of the FDCPA.

Schlosser v. Fairbanks Capital Corp., 323 F.3d 534 (7th Cir. 2003). The validation provision is aimed at preventing collection efforts based on mistaken information.

Marshall-Mosby v. Corporate Receivables, Inc., 205 F.3d 323 (7th Cir. 2000). The court vacated its earlier decision dismissing the complaint (194 F.3d 830 (7th Cir. 1999) because (only in the Seventh Circuit) whether a letter can be confusing or contradictory about § 1692g dispute rights to the least sophisticated consumer was a question of fact, not law.

Chaudhry v. Gallerizzo, 174 F.3d 394 (4th Cir. 1999). The collector is only required to verify that the creditor is demanding the amount claimed and is not required to keep detailed files of the debt. When a consumer is represented by an attorney, the validation of the debt should be sent to the attorney.

Johnson v. Revenue Mgmt. Corp., 169 F.3d 1057 (7th Cir. 1999). Dismissals of two separate class actions based on validation notices reversed. Appellate court held: (1) a contention that a validation notice was confusing was a recognized legal claim and no more was needed to survive a motion under Rule 12(b)(6) and (2) courts should allow plaintiffs to supplement a complaint or provide legal arguments before dismissing under Fed. R. Civ. P. 12(c).

Smith v. Computer Credit, Inc., 167 F.3d 1052 (6th Cir. 1999). Applies least sophisticated consumer standard to validation notice analysis.

Goldberg v. Transworld Sys., Inc., 164 F.3d 617 (2d Cir. 1998) (text at 1998 WL 650793). Applies least sophisticated consumer standard.

Bartlett v. Heibl, 128 F.3d 497 (7th Cir. 1997). Applies unsophisticated consumer standard.

Terran v. Kaplan, 109 F.3d 1428 (9th Cir. 1997). Applies least sophisticated consumer standard.

Russell v. Equifax A.R.S., 74 F.3d 30 (2d Cir. 1996). Applies least sophisticated consumer standard. The "least sophisticated consumer" lacks the astuteness of an attorney and even the sophistication of the average consumer.

Smith v. Transworld Sys., Inc., 953 F.2d 1025 (6th Cir. 1992). Applies least sophisticated consumer standard.

Swanson v. S. Oregon Credit Serv., 869 F.2d 1222 (9th Cir. 1988). Applies least sophisticated consumer standard.

Baker v. G.C. Servs. Corp., 677 F.2d 775 (9th Cir. 1982). Applies unsophisticated consumer standard. Also, a consumer need not dispute the validity of a debt to recover for a failure to provide a proper notice of validation rights provided by § 1692g.

California

Masuda v. Thomas Richards & Co., 759 F. Supp. 1456 (C.D. Cal. 1991). Applies least sophisticated consumer standard.

Connecticut

Gaudette v. G.C. Servs., 1999 U.S. Dist. LEXIS 21532 (D. Conn. Sept. 7, 1999). Applied least sophisticated consumer standard.

Macarz v. Transworld Sys., Inc., 26 F. Supp. 2d 368 (D. Conn. 1998). Applies least sophisticated consumer standard.

Colmon v. Payco-G.A.C., Inc., 1992 U.S. Dist. LEXIS 22733 (D. Conn. Jan. 22, 1992). Applied least sophisticated consumer standard.

Florida

In re Hathcock, 437 B.R. 696 (Bankr. M.D. Fla. 2010). The court stated that although there is a split among the circuit courts as to whether the effectiveness of a validation notice is an issue of law or fact, courts that apply the least sophisticated consumer standard treat these issues as questions of law.

Georgia

Mullis v. McDowell Servs., Inc., Clearinghouse No. 51,951 (N.D. Ga. 1997). Applies least sophisticated consumer standard.

Zoeckler v. Credit Claims & Collection, Inc., 1982 U.S. Dist. LEXIS 18384 (N.D. Ga. Sept. 30, 1982). Applies reasonable consumer standard.

Hawaii

Sakuma v. First Nat'l Credit Bureau, 1989 U.S. Dist. LEXIS 19120 (D. Haw. Nov. 15, 1989). Applies least sophisticated consumer standard.

Illinois

Crowder v. Kelly, 1999 U.S. Dist. LEXIS 4767 (N.D. Ill. Mar. 31, 1999). Applies least sophisticated consumer standard.

Seplak by Seplak v. IMBS, Inc., 1999 U.S. Dist. LEXIS 2106 (N.D. Ill. Feb. 22, 1999). Applies least sophisticated consumer standard.

Jenkins v. Union Corp., 999 F. Supp. 1120 (N.D. Ill. 1998). Applies unsophisticated consumer standard.

Francisco v. Doctors & Merchants Credit Serv., Inc., 1998 WL 474107 (N.D. Ill. Aug. 3, 1998). Courts may determine whether an alleged contradiction of a validation notice violates § 1692g without reference to evidence of actual consumer confusion.

Ozkaya v. Telecheck Servs., Inc., 982 F. Supp. 578 (N.D. Ill. 1997). Applies least sophisticated consumer standard.

Trull v. G.C. Servs. Ltd. P'ship, 961 F. Supp. 1199 (N.D. Ill. 1997). Applies unsophisticated consumer standard.

Flowers v. Accelerated Bureau of Collections, 1997 WL 224987 (N.D. Ill. Apr. 30, 1997). Applies unsophisticated consumer standard.

Cortright v. Thompson, 812 F. Supp. 772 (N.D. Ill. 1992). Applies least sophisticated consumer standard.

Kansas

Rachoza v. Gallas & Schultz, 1998 WL 171280 (D. Kan. Mar. 23, 1998). Applies least sophisticated consumer standard.

Louisiana

Garner v. Kansas, 1999 U.S. Dist. LEXIS 6430 (E.D. La. Apr. 29, 1999). Applies least sophisticated consumer standard.

Badon v. Transworld Sys., Inc., 1997 WL 149986 (E.D. La. Mar. 26, 1997). Applies least sophisticated consumer standard.

Bukumirovich v. Credit Bureau, Inc., 155 F.R.D. 146 (M.D. La. 1994). Applies least sophisticated consumer standard.

Michigan

Gradisher v. Check Enforcement Unit, Inc., 210 F. Supp. 2d 907 (W.D. Mich. 2002). In determining whether a debt collector violated the FDCPA, courts in the Sixth Circuit apply the "least sophisticated consumer" standard which focuses upon whether the debt collector's actions would mislead or deceive the least sophisticated consumer.

Stojanovski v. Strobl & Manoogian, 783 F. Supp. 319 (E.D. Mich. 1992). Applies least sophisticated consumer standard.

Nevada

Edwards v. Nat'l Bus. Factors, Inc., 897 F. Supp. 455 (D. Nev. 1995). Applies least sophisticated consumer standard.

New Jersey

Rosamilia v. ACB Receivables Mgmt., Inc., 2009 WL 1085507 (D.N.J. Apr. 22, 2009). Because the FDCPA is a strict liability statute, a debt collector violates the act by failing to provide a proper validation notice, even if there was little or no harm to the consumer.

New York

Weber v. Computer Credit, Inc., 259 F.R.D. 33 (E.D.N.Y. 2009). "The law must assume that the least sophisticated consumer— even one under financial or other stresses—is not so irresponsible as to throw away a serious letter affecting her finances, such as [the debt collector's] first communication, instead of saving it for future reference or action."

Shami v. United Collection Bureau, Inc., 2009 WL 3049203 (E.D.N.Y. Sept. 25, 2009). Judgment on the pleadings granted to the defendant where the plaintiff claimed that a Kansas notice would confuse the least sophisticated New York consumer as to his rights. The court held that FDCPA protects not just consumers, but also debt collectors from unreasonable constructions of debt collector's communications.

Johnson v. Equifax Risk Mgmt. Servs., 2004 WL 540459 (S.D.N.Y. Mar. 17, 2004). That the consumer failed to object at the time to the offending dun "is beside the point, as the FDCPA strictly imposes liability for violations of the statute, without regard to whether the consumer was actually confused."

In re Risk Mgmt. Alternatives, Inc., 208 F.R.D. 493 (S.D.N.Y. 2002). The court declined to follow *Graziano v. Harrison,* 950 F.2d 107 (3d Cir. 1991), and held that a jury must determine whether the least sophisticated consumer could believe that any challenge to the debt must be in writing.

Cavallaro v. Law Office of Shapiro & Kriesman, 933 F. Supp. 1148 (E.D.N.Y. 1996). Applies least sophisticated consumer standard.

Beeman v. Lacy, Katzen, Ryen & Mittleman, 892 F. Supp. 405 (N.D.N.Y. 1995). Applies least sophisticated consumer standard.

Tsenes v. Trans-Continental Credit & Collection Corp., 892 F. Supp. 461 (E.D.N.Y. 1995). Applies least sophisticated consumer standard.

Rabideau v. Mgmt. Adjustment Bureau, 805 F. Supp. 1086 (W.D.N.Y. 1992). Applies least sophisticated consumer standard.

Oregon

Peters v. Collection Tech. Inc., 1991 U.S. Dist. LEXIS 21810 (D. Or. Dec. 5, 1991). Applies least sophisticated consumer standard.

Furth v. United Adjusters, Inc., 1983 U.S. Dist. LEXIS 20368 (D. Or. Nov. 17, 1983). Applies least sophisticated consumer standard.

Texas

Youngblood v. G.C. Servs. Ltd. P'ship, 186 F. Supp. 2d 695 (W.D. Tex. 2002).

Virginia

Talbott v. G.C. Servs. Ltd. P'ship, 53 F. Supp. 2d 846 (W.D. Va.

1999). Applies least sophisticated consumer standard.

Morgan v. Credit Adjustment Bd., Inc., 999 F. Supp. 803 (E.D. Va. 1998). Applies least sophisticated consumer standard.

West Virginia

Chapman v. ACB Bus. Servs., 1997 U.S. Dist. LEXIS 23743 (S.D. W. Va. Feb. 13, 1997). Applied least sophisticated consumer standard.

Wisconsin

Booth v. Collection Experts, Inc., 969 F. Supp. 1161 (E.D. Wis. 1997). Section 1692g debt validation is a strict liability provision; an unintentional violation of the validation requirements was a violation.

Tychewicz v. Dobberstein, 1996 U.S. Dist. LEXIS 22555 (W.D. Wis. Aug. 28, 1996). Applied least sophisticated consumer standard.

K.2.6.2 Duns Overshadow Validation Notice

Ellis v. Solomon & Solomon, P.C., 591 F.3d 130 (2d Cir. 2010). The § 1692g validation notice that the debt collector disclosed in its dunning letter was overshadowed by its service on the consumer later during the thirty-day validation period of its collection lawsuit since the collector failed to explain or clarify in either the dun or "in a notice provided with the summons and complaint" that "that commencement of the lawsuit has no effect on the information conveyed in the validation notice . . . Defendants did not have to serve [plaintiff] during the validation period; they could have waited until the validation period expired. It is difficult to discern what tactical advantage was gained by commencing a lawsuit when the validation period had only two weeks to run . . . Of course, debt collectors may continue collection activities, including commencing litigation, during the validation period; but in doing so the debt collector must not transgress § 1692g(b)'s proscription of collections activities that 'overshadow or . . . [are] inconsistent with' the validation notice . . . If the debt collector chooses not to wait until the end of the validation period to commence debt collection litigation, an explanation of the lawsuit's impact . . . be provided . . . The best practice is to provide an explanation in both the validation notice and the summons and complaint."

McKinney v. Cadleway Properties, Inc., 548 F.3d 496 (7th Cir. 2008). Collector's otherwise complaint validation disclosure met the requirements of § 1692g(a) since the unsophisticated consumer would not be confused by the accompanying request to confirm or dispute the amount owed.

Jacobson v. Healthcare Fin. Serv., Inc., 516 F.3d 85 (2d Cir. 2008). Language unlawfully overshadowed or contradicted the debt validation rights notice when it would make the least sophisticated consumer uncertain as to her rights, regardless of whether the plaintiff was actually confused. The 2006 amendment to § 1692g(b): "[The debt collector] . . . has the obligation, not just to convey the information, but to convey it clearly . . . Any collection activities and communication during the 30-day period may not overshadow or be inconsistent with the disclosure of the consumer's right to dispute the debt or request the name and address of the original creditor." Congress "codified" the overshadowing/contradiction doctrine as it had been developed over the years by the courts. The initial dun at issue was not inconsistent with and did not overshadow the validation notice because it clearly and prominently explained that that the consumer could dispute the debt notwithstanding its demand for payment and thus "even the least sophisticated debtor would understand that she had the option to submit a notice of dispute, rather than pay the claimed sum." The omission of the starting date of the thirty-day validation period in one portion of the dun and the resulting ambiguity were sufficiently clarified by the validation notice's explicit statement elsewhere in the dun that the period began upon receipt of the notice. The collector contradicted the validation disclosure when it stated that the dispute must be "received" within the thirty-day period, since § 1692g requires that the consumer only send a validation request within the thirty-day period.

Van v. Grant & Weber, 308 Fed. Appx. 46 (9th Cir. 2008). Collection letter containing reminder of a state law requiring debtors to provide new contact information, while warning debtors that the information will be used for purposes of debt collection, did not conflict with §§ 1692e, 1692f, 1692g.

Sims v. GC Servs. L.P., 445 F.3d 959 (7th Cir. 2006). A validation notice on the reverse in light gray type on white background did not violate the notice requirement, where the consumer's attention to it was drawn by a red notice on the front of the dun. "The statement that the collection agency would continue with collection efforts until the matter is handled does not obscure the debtor's statutory entitlement to a thirty-day period in which to dispute the debt."

Durkin v. Equifax Check Servs., Inc., 406 F.3d 410 (7th Cir. 2005). Two letters and a phone call within the thirty-day validation period did not overshadow or contradict the validation notice. "[T]he simple act of demanding payment in a collection letter during the validation period does not automatically create an unacceptable level of confusion so as to entitle the plaintiffs to summary judgment." The debt collector need not remind the consumer of the dispute right. The toll-free number in the follow-up letters did not detract from the disclosure regarding written disputes. Extrinsic evidence of confusion, such as a consumer survey, was necessary in the Seventh Circuit where the letter did not violate the FDCPA on its face. The court properly applied *Daubert* to exclude plaintiffs' linguist as an expert. The expert's opinion as to overall readability was irrelevant as to the particular language at issue, as to which it was conclusory.

Olson v. Risk Mgmt. Alternatives, Inc., 366 F.3d 509 (7th Cir. 2004). The words "Now Due," do not eviscerate the message conveyed in the debt validation notice. "The phrase 'Now Due,' even to an unsophisticated consumer, simply means that the debt collector is willing to accept less than the total amount of the debt to bring the account to a current status. The consumer has the option of paying the amount due, paying the total balance, or doing neither and contesting the debt. These options do not contradict one another. When used in conjunction with a "Balance" figure, simply listing an amount 'Now Due' does not contradict or overshadow the validation notice."

Taylor v. Calvary Inv., L.L.C., 365 F.3d 572 (7th Cir. 2004). The validation notice was not contradicted, nor was the unsophisticated consumer confused, by language that interest would continue to accrue contained in collection letters stating the principal balance, the interest owed, and the total balance due. Language stating " 'Act now to satisfy your debt' was in the nature of puffing."

Shapiro v. Riddle & Assocs., P.C., 351 F.3d 63 (2d Cir. 2003). The threat of suit did not overshadow the debt validation notice where the collector disclosed that no decision on suit had been made and that a request for validation would suspend collection efforts by suit or otherwise.

Miller v. Wolpoff & Abramson, L.L.P., 321 F.3d 292 (2d Cir. 2003). Where a validation notice was provided on the back of the collection letter, it was not obscured by multiple requests on the front to call or write the collection attorney where the front of the letter also twice instructed the consumer to read the validation notice on the back. The argument that the validation notice implied that it provided the consumer's exclusive legal protections under the FDCPA did not state a claim under the FDCPA as the consumer was not entitled to a notice of his other rights under the FDCPA.

Shapiro v. Dun & Bradstreet Receivable Mgmt. Servs., Inc., 2003 WL 1025581 (2d Cir. Mar. 7, 2003). The question of whether language in a debt collection letter overshadows or contradicts required disclosures is a question of law. An initial dun that refers the consumer to the creditor to make payments or for additional information but which clearly tells the consumer to contact the collector to dispute the debt and seek verification does not unlawfully contradict the verification notice by encouraging the debtor to dispute the debt with the creditor rather than with the debt collector. The statement that the debtor could "disregard this letter" if payment had been made is not at odds with the validation notice and is not reasonably susceptible to misinterpretation or likely to cause a debtor to misunderstand his rights.

Peter v. G.C. Servs. L.P., 310 F.3d 344 (5th Cir. 2002). The language, "FULL COLLECTION ACTIVITY WILL CONTINUE UNTIL THIS ACCOUNT IS PAID IN FULL. . . . TO AVOID FURTHER COLLECTION ACTIVITY, YOUR STUDENT LOAN MUST BE PAID IN FULL" did not violate § 1692g.

McStay v. I.C. Sys., Inc., 308 F.3d 188 (2d Cir. 2002). There was no violation of § 1692g when any ambiguities in the statement of the thirty-day period in which to request validation on the front side of the collection letter were overcome by a statement seven lines beneath, printed in bold and all capital letters, referring the consumer to the reverse side where the validation notice was printed in a font three times that of the front page.

Renick v. Dun & Bradstreet Receivable Mgmt. Servs., 290 F.3d 1055 (9th Cir. 2002). The FDCPA thirty-day validation notice was not overshadowed by collector's letter stating "send your payment today" and "PROMPT PAYMENT IS REQUESTED" because it was in the same font as the surrounding text, was not emphasized in any other way, was in the nature of a request rather than a demand, and carried no sense of urgency.

DeSantis v. Computer Credit, Inc., 269 F.3d 159 (2d Cir. 2001). Debt collector's initial dun demanding payment or a "valid reason" for nonpayment was unlawfully contradictory or confusing with regard to the § 1692g notice. Section 1692g allowed consumers to exercise the right to dispute the debt and seek validation whether or not they have a "valid reason" to do so.

Wilson v. Quadramed Corp., 225 F.3d 350 (3d Cir. 2000). Offer to accept immediate payment was found to not contradict or overshadow the debt validation notice that followed on the same side of the letter in the same font. Although acknowledging it was a close question, the court held that the option to pay immediately and the option to request debt validation were not presented in an apparent contradictory manner.

Marshall-Mosby v. Corporate Receivables, Inc., 205 F.3d 323 (7th Cir. 2000). The court vacated its earlier decision dismissing the complaint (194 F.3d 830 (7th Cir. 1999)) because (only in the Seventh Circuit) whether a letter can be confusing or contradictory about § 1692g dispute rights to the least sophisticated consumer was a question of fact, not law.

Walker v. Nat'l Recovery, Inc., 200 F.3d 500 (7th Cir. 1999). Confusion is a matter of fact rather than law. Therefore, district court improperly dismissed case where validation letter confusingly stated that past-due account had been placed with collector for "immediate payment" when the consumer had thirty days to request validation. Court suggested that survey could show "that four out of five high school dropouts would take the reference to "immediate collection" to demand "immediate payment."

Johnson v. Revenue Mgmt. Corp., 169 F.3d 1057 (7th Cir. 1999). Collection letters which requested "prompt payment" or "call our office immediately" stated a cause of action under § 1692g sufficient to withstand a Rule 12(b)(6) motion to dismiss.

Smith v. Computer Credit, Inc., 167 F.3d 1052 (6th Cir. 1999). A subsequent dun within the initial thirty-day dispute period that threatens or encourages the least sophisticated consumer to ignore his validation rights does not effectively convey the validation notice and therefore violates the Act. The dun under scrutiny, which purported to "advise [the consumer] of our final position" prior to the expiration of the thirty-day period failing payment or dispute, effectively conveyed the validation notice. Court held that this was not a threat, where it mentioned the possibility of disputing the debt and where the collector's final action was, in fact, to send the debt back to the original creditor.

Goldberg v. Transworld Sys., Inc., 164 F.3d 617 (2d Cir. 1998) (text at 1998 WL 650793). The language "grace period about to expire" does not suggest to the least sophisticated consumer that he has less than thirty days to dispute the debt. In addition, stating that the consumer "may eliminate the possibility of additional costs" is "no threat whatsoever, false or otherwise."

Savino v. Computer Credit, Inc., 164 F.3d 81 (2d Cir. 1998). Defendant's demand for immediate payment alone does not eliminate right to validate. Defendant's violation of the FDCPA "consisted of its decision to ask for immediate payment without also explaining that its demand did not override the consumer's rights under Section 1692g to seek validation of the debt."

Bartlett v. Heibl, 128 F.3d 497 (7th Cir. 1997). Demand for payment or making suitable arrangements within ten days to forestall collection litigation, together with recitation of thirty-day validation notice, was confusing to the unsophisticated consumer and thus contradicted and overshadowed the validation notice.

Chauncey v. JDR Recovery Corp., 118 F.3d 516 (7th Cir. 1997). The statement in the collector's letter—"Unless we receive a check or money order for the balance, in full within thirty (30) days from receipt of this letter, a decision to pursue other avenues to collect the amount due will be made"—contradicted, the language in the letter explaining the plaintiff's validation rights.

Terran v. Kaplan, 109 F.3d 1428 (9th Cir. 1997). A demand that the consumer telephone the collection lawyer's office immediately did not make the notice of validation rights that followed in the letter ineffective. The type for both messages was the same and the request for a telephone call from the consumer was not contradictory of the right to request validation in writing. The question of whether the validation notice was conveyed effectively to a least sophisticated consumer was a question of law where the decision did not require reference to extrinsic facts.

United States v. Nat'l Fin. Servs., Inc., 98 F.3d 131 (4th Cir. 1996). The debt collectors violated the debt validation requirements by sending the validation notice on the back of a demand letter which contained conflicting deadlines and overshadowed the notice by being in larger typeface.

Avila v. Rubin, 84 F.3d 222 (7th Cir. 1996). To be effective a debt validation notice must not be undermined by inconsistent and contradictory language which eviscerated its message. The statement that if the debtor was not disputing the debt the debtor must pay in ten days or risk a lawsuit violated this standard. Further, it was proper to find the defendant violated § 1692g without extrinsic evidence, e.g., a survey of class members, to show actual deception of class members.

Russell v. Equifax A.R.S., 74 F.3d 30 (2d Cir. 1996). FDCPA was violated by a validation notice printed on the back of the collection letter which was contradicted and overshadowed by the warning on the front, which stated that the collection would be "posted on the consumer's files unless the consumer chose not to dispute the debt and paid it within ten days." The internal contradiction in the validation notice need not have been "threatening" to have violated the FDCPA. A notice is overshadowing or contradictory if least sophisticated consumer would be confused as to the consumer's rights. A second collection notice demanding payment within five days, which was sent only twenty-five days from the first communication, violated §§ 1692g and 1692e(10).

Graziano v. Harrison, 950 F.2d 107 (3d Cir. 1991). Threat to sue, if payment was not received within ten days, contained on the front of a letter that provided notice of the consumer's right to request verification of the debt, within thirty days, rendered the verification notice ineffective, violating § 1692g, and was confusing, violating § 1692e(10).

Miller v. Payco-Gen. Am. Credits, Inc., 943 F.2d 482 (4th Cir. 1991). "Congress included the debt validation provisions in order to guarantee that consumers receive adequate notice of their legal rights." "Screaming headlines, bright colors and huge lettering" in the debt collector's initial correspondence to the consumer contradicted and overshadowed the validation notice in violation of § 1692g. A debt collector need not cease its collection efforts, but it must effectively convey the validation notice without using collection efforts contradicting it. The debt collector's letter commanding the consumer to telephone immediately could cause the consumer to overlook his right to verification and cessation of collection efforts upon written request.

Swanson v. S. Oregon Credit Serv., 869 F.2d 1222 (9th Cir. 1988). The placement of a validation notice at the bottom of a dunning message, by which it was dwarfed and contradicted, violated § 1692g. The implicit threat to damage the consumer's credit reputation in ten days contradicted the consumer's right to request validation for thirty days.

Arizona

Gostony v. Diem Corp., 320 F. Supp. 2d 932 (D. Ariz. 2003). Invitation to call about questions or concerns, or about the methods available for payment, did not overshadow or contradict the thirty-day validation notice. Suggestion, twenty days into dispute period, that the consumer consult with an attorney, and threat of litigation, did not contradict validation notice or create a false sense of urgency.

California

Elliott v. Credit Control Servs., Inc., 2010 WL 1495402 (S.D. Cal. Apr. 14, 2010). A letter containing the heading "Warning Notice-Warning Notice" in white letters against a solid black background did not overshadow the § 1692g disclosures.

Durham v. Continental Cent. Credit, 2009 WL 3416114 (S.D. Cal. Oct. 20, 2009). A second collection letter, which did not reiterate the consumer's right to dispute the debt, sent within the thirty-day validation period demanding immediate payment, violated § 1692g.

Robertson v. Richard J. Boudreau & Assocs., L.L.C., 2009 WL 5108479 (N.D. Cal. Dec. 18, 2009). Collection letter disclaiming a review of the account by an attorney was contradicted and overshadowed by the remainder of the collection letter on a letterhead stating "Attorneys at Law" and signed by the law firm, using increasingly threatening legal language violating § 1692e(5) because none of the lawyers were admitted to practice in California.

Wan v. Commercial Recovery Sys., Inc., 369 F. Supp. 2d 1158 (N.D. Cal. 2005). The collector's letter to the consumer did not overshadow the debt validation notice simply because it suggested that the consumer "consult with [her] attorney about what the laws in [her] state will allow our client to do to recover the moneys owed to it and further consequences of nonpayment."

Hipolito v. Alliance Receivables Mgmt., Inc., 2005 WL 1662137 (N.D. Cal. July 15, 2005). The statement in the initial dun to "pay in full to [stop] all collection activity" was not a demand for payment in fewer than thirty days and thus did not overshadow or contradict the verification notice.

Palmer v. Stassinos, 348 F. Supp. 2d 1070 (N.D. Cal. 2004). The threat of litigation made within the validation period did not cause a debtor confusion regarding her right to validate the amount of debt where there was no statement that could be construed to shorten the thirty-day validation period. A second dun sent within the validation period did not overshadow the § 1692g verification notice or cause confusion since its demand for payment did not state a time period within which to pay and thus could not be construed as shortening the available thirty-day period.

Valdez v. Hunt & Henriques, 2002 U.S. Dist. LEXIS 4575 (N.D. Cal. Mar. 19, 2002). An initial collection letter that referred the consumer to the creditor to make payment arrangements and then continued with the standard verification language inviting any dispute to be directed to the collector would not unlawfully confuse or mislead as to whom to direct any verification request.

Baker v. Citibank (South Dakota) N.A., 13 F. Supp. 2d 1037 (S.D. Cal. 1998). Collection letter which threatened "trouble of litigation" and "legal and/or attorney fees" unless the debt was paid "now" contradicted the validation notice.

Newman v. CheckRite California, Inc., 912 F. Supp. 1354 (E.D. Cal. 1995). The adequacy of a validation notice in minuscule print following a big, bold threat of suit would be determined by trial.

Masuda v. Thomas Richards & Co., 759 F. Supp. 1456 (C.D. Cal. 1991). Collector's initial letter informing the consumer that, if claim was insurable, insurance form must be submitted in one week would imply to the least sophisticated consumer that he did not have thirty days to dispute the validity of the debt in violation of § 1692g.

Connecticut

Gervais v. Riddle & Assoc., P.C., 363 F. Supp. 2d 345 (D. Conn. 2005), *c.f., later op.* 479 F. Supp. 2d 270 (D. Conn. 2007). Where the debt collector's letter presented the consumer with the opportunity to satisfy the outstanding balance at a fifty-percent discount of over $4000 if paid within thirty days of the date of the letter, it violated § 1692g because the consumer was entitled to the full thirty days from receipt of the collection letter to request debt validation and the shorter period for the discount overshadowed and contradicted the validation notice.

Gaudette v. G.C. Servs., 1999 U.S. Dist. LEXIS 21532 (D. Conn. Sept. 7, 1999). Statement in validation notice that plaintiff's debt was legally binding and collection activity was lawful implied that legal validity of debt had been decided and therefore overshadowed and obscured notice by deterring the plaintiff from disputing debt.

Macarz v. Transworld Sys., Inc., 26 F. Supp. 2d 368 (D. Conn. 1998). Transworld overshadowed or contradicted § 1692g when the notice was at the bottom of the page in passive voice and small print "where it appears to look purposefully insignificant," combined with the main text directing the consumer to "contact your creditor" if there is a dispute. Transworld further overshadowed or contradicted § 1692g by its admonition to "discuss" any dispute, which could induce the least sophisticated consumer to call instead of write, waiving important § 1692g rights.

Madonna v. Acad. Collection Serv., Inc., 1997 WL 530101 (D. Conn. Aug. 12, 1997). Request that consumer "contact" the collector within the validation period and other language which did not demand payment in less than thirty days did not contradict the validation notice.

Young v. Dey, 1994 U.S. Dist. LEXIS 21484 (D. Conn. July 5, 1994). Court granted the consumer's motion for summary judgment in part holding that the debt collector's filing of a summons with a return date before the expiration of the thirty day validation period without any notice or warning as to the consumer's continued validation rights violated § 1692g(a).

Colman v. Payco-GAC Inc., 1992 U.S. Dist. LEXIS 22733 (D. Conn. Jan. 22, 1992), *rev'g* 774 F. Supp. 691 (D. Conn. 1990). In light of *Miller v. Payco-Gen. Am. Credits, Inc.*, 943 F.2d 482 (4th Cir. 1991), the court granted consumer's motion for reconsideration, reversed its earlier decision, and held that debt collector's demand of immediate action by the consumer contradicted and overshadowed the thirty-day validation notice in violation of § 1692g.

Kizer v. Am. Credit & Collection, Clearinghouse No. 45,928 (D. Conn. 1991). The collector failed to provide adequate notice of validation rights when the dunning letter containing the notice, and one sent shortly afterward, urged the consumer to phone the collector, obscuring the requirement that validation requests be in writing.

Stebbins v. Allied Account Servs., 1991 U.S. Dist. LEXIS 21778 (D. Conn. Sept. 9, 1991). Collector violated the debt validation notice requirement by sending a dunning letter that requested the consumer to telephone the collector, a demand contradicting the requirement that the consumer *write* to obtain validation of the debt, one week after it sent the debt validation notice. The validation notice was not made inadequate by failing to fully paraphrase § 1692g(a)(4).

Woolfolk v. Van Ru Credit Corp., 783 F. Supp. 724 (D. Conn. 1990). A validation notice was inadequate when it stated, but did not emphasize, the requirement that the consumer's request for validation of the debt must be in writing because the front of the dunning letter emphasized that consumer may telephone the collector. The consumer's evidence was insufficient to show prohibited collection contacts after the request for validation and before validation was made.

Gaetano v. Payco, Inc., 774 F. Supp. 1404 (D. Conn. 1990). The request in a dunning letter to phone the collector if there was a valid reason for nonpayment, a statement repeated in a second letter sent eight days later, violated the FDCPA because it contradicted the language of the validation notice in the first letter that any dispute must be in writing in order to obtain verification of the debt. Notice on the front of a dunning letter to "SEE REVERSE SIDE FOR IMPORTANT INFORMATION" sufficed to alert a consumer to a § 1692g notice on the back. Threatening language on the front and back of the letter did not obscure the § 1692g notice.

Weber v. Payco-Gen. Am. Credits, 1990 U.S. Dist. LEXIS 20978 (D. Conn. Dec. 13, 1990). Request to "phone us today" and the rapidity with which the second and third notices followed the first (one and three days) overshadowed the validation notice.

Thomas v. Nat'l Bus. Assistants, Inc., 1984 U.S. Dist. LEXIS 24876, 1984 WL 585309 (D. Conn. Oct. 5, 1984) (slip copy). A validation notice that is inconspicuous and grossly overshadowed by demand for payment in three days violates § 1692g.

Delaware

Smith v. Fin. Collection Agencies, 770 F. Supp. 232 (D. Del. 1991). Language in debt collector's letter was much milder than that in *Swanson* and did not stand in threatening contradiction to validation notice.

Higgins v. Capitol Credit Servs., Inc., 762 F. Supp. 1128 (D. Del. 1991). Language of "IMMEDIATE SETTLEMENT NOTICE" stating that "Your Account Must Be Settled Now" merely encouraged payment and did not overshadow validation notice, nor did letter almost thirty days later stating "Payment in full within ten days will stop all recommended action" violate the Act.

Florida

Gaalswyk-Knetzke v. Receivable Mgmt. Serv. Corp., 2008 WL 2224833 (M.D. Fla. May 27, 2008). Factual question whether light grey ink and poor quality paper effectively conveyed disputed rights.

Law Offices of David J. Stern, P.A. v. Martinez, 271 B.R. 696 (S.D. Fla. 2001), *aff'd*, 311 F.3d 1272 (11th Cir. 2002). The validation notice was confusing where it was inserted as page eight of a sixteen page foreclosure suit package.

In re Hathcock, 437 B.R. 696 (Bankr. M.D. Fla. Oct. 1, 2010). Utilizing the least sophisticated consumer standard, the court found that the five references to the debt collector and the three references to the creditor in the collection letter were not confusing, since the letter clearly stated that the account had been placed with the former for collection. The court explicitly rejected the argument that the references would somehow confuse the recipient regarding the triggering of the thirty-day period to dispute the debt.

Georgia

Gilmore v. Account, Mgmt., Inc., 2009 WL 2848278 (N.D. Ga. Apr. 27, 2009). Court held plaintiff had sufficiently pleaded a violation of § 1692g(a) when defendant's second collection letter overshadowed the required notice of the thirty-day period for disputing the debt in the previously sent letter because it demanded full payment of the debt on a date before the thirty-day period for disputing the debt concluded.

Schimmel v. Slaughter, 975 F. Supp. 1357 (M.D. Ga. 1997). Threat that "suit will follow after thirty (30) days" (from the date of the letter) did not deceptively shorten or contradict the validation period.

Mullis v. McDowell Servs., Inc., Clearinghouse No. 51,951 (N.D. Ga. 1997). The court granted the consumer's motion for summary judgment finding that collection agency's first two dunning letters contained language that contradicted and overshadowed the validation notice by emphasizing immediate payment and warning that failure to act immediately could result in further embarrassment. Those statements could easily confuse or mislead a least sophisticated consumer about the right to contest the validity of debt.

Zoeckler v. Credit Claims & Collection, Inc., 1982 U.S. Dist. LEXIS 18384 (N.D. Ga. Sept. 30, 1982). Using a "reasonable consumer" standard, the court found the collector's first dunning letter not violative of the FDCPA, although the validation notice was in a noticeably smaller print size. The collector's second dunning letter violated the FDCPA in two respects. An ambiguous sentence in it could reasonably give the false impression the suit had been filed although literally read the sentence stated that advice to file a suit was pending. The second letter also violated FDCPA by falsely giving the impression that the consumer's

§ 1692g rights to dispute the debt had terminated before the statutory thirty-day dispute period expired.

Blackwell v. Prof'l Bus. Servs., 526 F. Supp. 535 (N.D. Ga. 1981). The placement of the validation notice on the back of the initial dunning letter was not a violation of FDCPA.

Williams v. Rash, Curtis & Assocs., 1978 U.S. Dist. LEXIS 20395 (N.D. Ga. Dec. 13, 1978). Motion to dismiss was denied. Plaintiff alleged that threats of action during the thirty-day period for requesting validation violated the validation provisions or were unfair.

Hawaii

Keli v. Universal Fid. Corp., 1997 U.S. Dist. LEXIS 23940 (D. Haw. Feb. 25, 1997). Validation notice on back of dunning letter was overshadowed by language on front page of letter regarding collector's threats to collect the debt and was obscured by being placed on back of letter.

Bailey v. TRW Receivables Mgmt. Servs., Inc., 1990 U.S. Dist. LEXIS 19638 (D. Haw. Aug. 16, 1990). A request for immediate payment did not contradict the notice of § 1692g rights.

Sakuma v. First Nat'l Credit Bureau, 1989 U.S. Dist. LEXIS 19120 (D. Haw. Nov. 15, 1989). Collection letter violated the § 1692g(a) validation notice requirements because it included a demand for payment within seven days which would be contradictory of the thirty-day right to validate and confusing to least sophisticated consumers.

Illinois

Quiroz v. Revenue Prod. Mgmt., Inc., 252 F.R.D. 438 (N.D. Ill. 2008). The court certified the class on the basis of a form letter, which had not mislead or confused the named plaintiff although it was alleged that the letter contained a defective FDCPA notice because the court held that "the test for determining a violation of the FDCPA is not whether the individual who received the letter was misled, but whether an unsophisticated consumer would be misled."

Francis v. Snyder, 389 F. Supp. 2d 1034 (N.D. Ill. Sept. 30, 2005). The collection letter to the consumer that the balance will be pursued in full if she did not call the collector "on receipt of this letter" while at the same time allowing her thirty days to dispute the validity of that debt presented two statements that an unsophisticated consumer could reasonably find contradictory or confusing and violated § 1692g.

Hernandez v. Attention, L.L.C., 429 F. Supp. 2d 912 (N.D. Ill. Sept. 28, 2005). The language "[y]our failure to remit the balance due will result in our agency continuing our collection efforts" was a truism and did not contradict or overshadow the FDCPA's validation notice. The consumer's survey as to consumers' interpretation of letter was fatally flawed as it lacked a control group focused solely on the confusion that might be caused by the § 1692g notice alone.

Allen v. ATG Credit L.L.C., 2004 WL 2931298 (N.D. Ill. Dec. 14, 2004). Consumer received both initial letter (with thirty-day notice) and follow up letter (with one day deadline) on the same day. Since this could confuse the unsophisticated consumer, defendant's

motion for summary judgment was denied.

Carbajal v. Capital One, F.S.B., 219 F.R.D. 437 (N.D. Ill. Jan. 20, 2004). Plaintiffs received solicitations from the defendants to transfer delinquent debts owed to other creditors to a new Capital One Visa credit card account. They contend that this constituted debt collection activity subject to the FDCPA, and they assert that Capital One's solicitation improperly obscured the FDCPA-required "validation" notice and misleadingly advised debtors that they would still be able to dispute the old debt after its transfer to Capital One. Two state classes certified.

Levin v. Kluever & Platt, L.L.C., 2003 WL 22757763 (N.D. Ill. Nov. 19, 2003). Whether the presentation of the validation disclosure on the eighth page of a sixteen page foreclosure document was unlawfully confusing to the unsophisticated consumer is a question of fact unsuitable for summary judgment.

Carbajal v. Capital One, F.S.B., 2003 WL 22595265 (N.D. Ill. Nov. 10, 2003). Allegation that an otherwise proper validation notice was "buried" among a "flurry of papers" so as to obscure its message stated a claim for relief for violating § 1692g(a).

Blum v. Lawent, 2003 WL 22078306 (N.D. Ill. Sept. 8, 2003). A threat of a lawsuit within thirty days of receipt was confusing for an unsophisticated consumer in the letter containing the validation notice, and did not fall within the *Bartlett* decision's safe harbor.

Mistretta v. Babb, 2003 WL 1868717 (N.D. Ill. Apr. 9, 2003). Initial dun which requested payment of the debt "at this time" to avoid "further expense" stated a claim for relief as a violation of § 1692g(a) for being capable of confusing the unsophisticated consumer concerning the right to seek verification of the debt for thirty days.

Taylor v. Cavalry Inv., L.L.C., 210 F. Supp. 2d 1001 (N.D. Ill. 2002). Collector's initial dun which recited the required § 1692g verification language and also instructed the consumer to "act now to satisfy this debt" did not violate the FDCPA since the latter statement was not accompanied by any threat of action and did not demand payment with a threat of action if the debt was not satisfied in a certain amount of time.

McCabe v. Crawford & Co., 210 F.R.D. 631 (N.D. Ill. 2002). Collector's letter which stated in part "you became obligated to pay for any and all damages to the vehicle" did not violate § 1692g.

Allen v. NCO Fin. Servs., Inc., 2002 U.S. Dist. LEXIS 10513 (N.D. Ill. June 10, 2002). Defendant's second collection letter, sent only four days after its initial letter, clearly overshadowed the validation notice provided in the first letter.

Durkin v. Equifax Check Servs., Inc., 2001 U.S. Dist. LEXIS 15474 (N.D. Ill. Sept. 27, 2001). Whether a series of letters was confusing or misleading was a question of fact for the jury. One such question is whether, because defendant's letters did not explain the significance of written disputes compared with oral disputes, a reasonable jury could find consumer confusion.

Cyborski v. Computer Credit, Inc., 2001 U.S. Dist. LEXIS 15344 (N.D. Ill. Sept. 26, 2001). Defendant's validation notice, which varied only technically from the model of *Bartlett*, did not overshadow the validation notice, and the dun referenced important information on the reverse.

Riddle & Assocs., P.C. v. Kelley, 2001 U.S. Dist. LEXIS 15712 (N.D. Ill. Sept. 28, 2001). Since the collection letter was virtually identical to the "safe harbor" language in *Bartlett*, it was not overshadowing or confusing.

Matthews v. First Revenue Assurance, L.L.C., 2001 U.S. Dist. LEXIS 11091 (N.D. Ill. July 31, 2001). Collector's first dun with proper validation notice together with the statement to "please submit payment in the enclosed envelope for proper credit or contact our office today to set up an autopay for immediate credit to your account" overshadowed the validation notice. Summary judgment establishing liability for overshadowing the validation notice was appropriate without any expert or other supporting evidence where the message was contradictory on its face.

Weinstein v. Fink, 2001 U.S. Dist. LEXIS 2075 (N.D. Ill. Feb. 21, 2001). The inclusion of the validation notice with the summons and complaint that required a much quicker response did not violate the FDCPA.

Nance v. Lawrence Friedman P.C., 2000 WL 1230462 (N.D. Ill. Aug. 28, 2000). On summary judgment on the plaintiffs' § 1692g overshadowing and contradiction claim, the court stated, "The letter does not require immediate or prompt action, nor does it set forth a time period contrary to the thirty-days given in the letter. The Friedman letter therefore does not suffer from the usual defects that support an overshadow or dilution claim." Notwithstanding that holding, the court recognized that the plaintiff may still prevail if the letter was "confusing": "Confusion is an issue of fact, not a question of law. On summary judgment, this meant that the plaintiffs must offer some evidence to create a triable issue as to whether the letter was likely to confuse the unsophisticated debtor." Since there was no outright contradiction, which could be determined by the court without the aid of extrinsic evidence, the court held on the basis of binding Seventh Circuit precedent that the plaintiffs' own deposition testimony that they were "baffled" by the letter was inadequate to create a triable issue and the absence of any other evidence, such as "expert testimony, the opinions of an objective observer, or survey evidence or testimony," required entry of summary judgment dismissing the claim.

Rosenburg v. Transworld Sys., Inc., 2000 U.S. Dist. LEXIS 5486 (N.D. Ill. Apr. 13, 2000). The court found summary judgment inappropriate where the dunning letter's capacity to mislead unsophisticated consumers about their validation rights was apparent— the letter stated the consumer should contact the creditor about disputes. However, the collector showed that it was frequently contacted by consumers requesting validation suggesting the letter was not confusing—an issue of fact for a jury.

Wollert v. Client Servs., Inc., 2000 U.S. Dist. LEXIS 6485 (N.D. Ill. Mar. 24, 2000). The court certified a class action of all Illinois residents who received a collection letter requesting they phone the collector creating potential confusion about the requirement that they write to obtain validation of the debt.

Perdue v. United Credit Mgmt. Corp., 2000 U.S. Dist. LEXIS 1502 (N.D. Ill. Feb. 9, 2000). Court denied motion to dismiss in an overshadowing case where the letter asked the debtor to remit "immediately" or call to set up payment arrangements and implied that debtor's credit would be adversely affected by stating, "Good credit is a valuable asset" and by notice that the debt would be reported to a consumer reporting agency. "The combination of

making the print smaller, limiting mention of possible invalidity of the debt to only one sentence; and using bold, italicized and underscored text in only the aspects of the letter related to paying the debt, rendered it genuinely debatable whether overshadowing has taken place."

Withers v. Equifax Risk Mgmt. Servs., 40 F. Supp. 2d 978 (N.D. Ill. 1999). The second letter sent within the thirty day dispute period referred to Equifax's check authorization service. The reference would lead the unsophisticated consumer to surmise that her ability to write checks would be impaired. The reference was confusing, in violation of § 1692g.

Farley v. Diversified Collection Servs., 1999 U.S. Dist. LEXIS 16174 (N.D. Ill. Sept. 28, 1999). A statement that the account had been referred for "immediate collection" did not merely request an immediate communication from the debtor and therefore unlawfully contradicted the validation notice.

Frey v. Satter, Beyer & Spires, 1999 WL 301650 (N.D. Ill. May 3, 1999). The assertion by a collection agent that "the law does not require me to wait until the end of the thirty day period before suing you to collect this debt" violated the FDCPA because, absent explanation, it contradicted the validation notice.

Phillips v. N. Am. Capital Corp., 1999 U.S. Dist. LEXIS 7000 (N.D. Ill. Apr. 29, 1999). An oral demand for immediate payment, which preceded the validation notice by no more than five days, did not violate the FDCPA.

Crowder v. Kelly, 1999 U.S. Dist. LEXIS 4767 (N.D. Ill. Mar. 31, 1999). A demand letter contained the § 1692g notice as well as the statements, "Please contact me as soon as possible to discuss this matter. A quick settlement of this debt may help prevent additional amounts being added to the balance listed above." This statement could lead the unsophisticated consumer to believe that she must pay in advance of the thirty-day validation period and therefore unlawfully contradicted the § 1692g notice.

Kaczor v. TRSI, Inc., 1999 U.S. Dist. LEXIS 4252 (N.D. Ill. Mar. 15, 1999). Complaint alleged that the collection agency violated the FDCPA because some of the language in its collection letter demanding immediate payment contradicted and overshadowed the notice required by § 1692g. This was sufficient to state a claim for a violation of the FDCPA under the minimal requirements of notice pleading. At this stage, the court could not, as TRSI urged, find that the collection letter was not confusing as a matter of law.

Laws v. Cheslock, 1999 U.S. Dist. LEXIS 3416 (N.D. Ill. Mar. 8, 1999). A collection agency's threat to sue after seven days misled the consumer about her right to dispute the debt.

Seplak by Seplak v. IMBS, Inc., 1999 U.S. Dist. LEXIS 2106 (N.D. Ill. Feb. 22, 1999). The suggestion in a collection agency's first letter, "if you do not feel you owe this amount, please call us," could cause consumer confusion and clearly contradicted the statute. The letters did not explain how the telephone call would fit in the statutory scheme set forth in the validation notice. Violation of § 1692g can result from contradiction, overshadowing, or confusion about the thirty-day dispute right. Confusion resulted from a mistaken impression that some action must be taken before the end of the thirty-day validation period. The second letter, issued only twenty-eight days after the first, was confusing since it told the consumer she could avoid "accelerated collection activity by paying the balance at this time." The statement was not an unlawful threat, but could still be confusing. "Even a statement of intention to act in an entirely legal manner, absent an explanation of how that intention fits within the statutory validation period, can render the communication confusing to the unsophisticated consumer." The second letter was also confusing because it contained another thirty-day notice.

Veillard v. Mednick, 24 F. Supp. 2d 863 (N.D. Ill. 1998). Dun which requests the consumer to "resolv[e] this matter as soon as possible as our client shows this obligation to be due immediately," contradicts the thirty-day validation notice as a matter of law.

Young v. Meyer & Njus, P.A., 183 F.R.D. 231 (N.D. Ill. 1998). Letter which instructed the consumer to send payment by "return mail" could not reasonably mean immediate payment or payment within the thirty day validation period.

Jenkins v. Union Corp., 999 F. Supp. 1120 (N.D. Ill. 1998). Rejects threatening contradiction in favor of standard based on creation of consumer confusion. No visual overshadowing merely from smaller type size, where disclosures were easily readable, not printed in lighter type, and not juxtaposed with screaming headlines. Demand in first letter to make immediate payment or arrangements with the creditor contradicted the validation notice. Letter that began with "URGENT" and informed consumer that the account has been "assigned to our agency for immediate collection," was likely to be understood by the unsophisticated consumer to be a demand for immediate payment and thus contradicts the validation notice even in absence of express demand for immediate payment. Follow-up letter within validation period stating "IMPERATIVE—Grace period about to expire" and requesting consumer to "contact your creditor at once" created no false sense of urgency and did not contradict validation notice timeframe. Follow-up letter stating that the verification period would expire within ten days and demanding timely payment did not contradict verification notice, but a question of disputed fact regarding timing of the letter barred summary judgment on a claim that consumer had more than ten days left from receipt of first notice to dispute the debt.

Keen v. Omnibus Int'l, Inc., 1998 WL 485682 (N.D. Ill. Aug. 12, 1998). Language in the collection letter stating that "you should notify us in writing immediately" if the debt was invalid or discharged in bankruptcy did not contradict or overshadow the validation notice.

Wollert v. Client Servs., Inc., 1998 WL 474118 (N.D. Ill. Aug. 4, 1998). The validation notice was not contradicted nor overshadowed by this statement: "The above account has been placed with our firm for payment in full. Call our office immediately on receipt of this letter."

Shaver v. Trauner, 1998 U.S. Dist. LEXIS 19647 (C.D. Ill. May 29, 1998), *adopted by* 1999 U.S. Dist. LEXIS 19648 (C.D. Ill. July 31, 1998). Motion to dismiss denied where the attorney's letter allegedly violated the validation notice requirement by including "the Federal Trade Commission has stated that the Fair Debt Collection Practices Act does not preclude institution of a legal action prior to the expiration of the aforementioned thirty-day period. Legal action may be instituted forthwith in the absence of payment or satisfactory payment arrangements."

Blair v. Collectech Sys., Inc., 1998 WL 214705 (N.D. Ill. Apr. 24, 1998). Consumer stated a claim for relief for contradictory validation notice disclosure where collector in bold face type on front of dun requested the consumer to pay and contact the creditor and stated on the reverse side in regular typeface that the consumer must write to the collector to dispute the debt.

Vasquez v. Gertler & Gertler, Ltd., 987 F. Supp. 652 (N.D. Ill. 1997). A request for the consumer's immediate attention by sending a payment or contacting the collection attorney did not contradict or overshadow or create confusion about the validation notice that immediately preceded the request.

Ozkaya v. Telecheck Servs., Inc., 982 F. Supp. 578 (N.D. Ill. 1997). Telecheck's warning that "any delay" in payment "may affect your ability to use checks" may have been deceptive because it could confuse the unsophisticated consumer by failing to explain how this comports with her thirty-day right to contest the debt.

Trull v. G.C. Servs. Ltd. P'ship, 961 F. Supp. 1199 (N.D. Ill. 1997). Dunning notice containing the statement, "Since you ignored our previous notice, we assume this debt is correct," sent within the thirty day validation period could mislead the unsophisticated consumer about his validation rights, even where the reverse of the letter explained that the letter did not affect such rights. Debt validation notice must be effective and cannot be treated in a way which destroys its message.

Young v. Meyer & Njus, P.A., 953 F. Supp. 238 (N.D. Ill. 1997). The consumer did not state a claim that the validation notice was overshadowed by a request for payment by return mail and a threat of suit. The demand letter from the collection lawyer was reasonable and had no offensive elements. It merely explained to the consumer the reason the law firm was retained, set forth consumer's validation rights properly, and gave instructions for payment. The request for payment by return mail was held not to be a request for immediate payment.

Chapman v. Ontra, Inc., 1997 WL 321681, RICO Bus. Disp. Guide 9319 (N.D. Ill. June 6, 1997). FDCPA claim was dismissed with leave to amend where it did not allege that the letter from defendants was an initial communication or was sent within the validation period. The consumer could amend to plead facts showing: (1) the letter was an initial communication, or (2) the date of the initial communication indicating that the letter was sent during the validation period.

Flowers v. Accelerated Bureau of Collections, 1997 WL 224987 (N.D. Ill. Apr. 30, 1997). Upon debtor's motion to reconsider, court determined that language requesting that the debtor contact the collector immediately, without mentioning the debtor's validation rights, could lead an unsophisticated consumer to believe that these rights no longer existed, when, in fact, there were thirteen days remaining in the validation period, even where the communication did not demand payment. Therefore, collector's motion to dismiss was denied.

Gammon v. Belzer, 1997 WL 189291 (N.D. Ill. Apr. 11, 1997). Statement that "Your immediate attention to this matter is in your best interest" did not contradict or overshadow the validation notice.

Gordon v. Fink, 1995 WL 55242 (N.D. Ill. Feb. 8, 1995). Statement, that if payment arrangements were not made within ten days the attorney collector would be compelled to take appropriate action, contradicted the thirty-day validation notice in violation of § 1692g.

Vaughn v. CSC Credit Servs., Inc., 1995 WL 51402 (N.D. Ill. Feb. 3, 1995). Demand for immediate action on threat of adverse report to credit bureau contradicted thirty-day validation notice in violation of § 1692g. Whether the warnings required by §§ 1692g and 1692e(11) were legible was a question of fact for the jury to determine.

Taylor v. Fink, 1994 WL 669605 (N.D. Ill. Nov. 25, 1994). Validation notice on the second page was contradicted and overshadowed by language on first page that consumer must pay within ten days or legal action would begin immediately.

Beasley v. Blatt, 1994 WL 362185 (N.D. Ill. July 11, 1994). Debt collector's letter stated that failure to remit the amount due in five days would result in the review of the consumer's file which might result in the preparation and filing of a law suit without further notice. Whether that violated § 1692g by contradicting or overshadowing the validation notice was a matter for the jury to decide.

Philipps v. G.C. Servs., 1994 WL 127283 (N.D. Ill. Apr. 7, 1994). Consumer's complaint alleging that the debt collector's collection letters directed consumers to two different addresses where they could mail their request for validation failed to state a claim under § 1692g, and the debt collector's motion to dismiss was granted. Collection letters which stated, "Remit your balance in full promptly or phone the number listed above," without highlighting that a phone call would not protect the consumer's validation rights did not violate § 1692g when a statement that the consumer must contest the validity of the debt in writing within thirty days or the loan would be presumed valid was contained elsewhere in the letter.

Vaughn v. CSC Credit Servs., 1994 WL 449247 (N.D. Ill. Mar. 1, 1994). Whether the legally required validation notice which was printed on the back of the debt collector's form collection letter in grey ink which was difficult or impossible to read and thereby violated § 1692g was an issue of fact and would not be decided on summary judgment.

Cortright v. Thompson, 812 F. Supp. 772 (N.D. Ill. 1992). Applying the least sophisticated consumer standard, the court found that the attorney collector's letter, which demanded immediate payment suggesting that possible legal action would result if the balance due was not paid within ten days, contradicted and overshadowed the validation notice in violation of § 1692g(a).

American Mgmt. Consultant, L.L.C. v. Carter, 915 N.E.2d 411 (Ill. App. Ct. 2009). FDCPA applied to forcible entry and detainer action that also sought back rent. Notice posted on door did not comply with § 1692g.

Indiana

Collins v. Feiwell & Hannoy, P.C., 2008 WL 4810550 (S.D. Ind. Oct. 30, 2008). Debt collector's motion to dismiss was denied where the consumer alleged that that the collector's collection notice violated § 1692g(a)(1) by failing to include the *Miller v. McCalla* safe harbor language regarding the continuing accrual of interest.

Hall v. Leone Halpin & Konopinski, L.L.P., 2008 WL 608609 (N.D. Ind. Feb. 28, 2008). Consumer failed to offer evidence that a debt validation notice was overshadowed by a summons sent at the same time and requiring an answer in twenty days.

Roudebush v. Collecto, Inc., 2004 WL 3316168 (S.D. Ind. Nov. 12, 2004). A reasonable jury could find that the debt collector's validation notice on the reverse side of the initial dun seeking payment on an underlying telephone bill was physically overshadowed and thus not effectively conveyed where the front side referred the debtor to "important rights" on the reverse side, yet the validation notice on the reverse side appeared under an unrelated heading "FOR MEDICAL USE ONLY" and not under the heading "NOTICE OF IMPORTANT RIGHTS." Where the initial dun demanded payment "today" while at the same time disclosed the standard thirty-day verification notice, the court held that the demand for payment did not unlawfully confuse or contradict the validation notice because the accompanying disclosure of the § 1692g notice "met the standard outlined in *Johnson v. Revenue Mgmt. Corp.*, which said that a demand for immediate payment does not violate the FDCPA when it is 'accompanied by additional reconciling language, such as that payment is due "immediately" only when the payment is uncontested.' " The court's holding that disclosure of the § 1692g notice necessarily meets the *Johnson* standard to reconcile an apparent temporal contradiction is mistaken since the basis for the doctrine is always the presence of a shortened demand for payment along with disclosure of the normal thirty-day validation notice.

Bernstein v. Howe, 2003 WL 1702254 (S.D. Ind. Mar. 31, 2003). A collection letter instructing the consumer that payment or payment arrangements should be made by a date prior to the expiration of the thirty-day validation period without the threat of legal or other serious consequences did not violate the FDCPA.

Spears v. Brennan, 745 N.E.2d 862 (Ind. Ct. App. 2001). Scheduling a hearing date in small claims court and obtaining a default judgment within the thirty-day validation period infringed on the consumer's right to have the complete thirty days in which to dispute the debt.

Kansas

Rachoza v. Gallas & Schultz, 1998 WL 171280 (D. Kan. Mar. 23, 1998). Collection letters which include the required statutory thirty-day validation notice and statements that payment must be made within a period less than thirty days or a lawsuit may be commenced did not comply with the requirements of § 1692g(a) as a matter of law. The potentially conflicting deadlines in the collection letter would be misleading to a hypothetical least sophisticated consumer and violate the FDCPA.

Louisiana

Garner v. Kansas, 1999 U.S. Dist. LEXIS 6430 (E.D. La. Apr. 29, 1999). An unqualified and unexplained demand for payment in seven days, failing which a lien would be perfected and suit filed, in the same letter as the § 1692g verification notice, was confusing to the least sophisticated consumer and therefore unlawfully contradicted the verification notice. Whether a dun contradicted or overshadowed the § 1692g validation notice was a question of law.

Badon v. Transworld Sys., Inc., 1997 WL 149986 (E.D. La. Mar. 26, 1997). Dunning letter stating "Imperative—Grace Period About to Expire," as well as other letters sent, could, but not necessarily would, lead a reasonable jury to believe the least sophisticated consumer might believe he must act immediately and disregard his validation rights.

Johnson v. Eaton, 873 F. Supp. 1019 (M.D. La. 1995). Threat of suit after seven days contradicted the thirty-day validation notice in violation of § 1692g.

Bukumirovich v. Credit Bureau, Inc., 155 F.R.D. 146 (M.D. La. 1994). When assessing whether a validation statement is sufficiently communicated to a consumer under § 1692g(a), the "least sophisticated consumer" standard should be applied. Validation statement violated § 1692g(a)(3) because it did not give consumer notice that the dishonored check charge added by the collector could be disputed. Because there were disputed issues of fact as to whether the notice otherwise met the requirements of § 1692g, both consumer's and debt collector's motions for summary judgment on these counts were denied.

Maryland

Wallace v. Capital One Bank, 168 F. Supp. 2d 526 (D. Md. 2001). Inviting the debtor to call with questions did not overshadow the validation notice because of its font, language, tenor, and placement.

United States v. Nat'l Fin. Servs., Inc., 820 F. Supp. 228 (D. Md. 1993), *aff'd* 98 F.3d 131 (4th Cir. 1996). Demand for payment within the thirty day period to request verification and reference in smaller print to see the reverse side containing the validation notice, printed in light gray ink which made it difficult to read, undercut and overshadowed the validation notice in violation of § 1692g.

Michigan

West v. Check Alert Sys., 2001 U.S. Dist. LEXIS 22122 (W.D. Mich. Sept. 7, 2001). The following statement in a collection letter did not contradict or overshadow the debt validation notice on the back of the letter: "Please be advised that, if after 30 days your account is not paid in full or otherwise closed, the account information will be forwarded to the National Credit Reporting Agencies. This may hinder your ability to obtain credit in the future."

Latimer v. Transworld Sys., Inc., 842 F. Supp. 274 (E.D. Mich. 1993). Although the validation notice and debt collection warning were in smaller print than other portions of the letter, §§ 1692g and 1692e(11) were not violated.

Burns v. Accelerated Bureau of Collections, 828 F. Supp. 475 (E.D. Mich. 1993). Collector's request for payment "today" in slightly larger and bolder print did not violate the FDCPA by overshadowing or standing in threatening contradiction to the thirty day validation notice which immediately followed.

Minnesota

Owens v. Hellmuth & Johnson, P.L.L.C., 550 F. Supp. 2d 1060 (D. Minn. 2008). Demand for payment within thirty days of the date of the letter overshadowed its validation notice and dispute rights where it did not include additional explanatory language that the demand did not override the consumer's dispute rights. Whether the language overshadowed the dispute right is a question of law for the court.

Bishop v. Global Payments Check Recovery Servs., Inc., 2003 WL 21497513 (D. Minn. June 25, 2003). Initial dun that threatened state authorized dishonored check penalties if the debt were not paid within thirty days from the date of the dun unlawfully overshadowed the FDCPA validation notice's requirement that the consumer be given thirty days from receipt of the notice to dispute the debt.

Missouri

Terry v. C & D Complete Bus. Solutions, 2011 WL 144920 (W.D. Mo. Jan. 18, 2011). The debt collector's letter violated the FDCPA by demanding payment under threat of a lawsuit within ten days, even though it contained an otherwise correct validation statement. "Applying the unsophisticated consumer standard, such a person would be confused by the contradictory dates."

Nevada

Edwards v. Nat'l Bus. Factors, Inc., 897 F. Supp. 455 (D. Nev. 1995). Applying the least sophisticated consumer standard, the sentence "FULL PAYMENT OF UNDISPUTED AMOUNTS MUST BE MADE WITHIN FIVE DAYS or our attorney will be authorized to proceed with action without further notice" contradicted and overshadowed the validation notice.

New Jersey

Watson v. Certified Credit & Collection Bureau, 2009 WL 3068387 (D.N.J. Sept. 23, 2009). The language at issue, "if you believe that these services should have been covered by your insurance company please call your insurance carrier immediately," is sufficient to provide notice of the debt and insufficient upon which to build an actionable violation of the FDCPA. The language does not appear overly antagonistic or intimidating so as to overshadow the § 1692g notice.

Stair ex rel. Smith v. Thomas & Cook, 254 F.R.D. 191 (D.N.J. 2008). The court granted the plaintiff class summary judgment for defendant's violation of § 1692g (a) in an initial dun that disclosed the complete validation notice but then stated a two week response time to avoid suit, since an "unsophisticated debtor, confronted with repeated threats of litigation and a two-week deadline, would be induced to overlook his statutory right to dispute the debt within thirty days."

Smith v. Paramount Recovery Sys., 2008 WL 4951227 (D.N.J. Nov. 18, 2008). The debt collector's motion to dismiss was denied because the complaint which alleged that a second collection letter stated "[a]ll questions regarding the insurance filings should be directed to your insurance company" stated a cause of action for violation of § 1692g.

Casterline v. I.C. Sys., Inc., 1991 U.S. Dist. LEXIS 21728 (D.N.J. June 26, 1991). Validation notice violated the Act because it was not effectively provided when it was placed in small print at the bottom of a dunning letter that contradicted the validation notice. After the consumer's request for verification of the debt, the collector failed to provide any basis for the collector's claim to $729.19 in late fees for failing to return a $50.00, rented videotape. The collector thus violated the requirement that the collector verify the debt upon written request of the consumer. A dunning letter sent with the collector's attempted verification of the debt violated the requirement that the collector stop communicating with the consumer until it verifies the debt.

New Mexico

Russey v. Rankin, 911 F. Supp. 1449 (D.N.M. 1995). Validation notice overshadowed by threat of suit within thirty days.

New York

Ellis v. Cohen & Slamowitz, L.L.P., 701 F. Supp. 2d 215 (N.D.N.Y. 2010). Allegations that a second letter sent after the initial letter containing the validation notice would have allowed the consumer to pay a discounted amount after the validation deadline and that a third letter asserted that the debt collector had authority to commence a lawsuit could confuse and overshadow the consumer's right to seek validation adequately pleaded violations of §§ 1692f and 1692g.

Ehrich v. I.C. Sys. Inc., 681 F. Supp. 2d 265 (E.D.N.Y. 2010). A Spanish language sentence, which was placed in an otherwise compliant English language validation notice immediately following the § 1692g(a)(4) written dispute disclosure and which advised consumers to telephone the debt collector at the listed toll-free number if they had any questions regarding the debt, would leave "the Spanish-speaker uncertain as to his or her rights" and "encouraged the Spanish-speaking consumer to call and potentially waive his or her rights to challenge the validity of the debt," and thus unlawfully "created a particular emphasis on the phone number, thereby overshadowing the rest of the letter."

Weiss v. Zwicker & Assocs., P.C., 664 F. Supp. 2d 214 (E.D.N.Y. 2009). A debt collector has no obligation to explain why a consumer's debt has increased five percent from the time that the initial dun was sent: "The Court finds that there is nothing confusing or misleading about the increased amount of debt stated [in the second dun] as even the most unsophisticated consumer would understand that credit card debt accrues interest."

Day v. Allied Interstate, Inc., 2009 WL 1139474 (E.D.N.Y. Apr. 27, 2009). The mere inclusion of a payment coupon would not confuse the least sophisticated consumer about the right to dispute the debt and did not violate the FDCPA.

Stark v. RJM Acquisitions L.L.C., 2009 WL 605811 (E.D.N.Y. Mar. 9, 2009). The FDCPA disclosures on the reverse side of the dun were not overshadowed by "the placement and length of the settlement offers presented on the front page of the collection letter" since "even the least sophisticated consumer would not read a collection letter so carelessly so as not to notice a bolded instruction in larger type to 'see reverse side of this letter for important information.' " The various non-FDCPA-mandated disclosures printed in the largest print on the reverse side did not overshadow the accompanying § 1692g(a) notice that was printed in smaller print since the validation disclosure "appears squarely at the top of the page and is among the first things the consumer is likely to read. Given the validation notice's prominent placement, no reasonable juror could conclude that the inclusion of other notices on the same page overly distracts from the validation notice."

Larsen v. JBC Legal Group, P.C., 533 F. Supp. 2d 290 (E.D.N.Y. 2008). The threat of suit before expiration of the consumer's right to seek validation of the debt violated the FDCPA.

Foti v. NCO Fin. Sys., Inc., 424 F. Supp. 2d 643 (S.D.N.Y. 2006). An initial communication telling the debtor that the matter required "immediate attention" did not overshadow or contradict the § 1692g disclosures since there was "no suggestion that the thirty-day validation period should be disregarded, or that immediate payment is required." Court denied the collector's motion to dismiss the consumer's claim that the collector's telephone calls overshadowed or contradicted the § 1692g disclosures since the allegations that the collector repeatedly demanded payment and threatened continuous demands for payment absent immediate payment during the thirty-day validation period stated a claim for relief. Claims that properly allege a § 1692g overshadowing violation and a § 1692e misrepresentation do not by themselves also state claim for engaging in unfair practices in violation of § 1692f.

Jackson v. Immediate Credit Recovery, Inc., 2006 U.S. Dist. LEXIS 85928 (E.D.N.Y. Nov. 28, 2006). Letter sent on the 31st day after initial letter was not confusing or misleading as to validation rights.

Delmoral v. Nationwide Recovery Sys., 2006 U.S. Dist. LEXIS 71084 (E.D.N.Y. Sept. 29, 2006). The court granted the defendant's motion to dismiss the plaintiff's claim that the initial letter violated § 1692g(a), finding that the letter contained no demand for payment in fewer than the statutory thirty days and no language that had two or more different meanings that could create a claim for deception.

Rios v. Pinnacle Fin. Group, Inc., 2006 WL 2462899 (S.D.N.Y. Aug. 23, 2006). Collectors' motion to dismiss FDCPA complaint alleging that the validation notice was overshadowed was granted because the letter directed the consumer to the validation notice on the reverse side printed at least as large as any other language on the page and was accentuated in capitals.

Lawrence v. Borah, Goldstein, Altschuler, Schwartz & Nahins, P.C., 2005 WL 2875383 (S.D.N.Y. Nov. 1, 2005). Consumer stated a claim for confusion about the thirty-day validation right, when three-day rent demand which referred to an upcoming notice that would give rights under the FDCPA.

Vega v. Credit Bureau Enters., 2005 U.S. Dist. LEXIS 4927 (E.D.N.Y. Mar. 29, 2005). Collector's explicit instruction to the consumer that she must dispute the validity of the debt in writing clearly overshadowed the validation notice below that statement in violation of § 1692g(a)(3).

Swift v. Maximus, Inc., 2004 WL 1576618 (E.D.N.Y. July 15, 2004). Defendant's motion for summary judgment was denied, where letter demanded payment within thirty days of date of initial letter to avoid further collection activities. "Even the least-sophisticated consumer would calculate that payment must be mailed in advance of a deadline in order to be received by that deadline." "The least sophisticated consumer is capable of conjuring a host of frightening actions approximating the vague 'further collection activities' phrase contained in the letter."

Johnson v. Equifax Risk Mgmt. Servs., 2004 WL 540459 (S.D.N.Y. Mar. 17, 2004). Collector's dun to collect a dishonored check, while not expressly demanding immediate payment, overshadowed the thirty-day validation period by effectively threatening that the consumer's check-writing privileges within the collector's national network could only be restored by tendering full payment.

Lerner v. Forster, 240 F. Supp. 2d 233 (E.D.N.Y. 2003). A dun requesting full payment or a call to the creditor to arrange partial payment did not contradict or overshadow the debt validation notice in the following paragraph.

Rumpler v. Phillips & Cohen Assocs., Ltd., 219 F. Supp. 2d 251 (E.D.N.Y. 2002). Requesting the debtor to "immediately contact this office" after language stating that "it was not in your best interest to neglect this account any further" did not overshadow the thirty-day validation period.

Hillaire v. Delta Funding Corp., 2002 WL 31123860 (E.D.N.Y. Sept. 26, 2002). The district court held that the debt collector's letter adequately explained how the two ideas—that the consumer retained the right to dispute the validity of the debt, but that such right did not affect the creditor's right to initiate a lawsuit—fit together and did not confuse even the least sophisticated consumer.

Orenbuch v. Computer Credit, Inc., 2002 WL 1918222 (S.D.N.Y. Aug. 19, 2002). A debt collector that had not received a request for validation or other reply from a consumer may continue to attempt to collect the debt during the thirty-day validation period so long as it does not create the impression that the consumer has less than thirty days in which to dispute the debt. Collector's second notice sent within the thirty-day validation period stating that it was returning the account to the creditor did not contradict or overshadow the initial thirty-day verification disclosure or render it false.

Kramsky v. Mark L. Nichter, P.C., 166 F. Supp. 2d 912 (S.D.N.Y. 2001). The validation notice was not overshadowed by the language that a collection law firm "has been engaged to proceed against you because of your failure to make payment," that it "will not permit this debt to be ignored," and that "it would definitely be in your best interest to satisfy in full your outstanding balance."

Kramsky v. Trans-Continental Credit & Collection Corp., 166 F. Supp. 2d 908 (S.D.N.Y. 2001). The validation notice was not contradicted or overshadowed by the statement: "This past due statement reflects a balance due the above stated creditor. This account has been referred to collection and we must ask that you remit the balance shown in full using the enclosed envelope."

Unger v. Nat'l Revenue Group, Ltd., 2000 U.S. Dist. LEXIS 18708 (E.D.N.Y. Dec. 8, 2000). The collection agency's validation notice was confusing and ineffective, violating § 1692e(10) and 1692g, as a result of the statement in the same letter that full payment was due now and a second letter a few weeks later assuming the debt was valid.

Laster v. Cole, 2000 U.S. Dist. LEXIS 3771 (E.D.N.Y. Mar. 20, 2000). Lawyer's initial letter, which said he would hold litigation advice in abeyance for seven days, conflicted with the thirty-day validation notice violating §§ 1692e and 1692g.

Castro v. ARS Nat'l Servs., Inc., 2000 U.S. Dist. LEXIS 2618 (S.D.N.Y. Mar. 8, 2000). ARS's letter listing examples of "suitable

dispute documentation" violated § 1692g, since the section does not require the consumer to specify the nature of any dispute, or that the consumer's dispute be "suitable," to obtain validation of the debt. "I dispute the debt" suffices. The defendant's letter could therefore have hampered a consumer's efforts to communicate the fact that she disputed a debt, thereby depriving her of the statutory protection afforded consumers who notify a collector that the validity of a debt is contested.

Tipping-Lipshie v. Riddle, 2000 U.S. Dist. LEXIS 2477 (E.D.N.Y. Mar. 1, 2000). Demand for payment or a call to make payment arrangements within one week overshadowed the thirty-day validation period which was also set forth in the letter. The Seventh Circuit safe harbor letter in *Bartlett v. Heibl* conflicts with Second Circuit authority, so the court did not find the safe harbor available. The request for the consumer to telephone the collection firm's "800" number did not overshadow the FDCPA requirement that a consumer must give the notice of a dispute in writing to be entitled to a validation of the debt. Defendant's argument that a prior collection agency had already given the validation notice was rejected. The initial communication from each collector must contain the notice.

Sokolski v. Trans Union Corp., 53 F. Supp. 2d 307 (E.D.N.Y. 1999). A collector's request that payment be "at once" overshadowed the thirty-day validation notice.

DeSantis v. Roz-Ber, Inc., 51 F. Supp. 2d 244 (E.D.N.Y. 1999). Statutory damages of $750 awarded for language that overshadowed the thirty-day dispute right. The letter used "IMMEDIATE ATTENTION!" in bold letters, and implicitly threatened that if the consumer did not remit payment in full or call to arrange settlement, he would not receive "cooperation" from the collection agency. The court found the "options" clearly more onerous than in *Terran*. The court distinguished other cases that "were clearly less intrusive and did not call for immediate payment in exchange for cooperation from the collection agency."

Ong v. Am. Collections Enter., Inc., 1999 U.S. Dist. LEXIS 409 (E.D.N.Y. Jan. 15, 1999). Collection agency's letter to consumer violated § 1692g(a)(3) of the FDCPA by requiring that consumer notify collection agency in writing that he disputes the validity of the debt.

Hairston v. Whitehorn & Delman, 1998 WL 35112 (S.D.N.Y. Jan. 30, 1998). The expedited twenty-day period afforded under the N.Y. Real Property Actions and Proceedings Law when given with the thirty-day validation notice violated the FDCPA.

Monokrousos v. Computer Credit, Inc., 984 F. Supp. 233 (S.D.N.Y. 1997). A claim was stated for a violation of § 1692g by a letter demanding that the consumer pay or dispute the debt on a date shortly before the expiration of the thirty day validation period.

Harrison v. NBD Inc., 968 F. Supp. 837 (E.D.N.Y. 1997). An offer to accept payment of 65% of the balance for a period slightly shorter than the validation period did not obscure or contradict the validation notice.

Cavallaro v. Law Office of Shapiro & Kriesman, 933 F. Supp. 1148 (E.D.N.Y. 1996). The debt collector violated § 1692g(a)(3) by misstating on the validation notice the time the debtor had to respond as thirty days from date of notice rather than the statutorily required thirty days from receipt of notice. The debt validation notice on a separate page sent to plaintiff in the same envelope as a collection letter was effectively provided because there was no concealment of the notice where it was the same size as the collection letter, was marked "Notice," was addressed to plaintiff, and named the creditor and amount of the debt. There was no violation of § 1692g(a)(5) since the debt collector supplied the name and address of the original creditor in its debt validation notice so it did not need to offer to supply the name and address of the original creditor. Dunning language in a validation notice that overshadowed or contradicted the notice and would make a least sophisticated consumer unsure of his rights would violate § 1692g. However, the court left the question whether this was a violation to the jury, since the debt collector said it "may" sue during the validation period, not that it would sue.

Brown v. ACB Bus. Servs., 1996 WL 469588 (S.D.N.Y. Aug. 16, 1996). Mere "possibility of confusion" was not sufficient to overshadow required disclosures. Where required debt validation disclosures were made, and the letter mentioned that the collection agency would contact consumer "shortly" if payment was not made, the debt validation notice was not overshadowed, even though the consumer might wait for contact and miss the debt validation deadline. The court was reluctant to find liability for this confusing statement without allegations of actual damages.

Wiener v. Bloomfield, 901 F. Supp. 771 (S.D.N.Y. 1995). Conflicting deadlines which overshadowed the validation notice violated § 1692g.

Tsenes v. Trans-Continental Credit & Collection Corp., 892 F. Supp. 461 (E.D.N.Y. 1995). Follow-up letter, received by consumer one to two weeks after initial letter, threatened action within ten days which could "hurt [consumer's] ability to obtain credit for many years," contradicted the validation notice, and might induce the least sophisticated consumer "to overlook his statutory right to dispute the debt within thirty days." Complaint stated a cause of action under § 1692e(10) on grounds that the juxtaposition of inconsistent statements of validation rights in the initial letter and demanding payment in five days in a follow-up letter constituted a "false representation or deceptive means to collect . . . any debt."

Beeman v. Lacy, Katzen, Ryen & Mittleman, 892 F. Supp. 405 (N.D.N.Y. 1995). Contradiction of the validation notice need not be threatening in order to state a claim for violation of § 1692g. To survive a Fed. R. Civ. P. 12(b)(6) motion to dismiss a § 1692g claim, complaint must plead (1) that a contradiction exists between the demand language and the validation notice and (2) that the contradiction could mislead the least sophisticated consumer into disregarding his or her rights under the validation notice. The finder of fact must determine that the contradiction between the demand and the validation notice would induce the least sophisticated consumer to overlook the procedures contained in the validation notice. Expert testimony may be presented by both parties to demonstrate the contradiction between the demand and the validation notice and the effect on the least sophisticated consumer.

Robinson v. Transworld Sys., Inc., 876 F. Supp. 385 (N.D.N.Y. 1995). Letter stating that debt was considered valid, sent twenty days after the validation notice, contradicted the thirty-day period within which to request validation information in violation of §§ 1692g and 1692e(10). Whether cumulative effect of language in letters violated §§ 1692g and 1692e(10) was a question for the jury.

Washington v. Mercantile Adjustment Bureau, 1994 WL 263452 (W.D.N.Y. May 25, 1994). Whether debt collector's statements that the balance was due and payable immediately in order to avoid further collection activity overshadowed or contradicted the legible validation statement included in a separate part of the letter or constituted a deceptive statement or false representation pursuant to § 1692e(10) was a question for the jury and the consumer's motion for summary judgment was denied.

Rabideau v. Mgmt. Adjustment Bureau, 805 F. Supp. 1086 (W.D.N.Y. 1992). Although the reader was directed to information on the back, placement of the validation notice on the reverse side of the collector's letter in dot matrix print smaller than the explanation of payment by credit card which appeared in larger print did not effectively convey the information required by §§ 1692g and 1692e(11) to the least sophisticated consumer. Statement that immediate payment would avoid further contact contradicts the validation notice because it would mislead the consumer to believe payment was the only way to avoid future contact. Sent fifteen days after the initial communication, second notice, which advised the debt must be paid in five days "to avoid further collection measures," could create the impression that it shortened the thirty-day period to request validation of the debt and violated § 1692g(b). At trial plaintiff utilized an expert in organizational communication to testify that the format and placement of the validation notice discouraged reading of the validation notice. The language "SEE REVERSE SIDE FOR IMPORTANT INFORMATION" on the front would draw the recipient's attention to the larger type describing payment by credit card.

Phillips v. Amana Collection Servs., 1992 WL 227839 (W.D.N.Y. Aug. 25, 1992). Notices on the reverse of the collection letter without reference to it on the front were insufficient to place a consumer on notice of his legal rights and violated §§ 1692g and 1692e(11).

Siler v. Mgmt. Adjustment Bureau, 1992 WL 32333 (W.D.N.Y. Feb. 18, 1992). Debt collector's initial communication to the consumer which contained the validation notice and debt collection warning required by §§ 1692g(a) and 1692e(11) respectively on the reverse side, with reference thereto on the front, "in a smaller, lighter typeface than any on the front," with larger print below soliciting credit card information if the consumer chose to pay the debt in this method, was not in compliance with FDCPA.

Read v. Amana Collection Servs., 1991 U.S. Dist. LEXIS 21773 (W.D.N.Y. Jan. 15, 1991). Placing the notices required by §§ 1692e(11) and 1692g on the back of a dunning letter, in smaller type size, and with no reference to the notices on the front of the letter was a strategic placement violating those provisions.

Riveria v. MAB Collections, Inc., 682 F. Supp. 174 (W.D.N.Y. 1988). Validation notice on back of dunning letter in gray ink, smaller type, without salutation was no notice at all; the collector should have referenced it on the front.

North Dakota

Ost v. Collection Bureau, Inc., 493 F. Supp. 701 (D.N.D. 1980). A five day demand for payment was misleading when consumer had a thirty-day validation right. If the validation notice is put on reverse of a collection letter, the front of the letter must refer to the validation notice.

Ohio

Richeson v. Javitch, Block & Rathbone, L.L.P., 576 F. Supp. 2d 861 (N.D. Ohio 2008). Additional sentence, "Our request that you contact us by telephone does not affect the requirement under federal law that to obtain verification of the debt, you are required to notify us of a dispute in writing" merely explains that written notice of a dispute is what triggers the debt collector's obligation to provide written verification. Debt collector did not violate § 1692g by clarifying the difference between subsections (a)(3) and (a)(4).

Kelly v. Montgomery Lynch & Assocs., Inc., 2008 WL 1775251 (N.D. Ohio Apr. 15, 2008). Cross motions for summary judgment denied on the § 1692g(a) claim because whether the dun's demand for payment of the dishonored check within the state dishonored check statute's ten-day period overshadowed or contradicted the thirty-day validation right and, if so, whether the violation was a bona fide error were triable issues of material fact.

Kafele v. Lerner, Sampson & Rothfuss, L.P.A., 2005 WL 1379107 (S.D. Ohio June 9, 2005), *aff'd on other grounds*, 2005 Fed. Appx. 1006N (6th Cir. Dec. 22, 2005). The defendants, the prosecuting attorneys in the underlying state-court foreclosure action, conceded liability for their disclosure of the FDCPA thirty-day verification notice as an attachment to the state court summons and complaint that disclosed an inconsistent twenty-eight-day answer deadline, thus failing to effectively convey the § 1692g notice under the contradiction/confusion doctrine.

Sprouse v. City Credits Co., 126 F. Supp. 2d 1083 (S.D. Ohio 2000). Applying binding Circuit authority from *Smith v. Computer Credit, Inc.*, 167 F.3d 1052 (6th Cir. 1999), court found no threatening § 1692g contradiction.

Powell v. Computer Credit, Inc., 975 F. Supp. 1034 (S.D. Ohio 1997), *aff'd*, 1998 U.S. App. LEXIS 26797 (6th Cir. Oct. 15, 1998). Demand for "immediate payment or a valid reason for" nonpayment was consistent with the validation rights notice.

Smith v. Transworld Sys., 1997 U.S. Dist. LEXIS 23775 (S.D. Ohio July 31, 1997). Request in second collection letter that debtor telephone the collection agency "at once" did not contradict earlier notice that debtor had thirty days to contest the validity of the debt because the language merely encouraged communication rather than threatening or encouraging the consumer to waive the statutory right to challenge the validity of the debt.

Lee v. CBC Co., 1996 U.S. Dist. LEXIS 21993 (S.D. Ohio Sept. 26, 1996). Demand for immediate payment and threat to credit report overshadowed validation notice.

Oklahoma

Osborne v. RJM Acquisitions Funding, L.L.C., 2010 WL 5079482 (W.D. Okla. Dec. 1, 2010). The court found that the bold notice directing plaintiff to view the verification language on the back met the requirements of § 1692g. Found no reason to distinguish between notice directing the reader to another piece of paper and directing the reader to the back side.

Mendus v. Morgan & Assoc., 994 P.2d 83 (Okla. Ct. App. 1999). Where the thirty-day debt validation notice was included in the summons along with the state code's admonition that a judgment could be rendered in twenty days if no answer was on file, an unsophisticated consumer would be confused as to her rights.

Oregon

Dunn v. Derrick E. McGavic, P.C., 653 F. Supp. 2d 1109 (D. Or. 2009). The collector's unexplained threat to immediately file suit overshadowed and contradicted the § 1692g(a) disclosure: "Without a clear explanation of the simple concept that must cease litigation if [plaintiff] disputes the debt, the least sophisticated consumer is likely to wonder what good it would do him to dispute the debt if he cannot stave off a lawsuit. Consequently, [defendant's] threat of immediate lawsuit, court costs, and attorney fees may well encourage the least sophisticated consumer to make a hasty payment rather than dispute the debt. [Defendant's] letter therefore violates § 1692g."

Peters v. Collection Tech. Inc., 1991 U.S. Dist. LEXIS 21810 (D. Or. Dec. 5, 1991). Under the least sophisticated debtor standard, letter demanding immediate payment and informing the consumer that debt collector reported all unpaid debts to a credit reporting agency within thirty days was held to be a "sharp contradiction" to rights explained in validation notice in violation of § 1692g.

Furth v. United Adjusters, Inc., 1983 U.S. Dist. LEXIS 20368 (D. Or. Nov. 17, 1983). A collector did not fulfill its obligations by including a photocopy of § 1692g in its initial communication with the debtor. The initial communication did not state the full amount of the debt. The initial communication did not alert the consumer to the separate notice of validation rights. The collector did not provide the validation notice language in a form calculated to be understandable to the least sophisticated readers.

Pennsylvania

Greer v. Shapiro & Kreisman, 152 F. Supp. 2d 679 (E.D. Pa. 2001). The juxtaposition of the statutory verification rights with an indication that legal proceedings had been instituted (or will be instituted as soon as possible) would make the least sophisticated consumer uncertain as to her rights.

Adams v. Law Offices of Stuckert & Yates, 926 F. Supp. 521 (E.D. Pa. 1996). A debt collection letter violated § 1692g because the demand to the plaintiff for immediate or prompt payment to avoid a negative credit report and threatening suit and "trouble" contradicted the required thirty-day period in the validation notice. The validation notice violated the Act by stating that the thirty-day period started on the date of the letter. Sending separate validation notices to the consumer's home and office was confusing and violated the Act. As the court had found defendant liable for this action under § 1692g, it declined to find the defendant liable for the same acts under § 1692f as it found the violations not to reflect an abuse of a superior economic position.

In re Belile, 209 B.R. 658 (Bankr. E.D. Pa. 1997). The validation notice was not overshadowed where there was a notice on the front of the letter referring to the validation notice on the back, and the type size for the notices and the other text was the same, although the dunning language was in red type and the notices were in black type.

Puerto Rico

In re Almodovar, 2011 WL 381742 (Bankr. D. P.R. Feb. 3, 2011). The court granted summary judgment to the consumer on the § 1692g claim where the defendant's collection letter contradicted the thirty-day verification right by insisting that it was extremely important for the consumer to contact the defendant within five days of receipt of the letter and failed to make the statutorily mandated disclosures.

Texas

Youngblood v. G.C. Servs. Ltd. P'ship, 186 F. Supp. 2d 695 (W.D. Tex. 2002). § 1692e(11) and § 1692g notices in gray type on gray background were sufficiently legible. § 1692e(11) and § 1692g notices on reverse were proper where face of dun prominently referenced the notice on reverse.

Virginia

McCormick v. Wells Fargo Bank, 640 F. Supp. 2d 795 (S.D. W. Va. 2009). The district court held that the Fourth Circuit would find the contradiction/overshadowing issue a question of law.

Turner v. Shenandoah Legal Group, P.C., 2006 WL 1685698 (E.D. Va. June 12, 2006). A collection letter which contained two different thirty day periods: (1) thirty days from the date of the letter and (2) thirty days from the receipt of the letter, as well as reference to an adversarial proceeding in the "re" line, raised a question of fact whether the letter contradicted or overshadowed the validation notice or contained a misleading statement in violation of the FDCPA.

Talbott v. G.C. Servs. Ltd. P'ship, 53 F. Supp. 2d 846 (W.D. Va. 1999). G.C. Services' collection letter demanding payment within ten days in order to avoid additional collection fees could mislead or confuse the least sophisticated debtor as to his rights, and overshadowed the validation notice.

Morgan v. Credit Adjustment Bd., Inc., 999 F. Supp. 803 (E.D. Va. 1998). That the consumer never read the collection letter had no bearing on whether a violation of the FDCPA occurred. Under overshadowing/contradiction doctrine the FDCPA was violated by either (1) format overshadowing—i.e., the thirty-day validation notice is not effectively conveyed to the least sophisticated consumer—or (2) contradiction—i.e., language accompanying the thirty-day validation notice is inconsistent and therefore contradicts the substance of the rights and duties imposed by § 1692g(a).

Creighton v. Emporia Credit Serv., Inc., 981 F. Supp. 411 (E.D. Va. 1997). Demand for payment in full upon receipt of dun or debt will be reported on the consumer's credit report contradicted the validation notice as a matter of law and was a false representation of urgency where collector's policy was not to report a debt to a credit reporting agency for sixty days.

Withers v. Eveland, 988 F. Supp. 942 (E.D. Va. 1997). The letter's demand for "payment IN FULL WITHIN FIVE (5) DAYS" directly conflicted with the thirty days allowed in the debt validation notice. In addition, the collection letter instructed the consumer to either "contact" the debt collection agency or make payment in full, and that could easily lead to confusion about the response time and the need to dispute the debt in writing in order to obtain verification of the debt.

West Virginia

Rhoades v. W. Virginia Credit Bureau Reporting Servs., 96 F. Supp. 2d 528 (S.D. W. Va. 2000). A dun which demanded "immediate payment," said "Pay the full amount today" and "Call us today" in large type overshadowed and contradicted "the tiny-type rendering of the validation notice." The statutory validation notice applied to all consumers because all consumers must get notice of their right to validation even if they do not dispute the debt. An issue of fact as to whether the debt was a consumer debt required denial of summary judgment even though the validation notice requirements were violated.

Chapman v. ACB Bus. Servs., 1997 U.S. Dist. LEXIS 23743 (S.D. W. Va. Feb. 13, 1997). Language on the front of validation notice such as "should we not hear from you within 72 hours" and "please call today" implied coercive measures, and contradicted and overshadowed a validation notice in small print on the back of the notice.

Wisconsin

Borcherding-Dittloff v. Corporate Receivables, Inc., 59 F. Supp. 2d 822 (W.D. Wis. 1999). A second letter sent only fourteen days after first letter overshadowed the thirty day validation notice because it did not explain how the threat affected the period for requesting debt validation. The court compared this letter with the one in *Jenkins v. Union Corp.*, 999 F. Supp. 1120, 1133 (N.D. Ill. 1998) where the second letter was sent fourteen days after the notice and was held to not overshadow the notice. The Union Corp. second letter warned "IMPERATIVE—Grace period about to expire." In this case the second letter said, "PROTECT YOUR CREDIT AS IT COULD BE YOUR MOST VALUABLE ASSET. TO DATE YOU HAVE IGNORED OUR NOTICE OF COLLECTION AGENCY ASSIGNMENT. SHOULD WE INTERPRET THIS TO MEAN THAT YOU DO NOT INTEND TO PAY VOLUNTARILY? YOUR SILENCE MAY COMPEL US TO SEEK FURTHER REMEDIES" but did not mention the continuing right to dispute.

Booth v. Collection Experts, Inc., 969 F. Supp. 1161 (E.D. Wis. 1997). A letter sent during the thirty-day validation period violated the Act because it conflicted with the notice of validation rights by stating that the consumer had to pay the debt within five days or face "more extreme measures." An acknowledgment of the debt would not be a waiver of that claim.

Sturdevant v. Jolas, P.C., 942 F. Supp. 426 (W.D. Wis. 1996). A validation notice that required a consumer to dispute a debt in writing did not violate § 1692g. The lawyer sent a demand letter with a validation notice and, before the end of the thirty day period, sent another letter stating payment in full must be received within ten days. As the ten day period would expire at least the day after the thirty day validation period, the court found no violation as a debt collector could legally demand payment of a debt immediately after the thirty day validation period.

Tychewicz v. Dobberstein, 1996 U.S. Dist. LEXIS 22555 (W.D. Wis. Aug. 28, 1996). The concept of overshadowing was not limited to language contained within a single document, and the likelihood of an unsophisticated consumer being misled was greater when the conflicting language was in different documents.

K.2.6.3 Oral Validation Requests and Disputes

Camacho v. Bridgeport Fin. Inc., 430 F.3d 1078 (9th Cir. 2005). Collectors could not notify consumers that they will assume that a debt is valid unless they receive a written notice of dispute—instead, the consumer can dispute the debt's validity in writing or orally, under § 1692g(a)(3). In reaching this conclusion, the Ninth Circuit noted that there are at least three other FDCPA provisions only requiring oral notice by the consumer.

Brady v. Credit Recovery Co., 160 F.3d 64 (1st Cir. 1998). Section 1692e(8)'s requirement that a debt collector, when communicating credit information to a third party (here, a credit reporting agency), must communicate that a debt is disputed when a debt is known or should be known to be disputed applies when the disputed nature of the debt is conveyed orally and is not limited to written disputes.

Graziano v. Harrison, 950 F.2d 107 (3d Cir. 1991). Debt verification notice which stated that a consumer's dispute must be in writing to overcome the collector's presumption that the debt was valid did not violate the FDCPA. While § 1692g(a)(3), unlike § 1692g(a)(4) and (5), does not state that a written dispute is necessary, the overall structure of that section must be read to require written notice by the consumer.

Alabama

In re Turner, 2010 WL 3211030 (M.D. Ala. Aug. 13, 2010). The collector's validation notice that limited disputes to those in writing violated § 1692g(a)(3).

Arizona

Bogner v. Masari Invs., L.L.C., 257 F.R.D. 529 (D. Ariz. 2009). Class certified on a *Camacho* claim where the collector's § 1692g(a) notice stated that any dispute must be made in writing.

California

Hipolito v. Harris & Zide, 2004 WL 3563366 (N.D. Cal. Dec. 16, 2004). A debt collector must make the § 1692g(a)(3) disclosure without limiting the assumption of a debt's validity unless it is disputed in writing.

Forsberg v. Fidelity Nat'l Credit Servs., 2004 U.S. Dist. LEXIS 7622 (S.D. Cal. Feb. 25, 2004). It was not a violation to fail to state the oral disputes would overcome the collector's assumption of validity.

Sanchez v. Weiss, 173 F. Supp. 2d 1029 (N.D. Cal. 2001). The plain language of § 1692g(a)(3) does not require that a dispute be "in writing."

Georgia

Young v. McDowell Servs., Inc., 1991 U.S. Dist. LEXIS 21814 (N.D. Ga. Apr. 30, 1991). Debt collector's statement that the consumer must dispute the debt "in writing" within thirty days (otherwise it would be assumed to be valid) violated § 1692g(a)(3).

Hawaii

Sambor v. Omnia Credit Servs., 183 F. Supp. 2d 1234 (D. Haw. 2002). An initial dun containing the required § 1692g disclosure but reciting examples of "suitable dispute documentation" unlawfully suggested to the least sophisticated consumer that a dispute under § 1692g must be in writing, that some supporting documentation might be unsuitable, and that any documentation at all was required.

King v. Int'l Data Servs., 2002 WL 32345923 (D. Haw. Aug. 5, 2002). Collection agency's § 1692g notice violated the Act because it was likely to cause the least sophisticated consumer to believe that a dispute must be in writing, explained and supported by documentation.

Bailey v. TRW Receivables Mgmt. Servs., Inc., 1990 U.S. Dist. LEXIS 19638 (D. Haw. Aug. 16, 1990). A consumer should not lose the validation right by paying before the request. The collector also violated § 1692g by stating that the debt will be assumed valid unless disputed in writing when no writing is required by § 1692g(a)(3) for avoiding this assumption of validity. A written request for validation is required by § 1692g(a)(4) only to obtain verification from the collector.

Illinois

Jolly v. Shapiro, 237 F. Supp. 2d 888 (N.D. Ill. 2002). Court sides with the Third Circuit position in *Graziano* in the current split on whether a proper § 1692g notice may require that any dispute must be in writing.

Ingram v. Corporate Receivables, Inc., 2003 WL 21018650 (N.D. Ill. May 5, 2003). Court followed the Third Circuit in *Graziano* and held that a § 1692g(a) verification disclosure that required any consumer dispute to be in writing comported with the intent of Congress.

Indiana

Campbell v. Hall, 624 F. Supp. 2d 991 (N.D. Ind. 2009). The court sided with the Ninth Circuit in *Camacho* and rejected the Third Circuit in *Graziano* and held that the defendant's initial dunning letters violated "§ 1692g(a)(3) insofar as they state that disputes regarding the validity of a debt must be made in writing."

Chung v. Nat'l Check Bureau, Inc., 2005 WL 1541030 (S.D. Ind. June 30, 2005). Defendant's motion to dismiss complaint denied, because its validation notice improperly limited any dispute to a written dispute.

Rosado v. Taylor, 324 F. Supp. 2d 917 (N.D. Ind. 2004). The collection attorney violated the § 1692g(a)(3) by requiring that disputes be in writing to prevent the collector from considering the debt valid. The court noted that oral disputes impose the requirement under § 1692e(8) that the debt collector report the dispute if reporting the debt to third parties.

Spearman v. Tom Wood Pontiac-GMC, Inc., 2002 WL 31854892 (S.D. Ind. Nov. 4, 2002). Court parts with the Third Circuit position in *Graziano* in the current split on whether a proper § 1692g notice may require that any dispute must be in writing and holds in a comprehensive analysis that the validation notice must disclose the consumer's right to dispute orally.

Castillo v. Carter, 2001 U.S. Dist. LEXIS 2686 (S.D. Ind. Feb. 28, 2001). A collection letter did not violate § 1692g(a)(3) by stating that a dispute of the debt's validity should be in writing.

Louisiana

Reed v. Smith, 1994 U.S. Dist. LEXIS 21463 (M.D. La. July 25, 1994). There is no requirement for a writing to dispute a debt for the purposes of § 1692g(a)(3), and the jury should decide whether the collector's validation notice was inadequate in this regard. The court distinguished between requests for verification under § 1692g(a)(4) which must be in writing and a dispute under § 1692g(3) which does not expressly require a written dispute.

Maryland

Wallace v. Capital One Bank, 168 F. Supp. 2d 526 (D. Md. 2001). Limiting the debtor's dispute to a written dispute did not violate the debtor's validation rights; the court recognized the conflict of authority on this issue.

Michigan

Diamond v. Corcoran, 1992 U.S. Dist. LEXIS 22793 (W.D. Mich. Aug. 3, 1992). Collection letter which stated that all disputes must be in writing did not render the validation notice invalid.

Minnesota

Burke v. Messerli & Kramer P.A., 2010 WL 3167403 (D. Minn. Aug. 9, 2010). While the court noted that an orally communicated dispute of the debt within thirty days of the initial communication is sufficient under § 1692g, it also noted that the consumer's provision of prior correspondence during the period could have been a sufficient written dispute of the paid debt.

Silbert v. Asset Res., Inc., 2000 U.S. Dist. LEXIS 6453 (D. Minn. Feb. 14, 2000). Consumer's allegation that debt collector hung up in response to consumer's request for information during initial telephone communication precluded finding upon motion for judgment on the pleadings that debt collector provided an oral validation notice.

Montana

Blome v. Johnson, Rodenburg & Lauinger, 2007 WL 4374498 (D. Mont. Dec. 11, 2007). Without some evidence that the *pro se* consumer disputed the debt, he could not prevail on a claim that the debt collector violated the debt validation notice requirements by stating all disputes must be in writing.

New Jersey

Bodine v. First Nat'l Collection Bureau, Inc., 2010 WL 5149847 (D.N.J. Dec. 13, 2010). Where the plaintiff acknowledged that she did not request verification of the debt in writing but nevertheless asserted that her oral dispute obligated the collector to provide verification of the debt, defendant was entitled to judgment.

Smith v. Lyons, Doughty & Veldhuius, P.C., 2008 WL 2885887 (D.N.J. July 23, 2008). Use of the word "we" to refer to the debt collector in the validation notice would not confuse the least sophisticated consumer or violate § 1692g(a)(3).

New York

Nero v. Law Office of Sam Streeter, P.L.L.C., 655 F. Supp. 2d 200 (E.D.N.Y. 2009). The validation notice clearly omitted an impor-

tant term—that the consumer must inform the debt collector *in writing* to be entitled to verification of the debt. It makes no difference whether defendant would have honored an oral request.

In re Risk Mgmt. Alternatives, Inc., 208 F.R.D. 493 (S.D.N.Y. 2002). The court declined to follow *Graziano v. Harrison*, 950 F.2d 107 (3d Cir. 1991), and held that a jury must determine whether the least sophisticated consumer could believe that the language of the letter at issue implied that any challenge to the debt must be in writing.

Nasca v. G.C. Servs., Ltd., 2002 WL 31040647, 53 Fed. R. Serv. 3d 1089 (S.D.N.Y. Sept. 12, 2002). A debt collector was not required to provide debtors with a telephone number in order to assist debtors in disputing the debt orally.

Barrientos v. Law Offices of Mark L. Nichter, 75 F. Supp. 2d 510 (S.D.N.Y. 1999). A letter sent after the validation notice but before the expiration of the thirty-day validation period violated § 1692g by stating that the attorney collector was authorized "to take any lawful action we deem necessary to collect this debt" and urged plaintiff "to make payment today so we can put this matter to rest."

Fasten v. Zager, 49 F. Supp. 2d 144 (E.D.N.Y. 1999). A collection agent who refused to verify a debt orally disputed by the consumer over the telephone did not violate § 1692g(4), since that section requires any request for verification to be in writing. Accordingly the same conduct did not violate § 1692e.

Ong v. Am. Collections Enter., Inc., 1999 U.S. Dist. LEXIS 409 (E.D.N.Y. Jan. 15, 1999). The initial collection notice must contain the non-writing dispute notice of § 1692g(a)(3). Debt collection letter requiring that debt be disputed in writing or collector would presume it valid, violated the FDCPA.

Young v. Credit Bureau Inc., 729 F. Supp. 1421 (W.D.N.Y. 1989). Same holding as *Spencer v. Credit Bureau, Inc.*, *supra*.

Spencer v. Credit Bureau Inc., Clearinghouse No. 45,350 (W.D.N.Y. 1989). Statement in validation notice that debt will be presumed valid unless the consumer disputes it in writing violates FDCPA, since § 1692g(a)(3) does not require a writing.

Henderson v. Credit Bureau Inc., Clearinghouse No. 45,349 (W.D.N.Y. 1989). Same holding as *Spencer v. Credit Bureau, Inc.*, *supra*.

Castillo v. Frenkel, 2010 WL 5507904 (N.Y. App. Div. Dec. 23, 2010). The lower court should not have dismissed the claim where the plaintiff's amended complaint stated a cause of action by alleging that the defendant's dunning letter improperly included a notice that in the event plaintiff sought to dispute the debt, he was required to do so in writing.

Ohio

Jerman v. Carlisle, 464 F. Supp. 2d 720 (N.D. Ohio 2006). The court agreed with *Camacho v. Bridgeport Fin., Inc.*, 430 F.3d 1078 (9th Cir. 2005) and held that the plain meaning of § 1692g(a)(3) did not impose a writing requirement on the consumer to dispute the debt.

Damsel v. Shapiro, 2001 Ohio App. LEXIS 4052 (Ohio Ct. App. Sept. 13, 2001). Collector's tardy reply to consumers' oral request for mortgage reinstatement amount was not subject to § 1692g, since requesting the reinstatement amount was not in the nature of a dispute or seeking verification of the debt itself and, in any event, the request was not in writing.

Oregon

Harvey v. United Adjusters, 509 F. Supp. 1218 (D. Or. 1981). The collector's verification notice violated the Act in that if it was sent, it did not state the right to dispute a portion of the debt and erroneously required any dispute to be in writing.

Check Cent., Inc. v. Barr, Clearinghouse No. 37,497 (Bankr. D. Or. 1984). A statement in the collector's validation notice that consumer must notify collector in writing in thirty days does not violate FDCPA.

Puerto Rico

In re Almodovar, 2011 WL 381742 (Bankr. D. P.R. Feb. 3, 2011). The court granted summary judgment to the consumer on the § 1692g claim where the collector failed to advise the consumer that he had the option of disputing the debt orally. Rejecting the Third Circuit's rationale in *Graziano*, the court stated: "Such a scheme seems not only coherent, but progressive, and perhaps intended to benefit undereducated or handicapped consumers who are unable to communicate in writing."

Virginia

Turner v. Shenandoah Legal Group, P.C., 2006 WL 1685698 (E.D. Va. June 12, 2006). Following *Camacho v. Bridgeport Fin., Inc.*, 430 F.3d 1078 (9th Cir. 2005), the magistrate judge recommended that the dispute of a debt pursuant to § 1692g(a)(3) need not be in writing.

Wisconsin

Sturdevant v. Jolas, P.C., 942 F. Supp. 426 (W.D. Wis. 1996). A validation notice that required the consumer to dispute the debt in writing did not violate § 1692g.

K.2.6.4 Proper Verification of the Debt

Madura v. Lakebridge Condo. Ass'n Inc., 2010 WL 2354140 (11th Cir. June 14, 2010). Where the defendant sent verification of the debt with its "Notice of Intent to File Lien," updated that verification in later correspondence, and again sent the consumers a current statement in verification of the debt contemporaneously with the filing of the lien, the defendant did not violate § 1692g(b).

Clark v. Capital Credit & Collection Servs., Inc., 460 F.3d 1162 (9th Cir. 2006). In *Mahon v. Credit Bureau of Placer County Inc.*, 171 F.3d 1197, 1203 (9th Cir. 1999), the court described one way to provide proper verification:

> [T]he Credit Bureau, when it received the [verification] request, promptly contacted [the creditor's] office, verified the nature and balance of the outstanding bill, learned that monthly statements had been sent from [the creditor's] office to the[debtors] for over two years, and established

that the balance was still unpaid. The Credit Bureau then promptly conveyed this information to the [debtors], along with an itemized statement of the account. We decline to impose such a high threshold. Rather, we adopt as a baseline the more reasonable standard articulated by the Fourth Circuit in *Chaudhry v. Gallerizzo,* 174 F.3d 394 (4th Cir. 1999). At the minimum, "verification of a debt involves nothing more than the debt collector confirming in writing that the amount being *1174 demanded is what the creditor is claiming is owed." Undisputed facts demonstrate that, upon the Clarks' request for verification, Capital obtained information from Dr. Evans about the nature and balance of the outstanding bill and provided the Clarks with documentary evidence in the form of the itemized statement . . . Capital's and Hasson's actions, then, satisfied the requirement that they confirm with their client the particular amount being claimed.

Jang v. A.M. Miller & Assocs., 122 F.3d 480 (7th Cir. 1997). The policy of the debt collectors to return to the creditor all debts in which the consumer requests validation was not deceptive or unconscionable in light of the § 1692g validation notice statement that the collectors would validate the debt. § 1692g allowed the collector to either validate or cease collection. These collectors chose to cease collecting the debt. They could not be found to violate the FDCPA by providing the notice required by the FDCPA.

Dikeman v. Nat'l Educators, Inc., 81 F.3d 949 (10th Cir. 1996). The jury had found the debt had not been verified when the verification given was inadequate because it overstated the collector's claim, but the jury excused the violation as a bona fide error.

Graziano v. Harrison, 950 F.2d 107 (3d Cir. 1991). Computer printout showing the amounts of the debts, the services provided and the dates of the debts met the collector's verification obligation.

Alabama

Quale v. Unifund CCR Partners, 682 F. Supp. 2d 1274 (S.D. Ala. 2010). Consumer's allegations that debt collector, after receiving request for verification, failed to verify the debt and, instead, reported it to consumer reporting agencies without notifying the agencies that the debt was disputed, were sufficient to state a claim.

Arkansas

Marshall v. Deutsche Bank Nat'l Trust Co., 2011 WL 345988 (E.D. Ark. Feb. 1, 2011). Issue preclusion barred the § 1692g claims since prior adjudications had conclusively established the validity of the debt: "By overruling Plaintiff's objections to Wells Fargo's proof of claims in her second and third bankruptcies and confirming Plaintiff's Chapter 13 plan, the bankruptcy court validated Wells Fargo's claim, inherently finding that Wells Fargo had a right to collect the debt. . . . If confirmed plans do not have preclusive effect then debtors would be able to make bad faith claims to 'effectively prevent the collection of a debt, despite a court of competent jurisdiction having already adjudicated the dispute.' Thus Plaintiff's claim that Wells Fargo failed to provide

§ 1692g(a) notice, and violated § 1692g(b) by attempting to collect an unverified debt that it knew was disputed are also precluded because those claims depend on the underlying issue of the disputed mortgage debt."

Dunham v. Portfolio Recovery Assocs., L.L.C., 2009 WL 3784236 (E.D. Ark. Nov. 10, 2009). Defendant debt buyer's Rule 12(c) motion denied on the consumer's § 1692g(b) inadequate verification claim where the pleadings established that the defendant merely repeated the information in its own file and failed to take any steps to confirm the debt with the original creditor: "The verification requirement demands more than that the debt collector merely repeat its assertion that a debt is due. . . . Simply repeating second—or third-hand information in the debt collector's file is insufficient under the statute."

California

Consumer Solutions REO, L.L.C. v. Hillery, 658 F. Supp. 2d 1002 (N.D. Cal. 2009). A request for verification pursuant to the FDCPA does not require the debt collector to take any action within five days.

Hernandez v. Downey Sav. & Loan Ass'n, 2009 WL 667406 (N.D. Cal. Mar. 13, 2009). The consumers failed to state a claim for relief for the defendants' violation of § 1692g(b), since they did "not allege any facts demonstrating that Defendants continued their efforts to collect the debt" following receipt of the consumer's verification request.

Casas v. Midland Credit Mgmt., Inc., 2009 WL 249992 (S.D. Cal. Jan. 30, 2009). Debt collector failed to verify the debt by providing three pages listing charges made in Texas when the consumer had stated that she never had that type of credit card, had provided her California addresses for the last twelve years, and had requested a copy of a credit application with her signature. The debt collector made no effort to verify the debt in the face of the consumer's dispute.

Shubin v. Midland Credit Mgmt., Inc., 2008 WL 5042849 (C.D. Cal. Nov. 24, 2008). Upon receipt of a consumer's request for verification, a debt collector may simply confirm with the creditor that the amount of the debt being collected is correct, it is not required to obtain detailed evidence of the debt.

Holsinger v. Wolpoff & Abramson, L.L.P., 2006 U.S. Dist. LEXIS 55406 (N.D. Cal. July 27, 2006). The NAF MBNA claim sent to consumer constituted sufficient verification even though it listed attorney fees that could have been unreasonably high.

Colorado

Smith v. Argent Mortgage Co., L.L.C., 447 F. Supp. 2d 1200 (D. Colo. 2006). Debt collector's motion to dismiss *pro se* plaintiffs' complaint was denied because the consumer sufficiently alleged the collector's failure to verify the debt upon his dispute.

District of Columbia

Antoine v. J.P. Morgan Chase Bank, 2010 WL 5313309 (D.D.C. Dec. 28, 2010). Where the debt collector established that it sent the § 1692g notice, there remained a question of fact for the jury as to whether or not the consumer timely faxed his dispute letters.

Johnson v. Chase Manhattan Mortgage Corp., 2006 WL 2506598 (D.D.C. Aug. 28, 2006). The plaintiff's claim that the defendants had unlawfully failed to provide verification of her debt as required by the FDCPA was barred by res judicata as a result of the final adverse adjudication in state court of an earlier case between the same parties contesting the validity of the underlying home mortgage and foreclosure sale.

Florida

Lee v. Security Check, L.L.C., 2010 WL 3075673 (M.D. Fla. Aug. 5, 2010). Noted that the debt collector had no duty to investigate what the creditor reported to it since the FDCPA does not impose any duty of independent investigation regarding a disputed debt that has been referred for collection.

Sandlin v. Shapiro & Fishman, 919 F. Supp. 1564 (M.D. Fla. 1996). The debt collector did not violate the § 1692g validation notice requirement by charging consumers a $60 fee for providing payoff figures on delinquent loans as the FDCPA did not address the imposition of fees and the fee did not prevent the debtors from disputing the debt.

Georgia

Milton v. LTD Fin. Servs., 2011 WL 291363 (S.D. Ga. Jan. 25, 2011). A consumer wishing to sue a collector for misrepresenting the amount of the debt must first utilize § 1692g's dispute procedure, but summary judgment was denied on the plaintiff's purported failure since a genuine issue of material fact remained as to whether the plaintiff properly utilized the debt validation procedure prior to filing suit.

Anderson v. Frederick J. Hanna & Assocs., 361 F. Supp. 2d 1379 (N.D. Ga. 2005). In providing that the consumer may obtain verification by disputing the debt within thirty days of receipt of the initial communication, the FDCPA clearly contemplates that the verification is separate and distinct from the initial communication. Verification of a debt involves nothing more than the debt collector confirming in writing that the amount being demanded is what the creditor is claiming is owed.

Hawaii

Bailey v. TRW Receivables Mgmt. Servs., Inc., 1990 U.S. Dist. LEXIS 19638 (D. Haw. Aug. 16, 1990). Another violation occurred when the collector failed to validate the debt when requested to do so, and even though the debt had been paid.

Illinois

Allen v. ATG Credit L.L.C., 2004 WL 2931298 (N.D. Ill. Dec. 14, 2004). Whether verification was defective, by not accounting for cancellation of the school enrolment, was question for jury. The failure to provide the address of the original creditor was not a violation because it was not requested.

Bradley v. Fairbanks Capital Corp., 2003 WL 21011801 (N.D. Ill. May 5, 2003). Allegation that it violated the FDCPA for an attorney to verify a complaint based upon information supplied by the plaintiff (which was permitted by state law), failed to state a claim.

Indiana

Recker v. Cent. Collection Bureau, Inc., 2005 WL 2654222 (S.D. Ind. Oct. 17, 2005). Executed contracts in combination with an itemized statement showing the medical services provided, interest, and fees was sufficient verification under the FDCPA where the consumer did not specify a reason for disputing the debt. Attaching verification of a debt to a small claims complaint was insufficient verification because the FDCPA requires that once requested, verification must be provided before any further steps are taken to collect the debt.

Monsewicz v. Unterberg & Assocs., P.C., 2005 WL 756433 (S.D. Ind. Jan. 25, 2005). Having mailed the verification of the debt to the consumer with the initial communication, the debt collector was not required by § 1692g(b) to cease collection of the debt. Nor was the debt collector obligated under the FDCPA to answer the consumer's letters.

Zaborac v. Mutual Hosp. Serv., Inc., 2004 WL 2538643 (S.D. Ind. Oct. 7, 2004). Debt verification requires only a written confirmation that the debt collector is demanding what the creditor claims is owed.

Kansas

McCammon v. Bibler, Newman & Reynolds, P.A., 515 F. Supp. 2d 1220 (D. Kan. 2008). A dispute made outside the thirty-day validation period did not trigger the collector's duty to verify the debt pursuant to § 1692g(b). An oral dispute did not trigger the collector's duty to verify the debt pursuant to § 1692g(b).

Maine

Poulin, Jr. v. Thomas Agency, 2011 WL 159889 (D. Me. Jan. 13, 2011). FDCPA does not require a debt collector to independently investigate the merit of the debt disputed under 1692g; a debt collector can rely on its clients' representations regarding the validity of the debt; verification of a debt by merely confirming of the amount of the debt and the identity of the creditor is sufficient.

Poulin v. The Thomas Agency, 2011 WL 140477 (D. Me. Jan. 13, 2011). The FDCPA does not require a debt collector to conduct its own investigation into the amount or validity of the underlying loan. Confirmation of the amount of the debt and the identity of the creditor, which is then relayed to the debtor, is sufficient.

Maryland

Senftle v. Landau, 390 F. Supp. 2d 463 (D. Md. 2005). A collector is under no duty to verify a debt which the consumer disputes after the expiration of the thirty-day validation period.

Shah v. Collecto, Inc., 2005 WL 2216242 (D. Md. Sept. 12, 2005). Consumer's request for validation outside the notice period did not impose liability under § 1692g.

Michigan

King v. Ocwen, 2008 WL 2063553 (E.D. Mich. Apr. 14, 2008), *report and recommendation adopted by*, 2008 WL 2063551 (E.D. Mich. May 14, 2008). *Pro se* plaintiffs' motion for summary judgment on § 1692g(b) claim denied because there remained unresolved the material fact whether the defendant mailed verification of the debt to the plaintiffs.

Minnesota

Burke v. Messerli & Kramer P.A., 2010 WL 3167403 (D. Minn. Aug. 9, 2010). The thirty-day period for requesting verification begins when the consumer receives the debt verification notice and ends thirty days later, the last day the consumer may send a dispute notice to the debt collector. The debt collector need not receive the dispute notice in that period. A consumer need not use particular language to dispute a debt as long as she conveyed that she was questioning the existence, validity, or extent of the debt. The transmission of a demand letter with the handwritten notation: "THIS DEBT IS PAID IN FULL AS PER THE SETTLEMENT AGREEMENT. DO NOT CONTACT ME AGAIN!" clearly showed that the consumer disputed the debt.

Erickson v. Johnson, 2006 WL 453201 (D. Minn. Feb. 22, 2006). Where the debt collector provided statements of account sent to plaintiff and his spouse, and canceled checks drawn on the marital joint account, the verification was "minimally sufficient" since the FDCPA does not require an investigation and does not require the collector to ascertain the legality of the debt. Where the plaintiff did not request verification of the attorney fee component of the amount demanded, the collector had no obligation to verify it. The court dismissed the verification claims, noting, "However, the Court is gravely disappointed by the actions of Defendants [collection attorneys]and the creditor. Defendants did the bare minimum to comply with the FDCPA's verification requirements. Had they investigated Kermit Erickson's identity theft allegations further before continuing with the state court lawsuit, they could have saved considerable time and effort by the parties and the state and federal court systems." "Although the FDCPA does not punish Defendants for continuing to attempt to collect this debt when their proof of verification was weak, the Court admonishes Defendants and their clients that both good business practices and good citizenship require them to do their part to prevent identity theft."

Mississippi

Hennis v. Trustmark Bank, 2010 WL 1904860 (S.D. Miss. May 10, 2010). Where defendant did not show beyond doubt that the *pro se* consumers could prove no set of facts to support their FDCPA claim for failure to validate the debt, it survives the motion to dismiss.

Weathersby v. Citibank, N.A., 928 So. 2d 941 (Miss. Ct. App. 2006). Without discussing the fact that Citibank is a creditor and not subject to the FDCPA, court held that sending copies of periodic statements and employee affidavits stating they were sent to the *pro se* cardholders was sufficient verification within § 1692g despite not providing the requested signed agreement.

Missouri

Settle v. Bank of Am., 2010 WL 682296 (E.D. Mo. Feb. 23, 2010). Where the *pro se* consumer requested verification prior to the receipt of defendant's initial debt collection communication, the mortgagee's alleged failure to respond did not amount to a § 1692g violation.

Montana

Blome v. Johnson, Rodenburg & Lauinger, 2007 WL 4374498 (D. Mont. Dec. 11, 2007). Verification information regarding a car deficiency claim which included a retail installment contract, a loan application, and a notice of sale and an accounting of the sale met the § 1692g requirements of the FDCPA.

Nebraska

Uche v. Brumbaugh & Quandahl, P.C., 2010 WL 5256351 (D. Neb. Dec. 15, 2010). Where a debt collector did not provide all of the information the *pro se* consumer believed was required to verify the debt, but instead provided enough information to show that it was not attempting to collect the debt from "the wrong person" or attempting "to collect debts which the consumer has already paid," the FDCPA verification requirement was met.

Uche v. North Star Capital Acquisition, L.L.C., 2010 WL 5256350 (D. Neb. Dec. 15, 2010). Where a debt collector did not provide all of the information the *pro se* consumer believed was required to verify the debt, but instead provided enough information to show that it was not attempting to collect the debt from "the wrong person" or attempting "to collect debts which the consumer has already paid," the FDCPA verification requirement was met.

Nevada

Karony v. Dollar Loan Ctr., L.L.C., 2010 WL 5186065 (D. Nev. Dec. 15, 2010). The court dismissed the § 1692g claim, since the plaintiff alleged no facts indicating that the defendants failed to send him the required § 1692g(a) disclosures in a timely manner or that he disputed the debt in writing within thirty days to trigger the defendants' § 1692g(b) responsibility to verify the debt.

New Jersey

Huertas v. Galaxy Asset Mgmt., 2010 WL 936450 (D.N.J. Mar. 9, 2010). Because the alleged running of the statute of limitations did not extinguish the debt, debt buyer's alleged failure to verify the debt as uncollectible did not violate the § 1692g.

Bass v. Palisades Collections, L.L.C., 2008 WL 4513812 (D.N.J. Sept. 26, 2008). Failure to validate the debt within the ninety-day estimated time frame did not violate the FDCPA because § 1692g does not establish a time limit.

New York

Davis v. Countrywide Home Loans, 2010 WL 3219306 (S.D.N.Y. July 23, 2010). Dismissed the *pro se* complaint because although it alleged that defendants failed to provide consumer with verification of his debt, it failed to allege that they were engaged in collection efforts, and thus the defendants' alleged failure was not actionable.

Bascom v. Dubin, 2007 WL 210387 (W.D.N.Y. Jan. 25, 2007). Bank's collection attorney adequately provided verification of the debt where he provided plaintiffs copies of original billing statements that showed that the amount being demanded was what was claimed to be owed and that showed the dates on which charges were incurred, together with the current bank's supporting "Affidavit of Claim and Certification of Amount Due."

Dowling v. Kucker Kraus & Bruh, L.L.P., 2005 WL 1337442 (S.D.N.Y. June 6, 2005). Debt collectors could not evade the notice requirements of the FDCPA merely by having a creditor sign a demand for rent that the collector prepared and mailed.

Johnson v. Equifax Risk Mgmt. Servs., 2004 WL 540459 (S.D.N.Y. Mar. 17, 2004). Because the consumer had both disputed the debt as based on a forged check and specifically demanded the address of the payee merchant in his § 1692g verification request, the collector's transmittal to the consumer of only a copy of the dishonored check but not the payee's address as requested failed to comply with § 1692g(b).

Stonehart v. Rosenthal, 2001 U.S. Dist. LEXIS 11566 (S.D.N.Y. Aug. 13, 2001). Provision of the computer printout of the dentist's Account Statement to the consumer satisfied the verification requirement of § 1692g(b) where the consumer argued that she should not have been billed for a negligent treatment that necessitated a root canal.

North Carolina

Gough v. Bernhardt & Strawser, P.A., 2006 WL 1875327 (M.D.N.C. June 30, 2006). The collection lawyers did not violate § 1692g(b) when they continued to litigate after the debtor had submitted a timely written verification request once served with the summons and complaint because the collection complaint and its attachments already provided the consumer with adequate verification information.

Ohio

Asset Acceptance L.L.C. v. Davis, 2004 WL 2940747 (Ohio Ct. App. Dec. 13, 2004). The court held that the debt collector's failure to provide validation, which was requested by the consumer more than three years after the collector sent its initial communication containing the § 1692g notice, was not unlawful since that section requires a collector to comply only with such requests lodged within thirty days after the consumer's receipt of the communication containing the validation notice.

Damsel v. Shapiro, 2001 Ohio App. LEXIS 4052 (Ohio Ct. App. Sept. 13, 2001). Summary judgment for the defendant affirmed on the consumers' claim that the defendant failed to send verification in response to their § 1692g request when the evidence was uncontroverted that the defendant mailed the response in accordance with ordinary business practices and received no indication that the response was returned or undeliverable. Consumers' mere denial of receipt of the collector's verification response was insufficient to create an issue of fact for trial since § 1692g requires only that the collector send such verification.

Oregon

McNall v. Credit Bureau, 689 F. Supp. 2d 1265 (D. Or. 2010). Credit bureau obtained and sent to consumers the RVMC invoice and an "admissions statement" signed by consumer. Under *Clark*, the itemized invoice alone satisfied the verification requirements of § 1692g.

Pennsylvania

Jarzyna v. Home Prop., L.P., 2011 WL 382367 (E.D. Pa. Feb. 4,

2011). The plaintiff stated a claim for a § 1692g(b) violation by alleging that the defendant verified the debt merely by sending a copy of the invoice that had already been enclosed in the original dunning letter and failed to show it was pursuing a colorable claim.

Harris v. NCO Fin., Sys., 2009 WL 497409 (E.D. Pa. Feb. 26, 2009). Because a genuine issue of fact existed as to whether plaintiff disputed the debt as set forth in that section—obligating the debt collector to submit evidence of the origin and validity of the debt—summary judgment must be denied.

Tennessee

Rudek v. Frederick J. Hanna & Assocs., P.C., 2009 WL 385804 (E.D. Tenn. Feb. 17, 2009). The collection lawyer's confirmation of the debt with the creditor was all that was required in response to the consumer's valid request for verification under § 1692g.

Texas

Crain v. Credit Prot. Ass'n, 2010 WL 2976127 (N.D. Tex. June 30, 2010). Where the *pro se* consumer did not allege that he sought verification of his debt either verbally or in writing, he failed to allege sufficient facts to support a cause of action under § 1692g(b).

Tesi v. Chase Home Fin., L.L.C., 2010 WL 2293177 (N.D. Tex. June 7, 2010). The court rejected the *pro se* consumer's argument that the defendants had refused to produce a "genuine verified original note" for his inspection. "[S]ection 1692g(a), while requiring a debt collector to send a consumer from whom it is attempting to collect a debt a notice containing specified information, does not require that the debt collector produce a copy of the original loan obligation."

Alexander v. U.S. Bank, 2008 WL 3152989 (N.D. Tex. July 30, 2008). *Pro se* consumer failed in his argument that § 1692g required that defendants provide the original signed mortgage note to plaintiff.

Weissman v. Unifund CCR Partners Assignee of Discover, 2009 WL 6407538 (Tex. Ct. App. Apr. 2, 2009). The debt collector provided the *pro se* consumer adequate verification information to confirm the debt and comply with § 1692g when it sued her and provided some monthly statement.

Utah

Reed v. AFNI, Inc., 2011 WL 112430 (D. Utah Jan. 13, 2011). Verification of a debt involves nothing more than the collector confirming in writing that the amount being demanded is what the creditor claims is owed; the collector is not required to keep detailed files of the alleged debt. Debt collectors do not have to vouch for the validity of the underlying debt.

Maxwell v. Barney, 2009 WL 1707959 (D. Utah June 17, 2009). Collector's providing ambulance trip ticket to plaintiff in response to her request to validate her debt did not violate FDCPA.

Maynard v. Bryan W. Cannon, P.C., 650 F. Supp. 2d 1138 (D. Utah 2008). After a request for validation, the consumer should not be left guessing as to the amount of the debt.

Washington

Semper v. JBC Legal Group, 2005 WL 2172377 (W.D. Wash. Sept. 6, 2005). Simply repeating the second- or third-hand information in the debt collector's file was insufficient validation.

K.2.6.5 Proper Debt Validation Rights Notice [*See also* K.2.6.2, Duns Overshadow Validation Notice]

Wilhelm v. Credico, Inc., 519 F.3d 416 (8th Cir. 2008). A categorical threat to sue made in a letter failed to disclose that the debt buyer would not sue any consumer who timely disputed the debt as permitted by § 1692g, as the debt buyer then must cease collection until the debt is verified: "That appears to be a threat to take action 'that cannot legally be taken' within the meaning of § 1692e(5). A reasonable jury might also find that an unequivocal threat to sue in these circumstances constituted use of a 'deceptive means to collect or attempt to collect' a debt that is prohibited by § 1692e(10)."

Jacobson v. Healthcare Fin. Servs., Inc., 516 F.3d 85 (2d Cir. 2008). Debt validation notice violated the FDCPA by shortening the time for the consumer to respond. The notice required that the debt collector receive the debt validation request within thirty days of the consumer's receipt of the notice when the FDCPA gives the consumer thirty days from to receipt of the notice to mail the request.

Volden v. Innovative Fin. Sys., Inc., 440 F.3d 947 (8th Cir. 2006). Identifying the stores and their location as the creditors to whom the debt is owed provided all the information required by § 1692g(a)(5). While the collector did not provide the wording specified in § 1692g(a)(5), there was "substantial compliance." "The technical and meaningless omission by IFS could not have been seen by Congress as a purposeful violation of the FDCPA."

Greco v. Trauner, Cohen & Thomas, L.L.P., 412 F.3d 360, 363 (2d Cir. 2005). Debt collector's addition to the debt validation notice that the creditor would also assume that the debt was valid if the consumer did not dispute the in thirty days was not a violation of the FDCPA.

Thomas v. Law Firm of Simpson & Cybak, 354 F.3d 696 (7th Cir. Jan. 13, 2004) (2-1 split decision), *vacated*, 358 F.3d 446 (7th Cir. 2004). Law firm's filing of summons and complaint on behalf of creditor in state court after debtor missed payment on installment contract was an "initial communication."

Horkey v. J.V.D.B. & Assocs., 333 F.3d 769 (7th Cir. 2003). The collection agency failed to provide a validation notice to the consumer, violating the FDCPA. The provision of a validation notice by the collector's attorney did not excuse the agency as the notice did not refer to the agency. The collection agency's ignorance of the consumer's new address was not an excuse when it could have sent the validation notice to the consumer's old address, asked the post office for her forwarding address, or mailed it to the debtor's attorney.

Buckley v. Bass & Assocs., P.C., 249 F.3d 678 (7th Cir. 2001). Letter inquiring about bankruptcy status, with no demand for payment, and not giving the §§ 1692e(11) or 1692g notices was not an effort to collect a debt. "[T]he inclusion of the language plaintiff claims was required under the FDCPA was forbidden by the Bankruptcy Code."

Mahon v. Credit Bureau, 171 F.3d 1197 (9th Cir. 1999). Debt collection agency must prove only that the § 1692g notice was sent, not received by the consumer. Absent any evidence other than the consumer's bare denial of receipt, the common law mailbox rule controlled where uncontroverted evidence showed that the collection agency properly mailed the notice. The court additionally found that a debt collector was under no duty to verify a debt which the consumer disputed after the thirty-day validation period.

Huff v. Dobbins, Fraker, Tennant, Joy & Perlstein, 1999 U.S. App. LEXIS 12055 (7th Cir. June 2, 1999). Collection attorney's violation of the § 1692g validation notice requirements was not changed by the consumer hiring an attorney within five days of receipt of the violating letter. The court was bound to follow the plain language of the FDCPA.

Schnitzspahn v. F.A.B., Inc., 156 F.3d 1232 (6th Cir. 1998) (unpublished) (text at 1998 WL 466109). The court summarily found no FDCPA violations. The defendant's debt validation notice contained all the necessary information required under § 1692g.

Ferree v. Marianos, 129 F.3d 130 (10th Cir. 1997) (unpublished) (text at 1997 WL 687693). The validation notice provided the information required by the FDCPA.

Frey v. Gangwish, 970 F.2d 1516 (6th Cir. 1992). The validation notice must be provided within five days of the initial communication even where the first communication was an attorney's post-judgment letter to the consumer.

Smith v. Transworld Sys., Inc., 953 F.2d 1025 (6th Cir. 1992). Debt collector's letter, which stated that "all portions of this claim shall be assumed valid unless disputed within thirty days of receiving this notice," satisfied § 1692g(a)(3) under the least sophisticated consumer standard.

Baker v. G.C. Servs. Corp., 677 F.2d 775 (9th Cir. 1982). A validation notice that does not notify the consumer that a portion of a debt may be disputed violates § 1692g. The collector's validation notice was not sufficient to put unsophisticated consumers on notice as to their rights. The consumer need not dispute the validity of the debt to recover for this violation.

Alabama

In re Turner, 2010 WL 3211030 (M.D. Ala. Aug. 13, 2010). The court rejected the collector's de minimis defense to its violation for sending a validation notice requiring that disputes must be sent within thirty days from its date rather than the required thirty days from the consumer's receipt.

In re Turner, 2008 WL 4168488 (Bankr. M.D. Ala. Sept. 5, 2008). If the defendant is not the assignee, the letters do not identify the creditors to whom the debts are owed as required by § 1692g(a)(2). Because § 1692g(a)(3) does not require written notice of dispute, defendant's letter requiring writing dispute violated the FDCPA. Defendant violated § 1692g(a)(4) by requiring dispute within thirty days of the date of the letter, rather than its receipt.

Arizona

Horvath v. Premium Collection Servs., Inc., 2010 WL 1945717 (D. Ariz. May 13, 2010). Where the debt collector has made no communication to the consumer, there is no liability under the FDCPA for failure to provide the validation notice.

Nichols v. GC Serv., L.P., 2009 WL 3488365 (D. Ariz. Oct. 27, 2009). Summary judgment granted to the debt collector on the consumer's claim that the collector failed to send the required validation disclosure since, notwithstanding the consumer's claim that he never received the notice, the evidence showed that defendant complied with § 1692g by sending it.

Thweatt v. Law Firm of Koglmeier, Dobbins, Smith & Delgado, P.L.C., 425 F. Supp. 2d 1011 (D. Ariz. 2006). Since the summons and complaint served in the state court action may be an "initial communication" under the FDCPA, plaintiffs' allegation that the defendants failed to include the required § 1692g(a) validation disclosure in those pleadings stated a claim for relief.

Beuter v. Canyon State Prof'l Servs., 2005 U.S. Dist. LEXIS 12281 (D. Ariz. June 13, 2005), aff'd, 261 Fed. Appx. 14 (9th Cir. 2007). The court found disputed issues of fact precluding entry of summary judgment for either party where the consumer denied that she received the collector's initial dun containing the required debt validation notice and the collector submitted only a conclusory statement that it had sent the initial dun but without any supporting evidence of the ordinary business practices through which the dun was purportedly sent.

Arkansas

Marshall v. Deutsche Bank Nat'l Trust Co., 2011 WL 345988 (E.D. Ark. Feb. 1, 2011). The § 1692g(a) claim against the defendant was dismissed since a prior collector had already provided the § 1692g(a) disclosure. The court found that the defendant who had been "hired to litigate for collection of that same debt need not supply a second validation notice" and "a § 1692g(a) notice by one debt collector serves as notice for subsequent attempts by different debt collectors to collect on the same debt."

California

Welker v. Law Office of Daniel J. Horwitz, 699 F. Supp. 2d 1164 (S.D. Cal. 2010). Defendant violated § 1692g(a)(4) and (5) because his dunning letter failed to advise the debtor that to be entitled to a verification of the debt or to obtain the name and address of the original creditor under the request had to be in writing.

Riggs v. Prober & Raphael, 2010 WL 3238969 (N.D. Cal. Aug. 16, 2010). The defendant's § 1692g disclosure adequately informed the least sophisticated consumer of the right to dispute the debt both in writing and orally.

del Campo v. Am. Corrective Counseling Serv., Inc., 2010 WL 2473586 (N.D. Cal. June 3, 2010). The court granted summary judgment to the consumers on their §§ 1692e(11) and 1692g claims since the defendant's duns entirely omitted the FDCPA-mandated disclosures.

Johnson v. Professional Collection Consultants, 2010 WL 2196571 (S.D. Cal. May 28, 2010). Consumer's evidence that he had never resided at or received mail at the address listed on the envelope in which the debt collector sent the validation notice, or otherwise had any affiliation with such address, created an issue of fact as to whether the letter was properly sent in compliance with § 1692g.

Welker v. Law Office of Horwitz, 626 F. Supp. 2d 1068 (S.D. Cal. 2009). Letter did not comply with § 1692g(a)(4) and (5) because it did not inform plaintiffs that their entitlement to verification of the debt under § 1692(a)(4), as well as their right to the name and address of the original creditor under § 1692g(a)(5), was contingent on the submission of their disputes in writing.

Robertson v. Richard J. Boudreau & Assocs., L.L.C., 2009 WL 5108479 (N.D. Cal. Dec. 18, 2009). Debt validation notice violated § 1692g by implying in one paragraph that the consumer had no right to dispute the debt and then attempted to cure that violation in the next paragraph by stating that the consumer had such a right.

Basinger-Lopez v. Tracy Paul & Assocs., 2009 WL 1948832 (N.D. Cal. July 6, 2009). Default judgment entered on well pleaded facts showing that the defendants failed to provide a § 1692g notice.

Cassady v. Union Adjustment Co., 2008 WL 4773976 (N.D. Cal. Oct. 27, 2008). The FDCPA requires only that the debt collector send the validation notice within five days of its initial communication, not that the consumer receive the validation notice.

Taylor v. Quall, 471 F. Supp. 2d 1053 (C.D. Cal. 2007). Collector's detailed evidence showed compliance in this case with the regular procedure for sending the § 1692g notice and the plaintiff's only contrary evidence was that he never received it.

Weiner v. McCoon, 2007 WL 2782843 (S.D. Cal. Sept. 24, 2007). The consumer's mere failure to receive the defendant's § 1692g notice in the mail failed to rebut the defendant's evidence that he mailed the notice and thus complied with § 1692g(a).

Holsinger v. Wolpoff & Abramson, L.L.P., 2006 U.S. Dist. LEXIS 55406 (N.D. Cal. July 27, 2006). Inclusion of a partial validation rights notice in a letter sent subsequent to the initial notice obligated the debt collector to comply with the parts of § 1692g(a) included in the second notice but the failure of the second notice to state the amount of the debt would not be a violation.

Foresberg v. Fidelity Nat'l Credit Servs., Ltd., 2004 WL 3510771 (S.D. Cal. Feb. 26, 2004). The collector's omission from the validation notice of the consumer's right to dispute any portion of the debt violated the Act. The collector's disclosure that unless the consumer disputed the debt pursuant to the validation notice, it would assume the debt to be "valid and enforceable," when the statute states only that it would then be assumed "valid," created ambiguity that rendered the disclosure in violation of § 1692g(a). The court held that any attempt to request validation of the debt under § 1692g(a) must be in writing. The collector's validation disclosure that omitted the entirety of § 1692g(a)(4) violated the Act. Since the collector's initial dun identified the original creditor, it was under no obligation to make the § 1692g(a)(5) disclosure to offer to again identify that creditor. The collector's instruction to "please include documentation" along with any verification request unlawfully confused the least sophisticated consumer that supporting documentation was a requirement in order to lodge a dispute.

Forsberg v. Fidelity Nat'l Credit Servs., 2004 U.S. Dist. LEXIS 7622 (S.D. Cal. Feb. 25, 2004). Debt validation rights notice violated § 1692g by failing to state a portion of the debt could be disputed, by failing to state that debt verification would be provided by the collector, by requesting documentation with a dispute. It was not a violation to fail to state the oral disputes would overcome the collector's assumption of validity and to fail to offer to provide the creditor's name when it was provided in the letter.

Bush v. Loanstar Mortgage Servs., L.L.C., 286 F. Supp. 2d 1210 (N.D. Cal. 2003). Section 1692g(a)(1) was not violated by a document which contained both the total amount of the mortgage and a lesser amount to reinstate normal terms of the mortgage without explanation of their relationship. Although the defendant was precluded by California Civil Code § 2924(c) from taking legal action to collect the total amount of the mortgage until after the thirty-day validation period, the FDCPA was not violated. Defendant was not required to explain in its validation notice that plaintiffs' obligation to repay the loan would be extinguished if the creditor ultimately exercised its right to sell plaintiffs' home.

Irwin v. Mascott, 96 F. Supp. 2d 968 (N.D. Cal. 1999). Sending an unlawful notice imposed liability; whether the notice was received was irrelevant.

Newman v. CheckRite California, Inc., 912 F. Supp. 1354 (E.D. Cal. 1995). It was a question of fact whether the validation notice was properly conveyed, given the font and positioning of such notice.

Colorado

Ray v. Int'l Bank, Inc., 2005 WL 2305017 (D. Colo. Sept. 21, 2005). On the defendant's motion to dismiss, the court examined the split between the Eleventh Circuit in *Vega* and the Seventh Circuit in *Thomas* on whether a pleading can be an initial FDCPA communication but refused to rule on the issue "at this juncture."

Connecticut

Derisme v. Hunt Leibert Jacobson, P.C., 2010 WL 4683916 (D. Conn. Nov. 10, 2010). The court rejected the *pro se* plaintiff's theory of multiple § 1692g violations, since only the initial communication was at issue. Found claim stated for § 1692g(a) but not § 1692g(b) or § 1692e.

Krueger v. Ellis, Crosby & Assocs., Inc., 2006 WL 3791402 (D. Conn. Nov. 9, 2006). Defendant violated the FDCPA by not sending required notices.

Cirkot v. Diversified Fin. Sys., 839 F. Supp. 941 (D. Conn. 1993). Provision of the validation notice more than five days after the initial communication violated § 1692g.

Delaware

Sutton v. Law Offices of Alexander L. Lawrence, 1992 U.S. Dist. LEXIS 22761 (D. Del. June 17, 1992). Even though initial communication satisfied notice requirements, a follow-up letter, which did not, violated § 1692g if it was clearly sent by a separate entity.

Beattie v. D.M. Collections, Inc., 754 F. Supp. 383 (D. Del. 1991). If a debt collector ceases debt collection and informs the consumer of this fact within five days of the initial communication, the debt collector need not send a § 1692g validation notice.

Florida

Sanz v. Fernandez, 633 F. Supp. 2d 1356 (S.D. Fla. 2009). Allegations that the defendants were debt collectors who failed to make §§ 1692e(11) and 1692g(a) disclosures stated a claim for relief.

Acosta v. Campbell, 2006 WL 146208 (M.D. Fla. Jan. 18, 2006). The FDCPA does not impose on a debt collector an obligation to disclose to a consumer the right to dispute the debt prior to filing suit. Pursuant to binding circuit authority (*Vega*), a summons and complaint does not constitute a "communication" in connection with collection of a debt, and thus neither the omission of the § 1692g disclosures nor service of these documents at 7:20 a.m. in alleged violation of § 1692c(a)(1) stated a claim for relief. "A debt collector is free to file suit when collecting on a debt *unless* the debtor timely disputes the debt" (Emphasis in original). Consumer stated a claim for the collection attorney's violation of § 1692g(b) where the complaint alleged that the attorney filed suit after having received the consumer written validation request earlier on the same day.

McKnight v. Benitez, 176 F. Supp. 2d 1301 (M.D. Fla. 2001). Neither a summons, complaint, nor other papers served on a consumer in conjunction with the initiation of a lawsuit was a "communication" and, therefore, the plaintiff's claim that the papers failed to comply with § 1692g was dismissed.

In re Hathcock, 437 B.R. 696 (Bankr. M.D. Fla. 2010). The disclosure in the collection letter of the consumer's right to dispute the debt within thirty days of receipt of the "initial written notice to you concerning this debt" would not confuse the least sophisticated consumer who "would understand that the thirty day period to dispute the debt commenced upon receipt of the collection letter."

Georgia

Thomas v. LDG Fin. Servs., Inc., 463 F. Supp. 2d 1370 (N.D. Ga. 2006). Stated a claim for violation of § 1692g where the complaint specifically alleged that the debt collector did not send plaintiff a validation notice. The court declined to convert defendant's motion to dismiss to a motion for summary judgment and to consider the affidavit submitted by the defendant alleging that it had sent a validation notice.

Maloy v. Phillips, 197 B.R. 721 (M.D. Ga. 1996). A collection attorney who before he learned of the bankruptcy, mailed a collection letter to a chapter 13 debtor was prohibited by the automatic stay under the Bankruptcy Code from subsequently mailing a validation notice under § 1692g. The attorney was not liable for his FDCPA violation.

Johnson v. Ardec Credit Servs., Inc., 1984 U.S. Dist. LEXIS 24889 (N.D. Ga. Mar. 21, 1984). The debtor is entitled to summary judgment where the notice of validation rights was neither contained in collector's initial phone communication nor given to debtor in writing within five days of that communication.

Florence v. Nat'l Sys., 1983 U.S. Dist. LEXIS 20344 (N.D. Ga. Oct. 14, 1983). The collector violated the FDCPA by failing to provide a validation notice.

Wright v. Credit Bureau of Ga., Inc., 548 F. Supp. 591 (N.D. Ga. 1982), *modified on other grounds,* 555 F. Supp. 1005 (N.D. Ga.

1983). When the consumer did not contest the collector's statement that it had provided notice of validation rights, the collector was entitled to summary judgment on that issue.

Blackwell v. Prof'l Bus. Servs., 526 F. Supp. 535 (N.D. Ga. 1981). The placement of the validation notice on the back of the initial dunning letter was not a violation of FDCPA. The inclusion of the word "judgment" in the validation notice when there was no judgment on the claim did not violate the FDCPA.

Carrigan v. Cent. Adjustment Bureau, Inc., 494 F. Supp. 824 (N.D. Ga. 1980). No validation notice was sent violating the FDCPA.

Hawaii

Sambor v. Omnia Credit Servs., 183 F. Supp. 2d 1234 (D. Haw. 2002). An initial dun containing the required § 1692g disclosure but reciting examples of "suitable dispute documentation" unlawfully suggested to the least sophisticated consumer that a dispute under § 1692g must be in writing, that some supporting documentation might be unsuitable, and that any documentation at all was required.

Bailey v. TRW Receivables Mgmt. Servs., Inc., 1990 U.S. Dist. LEXIS 19638 (D. Haw. Aug. 16, 1990). The § 1692g notice did not have to refer to any judgment where there was none. The failure to notify the consumer that any portion of the debt could be disputed and verified violated § 1692g.

Illinois

Shapiro v. United Recovery Serv., L.L.C., 2009 WL 1313194 (N.D. Ill. May 12, 2009). The collector's initial dun that stated that the debt would be assumed to be valid unless disputed did not violate § 1692g(a)(3) for the reason it failed to disclose that it was the debt collector and not another entity, such as the creditor, who would make that assumption: "Although the letter does not expressly include the language 'by the debt collector,' even unsophisticated consumers would recognize that [the defendant] is the entity that will assume the debt is valid. [Plaintiff's] perception that the letter is deceptive on this basis only and that she is entitled to statutory relief is an unrealistic expectation. As such, [plaintiff] fails to state a cognizable claim under Fed. R. Civ. P. 12(b)(6)."

Krawczyk v. Centurion Capital Corp., 2009 WL 395458 (N.D. Ill. Feb. 18, 2009). The debt collector satisfied its burden of establishing it mailed the § 1692g notice—all that is required.

Davis v. World Credit Fund I, L.L.C., 543 F. Supp. 2d 953 (N.D. Ill. 2008). Summary judgment denied on § 1692g(a) claim in view of conflicting evidence whether the defendant in fact sent plaintiff a communication containing the validation notice.

Moore v. Blatt, Hasenmiller, Leibsker & Moore, L.L.C., 2006 WL 1806195 (C.D. Ill. June 29, 2006). Defendant's testimony as to its regular mailing practices was sufficient to invoke the mailbox rule, even though consumer denied receiving the initial notice.

Ruth v. M.R.S. Assocs., Inc., 2006 WL 1207926 (N.D. Ill. Apr. 4, 2006). FDCPA was not violated by language, "if for some reason you believe the debt is not valid" which referred consumer to validation notice but did not ask for explanation.

Mendez v. M.R.S. Assocs., 2005 WL 1564977 (N.D. Ill. June 27,

2005). The consumer's motion for summary judgment was granted where the collector's letter instructed the consumer to contact the sender and "explain the nature of the dispute" because of that statement suggested that the consumer must have a specific reason in order to demand verification of the debt.

Mendez v. M.R.S. Assocs., 2004 WL 1745779 (N.D. Ill. Aug. 3, 2004). A class action was certified in an FDCPA case alleging that debt collection letter added an additional § 1692g step that the consumer explain the nature of the dispute in violation of § 1692g.

Collins v. Sparacio, 2004 WL 555957 (N.D. Ill. Mar. 19, 2004). A prayer in a collection suit for an unspecified amount for court costs was not a confusing presentation of the amount of the debt since the amount of the court costs that might be awarded was not knowable as a practical matter when suit was filed.

McCabe v. Crawford & Co., 272 F. Supp. 2d 736 (N.D. Ill. 2003). Failure to specify that any portion of the debt may be disputed also violated § 1692g(a). Omitting the words "in writing" from the validation notice violated § 1692g(a). The court was unable to determine as a matter of law that the language "Federal Law provides that this debt will be assumed to be valid and owing" violated § 1692e(10) and required additional proof such as a consumer survey.

Carbajal v. Capital One, F.S.B., 2003 WL 22595265 (N.D. Ill. Nov. 10, 2003). The consumer stated a claim for relief for violating § 1692g(a) where the debt collector's validation notice stated that if the debtors made a payment, they still retained their right to dispute the debt for the full thirty-day validation period in view of the allegation that making the payment itself could extinguish the dispute (e.g., revival of a debt disputed as time barred).

McGinley v. Law Office of Shapiro & Kreisman, 2003 WL 21466936 (N.D. Ill. June 24, 2003). Court granted summary judgment dismissing consumer claim that the debt collector failed to send the required initial validation notice, where the consumer's only evidence was that he did not receive the notice and the debt collector produced a facsimile of the initial dun and electronic records showing that it was in fact mailed to the consumer.

McCabe v. Crawford & Co., 210 F.R.D. 631 (N.D. Ill. 2002). A claim was stated where the collector's letter failed to inform the consumer that a dispute must be "in writing." A claim was stated where the collector's letter failed to inform the consumer that he may dispute "any portion" of the debt.

Whitten v. ARS Nat'l Servs., Inc., 2002 U.S. Dist. LEXIS 10828 (N.D. Ill. June 17, 2002). Court affirmed prior ruling and held that no evidence other than the collection letter was required in order for the court to determine that the letter violated the FDCPA because the additional phrase "suitable dispute documentation could include . . ." and attendant list, juxtaposed with the statutory right to dispute a debt within thirty days, created more than the mere potential for confusion and was as bad as an outright contradiction or inconsistency.

Whitten v. ARS Nat'l Servs., Inc., 2002 U.S. Dist. LEXIS 9385 (N.D. Ill. May 23, 2002). The FDCPA was violated because the collection letter on its face impermissibly imposed a requirement that the consumer submit "suitable dispute documentation" to dispute a debt in contradiction to the plain language of § 1692g(a), which makes no such requirement.

Shula v. Lawent, 2002 WL 31870157 (N.D. Ill. Dec. 23, 2002). Collector's letter demanding payment of court costs was required to include the statutory validation notice pursuant to § 1692g.

Thomas v. Law Firm of Simpson & Cybak, 2001 U.S. Dist. LEXIS 19456 (N.D. Ill. Nov. 16, 2001). A verified complaint filed by the creditor's law firm did not violate § 1692g because it was not the initial communication.

Young v. Manley, 2000 U.S. Dist. LEXIS 13035 (N.D. Ill. Sept. 6, 2000). Defendant law firm sent a letter to plaintiff's bankruptcy attorney threatening a dischargeability proceeding based on the amount of credit card charges just before bankruptcy. The letter contained neither of the required FDCPA notices. The consumer's attorney was not a "consumer" within the FDCPA and did not need its protections; a collector was, indeed, required to communicate with the attorney who represented the debtor. The letter was not an indirect collection effort. The §§ 1692e(11) and 1692g counts were dismissed.

DiRosa v. N. Shore Agency, 56 F. Supp. 2d 1039 (N.D. Ill. 1999). Without discussing any standard of deception, court concluded that it failed to see how plaintiff could be confused by receiving subsequent validation notices. The court failed to consider that the subsequent notices misrepresented that the consumer's validation rights extended beyond the first thirty days.

Johnson v. Revenue Mgmt. Corp., 52 F. Supp. 2d 889 (N.D. Ill. 1999). Well after the litigation was commenced, based on consumer's allegation that the collection letter violated § 1692g, the collection agency disclosed that it had sent a previous letter that complied with the law. The consumer moved to withdraw the complaint, and for sanctions against the collection agency for not revealing the letter upon request. Sanctions were denied, on the basis that both parties were partially at fault, since the consumer presumably received the first letter.

Frey v. Satter, Beyer & Spires, 1999 WL 301650 (N.D. Ill. May 3, 1999). Collection agency's omission of the words "after receipt" from the thirty-day validation notice may be de minimis but it set forth a valid legal claim and survived a motion to dismiss. Collection attorney's request that the consumer indicate the nature of the dispute was contrary to the plain language of § 1692g.

Ozkaya v. Telecheck Servs., Inc., 982 F. Supp. 578 (N.D. Ill. 1997). Since the consumer's right to obtain validation of a debt runs from the date the validation notice was received, obscuring the date on the notice did not affect her rights or result in an FDCPA violation.

Trull v. G.C. Servs. Ltd. P'ship, 961 F. Supp. 1199 (N.D. Ill. 1997). Validation notice received twice in letters less than thirty days apart, where each notice informed debtor that the thirty-day validation period commenced upon receipt of initial notice, would not confuse an unsophisticated consumer into believing that validation period had been extended.

Villarreal v. Snow, 1996 WL 28308 (N.D. Ill. Jan. 19, 1996). A lawyer's collection letter violated § 1692g by failing to include the validation notice.

Altergott v. Modern Collection Techniques, 1994 WL 319229 (N.D. Ill. June 23, 1994). Debt collector's letter which omitted two of the five pieces of information required by § 1692g(1)–(5) violated the notice requirements of the section.

Indiana

Campbell v. Hall, 624 F. Supp. 2d 991 (N.D. Ind. 2009). The omission of the "receipt" language from the start of the thirty-day dispute period did not violate § 1692g(a)(3): "The Court finds that the language contained in the debt collection letter in *Chauncey* is distinguishable from the language contained in the instant letters. Specifically, the language contained in Defendant's letters stating 'IF YOU DISPUTE THIS DEBT, or any portion thereof, you must notify this office in writing of that fact within 30 days of this letter' does not require that a dispute regarding the validity of a debt be *received* by Defendant within thirty days of the date of the letters. Rather, the language in the debt collection letters states that any dispute by Plaintiffs must be made 'within 30 days of this letter.' On the basis of this language, it is reasonable to assume that Plaintiffs had thirty days from when they received the letters to dispute the validity of their debts. Therefore, the letters do not require that Plaintiffs provide notice of a debt dispute within thirty days of the date of the letters. Accordingly, because *Chauncey* does not support Plaintiffs' contention that Defendant's debt collection letters violate § 1692g(a)(3) by shortening the statutory thirty-day period in which they are permitted to dispute their debts, Defendant is entitled to summary judgment on this issue."

Kaiser v. Braje & Nelson, L.L.P., 2006 WL 1285143 (N.D. Ind. May 5, 2006). Court filings and letters sent only to consumer's lawyer were not communications with the consumer for the purpose of validation notice requirement.

Monsewicz v. Unterberg & Assocs., P.C., 2005 WL 756433 (S.D. Ind. Jan. 25, 2005). The FDCPA does not require a debt collector to provide the original, a certified, or an attested copy of the document creating a debt as part of the verification. Documents such as computer printouts of itemized statements of account may be sufficient to verify the debt pursuant to § 1692g.

Walters v. PDI Mgmt. Servs., 2004 WL 1622217 (S.D. Ind. Apr. 6, 2004). The collector's validation notice that required that the consumer's dispute be sent by certified mail was an additional, unauthorized burden that violated the FDCPA.

Spears v. Brennan, 745 N.E.2d 862 (Ind. Ct. App. 2001). Failure to disclose clearly in § 1692g notice that the consumer had the right to dispute the debt and stating that the consumer had thirty days to act but without stating that the thirty days is calculated from receipt of the notice violated § 1692g.

Kentucky

Campbell v. Credit Bureau Sys., Inc., 2009 WL 211046 (E.D. Ky. Jan. 27, 2009). The *pro se* consumer adequately rebutted the debt collectors' affidavits that they had mailed a debt verification notice with his affidavit that he was changing addresses at the time of the mailing. The debt collectors' affidavits failed to say the notices were not returned by the post office.

Louisiana

Kahn v. Rowley, 968 F. Supp. 1095 (M.D. La. 1997) (withdrawn from hard cover publication). Question of fact precluded summary judgment on issue whether consumer's attorney telephoned collector's office within five days of initial communication to demand

that communications cease, and thereby waived debt validation notice requirement.

Maryland

Robinson v. TSYS Total Debt Mgmt., Inc., 447 F. Supp. 2d 502 (D. Md. 2006). Collector's request for a collection score from a credit reporting agency did not trigger FDCPA coverage because it was not a communication with a consumer, who was proceeding *pro se* in this action.

Senftle v. Landau, 390 F. Supp. 2d 463 (D. Md. 2005). A court summons and collection complaint may be an "initial communication" under § 1692g(a) if those pleadings are the first communication to a debtor relating to the particular debt. When a collection agency had provided the validation rights notice, a collection law firm that subsequently collected the debt was not required to send its own validation rights notice.

Spencer v. Hendersen-Webb, 81 F. Supp. 2d 582 (D. Md. 1999). Debt collector's fax of a bill to the father of the consumer's boyfriend in response to his request for information on the debt was deemed to be an attempt to collect a debt since debt collector believed the father was consumer's attorney and that information would reach consumer indirectly. Court determined that fax was debt collector's initial communication and thus the failure to provide a validation notice in connection with the fax violated the FDCPA. Therefore, debt collector violated § 1692g(b) making the offer and by failing to cease collection until debt was verified.

Ransom v. Telecredit Serv. Corp., 1992 U.S. Dist. LEXIS 22738 (D. Md. Feb. 5, 1992). Failure to provide the consumer with the validation notice violated § 1692g(a).

Dorsey v. Morgan, 760 F. Supp. 509 (D. Md. 1991). If an attorney is a debt collector, failure of his correspondence to contain the validation notice and debt collection warning violates §§ 1692g and 1692e(11).

Michigan

South v. Midwestern Audit Servs., Inc., 2010 WL 5089862 (E.D. Mich. Dec. 8, 2010). Following *Bailey* and *Gburek*, the court found a debt collection agency's sending an obtuse letter to the consumer indicating that the utility bill balance from her boyfriend's prior account was being transferred to her utility account and not demanding payment was not sent "in connection with the collection of a debt" and not subject to the FDCPA.

McLehan v. Chase Home Fin., L.L.C., 2010 WL 3518021 (E.D. Mich. Aug. 17, 2010). Because the *pro se* plaintiffs could not show that the debt collector law firm was noncompliant with the requirements of § 1692g, dismissal of the FDCPA claim was appropriate.

Gradisher v. Check Enforcement Unit, Inc., 210 F. Supp. 2d 907 (W.D. Mich. 2002). A debt collector violated § 1692g(a) by failing to provide the validation notice to the debtor.

Stojanovski v. Strobl & Manoogian, 783 F. Supp. 319 (E.D. Mich. 1992). Debt collector's letter, which stated that it will assume the amount stated is correct unless the consumer advises otherwise within thirty days of the date of the letter, in which case the collector will forward a verification of the debt to the consumer, was sufficient to comply with § 1692g(a)(3) and (4). Where original creditor's name is provided in the initial letter, debt collector's failure to include the language of § 1692g(a)(5) did not violate FDCPA.

Minnesota

Gray v. Four Oak Court Ass'n, Inc., 580 F. Supp. 2d 883 (D. Minn. 2008). The court rejected the consumer's § 1692g(a) claim based on not receiving the verification disclosure that the putative collector sent since that section requires only that the collector show that the notice was sent, not that it was received.

Mississippi

Shakir v. Nationwide Tr. Servs., Inc., 2010 WL 1529224 (N.D. Miss. Apr. 15, 2010). The court dismissed the *pro se* consumer's claims since the defendant showed that it had the right to foreclose on the subject property as the current assignee of the debt and that it had complied with § 1692g because it ceased foreclosure proceedings during the pendency of the action and sent the consumer verification of the loan—albeit belatedly.

Missouri

Lewis v. Hanks, 1991 U.S. Dist. LEXIS 21807 (E.D. Mo. Feb. 26, 1991). Debt collector's letter failed to contain the information required by § 1692g(a)(3) and (4).

Nebraska

Beaulieu v. Am. Nat'l Educ. Corp., Clearinghouse No. 30,892 (D. Neb. 1981). Collector's failed to provide notice of validation rights and failed to disclose that information obtained will be used for collecting the debt.

Nevada

Karony v. Dollar Loan Ctr., L.L.C., 2010 WL 5186065 (D. Nev. Dec. 15, 2010). The court dismissed the § 1692g claim, since the plaintiff alleged no facts indicating that the defendants failed to send him the required § 1692g(a) disclosures in a timely manner or that he disputed the debt in writing within thirty days to trigger the defendants' § 1692g(b) responsibility to verify the debt.

Nichols v. Byrd, 435 F. Supp. 2d 1101 (D. Nev. 2006). The initiation of a lawsuit seeking to recover a debt may be an initial communication triggering the validation notice requirement under § 1692g. Where a validation notice had been sent by the collection agency, a lawyer hired by the collection agency to collect the debt need not supply a second validation notice. The lawsuit was a subsequent communication that did not trigger the requirements of § 1692g. A validation notice must simply be sent, and need not be received, in order to fulfill the requirements of the FDCPA.

New Jersey

Nicholls v. Portfolio Recovery Assocs., L.L.C., 2010 WL 1257738 (D.N.J. Mar. 29, 2010). Nothing in § 1692g requires a debt collector to either include or omit an e-mail address by which a debtor may contact the collector.

Rosamilia v. ACB Receivables Mgmt., Inc., 2009 WL 1085507 (D.N.J. Apr. 22, 2009). Cessation of communications by the debt

collector after it received a request for validation does not relieve it from the requirement to provide a proper validation notice pursuant § 1692g. Because the FDCPA is a strict liability statute, a debt collector violates the act by failing to provide a proper validation notice, even if there was little or no harm to the consumer.

Stair ex rel. Smith v. Thomas & Cook, 254 F.R.D. 191 (D.N.J. 2008). Each subsequent debt collector must provide a § 1692g validation notice even if the notice was provided by a previous debt collector.

Kaschak v. Raritan Valley Collection Agency, 1989 U.S. Dist. LEXIS 19103 (D.N.J. May 22, 1989). Validation notice was required even though the consumer had actually paid the debt. Collector was liable where collection letter did not completely comply with § 1692g(a)(3).

Hodges v. Feinstein, Raiss, Kelin & Booker, L.L.C., 893 A.2d 21 (N.J. Super. Ct. App. Div. Mar. 8, 2006), *aff'd sub nom. Hodges v. Sasil Corp.*, 915 A.2d 1 (N.J. 2007). FDCPA and state requirements for eviction notices were not inconsistent, and court sets out special instructions to avoid any possible inconsistency, pending amendment of the state requirements.

Loigman v. Kings Landing Condo. Ass'n, 734 A.2d 367 (N.J. Super. Ct. App. Div. 1999). Validation notice which recited all notice requirements of § 1692g was in compliance with the FDCPA notwithstanding the fact that it did not cite the FDCPA.

New Mexico

Toledo v. McNeel, Clearinghouse No. 50,433 (D.N.M. 1995). Collection attorney's letter failed to provide validation notice in violation of § 1692g and entitled plaintiff to statutory damages of $1000 and actual damages of $200.

New York

Sarno v. Midland Credit Mgmt., Inc., 2011 WL 349974 (S.D.N.Y. Jan. 31, 2011). The disputed sentence—"Please remember, even if you make a payment within 30 days after receiving this notice, you still have the remainder of the 30 days to exercise the rights described above."—could be reasonably read as having only one meaning: that the rights stated in the validation notice, and only those rights, would not be waived by the act of payment. The sentence made no reference to rights beyond those enumerated in § 1692g. Accordingly, the court found that the disputed sentence did not overshadow or contradict the validation notice.

Weiss v. Zwicker & Assocs., P.C., 664 F. Supp. 2d 214 (E.D.N.Y. 2009). Summary judgment granted to the plaintiff on his § 1692g(a) (1) claim where the initial dun stated that the disclosed amount of the debt "may include additional charges including delinquency charges, as applied at the direction of American Express, if said charges are permissible in accordance with the terms of the parties' agreement," since it was unclear and confusing whether the additional charges were already included in the total balance. A debt collector who, after having sent a § 1692g(a) compliant initial disclosure, sent a subsequent dun demanding an increased balance had no duty to provide new § 1692g(a) disclosures regarding the increased balance.

Kamen v. Steven J. Baum, P.C., 659 F. Supp. 2d 402 (E.D.N.Y. 2009). Plaintiff received the § 1692g notice within five days after receiving the summons and complaint, even if the summons and complaint were the initial communication.

Weber v. Computer Credit, Inc., 259 F.R.D. 33 (E.D.N.Y. 2009). The FDCPA is not violated simply because the validation notice is placed on the back side of the collection letter.

Schwartz v. Resurgent Capital Servs., L.P., 2009 WL 3756600 (E.D.N.Y. Nov. 9, 2009). The plaintiff was not a "consumer" with standing to sue for the alleged § 1692g(a) disclosure violation where the collector sent the dun to an unknown individual "in care of" the plaintiff at the plaintiff's address.

Sebrow v. NCO Fin. Sys., Inc., 2009 WL 2707341 (E.D.N.Y. Aug. 27, 2009). The collector's validation disclosure informing the consumer that "[u]nless you notify this office within 30 days after receiving this notice that you dispute the debt or any portion thereof" did not unlawfully limit disputes to those that are received by the collector within thirty days of the consumer's receipt of the notice and fully complied with § 1692g(a).

Stark v. RJM Acquisitions L.L.C., 2009 WL 605811 (E.D.N.Y. Mar. 9, 2009). Based on the following § 1692g notice: "Unless you dispute the validity of all or part of this debt within 30 days after receipt of this notice, we will assume the debt is valid. If you notify us in writing within the 30-day period, we will mail a copy of verification of the debt or the judgment to you and will provide you with the name and address of the original creditor for this debt." The court granted in part and denied in part defendant's motion for summary judgment, holding that 1) the disclosure complied with § 1692g(a)(4), even though the second sentence makes no reference to disputing the debt as required by that subsection, since the least sophisticated consumer would understand she needed to dispute the debt as stated in the first sentence and would not believe that the right to receive verification could be triggered merely upon written request; however, 2) because of the same natural reference to the first sentence, "a reasonable juror could find that the language of the notice at issue here could lead the least sophisticated consumer to believe she must dispute the debt in order to obtain the name and address of the original creditor" when § 1692g(a)(5) requires a collector to so identify the original creditor merely upon written request.

Sorey v. Computer Credit, Inc., 2006 WL 1896401 (S.D.N.Y. July 7, 2006). The court granted judgment to the defendant collector following a bench trial when it found as a matter of fact and law that the § 1692g disclosure on the reverse side of the dun was in a print, color, and format sufficiently prominent and readable to comply with the applicable *Swanson* standard.

Scott v. Enhanced Recovery Corp., 2006 WL 1517755 (E.D.N.Y. May 31, 2006). Allegations that the collector's use of light grey ink to print the validation notice on the reverse side of the initial dun was illegible and/or was so light that it signaled to consumers that they should not bother reading it stated a claim for relief since the contention "is not a legal issue but a factual matter to be determined by the fact finder."

Hernandez v. Affiliated Group, Inc., 2006 WL 83474 (E.D.N.Y. Jan. 12, 2006). Summary judgment for defendant in class action alleging that defendant had not provided the name of the creditor under § 1692g, where the creditor's name was on the reverse, and the front of the letter referred the reader to the reverse.

Sparkman v. Zwicker & Assocs., P.C., 374 F. Supp. 2d 293 (E.D.N.Y. 2005). Summary judgment was granted for the consumer for violation of § 1692g(a)(2) where the collector failed to clearly identity the current creditor.

Acheampongtieku v. Allied Interstate, Inc., 2005 WL 2036153 (S.D.N.Y. Aug. 24, 2005). Summary judgment was granted for the debt collector where its letter mirrored the safe harbor letter set forth in *Bartlett v. Heibl*, 128 F.3d 497 (7th Cir. 1997), did not threaten to report information to a credit bureau without providing plaintiff with a meaningful opportunity to dispute the debt, and set forth a bona fide error defense.

Franzos v. Pinnacle Credit Servs. L.L.C., 332 F. Supp. 2d 682 (S.D.N.Y. 2004). Language at bottom of letter listing documents to submit as proof that debt was not owed did not overshadow the validation notice and would not have confused the least sophisticated consumer as to dispute rights.

Brenker v. Creditors Interchange, Inc., 2004 WL 594502 (S.D.N.Y. Mar. 25, 2004). The collector's second dun that stated the name of the original creditor and that was sent five days after the first dun which omitted that identification violated no provision of the FDCPA, since § 1692g does not require disclosure of the identity of the original creditor and only requires that debtors be advised of their right to request that identity.

Vera v. Trans-Continental Credit & Collection Corp., 1999 U.S. Dist. LEXIS 6937 (S.D.N.Y. May 10, 1999). A collector's § 1692g notice, which stated that the consumer had thirty days to dispute the debt but which omitted the statutory language indicating that the thirty days ran from the date of receipt, was inadequate and therefore violated § 1692g and § 1692e, since it could confuse a consumer to believe that the thirty days ran from the date of the notice.

Prevete v. Margolin & Meltzger, 1998 WL 426700 (E.D.N.Y. May 19, 1998). Failure to include the information required by § 1692g(a)(4) violated the FDCPA.

Goldberg v. Winston & Morrone, 1997 WL 139526 (S.D.N.Y. Mar. 26, 1997). Whether statement that dispute must be "in writing" violated § 1692g(a)(3) was a question for the jury.

Cavallaro v. Law Office of Shapiro & Kriesman, 933 F. Supp. 1148 (E.D.N.Y. 1996). It was a factual question as to whether defendants disclosed they were attempting to collect a debt in the collection letter and had sent validation notice to plaintiff.

Beeman v. Lacy, Katzen, Ryen & Mittleman, 892 F. Supp. 405 (N.D.N.Y. 1995). Where no judgment exists, debt collector was not required to include statement in the validation notice that it would obtain and send a copy of a judgment to the consumer in order to comply with § 1692g.

Grammatico v. Sterling, Inc., Clearinghouse No. 47,976 (N.D.N.Y. 1991). Failure to provide validation notice required by § 1692g violated FDCPA.

Wegmans Food Mkts., Inc. v. Scrimpsher, 17 B.R. 999 (Bankr. N.D.N.Y. 1982). The failure to include the collector's address in the dunning letters (the address appeared on the envelope) was unfair since it nullified the consumer's rights under § 1692g(b). The collector also failed to provide complete notice of validation rights.

North Carolina

Beasley v. Sessoms & Rogers, P.A., 2010 WL 1980083 (E.D.N.C. Mar. 1, 2010). Defendants did not unlawfully limit the consumer's right to dispute the debt at any time in violation of § 1692e since their statement that "you must advise us within thirty days" of a dispute was limited to the § 1692g validation disclosure and "[d]efendants did not state (expressly or implicitly) that consumer would not, thereafter, be able to dispute her debt." Omission of the requirement that the consumer request verification in writing violated § 1692g(a). The court concluded that the least sophisticated debtor would plausibly interpret the defendants' request for information regarding the nature of the dispute to require some reason for the debtor to dispute the debt. Since a consumer need not state any reason to dispute a debt under § 1692g, defendants' directive that the consumer state "the nature of your dispute" stated a claim for unlawfully overshadowing or contradicting § 1692g(a). Defendants' validation notice that stated that the consumer could dispute the debt "in whole or in part" complied with § 1692g(a)(4) since that language conveyed to the least sophisticated debtor the required disclosure The court rejected defendants' argument that the validation notice "clearly implies receiving written notification" and found that the notice violated § 1692g(a)(4) by omitting the "in writing" requirement that she could dispute any portion of the debt.

North Dakota

Bingham v. Collection Bureau, Inc., 505 F. Supp. 864 (D.N.D. 1981). The collector failed to give timely notice of validation rights.

Ost v. Collection Bureau, Inc., 493 F. Supp. 701 (D.N.D. 1980). Where two collectors acted as a unit, one sending a series of letters demanding payment to the creditor and the second collector sending a series of letters demanding payment to it, the failure of the first collector to include a notice of validation rights was attributed to the second collector.

Ohio

Hill v. Javitch, Block & Rathbone, L.L.P., 574 F. Supp. 2d 819 (S.D. Ohio 2008). Since a summons/complaint need not contain statutory notices, court dismissed plaintiff's complaint based on failure to give notices therein.

Zamos v. Asset Acceptance, L.L.C., 423 F. Supp. 2d 777 (N.D. Ohio 2006). Section 1692g(a) requires only that a collector timely send the validation disclosures, not that the consumer ever receive them.

Johnson v. Midland Credit Mgmt. Inc., 2006 WL 2473004 (N.D. Ohio Aug. 24, 2006). Since the post office had returned as undeliverable the initial dun containing the validation notice which the debt collector had attempted to send to the consumer, the collector violated § 1692g(a) when it failed to send an effective validation notice once it thereafter communicated with the consumer at the proper address; a debt collector who knows that its initial valida-

tion notice was not received by the consumer cannot claim to have "sent" the notice to the consumer as required by § 1692g(a).

Edwards v. McCormick, 136 F. Supp. 2d 795 (S.D. Ohio 2001). The debt collector violated § 1692g(a) by failing to send the consumer the validation notice as mandated by the FDCPA.

Sprouse v. City Credits Co., 126 F. Supp. 2d 1083 (S.D. Ohio 2000). A lawsuit to collect a debt is a "communication" as defined by the FDCPA and, since the suit involved here was the initial communication from the attorney collector, the validation notice attached to the complaint met the requirements of 1692g.

Boyce v. Attorney's Dispatch Serv., 1999 U.S. Dist. LEXIS 1124 (S.D. Ohio Feb. 2, 1999). Collection agent violated the §§ 1692g and 1692e(11) notice requirements where the collection letter did not contain the requisite notices.

Lamb v. M & M Assoc., 1998 WL 34288694 (S.D. Ohio Sept. 1, 1998). Collection letter which failed to include the § 1692g(a)(4) language violated § 1692g(a).

Sampson v. Banchek, 1991 U.S. Dist. LEXIS 21815 (N.D. Ohio Jan. 8, 1991). An attorney violated the debt validation notice requirement when he failed to send the notice after a phone call regarding a debt.

United States v. First Fed. Credit Control, Inc., Clearinghouse No. 33,811 (N.D. Ohio 1982). The collector violated the FDCPA by failing to provide a validation notice.

Oregon

Saccato v. Gordon, 2010 WL 3395295 (D. Or. Aug. 26, 2010). Even if the court were to allow the *pro se* consumer to amend his complaint to allege that the defendant violated the FDCPA it would be futile, since the request for validation occurred five and one half months after receipt of the § 1692g notice, which was well beyond the statutory thirty-day period.

Van Westrienen v. Americontinental Collection Corp., 94 F. Supp. 2d 1087 (D. Or. 2000). The consumer need not receive the validation notice; the requirement was that it must be *sent* by the debt collector. Testimony that it was not received did not rebut evidence that it was sent.

Griswold v. J&R Anderson Bus. Servs., Inc., 1983 U.S. Dist. LEXIS 20365 (D. Or. Oct. 21, 1983). When a second collection agency began collecting a debt for which the first collection agency had provided a validation notice, the second collection agency was also required to provide a validation notice since there is no exemption in § 1692g for subsequent collection agencies.

Check Cent., Inc. v. Barr, Clearinghouse No. 37,497 (Bankr. D. Or. 1984). Use of the word "judgment" in validation notice, when there is none, does not violate FDCPA.

Pennsylvania

Harlan v. NRA Group, L.L.C., 2011 WL 500024 (E.D. Pa. Feb. 9, 2011). Disclosure—"Unless you dispute this debt or any part thereof within 30 days after receiving this notice, the debt will be presumed to be valid"—violated §§ 1692g(a)(3) and 1692e(10), since the replacement of the statutorily mandated word "assumed" with "presumed" and the failure to state that it was the debt collector who makes the assumption could mislead the least sophisticated debtor to "reasonably believe that failure to dispute the debt would create an evidentiary presumption of validity by a court or other entity of authority in a subsequent collection proceeding."

Dutterer v. Thomas Kalperis Int'l, Inc., 2011 WL 382575 (E.D. Pa. Feb. 4, 2011). A validation notice that could be "reasonably read to have two or more different meanings, one of which is inaccurate," is considered deceptive.

Jarzyna v. Home Prop., L.P., 2011 WL 382367 (E.D. Pa. Feb. 4, 2011). The plaintiff stated a claim under § 1692g(a) where the required disclosure that appeared in small print on the bottom of the letter was overshadowed by the prominent bold printed statement, "Pay in full online anytime." The court found that the least sophisticated debtor, upon receipt of the letter, "would not know he or she had a right to dispute the debt and was not required to pay it in full as soon as possible."

Pierce v. Carrington Recovery Servs., L.L.C., 2009 WL 2525465 (W.D. Pa. Aug. 17, 2009). Motion to dismiss denied where complaint alleged that "by the debt collector" was omitted from the § 1692g(a)(3) language.

Harris v. NCO Fin. Sys., 2009 WL 497409 (E.D. Pa. Feb. 26, 2009). Because genuine issues of fact existed as to (1) whether a validation notice was given as required by § 1692g and (2) whether plaintiff disputed the debt as set forth in that section—obligating the debt collector to submit evidence of the origin and validity of the debt—summary judgment was denied.

Oppong v. First Union Mortgage Corp., 566 F. Supp. 2d 395 (E.D. Pa. 2008), *aff'd*, 326 Fed. Appx. 663 (3d Cir. 2009). The 2006 § 1692g(d) amendment that a "communication in the form of a formal pleading in a civil action shall not be treated as an initial communication for purposes of subsection (a) of this section" did not apply retroactively. Under the pre-§ 1692g(d) amendment, the filing of the state court foreclosure complaint was the "initial communication" triggering the § 1692g(a) disclosures. A state court complaint that in a separate paragraph recited the thirty-day verification disclosures complied with § 1692g(a) because the potentially conflicting recitation of the twenty-days in which to file a responsive pleading was adequately explained so as not to confuse the least sophisticated consumer. A mortgage servicer that "did not undertake any debt collection action" was not a debt collector; and even assuming that it was a debt collector, the servicer did not violate the FDCPA by failing to send a § 1692g(a) validation notice because subsequent collectors need not send a second validation notice once the first debt collector has done so.

Galuska v. Collectors Training Inst., Inc., 2008 WL 2050809 (M.D. Pa. May 13, 2008). Dismissal denied where the dun said "this debt will be assumed to be valid" but did not include "by the debt collector," as the omission could be confusing or misleading.

Smith v. Hecker, 2005 U.S. Dist. LEXIS 6598 (E.D. Pa. Apr. 18, 2005). The court held that the collector's verification notice violated § 1692g(a)(3) because it used the phrase "will be assessed valid" instead of the statutory phrase "will be assumed to be valid" and omitted the statutory phrase "by the debt collector" since this embellished disclosure "would confuse or deceive the least sophisticated debtor into believing that the debt will be determined to be valid by some entity of authority, rather than

informing the least sophisticated debtor that the debt will be assumed to be valid for collection purposes unless disputed."

Bezpalko v. Gilfillan, Gilpin & Brehman, 1998 WL 321268 (E.D. Pa. June 17, 1998). Omission from validation notice of right to dispute "any portion" of the debt did not violate FDCPA "[c]onsidering the letter in its entirety, and given the circumstances surrounding the letter as well as the prior dealings between the parties."

Rhode Island

In re Mason, 167 B.R. 327 (Bankr. D.R.I. 1994). Consumer failed to establish that the debt collector did not include required § 1692g notice in initial telephone communication in connection with the collection of the debt as alleged.

South Carolina

Moore v. Ingram & Assocs., Inc., 805 F. Supp. 7 (D.S.C. 1992). Use of the word "judgment" in the validation notice pursuant to § 1692g was not misleading even though a judgment had not been obtained.

Duncan v. Nichols, 451 S.E.2d 24 (S.C. Ct. App. 1994). Attorney's letter to consumer which repeats the language of § 1692g(a)(4), even though a judgment does not exist, is not misleading in violation of § 1692e.

Tennessee

Spangler v. Conrad, 2010 WL 2389481 (E.D. Tenn. June 9, 2010). Identifying the current creditor together with a reference to the name of the original creditor with whom the consumer dealt would not confuse the least sophisticated consumer and thus did not violate § 1692g(a)(2).

Texas

Flores v. Millennium Interests, Ltd., 273 F. Supp. 2d 899 (S.D. Tex. 2003). Information required to be disclosed by § 1692g(a) needed only be in the initial communication and not in subsequent letters.

Youngblood v. G.C. Servs. Ltd. P'ship, 186 F. Supp. 2d 695 (W.D. Tex. 2002). § 1692e(11) and § 1692g notices in gray type on gray background were sufficiently legible. § 1692e(11) and § 1692g notices on reverse were proper where face of dun prominently referenced the notice on reverse.

Utah

Ditty v. CheckRite, Ltd., 973 F. Supp. 1320 (D. Utah 1997). Section 1692g does not require another debt collector, undertaking collection efforts after a validation notice has been timely sent, to provide additional notice and another thirty-day validation period.

Virginia

Sunga v. Rees Broome, P.C., 2010 WL 1138319 (E.D. Va. Mar. 18, 2010). Even though the demand letter used the words "intent to dispute" instead of the word "dispute," the court found, after applying the least sophisticated consumer standard, that the letter clearly and effectively conveyed to the consumer her duty to dispute the debt within thirty days after receipt of the notice if she wanted it verified.

McCormick v. Wells Fargo Bank, 640 F. Supp. 2d 795 (S.D. W. Va. 2009). There was no violation of § 1692g(a) where the debt collector did not include the § 1692g(b) rights in its dunning letter.

Cappetta v. GC Servs., Ltd. P'ship, 654 F. Supp. 2d 453 (E.D. Va. 2009). Plaintiff's allegation that the defendant "failed to give initial notice, as required by § 1692g, that she had a right to validate the debt" stated a claim for relief.

Turner v. Shenandoah Legal Group, P.C., 2006 WL 1685698 (E.D. Va. June 12, 2006). The magistrate judge recommended that the definition of "initial communication" be interpreted to require subsequent debt collectors (attorneys) to provide the validation notice although it may have been provided by an earlier debt collector.

Dikun v. Streich, 369 F. Supp. 2d 781 (E.D. Va. 2005). Debt collector's identification of its creditor in its initial dun by a name that differed slightly from the creditor's actual name was not inaccurate as tested by the least sophisticated consumer standard. Collector's validation notice tracked the language of § 1692g(a) and therefore was in full compliance with that section. The § 1692g validation notice needed only be disclosed in the initial communication with the consumer, and until the consumer disputed the debt, the debt collector was under no obligation to verify it.

Washington

McLain v. Gordon, 2010 WL 3340528 (W.D. Wash. Aug. 24, 2010). Section 1692g(a) does not require that a validation of debt notice must be received by a debtor, but only that it was sent to a debtor.

Wisconsin

Anderson v. CBCS Collection Agency, 2010 WL 4024926 (E.D. Wis. Oct. 13, 2010). The court granted summary judgment to a defendant who produced evidence that it provided the *pro se* plaintiff with the requisite validation notice in an earlier correspondence.

Robbins v. Wolpoff & Abramson L.L.P., 422 F. Supp. 2d 1011 (E.D. Wis. 2006). The court granted the collector's motion to dismiss and rejected the consumer's claim that the validation notice was unlawfully confusing where the collector's disclosure tracked the actual convoluted § 1692g(a) statutory language with only minor variations including extraneous information.

Schneider v. TSYS Total Debt Mgmt., Inc., 2006 WL 1982499 (E.D. Wis. July 13, 2006). The collector must make all of the § 1692g(a) disclosures in a non-confusing manner, and accordingly the allegation that the collector disclosed the name of the current creditor, as required by § 1692g(a)(2), in a confusing shorthand fashion, using only its first name, "Target," that the unsophisticated consumer would not recognize because it identifies several unrelated business entities with the same first name, e.g., Target National Bank, Target Stores, stated a claim for relief.

Berres v. Attention, L.L.C., 2006 U.S. Dist. LEXIS 67059 (E.D. Wis. Feb. 14, 2006). Following Seventh Circuit precedent, the court denied the defendant's motion for judgment on the pleadings that claimed that the plaintiff's allegation that the subject dun violated § 1692g(a) was facially insubstantial because the "plain-

tiff has indicated that he will introduce extrinsic evidence that defendant's letter is confusing."

Hartman v. Meridian Fin. Servs., Inc., 191 F. Supp. 2d 1031 (W.D. Wis. 2002). The third party debt collector's initial communications with consumers in the name of the creditor failed to contain the validation notice, thus violating § 1692g.

K.2.6.6 Amount of Debt [*See also* K.2.4.10, Disclosing the Amount of the Debt]

Olson v. Risk Mgmt. Alternatives, Inc., 366 F.3d 509 (7th Cir. 2004). An unsophisticated consumer would understand the amount of the debt is the "Balance" and that the amount "Now Due" is a portion of the balance that the creditor will accept for the time being until the next bill arrives.

Taylor v. Calvary Inv., L.L.C., 365 F.3d 572 (7th Cir. 2004). The validation notice was not contradicted, nor was the unsophisticated consumer likely to be confused, by language that interest would continue to accrue contained in collection letters stating the principal balance, the interest owed, and the total balance due.

Chuway v. National Action Fin. Servs., Inc., 362 F.3d 944 (7th Cir. 2004). Demand letter unclear due to references to both a "balance due" and a procedure for obtaining a "current balance."

Shula v. Lawent, 359 F.3d 489 (7th Cir. 2004). Where no judgment for costs had been entered against the consumer, the collecting attorney's letter demanding payment of such costs violated of §§ 1692e and 1692f(1), and failure to send a follow-up letter violated § 1692g(a).

California

Welker v. Law Office of Daniel J. Horwitz, 699 F. Supp. 2d 1164 (S.D. Cal. 2010). Where the dunning letter demanded payment for the outstanding balance plus "interest at the legal rate, and reimbursement of court costs," the defendant violated § 1692g(a)(1) since the unpaid principal balance is only part of the debt.

Hutton v. Law Offices of Collins & Lamore, 668 F. Supp. 2d 1251 (S.D. Cal. 2009). The § 1692g(a)(1) claim was dismissed for failure to state a claim where the initial dun stated that "the outstanding balance due in the amount of $22,519.17 . . . may not include accruing interest (and does not account for changing exchange rates after the date of this letter, for accounts originated in a foreign country)," since the dun properly disclosed the entire amount then owed and the additional language would not confuse or mislead the least sophisticated consumer as to the amount owing.

Welker v. Law Office of Horwitz, 626 F. Supp. 2d 1068 (S.D. Cal. 2009). Letter did not adequately disclose the amount of the debt within § 1692g where it disclosed the outstanding balance but asked for additional unspecified interest and costs.

Delaware

U.S. Bank Nat'l v. Swanson, 918 A.2d 339 (Del. Super. Ct. 2006). Where the consumer relied on the payoff amount of the debt in the debt validation notice, the bank was estopped from recovering any additional payoff costs on the mortgage.

Florida

Hepsen v. J.C. Christensen & Assocs., Inc., 2009 WL 3064865 (M.D. Fla. Sept. 22, 2009). A dunning letter must state the exact and correct amount of the debt in order to comply with § 1692g(a)(1). Defendant overstated the amount of the debt, when compared with a later letter from the debt collector.

Hawaii

Sambor v. Omnia Credit Servs., 183 F. Supp. 2d 1234 (D. Haw. 2002). The recitation on different dates of differing amounts owing in a telephone dun and a letter did not violate § 1692e or § 1692g as the discrepancy correctly resulted from the accrual of interest and fees.

Illinois

Ingram v. Corporate Receivables, Inc., 2003 WL 21018650 (N.D. Ill. May 5, 2003). Initial demand letter that disclosed an exact amount allegedly owing did not comply with § 1692g(a)(1) where the amount included interest that changes periodically and the letter did not expressly state as of what date that amount was due or what impact payment of the stated amount would have on the consumer's obligation to pay later-accruing interest.

Chuway v. Nat'l Action Fin. Servs., Inc., 2003 WL 943949 (N.D. Ill. Mar. 7, 2003). Summary judgment granted defendant in FDCPA class action; reference in text to "most current balance" did not on its face contradict the dollar amount stated. Plaintiff did not submit evidence that letter would be confusing to least sophisticated consumer.

Taylor v. Fink, 1994 WL 669605 (N.D. Ill. Nov. 25, 1994). Failure to disclose the amount of the debt violated § 1692g(a)(1).

Indiana

Campbell v. Hall, 624 F. Supp. 2d 991 (N.D. Ind. 2009). The defendant did not violate § 1692g(a)(1) by failing to disclose the "amount of the debt" as a "sum certain" since "[i]t would not be unreasonable to expect an unsophisticated consumer or debtor to be able to add three figures together and come up with the $550.00 figure" that was the total of the listed components.

Dechert v. Cadle Co., 2003 WL 23008969 (S.D. Ind. Sept. 11, 2003). Initial demand letter violated § 1692g(a) by failing to disclose the full amount of the debt and instead disclosing the unpaid principal balance and directing the debtor to call the collector to learn the total amount owed, including the additional accrued interest, late charges, and other fees.

Bernstein v. Howe, 2003 WL 1702254 (S.D. Ind. Mar. 31, 2003). A collection letter demanding payment of a specific amount "plus interest and attorneys fees" violated § 1692g(a)(1) by failing to state the amount due when the letter was sent.

Michigan

Richard v. Oak Tree Group, Inc., 614 F. Supp. 2d 814 (W.D. Mich. 2008). The inclusion of unaccrued collection agency fees hidden within the stated amount of the debt did not violate § 1692g(a)(1) but did violate §§ 1692e(2)(A), (B), and 1692f(1).

New York

Golubeva v. GC Serv. Ltd. P'ship, 2010 WL 4340465 (E.D.N.Y. Oct. 22, 2010). The court denied a motion to dismiss regarding the following disclaimer included in three successive letters: "As of the date of this letter, you owe [$X.XX]. Because of interest, late charges, and other charges that may vary from day to day, the amount due on the day you pay may be greater. Hence, if you pay the amount shown above, an adjustment may be necessary after we receive your check, in which event we will inform you" While the court acknowledged the defendant's argument that the disclaimer in the letters, standing alone, was not deceptive, the court nevertheless concluded that the plaintiff alleged sufficient facts to state a claim that the second letter violated § 1692g(a)(1) as it may have omitted added charges. In addition, the fact that the third letter set forth a higher balance could confuse a consumer as to the amount actually owed and the method for how or when additional interest and fees would be calculated.

Weiss v. Zwicker & Assocs., P.C., 664 F. Supp. 2d 214 (E.D.N.Y. 2009). Summary judgment was granted to the consumer on his § 1692g(a)(1) claim where the initial dun stated that the disclosed amount of the debt "may include additional charges including delinquency charges, as applied at the direction of American Express, if said charges are permissible in accordance with the terms of the parties' agreement," since it was unclear and confusing whether the additional charges were already included in the total balance. A debt collector has no obligation to explain why a consumer's debt has increased five percent from the time that the initial dun was sent: "The Court finds that there is nothing confusing or misleading about the increased amount of debt stated [in the second dun] as even the most unsophisticated consumer would understand that credit card debt accrues interest."

Larsen v. JBC Legal Group, P.C., 533 F. Supp. 2d 290 (E.D.N.Y. 2008). The debt validation notice failed to state the amount of the debt where it did not state face amount of the check and requested a fee of $20 in one place and $25 in another.

North Carolina

Woody v. Bank of Am. Corp., 2010 WL 2332732 (E.D.N.C. June 9, 2010). The *pro se* complaint alleging that defendants violated the FDCPA because the "payoff balance" of the loan was "inaccurate" and "based on predatory lending practices" was dismissed in the absence of any factual support for any such violation.

Beasley v. Sessoms & Rogers, P.A., 2010 WL 1980083 (E.D.N.C. Mar. 1, 2010). A § 1692g(a)(1) disclosure was compliant notwithstanding the additional statement that "interest may still be continuing to accrue" since defendants were not required to estimate the total amount of debt as of when consumer actually received or read the letter, and language would not confuse the least sophisticated debtor as to the amount of the debt.

Oregon

Clark v. Schwabe, Williamson & Wyatt, Clearinghouse No. 44,831 (D. Or. 1990). Validation notice sufficiently stated the amount of the debt by referring to another document that was enclosed. It did not have to compute the interest and charges to date.

K.2.6.7 Ceasing Collection of Unverified Debt

Hepsen v. Resurgent Capital Servs., L.P., 2010 WL 2490734 (11th Cir. June 17, 2010). Because § 1692g(b) does not modify § 1692e, which prohibits a debt collector from attempting to collect an inaccurate debt, the collector could still be liable for sending an inaccurate demand letter to the consumer even if the FDCPA does not explicitly require that a collector verify the debt before sending a demand.

Jacobson v. Healthcare Fin. Serv., Inc., 516 F.3d 85 (2d Cir. 2008). If the consumer disputes the debt or any portion in writing per § 1692g, the debt collector must "cease collection" and "may resume collection activities only when it has obtained verification of the debt, and has mailed a copy of the verification to the consumer."

Shimek v. Weissman, Nowack, Curry & Wilco, P.C., 374 F.3d 1011 (11th Cir. 2004). The FDCPA does not preclude a debt collector from contemporaneously filing a lien with the state clerk of the court at the same time it sends a letter of demand to the consumer, so long as the initial filing of the lien was permitted by state law, even though the consumer did not first have the opportunity to dispute or verify the debt. The FDCPA does not create an affirmative duty on the debt collector to prevent the clerk of the court from filing the lien after verification has been requested.

Kazen v. Premier Mortgage Servs., Inc., 2003 WL 22359610 (9th Cir. Oct. 16, 2003). The absence of any further collection efforts precluded the claimed violation of § 1692g(b).

Peter v. G.C. Servs. L.P., 310 F.3d 344 (5th Cir. 2002). The FDCPA does not require the debt collector to inform the consumer of the obligation to stop collection until the requested verification has been provided.

Jang v. A.M. Miller & Assocs., 122 F.3d 480 (7th Cir. 1997). Where a debt collector could not verify the debt and ceased collection efforts, the debt collector's initial collection letter promising a debt verification if requested was not deemed misleading. The FDCPA only requires that the debt collector verify the debt or cease collection activity.

Smith v. Transworld Sys., Inc., 953 F.2d 1025 (6th Cir. 1992). Where debt collector ceased collection activities, it did not violate § 1692g(b) by failing to provide verification of the debt upon the consumer's written request.

Alabama

In re Young, 280 B.R. 864 (Bankr. S.D. Ala. 2001). Consumer awarded $1000 where the student loan collector violated the FDCPA by imposing an administrative garnishment without responding to a § 1692g dispute letter.

California

McClenning v. NCO Fin. Sys., Inc., 2010 WL 4795269 (C.D. Cal. Nov. 15, 2010). A question of fact was raised as to whether or not the defendant failed to cease collection of the debt in violation of § 1692g(b) when it made a soft-pull credit inquiry.

Casas v. Midland Credit Mgmt., Inc., 2009 WL 249992 (S.D. Cal. Jan. 30, 2009). The debt collector violated § 1692g by continuing to demand payment before it verified the debt.

Wood v. Midland Credit Mgmt., Inc., 2005 WL 3159639 (C.D. Cal. July 29, 2005), *aff'd on reconsideration*, 2005 WL 3159637 (C.D. Cal. Sept. 21, 2005). The plaintiff adequately pleaded that the debt collector failed to comply with its § 1692g obligation to cease collection activity when requested in writing within thirty days of receipt of the first dun to verify the debt. A debt collector's continued collection of the debt when the consumer disputed it after the thirty-day validation request period did not violate § 1692g, nor was the same conduct an unfair practice in violation of § 1692f.

Palmer v. Stassinos, 348 F. Supp. 2d 1070 (N.D. Cal. 2004). A debt collector is not required to suspend debt collection activities, including pursuing litigation options, during the period for requesting validation.

Connecticut

Young v. Dey, 1994 U.S. Dist. LEXIS 21484 (D. Conn. July 5, 1994). Summary judgment motions of both parties were denied in part because there existed genuine issues of fact as to whether the debt collector continued efforts to collect a debt after the debt collector received a request for validation from the consumer.

Woolfolk v. Van Ru Credit Corp., 783 F. Supp. 724 (D. Conn. 1990). The consumer's evidence was insufficient to show prohibited collection contacts after the request for validation and before validation was made.

Florida

Lee v. Security Check, L.L.C., 2010 WL 3075673 (M.D. Fla. Aug. 5, 2010). In dicta the court noted that liability under the FDCPA attaches when a debt collector continues to communicate or attempts to collect a disputed debt from the consumer until the debt is verified and the consumer notified. The statute does not impose liability for furnishing erroneous information to a credit reporting agency or for failing to correct erroneous information provided to a credit reporting agency. The check collector furnished correct information which attached someone else's dishonored check to the plaintiff's consumer's credit file through an existing erroneous prior address and the last names. The FDCPA did not apply because the check collector did not seek payment from the plaintiff consumer.

Hepsen v. J.C. Christensen & Assocs., Inc., 2009 WL 3064865 (M.D. Fla. Sept. 22, 2009). Where a debt collector could not verify the debt and ceased collection efforts, it was not required to provide the consumer with the name of the original creditor requested by the consumer.

Martinez v. Credit Bureau, 2005 WL 1972538 (S.D. Fla. Aug. 12, 2005). The allegation that the debt collector sent to the consumer a second demand letter after it had received the consumer's written § 1692g dispute and before it had provided any verification stated a claim for violation of § 1692g(b).

Georgia

Milton v. LTD Fin. Servs., 2011 WL 291363 (S.D. Ga. Jan. 25, 2011). When a collection agency ceased all collection activities in response to a request for validation of an alleged debt, it was in compliance with the FDCPA. The defendant was not obligated to send a separate validation of the debt to plaintiff.

Gilmore v. Account, Mgmt., Inc., 2009 WL 2848278 (N.D. Ga. Apr. 27, 2009). Continuation of collection efforts after plaintiff disputed the validity of the debt and sought verification violated § 1692g(b).

Hawaii

Sambor v. Omnia Credit Servs., 183 F. Supp. 2d 1234 (D. Haw. 2002). Debt collector's cessation of further collection activity after receiving the § 1692g dispute, without first verifying the debt, fully complied with § 1692g.

Illinois

Gulley v. Pierce & Assocs., 2010 WL 5060257 (N.D. Ill. Dec. 6, 2010). The *pro se* consumer's § 1692g(b) claim that the defendant continued to collect the debt without responding to his verification request was not time barred, since although the verification request was made more than one year before suit was filed, the defendant's alleged violation of § 1692g(b) by continuing to collect the debt occurred within the one year period.

Moore v. Blatt, Hasenmiller, Leibsker & Moore, L.L.C., 2006 WL 1806195 (C.D. Ill. June 29, 2006). Consumer's answer filed in court disputing the debt was not a § 1692g notice that required the debt collector to cease collection.

Jeffries v. Dutton & Dutton, P.C., 2006 WL 1343629 (N.D. Ill. May 11, 2006). Section 1692g(b) gives debt collectors two options when they receive requests for validation, the debt collectors may provide the requested validation and continue their collection activities or they may cease all collection activities.

Luxenburg v. Equifax Credit Info. Servs., 2005 WL 78947 (N.D. Ill. Jan. 12, 2005). A claim was stated by the allegation that the collection agency failed to cease collecting a debt after receiving a request to validate a debt that was not owed when agency requested payment in a telephone call initiated by the consumer requesting that its delinquent debt be deleted from his credit report.

Allen v. ATG Credit L.L.C., 2004 WL 2931298 (N.D. Ill. Dec. 14, 2004). The collector asserted it called the consumer five times to confirm that the validation information was received, not to collect the debt. Whether defendant's motivation excused its continuing to try to contact plaintiff after a validation request was question for jury.

Levin v. Kluever & Platt, L.L.C., 2003 WL 22757763 (N.D. Ill. Nov. 19, 2003). If the consumer seeks verification of a debt pursuant to § 1692g, the debt collector must cease all collection efforts, including pursuing any legal action as well as seeking a default judgment in a pending court proceeding.

Trull v. G.C. Servs. Ltd. P'ship, 961 F. Supp. 1199 (N.D. Ill. 1997). Debt collector must only cease collection activity if debtor disputes the debt or requests creditor's name and address during the validation period, and then only until it sends a verification to the debtor.

Taylor v. Fink, 1994 WL 669605 (N.D. Ill. Nov. 25, 1994). A request for validation would postpone the filing of a legal action until validation was given.

Hoffman v. Partners In Collections, Inc., 1993 WL 358158 (N.D. Ill. Sept. 14, 1993). In order to plead a violation of § 1692g(b) the consumer must plead that the collector was notified in writing that the debt or a portion of it was disputed, and that the collector failed to cease communication until verification was provided; consumer's statement of an invalid reason for disputing liability did not undermine this FDCPA claim.

Indiana

Campbell v. Hall, 624 F. Supp. 2d 991 (N.D. Ind. 2009). The defendant complied with § 1692g(b) by ceasing all collection efforts and further communication "once Defendant was notified by [the consumer] that the debt was disputed because it had been discharged in bankruptcy."

Zaborac v. Mutual Hosp. Serv., Inc., 2004 WL 2538643 (S.D. Ind. Oct. 7, 2004). Once the consumer's attorney has requested verification of the debt, the collector has two choices: (1) provide verification to the attorney or (2) cease attempts to collect the debt.

Spears v. Brennan, 745 N.E.2d 862 (Ind. Ct. App. 2001). Providing a copy of the original signed contract is not a sufficient verification to a general § 1692g dispute, since it cannot show basic necessary information such as an accounting of payments made and interest and fees charged; therefore, attorney collector's continuing to collect the debt by procuring a default judgment after the dispute and inadequate verification violated § 1692g(b).

Kansas

McDaniel v. South & Assocs., P.C., 325 F. Supp. 2d 1210 (D. Kan. 2004). Collector violated FDCPA by initiating judicial foreclosure action seeking a money judgment as well as foreclosure after receiving a timely validation request but before responding to it. The court distinguished cases holding that non-judicial foreclosure was not debt collection.

Clark's Jewelers v. Humble, 823 P.2d 818 (Kan. Ct. App. 1991). Consumer or his attorney may dispute the debt pursuant to § 1692g without using the word "dispute." Debt collector violated § 1692g(b) where it failed to provide verification of the debt but continued to send dunning letters in care of consumers' attorney.

Louisiana

Ford Motor Credit Co. v. Dunham, 2009 WL 4981913 (La. Ct. App. Dec. 23, 2009) (unpublished). The court stated that the creditor was obligated on the basis of § 1692g to stop collection efforts and investigate the consumer's dispute that her signature was forged on the underlying sales contract, without noting that the FDCPA was inapplicable to a creditor as here and oblivious to the requirement that the § 1692g duty was limited to disputes submitted within the thirty-day verification window.

Maryland

Humphrey v. Brown, 2011 WL 53081 (D. Md. Jan. 7, 2011). The court found that a *pro se* consumer who claimed to have been a victim of a home equity fraud scam failed to state a § 1692g(b) claim where the defendant ceased all collection activity once the consumer disputed the debt and provided notice of the alleged underlying forgery of the deed that transferred ownership in the subject property, even though it did not take any steps to unwind the transfer: "§ 1692g(b) of the FDCPA merely prohibits debt collectors from engaging in certain debt collection activity; it does not impose on debt collectors an affirmative obligation to interfere with or cancel debt collection activity undertaken before the debt was disputed."

Spencer v. Hendersen-Webb, 81 F. Supp. 2d 582 (D. Md. 1999). Debt collector's fax of a bill to the father of the consumer's boyfriend in response to his request for information on the debt was deemed to be an attempt to collect a debt since debt collector believed the father was consumer's attorney and that information would reach consumer indirectly. Court determined that fax was debt collector's initial communication and thus the failure to provide a validation notice in connection with the fax violated the FDCPA. Therefore, debt collector violated § 1692g(b) making the offer and by failing to cease collection until debt was verified.

Michigan

Bond v. U.S. Bank Nat'l Ass'n, 2010 WL 1265852 (E.D. Mich. Mar. 29, 2010) (*pro se* consumer). The FDCPA places no time limit on verification of a disputed debt. A debt collector who receives a demand for verification is under no obligation to respond, but must either do so or abandon the debt collection activity.

Taylor v. Countrywide Home Loans, 2010 WL 750215 (E.D. Mich. Mar. 3, 2010). Plaintiffs neither alleged nor offered any evidence showing that defendant collector took any further collection activity after receiving plaintiffs' request for validation. Plaintiffs offer no legal basis for attributing any communications by defendant to the collector.

Minnesota

Edeh v. Midland Credit Mgmt., Inc., 2010 WL 3893604 (D. Minn. Sept. 29, 2010). Summary judgment for the *pro se* plaintiff was proper, since the defendant was engaged in "collection of the debt" in violation of § 1692g(b) when it reported the disputed debt to the CRAs before sending verification of that debt to the plaintiff.

Burke v. Messerli & Kramer P.A., 2010 WL 3167403 (D. Minn. Aug. 9, 2010). By including the § 1692e(11) disclosure, the collection attorney expressly conveyed that the letter was "an attempt to collect a debt." The argument that the letter was not a communication in connection with the collection of a debt when the language of the letter is directly to the contrary was unconvincing.

Mississippi

Shakir v. Nationwide Tr. Servs., Inc., 2010 WL 1529224 (N.D. Miss. Apr. 15, 2010). The court dismissed the *pro se* consumer's claims since the defendant showed that it had the right to foreclose on the subject property as the current assignee of the debt and that it had complied with § 1692g because it ceased foreclosure proceedings during the pendency of the action and sent the consumer verification of the loan—albeit belatedly.

Nebraska

Moriarty v. Capital Mgmt. Servs., Inc., 2005 WL 2042302 (D. Neb. Aug. 24, 2005). Where the debt collector's letter to the consumer's lawyer stated that it had requested verification (after the consumer disputed the debt and told the collector to cease collection) but also stated it was attempting to collect an "obligation." The court denied the collector's Rule 12(b)(6) motion to dismiss finding that the complaint stated a cause of action.

Beaulieu v. Am. Nat'l Educ. Corp., Clearinghouse No. 30,892 (D. Neb. 1981). Collector failed to cease collection efforts after a request for validation was answered by the creditor but not the collector as required by the Act.

New Jersey

Citibank v. Razvi, 2008 WL 2521082 (N.J. Super. Ct. App. Div. June 26, 2008). Collection attorneys did not violate § 1692g(b) when they failed to validate the debt, where the consumer sent to the collection attorney's creditor client at its address, rather than to the attorneys at their disclosed address, a cryptic "valid verified firm offer" requesting "an affidavit signed by you in your unlimited commercial capacity showing what goods and services were provided establishing a liability equal to the 'alleged' balance [of the account]."

Bey v. Daimler Chrysler Servs., L.L.C., 2006 WL 1344080 (D.N.J. May 15, 2006). *Pro se* plaintiff's claim that the debt collector did not send verification within seven days after the plaintiff disputed the debt was dismissed because a debt collector need not send verification so long as the collector ceases collection activity, and summary judgment was entered for defendants.

Bey v. Daimler Chrysler Servs., L.L.C., 2006 WL 361385 (D.N.J. Feb. 15, 2006). The attorney defendants' filing of a replevin action within the thirty-day dispute period did not violate the FDCPA. The attorney defendants' efforts to serve a filed replevin action after receiving a dispute letter did not violate the FDCPA. The court said, "[R]eading the FDCPA to prohibit parties from acting to preserve a previously-filed lawsuit interferes with state remedies in a manner unanticipated by the FDCPA." A verification which was higher than the amount initially demanded did not violate the FDCPA, since the higher amount was merely interim accrued attorney fees.

Kaschak v. Raritan Valley Collection Agency, 1989 U.S. Dist. LEXIS 19103 (D.N.J. May 22, 1989). Collector did not violate § 1692g(b) by sending the debtor another collection letter the day or the day after it received the debtor's request for validation, since notification is not presumed upon receipt. Collector was liable for failing to provide the requested verification.

New York

Johnson v. Equifax Risk Mgmt. Servs., 2004 WL 540459 (S.D.N.Y. Mar. 17, 2004). The collector's dun sent after the consumer had written a timely verification dispute violated §§ 1692e and 1692g by implying that the dispute was ineffective.

North Carolina

Gough v. Bernhardt & Strawser, P.A., 2006 WL 1875327 (M.D.N.C. June 30, 2006). The collection lawyers did not violate § 1692g(b) when they continued to litigate after the debtor had submitted a timely written verification request once served with the summons and complaint because the collection complaint and its attachments already provided the consumer with adequate verification information.

Jolly v. Academy Collection Serv., Inc., 400 F. Supp. 2d 851 (M.D.N.C. 2005). Debt collector's failure to respond to a request to validate debt within thirty days did not lead to Fair Credit Reporting Act obligations to stop listing the debt on the consumer's credit report.

Ohio

Kelly v. Montgomery Lynch & Assocs., Inc., 2008 WL 1775251 (N.D. Ohio Apr. 15, 2008). Summary judgment granted to the defendant on the § 1692g(b) claim since the written dispute was sent to the defendant outside the thirty-day statutory validation period thus validating the defendant's efforts to continue to collect a previously undisputed debt.

Sprouse v. City Credits Co., 126 F. Supp. 2d 1083 (S.D. Ohio 2000). Only if the consumer disputes the debt is the collector barred from filing suit under § 1692g; since consumer did not so dispute, collector was free to file suit within the thirty-day validation period.

Lamb v. M & M Assoc., 1998 WL 34288694 (S.D. Ohio Sept. 1, 1998). Section 1692g(b) does not require that a debt collector provide validation; however, the debt collector must cease all further collection activity until it does so.

Oklahoma

Mendus v. Morgan & Assoc., 994 P.2d 83 (Okla. Ct. App. 1999). Where the initial communication was the summons and petition, the collector would be required to pause its suit if validation was requested.

Oregon

McNall v. Credit Bureau, 2008 WL 1881796 (D. Or. Apr. 18, 2008). Consumers stated a claim for relief for defendant's violation of § 1692g(b) by alleging that the defendant did not validate the debt after receiving a timely, written dispute but instead continued to pursue collection, including filing suit and reporting a negative collection account to a credit bureau.

Pennsylvania

Cowell v. Creditors Interchange Receivable Mgmt., L.L.C., 2009 WL 465580 (W.D. Pa. Feb. 25, 2009). Where the complaint alleged that the plaintiff's attorney was, in fact, authorized to dispute the debt on plaintiff's behalf and did so, the debt collector who nonetheless continued to call and send dunning letters to the plaintiff was denied dismissal of the claim for violation of § 1692g.

Mumma v. Burton & Neil Assocs., P.C., 2006 WL 1094548 (M.D. Pa. Apr. 24, 2006). Defendant did not violate § 1692g by not responding to consumer's dispute letter, sent several months after *pro se* consumer received validation notice.

Texas

Cunningham v. Credit Mgmt., L.P., 2010 WL 3791104 (N.D. Tex. Aug. 30, 2010). Where the *pro se* plaintiff admitted that the letter he wrote to the debt collector did not represent a dispute, but rather

a "reject [ion] of Defendants [sic] purported validation," he failed to establish a claim that the defendants violated the FDCPA by continuing collection efforts after he disputed the debt and before the defendants verified the debt. "While the FDCPA does give debtors an opportunity to dispute the validity of a debt, it does not give a 'debtor's veto' that allows debtors to cease all collection efforts by rejecting a debt collector's verification."

United States v. Cent. Adjustment Bureau, Inc., 667 F. Supp. 370 (N.D. Tex. 1986). The collector violated § 1692g by failing to validate debts and by continuing efforts after receiving written notice of a dispute requesting validation.

Utah

Reed v. AFNI, Inc., 2011 WL 112430 (D. Utah Jan. 13, 2011). Where the collector verified the debt and did not continue with collection efforts after providing the plaintiff the verification, the FDCPA was not violated.

Maynard v. Cannon, 2006 WL 2403591 (D. Utah Aug. 21, 2006). A debt collector who had filed in the public record a mortgage default notice containing an incorrect amount owed and who thereafter did not verify the amount of the debt as the consumer requested did not comply with § 1692g(b) by failing to withdraw or correct the public notice attempting to collect the debt.

Lietz v. Mikel M. Boley Attorney at Law, 2006 WL 335854 (D. Utah Feb. 14, 2006). An FDCPA claim was stated where defendant filed a complaint and summons after verification was requested and before it had been provided to the consumer.

Ditty v. CheckRite, Ltd., 973 F. Supp. 1320 (D. Utah 1997). Section 1692g did not prohibit all collection efforts until the thirty-day validation period has passed.

Virginia

Dikun v. Streich, 369 F. Supp. 2d 781 (E.D. Va. 2005). Consumer's allegation that the collector continued to collect the debt without providing any verification after it received a validation request stated a claim for relief for violating § 1692g(b).

Marro v. Crosscheck, Inc., 2004 WL 3688137 (E.D. Va. Aug. 6, 2004), *aff'd*, 115 Fed. Appx. 168 (4th Cir. 2004). Upon receipt of the consumer's vaguely written purported dispute letter, the collector's reply asking for clarification, including supporting documentation, but not demanding payment, was not an unlawful attempt to continue collecting the debt.

Wyoming

Johnson v. Statewide Collections, Inc., 778 P.2d 93 (Wyo. 1989). Collector must cease collection from date it receives consumer's attorney's request for validation until it provides written verification of the debt. Verification is mandatory even though the consumer may have had adequate prior notice of the debt.

K.2.6.8 Other

Goldman v. Cohen, 445 F.3d 152 (2d Cir. 2006). Failure to include the validation notice with or within five days of the initial communication, which was a legal pleading, violated § 1692g(a).

Durkin v. Equifax Check Servs., Inc., 406 F.3d 410 (7th Cir. 2005). The validation period is not a grace period.

Vega v. McKay, 351 F.3d 1334 (11th Cir. 2003). The court deferred to the nonbinding FTC Staff Commentary's conclusion that a summons and complaint was not a communication requiring that § 1692g informal dispute rights be given the consumer. The court did not refer to the FTC's Advisory Opinion (Mar. 31, 2000) overruling that part of the Staff Commentary.

California

Yee v. Ventus Capital Servs., Inc., 2006 WL 1310463 (N.D. Cal. May 12, 2006). Collection agency's motion for partial summary judgment was denied because the record was insufficient to demonstrate when plaintiff disputed the debt.

Palmer v. I.C. Sys., Inc., 2005 WL 3001877 (N.D. Cal. Nov. 8, 2005). Since the consumer did not dispute the debt within the thirty-day time frame, the collector could presume its validity. Consumer's inquiry about the basis for the additional client charges, was an oral dispute that she owed the amount sought; defendant could not thereafter report to the credit bureaus without also reporting the account as disputed.

Delaware

Anthes v. Transworld Sys., Inc., 765 F. Supp. 162 (D. Del. 1991). Whether collector's letter stating that the debt was now assumed to be valid was received within thirty days of receipt of collector's initial communication raised a fact question which precluded summary judgment.

Florida

Andrade v. Erin Capital Mgmt. L.L.C., 2010 WL 1961843 (S.D. Fla. May 17, 2010). A letter from the consumer's attorney to the defendant protesting the defendant's debt collection strategy and seeking certain documents but failing to dispute the debt or request the name and address of the original creditor failed to state a claim to relief under § 1692g.

Illinois

Miller v. Midland Credit Mgmt., Inc., 621 F. Supp. 2d 621 (N.D. Ill. 2009). The defendants' allegedly false statement concerning the plaintiffs' rights to privacy, though sent only to comply with the requirements of a federal privacy law and enclosed as a separate second page with a dunning letter, was nonetheless sent "in connection with the collection of a debt," was not excluded by § 1692g(e), and was therefore subject to the FDCPA.

Indiana

Thompson v. BAC Home Loans Serv., L.P., 2010 WL 1286747 (N.D. Ind. Mar. 26, 2010). The court found that the notice from the defendants informing the consumer that his mortgage loan was transferred to a new servicer was not made "in connection with the collection of any debt" and thus "it was not a communication that triggered the requirement to send a Validation Notice."

Spears v. Brennan, 745 N.E.2d 862 (Ind. Ct. App. 2001). Consumers may not waive their rights under the FDCPA. The "FDCPA is a

strict liability statute and that a consumer need not show intentional conduct by the debt collector to be entitled to damages."

Kansas

Burdett v. Harrah's Kansas Casino Corp., 294 F. Supp. 2d 1215 (D. Kan. 2003). The failure to dispute a debt was not an admission of liability.

Kentucky

Olson v. J.J. Marshall & Assoc., 2008 WL 2794655 (E.D. Ky. July 16, 2008). The magistrate judge approved this *pro se* prisoner's *in forma pauperis* request in a pre-filing screening order because the plaintiff alleged an FDCPA violation on the basis that the defendant collectors continued collection activity in violation of § 1692g(b) after receiving the plaintiff's written dispute and demand for information when they "either failed to respond to his letter or gave only a partial response."

Michigan

Kaniewski v. Nat'l Action Fin. Servs., 678 F. Supp. 2d 541 (E.D. Mich. 2009). One who knows that he is not alleged to owe the debt is not a "consumer" and does not have standing to bring claims under § 1692e or § 1692g, but does have standing as "any person" to bring claims pursuant to § 1692d.

Ruthenberg v. Bureaus, Inc., 2008 WL 3979507 (E.D. Mich. Aug. 25, 2008). Where the consumer did not dispute the data or request verification until after thirty days from the receipt of the debt collector's initial communication, the time period in which to obtain debt verification had elapsed and the debt collector was awarded summary judgment on the § 1692g claim.

Minnesota

Wald v. Morris, Carlson, & Hoelscher, P.A., 2010 WL 4736829 (D. Minn. Nov. 16, 2010). "Defendants claim, however, that Plaintiff's failure to respond to the September 2003 and August 2008 letters [containing debt verification notices] validated the debt, therefore the debt is not time-barred . . . Such assertion is not supported by the FDCPA, which provides '[t]he failure of a consumer to dispute the validity of a debt under [15 U.S.C. § 1692g] may not be construed by any court as an admission of liability by the consumer.' 15 U.S.C. § 1692g(c)."

Missouri

Settle v. Southwest Bank, 2010 WL 2041366 (E.D. Mo. May 21, 2010). Because the *pro se* consumers failed to allege that there was an initial communication from defendant, they failed to state a claim for relief under § 1692g.

New Jersey

Christion v. Pressler & Pressler L.L.P., 2010 WL 988547 (D.N.J. Mar. 12, 2010). Where a consumer failed to allege that she timely disputed the debt in writing, the debt collector was not required to verify the debt, and § 1692g(b) was not violated.

D'Allesandro v. Vision Fin. Corp., 2009 WL 816082 (N.J. Super. Ct. App. Div. Mar. 31, 2009). The collector's third dun—which stated that it was now collecting "on a valid debt" and was sent after the consumer had not responded to the thirty-day verification disclosure—did not falsely or deceptively "impl[y] that the debt had been deemed legally enforceable by a third party and no longer subject to challenge by plaintiff;" in response to the consumer's proffer of the dictionary meaning of the word "valid" to show that the usage here was misleading, the court said: "We reject this argument because based on a plain reading of 15 U.S.C.A. § 1692g(a)(3), was statutorily authorized to state to plaintiff: 'Unless you notify this office within 30 days after receiving this notice that you dispute the validity of this debt or any portion thereof, this office will assume this debt is valid.' The word 'valid' in this context was not selected by ; Congress specifically included the word in the statute as a means of apprising the consumer of his or her obligation to respond to the notice. Under the Act, plaintiff's inactions have legal consequences. One of those consequences is the right of a creditor to assume that the debt is valid."

New York

Kamen v. Steven J. Baum, P.C., 659 F. Supp. 2d 402 (E.D.N.Y. 2009). Summons and complaint constituted a single "legal pleading" excluded from the definition of an initial communication and thereby not required to contain a debt validation notice.

Weber v. Computer Credit, Inc., 259 F.R.D. 33 (E.D.N.Y. 2009). The thirty day validation period is not a grace period, and, unless the debt is disputed, the debt collector may demand immediate payment and continue collection activity.

Stark v. RJM Acquisitions L.L.C., 2009 WL 605811 (E.D.N.Y. Mar. 9, 2009). Summary judgment granted to the defendant regarding plaintiff's challenge to an allegedly confusing sentence that appeared immediately after the validation disclosure since the "plaintiff does not suggest that the language [at issue] confuses the least sophisticated consumer as to her rights under the FDCPA."

Johnson v. Equifax Risk Mgmt. Servs., 2004 WL 540459 (S.D.N.Y. Mar. 17, 2004). A check collector whom the consumer had notified of the consumer's dispute that the underlying check was a forgery did not impose an unlawful additional burden on the consumer in violation of § 1692g to dispute the debt when it subsequently sent him an affidavit of forgery to sign; however, sending the affidavit of forgery falsely implied that the consumer's verification dispute was ineffective, in violation of § 1692e.

Bleich v. Revenue Maximization Group, Inc., 233 F. Supp. 2d 496 (E.D.N.Y. 2002). Summary judgment is proper for the defendant where the consumer shows only that the collector was unwittingly collecting an invalid debt that the underlying creditor referred to it, and the collector complied with the validation disclosures and received no dispute.

Garmus v. Borah, Goldstein, Altschuler & Schwartz, P.C., 1999 WL 46682 (S.D.N.Y. Feb. 1, 1999). The FDCPA's thirty-day verification provision preempts the less stringent state law allowing a three-day rent demand notice.

Deutsche Bank Nat'l Trust Co. v. Gillio, 881 N.Y.S.2d 362 (table), 2009 WL 595560 (N.Y. Sup. Ct. 2009) (unpublished). Where the defendant, in order to have his default judgment vacated, claimed that the collector did not provide a timely validation notice pursuant to § 1692g(a), the court held that it did not constitute a valid defense to plaintiff's claim of collection of the debt or foreclosure on the secured property.

Finlayson v. Yager, 873 N.Y.S.2d 511 (table), 2008 WL 4571562 (N.Y. Civ. Ct. 2008). "[T]he FDCPA notice provisions do not apply where the creditor, rather than a debt collector, directly attempts to collect the debt. As such, if the landlord sends the demand for rent, then the landlord, as a creditor directly trying to collect a debt, would not have to wait the 30-days before commencing his eviction proceedings." Accordingly, "where the petitioner's attorney signs the notice to quit, or where the attorney's name appears with the landlord's name on a notice to quit, then the petitioner must wait the 30-day period to expire before commencing a summary proceeding." Because "the summary proceeding was filed only six (6) days after the notice to quit was served, . . . it was prematurely filed, for the proceeding could not be legally commenced prior to 30-days expiring."

North Carolina

Gough v. Bernhardt & Strawser, P.A., 2006 WL 1875327 (M.D.N.C. June 30, 2006). The court held that a summons and complaint in the state court collection action may qualify as an initial § 1692g communication.

Ohio

National Check Bur. v. Patel, 2005 WL 3454694, 2005 Ohio 6679 (Ohio Ct. App. Dec. 16, 2005). Where a credit card debt buyer sued the consumer on the incorrect but reasonable belief that he was the obligor of the subject account and dismissed the collection action once it ascertained that it had mistakenly mismerged the consumer's identification with the actual debtor, the appellate court affirmed the lower court's denial of sanctions against the debt buyer, holding that the lower court acted within its discretion in finding that the debt buyer's conduct did not rise to the level harassment or malice required by state law to impose such sanctions, based, *inter alia*, on the fact that the debt buyer had sent the consumer a § 1692g notice and the consumer had not responded to it, thus contributing to the reasonableness of the debt buyer's mistaken assumption that this consumer was the debtor.

Pennsylvania

Harris v. NCO Fin. Sys., 2009 WL 497409 (E.D. Pa. Feb. 26, 2009). Because a genuine issue of fact existed as to (1) whether a validation notice was given as required by § 1692g and (2) whether plaintiff disputed the debt as set forth in that section—obligating the debt collector to submit evidence of the origin and validity of the debt—summary judgment was denied.

Gigli v. Palisades Collection, L.L.C., 2008 WL 3853295 (M.D. Pa. Aug. 14, 2008). Failure of the consumer to dispute the debt within thirty days of the initial communication does not prevent the consumer from asserting an FDCPA claim.

Texas

Eads v. Wolpoff & Abramson, L.L.P., 538 F. Supp. 2d 981 (W.D. Tex. 2008). The consumer stated a legally cognizable claim against the collection law firm by alleging it violated § 1692g by failing to provide a validation notice.

K.2.7 Distant Forums, 15 U.S.C. § 1692i

Addison v. Braud, 105 F.3d 223 (5th Cir. 1997). Attorney, who failed to bring action in the judicial district where the debtors resided or had signed the promissory note, violated § 1692i.

Newsom v. Friedman, 76 F.3d 813 (7th Cir. 1996). Under the § 1692i(a)(2) venue provisions, the Illinois Circuit Courts constitute "a judicial district or similar legal entity."

Wadlington v. Credit Acceptance Corp., 76 F.3d 103 (6th Cir. 1996). Attorneys who filed suit on behalf of a financer were debt collectors and subject to liability under the FDCPA for filing suit in a venue not permitted by § 1692i(a)(2), but the court remanded the issue of whether the venue protection was waived by the sales contract.

Fox v. Citicorp Credit Servs., Inc., 15 F.3d 1507 (9th Cir. 1994). Rejecting the collection attorney's theory that the FDCPA does not apply to "purely legal activities," the filing of an application for a writ of garnishment in a county other than where the consumers resided or the contract was signed violated § 1692i. Application for a writ of garnishment is a "legal action on a debt" covered by § 1692i restrictions. Where the state has provided a formal transfer mechanism between courts in different counties, the county is the "judicial district or similar legal entity" addressed by § 1692i. A collector may be held liable for violation of § 1692i where its attorney filed in an improper forum.

Scott v. Jones, 964 F.2d 314 (4th Cir. 1992). Lawyer filing suits in a distant forum was covered by the Act.

Alabama

In re Barnes, 397 B.R. 149 (Bankr. N.D. Ala. 2008). 15 U.S.C. § 1692i "has the effect of invalidating any forum-selection clause that the parties to a debt contract might agree to."

Arizona

Randall v. Nelson & Kennard, 2010 WL 3636258 (D. Ariz. Sept. 20, 2010). Because the collection action was filed in Riverside County, California, where the consumer did not live when he entered into the contract with the creditor and when the debt collection suit was filed, the defendants violated § 1692i(a)(2).

California

Dale v. Johnson, 1997 WL 797913 (N.D. Cal. Dec. 12, 1997) *(pro se)*. A § 1692i claim that the court action to enforce an arbitration award should have been instituted in another county should have been raised in the state court proceeding and not in federal court.

Colorado

Shapiro & Meinhold v. Zartman, 823 P.2d 120 (Colo. 1992), *aff'g Zartman v. Shapiro & Meinhold*, 811 P.2d 409 (Colo. App. 1990). Attorney collector, who brought foreclosure action in a county other than that where the real estate was situated, violated § 1692i(a)(1) even though state statute allows such venue.

Connecticut

First Trust Nat'l v. Crespo, 1996 WL 383437 (Conn. Super. Ct. June 14, 1996). A foreclosure action was filed in the wrong county but transferred to the correct county. The homeowner then opposed summary judgment for foreclosure by arguing that the mortgagee had violated the FDCPA by filing the foreclosure in the wrong county. Summary judgment was granted the mortgagee because the homeowner failed to file the FDCPA claim as a counterclaim, the mortgagee was a creditor exempt from the FDCPA, and the FDCPA violation was not a defense to the foreclosure.

Marina Assocs. v. Mase, 1994 WL 669635 (Conn. Super. Ct. Nov. 10, 1994). Section 1692i was not a valid defense to a judgment transferred from New Jersey to Connecticut.

Delaware

Dutton v. Wolhar, 809 F. Supp. 1130 (D. Del. 1992), *aff'd*, 5 F.3d 649 (3d Cir. 1993). The term "judicial district or similar legal entity" in § 1692i refers to state, rather than federal, divisions when the suit is filed in state court. Although the State of Delaware provides for statewide jurisdiction of civil actions, an attorney must bring suit in the county in which the consumer resides or where the contract was signed to avoid violating § 1692i(2). Section 1692f is violated where an attorney collector brings an action, seeking costs as well as damages, in a county other than where the consumer resides, when recovery of costs of suit filed in an inconvenient forum is prohibited by Delaware statute.

Hsu v. Great Seneca Fin. Corp., 2010 WL 2635771 (Del. Super. Ct. June 29, 2010). The court rejected the *pro se* consumer's argument that a debt buyer violated § 1692i when it sued in its own name, noting that was permitted by Delaware law. The debt buyer complied with § 1692i by suing in the judicial district of the consumer's home.

Florida

McKnight v. Benitez, 176 F. Supp. 2d 1301 (M.D. Fla. 2001). Initiation of a replevin action on behalf of the secured creditor, as required by state law in the judicial district where the secured vehicle was being held by the local sheriff as allegedly having been used in a drug deal, violated § 1692i when the action also sought money damages against the consumer, since the additional request for damages constitutes a "legal action on a debt" and the district where the action was filed was not where the consumer resided or signed the contract.

Georgia

Canady v. Wisenbaker Law Offices, P.C., 372 F. Supp. 2d 1379 (N.D. Ga. 2005). Attorney collection firm violated the FDCPA by filing its collection suit in a venue prohibited by § 1692i. The consumer's failure to notify the attorney collection firm of its violation of the FDCPA venue provision or otherwise object to its filing in an improper venue was irrelevant as to the firm's defense to the violation or its establishment of its putative the bona fide error defense.

Pickens v. Collection Servs., Inc., 165 F. Supp. 2d 1376 (M.D. Ga. 2001), *aff'd without op.* 273 F.3d 1121 (11th Cir. 2001). A post-judgment garnishment action was against the garnishee, and the consumer was not a party. Therefore, defendants did not violate the FDCPA's venue provisions, which applied to actions against a consumer. The court relied, in part, on the FTC Staff Commentary, Appx. C, *supra*, and refused to follow *Fox v. Citicorp Credit Servs., Inc.*, 15 F.3d 1507, 1511 (9th Cir. 1994), because it did not consider whether the garnishment action was against the consumer.

Lord v. Carragher, 270 B.R. 787 (Bankr. M.D. Ga. 1998). Collection attorney's post-judgment garnishment was a legal action within the venue provision of the FDCPA, § 1692i, and it was a violation to file the garnishment in the county of the consumer's employer because it was not the county in which the consumer resided or signed the contract.

Idaho

Coultson v. United Serv. Bureau, Inc., Clearinghouse No. 27,718 (D. Idaho 1979). Preliminary injunction granted against distant forum abuses.

Illinois

Lawson v. Mgmt. Adjustment Bureau, Inc., 1997 WL 283027 (N.D. Ill. May 15, 1997). Collector's assertion to debtor in a collection letter that pre-wage garnishment hearings would be held in Colorado when the debt originated in, and the debtor resided in, Illinois, was not in violation of § 1692i(a)(2) because the hearing was not a "legal action" for the purposes of the FDCPA.

Holloway v. Pekay, 1996 WL 19580 (N.D. Ill. Jan. 18, 1996). Where state law authorized lender to recover costs and attorney fees in collection action and the underlying debt was not contested, the collection attorney fee recovery did not constitute actual damages for filing the collection action in an improper distant forum.

Narwick v. Wexler, 901 F. Supp. 1275 (N.D. Ill. 1995). Class certification was denied for failure to demonstrate numerosity; affidavit of plaintiffs' attorney, based on a 7% sampling of defendants' court filings to collect a debt, which examined the residence of the debtor, but failed to consider the location of the signing of the contract, was inadequate. "Judicial district or similar legal entity" referred to the Circuit Court of Cook County, Illinois, rather than its sub-county divisions, the Municipal Courts.

Blakemore v. Pekay, 895 F. Supp. 972 (N.D. Ill. 1995). The FDCPA venue provision prohibited debt collectors from filing legal actions on debts in counties other than where the debtor resided or where the contract was signed. It was not a violation of the FDCPA venue provision to file a collection action in a sub-county "judicial district" where the debtor neither resided nor signed the contract so long as the lawsuit was filed in the county where the debtor resided or signed the contract. The debtor does not waive his FDCPA venue claims by appearing in a "judicial district" other than where he resided or signed the contract.

Oglesby v. Rotche, 1993 WL 460841 (N.D. Ill. Nov. 5, 1993). The collector's argument that the debtors had waived any claim pursuant to § 1692i when debtors had entered their defense in the distant forum was rejected because the "least sophisticated consumer" should not be forced to exercise his FDCPA rights immediately or lose them.

Kansas

Farmers Nat'l Bank v. Hall, 791 P.2d 752 (Kan. Ct. App. 1990). Creditors were exempt from the FDCPA and were not required to file suit in a venue provided by § 1692i.

Louisiana

Chase Bank v. Roach, 978 So. 2d 1103 (La. Ct. App. Mar. 5, 2008). The FDCPA requires confirmation of an arbitration award be filed where the contract was signed or the debtor resides.

Michigan

Asset Acceptance Corp. v. Robinson, 625 N.W.2d 804 (Mich. Ct. App. 2001). The FDCPA does not prohibit a debt collector from filing suit on a debt, only from filing suit in an inconvenient forum as stated in § 1692i.

Minnesota

Fischbach v. Capital One Bank (USA), N.A., 2011 WL 71207 (D. Minn. Jan. 7, 2011). The defendants were permitted to file a third-party complaint against the daughter of the plaintiff, who co-signed for his daughter's credit card and who alleged that the defendant lawyers sued him in a distant forum prohibited by § 1692i, since the defendants alleged that the daughter's failure to update her address as required by the cardholder agreement was somehow the cause of their violation.

Missouri

Smith v. Kramer & Frank, P.C., 2009 WL 4725285 (E.D. Mo. Dec. 2, 2009). An application for writ of garnishment, as an action in enforcement of a previously obtained judgment, is a "legal action" which falls within § 1692i.

Nevada

Nichols v. Byrd, 435 F. Supp. 2d 1101 (D. Nev. 2006). The Ninth Circuit has held that separate county courts within a judicial district were separate venues for the purpose of the FDCPA. A collection attorney's review of post office address correction forms was found to be a reasonably sufficient preventive procedure to establish the bona fide error defense to a violation of the venue requirements of § 1692i.

New Jersey

Bey v. Daimlerchrysler Servs., L.L.C., 2005 WL 2090207 (D.N.J. Aug. 29, 2005). Section 1692i does not prohibit debt collectors from bringing a suit where they are entitled to do so under state law; rather, it clarifies that it does not extend the circumstances under which a collector can bring a suit.

Rutgers v. Fogel, 958 A.2d 1014 (N.J. Super. Ct. App. Div. 2008). Law firm violated the FDCPA's venue provision § 1692i by bringing the action in the creditor's county, rather than the county of the student's residence. "Judicial district" has generally been construed as referring to the geographic units into which a state divides its judiciary, rather than the federal judicial district. The FDCPA sets forth a bright-line venue rule. It does not require a case-by-case inquiry into the relative sophistication of each debtor (here, the debtor was a lawyer), nor into the relative hardship posed by the collection attorney's choice of venue.

New Mexico

Kolker v. Sanchez, 1991 WL 11691589 (D.N.M. Dec. 10, 1991). Section 1692i does not authorize debt collectors to file any lawsuits.

Martinez v. Albuquerque Collection Servs., 867 F. Supp. 1495 (D.N.M. 1994). There is no exemption under the FDCPA for an action brought to enforce a judgment and such activities are subject to the venue requirements of § 1692i. Where the state had developed formal transfer mechanisms between courts in two counties, each county was a "judicial district or similar legal entity" for the purposes of § 1692i. Debt collection agencies may be held vicariously liable under § 1692i for venue decisions made solely by the debt collector's attorney. The collection agency violated § 1692e by not filing its debt collection suit in a state court in the county where the consumer resided. That was the only proper venue when the contract was oral. The proper state court is determined by state, not federal, court districts.

New York

Hess v. Cohen & Slamowitz, L.L.P., 2010 WL 60322 (N.D.N.Y. Jan. 7, 2010). Summary judgment under § 1692i in favor of debt collector where he brought suit in the consumer's county of residence even though the specific court did not have jurisdiction. Requiring suit to be brought in the court of proper jurisdiction would impose undue restrictions on the actions of ethical debt collectors.

Howell v. Citibank (South Dakota), 2009 WL 152700 (W.D.N.Y. Jan. 21, 2009). *Pro se* allegation of venue violation dismissed where two courts in question were located less than ten miles apart; the distance did not present a substantial burden upon the debtor; nor did the distance support the argument that the defendants were attempting to secure a default judgment by filing in a distant venue. Courts have concluded that for purposes of the FDCPA, "judicial district," has been held to mean "county" when determining whether a state court action has been filed in the proper judicial district.

Wiener v. Bloomfield, 901 F. Supp. 771 (S.D.N.Y. 1995). Threat of filing in an improper venue did not violate § 1692i; however, it did violate § 1692e(5) by threatening action that legally could not be taken.

Scott v. Jones, 1991 WL 156060 (W.D. Va. Mar. 1, 1991), *aff'd on other grounds*, 964 F.2d 314 (4th Cir. 1992). A lawyer who filed a high volume of suits in a forum distant from the consumer defendants' residences violated § 1692i(a)(2). The court rejected the FTC staff and judicial opinion that a lawyer only filing suit was not covered by the FDCPA.

Nat'l Union Fire Ins. Co. v. Hartel, 741 F. Supp. 1139 (S.D.N.Y. 1990). A law firm was not a debt collector under the FDCPA where the debt was not incurred for a consumer purpose, and the firm only engaged in legal activities, i.e., filing a suit in a distant forum. The latter was overruled by *Heintz v. Jenkins*, 514 U.S. 291, 115 S. Ct. 1489, 131 L. Ed. 2d 395 (1995).

Jack Mailman & Leonard Flug D.D.S., P.C. v. Whaley, 2002 WL 31988623 (N.Y. Civ. Ct. Nov. 25, 2002). Attorney for dentist suing on unpaid account was required by § 1692i to bring the action where the consumer signed the contract sued upon or where the consumer resided at the commencement of the action.

Ohio

Lamb v. Javitch, Block & Rathbone, L.L.P., 2005 WL 4137778 (S.D. Ohio Jan. 24, 2005). The court found that MBNA's law firm did not violate § 1692i when it commenced arbitration by filing a claim with NAF which is located in Minnesota as required by the contractual agreement, when the arbitration would be conducted in the consumer's locale.

Candlewood Lake Assoc. v. Scott, 2001 Ohio App. LEXIS 5917 (Ohio Ct. App. Dec. 27, 2001). Venue in a suit for unpaid condominium assessments was proper in the location of the real estate, since the attorney for the condominium association was enforcing its interest in real property.

Durve v. Oker, 679 N.E.2d 19 (Ohio. Ct. App. 1996). The trial court erred by granting summary judgment to collectors against the consumer's claim under § 1692i that the collectors had filed their collection action in an improper venue.

Celebrezze v. United Research, Inc., 482 N.E.2d 1260 (Ohio Ct. App. 1984). Lower court enjoined distant forum abuse based on FDCPA as well as on state UDAP statute.

Oregon

Flores v. Quick Collect, Inc., 2007 WL 2769003 (D. Or. Sept. 18, 2007). Applying *Fox v. Citicorp Credit Servs., Inc.*, 15 F.3d 1507 (9th Cir. 1994), the court held that, separate from filing the collection suit itself, "issuing a writ of garnishment and seeking a debtor examination are considered 'legal actions on a debt' in the Ninth Circuit and subject to the venue provision under § 1692i," and therefore "defendants may bring enforcement actions against plaintiff 1) in the county in which she resides when the action is commenced, or 2) in the county in which the underlying loan agreement was signed."

Flores v. Quick Collect, Inc., 2007 WL 433239 (D. Or. Jan. 31, 2007). Filing suit in a county where the debtor neither resided nor signed the contract violated § 1692i.

South Dakota

Crawford v. Credit Collection Servs., 898 F. Supp. 699 (D.S.D. 1995). A signed "Patient Registration Form" reciting credit terms constituted a contract, and collection action was properly filed within the judicial district where it was signed. "Judicial district or similar legal entity" means the state judicial circuits, not counties. Although spouse may be liable for a medical debt as necessities under state law, collection action may only be filed in the "judicial district or similar legal entity" where that spouse resided when she did not join in signing contract for her husband's health care contract.

Action Prof'l Serv. v. Kiggins, 458 N.W.2d 365 (S.D. 1990). Filing a debt collection action against a consumer in a state circuit court for a circuit in which the consumer did not reside violated § 1692i.

The fact that the consumer resided in the same federal district as where the suit was filed made no difference, since the suit was not filed in the federal district court, but in the wrong state circuit court.

Texas

Geffrard v. Rolfe & Lobello, P.A., 2010 WL 1924434 (S.D. Tex. May 11, 2010). Garnishment is not a separate legal action triggering the venue requirements of § 1692i.

Beeler-Lopez v. Dodeka, L.L.C., 2010 WL 1889428 (E.D. Tex. May 7, 2010). Any violation of the FDCPA's venue provision occurs when the suit is brought. If the consumer does not object to venue, then merely continuing to pursue the action is not a violation of §§ 1692i, 1692d, or 1692e. Where the successor attorneys did not "bring" the action (i.e., "sue or institute any legal proceedings") in the wrong legal venue, they were not vicariously liable for the wrongdoing of the original attorneys.

McNeill v. Graham, Bright & Smith, P.C., 2006 WL 1489502 (N.D. Tex. May 26, 2006). Defendant collection attorneys violated the FDCPA distant forum provision by filing the state collection case in a court other than in the district where the consumer signed the underlying contract and resided when sued. The filing of a counterclaim in the federal FDCPA case in order to collect the underlying debt "is not the same thing as filing a lawsuit in a distant forum" and therefore did not violate the FDCPA distant forum provision.

Hester v. Graham, Bright & Smith, 2005 WL 994704 (E.D. Tex. Apr. 1, 2005). Summary judgment was granted for violation of § 1692i where defendants filed suit in a county other than where the consumer resided or signed the contract.

Washington

Unifund CCR v. Ayhan, 146 Wash. App. 1026 (Wash. Ct. App. 2008). Venue in this collection suit was proper under § 1692i(a)(2)(B) since the action was brought in the county in which the consumer resided.

K.2.8 Furnishing Deceptive Forms, 15 U.S.C. § 1692j [See also K.1.3, Flat Rate Debt Collection]

Taylor v. Perrin, Landry, deLaunay & Durand, 103 F.3d 1232 (5th Cir. 1997). The law firm was liable under § 1692j as it knowingly furnished forms to a creditor for use in a deceptive manner so that a consumer would think a law firm was involved in collection of a debt when it was not.

Delaware

Anthes v. Transworld Sys., Inc., 765 F. Supp. 162 (D. Del. 1991). Letter sent by outside attorney retained by debt collector was neither impersonation of attorney, nor use of a name other than its own, nor "flat-rating" in violation of §§ 1692e(3), 1692e(14) or 1692j(a), respectively.

Illinois

Nielsen v. Dickerson, 1999 WL 754566 (N.D. Ill. Sept. 9, 1999). Court granted the consumer summary judgment on § 1692e(3) and (5) claims, since the collection law firm had never actually filed a collection lawsuit on behalf of creditor. Court also found the collection law firm liable under § 1692j.

Michigan

South v. Midwestern Audit Servs., Inc., 2010 WL 5089862 (E.D. Mich. Dec. 8, 2010). The FDCPA's flat-rating prohibition is limited to preventing the deceptive suggestion that a debt collector is participating in the collection of a debt when in fact it is not so participating. The collection agency's matching two utility accounts to roommates for a 10% collection fee was enough for the court to find sufficient participation.

New York

Sokolski v. Trans Union Corp., 53 F. Supp. 2d 307 (E.D.N.Y. 1999). A "flat-rater" is a collection agency that sells a creditor a series of dunning or demand letters, bearing the letterhead of the collection agency, which are sued by the creditor without the collection agency's involvement. An unlawful flat-rating arrangement was found where the collection agency's activities were limited to furnishing collection letters, and the creditor was found liable under § 1692a(6).

Ohio

Canterbury v. Columbia Gas of Ohio, 2000 WL 1460080 (S.D. Ohio Sept. 29, 2000). Relying on and adopting the factors enunciated in *Larson v. Evanston Northwestern Healthcare Corp.*, 1999 U.S. Dist. LEXIS 11380 (N.D. Ill. July 19, 1999). Plaintiff's complaint dismissed without prejudice to file an amended complaint to allege the supporting basis for the conclusory allegation that the defendant creditor was acting as a flat rater and collecting its own debts in another name in violation of the FDCPA.

K.2.9 Miscellaneous

Evory v. RJM Acquisitions Funding, 505 F.3d 769 (7th Cir. 2007). The court held that a communication to the plaintiff's lawyer is subject to the FDCPA as a communication to the debtor.

Sims v. GC Servs. L.P., 445 F.3d 959, 964 (7th Cir. 2006). The court found that "analysis of the text design and readability of dunning letters admittedly similar to the letters at issue here does not by itself create an issue of material fact that survives summary judgment." It called for "objective" consumer survey evidence.

Lewis v. ACB Bus. Servs., Inc., 135 F.3d 389 (6th Cir. 1998). Collector's retaliatory suit to collect the debt did not violate the Equal Credit Opportunity Act.

Phillips v. Bergland, 586 F.2d 1007 (4th Cir. 1978). *In dictum* the court indicated that another employee's behavior in hounding the plaintiff for a business debt would have violated the Act if covered.

Connecticut

Silver v. Law Offices of Howard Lee Schiff, P.C., 2010 WL 3000053 (D. Conn. July 28, 2010). Questions about the clarity of the consumer's directions to apply two payments to separate accounts pursuant to § 1692h required the issue to be tried.

Florida

Pollock v. Bay Area Credit Serv., L.L.C., 2009 WL 2475167 (S.D. Fla. Aug. 13, 2009). A single violation subjects the collector to liability.

Illinois

Sorrell v. Illinois Student Assistance Comm'n, 314 F. Supp. 2d 813 (C.D. Ill. 2004). *Pro se* plaintiff's FDCPA and FCRA claims against the Illinois Student Assistants Commission were dismissed on the basis of 11th Amendment sovereign immunity.

Robles v. Corporate Receivables, Inc., 220 F.R.D. 306 (N.D. Ill. Mar. 2, 2004). FDCPA violations occur when the letter is sent, not when it is received.

Wilson v. Collecto, Inc., 2004 WL 432509 (N.D. Ill. Feb. 25, 2004). FDCPA violations occur when the letter is sent, not when it is received.

Indiana

Zaborac v. Mutual Hosp. Serv., Inc., 2004 WL 2538643 (S.D. Ind. Oct. 7, 2004). The Health Insurance Portability and Accountability Act (HIPAA) allows a collection agency to disclose protected health information as necessary to obtain payment for health care services.

Northern Mariana Islands

Tenorio v. Reliable Collection Agency, Inc., 2003 WL 23150110 (D. N. Mar. I. Dec. 31, 2003). After bench trial, the court entered judgment in favor of the debt collector because the consumer failed to present evidence showing that the debt collector had violated §§ 1692b(3), 1692c(a)(1), 1692d, or 1692e(11).

Ohio

Kistner v. Law Offices of Michael P. Margelefsky, L.L.C., 2007 U.S. Dist. LEXIS 1925 (N.D. Ohio Jan. 10, 2007), *cf. later op.*, 518 F.3d 433 (6th Cir. 2008) (reversing summary judgment; attorney possibly liable under FDCPA as "debt collector"). Refused to consider as violations of § 1692f the attorney collector's putative violations derived from alleged violations of the lawyer canons of ethics.

Dowling v. Litton Loan Serv., L.P., 2006 WL 3498292 (S.D. Ohio Dec. 1, 2006). The defendant did not violate § 1692h when it failed, as instructed by the consumer, to apply payments to certain components of the loan and not to other disputed components because § 1692h is applicable only when a consumer allegedly owes multiple debts and does not apply to payment allocations within a single obligation.

Oklahoma

Bynum v. Cavalry Portfolio Servs., L.L.C., 2006 WL 1047035

(N.D. Okla. Apr. 13, 2006). Defendant's motion for reconsideration was denied with the court holding that expert testimony was not required to establish actual damages for emotional distress or lost wages and the consumer could testify on those issues.

Pennsylvania

Paoletta v. Stock & Grimes, L.L.P., 2005 WL 3543190 (M.D. Pa. Dec. 27, 2005). The court rejected the debt collectors' argument that the only debt collection litigation misconduct that the FDCPA prohibits is for filing an action in an improper venue.

K.3 Remedies and Litigation

K.3.1 Damages

K.3.1.1 Actual Damages

Bartlett v. Heibl, 128 F.3d 497 (7th Cir. 1997). A consumer's admission that he did not read the collection letter violating § 1692g did not affect his claim for statutory damages but would have defeated a claim for actual damages if they had been sought.

Anunciation v. West Capital Fin. Servs. Corp., 97 F.3d 1458 (9th Cir. 1996) (table, text at 1996 WL 534049). Plaintiff filed and properly served a complaint for violation of FDCPA, then filed an amended complaint with invasion of privacy claims but failed to serve a summons with it. The defendant defaulted. The court awarded $1000 statutory damages, actual damages of $9500, and $5289 costs and attorneys fees for obtaining the default judgment. On appeal the court held there was personal jurisdiction over defendant for all causes of action in the properly served initial complaint. Additional attorney fees were to be awarded to the consumer for the appeal.

Emanuel v. Am. Credit Exch., 870 F.2d 805 (2d Cir. 1989). Actual damages would not be considered where no specific loss was pleaded.

Crossley v. Lieberman, 868 F.2d 566 (3d Cir. 1989). In the circumstances of this case an attack on the award of actual damages of $1000 would be fruitless.

Alabama

McGrady v. Nissan Motor Acceptance Corp., 40 F. Supp. 2d 1323 (M.D. Ala. 1998). Actual damages for mental anguish available under FDCPA.

Arizona

Perkons v. American Acceptance, L.L.C., 2010 WL 4922916 (D. Ariz. Nov. 29, 2010). While the FDCPA does not define what constitutes "actual damages," it is commonly accepted that damages stemming from emotional distress are compensable under the Act. The consumer does not have to prove the elements of Arizona's tort of intentional infliction of emotional distress in order to be entitled to emotional distress damages under the FDCPA. Emotional distress damages can be awarded pursuant to the FDCPA without corroborative evidence.

California

Carrizosa v. Stassinos, 2010 WL 4393900 (N.D. Cal. Oct. 29, 2010). Where the debt collector collected $150,154.08 in unlawful interest charges from class members, the class was entitled to that amount in actual damages and restitution.

Owings v. Hunt & Henriques, 2010 WL 3489342 (S.D. Cal. Sept. 3, 2010). The court rejected the argument that the plaintiff's failure to pay the debt rather then the default judgment against him was what caused him injury, since it is irrelevant whether he paid the debt.

Morisaki v. Davenport, Allen & Malone, Inc., 2010 WL 3341566 (E.D. Cal. Aug. 23, 2010). The consumer need only offer evidence that she suffered emotional distress as a result of the defendant's FDCPA violations in order to recover emotional distress damages. Awarded $73,000 in actual damages for emotional distress under federal and state law.

Brablec v. Paul Coleman & Assocs. P.C., 2010 WL 235062 (E.D. Cal. Jan. 21, 2010). The court awarded $25,000 actual damages following the debt collection law firm's default on the consumer's claim alleging harassing telephone calls and threats of legal action resulting in severe emotional distress.

Molina v. Creditors Specialty Serv. Inc., 2010 WL 235042 (E.D. Cal. Jan. 21, 2010). The court refused the plaintiff's proffer of emotional distress actual damages and set that issue for an evidentiary hearing.

Basinger-Lopez v. Tracy Paul & Assocs., 2009 WL 1948832 (N.D. Cal. July 6, 2009). Court denied award of emotional distress damages on default judgment where the consumer's declaration that "Defendant's actions caused [her] to suffer damages, including emotional distress, embarrassment, humiliation, invasion of privacy, harassment, stress and anxiety, sleeplessness, and medical issues" was "too vague to establish that Plaintiff suffered significant emotional harm. . . ." "While Plaintiff's declaration shows that she understandably suffered general anxiety resulting from Defendant's conduct, the law requires a more specific and substantial showing before emotional damages may be awarded."

Hartung v. J.D. Byrider, Inc., 2009 WL 1876690 (E.D. Cal. June 26, 2009). The California intentional infliction of emotional distress standard was applied to determine actual damages for emotional distress arising under the FDCPA. Report recommended entry of default judgment for the consumer in the amount of $25,000 in FDCPA actual damages. The consumer's testimony about her severe distress was sufficient without corroboration.

Bolton v. Pentagroup Fin. Servs., L.L.C., 2009 WL 734038 (E.D. Cal. Mar. 17, 2009). The court adopted the *Costa* holding that emotional distress damages under the FDCPA must be proven under the standard for the state's law tort of intentional infliction of emotional distress.

Myers v. LHR, Inc., 543 F. Supp. 2d 1215 (S.D. Cal. 2008). Default judgment was entered against the collector for $92,000 in damages. Plaintiff did not owe the debt, suffered repeated and abusive collection efforts and suffered sleeplessness, upset, and embarrassment. Furthermore, she sought medical treatment for the stress. In addition to over-the-counter medications, plaintiff was prescribed Flexeris to relieve pain, and underwent steroid injections for back pain. She also testified to the extreme emotional distress caused by the erroneous reporting of the debt on plaintiff's credit report hindering her ability to timely purchase a home.

Lowe v. Elite Recovery Solutions L.P., 2008 WL 324777 (E.D. Cal. Feb. 5, 2008). The court awarded as actual damages ($2560) the amount of attorney fees incurred by the consumer in defending the underlying state collection action in which the FDCPA violations at issue occurred (the action was barred by the statute of limitations and sought an incorrect principal balance, an unauthorized amount of interest, and unauthorized attorney fees). The consumer's actual damages in the amount of the attorney fees incurred in defending the underlying state collection action was sufficiently proven by the declarations of the consumer and his attorney, "and further evidence such as attorney's bills or cancelled checks is not necessary." The court found that the plaintiff failed to establish emotional distress damages where he testified that the filing of the unlawful, underlying collection action against him caused him "a great deal of stress and worry" and that "he felt helpless as he knew little about the legal system, but learned that if he lost the lawsuit he could have his bank account cleaned out, his wages garnished or even property repossessed;" "as a result, plaintiff states that he lost sleep, and suffered from irritability, and could not get the lawsuit out of his mind." This evidence was insufficient under the standard that the court applied that "a plaintiff must demonstrate more than transitory symptoms of emotional distress, and unsupported self-serving testimony by a plaintiff is not sufficient."

Costa v. Nat'l Action Fin. Servs., 634 F. Supp. 2d 1069 (E.D. Cal. 2007). In order to sustain a claim for emotional distress damages under the FDCPA and the California FDCPA, the consumer must establish the elements of a claim for intentional infliction of emotional distress under California law.

Young v. Martini, Hughes & Grossman, 2006 U.S. Dist. LEXIS 79512 (S.D. Cal. Oct. 31, 2006). The court entered default judgment for the consumer but denied his request for $6000 in damages and instead awarded $300 in statutory damages under the FDCPA and $300 in statutory damages under the California Rosenthal Act for a total of $600.

Ballard v. Equifax Check Servs., 158 F. Supp. 2d 1163 (E.D. Cal. 2001). For violations of the FDCPA and the California Unfair Business Practices Act, damages were equal to all amounts collected above the face value of the dishonored checks plus prejudgment interest.

Colorado

O'Connor v. Check Rite, 973 F. Supp. 1010 (D. Colo. 1997). Because no damages arising from a § 1692c(b) violation could be shown, judgment in the amount of $0.01 was entered against the defendant.

Connecticut

Chiverton v. Fed. Fin. Group, Inc., 399 F. Supp. 2d 96 (D. Conn. 2005). After entry of a default judgment, the magistrate judge recommended the award of $5000 actual damages, $1000 statutory damages, and punitive damages of $7500 for a UDAP claim, to each of two plaintiffs plus costs and attorney fees of $4613.54.

One consumer had worried about losing his job or a promotion. The other consumer was frightened and embarrassed by threats of arrest.

Gervais v. O'Connell, Harris & Assocs., Inc., 297 F. Supp. 2d 435 (D. Conn. 2003). Court awarded $2500 for the return of funds sent to pay a debt misrepresented as not barred by the statute of limitations, $1500 for emotional distress resulting from FDCPA violations, $8000 punitive damages under the state UDAP, and $5000 in attorney fees for twenty-seven hours at $200 on default.

Evanauskas v. Strumpf, 2001 U.S. Dist. LEXIS 14326 (D. Conn. June 27, 2001). Attorney fees incurred by the consumer in a state court collection suit were recoverable FDCPA damages only if the consumer met her burden of proving that incurring the fees was caused by the FDCPA violations. The court denied actual damages for emotional distress when the consumer did not meet her burden to show that any distress that she suffered was a result of the defendants' FDCPA violations as opposed to a result of the stress of having a judgment issued against her for the debt she owed.

Thomas v. Nat'l Bus. Assistants, Inc., 1984 U.S. Dist. LEXIS 24876, 1984 WL 585309 (D. Conn. Oct. 5, 1984) (slip copy). Plaintiffs entitled to actual damages for humiliation, mental anguish or distress and the like. Couple who received notices during period of marital strain, bankruptcy, and pregnancy entitled to $200 each, although there "was no permanent injury except to strained marriage." Third plaintiff entitled to $500 where she suffered shortness of temper with family, abandoned attempt to settle financial affairs and sought bankruptcy. Fourth consumer awarded $750 to compensate for resulting perception of herself as failure as family provider, fear of government sanctions, including jail or firing, embarrassment, isolation and fear of her elderly mother's reaction to road adjuster.

Delaware

Langley v. Scanlon, 1993 U.S. Dist. LEXIS 17278 (D. Del. Feb. 5, 1993). "Where a specific act is prohibited by the FDCPA and a debt collector performs such an act, a violation of the FDCPA has occurred and consideration of other factors must be reserved until consideration of what damages are appropriate for the violation."

Smith v. Law Offices of Mitchell N. Kay, 124 B.R. 182 (D. Del. 1991). Jury award of $15,000 actual damages was grossly excessive and a new trial was ordered if the consumer did not accept the reduction of the award to $3000 actual damages. The larger award was an abuse of discretion and failed to distinguish between suffering caused by the collector and the consumers' severe distress caused by other substantial health, financial and legal problems. After lengthy analysis, the court determined that actual damages for emotional distress may be recovered under the FDCPA independent of state requirements for the tort of intentional infliction of mental distress.

Florida

Ortega v. Collectors Training Inst. of Illinois, Inc., 2011 WL 241948 (S.D. Fla. Jan. 24, 2011). Emotional distress is considered a form of actual damages under the FDCPA. While it was undisputed that the plaintiff never sought medical treatment for emotional distress, the defendant cited no cases suggesting that such a requirement exists and, in fact, another court within the circuit found that failing to seeking medical treatment, *inter alia*, did not preclude the recovery of emotional distress damages under the FDCPA. Awarding actual damages in an FDCPA case is not suitable for summary judgment.

Newsome v. Regent Asset Mgmt. Solutions, Inc., 2010 WL 3447536 (M.D. Fla. Aug. 30, 2010). The court entered a default judgment for the consumer consisting of $25,000 for a lost employment opportunity and emotional distress, $1000.00 in statutory damages, and attorney fees of $2707.50.

Rodriguez v. Florida First Fin. Group, Inc., 2009 WL 535980 (M.D. Fla. Mar. 3, 2009). The court awarded $1000 FDCPA statutory and $1000 actual damages (plus $1000 state law punitive and $1000 statutory damages) where the defendant knowingly misrepresented the identity of its agents, falsely threatened to have the plaintiff arrested, and engaged in other false and deceptive conduct.

Laufman v. Phillips & Burns, Inc., 2008 WL 190604 (M.D. Fla. Jan. 22, 2008). Emotional distress and punitive damages under state claim were supported where the consumer was upset that the debt collector threatened his eight-year-old daughter with the sheriff coming to the house.

Barker v. Tomlinson, 2006 WL 1679645 (M.D. Fla. June 7, 2006). Consumer awarded actual damages of $10,000 under both the Florida Consumer Collection Practices Act and FDCPA.

McKnight v. Benitez, 176 F. Supp. 2d 1301 (M.D. Fla. 2001). The additional attorney fees incurred by a consumer to change venue in a case filed in a judicial district unlawful under § 1692i were actual damages.

Merchant v. Nationwide Collection Serv., Inc., Clearinghouse No. 43,382 (Fla. Cir. Ct. 1988). Two plaintiffs each awarded $2500 actual damages, $1000 statutory damages and $50,000 punitive damages for late night phone calls, threats of arrest, and a third-party contact.

Georgia

Schimmel v. Slaughter, 975 F. Supp. 1481 (M.D. Ga. 1997). The collector's fee was not considered as actual damages under an unjust enrichment approach where the FDCPA violations were not related to the fee.

Florence v. Nat'l Sys., 1983 U.S. Dist. LEXIS 20344 (N.D. Ga. Oct. 14, 1983). The court awarded $4000 in actual damages.

Carrigan v. Cent. Adjustment Bureau, Inc., 502 F. Supp. 468 (N.D. Ga. 1980). Entitlement to actual damages for harassing contacts where there is no physical injury or out-of-pocket loss depends upon the availability of mental anguish damages under the state law regarding intentional infliction of mental distress. Since the consumer (a lawyer) only received a few short phone calls and his reaction was mere "indignation," $100 actual damages were awarded.

Lord v. Carragher, 270 B.R. 787 (Bankr. M.D. Ga. 1998). Where a garnishment was filed in a venue not permitted by § 1692i, the amount garnished was the consumer's actual damages.

Vidrine v. Am. Prof'l Credit, Inc., 477 S.E.2d 602 (Ga. Ct. App.

1996). The consumer may recover actual damages including emotional distress without proving the elements of the state law of intentional infliction of emotional distress.

Faust v. Texaco, 270 B.R. 310 (Bankr. M.D. Ga. 1998). Where G.C. Services violated § 1692e(1) by implying that it was vouched for by the government, the consumer was entitled to $500 for emotional distress and $1000 statutory damages for this attempt to intimidate the consumer.

Illinois

Bassett v. I.C. Sys., Inc., 2010 WL 2179175 (N.D. Ill. June 1, 2010). The consumer's allegations regarding emotional distress damages were insufficient because his conclusory statements fail to contain enough detail "to overcome the Seventh Circuit's strict standard in proving emotional damages." The facts underlying the case were not so inherently degrading as a matter of law "that it would be reasonable to infer that a person would suffer emotional distress from the defendant's action."

Clodfelter v. United Processing, Inc., 2008 WL 4225557 (C.D. Ill. Sept. 12, 2008). The court awarded $100,000 of emotional distress FDCPA actual damages following entry of default where the evidence showed that the defendants, consistent with pattern and practice evidence that the same type of misconduct conducted regarding several other consumers, made multiple unlawful third party contacts and threats of criminal prosecution to collect a $400 loan.

Davis v. Suran, 1998 WL 378420 (N.D. Ill. July 1, 1998). The legal definition of actual damages does not encompass nominal damages. Nominal damages are distinct and separate from actual injury or damages.

Holloway v. Pekay, 1996 WL 19580 (N.D. Ill. Jan. 18, 1996). Where state law authorized lender to recover costs and attorney fees in collection action and the underlying debt was not contested, the collection attorney fee recovery did not constitute actual damages for filing the collection action in an improper distant forum.

Rutyna v. Collection Accounts Terminal, Inc., Clearinghouse No. 25,556 (N.D. Ill. 1979) (excerpt of proceedings). A consumer who was a non-wage earner, a nervous person, substantially bedridden and unable to eat for three days was awarded $750 actual damages for her physical and emotional suffering calculated at $250 per day.

Indiana

Thomas v. Boscia, 2009 WL 2778105 (S.D. Ind. Aug. 28, 2009). Summary judgment dismissed the consumer's claim of actual damages since her supporting evidence was no more than "conclusory statements of emotional distress" that were insufficient "unless the facts underlying the case [unlike here] are so inherently degrading that it would be reasonable to infer the person suffered emotional distress."

Gastineau v. UMLIC VP L.L.C., 2006 WL 1131768 (S.D. Ind. Apr. 25, 2006). Plaintiff had demonstrated actual damages by showing anxiety, diminished libido, shortness of breath, fatigue, and weakness as well as loss of income attending court hearings and visiting doctors, and court expenses and mileage costs incurred successfully defending a state foreclosure action.

Louisiana

S. Siding Co. v. Raymond, 703 So. 2d 44 (La. Ct. App. 1997). Consumers suffered depression and anxiety compensable under FDCPA absent medical evidence for attorney's dun threatening civil suit on rescinded home repair contract and criminal prosecution for stopping payment on their down payment check; but award of general damages of $12,500 and $5000 to husband and wife was excessive as matter of law, with court reducing amount to $5000 and $3000; award of $1000 each in statutory damages affirmed.

Maine

Sweetland v. Stevens & James, Inc., 563 F. Supp. 2d 300 (D. Me. 2008). Default judgment in the amount of $2500 actual damages plus $250 additional damages and $3520 attorney fees and costs was entered for consumer's FDCPA claims that the debt collector had made harassing telephone calls.

Maryland

Keane v. Nat'l Bureau of Collections, Clearinghouse No. 35,923 (D. Md. 1983). The evidence was sufficient to support an award of $5000 actual damages. Neither proof of physical injury nor extreme or outrageous conduct is necessary to support damages for emotional distress under the FDCPA where the violation was intentional.

Massachusetts

In re Maxwell, 281 B.R. 101 (Bankr. D. Mass. 2002). Actual damages may include emotional distress; proof need not meet state law negligent or intentional infliction of emotional distress standards.

In re Hart, 246 B.R. 709 (Bankr. D. Mass. 2000). The consumer was entitled to $3000 damages for emotional distress caused by the FDCPA violation. He was not required to establish intentional infliction of emotional distress or actual illness as required to recover under state tort law.

Michigan

Stolicker v. Muller, Muller, Richmond, Harms, Myers, Sgroi, P.C., 2006 WL 3386546 (W.D. Mich. Nov. 22, 2006). Pursuant to § 1692k(a), members of a class action may recover actual damages without any cap.

Shoup v. Illiana Recovery Sys., Inc., 2002 U.S. Dist. LEXIS 674 (W.D. Mich. Jan. 8, 2002). Upon repossessor's default, the court awarded damages of $53,000 to owner of wrongfully repossessed car, including $12,500 as mental distress, for violations of FDCPA and state law including Michigan's conversion statute which provided for treble damages. Court also awarded $10,000 to car owner's father, and $5000 to car owner's mother for mental distress.

Minnesota

Edeh v. Midland Credit Mgmt., Inc., 2010 WL 3893604 (D. Minn. Sept. 29, 2010). The FDCPA authorizes recovery of "any actual damage," including emotional distress that was not severe.

Venes v. Prof'l Serv. Bureau, Inc., 353 N.W.2d 671 (Minn. Ct. App. 1984). Jury awarded $6000 for emotional distress resulting from repeated phone calls, abusive language and taking judgment for interest not owed. The jury's finding that conduct was outrageous, intentional, and caused severe distress was not error. Attorney fees of $3900 were properly awarded by the jury as actual damages since they were caused by having to reopen the collector's judgment in a prior suit claiming interest not owed and thus taken in violation of the FDCPA. Jury award for $1000 travel expenses to consult with lawyer to reopen prior judgment proper.

Missouri

Poniewaz v. Regent Asset Mgmt. Solutions, Inc., 2010 WL 3584368 (E.D. Mo. Sept. 7, 2010). In a default judgment, the court awarded $500 in actual damages for the mental distress caused by two brief phone calls initiated by the debt collector.

Jenkins v. Eastern Asset Mgmt., L.L.C., 2009 WL 2488029 (E.D. Mo. Aug. 12, 2009). On default, court awarded $1000 statutory damages, $2000 emotional distress damages, and $3250 fees and costs for multiple calls to place of employment threatening suit after being told plaintiff could not accept personal calls at work.

Montana

McCollough v. Johnson, Rodenburg & Lauinger, 645 F. Supp. 2d 917 (D. Mont. June 3, 2009). Jury verdict awarded consumer $250,000 in compensatory damages, $1000 FDCPA statutory damages, and $60,000 in state law punitive damages and the court awarded attorney fees in the full amount requested of over $93,000 commenting, *inter alia,* that the litigation "confers a meaningful public benefit by discouraging illegal debt collection" in the state. "[Plaintiff's] testimony, corroborated by [its] expert testimony . . . provides a legally sufficient evidentiary basis for the jury's award. [Plaintiff] testified that the lawsuit prosecuted against him 'definitely' caused him anxiety, increasing his temper, pain, adrenalin, and conflict with his wife. . . . The lawsuit caused him to spend more time 'down' in bed with severe headaches. . . . He thought that the lawsuit was 'frivolous' and 'an insult,' and he was 'being shoved around. . . .' The lawsuit 'was the straw that broke the camel's back. I got mad. I'm still mad.' "

Nevada

Anunciation v. West Capital Fin. Servs. Corp., Clearinghouse No. 50,452 (D. Nev. 1995). After entry of default and hearing on damages, the court awarded $1000 in statutory damages and $9500 in actual damages.

New Mexico

Toledo v. McNeel, Clearinghouse No. 50,433 (D.N.M. 1995). Collection attorney's letter failed to provide validation notice in violation of § 1692g and entitled plaintiff to statutory damages of $1000 and actual damages of $200. Consumer must elect between accepting $200 actual plus $1000 punitive damages for tortious debt collection, or up to treble her actual damages for unfair practices, or $200 actual damages under the FDCPA.

Vigil v. Burdge Enters., Clearinghouse No. 31,109 (D.N.M. 1981). One spouse was awarded $1013 and the other $1000.

New York

Henneberger v. Cohen & Slamowitz, L.L.P., 2010 WL 1405578 (W.D.N.Y. Mar. 31, 2010). Actual damages are intended to compensate a consumer for out-of-pocket expenses, personal humiliation, embarrassment, mental anguish, and emotional distress resulting from defendant's violation of the FDCPA.

Annis v. Eastern Asset Mgmt., L.L.C., 2010 WL 1035273 (W.D.N.Y. Mar. 18, 2010). After entry of default, the court entered judgment for $3000.00 in statutory damages, $6500.00 in actual damages, $4240.50 in attorney fees, and $410.00 in costs, for a total award of $14,150.50.

Pearce v. Ethical Asset Mgmt., Inc., 2010 WL 932597 (W.D.N.Y. Mar. 11, 2010). Actual damages of $750 awarded for one plaintiff and $1079 for the other.

Clayson v. Rubin & Rothman, L.L.C., 2010 WL 547476 (W.D.N.Y. Feb. 11, 2010). The court denied the defendant's motion for summary judgment claiming that the consumer could not sustain her claim for emotional distress damages as a matter of law on the basis of the supporting deposition testimony and affidavits of her and her mother: "Further, consumer must be permitted the opportunity to prove even nominal actual damages, even if the only evidence of such damages is her testimony." The defendant's argument that had the consumer advised it in writing that she had legal representation would have caused it to cease communication with her and would have prevented any emotional distress actual damages was without merit. Nothing in the FDCPA requires a debtor to provide written notice to a debt collector advising of such legal representation.

Mostiller v. Chase Asset Recovery Corp., 2010 WL 335023 (W.D.N.Y. Jan. 22, 2010). The court awarded $250 actual damages following the debt collector's default on the consumer's claim of false threats of legal and other action.

Shepherd v. Law Offices of Cohen & Slamowitz, L.L.P., 668 F. Supp. 2d 579 (S.D.N.Y. 2009). The attorney fees incurred by the consumer to vacate an improperly obtained default judgment in the underlying state collection action, the "additional fees to right her credit rating," and the charges that she paid to her bank in connection with the defendant's allegedly wrongful attachment of her bank account were among the recited actual damages that a Rule 68 offer would have to satisfy in order to moot the case.

Berry v. Nat'l Fin. Sys., Inc., 2009 WL 2843260 (W.D.N.Y. Aug. 27, 2009). In this FDCPA case, upon entry of default and after a hearing to establish damages, husband and wife were awarded actual damages of $3000, statutory damages of $2000, and attorney fees of $5999.

DeGeorge v. LTD Fin. Servs., L.P., 2008 WL 905913 (W.D.N.Y. Mar. 31, 2008). Defendant's motion for partial summary judgment to dismiss the plaintiff's claim for emotional distress damages were denied because the jury could find the recited evidence adequate, although admittedly "fairly weak" based on the plaintiff's and his relative's testimony as to the adverse effect the alleged misconduct had on him and the strain it allegedly caused between himself and his family members. This notwithstanding the fact that the plaintiff himself is employed as a debt collector.

Johnson v. Equifax Risk Mgmt. Servs., 2004 WL 540459 (S.D.N.Y.

Mar. 17, 2004). The consumer's wasted time and distress from responding to the collector's misconduct may be compensated as actual damages.

Sibersky v. Borah, Goldstein, Altschuler & Schwartz, P.C., 2000 U.S. Dist. LEXIS 14043 (S.D.N.Y. Sept. 22, 2000). An FDCPA complaint need not allege actual damages.

Miele v. Sid Bailey, Inc., 192 B.R. 611 (S.D.N.Y. 1996). The maximum award of $1000 statutory damages was warranted because of the collection agency's numerous communications with the consumer after being advised by the consumer and his counsel that the debt had been discharged in bankruptcy. $1153.43 actual and $60,000 punitive (for a state law claim) damages also awarded. Actual damages included tax refund intercepted to pay a student loan that had been discharged in bankruptcy and accountant fees for filing for return of the intercepted funds.

Donahue v. NFS, Inc., 751 F. Supp. 188 (W.D.N.Y. 1991). After default in a nonjury determination, actual damages were assessed against Defendant NFS, Inc. at $33.33 and Defendant Lanocha at $66.67 based on the consumer's emotional distress and apportionment between these and other collectors.

Bish v. Credit Control Sys., Inc., 1991 WL 165035 (W.D.N.Y. Aug. 14, 1991) (default judgment). Request for $500 actual damages denied where no evidence whatsoever offered of actual damages.

Read v. Amana Collection Servs., 1991 WL 165033 (W.D.N.Y. Aug. 12, 1991). Actual damages for emotional distress were not established by consumer's testimony that she was angry, tense, and forced to increase her asthma medication (which did not require a medical examination).

North Dakota

Wilhelm v. Credico, Inc., 2008 WL 5156660 (D.N.D. Dec. 5, 2008). Despite its opinion that plaintiff's claim for "inconvenience" damages was "extremely weak," court reserved the issue for the jury, after surveying "emotional distress" cases.

Bingham v. Collection Bureau, Inc., 505 F. Supp. 864 (D.N.D. 1981). $1000 actual damages were awarded to a consumer for loss of happiness, interest in housework, and sleep, and for nightmares, headaches, sensitive stomach, and crying spells, but no permanent ill effects. Her husband was awarded $100 actual damages for loss of consortium.

Ohio

Davis v. Creditors Interchange Receivable Mgmt., L.L.C., 585 F. Supp. 2d 968 (N.D. Ohio 2008). Rejecting *Costa v. Nat'l Action Fin. Servs.*, 634 F. Supp. 2d 1069 (E.D. Cal. 2007), "which required the plaintiffs to show the elements of intentional infliction of emotional distress under California law to collect emotional distress damages for an FDCPA violation," the court held that an FDCPA plaintiff need only meet the "more lenient standard for proving emotional damages" established by federal law irrespective of the rules established by state tort law.

Royster v. Pacific Creditors Ass'n, 2008 WL 4693411 (S.D. Ohio Oct. 23, 2008). On the consumer's motion for default judgment, where the complaint established that the collector breached the parties' prior settlement agreement by failing to remove derogatory information from the consumer's credit report on a non-existent debt supposedly owed by the consumer, the court awarded actual damages of $61,500, comprised of $1000 for emotional distress and $60,500 based on the 2.75% higher interest rate for a $100,000/30-year mortgage caused by the resulting lower FICO score.

Lee v. Javitch, Block & Rathbone, L.L.P., 2008 WL 1886178 (S.D. Ohio Apr. 25, 2008). The plaintiff proved "the causal link between the lack of the 'reasonable basis' and Plaintiff's resulting damages" to sustain the jury's award of economic and non-economic damages. The court rejected the defendant's contention "that higher standards applicable to intentional infliction of emotional distress damages, or the standards imported from the common law claim for 'wrongful attachment' (requiring malice or something akin to it) should apply to FDCPA claims" and instead applied the rule applicable to other federal damage claims: "An injured person's testimony alone may suffice to establish damages for emotional distress provided that she reasonably and sufficiently explains the circumstances surrounding the injury and does not rely on mere conclusory statements."

Dowling v. Litton Loan Servicing, L.P., 2008 WL 906042 (S.D. Ohio Mar. 31, 2008), *aff'd on other grounds*, 320 Fed. Appx. 442 (6th Cir. 2009). Following a successful bench trial the court awarded the plaintiff $25,000 in actual damages.

Foster v. D.B.S. Collection Agency, 463 F. Supp. 2d 783 (S.D. Ohio 2006). Court, applying the "extreme and outrageous" standard for actual damages, found a genuine issue of material fact as to whether class members could get mental distress damages.

Becker v. Montgomery, Lynch, 2003 WL 23335929 (N.D. Ohio Feb. 26, 2003). "The imposition of actual damages should be interpreted as a message to other debt collectors that such conduct is inappropriate. To not award actual damages would encourage 'a race to the bottom' as debt collectors could operate in an inappropriate manner with little consequence."

Boyce v. Attorney's Dispatch Serv., 1999 U.S. Dist. LEXIS 12970 (S.D. Ohio Apr. 27, 1999). The court noted that the defendants' violations (threats of criminal prosecution), were "the most egregious conduct of any defendant" in an FDCPA action previously before the court. It awarded the two newlywed, pregnant consumers $10,000 actual damages for nausea and sleeplessness, but not the full amount requested, since soon after the egregious conduct began, the consumers engaged a lawyer who could "still their fears."

Lamb v. M & M Assoc., 1998 WL 34288694 (S.D. Ohio Sept. 1, 1998). If the telephone conversation in question constituted a violation of the FDCPA, the consumer was entitled to recover compensatory damages for any harm she suffered as a direct and proximate result thereof.

Minick v. First Fed. Credit Control, Inc., 1981 U.S. Dist. LEXIS 18622 (N.D. Ohio June 9, 1981). Damages other than emotional distress are not necessary to state a cause of action.

Oregon

Clark v. Quick Collect, Inc., 2006 WL 572157 (D. Or. Mar. 6, 2006). Plaintiff was awarded $4000 actual damages and $1000 in statutory damages for abusive collection.

Hooper v. Capital Credit & Collection Servs., Inc., 2005 WL 2297062 (D. Or. Sept. 20, 2005). Following a jury trial, which resulted in a $1570 actual damage award against the collection agency and a defense verdict for the agency's named employee, the court denied any additional statutory damages, awarded the plaintiff $17,467 in attorney fees, and denied any fees to the exonerated employee since the claims against her were not "brought in bad faith and for the purpose of harassment."

Grassley v. Debt Collectors, Inc., 1992 U.S. Dist. LEXIS 22782 (D. Or. Dec. 14, 1992). Under the FDCPA actual damages for emotional distress may be proved independently of the state law requirements of proof for the tort of intentional infliction of emotional distress. Although the collector's violations of the FDCPA caused the debtor's distress, actual damages were "quite small"—$1000 per plaintiff in light of preexisting health, marital and financial problems.

Baker v. G.C. Servs. Corp., Clearinghouse No. 31,230 (D. Or. 1981), *aff'd*, 677 F.2d 775 (9th Cir. 1982). Claim for general damages for emotional distress was denied as "belated and unfounded" although the court recognized this was a proper element of general damages, unlike the consumer's claim for $1.25 in parking and gasoline expenses to visit an attorney's office.

Lambert v. Nat'l Credit Bureau, Inc., 1981 U.S. Dist. LEXIS 18623 (D. Or. Apr. 8, 1981). Actual damages of $500 were awarded where the consumer cried upon receiving the dunning letter, actually feared suit, and worried and was sleepless for two days.

Dixon v. United Adjusters, Inc., 1981 U.S. Dist. LEXIS 18392 (D. Or. Feb. 19, 1981). The debtor may recover statutory damages in the absence of proof of actual damages.

Pennsylvania

Lavelle v. Phoenix Acquisition Group, L.L.C., 2010 WL 5014347 (M.D. Pa. Dec. 3, 2010). Upon a default judgment, consumer was awarded actual damages in the amount of $2500 to compensate her for the exacerbation of her anxiety, the emotional trauma, embarrassment, and humiliation caused by the calls to her home and workplace.

McNally v. Client Servs., Inc., 2008 WL 2397489 (W.D. Pa. June 11, 2008), *report and recommendation adopted*, 2008 WL 2987199 (W.D. Pa. July 31, 2008). Plaintiff's credible testimony alone can support emotional distress actual damages.

O'Brien v. Valley Forge Specialized Educ. Servs., 2004 WL 2580773 (E.D. Pa. Nov. 10, 2004). In *dicta* the court considered restitution of wrongfully taken funds as FDCPA actual damages.

Wenrich v. Robert E. Cole, P.C., 2000 U.S. Dist. LEXIS 18687 (E.D. Pa. Dec. 22, 2000). Damages for emotional distress may be recovered under the FDCPA without proving the elements of a state tort.

Littles v. Lieberman, 90 B.R. 700 (E.D. Pa. 1988). Nominal actual damages of $1 awarded where evidence of actual harm was not strong, and the collector was not given an opportunity to participate in the settlement of a related FDCPA claim against another collector.

Crossley v. Lieberman, 90 B.R. 682 (E.D. Pa. 1988), *aff'd*, 868 F.2d 566 (3d Cir. 1989). District court increased bankruptcy judge's award of $100 to $1000 actual damages for a letter falsely threatening imminent suit where the impoverished, seventy-year-old consumer, desperately trying to maintain her independence, lost sleep and weight, immediately called the collection lawyer and her lawyer, borrowed money and quit her job to cash in her pension.

In re Belile, 209 B.R. 658 (Bankr. E.D. Pa. 1997). The consumer was awarded actual damages of $100 against each of two defendants, statutory damages of $100 and $750, and treble state damages of $300.

In re Littles, 75 B.R. 240 (Bankr. E.D. Pa. 1987), *rev'd on other grounds*, 90 B.R. 700 (E.D. Pa. 1988). Emotional distress under FDCPA need not meet the requirements for tortious infliction of emotional distress.

South Carolina

Meredith v. Pathfinders Detective & Recovery, Inc., 1983 U.S. Dist. LEXIS 11860, 20367 (D.S.C. Nov. 9, 1983). Where a repossession company repossessed the consumer's car worth $7000 in violation of § 1692f(6) causing emotional distress and a loss of transportation, the court awarded $7500 in actual damages and $7500 punitive damages in connection with a pendent, common law conversion claim.

South Dakota

Ewing v. Messerli, Clearinghouse No. 44,331 (D.S.D. 1988). After a bench trial in which the collector failed to appear or defend, the consumer was awarded $5000 "punitive" or statutory damages for five intentional and separate violations in three communications: $2340 actual damages (for pain and suffering, mental anguish, loss of income and medical expenses) for one spouse and $611 (loss of income and consortium, pain and suffering, transportation expenses) for other spouse, and $3948.85 attorney fees for a total $11,899.85 liability.

Tennessee

Sewell v. Allied Interstate, Inc., 2011 WL 32209 (E.D. Tenn. Jan. 5, 2011). Debt collector may raise the "speculation" defense to the plaintiffs' request for actual damages.

Greene v. Rash, Curtis & Assoc., 89 F.R.D. 314 (E.D. Tenn. 1980). Noting the lack of a definition of the term "actual damages," the lack of legislative history on its meaning, the purposes and provisions of the FDCPA, and interpretations of the term in other chapters of the Consumer Credit Protection Act, the judge reversed the magistrate and postponed until trial the issue of whether damages related to mental anguish were recoverable under FDCPA in the absence of physical injury. Where undisputed medical evidence showed no causal link between plaintiff's aggravated heart problems and defendant's conduct, summary judgment was granted to the defendant on that part of the claim.

Texas

Toomer v. Alliance Receivables Mgmt., Inc., 2010 WL 5071778 (W.D. Tex. Dec. 9, 2010). Where the parties agreed to voluntary arbitration, the arbitrator awarded the consumer $25,000 in actual FDCPA damages for emotional distress finding that only part of her distress was related to the debt collection.

Bullock v. Abbott & Ross Credit Servs., L.L.C., 2009 WL 4598330 (W.D. Tex. Dec. 3, 2009). Recommended a default judgment award of $2000 actual damages for mental anguish.

McNeill v. Graham, Bright & Smith, P.C., 2006 WL 1489502 (N.D. Tex. May 26, 2006). The consumer incurred, and the court awarded actual damages in connection with the defendant's violation of the FDCPA distant forum provision of $64, comprised of the costs of filing in state court a *pro se* motion to transfer venue and of filing a consumer complaint with the state consumer protection agency.

In re Eastman, 419 B.R. 711 (Bankr. W.D. Tex. 2009). Denied actual damages for loss of military career as speculative and for emotional distress for lack of evidence.

Chislum v. Home Owners Funding Corp., 803 S.W.2d 800 (Tex. App. 1991). State trial court, which held that consumer was not damaged by violations of FDCPA deemed admitted, and thus not entitled to actual or statutory damages, was affirmed by state appellate court.

Virginia

Carter v. Countrywide Home Loans, Inc., 2009 WL 1010851 (E.D. Va. Apr. 14, 2009). Section 1692k allows for recovery of emotional distress damages.

McHugh v. Check Investors, Inc., 2003 WL 21283288 (W.D. Va. May 21, 2003). On damage hearing following entry of default, court awarded consumer maximum statutory damages of $1000 and emotional distress damages of over $10,000 for series of abusive and threatening communications.

Washington

Heib v. Arches Fin., 2008 WL 4601602 (E.D. Wash. Oct. 14, 2008). In this FDCPA action, actual damages of $151,900 were awarded against defendants plus costs and attorney fees for abusive debt collection tactics against a husband and wife, both of whom had heart attacks in connection with their resulting distress.

Wisconsin

Crass v. Marval & Assocs. L.L.C., 2010 WL 2104174 (E.D. Wis. May 25, 2010). Upon entry of default in this FDCPA case, the court denied the consumer's request for $3500 in actual damages because she failed to provide a reasonably detailed explanation of the emotional injuries suffered.

Suszka v. Capital Collections, L.L.C., 2009 WL 959798 (E.D. Wis. Apr. 8, 2009). Plaintiff awarded $1000 statutory damages, $2380 fees and costs upon defendant's default, but no actual damages. Conclusory allegations of an emotional injury were insufficient to establish damages, and the court did not consider defendant's conduct so inherently degrading that emotional distress could be reasonably inferred.

K.3.1.2 Statutory Damages in Individual Actions

Ellis v. Solomon & Solomon, P.C., 591 F.3d 130 (2d Cir. 2010). "To recover damages under the FDCPA, a consumer does not need to show intentional conduct on the part of the debt collector."

Edwards v. Niagara Credit Solutions, Inc., 584 F.3d 1350 (11th Cir. 2009). The court awarded the maximum $1000 statutory damages for the defendant's §§ 1692d(6) and 1692e(11) violations since the misconduct was "measured and calculated" as it was undertaken in conformity with "company policy."

Beaudry v. TeleCheck Servs., Inc., 579 F.3d 702 (6th Cir. 2009). FCRA case held that consumer may recover statutory damages if the debt collector violates the FDCPA, even if the consumer suffered no actual damages.

Lester E. Cox Med. Ctr. v. Huntsman, 408 F.3d 989 (8th Cir. 2005). The district court properly exercised its discretion to award nominal damages of $1 and no statutory damages where the violation was not frequent, persistent, or intentional, and minor in nature.

King v. International Data Servs. (IDS), 100 Fed. Appx. 681 (9th Cir. 2004). The district court did not abuse its discretion in awarding maximum statutory damages pursuant to § 1692k(a)(2)(A).

Kobs v. Arrow Serv. Bureau, Inc., 134 F.3d 893 (7th Cir. 1998). The FDCPA provided for trial by jury in determining statutory damages. The word "court," in § 1692k(a)(2)(A) authorizing "such additional damages as the court may allow," should be interpreted to permit trial by both judge and jury, finding that such an interpretation avoided the serious constitutional issues that would be raised under the Seventh Amendment if the Act was construed to prohibit trial by jury.

Bartlett v. Heibl, 128 F.3d 497 (7th Cir. 1997). A consumer's admission that he did not read the collection letter violating § 1692g did not affect his claim for statutory damages but would have defeated a claim for actual damages if they had been sought.

Chauncey v. JDR Recovery Corp., 118 F.3d 516 (7th Cir. 1997). Statutory damages of $1000 were awarded to plaintiff plus $1475 in attorney fees by the district court.

Anunciation v. West Capital Fin. Servs. Corp., 97 F.3d 1458 (9th Cir. 1996) (text at 1996 WL 534049). Plaintiff filed and properly served a complaint for violation of FDCPA, then filed an amended complaint with invasion of privacy claims but failed to serve a summons with it. The defendant defaulted. The court awarded $1000 statutory damages, actual damages of $9500, and $5289 costs and attorneys fees for obtaining the default judgment. On appeal the court held there was personal jurisdiction over defendant for all causes of action in the properly served initial complaint. Additional attorney fees were to be awarded to the consumer for the appeal.

Russell v. Equifax A.R.S., 74 F.3d 30 (2d Cir. 1996). FDCPA imposes strict liability; thus, the consumer need not have shown intentional conduct by the collector to prove damages.

Wright v. Fin. Serv., Inc., 22 F.3d 647 (6th Cir. 1994). Executrix of deceased consumer's estate was limited to total statutory damages of $1000 for the debt collector's multiple FDCPA violations rather than $1000 for each violation.

Bentley v. Great Lakes Collection Bureau, 6 F.3d 60 (2d Cir. 1993). A single violation is sufficient to establish liability under the FDCPA. "The FDCPA is a strict liability statute, . . . and the degree of a defendant's culpability may only be considered in computing damages."

Clomon v. Jackson, 988 F.2d 1314 (2d Cir. 1993) "The decision on whether to award 'additional damages' and on the size of any such award is committed to the sound discretion of the district court."

Harper v. Better Bus. Servs., Inc., 961 F.2d 1561 (11th Cir. 1992). FDCPA authorizes statutory damages up to $1000 per action, not per violation, communication, or debt.

Pipiles v. Credit Bureau, Inc., 886 F.2d 22 (2d Cir. 1989). Court awarded attorney fees and costs, but no statutory damages, where the collector did not intend to deceive or harass the consumer and there was no evidence that the collector's violations were frequent or persistent.

Emanuel v. Am. Credit Exch., 870 F.2d 805 (2d Cir. 1989). No statutory damages awarded for failure to include part of the § 1692e(11) notice, since the noncompliance was not frequent, persistent or intentional, and no actual damages demonstrated.

Crossley v. Lieberman, 868 F.2d 566 (3d Cir. 1989). Awarding $1000 was appropriate for the egregious tactics of a lawyer trying to scare the consumer into paying a debt and then denying the nature of his business and the plain language of the letter when sued under the FDCPA.

Baker v. G.C. Servs. Corp., 677 F.2d 775 (9th Cir. 1982). Statutory damages are available without proof of actual damages. $100 in statutory damages were awarded.

Alabama

In re Turner, 2010 WL 3211030 (M.D. Ala. Aug. 13, 2010). The court remanded to the bankruptcy court its statutory damage recommendation for an explanation of its summary exercise of discretion in awarding the maximum $1000 statutory damages.

In re Lisenby, 2006 WL 802392 (Bankr. M.D. Ala. Feb. 22, 2006). Debt collector and its attorneys were held liable for violation of both the bankruptcy automatic stay and the FDCPA for continuing to withdraw funds from the consumer's bank account after they were notified of the bankruptcy filing, for which violations the court awarded the consumer actual damages of $287.50, $1000 punitive damages for violation of the automatic stay, $1000 additional FDCPA damages, plus fees and costs.

In re Young, 280 B.R. 864 (Bankr. S.D. Ala. 2001). Consumer awarded $1000 where the student loan collector violated the FDCPA by imposing an administrative garnishment without responding to a § 1692g dispute letter.

Arizona

Perkons v. American Acceptance, L.L.C., 2010 WL 4922916 (D. Ariz. Nov. 29, 2010). On the motion for default judgment against the debt collector involving multiple violations of the FDCPA, the plaintiff was awarded statutory damages of $1000.

Hill v. First Integral Recovery, L.L.C., 2009 WL 3353012 (D. Ariz. Oct. 16, 2009). Default judgment was granted the consumer awarding $1000 in FDCPA statutory damages.

California

Carrizosa v. Stassinos, 2010 WL 4393900 (N.D. Cal. Oct. 29, 2010). The defendants were jointly and severally liable for $1000 statutory damages to each plaintiff.

Morisaki v. Davenport, Allen & Malone, Inc., 2010 WL 3341566 (E.D. Cal. Aug. 23, 2010). Statutory damages may be awarded cumulatively under both the FDCPA and the RFDCPA (Rosenthal Act).

Bretana v. International Collection Corp., 2010 WL 1221925 (N.D. Cal. Mar. 24, 2010). The court found that full statutory damages were appropriate where the defendants had not put in place any system or procedure to protect against errors in the debt collection process, sent multiple letters to the consumer citing liability for interest and fees that did not apply, and improperly sued the consumer in a California state court. "These actions show a persistence of improper collection techniques, which Defendants easily could have prevented."

Jamal v. Thompson & Assocs., P.C., 2010 WL 678925 (N.D. Cal. Feb. 25, 2010). Since only one violation was well-pleaded, court awarded statutory damages of $300 under FDCPA and $300 under state law on default.

Brablec v. Paul Coleman & Assocs. P.C., 2010 WL 235062 (E.D. Cal. Jan. 21, 2010). The court awarded $1000 FDCPA statutory damages following the debt collection law firm's default on the consumer's claim alleging harassing telephone calls and threats of legal action resulting in severe emotional distress.

Molina v. Creditors Specialty Serv. Inc., 2010 WL 235042 (E.D. Cal. Jan. 21, 2010). The court awarded $1000 FDCPA statutory damages plus fees and costs following the debt collector's default on the consumer's claim of harassing telephone calls and false threats of legal action.

Jones v. Morgan Stone Assocs., 2010 WL 55884 (N.D. Cal. Jan. 4, 2010). $2000 statutory damages at $1000 per count awarded on default judgment.

Riley v. Giguiere, 631 F. Supp. 2d 1295 (E.D. Cal. 2009). For the purpose of determining if defendant's acts violated §§ 1692d and 1692f, and for the purpose of award of maximum statutory damages of $1000, which is awarded per action and not per violation, several acts of defendant, including some acts outside of the statute of limitations, were viewed as a single course of conduct.

Dabu v. Becks Creek Indus., 2009 WL 5178263 (N.D. Cal. Dec. 22, 2009). Consumer's motion for default judgment was granted awarding $2000 in statutory damages ($1000 per FDCPA and $1000 per Rosenthal Act).

Cruz v. Int'l Collection Corp., 2009 WL 5108486 (N.D. Cal. Dec. 18, 2009). Consumer's motion to alter or amend judgment was granted to award plaintiff $1000 in damages as well as reasonable attorney fees and costs.

Robertson v. Richard J. Boudreau & Assocs., L.L.C., 2009 WL 5108479 (N.D. Cal. Dec. 18, 2009). Awarded $1000 under the FDCPA and $1000 under the Rosenthal Act.

Harrington v. Creditors Specialty Serv., Inc., 2009 WL 1992206 (E.D. Cal. July 8, 2009). Default judgment entered, as requested for both FDCPA and Rosenthal Act violations, of statutory damages in the total amount of $2000, fees in the amount of $3029, and costs of $400, arising from the defendant's false threat of suit and garnishment in violation of § 1692e(5).

Basinger-Lopez v. Tracy Paul & Assocs., 2009 WL 1948832 (N.D. Cal. July 6, 2009). Maximum $1000 statutory damages awarded on default judgment.

Hartung v. J.D. Byrider, Inc., 2009 WL 1876690 (E.D. Cal. June 26, 2009). The report recommended entry of default judgment for the consumer in the amount of $1000 in FDCPA statutory damages.

Bankston v. PhyCom Corp., 2008 WL 4412252 (N.D. Cal. Sept. 25, 2008). On an opposed motion to set FDCPA damages following entry of default, the court awarded $1000 in statutory damages—$500 each for two separate violations, one for falsely threatening to sue and the other for failing to disclose in the initial dun that a formal dispute must be in writing.

Miller v. Midland Funding L.L.C., 2008 WL 4093004 (C.D. Cal. Sept. 4, 2008), *vacated in part on other grounds,* 2008 WL 5003042 (C.D. Cal. Nov. 20, 2008). The court found that FDCPA statutory damages were limited to up to $1000 per lawsuit, not $1000 per defendant, and having accepted one defendant's offer of judgment of $1000 plaintiff had no further statutory damages claims against the other defendants.

Napier v. Titan Mgmt. Servs., L.L.C., 2008 WL 2949274 (N.D. Cal. July 25, 2008). In this FDCPA action default judgment was entered against the debt collector for statutory damages of $500.

Lowe v. Elite Recovery Solutions L.P., 2008 WL 324777 (E.D. Cal. Feb. 5, 2008). FDCPA statutory damages are limited to $1000 per action, not $1000 per defendant.

Costa v. Nat'l Action Fin. Servs., 634 F. Supp. 2d 1069 (E.D. Cal. 2007). Statutory damages in the amount of $1000 were awarded to the consumer for the debt collector's violation of §§ 1692d(6) and 1692e(11).

Masuda v. Thomas Richards & Co., 759 F. Supp. 1456 (C.D. Cal. 1991). Statutory damages of $1000 were awarded, but the court did not decide whether multiple awards could be made.

Colorado

O'Connor v. Check Rite, 973 F. Supp. 1010 (D. Colo. 1997). Where the noncompliance with the FDCPA was merely technical and neither frequent, persistent, nor intentional, no statutory damages were awarded.

Connecticut

Ellis v. Solomon & Solomon, P.C., 599 F. Supp. 2d 298 (D. Conn. 2009). Based upon the debt collectors' filing and service of collection suits within the thirty-day validation period, the court determined that the frequency and persistence of defendants' conduct existed such that the maximum statutory damages of $1000 should be awarded.

Krueger v. Ellis, Crosby & Assocs., Inc., 2006 WL 3791402 (D. Conn. Nov. 9, 2006). Plaintiff was awarded the maximum statutory damages for the failure to have a license, since lack of a license potentially has more widespread illegality. Statutory damages awards do not require proof of actual injury.

Evanauskas v. Strumpf, 2001 U.S. Dist. LEXIS 14326 (D. Conn. June 27, 2001). A single plaintiff's FDCPA statutory damages are limited to $1000 per action, not $1000 per defendant. In this case, the court awarded $750 in statutory damages based on its assessment of the factors recited in § 1692k(b), notwithstanding absence of any actual damage award.

Madonna v. Acad. Collection Serv., Inc., 1997 WL 530101 (D. Conn. Aug. 12, 1997). No additional damages warranted where collector corrected the isolated misrepresentation in its subsequent letter.

Cirkot v. Diversified Fin. Sys., 839 F. Supp. 941 (D. Conn. 1993). Only one violation need be shown to recover under the FDCPA.

Austin v. Great Lakes Collection Bureau, Inc., 834 F. Supp. 557 (D. Conn. 1993). A single violation of the FDCPA is sufficient to establish liability.

Kimberly v. Great Lakes Collection Bureau, Inc., 1993 WL 13651243 (D. Conn. June 2, 1993). The form demand letter was sent from the defendant company, computer generated, and dispatched under the name of a person, identified in the letter as "Attorney At Law," and "Corporate Counsel" for defendant. That communication, obviously suggesting that the dunning letter was from an attorney and had received her personal attention, is precisely the misleading mass mailing technique condemned in *Clomon v. Jackson*. Because that form communication was plainly fashioned as a matter of company policy, plaintiff is clearly and properly entitled to the maximum $1000 in statutory "additional" damages, together with costs and a reasonable attorney fee.

Bishop v. Nat'l Accounts Sys., Inc., Clearinghouse No. 49,175 (D. Conn. 1993). Showing of only one false or misleading representation is sufficient to support a finding of liability, as the FDCPA is a strict liability statute.

Latella v. Atl. Advisors, Inc., 1992 U.S. Dist. LEXIS 22849 (D. Conn. May 11, 1992). The FDCPA is a strict liability statute requiring proof of only one violation for entry of summary judgment in favor of the consumer.

Kizer v. Am. Credit Collection, Clearinghouse No. 45,928 (D. Conn. 1991). Maximum statutory damage of $1000 justified by thinly veiled threat that the consumer may not receive prompt medical care.

Woolfolk v. Van Ru Credit Corp., 783 F. Supp. 724 (D. Conn. 1990). An award of actual damages is not a prerequisite to statutory damages.

Cacace v. Lucas, 775 F. Supp. 502 (D. Conn. 1990). Maximum statutory damages of $1000 awarded against an attorney who violated the Act in several respects and continued to use the violative collection letter after its impropriety was brought to his attention.

Woolfolk v. Rubin, 1990 U.S. Dist. LEXIS 20964 (D. Conn. Feb. 2, 1990). Full $1000 FDCPA statutory damages awarded against attorney for the failure to provide § 1692e(11) notices and for threatening to sue without authority, intent, or capability. *Emanuel* did not require actual damages before statutory damages may be awarded.

Traverso v. Sharinn, Clearinghouse No. 44,332 (D. Conn. 1989). Statutory damages of $1000 awarded for failure to make the disclosures required by § 1692e(11).

Thomas v. Nat'l Bus. Assistants, Inc., 1984 U.S. Dist. LEXIS 24876, 1984 WL 585309 (D. Conn. Oct. 5, 1984) (slip copy). In consolidated cases against the same collector for the same activities, $500 statutory damages were awarded to two plaintiffs and $250 to two others. Court considered that each letter was flawed, the egregiousness of false threat to send out "road adjuster," and deliberate writing of validation notice to obscure statutory purpose.

Delaware

Langley v. Scanlon, 1993 U.S. Dist. LEXIS 17278 (D. Del. Feb. 5, 1993). "Where a specific act is prohibited by the FDCPA and a debt collector performs such an act, a violation of the FDCPA has occurred and consideration of other factors must be reserved until consideration of what damages are appropriate for the violation."

Anthes v. Transworld Sys., Inc., 765 F. Supp. 162 (D. Del. 1991). Collection agency was not responsible for alleged violations of FDCPA found in its attorney's correspondence.

Beattie v. D.M. Collections, Inc., 754 F. Supp. 383 (D. Del. 1991). Section 1692k(a)(2)(A) provides for a single recovery for statutory damages of up to $1000 per plaintiff, per lawsuit.

Smith v. Law Offices of Mitchell N. Kay, 124 B.R. 182 (D. Del. 1991). A default judgment was entered against a law firm which failed to respond to an FDCPA complaint, and a jury trial on actual and statutory damages was ordered. Upon granting a new trial on the basis of an excessive jury verdict for actual damages, the court held that the issue of statutory damages should be retried since the two were not separate and distinct issues. Jury awarded $15,000 actual damages (remitted to $3000 later) and the maximum $1000 statutory damages, and the court awarded $1365 attorney fees after a default judgment and uncontested trial on damages.

District of Columbia

Bard v. W.J. Cohan, Ltd., 43 Antitrust & Trade Reg. Rep. (BNA) 695 (D.D.C. 1982) (default judgment). Court declined to determine whether consumer could recover the maximum statutory award for each violation of the Act, instead awarding $400 for the six violations.

Florida

Sampson v. Brewer, Michaels & Kane, L.L.C., 2010 WL 2432084 (M.D. Fla. May 26, 2010). Although the record was "sparse, in view of the verified allegation that the calls were 'constant and continuous,'" the court found an award of $1000 to be appropriate in this default judgment.

Beeders v. Gulf Coast Collection Bureau, 632 F. Supp. 2d 1125 (M.D. Fla. 2009). Where the consumer filed multiple FDCPA lawsuits, one for each identical telephone message left, the lawsuits were joined into a single action with statutory damages limited up to $1000 pursuant to § 1692k. "These claims, which seek the same remedy and share the same nucleus of operative fact, are parts of the same cause of action and, therefore, should be joined in the same suit as separate claims within the same cause of action."

Rodriguez v. Florida First Fin. Group, Inc., 2009 WL 535980 (M.D. Fla. Mar. 3, 2009). The court awarded $1000 FDCPA statutory damages and $1000 actual damages (plus $1000 state law punitive and $1000 statutory damages) where the defendant knowingly misrepresented the identity of its agents, falsely threatened to have the plaintiff arrested, and engaged in other false and deceptive conduct.

Ugarte v. Sunset Constr., Inc., 2008 WL 4723600 (M.D. Fla. Oct. 21, 2008). The consumer was awarded $1000 statutory damages for the debt collector's violation of the FDCPA and $1000 statutory damages for the debt collector's violation of the Florida Consumer Collection Practices Act.

Barker v. Tomlinson, 2006 WL 1679645 (M.D. Fla. June 7, 2006). Plaintiff was awarded damages in the amount of $22,000 under the Florida Consumer Collection Practices Act (FCCPA) and the federal Fair Debt Collection Practices Act (FDCPA), including: statutory damages of $1000 under the FCCPA; statutory damages of $1000 under the FDCPA; actual damages of $10,000 under both the FCCPA and FDCPA; and punitive damages of $10,000 under the FCCPA.

Shorr v. Am. Collection Sys., Inc., Clearinghouse No. 29,301 (S.D. Fla. 1980) (default judgment). Statutory damages of $1000 plus $585 attorney fees to legal services program awarded.

Merchant v. Nationwide Collection Serv., Inc., Clearinghouse No. 43,382 (Fla. Cir. Ct. 1988). Two plaintiffs each awarded $2500 actual damages, $1000 statutory damages and $50,000 punitive damages for late night phone calls, threats of arrest, and a third-party contact.

Georgia

Gilmore v. Account Mgmt., Inc., 2009 WL 2848278 (N.D. Ga. Apr. 27, 2009). After entry of default the magistrate judge recommended an award of $1000 as FDCPA statutory damages.

Schimmel v. Slaughter, 975 F. Supp. 1357 (M.D. Ga. 1997). Although a single violation of the FDCPA establishes liability, the number and extent of violations are relevant to damages, and court therefore will consider each allegation of separate violations.

Harper v. Better Bus. Servs., Inc., 768 F. Supp. 817 (N.D. Ga. 1991) (default judgment), *aff'd*, 961 F.2d 1561 (11th Cir. 1992). $1000 statutory damages awarded for seven violations of the FDCPA, including misrepresenting that there was judgment, misrepresenting liability for attorney fees and contacting a consumer known to be represented by a lawyer. Multiple statutory damages in excess of $1000 may not be awarded for multiple violations.

Hollis v. Roberts, Clearinghouse No. 46,784 (N.D. Ga. 1991). Having ruled in another case that the award of statutory damages may not exceed $1000 regardless of the number of violations, the court held that the FDCPA provides for a maximum statutory damages of $1000 per debt. Statutory damages of $1500 were awarded, $750 for each of two debts.

Phillips v. Stokes & McAtee, Clearinghouse No. 47,747A (N.D. Ga. 1991). Statutory damages were limited in this action, where only one communication was in issue, to $1000, but no ruling as to whether repeated communications may result in an award of statutory damages for each infraction. Statutory damages of $500 were awarded for falsely threatening suit and failing to include the notice required by § 1692e(11).

Yelvington v. Buckner, Clearinghouse No. 36,581 (N.D. Ga. 1984). Statutory damages of $1000 awarded to each of two plaintiffs based upon the nature, frequency, persistence and intentionality of the violations.

Florence v. Nat'l Sys., 1983 U.S. Dist. LEXIS 20344 (N.D. Ga. Oct. 14, 1983). The court awarded $4000 in statutory damages against a single collector for multiple FDCPA violations while collecting a single debt (although the collector mistakenly believed there were two debts) from a single consumer in consideration of the frequency, persistence and nature of the collector's noncompliance.

Zoeckler v. Credit Claims & Collections, Inc., 1983 U.S. Dist. LEXIS 20364 (N.D. Ga. Jan. 19, 1983). Actual damages are not required to recover statutory damages. In cases of aggravated or persistently illegal practices, the full $1000 of statutory damages should be awarded. In other cases, the court has discretion to award nothing or an amount less than $1000. In this case, $500 statutory damages was an appropriate deterrent considering it involved a single collection letter, the collector ceased collection efforts when it was informed the creditor had been paid, and the consumer's suffering was indignation rather than emotional or physical injury.

Whatley v. Universal Collection Bureau, Inc., 525 F. Supp. 1204 (N.D. Ga. 1981). The parties stipulated that statutory damages are limited to one award of $1000 to each plaintiff. Not just a "consumer" (a person allegedly indebted), but "any person" harmed by a violation (the parents of the consumer in this case) has standing under the FDCPA for damages.

Carrigan v. Cent. Adjustment Bureau, Inc., 502 F. Supp. 468 (N.D. Ga. 1980). The court awarded $250 statutory damages to the consumer (a lawyer) considering the violation occurred in the first year of the Act, the absence of specific intent to injure, the limited nature of the contact, and the collector's ready access to legal counsel. $500 statutory damages on a pendent state claim and attorneys fees were also awarded.

Faust v. Texaco, 270 B.R. 310 (Bankr. M.D. Ga. 1998). Where G.C. Services violated § 1692e(1) by implying that it was vouched for by the government, the consumer was entitled to $500 for emotional distress and $1000 statutory damages for this attempt to intimidate the consumer.

Hawaii

Sakuma v. First Nat'l Credit Bureau, 1989 U.S. Dist. LEXIS 19120 (D. Haw. Nov. 15, 1989). FDCPA damages of $1034 awarded for two notice violations and $1000 minimum UDAP damages awarded on a pendent state claim. Attorney fees awarded and settled for $12,500 to legal aid.

Illinois

Donnelly v. NCO Fin. Sys., Inc., 263 F.R.D. 500 (N.D. Ill. 2009). Section 1692k(c) frequency and persistence of noncompliance in an individual action does not relate to other consumers.

Clodfelter v. United Processing, Inc., 2008 WL 4225557 (C.D. Ill. Sept. 12, 2008). The court awarded $1000 in FDCPA statutory damages (plus $250,000 in state law-based punitive damages) following entry of default where the evidence showed that the defendants, consistent with pattern and practice evidence that the same type of misconduct conducted regarding several other consumers, made multiple unlawful third party contacts and threats of criminal prosecution to collect a $400 loan.

Francis v. Snyder, 2006 WL 1236052 (N.D. Ill. May 4, 2006). Maximum statutory damages awarded against attorney who committed two letter violations and did not use the safe harbor language. Attorney fees reduced for block billing and vague entries.

Gammon v. G.C. Servs. Ltd. P'ship, 162 F.R.D. 313 (N.D. Ill. 1995). Where the FDCPA plaintiff prevailed on issue of liability, statutory damages flowed from the award of declaratory relief.

Altergott v. Modern Collection Techniques, 1994 WL 319229 (N.D. Ill. June 23, 1994). Where none of the violations of the FDCPA were egregious, the tone and substance of the offending letters was not particularly threatening or overreaching, and where the ownership of the debt collection agency had changed hands since the offending letters were sent out, the court awarded the consumer $300 in statutory damages.

Strange v. Wexler, 796 F. Supp. 1117 (N.D. Ill. 1992). "One purpose of statutory damages is to create an incentive to obey the law."

Rutyna v. Collection Accounts Terminal, Inc., Clearinghouse No. 25,556 (N.D. Ill. 1979) (excerpt of proceedings). Finding the violations not the most egregious, the court awarded $500 statutory damages noting that anything less would not deter violations.

Indiana

Owens v. Howe, 365 F. Supp. 2d 942 (N.D. Ind. 2005). After the consumer settled for $1000 in statutory damages for five violations, the court awarded attorney fees in the amount of $12,037.50 and costs of $534.13.

Hill v. Priority Fin. Servs., Inc., 2001 U.S. Dist. LEXIS 16900 (S.D. Ind. Sept. 28, 2001). Consumers may be entitled to damages under the FDCPA regardless of actual harm.

Kansas

Whayne v. U.S. Dep't of Educ., 915 F. Supp. 1143 (D. Kan. 1996). Statutory damages of $500,000 or one percent of debt collector's net worth were only available in class actions.

Clark's Jewelers v. Humble, 823 P.2d 818 (Kan. Ct. App. 1991). In awarding statutory damages the court must consider the frequency and persistence of noncompliance, the nature of the noncompliance, and the extent to which the noncompliance was intentional.

Louisiana

McDaniel v. Asset Retrieval, Inc., 1996 WL 7001 (E.D. La. Jan. 5, 1996). The court awarded the consumer FDCPA statutory damages of $1000 on a default judgment. No actual damages were awarded as plaintiff's complaint did not request any, and the motion for default judgment did not specify any. The court found that the maximum statutory damages were per proceeding and not per violation.

Byes v. Credit Bureau Enters., Inc., 1995 WL 540235 (E.D. La. Sept. 11, 1995). Discovery of debt collector's practices regarding persons other than plaintiff was not relevant to the issue of additional damages; nothing in § 1692k(b)(1) suggests that additional damages may be based on anything other than debt collector's conduct toward the plaintiff.

S. Siding Co. v. Raymond, 703 So. 2d 44 (La. Ct. App. 1997). General damages of $12,500 and $5000 to husband and wife was excessive as matter of law, with court reducing amount to $5000 and $3000; award of $1000 each in statutory damages affirmed.

Maryland

Keane v. Nat'l Bureau of Collections, Clearinghouse No. 35,923 (D. Md. 1983). It was unnecessary to determine whether multiple violations of the FDCPA by a collection agency and its employee with regard to a single plaintiff and a single debt would support multiple awards of statutory damages since the jury awarded $1000 statutory damages for the defendants' several misrepresentations that she knew the whereabouts of her ex-husband.

Michigan

Richard v. Oak Tree Group Inc., 614 F. Supp. 2d 814 (W.D. Mich. 2008). The FDCPA does not require proof of actual damages to recover statutory damages. The "frequency and persistence of noncompliance" consideration for statutory damages under § 1692k does not include a debt collector's actions with respect to non-parties. Awarded $50 in statutory damages.

Diamond v. Corcoran, 1992 U.S. Dist. LEXIS 22793 (W.D. Mich. Aug. 3, 1992). Where the attorney collector did not intend to deceive or harass consumers and that the violations were technical but not frequent and persistent, statutory damages were denied.

Minnesota

Nelson v. Eastern Asset Mgmt., L.L.C., 2009 WL 3255244 (D. Minn. Oct. 7, 2009). Default judgment for $1000 FDCPA statutory damages.

Armstrong v. Rose Law Firm, P.A., 2002 U.S. Dist. LEXIS 4039 (D. Minn. Mar. 7, 2002). The circumstances surrounding the debt collector's violations warranted imposition of the maximum $1000 statutory damages.

Venes v. Prof'l Serv. Bureau, Inc., 353 N.W.2d 671 (Minn. Ct. App. 1984). Statutory damages of $2000 awarded where there were two consumer-plaintiffs and at least two FDCPA violations.

Missouri

Terry v. C & D Complete Bus. Solutions, 2011 WL 144920 (W.D. Mo. Jan. 18, 2011). Actual damages are not a prerequisite to statutory damages.

Jenkins v. Eastern Asset Mgmt., L.L.C., 2009 WL 2488029 (E.D. Mo. Aug. 12, 2009). On default, court awarded $1000 statutory damages, $2000 emotional distress damages, and $3250 fees and costs for multiple calls to place of employment threatening suit after being told plaintiff could not accept personal calls at work.

Montana

McCollough v. Johnson, Rodenburg & Lauinger, 645 F. Supp. 2d 917 (D. Mont. June 3, 2009). Jury verdict awarded consumer $250,000 in compensatory damages, $1000 FDCPA statutory damages, and $60,000 in state law punitive damages and the court awarded attorney fees in the full amount requested of over $93,000 commenting, *inter alia*, that the litigation "confers a meaningful public benefit by discouraging illegal debt collection" in the state. While evidence of the debt collector's pattern or practice of violations may not have been admissible in support of FDCPA statutory damages, it was admissible to support the state law punitive damages.

Nebraska

Page v. CheckRite, Ltd., Clearinghouse No. 45,759 (D. Neb. 1984). Five consumers were each awarded $150 statutory damages and attorney fees of $19,700 for the failure to provide § 1692e(11) notices.

Hulshizer v. Global Credit Servs., Inc., Clearinghouse No. 36,146 (D. Neb. 1983), *aff'd on other grounds*, 728 F.2d 1037 (8th Cir. 1984). $200 statutory damages proper where collector failed to provide the § 1692e(11) warning in one letter. The frequency of this violation with regard to other consumers is not relevant in an individual action.

Nevada

Annunciation v. West Capital Fin. Servs. Corp., Clearinghouse No. 50,452 (D. Nev. 1995). After entry of default and hearing on damages, the court awarded $1000 in statutory damages and $9500 in actual damages.

New Jersey

Kaschak v. Raritan Valley Collection Agency, 1989 U.S. Dist. LEXIS 19103 (D.N.J. May 22, 1989). $1000 statutory damages limit applied to each violation; the number of incidents was relevant to the amount of damages. Consumer's executrix was awarded $900 for five violations in two letters, where the violations were clear but the collector's conduct was not intentional or egregious and caused no actual harm.

New Mexico

Toledo v. McNeel, Clearinghouse No. 50,433 (D.N.M. 1995). Collection attorney's letter failed to provide validation notice in violation of § 1692g and entitled plaintiff to statutory damages of $1000 and actual damages of $200.

Shelden v. J-K Collections, Inc., Clearinghouse No. 45,772 (D.N.M. 1990). The collector should have responded to the consumer's interrogatory requesting the number of other persons to whom had been sent the dunning form letter received by the consumer. Courts have held that the frequency and persistence of noncompliance with regard to all consumers is relevant to the amount of statutory damages awarded to a single consumer plaintiff.

Vigil v. Burdge Enters., Clearinghouse No. 31,109 (D.N.M. 1981). One spouse was awarded $1013 and the other $1000.

New York

Fajer v. Kaufman, Burns & Assocs., 2011 WL 334311 (W.D.N.Y. Jan. 28, 2011). In this default action, the court awarded $500 in statutory damages where the collector was deemed to have admitted calling the consumer more than once, improperly communicated with a third party about the consumer, called the consumer at her workplace despite being told not to call her there, made multiple false representations to the consumer, and sought payment of an unauthorized amount. "Although these acts violate the FDCPA, they were not so persistent or egregious as to warrant the statutory maximum penalty."

Copper v. Global Check & Credit Servs., L.L.C., 2010 WL 5463338 (W.D.N.Y. Dec. 29, 2010). In this default judgment, the court awarded $250 in statutory damages. While the defendant was deemed to have admitted calling the plaintiff's daughter more than once, disclosing the debt, and failing to provide proper notice of her debt, these acts were not so persistent or egregious as to warrant the statutory maximum penalty.

Hoover v. Western New York Capital, 2010 WL 2472500 (W.D.N.Y. June 16, 2010). In a default judgment, the court awarded $500 in statutory damages in a case involving the defendant's failure to provide required debt validation information.

Taylor v. Morgan Stone & Assocs., L.L.C., 2010 WL 1816675 (W.D.N.Y. May 4, 2010). The court entered default judgment, finding that the facts as alleged showed that the defendant failed to send a validation notice, made unlawful false threats of legal action and arrest, and illegally contacted a third party. The court awarded $250 statutory damages.

Annis v. Eastern Asset Mgmt., L.L.C., 2010 WL 1035273 (W.D.N.Y. Mar. 18, 2010). After entry of default, the court entered judgment for $3000.00 in statutory damages, $6500.00 in actual damages, $4240.50 in attorney fees, and $410.00 in costs, for a total award of $14,150.50.

Pearce v. Ethical Asset Mgmt., Inc., 2010 WL 932597 (W.D.N.Y. Mar. 11, 2010). Statutory damages of $250 awarded on default where defendant called plaintiffs multiple times, improperly disclosed a debt, and made unauthorized withdrawals from a bank account.

Healy v. Midpoint Resolution Group, L.L.C., 2010 WL 890996 (W.D.N.Y. Mar. 10, 2010). The court awarded maximum $1000 statutory damages; denied request for $1000 per violation.

Mostiller v. Chase Asset Recovery Corp., 2010 WL 335023 (W.D.N.Y. Jan. 22, 2010). Awarded $150 statutory damages following the debt collector's default on the consumer's claim of false threats of legal and other action.

Nero v. Law Office of Sam Streeter, P.L.L.C., 655 F. Supp. 2d 200 (E.D.N.Y. 2009). Court awarded $500 statutory damages on default.

Weiss v. Zwicker & Assocs., P.C., 664 F. Supp. 2d 214 (E.D.N.Y. 2009). The court awarded statutory damages of $500 for the defendant's § 1692g(a)(1) violation.

Estay v. Moren & Woods L.L.C., 2009 WL 5171881 (W.D.N.Y. Dec. 22, 2009). On entry of default, $250 in statutory damages awarded.

Dayton v. Northeast Fin. Solutions, 2009 WL 4571819 (W.D.N.Y. Dec. 7, 2009). Award on default judgment in this non-actual damage case of $750 statutory damages.

Clark v. Brewer, Michaels & Kane, L.L.C., 2009 WL 3303716 (W.D.N.Y. Oct. 14, 2009). Default judgment was entered for $500 as FDCPA statutory damages and $2386 as attorney fees.

Berry v. Nat'l Fin. Sys., Inc., 2009 WL 2843260 (W.D.N.Y. Aug. 27, 2009). Upon entry of default and after a hearing to establish damages, husband and wife were awarded FDCPA actual damages of $3000, statutory damages of $2000, and attorney fees of $5999.

Overcash v. United Abstract Group, Inc., 549 F. Supp. 2d 193 (N.D.N.Y. 2008). $2000 in statutory damages awarded as there are two defendants in this case, because the limitation that § 1692k(a) imposes "is cast not in terms of the plaintiff's recovery, but in terms of the defendant's liability," and thus "in the case of multiple defendants, each may be liable for additional damages of up to $1,000."

Leyse v. Corporate Collection Serv., Inc., 545 F. Supp. 2d 334 (S.D.N.Y. 2008), *report and recommendation adopted*, 557 F. Supp. 2d 442 (S.D.N.Y. 2008). The court awarded $1000 in statutory damages.

Hall v. Salt City Recovery Sys., 2006 U.S. Dist. LEXIS 60472 (N.D.N.Y. Aug. 25, 2006). In the absence of any evidence that the violation was frequent, persistent, abusive, or threatening, the court awarded $500 in statutory damages for the defendant's violation of § 1692g(a)(4) in omitting from its disclosure the writing requirement to dispute the debt.

Williams v. Goldman & Steinberg, Inc., 2006 U.S. Dist. LEXIS 50222 (E.D.N.Y. July 21, 2006). FDCPA was violated because the debt collector did not have a required city license when it sent its collection letter; consumer awarded 1000 in statutory damages and attorney fees for individual claims in the amount of $995.

Johnson v. Equifax Risk Mgmt. Servs., 2004 WL 540459 (S.D.N.Y. Mar. 17, 2004). The amount of statutory damages is best decided at trial and not on summary judgment.

Padilla v. Payco Gen. Am. Credits, Inc., 161 F. Supp. 2d 264 (S.D.N.Y. 2001). Without reference to a contrary decision in *Kobs v. Arrow Serv. Bureau, Inc.*, 134 F.3d 893 (7th Cir. 1998), the court held that statutory damages under § 1692k are to be set by the court, not a jury.

Miele v. Sid Bailey, Inc., 192 B.R. 611 (S.D.N.Y. 1996). The maximum award of $1000 statutory damages was warranted because of the collection agency's numerous communications with the consumer after being advised by the consumer and his counsel that the debt had been discharged in bankruptcy. $1153.43 actual and $60,000 punitive (for a state law claim) damages also awarded.

Actual damages included tax refund intercepted to pay a student loan that had been discharged in bankruptcy and accountant fees for filing for return of the intercepted funds.

Wiener v. Bloomfield, 901 F. Supp. 771 (S.D.N.Y. 1995). Court awarded consumer $350 in statutory damages for several deceptive statements despite consumer's failure to plead any actual damages.

Rabideau v. Mgmt. Adjustment Bureau, 805 F. Supp. 1086 (W.D.N.Y. 1992). Statutory damages of $500 for each of two violations, totaling $1000, was awarded at non-jury trail.

Siler v. Mgmt. Adjustment Bureau, 1992 WL 32333 (W.D.N.Y. Feb. 18, 1992). Statutory damages of $200, $100 each for violation of the notice provisions of §§ 1692e(11) and 1692g, were awarded in bench trial.

Donahue v. NFS, Inc., 751 F. Supp. 188 (W.D.N.Y. 1991). Only up to $1000 per suit as a maximum could be awarded as additional damages pursuant to § 1692k(a)(2)(A). The factors set forth in § 1692k(b)(1) must be considered in awarding additional damages. After default in two cases in a nonjury proceeding, statutory damages were assessed against one defendant at $250 and the other at $525.

Lauderback v. Master Collectors, Inc., 1991 U.S. Dist. LEXIS 21817 (D. Or. Oct. 22, 1991). Statutory and punitive damages may be recovered for multiple violations but may not exceed $1000 in any case.

Bish v. Credit Control Sys., Inc., 1991 WL 165035 (W.D.N.Y. Aug. 14, 1991) (default judgment). Statutory damages of $200 ($100 per claimed violation) awarded.

Read v. Amana Collection Servs., 1991 WL 165033 (W.D.N.Y. Aug. 12, 1991). Statutory damages of $100 for each of two violations was appropriate. One of the violations was an inconspicuous validation notice.

Young v. Credit Bureau Inc., 729 F. Supp. 1421 (W.D.N.Y. 1989). Same holding as *Spencer v. Credit Bureau Inc.*, *supra*.

Spencer v. Credit Bureau Inc., Clearinghouse No. 45,350 (W.D.N.Y. 1989). Court awarded $100 statutory damages, plus attorney fees and costs, for technical, nonegregious violations of validation notice requirement.

Henderson v. Credit Bureau, Inc., Clearinghouse No. 45,349 (W.D.N.Y. 1989). $500 statutory damages awarded for misstatement of consumer's validation rights, implied threat to contact consumer's employer, and harassing statement in collection letter.

Riveria v. MAB Collections, Inc., 682 F. Supp. 174 (W.D.N.Y. 1988). Statutory damages of $1000 awarded for a validation notice placed on the reverse of a collection letter because the violation occurred routinely and the collector was intentionally circumventing the Act by hiding the notice.

Wegmans Food Mkts., Inc. v. Scrimpsher, 17 B.R. 999 (Bankr. N.D.N.Y. 1982). Statutory damages were awarded where no actual damages were sought. Statutory damages were set at $300 on the basis of several less than egregious abuses. $50 statutory damages under a state statute were also awarded.

North Dakota

Bingham v. Collection Bureau, Inc., 505 F. Supp. 864 (D.N.D. 1981). $400 in statutory damages were awarded for false statements in letters and abusive telephone calls where the violations were intentional but not frequent and persistent.

Ohio

Royster v. Pacific Creditors Ass'n, 2008 WL 4693411 (S.D. Ohio Oct. 23, 2008). Section 1692k(a)(2)(A) limits a plaintiff's additional damages to $1000 per proceeding rather than per violation.

Dowling v. Litton Loan Servicing, L.P., 2008 WL 906042 (S.D. Ohio Mar. 31, 2008), *aff'd on other grounds*, 320 Fed. Appx. 442 (6th Cir. 2009). Following a successful bench trial the court awarded the plaintiff $1000 in statutory damages.

Dowling v. Litton Loan Serv., L.P., 2006 WL 3498292 (S.D. Ohio Dec. 1, 2006). The court awarded maximum statutory damages of $1000.

Mann v. Acclaim Fin. Servs., Inc., 348 F. Supp. 2d 923 (S.D. Ohio 2004). The court awarded the maximum statutory damages of $1000 pursuant to the FDCPA and $200 pursuant to the Ohio Consumer Sales Practices Act (OCSPA) for dun that overshadowed the notice of validation rights.

Becker v. Montgomery, Lynch, 2003 WL 23335929 (N.D. Ohio Feb. 26, 2003). Court awarded full statutory damages, plus $250 for the particularly offensive implication that the failure to pay the amount will cause hard feelings and implying that consumer (who worked in the collection business) should display the "proper attitude" when dealing with Montgomery, Lynch. "This is sufficient to cause anyone embarrassment, humiliation and upset."

Boyce v. Attorney's Dispatch Serv., 1999 U.S. Dist. LEXIS 12970 (S.D. Ohio Apr. 27, 1999). The court noted that the defendants' violations (threats of criminal prosecution) were "the most egregious conduct of any defendant" in an FDCPA action previously before the court. It awarded the two consumers the $1000 statutory damages each and punitive damages of $2500 each under a state UDAP claim. The court declined to award punitive damages under the FDCPA, ruling that they were not expressly authorized under the act and would be duplicative of statutory damages.

Boyce v. Attorney's Dispatch Serv., 1999 U.S. Dist. LEXIS 1124 (S.D. Ohio Feb. 2, 1999). The court declined to award the maximum statutory damages of $1000 against an employee of a collection agency who was only employed for three months and who had no prior experience collecting debts. The employee was "merely an employee ignorant of the requirements of the FDCPA, who followed the instructions of his superiors." The amount of damages, if any, to award against this defendant was a factual matter not susceptible to summary judgment.

Minick v. First Fed. Credit Control, Inc., 1981 U.S. Dist. LEXIS 18622 (N.D. Ohio June 9, 1981). Damages other than emotional distress are not necessary to state a cause of action.

Oregon

McNall v. Credit Bureau of Josephine County, Inc., 2010 WL 3806143 (D. Or. Sept. 23, 2010). The court awarded $250 in statutory damages for defendant's violation of § 1692e(8):

"There is nothing in the record which suggests that defendant's decision not to report the debt as disputed was other than a good faith misinterpretation of statutory requirements. And there is nothing which suggests that the decision was other than an isolated decision made on the unique facts where plaintiff had already notified the credit agencies that they disputed the debt."

Dunn v. Derrick E. McGavic, P.C., 653 F. Supp. 2d 1109 (D. Or. 2009). The court awarded maximum statutory damages of $1000. "Relevant to the statutory damages inquiry is that knowingly walked perilously close to the edge of the law. Although [plaintiff] has not shown these letters were sent to other consumers, the abusive collection practices evidenced here should be deterred." Although "actual damages would be inappropriate, as [plaintiff] alleges no emotional distress or other basis for such an award in his complaint, [t]his does not bar his request for statutory damages."

Hooper v. Capital Credit & Collection Servs., Inc., 2005 WL 2297062 (D. Or. Sept. 20, 2005). Following a jury trial, which resulted in a $1570 actual damage award against the collection agency and a defense verdict for the agency's named employee, the court denied any additional statutory damages, awarded the plaintiff $17,467 in attorney fees, and denied any fees to the exonerated employee since the claims against her were not "brought in bad faith and for the purpose of harassment."

Grassley v. Debt Collectors, Inc., 1992 U.S. Dist. LEXIS 22782 (D. Or. Dec. 14, 1992). Statutory damages are not allowed per violation, but per action, such that $1000 was the maximum recoverable in a single action involving more than one violation. Collector was not entitled to a set-off for amounts previously paid in settlement by two other debt collection agencies.

Wolfe v. Collection Tech., Inc., 1991 U.S. Dist. LEXIS 21852 (D. Or. May 3, 1991). Collector's unintentional misrepresentation of collection fees as $95.54, instead of the $83.38 provided by the contract, entitled the consumer to $1 statutory damages under the FDCPA and $200 minimum damages under the state debt collection law.

Clark v. Schwabe, Williamson & Wyatt, Clearinghouse No. 44,831 (D. Or. 1990). Court awarded no statutory damages for a technical violation in the attempt to comply with § 1692e(11). It awarded $100 for a violation of the rule against communication with consumers who are represented by attorneys, which demonstrated a more fundamental misunderstanding of the FDCPA's consumer rights.

Furth v. United Adjusters, Inc., 1983 U.S. Dist. LEXIS 20368 (D. Or. Nov. 17, 1983). The full $500 statutory damages sought by the consumer were awarded where there were no actual damages, there were violations of three provisions of the Act, the violations were intentional, and the collector had been twice previously found liable for one of the violations.

Zurcher v. Credit Bureau, Inc., 1983 U.S. Dist. LEXIS 20366 (D. Or. Nov. 8, 1983). Statutory damages of $200 granted for failure to include § 1692e(11) notice in dunning letter.

Griswold v. J&R Anderson Bus. Servs., Inc., 1983 U.S. Dist. LEXIS 20365 (D. Or. Oct. 21, 1983). Statutory damages of $200 to a consumer for failure by second of two collectors to provide a second validation notice.

Harvey v. United Adjusters, 509 F. Supp. 1218 (D. Or. 1981). The consumer was entitled to $500 statutory damages for multiple violations of the Act. There was no proof of actual damage. The $1000 maximum applies to each "action" and not each violation. An award of statutory damages is not conditioned upon the award of pecuniary damages (distinguishing between mental anguish and pecuniary harm). The full $1000 is to be reserved for an aggravated case of persistent and repeated illegal practices.

Lambert v. Nat'l Credit Bureau, Inc., 1981 U.S. Dist. LEXIS 18623 (D. Or. Apr. 8, 1981). $100 statutory damages were awarded where the two violations stemmed from a single letter, were not among the "more serious" types of violations, and the collector had sought legal advice to avoid violations.

Dixon v. United Adjusters, Inc., 1981 U.S. Dist. LEXIS 18392 (D. Or. Feb. 19, 1981). Citing the number of contacts and the seriousness of the violation, the court awarded $300 in statutory damages. The debtor may not recover more than $1000 and may recover statutory damages in the absence of proof of actual damages.

Check Cent., Inc. v. Barr, Clearinghouse No. 37,497 (Bankr. D. Or. 1984). Statutory damages of $100 awarded for failure to include a § 1692e(11) notice in dunning letters.

Pennsylvania

Lavelle v. Phoenix Acquisition Group, L.L.C., 2010 WL 5014347 (M.D. Pa. Dec. 3, 2010). Upon a default judgment, the plaintiff was awarded $1000 in statutory damages.

Armbruster v. Hecker, 2010 WL 1643599 (M.D. Pa. Apr. 22, 2010). A jury could award the maximum $1000 statutory damages to each of the two consumers.

Campbell v. Watson, 2009 WL 4544395 (E.D. Pa. Nov. 30, 2009). Additional damages may not exceed $1000.

Holliday v. Cabrera & Assocs., P.C., 2007 U.S. Dist. LEXIS 161 (E.D. Pa. Jan. 3, 2007). The court awarded the maximum statutory damages upon default, where plaintiff demonstrated at least three violations of the FDCPA and two exacerbating factors.

Nelson v. Select Fin. Servs., Inc., 2006 WL 1672889 (E.D. Pa. June 9, 2006). The court awarded statutory damages of $1000. The maximum statutory damages were justified in part by defendant's characterizing its FDCPA violation as "hyper-technical"; its "dismissive characterization—which alone confirms that what it did here was no accident but part of its low regard for the law that governs its business—underscores the continuing need for citizens like Nelson to step forward, as Congress intended, and act as private attorneys general to challenge debt collectors who use deceptive collection methods. . . ."

Littles v. Lieberman, 90 B.R. 700 (E.D. Pa. 1988). Statutory damages of $100 appropriate where the collector was careless and his knowledge was imputed.

Crossley v. Lieberman, 90 B.R. 682 (E.D. Pa. 1988), *aff'd*, 868 F.2d 566 (3d Cir. 1989). Statutory damages raised to $1000 by district court reviewing bankruptcy court's $100 award based on collection attorney's dilatory defense of FDCPA suit which indicated his intent to continue to use a deceptive collection letter which in this action was sent once, soon after expanded FDCPA coverage of lawyers.

In re Belile, 209 B.R. 658 (Bankr. E.D. Pa. 1997). The consumer was awarded actual damages of $100 against each of two defendants, statutory damages of $100 and $750, and treble state damages of $300. The statutory damages of $750 were justified by the collector's failure to admit its violation, by its extreme resistance to discovery, and by the fact that the letter was a form letter mailed to numerous other consumers.

South Dakota

Crawford v. Credit Collection Servs., 898 F. Supp. 699 (D.S.D. 1995). Statutory damages of $500 and attorney fees of $4000 were awarded.

Ewing v. Messerli, Clearinghouse No. 44,331 (D.S.D. 1988). After a bench trial in which the collector failed to appear or defend, the consumer was awarded $5000 "punitive" or statutory damages for five intentional and separate violations in three communications, plus $2951 actual damages and attorney fees.

Tennessee

Sewell v. Allied Interstate, Inc., 2011 WL 32209 (E.D. Tenn. Jan. 5, 2011). A consumer may recover statutory damages if the debt collector violates the FDCPA even if the consumer suffered no actual damages. Because the FDCPA is a strict liability statute, the debt collector may not raise a "speculation" defense to a plaintiffs' request for statutory damages under the FDCPA as opposed to actual damages.

Texas

Toomer v. Alliance Receivables Mgmt., Inc., 2010 WL 5071778 (W.D. Tex. Dec. 9, 2010). Where the parties agreed to voluntary arbitration, the arbitrator awarded the consumer $500 in statutory damages.

Bullock v. Abbott & Ross Credit Servs., L.L.C., 2009 WL 4598330 (W.D. Tex. Dec. 3, 2009). Recommended a default judgment award of $1000 statutory damages.

Brown v. Sterling & King, Inc., 2009 U.S. DIST. LEXIS 15599 (S.D. Tex. Feb. 27, 2009). Default judgment was entered in the amount of $1000 FDCPA statutory damages and $3756 attorney fees.

Molinar v. Coleman, 2009 WL 435274 (N.D. Tex. Feb. 20, 2009). Plaintiff's motion for entry of judgment by default was entered awarding no actual damages, $250 statutory damages, $2800 costs and attorney fees.

McNeill v. Graham, Bright & Smith, P.C., 2006 WL 1489502 (N.D. Tex. May 26, 2006). The court declined to award statutory damages for a violation of § 1692i where the consumer only established $64 in actual damages.

In re Eastman, 419 B.R. 711 (Bankr. W.D. Tex. 2009). Plaintiff need not establish actual damages to recover FDCPA statutory damages.

Agueros v. Hudson & Keyse, L.L.C., 2010 WL 3418286 (Tex. App. Aug. 31, 2010). The consumer was not required to prove actual damages in order to recover "additional" damages under § 1692k.

Virginia

In re Accelerated Recovery Sys., Inc., 431 B.R. 138 (W.D. Va. 2010). In light of the collector's own admission of a fifteen-year history of sending these letters, the bankruptcy court should award at least some amount in statutory damages.

Coles v. Land's Towing & Recovery, Inc., 2010 WL 5300892 (E.D. Va. Dec. 22, 2010). In this default judgment matter involving an improper threat of repossession, the court awarded $750 in statutory damages.

Sears v. Federal Credit Corp., 2009 WL 2601378 (W.D. Va. Aug. 18, 2009). Court awarded $1000 based on the nature of the violation, but per proceeding, not per violation.

McHugh v. Check Investors, Inc., 2003 WL 21283288 (W.D. Va. May 21, 2003). On damage hearing following entry of default, court awarded consumer maximum statutory damages of $1000 and emotional distress damages of over $10,000 for series of abusive and threatening communications.

Jones v. Vest, 2000 U.S. Dist. LEXIS 19026 (E.D. Va. Dec. 27, 2000). Three prior FDCPA claims against the collector in only four years indicated that its noncompliance was frequent and persistent requiring $1000 statutory damages.

Morgan v. Credit Adjustment Bd., Inc., 999 F. Supp. 803 (E.D. Va. 1998). Statutory damages of $300 were awarded to each plaintiff for a total of $600.

Withers v. Eveland, 988 F. Supp. 942 (E.D. Va. 1997). The collection agency was required to do more than follow "the spirit of the law." Because collector failed to do so, a $1000 civil sanction was awarded, an amount that would deter collector from engaging in future improper collection practices.

Creighton v. Emporia Credit Serv., Inc., 981 F. Supp. 411 (E.D. Va. 1997). Court awarded $750 in statutory damages plus fees and costs.

Washington

Francis v. J.C. Penney Corp., 2010 WL 715535 (W.D. Wash. Feb. 24, 2010). The court awarded $1000 statutory damages plus attorney fees on motion for default judgment.

Heib v. Arches Fin., 2008 WL 4601602 (E.D. Wash. Oct. 14, 2008). Statutory damages of $1000 for each spouse against each of two debt collectors awarded for extreme telephone harassment. $3900, treble the out-of-pocket damages awarded under the state consumer protection law.

Watkins v. Peterson Enters., 57 F. Supp. 2d 1102 (E.D. Wash. 1999). Consumers were entitled to full statutory damages where collection agency improperly included costs of unsuccessful writs of garnishment in collection efforts.

In re Hodges, 342 B.R. 616 (Bankr. E.D. Wash. 2006). The court awarded husband and wife plaintiffs each $1000 of additional damages, plus fees and costs.

West Virginia

Clements v. HSBC Auto Fin., Inc., 2010 WL 4281697 (S.D. W. Va. Oct. 19, 2010). Failure to mitigate damages as an affirmative defense is not applicable to the imposition of statutory damages.

Chapman v. ACB Bus. Servs., 1997 U.S. Dist. LEXIS 23743 (S.D. W. Va. Feb. 13, 1997). Letter purporting to demand full payment within seventy-two hours and which contradicted and overshadowed validation notice in small print on the reverse side warranted statutory damages of $1000 as well as statutory damages under a state consumer statute.

Wisconsin

Hartman v. Meridian Fin. Servs., Inc., 191 F. Supp. 2d 1031 (W.D. Wis. 2002). The FDCPA was a strict liability statute, and proof of one violation was sufficient to support summary judgment; however, the number of separate violations was a factor in determining statutory damages, thus requiring adjudication of remaining theories of liability.

Barber v. Nat'l Revenue Corp., 932 F. Supp. 1153 (W.D. Wis. 1996). Statutory damages under § 1692k(a)(2)(A) were limited to $1000 per proceeding rather than for each statutory violation.

Dewey v. Associated Collectors, Inc., 927 F. Supp. 1172 (W.D. Wis. 1996). Under § 1692k, plaintiffs were limited to the statutory damages per proceeding instead of per violation. Court denied plaintiff's wife any recovery as there was no evidence that she saw the letter directed to her husband, and unlike other cases that allowed someone to sue in the place of the debtor, there was no need to in this case. In determining damages, the statutory language "frequency and persistence of noncompliance" referred only to acts by the defendant in this case and not in other cases. As defendant had admitted liability, plaintiff did not have a right to a jury trial to determine statutory damages because he was not claiming actual damages and the FDCPA leaves the determination of statutory damages to the court.

White v. Bruck, 927 F. Supp. 1168 (W.D. Wis. 1996). Statutory damages under § 1692k(a)(2)(A) were limited to $1000 per proceeding rather than $1000 per statutory violation.

K.3.1.3 Other Damages Issues

California

Kindley v. Flagstar Bank, 2004 WL 5631084 (S.D. Cal. Oct. 28, 2004). The court denied the defendant's motion to strike the demand for FDCPA punitive damages since "a motion to strike should not be granted unless it is clear that the matter to be stricken could have no possible bearing on the subject matter of the litigation [and the defendant] has failed to demonstrate that the award of punitive damages under the FDCPA is definitively barred as a matter of law," stating the following: "It is not clear whether punitive damages are recoverable for a violation of the FDCPA; the availability of punitive damages is not addressed in the statute itself, and the issue has not yet been addressed in any reported case. 41 Am. Jur. Proof of Facts 3d. §§ 34, 49 (updated Aug. 2004) (stating that there are valid arguments both in favor of and against the award of punitive damages under the FDCPA)."

Colorado

Kittle v. Accredited Collection Agency Inc., 2010 WL 2650479 (D. Colo. June 30, 2010). The court awarded statutory damages of $1000 in a default judgment, but found that "conclusory, general and uncorroborated" allegations were insufficient to establish emotional distress where the consumer provided "no details of any kind about her claimed emotional distress, including the forms, timing, duration, and frequency of her claimed distress, or whether she sought treatment for her claimed distress."

Connecticut

Evanauskas v. Strumpf, 2001 U.S. Dist. LEXIS 14326 (D. Conn. June 27, 2001). On defendant's default, only factual assertions were deemed admitted, and the court still must conclude that the allegations stated a claim for relief as a matter of law and must independently establish the amount of damages. Admitted factual allegations established FDCPA violations of communicating with a consumer known to be represented by counsel, threatening repossession of assets that were either exempt or not owned by the consumer, and including the consumer's mother's name in the subject line of the dun when the mother was not liable for any part of the consumer's debt.

Florida

Pollock v. Bay Area Credit Serv., L.L.C., 2009 WL 2475167 (S.D. Fla. Aug. 13, 2009). Defendant admitted *Foti* violation, but court ruled that damages had to be assessed by the jury.

Lee v. Security Check, L.L.C., 2009 WL 2044687 (M.D. Fla. July 10, 2009). The FDCPA does not permit the award of punitive damages.

Laufman v. Phillips & Burns, Inc., 2008 WL 190604 (M.D. Fla. Jan. 22, 2008). Emotional distress and punitive damages under state claim were supported where the consumer was upset that the debt collector threatened his eight-year-old daughter with the sheriff coming to the house.

Georgia

Gilmore v. Account Mgmt., Inc., 2009 WL 2848278 (N.D. Ga. Apr. 27, 2009). After entry of default, the magistrate recommended an award of general damages for mental distress of $10,000 as a result of stress caused by dunning for a fully disputed debt during a time when the consumer was having heart problems and recovering from open heart surgery, trebled to $30,000 pursuant to the state consumer protection statute.

Thomas v. Pierce, Hamilton & Stern, Inc., 967 F. Supp. 507 (N.D. Ga. 1997). Punitive damages not available under the FDCPA.

Illinois

Scott v. Universal Fid. Corp., 1999 U.S. Dist. LEXIS 14339 (N.D. Ill. Aug. 26, 1999). Motion to compel discovery of documents relating to defendants' fair market value granted. Defendant's argument that the appropriate measure of defendant's net worth was its book value was rejected because book value results in low estimations of businesses. The proper measure of defendant's value was its fair market value since FDCPA's purpose is to eliminate abusive debt collection practices.

Michigan

Gradisher v. Check Enforcement Unit, Inc., 2003 WL 187416 (W.D. Mich. Jan. 22, 2003). The consumer also recovered her attorney's out-of-pocket expenses of $7808.44.

Mississippi

Harris v. Everhome Mortgage Co., 2008 WL 2902154 (S.D. Miss. July 23, 2008). The FDCPA does not authorized equitable relief.

Odom v. Trustmark Nat'l Bank, 1995 U.S. Dist. LEXIS 22261 (S.D. Miss. Nov. 9, 1995). FDCPA statutory damages are punitive in effect and an award of punitive damages should be determined in light of the award of statutory damages among other factors.

New Jersey

Stair ex rel. Smith v. Thomas & Cook, 254 F.R.D. 191 (D.N.J. 2008). Based on stipulated facts, the court granted summary judgment on damages of $1000 to the named plaintiff and 1% of the defendant collector's net worth of $275,000, or $2750, to the class.

Smith v. Lyons, Doughty & Veldhuius, P.C., 2008 WL 2885887 (D.N.J. July 23, 2008). The FDCPA contains no provision for equitable relief in private actions.

New York

Miller v. Midpoint Resolution Group, L.L.C., 608 F. Supp. 2d 389 (W.D.N.Y. 2009). Bench trial resulted in $500 for emotional distress, $1000 in statutory damages (multiple violations), and $7000 in fees.

Dowling v. Kucker Kraus & Bruh, L.L.P., 2005 WL 1337442 (S.D.N.Y. June 6, 2005). Maximum statutory damages is limited to $1000 per plaintiff per proceeding. The maximum did not apply per defendant. Court awarded $550 per plaintiff.

Laster v. Cole, 2000 U.S. Dist. LEXIS 3771 (E.D.N.Y. Mar. 20, 2000). $100 awarded to each of two plaintiffs, absent evidence that the violation was intentional, frequent, persistent, or abusive.

North Carolina

Tye v. Brock & Scott, P.L.L.C., 2010 WL 428964 (M.D.N.C. Feb. 1, 2010). Fees are not part of costs under the FDCPA.

Ohio

Byrd v. Law Offices of John D. Clunk Co., 2010 WL 816932 (S.D. Ohio Mar. 8, 2010). Law firm not vicariously liable for acts of independent contractor who served process.

Boyce v. Attorney's Dispatch Serv., 1999 U.S. Dist. LEXIS 12970 (S.D. Ohio Apr. 27, 1999). Punitive damages are not recoverable under the FDCPA, although they were awarded in a pendent UDAP claim.

Pennsylvania

Campbell v. Watson, 2009 WL 4544395 (E.D. Pa. Nov. 30, 2009). Punitive and treble damages above $1000 are not authorized by the FDCPA.

Parks v. Portnoff Law Assocs., 243 F. Supp. 2d 244 (E.D. Pa. Jan. 22, 2003). Class action settlement approved after a ten part fairness analysis. The class was to receive a minimum of $250 per claimant (about $13,500 total) with the two named plaintiffs receiving $1000 each and the consumers' attorneys receiving $56,000 in fees and costs.

Piper v. Portnoff Law Assocs., 216 F.R.D. 325 (E.D. Pa. 2003). While the FDCPA limits statutory damages to $1000 per action rather than per violation, the federal statute does not limit recovery for other causes of action arising from the same set of facts.

Texas

Quesenberry v. Alliant Law Group, P.C., 2010 WL 1189457 (E.D. Tex. Mar. 5, 2010), *report and recommendation adopted*, 2010 WL 1189481 (E.D. Tex. Mar. 24, 2010). Where debt collector asked law firm to send the facsimile that charged allegedly illegal interest, debt collector was also liable.

Washington

Campion v. Credit Bureau Servs., 206 F.R.D. 663 (E.D. Wash. 2001). Net worth information was useful, but not determinative, in considering a motion for class certification.

Wisconsin

Ganske v. Checkrite, Ltd., 1997 WL 33810208 (W.D. Wis. Jan. 6, 1997). Each defendant who independently violated the FDCPA is liable for a separate award of maximum $1000 statutory damages even if they are sued by the consumer in the same case.

K.3.2 Class Actions

Hunt v. Imperial Merchant Servs., Inc., 560 F.3d 1137 (9th Cir. 2009). Shifting cost of notice in class action to defendant after consumer obtained summary judgment was not an abuse of discretion.

Liles v. Del Campo, 350 F.3d 742 (8th Cir. 2003). District court's injunction of all related proceedings in other federal courts involving certain conduct of American Corrective Counseling Servs., Inc., was upheld on appeal brought pursuant to 28 U.S.C. § 1292 because injunction of other litigation was necessary to ensure the enforceability of the order granting the preliminary approval of a nationwide FDCPA class action settlement and to prevent further draining of the limited settlement fund. Objectors' appeal of class certification pursuant to Rule 23(f) in a proposed nationwide FDCPA class action settlement was denied as premature.

Davis v. Hutchins, 321 F.3d 641 (7th Cir. 2003). Decision awarding class damages by default judgment in FDCPA case vacated because no class had been certified. Awards of individual actual and statutory damages as well as attorney fees of $18,861 by default were upheld.

Sanders v. Jackson, 209 F.3d 998 (7th Cir. 2000). To calculate FDCPA class statutory damages, the debt collector's net worth should be determined by book value, not the fair market value; goodwill was not part of net worth. Conclusion was based on the ordinary meaning of the term net worth, generally accepted accounting principles, the protection of debt collectors from insolvency, construction of analogous statutes, and the deterrence provided by FDCPA fee shifting and actual damages.

Crawford v. Equifax Payment Servs., 201 F.3d 877 (7th Cir. 2000). Class settlement could not survive because (1) it provided no notice and opt-out rights to pursue class action and (2) unnamed class members received nothing yet lost their rights to pursue a class action.

Blair v. Equifax Check Servs., 181 F.3d 832 (7th Cir. 1999). Class certification affirmed in interlocutory appeal. Issues concerning the relation among multiple suits deemed appropriate situation for court to accept interlocutory appeal and certifying class was in discretion of judge where another class action involving superset of class at issue had not reached final judgment.

Savino v. Computer Credit, Inc., 164 F.3d 81 (2d Cir. 1998). Court affirmed the decisions below denying class certification because of inadequacy of representation where the consumer changed his denial of receipt of the dunning letter at issue [173 F.R.D. 346 (E.D.N.Y. 1997)].

Keele v. Wexler, 149 F.3d 589 (7th Cir. 1998). Because the injury under the FDCPA was the receipt of the letter threatening suit if an illegal $12.50 collection fee was not paid to the collection law firm, the consumer had standing to represent the class of consumers receiving the letter and seeking actual damages in the amount of the fee, regardless of whether she had paid the fee which she alleged she paid involuntarily. The consumer met the commonality and typicality requirements to represent the class of consumers receiving the letter and seeking actual damages in the amount of the fee, regardless of whether she had paid the fee, which she alleged she paid involuntarily.

Mace v. Van Ru Credit Corp., 109 F.3d 338 (7th Cir. 1997). FDCPA does not require a multistate class by virtue of its cap on class statutory damages. Denial of certification of a statewide FDCPA class action was error. Recovery per class member need not always be more than de minimis for the lawsuit to go forward. The attorney fees provision is designed in part to correct the disincentive created by the possibility of a small recovery. *Cy pres* recovery should be reserved only for those unusual situations where victims are unidentifiable or disbursement would be impossible or inappropriate for some other reason. By contrast, the FDCPA specifically requires that damages (that may consist of more than actual monetary loss) be paid. The notice requirement of the Wisconsin Consumer Act was procedural, not substantive. Therefore Fed. R. Civ. P. 23, with no notice provision, applied to a supplementary state class claim.

Dugas v. Trans Union Corp., 99 F.3d 724 (5th Cir. 1996). Plaintiff who had settled his individual FDCPA suit by accepting defendant's offer of judgment and had not reserved the right to appeal the prior denial of class certification was barred from doing so after settlement.

Smith v. Transworld Sys., Inc., 953 F.2d 1025 (6th Cir. 1992). Denial of consumer's motion to amend the complaint to add class action allegations was not error where the proposed amended complaint was insufficient to satisfy the prerequisites of Rule 23(a).

Alabama

Jones v. Roy, 202 F.R.D. 658 (M.D. Ala. 2001). Class certification denied because most potential class members received a collection letter that was slightly different from the one plaintiff received. Only about twenty people received the identical letter.

Arizona

Garo v. Global Credit & Collection Corp., 2011 WL 251450 (D. Ariz. Jan. 26, 2011). In certifying the class, the court rejected the argument that individual issues predominated, distinguishing *Hutton v. D.B. Accounts, Inc.*, 2010 WL 5070882 (C.D. Ill. Dec. 3, 2010).

Bogner v. Masari Inv., L.L.C., 257 F.R.D. 529 (D. Ariz. 2009). Class certified on a *Camacho* claim where the collector's § 1692g(a) notice stated that any dispute must be made in writing.

Brink v. First Credit Res., 185 F.R.D. 567 (D. Ariz. 1999). The court certified the class: (a) variability of damages was not a basis for denying class certification; (b) the named plaintiff's lack of actual damages did not preclude him from representing a class of persons who suffered actual damages; (c) the named plaintiff's willingness to pay only his pro-rata share of the litigation expenses was all that was required; (d) the named plaintiff only needed to be marginally familiar with the facts of his case and need not fully understand the legal theories; and (e) a statewide rather than national class was approved.

Duran v. Credit Bureau of Yuma, Inc., 93 F.R.D. 607 (D. Ariz. 1982). A 23(b)(3) class action for statutory damages was certified.

Arkansas

Cheqnet Sys., Inc. v. Montgomery, 911 S.W.2d 956 (Ark. 1995). Certification of class upheld where class was defined as persons from whom debt collection agency collected, or attempted to collect, a $25 service fee per returned check. Class representative's failure to pay alleged illegal service charge did not defeat the typicality requirement of class certification.

California

Carrizosa v. Stassinos, 2010 WL 4393900 (N.D. Cal. Oct. 29, 2010). Where the debt collector collected $150,154.08 in unlawful interest charges from class members, the class was entitled to that amount in actual damages and restitution.

Janti v. Encore Capital Group, Inc., 2010 WL 3058260 (S.D. Cal. Aug. 3, 2010). A motion to dismiss is not the proper forum to challenge class allegations.

Durham v. Continental Cent. Credit, 2010 WL 2776088 (S.D. Cal. July 14, 2010). The court certified a class regarding overshadowing or contradicting the § 1692g notice consisting of persons with California addresses to whom two form letters in an attempt to collect a debt allegedly due for a vacation owners association.

Ybarrondo v. NCO Fin. Sys., Inc., 2009 WL 3612864 (S.D. Cal. Oct. 28, 2009). Settlement of the class action, arising from the defendant's unlawful threats to report obsolete debts to a credit bureau, approved on terms that included a cash payment to the class members and a stipulation that each class members' debt was forgiven and "[b]ecause the debt is disputed, no IRS 1099 tax forms will be submitted to the Internal Revenue Service or any Class members as a result of the Settlement."

Ybarrondo v. NCO Fin. Sys., Inc., 2009 U.S. Dist. LEXIS 55424 (S.D. Cal. June 30, 2009). Denied final FDCPA class action approval, without prejudice, based on the failure to provide adequate notice to the class and ordered that new notice be sent.

Palmer v. Stassinos, 2009 WL 86705 (N.D. Cal. Jan. 9, 2009). The FDCPA assumes that class actions may be appropriate. Class redefinition required before certification.

Palmer v. Far West Collection Servs., Inc., 2008 WL 5397140 (N.D. Cal. Dec. 18, 2008). The court approved an award of reasonable attorney fees in accordance with the parties' class action settlement agreement.

Del Campo v. American Corrective Counseling Servs., Inc., 254 F.R.D. 585 (N.D. Cal. Dec. 3, 2008). FDCPA case was certified to proceed as a hybrid class action pursuant to Rules 23(b)(2) and 23(b)(3) with the class consisting of all persons who were mailed at least one demand letter purporting to be from a district attorney's office in California attempting to collect a dishonored check, which had not been returned.

Abels v. JBC Legal Group, P.C., 2008 WL 782527 (N.D. Cal. Mar. 21, 2008). On the parties' stipulation and prior to the plaintiff having sent class notice, the court decertified the class and dismissed the plaintiff's individual claims with prejudice, each party to bear its own costs and fees, since entering the stipulation would "not prejudicially affect any claims of members of the class as to which notice was never sent" and "the statute of limitations would have been tolled as to any such claims during the pendency of this action," citing *American Pipe & Const. Co. v. Utah*, 414 U.S. 538 (1974).

Hunt v. Check Recovery Sys., Inc., 2008 WL 754991 (N.D. Cal. Mar. 21, 2008). Following its earlier interlocutory ruling that the defendant pay the plaintiff's costs in providing class notification, the court stayed that order and instead directed the defendant to post a bond of $9000 in connection with its appeal of that ruling.

Ybarrondo v. NCO Fin. Sys., Inc., 2008 WL 183714 (S.D. Cal. Jan. 18, 2008). Plaintiff's motion for preliminary approval of class action settlement was denied without prejudice, on renewal the parties to show: (1) fairness of the settlement; (2) why the named plaintiff would received $2000 but the class members would receive $23 each; and (3) why $7000 is allocated as a *cy pres* award instead of distributing the funds to the class.

Palmer v. Stassinos, 236 F.R.D. 460 (N.D. Cal. 2006). Class certification was granted in this FDCPA action and the class was defined to include persons who were sent at least one form computer generated or otherwise mass-produced collection letter similar to that sent to plaintiff. Class certification was denied for another proposed class in this FDCPA action where the consumers' interest in and ability to pursue actual damage claims prevented the action from being the superior vehicle for adjudicating the claims of the proposed class.

Schwarm v. Craighead, 233 F.R.D. 655 (E.D. Cal. 2006). Court certified this class action for both injunctive relief and damages based on alleged violations of the FDCPA, 42 U.S.C. § 1983, and state law in the collection of dishonored checks by the defendant private debt collector acting under contract and in cooperation with local government law enforcement entities.

Palmer v. Stassinos, 233 F.R.D. 546 (N.D. Cal. 2006). A proposed class definition must specify the alleged infirmities of the letters that are the subject of plaintiffs' FDCPA complaint in order to meet the typicality requirement of Rule 23. The court denied without prejudice plaintiffs' motion for class certification because the proposed class definition was vague making it impossible to determine whether plaintiffs' claims were typical of the proposed class. Filing of a putative class action for violations of the FDCPA cannot toll the statute of limitations for a state debt collection statutory claim for which the plaintiffs lacked standing.

Guevarra v. Progressive Fin. Servs., Inc., 2006 WL 3613742 (N.D. Cal. Nov. 30, 2006). Denial of class certification limited to only one of the many creditors on whose behalf the same letter was sent. It appears to the court that counsel have divided this class action in order to maximize attorney fees without significant benefit to their clients.

Nutter v. NCO Fin. Sys., Inc., 2006 U.S. Dist. LEXIS 79375 (S.D. Cal. Oct. 3, 2006). Debt collector that sold debts subject to this class action during the pendency of the litigation and before the collector had the opportunity to credit the accounts in accordance with the class settlement was allowed to now post the credits to those accounts to cure that breach.

Fabiani v. Oreck Corp., 2006 WL 1390458 (N.D. Cal. May 19, 2006). The court approved the proposed settlement of this class action which included forgiveness of all debts.

Abels v. JBC Legal Group, P.C., 233 F.R.D. 645 (N.D. Cal. Mar. 9, 2006). Court denied class defendant's motion to compel production of the plaintiff's fee agreement since (1) the case had no yet proceeded to the fee stage where fee information might be relevant and (2) the assertion that the fee agreement contained unethical provisions which would be relevant in determining the suitability of the plaintiff and counsel as class representatives was merely unsubstantiated hearsay from which the court could not conclude that production of the agreement was "reasonably calculated to lead to the discovery of admissible evidence." Federal Rule of Civil Procedure 26(b)(1). Though the court found it "not necessary" in reaching its conclusion, but in order to "put the issue to rest," the court accepted for filing class counsel's declaration stating that the fee agreement did not contain the alleged unethical provisions. Court denied discovery of class plaintiff's retainer agreement.

Gonzales v. Arrow Fin. Servs., L.L.C., 233 F.R.D. 577 (S.D. Cal. Feb. 7, 2006). Class certified of consumers who were offered a settlement of seven-year-old claims to have the claims removed from their credit reports.

Palmer v. Stassinos, 2006 WL 83059 (N.D. Cal. Jan. 12, 2006). The court found that plaintiffs had met the requirements of Rule 23(a)(1), (2), and (4) but required further briefing on the typicality of the class representatives and (b)(3) requirements of predominance and superiority.

Campos v. W. Dental Servs., Inc., 404 F. Supp. 2d 1164 (N.D. Cal. 2005). Finding that a countywide class was not "superior" the court denied class certification without prejudice.

Abels v. JBC Legal Group, P.C., 227 F.R.D. 541 (N.D. Cal. 2005). FDCPA class action for deceptive threats and unauthorized charges certified.

Abels v. JBC Legal Group, P.C., 2005 WL 3839309 (N.D. Cal. Nov. 30, 2005). Court refused the consumer's request to further limit the certified class of California consumers to consumers who had written check to two particular merchants in order to greatly reduce the size of the class making it more manageable.

Wyatt v. Creditcare, Inc., 2005 WL 2780684 (N.D. Cal. Oct. 25, 2005). Class certified alleging misrepresentation of interest owed.

Chapman v. Worldwide Asset Mgmt., L.L.C., 2005 WL 2171168 (N.D. Ill. Aug. 30, 2005). Class certified alleging that the debt buyers' form privacy statement violated the FDCPA. Numerosity was inferred from the defendant's large annual revenues and use of a bulk mailing indicating a minimum of 200 pieces mailed. Sanctions in three cases against the consumer's counsel did not mean he was inadequacy as class counsel.

Irwin v. Mascott, 2001 U.S. Dist. LEXIS 3285 (N.D. Cal. Feb. 27, 2001). Although summary judgment had been entered in an FDCPA action, the court retained discretion pursuant to Rule 23(c)(1) to modify the class definition prior to the entry of final judgment. After the entry of summary judgment, the court modified the class definition under Rule 23(b)(3) to limit the class to those persons who received collection letters prior to the date of summary judgment. The class definition under Rule 23(b)(2) was not modified and remained open-ended.

Littledove v. JBC & Assocs., 2001 U.S. Dist. LEXIS 139 (E.D. Cal. Jan. 10, 2001). Rule 23b(2) and (3) classes certified under the FDCPA and state consumer protection laws against check collector who sent form collection letters seeking excessive fees.

Irwin v. Mascott, 96 F. Supp. 2d 968 (N.D. Cal. 1999). The fact that the named plaintiffs had attorneys and may have received advice from their attorneys did not render their claims atypical. The least sophisticated consumer standard is an objective standard that applies even to those who have lawyers. Nor did fact that they did not have damages (did not pay the service charge) render their claims atypical.

Ballard v. Equifax Check Servs., Inc., 186 F.R.D. 589 (E.D. Cal. 1999). Court rejected Equifax's argument that the issue of whether each check constituted a "consumer debt" involved a case by case determination precluding class certification. After the court granted summary judgment under FDCPA to a named plaintiff, it reconsidered its earlier denial of certification and certified the class based on the following: (a) the assertion by Equifax of a counterclaim against the named plaintiff was not of itself grounds to deny class certification; (b) because the court had ruled that a service charge was not recoverable as an "incidental damage" by the holder of a check (as opposed to the seller), its earlier conclusion that the circumstances of each class member's transaction needed to be reviewed and thus individual issues predominated was no longer applicable; (c) Equifax's internal system of identifying returned checks as personal and business eliminated any individualized inquiry into the nature of each class member's transaction; and (d) court declined to exercise supplemental jurisdiction over the defendant's counterclaims against each class member to recover the service charge for the "compelling reasons of public

policy embodied in the FDCPA" and thus eliminated the counterclaims as a bar to certification.

Asset Acceptance, L.L.C. v. Hanson, 2009 WL 840047 (Cal. Ct. App. Apr. 1, 2009) (unpublished). Denial of class certification affirmed on the basis of the trial court's "finding that there was no well-defined community of interest among the purported class members;" this state law based class certification decision was decided in the context of the plaintiff's substantive claim, which the court assumed to be true, that "[debt collector's] standard corporate policy of concealing from, and willfully failing to disclose to, debtors that any payment made towards a debt the enforcement of which is barred by the statute of limitations may create a new, distinct and enforceable legal obligation is a false, deceptive and misleading practice in violation of the FDCPA. . . ."

Connecticut

Wise v. Cavalry Portfolio Servs., L.L.C., 2010 WL 3724249 (D. Conn. Sept. 15, 2010). The court certified an FDCPA class consisting of: "All persons with Connecticut addresses at the time to whom Cavalry sent, since the period that is one year prior to the filing of the Complaint, one or more letters or other communications in an attempt to collect a debt that was incurred for personal, family, or household purposes and which was subject to being increased by reason of interest, late charges, or other charges, and Cavalry failed in the initial letter to notify them that the debt might vary from day to day or failed to notify them that they could contact Cavalry to obtain an up-to-date amount of the debt allegedly due."

O'Connor v. AR Res., Inc., 2010 WL 1279023 (D. Conn. Mar. 30, 2010). Certification of an FDCPA settlement class was granted, but preliminary approval of the class settlement was denied without prejudice.

Aramburu v. Healthcare Fin. Servs., 361 F. Supp. 2d 21 (D. Conn. 2005). The court granted class certification stating that suits brought pursuant to the FDCPA regularly satisfy the superiority requirement of Rule 23(b)(3).

Petrolito v. Arrow Fin. Servs., L.L.C., 221 F.R.D. 303 (D. Conn. 2004). Class certified despite named plaintiff's lack of actual damages from the collection efforts.

Macarz v. Transworld Sys., Inc., 201 F.R.D. 54 (D. Conn. 2001). The court approved notice by publication to 56,000 Connecticut class members.

Macarz v. Transworld Sys., Inc., 193 F.R.D. 46 (D. Conn. 2000). Class certification was granted over objection that plaintiff was atypical as an attorney capable of recognizing FDCPA violations who suffered no actual damages. "Indeed, if a notice was violative as to the prototypical 'least sophisticated consumer,' it was violative as to all recipients, without a subjective inquiry into the sophistication of those recipients. Further, a law degree was no guarantee of sophistication or familiarity with the complex requirements of consumer law." The court rejected the small recovery per class member as a reason to deny class certification. "Defendant would no doubt benefit from such result, as the vast majority, if not all, of those potential plaintiffs would fail to pursue what this Court has already determined are meritorious claims. But defendant's desire to limit its exposure in damages cannot be a criteria for assessing the appropriateness of a class action." The court rejected defendant's arguments that it could not identify whether class members were consumers or businesses. "Should a debt collection company as large and as sophisticated as Transworld be able to avoid class action liability by mere fact of inadequate record-keeping, the Congressional purpose behind the statute would indeed be thwarted."

Bolden v. G.H. Perkins Assocs., Inc., Clearinghouse No. 31,470 (D. Conn. 1983). FDCPA class action for damages and equitable relief was provisionally certified as meeting Fed. R. Civ. P. 23(a) and (b) requirements and as within the purposes of the FDCPA. The complaint alleged that the collector demands a 1/3 collection fee in violation of the FDCPA. The case was settled with an agreed injunction and dismissal of the class.

Florida

Arlozynski v. Rubin & Debski, P.A., 2010 WL 2243817 (M.D. Fla. June 4, 2010). The court granted the parties' joint motion for class certification.

Capote v. United Collection Bureau, Inc., 2010 WL 966859 (S.D. Fla. Mar. 12, 2010). In the early stages of an individual FDCPA case seeking statutory damages where the defendant offered to settle for payment of $1001 plus costs and reasonable attorney fees, the court granted the consumer's motion to amend the complaint to assert claims on behalf of a class. The court also denied the defendant's motion to dismiss, stating that even assuming the defendant's offer rendered moot consumer's FDCPA claim, the offer did not include consumer's state law claims, and therefore did not extinguish the entire case.

Hicks v. Client Servs., Inc., 257 F.R.D. 699 (S.D. Fla. 2009). Defendant's motion to decertify the class on the basis that any recovery to its members would be de minimis, thus defeating the superiority requirement of Rule 23, was denied, with the court explaining that they found the reasoning of the cases supporting an FDCPA class action despite de minimis recovery by the class members to be more persuasive. The court also noted that decertifying the class would (theoretically) create a perverse incentive for debt collectors using unfair practices to use them as widely as possible, in order to prevent a class action from being certified, and thus held that class action was the superior method of adjudication.

Drossin v. Nat'l Action Fin. Servs., Inc., 255 F.R.D. 608 (S.D. Fla. 2009). Person who received a prerecorded voicemail without disclosure that the caller was a debt collector had standing to bring an FDCPA claim under § 1692e(11) even if she was not the person the debt collector was trying to reach. The debt collector's conduct would have indicated to an unsophisticated consumer that it was collecting from her. The numerosity requirement could not be defeated by the defendant's poor record keeping and was satisfied by evidence that could evidence more than eighty similar calls within a few days. The court certified the Rule 23(b)(3) class but refused to certify a state claim class for lack of commonality.

Hicks v. Client Servs., Inc., 2008 WL 5479111 (S.D. Fla. Dec. 11, 2008), *later decision*, 257 F.R.D. 699 (S.D. Fla. 2009) (denying motion to decertify). Class certified in this case alleging that the defendant routinely left voice mail messages that did not disclose the defendant's identity, status as a debt collector, and purpose of the call as required by §§ 1692d(6) and 1692e(11).

Gaalswijk-Knetzke v. Receivables Mgmt. Servs. Corp., 2008 WL 3850657 (M.D. Fla. Aug. 14, 2008). Certified an FDCPA class defined as "all residents of State of Florida who received debt collection notices and/or letters from relating to a consumer debt on or after Mar. 14, 2006" and rejected the defendant's argument that the class should not be certified because class members would receive *de minimis* recovery of only $3.20 each.

Tyrell v. Robert Kaye & Assocs., P.A., 223 F.R.D. 686 (S.D. Fla. 2004). Class was certified where the defendant sent dunning letters to members of between 100 and 400 condo associations and failed to include required FDCPA notices; however, where another claim was that the defendant improperly charged attorney fees and expenses to these consumers but the underlying condo contracts differed among the various associations, individual issues pertinent to the terms of each association contract made class certification inappropriate.

Wilson v. Transworld Sys., Inc., 2002 U.S. Dist. LEXIS 10891 (M.D. Fla. Mar. 29, 2002). Because of "profound difficulties in defining and identifying the constituent members of the class, or possible subclasses, for purposes of an action for damages," and because allowing declaratory and injunctive relief was a superior remedy, the putative damages class was not certified but an injunctive class was certified.

Fuller v. Becker & Poliakoff, P.A., 197 F.R.D. 697 (M.D. Fla. 2000). Showing allegedly deceptive dunning letters were sent to 200 families satisfied numerosity, commonality and typicality requirements.

Swanson v. Mid Am, Inc., 186 F.R.D. 665 (M.D. Fla. 1999). Court refused to certify case under Rule 23(b)(3) because one of the defendant collection agencies was unable to identify the names and addresses of specific class members. Therefore, the court could not notify individual class members, but ruled that the case qualified under Rule 23(b)(2) because any monetary damages were incidental to the injunctive relief requested, and all flowed from the same notice letters sent by defendants. Similar letters sent to class plaintiffs by defendant collection agency satisfied the numerosity requirement. To satisfy the commonality requirement, the class plaintiffs did not need to show at the certification stage that the underlying debts were consumer debts, or that the class members read or were confused by the letters sent. It was sufficient that the class plaintiffs alleged they received the same letter.

Sandlin v. Shapiro & Fishman, 1997 WL 155418 (M.D. Fla. Mar. 18, 1997). Court denied request for reconsideration of denial of class certification. Plaintiff met burden concerning commonality of claims where debt collector charged fee for payoff statements, but did not establish numerosity, typicality, or adequacy of representation required under Rule 23.

Sandlin v. Shapiro & Fishman, 168 F.R.D. 662 (M.D. Fla. 1996). The court denied class certification for an FDCPA suit finding that while there was a common question of whether unauthorized mortgage payoff fees were charged and imposed, the consumers did not meet the numerosity requirement as the consumers offered no proof or estimate of the size of the proposed class. Furthermore, the plaintiffs did not meet the typicality requirement because they failed to differentiate between class members who actually paid the payoff fees and those who did not. Nor was representation adequate as plaintiff lacked the funds to finance the class action resulting in plaintiffs' counsel advancing costs which could cause a conflict of interest between counsel and the class.

Dalton v. FMA Enters., Inc., 1996 WL 684441 (M.D. Fla. Nov. 25, 1996). The court denied the consumer's motion for reconsideration of the denial of class certification. The consumer did not establish numerosity as the defendant's statement that the offending letters may have been sent to over 1000 consumers was too indefinite a basis for certification. The consumer also tried to show typicality by stating a conclusion that all proposed members received the same form letters rather than making detailed allegations of the fact that they received the letters.

Hall v. Nat'l Recovery Sys., 1996 WL 467512 (M.D. Fla. Aug. 9, 1996). Motion for class certification denied. Plaintiff alleged various violations of FDCPA in form letters sent out in an attempt to collect on bad checks. Evidence that 3100 form letters were sent was sufficient to establish numerosity. Common issues regarding service charges and threats to take action not intended to be taken were sufficiently pleaded. Typicality was not established where collectors dealt differently with debtors as a result of different possibilities for referral for criminal prosecution. Where named plaintiff had a criminal record (including writing numerous worthless checks and armed robbery), relocated frequently, and was presently living in a motel, he was an inadequate representative due to his low credibility.

Dalton v. FMA Enters., Inc., 1996 WL 379105 (M.D. Fla. July 1, 1996). Court refused to certify FDCPA class action. The consumer plaintiff failed to establish numerosity. The fact that a form collection letter with a lawyer's facsimile signature was used was not sufficient. The consumer must be able to establish the number of class members. Commonality and typicality were not established where three different letters were sent to various consumers, there were phone calls to others, and it would be necessary to determine which credit card debts were for consumer and business purposes. Adequacy of class representation was not established where the plaintiff erroneously thought Texas claims had been filed and was not financially able to pay for class notice, and funds advanced by counsel were likely to create conflict of interest.

Georgia

Stewart v. Slaughter, 165 F.R.D. 696 (M.D. Ga. 1996). The defendant was the majority owner and the chief executive officer of a credit bureau. The court certified a class action suit for the purpose of determining whether the defendant's modus operandi violated the FDCPA. The defendant held himself out as an independent attorney for the purpose of collecting debts by sending letters on letterhead purporting to be from William Slaughter, Attorney at Law. The letters claimed that he brought a hundred suits a month. While he was a member of the state bar, he did not actually bring any debt collection cases but retained outside counsel to do so and maintained no other law "practice." The numerosity requirement was met as there were hundreds of class members which made joinder impossible, liability was common to all who received the letters, the class representatives asserted essentially the same claim held as class members thus meeting the typicality requirement, the class interests were protected, and class certification protected against inconsistent adjudication.

Illinois

Hutton v. C.B. Accounts, Inc., 2010 WL 5463108 (C.D. Ill. Dec. 29, 2010). The court denied the plaintiff's motion to reconsider its earlier denial of class certification. The earlier denial was based upon the court's finding that individual issues of proof would predominate over class issues because some of the class members may already have known who the collector was and why it was calling. "[S]ome of the approximately 62,093 putative class members may have received debt collection calls and letters from CBA prior to getting any offending voicemails. Individuals who received calls and letters which satisfied § 1692e(11)'s disclosure requirements prior to receiving offending calls and letters may not have actionable FDCPA claims."

Smith v. Greystone Alliance L.L.C., 2010 WL 2680147 (N.D. Ill. June 30, 2010). The court certified a class comprised of consumers for whom the defendant left voicemail messages without identifying itself as a debt collector as required by § 1692e(11).

Miller v. Midland Credit Mgmt., Inc., 621 F. Supp. 2d 621 (N.D. Ill. 2009). In this FDCPA litigation, a class of 135,571 Cook County residents was certified.

Hale v. AFNI, Inc., 264 F.R.D. 402 (N.D. Ill. 2009). Class certified where the plaintiffs alleged §§ 1692e and 1692g violations from the defendant's failure to provide the required verification notice, falsely claimed that it had insufficient information to verify the debt, and falsely implied that consumers bore an obligation to prove that they did not owe the debt.

Sadler v. Midland Credit Mgmt, Inc., 2009 WL 901479 (N.D. Ill. Mar. 31, 2009). For the purpose of a class statutory damages claim, defendants' simple act of mailing letters with allegedly misleading information constitutes a "use" of deceptive means, irrespective of whether the letters were read by the consumer.

Buford v. Palisades Collection, L.L.C., 552 F. Supp. 2d 800 (N.D. Ill. 2008). Provision in underlying contract waiving class action was not shown to be part of the rights assigned to a debt buyer.

Randolph v. Crown Asset Mgmt., L.L.C., 254 F.R.D. 513 (N.D. Ill. 2008). FDCPA class certified on the basis of state court collection complaints that allegedly failed to attach a copy of an assignment that complied with state law as required for licensed debt collectors and where business records affidavits were filed in state collection suits allegedly falsely verifying that the collector was a holder in due course.

Ramirez v. Palisades Collection L.L.C., 250 F.R.D. 366 (N.D. Ill. 2008). The court certified the class based on the collector's alleged FDCPA violation of suing consumers in state court more than five years after last payment or charge-off in cases where the collector subjected itself to the state's shortened five-year statute of limitations as a consequence of failing to attach a copy of the underlying contract to its collection complaints.

Herkert v. MRC Receivables Corp., 254 F.R.D. 344 (N.D. Ill. Dec. 1, 2008). Class certification was granted in an FDCPA case claiming that the debt collectors had filed time-barred collection actions.

Rosales v. Unifund CCR Partners, 2008 WL 4976223 (N.D. Ill. Nov. 19, 2008). Class certification was denied in this FDCPA litigation because individual inquiries would be required to establish commonality and predominance of claim that a debt buyer had filed state debt collection suits with false affidavits attesting to the claim.

Acik v. I.C. Sys., Inc., 251 F.R.D. 332 (N.D. Ill. June 11, 2008). FDCPA case certified as class action where collection agency sought unspecified fees and interest and failed to include contact information.

Warcholek v. Medical Collections Sys., 241 F.R.D. 291 (N.D. Ill. 2006). The court certified a class of Illinois residents who were sent a letter from defendants to recover a debt incurred for medical care provided by Parkview Orthopedic Group SC.

Hernandez v. Midland Credit Mgmt., 236 F.R.D. 406 (N.D. Ill. 2006). Class certified for providing a deceptive privacy notice.

Thomas v. Arrow Fin. Servs., L.L.C., 2006 WL 2438346 (N.D. Ill. Aug. 17, 2006). Class certification was granted regarding the FDCPA claims for requesting location information from an employer when the collector already had the consumer's location information, but denied with regard to the Illinois UDAP and state debt collection statutory claims.

Nichols v. Northland Groups, Inc., 2006 WL 897867 (N.D. Ill. Mar. 31, 2006). Neither Rule 23 nor the FDCPA prohibits plaintiffs from engaging in multiple class actions to deter continuing FDCPA violations. The court concluded that neither the FDCPA nor Rule 23 require a larger class than the plaintiff proposed to certify, Illinois residents receiving a collection letter during the three-month period after the collector was previously sued for the deceptive letter and when it stopped using the letter. Although attorneys are necessarily the driving force behind class action claims, that fact does not by itself detract from the plaintiff's ability to adequately represent the class.

Longo v. Law Offices of Gerald E. Moore & Assocs., P.C., 2006 WL 897800 (N.D. Ill. Mar. 30, 2006). The Seventh Circuit has made it clear that a consumer who is eligible only for statutory damages can represent a class of persons who are eligible for both actual and statutory damages. The class representative need only be conscientious and have a basic understanding of the litigation.

Murray v. Sunrise Chevrolet, Inc., 2006 WL 862886 (N.D. Ill. Mar. 30, 2006). There is nothing about an FDCPA consumer's frequency of litigation that implies that she is less suited to represent a class than someone who has engaged in litigation only on a single occasion. A consumer who has engaged in repeated class action litigation may be better suited to monitor the conduct of class counsel.

Thompson v. Spinelli, 2005 WL 2483376 (N.D. Ill. Oct. 5, 2005). Motion for class certification was denied because the court would be required to examine approximately 4900 agreements to determine if the $8 credit card processing fee was authorized.

Dawson v. Allied Interstate, Inc., 2005 WL 1692606 (N.D. Ill. July 13, 2005). Class certified on form collection letters giving limited time to accept discounted settlement.

Mendez v. M.R.S. Assocs., 2004 WL 1745779 (N.D. Ill. Aug. 3, 2004). A class action was certified in an FDCPA case alleging that the debt collection letter added an additional § 1692g step that the consumer explain the nature of the dispute in violation of § 1692g.

Maxwell v. Arrow Fin. Servs., L.L.C., 2004 WL 719278 (N.D. Ill. Mar. 31, 2004). Court certified the class where the evidence showed that more than 500 persons received a form letter that stated that payment of debts which were more than seven years old would result in the collector informing credit bureaus that the debts were fully paid, thus allegedly suggesting that nonpayment would result in reporting obsolete debts in violation of the Fair Credit Reporting Act.

Robles v. Corporate Receivables, Inc., 220 F.R.D. 306 (N.D. Ill. Mar. 2, 2004). Class certified consisting of 102 Illinois consumers who received two collection letter overshadowing the debt validation notice.

Carbajal v. Capital One, F.S.B., 219 F.R.D. 437 (N.D. Ill. Jan. 20, 2004). Plaintiffs received solicitations from the defendants to transfer delinquent debts owed to other creditors to a new Capital One Visa credit card account. They contend that this constituted debt collection activity subject to the FDCPA, and they assert that Capital One's solicitation improperly obscured the FDCPA-required "validation" notice and misleadingly advised debtors that they would still be able to dispute the old debt after its transfer to Capital One. Two state classes certified.

Pleasant v. Risk Mgmt. Alternatives, Inc., 2003 WL 22175390 (N.D. Ill. Sept. 19, 2003). The district court granted plaintiff's motion for class certification with the class defined as: (a) all natural persons in Illinois; (b) to whom Defendant Risk Management Alternatives, Inc. sent a letter; (c) on behalf of Bank One Credit Company; (d) offering a settlement at fifty percent or more of the balance due; (e) that must be accepted in a limited period; (f) which letter was sent on or after September 26, 2001 (one year prior to the filing of this action).

Whaley v. Shapiro & Kreisman, L.L.C., 2003 WL 22232911 (N.D. Ill. Sept. 16, 2003). In dicta the court noted that an FDCPA claim regarding unreasonable or an unearned attorney fee would doom any effort to pursue the case as a class action, presumably because of individual questions.

Weiss v. Coldata, Inc., 2003 WL 22118936 (N.D. Ill. Sept. 11, 2003). Plaintiff's motion for class certification was granted with the class defined as: (a) all natural persons with Illinois addresses who, according to the books and records of defendant; (b) were sent a letter containing a settlement offer of 50% or more with a purported deadline; (c) which was not returned by the Postal Service; (d) seeking to collect a purported credit card debt; (e) which letter was sent on or after a date one year prior to the filing of this action.

Ingram v. Corporate Receivables, Inc., 2003 WL 21982152 (N.D. Ill. Aug. 19, 2003). The court certified an FDCPA 23(b)(3) class. Despite some discomfort the court inferred that numerosity would be met because of the debt collector's general volume of collections.

Jones v. Risk Mgmt. Alternatives, Inc., 2003 WL 21654365 (N.D. Ill. July 11, 2003). In an FDCPA challenge to a collector's limited time offer letter alleging that repeated identical letters to consumer offering alleged "one time" settlement offer for limited time violated § 1692(e), the court certified a class action pursuant to Rule 23(a) and (b)(3).

Seidat v. Allied Interstate, Inc., 2003 WL 21468625 (N.D. Ill. June

19, 2003). A statistical estimate of the number of class members (50) was sufficient evidence to meet the numerosity requirement since discovery was forthcoming which would determine the exact number of members of the class.

McCabe v. Crawford & Co., 210 F.R.D. 631 (N.D. Ill. 2002). The court granted plaintiff's motion for class certification pursuant to Rule 23(a) and (b)(3).

Parker v. Risk Mgmt. Alternatives, Inc., 206 F.R.D. 211 (N.D. Ill. 2002). Class certified where evidence showed that there were between 39 and 97 members and all criteria for certification were met.

Thompson v. Doctors & Merchants Credit Serv., Inc., 2002 WL 31854974 (N.D. Ill. Dec. 19, 2002). Court held that the criteria of Rule 23(a) and (b) were satisfied and certified the matter to proceed as a class action.

Rogers v. Simmons, 2002 U.S. Dist. LEXIS 5457 (N.D. Ill. Mar. 28, 2002). Where the only remaining issue was whether the attorney fee request was bona fide and reasonable, the consumer did not meet the predominance requirement of Rule 23(b)(3), and her motion for class certification was denied.

Bigalke v. Creditrust Corp., 162 F. Supp. 2d 996 (N.D. Ill. 2001). The fact that the debt collector could not admit or deny a request for admissions asking whether it sent 500 letters similar to the one sent to plaintiff suggested that the numerosity requirement was met. A debt collector's standardized conduct of mailing form letters to members of the proposed class is frequently determined to be a common nucleus of operative fact sufficient to satisfy the commonality requirement of Rule 23(a). It is the norm in a class action that the representative plaintiff will know little about the case and will give free reign to class counsel to prosecute it. The class representative must understand the basic facts underlying his or her claim. General knowledge and participation in discovery are sufficient to meet the representativeness standard.

Parker v. Risk Mgmt. Alternatives, Inc., 204 F.R.D. 113 (N.D. Ill. 2001). Debt collector's offer of judgment expired when plaintiff filed his motion for class certification within ten days of the offer. A Rule 68 offer to plaintiff individually could not have been accepted by him at any time during the ten-day period without approval of the court pursuant to Fed. R. Civ. P. 23(e).

Wilkerson v. Bowman, 200 F.R.D. 605 (N.D. Ill. 2001). Whether the form collection letter violated the FDCPA was a common question of law and fact. The need to show that the transactions involved are consumer transactions is inherent in many FDCPA class actions. Where there is genuine question of whether debts are for business or consumer purposes, class members can be asked a single question to determine their eligibility for class membership. The modest recovery available to an individual in an FDCPA case was an argument in favor of class certification, not a basis for denial: "Indeed, the class action is not only the superior method, but the best one for pursuing remedies under the FDCPA."

Miller v. McCalla, Raymer, Padrick, Cobb, Nichols & Clark, L.L.C., 198 F.R.D. 503 (N.D. Ill. 2001). "[I]f class actions can be said to have a main point, it is to allow the aggregation of many small claims that would otherwise not be worth bringing, and thus to help deter lawless defendants from committing piecemeal highway robbery, a nickel here and a nickel there, that adds up to real

money, but which would not be worth the while of an individual plaintiff to sue on." The court awarded the maximum allowable statutory damages of $1000 for the plaintiff and either $500,000 or 1% of the collector's net worth, whichever is less, for the absent class members.

Kort v. Diversified Collections Servs., Inc., 2001 U.S. Dist. LEXIS 20988 (N.D. Ill. Dec. 17, 2001). Class certification was granted for Count II of the FDCPA complaint regarding student claims arising from collector's form letter, reversing the burden required to establish an exemption from garnishments, but denied for Count I claims regarding advance notice of garnishment, which would require demonstration of the date of mailing and receipt of the letter.

Hamid v. Blatt, Hasenmiller, Leibsker, Moore & Pellettieri, 2001 U.S. Dist. LEXIS 20012 (N.D. Ill. Nov. 30, 2001). Two FDCPA classes were certified regarding the collection of old Montgomery Ward accounts, but the subclasses relating to state court judgments were denied due to application of the *Rooker-Feldman* doctrine.

Valentine v. ECC Mgmt. Servs., Inc., 2001 U.S. Dist. LEXIS 16887 (N.D. Ill. Oct. 16, 2001). Plaintiff's motion for class certification was granted where the collection agency's letter stated that other charges may be added to the stated amount of the debt.

Whitten v. ARS Nat'l Servs., Inc., 2001 U.S. Dist. LEXIS 15472 (N.D. Ill. Sept. 26, 2001). Class certification granted based on form letter. Motion to dismiss based on Rule 68 offer to the named plaintiff, made while motion for class certification was pending denied.

Asch v. Teller, Levit & Silvertrust, P.C., 2001 U.S. Dist. LEXIS 13160 (N.D. Ill. Aug. 27, 2001). For the purposes of determining typicality, the court need only ask whether plaintiffs have asserted that (1) their purported claims stem from the same conduct that gives rise to claims alleged on behalf of class members and (2) whether the claims of the two groups are asserted under the same legal theories. Individualized damage calculations alone will not defeat a motion for class certification.

Sanders v. OSI Educ. Servs., 2001 U.S. Dist. LEXIS 12578 (N.D. Ill. Aug. 2, 2001). Evidence that at least ninety-one persons qualified as class members met numerosity requirement. Defendant's standardized conduct met commonality and typicality requirements; defendant's claim to the contrary involved inquiry into the plaintiff's method of proof, an inquiry that was not allowed at the class certification stage.

Lang v. Winston & Winston, P.C., 2001 U.S. Dist. LEXIS 7480 (N.D. Ill. May 31, 2001). The court certified a class action alleging that attorneys were not personally involved in reviewing the file or sending out any particular letter and exercised no judgment about whether any particular letter should be sent.

Thomas v. Kunin, 2001 WL 34610463 (S.D. Ill. Feb. 28, 2001). Court certified the class in accordance with the parties' settlement agreement.

Daley v. Provena Hosps., 193 F.R.D. 526 (N.D. Ill. 2000). The court certified three separate subclasses because defendants sent three separate form collection letters. Rule 23(c)(4)(B) provides for multiple classes in a single case, the basis for plaintiffs' request for subclasses was standing which required that the class representative suffer the same injury by members of the class, and the named plaintiffs may not have suffered the same injury as a debtor who received a different collection letter.

Campos v. Sethness, 2000 U.S. Dist. LEXIS 5491 (N.D. Ill. Apr. 11, 2000). Pursuant to Rule 23(e) notice need not be sent to the putative class members where the class has not been certified and the litigation was being dismissed because it was not economically feasible given the death of one defendant and the bankruptcy of another.

Shea v. Codilis, 2000 U.S. Dist. LEXIS 4131 (N.D. Ill. Mar. 27, 2000). A class was certified against a collection law firm that violated the § 1692g requirement that it state the amount of the debt. The collector stated the principal due without stating the balance that included accrued interest.

Nance v. Lawrence Friedman, P.C., 2000 U.S. Dist. LEXIS 2721 (N.D. Ill. Feb. 22, 2000). The court denied the consumer's motion to redefine the class more narrowly to encompass only the members which had originally dealt with two of the creditors which the collection firm collected, so that class members would number fewer than 2500 rather than 25,000. The difference between an $1 recovery and a $10 recovery was not too little to be material and the redefinition was denied. Individual class members could opt out after reading the class notice if they preferred to pursue their individual claim.

Perdue v. United Credit Mgmt. Corp., 2000 U.S. Dist. LEXIS 1502 (N.D. Ill. Feb. 9, 2000). Class certification granted.

Raimondi v. McAllister & Assocs., Inc., 50 F. Supp. 2d 825 (N.D. Ill. 1999). Statutory damages are limited to an award of up to $1000 to the consumer. The court awarded the consumer the full $1000 statutory damages where the collection agency threatened to contact the consumer's employer.

Scott v. Universal Fid. Corp., 42 F. Supp. 2d 837 (N.D. Ill. 1999). FDCPA statutory damages, like punitive damages, are designed to deter abusive collection practices that are a violation of the law.

Vines v. Sands, 188 F.R.D. 302 (N.D. Ill. 1999). Class action filed alleging that the inclusion of the notice of Massachusetts residents' rights to stop calls to the consumer's place of employment overshadowed the recitation of the § 1692c(a)(3) right to be free at work from collection calls if receiving such calls was prohibited by the employer. Court found that commonality and typicality were satisfied because the same form letter was sent to each class member, and the claims regarding those letters made by the named class members raised the same issues of fact and law common to all class members.

Clark v. Retrieval Masters Creditors Bureau, Inc., 185 F.R.D. 247 (N.D. Ill. 1999). Class plaintiff met typicality requirement even if he denied owing the debt, since the FDCPA applies regardless of whether the debt is valid.

Nance v. Lawrence Friedman P.C., 1999 U.S. Dist. LEXIS 16524 (N.D. Ill. Oct. 18, 1999). Plaintiffs were adequate class representatives. The fact that plaintiff may not have actually been deceived by a form validation notice was irrelevant since liability is determined by the objective "unsophisticated consumer" test. Also, one plaintiff's conviction of a misdemeanor for a "youthful impropriety" and the other plaintiff's failure to recall being a party to a prior

lawsuit did not render them inadequate class representatives. Defendants' objection that a small law firm did not have staff sufficient to prosecute a class action was rejected since court believed plaintiffs' firm to be competent and qualified and could contract with others to handle administrative tasks if necessary.

Roe v. Publishers Clearing House, Inc., 1999 U.S. Dist. LEXIS 16249 (N.D. Ill. Sept. 30, 1999). The court rejected defendant's claims that plaintiff was not an adequate class representative, plaintiff had not shown that common questions predominate, and a class action was not a superior method of adjudication. Plaintiff may serve as a class representative even if she delegated factual and legal investigation to her attorneys, as long as she was able to consult with counsel and make decisions on the advice of counsel. Common questions predominated. Plaintiff was a class representative in *Roe*, and a class member in *Randle*. The two actions were based on the same letters, but alleged different violations. The court ruled that the class members could recover in each proceeding: "Were this court to find that defendant is a debt collector and is liable for violating other provisions of the FDCPA, defendant would be liable as a debt collector as well, and both defendant and G.C.S. would be liable for statutory damages. A plaintiff who belonged both to the Randle class and to the putative Roe class would therefore be able to recover statutory damages against both defendants." Class was superior. "A class action will also allow the individual class members to avoid the costs and inconvenience of bringing individual actions against defendant. Finally, a successful class action will have a stronger deterrent effect on defendant than would the handful of individual actions that might otherwise be filed."

Davis-Holden v. Merchant's Legal Servs., 1999 WL 703293 (N.D. Ill. Aug. 25, 1999). In determining whether to certify a class, the court may properly look at the plaintiff's counsel's track record as class counsel in evaluating the adequacy of representation requirement of Rule 23(a).

Kane v. Shapiro, 1999 U.S. Dist. LEXIS 12679 (N.D. Ill. Aug. 16, 1999). Typicality requirement met where claim based on form letter received in connection with mortgage loans.

Morency v. Evanston Northwestern Healthcare Corp., 1999 U.S. Dist. LEXIS 11019 (N.D. Ill. July 14, 1999). The court approved an agreement between the plaintiff and the defendant collection agencies dismissing her putative class claims against them in exchange for modifying the collection letter at issue. The court disagreed with the creditor who objected to the settlement on the basis that the putative class members had to be notified and given the opportunity to object. Subsequently, in *Morency v. Evanston Northwestern Healthcare Corp.*, 1999 U.S. Dist. LEXIS 14744 (N.D. Ill. Sept. 13, 1999), the court dismissed the case against the creditor.

Nielsen v. Dickerson, 1999 WL 350649 (N.D. Ill. May 20, 1999), *aff'd on other grounds*, 307 F.3d 623 (7th Cir. 2002). Court granted class certification: (a) finding typicality despite the collection agency's claim that the named plaintiff was not confused by the offending letter until class counsel colored her opinion; (b) holding that the named plaintiff had standing to sue despite her failure to identify each defendant in her bankruptcy schedule while identifying the cause of action and other co-defendants; (c) finding the named plaintiff to be an adequate representative given her limited but sufficient knowledge and understanding of the suit; and (d) rejecting claim that class counsel was not an adequate representative because of purported solicitation of the named plaintiff and delay in seeking class certification.

Chancellor v. Nationwide Credit, Inc., 1999 WL 259951 (N.D. Ill. Apr. 6, 1999). A prior class action against Nationwide challenging its "Colorado" notice was settled by injunctive and monetary relief. This plaintiff and the class she represented were not included in the prior class action either as parties or class representatives. Res judicata did not bar the class. The court questioned whether the collection agency should get two settlements for the price of one and free releases from every potential plaintiff who did not benefit from the prior action. The court suggested an early Rule 68 offer of judgment by the collection agency.

Kaczor v. TRSI, Inc., 1999 U.S. Dist. LEXIS 4251 (N.D. Ill. Mar. 22, 1999) (Note: This decision follows the *Kaczor* decision in 1999 U.S. Dist. LEXIS 4252.) Defendant collection agency alleged that the named plaintiff was not an adequate class representative. The court disagreed, noting that the collection agency cited no authority that a prospective class plaintiff must do more than retain counsel and file a lawsuit to demonstrate that he or she is an interested party. "Thus, absent any hint whatsoever that Kaczor is a disinterested figurehead for counsel, the court will not require Kaczor to further demonstrate her interest in the litigation."

Scott v. Universal Fid. Corp., 1999 WL 138868 (N.D. Ill. Mar. 5, 1999). Pursuant to Rule 23(b)(3), the magistrate judge recommended certification of a class of all Illinois residents who met the following criteria: (1) on or after July 1, 1997 (2) they were sent collection letters in the form identical to the letter sent to Mr. Scott (3) by Universal Fidelity Corp. (4) in connection with the attempted collection of debts for non-business purposes, and (5) which letters were not returned as undeliverable by the Post Office. Assessing damages based on a debt collection agency's fair market value is consistent with the FDCPA's purpose of eliminating abusive debt collection practices without harming ethical debt collectors. Court was not persuaded that a de minimis recovery automatically barred class certification. The meaning of "net worth" under the FDCPA is fair market value.

Blair v. Equifax Check Servs., Inc., 1999 WL 116225 (N.D. Ill. Feb. 26, 1999), *aff'd on other grounds*, 181 F.3d 832 (7th Cir. 1999). The court certified a class consisting of all Illinois residents: (1) who were sent a demand letter by the collection agency on or after that date one year prior to the filing of this action; (2) in the form represented by the exhibit to plaintiffs' complaint; (3) in connection with an attempt to collect a check written to Champs or TJ Maxx for personal, family, or household purposes; and (4) where the letter was not returned by the Post Office. *Ballard* chart produced by Equifax showing 1790 persons in the class and 696 in the subclass was sufficient to satisfy numerosity. Because each instance of the alleged FDCPA violation required the court to determine whether the language in the collection agency's form documents sent to the class and subclass misled or confused the named plaintiffs in violation of the FDCPA's notice requirement, commonality was satisfied. Where the named plaintiffs' claims arose from the use of certain language in form collection letters, which language gave rise to the claims of the other class members based on the same legal theory, the typicality requirement was met. Although the named plaintiffs had undergone chapter 7 bankruptcy

proceedings, the court refused to hold that they were inadequate class representatives simply because they could not finance the present litigation. The mere fact that the consumer had written several bad checks did not make her incapable of fairly and adequately protecting the interests of the class. That Equifax may, in the future, assert a counterclaim against other class members did not create antagonism between the named plaintiffs and any other class members. A successful counterclaim against any class member would not affect the named plaintiff's representation of the class under the FDCPA, but would merely offset statutory damages. The court rejected Equifax's argument that it could not distinguish between checks written for personal or business purposes. Those few purchases made with a check written on a business entity's checking account could be easily segregated and excluded from the class. Because of the nature of this FDCPA dispute, the numerosity of the plaintiffs, and the fact that the named plaintiffs and their counsel adequately represented the interests of other members of the class, a class action was the best vehicle for the fair and efficient adjudication of the controversy.

Young v. Meyer & Njus, P.A., 183 F.R.D. 231 (N.D. Ill. 1998). Motion by defendant to decertify class, who had previously stipulated to class certification, was denied because the requirements for Rule 23(b)(2)class certification had been met.

Sledge v. Sands, 182 F.R.D. 255 (N.D. Ill. 1998). Based on debt collector's size and frequency with which it sent collection letters, numerosity was demonstrated for the purposes of Rule 23(a). Court rejected defendant's argument that because a few business debts may be included in the class receiving its dunning letters that there was a lack of commonality. "Such a finding would be contrary to the clear remedial goals of the FDCPA."

Randle v. G.C. Servs. L.P., 181 F.R.D. 602 (N.D. Ill. 1998). A Rule 23(b)(3) class was certified and defined as all Illinois residents who were sent a specific form collection letter concerning a debt which, from the records of the defendant or creditor or the nature of the debt, was a non-business debt allegedly owed to Publishers Clearing House; the letter was sent on or after November 18, 1996; and was not returned by the Postal Service. As long as class representatives' interests did not conflict with those of the proposed class, they need only have a marginal familiarity with the facts of the case and need not understand the larger legal theories upon which the case was based.

In re CBC Cos., 181 F.R.D. 380 (N.D. Ill. 1998). The named plaintiffs were adequate representatives of the three classes. The fact that some of the proposed class members may not ultimately meet the requirements to be part of the class did not defeat commonality.

Wilborn v. Dun & Bradstreet Corp., 180 F.R.D. 347 (N.D. Ill. 1998). Commonality existed regarding collection letters seeking to collect accounts of $5000 or less. Plaintiff's claims were typical of the class because they were not based on the debt which he allegedly owed; the claims were based on his receipt of an allegedly illegal collection letter from defendant. Defendant's alleged concern that individual class members may be able to recover more in individual actions was adequately addressed by the use of the Rule 23(b)(3) opt-out procedure.

Peters v. AT&T Corp., 179 F.R.D. 564 (N.D. Ill. 1998). Class certified as all elements of Rule 23, including adequacy of representation of the named plaintiff in face of charges of his lack of interest in the case, of understanding of the claims, and of monetary injury.

Augelli v. Googins & Lavintman, P.A., 1998 WL 842348 (N.D. Ill. Nov. 30, 1998). Motion to modify order certifying class or to be excluded from the class was denied because the letter in question was substantially "similar" to letter described in the class definition. Rule 60(b) does not provide authority for post-judgment modification of the class definition.

Brider v. Nationwide Credit, Inc., 1998 WL 729747 (N.D. Ill. Oct. 14, 1998). Alleged class of consumers who had not received prior communications from the defendant failed to meet the requirements of commonality and typicality because some proposed class members could have received letters or phone calls. Contradictions in the plaintiff's deposition testimony raised concerns about her credibility, resulting in a finding that the named plaintiff would not be an adequate class representative.

Trull v. Plaza Assocs., 1998 WL 578173 (N.D. Ill. Sept. 3, 1998). Even though a default judgment was entered against the defendant, plaintiff must present some evidence to allow the court to make the findings required by Rule 23, including the determination related to numerosity.

Francisco v. Doctors & Merchants Credit Serv., Inc., 1998 WL 474107 (N.D. Ill. Aug. 3, 1998). Adequacy of representation pursuant to Rule 23(a)(4) has three elements: (1) the chosen class representative cannot have antagonistic or conflicting claims with any other members of the class; (2) the named representative must have a sufficient interest in the outcome of the litigation to ensure vigorous advocacy; and (3) counsel for the named plaintiff must be competent, experienced, qualified, and generally able to conduct the proposed litigation vigorously.

Davis v. Suran, 1998 WL 474105 (N.D. Ill. Aug. 3, 1998). Sending more than 1000 letters in the same form met the numerosity requirement of Rule 23(a)(1). Sending a form collection letter met the commonality and typicality requirements of Rule 23(a)(2) and (3). A class action was the most efficient method of adjudicating the claims of numerous class members who, largely unsophisticated and uninformed of their rights, might not otherwise possess the initiative to commence an action on their own behalf.

Arellano v. Etan Indus., Inc., 1998 WL 417599 (N.D. Ill. July 20, 1998). Named plaintiff had sufficient knowledge of the facts and his duties as class representative to meet the requirements of representativeness pursuant to Rule 23(a)(4). Named plaintiff's conviction of misdemeanor theft in 1991 would not bar him from acting as the class representative.

Arango v. G.C. Servs., L.P., 1998 WL 325257 (N.D. Ill. June 11, 1998). Class certified over defendant's objections that the named plaintiff was an inadequate class representative because he lacked a basic understanding of the claims, could not speak English, and suffered no monetary injury.

Wells v. McDonough, 1998 WL 160876 (N.D. Ill. Mar. 31, 1998), *motion to decertify denied*, 188 F.R.D. 277 (N.D. Ill. 1999). Class certified. Fact that the named plaintiff disputed the underlying debt while other class members did not was irrelevant. Named plaintiff's marginal understanding of the class issues did not prevent him from being class representative, since the FDCPA was designed to protect unsophisticated consumers and the plaintiff's lack of understanding simply confirmed that he was unsophisticated.

Miller v. Wexler & Wexler, 1998 WL 60798 (N.D. Ill. Feb. 6, 1998). Class certified. Named plaintiff's failure to pay the allegedly inflated sums that were added to the amount of the dishonored check and that formed the basis for the substantive violations did not deprive her of standing. Whether some class members wrote the checks with the intent not to pay was irrelevant under *Bass* and therefore could not be a basis to deny certification.

McFarland v. Bass & Assocs., 1998 WL 42286 (N.D. Ill. Jan. 30, 1998). Class certification denied, but with suggestion that additional facts would permit certification at a later date. Class was defined as all consumers who were dunned by the defendant lawyers for payment under a bankruptcy reaffirmation agreement that was never approved by the bankruptcy court. The court found all requirements of Rule 23 were met, except numerosity. On that issue, the plaintiff provided some evidence suggesting a pool of 500 persons within the class, but without showing the relevant timeframe of their circumstances. The court would not speculate as to the actual numbers in the relevant period.

Perovich v. Humphrey, 1997 WL 674975 (N.D. Ill. Oct. 28, 1997). The consumers having shown no monetary injury and no particular desire to obtain monetary relief were inadequate class representatives, and the court refused to certify the class action. Principle was an insufficient basis for acting as class representative.

Drennan v. Van Ru Credit Corp., 1997 WL 305298 (N.D. Ill. June 2, 1997). Pursuant to Rule 23(b)(2) the court certified a class defined as (i) all persons with addresses in the state of Minnesota (ii) to whom collection letters entitled "LEGAL REVIEW NOTIFICATION" or "NOTICE OF POSSIBLE WAGE GARNISHMENT" were sent (iii) in an attempt to collect a debt incurred for student loans (iv) which were not returned as undelivered by the U.S. Post Office. In a Rule 23(b)(2) class action, damages for the class were distributed in a *cy pres* remedy to a legal aid program.

Lawson v. Mgmt. Adjustment Bureau, Inc., 1997 WL 283027 (N.D. Ill. May 15, 1997). Debtor's motion for class certification was granted where the debtor had demonstrated sufficient knowledge about her claim, had no interests adverse to those of potential class members, and was willing to participate in the litigation, thereby meeting the adequacy of representation requirement of Fed. R. Civ. P. 23(a). Class certification was also warranted under Fed. R. Civ. P. 23(b) because the question of whether defendant's notice violated the FDCPA was a question of law common to all the potential members.

Drennan v. Van Ru Credit Corp., 1997 WL 160757 (N.D. Ill. Apr. 3, 1997). Where the class representative's deposition indicated that the collector actually had garnished his wages contrary to the allegations of the FDCPA complaint, the consumer would have to show a basis for the surviving claim, that the garnishment was illegal, before the court would consider certifying the class action.

Kohlenbrener v. Dickenson, 1996 WL 131736 (N.D. Ill. Mar. 15, 1996). A class action was not superior to individual actions where only statutory damages were sought and defendant had negative or very small net worth. Motion for class certification was denied, but plaintiff may try again if discovery in the individual action indicated that defendants' net worth was larger than they claimed.

Villarreal v. Snow, 1996 WL 28254 (N.D. Ill. Jan. 19, 1996). Motion for class certification was allowed as to FDCPA claims against Beneficial Illinois and its attorney. Plaintiff had standing where she had signed the loan agreement as co-owner of real estate used to secure the other co-owner's loan. Numerosity and commonality were satisfied where the lender sent out form letters which allegedly violated notice requirements of FDCPA. Where the consumer's claim resulted from the same course of conduct as other claims, typicality was present. Plaintiff was adequate representative, even though she was seeking only statutory, not actual damages. In determining that counsel would adequately represent class, the court looked to counsel's performance in other class action cases. A class action was superior because individual claims were small, most claimants were consumers, and a class action was convenient and efficient way to challenge legality of document sent to all class members.

Narwick v. Wexler, 901 F. Supp. 1275 (N.D. Ill. 1995). Class certification was denied for failure to demonstrate numerosity; affidavit of plaintiffs' attorney, based on a 7% sampling of defendants' court filings to collect a debt, which examined the residence of the debtor but failed to consider the location of the signing of the contract, was inadequate.

Gammon v. G.C. Servs. Ltd. P'ship, 162 F.R.D. 313 (N.D. Ill. 1995). Plaintiff was adequate class representative despite defendant's challenge that he was uninformed as to the substance and status of the litigation, where plaintiff testified at deposition that he had read the letter at issue and found it threatening because the defendant was somehow connected with "the government and taxes," that the purpose of the litigation was to require the defendant to change the letter, that he understood the nature of a class action and his duties as class representative, that he had spoken with his attorney before the filing of the complaint, that he was familiar with the status of the lawsuit and that damages would be awarded at the discretion of the court. Defendant's assertion that plaintiff's attorneys were inadequate as class counsel because they had filed numerous FDCPA class actions was rejected, since appointment as class counsel demonstrated their expertise. To certify a class under Fed. R. Civ. P. 23(b)(2), nonmonetary relief must predominate over money damages. Where the FDCPA plaintiff prevailed on issue of liability, statutory damages flowed from the award of declaratory relief. Because the amount of statutory damages each class member would receive was de minimis, statutory damages would flow from the award of declaratory judgment, and the amount of statutory damages were readily calculated, non-monetary relief predominated over the request for damages. Class certification was not barred simply because some class members may recover lesser statutory damages than they would have had they brought their claims individually.

Holloway v. Pekay, 1995 WL 736925 (N.D. Ill. Dec. 11, 1995). "At least 310 non-student-loan debtors" met the numerosity requirement for class certification. Plaintiff, who was not a student loan debtor, was not a proper representative of the class comprised of student loan debtors. Circuit court certified a class consisting of all persons against whom defendants had filed an action in the county where the class member did not reside or had not signed the contract giving rise to the action. All class members had such a debt related to the purchase of a used car.

Vaughn v. CSC Credit Servs., Inc., 1995 WL 51402 (N.D. Ill. Feb.

3, 1995). Court approved limiting the class to those consumers who received a collection letter concerning deficiency claims on automobile contracts. A class was certified consisting of "all persons who, between July 12, 1992 and July 12, 1993, were sent by CSC form documents similar to Exhibit A to the Complaint in connection with purported debts consisting of alleged deficiencies on contracts for the purchase or lease of motor vehicles."

Avila v. Van Ru Credit Corp., 1995 WL 41425 (N.D. Ill. Jan. 31, 1995), *aff'd* 84 F.3d 222 (7th Cir. 1996). "Unlike TILA, the FDCPA's civil liability provision does not make the $500,000 limitation an absolute liability cap if a series of class actions were brought on the same violation." FDCPA litigation arising from a collector's standardized procedures or forms is particularly appropriate for class action treatment. The ability of consumers who are members of an FDCPA class action, to bring individual FDCPA suits for more damages was preserved by ample notice and use of the Fed. R. Civ. P. 23(b)(3) opt-out procedure. FDCPA case was certified as a class consisting of all persons (a) in Connecticut to whom collectors sent demand letters (b) using the forms represented by the exhibits to the complaint (c) which were not returned undelivered by the post office and (d) in connection with attempts to collect debts arising from student loans and medical or hospital bills.

Beasley v. Blatt, 1994 WL 362185 (N.D. Ill. July 11, 1994). A class of all persons who received debt collector's form documents in connection with purported debts arising from automobile leases satisfied the Fed. R. Civ. P. 23 requirements and class certification was granted.

Oglesby v. Rotche, 1994 WL 142867 (N.D. Ill. Apr. 18, 1994). Where the court granted the debt collector's motion asking the court to review the merits of the debt collector's summary judgment motion before considering class certification issues on the condition that the debt collector agree to waive any objections to future class certification based on the fact that the merits of the case had already been decided, the debt collector could not object to the consumers' motion to expand the class after summary judgment was entered for the consumer.

Vaughn v. CSC Credit Servs., 1994 WL 449247 (N.D. Ill. Mar. 1, 1994). Consumer's motion for class certification for consumers who had received the debt collector's form collection letter in connection with motor vehicle loans or leases was granted even though other types of consumers had received the form letter and the class could have been defined more broadly. Consumer's motion for class certification for a class of consumers who had received a second demand letter from the debt collector within two weeks of the first was denied because the named plaintiff had not received a second demand letter.

Brewer v. Friedman, 152 F.R.D. 142 (N.D. Ill. 1993). Class defined as all persons from whom attorney collector collected or attempted to collect a consumer debt by use of documents identical to or similar in form to those received by the named plaintiffs was certified.

Broome v. Feingold, Lang & Levy, 1991 WL 214159 (N.D. Ill. Oct. 17, 1991). Class action certification was denied without prejudice because alleged class and subclass were vaguely defined, making determination of numerosity and commonality impossible. Plaintiffs were given ninety days in which to file a Motion for Class Certification after appropriate discovery has been completed.

Zanni v. Lippold, 119 F.R.D. 32 (C.D. Ill. 1988). 151 member FDCPA class for damages certified; injunctive relief denied.

Smith v. Mikell, Clearinghouse No. 34,362C (N.D. Ill. 1982). Determination of right of the putative consumer class to actual damages should await the consumers' opportunity to adduce evidence.

Indiana

Rayl v. Moores, 2010 WL 468096 (S.D. Ind. Feb. 4, 2010). Because it is not clear if the class representative heard the prerecorded message by the debt collection attorney at the attorney's phone number listed on a small claims court collection suit, the court denied class certification pending clarification.

Hubbard v. Midland Credit Mgmt., Inc., 2008 WL 5384219 (S.D. Ind. Dec. 19, 2008). Class certified in this case alleging that the defendant's form letter offering "a 50 percent discount before a specified date" was false, deceptive, or misleading in violation of § 1692e, "because the defendants would have been willing to settle the debt at any time and for less than the amount they said they were willing to accept." This claim was sustained in the earlier appeal of this case when the Seventh Circuit "held that such a claim could be viable if a plaintiff is able to demonstrate using a survey that comports with the principles of professional survey research that a sufficiently large segment of the unsophisticated public is likely to be deceived by such language. *See Evory v. RJM Acquisitions Funding L.L.C.*, 505 F.3d 769 (7th Cir. 2007)."

Evory v. RJM Acquisitions Funding, L.L.C., 2008 WL 4890591 (S.D. Ind. Nov. 12, 2008). Plaintiff's motion to dismiss an FDCPA case certified as a class action was granted on the basis that the projected expense of $25,000 or more to conduct a survey to prove that the merits of the case was not warranted.

Stavroff v. Midland Credit Mgmt., 2005 U.S. Dist. LEXIS 11640 (N.D. Ind. June 8, 2005). The court exercised its discretion to bifurcate class certification from the merits and ordered the class determination stayed until resolution of liability.

Sheets v. Nat'l Action Fin. Servs., 2005 U.S. Dist. LEXIS 8439 (N.D. Ind. May 9, 2005). The court exercised its discretion to bifurcate class certification from the merits and ordered the class determination stayed until resolution of liability.

Woolley v. Krisor & Assoc., 2000 U.S. Dist LEXIS 7069 (S.D. Ind. May 15, 2000). FDCPA class certified based on excessive attorney fee claim despite their limited recovery under the Act. "In keeping with the principles espoused in Mace and in recognition that Congress expressly authorized class actions notwithstanding the damages 'cap,' the court finds the appropriate remedy was simply to include an explanation of the right to bring an individual action in the notice to the class. . . . Moreover, class members were free to opt out of the class to pursue an individual action."

Iowa

Liles v. American Corrective Counseling Servs., Inc., 231 F.R.D. 565 (S.D. Iowa 2005). In this case alleging violations of the FDCPA by a check collection agency, the court certified a class consisting of persons in ten states.

Louisiana

Henderson v. Eaton, 2002 WL 31415728 (E.D. La. Oct. 25, 2002). The court found the class settlement fair and reasonable which provided $20,000 in attorney fees, $3000 to the named plaintiff as an incentive award, and $3000 to be divided among 142 class members.

Henderson v. Eaton, 2002 U.S. Dist. LEXIS 274 (E.D. La. Jan. 2, 2002). FDCPA class action certified. Defendant's statement that the letter in issue had been sent over 250 times was sufficient to satisfy the numerosity requirement.

Byes v. Telecheck Recovery Servs., Inc., 173 F.R.D. 421 (E.D. La. 1997). If all proposed class members received at least one of the five letters in issue, commonality was satisfied. The named plaintiff's claim was typical if it was based on the same legal theories and arose from the same event or practice or course of conduct that gave rise to the claims of the other class members. Where each collection letter was different, all class members did not receive all five letters, and the class was defined as persons who were "sent" the letters instead of those who received the letters, the plaintiff's claims were not typical of those of the class. While the class representative was not required to understand the meaning of complex legal terms or to direct litigation strategies, he or she should have had some awareness of the basic facts underlying the suit. A criminal record of the named plaintiff was not per se disqualifying. Where named plaintiff signed affidavit which stated that she understood each specific claim in the lawsuit, the class definitions, and her duties as class representative, but her deposition testimony demonstrated she did not, the affidavit indicated that she had placed blind faith in her attorneys. Class counsel undertakes a responsibility to give the class representative sufficient information to participate intelligently in settlement and/or settlement negotiations. Where the named plaintiff was unaware of her duties as class representative and her attorneys failed to communicate settlement offers to her, representation was not adequate.

Byes v. Accelerated Cash Flow, 1997 WL 285004 (E.D. La. May 27, 1997). Debtor's motion for class certification was denied because debtor's evidence regarding the potential size of the class was insufficient to meet the numerosity requirement of Fed. R. Civ. P. 23(a)(1) where the debt collector stated only five of 4000 Louisiana consumers received the letters which were the basis of the class complaint.

Byes v. Kelly & Kano, Inc., 1997 U.S. Dist. LEXIS 7358 (E.D. La. May 22, 1997). Five letters included a $20 service fee for each NSF check. Whether this fee was legally collectable depended on an individual factual determination of whether the collection of the fee was authorized by agreement creating the debt or by law under § 1692f(1). Individual factual assessments did not prevent finding of commonality. One common legal or factual issue was sufficient to satisfy commonality. The class was defined as persons who were sent the letters. Class members who never received their letters would not have claims typical of Byes who received all five letters. Considering these facts, Byes failed to show that her claims were typical. Byes was admittedly unaware that she had some duties as a class representative. Her attorneys submitted an affidavit which defendants showed to be inaccurate. Her attorneys failed to communicate settlement offers to her. Any one of these factors standing alone might not have rendered representation inadequate but in combination they made representation inadequate.

Maryland

Peoples v. Wendover Funding, Inc., 179 F.R.D. 492 (D. Md. 1998). Rule 23(b)(3) class certified as to question of liability, reserving issue of damages that may be owing to each class member.

Massachusetts

Pettway v. Harmon Law Offices, P.C., 2005 WL 2365331 (D. Mass. Sept. 27, 2005). Class certification was granted in an FDCPA action alleging that attorney fees were overstated and the collection letter was false and deceptive.

Michigan

Stolicker v. Muller, Muller, Richmond, Harms, Myers & Sgroi, P.C., 2006 WL 1547274 (W.D. Mich. June 2, 2006). The court followed the Seventh Circuit in *Sanders* and held that "net worth" is limited to book value or balance sheet net worth and does not include goodwill.

Gradisher v. Check Enforcement Unit, Inc., 2003 WL 187416 (W.D. Mich. Jan. 22, 2003). Consumers prevailed on summary judgment but decertified their class action when it became apparent that the debt collector's net worth for calculating class damages was negligible.

Gradisher v. Check Enforcement Unit, Inc., 210 F.R.D. 907 (W.D. Mich. 2002). The court granted the plaintiff's motion to decertify the class previously approved because of the *de minimis* recovery ($0.06 per identified class member) available as a result of the 1% of net worth statutory damage cap and ordered the parties to split the cost of notice to the class of the decertification.

Gradisher v. Check Enforcement Unit, Inc., 203 F.R.D. 271 (W.D. Mich. 2001). The court certified a class under Rule 23(b)(3) but declined to certify under Rule 23(b)(2).

Case v. Whetstone, 1998 WL 276088 (W.D. Mich. May 7, 1998). Class certification denied as one of the violations may have been a result of an isolated error, and there was conflicting evidence about the attorney's role in sending a form letter threatening suit to at least hundreds of consumers. None of the Rule 23(a) requirements—numerosity, commonality, typicality or adequacy of representation—were met. Individual questions predominated and separate inquiry into circumstances of each class member was required to determine defendants' alleged violations for, *inter alia*, falsely threatening suit and sending an attorney letter without the prior review by the attorney.

Minnesota

Mund v. EMCC, Inc., 259 F.R.D. 180 (D. Minn. 2009). On meeting all requirements, class certification was granted in an FDCPA case claiming that the debt collector violated § 1692f(1) by adding a collection fee based on a percentage rather than actual costs of collection.

Knoll v. Intellirisk Mgmt., 2006 WL 2974190 (D. Minn. Oct. 16, 2006). Denied debt collector's motion to dismiss class action where debt collector used the false name, Jennifer Smith, as the Caller ID finding a claim was stated under §§ 1692d, 1692e, 1692f.

Munoz v. Pipestone Fin., L.L.C., 2006 WL 2786911 (D. Minn. Sept. 26, 2006). Class certification was denied because the proposed class definition did not distinguish between receivables and other accounts which would necessarily proceed on different legal theories.

Thinesen v. JBC Legal Group, P.C., 2005 WL 2346991 (D. Minn. Sept. 26, 2005). FDCPA class certified claiming threats to sue on time-barred checks and asserting excessive check fees.

Egge v. Healthspan Servs. Co., 208 F.R.D. 265 (D. Minn. 2002). Based on evidence gleaned from the files of a sample of 50 putative class members, the court certified the requested class as meeting each of the requirements of Rule 23.

Sonmore v. CheckRite Recovery Servs., 206 F.R.D. 257 (D. Minn. 2001). The two named plaintiffs were not adequate class representatives where, with summary judgment having already been entered on liability, each would be entitled to a maximum $1000 individual statutory damage recovery immediately and therefore would not seem to have a sufficient incentive to pursue the absent class members' interests vigorously, since they would not receive any larger recovery later than that to which they were now entitled. Class action was not superior because class treatment would be detrimental to absent class members as it would substantially limit their recovery from $1000 each in an individual action to between 15 cents and $25 per class member depending on the defendant's net worth.

Sonmore v. CheckRite Recovery Servs., Inc., 2001 U.S. Dist. LEXIS 18224 (D. Minn. Oct. 26, 2001). Joint motion for class certification was denied because the superiority requirement of Rule 23(b)(3) was not met where 150,000 potential class members would receive a maximum potential recovery of 25 cents each and there were questions about the adequacy of the representation.

Mississippi

Harrell v. Checkagain, L.L.C., 248 F.R.D. 199 (S.D. Miss. May 2, 2006). Class certification denied where claim of illegality of bounced check fees involved individualized issues such as whether there was a point of sale sign or an express agreement.

Walton v. Franklin Collection Agency, Inc., 190 F.R.D. 404 (N.D. Miss. 2000). As part of its analysis of the adequacy of representation, court reviewed zeal and competency of counsel. Court found that solo practitioner met his burden where he had substantial litigation experience, a familiarity with the issues, and had competently and vigorously maintained the suit to date. Because the potential class included hundreds of plaintiffs, in the future, counsel could find it necessary to associate outside counsel to assist. At such time, counsel would be required to file a motion detailing the qualifications of the proposed co-counsel. One of the three named plaintiffs could not be a class member in a case against a debt collector who sought attorney fees for services rendered by a non-attorney since his judgment was amended so that he was not assessed attorney fees as part of his final judgment. Court certified class but the individual plaintiff's case was dismissed without prejudice. Although the amount of damage suffered by each member of the class may have to be proven on an individual basis, the fact of injury was common to the class. Small differences in the amount of damage suffered by each class member would not preclude class certification.

Lyles v. Rosenfeld Attorney Network, 2000 U.S. Dist. LEXIS 8543 (N.D. Miss. May 19, 2000). Court denied certification of a class of some 27,000 persons as not superior to individual actions due to the court's misreading of the plain language of the Act leading it to conclude that the 1% of net worth statutory limits on recovery of statutory damages applied to the class recovery of actual damages as well. As a result the court believed consumers consequently had in prosecuting separate claims for their average of nearly $300 paid for decedent estates' debts which the relatives who were dunned did not owe.

Nebraska

Harris v. D. Scott Carruthers & Assoc., 2010 WL 2773891 (D. Neb. July 13, 2010). Certified a class action of Nebraska residents to whom defendants sent specific form letters for violations of §§ 1692e, 1692f, 1692g. Certification under Rule 23(b)(2) is improper for a class action brought pursuant to the FDCPA because neither equitable nor injunctive relief was available to the class. Where the defendants argued (against superiority) in an FDCPA class action case that the class members would receive no statutory damages under the FDCPA, the defendants had the burden of demonstrating their negative net worth.

Jenkins v. General Collection Co., 2008 WL 4104677 (D. Neb. Aug. 28, 2008). Class certification denied because the defendants could argue that their state court collection actions could have been based on written contracts which would require an individual inquiry to determine membership in the class.

Evans v. American Credit Sys., Inc., 222 F.R.D. 388 (D. Neb. 2004). The district judge adopted the magistrate's recommendation certifying the class and overruled the defendant's objections that the time periods for the classes were not sufficiently definite and that the named plaintiffs in one subclass were not representative of the class.

Valderrama v. Nat'l Revenue Corp., 1981 U.S. Dist. LEXIS 18627 (D. Neb. Sept. 28, 1981). Amendments to complaint allowed consumers to delete Rule 23(b)(3) class allegation and substitute a Rule 23(b)(2) injunctive class allegation when discovery indicated that the debt collector's net worth was insufficient for a significant recovery of statutory damages. Class injunctive action for FDCPA violations certified. Protective orders granted to collector which alleged expenses greatly in excess of the amount in controversy in order to respond to certain interrogatories and requests for admissions.

Nevada

Santoro v. Aargon Agency, Inc., 252 F.R.D. 675 (D. Nev. 2008). Class certified where the plaintiff showed that the defendant collector sent to 10,000 consumers an initial dunning letter that allegedly (1) failed to notify consumers of their right to receive verification of the debt by sending the debt collector written notice that they dispute the debt, in violation of §§ 1692g(a)(4) and 1692g(b); (2) failed to itemize, and attempted to collect, additional charges or interest added by the debt collector to the amount claimed by the creditor, in violation of §§ 1692e(2), 1692e(5),

1692f(1), and 1692g(a)(1); and (3) listed the name of the debt collector as the "original creditor," in violation of §§ 1692g(a)(1), 1692e, 1692e(2), 1692e(10), and 1692f.

New Hampshire

Silva v. Nat'l Telewire Corp., 2000 U.S. Dist. LEXIS 13986 (D.N.H. Sept. 22, 2000). Rule 23(b)(2) class denied because monetary claims predominated.

New Jersey

Zimmerman v. Zwicker & Assocs., P.C., 2011 WL 65912 (D.N.J. Jan. 10, 2011). The parties' joint motion for conditional certification and preliminary approval of amended class action settlement agreement was denied because: (1) the proposed class definition was indefinite and overbroad, e.g., "collection letter" was undefined; (2) there was a phantom benefit, i.e., $32,289.44 paid as a *cy pres* award to United Way for financial education activities to a nationwide class of approximately 800,000 members but the class was required to release all their FDCPA claims; and (3) the scope of the proposed release and agreement not to sue was over-inclusive.

Agostino v. Quest Diagnostics Inc., 2010 WL 5392688 (D.N.J. Dec. 22, 2010). The court denied class certification: "The absence of any proof that putative class members received a common debt collection letter frustrates commonality and typicality in an action pursuing relief under the Fair Debt Collection Practices Act for a debt collector's communication that it will take action that it is illegal or otherwise unauthorized."

Richardson v. Allied Interstate, Inc., 2010 WL 3404978 (D.N.J. Aug. 26, 2010). The district court rejected as clearly erroneous the magistrate judge's recommended ruling to deny the plaintiff leave to file an amended complaint to expand the putative FDCPA statewide class to a national class.

Nicholas v. CMRE Fin. Servs, Inc., 2010 WL 1049935 (D.N.J. Mar. 16, 2010). Defendant's motion to dismiss the putative class based on an alleged de minimis recovery was denied.

Agostino v. Quest Diagnostics Inc., 256 F.R.D. 437 (D.N.J. 2009). Injunctive relief is not available in FDCPA actions. Because a court would have to engage in a transaction-by-transaction analysis of the alleged billing improprieties, defendants conclude that the class lacks the requisite cohesiveness and, therefore, certification under Rule 23(b)(2) should be denied. Individual questions of medical coverages and damages required denial of certification under Rule 23(b)(3).

Hurwitz v. Hecker, 2009 WL 4282194 (D.N.J. Nov. 30, 2009). Putative class case dismissed based on conclusory allegation that state required Kansas and Utah notices violated FDCPA.

Stair ex rel. Smith v. Thomas & Cook, 254 F.R.D. 191 (D.N.J. 2008). The court certified a class comprised of the 227 individuals who received the same form dunning letter containing the same alleged violation of disclosing the complete validation notice but followed by an allegedly contradictory two-week response demand to avoid suit. The court ordered class notice detailing the pro-rata distribution of $12.11 per member and disclosing class counsel's entitlement to attorney fees to be awarded against the defendant as a lodestar calculation and not from the class recovery/common fund.

Smith v. Lyons, Doughty & Veldhuius, P.C., 2008 WL 2885887 (D.N.J. July 23, 2008). The consumer failed to state a classwide cause of action for violation of §§ 1692c(a)(2) and 1692c(c) because an individual inquiry of each class member would be required; plaintiff was granted leave to amend the complaint.

Barkouras v. Hecker, 2006 WL 3544585 (D.N.J. Dec. 8, 2006). Class action certified despite collection lawyer's and debt buyer's arguments that the class action was not superior because they had negative net worth.

Weiss v. Regal Collections, 2006 U.S. Dist. LEXIS 48995 (D.N.J. July 18, 2006). Final approval of this FDCPA class action settlement with $157.38 distributed to the 413 class members, and any remainder a *cy pres* distribution to the Nclcccccc, and counsel sought attorney fees of only $60,000 when the lodestar was over $108,000.

New York

Huntley v. Law Office of Richard Clark, P.L.L.C., 262 F.R.D. 203 (E.D.N.Y. 2009). Class certification denied where the plaintiff, who allegedly received a threatening phone call from defendant, submitted "no evidence in the record—other than the Plaintiff's speculative allegation—to suggest that other consumers received threatening phone calls."

Leone v. Ashwood Fin., Inc., 257 F.R.D. 343 (E.D.N.Y. 2009). The court modified and approved the FDCPA class notice.

Gravina v. Client Servs., Inc., 2009 U.S. Dist. LEXIS 78204 (E.D.N.Y. Aug. 25, 2009). Settlement of nationwide class claims arising from messages left by defendant for settlement class members on telephone answering device included an injunction permanently enjoining defendant as follows: all telephone voice messages left by defendant for consumers on telephone answering devices will meaningfully identify the defendant as the caller, state the purpose or the nature of the communication, and disclose that the communication is from a debt collector.

Anderson v. Nationwide Credit Inc., 2009 U.S. Dist. LEXIS 57157 (E.D.N.Y. June 25, 2009). FDCPA class settlement permanently enjoined the defendant as follows: "All telephone voice messages left by Defendant for consumers on telephone answering devices will meaningfully identify the Defendant as the caller, state the purpose or nature of the communication, and disclose that the communication is from a debt collector."

Aramburu v. Healthcare Fin. Servs., Inc., 2009 WL 1086938 (E.D.N.Y. Apr. 22, 2009). The court approved this FDCPA class action settlement finding it to be fair, adequate, and reasonable.

Fainbrun v. Southwest Credit Sys., L.P., 2008 WL 750550 (E.D.N.Y. 2008). The class was decertified on the joint motion of the parties in light of the de minimis recovery available ($5000 net worth and $50 available to the 140,000 member nationwide class) and the court's resulting finding that class superiority was no longer present.

Fainbrun v. Southwest Credit Sys., L.P., 246 F.R.D 128 (E.D.N.Y. 2007). The court certified a nationwide class of all consumers who received the form dun containing the offending language misrepresenting that additional late payments would provide additional harm to the person's credit report.

Ayzelman v. Statewide Credit Servs. Corp., 238 F.R.D. 358

(E.D.N.Y. 2006). Approved the class action settlement and the form of the class notice.

Reade-Alvarez v. Eltman, Eltman & Cooper, P.C., 237 F.R.D. 26 (E.D.N.Y. 2006). The court certified a settlement class and granted preliminary approval of the proposed settlement where collection attorneys agreed to exercise supervision and control over nonattorney staff in compliance with the FDCPA and state bar ethics rules, payment of $15,000 as a *cy pres* payment to Queens County Legal Aid Society, $1000 to each named plaintiff as statutory damages, $1000 to each named plaintiff for their services as class representatives, and $50,000 for costs and attorney fees.

Cinelli v. MCS Claim Servs., Inc., 236 F.R.D. 118 (E.D.N.Y. 2006). Court approved the proposed settlement of this small class action alleging a defective § 1692g notice.

Larsen v. JBC Legal Group, P.C., 235 F.R.D. 191 (E.D.N.Y. 2006). Plaintiff's motion for leave to move simultaneously for summary judgment and Rule 23(b)(3) class certification for purposes of shifting the cost of notice to the defendants who were allegedly not paying outstanding judgments, was denied. The FDCPA claims included failure to state the amount of the debt and threatening suit on time-barred claims.

Leyse v. Corporate Collection Servs., Inc., 2006 WL 2708451 (S.D.N.Y. Sept. 18, 2006). Where the number of prerecorded messages to consumers were not restricted the number to calls placed on behalf of the creditor in the class definition within the class period, the numerosity requirement of Rule 23(a)(1) was not satisfied and resulted in a denial of class certification of this FDCPA case.

Reade-Alvarez v. Eltman, Eltman & Cooper, P.C., 2006 WL 941765 (E.D.N.Y. Apr. 12, 2006). The court held that certification of a class pursuant to Rule 23(b)(1)(A) was inappropriate and granted class certification pursuant to Rule 23(b)(3). Plaintiff was required to bear the cost of individual class notice.

Gross v. Washington Mut. Bank, F.A., 2006 WL 318814 (E.D.N.Y. Feb. 9, 2006). The court certified a class action and found the proposed settlement to be well within the range of reasonableness. The court approved a 100% multiplier for the attorney's hourly rate and awarded $115,000 in attorney fees. The court approved a $5000 incentive award for the named plaintiff.

Vega v. Credit Bureau Enters., 2005 U.S. Dist. LEXIS 4927 (E.D.N.Y. Mar. 29, 2005). Certification of an FDCPA action for statutory damages where the class numbered in excess of 1.6 million was granted pursuant to Rule 23(b)(3), but not Rule 23(b)(2).

In re Risk Mgmt. Alternatives, Inc., 208 F.R.D. 493 (S.D.N.Y. 2002). The court certified a class action defined as "All persons to whom Defendant and its agents sent initial communications in the form of the April 9, 2001 letter mailed to plaintiff Gerda Schaake, or otherwise containing the identical subject language, in an attempt to collect a consumer debt, as reflected by Defendant's records, on or after May 23, 2000." "Suits brought under the FDCPA such as this case regularly satisfy the superiority requirement of Rule 23."

Weiss v. Fein, Such, Kahn & Shepard, P.C., 2002 U.S. Dist. LEXIS 4783 (S.D.N.Y. Mar. 21, 2002). Class certification denied where the sole evidence of numerosity was the consumer's speculation "on information and belief" that the subject dun had been sent to anyone other than the named plaintiff.

Mailloux v. Arrow Fin. Servs., L.L.C., 2002 U.S. Dist. LEXIS 3314 (E.D.N.Y. Feb. 21, 2002). Plaintiff in class action was entitled to discover defendant's tax returns and other financial information relevant to statutory damage determination of the defendant's net worth, notwithstanding defendant's offer to provide an affidavit of net worth, since the plaintiff was entitled to examine the underlying data to test the defendant's calculations. Motion to compel granted.

Mailloux v. Arrow Fin. Servs., L.L.C., 204 F.R.D. 38 (E.D.N.Y. 2001). Proposed class of Sears customers who received its collection agency's letter threatening a broad inquiry into their assets satisfied the requirements of Rule 23(a) and (b)(3) and was certified.

Edge v. C. Tech Collections, Inc., 203 F.R.D. 85 (E.D.N.Y. 2001). Class certification was denied when, because of lack of discovery, plaintiff could not establish numerosity.

Wilner v. OSI Collection Servs., Inc., 201 F.R.D. 321 (S.D.N.Y. 2001). The court denied class certification pending additional information about the qualification of the class representative after reversing an earlier decision dismissing the action as moot based on an offer of judgment found to be less than complete on reconsideration.

Wilner v. OSI Collection Servs., 198 F.R.D. 393 (S.D.N.Y. 2001). Evidence of numerosity must be presented to obtain class certification; the obviousness of numerous duns by MCI's multistate collection agency was not enough.

Kupfer v. Goodman, 2000 U.S. Dist. LEXIS 7951 (E.D.N.Y. May 17, 2000). Where the named plaintiff entered into a new retainer agreement assuming responsibility for his pro rata share of costs of the action as required by state disciplinary rules, he became an adequate class representative and the class attacking excessive attorney collection fees was certified.

Weber v. Goodman, 9 F. Supp. 2d 163 (E.D.N.Y. 1998). While court found all other elements of Rule 23 were met, class certification denied on basis of inadequacy of class representation because (1) counsel, not the named plaintiff, was the real decision maker in the case, and (2) named plaintiff was not obligated by the fee agreement to pay even his pro rata share of costs. Reconsideration was granted and class certification was allowed after counsel modified its fee agreement with named plaintiff, see 1998 WL 1807355 (E.D.N.Y. June 1, 1998).

Sokolski v. Trans Union Corp., 178 F.R.D. 393 (E.D.N.Y. 1998). Leave to amend complaint to add a class action was granted, rejecting the defendant's argument that the class action was time barred, since the class amendment related back to the filing of the original complaint because it was based on the same claim.

Berrios v. Sprint Corp., 1998 U.S. Dist. LEXIS 22833 (E.D.N.Y. Sept. 10, 1998). Plaintiff's renewed motion for class certification was allowed because plaintiff had since met the requirement under Rule 23(a) of adequacy of representation by entering into a fee agreement under which plaintiff made an initial contribution of $1 toward litigation expenses rather than no responsibility at all, and

any attorney fee award would be split among counsel in proportion to their respective work and costs rather than equally.

Villari v. Performance Capital Mgmt., Inc., 1998 WL 414932 (S.D.N.Y. July 22, 1998). Because plaintiff's claim was subject to a bona fide error defense, it was not typical, and a Rule 23(b)(3) class could not be certified.

Weber v. Goodman, 1998 U.S. Dist. LEXIS 22832 (E.D.N.Y. May 26, 1998). Plaintiff's motion for reconsideration of denial of motion for class certification (*Weber v. Goodman*, 9 F. Supp. 2d 163 (E.D.N.Y. 1998)) was allowed because plaintiff had since entered into a fee agreement under which plaintiff made an initial contribution of $1 toward litigation expenses rather than no responsibility at all, and named plaintiff's strategic decision not to seek actual damages on behalf of himself or the class did not undermine named plaintiff's adequacy as class representative or suggest lack of control over counsel.

Berrios v. Sprint Corp., 1998 U.S. Dist. LEXIS 6579 (E.D.N.Y. May 16, 1998). The party seeking class certification has the burden of demonstrating that all of the criteria of Rule 23(a) were met. Individual counterclaims for the debt might overwhelm common questions, but such counterclaims are not within the court's supplemental jurisdiction because they arise from a distinct set of facts. The need to determine the consumer nature of a debt for coverage by the FDCPA did not preclude class certification where the defendant Sprint distinguished between residential and business customers. Courts have been satisfied with the plaintiff's financial responsibility for class expenses if plaintiff's counsel agreed to pay all necessary costs and if the class representative agreed to pay a pro rata share of the costs should the suit be unsuccessful. Plaintiff was not an adequate class representative because plaintiff had not agreed to bear ultimate liability for her pro rata share of costs and expenses of the lawsuit estimated at $.40. Counsel for plaintiff was an inadequate representative because it continued to miscite authority even after its error was pointed out in defendant's memo of law.

Deflumer v. Overton, 176 F.R.D. 55 (N.D.N.Y. 1997). An FDCPA class action would not be certified where the consumers failed to obtain timely discovery in support of their allegation of numerosity.

Harrison v. Great Springwaters of Am., Inc., 1997 WL 469996 (E.D.N.Y. June 18, 1997). The Second Circuit favors the liberal construction of Rule 23 and courts may exercise broad discretion when they determine whether to certify a class. Where FDCPA plaintiffs received similar debt collection letters from defendants, there are common questions of law or fact. If the named plaintiff was subject to unique defenses, her claims may be atypical and she may not be a suitable class representative. Even if the named plaintiff failed to read the collection letter at issue, that fact would not defeat typicality because it is not a complete defense, but it may affect her damages. Because defendant's unclean hands argument goes to the merits of the lawsuit, it was inappropriate for consideration in the context of a motion for class certification. A named plaintiff is generally an adequate class representative if her interests are not adverse to the interests of other class members and she has some basic knowledge of the lawsuit and is capable of making intelligent decision based upon her lawyer's advice. If a proposed representative was ignorant of events central to the plaintiff's case, or if his testimony on important issues was so inconsistent as to call his credibility into question, courts will frequently deny a motion to certify on adequacy grounds. The class representative was required to pay only her pro rata share of the costs of the action. For purposes of (b)(3) of Rule 23, common questions of law and fact predominated in the case as it related to the legality of standardized documents and practices. The interests of members of the class in individually controlling the prosecution or defense of separate actions was typically lower in actions like this one to enforce compliance with the consumer protection laws, since damage awards in such cases were generally too small to permit a single consumer to bring suit. It was desirable to concentrate the litigation of the claims in this forum since one of the proposed classes was composed of residents in the state.

Goldberg v. Winston & Morrone, 1997 WL 139526 (S.D.N.Y. Mar. 26, 1997). Finding that the FDCPA suit primarily sought damages, not declaratory relief, the court denied certification of a Rule 23(b)(2) class.

Labbate-D'Alauro v. G.C. Servs. Ltd. P'ship, 168 F.R.D. 451 (E.D.N.Y. 1996). The court certified a statewide class action holding that the FDCPA does not prohibit certification of a state class action when multistate activities occurred. The proposed class members received the two identical collection letters so the alleged violations were common to all proposed class members even though some members also received telephone calls. The alleged unlawful conduct was directed at the named plaintiff and class members alike so that the plaintiff's claim was typical of the claim. The consumer's attorney was adequate to represent plaintiff as he had represented plaintiffs in more than fifty FDCPA actions. Common questions of law and fact surrounding the letters predominated over individual issues and a class action was the superior method of resolution as most proposed members were not likely to bring suit on their own. Cases regarding the legality of standardized documents and practices are generally appropriate for resolution by class action.

North Carolina

Goetsch v. Shell Oil Co., 197 F.R.D. 574 (W.D.N.C. 2000). Class certification was denied because the named plaintiff failed to show he was an adequate representative where he failed in this and prior suits to move for class certification.

Woodard ex rel. Woodard v. Online Info. Servs., 191 F.R.D. 502 (E.D.N.C. 2000). Class action certified under 23(b)(2) and (3) in overshadowing case. Consumer plaintiff's representation by a guardian did not render him an inadequate class representative.

North Dakota

Wilhelm v. Credico Inc., 2008 WL 5110938 (D.N.D. Dec. 2, 2008). Denied class certification: whether defendant intended to sue plaintiff and the putative class members when it sent the individual "Notice of Lawsuit" letters would require an individual inquiry into defendant's intent when it sent each letter.

Ohio

Passa v. City of Columbus, 266 F.R.D. 197 (S.D. Ohio 2010). Finding that the requirements of both Rule 23(b)(2) and (b)(3)

were satisfied, the court certified an FDCPA and OCSPA class consisting of all persons who were or would be the subject of a debt collection communication from and through the City of Columbus' Check Resolution Program in connection with an attempt to obtain payment of payday loans allegedly owed to Check$mart, Quick Cash USA, or Always Payday under a loan agreement governed by Ohio state law.

Jerman v. Carlisle, McNellie, Rini, Kramer & Ulrich, 2010 WL 5140850 (N.D. Ohio Dec. 14, 2010). In certifying the class, the court rejected as a matter of law, and as against FDCPA policy, the defendants' argument that "a class certification would create such a large discrepancy in potential recovery (i.e., each proposed class member pursuing an individual claim could potentially recover up to $1,000, while each member of the class would recover only $3.10)." The court found that the class action was the superior method for handling this case.

Kelly v. Montgomery Lynch & Assocs., Inc., 2008 WL 4560744 (N.D. Ohio Oct. 8, 2008). Where class recovery was $5200, counsel were awarded $101,275 fees at the local rate of $300/hour, plus costs.

Todd v. Weltman Weinberg & Reis Co., L.P.A., 2008 WL 419943 (S.D. Ohio Feb. 14, 2008). Individual factual issues on whether the collection lawyer's affidavit for garnishment misrepresented that the affiant had a reasonable basis to believe there were nonexempt funds in the accounts of judgment debtors precluded certification of a class as common questions did not predominate.

Griffith v. Javitch, Block & Rathbone, L.L.P., 358 B.R. 338 (S.D. Ohio 2007), *reconsideration granted*, 241 F.R.D. 600 (S.D. Ohio 2007). A named plaintiff in an FDCPA class action filed bankruptcy before certification of the FDCPA class; her FDCPA claim was settled by the bankruptcy trustee; and the federal court dismissed the FDCPA claim. The court reversed its prior ruling and held that the named plaintiff need not send notice of the settlement to the class, as the class action had not received publicity and the settlement was without collusion or bad faith.

Tedrow v. Cowles, 68 Fed. R. Serv. 3d 1564 (S.D. Ohio 2007). The court certified a class action based on defendant's filing of collection suits in venues prohibited by § 1692i against consumers who neither lived nor signed contracts in the judicial district where suit was filed.

Johnson v. Midland Credit Mgmt. Inc., 2006 U.S. Dist. LEXIS 60133 (N.D. Ohio Aug. 23, 2006). Granted consumers leave to amend their FDCPA complaint to narrow the class to consumers who did not receive a § 1692g notice because it was returned by the post office, but denied leave to add a proposed class of consumers who were contacted after disputing the debt as it was untimely.

Passa v. City of Columbus, 2006 WL 642492 (S.D. Ohio Mar. 9, 2006). Class action plaintiff had standing to pursue FDCPA claims against various defendants' operation of the City of Columbus' Check Resolution Program where plaintiff and the putative class alleged similar injury by operation of the concerted practice.

Fahey v. Encore Fin., 2005 WL 2739323 (N.D. Ohio Oct. 24, 2005) (slip copy). General information about the debt collector's volume of business was insufficient for the court to determine numerosity resulting in the denial of class certification.

Pennsylvania

Dotson v. Portfolio Recovery Assocs., L.L.C., 2009 WL 1559813 (E.D. Pa. June 3, 2009). Class certification denied where the named plaintiff's lack of credibility ("having given false testimony under oath by denying his prior claims under the FDCPA"), his admitted post traumatic stress syndrome and resulting cognitive disabilities ("I forget a lot of things. I can't remember faces, people's names, things of that nature. I think about it but I can't recall."), and his "demonstrate[d] lack of involvement or understanding of the claims asserted on his behalf by his attorney" prevented him from adequately representing the proposed class.

Richburg v. Palisades Collection L.L.C., 247 F.R.D. 457 (E.D. Pa. 2008). Class certification was denied in this case alleging FDCPA violations for filing time-barred debts since evidence that the named plaintiff had acknowledged the putative time-barred debt would toll the statute of limitations as to her in accordance with state law and thus rendered her not a typical or adequate class representative.

McCall v. Drive Fin. Servs., L.P., 440 F. Supp. 2d 388 (E.D. Pa. 2006). Pursuant to § 1692k(a)(2)(B) in a class action under the FDCPA for statutory damages the debt collector may be liable for up to $1000 for the named plaintiff and up to $500,000 for the class. The cap on statutory damages for an individual pursuant to § 1692k(a) of $1000 does not limit the share of the class award that any class member, including a named plaintiff, may receive.

Jordan v. Commonwealth Fin. Sys., Inc., 237 F.R.D. 132 (E.D. Pa. 2006). The court found all required elements present and certified an FDCPA class on the basis of alleged violations in the defendants' standardized collection letters. In certifying this FDCPA class action, the court rejected the defendants' argument that, because of their extremely small net worth, "a class action is an inferior method for adjudicating the controversy because members of the proposed classes would enjoy a greater financial recovery through individual actions."

McCall v. Drive Fin. Servs., L.P., 236 F.R.D. 246 (E.D. Pa. 2006). Class certified against finance company allegedly using bogus attorney stationary. Plaintiff's fifteen-year-old armed robbery conviction did not disqualify him as an adequate representative.

Seawell v. Universal Fid. Corp., 235 F.R.D. 64 (E.D. Pa. 2006). Court certified this nationwide FDCPA class action for both injunctive relief and damages based on the alleged unlawful misrepresentation that the debt collector's misrepresented itself as an arm of the U.S. government through its placement of the American flag in the letterhead of its form duns.

Wesley v. Cavalry Inv., L.L.C., 2006 WL 2794065 (E.D. Pa. Sept. 27, 2006). Court refused to certify a class of consumers who had disputed their debt and the debt buyer failed to inform the credit reporting agencies of the disputes that did not involve fraud or true identity theft. Individual issues of fact involving oral conversations between the debt buyer and the credit reporting agencies undermined the commonality and typicality requirements.

Kondratick v. Beneficial Consumer Discount Co., 2006 WL 305399 (E.D. Pa. Feb. 8, 2006). Class certification was denied in a case including FDCPA claims where determination of membership in the class would require mini-trials of whether Beneficial failed to stop its foreclosure when it entered into a mortgage reinstatement agreement with a state homeowner assistance program.

Wisneski v. Nationwide Collections, Inc., 227 F.R.D. 259 (E.D. Pa. 2004). In this FDCPA action the court certified a class consisting of all persons in the Commonwealth of Pennsylvania who at any time or from March 3, 2003 through and including March 3, 2004, received a debt collection letter from defendant as a part of an attempt to collect a non-business debt. The court rejected the debt collector's argument that the superiority requirement of Rule 23(b)(3) had not been satisfied because it had a net worth of zero, stating "I do not believe that Congress intended to allow a company to avoid a class action litigation arising under the FDCPA by presenting a balance sheet which shows that assets equal liabilities; such a demonstration is the nature of a balance sheet. I would include equity, capital stock, and goodwill into the calculation of a company's net worth for these purposes."

Buzoiu v. Risk Mgmt. Alternatives, Inc., 2004 WL 1505061 (E.D. Pa. June 14, 2004). Class certification was denied on the basis that the named plaintiff was not an adequate representative and the case was ordered to proceed only on the named plaintiff's individual claim since the defendant's liability for the alleged misrepresentation in its form dunning letter hinged entirely on the named plaintiff's credibility in her uncorroborated contention that the collector's telephone call contradicted the contents of the letter.

Orloff v. Syndicated Office Sys., 2004 WL 870691 (E.D. Pa. Apr. 20, 2004). District court approved class action settlement of FDCPA and CROA claims first ensuring the requirements of Rule 23 were met and second evaluating the fairness of the settlement. The court applied the Third Circuit's nine factors in analyzing the fairness of the settlement. *See also Girsh v. Jepson,* 521 F.2d 153 (3d Cir. 1975).

Thomas v. NCO Fin. Sys., Inc., 2004 WL 727071 (E.D. Pa. Mar. 31, 2004). On resubmission following its earlier rejection, the court approved a settlement class, finding that notice to the class through publication was a superior method of notice than individualized mailings.

Parks v. Portnoff Law Assocs., 243 F. Supp. 2d 244 (E.D. Pa. 2003). Class action settlement approved as fair and reasonable. Where there was a contest of the coverage of the debts, municipal assessments for trash, water and sewer services, a $75,000 settlement fund was fair and reasonable. $1000 was distributed to the each of the named plaintiffs, at least $250 to each of fifty-two class claimants, and $13,500 to consumer's counsel.

Piper v. Portnoff Law Assocs., 216 F.R.D. 325 (E.D. Pa. 2003). Documentation of 148 individuals who paid attorney fees to the collector satisfied the numerosity requirement. At the certification stage the exact class size or identity of class members is not required.

Oslan v. Collection Bureau, 206 F.R.D. 109 (E.D. Pa. 2002). Class certified in case involving form letter which implied that recipients' credit could be "restored" by paying debt where all criteria for certification were met.

Tenuto v. Transworld Sys., Inc., 2002 U.S. Dist. LEXIS 1764 (E.D. Pa. Oct. 31, 2002). Upon consideration of the complexity, expense and duration of any litigation, the reaction of the class, the extent of discovery and the stage of the proceedings, the risk of establishing liability, the risk of establishing damages, and the reasonableness of the settlement in view of the best recovery and in view of the attendant risks, the district court concluded that the settlement was fair, adequate, and reasonable under the circumstances, and the class action settlement was approved and a $2000 incentive payment was awarded to the estate of the named plaintiff.

Schilling v. Let's Talk Cellular & Wireless, 2002 U.S. Dist. LEXIS 3352 (E.D. Pa. Feb. 5, 2002). FDCPA class certified in case involving collection form letter but class certification denied as to state law claims because plaintiff had not undertaken a conflict of laws analysis demonstrating which state's law should apply.

Greer v. Shapiro & Kreisman, 2001 U.S. Dist. LEXIS 21114 (E.D. Pa. Dec. 18, 2001). The court denied a motion for approval of a class settlement with leave to renew requesting clarification and information regarding the reasonableness of the settlement, including the defendant's net worth, the amounts likely to be paid to each class member, the basis for the named plaintiff's recovery, the attorney fees, and the adequacy of notice to class members for whom no current address was known.

Tenuto v. Transworld Sys., Inc., 2001 U.S. Dist. LEXIS 17694 (E.D. Pa. Oct. 30, 2001). Touchstone for approval of a class action settlement was a determination that it was fair, adequate, and reasonable. In evaluating a class action settlement for preliminary approval, the court determined whether the proposed settlement disclosed grounds to doubt its fairness or other obvious deficiencies such as unduly preferential treatment of the class representatives or segments of the class, excessive compensation of attorneys, and whether it appeared to fall within the range of possible approval.

In re Mortgagors of Temple-Inland Mortgage Corp., 2001 U.S. Dist. LEXIS 1918 (E.D. Pa. Jan. 23, 2001). Where no class had yet been certified and the original plaintiffs had been dismissed (not the result of the defendant's actions or mootness), the case or controversy requirement of Article III was not met, and the FDCPA case was dismissed without prejudice. Plaintiffs failed to timely obtain a substitute representative.

Fry v. Hayt, 198 F.R.D. 461 (E.D. Pa. 2000). Where collection law firm asserted its net worth to be $137,000 and there were uncertainties about insurance coverage and the state claims, a settlement of an FDCPA and state consumer protection class claims for $500,000 and injunctive relief (about 1/3 or $150,000 for attorney fees and $80,000 for notice) appeared fair and reasonable.

Carr v. Trans Union Corp., 1995 WL 20865 (E.D. Pa. Jan. 12, 1995). "Class actions are often the most suitable method for resolving suits to enforce compliance with consumer protection laws because the awards in an individual case are usually too small to encourage the lone consumer to file suit." In an FDCPA case, a class was certified consisting of all Pennsylvania residents who, during the relevant period, received from the collector, collecting on behalf of this creditor, a debt collection notice similar to that attached to the complaint.

Colbert v. Trans Union Corp., 1995 WL 20821 (E.D. Pa. Jan. 12, 1995). Same holding as *Carr v. Trans Union Corp.*, *supra*.

Rhode Island

Gordon v. Corporate Receivables, 2010 WL 376386 (D.R.I. Jan.

27, 2010). Where the consumer challenged the debt collector's requirement that any dispute must be "in writing" as violative of § 1692g(a)(3), a class action was certified.

Texas

Eatmon v. Palisades Collection, L.L.C., 2010 WL 1189571 (E.D. Tex. Mar. 5, 2010), *report and recommendation adopted*, 2010 WL 1189574 (E.D. Tex. Mar. 24, 2010). Recommended a class of consumers whose motor vehicle retail installment credit contract was sold to the debt buyer which was suing on the contract without a Texas license to hold such contracts.

Castro v. Collecto, Inc., 256 F.R.D. 534 (W.D. Tex. 2009). This FDCPA case was certified to proceed as a class action defined as (a) all individuals with Texas addresses (b) who were sent a letter in the form represented by Exhibit A to plaintiff's complaint, (c) seeking to collect a cellular telephone debt, (d) which became delinquent more than two years prior to the sending of the letter, (e) which letter was sent between June 16, 2007 and July 6, 2008.

Gutierrez v. LVNV Funding, L.L.C., 2009 U.S. Dist. LEXIS 54479 (W.D. Tex. Mar. 16, 2009). Class action certified alleging that the defendant debt buyer violated § 1692e, 1692e(2), and 1692e(10) by filing all of its state court collection complaints with an attached "Affidavit of Account" that falsely attested that the affiant had "personal knowledge" of the supporting account documents.

Barnett v. Experian Info. Solutions, Inc., 236 F.R.D. 307 (E.D. Tex. 2006). The court, *sua sponte*, decertified the class claims as a result of the defendant debt buyer's bankruptcy and limited assets in this FDCPA case and directed class counsel to publish notice of the decertification of the claim that the debt buyer had been re-aging debts on consumers' credit reports on its web site for thirty days.

Purdie v. Ace Cash Express, Inc., 2003 WL 22976611 (N.D. Tex. Dec. 11, 2003). The district court certified the class, found that the class settlement was fair, adequate, and reasonable, approved an award of incentive compensation to the named plaintiffs, and granted attorney fees and expenses in the amount of $2.1 million. In determining whether a class settlement is fair, adequate, and reasonable, the court should consider the following six factors: (1) whether the settlement was a product of fraud or collusion; (2) the complexity, expense and likely duration of the litigation; (3) the stage of the proceedings and the actual amount of discovery completed; (4) the probability of plaintiffs' success on the merits (or, the factual and legal obstacles to prevailing on the merits); (5) the possible range of recovery and certainty of damages; and (6) the respective opinions of the participants, including class counsel, class representative, and the absent class members.

Sibley v. Diversified Collection Servs., 1998 WL 355492 (N.D. Tex. June 30, 1998). Class certification pursuant to Rule 23(b)(2) of a proposed FDCPA national class was denied because declaratory relief did not predominate: the declaratory relief was for declaring defendant's act violative of the FDCPA, not for an injunctive like purpose, and the lawsuit sought actual damages.

Utah

Ditty v. Check Rite, Ltd., 182 F.R.D. 639 (D. Utah 1998). Rule 23(b)(3) class action certified regarding DeLoney & Associates' letters seeking payment of dishonored checks in exchange for a "covenant not to sue." Defendants sent about 15,000 letters per year, so joinder was impracticable. The mailing of a standard debt collection letter satisfied commonality, and fact pattern was also typical. That some people paid the "covenant not to sue" fee and some did not was immaterial. Named plaintiffs' understanding of the lawsuit was given little weight; competence of counsel was the significant factor showing adequacy of representation. Adequacy of representation was challenged because class counsel kept bringing class actions when defendants continued using letters which the court had declared illegal. Since "injunctive relief is not available under the FDCPA, successive class actions provide the only remedy to plaintiffs who believe they have been the victims of ongoing illegal behavior by the defendants." Defendants' attacks on the personal integrity of plaintiffs or their ability to finance the lawsuit were rejected.

Virginia

Cappetta v. GC Servs., L.P., 2009 WL 482474 (E.D. Va. Feb. 24, 2009). Consumer's motion to file an amended FDCPA complaint to add allegations for class certification was denied without prejudice to renew her motion after completion of extended discovery to establish the validity of class certification.

Talbott v. G.C. Servs. Ltd. P'ship, 191 F.R.D. 99 (W.D. Va. 2000). A 23(b)(3) class action limited to Virginia consumers was certified in an overshadowing case. Whether a consumer received the letter was not a barrier to certification, since the consumer need not actually read the letter for liability to attach.

Health Plan, Inc. v. DeGarmo, 1996 WL 780508 (N.D. W. Va. Oct. 28, 1996). A class action was certified in a counterclaim against a HMO for improperly requesting more than its costs in its subrogation and reimbursement claims against its patients. The class consisted of all group enrollees in the HMO. RICO and FDCPA violations were alleged.

West v. Costen, 558 F. Supp. 564 (W.D. Va. 1983). A class action for statutory damages was certified for certain issues against a collection agency and its owner, but not against individual employees. The class proceeded on an allegation of a failure to provide § 1692g(a) validation notices and for collecting service charges on NSF checks in violation of §§ 1692e(2) and 1692f(1). Class certification was withdrawn for claims of illegal third-party contacts and threats of arrest as involving more individual than common issues. Summary judgment was entered on the validation notice claim but denied on the service charge claim because of remaining factual issues.

Washington

Hansen v. Ticket Track, Inc., 213 F.R.D. 412 (W.D. Wash. 2003). Class certified of those consumers who were charged an amount in addition to the parking fee by the collection agency for parking lot owners.

Clark v. Bonded Adjustment Co., 204 F.R.D. 662 (E.D. Wash. 2002). In the course of granting class certification based on charging excessive process server fees, the court recognized that the FDCPA applied whether the fee was actually collected or whether the debt collector merely attempted to collect it. Consum-

ers could serve as class representatives even if they did not actually pay the fee.

Campion v. Credit Bureau Servs., 206 F.R.D. 663 (E.D. Wash. 2001). Defendant's motion to dismiss was denied because a consumer in a chapter 13 bankruptcy had the right to proceed with an FDCPA class action. The court found that plaintiff had satisfied the requirements of Rule 23(a) and certified class pursuant to subsection (b)(3) but declined certification pursuant to (b)(2) because the claim for monetary damages predominated over any claim for equitable relief.

Connor v. Automated Accounts, Inc., 202 F.R.D. 265 (E.D. Wash. 2001). Class action alleging that collector sent initial dun demanding payment in fifteen days in violation of § 1692g was certified as a Rule 23(b)(3) but not as a (b)(2) class over collector's objections that the named plaintiff incurred no actual damages and that class members could not be determined to have incurred consumer, rather than commercial, debts.

Wisconsin

Drinkman v. Encore Receivable Mgmt., Inc., 2007 WL 5404595 (W.D. Wis. Dec. 3, 2007). The court cured the "indefiniteness" of the proposed class description by re-writing and certifying a statewide class for this alleged *Foti* violation as follows: "All Wisconsin 'consumers' (as that term is defined by § 1692a(3)) that received pre-recorded messages from Defendant, within one year prior to July 3, 2007, in which Defendant included nothing more than the caller's name, a phone number and a reference to some important matter."

Drinkman v. Encore Receivable Mgmt., Inc., 2007 WL 4458307 (W.D. Wis. Dec. 7, 2007). FDCPA case involving prerecorded telephone messages was certified as a class action pursuant to Rule 23(b)(2).

Robbins v. Wolpoff & Abramson, 2006 U.S. Dist. LEXIS 77236 (E.D. Wis. Oct. 19, 2006). A low level of commitment is sufficient to be an adequate class representative, given the Act's purpose to protect unsophisticated consumers.

Wanty v. Messerli & Kramer, P.A., 2006 WL 2691076 (E.D. Wis. Sept. 19, 2006). Class certified of Wisconsin consumers who received a letter from an attorney allegedly not involved in the collection as an attorney. The named plaintiff's bankruptcy had no effect on their adequacy as a representative.

Seeger v. AFNI, Inc., 2006 WL 2290763 (E.D. Wis. Aug. 9, 2006). FDCPA and Wisconsin Consumer Act case against a debt buyer for adding a 15% fee to Cingular bills was certified to proceed is a class action.

Beattie v. Capital One, 2006 WL 1519087 (E.D. Wis. May 30, 2006). The court certified a Rule 23(b)(3) a statewide class on the alleged §§ 1692e and 1692g letter violations.

Borcherding-Dittloff v. Transworld Sys., Inc., 185 F.R.D. 558 (W.D. Wis. 1999). Pursuant to Rule 23(b)(2), the court certified a class defined as (1) all persons with addresses in the state of Wisconsin (2) to whom letters were sent by the collection agency (3) containing a notification of rights under the heading "COLORADO," (4) in attempt to collect a debt incurred for personal, family, or household purposes, (5) which letters were not returned undelivered by the Post Office, and (6) which were sent during the one-year period prior to the filing of the complaint in this action. A collection agency's response to interrogatories that over 50,000 people had probably been sent letters satisfied the numerosity requirement. A collection agency's standardized practice of sending collection letters satisfied the commonality requirement. Counsel's use of the FDCPA as a fee generating mechanism did not adversely reflect on the ability to adequately represent the interest of the class. The consumer's financial position, inability to pay legal fees and counsel's advancement of costs, did not render the named plaintiff inadequate as class representative. Despite collection agency's contention that the class should be national in scope, certification of a statewide class was appropriate.

Wyoming

Versteeg v. Bennett, Deloney & Noyes, P.C., 2011 WL 159805 (D. Wyo. Jan. 13, 2011). Where there was no dispute that the defendants had limited financial ability to pay a recovery in this case, there was little chance for recovery by the individual class members. Thus the court found that a class action was not superior to other means of handling the FDCPA claims.

K.3.3 Consumer's Attorney Fees and Costs

K.3.3.1 Standards for Award of Attorney Fees

Farrar v. Hobby, 506 U.S. 103, 113 S. Ct. 566, 121 L. Ed. 2d 494 (1992). Pursuant to 42 U.S.C. § 1988 a plaintiff who was awarded nominal damages was a prevailing party. Plaintiff who was granted only nominal damages in civil rights litigation, where compensatory damages of $17 million were sought, was not entitled to an award of attorney fees. In her concurring opinion Justice O'Connor writes: "When the plaintiff's success is purely technical or de minimis, no fees can be awarded." *Id.* at 576. "That is not to say that *all* nominal damages awards are de minimis. Nominal relief does not necessarily a nominal victory make." *Id.* at 578. Justice O'Connor stated that the difference between the amount sought and the amount recovered was not the only inquiry; other factors such as the significance of the legal issue must be considered.

City of Burlington v. Dague, 505 U.S. 557, 112 S. Ct. 2638, 120 L. Ed. 2d 449 (1992). Enhancement of award of attorney fees on the basis of contingency was not permitted in a non-FDCPA decision.

Anchondo v. Anderson, Crenshaw & Assocs., L.L.C., 616 F.3d 1098 (10th Cir. 2010). The appellate court affirmed in all respects the district court's award to the prevailing consumer of some $63,000 in fees. The court rejected the collection agency's argument that the lower court abused its discretion by not considering the twelve factors for determining the lodestar in *Johnson v. Georgia Highway Express, Inc.* The primary lodestar analysis is the amount of reasonable fees and reasonable hours undertaken by the court below and approved in *Perdue*. That could be adjusted using *Johnson* factors but it was not error to do not do so. The court rejected the argument that all the hours of prominent national co-counsel should be struck because the case did not require co-counsel. The collection agency offered no precedent for that argument. The court rejected the collection agency's arguments that counsel spent unnecessary time on specific parts of the case

deferring to the lower court's finding that they showed proper billing judgment and that the hours expended were reasonable.

Hepsen v. J.C. Christensen & Assocs., Inc., 2010 WL 3329836 (11th Cir. Aug. 25, 2010). The lower court did not abuse its discretion in reducing the prevailing plaintiff's attorney fees based on its evaluation of the reasonable time required to prosecute the case and its determination that that the results obtained were a fraction of the amount originally sought.

Schlacher v. Law Offices of Phillip J. Rotche & Associates, P.C., 574 F.3d 852 (7th Cir. 2009). Award of reasonable FDCPA attorney fees affirmed since the district court adequately explained both its reduction of the attorney's requested time as well as its determination of an appropriate, lower hourly rate, and thus did not abuse its discretion. Courts normally begin with the lodestar rate and may then adjust for various factors, such as duplicative work, excessive billing, and proportionality. The attorneys who referred the case to an FDCPA specialist should have relinquished their involvement in the case.

Dowling v. Litton Loan Servicing L.P., 320 Fed. Appx. 442 (6th Cir. 2009). The district court did not abuse its discretion in refusing to adjust the lodestar downward on the basis of the plaintiff's refusal to accept pretrial settlement offers where the settlement offers never exceeded plaintiff's ultimate recovery plus the attorney fees that had accrued at the time when each of the offers was made. No downward adjustment in the lodestar was warranted for the plaintiff's unsuccessful claims since where, as here, "the claims are related, the fact that some claims ultimately fail while others succeed is not reason to reduce the fee award." The plaintiff was entitled to reasonable attorney fees incurred for successfully defending the appeal.

Camacho v. Bridgeport Fin., Inc., 523 F.3d 973 (9th Cir. 2008). Court abused its discretion in determining that $200 was reasonable hourly rate in FDCPA action, instead of requested hourly rates of $425 to $500, because it failed to identify the relevant community or explain the prevailing hourly rate in that community for similar services by attorneys of reasonably comparable skill, experience and reputation. The party opposing the application for an attorney fee award has a burden of rebuttal that requires submission of evidence to the district court challenging the accuracy and reasonableness of the facts asserted by the prevailing party. Fees are properly awarded for time expended in connection with the fee application.

Jacobson v. Healthcare Fin. Serv., Inc., 516 F.3d 85 (2d Cir. 2008). Award of attorney fees to the prevailing consumer is mandatory: "In this way, the FDCPA enlists the efforts of sophisticated consumers like [plaintiff] as 'private attorneys general' to aid their less sophisticated counterparts, who are unlikely themselves to bring suit under the Act, but who are assumed by the Act to benefit from the deterrent effect of civil actions brought by others."

Thornton v. Wolpoff & Abramson, L.L.P., 312 Fed. Appx. 161 (11th Cir. 2008). "The difference between zero dollars and one dollar is the difference between an unsuccessful action and a successful action" for purpose of awarding a consumer FDCPA attorney fees. The district court retained discretion to award attorney fees when damages were nominal. Where the consumer was awarded a nominal $1 in statutory damages by the jury, the court did not abuse its discretion by drastically reducing the consumer's attorney fees award to a small portion of the lodestar as the success was "technical" or "de minimis."

Moton v. Nathan & Nathan, P.C., 297 Fed. Appx. 930 (11th Cir. 2008). Trial court erred by awarding a "flat fee" of $500 to the prevailing FDCPA consumer, requiring remand for re-calculation of fees using the required lodestar method.

Hester v. Graham, Bright & Smith, P.C., 289 Fed. Appx. 35 (5th Cir. 2008). The award of attorney fees is to be made to the prevailing FDCPA plaintiff and not in the name of the plaintiff's attorney.

Defenbaugh v. JBC & Assocs. P.C., 2006 U.S. App. LEXIS 19930 (9th Cir. July 24, 2006). The court affirmed the award to the prevailing consumer of fees calculated pursuant to the lodestar method, rejecting the defendant's contention that the court "should 'readjust' the lodestar approach in non-complex FDCPA cases."

Dechert v. Cadle Co., 2006 WL 647715 (7th Cir. Mar. 16, 2006), *rev'd*, 441 F.3d 474 (7th Cir. 2006). Plaintiff was not a prevailing party merely because of a discovery sanctions award, so the award of fees to plaintiff was reversed. Fees were not awarded to defendant on its cross-appeal; the denial of fees to plaintiff was "sanction enough."

King v. International Data Servs. (IDS), 100 Fed. Appx. 681 (9th Cir. 2004). Additional costs and attorney fees were awarded for work on the appeal by consumer's attorney.

Ferland v. Conrad Credit Corp., 244 F.3d 1145 (9th Cir. 2001). Reducing the lodestar hours by more than 140 hours or 50% based on the consumer attorney's inexperience, inefficiency, and the lack of complexity of the case was not a sufficiently clear and nonduplicative reason for a reduction where the court had already reduced the hourly rate from the $195 requested to $160 based on the consumer attorney's experience level.

Savino v. Computer Credit, Inc., 164 F.3d 81 (2d Cir. 1998). The court reversed the trial court's reduction of fees by 90% because it was without explanation. The court noted that the fact that Savino ultimately succeeded on his claim "undermines any contention that he brought this action in bad faith and for the purpose of harassment."

Zagorski v. Midwest Billing Servs., Inc., 128 F.3d 1164 (7th Cir. 1997). It was an abuse of discretion to not award attorney fees where the collector had admitted liability for $100. The Seventh Circuit had held that fees sufficient to compensate the attorney for the time spent on the case must be awarded to encourage enforcement of the FDCPA.

Lee v. Thomas & Thomas, 109 F.3d 302 (6th Cir. 1997). Additional consumer's attorney fees were properly denied for work done after an offer of judgment where the offer was sufficient except for the consumer's attorney's refusal to disclose his hours spent on the case to defense counsel. Fees of $1106.85 were awarded but the consumer sought $12,759 in fees, mostly for work performed after the rejected offer of judgment.

Johnson v. Eaton, 80 F.3d 148 (5th Cir. 1996). Award of costs and fees is available only where defendant is liable for actual or additional damages.

Carroll v. Wolpoff & Abramson, 53 F.3d 626 (4th Cir. 1995).

Review of attorney fees pursuant to the Fair Debt Collection Practices Act was made under the abuse of discretion standard. The language of the FDCPA established an intent to allow trial courts wide latitude in calculating fee awards. Section 1692k does not mandate a fee award in the lodestar amount. Where the consumer abandoned her claim to actual damages, on remand from the appellate court, and receive only $50 of a possible maximum of $1000 in statutory damages for a technical violation of the FDCPA, the district court did not abuse its discretion in limiting the award of attorney fees to $500.

Tolentino v. Friedman, 46 F.3d 645 (7th Cir. 1995). "The reason for mandatory fees is that Congress chose a 'private attorney general' approach to assume enforcement of the FDCPA." Several factors are to be considered in calculating attorney fees: (1) the time and labor required, (2) the novelty and difficulty of the question, (3) the skill requisite to perform the legal service properly, (4) the preclusion of employment by the attorney due to acceptance of the case, (5) the customary fee, (6) whether the fee is fixed or contingent, (7) any time limitations imposed by the client or the circumstances, (8) the amount involved and the results obtained, (9) the experience, reputation, and ability of the plaintiff's attorney, (10) the "undesirability" of the case, (11) the nature and length of the professional relationship with the client, and (12) awards in similar cases. Consumer who prevailed on summary judgment and received the maximum award of statutory damages obtained a high degree of success. "Paying counsel in FDCPA cases at rates lower than those they can obtain in the marketplace is inconsistent with the congressional desire to enforce the FDCPA through private actions, and therefore misapplies the law."

Joe v. Payco-Gen. Am. Credits, Inc., 34 F.3d 1072 (9th Cir. 1994). Where maximum statutory damages were awarded pursuant to the FDCPA, consumer was "completely successful" and entitled to an award of reasonable attorney fees. Consumer's success on FDCPA appeal entitled him to an award of attorney fees and cost.

Hollis v. Roberts, 984 F.2d 1159 (11th Cir. 1993). Where the record demonstrates that a prepaid legal services organization is separate and distinct from the union whose members were provided legal services and attorney fees awarded to the legal services organization were not shared with the union, fees were to be awarded at the prevailing market rate to lawyer employed by prepaid legal services.

Harper v. Better Bus. Servs., Inc., 961 F.2d 1561 (11th Cir. 1992). Where the record failed to disclose the independence of a prepaid legal plan from the union, the district court's award of fees on a cost basis rather than at the prevailing market rate was affirmed.

Graziano v. Harrison, 950 F.2d 107 (3d Cir. 1991). In a typical case under the Act, reasonable attorney fees to a successful consumer are mandated. Only in unusual cases may a court decline to award a fee.

Pipiles v. Credit Bureau, 886 F.2d 22 (2d Cir. 1989). Plaintiff was entitled to award of fees and costs despite failure to establish actual or additional damages.

Emanuel v. Am. Credit Exch., 870 F.2d 805 (2d Cir. 1989). Attorney fees are mandatory to a successful consumer even if actual and statutory damages are not awarded.

Arizona

Pearson v. National Credit Sys., Inc., 2010 WL 5146805 (D. Ariz. Dec. 13, 2010). Where the offer of judgment clearly stated that the defendant was offering "Plaintiff's cost and reasonable attorney fees now accrued," the plaintiff was entitled only to those fees incurred prior to his acceptance of the offer of judgment.

St. Bernard v. State Collection Serv., Inc., 2010 WL 2743327 (D. Ariz. July 12, 2010). "[F]or Congress's private attorney general approach to succeed in the context of FDCPA cases, attorney fees must not hinge on a percentage of actual damages awarded. Consumer's fee request is therefore not per se unreasonable simply because it is nearly six times greater than the actual damages."

Savage v. NIC, Inc., 2010 WL 2347028 (D. Ariz. June 9, 2010). "The specific number of claims on which Consumers prevailed does not control whether the Court awards an attorneys' fee. Any violation of the FDCPA requires awarding an attorneys' fee, regardless of the number of prevailing claims."

Winn v. Unifund CCR Partners, 2007 WL 2701941 (D. Ariz. Sept. 14, 2007). The court denied attorney fees to the prevailing defendant, since neither the fact that the plaintiff's claim was novel or that the plaintiff's attorney had sued the defendant on five occasions established the defendant's burden that the plaintiff's claim was meritless and that the case was brought for the purpose of harassment.

California

Jamal v. Thompson & Assocs., P.C., 2010 WL 678925 (N.D. Cal. Feb. 25, 2010). Request for anticipated collection costs of $750 denied.

Middlesworth v. Oaktree Collections Inc., 2009 WL 3720884 (E.D. Cal. Nov. 3, 2009). Consumer's request for fees for anticipated $750 costs of collection of a default FDCPA judgment denied as unprecedented.

Tomovich v. Wolpoff & Abramson, L.L.P., 2009 WL 2447710 (S.D. Cal. Aug. 7, 2009). Court reduced claimed hourly rates from $385 to $300, noting that this was a simple case not justifying the rate used by the consumer attorney in a class action. Reduced the hours compensated by about half because of the simplicity of the case and the experience of the counsel.

Costa v. Nat'l Action Fin. Serv., 2008 WL 1925235 (E.D. Cal. Apr. 30, 2008). Attorney fees are not part of costs within the FDCPA and thus a Rule 68 offer does not result in fee-shifting. In determining the reasonableness of an attorney fees award post-Rule 68 offer, the court must consider: (1) the amount of the Rule 68 offer; (2) the stage of the litigation at which the offer was made; (3) what services were rendered thereafter; (4) the amount obtained by the judgment; and (5) whether it was reasonable to continue litigation after the Rule 68 offer was made. Court has discretion to refuse to award post-offer fees since it was unreasonable to continue litigation and ultimate award was less than Rule 68 offer. Awarded $315/hour for sixteen hours expended pre-Rule 68 offer.

Lowe v. Elite Recovery Solutions L.P., 2008 WL 324777 (E.D. Cal. Feb. 5, 2008). An award of attorney fees to the prevailing FDCPA plaintiff is mandatory.

Kinh Tong v. Capital Mgmt. Servs. Group, Inc., 2008 WL 171035 (N.D. Cal. Jan. 18, 2008). The court awarded attorney fees of $4500 for ten hours of attorney and eight hours of law clerk time to obtain a favorable settlement on technical claim of contacting the husband of a represented consumer which involved little more than a complaint, a motion to strike the answer, and settlement negotiations.

Langley v. Check Game Solutions, Inc., 2007 WL 2701345 (S.D. Cal. Sept. 13, 2007). Time expended in an FDCPA suit to defend against debt collector's state law counter claims for abuse of process and emotional distress was not compensable to the prevailing consumer under § 1692k(a)(3).

Colorado

O'Connor v. Check Rite, 973 F. Supp. 1010 (D. Colo. 1997). Where no actual or statutory damages were awarded, the court agreed with *Johnson v. Eaton* and declined to award attorney fees.

Connecticut

Rivera v. Corporate Receivables, Inc., 540 F. Supp. 2d 329 (D. Conn. 2008). In determining the reasonable attorney fees after the jury awarded the consumer $1000 statutory damages, the court found that the consumer's rejection of the defendant's pre-trial offer of judgment in the total amount of $4000 was reasonable because the consumer's reasonable fees at the time of the offer were more than $3000. The court made the following insightful comment that this case helps illustrate: "A defendant who discovers a technical violation of the FDCPA should consider the economics of an immediate filing of an offer of judgment 'up to $1,000 statutory damages plus reasonable fees to be decided by the court.' Courts are capable of exercising sound discretion in determining how much statutory damages are appropriate, and what hourly rate is reasonable in the locality among lawyers of comparable skill and experience. Leaving the amount of attorney's fees to the discretion of the court avoids the pitfall of offering acceptable damages but fees that are unreasonably low, though only barely so."

Goins v. JBC & Assocs., 2005 WL 3536147 (D. Conn. Nov. 28, 2005). "When a party advocates that the lodestar amount should be reduced, he or she bears the burden of establishing that a reduction is justified . . . [A]n award of attorney's fees under the FDCPA is designed not only for plaintiff's benefit but also to serve as a deterrent to defendants and others similarly situated." The court took note of other FDCPA cases against the debt collector in declining to reduce the lodestar.

Evanauskas v. Strumpf, 2001 U.S. Dist. LEXIS 14326 (D. Conn. June 27, 2001). Consumer's attorney was entitled to a fee award based on the reasonable rate of $275 per hour.

Chambers v. Manning, 169 F.R.D. 5 (D. Conn. 1996). The court found that if the collector had intended his Fed. R. Civ. P. 68 offer of a $10,000 FDCPA judgment to include the consumer's attorney fee award, he could had said so explicitly and his failure to do would be construed against him. Attorney fees of $4004 were awarded.

Delaware

Smith v. Law Offices of Mitchell N. Kay, 762 F. Supp. 82 (D. Del. 1991). Consumers are prevailing parties entitled to an award of attorney fee for time expended opposing debt collector's motion for new trial or remittitur even though remittitur was awarded reducing actual damages from $15,000 to $3000. Reasonable attorney fees arising from work performed after entry of judgment, in an effort to protect the judgment or enforce the court's decree, are compensable pursuant to the FDCPA's fee shifting provision.

Florida

Selby v. Christian Nicholas & Assocs., Inc., 2010 WL 745748 (M.D. Fla. Feb. 26, 2010). Awarded $1000 statutory damages on default and fees at $200 per hour. Denied request for anticipated fees in enforcing judgment; "Future, anticipated sums, which may or may not be incurred in enforcing any resulting judgment, are not part of the costs and attorney's fees incurred in enforcing liability under the FDCPA in this action."

Valencia v. Affiliated Group, Inc., 674 F. Supp. 2d 1300 (S.D. Fla. 2009). Awarding attorney fees to prevailing FDCPA consumers is mandatory. The court found that an across-the-board reduction of 60% in requested attorney fees was appropriate where the consumer continued litigating and "tenaciously clinging to an unsupportable position, namely, that she was entitled to equitable relief, despite clear and unmistakable case law to the contrary" after rejecting an offer that was $1 higher than final settlement. While recognizing the national problem of debt collection abuse, the court also criticized the plaintiff for prolonging the case to increase fees.

Danow v. Law Office of David E. Borback, P.A., 634 F. Supp. 2d 1337 (S.D. Fla. 2009). Court rejected "bad faith" and "limited success" arguments to reduce fees. "The fact that plaintiff brought and pursued related claims later dismissed or dropped before trial, does not imply bad faith or improper purpose, or lead to the conclusion that plaintiff had only 'limited success.'"

Sandin v. United Collection Bureau, Inc., 2009 WL 2500408 (S.D. Fla. Aug. 14, 2009). The rates for a consumer advocate will not necessarily mirror those for a defense attorney, who does not work on a contingency basis. The court awarded $300 per hour for attorney and $175 per hour for first year associate. "Consumer law" is a term that encompasses areas of practice ranging from the open-and-shut FDCPA case to complex litigation involving anything from fraud to personal injury. Thus, there is presumably not a single, reasonable hourly rate for all of "consumer law."

Conner v. BCC Fin. Mgmt. Servs., Inc., 597 F. Supp. 2d 1299 (S.D. Fla. 2008). Defendant's motion for attorney fees was granted in part with 15% reduction in hours requested where the law firm's invoice failed to specify how much time was spent on listed tasks.

Gaisser v. Portfolio Recovery Assocs., L.L.C., 571 F. Supp. 2d 1273 (S.D. Fla. 2008). The defendants did not violate §§ 1692e or 1692f(1) as alleged because of the defendants' request in the underlying state collection case for attorney fees in a specific amount: "[the collection attorney] did not state the reasonable fees as a sum certain in the state complaint or affidavit. Instead, the amounts were recommendations or suggestions, and the state court had discretion to award fees based on its own evaluation of the facts. Because [the collection attorney] did not mischaracterize the fees as part of the debt or as required under the agreement, Plaintiff has failed to state a claim with respect to the requests for attorney's fees."

Georgia

Kim v. Barro, 2009 WL 1616271 (N.D. Ga. June 9, 2009). In light of the FDCPA statutory maximum amount of $1000 in damages, consumer who accepted a $250 offer of judgment was a prevailing party and obtained more than the "nominal" damages awarded to the civil rights plaintiff in *Farrar*.

Phillips v. Stokes, 1992 U.S. Dist. LEXIS 22731 (N.D. Ga. Jan. 8, 1992). Factors enumerated in § 1692k(b)(1) are applicable only to damages, not to an award of attorney fees. Attorney fees of $3390, at the hourly rate of $150 per hour, were awarded to consumer.

Illinois

Francis v. Snyder, 2006 WL 1236052 (N.D. Ill. May 4, 2006). Attorney fees reduced for block billing, grouping time for different tasks together, and vague entries.

Shula v. Lawent, 2004 WL 2044279 (N.D. Ill. Sept. 2, 2004). Consumer's attorneys were awarded reasonable fees for their work on their successful defense of the defendant's appeal. The award for the appellate work was $15,350 ($12,375 covering the 55.0 hours reasonably expended by one attorney, plus $2975 covering the 8.5 hours reasonably expended his co-counsel in a case considered rather simple by the court). $32,165 in fees were awarded before the appeal.

Shula v. Lawent, 2004 WL 1244030 (N.D. Ill. June 7, 2004), *aff'd on other grounds*, 359 F.3d 489 (7th Cir. 2004). Where the parties litigated for over three years over claims worth only $1200, the court refused to reduce the lodestar, noting that defendant's refusal to settle early on, in the face of blatant violations, prolonged the matter. In a detailed opinion providing a road map for fee applications, the court reduced the fee request by about half, reducing both the hourly rate and time expended.

Riter v. Moss & Bloomberg, Ltd., 2000 U.S. Dist. LEXIS 14470 (N.D. Ill. Sept. 26, 2000). Case sets forth lodestar standards for determining an FDCPA fee petition, including that fees are mandatory, and the amount of attorney fees requested need not be proportionate to the settlement amount as that would defeat the public benefit advanced by the litigation.

Jackson v. Bellsouth Telcoms, Inc., 2000 U.S. Dist. LEXIS 7674 (N.D. Ill. June 1, 2000). Fee application of $12,500 reduced more by than half, by reducing hourly rate, eliminating time spent on meritless venue dispute, and eliminating other hours. Fees were awarded where plaintiff settled for $1000 statutory damages after dropping class claims, even though the defendant in the settlement agreement expressly denied liability and all wrongdoing. "First, Jackson's lawsuit was clearly causally linked to the damages that he received. Second, the court does not find that defendants acted gratuitously in settling the lawsuit. After Jackson dropped the class action, defendants settled with him for the maximum individual amount allowed under the FDCPA. Consequently, the court does not find that defendants settled with Jackson for wholly gratuitous reasons." "A defendant settles gratuitously if the lawsuit was 'frivolous, unreasonable, or groundless.'"

Komperda v. Turcy, 1999 U.S. Dist. LEXIS 6329 (N.D. Ill. Apr. 14, 1999). Consumers' attorney fees were reduced from over $9000 to just under $3000 because of excessive and duplicative billing where the consumers prevailed on some of their FDCPA claims and settled others.

Strange v. Wexler, 796 F. Supp. 1117 (N.D. Ill. 1992). Attorney fees may not be awarded to a *pro se* plaintiff who happens to be a lawyer.

In re Vasquez, 221 B.R. 222 (Bankr. N.D. Ill. 1998). Successful *pro se* attorney plaintiff not entitled to award of attorney fees.

Indiana

Dieske v. CCS Commercial, L.L.C., 2010 WL 3909868 (N.D. Ind. Oct. 1, 2010). Fees do not include those expended after the offer of judgment, since such fees would not be reasonably incurred.

Holmes v. Lockhart Morris Montgomery, Inc., 2010 WL 3719743 (N.D. Ind. Sept. 14, 2010). The court awarded $1000 in statutory damages on a default motion, but reduced the requested attorney fees and costs since they were not fully supported by the billing invoice, which showed a lesser amount.

Dechert ex rel. Estate of Oyler v. The Cadle Co., 2004 WL 2999112 (S.D. Ind. Nov. 10, 2004). Fees were reduced for duplication, "given that this was a matter arising under a strict liability statute and given that there are an ample number of local practitioners well versed and experienced in the FDCPA and consumer law arena," including multiple attorney attendance at hearings and conferences before the magistrates and this court and joint attendance at depositions.

Payday Today, Inc. v. Hamilton, 911 N.E.2d 26 (Ind. Ct. App. 2009). The lender and attorney were liable for attorney fees pursuant to the FDCPA and state law even though the borrower was represented by law school clinic and student interns.

Kansas

Caputo v. Prof'l Recovery Servs., Inc., 2004 WL 1503953 (D. Kan. June 9, 2004). The court refused to order the defendant to disclose the hourly rate and total paid to its out-of-state attorney in its unsuccessful defense on the merits as the court determined that the information would not be significant to determine the rate or total fees to be awarded the prevailing plaintiff for reasonable attorney fees.

Louisiana

Sanders v. Washington Mut. Home Loans, Inc., 2009 WL 365683 (E.D. La. Feb. 10, 2009). Consumer not entitled to fees against other parties from the collection attorneys joined late in the case. Ninety-two hours were reasonably expended in case settled after discovery.

Cope v. Duggins, 203 F. Supp. 2d 650 (E.D. La. 2002). Court approved class settlement requiring payment to class members of 60% of the maximum net worth calculation that the defendant could be assessed as reasonable in view of the vagaries of continued litigation. Court awarded class counsel reasonable attorney fees equal to several times the amount of the class recovery, recognizing that federal courts reject any proportionality require-

ment and observing that "this imbalance was principally attributable to the design of the FDCPA damages provision" that limits the class recovery to 1% of the defendant's net worth but places no cap on fees.

Hagan v. MRS Assocs., 2001 U.S. Dist. LEXIS 6789 (E.D. La. May 15, 2001). In a detailed analysis, the court reduced plaintiff's fee application on a $6000 settlement to $19,500 plus expenses (finding $200 per hour reasonable) by deducting 10% for lumping different tasks; allowing 10 hours as reasonable for settlement efforts; 25 hours for discovery; 14.25 hours for legal research; and 5 hours for opening the matter and preparing the complaint.

Addison v. Braud, 34 F. Supp. 2d 407 (M.D. La. 1998). Following *Johnson v. Eaton,* 80 F.3d 148 (5th Cir. 1996) the plaintiff must prove either actual or additional damages to be eligible for an award of attorney fees. Court's advising jury that no attorney fees can be awarded to plaintiff if jury failed to return verdict of money damages was not so prejudicial as to warrant granting a new trial.

Johnson v. Eaton, 958 F. Supp. 261 (M.D. La. 1997). Attorney fees awarded to a successful consumer for fees incurred during FDCPA suit and defendant's appeal. The court stated that the intent of FDCPA was for plaintiffs to recover reasonable attorney fees regardless of size of judgment as a way to encourage FDCPA claims.

Massachusetts

Nelson v. Hecker, 2010 WL 1741072 (D. Mass. Apr. 28, 2010). Following entry of Rule 68 judgment, the court rejected the defendant's request to reduce the award of attorney fees due to the claimed "unexceptional nature of the work required" and awarded $10,385 lodestar fees.

Michigan

Richard v. Oak Tree Group Inc., 2009 WL 3234159 (W.D. Mich. Sept. 30, 2009). Fee award reduced substantially to twelve hours at $250 per hour; fee entries were unintelligible; case was simple with small recovery.

Pietrowski v. Merchants & Med. Credit Corp., 256 F.R.D. 544 (E.D. Mich. 2008). Where the jury found defendants liable for violations of the FDCPA but awarded no damages, plaintiff was not "successful" and attorney fees would not be awarded to her counsel.

Gradisher v. Check Enforcement Unit, Inc., 2003 WL 187416 (W.D. Mich. Jan. 22, 2003). While there was some duplication of attendance by local and out-of-state counsel, it was necessary for them to confer on the case, the use of local counsel reduced the total hours spent, and the duplication would not be the basis for reducing the award. Attorney fees in the amount of $69,872.00 (out of a $92,401 lodestar) and expenses in the amount of $7808.44 were awarded in case where consumers prevailed on summary judgment but decertified their class action when it became apparent that the debt collector's net worth for calculating class damages was negligible. Although an hourly rate of $400 was approved by another court for one counsel, the court believed the $300 rate originally sought was more in line with local rates. A defendant which litigates a case vigorously cannot later complain about the resulting hours that consumer's counsel needed to respond. While there was some duplication of attendance by local and out of state counsel, that was necessary for them to confer on the case and the use of local counsel reduced the total hours spent. Where a class was decertified, the success was partial, and the lodestar was reduced by the time spent on class issues. Expenses of consumer's attorneys including some copying, travel expenses, and computer research fees were shifted to the defendant.

Diamond v. Corcoran, 1992 U.S. Dist. LEXIS 22793 (W.D. Mich. Aug. 3, 1992). Although no actual or statutory damages were awarded, the FDCPA requires an award of costs and attorney fees to the successful consumer. "An award of attorney's fees fulfills Congress's intent that the Act be enforced by debtors acting as private attorneys general."

Minnesota

Bankey v. Phillips & Burns, L.L.C., 2008 WL 2405773 (D. Minn. June 11, 2008). Reduced fee award from $50,000 requested to $33,000, detailed analysis of time records, where an offer of judgment was accepted after discovery.

Missouri

Liggens v. Unger & Assocs., Inc., 1990 WL 34188 & 34191 (W.D. Mo. Jan. 4, 1990). Where the consumer had accepted the collector's Fed. R. Civ. P. 68 offer of judgment of $500 and "costs," the consumer was not entitled to attorney fees since § 1692k does not consider attorney fees to be costs. Subsequently, the court refused to rescind the agreed judgment.

Montana

McCollough v. Johnson, Rodenburg & Lauinger, 2009 WL 2476543 (D. Mont. June 3, 2009). Where there was a large jury verdict for the consumer, the FDCPA attorney fees would not be reduced because the closing argument to the jury asked for a much higher amount or because the verdict was based on two tort claims in addition to the FDCPA claim. The consumer is entitled to out-of-pocket expenses "[e]ven though not normally taxable as costs . . . that would normally be charged to a fee paying client." However, expert witness fees were not recoverable as costs in excess of $40 per day.

Nebraska

Jenkins v. General Collection Co., 2009 WL 3631014 (D. Neb. Oct. 26, 2009). The court reduced the $419,715.67 attorney fees requested for based on 1667 hours to $50,000. The reduction was based on the plaintiffs' failure to achieve class certification and the limited value of the settlement to the three individual plaintiffs, $21,000. The defendant's recommendations of $45,000 and to exclude fees for the two out-of-state attorneys were rejected.

New Hampshire

Silva v. Nat'l Telewire Corp., 2001 U.S. Dist. LEXIS 20717 (D.N.H. Dec. 12, 2001). Attorney fees may be based on a nonlocal rate if it was reasonable for the plaintiff to hire a nonlocal specialist. A plaintiff reasonably hires a nonlocal specialist when there are no attorneys available in the local area with the required skill to handle the case. Generally, travel time is not compensated at a full professional rate and, in this case, fifty percent of the professional rate would be reasonable.

New Jersey

Norton v. Wilshire Credit Corp., 36 F. Supp. 2d 216 (D.N.J. 1999). In an FDCPA jury trial, plaintiff won $5800 on a § 1692g claim, and defendant won $1651.63 on its counterclaim for the debt. Plaintiff's counsel sought fees and costs of $67,697.56, and was awarded $57,206.34 at his current rate of $215 per hour. The court rejected the argument that there must be proportionality between the damages and the fee. The hours were high because there was an arbitration and an appeal to the Third Circuit. Because plaintiff prevailed on only one of his five claims the fee petition was reduced by five percent. The court also excluded ten percent of the sixty-eight hours spent on summary judgment, when the attorney had already spent thirty-four hours preparing for arbitration on the same subject.

New York

Ostrander v. Dentistry by Dr. Kaplansky, P.L.L.C., 2010 WL 1407300 (W.D.N.Y. Mar. 30, 2010). A *pro se* consumer who prevails on an FDCPA claim cannot recover attorney fees for representing himself.

Aslam v. Malen & Assocs., P.C., 669 F. Supp. 2d 275 (E.D.N.Y. 2009). The court found that a consumer who settled for $1000 statutory damages and $278 actual damages obtained "both forms of relief sought" and "achieved a high degree of success". Therefore, the court refused to reduce attorney fees on the basis of degree of success. "The proposed jury instructions submitted by the lawyer were lifted, almost verbatim, from *Fair Debt Collection*, a popular manual published by the Nclcccccc. The Court finds it difficult to accept that a relatively experienced consumer rights lawyer required more than 13 hours to lift jury instructions from the most widely used manual in the field." Accordingly, the court reduced the time on the proposed jury instructions from 13.2 hours to 2 hours. An hourly rate of $250 (rather than $425) was reasonable as compared to for similar attorneys in the region. After some reduction in requested hours, the court awarded over $63,000 in fees.

Aslam v. Malen & Assocs., P.C., 669 F. Supp. 2d 275 (E.D.N.Y. 2009). No reduction of fees for degree of success where plaintiff settled for $1000 statutory damages and $278 actual damages.

Miller v. Midpoint Resolution Group, L.L.C., 608 F. Supp. 2d 389 (W.D.N.Y. 2009). $7000 in fees awarded, a reduction from the unopposed $18,000 requested because plaintiff had requested $10,000 for emotional distress but recovered only $500.

Barrows v. Tri-Financial, 2009 WL 3672069 (W.D.N.Y. Oct. 30, 2009). Fourteen hours ranging from $250 to $400 excessive for a default. Court awarded half the requested rate and noted that the $1855 was proportional to the $1000 statutory damage award.

Cole v. Truelogic Fin. Corp., 2009 WL 261428 (W.D.N.Y. Feb. 4, 2009). 15.4 hours were reasonably expended to obtain a default judgment.

Larsen v. JBC Legal Group, P.C., 588 F. Supp. 2d 360 (E.D.N.Y. 2008). Time was not compensable where it involved a phone call to named persons without designating the topic.

Leyse v. Corporate Collection Servs., Inc., 557 F. Supp. 2d 442 (S.D.N.Y. 2008), *report and recommendation adopted*, 557 F. Supp. 2d 442 (S.D.N.Y. 2008). With a reduction of the hours by 40% the court awarded attorney fees of $12,735 and $302.50 in costs in this FDCPA case determined by summary judgment.

Dowling v. Kucker Kraus & Bruh, L.L.P., 2005 WL 1337442 (S.D.N.Y. June 6, 2005). Court reduced fee application to just over half, based on perception that experienced FDCPA counsel need not have expended so many hours on various tasks.

Padilla v. Payco Gen. Am. Credits, Inc., 161 F. Supp. 2d 264 (S.D.N.Y. 2001). *Pro se* litigant was not entitled to an award of reasonable attorney fees.

Cooper v. Sunshine Recoveries, Inc., 2001 U.S. Dist. LEXIS 8938 (S.D.N.Y. June 27, 2001). Granting plaintiff's attorney fee application, as adjusted, the court ruled that (1) out-of-state counsel, who was admitted *pro hac vice* only once the fee application was submitted and who otherwise appeared with local counsel, was entitled to compensation; (2) the recovery of $750 in statutory damages was full success, particularly when the damage ceiling itself of $1000 is "exceedingly low;" (3) elimination of the time spent on the unsuccessful class claims was warranted; and (4) reduction was appropriate for duplicative and excessive time.

Laster v. Cole, 2000 U.S. Dist. LEXIS 8672 (E.D.N.Y. June 23, 2000). Where counsel admitted that he overstated his hours for preparing for summary judgment as nine hours when he only spent six, his fee would be reduced by that amount, any multiplier for success was denied, and he was ordered to show why the court should not sanction him in that amount for falsely certifying his hours. $200 per hour was a reasonable rate and $5490 a reasonable fee for the case, but the retainer agreement that the client would pay 50% of the recovery to the attorney provided double payment and the attorney fee was reduced by the $100 the consumer was to pay out of the recovery.

Shapiro v. Credit Prot. Ass'n I, Inc., 53 F. Supp. 2d 626 (S.D.N.Y. 1999). FDCPA attorney fees are not part of costs. Therefore, since the collection agency accepted the consumer's Rule 68 offer of judgment, which included costs but made no mention of fees, the court was required to award an additional amount as attorney fees. The court reluctantly did so, awarding only a fraction of the amount requested.

Vera v. Trans-Continental Credit & Collection Corp., 1999 U.S. Dist. LEXIS 6937 (S.D.N.Y. May 10, 1999). Attorney fees of $3500 were awarded, reduced from a $10,750 application. The court used factors more appropriate to determination of statutory damages: the technical nature of the violation, the $8 amount of the debt, and the consumer's rejection of a $950 offer of judgment made at the outset.

Berrios v. Sprint Corp., 1998 WL 199842 (E.D.N.Y. Mar. 16, 1998). Fees may be paid only to those attorneys who actually had some responsibility for the case performing some work for the case.

Siler v. Mgmt. Adjustment Bureau, 1992 WL 170699 (W.D.N.Y. July 6, 1992). Where prepaid legal plan representing the consumer demonstrated that it was financially independent from the union, the court rejected the collector's contention that attorney fees should be awarded on a cost basis and awarded fees at the prevailing market rate.

Gutierrez v. Direct Mktg. Credit Servs., 701 N.Y.S.2d 116 (N.Y. App. Div. 1999). Affirmation from another attorney regarding his law firm's billing rate failed to indicate that the rate was the prevailing market rate in the community for similar services provided by plaintiff's attorney.

North Carolina

O'Fay v. Sessoms & Rogers, P.A., 2010 WL 3210948 (E.D.N.C. Aug. 9, 2010). Fees awarded at $225 per hour, but the court reduced the requested fees by two thirds based on a finding of limited success where consumer prevailed on one of three claims.

Ohio

Dobina v. Carruthers, 2010 WL 1796345 (N.D. Ohio May 3, 2010). The court followed the circuit's rule limiting the time compensable for obtaining the attorney fee award to 3% of the prior compensable time.

Wamsley v. Kemp, 2010 WL 1610734 (S.D. Ohio Apr. 20, 2010). The full amount of attorney fees requested, $3,751.50, was granted. The court found that the stipulated award of $750.00 to the consumer was "an excellent result" (75% of the maximum statutory damages available), and the extent of success is a "crucial factor" to consider when awarding attorney fees.

Mann v. Acclaim Fin. Servs., Inc., 348 F. Supp. 2d 923 (S.D. Ohio 2004). Where the consumer achieved only partial success, the court reduced the award of attorney fees by one-third.

Cook v. VFS, Inc., 2000 U.S. Dist. LEXIS 15621 (S.D. Ohio Sept. 27, 2000). Court rejected, as basis for reducing fee request, the argument that recovery of $1000 statutory damages was a mere technical victory. Court declined to reduce fee application merely because plaintiff did not prevail on all claims. However, it applied a 50% reduction to the time distinctly spent on a losing issue. Court restricted claimed costs to those allowed by statute.

White v. Cadle Co., 1999 U.S. Dist. LEXIS 15760 (S.D. Ohio Sept. 30, 1999). Where consumer achieved only limited success under the FDCPA, with the jury awarding only a fraction of the damages and none of the $400,000 punitive damages requested and found no liability for fraud and no liability for one defendant, consumer's attorney fees reduced by thirty percent. Consumers received only $800 in actual and statutory FDCPA damages and $900 for a state claim, but plaintiffs' attorney was awarded over $13,000 in costs and fees.

Boyce v. Attorney's Dispatch Serv., 1999 U.S. Dist. LEXIS 12970 (S.D. Ohio Apr. 27, 1999). In a case involving overt threats of bad check prosecution, which the court called "the most egregious conduct of any defendant" in any FDCPA case before it, the court nevertheless declined to award the consumer's attorney all the attorney fees sought since they were high considering one defendant had defaulted and the other defendants settled.

Oregon

Daley v. A & S Collection Assocs., Inc., 2010 WL 5137834 (D. Or. Dec. 10, 2010). The court found that the unsuccessful claims were related to the successful claims because they were premised on the same actions by the defendant. Because the plaintiff recovered her statutory penalty plus $2500 in actual damages, the court saw no need to reduce the time due to the lack of success on some of her claims. The court reduced the hourly rate and deducted another 20% from the award of attorney fees due to the settlement approach: "In sum, this case is an example of litigation gone amok because plaintiff's counsel did not engage in a good faith attempt to settle the case. Given the low amount of damages available to plaintiff if she prevailed, the only reasons to reject ADR at an early stage in the litigation were to increase the fees recoverable by plaintiff's attorneys and/or to punish the debt collector. Neither motive can be condoned by this court. Of course, plaintiff's counsel is not entirely to blame since defendant failed to make a reasonable offer after plaintiff unreasonably rejected ADR. Therefore, this court is not inclined to exclude all fees expended by plaintiff after rejecting ADR, but concludes that a sizeable portion must be excluded as being far in excess of those needed to obtain the results obtained."

Pennsylvania

Jackson v. National Credit Adjusters, L.L.C., 2009 WL 367408 (M.D. Pa. Feb. 13, 2009). Requested attorney fees were reduced to thirty hours in a case that was settled with the court disallowing time in initially conferring with the client and reducing time in conferring with law partners.

Hensley v. Berks Credit & Collections, Inc., 1997 WL 725367 (E.D. Pa. Nov. 18, 1997). Consumer's attorney fee request of $9450 was reduced to $4050 based on the attorney's failure to justify the time claimed, overbilling of time, keeping time in 15 minute increments, and billing for time spent on support work. The court reluctantly used the $200 per hour rate for the fee for an attorney with twenty-five years' experience.

Vandzura v. C & S Adjusters, Inc., 1997 WL 56927 (E.D. Pa. Feb. 10, 1997). Part of the consumer's attorney fee award was reduced 45% (from $17,005 to $9352.75) reflecting time spent litigating unsuccessful claims and the consumer's limited success. Post trial fees of $3140 were awarded. In addition, debtor's request of 10% upward adjustment for the delay between filing and judgment was granted due to the collector's failure to object.

Texas

Guerrero v. Hudson & Keyse, L.L.C., 2009 U.S. Dist. LEXIS 4921 (W.D. Tex. Jan. 20, 2009). Plaintiff was entitled to reasonable attorney fees for thirty hours at $275 an hour. Where the offer of judgment provided for the consumer's attorney fees, none were awarded for the fee petition after the offer was accepted, as that is the ordinary rule if not addressed in the offer. Consumer's requested thirty hours were reduced to ten because the disallowed time had been spent by the attorney after the offer of judgment was made. Thus, attorney fees in the amount of only $8676 were awarded.

Virginia

Randle v. H&P Capital, Inc., 2010 WL 2944907 (E.D. Va. July 21, 2010). There is nothing inherently unreasonable about having multiple attorneys, and the use of two attorneys to represent a party is the norm for federal court litigation. In light of the congressional intent in the FDCPA, the court will not reduce an award of attorney fees merely because the consumer's recovery appears. Where the record indicated that the specific FDCPA violation alleged constitutes a topic of debate among practitioners who specialize in consumer law such that the defendants raised constitutional challenges to the issue presented in the complaint, the complexity of the issues involved in this case supported the finding that counsel expended a reasonable number of hours on this matter. proportionally lower than the total amount of fees requested. The time expended by counsel to adapt discovery from another case to the needs in the present matter was reasonable.

Zhang v. GC Serv., L.P., 537 F. Supp. 2d 805 (E.D. Va. 2008). Fee application reduced from $24,000 to about $18,000 based on duplication of efforts, billing attorney time for clerical or paralegal work, unexplained time entries. The court found forty-six hours reasonably expended by the lead counsel in this uncomplicated case settled fairly early after filing. Court denied post-judgment request for defendants' time records. "Such production would be of marginal assistance to the Court, at best, while placing an undue burden on the defense."

Jones v. Vest, 2000 U.S. Dist. LEXIS 19026 (E.D. Va. Dec. 27, 2000). The consumer attorney's twenty-four years experience in public interest law justified the rate.

Wisconsin

Sweet v. Corporate Receivables, Inc., 2008 WL 2953572 (E.D. Wis. July 29, 2008). Reasonable attorney fees include travel time billed at the same hourly rate as the lawyer's normal working time but travel expenses are not reimbursed. Attorney fee in the amount of $30,922.69 and expenses of $1279.14 was awarded in this FDCPA case filed as a class action but settled as an individual claim after limited discovery.

Klewer v. Cavalry Invs., L.L.C., 2002 U.S. Dist. LEXIS 9289 (W.D. Wis. May 17, 2002). Following entry of judgment against the debt collector, the consumer's attorney was awarded reasonable fees at the requested rate of $200 per hour with various reductions totaling approximately 25% of the hours sought as excessive or unnecessary.

Booth v. Collection Experts, Inc., 969 F. Supp. 1161 (E.D. Wis. 1997). The statutory language of the FDCPA makes an award of attorney fees to the successful consumer mandatory.

K.3.3.2 LSC Programs

Arizona

Nunez v. Interstate Corporate Sys., Inc., Clearinghouse No. 36,156 (D. Ariz. 1984). $8452 attorney fee awarded for 90.8 hours at $75 and $80 per hour for two legal aid lawyers in successfully settled FDCPA class action. A multiplier of 1.2 was granted without objection of the defendant based on innovative nature of suit, class relief, preclusion of other legal aid work during declining funding period, and degree of success and public service.

Nunez v. Interstate Corporate Sys., Inc., 799 P.2d 30 (Ariz. Ct. App. 1990). Attorney fees under § 1692k(a)(3) awarded in an action in state court action based on the defendant's fraudulent conveyance to avoid the enforcement of a prior FDCPA judgment.

Florida

Shorr v. Am. Collection Sys., Inc., Clearinghouse No. 29,301 (S.D. Fla. 1980) (default judgment). $585 LSP attorney fees awarded and $1000 statutory award.

Hawaii

Sakuma v. First Nat'l Credit Bureau, 1989 U.S. Dist. LEXIS 19120 (D. Haw. Nov. 15, 1989). FDCPA damages of $1034 awarded for two notice violations and $1000 minimum UDAP damages awarded on a pendent state claim. Attorney fees awarded and settled for $12,500 to legal aid.

Illinois

Rutyna v. Collection Accounts Terminal, Inc., Clearinghouse No. 25,556 (N.D. Ill. 1979) (excerpt of proceedings). Attorney fees were awarded to legal services lawyers with the court suggesting that the level of the award would be based upon the salary level of the staff attorneys not the level of compensation for private practitioners.

Nebraska

Page v. CheckRite, Ltd., Clearinghouse No. 45,759 (D. Neb. 1984). Attorney fees of $19,700 in case involving failure to provide § 1692e(11) notices.

New Mexico

Vigil v. Burdge Enters., Clearinghouse No. 31,109 (D.N.M. 1981). One spouse was awarded $1013 and the other $1000. $5279 in attorney fees was awarded to two legal services attorneys using hourly rates of $40 and $50.

North Dakota

Bingham v. Collection Bureau, Inc., 505 F. Supp. 864 (D.N.D. 1981). Attorney fees were awarded to a legal services program.

Oregon

Furth v. United Adjusters, Inc., 1983 U.S. Dist. LEXIS 20368 (D. Or. Nov. 17, 1983). Attorney fees were awarded to a consumer represented by a law school clinic.

South Dakota

Ewing v. Messerli, Clearinghouse No. 44,331 (D.S.D. 1988). The consumer was awarded $7955 in damages and $3948.85 attorney fees.

Tennessee

Whitehorn v. Fisher, Clearinghouse No. 35,740 (Tenn. Ch. Ct. 1982). Attorney fees of $1172.50 was awarded after a trial of FDCPA claims.

K.3.3.3 Examples of Attorney Fee Awards

Danow v. Law Office of David E. Borack, P.A., 2010 WL 597213 (11th Cir. Feb. 22, 2010). The court found that the defendant law firm's offer of judgment of $1000 in damages, $2000 in attorney fees and costs, and confidentiality was not more favorable than the judgment entered in consumer's FDCPA action, in which consumer was awarded statutory damages of $1000, attorney fees and costs, and no confidentiality. Attorney fees in the amount of $62,895.00 plus costs of $715.60 awarded.

Schlacher v. Law Offices of Phillip J. Rotche & Assocs., P.C., 574 F.3d 852 (7th Cir. 2009). Court affirmed award of $6500 in fees where case settled in three months with no discovery; reduced from a fee application of some $12,500 by four attorneys.

Dowling v. Litton Loan Servicing L.P., 320 Fed. Appx. 442 (6th Cir. Apr. 9, 2009). The district court did not abuse its discretion in awarding the prevailing plaintiff, who had recovered at a bench trial over three days $1000 in statutory damages and $25,000 in emotional distress actual damages, attorney fees of $49,460 calculated at the lodestar rate of $300 per hour over 165.2 reasonably expended hours.

Savino v. Computer Credit, Inc., 164 F.3d 81 (2d Cir. 1998). Slight reduction of requested fee rate to $135 and $200 within lower court's discretion.

Chauncey v. JDR Recovery Corp., 118 F.3d 516 (7th Cir. 1997). Statutory damages of $1000 were awarded to plaintiff plus $1475 in attorney fees by the district court.

Bass v. Stopler, Koritzinsky, Brewster & Neider, S.C., 1997 U.S. App. LEXIS 41397 (7th Cir. June 6, 1997). $275 per hour was a reasonable fee for an attorney specializing in consumer law with a national reputation and experience.

Anunciation v. West Capital Fin. Servs. Corp., 97 F.3d 1458 (9th Cir. 1996) (text at 1996 WL 534049). Plaintiff filed and properly served a complaint for violation of FDCPA, then filed an amended complaint with invasion of privacy claims but failed to serve a summons with it. The defendant defaulted. The court awarded $1000 statutory damages, actual damages of $9500, and $5289 costs and attorney fees for obtaining the default judgment. On appeal the court held there was personal jurisdiction over defendant for all causes of action in the properly served initial complaint. Additional attorney fees were to be awarded to the consumer for the appeal.

Johnson v. Eaton, 80 F.3d 148 (5th Cir. 1996). Where jury found that a lawyer's assistant had violated FDCPA, but that the consumer had sustained no actual or statutory damages as a result of that violation, an award of attorney fees to the consumer for the legal assistant's violation was improper. The consumer was awarded $500 statutory damages, against the collection lawyer and the fee award against him was proper.

Hulshizer v. Global Credit Servs., Inc., 728 F.2d 1037 (8th Cir. 1984). District court awarded $1795.50 in attorney fees.

Baker v. G.C. Servs. Corp., 677 F.2d 775 (9th Cir. 1982). The district court awarded attorney fees of $800.

Alabama

Dempsey v. Palisades Collection, Inc., 2010 WL 923473 (S.D. Ala. Mar. 11, 2010). The consumer was awarded reasonable attorney fees in the amount of $2400.00 and costs in the amount of $355.75.

Arizona

Perkons v. American Acceptance, L.L.C., 2010 WL 4922916 (D. Ariz. Nov. 29, 2010). On the motion for default judgment against the debt collector, the plaintiff was awarded $7388.38 in attorney fees and costs.

Blair v. Viking Recovery Servs., 2010 WL 3522284 (D. Ariz. Aug. 10, 2010). On motion for entry of default judgment, the court recommended granting the plaintiff $1000 in statutory damages under § 1692k(a)(2)(A), $5275.00 in attorney fees and $425.30 in costs under § 1692k(a)(3), but no actual damages.

St. Bernard v. State Collection Serv., Inc., 2010 WL 2743327 (D. Ariz. July 12, 2010). Where consumer had accepted an offer of judgment for $1001.00, the court found that counsel's fees in the amount of $3010.71 (at a rate of $350.00 per hour) were reasonable. Counsel worked on procedural motions, assisted with discovery, and engaged in settlement discussions with defense counsel. Six hours were reasonable not the 9.7 requested.

Savage v. NIC, Inc., 2010 WL 2347028 (D. Ariz. June 9, 2010). The court awarded $17,442.30 in fees for sixty-one hours of work prior to settlement over the defendant's objections based on unsuccessful claims, the attorney's use of form pleadings, and the limited success (two out of seven claims) of a $2000 recovery.

Hill v. First Integral Recovery, L.L.C., 2009 WL 3353012 (D. Ariz. Oct. 16, 2009). Motion for default judgment by the consumer was granted awarding $1889.50 in FDCPA attorney fees.

Shelago v. Marshall & Ziolkowski Enter., L.L.C., 2009 WL 1097534 (D. Ariz. Apr. 22, 2009). Attorney fees of $17,175.33 for about sixty hours at $300 to $400 per hour to obtain a default judgment plus costs of $1177.58 was awarded in this FDCPA action.

Nunez v. Interstate Corporate Sys., Inc., 799 P.2d 30 (Ariz. Ct. App. 1990). Attorney fees under § 1692k(a)(3) awarded in an action in state court action based on the defendant's fraudulent conveyance to avoid the enforcement of a prior FDCPA judgment.

California

Johnson v. JP Morgan Chase Bank, N.A., 2010 WL 4977648 (E.D. Cal. Dec. 2, 2010). The court awarded the prevailing FDCPA plaintiff $56,770 in attorney fees following a $7450 jury verdict. The court made some reductions due to excessive hours, but rejected the defendant's "partial success" argument, finding instead that the plaintiff "obtained excellent results in this case warranting a full compensatory fee [less the reductions] because although she was only successful on one of the three causes of action, Plaintiff obtained relief in the form of emotional distress, statutory and other damages."

Jamal v. Thompson & Assocs., P.C., 2010 WL 678925 (N.D. Cal. Feb. 25, 2010). Fees awarded at $290; reduced by an hour for carelessly drafted documents.

Brablec v. Paul Coleman & Assocs. P.C., 2010 WL 235062 (E.D. Cal. Jan. 21, 2010). The court awarded $5120 in fees and $580 in costs.

Jones v. Morgan Stone Assocs., 2010 WL 55884 (N.D. Cal. Jan. 4, 2010). $2312.40 in attorney fees awarded on default.

Dabu v. Becks Creek Indus., 2009 WL 5178263 (N.D. Cal. Dec. 22, 2009). Consumer's motion for default judgment was granted awarding $3350 in attorney fees and costs.

Dudek v. Law Office of Scott Carruthers, 2009 WL 4981165 (N.D. Cal. Dec. 15, 2009). Court concluded that the consumer was the prevailing party in this settled case where the issue of fees was left to the court's jurisdiction and awarded $4000 for attorney fees and costs.

Hicke v. Marauder Corp., 2009 WL 4641724 (S.D. Cal. Dec. 1, 2009). Court awarded attorney fees of $3498 on default.

Middlesworth v. Oaktree Collections Inc., 2009 WL 3720884 (E.D. Cal. Nov. 3, 2009). Fee award on default ranging from $394 per hour to $250 per hour. Less than thirteen hours is a reasonable expenditure of time to, among other things, draft, serve, and file a complaint, an amended complaint, and move for entry of default judgment.

Tomovich v. Wolpoff & Abramson, L.L.P., 2009 WL 2447710 (S.D. Cal. Aug. 7, 2009). As the court found it unreasonable, plaintiff's claim for $80,777.45 attorney fees and litigation expenses was reduced to $42,725.95 by reducing the number of hours expended and reducing claimed hourly rates from $420 to $350 and from $385 to $300. The case settled after some discovery.

Basinger-Lopez v. Tracy Paul & Assocs., 2009 WL 1948832 (N.D. Cal. July 6, 2009). Attorney fees of full lodestar of $4002 awarded on default judgment, based on billing rates ranging from $225 to $355 per hour for 15.3 hours for the attorneys and about an hour of paralegal time at $125 per hour.

Hartung v. J.D. Byrider, Inc., 2009 WL 1876690 (E.D. Cal. June 26, 2009). Recommends entry of default judgment for the consumer in the amount of $27,000 damages and attorney fees for 23.8 hours at $250 per hour, totaling $5962.

Myers v. LHR, Inc., 543 F. Supp. 2d 1215 (S.D. Cal. 2008). Attorney fee in the amount of $24,934.50 was awarded in a default judgment.

Owens v. Brachfeld, 2008 WL 5130619 (N.D. Cal. Dec. 5, 2008). Court approved $325 hourly for attorney and $125 hourly rate for law clerk in the San Francisco area. Court reduced the time for the award to about twenty hours to obtain an unopposed summary judgment since the documents were virtually identical to documents used by counsel in other cases.

Bankston v. PhyCom Corp., 2008 WL 4412252 (N.D. Cal. Sept. 25, 2008). The court awarded $5580 in attorney fees calculated at $300 per hour for obtaining a default judgment and contested damages.

Bankston v. Patenaude & Felix, 2008 WL 4078451 (N.D. Cal. Aug. 29, 2008). FDCPA plaintiff's motion for attorney fees and costs was granted in the amount of $8372.50 at $300 per hours in fees and $58.62 in costs for twenty-three hours to obtain summary judgment plus additional hours to support the motion for fees.

Napier v. Titan Mgmt. Servs., L.L.C., 2008 WL 2949274 (N.D. Cal. July 25, 2008). Default judgment entered for consumer's attorney fees of $3960.00 and costs of $494.71.

Camacho v. Bridgeport Fin., Inc., 2008 WL 2951290 (N.D. Cal. July 24, 2008). On remand of *Camacho v. Bridgeport Fin.*, 523

F.3d 973, 978 (9th Cir. 2008), the district court recalculated the award of attorney fees at the rate of $375 per hour.

Sial v. Prof'l Collection Consultants, 2008 WL 2415037 (C.D. Cal. June 12, 2008). Fee request for twenty-two hours at $250/hour cut in half because of overzealous lawyering. For instance, the complaint should have taken no more than five hours to draft, rather than ten. The case was quickly settled by the acceptance of an offer of judgment.

Lowe v. Elite Recovery Solutions L.P., 2008 WL 324777 (E.D. Cal. Feb. 5, 2008). The court awarded $300 per hour to one attorney, $250 per hour to another, $115 for the work of a paralegal, and $90 for the work of a legal assistant, for a total fee award of $4100.

Langley v. Check Game Solutions, Inc., 2007 WL 2701345 (S.D. Cal. Sept. 13, 2007). After reductions in the number of hours claimed, the court awarded the plaintiff, who recovered the maximum $1000.00 in statutory damages and $91.00 in actual damages, $39,049.00 in reasonable attorney fees and $7075.77 in costs based on an lodestar rate of $350.00 per hour for the work of her attorney, who had eight years of legal experience, and about fifty hours in case settled by an offer of judgment after discovery.

Young v. Martini, Hughes & Grossman, 2006 U.S. Dist. LEXIS 79512 (S.D. Cal. Oct. 31, 2006). Upon the entry of default judgment for the consumer, awarded attorney fees in the amount of $1000 consisting of twenty hours at $50 per hour.

Giovannoni v. Bidna & Keys, P.L.C., 2006 WL 279345 (N.D. Cal. Feb. 3, 2006), *aff'd*, 255 Fed. Appx. 124 (9th Cir. 2007). Court found that about 12 attorney and 3 law clerk hours were reasonably expended where the consumer rejected the first but accepted the second offer of judgment for $1001.

Cancio v. Financial Credit Network, Inc., 2005 WL 1629809 (N.D. Cal. July 6, 2005). Some $10,000 in fees and costs were awarded on a $1000 offer of judgment, at $345 and $435 per hour. However, the court reduced the compensable hours to 8 for the complaint, 7 for case management, 8 for discovery, 1 for acceptance of the Rule 68 offer, and 7.8 for the attorney fee petition.

Defenbaugh v. JBC & Assocs., Inc., 2004 WL 1874978 (N.D. Cal. Aug. 10, 2004). Fee award decision in which the court rejected the defendant's principle attacks alleging lack of relative success and unnecessary time spent by the consumer's attorneys, awarded hourly rates at the requested amount for experienced counsel of $425 and $400 per hour, and exercised discretion to reduce the time requested on several individual items to reach an award of over $46,000.

Colorado

Harper v. Phillips & Cohen Assocs., Ltd., 2009 WL 3059113 (D. Colo. Sept. 21, 2009). Fee award of $9225 for 36.9 hours at $250 per hour on $2000 offer of judgment.

Ocker v. Nat'l Action Fin. Servs., Inc., 2008 WL 4964772 (D. Colo. Nov. 18, 2008). Attorney fees of $2712.50 for 10.85 hours (reduced from 13.85) at $250.00 per hour awarded in this FDCPA case.

Smith v. Argent Mortgage Co., L.L.C., 2008 WL 184072 (D. Colo. Apr. 22, 2008), *aff'd*, 331 Fed. Appx. 549 (10th Cir. 2009) (unpublished). The court awarded the prevailing foreclosure attorney defendants $18,600 in § 1692k attorney fees where the *pro se* plaintiffs vigorously litigated the case over two years, culminating in a bench trial where the plaintiffs "presented absolutely no evidence" that they had disputed the debt in a timely manner and that the defendants had unlawfully failed to verify the dispute, as alleged; the court explained that "the plaintiffs' actions concerning their FDCPA claim support strongly the inference that the plaintiffs brought their FDCPA claim with the primary purpose of harassing [defendants]. The record contains also strong indications that the plaintiffs pursued this litigation, including the FDCPA claim, with the goal of delaying foreclosure and other collection actions against them." "Pursuing litigation with the primary purposes of delay and harassment constitutes bad faith."

Connecticut

Silver v. Law Offices Howard Lee Schiff, P.C., 2010 WL 5140851 (D. Conn. Dec. 16, 2010). The court awarded $25777.50 based upon an hourly rate of $350.00 per hour. 73.65 hours was reasonably expended in case settled after a decision on summary judgment.

Ellis v. Solomon & Solomon, P.C., 2009 WL 3418231 (D. Conn. Oct. 20, 2009). FDCPA attorney fees at $350 per hour for ninety-nine hours were reasonable and the award totaled $34,720 plus costs of $1413 for successfully obtaining summary judgment, defeating defendant's motion for summary judgment, and taking several depositions. Travel time to the deposition was reasonably expended and compensated at the same hourly rate.

Rivera v. Corporate Receivables, Inc., 540 F. Supp. 2d 329 (D. Conn. 2008). Where the jury found for the consumer on only one of seven claimed separate violations, the court held that the consumer achieved only limited and partial success and reduced the $30,652 lodestar requested and awarded $9195. This was a 70% reduction of the total time in view of the limited success, but not a reduction based on the plaintiff's rejection of an early Rule 68 offer of judgment because the offer did not cover all of the plaintiff's attorneys fees incurred at the time as argued by the defendant.

Krueger v. Ellis, Crosby & Assocs., Inc., 2006 WL 3791402 (D. Conn. Nov. 9, 2006). Six hours at $300 per hour was reasonably expended to obtain a default judgment.

Sellers v. Boyajian Law Offices, P.C., 2006 WL 1668011 (D. Conn. June 14, 2006). 9.9 hours expended to investigate case, prepare suit, scheduling order, and fee petition was reasonable where an offer of judgment was accepted.

Goins v. JBC & Assocs., P.C., 2006 WL 540332 (D. Conn. Mar. 6, 2006). The court awarded some $23,000 in fees on a recovery of $1500 in a "hard-fought case" where seventy-eight hours was reasonably expended to obtain partial summary judgment, settlement of damages, and contested award of attorney fees.

Goins v. JBC & Assocs., 2005 WL 3536147 (D. Conn. Nov. 28, 2005). The court awarded attorney fees of $16,518 and costs of $156 for 55.06 hours of work at $300 per hour. "A review of the docket sheet in this case indicates that, during the three years this case has been pending, seventy-four (74) documents have been filed, including the following documents filed by plaintiff's counsel: the complaint, the 26(f) report, a revised 26(f) report, a motion for sanctions, a motion to compel discovery, a motion for reconsideration, a motion for partial summary judgment with supporting memorandum and two reply briefs, another motion for reconsideration with a supporting memorandum and a reply brief, a motion for costs and fees with a supporting affidavit and memorandum and a reply brief. Additionally, there were a number of status conferences held by the Court. Thus, a substantial amount of legal work was performed by plaintiff's counsel in this FDCPA case, for which she should be compensated.''

Gervais v. O'Connell, Harris & Assocs., Inc., 297 F. Supp. 2d 435 (D. Conn. 2003). Court awarded $2500 for the return of funds sent to pay a debt misrepresented as not barred by the statute of limitations, $1500 for emotional distress resulting from FDCPA violations, $8000 punitive damages under the state UDAP, and $5000 in attorney fees for twenty-seven hours at $200 on default.

Woolfolk v. Rubin, 1990 U.S. Dist. LEXIS 20964 (D. Conn. Feb. 2, 1990). Attorney fees of $2160 awarded to attorney with over twenty years consumer law experience (at $160 per hour).

Thomas v. Nat'l Bus. Assistants, Inc., 1984 U.S. Dist. LEXIS 24876, 1984 WL 585309 (D. Conn. Oct. 5, 1984) (slip copy). Attorney fees totaling $2787.50 awarded for three consolidated cases using rate of $125 per hour for one attorney and disallowing time for duplication by counsel, reducing time allowed to 0.25 hours for preparing duplicate fee affidavits and meeting ex-spouses separately. Since judgments were by default, no counsel appeared in opposition, hearing was routine, and efficiencies were gained from consolidation, court refused to increase or decrease lodestar.

Delaware

Smith v. Law Office of Mitchell N. Kay, 762 F. Supp. 82 (D. Del. 1991) (default judgment). Jury awarded $1000 statutory damages, $15,000 actual damages for emotional distress, and attorney fees of $1365. Court reduced actual damages to $3000 and awarded $1665 supplemental attorney fees for defending a motion for a new trial.

Perez v. Perkiss, 742 F. Supp. 883 (D. Del. 1990). Attorney fees of $10,110 were awarded for the services of two UAW Legal Services attorneys who brought this FDCPA claim and obtained a judgment after a brief jury trial, and the consumer was awarded $1200 ($200 actual and $1000 statutory) damages. The rates of $100 per hour for one attorney and $150 per hour for the second attorney were appropriate in light of the attorneys' experience, i.e., the second attorney had practiced for seventeen years. Several hours of services were disallowed for the second attorney to review the case upon the first attorney's withdrawal, and for the vagueness of the description of certain blocks of time. A downward adjustment of the lodestar was not warranted since the defendant's settlement offers were too low, the case was not too simple, and the disparity between damages and fees was irrelevant. $1610 of the fees awarded were for the services on the motion for attorney fees.

District of Columbia

Bard v. W.J. Cohan, Ltd., 43 Antitrust & Trade Reg. Rep. (BNA) 695 (D.D.C. 1982) (default judgment). $5635 for attorney fees awarded for seventy-four hours at $75 per hour, one hour at $85 per hour, and thirty-three law clerk hours at $25 per hour.

Florida

Bianchi v. Bronson & Migliaccio, L.L.P., 2011 WL 379115 (S.D. Fla. Feb. 2, 2011). The court awarded $14,259.00 for work performed in the underlying case at an hourly rate of $350.00; $1389.50 for work performed in the litigation over the award of fees and costs; and costs in the total amount of $4463.19 (including costs for a video deposition).

Crescenzo v. Law Offices of Douglas R. Burgess, L.L.C., 2010 WL 4509815 (S.D. Fla. Oct. 15, 2010). The court awarded fees at the rate of $350 per hour for 10.2 hours in this default matter.

Dennis v. Syndicated Office Sys., Inc., 2010 WL 3632478 (S.D. Fla. Sept. 14, 2010). The court awarded attorney fees at the rate of $300 per hour for 22.5 hours expended before settlement.

Newsome v. Regent Asset Mgmt. Solutions, Inc., 2010 WL 3447536 (M.D. Fla. Aug. 30, 2010). The court entered a default judgment for the consumer consisting of $25,000 for a lost employment opportunity and emotional distress, $1000.00 in statutory damages, and attorney fees of $2.707.50.

Renninger v. Phillips & Cohen Assocs., Ltd., 2010 WL 3259417 (M.D. Fla. Aug. 18, 2010). The court awarded attorney fees of $2379.41 as requested after the consumer accepted the defendant's Rule 68 offer of judgment.

Crescenzo v. ER Solutions, Inc., 2010 WL 3385978 (S.D. Fla. Aug. 9, 2010). In a case where the plaintiff was awarded $2000 in statutory damages, the court recommended an attorney fee award of $4449 and costs of $475.

Sampson v. Brewer, Michaels & Kane, L.L.C., 2010 WL 2432084 (M.D. Fla. May 26, 2010). In a default judgment case, the court awarded $2,415 in attorney fees.

Herber v. Professional Adjustment Corp., 2010 WL 2103025 (M.D. Fla. May 25, 2010). In this FDCPA case, default judgment was entered for the consumer in the amount of $4443.41 which included $3081.80 for attorney fees, and $361.61 for costs.

Zachloul v. Fair Debt Collections & Outsourcing, 2010 WL 1730789 (M.D. Fla. Mar. 19, 2010). A consumer was entitled to attorney fees in the amount of $8204 for thirty hours to obtain a settlement. A 20% reduction of the lodestar amount was necessary where the consumer ultimately settled for far less than her initial demand.

Sclafani v. I.C. Sys., Inc., 2010 WL 1029345 (S.D. Fla. Mar. 18, 2010). In case alleging violations of the FDCPA, FCCPA and TCPA, consumer may recover the time spent and billed after the parties agreed to settle the claims for $1000 each because until the district court judge ruled on the award, attorney fees were properly accruing. A one-third reduction of attorney fees was not appropriate because the consumer's attorney did not request any fees for time spent after the settlement of the FDCPA and the FCCPA claims. Consumer was awarded fees for 21.77 hours at $300.00 per hour for a total of $6,531.00, plus $566.60 in costs.

Danow v. Law Office of David E. Borback, P.A., 634 F. Supp. 2d 1337 (S.D. Fla. 2009). Fee award at $300 per hour for two of the attorneys; the third was "second chair" at trial and his services were superfluous. Awarded fees for 153.6 hours by one attorney, and 56.05 hours for a second for a total attorney fee of $62,895 for obtaining a favorable jury verdict.

Stone v. Nat'l Enter. Sys., 2009 WL 3336073 (M.D. Fla. Oct. 15, 2009). In this FDCPA case the hourly rate for one attorney was reduced to $300 and the paralegal to $95. Court awarded fee of $7850 for the nonduplicative work of twelve members of the firm on a simple case settled after a answer and one conference.

Sandin v. United Collection Bureau, Inc., 2009 WL 2500408 (S.D. Fla. Aug. 14, 2009). Fee application of $5132.40 reduced to $4096.20 award.

Rodriguez v. Florida First Fin. Group, Inc., 2009 WL 535980 (M.D. Fla. Mar. 3, 2009). The court awarded the entire $38,363.50 requested in attorney fees at $350 per hour, stating, *inter alia*, that "the overall amount of time spent is reasonable, considering that the case involved motion practice, evidentiary hearing and a particularly difficult defendant."

Gill v. Graham, Noble, & Assocs. L.L.C., 2008 WL 5069705 (S.D. Fla. Nov. 13, 2008). Magistrate recommended that attorney fees of $4480 (12.8 hours at $350 per hour) to obtain a default judgment be awarded.

Fulford v. NCO Fin. Sys., Inc., 2008 WL 2952859 (M.D. Fla. July 30, 2008). Reduced the fee request by 25% as a result of partial success and failure to investigate the collection agency's correction of a disputed credit report and awarded attorney fees of $5843.25 and costs of $395.

Armstrong v. The Cadle Co., 2006 WL 894914 (S.D. Fla. Apr. 3, 2006). Collector's motion for enlargement of time to file its notice of appeal was denied, and the consumer was awarded $550 in attorney fees for time spent responding to the motion.

Small v. Absolute Collection Serv., Inc., 2006 WL 6183287 (S.D. Fla. Mar. 23, 2006). After making some small deductions of time, the court awarded over $40,000 in fees for this settled FDCPA case, including all time spent on the contested fees issue.

Armstrong v. The Cadle Co., 2006 WL 540330 (S.D. Fla. Mar. 2, 2006). Fee award for eighty hours at $275 per hour, plus costs for obtaining a $2750 jury verdict.

Bernard v. Int'l Portfolio Mgmt., Inc., 2005 WL 1840157 (S.D. Fla. July 25, 2005). Fee award of $20,925.00 and costs of $885.80 upon settlement agreeing that plaintiff was the prevailing party. 83.7 hours was reasonably expended in this case that involved an out of state deposition and mediation.

Casden v. JBC Legal Group, P.C., 2005 WL 165383 (S.D. Fla. Jan. 7, 2005). Found $250 to be a reasonable hourly fee. Found 12.5 hours to be a reasonable time to spend on a filed FDCPA case before discovery that involved negotiations and an offer of judgment. Three hours was a reasonable amount of time on preparing and justifying the attorney fee petition.

Thorpe v. Collection Info. Bureau, Inc., 963 F. Supp. 1172 (S.D. Fla. 1996) (magistrate's recommendations). The court found $195 an hour to be a reasonable attorney fee rate and awarded $33,598.5 in attorney fees for 172.3 hours based on the lodestar method. The defendant had filed six defenses, there had been extensive discovery, a motion to dismiss was rejected, and the collector offered a judgment which was accepted after the consumer moved for summary judgment.

Georgia

Kim v. Barro, 2009 WL 1616271 (N.D. Ga. June 9, 2009). Fee award at $250 per hour for four hours; court denied $60 for service costs since plaintiff did not show a request for waiver of service.

Gilmore v. Account Mgmt., Inc., 2009 WL 2848278 (N.D. Ga. Apr. 27, 2009). After entry of default the magistrate recommended an award of attorney fees of $1858.50 ($295 per hour for 6.3 hours).

Smith v. Perimeter Credit, L.L.C., 2004 WL 1987231 (N.D. Ga. Aug. 27, 2004). Lengthy opposition papers and multiple motions to strike in response to plaintiff's fee application were patently frivolous. Fees of $6875 plus costs awarded on acceptance of offer of judgment for $1100.

Yelvington v. Buckner, Clearinghouse No. 36,581 (N.D. Ga. 1984). $5142.50 attorney fee award was based on 60.5 hours of work at $85 per hour. No adjustment was justified.

Florence v. Nat'l Sys., 1983 U.S. Dist. LEXIS 20344 (N.D. Ga. Oct. 14, 1983). The court awarded $750 attorney fees.

Zoeckler v. Credit Claims & Collections, Inc., 1983 U.S. Dist. LEXIS 20364 (N.D. Ga. Jan. 19, 1983). Following the twelve factors listed in *Johnson v. Georgia Highways Express*, 488 F.2d 714 (5th Cir. 1974), the court awarded $4832.40 in attorney fees calculated at $75 per hour for one attorney, $70 for another, and $30 for a paralegal. Only paralegal time engaged in work traditionally done by an attorney (legal research opposed to clerical work) is separately compensable. The court reduced the compensable attorney time believing it too long for the type of issues and work performed in light of the attorney's expertise in consumer law. The base fee was enhanced by 20% given the contingency of the fee and brief attorney client relationship. Costs were awarded for, *inter alia*, photocopies of documents but not travel expenditures and investigatory expenses.

Carrigan v. Cent. Adjustment Bureau, Inc., 502 F. Supp. 468 (N.D. Ga. 1980). Attorney fees were awarded.

Hawaii

Onishi v. Redline Recovery Servs., L.L.C., 2010 WL 5128723 (D. Haw. Nov. 12, 2010). After making reductions in the number of hours and reducing the reasonable hourly rate from $300 to $285, the court awarded $6797.25 in attorney fees.

Sakaria v. FMS Inv. Corp., 2009 WL 1322356 (D. Haw. May 12, 2009). Attorney fees of almost $4000 were awarded following settlement of this FDCPA case, based on $150 per hour for the plaintiff's attorney with five years of experience.

Illinois

Farrar v. Receivable Mgmt. Servs., 2010 WL 2720786 (S.D. Ill. July 8, 2010). In this FDCPA case, the court awarded attorney fees in the amount of $5586.20.

Shula v. Lawent, 2004 WL 1244030 (N.D. Ill. June 7, 2004). Fee award of some $32,000 on a recovery of $1200.

Riter v. Moss & Bloomberg, Ltd., 2000 U.S. Dist. LEXIS 14470 (N.D. Ill. Sept. 26, 2000). Court awarded five hours for drafting the five page complaint, since it was similar to a complaint used in an earlier proceeding; awarded fees for drafting the fee application, rejected most of defendants' claims about duplicate or unnecessary work; and granted $173,000 for fees and $14,000 for expenses.

Arevalo v. Nat'l Credit Sys., Inc., 1998 WL 456541 (N.D. Ill. July 31, 1998). Attorney fees of $33,362.25 and costs of $1611.39 were awarded to plaintiff's counsel.

Cortez v. Trans Union Corp., 1997 WL 7568 (N.D. Ill. Jan. 3, 1997). In this FDCPA class action, the court awarded attorney fees of $15,028.75 and costs of $7329.89.

Purnell v. Kovitz Shifrin & Waitzman, 1996 WL 521401 (N.D. Ill. Sept. 11, 1996). The consumer was successful in settling his FDCPA claim and was entitled to attorney fees of $19,867.50 based on the "lodestar" method. Rates of $180 to $240 per hour were reasonable for the consumer's counsel but excessive hours were trimmed by the court.

Avila v. Van Ru Credit Corp., 1995 WL 683775 (N.D. Ill. Nov. 16, 1995). The FDCPA mandates that a successful plaintiff be awarded reasonable attorney fees and costs. Court awarded plaintiff's attorneys $35,103.75 at hourly rates between $135 and $275 for attorneys and $75 per hour for legal assistants, plus an additional $1418.15 in costs. Fully documented amounts claimed for filing fees, photocopying, postage, telephone and delivery charges were properly recoverable as costs.

Indiana

Lemieux v. Guy, 2006 WL 3626555 (S.D. Ind. Nov. 20, 2006). Reduced $8000 fee request on an early offer of judgment to $2000, finding that four attorneys were not necessary; denying cost of service because of the mail service available under Federal Rule of Civil Procedure 4; denying time spent discussing retainer and state court defense with client.

Owens v. Howe, 365 F. Supp. 2d 942 (N.D. Ind. 2005). After the consumer recovered $1000 in statutory damages the court awarded attorney fees in the amount of $12,037.50 and costs of $534.13. The fees reflected fifty-three hours reasonably expended to obtain summary judgment in a hard fought case.

Dechert ex rel. Estate of Oyler v. The Cadle Co., 2004 WL 2999112 (S.D. Ind. Nov. 10, 2004). Plaintiff was awarded fees at the market rate in the local community. Despite substantial reduction, the court awarded some $54,000 in fees on a $1000 statutory recovery.

Kansas

Caputo v. Professional Recovery Servs., Inc., 2004 WL 1503953 (D. Kan. June 9, 2004). The court adjusted prevailing plaintiff's fee request in the exercise of discretion and awarded over $87,000 in fees to plaintiff on an offer of judgment of $15,000.

Mercy Reg'l Health Ctr., Inc. v. Brinegar, 223 P.3d 311 (Kan. Ct. App. 2010). The appellate court affirmed an award of attorney fee under state law against the losing debtor, a *pro se* lawyer who counterclaimed under both the FDCPA and state law in this collection action to recover for medical services performed for his minor child, where the trial court found that the state law counterclaim had been brought for an impermissible purpose under the applicable state law standard but that the unsuccessful FDCPA counterclaim did not warrant an award under the fee-shifting provision of § 1692k(a)(3).

Clark's Jewelers v. Humble, 823 P.2d 818 (Kan. Ct. App. 1991). District court's calculation of attorney fees at $100 per hour for forty hours was upheld.

Louisiana

Henderson v. Eaton, 2002 WL 31415728 (E.D. La. Oct. 25, 2002). The court found the class settlement fair and reasonable which provided $20,000 in attorney fees, $3000 to the named plaintiff as an incentive award, and $3000 to be divided among 142 class members.

McDaniel v. Asset Retrieval, Inc., 1996 WL 7001 (E.D. La. Jan. 5, 1996). The court awarded attorney fees of $6300 on a default judgment finding the fees of $200 per hour for one attorney and $100 per hour for the other and the hours claimed by both to be reasonable.

Johnson v. Eaton, 884 F. Supp. 1068 (M.D. La. 1995), *aff'd in part & rev'd in part*, 80 F.3d 148 (5th Cir. 1996). An award of attorney fees and costs was mandatory where the consumer has established that the collector violated any provision of the FDCPA. Time expended by the consumer's attorney found excessive and lodestar adjusted by reducing the number of hours compensated.

Maine

Sweetland v. Stevens & James, Inc., 563 F. Supp. 2d 300 (D. Me. 2008). Default judgment in the amount of $2500 actual damages plus $250 additional damages and $3520 attorney fees and costs was entered for consumer's FDCPA claims that the debt collector had made harassing telephone calls.

Maryland

Nicholes v. Advanced Credit Mgmt., Inc., 2010 WL 2998625 (D. Md. July 27, 2010). Nine hours (at $350 per hour) is a reasonable time to spend on a defaulted matter. Krohn conducted client intake, performed research to determine appropriate venue, and reviewed preliminary discovery. Court allowed three hours for that not 4.5 hours requested.

Michigan

Wells v. Corporate Accounts Receivable, 683 F. Supp. 2d 600 (W.D. Mich. 2010). Fees awarded at $300/$200 per hour based on each attorney's experience and qualifications.

Wells v. Corporate Accounts Receivable, 2010 WL 610258 (W.D. Mich. Feb. 18, 2010). The court awarded over $70,000 in fees to the prevailing consumer following entry of judgment for $2500 in FDCPA damages.

Kuhne v. Law Offices of Timothy E. Baxter & Assocs., P.C., 2009 WL 1798126 (E.D. Mich. June 23, 2009). Attorney fees for 5.85 hours at $265 per hour (for an attorney with almost twenty years of experience) for a total of $1550.25 was awarded.

Gomez v. Allied Interstate, Inc., 2007 WL 2710390 (E.D. Mich. Sept. 13, 2007). After reductions of the hours to six reasonably expended to file a complaint and reach a settlement after a pretrial meeting and reducing the hourly rate to $200 per hour, court awarded the plaintiff $1596.35 in reasonable attorney fees and costs following entry of Rule 68 judgment.

Dunaway v. JBC & Assocs., Inc., 2005 WL 3465665 (E.D. Mich. Dec. 19, 2005) (slip copy). The court approved plaintiff's request for 262.8 hours in winning summary judgment, preparing for trial on damages, and settling the case before trial. The court calculated the fee at $225 per hour and awarded attorney fees in the amount of $59,130 and costs of $3846.89. An expert's affidavit on the reasonableness of the hours was cited by the court.

Gradisher v. Check Enforcement Unit, Inc., 2003 WL 187416 (W.D. Mich. Jan. 22, 2003). Attorney fees in the amount of $69,872 (out of a $92,401 lodestar) and expenses in the amount of $7808.44 were awarded in case where consumers prevailed on summary judgment but decertified their class action when it became apparent that the debt collector's net worth for calculating class damages was negligible. Rates of $300 to $400 per hour were reasonable in 2002 for a lawyer with a great deal of experience handling FDCPA cases.

Minnesota

Nelson v. Eastern Asset Mgmt., L.L.C., 2009 WL 3255244 (D. Minn. Oct. 7, 2009). Default judgment entered for $4237 attorney fees and costs.

Young v. Diversified Consultants, Inc., 554 F. Supp. 2d 954 (D. Minn. 2008). Award of $3705.20 at $325 to $300 per hour for attorneys and $110 for paralegal approved after some time reduction and finding that 17.6 hours was reasonably expended to initiate the complaint in a case where the consumer accepted the offer of judgment.

Olson v. Messerli & Kramer, P.A., 2008 WL 1699605 (D. Minn. Apr. 9, 2008). Following plaintiff's acceptance of the defendant's Rule 68 offer in the amount of $1001 plus fees and costs, the court awarded plaintiff's three counsel over $36,000 in fees based on rates of $325, $300, and $275 per hour, plus additional amounts for paralegals and others, and awarded costs. The court rejected use of the *Laffey* matrix for setting fees in Minnesota. The court refused to award compensation for the time spent on the fee application because "a substantial reason for the parties' failure to settle the amount of the fees was [plaintiff's] counsel's refusal to provide any documentation in support of their claimed fees during the parties' negotiations. . . . Had [plaintiff's] counsel not engaged in this unreasonable conduct, it is quite likely that no fee petition would have been necessary." The court found that 134 hours were reasonably expended in a case that was decided after a motion for summary judgment and an offer of judgment that was accepted.

Armstrong v. Rose Law Firm, P.A., 2002 WL 31050583 (D. Minn. Sept. 5, 2002). Full lodestar fee request of over $43,000 at $250 per hour awarded where consumer was unsuccessful on her state collection law claim but prevailed on related FDCPA claim and received maximum statutory damages of $1000, with court rejecting any proportionality requirement and attributing the necessity of consumer's attorney's efforts entirely to the defendant's defense posture.

Venes v. Prof'l Serv. Bureau, Inc., 353 N.W.2d 671 (Minn. Ct. App. 1984). Attorney fees of $1500 awarded as well as fees of $3900

incurred as FDCPA actual damages in defending a prior collection action.

Missouri

Poniewaz v. Regent Asset Mgmt. Solutions, Inc., 2010 WL 3584368 (E.D. Mo. Sept. 7, 2010). In a default judgment against a debt collector, the court awarded fees of $2064 and costs of $405.

Daugherty v. Central Credit Servs., 2010 WL 1610388 (E.D. Mo. Apr. 21, 2010). The court awarded reasonable attorney fees of $9115.50 and costs following offer of judgment of $1001.00.

Alexander v. Boyajian Law Offices, 2006 U.S. Dist. LEXIS 49562 (E.D. Mo. July 20, 2006). In this FDCPA action the court reduced the requested attorney fees and costs from $9058.10 (which included among other items 23.5 hours at $325 per hour) to $3004.00 (which included among other items 13.3 hours at $150 per hour) for reasonable attorneys fees to obtain an acceptable offer of judgment after an inconclusive attempt at mediation.

Montana

McCollough v. Johnson, Rodenburg & Lauinger, 2009 WL 2476543 (D. Mont. June 3, 2009). Following a plaintiff's jury verdict that awarded $250,000 in compensatory damages, $1000 FDCPA statutory damages, and $60,000 in state law punitive damages, the court awarded attorney fees in the full amount requested of over $93,000, commenting, *inter alia*, that the litigation "confers a meaningful public benefit by discouraging illegal debt collection" in the state.

Nebraska

Keller v. Georgia Check Recovery, Inc., 2009 WL 5171815 (D. Neb. Dec. 18, 2009). Where the case was settled for $600, the court found the amount of time expended to be excessive in light of the claim and success achieved and thus awarded $2400 attorney fees and $350 costs.

Rockwell v. Talbott, Adams & Moore, Inc., 2006 WL 436041 (D. Neb. Feb. 21, 2006). The court awarded the plaintiff reasonable attorney fees of some $5000 for 200 hours of legal work, a substantial reduction from the amount sought due to the plaintiff's limited success following a two-day jury trial that resulted in a judgment of $250 in statutory damages and no actual damages, significantly less than the amounts that the plaintiff asked the jury to award.

Nevada

Edwards v. Nat'l Bus. Factors, Inc., 897 F. Supp. 455 (D. Nev. 1995). An award of attorney fees to the successful plaintiff in an FDCPA action was mandatory. Attorney fees were awarded to successful FDCPA litigant at attorney's usual rate of $175 per hour. Court criticized attorney's billing in segments of quarter hours rather than traditional tenth hour segments and reduced the lodestar by two hours.

Anunciation v. West Capital Fin. Servs. Corp., Clearinghouse No. 50,452 (D. Nev. 1995). Court must award attorney fees to successful plaintiffs in FDCPA actions. Court found that reasonable attorney fee award in an FDCPA case was twenty-nine hours at $175/hour for a total of $5075.

New Hampshire

Silva v. Nat'l Telewire Corp., 2001 U.S. Dist. LEXIS 20717 (D.N.H. Dec. 12, 2001). Plaintiff was awarded attorney fees in the amount of $59,288.50 and costs and expenses in the amount of $5338.45.

New Jersey

Ford v. Consigned Debts & Collections, Inc., 2010 WL 5392643 (D.N.J. Dec. 21, 2010). In this default judgment matter, the court awarded the plaintiff $350 in statutory damages, $250 in actual damages and attorney fees of nearly $4000 where the defendant "improperly failed to identify itself as a debt collector when it telephoned him, improperly threatened to sue plaintiff if he did not pay off the debt immediately, and improperly threatened plaintiff that it would contact his parole officer and have him thrown back in jail if he did not immediately pay his debt."

Stair ex rel. Smith v. Thomas & Cook, 2009 WL 1635346 (D.N.J. June 10, 2009). Distinguishing *Carroll*, court awarded $325 per hour, noting: "As was their right, Defendants litigated this case to the hilt, raising a wide array of arguments over multiple motions that ranged from innovative (but unavailing) to frivolous." "The upshot of Defendants' vigorous but unsuccessful litigation strategy was to significantly increase the resources necessary to litigate this case on all sides, notwithstanding the statutory cap on the potential damages at stake." "Defendants bear the responsibility for the disproportion between the attorney hours expended in litigating this case and the modest damages awarded." Award exceeded $36,000 in this class action. Ninety-nine attorney and eleven paralegal hours were reasonably spent to obtain summary judgment and class certification after defeating the collection attorney's motion for summary judgment.

New Mexico

Martinez v. Albuquerque Collection Serv., Clearinghouse No. 50,420 (D.N.M. 1995). Attorney fee of $35,000 awarded in class action resulting in award of actual and statutory damages and injunctive relief.

Toledo v. McNeel, Clearinghouse No. 50,433 (D.N.M. 1995). Successful consumer was entitled to costs and reasonable attorney fees pursuant to the FDCPA and N.M. Unfair Practices Act.

New York

Fajer v. Kaufman, Burns & Assocs., 2011 WL 334311 (W.D.N.Y. Jan. 28, 2011). In this default action, the court awarded attorney using the hourly rate of $215 for a partner and $175 for an associate with experience and expertise in FDCPA cases.

Copper v. Global Check & Credit Servs., L.L.C., 2010 WL 5463338 (W.D.N.Y. Dec. 29, 2010). In this default judgment, the court awarded $1545 in fees based upon an hourly rate of $175 per hour.

Shepherd v. Law Offices of Cohen & Slamowitz, L.L.P., 2010 WL 4922314 (S.D.N.Y. Nov. 29, 2010). In this FDCPA case the magistrate recommended that the plaintiff should be awarded $62,322.00 in fees and $5940.66 in costs.

Abbott v. Law Offices of Forster & Garbus, 2010 WL 4703407 (W.D.N.Y. Nov. 19, 2010). The award included fees at a rate of $200 per hour for a fifth year associate and $80 per hour for a paralegal.

Barksdale v. Global Check & Credit Servs., L.L.C., 2010 WL 3070089 (W.D.N.Y. Aug. 4, 2010). Fees awarded at the rate of $215 per hour for 8.8 hours. In view of the fee shifting provision of the FDCPA, the court found that a reasonable client would endorse that time expenditure to obtain default.

Hoover v. Western New York Capital, 2010 WL 2472500 (W.D.N.Y. June 16, 2010). In a default judgment, the court adjusted the consumer's request for attorney fees and awarded $2091.61 in fees and costs according to the following standards: "[R]ecent cases in this District set reasonable attorney rates in debt collection cases at $215 per hour for partners, $180 per hour for associates, and $50 per hour for paralegals."

Robbins v. Viking Recovery Servs. L.L.C., 2010 WL 1840318 (W.D.N.Y. May 7, 2010). In a default judgment, the court awarded the consumer $1569 in attorney fees and costs.

Taylor v. Morgan Stone & Assocs., L.L.C., 2010 WL 1816675 (W.D.N.Y. May 4, 2010). The court entered a default judgment and awarded attorney fees in the amount of $1634.50 and $350.00 in costs.

Annis v. Eastern Asset Mgmt., L.L.C., 2010 WL 1035273 (W.D.N.Y. Mar. 18, 2010). After entry of default, the court entered judgment $4240.50 in attorney fees and a total award of $14,150.50.

Healy v. Midpoint Resolution Group, L.L.C., 2010 WL 890996 (W.D.N.Y. Mar. 10, 2010). Court awarded one-third of damages for fees, as requested.

Mostiller v. Chase Asset Recovery Corp., 2010 WL 335023 (W.D.N.Y. Jan. 22, 2010). Awarded fees and costs of some $4100 following the debt collector's default on the consumer's claim of false threats of legal and other action.

Aslam v. Malen & Assocs., P.C., 669 F. Supp. 2d 275 (E.D.N.Y. 2009). An hourly rate of $250 was a reasonable rate for a lawyer of about five year's experience, and 259 hours were reasonably expended on a straightforward FDCPA case that was settled during the first day of trial. Total fee award was $63,927.50. Thirteen hours for preparing jury instructions were reduced to two where the instruction were "lifted, almost verbatim" from NCLC's *Fair Debt Collection.*

Nero v. Law Office of Sam Streeter, P.L.L.C., 655 F. Supp. 2d 200 (E.D.N.Y. 2009). Court awarded attorney fees for 9.2 hours at $200 per hour on default.

Estay v. Moren & Woods L.L.C., 2009 WL 5171881 (W.D.N.Y. Dec. 22, 2009). On entry of default, $1767.50 in costs and fees were awarded.

Dayton v. Northeast Fin. Solutions, 2009 WL 4571819 (W.D.N.Y. Dec. 7, 2009). Award on default judgment in this non-actual damage case of some $1200 in fees.

Clark v. Brewer, Michaels & Kane, L.L.C., 2009 WL 3303716 (W.D.N.Y. Oct. 14, 2009). Default judgment was entered for $500 FDCPA statutory damages and $2386 attorney fees at hourly rates of $180 to $215 for attorneys and $50 for paralegals.

Sievert v. Federal Credit Corp., 2009 WL 3165392 (W.D. Wis. Sept. 28, 2009). $15,791.20 fee award in a settled case.

Simmons v. Roundup Funding, L.L.C., 2009 WL 3049586 (S.D.N.Y. Sept. 23, 2009). Fees and costs awarded to debt collector in conclusory finding that the claim was frivolous, without referring to the § 1602k(a)(3) standards.

Berry v. Nat'l Fin. Sys., Inc., 2009 WL 2843260 (W.D.N.Y. Aug. 27, 2009). Upon entry of default and after a hearing to establish damages, husband and wife were awarded FDCPA actual damages of $3000, statutory damages of $2000, and $5999 in attorney fees: 25.1 hours at $215 per hour for the partner, 1.1 hours at $175 per hour for the associate, plus filing fees and costs.

Larsen v. JBC Legal Group, P.C., 588 F. Supp. 2d 360 (E.D.N.Y. 2008). Following entry of judgment for the maximum $1000 statutory damages, the court awarded reasonable attorney fees of $65,000, calculated at $300 per hour for the attorney with 227.7 reasonably expended to obtain summary judgment and a bench trial on damages.

Overcash v. United Abstract Group, Inc., 549 F. Supp. 2d 193 (N.D.N.Y. 2008). $2750 in attorney fees awarded for eleven hours of work at a rate of $250 per hour to obtain a default judgment against two debt buyers.

Leyse v. Corporate Collection Serv., Inc., 545 F. Supp. 2d 334 (S.D.N.Y. 2008), *report and recommendation adopted,* 557 F. Supp. 2d 442 (S.D.N.Y. 2008). The court awarded approximately $13,000 in attorney fees, deducting 40% from the fee request because of the "inefficiencies" of counsel's admitted status as a novice to the FDCPA.

McCarty v. Capital Mgmt. Servs., Inc., 2006 U.S. Dist. LEXIS 48645 (W.D.N.Y. July 17, 2006). About eighteen hours of attorney time reasonable where offer of judgment accepted.

Sparkman v. Zwicker & Assocs., P.C., 2006 WL 463939 (E.D.N.Y. Feb. 27, 2006). The court awarded the plaintiff reasonable attorney fees of some $1500 for about twenty-seven hours of work to obtain summary judgment, a substantial reduction from the amount sought due to the plaintiff's limited success, lack of acceptable time records, and the court's assessment that the plaintiff's attorney was "unprepared" in court.

Pinkham v. Professional Claims Bureau, Inc., 367 F. Supp. 2d 338 (E.D.N.Y. 2005). Court awarded fees for 7.3 hours of work prior to the accepting an offer of judgment and costs to the prevailing consumer in the amount requested.

Edge v. C. Tech Collections, Inc., 203 F.R.D. 85 (E.D.N.Y. 2001). Motion to dismiss based on Rule 68 offer to individual party denied: an offer of judgment ($1000 + $2500 fees and costs) that caps costs and fees did not represent more money than the plaintiff could receive under the FDCPA.

Miele v. Sid Bailey, Inc., 192 B.R. 611 (S.D.N.Y. 1996). $9818 attorney fees awarded.

Donahue v. NFS, Inc., 781 F. Supp. 188 (W.D.N.Y. 1991). Consumer was awarded attorney fees against Defendant NFS, Inc. at $95 per hour for 11.6 hours totaling $1102 plus $185 costs and Defendant Lanocha at $95 per hour for 5.1 hours totaling $484.50 plus $185 costs.

Bish v. Credit Control Sys., Inc., 1991 WL 165035 (W.D.N.Y. Aug. 14, 1991) (default judgment). Request for attorney fees at $140 per hour rejected and $90 rate used where the FDCPA claims were not novel or complex. Attorney fees of $594 awarded.

Read v. Amana Collection Servs., 1991 WL 165033 (W.D.N.Y. Aug. 12, 1991). Reasonable attorney fees of $2700 awarded (thirty hours at $90 per hour), and a claim for forty-six hours at $100 per hour rejected because it was on the high side for FDCPA cases and twenty hours for the summary judgment brief was excessive.

Young v. Credit Bureau, Inc., 1991 WL 37818 (W.D.N.Y. Mar. 12, 1991). In three FDCPA cases against the same debt collector, attorney fees were awarded for the work of consumers' prepaid legal counsel at $75 per hour for 38 hours totaling $2850 and $90 per hour for 11.5 hours totaling $1035.

North Carolina

Tye v. Brock & Scott, P.L.L.C., 2010 WL 428964 (M.D.N.C. Feb. 1, 2010). Fees awarded at $225 per hour, including travel time and time expended on fee motion.

Ohio

Dobina v. Carruthers, 2010 WL 1796345 (N.D. Ohio May 3, 2010). Following an answer but prior to discovery, the court entered a Rule 68 judgment, awarded $4860 in fees for 16.5 hours, and $350 in costs.

Davis v. Riddle & Assocs., P.C., 585 F. Supp. 2d 968 (N.D. Ohio 2008). Court awarded full $125,000 fee application in a class action where the class divided $2000 plus 1% of the collector's net worth.

Lee v. Javitch, Block & Rathbone, L.L.P., 568 F. Supp. 2d 870 (S.D. Ohio 2008). Following the plaintiff's successful jury trial, the court awarded reasonable attorney fees in the amount of $125,315, based on attorney rates of $265 per hour and $250 per hour with a 10% fee enhancement of the lodestar amount. "If believed that defense of [plaintiff's] case merited close to 800 hours of work, it seems entirely reasonable that Plaintiff's counsel would spend about 440 hours prosecuting her claims." The case involved a jury trial after extensive motions.

Mann v. Acclaim Fin. Servs., Inc., 348 F. Supp. 2d 923 (S.D. Ohio 2004). The hourly rate of $200 was reasonable.

Becker v. Montgomery, Lynch, 2003 WL 23335929 (N.D. Ohio Feb. 26, 2003). Court awarded $3600 for attorney fees at $200 per hour, plus awards paralegal's fees.

Oregon

Whitworth v. National Enter. Sys., 2010 WL 1924505 (D. Or. Apr. 21, 2010). Following settlement of the case for $2500, the court awarded the consumer attorney fees of $30,460.50, including a reduction of 25% from the lodestar because the consumer "received in settlement an amount significantly less than the amount of damages he prayed for" in the complaint. 197 hours were reasonable expended to obtain a settlement after the court rejected both of the defendant's motions for summary judgment.

Pierce v. Palisades Collection L.L.C., 2008 WL 4376883 (D. Or.

Sept. 25, 2008). Finding that "counsel's requested hourly rate of $225 and legal assistant rate of $80 to be reasonable for her community and the type of work," the court awarded $3689 for work associated with the consumer's application for a default judgment that was set aside on condition that the defendant pay fees and costs incurred.

Clark v. Capital Credit & Collection Servs., Inc., 561 F. Supp. 2d 1213 (D. Or. June 11, 2008). In this FDCPA case attorney fees (at $200 per hour for attorneys and $50 for paralegal) of $72,262 and costs of $2634.65 were awarded for a case settled after trial and appeal with the court reducing the fees 40% to reflect unsuccessful efforts to obtain summary judgment and a jury verdict. The court allocated the award between the collection agency and collection attorney defendants.

Clark v. Quick Collect, Inc., 2006 WL 572157 (D. Or. Mar. 6, 2006). Ninety-eight hours to prepare case that resulted in a $5000 verdict for the consumer reduced by 1/3, to $17,800, in view of limited success on only one of several of plaintiff's claims. The lodestar time was also reduced where some of the work could have been performed by an assistant and some of the time was spent for another plaintiff that were unsuccessful.

Hooper v. Capital Credit & Collection Servs., Inc., 2005 WL 2297062, 2005 WL 1899380 (D. Or. Sept. 20, 2005). Following a jury trial, which resulted in a $1570 actual damage award against the collection agency and a defense verdict for the agency's named employee, the court denied any additional statutory damages, awarded the plaintiff $17,467 in attorney fees, and denied any fees to the exonerated employee since the claims against her were not "brought in bad faith and for the purpose of harassment."

Check Cent., Inc. v. Barr, Clearinghouse No. 37,497 (Bankr. D. Or. 1984). Attorney fees of $400 awarded.

Pennsylvania

Lavelle v. Phoenix Acquisition Group, L.L.C., 2010 WL 5014347 (M.D. Pa. Dec. 3, 2010). Upon a default judgment, the plaintiff was awarded attorney fees in the amount of $7448.50.

Gryzbowski v. I.C. Sys., Inc., 2010 WL 2507516 (M.D. Pa. May 24, 2010). Attorney fees in the full amount requested of over $23,000 were granted to the prevailing consumer. Forty-nine hours was a reasonable expenditure on a successful motion for summary judgment.

Morris v. I.C. Sys., Inc., 2009 WL 1362594 (E.D. Pa. May 15, 2009). Following settlement of the two plaintiffs' FDCPA claims for a total of $18,500, the court awarded attorney fees of $64,684, based on rates ranging from $275 to $390 per hour and a paralegal's time at $120 per hour, reimbursement for computerized legal research expenses of $376, and a reduction of the requested lodestar hours by 15% to "correct for duplicative or unnecessary legal work," plus costs of $3782.

Holliday v. Cabrera & Assocs., P.C., 2007 U.S. Dist. LEXIS 161 (E.D. Pa. Jan. 3, 2007). The court awarded $5713 fees for about twenty hours obtaining a default judgment.

Nelson v. Select Fin. Servs., Inc., 2006 WL 1672889 (E.D. Pa. June 9, 2006). In this successful FDCPA action, the court awarded statutory damages of $1000 and attorney fees of $24,693.80 at hourly rates of $430, $295, and $115 for 67.9 hours of legal work to obtain summary judgment.

Moyer v. Turnbrook Assocs., Inc., 2005 WL 2660353 (E.D. Pa. Oct. 17, 2005). After entry of an arbitration award of $1000 for violation of the FDCPA, the district court awarded $6461.87 in attorney fees for twenty-seven hours spent on the client intake, research, pleadings, and the arbitration.

Parks v. Portnoff Law Assocs., 243 F. Supp. 2d 244 (E.D. Pa. 2003). Class action settlement approved as fair and reasonable. Where there was a contest of the coverage of the debts, municipal assessments for trash, water and sewer services, a $75,000 settlement fund was fair and reasonable. $1000 was distributed to the each of the named plaintiffs, at least $250 to each of fifty-two class claimants, and $13,500 to consumer's counsel.

Tenuto v. Transworld Sys., Inc., 2002 U.S. Dist. LEXIS 1764 (E.D. Pa. Jan. 31, 2002). Attorney fee of $140,950 or 35% of total settlement fund minus administrative costs was reasonable where lodestar was between $131,000 and $146,518.

Colbert v. Trans Union Corp., 1997 WL 550784 (E.D. Pa. Aug. 22, 1997). An attorney who received his J.D. in 1992 would be paid $105 per hour for work in a simple FDCPA class action in 1993, in 1994 $115, in 1995 $125, in 1996 $135, and in 1997 $145. Extensive experience in federal litigation supports the rate of $340 for a 1971 graduate of Villanova Univ. School of Law. The third attorney, who had twenty-five years of class action litigation experience and had co-authored a treatise on class actions, received $200 per hour. Rejecting the award of $129,209.60 sought, an award of $73,147.85 was granted after reducing for excessive hours billed.

South Dakota

Crawford v. Credit Collection Servs., 898 F. Supp. 699 (D.S.D. 1995). Statutory damages of $500 and attorney fees of $4000 were awarded.

Tennessee

Carroll v. United Compucred Collections, Inc., 2008 WL 3001595 (M.D. Tenn. July 31, 2008). Attorney fees amounting to $128,142.00 and costs amounting to $3147.01 was awarded for 335 hours of the litigation involving summary judgment, class certification, an interlocutory appeal, and two offers of judgment over a seven-year period in this FDCPA class action. The court also awarded $4536.00 in attorney fees and $1037.21 in costs incurred for twenty hours expended to obtain attorney fees.

Texas

Toomer v. Alliance Receivables Mgmt., Inc., 2010 WL 5071778 (W.D. Tex. Dec. 9, 2010). Where the parties agreed to voluntary arbitration, the arbitrator awarded the consumer attorney fees and costs through the date of the award of $45,000, additional attorney fees of $1500 for post-award motions in arbitration, additional attorney fees of $8000 for motions to enter judgment in federal court and to defend against any motions to vacate the arbitration award, additional attorney fees of $25,000 for appeals to the Fifth Circuit, and additional attorney fees of $35,000 for appeals to the United States Supreme Court.

Brown v. Phoenix Recovery Group, 2009 WL 4907302 (N.D. Tex. Dec. 21, 2009). After acceptance of an offer of judgment, $2732 in attorney fees and $410 in costs were awarded.

Bullock v. Abbott & Ross Credit Servs., L.L.C., 2009 WL 4598330 (W.D. Tex. Dec. 3, 2009). Recommended a default judgment award of $12,000 in attorney fees.

Brown v. Sterling & King, Inc., 2009 U.S. DIST. LEXIS 15599 (S.D. Tex. Feb. 27, 2009). Default judgment was entered in the amount of $1000 FDCPA statutory damages, $3756 attorney fees, and $425 costs.

Molinar v. Coleman, 2009 WL 435274 (N.D. Tex. Feb. 20, 2009). Plaintiff's motion for entry of judgment by default was entered for defendant's FDCPA violation with the court awarding no actual damages, $250 statutory damages, $2800 costs and attorney fees, and interest to run at 0.60% per annum.

Guerrero v. Hudson & Keyse, L.L.C., 2009 U.S. Dist. LEXIS 4921 (W.D. Tex. Jan. 20, 2009). "[A]ttorney should not have needed more than ten (10) hours to research, investigate, draft and file the complaint; five (5) hours to draft and respond to discovery; five (5) hours to draft Plaintiff's motion for partial summary judgment; and ten (10) hours for other miscellaneous work. . . ."

Turner v. Oxford Mgmt. Serv., Inc., 552 F. Supp. 2d 648 (S.D. Tex. 2008). The court rejected the overwhelming majority of the collector's objections to the plaintiff's fee request, otherwise reduced the requested amount by approximately 10% on several bases, and awarded reasonable attorney fees and costs in the amount of $56,143 for about 240 hours of work by co-counsel to reach a settlement for $17,000 one month prior to trial.

McNeill v. Graham, Bright & Smith, P.C., 2006 WL 1489502 (N.D. Tex. May 26, 2006). The court awarded only $600 in attorney fees to the consumer where the consumer only established $64 in actual damages.

Purdie v. Ace Cash Express, Inc., 2003 WL 22976611 (N.D. Tex. Dec. 11, 2003). The district court certified the class, found that the class settlement was fair, adequate, and reasonable, approved an award of incentive compensation to the named plaintiffs, and granted attorney fees and expenses in the amount of $2.1 million.

Virginia

Coles v. Land's Towing & Recovery, Inc., 2010 WL 5300892 (E.D. Va. Dec. 22, 2010). In this default judgment matter involving an improper threat of repossession, the court awarded $3000 in attorney fees.

Randle v. H&P Capital, Inc., 2010 WL 2944907 (E.D. Va. July 21, 2010). The report recommended the hourly rates of $425 and $450 per hour for experienced FDCPA counsel and attorney fees and costs in the amount of $85,966.59

Zhang v. GC Serv., L.P., 537 F. Supp. 2d 805 (E.D. Va. 2008). Granted hourly rate of $350 and $225 to lawyers, $105 to paralegal; award of over $18,000 on $1000 offer of judgment.

Kelly v. Jormandy, Inc., 2005 WL 3177730 (W.D. Va. Nov. 29, 2005). Experienced consumer entitled to fees for 2.5 hours at $300 per hour for enforcing a settlement agreement.

Jones v. Vest, 2000 U.S. Dist. LEXIS 19026 (E.D. Va. Dec. 27, 2000). An attorney fee award of $17,766.49 was entered for about 76 attorney hours ($200/hour) and eleven paralegal hours investigating, negotiating and obtaining summary judgment in the FDCPA case.

Washington

Francis v. J.C. Penney Corp., Inc., 2010 WL 715535 (W.D. Wash. Feb. 24, 2010). The court awarded $1000 in statutory damages plus $6750 in attorney fees on motion in a default judgment.

Wisconsin

Suleski v. Bryant Lafayette & Assocs., 2010 WL 1904968 (E.D. Wis. May 10, 2010). The court approved the rate of $394 per hour for an attorney who had been practicing consumer law since 1995, and awarded fees in a default judgment of $2432 on a $1000 statutory damage award.

Huse v. Bonded Credit Co., 2010 WL 1186331 (E.D. Wis. Mar. 19, 2010). The consumer was awarded $1000 in statutory damages and the court found reasonable her request for $23,366.59 in attorney fees and costs.

K.3.3.4 Costs, 15 U.S.C. § 1692k(a)(3)

Rouse v. Law Offices of Rory Clark, 603 F.3d 699 (9th Cir. 2010). Held in a matter of first impression that the FDCPA authorizes award of costs only upon finding that action was brought in bad faith and for purpose of harassment.

K.3.4 Injunctive or Declaratory Relief (Including Class Actions)

Weiss v. Regal Collections, 385 F.3d 337 (3d Cir. 2004). Injunctive relief is not available in a private action under the FDCPA.

Liles v. Del Campo, 350 F.3d 742 (8th Cir. 2003). District court's injunction of all related proceedings in other federal courts involving American Corrective Counseling Services, Inc. was upheld on appeal brought pursuant to 28 U.S.C. § 1292 because injunction of other litigation was necessary to ensure the enforceability of the order granting the preliminary approval of a nationwide FDCPA class action settlement and to prevent further draining of the limited settlement fund. Objectors' appeal of class certification pursuant to Rule 23(f) in a proposed nationwide FDCPA class action settlement was denied as premature.

Carroll v. Wolpoff & Abramson, 53 F.3d 626 (4th Cir. 1995). Failure to seek and obtain declaratory relief was factor in a reduced award of FDCPA attorney fees.

Alabama

Jones v. Sonic Auto., Inc., 391 F. Supp. 2d 1064 (M.D. Ala. 2005). Equitable relief is not an available private remedy under the FDCPA.

Alaska

Holmes v. Cornerstone Credit Servs., Inc., 2010 WL 1874903 (D. Alaska May 6, 2010). The court refused to remand the case where it claimed injunctive relief under the FDCPA, without discussing whether such relief was available. "Holmes' Complaint, although it does not expressly invoke a federal cause of action, requests injunctive relief under the FDCPA, a federal statue. Congress has provided for federal jurisdiction over such enforcement actions."

Arizona

Duran v. Credit Bureau of Yuma, Inc., 93 F.R.D. 607 (D. Ariz. 1982). Since the FDCPA allowed only damages to private persons and vests the FTC with enforcement authority, a federal court had no jurisdiction to issue an injunction in a private action or certify a Fed. R. Civ. P. 23(b)(2) class.

Arkansas

Strong v. Nat'l Credit Mgmt. Co., 600 F. Supp. 46 (E.D. Ark. 1984). No private right to injunctive relief under the FDCPA. Class seeking FDCPA injunctive relief not certified.

California

Holmes v. Collection Bureau of Am., Ltd., 2009 WL 3762414 (N.D. Cal. Nov. 9, 2009). Preliminary injunction to bar continued FDCPA violations denied in absence of showing irreparable harm since the collector had already ceased the allegedly offending misconduct.

Taylor v. Quall, 471 F. Supp. 2d 1053 (C.D. Cal. 2007). Injunctive relief not available under the FDCPA.

Schwarm v. Craighead, 233 F.R.D. 655 (E.D. Cal. Mar. 7, 2006). Court certified this class action for both injunctive relief and damages based on alleged violations of the FDCPA, 42 U.S.C. § 1983, and state law in the collection of dishonored checks by the defendant private debt collector acting under contract and in cooperation with local government law enforcement entities.

Palmer v. Stassinos, 233 F.R.D. 546 (N.D. Cal. 2006). Because the FDCPA does not allow private plaintiffs to obtain equitable relief, class certification pursuant to Rule 23(b)(2) was denied.

Ballard v. Equifax Check Servs., 158 F. Supp. 2d 1163 (E.D. Cal. 2001). For violations of the FDCPA and the California Unfair Business Practices Act, plaintiff and the class were entitled to declaratory and injunctive relief.

Ballard v. Equifax Check Servs., 27 F. Supp. 2d 1201 (E.D. Cal. 1998). The Declaratory Judgment Act, 28 U.S.C. § 2201(a), permits the court to enter declaratory judgment notwithstanding the absence of corresponding injunctive relief.

United States v. Trans Continental Affiliates, 1997 WL 26297 (N.D. Cal. Jan. 8, 1997). Where debt collection agency did not provide any evidence disputing alleged FDCPA violations, government's motion for partial summary judgment and injunctive relief was granted. Where the court had already found that the debt collection agency violated the FDCPA, the government was entitled to permanent injunctive relief against the primary officers of the agency who were in control of the company and bore the responsibility of prohibiting such violations.

Connecticut

Krueger v. Ellis, Crosby & Assocs., Inc., 2006 WL 3791402 (D. Conn. Nov. 9, 2006). Court awarded injunction against collecting in Connecticut without a license.

Williams v. Kason Credit Corp., Clearinghouse No. 44,837 (D. Conn. 1989). Court denied motion to dismiss plaintiff's prayer for injunctive and declaratory relief.

Bolden v. G.H. Perkins Assocs., Inc., Clearinghouse No. 31,470 (D. Conn. 1983). FDCPA class action for damages and equitable relief was provisionally certified as meeting Fed. R. Civ. P. 23(a) and (b) requirements and as within the purposes of the FDCPA. The complaint alleged that the collector demands a 1/3 collection fee in violation of the FDCPA. The suit was settled with an agreed injunction and damages paid by the collector.

Florida

Drossin v. Nat'l Action Fin. Servs., Inc., 255 F.R.D. 608 (S.D. Fla. 2009). No FDCPA injunctive relief available.

Valencia v. Affiliated Group, Inc., 2008 WL 4372895 (S.D. Fla. Sept. 24, 2008). Equitable relief is not available to an individual under the civil liability section of the FDCPA.

Wilson v. Transworld Sys., Inc., 2002 U.S. Dist. LEXIS 10891 (M.D. Fla. Mar. 29, 2002). Because of "profound difficulties in defining and identifying the constituent members of the class, or possible subclasses, for purposes of an action for damages," and because allowing declaratory and injunctive relief was a superior remedy, the putative damages class was not certified but an injunctive class was certified.

Georgia

Bates v. Novastar/Nationstar Mortgage L.L.C., 2008 WL 2622810 (N.D. Ga. June 24, 2008). FDCPA does not authorize injunctive relief.

Idaho

Coultson v. United Serv. Bureau, Inc., Clearinghouse No. 27,718 (D. Idaho 1979). Preliminary injunction granted protecting class of consumers against distant forum abuses.

Illinois

Gammon v. G.C. Servs. Ltd. P'ship, 162 F.R.D. 313 (N.D. Ill. 1995). Injunctive relief was not available to the private litigant under the FDCPA. Declaratory relief was appropriate in FDCPA litigation.

Zanni v. Lippold, 119 F.R.D. 32 (C.D. Ill. 1988). Court found injunctive FDCPA class inappropriate under Fed. R. Civ. P. 23(b)(2) since the suit was predominantly for money damages.

Chavez v. Northwest Collectors, Inc., 1985 U.S. Dist. LEXIS 14979 (N.D. Ill. Oct. 11, 1985). Request for injunctive relief did not become moot upon cessation of the practice by the collector since the practice could easily be resumed.

Smith v. Mikell, Clearinghouse No. 34,362C (N.D. Ill. 1982). A claim for future class injunctive relief should not be precluded by the collectors' discontinuance of the letters to be enjoined.

Iowa

Liles v. Am. Corrective Counseling Servs., 131 F. Supp. 2d 1114 (S.D. Iowa 2001). Injunctive relief not available under the FDCPA.

Kansas

Zsamba v. Cmty. Bank, 56 F. Supp. 2d 1207 (D. Kan. 1999). Court ruled that FDCPA does not specifically provide for injunctions, and that minor who sought to enjoin the sale of a horse she owned securing a debt of her parents' was not entitled to an injunction.

Michigan

Gradisher v. Check Enforcement Unit, Inc., 203 F.R.D. 271 (W.D. Mich. 2001). The court certified a class under Rule 23(b)(3) but declined to certify under Rule 23(b)(2).

Minnesota

Bishop v. Global Payments Check Recovery Servs., Inc., 2003 WL 21497513 (D. Minn. June 25, 2003). FDCPA permits no equitable relief.

Mississippi

Smith v. Tower Loan, Inc., 216 F.R.D. 338 (S.D. Miss. 2003), *aff'd on other grounds, sub nom. Smith v. Crystian*, 2004 WL 507572 (5th Cir. Mar. 16, 2004). Injunctive relief is not available under the FDCPA (dictum in discussion of whether injunctive relief predominated for purpose of class certification; court also ruled that defendant creditor was not subject to FDCPA).

Nebraska

Hampton v. Countrywide Home Loans, 2009 WL 1813648 (D. Neb. June 24, 2009). Injunctive relief is not an available remedy under the FDCPA.

Valderrama v. Nat'l Revenue Corp., 1981 U.S. Dist. LEXIS 18627 (D. Neb. Sept. 28, 1981). Amendments to complaint allowed consumers to delete Rule 23(b)(3) class allegation and substitute a Rule 23(b)(2) injunctive class allegation when discovery indicated that the debt collector's net worth was insufficient for a significant recovery of statutory damages. Protective orders granted to collector which alleged expenses greatly in excess of the amount in controversy in order to respond to certain interrogatories and requests for admissions.

New Jersey

Huertas v. Dep't of Educ., 2009 WL 3165442 (D.N.J. Sept. 28, 2009). Injunctive and declaratory relief is not available under the FDCPA.

Loigman v. Kings Landing Condo. Ass'n, 734 A.2d 367 (N.J. Super. Ct. 1999). Since the FDCPA does not prohibit the granting of equitable relief, the court ordered the discharge of an improperly placed lien.

New Mexico

Martinez v. Albuquerque Collection Serv., Clearinghouse No. 50,420 (D.N.M. 1995). Injunction issued against collection agency's de-ceptive practices, unauthorized practice of law, distant forum abuse, and collecting excessive fees.

New York

Gravina v. Client Servs., Inc., 2009 U.S. Dist. LEXIS 78204 (E.D.N.Y. Aug. 25, 2009). Settlement of nationwide class claims arising from messages left by defendant for settlement class members on telephone answering device included an injunction permanently enjoining defendant as follows: All telephone voice messages left by defendant for consumers on telephone answering devices will meaningfully identify the defendant as the caller, state the purpose or the nature of the communication, and disclose that the communication is from a debt collector.

Anderson v. Nationwide Credit Inc., 2009 U.S. Dist. LEXIS 57157 (E.D.N.Y. June 25, 2009). FDCPA class settlement permanently enjoined the defendant as follows: "All telephone voice messages left by Defendant for consumers on telephone answering devices will meaningfully identify the Defendant as the caller, state the purpose or nature of the communication, and disclose that the communication is from a debt collector."

Sparkman v. Zwicker & Assocs., P.C., 374 F. Supp. 2d 293 (E.D.N.Y. 2005). Neither injunctive nor declaratory relief is available to private litigants under the FDCPA.

In re Risk Mgmt. Alternatives, Inc., 208 F.R.D. 493 (S.D.N.Y. 2002). Claims for injunctive and declaratory relief were dismissed because the FDCPA cannot serve as the basis for such relief for private plaintiffs.

Weiss v. Fein, Such, Kahn & Shepard, P.C., 2002 U.S. Dist. LEXIS 4783 (S.D.N.Y. Mar. 21, 2002). Injunctive relief was not available under the FDCPA.

Sokolski v. Trans Union Corp., 178 F.R.D. 393 (E.D.N.Y. 1998). FDCPA contains no injunctive relief remedy.

North Dakota

Bray v. Portfolio Recovery Assoc. L.L.C., 2008 WL 4745220 (D.N.D. Oct. 27, 2008). The Anti-Injunction Act barred the *pro se* consumer's request for a "stay or a temporary restraining order enjoining the State district court from proceeding with debt collection action initiated by the Defendants."

Ohio

Midland Funding L.L.C. v. Brent, 644 F. Supp. 2d 961 (N.D. Ohio 2009). The consumer was not entitled to declaratory judgment or injunctive relief for the violations of the FDCPA; but was granted injunctive relief under the Ohio consumer protection act against filing false mass produced affidavits in support of debt collection suits that falsely claimed to be based on personal knowledge about the claimed debt.

Johnson v. Midland Credit Mgmt. Inc., 2006 U.S. Dist. LEXIS 60133 (N.D. Ohio Aug. 23, 2006). Plaintiffs are not entitled to injunctive relief under the FDCPA. The court also found that an individual is not entitled to declaratory relief under the FDCPA but would consider the availability of declaratory relief to the putative class.

Oregon

Grassley v. Debt Collectors, Inc., 1992 U.S. Dist. LEXIS 22782 (D. Or. Dec. 14, 1992). Absent proof that the collector poses an ongoing threat of continued unlawful debt collection practices, injunctive relief pursuant to state statute was denied.

Pennsylvania

Campbell v. Watson, 2009 WL 4544395 (E.D. Pa. Nov. 30, 2009). Declaratory relief not available under FDCPA.

Whiteman v. Burton Neil & Assocs., P.C., 2008 WL 4372842 (M.D. Pa. Sept. 19, 2008). Punitive damages, injunctive relief, and declaratory relief are not available under the FDCPA.

Seawell v. Universal Fid. Corp., 235 F.R.D. 64 (E.D. Pa. 2006). Court certified this nationwide FDCPA class action for both injunctive relief and damages based on the alleged unlawful misrepresentation that the debt collector's misrepresented itself as an arm of the U.S. government through its placement of the American flag in the letterhead of its form duns.

Tomes v. Gordon & Berger, P.C., 2004 WL 614525 (E.D. Pa. Mar. 10, 2004). The court refused to certify a class for injunctive relief since the FDCPA does not authorize private lawsuits for injunctive relief, a remedy which it held was reserved to the Federal Trade Commission.

Piper v. Portnoff Law Assocs., 262 F. Supp. 2d 520 (E.D. Pa. 2003). In an FDCPA action, the court enjoined the collector from proceeding with the sale of the consumer's residence to enforce a municipal water lien. The injunction was in aid of the federal court's jurisdiction and was an exception to the Anti-Injunction Act. In order to obtain a preliminary injunction, the court must consider whether: (1) the movant has shown a reasonable probability of success on the merits; (2) the movant will be irreparably injured by denial of relief; (3) granting preliminary relief will not result in an even greater harm to the non-moving party; and (4) granting the preliminary relief will be in the public interest.

Scarpino v. Allegheny Adjustment, Inc., Clearinghouse No. 25,743C (W.D. Pa. 1978). Class action certified.

Texas

Sibley v. Diversified Collection Servs., Inc., 1998 WL 355492 (N.D. Tex. June 30, 1998). Class certification pursuant to Rule 23(b)(2) of proposed FDCPA class was denied because declaratory relief did not correspond to injunctive relief and the lawsuit sought monetary damages.

Virginia

Vitullo v. Mancini, 684 F. Supp. 2d 760 (E.D. Va. 2010). The FDCPA "does not permit private litigants to seek injunctive or declaratory relief that has the effect of cancelling or extinguishing a debt in suing for violations of the Act. Instead, these litigants are limited to the damages remedy. . . ."

Utah

Ditty v. CheckRite, Ltd., 973 F. Supp. 1320 (D. Utah 1997). Private injunctive relief was not available under the FDCPA.

United States v. Utah Bureau of Collections, Inc., 15 F.T.C. Ct. Dec. 485 (D. Utah 1981). FTC obtained permanent injunction requiring collector to include disclosure in each written communication advising debtor of right to stop communication and register complaint with FTC. Collector also ordered to send debtor itemized statements and maintain records of all phone contacts and communications relating to debt collection for inspection by FTC and consumers.

Wisconsin

Klewer v. Cavalry Invs., L.L.C., 2002 U.S. Dist. LEXIS 3378 (W.D. Wis. Feb. 21, 2002). The court granted class certification for injunctive relief pursuant to Rule 23(b)(2) reversing its earlier denial of class certification at 2002 U.S. Dist. LEXIS 3379 (W.D. Wis. Jan. 18, 2002).

K.3.5 Statute of Limitations

Mader v. United States, 619 F.3d 996 (8th Cir. 2010). In refusing to apply in this non-FDCPA case its FDCPA statute of limitations rule from *Mattson v. U.S. W. Commc'ns, Inc.*, 967 F.2d 259 (8th Cir. 1992), the court signaled that the rule may no longer be persuasive even under the FDCPA.

Ruth v. Unifund CCR Partners, 604 F.3d 908 (6th Cir. 2010). The one-year limitations period for the consumer's FDCPA claim was not tolled by the debt collector's alleged concealment of misconduct by delaying discovery responses. The court found that the alleged concealment did not prevent the consumer from raising her FDCPA theory within the limitations period, as she had raised the theory before requesting discovery and seven months before the expiration of the statute of limitations.

Solomon v. HSBC Mortgage Corp., 2010 WL 3069699 (10th Cir. Aug. 6, 2010). Separate communications create separate causes of action arising from the collection of a single debt. Where the complaint could be read to allege at least three kinds of violations within the one-year statutory period, it was not evident that these claims were barred by the statute of limitations, even if the initial communication was outside the statute of limitations.

Mangum v. Action Collection Serv., Inc., 575 F.3d 935 (9th Cir. 2009). The FDCPA statute of limitations runs from the date the consumer discovered that the collection agency gave copies of her dishonored checks to her employer, rather than running from the earlier date that the checks were given to her employer. Because the FDCPA's statute of limitations does not address the issue, this allowed the court to use the Ninth Circuit's usual presumption that federal statutes of limitation begin to run on discovery of the injury. The majority opinion rejected the argument that the subsection establishing the FDCPA limitations period titled "Jurisdiction" makes the FDCPA statute of limitations jurisdictional since the title was added by the Law Revision Counsel after enactment, was not a part of the law as enacted by Congress, and therefore not to be given the deference reserved for Congressional language. A concurring opinion believed that the statutory language was clear that limitations period ran from the violation date, making the discovery rule inapplicable, but that the limitations period must then be equitably tolled from the date of the violation until its discovery.

Avery v. First Resolution Mgmt. Corp., 568 F.3d 1018 (9th Cir. 2009). The debt collector did not file a time-barred debt since it was filed within the Oregon statute of limitations. The shorter New Hampshire period of limitations prescribed by the contract was applicable under Oregon choice of law rules until the New Hampshire law was determined to be tolled as to an Oregon consumer, in which case Oregon law reverted to its own statute of limitations.

Kuehn v. Cadle Co., 335 Fed. Appx. 827 (11th Cir. 2009). Amendment to change name of defendant to closely related defendant related back to filing and was thus within the statute of limitations.

Purnell v. Arrow Fin. Servs., L.L.C., 303 Fed. Appx. 297 (6th Cir. 2008). FDCPA credit reporting "serial violations" which were part of the collector's multi-year collection activities were time barred to the extent the misconduct pre-dated the filing of the complaint by more than the one-year statute of limitations but were timely as to the discrete violations that occurred within one year before filing suit. Collector's allegedly false communication which was made to a credit bureau within one year prior to filing suit and which misrepresented that the consumer owed the subject debt stated a timely claim for violations of §§ 1692e(2)(A), 1692e(8), and 1692f(1), notwithstanding that the collector had been making the same alleged misrepresentations to the credit bureau for several years, since that last communication constituted a discrete violation of the Act within the statute of limitations. Collector who allegedly received the consumer's thirty-day written dispute request several years earlier and had never provided the required verification was liable for a non-time-barred violation of § 1692g(b) when it communicated information concerning the debt to a credit bureau within the previous year since "§ 1692g(b) dictates that each 'failure to cease' collection activity without having validated the debt—like each 'communication' of false credit information under § 1692e(8)—presents a discrete claim for violation of the FDCPA."

Khaliq v. Draper & Goldberg, P.L.L.C., 286 Fed. Appx. 72 (4th Cir. 2008). Where the district court dismissed the plaintiff's complaint for the plaintiff's failure to show good cause for not serving defendant with the FDCPA process pursuant to Rule 4(m) within the time period, the Fourth Circuit affirmed the decision and stated that "Plaintiffs who cannot successfully challenge a Rule 4(m) dismissal by showing good cause for their delay should not be allowed to avoid the consequence of that dismissal and the statute of limitations by simply filing a new complaint immediately."

Kaltenbach v. Richards, 464 F.3d 524 (5th Cir. 2006). People whose principal business is the enforcement of security interests are subject only to § 1692f(6) unless they satisfy § 1692a(6)'s general definition of a "debt collector" in which case they are responsible for compliance with the entire FDCPA even when enforcing security interests.

McCready v. Harrison, 2003 WL 21461755 (7th Cir. June 18, 2003). FDCPA claim was barred by the one-year statute of limitations pursuant to § 1692k(d). The court refused to find that an alleged misrepresentation that property would be auctioned would be a continuing violation until an auction was held.

Johnson v. Riddle, 305 F.3d 1107 (10th Cir. 2002). The consumer's claim of an FDCPA violation arising from a collector's lawsuit did not occur until she was served with the collection action, not when it was filed. The day of the FDCPA violation was not counted in

calculating the statute of limitations; the one-year statute of limitations began to run on the day following the event violating the FDCPA.

Marshall-Mosby v. Corporate Receivables, Inc., 205 F.3d 323 (7th Cir. 2000). The statute of limitations provision in the FDCPA was not a jurisdictional restriction.

Bygrave v. Van Reken, 2000 U.S. App. LEXIS 29377 (6th Cir. Nov. 14, 2000). Consumer's substantive claims of FDCPA violations were based on events that occurred several years before filing of suit and therefore were time barred.

Naas v. Stolman, 130 F.3d 892 (9th Cir. 1997). An FDCPA claim filed more than one year after the filing of a state collection suit was barred by the statute of limitations where the FDCPA claim arose from the filing of the state claim and the period was not extended by a state appeal.

Morgovsky v. Creditor's Collection Serv., 92 F.3d 1193 (9th Cir. 1996) (text at 1996 WL 441709). The court found that the plaintiff's FDCPA suit was barred by the § 1692k(d) statute of limitations.

Maloy v. Phillips, 64 F.3d 607 (11th Cir. 1995). The mailing date of the collection letter is the triggering date for the statute of limitations for FDCPA violations and the day after the mailing is the date from which the statute runs in accordance with Rule 6(a). Where the initial communication did not contain the validation notice, an additional five days is added to one year from the day after the mailing date to determine the limitation on a claim for violation of § 1692g(a).

James v. Ford Motor Credit Co., 47 F.3d 961 (8th Cir. 1995). Where a repossession company had possession of the car for one hour before the consumer retook the car, the statute of limitations under § 1692k(d) began running on that date and consumer's action brought more than one year after that date was barred, even though the consumers erroneously relied on the company's records that the event had occurred just within the year before filing.

Mattson v. U.S. West Communications, Inc., 967 F.2d 259 (8th Cir. 1992). The date of mailing the collection letter began the running of the FDCPA's statute of limitations rather than the date of receipt. Because Fed. R. Civ. P. 6(a) did not apply to the calculation of time because § 1692k(d) was a jurisdictional statute, the 365-day FDCPA statute of limitations began running on the date of mailing the collection letter. In his dissent Judge McMillian argued that pursuant to the "modern doctrine" federal statutes of limitations should be determined by applying Fed. R. Civ. P. Rule 6(a).

Arizona

Brink v. First Credit Res., 57 F. Supp. 2d 848 (D. Ariz. 1999). Motion to amend complaint granted. Plaintiff was not time barred from adding president and vice president to lawsuit since claims against the new defendants related back to the original complaint. Constructive notice was imputed since the president shared an identity of interest with the corporate defendant and the vice president ran the day-to-day operations. Because notice was imputed, the new defendants had the same amount of time to prepare as the corporate defendant and, therefore, would not suffer prejudice, a mistake concerning identity occurred because plaintiff was unaware of the new defendant's identity. The corporate defendant withheld the names of the new defendants during the discovery process until the statute of limitations had expired and amending in the new defendants was not futile. The court had jurisdiction over the new defendants since they chose to direct the collection letter to the forum state.

Maher v. Bank One, 2009 WL 2580100 (Ariz. Aug. 20, 2009). While the FDCPA claim may be tolled until plaintiff discovers that it has been violated, here plaintiff knew of factual basis of the violations and did not file suit within one year of the knowledge.

Arkansas

Marshall v. Deutsche Bank Nat'l Trust Co., 2011 WL 345988 (E.D. Ark. Feb. 1, 2011). The § 1692g(a) claim was time-barred since the action was filed more than one year after the defendant began collecting the debt.

California

Barker v. Avila, 2010 WL 3171067 (E.D. Cal. Aug. 11, 2010). The consumer's claims were time barred since all alleged violations occurred more than one year prior to filing the complaint.

Consumer Solutions REO, L.L.C. v. Hillery, 658 F. Supp. 2d 1002 (N.D. Cal. 2009). An alleged violation of the FDCPA taking place more than one year prior to the filing of the complaint was barred by the one-year statute of limitations.

Thoennes v. Masari Inv., L.L.C., 2009 WL 4282807 (N.D. Cal. Nov. 25, 2009). Suit brought in wrong federal jurisdiction transferred so plaintiff would not lose the benefit of initial filing within statute of limitations.

Gruen v. EdFund, 2009 WL 2136785 (N.D. Cal. July 15, 2009). Claims arising within one year from filing were timely: "The Court rejects [defendant's] proposed theory that unlawful conduct occurring within the statute of limitations is time barred if some unlawful conduct also occurred outside of the statutory limitation period. The only case that cites in support of this proposition, *Wilhelm v. Credico, Inc.*, 455 F. Supp. 2d 1006 (D.N.D. 2006), is not persuasive." Note that *Wilhelm* is not only not persuasive, but it was overruled in relevant part in *Wilhelm v. Credico, Inc.*, 519 F.3d 416 (8th Cir. 2008).

Cruz v. Int'l Collection Corp., 2008 WL 2263800 (N.D. Cal. June 2, 2008). Although suit was filed over a year after the date of the last communication, court refused to dismiss because conduct occurring outside the statute of limitations period is actionable under a continuing violation theory.

Weiner v. McCoon, 2007 WL 2782843 (S.D. Cal. Sept. 24, 2007). The statute of limitations on the consumer's claim that the defendant violated the disclosure requirements of §§ 1692e(11) and 1692g(a) runs from the date of the alleged violation—one day after the mailing of the § 1692e(11) notice and five days after the initial communication for the § 1692g(a) notice—and not from the date of receipt and regardless of whether the consumer actually received the notices. The court rejected any discovery rule regarding the statute of limitations and therefore held on summary judgment that the plaintiff's claim was time barred since the complaint was filed more than one year after the defendant allegedly violated the

FDCPA by filing in the public record an unlawful claim of lien on the consumer's property.

Palmer v. Stassinos, 236 F.R.D. 460 (N.D. Cal. 2006). Rule 15(c)(3) permits relation back if the defendants have had notice of the pending claims against them. Where the original plaintiffs lacked standing to assert state law claims, the newly added plaintiffs' state law claims were not tolled and would begin to run on the date their claims were brought before the court.

Roybal v. Equifax, 405 F. Supp. 2d 1177 (E.D. Cal. 2005). The consumer's FDCPA claim based on the collector furnishing false information to a consumer reporting agency was time barred since the suit was filed more than one year after the allegedly erroneous information was communicated to the reporting agency as well as more than one year after the consumer learned of the false report.

Clark v. Transpack Corp., 2005 WL 3080853 (E.D. Cal. Nov. 11, 2005). Defendant's motion for summary judgment was granted because the alleged violations of the FDCPA occurred more than one year prior to the filing of the action.

Morgovsky v. Creditors Collection Serv., 1995 WL 316970 (N.D. Cal. May 16, 1995), *aff'd without op.*, 92 F.3d 1193 (9th Cir. 1996). An FDCPA cause of action accrues on the date of the violation, not the date when the consumer discovers the violation. Thus, a cause of action for improperly reporting a disputed debt occurs when the report was made, not when the consumer learns of the report.

Colorado

Zimmerman v. The CIT Group, Inc., 2009 WL 900172 (D. Colo. Mar. 31, 2009). Dismissed based on statute of limitations, since state court service was made more than a year before the action was brought even though plaintiff claimed that he was never served.

Dyer-Andrews v. Acad. Collection Servs., Inc., 2005 WL 1871120 (D. Colo. Aug. 5, 2005). The FDCPA statute of limitations barred a claim based on the allegation that the debt collector made false representations during a telephone conversation to extract the consumer's personal checking account information where the complaint was filed more than one year after the call. But the allegation that the collector weeks later unlawfully withdrew a sum from the account from the information extracted during the earlier call was not time barred when the complaint was filed less than one year after that unauthorized withdrawal.

Connecticut

Sundwall v. Basil, 2006 WL 1699594 (D. Conn. June 16, 2006). *Pro se* litigant's claim arose more than ten years before lawsuit, so was barred by statute of limitations.

Egbarin v. Lewis, Lewis & Ferraro, L.L.C., 2006 WL 236846 (D. Conn. Jan. 31, 2006). Claims based on the filling of a lawsuit generally accrue when a claim is filed, not when judgment is rendered. While Lewis's allegedly extortionist threat to initiate the bar grievance action could potentially give rise to an FDCPA claim, once it was filed, the grievance could no longer be characterized as a violation of the FDCPA as the collection of a debt was not the subject of the grievance proceedings. The facts of the instant case do not support the application of the continuing violation doctrine to toll the FDCPA one-year bar. The alleged actions of the defendants were dissimilar, discrete acts that did not, by their very nature involve repeated conduct.

Evanauskas v. Strumpf, 2001 U.S. Dist. LEXIS 14326 (D. Conn. June 27, 2001). Consumer's claims founded on alleged violations arising from defendants' filing of a state court collection action more than one year before the filing of the federal FDCPA suit were time barred.

Deutsche Bank v. Lichtenfels, 48 Conn. L. Rptr. 133 (Conn. Super. Ct. 2009). FDCPA claim based on a complaint must be brought within a year of the filing or service.

Heim v. Cal. Fed. Bank F.S.B., 2001 Conn. Super. LEXIS 2355 (Conn. Super. Ct. Aug. 15, 2001). *Pro se* complaint dismissed as barred by the statute of limitations for failure to allege any activity that occurred less than one year prior to filing of suit.

Florida

Andrade v. Erin Capital Mgmt. L.L.C., 2010 WL 1961843 (S.D. Fla. May 17, 2010). The statute of limitations for the FDCPA does not begin to run until the consumer knew or should have known of the defendant's violation of the Act.

Amaya v. Pollack & Rosen, P.A., 2010 WL 724451 (S.D. Fla. Feb. 25, 2010). Applies equitable tolling but dismisses complaint for failure to state a cause of action.

Ortiz v. Accounts Receivable Mgmt., Inc., 2010 WL 547910 (S.D. Fla. Feb. 12, 2010). The defendant's motion to dismiss the complaint as time barred was denied where the consumer's FDCPA complaint based on telephone calls made both more and less than a year before filing was "allowed to proceed to the extent it alleges violations that occurred within one year from the date of the filing of the Complaint."

Hinkle v. Asset Acceptance, L.L.C., 2010 WL 298396 (S.D. Fla. Jan. 20, 2010). The court dismissed as untimely the consumer's FDCPA complaint which alleged that the debt collection firm filed a time-barred state court collection action because the federal case was filed more than one year after the consumer had notice of the state court filing.

Pincus v. Law Offices of Erskine & Fleisher, 617 F. Supp. 2d 1265 (S.D. Fla. 2009). The collection attorney defendants whose underlying state court collection suit was dismissed as barred by the statute of limitations were now collaterally estopped in this FDCPA affirmative suit from re-litigating that issue and from now arguing that the collection suit was not time barred.

Perez v. Bureaus Inv. Group No. II, L.L.C., 2009 WL 1973476 (S.D. Fla. July 8, 2009). Plaintiff's FDCPA claim that the defendant filed a state court collection suit on a time-barred debt was dismissed as time barred; the court stated that "service, not filing, constitutes the violation and triggers the statute of limitations period;" still, the plaintiff did not file the federal case until more than one year after both filing and service of the state case, so the federal suit was time barred in either event.

Bridgewater Prods., Inc. v. HSBC Mortgage Corp., 2008 WL 2813283 (S.D. Fla. July 18, 2008). *Pro se* complaint was time barred since the events occurred more than one year before filing.

Zenon v. Palisades Collection, L.L.C., 2008 WL 506231 (M.D. Fla. Feb. 21, 2008). FDCPA action brought one year and seven months after the alleged violation had occurred was time barred. FDCPA statute of limitations began to run when the lawsuit which allegedly violated the FDCPA was filed.

Danow v. Borack, 2006 WL 5516577 (S.D. Fla. Jan. 30, 2006), *rev'd in part and remanded on other grounds*, 197 Fed. Appx. 853 (11th Cir. 2006). Where one-year statute ran out on a Sunday, plaintiff was within the statute when he filed on Monday.

Georgia

McDaniel v. Smith, 2008 WL 4425305 (S.D. Ga. Sept. 30, 2008). The plaintiff "abandoned" his FDCPA claim, "conceding that it was not brought within the one year statute of limitations."

Waller v. Fricks, 2008 WL 2233570 (M.D. Ga. May 28, 2008). Any violation in foreclosure action was not within statute of limitations.

Moore v. Equifax Info. Servs., L.L.C., 333 F. Supp. 2d 1360 (N.D. Ga. 2004). The complaint was dismissed as time barred where the offending telephone calls to collect the debt occurred more than one year before suit was filed.

In re Gilleland, 2004 WL 5846255 (Bankr. N.D. Ga. Dec. 16, 2004). The bankruptcy trustee's FDCPA claim was time barred even after adding the additional time permitted by 11 U.S.C. § 108(a).

Brinson v. First Am. Bank, 409 S.E.2d 50 (Ga. Ct. App. 1991). Alleged violations of FDCPA raised more than one year after their occurrence were time barred.

Illinois

Gulley v. Pierce & Assocs., 2010 WL 5060257 (N.D. Ill. Dec. 6, 2010). The *pro se* consumer's § 1692g(b) claim that the defendant continued to collect the debt without responding to his verification request was not time barred, since although the verification request was made more than one year before suit was filed, the defendant's alleged violation of § 1692g(b) by continuing to collect the debt occurred within the one year period.

Collins v. Asset Acceptance, L.L.C., 2010 WL 3245072 (N.D. Ill. Aug. 13, 2010). The consumer did not present any basis to support equitable tolling based on fraudulent concealment.

Greenfield v. Kluever & Platt, L.L.C., 2010 WL 604830 (N.D. Ill. Feb. 16, 2010). The *pro se* consumer's FDCPA claims based on the defendants' filing of a state court foreclosure action more than one year before the filing of this FDCPA case was not time barred since the consumer did not learn of the foreclosure "until long after it was filed" and "the Seventh Circuit, like most federal courts of appeals, applies a discovery rule in cases such as these." The court distinguished contrary cases construing statutory language that, unlike the FDCPA, was not "silent on the issue."

Judy v. Blatt, Hasenmiller, Leibsker & Moore L.L.C., 2010 WL 431484 (N.D. Ill. Jan. 29, 2010). Where the collection action was filed two and half years before filing of the FDCPA suit, the violations alleged to arise from the filing of the collection action alone were dismissed as barred by the one-year statute of limitations.

Basile v. Blatt, Hasenmiller, Leibsker & Moore L.L.C., 632 F. Supp. 2d 842 (N.D. Ill. 2009). An "affidavit of the indebtedness" and monthly credit card statements did not provide sufficient evidence of a written agreement; thus, the state court collection action was based on a unwritten contract and the Illinois five-year statute of limitations applied. The debt collector violated §§ 1692e and 1692f by filing a time-barred debt collection suit, unless the violation was excusable as a bona fide error.

Kasalo v. Monco Law Offices, S.C., 2009 WL 4639720 (N.D. Ill. Dec. 7, 2009). Consumer's claim that the collector communicated with a credit reporting agency without disclosing that the debt was known to be disputed, in violation of § 1692e(8), was time barred to the extent that the communication occurred more than one year prior to filing of the complaint and otherwise was timely to extent that the communication occurred within the one-year limitations period.

Hoang v. Worldwide Asset Purchasing, L.L.C., 2009 WL 3669883 (S.D. Ill. Nov. 2, 2009). Where lawsuit was dismissed within one year, that was the final act in the course of a state court lawsuit. Under the continuing violation theory, the FDCPA lawsuit was timely.

Jenkins v. Centurion Capital Corp., 2009 WL 3414248 (N.D. Ill. Oct. 20, 2009). The debt collector's delay in dismissing its state court collection suit when the debt was sold to another collector was an issue best left to the state court and did not give rise to an FDCPA cause of action.

Kubiski v. Unifund CCR Partners, 2009 WL 774450 (N.D. Ill. Mar. 25, 2009). While the FDCPA statute of limitations started when the state lawsuit was filed, it was equitably tolled because the lawsuit was not served for two years.

Krawczyk v. Centurion Capital Corp., 2009 WL 395458 (N.D. Ill. Feb. 18, 2009). The debt buyers were entitled to rely on creditor's statement that a payment had been made within the statute limitations restarting the five-year period of limitations. Their violation, if any, was a bona fide error.

Wisniewski v. Asset Acceptance Capital Corp., 2009 WL 212155 (N.D. Ill. Jan. 29, 2009). Motion to dismiss FDCPA suit was defeated by the general allegation that abusive phone calls were continuing.

Feltman v. Blatt, Hasenmiller, Leibsker & Moore, L.L.C., 2008 WL 5211024 (N.D. Ill. Dec. 11, 2008). Although the specific debt collection practices complained of here were separate acts from those expressly alleged in the original complaint, the new claims were based on defendants' continued debt collection practices, were mentioned in the original complaint, and arose out of the same "conduct, transaction or occurrence" as those alleged in the original complaint; thus the claims related back to the original complaint. Only the first instance of filing the plaintiff's Social Security number in the state court proceedings was actionable; dismissed claim that Social Security number improperly was placed in the public record as time barred.

Cole v. Noonan & Lieberman, Ltd., 2005 WL 2848446 (N.D. Ill. Oct. 6, 2005). Statute of limitations on § 1692g notice was triggered five days after the initial communication was mailed.

Garrett v. Empire Cooler Serv., Inc., 2004 WL 2011399 (N.D. Ill. June 21, 2004). Because the FDCPA's limitation period is not jurisdictional and the *pro se* plaintiff's mental and physical illnesses prevented him, despite all due diligence, from obtaining vital information bearing on the existence of his claim, the court permitted equitable tolling of the otherwise time-barred claim.

Salgado v. Harvard Collection Servs., Inc., 2001 U.S. Dist. LEXIS 10302 (N.D. Ill. July 16, 2001). Where consumer alleged that the debt collector violated the FDCPA by accepting full payment of a debt and failing to notify its assignee (which then filed suit to collect the fully paid debt), the statute of limitations accrued, not when the consumer paid the debt but when the debt collector failed to notify its assignee.

Friedman v. Anvan Corp., 1998 WL 559779 (N.D. Ill. Aug. 28, 1998). For the purpose of determining the beginning of the statute of limitations period, the FDCPA violation occurred when the debt collector mailed letter.

Perperas v. United Recovery Sys., Inc., 1997 WL 136326 (N.D. Ill. Mar. 19, 1997). The complaint was limited to seeking relief for communications occurring less than one year before the filing of the complaint.

Aikens v. Talbot Hoevel & Assocs., P.C., 1996 WL 675780 (N.D. Ill. Nov. 19, 1996). The court denied the consumer's motion to add an attorney individually as a defendant to her FDCPA complaint as the claim was barred by the statute of limitations. The consumer could not show she was in any way mistaken as to the identity or potential liability of the attorney who had signed the letter on which the suit was based. The court also denied the consumer's motion to add a debt collection agency as a defendant as that claim was also barred by the statute of limitations, and there was no fraudulent concealment of the collection agency's identity.

Blakemore v. Pekay, 895 F. Supp. 972 (N.D. Ill. 1995). The date of filing of Affidavits for Wage Deduction Orders was the trigger-date for the running of the FDCPA one year statute of limitations.

Friedman v. HHL Fin. Servs., Inc., 1993 WL 286487 (N.D. Ill. July 29, 1993). "For an action to be timely under the FDCPA, it must be commenced by one day prior to the anniversary of the date the violating letter was mailed."

McLean v. Joel Acceptance Co., 1983 U.S. Dist. LEXIS 13630 (N.D. Ill. Sept. 19, 1983). When the original complaint alleged a TIL claim and the complaint was amended to add an FDCPA claim, the FDCPA claim related back to the time of the filing of the original complaint since it involved the same credit transaction.

Smith v. Mikell, Clearinghouse No. 34,362C (N.D. Ill. 1982). Where the original complaint contained a reference to a dunning letter attached as an exhibit and the amended complaint alleged specific FDCPA violations in the letter, the amended complaint related back to the time of the filing of the original complaint pursuant to Fed. R. Civ. P. 15(c). However, an FDCPA violation alleged to have occurred seventeen months prior to the filing of the original complaint was barred by the one year FDCPA statute of limitations.

Indiana

Fausset v. Mortgage First, L.L.C., 2010 WL 1212085 (N.D. Ind. Mar. 23, 2010). Claim that debt collector made harassing telephone calls more than one year prior to the filing of suit barred by the one-year statute of limitations.

Rosado v. Taylor, 324 F. Supp. 2d 917 (N.D. Ind. 2004). The statute of limitations began to run on the date the court mailed a foreclosure summons and complaint to the homeowner, not on the date the foreclosing attorney mailed the summons and complaint to the court for service.

Richmond v. Malad, 2001 U.S. Dist. LEXIS 10505 (S.D. Ind. July 6, 2001). Consumer's claims founded on alleged violations arising from defendants' filing of a state court collection action more than one year before the filing of the federal FDCPA suit were time barred. Claims founded on defendants' failure to provide a validation notice within five days of its initial collection communication, i.e., the filing of a state court collection action, however, were not time barred where the FDCPA suit was filed more than a year but less than a year and five days from the filing of that state court collection action.

Russell v. Bowman, Heintz, Boscia & Vician, P.C., 744 N.E.2d 467 (Ind. Ct. App. 2001). The FDCPA statute of limitations runs from "the date on which the violation occurs," which, for the failure to provide a § 1692g disclosure, is five days after the initial communication, not the date of the initial communication, since the law provides the debt collector with the extra five days within which to comply and there can be no violation for failure to disclose within those five days.

Kansas

Burdett v. Harrah's Kansas Casino Corp., 260 F. Supp. 2d 1109 (D. Kan. 2003). Where events occurred both before and after the one year date prior to the filing of the FDCPA complaint, the court required the plaintiff to amend the complaint to identify each FDCPA violation, the party who committed the violation, and the date of the violation.

Whayne v. United States Dep't of Educ., 915 F. Supp. 1143 (D. Kan. 1996) (*pro se*). The court lacked jurisdiction as the alleged harassment by the debt collector occurred more than a year prior to the filing of the suit so the action was barred by the statute of limitations.

Kentucky

Benjamin v. Citibank, 2008 WL 5192239 (W.D. Ky. Dec. 11, 2008). One-year statute of limitations began on the date of the defendants' last chance to comply with the FDCPA. *Pro se*'s case dismissed because the events at issue took place more than one year before the case was filed.

Mattingly v. Mapother & Mapother, P.S.C., 2008 WL 2622891 (W.D. Ky. June 30, 2008). *Pro se* complaint dismissed as time barred since the plaintiff "filed this lawsuit more than one year after defendant's last contacts with him."

Louisiana

Wagner v. BellSouth Telecomms. Inc., 2008 WL 348784 (M.D. La. Feb. 7, 2008). *Pro se*'s complaint about § 1692g violation was time barred.

Deaville v. Capital One Bank, 425 F. Supp. 2d 744 (W.D. La. 2006). Equitable tolling of the limitations does not apply to FDCPA cases.

Jackson v. Adcock, 2004 WL 1900484 (E.D. La. Aug. 23, 2004). *Pro se* consumer's amended FDCPA complaint against that the collection attorney who allegedly committed FDCPA violations in filing the underlying state court foreclosure action was not time barred, since the original complaint was timely and the amended complaint related back to that original filing.

Decker v. Hibernia Nat'l Bank & Inv. Corp., 1996 WL 696323 (E.D. La. Nov. 26, 1996). An FDCPA claim was barred by the statute of limitations as it was filed three years after any alleged act violating the FDCPA.

Byes v. Telecheck Recovery Servs., Inc., 1996 WL 22686 (E.D. La. June 19, 1996). Leave to amend complaint was proper, where class action consumer plaintiff sought to add additional FDCPA claims arising from four letters sent more than a year before date of amended complaint, where the original complaint had attached several letters and described the class as recipients of "letters similar to" the attached letters. Defendant was sufficiently on notice of the subject matter and size of the litigation, and it knew what letters it had sent to plaintiff and who else had received the letters.

Byes v. Accelerated Cash Flow, Inc., 1996 WL 337222 (E.D. La. June 18, 1996). Plaintiff was denied permission to add a related collection agency to her complaint as the statute of limitations for her FDCPA claims had run, and she failed to meet the Fed. R. Civ. P. 15(c) requirements for adding a party after the statute of limitations had run.

Maine

Poulin, Jr. v. Thomas Agency, 2011 WL 159889 (D. Me. Jan. 13, 2011). Once a debt has been disputed by a consumer, the FDCPA prohibits any debt collection activity until verification occurs. Therefore, a cause of action under the FDCPA does not arise until the illegal debt collection activity occurs, and the statute of limitations does not begin to run until that time.

Poulin v. The Thomas Agency, 2011 WL 140477 (D. Me. Jan. 13, 2011). A cause of action under the FDCPA does not arise until the illegal debt collection activity occurs, and the one year statute of limitations does not begin to run until that time.

Kueter v. Chrysler Fin. Corp., 2000 U.S. Dist. LEXIS 8061 (D. Me. Apr. 5, 2000). A state FDCPA complaint that had been filed with a filing fee waiver requested, dismissed for nonpayment of the fee, and refiled was then barred by the statute of limitations.

Maryland

Queen v. Walker, 2010 WL 2696720 (D. Md. July 7, 2010). The court deferred on ruling whether a discovery rule or equitable tolling based on fraudulent concealment was applicable pending the filing of an amended complaint alleging additional facts.

Zarwell v. King & Nordlinger, L.L.P., 2006 WL 5503909 (D. Md. June 6, 2006), *aff'd*, 254 Fed. Appx. 249 (4th Cir. 2007). *Pro se* complaint dismissed as outside the statute of limitations where the state court complaint did not contain the notices required by § 1692g, so the statute began to run for failure to provide the notice on the fifth day thereafter.

Shah v. Collecto, Inc., 2005 WL 2216242 (D. Md. Sept. 12, 2005).

The statute of limitations for violations of the FDCPA relating to credit agency reporting began to run when the consumer knew or should have known of the violation (i.e., when the consumer obtained a credit report containing a possible FDCPA violation).

Tani v. President/CEO, Salomon Bros. Realty Corp./Citigroup, 2005 WL 1334604 (D. Md. May 31, 2005), *aff'd*, 2005 WL 3232752 (4th Cir. Dec. 1, 2005). *Pro se* FDCPA claims were dismissed as time barred since events occurred more than one year before suit.

Kouabo v. Chevy Chase Bank, 336 F. Supp. 2d 471 (D. Md. 2004). *Pro se* plaintiff's FDCPA claim, alleging collection attorney misconduct in the procurement of a state court judgment, was barred by the one-year statute of limitations, since the claim accrued at the latest when the judgment was entered three years before the FDCPA suit was filed. Similar state claim was not time barred.

Massachusetts

Zimmerman v. Cambridge Credit Counseling Corp., 322 F. Supp. 2d 95 (D. Mass. 2004), *vacated and remanded on other grounds*, 409 F.3d 473 (1st Cir. 2005). An FDCPA claim against a credit counselor was barred by the one-year statute of limitation. The consumer's argument that the statute of limitations should have been equitably tolled was not supported by evidence that they were mislead about the statute of limitations.

Alger v. Ganick, O'Brien & Sarin, 35 F. Supp. 2d 148 (D. Mass. 1999). A collection agency's conduct which occurred more than one year prior to the filing of the complaint was time barred under the FDCPA.

In re Anderson, 2006 WL 2786974 (Bankr. D. Mass. Sept. 26, 2006). As the ultimate event which the consumer claimed violated the FDCPA occurred six months prior to filing the action, the court denied the defendant's motion to dismiss on the basis of the FDCPA's one-year statute of limitations.

In re Maxwell, 281 B.R. 101 (Bankr. D. Mass. 2002). The FDCPA statute of limitations was procedural, not jurisdictional, entitling the consumer to reduce the collector's claim in bankruptcy by the amount of FDCPA damages.

Michigan

Kevelighan v. Trott & Trott, P.C., 2011 WL 164539 (E.D. Mich. Jan. 18, 2011). Claims based on alleged violations that pre-dated the filing of the complaint by more than one year were time-barred.

Barthlow v. Trott & Trott, P.C., 2010 WL 3258362 (E.D. Mich. Aug. 17, 2010). An FDCPA complaint that was filed more than one year after the allegedly unlawful foreclosure was filed was time barred.

Stanton v. Federal Nat'l Mortgage Ass'n, 2010 WL 707346 (W.D. Mich. Feb. 23, 2010). The *pro se* complaint for failure of the defendant to provide adequate § 1692g verification was time barred since the action was filed more than one year after the date of the alleged violation.

Charbonneau v. Mary Jane Elliott, P.C., 611 F. Supp. 2d 736 (E.D. Mich. 2009). Defendant relied on the information provided by the selling creditor to determine the statute of limitations, which was sufficient to establish a bona fide error defense.

Davis v. Countrywide Fin. Corp., 2009 WL 2922896 (E.D. Mich. Sept. 9, 2009). Consumers' FDCPA claims alleging that the defendant wrongfully foreclosed on their home were time barred since the foreclosure proceedings were instituted and in fact concluded more than one year prior to filing the FDCPA suit.

Peralta v. Accept Acceptance, L.L.C., 2009 WL 723910 (W.D. Mich. Mar. 10, 2009). The portion of consumer's FDCPA amended complaint adding class claims, that the defendant debt buyer routinely used false and deceptive supporting affidavits and documents when suing consumers in state court, did not relate back to the original complaint which alleged only that the defendant had unlawfully sued the plaintiff on a known time-barred debt. Thus, since the new claims did not arise out of the same conduct, transaction, or occurrence as the claim in the original complaint, those claims that arose more than one year prior to the FDCPA filing were dismissed as time barred. Equitable tolling of the statute of limitations, assuming that it even applies to FDCPA claims, did not apply under these circumstances, since the fraudulent concealment needed to support equitable tolling was not met simply by the alleged use of deceptive practices. The court held that the portion of the amended complaint adding only the plaintiff's individual claim for the use of false and deceptive supporting affidavits and documents in the underlying state collection case did relate back to the original, as it rested on the same common core of operative facts that were alleged in his original complaint alleging FDCPA violation. The court also stated that the mere fact that "plaintiff's Amended Complaint adds a new theory does not negate the opportunity for relation back to the original complaint. Where the parties are the same, a court will permit a party to add a new legal theory that arises out of the same transaction or occurrence."

Griffin v. Reznick, 609 F. Supp. 2d 695 (W.D. Mich. 2008). Dismissed based on one-year statute of limitations; since the defense had been raised by co-defendants, plaintiff was on notice and it was not deemed waived.

Toma v. Gen. Revenue Corp., 2008 WL 302378 (E.D. Mich. Feb. 1, 2008). Dismissed on summary judgment as barred by the FDCPA statute of limitations since the plaintiff filed her complaint on July 19, 2007, and the evidence showed that the defendant did not "engage[] in any allegedly prohibited conduct on or after July 19, 2006."

Purnell v. Arrow Fin. Servs., L.L.C., 2007 WL 421828 (E.D. Mich. Feb. 2, 2007). For the purpose of the FDCPA statute of limitations, each monthly credit bureau report presented a separate harm to plaintiff and an independent opportunity for defendant to comply with the statute. Even if some of the reports were outside the one-year statute, the plaintiff could proceed based on the reports within the statute of limitations.

Minnesota

Grimsley v. Messerli & Kramer, P.A., 2009 WL 928319 (D. Minn. Mar. 31, 2009). Statute of limitations did not run from the initial demand letters sent when defendants did not know the debt had been paid, but from the filing of a lawsuit after receiving the consumer's notice that the debt had been paid.

Burgi v. Gurstel Law Firm, P.A., 2008 WL 4634984 (D. Minn. Oct. 17, 2008). *Pro se* plaintiffs' FDCPA claims which occurred outside the one-year statute of limitations were time barred.

Wyles v. Excalibur I, L.L.C., 2006 WL 2583200 (D. Minn. Sept. 7, 2006). Cause of action based on seeking excessive fees during state court lawsuit arose at service of lawsuit not when the default judgment was entered; plaintiff's action was time barred.

Kirscher v. Messerli & Kramer, P.A., 2006 WL 145162 (D. Minn. Jan. 18, 2006). *Pro se* attorney's misrepresentation claim against defendant attorneys was time barred; there is no continuing violation theory under the FDCPA.

Malm v. Household Bank (SB), N.A., 2004 WL 1559370 (D. Minn. July 7, 2004). Statute of limitations had not expired on FDCPA claim under allegation that collector continued its failure to report the claim as disputed through a time within the one-year statute.

James v. Ford Motor Credit Co., 842 F. Supp. 1202 (D. Minn. 1994), *aff'd*, 47 F.3d 961 (8th Cir. 1995). Where repossession occurred on June 29, 1992 but FDCPA action was not filed until July 7, 1993, suit was not brought within the one year statute of limitations.

Mississippi

Landry v. Green Tree Fin. Corp. of Alabama, 2010 WL 1445530 (S.D. Miss. Apr. 8, 2010). The FDCPA claims were not time barred under Rule 15's relation-back doctrine.

Missouri

Eckert v. LVNV Funding L.L.C., 647 F. Supp. 2d 1096 (E.D. Mo. 2009). Plaintiff's claim dismissed as it presented insufficient facts to support claim that defendant violated § 1692e(10) by filing the state court petition outside of the statute of limitations period.

Murphy v. MRC Receivables Corp., 2007 U.S. Dist. LEXIS 2929 (W.D. Mo. Jan. 12, 2007). The court rejected any reading of the "continuing violations" case law that "new communications concerning an old claim do not start a new period of limitations" and held to the contrary that each new communication or action that allegedly violated the FDCPA established an independent basis for liability; accordingly, the court denied the defendant's motion for summary judgment that asserted that the plaintiff's claims were time barred and held that those FDCPA claims based on communications and activities that occurred within one year of filing were timely.

Garrett v. DeLeve, 1990 U.S. Dist. LEXIS 20983 (W.D. Mo. July 31, 1990). A claim that the collector violated § 1692g by not informing the debtor of the amount of interest claimed on the debt could be brought more than one year after five days after the initial communication between the parties, when it should have been disclosed. The purposes of the FDCPA were best served by applying the doctrine of equitable tolling and allowing the FDCPA claim to be filed within one year of the later date when the collector disclosed the interest charges. Other claims were agreed to be limited to events occurring within one year of the filing of the complaint.

Montana

McCollough v. Johnson, Rodenberg & Lauinger, 587 F. Supp. 2d 1170 (D. Mont. 2008). "A debt collector violated the FDCPA by using the courts to attempt to collect a time-barred debt."

Nevada

Karony v. Dollar Loan Ctr., L.L.C., 2010 WL 5186065 (D. Nev. Dec. 15, 2010). Any allegedly unlawful collection activities that occurred more than one year before filing suit were time barred.

Pittman v. J.J. Mac Intyre Co., 969 F. Supp. 609 (D. Nev. 1997). The consumer's cause of action under the FDCPA was based only on those three communications by the defendant that occurred within one year of filing her original complaint. While the statute of limitations rendered those specific communications between the defendant and the plaintiff prior to that date unactionable, evidence of these prior communications was relevant to establishing whether the calls occurring within the limitations period were part of an abusive or harassing pattern violating § 1692d.

New Jersey

Parker v. Pressler & Pressler, L.L.P., 650 F. Supp. 2d 326 (D.N.J. 2009). Regardless of whether the FDCPA statute of limitations began to run from the date of filing the state court complaint or the date of service, the consumer's FDCPA complaint filed one year and three months after the alleged violation was barred by § 1692k(d).

Smith v. Rubin & Raine of New Jersey, L.L.C., 2009 WL 2143644 (D.N.J. July 14, 2009). New FDCPA claims alleged in the amended complaint were time barred since they raised new violations based on new facts "which differ in both time and type from the claims asserted in the Initial Complaint" and therefore did not relate back to the original pleading. "[T]he date the letters were sent [and not when they were received], is the relevant period from which the statute of limitations begins to run."

Bass v. Palisades Collections, L.L.C., 2008 WL 4513812 (D.N.J. Sept. 26, 2008). Plaintiff's claim that debt collector failed to inform creditor and later debt buyer, by proxy, that plaintiff's debt was disputed is beyond the statute of limitations as to debt collector, and meritless as a basis for imputing knowledge on the part of later debt buyer.

Sutton v. New Century Fin. Servs., 2005 WL 3544783 (D.N.J. Dec. 27, 2005). The putative FDCPA claim was time barred where the operative events pre-dated the filing of the complaint by more than one year.

New Mexico

Billsie v. Brooksbank, 525 F. Supp. 2d 1290 (D.N.M. 2007). Denied summary judgment due to issues of fact: whether statute of limitations runs from date of wrongful garnishment or date of refusal to return funds where both dates were in dispute.

New York

Boyd v. J.E. Robert Co., 2011 WL 477547 (E.D.N.Y. Feb. 2, 2011). Equitable tolling did not apply to save the FDCPA claims because the plaintiffs could not demonstrate due diligence.

Caldwell v. Gutman, Mintz, Baker & Sonnenfeldt, P.C., 701 F. Supp. 2d 340 (E.D.N.Y. 2010). The *pro se* consumers' FDCPA suit was time barred where last action in underlying state court collection action was more than a year prior to filing.

Sykes v. Mel Harris & Assocs., L.L.C., 2010 WL 5395712 (S.D.N.Y. Dec. 29, 2010). FDCPA claims are subject to equitable tolling.

Puglisi v. Debt Recovery Solutions, L.L.C., 2010 WL 376628 (E.D.N.Y. Jan. 26, 2010). The cause of action for the alleged violation is deemed to accrue at the time of the FDCPA violation itself.

Schuh v. Druckman & Sinel, L.L.P., 602 F. Supp. 2d 454 (S.D.N.Y. 2009). An FDCPA violation in a payout letter was not time barred. Rejected the argument that the letter was a continuing part of foreclosure that had been filed more than a year before the consumer's FDCPA suit.

Ehrich v. RJM Acquisitions L.L.C., 2009 WL 4545179 (E.D.N.Y. Dec. 4, 2009). The claims based on alleged violations in the initial dun, which predated the filing of the complaint by much more than one year, were time barred since "FDCPA violations accrue, at latest, on the date a debt collection communication is received." The court rejected the debt collector's contention that all of the consumer's FDCPA claims accrued when debt collector first attempted to collect the debt and could not be revived by subsequent communications for the same debt: "separate communications that violate the FDCPA can create separate causes of action" and thus the "[c]laims based on communications falling within the one-year statutory period are not necessarily time-barred."

Boyd v. J.E. Robert Co., 2008 WL 4415253 (E.D.N.Y. Sept. 24, 2008). Consumers' FDCPA time-barred claims that were based on events and alleged injuries which occurred after the filing of an earlier class action complaint in which these consumers were class members could not be considered as part of that class action and therefore were not subject to tolling under *American Pipe & Constr. Co. v. Utah*, 414 U.S. 538 (1974). Consumers were granted leave to amend to state claims which were allegedly within the prior class action and to which *American Pipe* tolling might apply and to allege facts that might allow equitable tolling.

Wright v. Zabarkes, 2008 WL 872296 (S.D.N.Y. Apr. 2, 2008), *aff'd*, 347 Fed. Appx. 670 (2d Cir. 2009). *Pro se* consumer's complaint dismissed *sua sponte* as time barred since the complaint only alleged events that occurred more than one year prior to the filing of the action.

Mascoll v. Strumpf, 2006 WL 2795175 (E.D.N.Y. Sept. 25, 2006). The court held that the FDCPA complaint was not time barred since the plaintiff only learned of the defendants' wrongful prosecution of the underlying state court collection action within one year of the filing of the federal FDCPA suit and some of defendants' misconduct in wrongfully pursuing execution in that state case occurred within the one-year period.

Louis Fink Realty Trust v. Harrison, 2003 WL 22595555 (S.D.N.Y. Nov. 7, 2003). Complaint with no material allegation of a violation occurring within one year of its filing was barred by the FDCPA statute of limitations.

Padilla v. Payco Gen. Am. Credits, Inc., 161 F. Supp. 2d 264 (S.D.N.Y. 2001). Events that occurred before the one-year statute of limitations were still admissible as any other evidence.

Sierra v. Foster & Garbus, 48 F. Supp. 2d 393 (S.D.N.Y. 1999). The court rejected application of "continuing violation" theory to extend statute of limitations.

Calka v. Kucker, Kraus & Bruh, L.L.P., 1998 WL 437151 (S.D.N.Y. Aug. 3, 1998). FDCPA action filed more than one year after the filing of the collection action alleged to violate the FDCPA was barred by the one year statute of limitations even though an amended complaint and motion for summary judgment containing the same violation had been filed by the debt collector within the one year.

Victori v. Accelerated Bureau of Collections, Inc., 1997 WL 9788 (W.D.N.Y. Jan. 2, 1997). New claims which did not arise from the conduct set forth in the original complaint but were instead predicated upon a distinct and separate set of operative facts did not fall with the relation-back doctrine, and motion to amend was denied.

Seabrook v. Onondaga Bureau of Med. Econ., Inc., 705 F. Supp. 81 (N.D.N.Y. 1989). An FDCPA claim based on a letter dated May 18, 1987 and received on May 20, 1987 was filed timely on May 17, 1988.

Bank of Boston Int'l v. Arguello Tefel, 644 F. Supp. 1423 (E.D.N.Y. 1986). An FDCPA counterclaim was dismissed as it was not filed within one year of the alleged violation.

Holder v. GMC, 732 N.Y.S.2d 545 (N.Y. Sup. Ct. 2001). Consumer's complaint that the defendant violated § 1692e(8) by reporting false information to a credit reporting agency years earlier, where the consumer learned of the violation only when denied credit within one year of filing suit, was barred by the statute of limitations since the FDCPA limitations language of one year "from the date on which the violation occurs" demonstrated a clear directive from Congress to reject a discovery rule that otherwise is incorporated in every federal statute.

North Carolina

Martin v. Sessoms & Rogers, P.A., 2010 WL 3200015 (E.D.N.C. Aug. 12, 2010). The consumer's claim was time barred since no discrete violation occurred one year prior to filing the FDCPA complaint.

North Dakota

Eaton v. Credit Bureau, Inc., 2007 WL 2781844 (D.N.D. Sept. 21, 2007). The cause of action to remedy defendant's demands for payment of unlawful dishonored check civil penalties were not time barred where the checks were written more than one year before the FDCPA suit was filed but the demands for payment were made within the one-year period.

Wilhelm v. Credico, Inc., 455 F. Supp. 2d 1006 (D.N.D. 2006), *aff'd in part, rev'd in part*, 519 F.3d 416 (8th Cir. 2008). Court rejected the "continuing violation" theory that each failure to report the debt as disputed when reporting it to a credit reporting agency was a new violation, and held that statute of limitations had expired.

Ohio

McNerney v. Mortgage Elec. Registration Sys., Inc., 2010 WL 3222044 (N.D. Ohio Aug. 13, 2010). FDCPA claim against foreclosing attorneys that was filed more than one year after the allegedly unlawful foreclosure was both filed and served was time barred.

Zigdon v. LVNV Funding, L.L.C., 2010 WL 1838637 (N.D. Ohio Apr. 23, 2010). A complaint alleging that the defendant unlawfully filed a state court collection suit without the legal capacity to do so was time barred since "where the alleged FDCPA violation is the filing of the state lawsuit," the "limitations period begins to run when the state court complaint was served on the debtor-defendant." The FDCPA statute of limitations is subject generally to equitable tolling, but the court found that the doctrine was unavailable in this case due to the absence of concealment by defendant of any elements of the claim.

Byrd v. Law Offices of John D. Clunk Co., 2010 WL 816932 (S.D. Ohio Mar. 8, 2010). No equitable tolling of statute of limitations where no fraudulent concealment and plaintiff did not show diligence in discovering the claim against the proposed new party.

Kline v. Mortgage Elec. Sec. Sys., 659 F. Supp. 2d 940 (S.D. Ohio 2009). The FDCPA claim predicated upon the proof of claim filed in their bankruptcy case under chapter 13 was dismissed as barred by the statute of limitations, since the proof of claim was filed more than one year before this litigation was initiated. However, another claim was not barred, based on allegation that the defendants continue to seek illegal late fees and the like outside of bankruptcy.

Midland Funding L.L.C. v. Brent, 644 F. Supp. 2d 961 (N.D. Ohio 2009). Court allowed relation back of new claim related to imposition of excessive interest since it arose out of the same collection circumstances.

Whittiker v. Deutsche Bank Nat'l Trust Co., 605 F. Supp. 2d 914 (N.D. Ohio 2009). Dismissed based on statute of limitations; equitable tolling not appropriate here where defendants did not conceal the state court action.

Ruth v. Unifund CCR Partners, 2009 WL 585847 (N.D. Ohio Mar. 6, 2009). FDCPA claims alleging that defendants filed state court collection litigation without legal capacity were time barred since the federal action was filed more than one year after the plaintiff was served with the collection complaint. Defendants' litigation of the collection action based on the filing of a complaint without legal capacity is not the type of "continuing wrong" to support a continuing violation theory to extend the statute of limitations. FDCPA claim alleging that defendants illegally assigned the debt was time barred since the action was filed more than one year after the alleged violation.

Ison v. Javitch, Block & Rathbone, 2007 WL 2769674 (S.D. Ohio Sept. 18, 2007). Faced with the question whether the FDCPA statute of limitations for violations arising from false statements contained in the underlying state court collection suit "begin[s] to run on the date of the filing of the complaint, the date of the mailing of the complaint or the date of the receipt of the complaint by the debtor," the court rejected the date of filing option and did not need to chose between the dates of mailing and receipt since each was within the one-year statute of limitations. The consum-

er's amended complaint related back to the filing of the first complaint pursuant to Rule 15 since the allegation in the amended complaint arose out of the same conduct, transaction, or occurrence as the original pleading.

Foster v. D.B.S. Collection Agency, 463 F. Supp. 2d 783 (S.D. Ohio 2006). Statute of limitations ran, not based on the filing date of the state court suits, but on the actions thereafter, including post-judgment collection efforts. Court alternatively applied equitable tolling to the statute of limitations due to the defendant's concealment of their lack of capacity to file lawsuits.

Sylvester v. Laks, 1991 U.S. Dist. LEXIS 21777 (N.D. Ohio Aug. 1, 1991). Statute of limitation had not run on Nov. 14, 1990 regarding a letter received on Nov. 14, 1989 and mailed on Nov. 13, 1989. The violation occurred when the letter was received, not when it was mailed.

Oklahoma

Scoles v. Spellings, 2008 WL 4372365 (W.D. Okla. Sept. 18, 2008). "Having reviewed the amended Complaint, the Court finds that plaintiff's Fair Debt Collection Practice Act claim is time-barred. Specifically, the Court finds that the limitations period was triggered in 2004 [when the student loan debt collector breached an alleged settlement agreement with the consumer], and the instant suit was filed more than three years later in 2007. Furthermore, the Court finds, in light of the authorities, that each individual collection or successive garnishment does not establish a continuing violation of the Fair Debt Collection Practice Act."

In re Commercial Fin. Servs., Inc., 2008 WL 2889703 (Bankr. N.D. Okla. July 21, 2008). Judgment for the defendant because the *pro se* consumer's claims were time barred as the complaint was filed more than one year after any collection activity occurred.

In re Commercial Fin. Servs., 238 B.R. 479 (Bankr. N.D. Okla. 1999). A *pro se* litigant did not have standing to raise an FDCPA claim in a collection company's bankruptcy because the FDCPA statute of limitations had run.

Oregon

Blue v. Bronson & Migliaccio, 2010 WL 4641666 (D. Or. Nov. 4, 2010). Telephone calls made outside the statute of limitations period were time barred, but they were still relevant in determining whether the calls within the limitations period were part of an abusive or harassing pattern.

Stewart v. Mortgage Elec. Registration Sys., Inc., 2010 WL61055131 (D. Or. Feb. 9, 2010). The *pro se* complaint was dismissed as time barred for failure to allege any violation that occurred within one year of filing.

Avery v. Gordon, 2008 WL 4793686 (D. Or. Oct. 27, 2008). One year for the FDCPA statute of limitations means one calendar year, not 365 days; a case filed on the anniversary date timely.

Hooper v. Capital Credit & Collection Servs., Inc., 2004 WL 825616 (D. Or. Jan. 16, 2004). One year statute of limitations is procedural, not jurisdictional, so suit filed on anniversary of date letter was sent was timely.

Peters v. Collection Tech. Inc., 1991 U.S. Dist. LEXIS 21810 (D.

Or. Dec. 5, 1991). Where FDCPA complaint was stamped "received" by the clerk on May 2, 1990, but not stamped as "filed" until May 18, 1990 after granting petition to proceed *in forma pauperis*, the complaint was constructively filed on May 2, 1990.

Christopherson v. Gross & Siegel, 1991 U.S. Dist. LEXIS 21730 (D. Or. July 3, 1991). Whether the consumer's claim against a collection agency was untimely filed more than a year after the alleged violation or tolled by concealment of the agency's involvement required factual determinations not appropriate on a motion to dismiss. While the agency's name was stated in the dunning letter on the agency's attorney's letterhead, received more than one year prior to the complaint, the agency's role was not revealed until later.

Pennsylvania

Kirby v. Burton Neil & Assocs., L.L.C., 2010 WL 1687425 (W.D. Pa. Apr. 26, 2010) The *pro se* consumer's claim was dismissed as time barred since the alleged FDCPA violations occurred more than one year prior to the filing of the complaint.

Lennon v. Penn Waste, Inc., 2009 WL 3255238 (M.D. Pa. Oct. 7, 2009). Where there was a pattern of similar continuing violations, some before and some after the FDCPA statute of limitations, the court would not enter summary judgment for the debt collector on the claims predating the statute limitations as it was premature, as some courts find that a continuing violation approach would preserve those claims.

Tucker v. Mann Bracken, L.L.C., 2009 WL 151669 (M.D. Pa. Jan. 21, 2009). Since mechanical application of the one-year limitations period could operate to defeat some of the remedial consumer protection goals of the FDCPA, court holds that a continuing violations theory may be applied to FDCPA claims, so that it applies to telephone harassment campaign that occurred partly within and partly outside the one-year statute of limitations. To base a claim on conduct alleged to be part of a continuing violation, a plaintiff must demonstrate two things: (1) at least one act occurred within the one-year filing period, and (2) the alleged conduct must be more than isolated, sporadic acts—in other words, the conduct "must be a persistent, on-going pattern."

Whiteman v. Burton Neil & Assocs., P.C., 2008 WL 4372842 (M.D. Pa. Sept. 19, 2008). Rule 12(b)(6) motion to dismiss allegedly time-barred FDCPA complaint denied since the *pro se* consumer's complaint alleged actions that took place within one year of the filing of the complaint.

Jones v. Select Portfolio Servicing, Inc., 2008 WL 1820935 (E.D. Pa. Apr. 22, 2008). FDCPA claim was time barred where the last allegedly violative communication was sent to the consumer twenty-two months before the complaint was filed.

Dixon v. Law Offices of Peter E. Meltzer & Assocs., P.C., 2007 WL 275877 (E.D. Pa. Jan. 26, 2007). Dismissed a portion of the plaintiff's complaint since "FDCPA claims must be filed 'within one year from the date on which the violation occurs,'" and "[t]his statute of limitations is not subject to waiver or tolling."

Kondratick v. Beneficial Consumer Disc. Co., 2005 WL 2314042 (E.D. Pa. Sept. 21, 2005). Consumers' FDCPA complaint, alleging violations arising from the defendant attorney's filing of the underlying state court collection suit, was dismissed as time barred,

since the FDCPA case was filed one day after the expiration of the FDCPA's jurisdictional one-year statute of limitations, which accrued on the date that the state collection suit was filed—the date of the violation—and not days later when the consumers were served or learned of the violation.

Agosta v. InoVision, Inc., 2003 WL 23009357 (E.D. Pa. Dec. 16, 2003). Because factual issues were in dispute, the court took no position on the split among the federal courts whether, in cases involving alleged violations of § 1692e based on letters sent to consumer, the statute of limitations began to run on the day when the debt collector mailed the letter or when the consumer received it.

Sullivan v. Equifax, Inc., 2002 U.S. Dist. LEXIS 7884 (E.D. Pa. Apr. 19, 2002). Statute of limitations can only be raised as an affirmative defense in a motion to dismiss if it was apparent on the face of the complaint. Where the complaint generally alleges a continuing violation of the FDCPA through ongoing credit reports, the collector cannot raise a statute of limitations defense via motion to dismiss by alleging that the last credit report it made was more than one year ago.

Maydwell v. Yoffe, 2001 U.S. Dist. LEXIS 13442 (E.D. Pa. Aug. 28, 2001). *Pro se* plaintiff's complaint was time barred and dismissed.

Zhang v. Haven-Scott Assocs., 1996 WL 355344 (E.D. Pa. June 21, 1996). Plaintiff's FDCPA claim was barred by the statute of limitations which was considered jurisdictional.

Woodside v. New Jersey Higher Educ. Assistance Auth., 1993 WL 56020 (E.D. Pa. Mar. 2, 1993). Only those alleged violations that are based on events that occurred within the year prior to the date of filing the action are cognizable under the FDCPA.

Tennessee

McKamey v. Financial Accounts Servs. Team, Inc., 2010 WL 3632192 (E.D. Tenn. Sept. 10, 2010). Due to the inconsistent telephone records submitted by the parties, the court denied the plaintiff's motion to strike the defendant's statute of limitations defense.

Geffrard v. Rolfe & Lobello, P.A., 2010 WL 1924434 (S.D. Tex. May 11, 2010). Because the complaint was silent about date the garnishment was filed, the consumer did not show that she has an FDCPA cause of action within the one-year limitations period.

Brandon v. Financial Accounts Servs. Team, Inc., 701 F. Supp. 2d 990 (E.D. Tenn. Mar. 24, 2010). Where the defendant sent four letters reporting incorrect information within the one-year limitations period, the letters, while involving the violation discovered outside of the limitations period, were separate communications that are alleged to have violated the FDCPA. "A finding that a consumer could not assert a violation of the FDCPA for any alleged communication sent so long as the violation was detected over one year from the date a consumer filed suit would serve to immunize debt collectors from liability."

Hunter v. Washington Mut. Bank, 2008 WL 4206604 (E.D. Tenn. Sept. 10, 2008). Defendant's motion to dismiss was granted with regard to the FDCPA claims occurring more than one year prior to filing this suit.

Dowdy v. Solutia Healthcare TAS, Inc., 2006 WL 3545047 (M.D. Tenn. Dec. 8, 2006). Action on a February 2005 letter in which the debt was deceptively doubled was not time barred, even though consumer first learned that the amount sought was too high as early as April 2004.

Drumright v. Collection Recovery, Inc., 500 F. Supp. 1 (M.D. Tenn. 1980). An FDCPA claim filed one year, four days after an allegedly deceptive letter was barred by § 1692k(d) one year statute of limitations, but the claim of the failure to provide notice of validation rights was not barred since that claim did ripen until five days after the letter which was the initial communication from the debt collector.

Texas

Naranjo v. Universal Sur. of Am., 679 F. Supp. 2d 787 (S.D. Tex. 2010). The complaint alleged that the violations of the FDCPA occurred within one year of its filing and therefore were not barred by the statute of limitations.

Arvie v. Dodeka, L.L.C., 2010 WL 4312907 (S.D. Tex. Oct. 25, 2010). For statute of limitations purposes, each discrete violation of the FDCPA should be analyzed on an individual basis. In dismissing a claim against a debt buyer who resold a consumer's account beyond the FDCPA statute of limitations after settling it, the court rejected the application of the discovery rule and equitable tolling.

Darocy v. Grand Lending Group, L.P., 2010 WL 3858724 (N.D. Tex. Sept. 30, 2010). The court dismissed the plaintiff's eleven-year-old claim as barred by the FDCPA statute of limitations.

Castro v. Collecto, Inc., 256 F.R.D. 534 (W.D. Tex. 2009). The ability to bring or threaten suit on the subject cell phone debts were governed by the Federal Communications Act's two-year limitations period. A class of consumers was certified in FDCPA suit for collecting time-barred debts.

Barnett v. Experian Info. Solutions, 2004 WL 4033379 (E.D. Tex. Sept. 28, 2004). The court held the one-year statute of limitations period for FDCPA claims to be procedural not jurisdictional.

Flores v. Millennium Interests, Ltd., 273 F. Supp. 2d 899 (S.D. Tex. 2003). Suit based on allegedly erroneous information that the debt collector reported to a credit bureau nearly three years before suit was filed and that the consumer discovered more than one year before filing suit was barred by the FDCPA's one-year statute of limitation.

Utah

Maxwell v. Barney, 2008 WL 1981666 (D. Utah May 2, 2008). Action was timely where collection letter was mailed outside the statute of limitations, but received within the one-year time period. The limitations period began to run when plaintiff knew or had reason to know of the existence and cause of her injury, and this happened when she received the letter.

Morgan v. N.A.R., Inc., 2008 WL 639128 (D. Utah Mar. 5, 2008). Applying a discovery rule found cited in state and Tenth Circuit authorities, the court held that this action arising from an allegedly wrongful garnishment was not barred by the FDCPA's one-year statute of limitations: "June 10, 2005 was the first date that

Plaintiff was on notice that funds were withheld from her paycheck. Therefore, the statute of limitations does not bar this claim, filed on June 9, 2006."

Maynard v. Bryan W. Cannon, P.C., 2006 U.S. Dist. LEXIS 59297 (D. Utah Aug. 21, 2006). The statute of limitations regarding the FDCPA is not jurisdictional. Failure to withdraw or correct the recorded notice of default was a continuing misrepresentation of the amount of the debt.

Virginia

Vitullo v. Mancini, 684 F. Supp. 2d 747 (E.D. Va. 2010). Plaintiff's second amended complaint related back to filing of original complaint for purposes of the FDCPA's one-year limitations period.

Saylor v. CACV of Colorado, L.L.C., 2005 WL 1745644 (W.D. Va. July 26, 2005). Summary judgment was granted for the defendant where the consumer waited for more than a year (measured from the date of filing the enforcement action) to file his FDCPA claim.

Chisolm v. Charlie Falk Auto Wholesalers Inc., 851 F. Supp. 739 (E.D. Va. 1994). The court had no jurisdiction to hear the consumer's FDCPA action which was filed more than one year after the date the violation occurred.

Washington

Malik v. Unifund CCR Partners, 2009 WL 519782 (W.D. Wash. Dec. 22, 2009). Consumer's FDCPA claim arising from garnishment which occurred roughly three months before filing his action was within one year of filing the complaint and was not barred by the statute of limitations. Nothing in the language of the FDCPA suggests that the statute of limitations runs from the first possible violation and encompasses all later-occurring and distinct violations of the Act. The filing of a writ of garnishment is a "legal action on a debt" which starts the FDCPA statute of limitations.

Barnett v. T.D. Escrow Servs., Inc., 2005 WL 1838623 (W.D. Wash. Aug. 1, 2005) Suit was time barred where last collection letter was fourteen months before suit.

Clark v. Bonded Adjustment Co., 204 F.R.D. 662 (E.D. Wash. 2002). In the course of granting class certification based on charging excessive process server fees, the court determined that the one year statute of limitations ran from October 21, 1999 to October 23, 2000 due to the leap year.

Clark v. Bonded Adjustment Co., 176 F. Supp. 2d 1062 (E.D. Wash. 2001). Rule 6(a) applies to the FDCPA statute of limitations; the one-year filing period began to run on the day after the last alleged violation of the Act. Because the last day of the leap year fell on a Saturday, the filing of the complaint on the following Monday was timely.

West Virginia

Givens v. Main Street Bank, 2008 WL 44154490 (N.D. W. Va. Sept. 25, 2008). *Pro se* consumer's FDCPA claim dismissed as time barred where the last events preceding the filing of the lawsuit in 2008 occurred in 2005.

Prade v. Jackson & Kelly, 941 F. Supp. 596 (N.D. W. Va. 1996), *aff'd without op.*, 135 F.3d 770 (4th Cir. 1998). An FDCPA suit was barred by the statute of limitations where the consumers filed the FDCPA suit more than one year after receiving a summons in a collection suit filed in an improper venue.

K.3.6 Debt Collector's Defenses and Counterclaims

K.3.6.1 Bona Fide Error Defense, 15 U.S.C. § 1692k(c)

Jerman v. Carlisle, McNellie, Rini, Kramer & Ulrich L.P.A., 130 S. Ct. 1605 (2010). The bona fide error defense is not available for errors of interpretation of the FDCPA, but is available for factual errors of debt collectors. The Court expressly did not reach the applicability of the defense to errors of state law or other federal law.

Owen v. I.C. Sys., Inc., 2011 WL 43525 (11th Cir. Jan. 7, 2011). To qualify for the bona fide error defense, the debt collector has an affirmative statutory obligation to maintain procedures reasonably adapted to avoid readily discoverable errors. In this case, the errors, including compounding interest, were discernible on the face of the collection documents. The procedures element of the bona fide error defense requires the debt collector to (1) maintain, i.e., actually employ or implement procedures (2) reasonably adapted to avoid the specific error at issue. The suspension of collection efforts once the consumer contested the debt, along with the debt collector's subsequent receipt and delivery of debt verification materials to the consumer, do not constitute procedures "reasonably adapted to avoid" interest errors; these are statutory requirements. The debt collector's letter requesting the consumer to contact its office if she continued to dispute her debt was not a procedure "reasonably adapted to avoid" errors, since the collector's previous letter had already sought collection of improper charges. At best, this after-the-fact procedure was adapted to prevent the error from occurring again. A debt collector does not fulfill its affirmative obligation to "maintain procedures" by delegating it entirely to creditors. In this case, the collector cited no internal controls it employed to reduce the incidence of improper debt collection but, rather, demonstrated that its procedure was to outsource its oversight task to its creditor, which must report only debts that are "validly due and owing."

Hepsen v. Resurgent Capital Servs., L.P., 2010 WL 2490734 (11th Cir. June 17, 2010). The bona fide error defense was not available where the collector's practice of naming its client (Resurgent) as the "creditor," even when it had information suggesting the debt might be owed to other entities (LVNV), was not reasonable. The collector could be liable for stating an inaccurate amount for the debt in a demand letter to plaintiff even if the FDCPA does not explicitly require that a collector verify the amount of the debt before sending a demand. The FDCPA does not impose an affirmative obligation on debt collectors to independently verify debts, but that lack of affirmative obligation does not protect a debt collector who attempts to collect an inaccurate debt. The difference between the amount demanded by the collector and the lower amount later demanded by Resurgent, on behalf of the creditor LVNV, supported a reasonable inference that the collector's demand was inaccurate.

Edwards v. Niagara Credit Solutions, Inc., 584 F.3d 1350 (11th Cir. 2009). The district court properly denied the bona fide error defense arising from the defendant's failure to identify itself as a debt collector as required by § 1692e(11) when leaving consumers an answering machine message; first, the violation was in fact intentional, the result of a deliberate policy decision to not comply with § 1692e(11) purportedly to avoid violating § 1692c(b) in the event that the message was heard by a third party who would then know that a collection agency was calling the consumer; second, to be bona fide "the mistake must be objectively reasonable," and "[i]t was not reasonable for to violate § 1692e(11) of the FDCPA with every message it left in order to avoid the possibility that some of those messages might lead to a violation of § 1692c(b)."

Ruth v. Triumph P'ships, 577 F.3d 790 (7th Cir. 2009). A defendant is entitled to the bona fide error defense only if it can show that the violation: (1) was unintentional; (2) resulted from a bona fide error; and (3) occurred despite the defendant's maintenance of procedures reasonably adapted to avoid such error. If a claimed error is legal, it is only available to debt collectors, if it is permissible, "who can establish that they reasonably relied on either: (1) the legal opinion of an attorney who has conducted the appropriate legal research, or (2) the opinion of another person or organization with expertise in the relevant area of law—for example, the appropriate government agency." (Dictum.) Although the debt collectors produced evidence that their employees attend training sessions on FDCPA compliance, and they had procedures in place to prevent violations of other provisions of the FDCPA, the debt collectors could not establish a bona fide error defense where no evidence in the record indicated that they had ever sought legal or regulatory advice as to whether the collection letter and notice were in compliance with the FDCPA.

Hartman v. Great Seneca Fin. Corp., 569 F.3d 606 (6th Cir. 2009). Summary judgment for the defendants on their bona fide error defense reversed where the district court had erred in concluding that it was sufficient that the defendant debt buyer had no intent to mislead or misrepresent, had "exhaustive procedures in place to verify financial information associated with debts," and had hired a law firm to manage its portfolio, and that the defendant attorneys had relied on their client's representations and "did not believe that calling Exhibit A an 'account' was prohibited by the FDCPA;" instead, the evidence supported the conclusion that the violation was intentional in order to circumvent state pleading rules, and the procedures in place—to insure accuracy of the data—were not procedures designed to avoid the violation at issue, i.e., the deceptive nature of the document itself.

Danow v. Borack, 346 Fed. Appx. 409 (11th Cir. 2009). Jury could properly reject bona fide error based on evidence that defendant trains its callers in the FDCPA and supervisors monitor the calls when an employee actually talks to a debtor, but defendant did not produce any written procedures concerning how it processes letters from consumers, how it determines whether to place a "cease and desist" on an account, or if anyone reviews the employees' actions to determine whether a letter has been properly processed, and also acknowledged that the firm never receives an itemized list of its outbound calls from the telephone company, and never compares its internal telephone logs with telephone-company records to "make sure that your employees are not making phone calls that you don't know about." Finally, when the firm's employees call consumers and leave tape-recorded messages, the firm does not record or monitor those calls.

Seeger v. AFNI, Inc., 548 F.3d 1107 (7th Cir. 2008). Assuming the bona fide error defense applies to mistakes of law, the collector's evidence that it misunderstood the law notwithstanding its ongoing compliance efforts to apprise itself of applicable legal requirements did not meet the reasonable preventive procedures prong; allowing the defense under these circumstances "would essentially reward a business's ignorance of the law."

Reichert v. Nat'l Credit Sys, Inc., 531 F.3d 1002 (9th Cir. 2008). The court held that the debt collector failed to establish a bona fide error defense. Although the FDCPA is a strict liability statute it makes an exception in case of the bona fide error defense and allows a debt collector to establish that its error was unintentional by a preponderance of evidence. Bona fide error defense is an affirmative defense for which the debt collector has the burden of proof. "To qualify for the bona fide error defense under the FDCPA, the debt collector has an affirmative obligation to maintain procedures designed to avoid discoverable errors, including, but not limited to, errors in calculation and itemization. The latter would include errors in claiming collection expenses of the creditor that could not legitimately be part of the debt owed by the debtor."

Johnson v. Riddle, 443 F.3d 723 (10th Cir. 2006). The intent element of the bona fide error defense focuses on whether the defendant intended to violate the FDCPA, not whether he intended to engage in the collection efforts giving rise to the violation. The bona fide element of the defense is an objective test to determine whether a reasonable debt collector in the defendant's position would be in violation of the Act.

Kort v. Diversified Collection Servs., Inc., 394 F.3d 530 (7th Cir. 2005). The use of a Department of Education required pre-garnishment notice form was excused as a bona fide error. The court did not address whether the form was deceptive because it may have misstated the student loan borrower's rights. The court avoided the question of the applicability of the bona fide error defense to legal errors as the collector relied on the legal judgment of the Department of Education rather than make its own.

Turner v. J.V.D.B. & Assocs., Inc., 330 F.3d 991 (7th Cir. 2003). Section 1692e generally prohibits "false, deceptive or misleading" collection activities without regard to intent. The collector's ignorance of the consumer's bankruptcy did not excuse its post-discharge violation of § 1692e in seeking collection of a discharged debt (reversing summary judgment in the debt collector's favor).

Nielsen v. Dickerson, 307 F.3d 623 (7th Cir. 2002). Court assumes, but does not decide, that a legal error can be a bona fide error, surveying case law. Court does not decide whether the bona fide error defense was applicable where the actions themselves were intentional, surveying case law. Bona fide error defense was not available where prior case law was reasonably clear. "*Avila,* which was decided nearly a year before [the creditor] retained [its collection attorney], made clear that an attorney must have some professional involvement with the debtor's file in order for the presence of his name on a delinquency not to be misleading." "[The collection attorney's] actions complied neither with the spirit nor the letter of *Avila;* no reasonable attorney, and for that matter, no reasonable creditor or debt collector, having read our opinion, could have failed to appreciate this."

Picht v. Jon R. Hawks, Ltd., 236 F.3d 446 (8th Cir. 2001). Bona fide error defense does not apply to errors of legal judgment.

Pollice v. Nat'l Tax Funding, L.P., 225 F.3d 379 (3d Cir. 2000). Whether a reliance on a municipal ordinance that was preempted by a state statute limiting late charges was the basis for a bona fide error defense was not decided.

Lewis v. ABC Bus. Servs., Inc., 135 F.3d 389 (6th Cir. 1998). Where the creditor returned a debt to a collection agency marked as "new" rather than returned, a bona fide error defense existed to the collector's contact of the debtor who had sent a cease communication letter.

Jenkins v. Heintz, 124 F.3d 824 (7th Cir. 1997). The collection firm established a bona fide error defense by showing that they did not know that the debt on which they brought suit included a charge for unauthorized forced placed automobile insurance. The attorney collector was not expected to understand the legal intricacies of the retail installment sale on which they brought suit.

Dikeman v. Nat'l Educators, Inc., 81 F.3d 949 (10th Cir. 1996). The jury had found the debt had not been verified when the verification given was inadequate because it overstated the collector's claim, but the jury excused the violation as a bona fide error.

Fox v. Citicorp Credit Servs., Inc., 15 F.3d 1507 (9th Cir. 1994). To establish a bona fide error defense the collector must demonstrate "the maintenance of procedures reasonably adopted to avoid any such error."

Scott v. Jones, 964 F.2d 314 (4th Cir. 1992). Reliance on informal FTC opinions and outside counsel does not establish a § 1692k(c) defense.

Smith v. Transworld Sys., Inc., 953 F.2d 1025 (6th Cir. 1992). Although debt collector did not plead the bona fide error defense as an affirmative defense in its answer, the court allowed the debt collector to raise this defense for the first time in opposition to motion for partial summary judgment because the consumer failed to demonstrate prejudice. Although the debt collector sent from its California headquarters a second letter to the consumer shortly after receiving the consumer's cease and desist letter to its Columbia, Ohio office, the debt collector demonstrated "procedures reasonably adapted to avoid any such error" and thereby established a bona fide error defense. Misstatement of the amount of the debt due to the creditor's erroneous referral was not a violation of § 1692e(2)(A) because the debt collector demonstrated procedures reasonably adapted to prevent such errors, and the resulting mistake was a bona fide error. An independent investigation by the debt collector of the accuracy of the debt is not required by FDCPA. Dissent argued that the debt collector "has intentionally structured and implemented a system that defies compliance with the absolute duty mandated by § 1692c(c)."

Pipiles v. Credit Bureau Inc., 886 F.2d 22 (2d Cir. 1989). The bona fide error defense did not excuse a mistaken view of the law.

Juras v. Aman Collection Serv., Inc., 829 F.2d 739 (9th Cir. 1987). Jury's finding in favor of collector who called consumer before 8:00 a.m. was upheld where there was evidence that collector erroneously failed to consider consumer's time zone and no damages were incurred from calls.

Hulshizer v. Global Credit Servs., Inc., 728 F.2d 1037 (8th Cir. 1984). The bona fide error defense was not available to a collector who intentionally disregarded the plain language of the FDCPA and relied on the mistaken legal advice of an FTC staff attorney and the American Collectors Association.

Baker v. G.C. Servs. Corp., 677 F.2d 775 (9th Cir. 1982). It was not a defense under § 1692k(c) that the collector relied on the advice of counsel or was mistaken about the law.

Alabama

Winberry v. United Collection Bureau, Inc., 697 F. Supp. 2d 1279 (M.D. Ala. 2010). The court found that there was a question of fact precluding summary judgment on this bona fide error defense where defendant could not remember statements he was alleged to have made and, if he made them, he could not state that they were unintentional, and the consumer's testimony allowed for a reasonable inference that the statements were intentional, not accidental.

Sparks v. Phillips & Cohen Assocs., Ltd., 641 F. Supp. 2d 1234 (S.D. Ala. 2008). The court denied summary judgment for the defendant's bona fide error defense where the plaintiffs alleged reprehensible collector misconduct: "The Court finds that there are genuine issues of fact as to, at a minimum, the first two prongs of the bona fide error defense. [Defendant] directs the Court to no evidence or testimony from [its employee] that she did not intend to violate the FDCPA; to the contrary, they tout her many years of experience and expertise in compliance with that statute. If that is true, and if plaintiffs' version of the facts is accepted as true, a reasonable jury could find that [defendant's employee] must have subjectively known that her acts of calling [plaintiffs'] home despite knowledge that [plaintiff] was not involved with the Glover matter, refusing to identify herself when calling [plaintiffs'] home telephone number, berating [plaintiff's daughter] even after [she] told her to call her mother, casting aspersions on [plaintiff's daughters] in her communications with [plaintiff], browbeating [plaintiff] with a statement that defendant had already investigated her, and going out of her way to denigrate and calumniate [plaintiff's daughter] to her boss were all outside the scope of permissible activity under the FDCPA. Even if [defendant's employee] were not well-versed in the FDCPA, an intent to violate the Act could reasonably be inferred by reference to the numerous inconsistencies between [defendant's employee's] course of conduct and that prescribed by in its training manuals for collection specialists. Moreover, on this evidence, a reasonable finder of fact could readily determine that the aforementioned conduct was not objectively reasonable, even if [defendant's employee's] violations of the FDCPA were unintentional."

Arizona

Thompson v. Crown Asset Mgmt., L.L.C., 2009 WL 3059123 (D. Ariz. Sept. 23, 2009). Defendants' affidavits entitle them to the bona fide error defense based on declarations that defendant unintentionally contacted plaintiff as a result of a clerical error, immediately corrected the error, and had policies and procedures in place to avoid such errors.

Gostony v. Diem Corp., 320 F. Supp. 2d 932 (D. Ariz. 2003). Bona

fide error defense was overruled. Defendants did not argue that they maintained reasonable procedures to avoid the error or that errors were unintentional clerical errors. Classes and FDCPA literature aimed at avoiding legal violations did not support a bona fide error defense.

Axtell v. Collections U.S.A. Inc., 2002 WL 32595276 (D. Ariz. Oct. 22, 2002). The bona fide error defense was not available for a merely unintentional violation and instead must also be established by showing the maintenance of procedures reasonably adapted to avoid such error and that the error occurred notwithstanding these procedural safeguards. The referring creditor's representation that it would assign only amounts legally due was not a preventive "procedure" sufficient to establish the bona fide error defense.

Marchant v. U.S. Collections West, Inc., 12 F. Supp. 2d 1001 (D. Ariz. 1998). Where collector failed to present evidence of the maintenance of procedures reasonably adapted to avoid violations of the FDCPA, issue of material fact remained as to whether a bona fide error defense could be established.

California

Welker v. Law Office of Daniel J. Horwitz, 699 F. Supp. 2d 1164 (S.D. Cal. 2010). The bona fide error defense is an affirmative defense, for which the defendant has the burden of proof. Even though the defendant's error was not intentional in this case, this was not by itself sufficient to entitle him to a bona fide error defense, as it also requires him to show he maintains "reasonably adapted" procedures to avoid such errors. None of the measures recited by the defendant demonstrated any procedures in place at the time the error occurred that were reasonably adapted to avoid the specific error at issue. "In the present case, Defendant's expertise and training notwithstanding, the record is devoid of explanation of any measures used to avoid computer glitches such as occurred in this case or of avoiding sending letters that accidentally omitted certain FDCPA required warnings."

McClenning v. NCO Fin. Sys., Inc., 2010 WL 4795269 (C.D. Cal. Nov. 15, 2010). With respect to an alleged violation of § 1692c(c), the defendant raised a triable issue of fact as to whether communications made by defendant to the plaintiff were the result of bona fide error where the debt was placed with it a second time by mistake by the creditor.

Owings v. Hunt & Henriques, 2010 WL 3489342 (S.D. Cal. Sept. 3, 2010). A debt collector must show that reliance on the creditor's information was reasonable "on the basis of procedures maintained to avoid mistakes" that were put into place. Where the collector provided no evidence of any procedures maintained to avoid mistakes and no reason for its reliance on the creditor's information, it failed to meet its burden for a summary judgment in its favor.

Arteaga v. Asset Acceptance, L.L.C., 2010 WL 3310259 (E.D. Cal. Aug. 23, 2010). Summary judgment was granted to the collector on § 1692e claims that the collector unlawfully threatened to attach the consumer's bank account since, even if a jury believed that the collector made the alleged threat, the defendant was entitled to the bona fide error defense. The consumer failed to controvert the defendant's evidence that it "had policies and procedures in place that were reasonably adapted to avoid false representations made to consumers, or implications that Asset would attach a consumer's bank account if a debt was not paid without the legal right to do so."

Johnson v. Professional Collection Consultants, 2010 WL 2196571 (S.D. Cal. May 28, 2010). Evidence establishing that the defendant monitored returned mail to determine whether or not a validation notice was returned was insufficient to satisfy its burden of showing the absence of a genuine issue of material fact as to the bona fide error defense. The defendant submitted no evidence of procedures designed to verify the accuracy of an address received from a creditor prior to mailing letters to the debtor.

Riley v. Giguiere, 631 F. Supp. 2d 1295 (E.D. Cal. 2009). Court rejected "intentional infliction" standard by reference to standards applied in FCRA cases, as well as reference to the factors listed in § 1692k(c).

Durham v. Continental Cent. Credit, 2009 WL 3416114 (S.D. Cal. Oct. 20, 2009). The fact that corrective procedures had been put into place suggests that there were no safeguards previously in place to establish a bona fide error defense. The fact that the debt collector's employees received training upon being hired does not establish that the collector had implemented policies and procedures to ensure compliance with the FDCPA.

Palmer v. Stassinos, 2009 WL 86705 (N.D. Cal. Jan. 9, 2009). In the Ninth Circuit a mistake of law cannot alone be the basis for a bona fide error defense.

Taylor v. Quall, 471 F. Supp. 2d 1053 (C.D. Cal. 2007). Granted the consumer's motion under Rule 56(f) for a continuance to conduct discovery on the underlying factual basis of the defendants' asserted bona fide error defense.

Holsinger v. Wolpoff & Abramson, L.L.P., 2006 U.S. Dist. LEXIS 55406 (N.D. Cal. July 27, 2006). Where the collection law firm had not presented any evidence that the inclusion or amount of attorney fees resulted from a bona fide error, the court granted the consumer partial summary judgment and barred the debt collector from asserting the bona fide error defense with respect to its collection of attorney fees.

Palmer v. I.C. Sys., Inc., 2005 WL 3001877 (N.D. Cal. Nov. 8, 2005). Where creditor is required to warrant that it is forwarding only amounts that are validly due and owing, collector successfully asserted the bona fide error defense.

Newman v. CheckRite California, Inc., 912 F. Supp. 1354 (E.D. Cal. 1995). The bona fide error defense was not available for following a collector's procedures that violated the Act.

Connecticut

Silver v. Law Offices of Howard Lee Schiff, P.C., 2010 WL 3000053 (D. Conn. July 28, 2010). The court found that it was a question for the jury as to whether the defendant could meet the four prongs of the bona fide error defense where the defendant posted the payment to the wrong account and consumer called the wrong posting to the defendant's attention at least twice.

Herbert v. Monterey Fin. Servs., Inc., 2001 U.S. Dist. LEXIS 17338 (D. Conn. Sept. 28, 2001). After bench trial, the court found that defendant's error in failing, for four years, to report to credit

bureaus that the debt was disputed was the type of "bona fide error" that was "bound to occur" despite a human procedure for calling the dispute to the attention of a manager who then had to specifically direct computer operators to enter a dispute code. Defendant's procedures were (1) training which directed the collector to call a dispute to the manager's attention and (2) managers walking around the collection floor to be sure that guidelines were followed. The court cited no authority for its conclusion, which is contrary to the statute and case law. Plaintiff moved for reconsideration and planned to appeal.

Stebbins v. Allied Account Servs., 1992 U.S. Dist. LEXIS 22760 (D. Conn. June 23, 1992). To establish a bona fide error defense the debt collector must prove that (1) the violation was unintentional; (2) it was a bona fide error; (3) it was not a legal error, e.g., the error did not result from ignorance of the law; and (4) collector maintained procedures reasonably adapted to avoid such error. Because the debt collector failed to demonstrate procedures to prevent violations, its assertion that the notices violated the FDCPA in less than 1% of the cases did not excuse the collector's violation.

Cacace v. Lucas, 775 F. Supp. 502 (D. Conn. 1990). An attorney who mistakenly demanded more than twice the actual amount owed could not establish a bona fide error defense where he did not show the maintenance of any procedures to avoid such errors.

Garrick v. Hosp. Collection Servs., 1990 U.S. Dist. LEXIS 20961 (D. Conn. Jan. 31, 1990). Only clerical errors, not mistakes of law, may constitute bona fide errors. A collector who failed to meet its burden of showing, by a preponderance of the evidence, procedures reasonably adapted to avoid such errors, cannot claim this defense.

Butler v. Int'l Collection Serv., Inc., 1989 U.S. Dist. LEXIS 19102 (D. Conn. June 6, 1989). While a collector made an error in claiming a $15 illegal charge added by the creditor to claim without the collector's knowledge, the debt collector's contractual agreement that the creditor not add illegal charges was not a procedure reasonably adopted to avoid the error.

Stewart v. Salzman, 1987 U.S. Dist. LEXIS 16865 (D. Conn. Nov. 2, 1987). The bona fide error defense was not available where there was no evidence of procedures reasonably adapted to avoid such error and the collector made a mistake of law.

Baker v. I.C. Sys., Inc., 2009 WL 1365002 (Conn. Super. Ct. May 11, 2009). No bona fide error defense where debt collector called third parties without the consumer's permission and after consumer provided location information.

Delaware

Sutton v. Law Offices of Alexander L. Lawrence, 1992 U.S. Dist. LEXIS 22761 (D. Del. June 17, 1992). Bona fide error defense did not apply where defendant law office failed to provide any evidence that the requisite disclosure under §§ 1692e(11) or 1692(g) were normally included in correspondence directed at debtors.

Hubbard v. Nat'l Bond & Collection Assocs., 126 B.R. 422, 427 (D. Del. 1991), aff'd, 947 F.2d 935 (3d Cir. 1991). "Bona fide error" defense was an affirmative defense applicable where debt collector's violation arose from an unintentional clerical error despite maintaining reasonable preventative measures.

Florida

Kelemen v. Professional Collection Sys., 2011 WL 31396 (M.D. Fla. Jan. 4, 2011). The court denied summary judgment to the defendant on its bona fide error defense with respect to the claim that it violated § 1692e(2)(A) by collecting an invalid debt. While the defendant stated that it acted based upon its reliance on information provided by the referring creditor, the court found that the defendant failed to explain its policies and procedures adequately and that therefore a genuine issue of material fact existed as to whether the policies were reasonable.

Bacelli v. MFP, Inc., 2010 WL 2985699 (M.D. Fla. July 28, 2010). Debt collector not entitled to summary judgment on bona fide error defense. Section 1692k(c) does not require debt collectors to take every conceivable precaution to avoid errors; rather, it requires only reasonable precaution. The required procedures must be reasonably adapted to avoid the specific error at issue. Moreover, the procedures, along with the manner in which they were adapted to avoid the error, must be explained. A conclusory declaration that the debt collector maintained procedures to avoid error is insufficient. The debt collector defendant presented no evidence of an agreement or understanding with the creditor that it would not refer accounts in bankruptcy and no evidence that its reliance on the creditor had proved effective in avoiding errors in the past.

Knighten v. Palisades Collections, L.L.C., 2010 WL 2696768 (S.D. Fla. July 6, 2010). The court found that the bona fide error defense was unavailable to a lawyer who filed a time-barred lawsuit for a party that lacked standing. Even though attorneys, legal assistants, and the clients themselves reviewed the documents of the lawsuit to confirm their accuracy, "[n]either the attorney nor the legal assistant noticed the error of filing suit in the name of an entity that never owned the account, as it would not be obvious from the pleadings and exhibits themselves. . . . If the error would not be obvious to those checking it, it cannot follow that the procedures in place were reasonable, nor sufficient to prevent this error from occurring."

Magnuson v. NCC Bus. Servs., Inc., 2010 WL 2366535 (M.D. Fla. June 11, 2010). The court denied the consumer's summary judgment motion on the claim that the defendant violated § 1692b(3) by calling the consumer's parents twice, since evidence that the collector did not know that the telephone number called was a second line at the parents' home presented a jury question on the bona fide error defense.

Rhinehart v. CBE Group, Inc., 2010 WL 2158282 (M.D. Fla. May 27, 2010). The court found that the bona fide error defense was available where the debt collector's error in calling a third party was unintentional and occurred despite procedures reasonably adapted to avoid an FDCPA violation. "[A]creditor's procedures need not be foolproof."

Nicholas v. Nationwide Credit, Inc., 2010 WL 503071 (S.D. Fla. Feb. 8, 2010). Summary judgment denied on bona fide error defense. "While has made a legal argument regarding this defense, it has presented no factual evidence that it actually relied on this mistaken belief, or that it maintained any procedures designed to avoid such an error. *Cf.* United States v. Smith, 918 F.2d 1551, 1562 (11th Cir. 1990) ('[S]tatements and arguments of counsel are not evidence.')."

Pincus v. Law Offices of Erskine & Fleisher, 2010 WL 286790 (S.D. Fla. Jan. 19, 2010). Debt collection law firm's motion for summary judgment on its bona fide error defense to having unlawfully filed a time-barred state court collection action was denied since its "intent or lack of intent is a question of fact which the Court is unable to determine on this record as a matter of law."

Gaisser v. Portfolio Recovery Assocs., L.L.C., 593 F. Supp. 2d 1297 (S.D. Fla. 2009). Attorney's bona fide error defense presented questions of fact as to whether he maintained procedures reasonably adapted to prevent the filing of collection suits in Florida barred by the New Hampshire statute of limitations, and whether his conduct was intentional was a question for the jury.

Hepsen v. J.C. Christensen & Assocs., Inc., 2009 WL 3064865 (M.D. Fla. Sept. 22, 2009). To avail itself of the bona fide error defense, a debt collector must maintain "reasonable preventive procedures" aimed at avoiding the errors. Reasonable preventive procedures by debt collectors include: publication of an in-house fair debt collection compliance manual, training seminars on compliance issues, detailed pre-litigation review process, and creditor's verification under oath regarding the accuracy of each charge. In addition the procedures must be reasonably adapted to avoid the specific error at issue. Furthermore, a debt collector's mere assertion that the procedures are reasonably adapted to avoid errors is not sufficient to satisfy the "procedures" requirement of the bona fide error defense. A debt collector must explain the procedures and the manner in which they were adapted to avoid error. No bona fide error where defendant elected to name its client as the creditor in demand letters. It followed this practice even when a client was a debt collector under the FDCPA. Defendant did not show that it maintained adequate safeguards designed to prevent the misstatement of the debt amount. It did not require its clients to certify that the account information is true and accurate. Its account balancing system merely verified that any adjustments received from a client were posted correctly. In light of the numerous interest adjustments to plaintiff's account, it might have been prudent to confirm the accuracy of the debt amount with its client. Nonetheless, defendant's policy did not require such confirmation. Thus, defendant did not establish that it maintained procedures reasonably adapted to avoid misstating the amount of debt in its demand letter to plaintiff. Defendant's reliance on debt information from its client may not act as substitute for the maintenance of adequate procedures to avoid future mistakes.

Brazier v. Law Offices of Mitchell N. Kay, P.C., 2009 WL 764161 (M.D. Fla. Mar. 19, 2009). Summary judgment denied where plaintiff contends that attorney acted in bad faith by placing the disclaimer on the back of the letter, out of sight from the letterhead and the initial impression of the letter's authority, which creates disputed issue of fact.

Berg v. Merchants Ass'n Collection Div., Inc., 586 F. Supp. 2d 1336 (S.D. Fla. 2008). The plaintiff's allegation that the defendant knew or had reason to know that unauthorized third parties might hear the pre-recorded voicemail message that disclosed that the plaintiff allegedly owed the subject debt created a factual dispute as to the defendant's intent that precluded ruling as a matter of law on the defendant's bona fide error defense.

Pescatrice v. Orovitz, 539 F. Supp. 2d 1375 (S.D. Fla. 2008). Because there was a split of opinion among the lower state courts and as a result the applicable statute of limitations rule was unsettled when the allegedly time-barred underlying state collection suit was filed, the court excused any resulting FDCPA violation as bona fide error of law.

McCorriston v. L.W.T., Inc., 536 F. Supp. 2d 1268 (M.D. Fla. 2008). Credit card agreement that specified that Delaware law applied to substantive matters, including the statute of limitations, controlled the time frame within which the debt collector may initiate the collection action. Although the debt collector was wrong in its choice of the applicable statute of limitations within which to bring its collection action, the debt collector's procedures were "reasonably adapted" to prevent a legal error and established a bona fide error defense pursuant to § 1692k(c).

Valencia v. Affiliated Group, Inc., 2008 WL 4372895 (S.D. Fla. Sept. 24, 2008). The court rejected the defendant's bona fide error defense because the defense requires that the procedures be "reasonably adapted to avoid the specific error at issue," yet here defendant's policy and decision to not identify the caller as a collection agency are "procedures [that] were not designed to avoid the specific errors at issue, i.e., failure to disclose status as debt collector and failure to make meaningful disclosure of identity" but "ather, Defendant's procedures for voicemail message content were designed to avoid a violation of another section of the FDCPA, § 1692c(b)."

Gill v. Kostroff, 82 F. Supp. 2d 1354 (M.D. Fla. 2000). Whether defendant attorney had reasonable procedures to avoid suing the wrong consumer (a victim of identity theft) in the wrong venue was issue of fact for the jury and appropriate for summary judgment. Defendant mailed dunning letters with express instructions to the post office to confirm and, if necessary, update the residential address of the debtors; and relied on information provided to him by the creditor FirstCard, which was normally reliable and accurate. Defendant relied on the most reliable process server to verify the consumer's address information.

Georgia

Sanchez v. United Collection Bureau, Inc., 649 F. Supp. 2d 1374 (N.D. Ga. 2009). The debt collector was entitled to summary judgment on its unrebutted assertion of the bona fide error defense for allegedly misrepresenting the amount of the debt where the collector relied on and restated the amount as represented to it by its client. For summary judgment purposes, [employee's] affidavit regarding the process and procedures utilized by debt collector to avoid making errors in transmitting to the debtor the amount due that it receives from its client rises to the level of a preponderance of the evidence. Plaintiff has offered no facts to rebut or challenge the procedures articulated by debt collector in the [employee] affidavit, or from which a jury could reasonably conclude that debt collector intentionally falsely represented the amount of plaintiff's debt. Accordingly, the bona fide error defense shields debt collector from liability for the FDCPA violation that plaintiff has alleged, and debt collector should be granted summary judgment on plaintiff's claim under the FDCPA."

Canady v. Wisenbaker Law Offices, P.C., 372 F. Supp. 2d 1379 (N.D. Ga. 2005). The court rejected as a matter of law the attorney collection firm's bona fide error defense since, once it had acquired actual knowledge from its process server that it had filed suit in an improper venue, it failed to follow its own internal procedures that required it to abandon the suit and instead intentionally continued to pursue the collection litigation, obtained a default, and pursued garnishment.

Teemogonwuno v. Todd, Bremer & Larsen, Inc., Clearinghouse No. 45,946A, B (N.D. Ga. 1991). Genuine issue of material fact precluded grant of summary judgment where debt collector raised bona fide error defense. Consumer demonstrated prima facie violations of §§ 1692e(2)(A) and (10), 1692f(1), and 1692c(a)(2), but debt collector's assertion of a bona fide error defense 1692c required trial.

Carrigan v. Cent. Adjustment Bureau, Inc., 494 F. Supp. 824 (N.D. Ga. 1980). Good faith error defense inapplicable due to lack of reasonable procedures and pendant state claim on lack of collector's license permitted. Partial summary judgment on liability for both claims for plaintiff.

Hawaii

Bailey v. TRW Receivables Mgmt. Servs., Inc., 1990 U.S. Dist. LEXIS 19638 (D. Haw. Aug. 16, 1990). Sending a dunning letter one day after crediting the payment of the full balance was an excusable, bona fide error.

Sakuma v. First Nat'l Credit Bureau, 1989 U.S. Dist. LEXIS 19120 (D. Haw. Nov. 15, 1989). Collector's incorrect statement that a balance remained on the consumer's VISA account was excused as a bona fide error.

Idaho

Mangum v. Bonneville Billing & Collections, Inc., 2010 WL 672744 (D. Idaho Feb. 20, 2010). The defendant's motion for summary judgment on its bona fide error defense was denied since whether the violation was intentional depended on the disputed fact of whether the defendant communicated debt-related information to the local police department because it thought it was required to respond to a police investigation or to further its attempt to collect the consumer's debt.

Illinois

Bassett v. I.C. Sys., Inc., 2010 WL 2179175 (N.D. Ill. June 1, 2010). The court granted the consumer's motion for summary judgment on the defendant's bona fide error defense for violating § 1692d(5) since the collector admittedly placed thirty-one calls to the consumer over twelve days and thus committed intentional acts rather than the "procedural or clerical errors" to which the defense is limited under the *Jerman* opinion.

Hale v. AFNI, Inc., 2010 WL 380906 (N.D. Ill. Jan. 26, 2010). Where the debt collector offered no indication that it obtained or relied upon (1) the legal opinion of an attorney who had conducted the appropriate legal research or (2) the opinion of another person or organization with expertise in the relevant area of law, for example, the appropriate government agency, the debt collector could not establish a bona fide error defense pursuant to § 1692k(c).

Majeski v. I.C. Sys., Inc., 2010 WL 145861 (N.D. Ill. Jan. 8, 2010). "With regard to pre-dispute procedures, debt collector is entitled to rely on its client's obligation to deliver accurate account information on reported debts." Whether a debt collector's procedures are reasonable is, by its nature, fact-intensive, and should therefore typically be left to the jury.

Herkert v. MRC Receivables Corp., 655 F. Supp. 2d 870 (N.D. Ill. 2009). If the bona fide error defense is available at all for legal errors, it is only available to debt collectors "who can establish that they reasonably relied on either: (1) the legal opinion of an attorney who has conducted the appropriate legal research, or (2) the opinion of another person or organization with expertise in the relevant area of law—for example, the appropriate government agency." Defendants' view of the law, in view of appellate decisions, was "at best wishful thinking." Defendants did not meet their burden to establish that they relied on the "legal opinion of an attorney who has conducted the appropriate legal research." The defendants refused to reveal their attorney's advice. Assertion of a bona fide error defense under the FDCPA acts as a waiver of the attorney-client privilege, since the privilege was not meant to be used "both as a sword and a shield." Applying the bona fide error defense here would essentially reward a business's ignorance of the law.

Acik v. I.C. Sys., Inc., 640 F. Supp. 2d 1019 (N.D. Ill. 2009). The debt collector could not establish a bona fide error defense where it was aware that the un-itemized "Additional Client Charges" contained $60.00 in collection fees and $18.50 in interest.

Basile v. Blatt, Hasenmiller, Leibsker & Moore L.L.C., 632 F. Supp. 2d 842 (N.D. Ill. 2009). Law firm's bona fide error defense to filing a collection action after the Illinois five-year statute of limitations ran presented a question of fact.

Berg v. Blatt, Hasenmiller, Leibsker & Moore L.L.C., 2009 WL 901011 (N.D. Ill. Mar. 31, 2009). Inaccurate and confusing statement of the amount of interest violated the FDCPA, unless excused subject to a bona fide error defense. Defendants offered some evidence of procedures in place to avoid errors in the filing of collection complaints, but were unable to explain how the errors in this case occurred or how their processes of review are reasonably designed to prevent these specific kinds of errors. There is, thus, a genuine issue of material fact as to whether defendants' procedures for reviewing collection complaints and accompanying affidavits were sufficient.

Ramirez v. Apex Fin. Mgmt., L.L.C., 567 F. Supp. 2d 1035 (N.D. Ill. 2008). The collector's § 1692c(c) violations committed over a seven-day period as it continued to contact the consumer while it processed the consumer's cease communication letter were not the result of a bona fide error, since the collector provided an address to which the consumer mailed the letter that required forwarding and built-in internal procedures that delayed activation of the cease communication: "This is not a 'clerical error,' but a loose procedure that resulted in a seven day delay in processing and twenty-one collection calls to Plaintiff."

Ramirez v. Palisades Collection L.L.C., 2008 WL 2512679 (N.D. Ill. June 23, 2008). Five-year statute of limitations for unwritten contracts, rather than ten-year statute for written contracts, applied to credit card account. A reasonable jury could reject or accept defendant's bona fide error defense procedures involving: (1) screening through a timeliness chart indicating which debt accounts were time barred under a ten-year statute of limitations; (2) automated screening by defendants' IT department to calculate

which debt accounts fell within the statute of limitations; (3) additional compliance measures indicating that an account with at least 120 days left on the statute of limitations would be outsourced to collection attorneys; and (4) relying on outsourced collection attorneys to exercise their independent judgment on whether to file suit.

Konewko v. Dickler, Kahn, Sloikowsi & Zavell, Ltd., 2008 WL 2061551 (N.D. Ill. May 14, 2008). Bona fide error defense stricken for failure to allege "the who, what, when, where, and how of the mistake."

Hernandez v. Midland Credit Mgmt., Inc., 2007 WL 2874059 (N.D. Ill. Sept. 25, 2007). The court granted the consumer summary judgment rejecting the defendant's claimed bona fide error defense that alleged that any violation was unintentional and resulted from its attempt to provide a complaint Gramm-Leach-Bliley Act privacy notice because no reasonable jury could find that the violation was in good faith or that the defendant maintained reasonable preventive procedures where the subject notice added language foreign to the Gramm-Leach-Bliley form notice and stated that the collector was collecting and disclosing the information "in connection with collecting on . . . your account."

Nichols v. Northland Groups, Inc., 2006 WL 897867 (N.D. Ill. Mar. 31, 2006). The Seventh Circuit indicated in dicta that it would apply the bona fide error defense to errors of law.

Ross v. RJM Acquisitions Funding, L.L.C., 2006 WL 752953 (N.D. Ill. Mar. 16, 2006). Defendant was granted summary judgment on its bona fide error defense for attempting to collect a debt discharged in bankruptcy where it was uncontroverted that the defendant's assignor undertook to not assign discharged debts, the defendant conducted a public records bankruptcy search before commencing collection, and the defendant immediately ceased collecting the debt once informed that the debt had been discharged.

Hernandez v. Midland Credit Mgmt., Inc., 2006 WL 695451 (N.D. Ill. Mar. 14, 2006). The defendant's claim of a bona fide error could not be granted on a motion to dismiss on the pleadings.

Cross v. Risk Mgmt. Alternatives, Inc., 374 F. Supp. 2d 649 (N.D. Ill. 2005). The debt collector's preventive procedures that it employed in only selective instances based on its evaluation of the character of the debt, whereby it conducted a public records search to determine prior to initiating collection of qualifying debts whether a consumer has filed for bankruptcy, was sufficient as a matter of law to entitle the defendant to establish its bona fide error defense where the underlying debt in the instant case had not meet its criteria and thus the defendant had unlawfully initiated collection efforts in violation of the bankruptcy stay.

Miller v. Allied Interstate, Inc., 2005 WL 1520802 (N.D. Ill. June 27, 2005). Affidavit from the debt collector that it utilized a procedure to search a database on Lexis-Nexis to uncover debtors in bankruptcy created a genuine issue of material fact precluding determination of the consumer's motion for summary judgment.

Gonzalez v. Lawent, 2005 WL 1130033 (N.D. Ill. Apr. 28, 2005). Attorney debt collector's evidence in support of his bona fide error defense for having misrepresented the amount of the alleged debt, including that he reasonably relied on the incorrect information supplied by his client and that the agreement with his client to provide only current and collectible debts, presented a question of fact for a jury to decide.

Kort v. Diversified Collection Servs., Inc., 270 F. Supp. 2d 1017 (N.D. Ill. 2003), *aff'd in part*, 394 F.3d 530 (7th Cir. 2005). The collector's use of letters drafted by the Department of Education was sufficient to establish a bona fide error defense.

Hyman v. Tate, 2003 WL 1565863 (N.D. Ill. Mar. 24, 2003). The debt collector's informal reliance on the creditor not to refer accounts in bankruptcy was sufficient to avoid violation of the FDCPA.

Shula v. Lawent, 2002 WL 31870157 (N.D. Ill. Dec. 23, 2002), *aff'd on other grounds*, 359 F.3d 489 (7th Cir. 2004). Although the collector failed to plead the bona fide error defense, use of a former lawyer's letterhead was not a violation of the FDCPA where the consumer failed to demonstrate any prejudice or harm suffered as a result of the erroneous substitution.

Allen v. NCO Fin. Servs., Inc., 2002 U.S. Dist. LEXIS 10513 (N.D. Ill. June 10, 2002). Collector failed to demonstrate a bona fide error defense where it produced no documents or affidavits of the procedures it had in place to avoid such computer errors.

Wilkerson v. Bowman, 200 F.R.D. 605 (N.D. Ill. 2001). The bona fide error defense was not available to the collector who failed to state the amount of the debt as required by § 1692g, even though the collector's policy was to not collect more than the amount stated. A mistaken view of the obligations imposed by the FDCPA would not support the bona fide error defense.

Taylor v. Unifund Corp., 2001 U.S. Dist. LEXIS 13915 (N.D. Ill. Aug. 31, 2001). Defendant's motion for summary judgment was denied because it failed to provide sufficient evidence to establish a bona fide error defense.

Fitzgerald v. Pekay & Blitstein, P.C., 2001 U.S. Dist. LEXIS 13017 (N.D. Ill. Aug. 9, 2001). Summary judgment entered for the debt collector when the court found that the collector did not waive its right to collect thousands of dollars of interest charges on a student loan previously not billed, had demonstrated that its error was unintentional, and had a computer system in place to prevent such errors.

Withers v. Equifax Risk Mgmt. Servs., 40 F. Supp. 2d 978 (N.D. Ill. 1999). Because the court had previously found the Colorado notice was confusing, and Equifax had previously agreed to discontinue using the Colorado notice, the bona fide error defense was not available to Equifax as to the Massachusetts notice.

Farley v. Diversified Collection Servs., 1999 U.S. Dist. LEXIS 16174 (N.D. Ill. Sept. 28, 1999). Bona fide error defense to excuse the legal error giving rise to the Colorado violation rejected, holding that general attempts to keep abreast of the law are insufficient procedural rechecking safeguards. Mere errors of legal judgment are not subject to the bona fide error defense; court limits the statement in *Jenkins II* that errors of law may be subject to the bona fide error defense to the facts in *Jenkins*, where the error was not one of legal judgment or advice but errors by third parties and thus reconciles *Jenkins II* with the majority rule.

Jenkins v. Union Corp., 999 F. Supp. 1120 (N.D. Ill. 1998). Attempt to collect $25 check service fee on a check on which the consumer stopped payment because of a dispute with the merchant is in violation of state law, which limits such fees to dishonored checks, but violation was not intentional and was excused by the bona fide error defense, since the collector reasonably relied on the creditor referral information which erroneously stated that the check was dishonored.

Cusumano v. NRB, Inc., 1998 WL 673833 (N.D. Ill. Sept. 23, 1998). Based on "clear error" standard, the district judge affirmed magistrate judge's denial of plaintiff's attempt to discover litigation and administrative action against National Recovery Bureau as not pertinent to establish routine practice, intentional nature or frequency and persistence of noncompliance; and not helpful for impeachment or to counter the bona fide error defense. Plaintiff could use the defendant's training manual and collection guidelines for such purposes.

Narwick v. Wexler, 901 F. Supp. 1275 (N.D. Ill. 1995). Bona fide error defense based on collector's affidavit that he reviewed each lawsuit to determine that it was filed in the proper jurisdiction, where the consumer resides or where the contract was signed, followed by a similar review by a clerk, was not sufficient for the court to rule on the issue as a matter of law and would be left for the jury to decide whether it was a sufficient procedure "reasonably adapted to avoid" violation of the FDCPA's venue provision.

Beasley v. Blatt, 1994 WL 362185 (N.D. Ill. July 11, 1994). The debt collector could not invoke the bona fide error defense on the basis that it believed that it was dealing with a commercial and not a consumer account when it was established that the debt collector regularly mailed the identical form collection letters to consumer and commercial debtors alike.

Altergott v. Modern Collection Techniques, 1994 WL 319229 (N.D. Ill. June 23, 1994). Because the debt collector failed to meet its burden of showing by a preponderance of the evidence that its violation of FDCPA was not intentional, that it resulted from error, and that the defendant maintained procedures to avoid such errors, consumers' motion for summary judgment was granted. The bona fide error defense is not available for a mistake of law or mistaken advice from legal counsel.

Oglesby v. Rotche, 1993 WL 460841 (N.D. Ill. Nov. 5, 1993). The mere assertion of good intent, absent a factual showing of actual safeguards reasonably adopted to avoid violations of the FDCPA, was insufficient to establish a bona fide error defense.

Rutyna v. Collection Accounts Terminal, 478 F. Supp. 980 (N.D. Ill. 1979). Mistake of law is not bona fide error.

Indiana

Campbell v. Hall, 2010 WL 3655867 (N.D. Ind. Sept. 9, 2010). Because mistakes of law do not entitle defendants to the FDCPA's bona fide error defense, the court did not excuse a defendant who had improperly required the plaintiffs to dispute their debts in writing.

Campbell v. Hall, 624 F. Supp. 2d 991 (N.D. Ind. 2009). The court held that the bona fide error defense applies to mistakes of law. The court withheld ruling on the defendant's bona fide error defense on the *Camacho* § 1692g(a)(3) violation to allow the defendant additional time to develop the factual record.

Thomas v. Boscia, 2009 WL 2778105 (S.D. Ind. Aug. 28, 2009). Summary judgment granted to the defendant debt collectors on their bona fide error defense to excuse their admitted violation of § 1692e when they sued the consumer after receiving notice of her bankruptcy filing. The defendants "employed numerous safeguards" to identify cases in bankruptcy, demonstrated that this case was the only one out of 3327 where the error occurred because a bankruptcy was not properly flagged, and immediately dismissed the collection case once alerted to the mistake. Summary judgment granted to the plaintiff on the defendants' bona fide error defense to excuse their admitted violation of § 1692c when they communicated directly with her once on notice of her attorney's representation. The defendants' only preventive procedures relied on information provided by the defendants' clients, and thus the procedures were inadequate as a matter of law since they were incapable of cross-checking for attorney representation when, as here, notification was received independently of their clients.

Reed v. AID Assocs., Inc., 573 F. Supp. 2d 1105 (S.D. Ind. 2008). To meet the bona fide error defense, debt collector must show that the violation was unintentional, not that the communication itself was unintentional. Debt collector need not employ a procedure that catches every error before it is made, rather it must have reasonable procedures to prevent errors to succeed in its defense.

Zaborac v. Mutual Hosp. Servs., Inc., 2005 WL 1690553 (S.D. Ind. July 19, 2005). The court found that mistakes of law may be a bona fide error. Where the collector offered evidence of the maintenance of procedures to avoid FDCPA violations which included employee testing, call procedures, and an in-house reference manual, the court found that issues of material fact existed and denied the parties cross motions for summary judgment.

Smith v. Am. Revenue Corp., 2005 WL 1162906 (N.D. Ind. May 16, 2005). Bona fide error defense was insufficient for several reasons, including utter absence of any manuals, memoranda or instructions that related to the FDCPA; conclusory reference to nonparticular attorney review; and existence of letters that could have been used that did itemize all accounts.

Bell v. Bowman, Heintz, Boscia & Vician, P.C., 370 F. Supp. 2d 805 (S.D. Ind. May 6, 2005). The court denied summary judgment to the law firm debt collector on its bona fide error defense for misstating the amount of the debt that resulted from its reliance on the amounts transmitted to it by the underlying creditor, since the law firm produced no information to indicate that it has taken reasonable preventative steps to avoid such incorrect data submissions or to establish that it utilized procedures designed to identify incomplete data submissions from creditors. When a debt collector has had no previous reason to doubt the validity of the debt information submitted to it by the creditor, the FDCPA did not require the collector to have independently verified the validity of the debt to qualify for the bona fide error defense; however, that rule did not apply in this case where there was evidence suggesting that the collector knew or should have know that the consumer debt information uploaded from the creditor was incomplete.

Nance v. Ulferts, 282 F. Supp. 2d 912 (N.D. Ind. 2003). The bona fide error defense does not apply to a mere mistaken understanding of existing law, an intervening state usury appellate court decision.

Dechert v. Cadle Co., 2003 WL 23008969 (S.D. Ind. Sept. 11, 2003). The court rejected the defendant's bona fide error defense because the collector's asserted general practices of staying current with the developing areas of FDCPA law and its broad efforts to comply with the law did not constitute the types of required "procedures reasonably adapted to avoid" violations necessary to sustain the defense.

Bernstein v. Howe, 2003 WL 1702254 (S.D. Ind. Mar. 31, 2003). With regard to the bona fide error defense, the majority view is that it is only available for clerical and factual errors. To the extent that the bona fide error defense is applicable to mistakes of law, the mistakes must not only be unintentional but also reasonable.

Frye v. Bowman, Heintz, Boscia & Vician, P.C., 193 F. Supp. 2d 1070 (S.D. Ind. 2002). Since the form of summons at issue matched summons forms approved by the court clerks, the bona fide error defense would apply to this type of error of law, provided that the collectors could meet the other conditions for bona fide error to apply. If the collectors did not intend to violate the FDCPA and had procedures in place to avoid violating the FDCPA, the error was unintentional, even if the violating act itself was intentional.

Wehrheim v. Secrest, P.C., 2002 WL 31427515 (S.D. Ind. Oct. 9, 2002). Defendant did not establish the bona fide error defense as a matter of law; factual issues remained for trial. "[T]he Defendant's evidence does not establish what person or persons reviewed and proofread the draft foreclosure complaint. The affidavits do not reveal whether Mr. Secrest undertook the drafting, reviewing and proofreading process all by himself, either as a general rule, or in this particular case, or whether he relied on others to perform all or some of these tasks. If he did rely on others, their identities are unknown, as are the kind of education or training they may have had relevant to the error at issue and whether and to what extent they were supervised by Mr. Secrest."

Wehrheim v. Secrest, 2002 WL 31242783 (S.D. Ind. Aug. 16, 2002). Where bona fide error defense was first raised in a reply memorandum in response to a summary judgment motion, the consumer would be given additional time to respond.

Hill v. Priority Fin. Servs., Inc., 2001 U.S. Dist. LEXIS 16900 (S.D. Ind. Sept. 28, 2001). The bona fide error defense did not shield those who simply misunderstood the obligations imposed by the FDCPA. The FDCPA clearly states that the debt collector bears the burden of establishing the bona fide error defense by a preponderance of the evidence.

Bawa v. Bowman, Heintz, Boscia & Vician, 2001 U.S. Dist. LEXIS 7842 (S.D. Ind. May 30, 2001). The attorneys' bona fide error defense failed because the error was intentional. "The form letter itself was prepared and reviewed by Defendants, attorneys in a sophisticated debt collection law practice. Attorneys at the firm routinely review each such letter before it is mailed." Defendant simply misunderstood its obligations under the FDCPA.

Kansas

McDaniel v. South & Assocs., P.C., 325 F. Supp. 2d 1210 (D. Kan. 2004). Whether collector's computerized case management system was reasonably adapted to avoid collection action after notice of a dispute, and whether the continued collection was a clerical error, were questions of fact for the jury.

Caputo v. Prof'l Recovery Servs., Inc., 261 F. Supp. 2d 1249 (D. Kan. 2003). In an opinion highly critical of the conduct of the attorneys in the case, the court rejected both sides' cross motions for summary judgment on the debt collector's bona fide error defense on the basis that neither party "carried its evidentiary burden" or adequately presented its claim in a manner that would permit the court to rule.

Ubben v. Kramer & Frank, P.C., 2003 WL 22472231 (D. Kan. Oct. 30, 2003). Defendant's preventive procedures (not described in the opinion) established its entitlement on summary judgment to the bona fide error defense.

Bieber v. Associated Collection Servs., Inc., 631 F. Supp. 1410 (D. Kan. 1986). Any representation that 75% of a consumer's wages were subject to garnishment was excused by § 1692k(c) since it was completely unintended and the collector's employee had been properly educated on wage garnishment restrictions.

Clark's Jewelers v. Humble, 823 P.2d 818 (Kan. Ct. App. 1991). Debt collector failed to demonstrate by a preponderance of the evidence a bona fide error defense.

Louisiana

Goodman v. S. Credit Recovery, Inc., 1999 WL 14004 (E.D. La. Jan. 8, 1999). Placement of collection letter in an envelope with an incorrect address was a bona fide error.

Sibley v. Firstcollect, Inc., 913 F. Supp. 469 (M.D. La. 1995). Error of law was not a bona fide error. No bona fide error where legal counsel gave bad advice about the need for a collection agency license twice and there was no evidence of procedures to avoid that bad advice.

Byes v. Credit Bureau Enters., Inc., 1995 WL 540235 (E.D. La. Sept. 11, 1995). Discovery regarding collector's policies and practices was relevant to the bona fide error defense.

Maine

Shapiro v. Haenn, 222 F. Supp. 2d 29 (D. Me. 2002). Assuming the subject obligation was a consumer debt, the uncontroverted evidence that defendant collection attorney relied on the loan documents and his client's representation that the underlying transaction was a commercial debt, together with the procedures in place to review such documentation, established the attorney's entitlement to prevail on the bona fide error defense for his failure to provide state and federal notices required to collect consumer debts. The court characterized the mistake as one of law.

Maryland

Sayyed v. Wolpoff & Abramson, L.L.P., 2010 WL 3313888 (D. Md. Aug. 20, 2010). The bona fide error defense protected the defendant collection attorneys from liability for allegedly misrepresenting the amount of the debt since they relied on documentation and a sworn affidavit attesting to its accuracy provided by the client.

Shah v. Collecto, Inc., 2005 WL 2216242 (D. Md. Sept. 12, 2005). To establish the bona fide error defense, debt collector need not prove it had procedures to avoid the mistake of a third party in placing an account that had been paid. Once the consumer brought this to the collector's attention, it promptly investigated and corrected the error.

Spencer v. Hendersen-Webb, 81 F. Supp. 2d 582 (D. Md. 1999). Debt collector's procedures were "woefully inadequate" where computer program automatically added a 15% attorney fee to every account regardless of the agreement on fees underlying the debt.

Parks v. Chlan, 1996 WL 243473 (D. Md. May 3, 1996). As a result of a clerical error, the lawyer sent out a dunning letter for a hospital bill which had already been paid; the letter indicated the amount due was $0.00. When the consumer called the law office, the office acknowledged the mistake and advised her to "tear up the letter." Summary judgment was entered for the collection lawyer on the basis of a bona fide error defense.

In re Creditrust Corp., 283 B.R. 826 (Bankr. D. Md. 2002). Court dismissed car dealer's bankruptcy proof of claim that buyer of his released debts violated FDCPA by attempting to collect on them. Debts were business debts. Bona fide error defense would have protected buyer, which did not know debts had been released and returned them to the seller and removed credit reporting promptly upon verification of their release.

Massachusetts

Gathuru v. Credit Control Serv., Inc., 623 F. Supp. 2d 113 (D. Mass. 2009). The debt collector failed to present evidence of reasonable procedures to avoid not claiming collection fees as owed before they were incurred sufficient to qualify for the bona fide error defense.

In re Maxwell, 281 B.R. 101 (Bankr. D. Mass. 2002). The bona fide error defense applies only to clerical errors. Purchaser of defaulted note relied only on the computerized information it had been given, and produced no evidence to substantiate the defense. "In view of the evidence that [collector] did not have the Debtor's payment history and did not have the Note executed by the Debtor, its utilization of wholly unsupported figures in the demand letters sent to the Debtor cannot be viewed as unintentional. There can be no suggestion of any computational or clerical errors because [collector] lacked sufficient information to make any computation at all as to the amount of the Debtor's obligation to it. Indeed, [collector's] employees strained to acquire information about the Note, going so far as to . . . ask her to get a copy of the Note from the Debtor. Its conduct was not the result of a bona fide error. Its conduct violated the FDCPA and was egregious and inexcusable." In addition to not providing evidence of a bona fide error, the collector was not entitled to the bona fide error defense because it had not raised it in its pleadings.

Michigan

Shields v. Merchants & Med. Credit Corp., Inc., 2010 WL 2613086 (E.D. Mich. June 28, 2010). The debt collector claimed to have reasonable procedures in place to avoid the violation at issue, but the bona fide error defense was unavailing since the collector did not address two essential elements of the defense, namely whether the errors were unintentional and whether they resulted from a bona fide error.

Charbonneau v. Mary Jane Elliott, P.C., 611 F. Supp. 2d 736 (E.D. Mich. 2009). Defendant relied on the information provided by the selling creditor to determine the statute of limitations, which was sufficient to establish a bona fide error defense.

Kujawa v. Palisades Collection, L.L.C., 614 F. Supp. 2d 788 (E.D. Mich. 2008). Debt collectors did not violate the FDCPA by recording a judgment lien on property of the plaintiff who had the same last name as the debtor and by mailing a garnishment release to plaintiff. Even if this were a violation of the FDCPA, the bona fide error defense would apply.

Pietrowski v. Merchants & Med. Credit Corp., 256 F.R.D. 544 (E.D. Mich. 2008). Where the jury found that the debt collector had violated the FDCPA in two of nine alleged violations and found further that that defendant had established a bona fide error defense with regard to these violations, the court stated that plaintiff's request for over $31,000 in attorney fees was "patently unreasonable."

Ruthenberg v. Bureaus, Inc., 2008 WL 3979507 (E.D. Mich. Aug. 25, 2008). The court found that the debt collector had established a bona fide error defense where its notations in the consumer's account history as well as the undisputed fact that the consumer was only contacted once after notifying the debt collector to cease and desist collections.

Dunaway v. JBC & Assocs., Inc., 2005 WL 1529574 (E.D. Mich. June 20, 2005). Collection agency's assertion of the bona fide error defense for its collector's abusive and deceptive telephone calls was rejected as a matter of law since there was no evidence that the collector acted unintentionally.

Moya v. Hocking, 10 F. Supp. 2d 847 (W.D. Mich. 1998). Defendants granted summary judgment on bona fide error defense for violations of suing on and reporting to credit reporting agencies debts barred by the applicable statute of limitations, where evidence showed that the violations were unintentional because the referral information provided by the creditors was inaccurate and the defendants maintained reasonable and adequate procedures to avoid such violations.

Stojanovski v. Strobl & Manoogian, 783 F. Supp. 319 (E.D. Mich. 1992). Where consumer failed to dispute the defense, debt collector's unintentional failure to include the debt collection warning required by § 1692e(11) would be excused by the bona fide error defense. Note, however, that the debt collector did not establish, and the court did not discuss, that such a violation "resulted from a bona fide error notwithstanding the maintenance of procedures reasonably adapted to avoid any such error."

Diamond v. Corcoran, 1992 U.S. Dist. LEXIS 22793 (W.D. Mich. Aug. 3, 1992). Attorney collector's position that he believed in good faith that his letter complied with the law did not establish a bona fide error defense because he failed to demonstrate maintenance of procedures reasonably adapted to avoid violations.

Minnesota

Burke v. Messerli & Kramer P.A., 2010 WL 3167403 (D. Minn. Aug. 9, 2010). An unintentional misrepresentation can be actionable under § 1692e; to rule otherwise would render the bona fide error defense superfluous. Once the consumer disputed the debt, the reasonable procedure to avoid a violation would have been for the debt collector to verify the nature and status of the debt *before*

sending another communication to the consumer expressly stating it was "an attempt to collect a debt." Had the collector followed contacted the bank to verify the debt, it presumably would have learned that the debt had been resolved. Instead of following such a procedure, the collector promptly sent a letter representing that the consumer still owed the debt. Thus the collector did not show that it followed procedures reasonably adapted to prevent the violation and was not entitled to summary judgment on the basis of the bona fide error defense.

Beckstrom v. Direct Merchant's Credit Card Bank, 2005 WL 1869107 (D. Minn. Aug. 5, 2005). Law firm did not violate FDCPA where it removed the mistaken levy upon learning of the mix-up of plaintiff with his judgment debtor son as the creditor provided the collector with the wrong Social Security number and the collector had no reason to know of the error.

Armstrong v. Rose Law Firm, P.A., 2002 U.S. Dist. LEXIS 4039 (D. Minn. Mar. 7, 2002). "The bona fide error defense was not available for a mistake about the law or a mistake in legal judgment."

Kojetin v. C.U. Recovery, 1999 U.S. Dist. LEXIS 1745 (D. Minn. Feb. 17, 1999), *adopted by Kojetin v. C.U. Recovery,* 1999 U.S. Dist. 10930 (D. Minn. 1999), *aff'd,* 212 F.3d 1318 (9th Cir. 2000). Bona fide error defense not available where the collection agency intentionally included in the amount demanded a fifteen percent collection fee not authorized by the consumer's contract with the creditor that only authorized reasonable fees.

Danielson v. Hicks, 1995 WL 767290 (D. Minn. Oct. 26, 1995). Bona fide error defense was established where attorney's letter stated that "attorney's fees of 33 1/3% would be added to the outstanding balance if not paid," in light of state cap of 15% as attorney fees, where error resulted from new computer system, error was not repeated, and error was corrected shortly after mailing of letter. Where consumers raised no evidence that they would be prejudiced by defendant's bona fide error defense in the answer, had it been pleaded, the court allowed the attorney to rely on the bona fide error defense in motion for summary judgment.

State ex rel. Hatch v. JBC Legal Group, P.C., 2006 WL 1388453 (Minn. Dist. Ct. Apr. 13, 2006). Because defendants' misstatement of the service charge continued for a year after it was brought to their attention, they may not be able to sustain a bona fide error defense.

Montana

McCollough v. Johnson, Rodenberg & Lauinger, 610 F. Supp. 2d 1247 (D. Mont. 2009). The FDCPA's bona fide error defense provides a narrow exception to the strict liability rule. The bona fide error defense does not protect a debt collector whose reliance on its creditor's representations is unreasonable. The debt collection law firm failed to establish adequate procedures to guard against prosecuting a time-barred suit. The firm did not have documents on protocol to be followed to avoid FDCPA violations, it did have procedural manuals to follow, or any regularly scheduled training on proper debt collection practices. It relied on the debt buyer's information unreasonably where the debt buyer refused to warrant the accuracy of its information and the collection law firm had previous difficulties with the particular portfolio.

Nebraska

Clark v. Brumbaugh & Quandahl, P.C., L.L.O., 2010 WL 3190587 (D. Neb. Aug. 12, 2010). Summary judgment was granted for the defendant on its bona fide error defense for unwittingly collecting a debt discharged in bankruptcy.

Page v. Checkrite, Ltd., Clearinghouse No. 45,759 (D. Neb. 1984). Check guarantee agencies' routine failure to provide § 1692e(11) notices could not be excused as a bona fide error.

New Jersey

Casterline v. I.C. Sys., Inc., 1991 U.S. Dist. LEXIS 21728 (D.N.J. June 26, 1991). Summary judgment was inappropriate for a § 1692e(8) claim (making a false credit report) as the collector belatedly reported to the credit reporting agency that the debt was disputed. The violation could be excused as a bona fide error.

Kaschak v. Raritan Valley Collection Agency, 1989 U.S. Dist. LEXIS 19103 (D.N.J. May 22, 1989). Even if its actions in a given case are reasonable, collector failed to establish bona fide error defense where it did not show that it had institutionalized reasonable procedures to avoid error.

New Mexico

Billsie v. Brooksbank, 525 F. Supp. 2d 1290 (D.N.M. 2007). Denied summary judgment due to issues of fact as to whether defendant can establish a bona fide error defense.

Bitah v. Global Collection Servs., Inc., 968 F. Supp. 618 (D.N.M. 1997). The bona fide error defense did not shield a collection attorney from the mistakes of a collection agency to which he had given his letterhead and form dunning letters without his close oversight to guard against them being sent out of state.

Martinez v. Albuquerque Collection Servs., 867 F. Supp. 1495 (D.N.M. 1994). Neither a misunderstanding of the law nor reliance on an attorney's inaccurate advice was sufficient to make out a bona fide error defense under the FDCPA.

New York

Henneberger v. Cohen & Slamowitz, L.L.P., 2010 WL 1405578 (W.D.N.Y. Mar. 31, 2010). The court rejected the defendant's attempt to impose upon the bank an obligation to assess the exemption of the funds contained in the consumer's account it sought to garnish. The court found defendant's attempt to restrict the restraint of consumer's bank account to nonexempt funds insufficient to demonstrate entitlement to the bona fide error defense. However, the court found that it was neither unfair nor unconscionable for defendant to utilize New York's post-judgment remedies, namely the restraint upon the consumer's account through the customary garnishment process, to attempt to enforce its judgment.

McMahon v. Credex Am. Inc., 2009 WL 5171888 (W.D.N.Y. Dec. 22, 2009). Viewing the facts in the light most favorable to the non-moving party, and considering the defendant debt collector's bona fide error defense that it has used the "tickler" procedure for ten years to deposit thousands of checks and the instant case was the first time that a post-dated check had been deposited improperly, a jury could find that the procedure employed by the defendant was reasonably adopted to avoid the error of prematurely depositing post-dated checks.

Elder v. David J. Gold, P.C., 2009 WL 2580320 (W.D.N.Y. Aug. 18, 2009), *report and recommendation adopted*, 2009 WL 3459880 (W.D.N.Y. Oct. 19, 2009). Court questioned validity of bona fide error defense where defendant continued prosecuting lawsuit in wrong venue after notice that it was wrong.

Katz v. Asset Acceptance, L.L.C., 2006 WL 3483921 (E.D.N.Y. Nov. 30, 2006). The consumer was sued in an improper venue as a result of a paralegal's erroneous entry of the wrong numerical code into the venue field of the law firm's file. The law firm's evidence of policies and procedures in place to avoid filing collection suits in venues other than where the consumer resides established an unintentional bona fide error, and judgment was entered for the law firm on the consumer's § 1692i claim.

Hernandez v. Affiliated Group, Inc., 2006 WL 83474 (E.D.N.Y. Jan. 12, 2006). Defendant had a bona fide error defense within § 1692k, based on a coding glitch in a mail merge letter, resulting in misplacement, not elimination, of required information, and the coding error was genuinely unintentional.

Johnson v. Equifax Risk Mgmt. Servs., 2004 WL 540459 (S.D.N.Y. Mar. 17, 2004). Collector's assertion of the bona fide error defense based on its reliance on and use of the "safe harbor" language suggested by Judge Posner in *Bartlett v. Heibl* was rejected since the offending language in the collector's dun was not the "safe harbor" language but a different part of the dun. Despite the collector's uncontroverted affidavits that the violations occurred notwithstanding the maintenance of reasonable procedures to avoid them, the court refused on summary judgment to sustain the bona fide error defense on the basis that the "procedures were clearly inadequate given the numerous errors and violations of the FDCPA" and instead consigned the issue to trial as a disputed fact.

Micare v. Foster & Garbus, 132 F. Supp. 2d 77 (N.D.N.Y. 2001). To determine that an FDCPA action was brought in bad faith for the purpose of harassment, the merits of the case must first be determined.

Arroyo v. Solomon & Solomon, P.C., 2001 U.S. Dist. LEXIS 21908 (E.D.N.Y. Nov. 7, 2001). Student loan collector not entitled to summary judgment on it bona fide error defense where its intention to engage in conduct violating the Act was contested.

Tipping-Lipshie v. Riddle, 2000 U.S. Dist. LEXIS 2477 (E.D.N.Y. Mar. 1, 2000). The bona fide error defense was not available; once the validation requirement was violated, strict liability was imposed.

Barrientos v. Law Offices of Mark L. Nichter, 76 F. Supp. 2d 510 (S.D.N.Y. 1999). Mere evidence of maintenance of procedures, absent a showing that the violation was unintentional and resulted from a bona fide error was insufficient.

Villari v. Performance Capital Mgmt., Inc., 1998 WL 414932 (S.D.N.Y. July 22, 1998). To prevail on a bona fide error defense, a defendant must prove both the existence of a bona fide error and the existence of procedures reasonably adapted to avoid such error. Defendant's failure to present evidence that it had procedures in place to prevent violations of the FDCPA left a question of fact to be decided, and summary judgment could not be granted for the debt collector.

Fava v. RRI, Inc., 1997 WL 205336 (N.D.N.Y. Apr. 24, 1997). Bona fide error defense rejected in absence of collector maintaining any procedures designed to avoid the error.

Robinson v. Worldwide Mgmt. Servs., Inc., 1993 WL 367081 (N.D.N.Y. Sept. 15, 1993). Collector's motion to vacate the entry of default judgment was granted where the collector promptly moved to vacate the default and alleged a bona fide error defense, and the plaintiff was not prejudiced.

Read v. Amana Collection Servs., 1991 U.S. Dist. LEXIS 21773 (W.D.N.Y. Jan. 15, 1991). Consumer was granted summary judgment on the collector's bona fide error defense because it relied on a court order and the defense does not encompass mistakes of law and because the violations occurred on forms routinely used by the collector.

Seabrook v. Onondaga Bureau of Med. Econ., Inc., 705 F. Supp. 81 (N.D.N.Y. 1989). The bona fide error defense was not available, absent evidence of procedures reasonably adopted to avoid any such error.

Howe v. Reader's Digest Ass'n, Inc., 686 F. Supp. 461 (S.D.N.Y. 1988). Collector not responsible for creditor's billing error where creditor maintained procedures reasonably adapted to avoid such errors.

Mendez v. Apple Bank for Sav., 143 Misc. 2d 915, 541 N.Y.S.2d 920 (N.Y. Civ. Ct. 1989). Bona fide error defense would probably apply to bank that erroneously garnished a person's wages, since he had the same name, address, and social security number as the actual debtor.

North Dakota

Wilhelm v. Credico, Inc., 426 F. Supp. 2d 1030 (D.N.D. 2006), *aff'd in part, rev'd in part on other grounds*, 519 F.3d 416 (8th Cir. 2008). The collector established a bona fide error defense by showing the amount of the assigned principal and assigned interest was mistakenly entered.

Bingham v. Collection Bureau, Inc., 505 F. Supp. 864 (D.N.D. 1981). The defense of bona fide error was rejected by the court where the collector failed to establish the violations were the result of "error." However, the proscribed use of aliases was excused as a bona fide error since the collector believed it was not violating the law.

LaFrombois v. Valley Collection Agency, Clearinghouse No. 26,295F (D.N.D. 1979). Unopposed motion granted for leave to amend to plead bona fide error defense.

Ohio

Midland Funding L.L.C. v. Brent, 644 F. Supp. 2d 961 (N.D. Ohio 2009). "It is unclear to this Court why such a patently false affidavit would be the standard form used at a business that specialized in the legal ramifications of debt collection. [Defendants] could easily prepare a form affidavit that achieved the same goals without being misleading, by reflecting the truth, plain and simple. Rather than basing the affidavit on false personal knowledge, they could base it on the accuracy of the records kept and the

accuracy of the data." No bona fide error defense where the affidavit form was "prepared by in-house counsel and then populated with data that was obtained from Citibank." "They have provided little or no explanation for how the mistake of preparing a form affidavit that asserts personal knowledge on the part of an affiant who could not possibly have it could be without intent." Defendants completely failed to show any procedure to avoid this error.

Miller v. Javitch, Block & Rathbone, 534 F. Supp. 2d 772 (S.D. Ohio 2008). Bona fide error defense would protect collection lawyers if their state collection action for money loaned was deceptive when it was really based on a credit card as their decision to use that claim was based on a colorable analysis of the law.

Kelly v. Montgomery Lynch & Assocs., Inc., 2008 WL 177525 (N.D. Ohio Apr. 15, 2008). Summary judgment against the defendant where it "vaguely assert[ed]" a bona fide error defense since the measures it had in place were inadequate to prevent the violations that occurred.

Foster v. D.B.S. Collection Agency, 463 F. Supp. 2d 783 (S.D. Ohio 2006). Defendant attorney submitted an affidavit in support of his bona fide error defense which consisted of legal conclusions and his subjective beliefs as to the ultimate legal questions, and was therefore was not entitled to any weight. A debt collector's reliance on the inaccurate advice of its attorney is not sufficient to prove a bona fide error defense under the FDCPA.

Johnson v. Midland Credit Mgmt., Inc., 2006 WL 2473004 (N.D. Ohio Aug. 24, 2006). The debt collector could not invoke the bona fide error defense when it failed to send a validation notice to the consumer after receiving back from the post office as undeliverable its initial communication containing the validation notice since the violation occurred as a result of a systemic failure which took no note of undeliverable returned mail: "The fact Midland does take steps to avoid sending out mail to incomplete addresses does not negate the fact Midland has no process in place to record when mail is returned as undeliverable and no process to send out a new validation notice to a different address."

Edwards v. McCormick, 136 F. Supp. 2d 795 (S.D. Ohio 2001). The Sixth Circuit has explicitly held that the bona fide error defense applies only to clerical errors. Though there is no doubt the principal may lawfully assign his agent the responsibility of performing the "error-catching" procedures required to invoke the protection of § 1692k(c), when the principal himself has an essential role in the actual procedure, an abdication of that responsibility necessarily destroys the effectiveness of the procedure itself. A debt collector may rely upon information provided by his client, and § 1692k(c) will protect from FDCPA liability a debt collector who is not willfully blind to the inaccuracy of such information directly attributable to mistakes of the client.

Taylor v. Luper, Sheriff & Niedenthal, 74 F. Supp. 2d 761 (S.D. Ohio 1999). Mistake of law was a bona fide error defense where attorney collecting for bank sought attorney fees from plaintiff where the state law authority for the collection of the fees was divided. Court reviewed the state's ethical rules requiring an attorney to zealously represent clients within the bounds of the law and to resolve all doubts as to the bounds of the law in favor of the clients. The court commented that an attorney would be presented with an irreconcilable ethical dilemma if an attorney who asserted a claim in litigation in good faith could be held personally liable under the FDCPA. In cases where the mistake of law defense was rejected, the mistake of law was as to the applicability of the FDCPA. Citing Supreme Court language in *Heintz v. Jenkins* and the differences in TILA, court concluded that the "bona fide error defense includes error of law relating to the character, amount to legal status of the debt and the debtor's liability for any interest, fee, charge or expense incidental to the principal obligation and that the defense is not limited to clerical or administrative errors . . . [a] lawyer may invoke the bona fide error defense where the lawyer unsuccessfully but in good faith asserts a claim on behalf of a client." Attorney's affidavit that he regularly attended seminars regarding the FDCPA, reviewed newsletters regarding the FDCPA, reviewed the contract that formed the basis for the complaint and reviewed state law on the issue was sufficient to satisfy his burden of proof that he maintained procedures adequate for a bona fide error defense.

Boyce v. Attorney's Dispatch Serv., 1999 U.S. Dist. LEXIS 1124 (S.D. Ohio Feb. 2, 1999). Section 1692k(c) "bona fide error" defense was not available where the collection agent acknowledged that he intentionally sent the letter to the consumer, but claimed he misunderstood the requirements of the FDCPA.

Sylvester v. Laks, 1991 U.S. Dist. LEXIS 21777 (N.D. Ohio Aug. 1, 1991). Summary judgment was denied the consumer partly because of a factual dispute and partly because of a bona fide error defense where the violation involved the failure of a dunning letter to refer to an alleged separate § 1692e(11) notice.

Gasser v. Allen County Claims & Adjustment, Inc., 1983 U.S. Dist. LEXIS 20361 (N.D. Ohio Nov. 3, 1983). The bona fide error defense failed as it was not supported on motion for summary judgment by any indication that the collector maintained procedures to avoid sending collecting postcards. It was no defense that the collector's false written representations were explained orally to the debtor.

United States v. First Fed. Credit Control, Inc., Clearinghouse No. 33,811 (N.D. Ohio 1983). Even if the bona fide error defense were available in an FTC enforcement suit, it was not available for violations that result from mistakes of law.

Minick v. First Fed. Credit Control, Inc., 1981 U.S. Dist. LEXIS 18622 (N.D. Ohio June 9, 1981). Looking to Truth in Lending Act decisions the court overruled the defendant's defense of bona fide error since the defense was available only for clerical errors despite a system for correcting them and was unavailable for mistakes of law.

Oklahoma

Rice v. Troon Co. Partners, L.L.C., 2009 WL 935745 (W.D. Okla. Apr. 3, 2009). Defendant did not establish the bona fide error defense for the purpose of summary judgment by an affidavit that it "monitors industry publications, attends conferences, and keeps abreast of court decisions regarding FDCPA, that all employees who perform debt collection complete a two-week training class on procedures and FDCPA compliance, and that the training covers company training and operations manuals as well as videos and written materials prepared by the American Collectors Associa-

tion." Defendant "does not explain the procedures used to generate letters to debtors or what procedures are in place to prevent the specific clerical error at issue—an employee of [defendant partnership] allegedly using the wrong computer template or otherwise printing a document on [co-defendant's] letterhead and, without noticing the error despite distinct letterheads, mailing a [co-defendant] letter to a [defendant partnership] debtor."

Bynum v. Cavalry Portfolio Servs., L.L.C., 2006 WL 850935 (N.D. Okla. Mar. 30, 2006). For an error on the part of the debt collector to be "bona fide," it must be made in good faith, inadvertently, without fraud or deceit and with faithfulness to the collector's duty or obligation. A genuine issue of material fact existed regarding the debt collector's bona fide error defense where the consumer's cease and desist the letter was allegedly not received and input into the collector's system for tracking debts in bankruptcy.

Bynum v. Cavalry Portfolio Servs., L.L.C., 2005 WL 2789199 (N.D. Okla. Sept. 29, 2005). The FDCPA does not require collectors to independently verify the debt was not discharged in bankruptcy in order to qualify for a bona fide error defense. Defendant law firm's review and reliance on affidavits that the debt was valid and withdrawal of collection suit upon learning of the consumer's bankruptcy established a bona fide error defense to the FDCPA claim.

Oregon

McNall v. Credit Bureau, Inc., 2010 WL 3306899 (D. Or. Aug. 19, 2010). The court denied the defendant's bona fide error defense. "Defendant CBJC made a conscious decision not to report Consumers' debt as disputed when it reported the debt to the credit agencies. Defendant CBJC was required to do so by the specific terms of 15 U.S.C. § 1692e(8). The failure to report was not an unintended factual or clerical mistake."

Hooper v. Capital Credit & Collection Servs., Inc., 2004 WL 825619 (D. Or. Apr. 13, 2004). Consumer's motion for summary judgment was denied where debt collector presented sufficient evidence of a bona fide error defense to create material issues of fact.

Clark v. Schwabe, Williamson & Wyatt, Clearinghouse No. 44,831 (D. Or. 1990). Secretary's error did not establish bona fide error defense where the procedure the secretary was supposed to follow would have resulted in the same violation.

Lambert v. Nat'l Credit Bureau, Inc., 1981 U.S. Dist. LEXIS 18623 (D. Or. Apr. 8, 1981). The bona fide error defense was to be construed the same as that in the Truth in Lending Act and was therefore available only for clerical errors and not mistakes of law.

Check Cent., Inc. v. Barr, Clearinghouse No. 37,497 (Bankr. D. Or. 1984). Bona fide error defense available only for clerical errors and not for mistakes of law.

Pennsylvania

Gryzbowski v. I.C. Sys., Inc., 691 F. Supp. 2d 618 (M.D. Pa. 2010). As defendant admitted that its violation was intentional, in order to guard against a potential violation of § 1692c(b), defendant did not present a valid bona fide error defense.

Holmes v. Mann Bracken, L.L.C., 2009 WL 5184485 (E.D. Pa.

Dec. 22, 2009). Where defendant sent the communication knowing that the contents could be "deceptive" because such communication could have "two or more different meanings, one of which is inaccurate," the court could not determine if defendant's alleged bona fide error was "unintentional" and/or whether defendant employed "procedures designed to avoid such errors" and denied defendant's motion for summary judgment.

Regan v. Law Offices of Edwin A. Abrahamsen & Assocs., P.C., 2009 WL 4396299 (E.D. Pa. Dec. 1, 2009). Extensive discussion of merits and drawbacks of software used to enter codes to prevent calls to person represented by attorney, but court found question of fact as to defense of bona fide error.

Richburg v. Palisades Collection L.L.C., 247 F.R.D. 457 (E.D. Pa. 2008). "[W]e side with a growing minority of courts that find mistakes of law can satisfy the FDCPA's bona fide error defense." Denied the defendant's motion for summary judgment on its bona fide error of law defense for filing suit on a time-barred debt where it claimed to have misjudged the applicable state law, because a reasonable jury could find that the putative preventive measures taken were insufficient since the collector "relie[d] exclusively on its own interpretation and efforts" in reaching its erroneous legal conclusion.

Cook v. Gen. Revenue Corp., 2001 U.S. Dist. LEXIS 11181 (E.D. Pa. Aug. 6, 2001). Debt collector's motion to dismiss was denied because the consumer alleged adequate facts to state a claim: that the debt had been paid, suit was time barred, and the collection lawyer wrote unobligated relatives about the alleged debt. The collector failed to demonstrate a bona fide error defense.

Pollice v. Nat'l Tax Funding, 59 F. Supp. 2d 474 (W.D. Pa. 1999), *aff'd in part, rev'd in part,* 225 F.3d 379 (3d Cir. 2000). Court had insufficient facts before it to determine if the collector could claim a bona fide error defense for charging more than ten percent interest on water bills, and therefore denied plaintiffs' motion for summary judgment on that issue.

Adams v. Law Offices of Stuckert & Yates, 926 F. Supp. 521 (E.D. Pa. 1996). The court found the bona fide error defense was not available to the collection firm for its failure to include the § 1692e(11) warning as the defendant offered no evidence of specific procedures followed to ensure compliance with the FDCPA. Posting a reminder to include the required language in correspondence next to a word processor, as opposed to a system of proofreading letters, was insufficient to qualify as an adequate procedure to guard against such errors.

Tennessee

Sewell v. Allied Interstate, Inc., 2011 WL 32209 (E.D. Tenn. Jan. 5, 2011). Where the plaintiffs failed to show that the defendants' bona fide error defense had "no possible relation to the controversy," the plaintiffs' motion to strike was denied.

Texas

Toomer v. Alliance Receivables Mgmt., Inc., 2010 WL 5071778 (W.D. Tex. Dec. 9, 2010). Where the parties agreed to voluntary arbitration, the arbitrator found that a collector continued to collect a debt after it was told that the debt was paid. The collector stated the consumer had to prove payment and negotiated a payout of $80

per month. Collector did not establish a bona fide error defense.

Castro v. Collecto, Inc., 668 F. Supp. 2d 950 (W.D. Tex. 2009). Bona fide error of law defense upheld where reasonable lawyers, as this case demonstrates, readily disagree on whether the federal (FCC two years) or state (four years) statute of limitations period applied.

CA Partners v. Spears, 274 S.W.3d 51 (Tex. App. 2008). Where the record contained no evidence that the debt collector instituted reasonable procedures to prevent the error which caused the violations of the Fair Debt Collection Practices Act, the collector was not entitled to the protection of the bona fide error defense.

Tennessee

Dowdy v. Solutia Healthcare TAS, Inc., 2006 WL 3545047 (M.D. Tenn. Dec. 8, 2006). Bona fide error defense is not available where error was not clerical and the collectors knew that the creditor always doubled the debt before referring it for collection.

Utah

Johnson v. Riddle, 296 F. Supp. 2d 1283 (D. Utah 2003). The intent element of the bona fide error defense focuses on whether the defendant intended to violate the FDCPA, not whether he intended to engage in the collection efforts giving rise to the violation. The bona fide element of the bona fide error defense is an objective test to determine whether a reasonable debt collector in the defendant's position would have appreciated that the collection conduct would be in violation of the Act. The defendant collection attorney was granted summary judgment on his bona fide error defense arising from his collection of excessive statutory shoplifting penalties from writers of dishonored check, a practice later determined by an appellate court to be unlawful, because the violation was subjectively unintentional since the attorney initially had thoroughly researched the issue and the practice had appeared to be approved by state trial judges entering default judgments in several cases. The error was a bona fide error that occurred notwithstanding the maintenance of procedures designed to avoid the violation.

Scott v. Riddle, 2000 WL 33980013 (D. Utah Dec. 4, 2000). The bona fide error defense applies to clerical mistakes, not mistakes of law such as whether the shoplifting law applies to dishonored checks.

Virginia

In re Accelerated Recovery Sys., Inc., 431 B.R. 138 (W.D. Va. 2010). Bona fide error defense rejected where collector offered no justification for sending out the letter threatening criminal prosecution on a dishonored check other than ignorance of the law, and offered no evidence that it had any procedures in place to qualify for the bona fide error exemption from liability. To qualify for the exemption, the collector had the burden to show, by a preponderance of the evidence, a greater degree of due diligence and effort than blind acceptance of software purchased fifteen years ago and "assur[ances]" allegedly received "that everything was in compliance." The bona fide error defense presents a mixed question of law and fact.

Clements v. HSBC Auto Fin., Inc., 2010 WL 4281697 (S.D. W. Va. Oct. 19, 2010). The court found that the bona fide error defense failed as a matter of law regarding the calls that were made to the consumer after notification of attorney representation. "[N]one of the measures recited by Defendant in this matter demonstrate that its procedures were reasonably adapted to avoid the specific error at issue in this case. Particularly, Defendant had no system to fix or correct its employee's failure to properly send Plaintiffs' attorney information to management."

Perk v. Worden, 475 F. Supp. 2d 565 (E.D. Va. 2007). Notwithstanding that the underlying obligations were incurred on a corporate credit card, since the consumer alleged that the defendant collection attorneys knew or should have known the debt was incurred for personal purposes, the court held that it "is not convinced that 'the face of the complaint clearly reveals the existence' of the bona fide error defense, as would be required for purposes of a motion to dismiss."

In re Jones, 2009 WL 2068387 (Bankr. E.D. Va. July 16, 2009). "Genuine issues of material fact regarding whether this violation resulted from a bona fide error notwithstanding the maintenance of procedures reasonably adapted to avoid any such error" precluded summary judgment on the defendant's bona fide error defense.

Washington

Kirk v. Gobel, 622 F. Supp. 2d 1039 (E.D. Wash. 2009). "The FDCPA is a strict liability statute, unless the debt collector can prove that it committed a bona fide error."

Campion v. Credit Bureau Servs., 206 F.R.D. 663 (E.D. Wash. 2001). Court found that the defendant's misapprehension of applicable state law was not the result of an official interpretation of state law and therefore was only an error of law that did not amount to a bona fide error defense.

In re Hodges, 342 B.R. 616 (Bankr. E.D. Wash. 2006). Debt collector did not prevail on the bona fide error defense to liability for sending a collection letter which showed the demand for payment through the address window since it maintained no procedures to avoid the impermissible disclosure of this confidential information. The bona fide error defense did not apply to an error of law; but even if it did, the collector had a duty to seek independent, objective legal advice, and the reliance instead on the erroneous advice of the attorney on whose behalf the debt was being collected was not reasonable in light of the attorney's patent personal interest.

Wisconsin

Brzezinski v. Vital Recovery Servs., Inc., 2006 WL 1982501 (E.D. Wis. July 12, 2006). Assuming that legal errors qualify as bona fide errors, the court held that the collector's professed "understanding" that "qualified attorneys" "reviewed and approved" the challenged dun was insufficient as a matter of law to establish that it maintained procedures reasonably adapted to avoid the legal error.

DeMars v. Plaza Assocs., 2005 WL 1847226 (W.D. Wis. Aug. 3, 2005). Defendant established bona fide error defense as a matter of law where it had checked public records for bankruptcy in the case, but the consumer used different middle name/initial in the bankruptcy filing. Defendant stopped collection once told of bankruptcy.

Hartman v. Meridian Fin. Servs., Inc., 191 F. Supp. 2d 1031 (W.D. Wis. 2002). Debt collector's purported misunderstanding of its legal obligations under the FDCPA did not qualify as an error for the bona fide error defense. Debt collector could not avail itself of the bona fide error defense since it did not have in place any relevant preventative procedures.

Borcherding-Dittloff v. Transworld Sys., Inc., 58 F. Supp. 2d 1006 (W.D. Wis. 1999). The collection agency's "Colorado" notice violated the FDCPA absent an explanatory phrase. Transworld had no bona fide error defense. First, it relied on state administrators who did not administer the FDCPA. Second, the district court decision in *Jenkins* was decided two months before TSI's first letter to plaintiff, so it knew of the error of law. Waiting in the hope that the Seventh Circuit would reverse *Jenkins* was a business decision, not a bona fide error. The technical delays associated with overhauling defendant's letters fell well outside the parameters of § 1692k(c).

Booth v. Collection Experts, Inc., 969 F. Supp. 1161 (E.D. Wis. 1997). The term "error" in § 1692k(c) does not include mistakes of law. A bona fide error defense must be supported by evidence that there was an error and it was unintentional. It is not enough to show procedures to guard against errors.

Wyoming

Johnson v. Statewide Collections, Inc., 778 P.2d 93 (Wyo. 1989). Collector could not establish bona fide error defense without proving the existence of procedures to avoid the error.

K.3.6.2 Other Defenses and Counterclaims

Kelly v. Great Seneca Fin. Corp., 447 F.3d 944 (6th Cir. 2006). Consistent with its earlier rejection of absolute immunity for attorneys prosecuting a state court collection case in *Todd v. Weltman, Weinberg & Reis Co.,* 434 F.3d 432, 434 (6th Cir. 2006), the court rejected the defendants' similar claim cast as "advocacy immunity."

Todd v. Weltman, Weinberg & Reis Co., L.P.A., 434 F.3d 432 (6th Cir. 2006). Collection attorneys who falsely misrepresented state of debtors' non-exempt assets in affidavits in support of state court garnishments, when they had no knowledge or information whatever concerning the matter, could not claim absolute immunity.

Delawder v. Platinum Fin. Servs. Corp., 198 Fed. Appx. 369 (6th Cir. 2006). In accordance with its earlier decision *in Kelly v. Great Seneca Fin. Corp.,* 447 F.3d 944 (6th Cir. 2006), the court held that it lacked jurisdiction to hear an interlocutory appeal that a debt buyer's state complaint alleged to misrepresent that a consumer owed a debt enjoyed absolute immunity from the FDCPA "as participants in the judicial process."

Riddle & Assocs., P.C. v. Kelly, 414 F.3d 832 (7th Cir. 2005). The court affirmed the award of sanctions pursuant to 28 U.S.C. § 1927 against the consumer's counsel for demanding $3000 to release a frivolous claim and continuing to pursue that claim which it knew to be improper. The appellate court reversed and remanded the district court's failure to award additional sanctions against the consumer's attorney pursuant to 28 U.S.C. § 1927 holding that the district court abused its discretion in declining to award sanctions for pursuing an unfounded FDCPA counterclaim against defendant's attorneys.

Kropelnicki v. Siegal, 290 F.3d 118 (2d Cir. 2002). The Second Circuit stated: "Where an attorney was interposed as an intermediary between a debt collector and the consumer, we assume the attorney, rather than the FDCPA, will protect the consumer from a debt collector's fraudulent or harassing behavior."

Cousins v. Duane St. Assoc., 2001 U.S. App. LEXIS 5645 (2d Cir. Apr. 2, 2001). FDCPA claims not barred as res judicata since they could not have been asserted defensively in state landlord-tenant proceeding.

Retzlaff v. Horgan, 168 F.3d 495 (8th Cir. 1999) (unpublished) (text in Westlaw). District court's dismissal of FDCPA claim pursuant to Rule 12(b)(6) was affirmed.

Lally v. Crawford Cty. Trust & Sav. Bank, 863 F.2d 612 (8th Cir. 1988). FDCPA *pro se* claim was properly dismissed by district court, perhaps for lack of specificity.

California

Smith v. Levine Leichtman Capital Partners, Inc., 2010 WL 2787549 (N.D. Cal. June 29, 2010). The allegations that the defendants failed to comply with the FDCPA's safe harbor provisions applicable to the subject bad check diversion program stated a claim for relief.

Hutton v. Law Offices of Collins & Lamore, 668 F. Supp. 2d 1251 (S.D. Cal. 2009). The California anti-SLAPP statute, which protects against retaliation for filing protected litigation, did not apply in this case since this FDCPA suit alleged a violation in the defendant's collection letter sent prior to its initiation of collection litigation in state court

Riley v. Giguiere, 631 F. Supp. 2d 1295 (E.D. Cal. 2009). Plaintiff alleged that collection attorney acted as the agent for the plaintiff's former lessor and used improper means in pursuing an unlawful detainer action against him and in seeking to recover a related debt violating §§ 1692d, 1692e, and 1692f. Court held that defendant was not liable, as he acted as an agent.

Welker v. Law Office of Horwitz, 626 F. Supp. 2d 1068 (S.D. Cal. 2009). The mere sending of a debt collection letter, without more, does not invoke anti-SLAPP protection.

Martin v. Law Offices of John F. Edwards, 262 F.R.D. 534 (S.D. Cal. 2009). Motion to dismiss debt collection counterclaim granted for sound public policy reasons, including entanglement in state law issues and involvement of limited resources in legal questions of no federal significance.

Koumarian v. Chase Bank USA, 2008 WL 5120053 (N.D. Cal. Dec. 3, 2008). Defendant removed state court FDCPA action and interposed a counterclaim for the underlying debt. Court assumed supplemental jurisdiction over the permissive collection counterclaim even though the counterclaim did not arise from the same "transaction or occurrence" as the FDCPA claim, because it derived from a "common nucleus of operative fact," in that both claims were related to a single debt allegedly owed to defendant.

Reyes v. Kenosian & Miele, L.L.P., 2008 WL 171070 (N.D. Cal. Jan. 18, 2008). Rejects collection lawyers' assertion that the First Amendment, as a matter of law, protects the filing of a state court complaint from the reach of the FDCPA.

Mello v. Great Seneca Fin. Corp., 526 F. Supp. 2d 1020 (C.D. Cal. 2007). Denied defendant collection lawyer's motion to dismiss finding although anti-SLAPP law could apply, plaintiff showed a reasonable prospect of success on his claim that suit was filed beyond the statute of limitations.

Reyes v. Kenosian & Miele, L.L.P., 525 F. Supp. 2d 1158 (N.D. Cal. 2007). California litigation privilege applies to communications in state court action, so that the state court lawsuit did not violate the state collection practices act. The court did not discuss the FDCPA in connection with the litigation privilege, but noted that the state collection practices act explicitly excludes attorneys from the definition of "debt collectors" while the FDCPA does not.

Rouse v. Law Offices of Rory Clark, 465 F. Supp. 2d 1031 (S.D. Cal. 2006). Court denied debt collectors' anti-SLAPP motion to dismiss the consumer's claims of collection harassment directed against him for a judgment obtained by the collectors against his estranged father. Debt collectors' rights to free speech and petition were not implicated-the suit against the father did not involve his son.

Gorman v. Wolpoff & Abramson, L.L.P., 435 F. Supp. 2d 1004 (N.D. Cal. 2006), *rev'd on other grounds*, 584 F.3d 1147 (9th Cir. 2009). Where plaintiff attorney made factual representations to the court on which it relied, and those representations had no evidentiary support in the record, the court invoked Rule 11.

Cohen v. Murphy, 222 F.R.D. 416 (N.D. Cal. 2004). Debt collector's Rule 60 motion to set aside default was denied because defendant's neglect was inexcusable, and it failed to demonstrate a potentially meritorious defense.

Bracken v. Harris & Zide, L.L.P., 219 F.R.D. 481 (N.D. Cal. 2004). Because the FDCPA is a remedial rather than penal statute, an FDCPA action survives the death of a debt collector and the trustee of the debt collectors could be substituted as defendants.

Irwin v. Mascott, 94 F. Supp. 2d 1052 (N.D. Cal. 2000). Denial of debt collector's motion to serve third-party malpractice complaint against its legal counsel was appropriate because the FDCPA was a strict liability statute, a plaintiff was not required to establish intentional conduct on the part of the debt collector, there was no affirmative defense of reliance on counsel under the FDCPA, and there was no express or implied right of action for either contribution or indemnity under the FDCPA.

Irwin v. Mascott, 96 F. Supp. 2d 968 (N.D. Cal. 1999). There is no fraud exception to the FDCPA. The consumer's intent was irrelevant.

Bochman v. Pugh, 2005 WL 288976 (Cal. Ct. App. Jan. 31, 2005). In rejecting the defendant debt collector's attempt to invoke the state anti-SLAPP statute to short circuit this FDCPA case, the court stated that the instant FDCPA case "would confer a significant benefit on the general public and an ever-growing large class of persons who are finding themselves unable to pay off their debts in a timely fashion. It is in the public's interest that debtors not be subjected to unlawful debt collection practices. Long ago society decided that debtors' prisons are wrong. While unlawful debt collection practices do not physically imprison debtors, they can have a similar effect by limiting the debtor's financial freedom and reputation."

Colorado

Harris v. Anderson, Crenshaw & Assocs., L.L.C., 2008 WL 1766572 (D. Colo. Apr. 14, 2008). The defendant collector's motion for summary judgment on its counterclaim to collect the underlying debt denied for lack of standing where the collector's affidavit provided no admissible evidence that it was the assignee of the obligation.

O'Neil v. Wolpoff & Abramson, L.L.P., 210 P.3d 482 (Colo. App. 2009). Appeals court reversed the lower court's entry of summary judgment that claim preclusion, resulting from the parties' earlier settlement of the consumer's FDCPA federal court case, barred the consumer's current TCPA claim; the appeals court held that outstanding issues of material fact as to the parties' intent and the interpretation of the scope and intent of the settlement agreement precluded summary judgment.

Connecticut

Murphy v. Equifax Check Servs., Inc., 35 F. Supp. 2d 200 (D. Conn. 1999). Defendant's offer to settle for the complete relief requested and available, $1000 statutory damages plus reasonable attorney fees and costs, eliminated any case or controversy and warranted dismissal for lack of subject matter jurisdiction, though court retained jurisdiction to determine amount of fees and costs.

Gonsalves v. Nat'l Credit Sys., Inc., 1990 U.S. Dist. LEXIS 20944 (D. Conn. Aug. 13, 1990). Failure to include the § 1692e(11) notice in three of five collection letters violated the Act and was not excused by reliance on *Pressley v. Capitol Credit & Collection Serv., Inc.,* 760 F.2d 922 (9th Cir. 1985), which was to the contrary.

University of Connecticut v. Wolf, 2004 WL 2666168 (Conn. Super. Ct. Oct. 26, 2004). Consumer's FDCPA cross-complaint was not barred by sovereign immunity as the state had waived the defense when it initiated a lawsuit against the consumer.

Delaware

McDuffy v. DeGeorge Alliance, Inc., 2000 U.S. Dist. LEXIS 4879, *27 n.15 (D. Del. Mar. 31, 2000). Plaintiffs' FDCPA claims were litigated in an earlier state court decision on the merits and were precluded by res judicata.

Hubbard v. AID Assocs., Inc., 135 F.R.D. 83 (D. Del. 1991). Inadvertence by consumer's attorney in improperly effecting service of process by mail on nonresident resulting in failure of consumer to complete service of process within 120 day period established by Rule 4(j) of the Federal Rules of Civil Procedure did not constitute "good cause" and did not prevent dismissal of FDCPA suit, even though defendant was not prejudiced.

Florida

Marin v. Alvarez, Armas & Borron, P.A., 2010 WL 338839 (S.D. Fla. Jan. 28, 2010). In a suit brought pursuant to the FDCPA and the FCCPA, the consumer's attorney was sanctioned pursuant to Rule 11, in the amount of $21,960 in defendants' attorney fees to be paid by plaintiffs' counsel only and not by the plaintiffs, for

failing to have investigated defendants' status as "debt collectors" before filing the suit.

Chalik v. Westport Recovery Corp., 677 F. Supp. 2d 1322 (S.D. Fla. 2009). A debt collector may still violate the FDCPA while simultaneously following an authorized state procedure.

Conner v. BCC Fin. Mgmt. Servs., Inc., 597 F. Supp. 2d 1299 (S.D. Fla. 2008). Plaintiff and her counsel held jointly liable for award of attorney fees for continuing to litigate the case in bad faith, even after being advised of defendant's valid registration as a debt collector. Court rejected plaintiff's argument that Florida Act prevented the imposition of fees against her (regardless of whether the case filed was frivolous) when she could not be held personally liable for fees under FDCPA.

Agan v. Katzman & Korr, P.A., 2004 WL 555257 (S.D. Fla. Mar. 16, 2004). The court refused to abstain pending resolution of the related state court declaratory judgment case since the two cases raised different legal and factual issues, governed by different bodies of law.

Beck v. Codilis & Stawiarski, P.A., 2000 U.S. Dist. LEXIS 22440 (N.D. Fla. Dec. 26, 2000). Absolute witness immunity protected collection attorneys from false claims in an affidavit of hours spent on prior collection suit.

Sandlin v. Shapiro & Fishman, 919 F. Supp. 1564 (M.D. Fla. 1996). Settlement negotiations which are privileged and inadmissible as evidence under Florida law may still be the basis for an FDCPA violation.

In re Cooper, 253 B.R. 295 (Bankr. N.D. Fla. 2000). Sanctions of $5000 granted to creditor's attorney against the consumers' attorney under Bankr. R. 9011 for the costs of defending against a groundless FDCPA claim.

Georgia

Bailey v. Clegg, Brush & Assocs., Inc., 1991 U.S. Dist. LEXIS 21591 (N.D. Ga. June 14, 1991). Court struck from debt collector's answer language alleging that law firm brought action to avoid consumer's legitimate debts as scandalous.

Illinois

Simmons v. Collection Prof'ls, Inc., 2010 WL 569889 (C.D. Ill. Feb. 12, 2010). Defendant's motion for sanctions against this *pro se* consumer denied with an admonition to treat defendant's attorney better in the future.

Taylor v. United Collection Bureau, Inc., 2009 WL 1708762 (S.D. Ill. June 17, 2009). Rejected defendant's efforts to put its answer and counterclaim under seal lest it violate state privacy laws. State law privileges and protections do not control in federal question cases.

Jensen v. Unifund CCR Partners, 2006 WL 1430214 (N.D. Ill. May 19, 2006). Collector's motion to transfer venue was denied because, unless the balance is strongly in favor of the defendant, plaintiff's choice of forum should rarely be disturbed.

Weniger v. Arrow Fin. Servs., L.L.C., 2004 WL 2609192 (N.D. Ill. Nov. 17, 2004). Defendant attorneys' argument that state court counterpart of Rule 11 was exclusive remedy for the debt collector's abusive litigation was frivolous. State common law litigation privilege did not apply to FDCPA claims.

Crawford v. Equifax Payment Servs., Inc., 1998 WL 704050 (N.D. Ill. Sept. 30, 1998). Defendant's set-off of the underlying debt was allowed because it would not contradict the public policy of the FDCPA or have a chilling effect on the potential claim.

Santino v. Alan H. Slodki & Assoc., 1997 WL 201602 (N.D. Ill. Apr. 18, 1997). Court had no jurisdiction to grant default judgment against defendant alleged to have violated FDCPA where defendant did not waive service under Federal Rules of Civil Procedure Rule 4(h) and was not otherwise properly served.

Brunn v. Gaines, 1995 WL 88799 (N.D. Ill. Mar. 1, 1995). Plaintiff's vague claims that unauthorized insurance had been added to his loan by the creditor failed to state a claim pursuant to the FDCPA against the assignee which sought only to collect the amount assigned.

Altergott v. Modern Collection Techniques, 1994 WL 319229 (N.D. Ill. June 23, 1994). Where consumer failed to show that individual debt collection employees participated in wrongdoing, the employee could not be held personally liable for the violations committed by the debt collection company.

Indiana

Pickard v. Lerch, 2005 WL 1259629 (S.D. Ind. May 26, 2005). Collection attorney could not set-off amount consumer received in a settlement with the collection attorney's client. "It would be unjust for this Court to reward [law firm] by giving it a setoff based on Calvary's independent FDCPA-related actions and settlement with [plaintiff]."

Conner v. Howe, 344 F. Supp. 2d 1164 (S.D. Ind. 2004). The FDCPA did not create an implied or express right of contribution, indemnification, or equitable credit running from the defendant payday lender which settled the state claims against it to its collection attorney who was also a defendant in this FDCPA suit.

Clark v. Pollard, 2000 U.S. Dist. LEXIS 18934 (S.D. Ind. Dec. 28, 2000). The FDCPA claim that the collection agency engaged in unauthorized practice of law in state court would not be permitted where the challenged conduct was permitted by the state courts and not challenged there by the consumer.

Spears v. Brennan, 745 N.E.2d 862 (Ind. Ct. App. 2001). Where the parties' agreement allowed the creditor to recover "reasonable attorney's fees" and state law established that a percentage-based fee negotiated between the creditor and its lawyer was not binding against the debtor, the consumer nevertheless was barred from collaterally challenging the one-third attorney fees requested and added to underlying debt in default judgment, and the mere request for a one-third fee did not violate §§ 1692e or 1692f(1). (*N.B.*: The default judgment in the collection action was entered after the consumer's attorney had entered his appearance.)

Kentucky

Etapa v. Asset Acceptance Corp., 373 F. Supp. 2d 687 (E.D. Ky. 2004). The doctrine of absolute witness immunity for statements made in the course of legal proceedings precluded any debt collector liability under the FDCPA for making allegedly false statement in an affidavit filed in the state court collection action.

Cobb v. Wells Fargo Home Mortgage, Inc., 2009 WL 1636281 (Ky. Ct. App. June 12, 2009). Possible FDCPA counterclaim did not constitute a relevant basis to vacate foreclosure.

Louisiana

Michael v. Banks, 1996 WL 3902 (E.D. La. Jan. 3, 1996). An FDCPA claim was dismissed without prejudice for insufficient service. The consumer mailed a copy of the complaint, along with an acknowledgment form and a prepaid envelope. When an acknowledgment was not received, the consumer failed to follow up with any other method of service. suit and were barred by res judicata in a subsequent suit.

Johnson v. Eaton, 873 F. Supp. 1019 (M.D. La. 1995), *aff'd in part rev'd in part on other grounds*, 84 F.3d 148 (5th Cir. 1996). Consumer's request for information on payment arrangements formed no basis in fact or law for the collector's waiver argument.

Byes v. Credit Bureau Enters., Inc., 1995 WL 540235 (E.D. La. Sept. 11, 1995). The court denied collector's motion to bifurcate liability and damages, finding that it was a tactic to postpone or prevent discovery on the issue of damages.

Maryland

Jones v. Fisher Law Group, P.L.L.C., 334 F. Supp. 2d 847 (D. Md. 2004). *Pro se* consumer filed a series of bizarre documents in connection with defendant law firm's state court foreclosure. Since the law firm was in privity with its clients, res judicata precluded re-litigation of claims concerning the same transaction that could have been raised in state court. Sanctions were appropriate because "[t]he defense of frivolous suits brought by disgruntled losers in properly conducted proceedings should not be an occupational hazard of the legal profession."

Sheahy v. Primus Auto. Fin. Servs., Inc., 284 F. Supp. 2d 278 (D. Md. 2003). Plaintiff's FDCPA and other claims regarding the deficiency on a motor vehicle debt were dismissed based on res judicata where the state court had previously entered default judgment, the claims could have been raised there, and allowing the claims would have the effect of nullifying the prior judgment.

Michigan

Wolfe v. GC Servs. Ltd. P'ship, 2009 WL 230637 (E.D. Mich. Jan. 30, 2009). Consumer's FDCPA claims dismissed when the court rejected his claims that his telephone call log offered as evidence of telephone harassment was mistaken in places and found the call log in no small part a fabrication made in bad faith.

Mabbitt v. Midwestern Audit Serv., Inc., 2008 WL 1840620 (E.D. Mich. Apr. 23, 2008). Following entry of summary judgment for the defendant in its earlier ruling (*Mabbitt v. Midwestern Audit Serv., Inc.*, 2008 WL 723507 (E.D. Mich. Mar. 17, 2008), previously summarized), the court awarded § 1927 sanctions of just over $10,000 against plaintiff's counsel "as Plaintiff's counsel knew or reasonably should have known that the claims asserted by Plaintiff were frivolous." Rule 11 sanctions were denied because the defendant had not sent a "safe harbor" letter, and § 1692k fees were not mentioned or apparently sought.

Smith v. Provident Consumer Fin. Servs., 2006 WL 1999227 (E.D. Mich. July 17, 2006). Consumers who had litigated, appealed, and lost their state court case were barred by res judicata from bringing a subsequent federal FDCPA action alleging the same misconduct since the federal claims "arise out of the same transaction and occurrence as their prior state court lawsuit, a final decision has been rendered in the state court action, plaintiffs' present claims could have been resolved in the state court action, and both actions involved [the same parties.]"

Stolicker v. Muller, Muller, Richmond, Harms, Myers & Sgroi, P.C., 387 F. Supp. 2d 752 (W.D. Mich. 2005). Federal suit alleging that the defendant collection attorney's allegedly false affidavit submitted in support of its claim for attorney fees on default judgment in the underlying state court collection action violated the FDCPA was not barred by collateral estoppel since the federal "allegations do not implicate and are not affected by the issues addressed in the state court proceeding" and the consumer's "liability for the debt does not affect whether the . . . law firm's collection practices violated the FDCPA."

Stolicker v. Muller, Muller, Richmond, Harms, Myers & Sgroi, P.C., 2005 WL 2180481 (W.D. Mich. Sept. 9, 2005). Witness immunity does not protect an attorney from FDCPA violations committed during litigation.

Minnesota

Egge v. Healthspan Serv. Co., 115 F. Supp. 2d 1126 (D. Minn. 2000). State debt collection suit did not bar, on res judicata grounds, claim that defendant violated the FDCPA by threatening to collect usurious interest. The FDCPA claim was not a mandatory counterclaim in state court and did not arise from the underlying debt, but from a different transaction, its collection.

Mississippi

Walton v. Franklin Collection Agency, Inc., 1999 U.S. Dist. LEXIS 7523 (N.D. Miss. May 5, 1999). Collection agency pleaded the affirmative defenses of claim preclusion and issue preclusion, arguing that the claims were already resolved in its state court collection action against the consumers. The federal court disagreed, noting that the FDCPA claims were unrelated to whether the consumers owed the debt, and had not in any event been litigated in the prior state collection suit.

Missouri

Kayira v. Hilco Receivables, L.L.C., 2009 WL 211952 (E.D. Mo. Jan. 26, 2009). FDCPA defendant did not reach a binding settlement agreement with the plaintiff who found the monetary offer satisfactory but refused to settle with a 1099 for the amount sent to her personally.

Nebraska

Jenkins v. General Collection Co., 538 F. Supp. 2d 1165 (D. Neb. 2008). A default judgment in a state collection suit was not res judicata to an FDCPA claim for filing a time-barred suit as the statute of limitations was not adjudicated in the state suit. The FDCPA applied to litigation, the collection suit in state court.

Cabrera v. Courtesy Auto, Inc., 192 F. Supp. 2d 1012 (D. Neb.

2002). Analogizing to an FDCPA case, creditor's counterclaim for the underlying debt in TILA case was permissive, not compulsory, and court dismissed it because it did not have an independent jurisdictional basis.

Nevada

Kuhn v. Account Control Tech., Inc., 865 F. Supp. 1443 (D. Nev. 1994). Collection attorney's counterclaim for bad faith must be dismissed because it was not mandatory and did not arise out of the same transaction or occurrence as the FDCPA case. Collector's argument that the consumer did not receive or did not read the communication was of no moment on the issue of whether a violation occurred.

New York

Raydos v. Cohen & Slamowitz, L.L.P., 2009 WL 2929166 (W.D.N.Y. Sept. 9, 2009). The court lacked jurisdiction under the Full Faith and Credit Clause of the U.S. Constitution to hear the consumer's claim that the defendant violated the FDCPA by filing its state court collection suit beyond the applicable statute of limitations, since that suit resulted in a default judgment that under state law had preclusive effect and constituted a waiver of the limitations defense.

Moore v. Diversified Collection Servs., Inc., 2009 WL 1873654 (E.D.N.Y. June 29, 2009). Debt collector's counterclaim for attorney fees pursuant to § 1692k(a)(3) was dismissed where the consumer had survived the debt collector's motion to dismiss.

Herman v. Nat'l Enter. Sys., Inc., 2008 WL 4186321 (W.D.N.Y. Sept. 10, 2008), *report and recommendation approved in part, rejected in part,* 2009 WL 1874197 (W.D.N.Y. June 29, 2009). In this FDCPA action defendant's affirmative defenses of lack of standing, improper party, reliance on false or misleading representation, unclean hands, and privilege were dismissed. Affirmative defenses of good faith reliance and latches were also dismissed.

Sparkman v. Zwicker & Assocs., P.C., 374 F. Supp. 2d 293 (E.D.N.Y. 2005). Judicial estoppel did not apply where the consumer listed as an asset in his chapter 7 bankruptcy a potential FDCPA claim of up to $1000 but valued it at $0.

Bohensky v. Hosp. Billing & Collection Servs., Ltd., 1999 WL 294726 (E.D.N.Y. Mar. 23, 1999). Court re-opened default judgment obtained by a consumer in an FDCPA action over a year after it was entered and filed in another state for enforcement. The court found that default by the collection agency was not willful, there was a meritorious defense, and delay alone did not establish prejudice, and could therefore be re-opened under Fed. Civ. P. 60. There must be a showing of loss of evidence, increased difficulties in discovery, or opportunity for fraud and collusion. [*Ed. Note:* Some collectors routinely purge their files after a year.]

Robinson v. Transworld Sys., Inc., 876 F. Supp. 385 (N.D.N.Y. 1995). Whether release waived all future FDCPA claims was a question of fact for the jury to decide.

Clovis v. Herald Co., 1993 WL 56017 (N.D.N.Y. Mar. 1, 1993). Motion for relief from judgment pursuant to Fed. R. Civ. P. 60(b) filed 3 1/2 years after entry of judgment denied as untimely.

Nat'l Union Fire Ins. Co. v. Hartel, 782 F. Supp. 22 (S.D.N.Y.

1992). Insurer was awarded attorney fees for time expended in action to enforce note and indemnity agreement including time expended in a declaratory judgment suit determining it was not in violation of the FDCPA.

In re Germain, 249 B.R. 47 (Bankr. W.D.N.Y. 2000). A claim of abuse of process or malicious prosecution for a groundless FDCPA suit would not be allowed against the consumers in whose name the suit was filed where the consumers were unaware of the FDCPA suit or that suit was authorized by their retainer agreement with the lawyer from whom they sought only help paying their bills.

North Carolina

Goetsch v. Shell Oil Co., 197 F.R.D. 574 (W.D.N.C. 2000). Court ordered parties to arbitrate in accordance with credit card stuffer agreement; the consumer alleged an FDCPA claim among many others.

Ohio

Whittiker v. Deutsche Bank Nat'l Trust Co., 605 F. Supp. 2d 914 (N.D. Ohio 2009). No *Younger* abstention where plaintiff does not ask the court to enjoin or otherwise interfere with the pending foreclosure action. Court did not reach issues of preclusion, estoppel, or waiver on a motion to dismiss since they are affirmative defenses.

Amadasu v. General Revenue Corp., 2008 WL 207936 (S.D. Ohio Jan. 24, 2008). *Pro se* plaintiff's FDCPA case be dismissed as a sanction for submitting forged documents.

Barany-Snyder v. Weiner, 2007 U.S. Dist. LEXIS 5137 (N.D. Ohio Jan. 24, 2007), *aff'd on other grounds*, 539 F.3d 327 (6th Cir. 2008). The court rejected the defendants' claim that the plaintiff was "subject to judicial estoppel because she failed to disclose the existence of her claims against defendants when she filed for bankruptcy" because that failure was "inadvertent," based on the finding that the plaintiff "lack[ed] knowledge of the factual basis of the undisclosed claims" and once she "did become aware of her claims she pursued them in a prompt manner." The court rejected the defendants' res judicata defense where the consumer alleged that the defendant collection attorneys had misrepresented in the underlying state court collection suit their clients' entitlement to attorney fees, holding that "the two actions do not involve a common nucleus of operative facts and thus res judicata is not applicable." The court rejected the collection attorneys' claim of litigation immunity for their FDCPA violations that allegedly occurred in the underlying state court collection action.

Foster v. D.B.S. Collection Agency, 463 F. Supp. 2d 783 (S.D. Ohio 2006). Court rejected argument of issue preclusion based on the default judgments the collectors obtained; no issue had actually been litigated. Court rejected claim preclusion because there were different sets of operative facts in state court (whether debt was owed) and in federal court (whether FDCPA was violated) and because the parties in the underlying action were different and not in privity.

Williams v. Javitch, Block & Rathbone L.L.P., 2006 WL 1672897 (S.D. Ohio June 12, 2006). Collection attorneys' motion for Rule 11 sanctions was denied where no authoritative case accepting or

rejecting the specific theory of FDCPA liability alleged in plaintiff's complaint against a debt buyer could be found. The district court's dismissal of several of the same claims against the debt buyer, one of which had been appealed, did not establish authoritative law on the issue.

Martin v. Select Portfolio Serving Holding Corp., 2006 U.S. Dist. LEXIS 24749 (S.D. Ohio Mar. 17, 2006). *Pro se* plaintiffs who were members of a settlement class against the defendant were not barred by the doctrines of res judicata or release from bringing FDCPA case since the violations alleged occurred after the period covered by the class settlement and were not within the scope of the class release.

Kelly v. Great Seneca Fin. Corp., 443 F. Supp. 2d 954 (S.D. Ohio 2005). Finding no "substantial ground for difference of opinion," the court refused to certify for immediate appeal its earlier ruling that rejected the defendant's putative common law witness/litigation immunity defense to its alleged misconduct in prosecuting the earlier state court collection action.

Gionis v. Javitch, Block & Rathbone, 405 F. Supp. 2d 856 (S.D. Ohio 2005), *aff'd*, 238 Fed. Appx. 24 (6th Cir. 2007). The First Amendment litigation privilege or common-law witness immunity does not shield lawyers from FDCPA litigation.

Foster v. Ford, 2005 WL 1645953 (N.D. Ohio July 13, 2005). *Pro se* plaintiff's claim for FDCPA violations was dismissed as barred by res judicata where the current federal claim was identical to the counterclaim asserted in the state collection case that was dismissed on the merits.

Hartman v. Asset Acceptance Corp., 467 F. Supp. 2d 769 (S.D. Ohio 2004). Court rejected theory of absolute witness immunity for false affidavit in state court collection case, analyzing the extant cases. The state law "litigation privilege" did not bar plaintiff's FDCPA complaint arising out of an affidavit filed in state court.

Blevins v. Hudson & Keyse, Inc., 395 F. Supp. 2d 662 (S.D. Ohio 2004). The district court held that attorneys and law firms are not immune from FDCPA claims under the state law litigation privilege or attorney immunity doctrines. The state law "litigation privilege" does not bar FDCPA claims against a collection agency which arise from an affidavit filed in a state court proceeding.

Hartman v. Asset Acceptance Corp., 2004 U.S. Dist. LEXIS 24845 (S.D. Ohio Sept. 29, 2004). Defendant's affidavit asserting holder-in-due-course status in an affidavit in a state collection action on a Citibank Mastercard was not immune from FDCPA claims under state witness or attorney immunity.

Scott v. Fairbanks Capital Corp., 284 F. Supp. 2d 880 (S.D. Ohio 2003). The voluntary-payment doctrine is not a defense to an FDCPA claims.

Sprouse v. City Credits Co., 126 F. Supp. 2d 1083 (S.D. Ohio 2000). Consumer's formal stipulation in state collection suit to judgment on the underlying debt bars him from claiming in federal action that the defendant collection attorney violated the FDCPA by suing him for a debt that he did not owe.

Oregon

Flores v. Quick Collect, Inc., 2007 WL 433239 (D. Or. Jan. 31, 2007). The existence of a default judgment did not bar the court from considering whether efforts to enforce the judgment violated the FDCPA. Issue preclusion does not apply in the case of default judgment.

Grassley v. Debt Collectors, Inc., 1992 U.S. Dist. LEXIS 22782 (D. Or. Dec. 14, 1992). Collector was not entitled to a set-off for amounts previously paid in settlement by two other debt collection agencies.

Pennsylvania

Skoczylas v. Atl. Credit & Fin., Inc., 2002 U.S. Dist. LEXIS 429 (E.D. Pa. Jan. 15, 2002). Collector's motion for summary judgment on consumer's complaint based upon consumer's failure to respond to request for admissions was denied, and consumer was granted permission to respond to request for admissions. Collector's motion for summary judgment on its counterclaim for the outstanding credit card debt was granted as to liability due to consumer's failure to reply to the counterclaim.

Littles v. Lieberman, 90 B.R. 700 (E.D. Pa. 1988). Collection lawyer was jointly and severally liable with collection agency since his violation was separate. The release of the agency did not release the lawyer. Where evidence showed the defendant did not send a dunning letter as alleged, but supplied the form for the letter violating § 1692j, the complaint's claim under § 1692 *et. seq.* was broad enough to cover the § 1692j claim.

Tennessee

Sewell v. Allied Interstate, Inc., 2011 WL 32209 (E.D. Tenn. Jan. 5, 2011). A comparative fault defense may not be raised as to FDCPA claims.

Texas

Naranjo v. Universal Sur., 679 F. Supp. 2d 787 (S.D. Tex. 2010). The consumer's federal action alleging that the debt collectors violated the FDCPA by obtaining a default judgment in the state court collection case when they knew that the debt was beyond the statute of limitations was not barred by claim preclusion since the consumer "is not asking this Court to review or reject the state default judgment itself [but] is complaining about Defendants' alleged practices of bringing time-barred collections actions."

Bray v. Cadle Co., 2010 WL 4053794 (S.D. Tex. Oct. 14, 2010). The court refused to abstain where an FDCPA claim of unfair garnishment was brought while an appeal of the state court's dismissal of the garnishment of Social Security funds was pending.

Burns v. Dodeka, L.L.C., 2010 WL 1903987 (N.D. Tex. May 11, 2010). In an FDCPA suit, defendant's affirmative defenses of proximate cause, failure to mitigate, and exemplary damages were stricken, but its bona fide error defense was not.

Gutierrez v. LVNV Funding, L.L.C., 2009 U.S. Dist. LEXIS 54479 (W.D. Tex. Mar. 16, 2009). FDCPA action, alleging that the defendant debt buyer violated the FDCPA by filing state court collection complaints with an attached false "Affidavit of Account," was not a compulsory counterclaim in the state collection action and therefore was not barred by res judicata.

Eads v. Wolpoff & Abramson, L.L.P., 538 F. Supp. 2d 981 (W.D. Tex. 2008). The collection law firm was not immune from liability under the FDCPA.

United States v. Cent. Adjustment Bureau, Inc., 667 F. Supp. 370 (N.D. Tex. 1986). The court's prior finding, for purposes of determining the amount of administrative civil penalties, that the collector was not in bad faith and undertook efforts to comply with the FDCPA was withdrawn upon the showing at a second trial that the collector's FDCPA testing of its employees was a sham, employees who were the worst offenders were not disciplined and sometimes promoted, and there was no effort to deal with consumer complaints.

Virginia

Cappetta v. GC Servs., L.P., 645 F. Supp. 2d 453 (E.D. Va. 2009). Voluntary payment doctrine is a state law defense that was not applicable, since the FDCPA claim arose under federal law, and to the extent that it was otherwise applicable, the defense was preempted "to the extent the doctrine afforded less protection to consumers than the FDCPA."

Neild v. Wolpoff & Abramson, L.L.P., 453 F. Supp. 2d 918 (E.D. Va. 2006). Res judicata did not bar the consumer's FDCPA claims because the same evidence that supported the debt collector's state court collection claims would not suffice to establish the consumer's FDCPA claims. Collateral estoppel did not bar the consumer's FDCPA claims because defendant had not shown the deception issues raised had been litigated in the state court action.

Washington

Dexter v. Tran, 654 F. Supp. 2d 1253 (E.D. Wash. 2009). In a state court collection action where plaintiff presented a counterclaim for violation of § 1692i and the state court ruled for the collector, plaintiff's subsequent FDCPA action in federal court was barred by claim preclusion and issue preclusion.

Sprinkle v. SB&C Ltd., 472 F. Supp. 2d 1235 (W.D. Wash. 2006). The validity of a state court garnishment could not be relitigated under claim preclusion concepts, but court had jurisdiction over whether events surrounding the attempt to garnish violated the FDCPA and other laws, because those issues had not been litigated in state court.

Sweatt v. Sunkidd Venture, Inc., 2006 WL 1418652 (W.D. Wash. May 18, 2006). Collector's motion to vacate order of default in FDCPA action was granted based on communications between the parties that local counsel for defendant was being sought.

Wisconsin

Braunschweig v. Banco Servs., Inc., 2010 WL 3984659 (Wis. Ct. App. Oct. 13, 2010). Citing *Jerman*, the court affirmed the trial court's refusal to award statutory damages on a mere "technical" violation of a disclosure requirement in light of recognition that the FDCPA was not intended to create a "cottage industry for the production of attorney's fees."

K.3.6.3 Offers of Judgment

K.3.6.3.1 Individual actions

Danow v. Law Office of David E. Borack, P.A., 2010 WL 597213 (11th Cir. Feb. 22, 2010). The court found that the defendant law firm's offer of judgment of $1000 in damages, $2000 in attorney fees and costs, and confidentiality was not more favorable than the judgment entered in consumer's FDCPA action, in which consumer was awarded statutory damages of $1000 without confidentiality. Attorney fees in the amount of $62,895.00 plus costs of $715.60 properly awarded

Basha v. Mitsubishi Motor Credit of Am., Inc., 336 F.3d 451 (5th Cir. 2003). Extraneous communications of counsel established their intent to include settlement of the consumer's attorney fees in an offer of settlement that was silent on consumers attorney fees. Another defendant's offer of judgment was properly rejected by the court where it did not specify the amount of actual damages to be paid the consumer leaving that to the agreement of counsel.

Hennessy v. Daniels Law Office, 270 F.3d 551 (8th Cir. 2001). The court must include an additional amount for the plaintiff's fees when the consumer accepted the offer of judgment that was silent regarding fees and costs.

Burrell v. G.M.F., Inc., 225 F.3d 661 (9th Cir. 2000) (text at 2000 WL 689587). An offer of judgment that was silent on attorney fees would be construed against the drafter defendant and the plaintiff was allowed to obtain an award of fees in addition to accepting the offer of judgment.

Alabama

Streeter v. Offices of Douglas R. Burgess, L.L.C., 2008 WL 508456 (M.D. Ala. Feb. 21, 2008). Offer of judgment in an FDCPA case which attempted to cap actual damages at an indeterminate amount did not moot the cause of action. Offer of judgment in an FDCPA case which attempted to cap attorney fees and costs at a certain amount was not valid because the fees could exceed that amount.

Arizona

Pearson v. National Credit Sys., Inc., 2010 WL 5146805 (D. Ariz. Dec. 13, 2010). Where the offer of judgment clearly stated that the defendant was offering "Plaintiff's cost and reasonable attorney fees now accrued," the plaintiff was entitled only to those fees incurred prior to his acceptance of the offer of judgment.

Tillman v. Calvary Portfolio Servs., L.L.C., 2009 WL 510921 (D. Ariz. Feb. 27, 2009). Because the validity of an offer of judgment ripens only after the entry of a judgment less favorable than the defendant's offer, plaintiff's motion to strike was procedurally improper.

California

Scott v. Federal Bond & Collection Serv., Inc., 2011 WL 176846 (N.D. Cal. Jan. 19, 2011). There is nothing improper about a Rule 68 offer that limits recoverable costs and fees to those incurred up to the date of the offer. Because it was not unreasonable for counsel to continue to accrue some limited fees after an offer of judgment, including those associated with the litigation of a fee motion, the defendant's motion to dismiss the FDCPA claims as moot was denied where the Rule 68 offer provided for costs and fees only up to the date of the offer. The court found that the Rule 68 offer, though "likely beneficial to the plaintiff," did not offer her all that she was legally entitled to recover.

Shaw v. Credit Collection Servs., 2009 WL 4981620 (S.D. Cal. Dec. 14, 2009). The court awarded fees and costs following acceptance of a Rule 68 offer of judgment, but eliminated fees for postjudgment work since the offer by its terms was limited to fees "incurred to date."

Bolton v. Pentagroup Fin. Servs., L.L.C., 2009 WL 734038 (E.D. Cal. Mar. 17, 2009). Even though the plaintiff failed to accept an offer of judgment that provided all of the relief available, the case would not be deemed to be moot since the court's instant ruling adopting the *Costa* standard of emotional distress that now eliminated the plaintiff's claim for actual damages could not have been known before and thus "[a]t the time the settlement offer was made, Plaintiff did not know if the offer was more than his maximum legal recovery."

Ardito v. Wolpoff & Abramson, L.L.P., 2009 WL 449159 (C.D. Cal. Feb. 23, 2009). In this FDCPA case an individual lawyer defendant was granted relief from a mistakenly entered offer of judgment but would not be dismissed from the reopened action.

Bankston v. Patenaude & Felix, 2008 WL 4078451 (N.D. Cal. Aug. 29, 2008). An offer of judgment did not cut off the claim to additional attorney fees where the offer was less than the accrued value of the consumer attorney fees at the time.

Reed v. Global Acceptance Credit Co., 2008 WL 3330165 (N.D. Cal. Aug. 12, 2008). The consumer's rejection of an early Rule 68 offer tendering the statutory damages, attorney fees, and costs requested but minus a set-off for the amount of the alleged debt did "not terminate plaintiff's interest in the outcome of the litigation" and did not render the case moot as "defendants are unable to setoff the underlying debt against plaintiff's FDCPA claims, [and therefore] the Rule 68 settlement offer was not a full settlement offer," since "setoff is an equitable remedy, setoff appears contrary to the established policies of FDCPA, and . . . a counterclaim for the underlying debt would likely be dismissed."

Colorado

Nelson v. Cavalry Portfolio Servs., L.L.C., 2010 WL 1258045 (D. Colo. Mar. 24, 2010). Where the consumer accepted an offer of judgment from the debt buyer's collection agency, his complaint against the debt buyer was dismissed as moot pursuant to agency principles. Consumer's only claim against Cavalry was based on Cavalry's alleged vicarious liability for the acts of National Action, and he did not contend that Cavalry independently violated the FDCPA.

Harper v. Phillips & Cohen Assocs., Ltd., 2009 WL 3059113 (D. Colo. Sept. 21, 2009). Fee award of $9225 at $250 per hour on $2000 offer of judgment.

Skaer v. Nat'l Action Fin. Servs., Inc., 2009 WL 724054 (D. Colo. Mar. 18, 2009). Fee award for 8.5 hours at $250 per hour, as requested, after acceptance of $4001 offer of judgment.

Harris v. Anderson, Crenshaw & Assocs., L.L.C., 2008 WL 1766572 (D. Colo. Apr. 14, 2008). Defendant's motion to dismiss the case as moot based on plaintiff's rejection of its offer of judgment of $1001 plus fees and costs denied since, even assuming the legal validity of the mootness premise, the defendant failed to offer complete relief as it omitted from its offer any recovery for the mental anguish damages that the plaintiff allegedly suffered.

Connecticut

Derisme v. Hunt Leibert Jacobson, P.C., 2011 WL 320302 (D. Conn. Jan. 27, 2011). An offer of judgment for the full amount of damages the plaintiff could recover moots an FDCPA case. However, the court denied the defendant's motion to dismiss the *pro se* plaintiff's complaint in this case where the defendant offered only statutory damages but the complaint also requested actual and "additional" damages.

Rivera v. Corporate Receivables, Inc., 540 F. Supp. 2d 329 (D. Conn. 2008). The trial was partially successful and the jury ruled for the plaintiff only on one of the seven FDCPA claims, which in fact was a claim that was conceded by the defendant, and awarded $1000 in statutory damages. The court then awarded $9200 in attorney fees based on an hourly rate of $325 per hour. This was a 70% reduction of the total time in view of the limited success, but not a reduction based on the plaintiff's rejection of an early Rule 68 offer of judgment because the offer did not cover all of the plaintiff's attorney fees incurred at the time as argued by the defendant.

Florida

Brown v. Kopolow, 2011 WL 283253 (S.D. Fla. Jan. 25, 2011). The court found the Rule 68 offer valid and rejected the argument that Rule 68 was not applicable to an informal settlement offer.

Ortega v. Collectors Training Inst. of Illinois, Inc., 2011 WL 241948 (S.D. Fla. Jan. 24, 2011). The debt collector's offer of judgment in the amount of $1001 did not moot the consumer's FDCPA claim because the complaint sought actual damages for emotional distress in addition to statutory damages.

Muldrow v. Credit Bureau Collection Servs., Inc., 2010 WL 2650906 (S.D. Fla. June 30, 2010). On an unaccepted Rule 68 offer for $1001, the consumer's claims became moot. Judgment in that amount was entered in favor of consumer and the FDCPA claims were dismissed.

Valencia v. Affiliated Group, Inc., 674 F. Supp. 2d 1300 (S.D. Fla. 2009). Rule 68 does not prevent an award of attorney fees if the consumer's ultimate recovery is less than the offer since the FDCPA's attorney fee provision explicitly distinguishes attorney fees from awardable "costs."

Danow v. Law Office of David E. Borback, P.A., 634 F. Supp. 2d 1337 (S.D. Fla. 2009). Court ignored $1000 offer of judgment as a basis to reduce fees because it was not "less favorable" than the $1000 jury award.

Pollock v. Bay Area Credit Serv., L.L.C., 2009 WL 2475167 (S.D. Fla. Aug. 13, 2009). The Rule 68 offer did not provide complete relief to plaintiff as it did not encompass attorney fees and costs incurred after the offer was made. Rule 68 offer did not offer complete relief, since plaintiff sought injunctive relief under state law. Rule 68 offer was ambiguous because of the scope of the release which included nonparties.

Moore v. Hecker, 250 F.R.D. 682 (S.D. Fla. 2008). Debt collector's motion to dismiss as moot after his offer of judgment was denied because the offer was ambiguous as to the persons released.

Illinois

Thomas v. Law Firm of Simpson & Cybak, 2006 WL 2037329 (N.D. Ill. July 17, 2006). *Pro se* FDCPA case would not be dismissed as moot where the defendant's offer of judgment did not make clear the consequences of not accepting the offer.

Letellier v. First Credit Serv., 2001 U.S. Dist. LEXIS 10288 (N.D. Ill. July 19, 2001). Clerical error in offer of judgment was resolved in accordance with contract formation principles and, once clarified as an effective offer of judgment that provided the complete relief to which the consumer would be entitled, following binding circuit authority, court dismissed case as moot.

Taylor v. Unifund Corp., 1999 WL 33541932 (N.D. Ill. Apr. 30, 1999). Motion to strike Rule 68 offer in class action denied. Consumer ordered to respond to offer.

Indiana

Dieske v. CCS Commercial, L.L.C., 2010 WL 3909868 (N.D. Ind. Oct. 1, 2010). Because the plaintiff made no claim for actual damages in her complaint, the defendant's offer of $1000 plus costs accrued and reasonable attorney fees represented the most she could hope to recover. Fees do not include those expended after the offer of judgment, since such fees would not be reasonably incurred.

Cooper v. Verifications, Inc., 2008 WL 5332190 (N.D. Ind. Dec. 18, 2008). The plaintiff who accepted an offer of judgment in this non-FDCPA case was the prevailing party entitled to statutory attorneys fees by, *inter alia,* referring to the parallel language in the FDCPA and the fact that "the Seventh Circuit has found that a party who accepted an offer of judgment in an FDCPA case was successful and entitled to attorney fees. *Zagorski v. Midwest Billing Servs. Inc.,* 128 F.3d 1164 (7th Cir. 1997)."

Gastineau v. UMLIC VP L.L.C., 2006 WL 1131768 (S.D. Ind. Apr. 25, 2006). Defendants tried to force the *pro se* plaintiffs to accept their offer of judgment for $1000 by moving to dismiss claims for actual damages and attorney fees. The court noted that plaintiffs had been represented by an attorney, and after he withdrew, were represented by another attorney. Accordingly, since they might be entitled to recover attorney fees, the motion to dismiss was denied. Since there was expert and personal testimony as to possible emotional distress damages, the motion to dismiss the actual damage claim was denied.

Kansas

Caputo v. Professional Recovery Servs., Inc., 2004 WL 1503953 (D. Kan. June 9, 2004). The court adjusted prevailing plaintiff's fee request in the exercise of discretion and awarded over $87,000 in fees to plaintiff on an offer of judgment of $15,000.

Michigan

Kuhne v. Law Offices of Timothy E. Baxter & Assocs., P.C., 2009 WL 861244 (E.D. Mich. Mar. 27, 2009). Court dismissed the case for lack of jurisdiction where plaintiff did not accept Rule 68 offer that would make her whole; but simultaneously entered judgment for plaintiff in the amount of the offer, and retained jurisdiction to determine attorney fees.

Kuhne v. Law Offices of Timothy E. Baxter & Assocs., P.C., 2009 WL 1798126 (E.D. Mich. June 23, 2009). In this FDCPA case, time expended by the consumer's attorney after receipt of defendant's offer of judgment and its motion to dismiss was not recoverable.

Pietrowski v. Merchants & Med. Credit Corp., 256 F.R.D. 544 (E.D. Mich. 2008). Upon reconsideration of an award of $38,215 as reasonable attorney fees to the defendant as part of costs on its offer of judgment, the court vacated its award of attorney fee to the defendant. Because the FDCPA defines "costs" without including attorney fees, such fees cannot be recovered in FDCPA action pursuant to Rule 68.

Minnesota

Young v. Diversified Consultants, Inc., 554 F. Supp. 2d 954 (D. Minn. 2008). Where accepted Rule 68 offer of judgment specified that fees would be awarded only for the time expended before receipt of the offer, plaintiff could not recover fees for the fee application.

Malm v. Household Bank (SB), N.A., 2004 WL 1559370 (D. Minn. July 7, 2004). Rule 68 Offer of $1001 plus attorney fees and costs for consumer's FDCPA claims did not moot suit that also sought relief under FCRA and state law.

Mississippi

Frascogna v. Security Check, L.L.C., 2009 WL 57102 (S.D. Miss. Jan. 7, 2009). Case dismissed as moot where the plaintiff had rejected the defendant's offer of judgment (in the amount of $2001 plus reasonable fees and costs) that provided all of the relief to which the plaintiff could have been entitled. The complaint's conclusory allegations of emotional distress damages without any "corroborating testimony or medical or psychological evidence in support of the damage award" were insufficient to meet his evidentiary burden once the court's subject matter jurisdiction was factually challenged.

New Jersey

Lorenzo v. Palisades Collection, L.L.C., 2006 WL 891170 (D.N.J. Apr. 5, 2006). Rule 68 offer of judgment of $2000 satisfied the *pro se* consumer's claims for statutory damages and costs (the court found that actual damages did not exist and a *pro se* litigant was not entitled to attorney fees), and the court entered summary judgment to enter the offer and dismiss the complaint.

New York

Clayson v. Rubin & Rothman, L.L.C., 2010 WL 547476 (W.D.N.Y. Feb. 11, 2010). The consumer's refusal to accept an offer of judgment could not support the defendant's claim that she failed to mitigate her damages.

Graffeo v. Revenue Assistance Corp., 2010 WL 502768 (W.D.N.Y. Feb. 10, 2010). Where consumer claimed actual damages, Rule 68 offer of statutory damages does not moot the case.

Shepherd v. Law Offices of Cohen & Slamowitz, L.L.P., 668 F. Supp. 2d 579 (S.D.N.Y. 2009). The attorney fees incurred by the consumer to vacate an improperly obtained default judgment in the underlying state collection action, the "additional fees to right her credit rating," and the charges that she paid to her bank in connection with the defendant's allegedly wrongful attachment of her bank account were among the recited actual damages that a Rule 68 offer would have to satisfy in order to moot the case. Defendant's rejected Rule 68 offer of judgment did not offer all relief requested so as to moot the plaintiff's case, since the offer provided only the maximum $1000 for statutory damages plus fees and costs and omitted any sum for plaintiff's alleged actual damages.

Kapoor v. Rosenthal, 269 F. Supp. 2d 408 (S.D.N.Y. 2003). Time spent defending against an unlawful post-judgment execution in state collection suit was compensable attorney fee after accepted offer of judgment in subsequent federal FDCPA suit successfully challenging that practice.

Greif v. Wilson, Elser, Moskowitz, Edelman & Dicker L.L.P., 258 F. Supp. 2d 157 (E.D.N.Y. 2003). Where the consumer had not filed a class certification motion for the twenty months that the case was pending, the collector's rejected make-whole Rule 68 offer of judgment made to the individual plaintiff mooted the case.

Wilner v. OSI Collection Servs., Inc., 198 F.R.D. 393, 394 (S.D.N.Y. 2001), *rev'd on reconsideration,* 201 F.R.D. 321 (S.D.N.Y. 2001). Judge McMahon initially wrote that she "agree[s] wholeheartedly with Judge Nickerson's reasoning in *Ambalu,*" but on reconsideration found the offer of judgment insufficient to moot the case, as it offered $3000 for damage and fees but the lodestar for the fees was likely to exceed the $2000 offered. Later, Judge McMahon joined the majority holding that a reasonably prompt filing of a motion to certify a class action avoided mootness in a putative class action where the defendant's offer of judgment provided full individual relief to the named plaintiff.

Johnson v. Equifax Credit Info. Servs., Inc., 2001 U.S. Dist. LEXIS 18445 (S.D.N.Y. July 24, 2001). Motion to dismiss based on Rule 68 offer of judgment for statutory $1000 plus fees and costs denied. Plaintiff's complaint sought actual damages in addition to statutory damages.

North Carolina

Tye v. Brock & Scott, P.L.L.C., 2010 WL 428964 (M.D.N.C. Feb. 1, 2010). Ambiguity based on not mentioning attorney fees in Rule 68 offer construed against debt collection law firm.

North Dakota

Wilhelm v. Credico, Inc., 2008 WL 5156660 (D.N.D. Dec. 5, 2008). Rule 68 Offer of Judgment for $1001, although more than reasonable, did not moot the case. The plaintiff was entitled to a trial on the merits and a jury determination on the issues of liability and damages, if any.

Wilhelm v. Credico, Inc., 426 F. Supp. 2d 1030 (D.N.D. 2006), *aff'd in part, rev'd in part on other grounds*, 519 F.3d 416 (8th Cir. 2008). Defendant's Rule 68 offer of judgment which did not include actual damages did not moot the case.

Ohio

Mann v. Acclaim Fin. Servs., Inc., 348 F. Supp. 2d 923 (S.D. Ohio 2004). Neither Rule 68 nor Sixth Circuit precedent precluded an award of fees for time expended after an offer of judgment was made. A $2000 offer of judgment intended to compensate for $1200 in damages plus $800 in attorney fees and expenses fell well short where the attorney fees expended to date was $4600.

Pennsylvania

Andrews v. Professional Bureau of Collections of Maryland, Inc., 270 F.R.D. 205 (M.D. Pa. Nov. 9, 2010). The offer of judgment for the maximum statutory damages, plus reasonable costs and attorney fees that "accrued as of the date of the offer" was not an offer of judgment in the maximum amount that the consumer could recover under the FDCPA, and did not moot the consumer's cause of action. By attempting to limit the consumer to attorney fees incurred up until date of offer of judgment, with no right to recover for time spent in preparing fee application, the collector offered the consumer less than the broad right to attorney fees available under the Act.

Armbruster v. Hecker, 2010 WL 1643599 (M.D. Pa. Apr. 22, 2010). The defendant's offer of judgment of $1000 statutory damages plus fees and costs did not render the case moot since a reasonable jury could find that the defendants' conduct caused the consumer "anxiety, nervousness, worry, and fear" resulting in actual damages for emotional distress.

Linko v. Nat'l Action Fin. Servs., 2007 WL 6882431 (M.D. Pa. Oct. 29, 2007). In this FDCPA action seeking recovery of actual damages, statutory damages, punitive damages, costs and attorney fees, the debt collector's motion for summary judgment, claiming that its offer of judgment in the amount of $4000 satisfied the consumer's claims, was denied because at the time of the offer of judgment what the actual damages were was unclear.

Minnick v. Dollar Fin. Group, Inc., 2002 U.S. Dist. LEXIS 9115 (E.D. Pa. May 20, 2002). Consumer, who accepted a Rule 68 offer of judgment that provided for a sum certain and accrued costs but that was silent as to attorney fees, was entitled under the FDCPA to an additional amount for fees, since the offer failed to exclude fees and since the defendant, if it had intended to exclude fees, should have done so explicitly. Defendant's proffer of extrinsic evidence of the parties' prior negotiations that it claimed would confirm that the parties had not intended an additional sum for fees was rejected, since the accepted offer unambiguously allowed for an additional sum for fees and such extrinsic evidence would only be allowed if the agreement were ambiguous.

Texas

Harrington v. Nat'l Enter. Sys., Inc., 2010 WL 890176 (E.D. Tex. Mar. 9, 2010). Even though defendant's Rule's 68 offer of $3000 was not accepted, court found it satisfied all plaintiff's statutory and actual damages claims, and entered judgment in favor of plaintiff for $3000.

Guerrero v. Hudson & Keyse, L.L.C., 2009 U.S. Dist. LEXIS 4921 (W.D. Tex. Jan. 20, 2009). Citing *Grissom v. The Mills Corp.*, 549 F.3d 313, 319–20 (4th Cir. 2008), the district court held that under Rule 68 any fees or expenses incurred after the making of an Rule 68 offer of judgment were not recoverable unless the offer so provided.

In re Tracy, 2010 WL 5462490 (Bankr. W.D. Tex. Dec. 29, 2010). In this non-FDCPA attorney fee case, the court relied on FDCPA jurisprudence (*Valencia v. Affiliated Group, Inc.*, 674 F. Supp. 2d 1300 (S.D. Fla. 2009)) in ruling that "the cost-shifting mechanism in Rule 68(d) is not triggered" when fees are not part of costs.

K.3.6.3.2 Class actions

Weiss v. Regal Collections, 385 F.3d 337 (3d Cir. 2004). A Rule 68 offer of judgment to the named plaintiff did not moot the class FDCPA claim even without a motion for class certification which would relate back to the filing complaint.

Colbert v. Dymacol, 305 F.3d 1256 (3d Cir. 2003). Third Circuit en banc reversed a Third Circuit panel decision which had held that a debt collector could moot an entire class action by offering full relief to the named plaintiff only through an offer of judgment. *Colbert v. Dymacol*, 302 F.3d 155 (3d Cir. 2002). The vacating of the earlier decision and dismissal of the appeal reinstated the district court decision striking the offer of judgment as inappropriate in a class action and certifying the class. *Colbert v. Dymacol, Inc.*, 2001 WL 34083813 (E.D. Pa. Oct. 2, 2001).

California

Littledove v. JBC & Assocs., 2001 U.S. Dist. LEXIS 139 (E.D. Cal. Jan. 10, 2001). Refusal to accept offers of judgments for individual claims did not make the representatives inadequate. Individual questions of the consumer purpose of their check or the amount of excessive fees paid did not predominate.

Littledove v. JBC & Assocs., 2000 U.S. Dist. LEXIS 18490 (E.D. Cal. Dec. 21, 2000). An offer of judgment to the named consumers in an FDCPA class action, which included injunctive relief and which the collector claimed provided for all relief sought, did not moot the action requiring dismissal because it was not accepted by the consumers. A contrary case was not binding and distinguishable because class certification had been sought in this case.

Florida

Capote v. United Collection Bureau, Inc., 2010 WL 966859 (S.D. Fla. Mar. 12, 2010). In the early stages of an individual FDCPA case seeking statutory damages where the defendant offered to settle for payment of $1001 plus costs and reasonable attorney fees, the court granted the consumer's motion to amend the complaint to assert claims on behalf of a class. The court also denied the defendant's motion to dismiss, stating that even assuming the defendant's offer rendered moot consumer's FDCPA claim, the offer did not include consumer's state law claims, and therefore did not extinguish the entire case.

Sampaio v. People First Recoveries, L.L.C., 2008 WL 509255 (S.D. Fla. Feb. 19, 2008). Rule 68 cannot be invoked where the plaintiff filed a class action complaint unless the motion for class certification was unduly delayed.

Illinois

Giblin v. Revenue Prod. Mgmt., Inc., 2008 WL 780627 (N.D. Ill. Mar. 24, 2008). Where the defendant in this putative class action made a make-whole offer of judgment to the named plaintiff and the plaintiff then moved for class certification within five days (and well within the ten-day Rule 68 pendency period), the motion for class certification invalidated the offer of judgment and kept the class action alive.

McCabe v. Crawford & Co., 272 F. Supp. 2d 736 (N.D. Ill. 2003). An offer of judgment must occur either before class certification is sought or after class certification is denied.

Wilson v. Collecto, Inc., 2003 WL 22299022 (N.D. Ill. Oct. 6, 2003). Motion for class certification within the ten-day period after defendant's offer of judgment prevented the mootness of plaintiff's claim.

Parker v. Risk Mgmt. Alternatives, Inc., 206 F.R.D. 211 (N.D. Ill. 2002). Debt collector's offer of judgment expired when plaintiff filed his motion for class certification within ten days of the offer. A Rule 68 offer to plaintiff individually could not have been accepted by him at any time during the ten-day period without approval of the court pursuant to Fed. R. Civ. P. 23(e).

Whitten v. ARS Nat'l Servs., Inc., 2001 U.S. Dist. LEXIS 15472 (N.D. Ill. Sept. 26, 2001). Class certification granted based on form letter. Motion to dismiss based on Rule 68 offer to the named plaintiff, made while motion for class certification was pending, was denied.

Indiana

Gibson v. Aman Collection Serv., 2001 U.S. Dist. LEXIS 10669 (S.D. Ind. July 23, 2001). Where the defendant in a putative FDCPA class action made an offer of judgment to the named plaintiff individually shortly after suit was filed and the plaintiff filed her motion for class certification within the following ten-day period when the offer of judgment was outstanding, the offer of judgment was stricken since it was in conflict with Rule 23 and could not be considered by the plaintiff.

Iowa

Liles v. Am. Corrective Counseling Servs., 201 F.R.D. 452 (S.D. Iowa 2001). The court denied a motion to dismiss a putative class action based on an individual Rule 68 offer for $1000 plus fees and costs.

Louisiana

Henderson v. Eaton, 2001 U.S. Dist. LEXIS 13243 (E.D. La. Aug. 23, 2001). Debt collector's motion to dismiss was denied because its offer of judgment was made after the motion for class certification was filed.

Minnesota

Harris v. Messerli & Kramer, P.A., 2008 WL 508923 (D. Minn. Jan. 2, 2008). Because the Rule 68 offer did not include any relief

for the putative class, the offer did not give plaintiffs everything that they sought and therefore did not moot the case.

Mississippi

Frascogna v. Security Check, L.L.C., 2009 WL 57102 (S.D. Miss. Jan. 7, 2009). The plaintiff's attempt to avoid the mootness caused by his rejection of a "complete relief" offer of judgment by amending the complaint to add class allegations was unavailing since the offer had been rejected and the case was already moot prior to his attempt to amend.

New Hampshire

Silva v. Nat'l Telewire Corp., 2000 U.S. Dist. LEXIS 13986 (D.N.H. Sept. 22, 2000). Motion to dismiss, based on individual offer of judgment made while motion for class certification was pending, denied.

New York

Morgan v. Account Collection Tech., L.L.C., 2006 WL 2597865 (S.D.N.Y. Sept. 6, 2006). Although the class-action complaint in this FDCPA case had been filed a year and a half before the offer of judgment, the court denied the debt collector's motion to compel acceptance of its offer of judgment of the maximum amount recoverable by an individual where the consumer had expressed the need for discovery (regarding the number of letters sent and the net worth of the defendant) relevant to the motion for class certification and allowed the consumer one month to file her motion for class certification.

McDowall v. Cogan, 216 F.R.D. 46 (E.D.N.Y. 2003). A Rule 68 offer of judgment to an individual plaintiff was not an offer to the adverse party when the adverse party consisted of a class. "[D]efendants should not be allowed to force plaintiffs into hastily-drafted certification motions by making offers of judgment." "[I]f a defendant wishes to make an offer of judgment prior to class certification in the interests of effecting a reasonable settlement and avoiding the costs and inefficiencies of litigation, it must do so to the putative class and not to the named plaintiff alone."

Vega v. Credit Bureau Enter., 2003 WL 21544258 (E.D.N.Y. July 9, 2003). The consumer's FDCPA claims should not be rendered moot by an offer of judgment submitted before counsel has a reasonable opportunity to compile a record necessary to support a motion for class certification.

Nasca v. G.C. Servs., Ltd., 2002 WL 31040647 (S.D.N.Y. Sept. 12, 2002). Debt collector's offer of judgment pursuant to Rule 68 at the initial stages of litigation prior to the filing of a motion for class certification would not moot the FDCPA class action.

Weiss v. Fein, Such, Kahn & Shepard, P.C., 2002 U.S. Dist. LEXIS 4783 (S.D.N.Y. Mar. 21, 2002). Defendant's unaccepted Rule 68 offer of judgment offering the full relief to which the named plaintiff could be entitled after class certification had been denied mooted the action.

Schaake v. Risk Mgmt. Alternatives, Inc., 203 F.R.D. 108 (S.D.N.Y. 2001). Since a Rule 68 offer was not proper in a putative class action, regardless of the pendency of a certification motion, defendant's motion to dismiss was denied.

Edge v. C. Tech Collections, Inc., 203 F.R.D. 85 (E.D.N.Y. 2001). Motion to dismiss based on Rule 68 offer to individual party denied: an offer of judgment ($1000 + $2500 fees and costs) that caps costs and fees did not represent more money than the plaintiff could receive under the FDCPA.

Wilner v. OSI Collection Servs., Inc., 198 F.R.D. 393, 394 (S.D.N.Y. 2001), *rev'd on reconsideration*, 201 F.R.D. 321 (S.D.N.Y. 2001). Judge McMahon initially wrote that she "agree[s] wholeheartedly with Judge Nickerson's reasoning in *Ambalu*," but on reconsideration found the offer of judgment insufficient to moot the case, as it offered $3000 for damage and fees but the lodestar for the fees was likely to exceed the $2000 offered. Later, Judge McMahon joined the majority holding that a reasonably prompt filing of a motion to certify a class action avoided mootness in a putative class action where the defendant offer of judgment provided full individual relief to the named plaintiff.

White v. OSI Collection Servs., 2001 U.S. Dist. LEXIS 19879 (E.D.N.Y. Nov. 5, 2001). Defendant's motion to dismiss pursuant to Rule 12(b)(1) was denied when defendant's offer of judgment came very early in the litigation and before plaintiff, who had indicated in her complaint her intention to pursue the claim in a representative manner, could reasonably bring a motion to certify. It was proper to apply the relation-back exception even though no motion for class certification had yet been filed.

Tratt v. Retrieval Masters Creditors Bureau, Inc., 2001 U.S. Dist. LEXIS 22401 (E.D.N.Y. May 23, 2001). Case dismissed for lack of subject matter jurisdiction as moot where defendant made individual Rule 68 offer of $1000 plus attorney fees and costs before class certification motion was filed. Court retained jurisdiction to determine costs and fees.

Ambalu v. Rosenblatt, 194 F.R.D. 451 (E.D.N.Y. 2000). Case dismissed for lack of subject matter jurisdiction as moot where defendant made individual Rule 68 offer of $1000 plus attorney fees and costs before class certification motion was filed.

Ohio

Stewart v. Cheek & Zeehandelar, L.L.P., 252 F.R.D. 384 (S.D. Ohio 2008). Motion to strike Rule 68 offer granted; defendant could not moot class certification by filing an offer of judgment after discovery and on the eve of the class motion.

Pennsylvania

Smith v. NCO Fin. Sys., Inc., 257 F.R.D. 429 (E.D. Pa. May 22, 2009). Consumer's motion to strike debt collector's offer of judgment to her individually in a purported FDCPA class action was granted.

Wisconsin

Sweet v. Corporate Receivables, Inc., 2008 WL 2953572 (E.D. Wis. July 29, 2008). A motion for class certification filed before expiration of an offer of judgment invalidates the offer of judgment and protects a class action from mootness.

Person v. Stupar, Schuster & Cooper, S.C., 2001 U.S. Dist. LEXIS 18203 (E.D. Wis. July 6, 2001). The court granted a motion to dismiss based on Rule 68 offer made before a class certification

motion was filed. The court ordered disclosure of plaintiff's fees and costs.

K.3.6.4 Debt Collector's Claim for Attorney Fees and Costs, 15 U.S.C. § 1692k(a)(3)

Guidry v. Clare, 584 F.3d 1147 (9th Cir. 2009). On the prevailing defendant's motion, the court held that "the standard for sanctions liability under the FDCPA essentially mirrors Rule 11's 'improper purpose' analysis." Where five of seven of the plaintiff's claims were "frivolous," "baseless," without "even a scintilla of evidence," and thus unsupported in fact or law, the court awarded the prevailing defendant debt collector sanctions under its inherent powers, Rule 11 and § 1692k finding harassment by the plaintiff.

Hyde v. Midland Credit Mgmt., Inc., 567 F.3d 1137 (9th Cir. 2009). Attorney fees and costs may not be awarded under § 1692k(a)(3) against an attorney for an unsuccessful and allegedly abusive consumer plaintiff.

Brooks v. Citibank (South Dakota), 345 Fed. Appx. 260 (9th Cir. 2009). Remanded for factual findings on whether lawsuit was filed in bad faith within § 1692k(a)(3).

Jacobson v. Healthcare Fin. Servs., Inc., 516 F.3d 85 (2d Cir. 2008). Reversed an award of attorney fees against the consumer as one of the consumer's claims was found meritorious on appeal and the consumer's subjective reaction to letter and lack actual damages did not indicate the FDCPA claim was brought in "bad faith," a requirement for shifting the defendant's costs to the consumer. The consumer acknowledged that the underlying debt was valid and admitted that he did not feel "harassed, threatened or misled by the letter." The trial court felt that reflected bad faith. The Second Circuit disagreed: "the FDCPA permits and encourages parties who have suffered no loss to bring civil actions for statutory violations. Jacobson's subjective reaction to the letter, therefore, is neither here nor there."

Ross v. RJM Acquisitions Funding, L.L.C., 480 F.3d 493 (7th Cir. 2007). Sanctions under § 1692k were denied where plaintiff's attorney did not get the details of the successful bona fide error defense until after summary judgment was filed.

Dechert v. Cadle Co., 441 F.3d 474 (7th Cir. 2006). Court had no authority to grant attorney fees to defendant, despite plaintiff's loss of class certification on appeal and unsuccessful sanctions motions. Plaintiff was not a prevailing party merely because of a discovery sanctions award, so the award of fees to plaintiff was reversed. Fees were not awarded to defendant on its cross-appeal; the denial of fees to plaintiff was "sanction enough."

Horkey v. J.V.D.B. & Assocs., Inc., 333 F.3d 769 (7th Cir. 2003). In order to recover attorney fees under the FDCPA, the collector had to show that the entire lawsuit was brought in bad faith and for the purpose of harassment pursuant to § 1692k(a)(3), not just one of the claims.

Huff v. Dobbins, Fraker, Tennant, Joy & Perlstein, 243 F.3d 1086 (7th Cir. 2001). Rule 11 sanctions for relitigating settled issues affirmed against consumer's attorney, who was representing her mother, was affirmed.

Chaudhry v. Gallerizzo, 174 F.3d 394 (4th Cir. 1999). Sanctions of

$5000 against the consumers under § 1692k(a)(3) and their attorney of $10,000 under Fed. R. Civ. P. 11 upheld for pursuing a frivolous claim of deception.

Huff v. Dobbins, Fraker, Tennant, Joy & Perlstein, 1999 U.S. App. LEXIS 12055 (7th Cir. June 2, 1999). Consumer's attorney (who was her daughter) abused legal process by repeated, vague, unclear filings and persistent re-argument of already litigated issues. Abuse of process was grounds for Rule 11 sanctions. Consumer carried the burden of persuasion on liability and was expected to attempt this without abusing legal process.

Morgovsky v. Creditor Collection Serv., 166 F.3d 343 (9th Cir. 1998) (unpublished) (text in Westlaw). District court did not abuse its discretion by awarding defendants attorney fees.

Savino v. Computer Credit, Inc., 164 F.3d 81 (2d Cir. 1998). Motion for sanctions against consumer's attorney properly denied, where counsel documented "reasonable inquiry" before filing of pleading to which consumer subsequently changed his testimony.

Welch v. Credit Adjustment Co., 161 F.3d 19 (10th Cir. 1998) (unpublished) (text in Westlaw). District court's finding that plaintiff did not bring the FDCPA suit in bad faith or for purpose of harassment was reviewed for clear error (citing *Swanson v. S. Or. Credit Serv.,* 869 F.2d 1222, 1229 (9th Cir. 1988)), and affirmed.

Terran v. Kaplan, 109 F.3d 1428 (9th Cir. 1997). Fed. R. Civ. P. 11 sanctions were upheld where FDCPA claims were made without adequate investigation.

Campbell v. Associated Bureaus, Inc., 125 F.3d 857 (9th Cir. 1997) (unpublished) (text at 1997 WL 599516). Court rejected unsuccessful consumer's claim that $5069 of the costs taxed against her were for nontaxable witness fee costs because three of the witnesses were collection employees and the nonemployee witness did not individually petition for reimbursement.

Wade v. Reg'l Credit Ass'n, 91 F.3d 158 (9th Cir. 1996) (text at 1996 WL 375037). Attorney fees were awarded to the collection agency under Fed. R. Civ. P. 11 by the trial and appellate courts.

Johnson v. Eaton, 80 F.3d 148 (5th Cir. 1996). Where jury found that a lawyer's assistant had violated FDCPA, but that the consumer had sustained no actual or statutory damages as a result of that violation, an award of attorney fees to the consumer for the legal assistant's violation was improper. The consumer was awarded $500 statutory damages, against the collection lawyer and the fee award against him was proper. The legal assistant did not prove that case was brought in bad faith or for harassment, where a violation was found and thus was not entitled to have her attorney fees paid by the consumer.

Rodriguez v. Credit Bureau, 1993 WL 535174 (6th Cir. Dec. 27, 1993). Where consumer at the request of his attorney asked his ex-wife whether earlier collection letters had been received and was informed that none were, a reasonable inquiry into the collector's compliance with § 1692g had been made and sanctions under Rule 11 were not appropriate.

Torres v. Am. Tel. & Tel. Co., 914 F.2d 260 (7th Cir. 1990) (table), 1990 U.S. App. LEXIS 16116, *aff'g,* 1989 U.S. Dist. LEXIS 454 (N.D. Ill. Jan. 17, 1989). District court did not abuse its discretion in ordering Fed. R. Civ. P. 11 sanctions for meritless FDCPA claim. Fed. R. App. P. 38 sanctions were not appropriate in the appellate

review of that order because the appeal was not patently frivolous.

Emanuel v. Am. Credit Exch., 870 F.2d 805 (2d Cir. 1989). A malicious prosecution counterclaim by a collector in an FDCPA action cannot succeed if the FDCPA claim was successful. Fed. R. Civ. P. 11 sanctions denied against collector.

Alabama

Maddox v. Auburn Univ. Fed. Credit Union, 2010 WL 4867983 (M.D. Ala. Dec. 1, 2010). The court denied the prevailing defendant fees as there was no basis for holding that the plaintiffs acted in bad faith or for the purpose of harassment.

Fields v. Law Offices of James West, P.C., 2010 WL 2245036 (M.D. Ala. June 4, 2010). The court denied the prevailing defendant's request for fees and costs since there was no evidence of bad faith or harassment, and the consumer's claims, "while ultimately not meritorious, are not sanctionable."

Arizona

Chavez v. Northland Group, 2011 WL 317482 (D. Ariz. Feb. 1, 2011). Section 1692k(a)(3) does not authorize the award of bad faith expenses (attorney fees and costs) against a plaintiff's counsel. The defendant must show more than conclusory assertions that the plaintiff acted in bad faith and for the purpose of harassment. Where the defendant did not cite any case law discussing the application of § 1692k(a)(3), but rather relied on the definitions of "bad faith" and "harassment" in *Black's Law Dictionary* and *Merriam-Webster Dictionary*, citation to these two dictionaries without further analysis did not satisfy the defendant's burden.

Parker v. Shaw & Lines, L.L.C., 2010 WL 1640963 (D. Ariz. Apr. 20, 2010). The prevailing defendants' request for § 1692k(a)(3) attorney fees and costs was denied in the absence of any evidence that consumers brought the action in bad faith or for the purpose of harassment.

Grismore v. Kenneth Eisen & Assocs. Ltd., 2008 WL 2561938 (D. Ariz. June 25, 2008), *aff'd,* 348 Fed. Appx. 292 (9th Cir. 2009). The court awarded the prevailing defendant $9000 in attorney fees against the losing *pro se* consumer following its findings recited earlier in open court that the action "was brought in bad faith and for the purpose of harassment."

Maldonado v. CACV, L.L.C., 2007 U.S. Dist. LEXIS 4461 (D. Ariz. Jan. 18, 2007). Rejected the prevailing defendant's request for fees pursuant to 28 U.S.C. § 1927, stating: "The Court finds no evidence that counsel for Plaintiff acted unreasonably or vexatiously in this matter."

DeBusk v. Wachovia Bank, 2006 WL 3735963 (D. Ariz. Nov. 17, 2006), *aff'd,* 291 Fed. Appx. 55 (9th Cir. 2008). Defendants were each awarded $10,000 in fees and costs where it was clear that business' FDCPA claims lacked any basis in law or fact because the debt was commercial. Plaintiff also failed to articulate any basis for his bare allegation of misrepresentation.

California

Geist v. Onewest Bank, 2011 WL 223727 (N.D. Cal. Jan. 24, 2011). In light of the plaintiffs' *pro se* status and the record, the court exercised its discretion and denied the prevailing defendants' motion for attorney fees and costs. "The Ninth Circuit has recognized that a *pro se* plaintiff's ignorance of the complexities of law does not necessarily indicate that the litigation was pursued in bad faith for the purpose of harassment under the FDCPA."

Anderson v. Asset Acceptance, L.L.C., 2010 WL 1752609 (N.D. Cal. Apr. 29, 2010). The court approved the consumer's voluntary dismissal of the action "because it [was] posing harmful effect to his physical and emotional wellbeing" and denied the defendant's motion for sanctions and fees against the consumer's attorneys.

Roybal v. Trans Union, 2009 WL 394290 (E.D. Cal. Feb. 17, 2009). Defendant failed to introduce evidence of harassment or bad faith supporting its claims for attorney fees under § 1692k(a)(3) and 28 U.S.C. § 1927 resulting in a dismissal of the claims.

Cala v. Bush, 2008 WL 4279699 (N.D. Cal. Sept. 12, 2008). Prevailing defendants' motion for an award of fees denied since they have "not shown that this action was brought in bad faith and for the purpose of harassing Defendants."

Gorman v. Wolpoff & Abramson, L.L.P., 435 F. Supp. 2d 1004 (N.D. Cal. 2006), *rev'd on other grounds*, 584 F.3d 1147 (9th Cir. 2009). Notwithstanding some evidence to the contrary, "the Court does not make an express finding that the entire suit was filed in bad faith and for the purposes of harassment as required for defendant to recover attorneys' fees under 1692k."

Tilton v. Eskanos & Adler, 2006 WL 2355468 (N.D. Cal. Aug. 14, 2006). The court denied debt collector's motion pursuant to Rule 11 and § 1692k(a)(3) for an award of attorney fees alleging the FDCPA action was brought in bad faith when it was brought after a settlement of a time-barred state collection suit, after which the collection law firm's mistaken recorded the previous judgment that had been set aside.

Lemieux v. Jensen, 2004 WL 302318 (S.D. Cal. Jan. 29, 2004). No attorney fees under § 1692k(a)(3) to a collection lawyer who did not regularly collect debts. The consumer could not determine whether the attorney regularly collected debts until he filed suit and when he found out his mistake he promptly dismissed the FDCPA suit.

Colorado

O'Connor v. Check Rite, 973 F. Supp. 1010 (D. Colo. 1997). Where consumer (an attorney) should have known his action was substantially frivolous and groundless, attorney fees were granted to the debt collector under the Colorado debt collection law.

Connecticut

Oliphant v. Simboski, 2005 WL 927169 (D. Conn. Apr. 19, 2005). Summary judgment was entered in favor of the debt collectors who moved pursuant to Rule 11 for an award of attorney fees. Defendants' motion was denied because: (1) defendants failed to comply with the "safe harbor" provisions of Rule 11; (2) although the lawsuit was unsuccessful it was not frivolous; and (3) the motion failed to demonstrate that the lawsuit was brought in bad faith and for the purpose of harassment.

Csugi v. Monterey Fin. Servs., Inc., 2001 U.S. Dist. LEXIS 21255 (D. Conn. Oct. 30, 2001). Section 1692k(a)(3) does not permit an award of costs to the prevailing FDCPA defendant unless defendant shows that plaintiff brought the action in bad faith and for purpose of harassment.

Traverso v. Sharinn, 1989 U.S. Dist. LEXIS 19095 (D. Conn. Apr. 9, 1989). Counterclaim for malicious prosecution in FDCPA suit based on allegation that the FDCPA suit was baseless must be dismissed because it was premature since one element of malicious prosecution was that the prior litigation must be terminated in favor of the claimant.

CUDA & Assocs., L.L.C. v. Evon, 2009 WL 5698132 (Conn. Super. Ct. Dec. 16, 2009). The FDCPA does not preempt a state law claim against a consumer and her attorney for allegedly filing a vexatious FDCPA case.

Yale New Haven Hosp. v. Orlins, 1992 WL 110710 (Conn. Super. Ct. May 11, 1992). Counterclaim for vexatious litigation dismissed where plaintiff's action had not been terminated in defendant's favor.

Delaware

Smith v. Med. Credit Servs., Clearinghouse No. 45,644 (D. Del. 1990). Counterclaim for debt collector's attorney fees improper under § 1692k(a)(3); such a request should be by motion after the collector prevails on the merits.

Florida

Ritchie v. Cavalry Portfolio Servs., L.L.C., 2011 WL 309055 (M.D. Fla. Jan. 27, 2011). In this unsuccessful FDCPA case, the debt collector's motion for an award of attorney fees and costs in the amount of $30,608 under Rule 11 and § 1692k was denied. Conduct warrants sanctions under Rule 11 when a party demonstrates a deliberate indifference to obvious facts but not when a claim merely has weak support.

Bacelli v. MFP, Inc., 2010 WL 4054107 (M.D. Fla. Oct. 5, 2010). The court disallowed costs where there was no finding of bad faith or harassment in bringing the FDCPA suit.

Andre v. CCB Credit Servs., Inc., 2010 WL 3222500 (S.D. Fla. July 21, 2010). Where the record was devoid of any evidence that consumer or her attorney filed the complaint to harass defendant, the magistrate recommended that the defendant's application for attorney fees and sanctions pursuant to § 1692k be denied. The fact that the defendant was entitled to summary judgment did not in and of itself provide the basis for sanctions, and the filing of an identical complaint against another credit company did not alone establish bad faith or harassment.

Rhinehart v. CBE Group, Inc., 2010 WL 2158282 (M.D. Fla. May 27, 2010). Where consumer's counsel failed to dismiss any of the FDCPA claims when it became clear during discovery that they had no factual basis whatsoever, thereby forcing the defendant to file its motion for summary judgment, the consumer and her Krohn & Moss attorneys were ordered to pay the defendant's attorney fees.

Tucker v. CBE Group, Inc., 2010 WL 1849034 (M.D. Fla. May 5, 2010). The court awarded fees against the consumer, who signed a boilerplate complaint and verified a claim with multiple allegations that contradicted his own deposition testimony, and against Krohn & Moss counsel, who did not retract any claims when they were contradicted by the consumer's deposition.

Hinds v. Credigy Receivables, Inc., 2008 WL 5381345 (M.D. Fla. Dec. 23, 2008). The court denied the prevailing defendants' motion for sanctions, including under § 1692k(a)(3):

> Defendants' Motion for Sanctions seeks an award of fees and costs pursuant to Section 1692k(a)(3), which is permitted if Plaintiff's action was brought in bad faith and for the purpose of harassment. The standard for bad faith is higher than the standard for mere frivolousness. In assessing whether Plaintiff's conduct in pursuing this action is tantamount to bad faith, this Court focuses primarily on Plaintiff's conduct and motives, and not on the validity of this case. This Court exercises its inherent powers with restraint and discretion. Reviewing the present record, the Court cannot say that Plaintiff has acted in bad faith, wantonly, or for oppressive reasons. It has not been shown that Plaintiff brought this action for the purpose of harassing Defendants, or to delay or disrupt the litigation. Although Plaintiff may have brought this case without good cause, the Court cannot find that she did so maliciously or in subjective bad faith.

Conner v. BCC Fin. Mgmt. Servs., Inc., 597 F. Supp. 2d 1299 (S.D. Fla. June 25, 2008). Award of some $20,000 fees against plaintiff under state law, but expressly not under FDCPA, and jointly against plaintiff's counsel under 28 U.S.C. § 1927, for continuing to litigate after it became clear that claim that defendant had no collection agency license was meritless. Court rejected plaintiff's argument that Florida Act prevented the imposition of fees against her (regardless of whether the case filed was frivolous) when she could not be held personally liable for fees under FDCPA.

Craig v. Park Fin. of Broward County, Inc., 390 F. Supp. 2d 1150 (M.D. Fla. 2005). The finance company that originally financed and was the current holder of the consumer's motor vehicle installment contract was an exempt creditor and not a debt collector subject to the FDCPA; nevertheless, the court denied the company's motion for fees and sanctions against the plaintiff for filing a frivolous suit.

Wilson v. Transworld Sys., Inc., 2003 WL 21488206 (M.D. Fla. June 10, 2003). Federal Rule of Civil Procedure 54(d)(1)'s general allowance for costs to the prevailing party "except when express provision is made" by statute is accordingly overridden by the FDCPA's provision of fees and costs to the prevailing defendant only when the losing plaintiff has acted in bad faith and for the purpose of harassment. Collector's motion for costs was denied since its conclusory allegations did not establish the FDCPA standard that the losing consumer plaintiff acted in bad faith and for the purpose of harassment.

Clayton v. Bryan, 753 So. 2d 632 (Fla. Dist. Ct. App. 2000). Fla. offer of judgment statute providing for fee award was preempted by FDCPA attorney fee provisions, § 1692k(3). The court found that only where there was an express finding of bad faith and purpose of harassment may attorney fees be awarded to the prevailing defendant in an FDCPA matter. Any state cause of action which was not "at least as broad, in its protection to the consumer, as" the FDCPA was preempted. Accordingly, the court refused to award defendant's attorney fees for defending an unsuccessful FDCPA action.

Georgia

Sanchez v. United Collection Bureau, Inc., 649 F. Supp. 2d 1374 (N.D. Ga. 2009). The prevailing defendant was not entitled to an award of attorney fees since it has provided no evidence of "bad faith and purposeful harassment."

Johnson v. Ardec Credit Servs., Inc., 1984 U.S. Dist. LEXIS 24889 (N.D. Ga. Mar. 21, 1984). Debt collector's claim for attorney fees under § 1692k(a)(3) could not be raised as counterclaim in FDCPA action. Only after trial on merits and judgment in its favor could collector make motion for costs and attorney fees.

Zoeckler v. Credit Claims & Collections, Inc., 1982 U.S. Dist. LEXIS 18384 (N.D. Ga. Sept. 30, 1982). The collector's counterclaims for abuse of process for filing a harassing FDCPA suit were dismissed as groundless.

Hawaii

Nakao v. Int'l Data Servs., 2007 WL 295537 (D. Haw. Jan. 29, 2007). Section 1692k(a)(3), permits an award of costs to the prevailing defendant pursuant to Rule 54(d)(1) "only upon" such a finding of bad faith and harassment, which was not present in this case.

Illinois

Hoang v. Worldwide Asset Purchasing, L.L.C., 2009 WL 3669883 (S.D. Ill. Nov. 2, 2009). Denied sanctions under § 1692k(a)(3), where plaintiff did not file a claim in bad faith by bringing a "clearly time-barred claim," nor has the claim created unnecessary costs. Thus, plaintiff is not subject to sanctions.

Beler v. Blatt, Hasenmiller, Leibsker & Moore, 2006 U.S. Dist. LEXIS 50279 (C.D. Ill. July 19, 2006). The court denied the debt collector's motion for sanctions pursuant to 28 U.S.C. § 1927 finding that the consumer's statement that she did not receive a validation notice provided a reasonable basis for her counsel to explore the issue although the claim was later withdrawn.

Gonzalez v. Lawent, 2004 WL 2036409 (N.D. Ill. Sept. 10, 2004). A debt collector's motion for attorney fees was premature where the collector had prevailed on one issue but other issues remained unresolved, since a finding of bad faith and harassment must be based on the entire lawsuit and cannot be granted if the consumer prevails on a single claim.

Strange v. Armor Sys. Corp., 2004 WL 46244 (N.D. Ill. Jan. 7, 2004). Attorney fees were not awardable to the debt collector for a consumer's time-barred FDCPA claim where the FDCPA claim had been joined with a Fair Credit Reporting Act claim that was not time barred. The court should look at the entire suit, not just the FDCPA claim.

Blum v. Lawent, 2003 WL 22078306 (N.D. Ill. Sept. 8, 2003). A collector who defeated one of three claimed violations of the FDCPA is not entitled to attorney fees under § 1692k(a)(3).

Turner v. J.V.D.B. & Assocs., Inc., 211 F. Supp. 2d 1108 (N.D. Ill. 2002), *aff'd in part, rev'd in part, remanded*, 330 F.3d 991 (7th Cir. 2003). Prevailing collector's motion for attorney fees under § 1692k(a)(3) was denied since the consumer's claims were not brought in bad faith or to harass but instead, though unsuccessful, "were a good faith interpretation of the subject statute and existing case law."

Johnson v. Revenue Mgmt. Corp., 52 F. Supp. 2d 889 (N.D. Ill. 1999). Well after the litigation was commenced, based on consumer's allegation that the collection letter violated § 1692g, the collection agency disclosed that it had sent a previous letter that complied with the law. The consumer moved to withdraw the complaint, and for sanctions against the collection agency for not revealing the letter upon request. Sanctions were denied, on the basis that both parties were partially at fault, since the consumer presumably received the first letter.

Riebe v. Juergensmeyer & Assocs., 979 F. Supp. 1218 (N.D. Ill. 1997). Collector's motion for award of attorney fees denied where consumer, though the losing party, did not bring action in bad faith to harass in view of unique nature of the claim and the current debate as to the scope of FDCPA coverage and the definition of the term "debt."

Villarreal v. Snow, 1997 WL 116801 (N.D. Ill. Mar. 12, 1997). Creditor's motion for an award of attorney fees pursuant to the FDCPA and the Illinois Consumer Fraud Act was denied because there was no improper purpose or bad faith in bringing the claims.

Friedman v. HHL Fin. Servs., Inc., 1994 WL 22969 (N.D. Ill. Jan. 25, 1994). Motion for sanctions pursuant to Fed. R. Civ. P. 11 and § 1692k(a)(3) denied where FDCPA complaint was neither frivolous nor brought for an improper purpose.

Galuska v. Blumenthal, 1993 WL 101464 (N.D. Ill. Apr. 2, 1993), *on reconsideration*, 1994 WL 323121 (N.D. Ill. June 26, 1994). Complaint was dismissed for plaintiff's failure to state an FDCPA cause of action, and sanctions were imposed upon plaintiff for her entirely frivolous proposed amendments to the complaint.

Kegley v. Miles Mgmt. Corp., 1992 WL 370251 (N.D. Ill. Dec. 3, 1992). Defendant's Rule 11 motion for costs and attorney fees was denied where the court found that the plaintiff's claims were brought in good faith.

Indiana

Kaiser v. Braje & Nelson, L.L.P., 2006 WL 1285143 (N.D. Ind. May 5, 2006). Court declined to award fees against consumer who had a colorable claim for the arguments made.

Young v. Reuben, 2005 WL 1484671 (S.D. Ind. June 21, 2005). The court dismissed the collector's counterclaim alleging that the FDCPA action had been brought in bad faith for the purpose of harassment, but reserved the issue for later resolution. The collector's bad faith and harassment allegations are not to be presented to the jury, but addressed, if at all, by the court following the jury's verdict on the merits of the consumer's claims and the collector's affirmative defenses.

Conner v. Instant Cash Advance, 2003 WL 446378 (S.D. Ind. Feb. 20, 2003). Counterclaim for libel against consumer and his counsel dismissed for failure to state a cause of action. Since counsel was not a party, no counterclaim or cross claim could be asserted against counsel. Consumer has an absolute privilege for statements made in pleadings, so libel counterclaim based on the suit itself did not state a cause of action. Counterclaim based on filing a frivolous suit was a permissive counterclaim; court dismissed counterclaim for lack of an independent basis for jurisdiction such as diversity, amount in controversy.

Veach v. Sheeks, 2002 U.S. Dist. LEXIS 7819 (S.D. Ind. Apr. 16, 2002). The prevailing collection attorneys' motion for attorney fees was denied, where on one issue the plaintiff established a violation of the law but the jury sustained the defendant's bona fide error defense and all other issues, though meritless, were not "outside the bounds of colorable argument."

Ziobron v. Crawford, 667 N.E.2d 202 (Ind. Ct. App. 1996). A malicious prosecution claim based on a dismissed FDCPA claim was not preempted by the terms of § 1692n, which was limited to conflicts between state and federal laws regulating debt collection. The court failed to consider whether there was a conflict between state and federal law under the Supremacy Clause of the U.S. Constitution. A claim against the consumer for malicious prosecution was stated by the bringing and voluntary dismissal of an FDCPA claim against a lawyer who did insufficient debt collection to be covered by the FDCPA. The complaint claimed he was covered and that he failed to provide the notices required by §§ 1692e(11) and 1692g, which the court considered entirely technical. The court decided the FDCPA suit was brought solely for the improper purpose of recovery of consumer's attorney fees.

Kansas

Dean v. Gillette, 2005 WL 2810539 (D. Kan. Oct. 27, 2005). The prevailing defendant was not entitled to an award of fees under § 1692k(c) since the plaintiff had an arguable, though ultimately unsuccessful, basis for alleging that the defendant was a covered debt collector. Fees may be awarded to defendant only if the action was objectively in bad faith; the consumer's colorable legal argument defeated a finding of bad faith.

Dean v. Gillette, 2005 WL 957043 (D. Kan. Apr. 25, 2005). An award of costs and attorney fees pursuant to § 1692k(a)(3) was granted finding that plaintiff brought the lawsuit in bad faith and for the purpose of harassment.

Mercy Reg'l Health Ctr., Inc. v. Brinegar, 223 P.3d 311 (Kan. Ct. App. 2010). Affirmed an award of attorney fees under state law against the losing debtor, a *pro se* lawyer, who counterclaimed under both the FDCPA and state law in this collection action to recover for medical services performed for his minor child, where the trial court found that the state law counterclaim had been brought for an impermissible purpose under the applicable state law standard but that the unsuccessful FDCPA counterclaim did not warrant an award under the fee-shifting provision of § 1692k(a)(3).

Louisiana

Murungi v. Mercedes Benz Credit Corp., 2001 U.S. Dist. LEXIS 19490 (E.D. La. Nov. 20, 2001). Court denied *pro se* consumers' request to reopen previously dismissed frivolous FDCPA suit but denied creditor's motion for sanctions because consumers were *pro se* litigants.

Franco v. Maraldo, 2000 U.S. Dist. LEXIS 3325 (E.D. La. Mar. 15, 2000). Prevailing defendant's request for attorney fees under § 1692k(3) and Rule 11 denied since plaintiff and his attorney could have "plausibly" believed that the defendant attorney was a debt collector (though ultimately held not to be) where attorney stated in conformity with § 1692e(11) in his letter to the consumer that the attorney was a debt collector.

Taylor v. Frost-Arnett Co., 1998 WL 472052 (E.D. La. Aug. 5, 1998). Motion to dismiss § 1692k counterclaim granted. The section does not provide a defense or a cause of action. It merely provides a means to seek attorney fees if the defendant prevails.

Johnson v. Eaton, 884 F. Supp. 1068 (M.D. La. 1995), *aff'd in part & rev'd in part*, 80 F.3d 148 (5th Cir. 1996). Debt collectors could not claim attorney fees under § 1692k(a)(3) for bad faith and harassment by the consumer unless the collector prevailed against all FDCPA claims. Withdrawal of an actual damages claim for emotional distress shortly before trial by the consumer did not constitute in itself a basis for finding of bad faith or harassment under § 1692k(a)(3).

Maryland

Shah v. Collecto, Inc., 2005 WL 2216242 (D. Md. Sept. 12, 2005). For fees to be awarded to the defendant under § 1692k, it must show not merely negligence or bad judgment, but actual dishonest purpose or ill will. Suit must be completely without merit or utterly without factual foundation.

McCarthy v. Rosenthal, 1996 WL 249991 (D. Md. Jan. 5, 1996). The collection lawyer was awarded attorney fees and costs under Fed. R. Civ. P. 11 where the consumer's claim of misrepresentation against the collection lawyer was based on an inadequate investigation and was dismissed shortly before trial.

Massachusetts

Argentieri v. Fisher Landscapes, Inc., 15 F. Supp. 2d 55 (D. Mass. 1998), *later opinion*, 27 F. Supp. 2d 84 (D. Mass. 1998). Consumer's attorney held liable for Rule 11 sanctions. Collection attorney did not violate the FDCPA by improperly attempting to collect attorney fees to which his client was not entitled merely because he included prayer for attorney fees in complaint which he filed in state court, when he immediately withdrew the fee claim once notified by consumer's attorney of the lack of legal basis therefore.

Michigan

Pietrowski v. Merchants & Med. Credit Corp., 256 F.R.D. 544 (E.D. Mich. 2008). Upon reconsideration of an award of $38,215 as reasonable attorney fees to the defendant as part of costs on its offer of judgment, the court vacated its award of attorney fees to the defendant.

Minnesota

Kirscher v. Messerli & Kramer, P.A., 2006 WL 145162 (D. Minn. Jan. 18, 2006). Defendant's § 1692k counterclaim seeking fees for plaintiff's bad faith was dismissed, with leave to apply for fees.

Phernetton v. First Revenue Assur., 2003 WL 21246037 (D. Minn. May 19, 2003). Collector's motion for fees and costs denied, since consumer did not bring the action in bad faith and for purpose of harassment.

Missouri

Eckert v. LVNV Funding L.L.C., 647 F. Supp. 2d 1096 (E.D. Mo. 2009). Defendant held not entitled to award of attorney fees under § 1692k(a)(3), as defendant only argued that only one claim of plaintiff, under § 1692e(10), was brought in bad faith for the purposes of harassment as opposed to the entire lawsuit as required for the award of fees, and also because plaintiff's § 1692e claim was sufficiently supported by facts in the complaint and thus not brought in bad faith for purposes of harassment.

Martens v. Countrywide Home Loans Serv. L.P., 2006 WL 544209 (E.D. Mo. Mar. 3, 2006). Sanctions pursuant to Rule 11 were awarded against *pro se* plaintiff where the court found that the FDCPA action was brought in an attempt to relitigate her unsuccessful bankruptcy appeal.

Lewis v. Hanks, 1991 U.S. Dist. LEXIS 21807 (E.D. Mo. Feb. 26, 1991). "The Act does not contain a de minimis exception for the principled debt collector who sends a letter in technical violation of the Act." Pursuant to § 1692k(a)(3), the court may award attorney fees to the debt collector if the consumer is found to have brought suit "in bad faith and for the purpose of harassment." The district judge stated that an award of fees to the collector would be considered if the evidence revealed that the consumer filed the action "to gain leverage in the dispute over a debt plaintiffs legitimately owe."

Vogler v. Grier Group Mgmt. Co., 309 S.W.3d 328 (Mo. Ct. App. 2010). Trial court did not abuse its discretion in finding that the action was brought in bad faith and for the purpose of harassment and in thus awarding fees to the prevailing defendant.

Nebraska

Randall v. Midland Funding, L.L.C., 2009 WL 2358350 (D. Neb. July 23, 2009). The defendant's motion for an award of § 1692k(a)(3) attorney fees was denied since the court found three claims stated by the complaint and no evidence of bad faith.

Nevada

Kuhn v. Account Control Tech., Inc., 865 F. Supp. 1443 (D. Nev. 1994). Collection attorney's counterclaim for bad faith must be dismissed because it was not mandatory and did not arise out of the same transaction or occurrence as the FDCPA case.

New Hampshire

Stoddard v. Nationwide Recovery Serv., Inc., 2003 WL 25273708 (D.N.H. Nov. 25, 2003). Consumer's motion to dismiss collector's § 1692k(a)(3) counterclaim that suit was brought in bad faith and for harassment was denied with the court stating that, whether brought as a counterclaim or by motion, a claim under § 1692k(a)(3) is decided by the court only after the litigation has been resolved against the plaintiff.

New Mexico

Kolker v. Duke City Collection Agency, 750 F. Supp. 468 (D.N.M.

1990). A counterclaim may not be based on § 1692k(a)(3); relief under that provision is by motion after a determination of the consumer's claim.

New York

Clayson v. Rubin & Rothman, L.L.C., 2010 WL 4628516 (W.D.N.Y. Nov. 16, 2010). The defendant collector's motion for fees under § 1692k and 28 U.S.C. § 1927 were denied.

Moore v. Diversified Collection Servs., Inc., 2009 WL 1873654 (E.D.N.Y. June 29, 2009). Debt collector's counterclaim for attorney fees pursuant to § 1692k(a)(3) was dismissed where the consumer had survived the debt collector's motion to dismiss.

Bank v. Cooper, 2009 WL 1491227 (E.D.N.Y. May 27, 2009), *aff'd on other grounds*, 356 Fed. Appx. 509 (2d Cir. 2009). Defendants' motion for an award of costs, disbursements, and attorney fees pursuant to § 1692k(a)(3) was denied where the court found that the action was not brought in bad faith or for the purpose of harassment.

Kuhne v. Cohen & Slamowitz, L.L.P., 2008 WL 608607 (S.D.N.Y. Mar. 5, 2008). Defendant's request for attorney fees and costs were denied because the court found that "Plaintiff's action was not brought in bad faith or for the purpose of harassment."

Jacobson v. Healthcare Fin. Servs., Inc., 434 F. Supp. 2d 133 (E.D.N.Y. 2006), *rev'd*, 516 F.3d 85 (2d Cir. 2008). The court found the plaintiff liable to pay the prevailing defendant's attorney fees, stating that, since the plaintiff admittedly did not dispute owing the debt and did feel harassed or misled by the challenged dun, the "mistaken belief that the alleged violation of the statute, arrived at merely by a strained construction of its language, constitutes per se harassment."

Sorey v. Computer Credit, Inc., 2006 WL 1896401 (S.D.N.Y. July 7, 2006). The court denied the prevailing defendant's request for attorney fees and expenses since the action was "not objectively baseless" and the claim was not brought in bad faith or for purposes of harassment and instead "presented a fair ground for litigation."

Degrosiellier v. Solomon & Solomon, P.C., 2001 U.S. Dist. LEXIS 15254 (N.D.N.Y. Sept. 27, 2001). Collector's motion for an award of attorney fees was denied based on the absence of proof that the consumer commenced the action in bad faith or for the purpose of harassment.

Jones v. Weiss, 95 F. Supp. 2d 105 (N.D.N.Y. 2000). Defendant's motion for fees, costs and sanctions asserting plaintiffs' lawsuit was instituted only to harass it, denied for inadequate evidence to support that allegation.

Filsinger v. Upton, 2000 U.S. Dist. LEXIS 1824 (N.D.N.Y. Feb. 17, 2000). The absence of evidence that the consumer believed his claim was without merit or was motivated by a desire to harass defendants prevented an award of attorney fees to the prevailing defendants under § 1692k(3); the mere fact the complaint was dismissed and the collector prevailed was insufficient to support an award.

Countryman v. Solomon & Solomon, 2000 U.S. Dist. LEXIS 1397 (N.D.N.Y. Feb. 7, 2000). Fees can be awarded to the defendant on a successful motion to dismiss. Mere dismissal is not enough, however; there must be sufficient evidence that plaintiffs believed their action to be without merit or were motivated purely by a desire to harass. Absent such evidence, defendant's motion for fees was denied. The court failed to notice the plain language of § 1692k requiring both bad faith *and* purpose of harassment.

Sierra v. Foster & Garbus, 48 F. Supp. 2d 393 (S.D.N.Y. 1999). Sanctions of $4586.60 were awarded against consumer and his attorney for bringing suit claiming that the addition of $507.92 in attorney fees violated the FDCPA even though the underlying agreement provided for reasonable fees, and for dismissing the FDCPA claims to avoid removal, and then re-filing them in federal court anyway.

Phillips v. Amana Collection Serv., 1992 WL 227839 (W.D.N.Y. Aug. 25, 1992). Because Congress authorized the award of additional damages and attorney fees for enforcement of the FDCPA by "private attorneys general," the award of sanction or costs to the collector would be inappropriate on the collector's contention that the consumer demonstrated only "technical" violations and did not seek actual damages.

Knowles v. Credit Bureau, 1992 WL 131107 (W.D.N.Y. May 28, 1992). Collector's motion for an award of attorney fees pursuant to § 1692k(a)(3) was denied because the collector failed to demonstrate that the consumer brought the suit in bad faith and for the purpose of harassment.

Cornett v. Bank of New York, 1992 WL 88197 (S.D.N.Y. Apr. 17, 1992). Rule 11 sanctions in the amount of $500 were levied against *pro se* plaintiff who had no basis in law or fact for claims which had been previously litigated in small claims court.

Hardin v. Folger, 704 F. Supp. 355 (W.D.N.Y. 1988). Debt collector's claim for § 1692k attorney fees was not an independent claim, and so was properly brought by motion rather than counterclaim.

Chevy Chase F.S.B. v. Lane, 716 N.Y.S.2d 110 (N.Y. App. Div. 2000). Trial court's sanctions against attorney Capoccia in asserting baseless TILA and FDCPA defenses to credit card collection action was supported by the record and therefore was not an abuse of discretion.

Mendez v. Apple Bank for Sav., 541 N.Y.S.2d 920 (N.Y. Civ. Ct. 1989). To recover attorney fees under § 1692k(a)(3), a creditor must show more than mere dismissal of plaintiff's FDCPA suit; a showing that plaintiff believed suit to be meritless or filed it purely for harassment is necessary.

Brown v. Solomon & Solomon, P.C., 694 N.Y.S.2d 843 (N.Y. Albany City Ct. 1999). Attorney Capoccia sued counsel for Citibank under § 1692f alleging that the debt was not in default when defense counsel sent a demand letter. In a flurry of cross-motions for sanctions/disqualification, the court imposed $5000 in sanctions against Capoccia after dismissing the complaint for failure to state a cause of action because it did not plead that counsel knowingly acted. Court cited *Ducrest v. Alco Collections, Inc.*, 931 F. Supp. 459 (M.D. La. 1996): "[T]o state a claim under § 1692f(1) plaintiff would have to show that defendant was knowingly attempting to collect a charge not authorized by the lease and not permitted by law"; that "a debt collector should be able to rely on the representation and implied warranty from its client that the amount was due under either the lease or the law"; and "FDCPA does not require an independent investigation of the information provided by clients when a debt collector tries to collect a debt" (citation omitted), "nor does it require the debt collector to dispute the creditor's construction of a contract." Sanctions awarded against Capoccia because "[T]here is a pattern of conduct by the Capoccia Law Firm which exhibits a complete disregard for the judicial system, in tying up its limited resources and preventing the system from addressing legitimate disputes, by bombarding it with meritless claims and defenses, apparently as some sort of tactic, the aim of which is to coerce settlement from the adversaries of its clients. Therefore, in determining the amount of the sanction to be awarded, the Court has placed substantial weight, not only on the nature of the conduct found to be frivolous, but also on the need for an appropriate deterrent with respect to similar future conduct."

North Carolina

Gough v. Bernhardt & Strawser, PA, 2006 WL 1875327 (M.D.N.C. June 30, 2006). The prevailing defendants were not entitled to an award of fees because they failed to show plaintiff's lawsuit was brought either in bad faith or for the purpose of harassment.

Ohio

Deere v. Javitch, Block & Rathbone, L.L.P., 413 F. Supp. 2d 886 (S.D. Ohio 2006). Dismissed the FDCPA claims but denied sanctions: "[T]he Court cannot conclude, based upon two district court opinions, that Plaintiff is acting in bad faith in filing this lawsuit. Nor can the Court conclude that her counsels' zealous advocacy about the parameters of FDCPA's consumer protection is bad faith, or intended solely to harass JB&R."

Miller v. Credit Collection Servs., 200 F.R.D. 379 (S.D. Ohio 2000). Prevailing defendant's motion for attorney fees under § 1692k is waived since the motion was not made within the mandatory fourteen-day period of Rule 54(d)(2).

Boyce v. Computer Credit, Inc., 1997 U.S. Dist. LEXIS 14879 (S.D. Ohio Sept. 2, 1997). A motion for sanctions was dismissed where it was based on an attack on consumer's counsel bringing numerous FDCPA suits against various debt collectors and not on the factual and legal merits of the consumer's claims. The collector's counsel was admonished not to make *ad hominem* attacks in the future in that court.

Oklahoma

Smith v. Rockett, 2006 U.S. Dist. LEXIS 72172 (W.D. Okla. Oct. 2, 2006). The court denied the prevailing defendants' motions for fees because they presented no "evidence that the plaintiff believed her action to be without merit or was motivated purely by a desire to harass the defendants."

Oregon

Hooper v. Capital Credit & Collection Servs., Inc., 2005 WL 2297062 (D. Or. Sept. 20, 2005). Following a jury trial, which resulted in a $1570 actual damage award against the collection agency and a defense verdict for the agency's named employee, the court denied any additional statutory damages, awarded the plaintiff $17,467 in attorney fees, and denied any fees to the exonerated employee since the claims against her were not "brought in bad faith and for the purpose of harassment."

Conley v. KCA Fin. Servs., Inc., 931 P.2d 808 (Or. Ct. App. 1997). Awarding attorney fees to the creditor and its collection agency was improper as there was no finding that the FDCPA action was brought by consumers in bad faith and for the purpose of harassment.

Pennsylvania

Bezpalko v. Gilfillan, Gilpin & Brehman, 1998 WL 321268 (E.D. Pa. June 17, 1998). Collector's request for attorney fees for bad faith prosecution under the FDCPA denied. Appellate court authority was contrary to the consumer's claim. The consumer's claim was not frivolous in view of right of the plaintiff to advance in good faith the need to change prevailing interpretations: "In order for such necessary adjustments in the law to be made, attorneys must bring to the attention of the courts the need and reasoning for such a change."

Martin v. Berke & Spielfogel, 1995 WL 214453 (E.D. Pa. Apr. 4, 1995). After dismissal of FDCPA cause of action debt collector was allowed to conduct additional discovery on its bad faith claim against a commercial debtor pursuant to § 1692k(a)(3).

Rhode Island

Egan v. Williams, 709 A.2d 1057 (R.I. 1998). In suit to enjoin foreclosure, plaintiff mortgagor included an FDCPA count against mortgagee's collection attorney. Mortgagee's attorney counterclaimed against plaintiff, citing plaintiff's attorneys as third party defendants, alleging abuse of process in bringing the FDCPA count. Abuse of process against plaintiff allowed to stand, but dismissed without prejudice as to plaintiff's attorneys. (*Contra Kuhn v. Account Control Tech., Inc.,* 865 F. Supp. 1443 (D. Nev. 1994).)

Tennessee

Brown v. Hosto & Buchan, P.L.L.C., 2010 WL 4352932 (W.D. Tenn. Nov. 2, 2010). The court denied the collector's motion for fees, finding that it failed to present any evidence of bad faith, and adding that the court was unable to find any, particularly given that two of the plaintiff's three claims survived the motion to dismiss.

Erickson v. Brock & Scott, P.L.L.C., 2009 WL 4884424 (W.D. Tenn. Dec. 8, 2009). Consumer's motion to dismiss the defendant's counterclaim seeking declaratory judgment that it did not violate the FDCPA, that the plaintiff brought the action in bad faith for purposes of harassment, and that it be awarded attorney fees incurred was denied since this counterclaim was not barred by the rule that a counterclaim that merely redundantly negates the allegations of the complaint is unavailable.

White v. Myers, 2001 Tenn. App. LEXIS 814 (Tenn. Ct. App. Oct. 31, 2001). Trial court did not abuse its discretion in imposing Rule 11 sanctions against consumer's attorney for bringing a frivolous FDCPA case against opposing counsel in a prior mortgage foreclosure dispute where the defendant did not engage in debt collection at all and the consumer's attorney failed to investigate the law or facts prior to filing suit.

Texas

Allen v. Scott, 2011 WL 219568 (N.D. Tex. Jan. 19, 2011). Section 1692k does not permit a bad faith counterclaim. The attorney fees available under that section can be obtained only after the merits of a plaintiff's claims have been resolved.

Cunningham v. Credit Mgmt., L.P., 2010 WL 3791049 (N.D. Tex. Sept. 27, 2010). The court found no basis for awarding § 1692k(a)(3) fees against the *pro se* consumer where the defendants did not affirmatively show that the plaintiff acted in bad faith and for the purpose of harassment. "The fact that the plaintiff holds himself out as an angry and litigious expert in debt collection says nothing about the merits of the plaintiff's claims in this particular case. A number of the plaintiff's claims fail only for a lack of *competent* evidence. More importantly, the defendants have not shown that the plaintiff's actions were motivated by a dishonest purpose or moral obliquity."

Vermont

Committe v. Dennis Reimer, Co., L.P.A., 150 F.R.D. 495 (D. Vt. 1993). Collector's motion for summary judgment on the basis of lack of personal jurisdiction, which had been waived by operation of Fed. R. Civ. P. 12(h)(1)(A), had no reasonable basis in law, warranting imposition of Fed. R. Civ. P. Rule 11 sanctions.

Virginia

In re Faulkner, 1998 WL 34342248 (Bankr. E.D. Va. May 12, 1998). Court denied an award of attorney fees to the prevailing defendant, finding that the consumer's FDCPA claim, though unsuccessful, had some basis in law and thus could not have been brought in bad faith or for purposes of harassment.

Washington

Dexter v. Tran, 2009 WL 5208800 (E.D. Wash. Dec. 22, 2009). Action was not brought in bad faith or for the purpose of harassment, and defendants were not entitled to recover their attorney fees and costs by virtue of the parties' reaffirmation agreement because the consumer brought this action pursuant to the FDCPA and did not allege a breach of the reaffirmation agreement.

Allers-Petrus v. Columbia Recovery Group, L.L.C., 2009 WL 1160061 (W.D. Wash. Apr. 29, 2009). The court, giving the plaintiff the benefit of the doubt that the action was not filed in bad faith and for the purpose of harassment, denied the debt collector's motion for attorney fees and costs pursuant to § 1692k(a)(3).

Hylkema v. Palisades Collection, L.L.C., 2008 WL 163617 (W.D. Wash. Jan. 15, 2008). Granted defendants' motion to amend their counterclaim for attorney fees and costs under § 1692k(3) to add additional support for their counterclaim that plaintiff has brought this action in bad faith and for the purpose of harassment.

Campion v. Credit Bureau Servs., Inc., 2000 U.S. Dist. LEXIS 20233 (E.D. Wash. Sept. 19, 2000). Because the court found merit in the plaintiff's claims, the defendant's request for fees and costs under § 1692k was denied.

Wisconsin

Bernegger v. Washington Mut., 2008 WL 472239 (E.D. Wis. Oct.

24, 2008). The defendant's interlocutory request for fees was denied without prejudice as premature since § 1692k(a)(3) requires a showing that the entire lawsuit, and not just a certain claim, was brought in bad faith and for harassment purposes.

Barrows v. Petrie & Stocking, S.C., 2008 WL 3540405 (W.D. Wis. Aug. 13, 2008). Although the court found one group of claims so "baseless, unreasonable and vexatious that they merit sanctions against plaintiff's counsel under § 1927," the fact that the consumer prevailed on a single FDCPA claim precluded an award of § 1692k attorney fees since such an award is "warranted only when the entire 'action' or lawsuit is brought in bad faith."

K.3.6.5 Arbitration

Sherer v. Green Tree Servicing L.L.C., 548 F.3d 379 (5th Cir. 2008). The creditor's arbitration agreement governed this FDCPA case against the non-signatory servicer/debt collector and arbitration was therefore compelled since the FDCPA claim was covered by "the broad language of that agreement's arbitration clause" that applied to any claims arising from "the relationships which result from [the agreement]."

Koch v. Compucredit Corp., 543 F.3d 460 (8th Cir. 2008). Court ordered arbitration where "[e]ven assuming that [plaintiff's] debt had been extinguished before the assignment, and that the collection attempts by the defendants were erroneous, the heart of the dispute—the occurrence and alleged payment of the debt—is one founded in the credit agreement."

Martin v. Wells Fargo Fin. Alaska, Inc., 2006 WL 2466945 (9th Cir. Aug. 25, 2006). The district court lacked jurisdiction to confirm the consumers' arbitration award against the defendant since "a petitioner seeking to confirm or vacate an arbitration award in federal court must establish an independent basis for federal jurisdiction;" and "although the consumers raised questions of federal law under the FDCPA, those claims are derivative of their petition for confirmation, which raises no question of federal law."

Carbajal v. H & R Tax Servs., Inc., 372 F.3d 903 (7th Cir. 2004). Arbitration clause in a form contract was not unconscionable and was enforced despite FDCPA claim.

Arizona

Starr v. The Hameroff Law Firm, P.C., 2008 WL 906822 (D. Ariz. Mar. 31, 2008). Defendants' motion to compel arbitration denied because the "Defendants failed to make the threshold showing that they are the 'employees, agents or assigns' of [creditor]," the persons to whom the subject arbitration agreement applied.

Arkansas

Webb v. MBNA Am. Bank, 2006 WL 618186 (E.D. Ark. Mar. 10, 2006). The court held that the MBNA arbitration agreement's stated applicability to, *inter alia*, the bank's "assigns" included the defendants in this action to whom the account was in fact assigned and thus granted the motion to arbitrate.

Webb v. MBNA Am. Bank, 2005 WL 2648019 (E.D. Ark. Oct. 13, 2005). Challenge to an arbitration award dismissed as it was not filed within ninety days of the award. FDCPA and state claims not barred by res judicata as the arbitration decision allowing the collection of the debt did not address the consumer's claims.

California

Gerber v. Citigroup, Inc., 2008 WL 596112 (E.D. Cal. Feb. 29, 2008), *report and recommendation adopted*, 2008 WL 756132 (E.D. Cal. Mar. 21, 2008). Defendant's motion to compel arbitration was denied because defendant failed to demonstrate that the plaintiff was bound by change in terms mailed to his home address under California law.

Nickoloff v. Wolpoff & Abramson, L.L.P., 511 F. Supp. 2d 1043 (C.D. Cal. 2007). The consumer failed to state a claim where he merely contested the sufficiency of the documentary evidence submitted in the underlying arbitration to establish the defendant's chain of title of the alleged debt, since the arbitrator's decision that the evidence was sufficient could not be attacked via a complaint for unlawful debt collection practices and could only be attacked "through a motion to vacate, modify, or correct the award pursuant to the Federal Arbitration Act or the plaintiff can seek to reopen the arbitration proceeding and ask the arbitrator to reconsider pursuant to the National Arbitration Code of Procedure, Rule 43." The court adapted the holding in *Harvey v. Great Seneca Fin. Corp.*, 453 F.3d 324 (6th Cir. 2006), to arbitration proceedings and held that the consumer failed to state a claim that the debt collector violated the FDCPA merely because it filed an arbitration claim without immediate means of proving the debt.

Ventura v. 1st Fin. Bank, 2005 WL 2406029 (N.D. Cal. Sept. 29, 2005). Although the cost of bringing an individual claim in arbitration for violation of the FDCPA would be $125 whereas the cost to bring a class claim would cost as much as $60,000 for the first two of four phases of arbitration, the court relied upon South Dakota law and granted defendant's motion to compel arbitration and stay litigation pending the arbitration.

Colorado

Kelly v. Wolpoff & Abramson, L.L.P., 634 F. Supp. 2d 1202 (D. Colo. 2008). Any FDCPA claim which may properly be based upon collection lawyers' alleged failure to seek an order compelling arbitration would necessarily constitute an impermissible collateral attack on the confirmed arbitration award.

Connecticut

Boran v. Columbia Credit Servs., 2006 U.S. Dist. LEXIS 84659 (D. Conn. Nov. 21, 2006). The debt collector's motion to dismiss or stay proceedings in favor of arbitration was denied where the consumer stated that she was a victim of fraud and did not sign the credit card agreement containing the arbitration clause.

Florida

Bolanos v. First Inv. Serv. Corp., 2010 WL 4457347 (S.D. Fla. Oct. 29, 2010). Statutorily created causes of action, such as those pursuant to the FDCPA, are not exempted from arbitration.

Cunningham v. MBNA Am. Bank, 8 So. 3d 438 (Fla. Dist. Ct. App. 2009). In this case, filed as an MBNA arbitration confirmation action, the dismissal of the consumer's FDCPA counterclaim,

alleging misuse of the NAF arbitration process to secure payment of a credit card debt, was not final and therefore not appealable; court rules would permit appeal under these circumstances only if the counterclaim were permissive, but here the FDCPA claim is a compulsory counterclaim under state law because it was "inextricably tied to the transaction or occurrence underlying MBNA's claim."

Georgia

Wilder v. Midland Credit Mgmt., 2010 WL 2499701 (N.D. Ga. May 20, 2010). Arbitration was compelled in accordance with the Beneficial loan contract signed by the consumer providing for arbitration by AAA or JAMS.

Illinois

Fox v. Nationwide Credit, Inc., 2010 WL 3420172 (N.D. Ill. Aug. 25, 2010). The defendant's motion to dismiss this FDCPA action and to compel arbitration was denied, as the arbitration agreement did not include third-party debt collectors.

Massachusetts

Hoefs v. CACV of Colorado, L.L.C., 365 F. Supp. 2d 69 (D. Mass. 2005). Defendants' motion to arbitrate this FDCPA case was granted where the underlying MBNA credit card agreement required arbitration of claims against the credit card issuer's assigns and its agents, and thus required arbitration of consumer's claims against debt collection agency, its attorney, and attorney's law firm. Court ruled that the mail box rule bound consumer where there was evidence that the arbitration agreement was mailed but not received.

Missouri

Nichelson v. Soeder, 2006 U.S. Dist. LEXIS 78448 (E.D. Mo. Oct. 27, 2006). The court granted defendants' motion to compel arbitration and dismiss plaintiff's claims that defendants violated the FDCPA by filing a state court petition rather than arbitrating the dispute.

Morrow v. Soeder, 2006 U.S. Dist. LEXIS 72073 (E.D. Mo. Oct. 3, 2006). Granted the collection attorneys' motion to compel arbitration and to dismiss action that alleges violations of the FDCPA in collector's representation of a payday lender in state collection court, holding that the lender's broad arbitration agreement which covered its agents included the collector, and the prosecution of the state collection suit did not waive the arbitration agreement since the consumer did not establish the necessary element of prejudice.

Kramer & Frank, P.C. v. Wibbenmeyer, 2006 WL 1134479 (E.D. Mo. Apr. 26, 2006). Law firm filed suit seeking declaratory judgment that their arbitration practices, including requests for attorney fees for out of state attorneys, etc. did not violate FDCPA.

McCracken v. Green Tree Servicing, L.L.C., 279 S.W.3d 226 (Mo. Ct. App. 2009). Mortgagors' FDCPA case against mortgage servicer alleging misapplication of their mortgage payments was ordered to arbitration pursuant to the arbitration agreement in the original mortgage documents. The lower court had denied arbitration because the agreement did not say that it applied to "successors and assigns." The appeals court reversed, holding that "[t]he scope of the arbitration provision is broad enough to include the relationship between [plaintiff and defendant] that resulted from the lender's assignment of its right to receive the loan payments." The relevant portion of the arbitration agreement states: "All disputes, claims or controversies arising from or relating to this contract or the relationships which result from this contract, or the validity of this arbitration clause or the entire contract, shall be resolved by binding arbitration by one arbitrator selected by *you* with consent of us. . . . The parties agree and understand that all disputes arising under case law, statutory law, and all other laws including but not limited to, all contract, tort, and property disputes, will be subject to binding arbitration in accord with this conduct."

New Jersey

Wood v. Palisades Collection, L.L.C., 2010 WL 2950323 (D.N.J. July 22, 2010). The debt collector's motion to compel arbitration and stay all proceedings pending completion of arbitration was granted because the court determined that the parties entered into a valid agreement to arbitrate in credit card contracts with First USA and then Chase.

Cohen v. Wolpoff & Abramson, L.L.P., 2008 WL 4513569 (D.N.J. Oct. 2, 2008). The arbitration provision only requires arbitration when the credit card company has been named as a co-defendant in a suit. Here, because plaintiff did not name either credit card company as a co-defendant in this suit, this case does not fall within the scope of the arbitration provision. Claims for the unauthorized practice of law (by pursuing an arbitration proceeding) do not give rise to a misrepresentation cause of action under the FDCPA. Plaintiff points to nothing within the FDCPA that would allow this court to find that an attorney licensed in one jurisdiction who engaged in debt collection in another jurisdiction is not an attorney within the meaning of the FDCPA. Nothing in the FDCPA, its purposes, or its legislative history, suggests that Congress included within the scope of abusive practices multi-jurisdictional collection efforts by attorneys.

Schiano v. MBNA, 2005 U.S. Dist. LEXIS 35606 (D.N.J. Dec. 19, 2005). Stayed suit pending arbitration, since attorneys Pressler and Wolpoff, also defendants, were agents or assigns within the MBNA arbitration clause.

New York

Fedotov v. Peter T. Roach & Assocs., P.C., 2006 WL 692002 (S.D.N.Y. Mar. 16, 2006). The court granted the defendant's unopposed motion to stay proceedings and grant arbitration under the authority of a credit card arbitration agreement that included "all claims" against, *inter alia,* the card issuer's "agent" or "representative" where FDCPA case was filed against the card issuer's law firm engaged in the collection of the credit card balance.

Ohio

Hodson v. Javitch, Block & Rathbone, L.L.P., 531 F. Supp. 2d 827 (N.D. Ohio 2008). Capital One did not waive its right to arbitrate by filing two credit card collection suit in state court against a consumer as that conduct was not completely inconsistent with an intent to arbitrate the dispute and not prejudicial to the consumer. The arbitration agreement was not unconscionable; it was conspicuous in the credit card agreement and allowed either party to elect arbitration.

Liedtke v. Frank, 2006 WL 625730 (N.D. Ohio Mar. 10, 2006). Household Bank's arbitration clause in it's "GM" credit card agreement was enforced.

Savage v. Hatcher, 2005 WL 1279244 (S.D. Ohio May 31, 2005). Arbitration ordered in an FDCPA claim against the collection lawyer on a payday loan.

Hawkins v. O'Brien, 2009 WL 50616 (Ohio Ct. App. Jan. 9, 2009). FDCPA claim is arbitrable.

Pennsylvania

Holmes v. Mann Bracken, L.L.C., 2009 WL 5184485 (E.D. Pa. Dec. 22, 2009). The amended Pennsylvania Rules of Civil Procedure which created a specific section governing arbitration of consumer credit transactions was not preempted by the FAA.

Baylis v. Wachovia Bank, 2008 WL 5055746 (E.D. Pa. Nov. 25, 2008). Court enforced defendant's arbitration agreement when consumer challenged validity of debt collector's garnishment of her accounts, but retained jurisdiction to determine independent FDCPA claims against debt collector.

Bontempo v. Wolpoff & Abramson, L.L.P., 2006 U.S. Dist. LEXIS 78160 (W.D. Pa. Sept. 20, 2006). In this putative class action alleging that "it is W&A's practice to obtain alleged arbitration awards through an invalid, non-participatory process, and to add costs and fees to any arbitral award, after which it uses those awards to attempt to collect debts," the magistrate judge recommended that the defendant's motion to compel arbitration be denied, citing and following the *Karnette* decision that the subject MBNA arbitration agreement did not cover MBNA's attorneys where, as here, they are sued separately from MBNA.

Texas

Adams v. Dell Computer Corp., 2006 WL 2670969 (S.D. Tex. Sept. 18, 2006). Since the *pro se* consumer and the creditor had entered into an arbitration agreement, the court granted the defendants' motion to compel arbitration on the consumer's debt collection misconduct claims against the creditor under state law and its debt collector under the FDCPA because the debt collector was entitled to enforce the arbitration agreement to which it was not a party in accordance with circuit authority that so holds when, as here, "a signatory raises allegations of substantially interdependent and concerted misconduct by both a non-signatory and one or more signatories to the contract."

Virginia

Karnette v. Wolpoff & Abramson, L.L.P., 444 F. Supp. 2d 640 (E.D. Va. 2006). The court denied the collection attorney's motion to compel arbitration in FDCPA action on the basis of its creditor's arbitration agreement with the consumer, since the agreement did not provide coverage to the attorney as the creditor's "agent" sued separately from the creditor. The attorney debt collector waived any right to invoke its creditor's arbitration agreement with the consumer by actively defending this FDCPA action before filing the motion.

Washington

Miller v. Northwest Tr. Servs., Inc., 2005 WL 1711131 (E.D. Wash. July 20, 2005). Because the promissory note for the purchase of real estate did not limit arbitration to disputes between the original parties to the agreement, the court found that the note contemplated that borrowers may have to arbitrate disputes with future assigned lenders. Green Tree, the servicer, was entitled to enforce the arbitration clause to arbitrate this FDCPA dispute.

K.3.6.6 Litigation Privilege, Witness and Other Immunity

Allen ex rel. Martin v. LaSalle Bank, N.A., 2011 WL 94420 (3d Cir. Jan. 12, 2011). Because the FDCPA does not contain an exemption from liability for common law privileges, a state's litigation privilege is not a defense to liability.

Hartman v. Great Seneca Fin. Corp., 569 F.3d 606 (6th Cir. 2009). Neither the Petition Clause of First Amendment or the *Noerr-Pennington* doctrine bars FDCPA suits based on intentional misrepresentations made in state court collection cases. The FDCPA was not unconstitutionally vague as applied to the misconduct in this case which was an alleged intentional misrepresentation of an exhibit because such false statements are not immunized by the Petition Clause.

California

Welker v. Law Office of Horwitz, 626 F. Supp. 2d 1068 (S.D. Cal. 2009). Litigation privilege should not be applied to claims arising under the FDCPA or California's Rosenthal Act.

Gerber v. Citigroup, Inc., 2009 WL 248094 (E.D. Cal. Jan. 29, 2009), *report and recommendation adopted*, 2009 WL 2058576 (E.D. Cal. July 14, 2009). Defendants are not protected from FDCPA claims by their prior filing of a state collection action under the *Noerr-Pennington* doctrine or California's litigation privilege. Supplemental state claims under the California debt collection statute and for intentional infliction of emotional distress were dismissed as barred by the state litigation privilege. The state anti-SLAPP suit statute did not bar the FDCPA claims.

Reyes v. Kenosian & Miele, L.L.P., 619 F. Supp. 2d 796 (N.D. Cal. 2008). Any common law or First Amendment-based litigation-immunity doctrine is trumped by the statutory language of the FDCPA.

Sial v. Unifund CCR Partners, 2008 WL 4079281 (S.D. Cal. Aug. 28, 2008). Relying on the reasoning in *Heintz v. Jenkins*, the court concluded that the *Noerr-Pennington* doctrine did not immunize the collection action conduct at issue in violation of the FDCPA and denied defendant's motion for judgment on the pleadings.

Mello v. Great Seneca Fin. Corp., 526 F. Supp. 2d 1020 (C.D. Cal. 2007). Rejected defendant lawyer's assertion of litigation privilege for state court pleadings under the FDCPA. State litigation exemption not applicable to protect state court pleadings under more specific provisions of the FDCPA.

Connecticut

Bolorin v. Borrino, 248 F.R.D. 93 (D. Conn. Feb. 11, 2008). Privilege log insufficiently detailed to protect attorney client communications in a foreclosure and attorney was compelled to produce documents for examination.

Deutsche Bank v. Lichtenfels, 48 Conn. L. Rptr. 133 (Conn. Super. Ct. 2009). There is no blanket common law litigation immunity from the requirements of the FDCPA.

Florida

North Star Capital Acquisitions, L.L.C. v. Krig, 2008 WL 346021 (M.D. Fla. Feb. 7, 2008). The complaint failed to affirmatively and clearly show the applicability of the litigation privilege, and as a result the privilege cannot be held to be available to the debt collector by a motion to dismiss.

Illinois

Herkert v. MRC Receivables Corp., 655 F. Supp. 2d 870 (N.D. Ill. 2009). Assertion of a bona fide error defense under the FDCPA acts as a waiver of the attorney-client privilege, since the privilege was not meant to be used "both as a sword and a shield."

Basile v. Blatt, Hasenmiller, Leibsker & Moore L.L.C., 632 F. Supp. 2d 842 (N.D. Ill. 2009). Collection lawsuits are not shielded from the FDCPA by the *Noerr-Pennington* doctrine.

Taylor v. United Collection Bureau, Inc., 2009 WL 1708762 (S.D. Ill. June 17, 2009). Rejected defendant's efforts to put its answer and counterclaim under seal lest it violate state privacy laws. State law privileges and protections do not control in federal question cases.

Michigan

Pasiud v. GMAC, 2008 WL 2008616 (E.D. Mich. May 8, 2008). Attorneys who are involved in debt collection are not entitled to absolute immunity, even from statements that they made as "participants in the judicial process."

Minnesota

Gallagher v. Gurstel, Staloch & Chargo, P.A., 645 F. Supp. 2d 795 (D. Minn. 2009). FDCPA claims are not barred by any common law immunity or common law privilege applicable to a lawyer's litigation activities.

Phillips v. Messerli & Kramer P.A., 2008 WL 5050127 (D. Minn. Nov. 20, 2008). The Minnesota litigation privilege did not bar the plaintiffs' FDCPA claim that the law firm had improperly levied upon their bank account.

Missouri

Eckert v. LVNV Funding L.L.C., 647 F. Supp. 2d 1096 (E.D. Mo. 2009). "Where only a debt collector can be held liable under the FDCPA, and the 'witness' at issue is that debt collector, who can control his or her own liability by not making knowingly false statements in attempting to collect a debt," the doctrine of witness immunity is inconsistent with the purpose of the statute to hold debt collectors liable for conduct related to the process of debt collection.

Reynolds v. Persolve, L.L.C., 2008 WL 379695 (E.D. Mo. Feb. 11, 2008). Unopposed motion to dismiss granted because collection lawyer was protected by absolute witness immunity as his affidavit stating the amount of the debt in the state court petition.

Nebraska

Jenkins v. General Collection Co., 538 F. Supp. 2d 1165 (D. Neb. 2008). Debt collectors are not entitled to common law litigation immunity from FDCPA claims.

New Jersey

Ogbin v. Fein, Such, Kahn & Shepard, P.C., 2009 WL 1587896 (D.N.J. June 1, 2009). The state litigation privilege applies to the FDCPA. Note that the court based its opinion on the plaintiffs' inadequate briefing, stating (correctly) that the plaintiffs' cited cases do not support their position.

New York

Schuh v. Druckman & Sinel, L.L.P., 602 F. Supp. 2d 454 (S.D.N.Y. 2009). "Attempting to collect on a judgment is not a step in the 'ascertainment of truth' that requires the protection that immunity from suit affords. Accepting [foreclosure attorney's] argument would mean that the FDCPA would not apply to efforts by debt collectors to collect debts based on judgments. The statute's definition of the term 'debt,' however, explicitly recognizes that it applies to obligations that have been 'reduced to judgment.'"

Ohio

Kline v. Mortgage Elec. Sys., 659 F. Supp. 2d 940 (S.D. Ohio 2009). Court rejected claim of attorney immunity.

Ison v. Javitch, Block & Rathbone, 2007 WL 2769674 (S.D. Ohio Sept. 18, 2007). The court summarily rejected the defendant's defenses based on "absolute immunity under the witness immunity doctrine, absolute immunity from statements made in the course of a judicial proceeding, qualified immunity under the First Amendment and the *Noerr-Pennington* doctrine."

South Carolina

Sain v. HSBC Mortgage Servs., Inc., 2009 WL 2858993 (D.S.C. Aug. 28, 2009). State law immunity doctrine that shielded the defendant attorney from liability based on his prosecution of the underlying state foreclosure action was not applicable to this federal FDCPA claim.

West Virginia

Stover v. Fingerhut Direct Mktg., Inc., 709 F. Supp. 2d 473 (S.D. W. Va. 2009). First Amendment challenge to West Virginia's debt collection laws rejected. Defendants' debt collection practice of calling debtors at home to discuss debts is entitled to only a modicum of First Amendment protection because it: (1) involves commercial speech; (2) pertains to a matter of purely private, rather than public, concern; (3) includes noncommunicative conduct; and (4) implicates plaintiffs' right to privacy in their home. "Defendants' debt collection activities interject commercial speech directly into Plaintiffs' home against their wishes. Defendants' right to engage in this manner of speech is in direct conflict with Plaintiffs' right to privacy in their home. Where these two rights are in the balance, it is the right to privacy that generally carries more weight."

K.3.7 Jurisdiction and Venue

K.3.7.1 Removal and Federal/State Jurisdiction Issues

Avery v. First Resolution Mgmt. Corp., 568 F.3d 1018 (9th Cir. 2009). The consumer's FDCPA claim that the defendant filed a state court collection suit on a time-barred debt was properly dismissed since the suit was not time barred under "the narrow statutory argument" based on "Oregon's choice of law regime," the sole basis for decision presented by the consumer's counsel.

Long v. Shorebank Dev. Corp., 182 F.3d 548 (7th Cir. 1999). Tenant whose state court eviction was allegedly procured by fraud by a collector was not precluded by the *Rooker-Feldman* doctrine from pursuing FDCPA damages for the resulting loss of her job, loss of custody of her daughter, and six months of homelessness. Shorebank attorney allegedly agreed that Long did not owe rent, represented that Long would have time to work this out with the landlord, that the document she was signing was not a court document (it was a consent to eviction) and she could ignore court proceedings. "The counts in Long's complaint alleging violations of the FDCPA are independent from the eviction, order and, therefore, *Rooker Feldman* does not apply to these claims." Long could not have raised the FDCPA claim in the state court action. Statute in order to state a claim for relief for violating the FDCPA.

Arkansas

Portfolio Recovery Assocs., L.L.C. v. Born, 2010 WL 3001996 (W.D. Ark. July 23, 2010). A state court suit to recover a credit card debt could not be removed to federal court on the basis of an FDCPA counterclaim.

California

Petracek v. American Home Mortgage Serv., 2010 WL 582113 (E.D. Cal. Feb. 11, 2010). "Consumers' statement [in their complaint] that their Rosenthal Act claim is 'subject to the remedies' of the Federal Fair Debt Collection Practices Act is insufficient to state a claim 'arising under' the Federal Fair Debt Collection Practices Act [and t]herefore . . . does not provide a basis for federal subject matter jurisdiction."

Cable v. Protection One, Inc., 2009 WL 2970111 (C.D. Cal. Sept. 9, 2009). State case that had been removed to federal court now remanded: "The only remaining causes of action are asserted under state law, including [the Rosenthal Act]. . . . To whatever extent the [Rosenthal Act] imports elements of the FDCPA, it remains a state claim, and does not invoke federal policies of such significance to warrant federal question jurisdiction."

Abad v. Diversified Adjustment Serv., Inc., 2009 WL 256381 (E.D. Cal. Feb. 3, 2009). Where the FDCPA claim against a collection agency was dismissed, the court remanded the state claim against the creditor to state court from which it was removed.

Moore v. Chase Bank, 2008 WL 314664 (N.D. Cal. Feb. 4, 2008). Denied the plaintiff's motion to remand to state court where, although the complaint was comprised only of state claims relating to the plaintiff's mortgage, "several of Plaintiff's causes of action contain predicate federal statutory violations."

Colorado

Chase Home Fin. v. Lanier, 2008 WL 2477598 (D. Colo. June 18, 2008). Remanded to state court; mortgage lenders collecting their own debts are not "debt collectors."

HSBC Bank USA Nat'l Ass'n v. Crowe, 2008 WL 1699758 (D. Colo. Apr. 9, 2008). State court foreclosure and unlawful detention case removed on the alleged basis of the FDCPA now remanded and *pro se* defendant ordered to show cause why restrictions and sanctions should not be imposed where this *pro se* defendant had previously removed the case and the court had previously remanded.

Connecticut

Massad v. Greaves, 554 F. Supp. 2d 163 (D. Conn. 2008). State case where the state defendant raised an FDCPA counterclaim and then removed to federal court remanded since the federal counterclaim provided no basis for removal.

Georgia

Barkwell v. Portfolio Recovery Assocs., L.L.C., 2010 WL 2012149 (M.D. Ga. May 20, 2010). A federal counterclaim, even when compulsory, does not establish " 'arising under' jurisdiction." Thus, the consumer's allegations of an FDCPA violation in his counterclaim did not confer federal question jurisdiction.

Farrell v. Poythress, 2010 WL 2411502 (N.D. Ga. May 11, 2010). The *pro se* tenant's case was remanded to state court after she had removed this state eviction proceeding on the unavailing basis that the eviction was occurring in violation of the FDCPA.

Idaho

Bonneville Billing & Collections, Inc. v. Chase, 2009 WL 1269738 (D. Idaho May 6, 2009). Where the basis of removal to federal court was the consumer's FDCPA counterclaim, the debt collector's motion to remand was granted.

Illinois

Matmanivong v. Unifund CCR Partners, 2009 WL 1181529 (N.D. Ill. Apr. 28, 2009). A claim challenging state court pleadings controlled by state court procedural and evidentiary law was not a valid claim under the FDCPA. If the consumer alleges more than merely state court deficiencies and, instead, alleges that a false representation was made in the pleadings, the violation may properly be considered under the FDCPA.

Berg v. Blatt, Hasenmiller, Leibsker & Moore L.L.C., 2009 WL 901011 (N.D. Ill. Mar. 31, 2009). The FDCPA applies to misrepresentations made in state court actions.

Norris v. Miller, 926 F. Supp. 776 (N.D. Ill. 1996). The court issued a stay under the US Supreme Court's "Colorado River" doctrine as there was a similar parallel concurrent state proceeding in Florida, both cases were dependent on a Florida analysis of the state statute of limitations, and the Florida case was further along. Therefore, it was more efficient to stay the federal proceeding in light of the ongoing Florida case where a decision could render the federal action moot. The consumer's FDCPA class action had alleged that the collectors violated the FDCPA by collecting time-barred debts.

Louisiana

Bauer v. Dean Morris, L.L.P., 2010 WL 4103192 (E.D. La. Oct. 18, 2010). A plaintiff who disclaimed all federal claims to avoid removal was judicially estopped from then asserting FDCPA claims for the first time when the case was removed on the basis of the FDIC's entry into the state case as a receiver for WaMu.

Rhodes Life Ins. Co. v. Mendy Prop., L.C., 2009 WL 1212476 (E.D. La. Apr. 30, 2009). The inclusion of the FDCPA validation notice in a state court pleading did not create federal jurisdiction, and plaintiff's motion to remand was granted.

Massachusetts

Dean v. Compass Receivables Mgmt. Corp., 148 F. Supp. 2d 116 (D. Mass. 2001). Consumer's claims of debt collection abuse filed in state court alleging solely state law violations and removed by the defendants to federal court were remanded back to state court for lack of federal jurisdiction, where, although the misconduct underlying the consumer's claims was also a violation of the FDCPA, no federal FDCPA claims were actually asserted or could be said to be present under the artful pleading doctrine.

Commonwealth v. V. & M. Mgmt., Inc., 752 F. Supp. 519 (D. Mass. 1990). The allegation of an FDCPA violation was removed to federal court even though the attorney general maintained that its state suit was based purely on the state UDAP statute and that the federal law violations were alleged merely as evidence of unfair and deceptive acts and practices violating the state UDAP statute.

Michigan

Gavitt v. NCO Fin. Sys., Inc., 2009 U.S. Dist. LEXIS 66120 (E.D. Mich. July 31, 2009). Court exercised its discretion and remanded the state law claims in this FDCPA case that the defendant properly removed to federal court: "The Court finds that the contemporaneous presentation of Plaintiff's parallel state claim for relief will result in the undue confusion of the jury . . . *see also* Padilla v. City of Saginaw, 867 F. Supp. 1309, 1315 (E.D. Mich. 1994)."

Credit Union One v. Tindall, 2008 WL 180533 (E.D. Mich. Apr. 11, 2008). State collection case which the *pro se* consumer removed to federal court now remanded for lack of federal jurisdiction since the consumer's claim that the prosecution of the state collection suit violated the FDCPA did not alter the fact that the state court complaint raised no federal question.

Hughes v. May Dep't Stores Co., 368 F. Supp. 2d 793 (E.D. Mich. 2005). State law debt collection tort complaint filed in state court could not be removed to federal court on the theory that the consumer had "artfully" pleaded only state claims to avoid federal jurisdiction over what was in essence a federal FDCPA claim.

Minnesota

Mason v. Messerli & Kramer, P.A., 2004 WL 898273 (D. Minn. Apr. 14, 2004). Where FDCPA action was filed in federal court and claim arising from the same facts was filed in state court, the district court applied the *Colorado River* doctrine and abstained, dismissing the FDCPA claim.

Knutsen v. Consumer Credit Counseling Serv. of Minnesota, Inc., 1999 WL 181404 (D. Minn. Jan. 26, 1999). Collection agency's effort to remove a state unfair practices claim to federal court was unsuccessful. While state law standards were the same as the FDCPA, the collection agency was specifically exempt from the FDCPA. Thus, there was no federal question to support jurisdiction.

Nebraska

General Collection Co. v. Meyer, 2008 WL 747001 (D. Neb. Mar. 17, 2008). State court collection case that was removed to federal court by the state defendant/consumer was remanded since neither the consumer's state court counterclaim under the FDCPA nor the state court complaint's recital of the § 1692e(11) mini-*Miranda* notice is a basis for making the requisite showing to support removal that the state complaint arose under federal question jurisdiction.

New Jersey

Apostolou v. Mann Bracken, L.L.C., 2009 WL 1312927 (D.N.J. May 1, 2009). Because the court had obtained jurisdiction over the FDCPA claim, the nonresident plaintiffs' claims could be heard under Rule 20 of Federal Rules of Civil Procedure, but jurisdiction over their state law claims was denied.

New York

Gerontis v. Schwartz, 1999 U.S. Dist. LEXIS 3992 (S.D.N.Y. Mar. 31, 1999). Bankruptcy court could properly remand case to state court pursuant to the discretionary abstention doctrines. Although plaintiff raised a federal issue by asserting the FDCPA as a defense to her eviction, bankruptcy court could remand post-judgment motion of the eviction proceeding where removal by defendant to federal court was an attempt to have the federal courts serve as appellate courts to the state courts.

North Carolina

De Los Santos v. Nieves, 2010 WL 2471894 (M.D.N.C. June 15, 2010). The court granted the unopposed motion to remand the case to state court once the consumer dismissed the federal claims that had been the basis for removal.

North Dakota

Weiss v. Collection Ctr., Inc., 667 N.W.2d 567 (N.D. 2003). An action under the Act may be maintained in either state or federal court.

Pennsylvania

Crooker v. Wachovia Bank, 2010 WL 1186147 (E.D. Pa. Mar. 25, 2010). The court dismissed with prejudice the *pro se* complaint

where the consumer made it clear that "he refuses to participate in this suit because it has been removed to federal court" and where the consumer apparently moved for voluntary dismissal only to avoid federal jurisdiction.

First Horizon Home Loans v. Gardner, 2009 WL 1107818 (W.D. Pa. Apr. 23, 2009). A consumer's counterclaim in a state court collection lawsuit asserting violations of the FDCPA did not form a basis for removal to federal court.

Fosnocht v. Demko, 438 F. Supp. 2d 561 (E.D. Pa. 2006). Debtor/defendant's removal to federal court of the state collection case based on the assertion of an FDCPA counterclaim was improper, and remand was ordered, since removal may not be founded on a counterclaim filed as part of an answer but must rest on the allegation of a federal claim in the plaintiff's complaint.

Smith v. Resorts U.S.A., Inc., 1999 U.S. Dist. LEXIS 17614 (E.D. Pa. Nov. 10, 1999). Claims under the FDCPA are substantial federal claims. Therefore, remand to state court denied, in part, because the original complaint stated a claim under the FDCPA.

South Carolina

Burbage v. Richburg, 417 F. Supp. 2d 746 (D.S.C. 2006). The court remanded the removal of the state court collection and foreclosure case since the debtor's purported defenses under the FDCPA to the state court case did not create federal question jurisdiction and the state complaint did not plead a federal claim.

Tennessee

Simmons v. Countrywide Home Loans, 2010 WL 670032 (M.D. Tenn. Feb. 19, 2010). The *pro se* consumers' motion to remand the removed action was denied since the complaint relied in part on the FDCPA in asserting its claims.

Texas

Jaimes v. Dovenmuehle Mortgage, Inc., 2008 WL 536644 (S.D. Tex. Feb. 27, 2008). Where the complaint did not state an FDCPA or other federal claim and specifically disclaimed any federal causes of action, the case was remanded to state court.

Greene Home Owners Ass'n, Inc. v. Vogel, 1999 U.S. Dist. LEXIS 5165 (N.D. Tex. Apr. 12, 1999). Motion to remand to state court file by defendants/counter-plaintiffs was granted where plaintiff/counter-defendant removed case to federal court based on FDCPA counterclaim. Although the FDCPA counterclaim was a federal question separate and independent from the original claim, an original state court plaintiff was not entitled to removal to federal court based on a federal counterclaim.

Virginia

McGilvray v. Hallmark Fin. Group, Inc., 891 F. Supp. 265 (E.D. Va. 1995). Although FDCPA authorized filing FDCPA claims in state courts, collector's removal of the action to federal court was proper. Federal and state claims for collection abuse were so interwoven that no separate and independent state claim existed which would permit federal court to return case to state court.

Mabe v. G.C. Servs., L.P., 1994 WL 6920 (W.D. Va. Jan. 6, 1994), *aff'd*, 32 F.3d 86 (4th Cir. 1994). Contract between collector and state requiring collector to abide by the FDCPA did not confer federal question jurisdiction upon the court for a breach of that agreement.

Wisconsin

Crown Asset Mgmt. L.L.C. v. Doyle, 2010 WL 1050243 (E.D. Wis. Mar. 18, 2010). The court lacked subject matter jurisdiction because no federal claim appeared on the face of the small claims complaint and because the consumer's FDCPA counterclaim could not establish § 1331 jurisdiction.

K.3.7.2 Collector's Counterclaims and Ancillary Jurisdiction

Arizona

Hart v. Clayton-Parker & Assocs., Inc., 869 F. Supp. 774 (D. Ariz. 1994). A debt collector's state law counterclaim to collect the debt underlying the consumer's FDCPA action was not sufficiently "logically related" to the FDCPA claim to constitute a compulsory counterclaim. Accordingly, federal court had no supplementary jurisdiction to hear the counterclaim under the federal supplementary jurisdiction statute, 28 U.S.C. § 1367.

California

Martin v. Law Offices of John F. Edwards, 262 F.R.D. 534 (S.D. Cal. 2009). In an FDCPA action, a counterclaim for the underlying debt is not a compulsory counterclaim but, instead, is permissive. The motion to dismiss a debt collection counterclaim was granted for sound public policy reasons, including entanglement in state law issues and involvement of limited resources in legal questions of no federal significance.

Gerber v. Citigroup, Inc., 2009 WL 248094 (E.D. Cal. Jan. 29, 2009), *report and recommendation adopted*, 2009 WL 2058576 (E.D. Cal. July 14, 2009). In light of all the state law claims plaintiff has raised including challenges to the terms of the card agreement, the card issuer's counterclaim for the balance of the debt was properly within the court's supplementary jurisdiction. Even if the credit card account was time barred, the card issuer could obtain relief by recoupment or setoff.

Langley v. Check Game Solutions, Inc., 2007 WL 2701345 (S.D. Cal. Sept. 13, 2007). Time expended to defend the collection of the underlying debt brought as a counterclaim to the federal FDCPA suit is not compensable to the prevailing consumer under § 1692k(a)(3).

Campos v. W. Dental Servs., Inc., 404 F. Supp. 2d 1164 (N.D. Cal. 2005). Although finding that supplemental jurisdiction pursuant to 28 U.S.C. § 1367(a) over defendant's counterclaim for the underlying debt existed, the court declined to exercise its discretion to hear it and dismissed the counterclaim as the collection counterclaim could predominate the litigation and allowing it would chill the consumers' FDCPA rights.

Sparrow v. Mazda Am. Credit, 385 F. Supp. 2d 1063 (E.D. Cal. 2005). Although the court found that it had supplemental jurisdiction over the collector's counterclaims for the underlying debt, the court declined pursuant to 28 U.S.C. § 1367(c)(4) to exercise

supplemental jurisdiction because of the chilling affect it would have on litigants pursuing their rights under the FDCPA.

Williams v. Trans-Continental Affiliated, C-93-2999, Clearinghouse No. 49,952 (N.D. Cal. 1994). Debt collector's state law counterclaims alleging consumer had committed fraud in her credit application and failed to notify the debt collector of a change of address in violation of California Civil Code §§ 1788.20, 1788.21, was not sufficiently "logically related" to the consumer's FDCPA claim for abusive, deceptive and unfair trade practices to constitute a compulsory counterclaim and therefore, federal court had no supplementary jurisdiction over collector's counterclaim under 28 U.S.C. § 1367.

Connecticut

Gervais v. Riddle & Assocs., P.C., 2004 WL 725332 (D. Conn. Mar. 23, 2004). The court held that the consumer failed to provide any support for his motion to strike the collector's counterclaim for declaratory relief that its collection efforts were all lawful and did not violate the federal and state laws that the complaint alleged were violated.

Florida

Ghazal v. RJM Acquisitions Funding, L.L.C., 2008 WL 2439508 (S.D. Fla. June 16, 2008). Motion to dismiss a counterclaim to collect the debt denied; supplemental jurisdiction was appropriate.

Idaho

Moore v. Old Canal Fin. Corp., 2006 WL 851114 (D. Idaho Mar. 29, 2006). Supplemental jurisdiction existed over counterclaim seeking to collect the same debt from which plaintiff's FDCPA claim arose, but the court declined to exercise supplemental jurisdiction over the counterclaim for the debt.

Illinois

Crawford v. Equifax Payment Servs., Inc., 1998 WL 704050 (N.D. Ill. Sept. 30, 1998). Defendant's counterclaims to collect on dishonored checks could be heard under the court's supplemental jurisdiction because there was a loose connection between the two the claims; however, due to the chilling effect on FDCPA claims and the burden which would be placed on the court by such counterclaims, the court declined to exercise jurisdiction over the counterclaims. Defendant's set-off of the underlying debt was allowed because it would not contradict the public policy of the FDCPA or have a chilling effect on the potential claim.

Nunez v. Etan Indus., Inc., 1999 WL 14483 (N.D. Ill. Jan. 6, 1998). Court on its own struck the defendant's answer which erroneously alleged that the court did not have jurisdiction to determine its own jurisdiction and that conclusory allegations did not belong in the complaint. The defendant's attorney ordered to send a letter to the client and the court stating that the defendant would not be billed for the time spent on drafting a proper answer.

Gutshall v. Bailey & Assocs., 1991 U.S. Dist. LEXIS 12153 (N.D. Ill. Feb. 11, 1991). A federal district court does not have jurisdiction over a counterclaim for the debt involved in an FDCPA suit since the counterclaim is permissive and would impede the expeditious enforcement of the federal debt collection claim.

Michigan

Tworek v. Asset Acceptance, L.L.C., 2010 WL 707365 (E.D. Mich. Feb. 23, 2010). Defendant's motion for summary judgment, asserting that the amount of its set-off of the debt allegedly exceeded the plaintiff's affirmative claims, was denied: "First, Defendant has no right to setoff until the parties are mutually indebted, and there are no mutual debt obligations until the value of Plaintiff's claims in this matter have been established. Second, [t]he right to setoff does not operate as a denial of the plaintiff's claim but allows the defendant to set off the debt that the plaintiff owes the defendant against the plaintiff's claim against the defendant."

Nebraska

Evans v. American Credit Sys., Inc., 2003 WL 23018529 (D. Neb. Dec. 10, 2003). Court dismissed the defendant's counterclaim to collect the underlying debt because it was permissive and therefore lacked an independent basis for federal jurisdiction.

Vernon v. BWS Credit Servs., Inc., Clearinghouse No. 27,693 (D. Neb. 1980). A counterclaim seeking to collect the underlying debt in a Fair Debt Collection Practices action is permissive, and the court did not have ancillary jurisdiction over the counterclaim.

Nevada

Kuhn v. Account Control Tech., Inc., 865 F. Supp. 1443 (D. Nev. 1994). Collection attorney's counterclaim for bad faith must be dismissed because it was not mandatory and did not arise out of the same transaction or occurrence as the FDCPA case.

New Mexico

Larranaga v. Mile High Collection & Recovery Bureau, Inc., Clearinghouse No. 46,775B, *rev'd on other grounds*, 807 F. Supp. 111 (D.N.M. 1992). In FDCPA action, district court dismissed third-party bank's cross-claim for deficiency after repossession against consumer because the two claims raised different factual issues and were governed by different bodies of law.

New York

Fentner v. Tempest Recovery Servs., Inc., 2008 WL 4147346 (W.D.N.Y. Sept. 2, 2008). Granted plaintiff's motion to dismiss debt collector's debt collection counterclaim on the basis that involved different issues and proof.

Berrios v. Sprint Corp., 1998 WL 199842 (E.D.N.Y. Mar. 16, 1998). Court noted that all reported decisions have found that a defendant's counterclaims for payment of an overdue debt are distinct from and not logically related to, a plaintiff's FDCPA claim based on improper debt collection practices.

Grammatico v. Sterling, Inc., Clearinghouse No. 47,976 (N.D.N.Y. 1991). Counterclaim for underlying debt was dismissed.

Leatherwood v. Universal Bus. Serv. Co., 115 F.R.D. 48 (W.D.N.Y. 1987). Court lacked ancillary jurisdiction over collector's counterclaim for debt since it was not a compulsory counterclaim to the plaintiff's FDCPA claim.

Oregon

Hashbun v. Credit Bureau, Inc., 37 Consumer Fin. L. Bull. (Am. Fin. Serv. Assoc.) 1 (D. Or. 1983). A counterclaim for the underlying debt was not compulsory in an FDCPA suit.

Darnall v. Crown Collections, Inc., Clearinghouse No. 37,498 (D. Or. 1983). Collector's permissive counterclaim on underlying debt in FDCPA suit dismissed for lack of federal jurisdiction.

Baker v. G.C. Servs. Corp., Clearinghouse No. 31,230 (D. Or. 1981), *aff'd on other grounds*, 677 F.2d 775 (9th Cir. 1982). The collector's counterclaim for the debt was dismissed as permissive and outside of the court's ancillary jurisdiction.

Pennsylvania

Kimmel v. Cavalry Portfolio Servs., L.L.C., 2010 WL 3860370 (E.D. Pa. Sept. 29, 2010). The debt buyer's counterclaim to the consumer's FDCPA suit was permissive, and therefore jurisdiction over it required an independent federal basis. Such a basis was present in this case due to diversity of citizenship and the fact that the alleged credit card debt was over the $75,000 amount in controversy threshold.

Orloff v. Syndicated Office Sys., 2003 WL 22100868 (E.D. Pa. Aug. 20, 2003). In an FDCPA class action defendant's counterclaim based on contract was dismissed as it was a permissive counterclaim raising different issues of law and fact and it would have a chilling affect on the consumer's pursuit of federal protections.

Tennessee

Parker v. Sadler, 2008 WL 2697376 (E.D. Tenn. July 1, 2008). Defendant collectors' malicious prosecution and other state law counterclaims alleging that filing the instant lawsuit based on the FDCPA and supplemental state causes of action was extortionate, abusive, and improper were not compulsory counterclaims and thus were dismissed for lack of independent federal subject matter jurisdiction.

Texas

Beard v. Aurora Loan Servs., L.L.C., 2006 WL 1350286 (S.D. Tex. May 17, 2006). Where plaintiff's state court complaint alleged only state law causes of action and specifically disclaimed any rights or causes of action under federal law, it was improperly removed to federal court and was remanded to state court.

K.3.7.3 Consumer's State Claims and Supplemental Jurisdiction

Stark v. Sandberg, Phoenix & von Gontard, P.C., 381 F.3d 793 (8th Cir. 2004). Arbitrator's award which included $6 million punitive damages reinstated as the district court failed to give the required deference to the arbitrator's award. The homeowner's claims involved tort and FDCPA claims for debt collection harassment and wrongful foreclosure.

Juras v. Aman Collection Serv., Inc., 829 F.2d 739 (9th Cir. 1987). State debt collection statute claims should be considered for pendent jurisdiction.

Alabama

Bice v. Merchants Adjustment Serv., Clearinghouse No. 41,265 (S.D. Ala. 1985). The consumer's pendent state tort claim failed to state an action for invasion of privacy or intentional infliction of mental distress in light of state precedent.

Prof'l Check Serv. v. Dutton, 560 So. 2d 755 (Ala. 1990). The fact that it was not illegal under the FDCPA for merchants to contract with a collector to attempt to initiate criminal prosecutions for worthless checks did not mean that it was proper under state law.

Arizona

Randall v. Nelson & Kennard, 2009 WL 2710141 (D. Ariz. Aug. 26, 2009). While the court had supplemental jurisdiction over the debt collector's counterclaim for the underlying debt, it chose not to exercise supple mental jurisdiction because to do so would increase both the complexity and length of time to resolve this narrow and straightforward FDCPA claim.

California

Welker v. Law Office of Daniel J. Horwitz, 699 F. Supp. 2d 1164 (S.D. Cal. 2010). The California litigation privilege did not protect the defendant's improper dunning letter; if it did, the privilege would in effect render the Rosenthal Act inoperable.

Owings v. Hunt & Henriques, 2010 WL 3489342 (S.D. Cal. Sept. 3, 2010). "[I]f the debt collector's representation is false, deceptive or misleading, it can constitute an FDCPA violation regardless of whether it also constitutes a violation of state law."

Morisaki v. Davenport, Allen & Malone, Inc., 2010 WL 3341566 (E.D. Cal. Aug. 23, 2010). A $75,000 default judgment was comprised of $73,000 in actual damages for emotional distress under federal and state law, $1000 in FDCPA statutory damages, and $1000 in California statutory damages.

Moya v. Chase Cardmember Serv., 661 F. Supp. 2d 1129 (N.D. Cal. 2009). Applying federal FDCPA standards to the California mini-FDCPA applicable to creditors, the court held that the creditor's collection letter, which failed to disclose that calling the listed toll-free number would connect the consumer with defendant's collection department, was not deceptive or unfair.

Castillo v. Chase Bank, Inc., 2009 WL 302757 (N.D. Cal. Feb. 5, 2009). Supplemental state claims dismissed as they predominated over the federal claim.

Lopez Reyes v. Kenosian & Miele, L.L.P., 525 F. Supp. 2d 1158 (N.D. Cal. 2007). Dismissed claim of violating state law parallel to FDCPA: contents of the state court complaint constituted a "communication" subject to the California statutory litigation privilege (based on facts involved, distinguishing split of authority).

Reyes v. Kenosian & Miele, L.L.P., 2008 WL 171070 (N.D. Cal. Jan. 18, 2008). California debt collection statute claim barred by litigation privilege.

Voris v. Resurgent Capital Servs., L.P., 494 F. Supp. 2d 1156 (S.D. Cal. 2007). Applying *Wade v. Regional Credit Ass'n*, 87 F.3d 1098 (9th Cir. 1996), the district court denied the consumer's §§ 1692e and 1692e(10) claims that violations of the California Fair Debt Collection Practices Act were per se violations of the FDCPA.

Khosroabadi v. N. Shore Agency, 439 F. Supp. 2d 1118 (S.D. Cal. 2006). The court declined to exercise supplemental jurisdiction over the state law claim where the claim asserting federal jurisdiction had been dismissed.

McDonald v. Bonded Collectors, L.L.C., 233 F.R.D. 576 (S.D. Cal. 2005). The California state debt collection statute was amended to allow class action claims.

Palmer v. Stassinos, 233 F.R.D. 546 (N.D. Cal. 2006). Class actions are permissible for violations of the Rosenthal California Fair Debt Collection Practices Act.

Joseph v. J.J. Mac Intyre Cos., L.L.C., 238 F. Supp. 2d 1158 (N.D. Cal. 2002). Consumer's state law invasion of privacy tort claims was not inconsistent with and therefore was not preempted by the FDCPA.

Newman v. CheckRite California, Inc., 912 F. Supp. 1354 (E.D. Cal. 1995). The court should exercise supplemental jurisdiction where state and federal claims arise out of the same facts and constitute a single case or controversy.

Connecticut

Derisme v. Hunt Leibert Jacobson, P.C., 2010 WL 4683916 (D. Conn. Nov. 10, 2010). The court sees no reason why a violation of the FDCPA could not also constitute conduct that "offends public policy as it has been established by statutes" for the purpose of state UDAP law.

Rivera v. Corporate Receivables, Inc., 2006 U.S. Dist. LEXIS 77122 (D. Conn. Oct. 20, 2006). In this FDCPA action, the court denied defendant's Rule 12(b)(6) motion to dismiss the consumer's state law claim of intentional infliction of emotional distress.

Chiverton v. Fed. Fin. Group, Inc., 399 F. Supp. 2d 96 (D. Conn. 2005). After entry of a default judgment, the magistrate judge recommended the award of $5000 actual damages, $1000 statutory damages, and punitive damages of $7500 for a UDAP claim, to each of two plaintiffs plus costs and attorney fees of $4613.54. One consumer had worried about losing his job or a promotion. The other consumer was frightened and embarrassed by threats of arrest.

Gervais v. O'Connell, Harris & Assocs., Inc., 297 F. Supp. 2d 435 (D. Conn. 2003). On default judgment district court awarded consumer $2500 for the return of funds sent to pay a debt misrepresented as not barred by the statute of limitations, and $1500 as emotional distress damages resulting from FDCPA violations, $8000 punitive damages under the state UDAP, and $5720 as costs and attorney fees for twenty-seven hours at $200 for violations of the FDCPA and Connecticut Unfair Trade Practices Act.

Johnson v. NCB Collection Servs., 799 F. Supp. 1298 (D. Conn. 1992) (settled upon collector's payment of $4000 for consumer to withdraw appeal). When all federal claims were eliminated before trial, the court should decline jurisdiction over any pendent state claims.

Porter v. Somers, 1993 WL 280118 (Conn. Super. Ct. July 12, 1993). Defendant attorney's three suits to collect an allegedly past due fee, adding unauthorized interest of 18% and unauthorized attorney fees for collection, alleging that plaintiff committed a larceny of services, and claiming treble damages was done to frighten and intimidate the plaintiff, in violation of the Conn. Unfair Trade Practices Act, entitling her to an amount in effect doubling her damages.

District of Columbia

Sterling Mirror, Inc. v. Gordon, 619 A.2d 64 (D.C. 1993). The D.C. Consumer Credit Protection Act was not involved because the transaction was neither a consumer credit sale nor a direct installment loan. The creditor's conduct was not so outrageous and extreme as to amount to the intentional infliction of emotional distress.

Florida

Beeders v. Gulf Coast Collection Bureau, 632 F. Supp. 2d 1125 (M.D. Fla. 2009). The consumer may recover a maximum of $1000 for each telephone message, if found to violate the Florida Consumer Collection Practices Act.

Drossin v. Nat'l Action Fin. Servs., Inc., 255 F.R.D. 608 (S.D. Fla. 2009). Class certification pursuant to the Florida Consumer Collection Practices Act was denied on the basis of individual questions of fact where claim involved debt collection messages left on answering machines.

North Star Capital Acquisitions, L.L.C. v. Krig, 2008 WL 346021 (M.D. Fla. Feb. 7, 2008). By alleging that inclusion of a stipulation of settlement and collection letter with the service of the summons and complaint was improper and misleading, consumers adequately stated an abuse of process claim as well as a claim that fell within the FDCPA.

Wright v. Bush Ross, P.A., 2008 WL 190466 (M.D. Fla. Jan. 18, 2008). Pursuant to the Florida Consumer Collection Practices Act, a condominium assessment is a "debt."

Williams v. Edelman, 408 F. Supp. 2d 1261 (S.D. Fla. 2006). Complaint alleging that defendants improperly filed suit against condominium owner and improperly filed lien against her property, notwithstanding knowledge that she did not owe any money stated a claim for violation of the Florida Deceptive and Unfair Trade Practices Act (FDUTPA), Fla. Stat. §§ 501.201–501.213.

Barker v. Tomlinson, 2006 WL 1679645 (M.D. Fla. June 7, 2006). Plaintiff was awarded damages in the amount of $22,000 under the Florida Consumer Collection Practices Act (FCCPA) and the federal Fair Debt Collection Practices Act (FDCPA), including: statutory damages of $1000 under the FCCPA; statutory damages of $1000 under the FDCPA; actual damages of $10,000 under both the FCCPA and FDCPA; and punitive damages of $10,000 under the FCCPA.

Kaplan v. Assetcare, Inc., 88 F. Supp. 2d 1355 (S.D. Fla. 2000). The court held that plaintiff had also stated a cause of action under the Fla. Consumer Collection Practices Act because knowledge could be imputed to the defendants. The court declined to exercise supplemental jurisdiction over plaintiff's Florida Insurance Code claim because it raised a novel or complex issue of state law.

Sandlin v. Shapiro & Fishman, 919 F. Supp. 1564 (M.D. Fla. 1996). Plaintiff claimed that the imposition of a $60 payoff disclosure fee for the mortgage loan violated § 1692f and the Florida debt collection statute by attempting to collect an unauthorized fee.

The court found the plaintiff had sufficiently stated a cause of action and denied defendant's motion to dismiss.

Georgia

Gilmore v. Account Mgmt., Inc., 2009 WL 2848278 (N.D. Ga. Apr. 27, 2009). After entry of default, the magistrate recommended an award of general damages for mental distress of $10,000 as a result of stress caused by dunning for a fully disputed debt during a time when the consumer was having heart problems and recovering from open heart surgery, trebled to $30,000 pursuant to the state consumer protection statute.

Carrigan v. Cent. Adjustment Bureau, Inc., 502 F. Supp. 468 (N.D. Ga. 1980). $500 statutory damages on a pendent state claim and attorney fees were awarded.

Carrigan v. Cent. Adjustment Bureau, Inc., 494 F. Supp. 824 (N.D. Ga. 1980). Pendent state claim on lack of collector's license permitted. Partial summary judgment on liability for plaintiff.

Hawaii

Bailey v. TRW Receivables Mgmt. Servs., Inc., 1990 U.S. Dist. LEXIS 19638 (D. Haw. Aug. 16, 1990). Pendent UDAP claim was dismissed as a matter of comity.

Sakuma v. First Nat'l Credit Bureau, 1989 U.S. Dist. LEXIS 19120 (D. Haw. Nov. 15, 1989). FDCPA damages of $1034 awarded for two notice violations and $1000 minimum UDAP damages awarded on a pendent state claim.

Illinois

Wisniewski v. Asset Acceptance Capital Corp., 2009 WL 212155 (N.D. Ill. Jan. 29, 2009). The Illinois debt collection agency law that was amended in 2008 to more clearly apply to debt buyers and their subsidiaries, was reasonably construed to apply to those entities before the amendment. Civil conspiracy claims were dismissed for failure to identify a conspirator who was not a principal or agent of the debt collectors. No claim stated for malicious prosecution for filing a second debt collection suit as first suit was dismissed without prejudice.

Asch v. Teller, Levit & Silvertrust, P.C., 2004 WL 2967441 (N.D. Ill. Nov. 24, 2004). In 2003, the court found that defendant's practice of not crediting payments when received falsely represented the amount of the debtors' payment obligations (by reporting a balance that was inflated by interest overcharges) and used those false representations to collect additional amounts which the debtors should not have had to pay. Since defendant had not adequately corrected its practices, an injunction issued under state law in favor of the class.

McCabe v. Crawford & Co., 272 F. Supp. 2d 736 (N.D. Ill. 2003). In order to state a violation of the Illinois Collection Agency Act, actual injury must be shown.

McCabe v. Crawford & Co., 210 F.R.D. 631 (N.D. Ill. 2002). To state claim for unjust enrichment under Illinois law, "a plaintiff must allege that defendant has unjustly retained a benefit to the plaintiff's detriment, and that the defendant's retention of the benefits violates the fundamental principles of justice, equity, a good conscience."

Kim v. Fayazi, 1998 WL 729753 (N.D. Ill. Oct. 14, 1998). Under local rule in Northern District of Illinois requiring that all cases under or relating to Title 11 be referred to the Bankruptcy Courts, judge dismissed bankruptcy claims with leave to refile in appropriate Bankruptcy Court. Motions to dismiss RICO claims were denied given that most details of the alleged scheme to trick plaintiff into repaying previously discharged credit card debts were within defendants' exclusive control and plaintiff's allegations were sufficiently particular.

Davis v. Suran, 1998 WL 378420 (N.D. Ill. July 1, 1998). The territorial reach of the Wisconsin Consumer Act was not statutorily limited to Wisconsin residents. In the absence of a conflict of law, the court was obliged to apply local state law to pendant statutory claims.

Perovich v. Humphrey, 1997 WL 674975 (N.D. Ill. Oct. 28, 1997). A claim under a California consumer protection law was dismissed where it conflicted with Illinois law, the suit was filed in Illinois, and the injury and significant relationships were in Illinois.

Sroka v. Bagnall, 1990 WL 114582 (N.D. Ill. July 20, 1990). Court refused to exercise its pendent party jurisdiction over law firm employer of a defendant collector where the consumer failed to thoroughly investigate case in a timely manner so that the employer was not timely joined as FDCPA defendant.

Torres v. Am. Tel. & Tel. Co., 1988 WL 121547 (N.D. Ill. Nov. 9, 1988). When the federal claims were dismissed, the court should decline jurisdiction over pendent state claims.

Indiana

Hamilton v. Am. Corrective Counseling Servs., 2006 WL 3332828 (N.D. Ind. Nov. 14, 2006). No abstention since civil rights claim does not affect any pending or future check prosecutions. No lack of notice and hearing where the consumers could refuse the diversion program and obtain a criminal court hearing if they were prosecuted. Informal dispute resolution in the district attorney's office also offered. Equal protection indigency claim dismissed.

Gastineau v. UMLIC VP L.L.C., 2006 WL 1131768 (S.D. Ind. Apr. 25, 2006). Consumers failed to establish that the collection attorney intentionally deceived the state court by proceeding to try to get judgment after learning of the claimed invalidity of the debt.

Wehrheim v. Secrest, 2002 WL 31242783 (S.D. Ind. Aug. 16, 2002). State UDAP claim denied for failure to establish that deception was intentional.

Kansas

Caputo v. Prof'l Recovery Servs., Inc., 2002 U.S. Dist. LEXIS 6514 (D. Kan. Mar. 11, 2002). Complaint alleged sufficient basis for claim against collection agency for employee's tortuous actions during collection attempts. Case discussed elements of claim for intentional infliction of emotional distress under Kansas law.

Rachoza v. Gallas & Schultz, 1998 WL 171280 (D. Kan. Mar. 23, 1998). Attorneys may be liable under the Kansas Consumer Protection Act for the same actions which would subject a creditor or another debt collector to liability.

Louisiana

Byes v. Telecheck Recovery Servs., Inc., 1997 WL 736692 (E.D. La. Nov. 24, 1997). Claims of negligence and violation of the UDAP statute were dismissed for failure to establish injury or damages resulting from the collection activities where the consumer could not recall opening the collector's letters.

Maine

Shapiro v. Haenn, 176 F. Supp. 2d 42 (D. Me. 2002). Financial institutions were not subject to Maine's UDAP statute.

Maryland

Taylor v. Mount Oak Manor Homeowners Ass'n, 11 F. Supp. 2d 753 (D. Md. 1998). Complaint stated a claim for relief against the attorneys as debt collectors as defined, and against the homeowners association for breach of duty of fair dealing and good faith under state law.

Massachusetts

Alger v. Ganick, O'Brien & Sarin, 35 F. Supp. 2d 148 (D. Mass. 1999). 28 U.S.C. § 1367(c)(1) allows the district court to refuse to exercise supplemental jurisdiction over a state claim that raises a novel or complex issue of state law. 28 U.S.C. § 1367(c)(2) expressly permits the district court to refuse supplemental jurisdiction if the state claim substantially predominates over the claim or claims over which the district court had original jurisdiction. 28 U.S.C. § 1367(d) tolls the running of the statute limitations on the state claims while the claim is pending and for thirty days after it is dismissed unless state law provides for a longer tolling period. State law claims dismissed without prejudice subject to allowing the defendant law firm an opportunity to file a motion for reconsideration demonstrating any unfair prejudice.

In re Vienneau, 410 B.R. 329 (Bankr. D. Mass. 2009). In this comprehensive review of bankruptcy court jurisdiction to hear the pending FDCPA and other claims, the court held that it "cannot exercise supplemental jurisdiction" over those claims and concluded as follows: "Although the Court could stop at this juncture and simply dismiss counts III through VIII, the Court will follow the procedure espoused by other courts, namely granting the Plaintiffs an opportunity to have the district court withdraw the reference. *See, e.g., In re* County Seat Stores, Inc., 2007 WL 4191946, *4 (Bankr. N.D. Tex. June 21, 2007). Should the district court then determine it has jurisdiction and chooses to withdraw the reference, the parties will still have a single forum in which to try this proceeding. Failing withdrawal of the reference, however, the Court will dismiss Counts III through VIII for lack of subject matter jurisdiction."

Burke v. Sun Am., Inc., 2000 Mass. Super. LEXIS 203 (Mass. Super. Ct. Apr. 19, 2000). Court dismissed consumers' FDCPA claims derived from and paralleling their alleged state law violations on the basis of its finding that the foreclosure that was the subject of the case was conducted in a commercially reasonable manner with required state law notices.

Michigan

Gavitt v. NCO Fin. Sys., Inc., 2009 U.S. Dist. LEXIS 66120 (E.D.

Mich. July 31, 2009). Court exercised its discretion and remanded the state law claims in this FDCPA case that the defendant properly removed to federal court: "The Court finds that the contemporaneous presentation of Plaintiff's parallel state claim for relief will result in the undue confusion of the jury. . . . *see also* Padilla v. City of Saginaw, 867 F. Supp. 1309, 1315 (E.D. Mich. 1994)."

Shaffer v. ER Solutions, 2006 WL 1547755 (E.D. Mich. May 31, 2006). The court declined to exercise supplemental jurisdiction over the supplemental state claims "so as to avoid jury confusion."

Glomson v. LVNV Funding, Inc., 2006 WL 1307708 (E.D. Mich. May 11, 2006). The Michigan Collection Practices Act claims were dismissed from this FDCPA action as the court declined to exercise supplemental jurisdiction mentioning avoiding jury confusion.

Walker v. Lynn M. Olivier, P.C., 2006 WL 467912 (E.D. Mich. Feb. 23, 2006). The court exercised its discretion not to hear the consumer's supplemental state claims for conversion and state debt collection statutory violations because those "state law claims would substantially expand the scope of this case beyond that necessary and relevant to the federal claims under the FDCPA" and thus "judicial economy, convenience, fairness, and comity counsel against exercising supplemental jurisdiction in this case."

Malik v. Asset Acceptance, L.L.C., 2006 WL 13148 (E.D. Mich. Jan. 3, 2006). Court unilaterally dismissed consumer's state law supplemental claims because of judicial inefficiency and comity.

Shoup v. Illiana Recovery Sys., Inc., 2001 U.S. Dist. LEXIS 4454 (W.D. Mich. Mar. 27, 2001). Defendants' motion to dismiss 13 state law claims from a fourteen-count complaint was denied as the court concluded that the balance of factors under 13 U.S.C. § 1367(c) strongly favored the exercise of jurisdiction over the state law claims.

Minnesota

Osborne v. Minn. Recovery Bureau, Inc., 59 U.C.C. Rep. Serv. 2d 879 (D. Minn. 2006). While dismissing the FDCPA claim, the court found the consumer stated claims for violation of the UCC, invasion of privacy, and assault where the repossession company was alleged to have breached the peace in seeking to repossess the consumer's truck from its closed garage at night.

Thinesen v. JBC Legal Group, P.C., 2005 WL 2346991 (D. Minn. Sept. 26, 2005). Debt collection activities were not within the general state consumer protection statutes.

Mississippi

Blair v. GMAC Mortgage, L.L.C., 2009 WL 324053 (N.D. Miss. Feb. 9, 2009). Temporary restraining order granted in a supplemental wrongful foreclosure claim to prevent the homeowner's eviction.

Freeman v. CAC Fin., Inc., 2006 WL 925609 (S.D. Miss. Mar. 31, 2006). Mississippi law requires a plaintiff to prove sufficient control by the creditor over an independent debt collector in order to sustain a claim of vicarious liability for a state claim for negligent supervision.

Moore v. Principal Credit Corp., 1998 WL 378387 (N.D. Miss.

Mar. 31, 1998). Because no private cause of action was available for telephone harassment under either state or federal criminal laws, the claims under those statutes were dismissed.

Montana

McCollough v. Johnson, Rodenberg & Lauinger, 610 F. Supp. 2d 1247 (D. Mont. 2009). The Montana UDAP applies to a debt collection law firm's collection activities in court. The lack of probable cause for a claim for malicious prosecution was supported where a debt collection law firm filed a debt collection action with very little information, its debt buyer client disclaimed any warranty of accuracy of that little information and left it up the collection lawyer to determine whether they could ethically file a suit. There was sufficient evidence of the collection lawyers' disregard of the likely injury to the brain injured consumer by proceeding to get the issue of malice to the jury. The collection law firm's motion for summary judgment on the consumer's claim for abuse of process was similarly denied on the basis of maintaining a suit after it knew its debt collection suit was time barred.

Nevada

Kuhn v. Account Control Tech., Inc., 865 F. Supp. 1443 (D. Nev. 1994). Punitive damages were available for collector's unreasonable intrusion upon consumer's seclusion.

New Mexico

Billsie v. Brooksbank, 525 F. Supp. 2d 1290 (D.N.M. 2007). Denied summary judgment on consumer's claims of conversion, deceptive practices, and unjust enrichment due to issues of fact whether defendant garnished the wrong person.

Toledo v. McNeel, Clearinghouse No. 50,433 (D.N.M. 1995). Collection attorney's violation of the N.M. Unfair Practices Act entitled consumer to $100 statutory damages and treble the amount of any actual damages. Collection attorney's invasion of consumer's privacy resulted in the award of $200 for unreasonable and tortious debt collection practices and $10,000 punitive damages.

Larranaga v. Mile High Collection & Recovery Bureau, Inc., 807 F. Supp. 111 (D.N.M. 1992), *rev'g in part* 780 F. Supp. 780 (D.N.M. 1991). Absent consent, the taking of unsecured property located within an automobile subject to a security agreement was conversion under New Mexico law.

New York

Herman v. Nat'l Enter. Sys., Inc., 2009 WL 1874202 (W.D.N.Y. June 29, 2009). Debt collector's motion for summary judgment on the consumer's state claim for intentional infliction of mental distress denied where the consumer presented facts indicating daily harassing telephone calls to the nondebtor plaintiff over a five-month period, multiple insults regarding her fitness as a mother, insults directed at her son's military service, false representations concerning her criminal liability, unauthorized withdrawals from the checking account, and other false representations.

Cannon v. Kelly, 2009 WL 1158695 (W.D.N.Y. Apr. 28, 2009). In this FDCPA case, the court exercised supplemental jurisdiction pursuant to § 1367 over the lender.

Colorado Capital v. Owens, 227 F.R.D. 181 (E.D.N.Y. 2005) (applying N.H. and N.Y. law). A claim was stated that a credit card issuer owed a duty to use reasonable care collect to its debt and not negligently hire collection agencies.

Miele v. Sid Bailey, Inc., 192 B.R. 611 (S.D.N.Y. 1996). $1153.43 actual and $60,000 punitive (for a state law claim) damages awarded where collection agency continued communications after being advised that debt had been discharged in bankruptcy. Actual damages included tax refund intercepted to pay a student loan that had been discharged in bankruptcy and accountant fees for filing for return of the intercepted funds.

Wegmans Food Mkts., Inc. v. Scrimpsher, 17 B.R. 999 (Bankr. N.D.N.Y. 1982). $50 statutory damages under state statute also awarded.

Dearie v. Hunter, 183 Misc. 2d 336, 705 N.Y.S.2d 519 (N.Y. Sup. Ct. 2000). The trial court erred in dismissing the petition for back rent on the grounds that the three-day rent demand by petitioner's attorney failed to comply with the FDCPA since the FDCPA authorizes only a suit for damages against the debt collector as the remedy for any such violation. FDCPA compliance was not a jurisdictional predicate to the commencement of the landlord-tenant proceeding.

North Carolina

Godfredson v. JBC Legal Group, P.C., 387 F. Supp. 2d 543 (E.D.N.C. Aug. 15, 2005). State debt collection statute incorporated state UDAP exemption for a collection mill run by a out-of-state collection law firm.

Ohio

Roache v. Huron Valley Fin., 2010 WL 1796099 (N.D. Ohio May 5, 2010). Because the *pro se*'s FDCPA claim against the foreclosing attorney was the only claim surviving and was "unsubstantial compared to the state claims," the court declined to exercise supplemental jurisdiction over other parties and claims.

Edwards v. McCormick, 136 F. Supp. 2d 795 (S.D. Ohio 2001). Where the foreclosure letter clearly exaggerated the remedies available to the creditor and the consequences to the debtor of nonpayment, the Ohio consumer protection statute was violated.

Taylor v. Luper, Sheriff & Niedenthal, 74 F. Supp. 2d 761 (S.D. Ohio 1999). After granting summary judgment in favor of collector, court declined to exercise supplemental jurisdiction over the remaining state claims where claims raised "novel, complex and important issues of state law."

Boyce v. Attorney's Dispatch Serv., 1999 U.S. Dist. LEXIS 12970 (S.D. Ohio Apr. 27, 1999). The court declined to award punitive damages under the FDCPA, ruling that they were not expressly authorized under the act and would be duplicative of statutory damages. Each plaintiff was awarded $5000 in punitive damages under Ohio law.

Oklahoma

Melvin v. Credit Collections, Inc., 2001 WL 34047943 (W.D. Okla. Apr. 5, 2001). It was not an unfair practice under state law for the creditor to refrain from telling the collection agency that the consumer had requested no calls.

Oregon

Grassley v. Debt Collectors, Inc., 1992 U.S. Dist. LEXIS 22782 (D. Or. Dec. 14, 1992). Only one recovery of actual damages was allowed where both the FDCPA and state law were violated. Pursuant to Or. Rev. Stat. 646.641(1) punitive damages of $2000 each were awarded to the debtors.

Lambert v. Nat'l Credit Bureau, Inc., 1981 U.S. Dist. LEXIS 18623 (D. Or. Apr. 8, 1981). Pendent jurisdiction was exercised over violations of a state debt collection statute, but the state claim was denied because there was no proof that those violations were willful.

Dixon v. United Adjusters, Inc., 1981 U.S. Dist. LEXIS 18392 (D. Or. Feb. 19, 1981). The court exercised pendent jurisdiction over the consumer's state claim that the collector violated the state debt collection statute.

Pennsylvania

Clark v. EMC Mortgage Corp., 2009 WL 229761 (E.D. Pa. Jan. 29, 2009). Under Pennsylvania's gist of the claim doctrine the consumer's fraud claim against the mortgagee was dismissed as a breach of the mortgage contract claim. However the consumer's UDAP claim was allowed to proceed.

Dougherty v. Wells Fargo Home Loans, Inc., 425 F. Supp. 2d 599 (E.D. Pa. 2006). The court exercised supplemental jurisdiction over plaintiff's state law claims for breach of contract and unfair trade practices.

Piper v. Portnoff Law Assocs., 216 F.R.D. 325 (E.D. Pa. 2003). The district court granted the consumer's renewed motion to certify state law counts in addition to the FDCPA claims in a case involving the collection of delinquent water and sewer bills. Although the consumer could not recover under both the state and federal laws, the law does not bar the consumer from proceeding under both statutes before he or she chooses the state or federal remedy.

Dawson v. DovenMuehle Mortgage, Inc., 2002 U.S. Dist. LEXIS 5688 (E.D. Pa. Apr. 3, 2002). When a district court has dismissed all federal claims within a complaint, and diversity jurisdiction did not exist over the remaining state statutory and/or common law claims, the court had discretion to retain, dismiss, or remand the remaining state law claims pursuant to 28 U.S.C. § 1367.

PNC Bank v. Millaway, 1996 WL 684245 (E.D. Pa. Nov. 21, 1996). Bank's motion to remand to state court was granted as there were no federal claims in the complaint as the homeowner had only asserted the FDCPA as a counterclaim.

Crossley v. Lieberman, 90 B.R. 682 (E.D. Pa. 1988), *aff'd*, 868 F.2d 566 (3d Cir. 1989). Court abstained under the Bankruptcy Code from deciding whether attorneys are covered by the Pennsylvania debt collection regulations where the issue of exclusive Supreme Court regulation of lawyers was raised.

In re Belile, 209 B.R. 658 (Bankr. E.D. Pa. 1997). The consumer was awarded actual damages of $100 against each of two defendants, statutory damages of $100 and $750, and treble damages of $300. The statutory damages of $750 were justified by the collector's failure to admit its violation, by its extreme resistance to discovery, and by the fact that the letter was a form letter mailed to numerous other consumers.

South Carolina

Meredith v. Pathfinders Detective & Recovery, Inc., 1983 U.S. Dist. LEXIS 11860, 20367 (D.S.C. Nov. 9, 1983). The consumer was awarded punitive damages in connection with his pendent, common law conversion claim in a suit for violation of § 1692f(6), relating to illegal repossessions.

Tennessee

Brown v. Hosto & Buchan, P.L.L.C., 2010 WL 4352932 (W.D. Tenn. Nov. 2, 2010). After extensive discussion, the court .exercised supplemental jurisdiction over the private TCPA claims for autodialer calls to the consumer's cell phone: "Exercising supplemental jurisdiction over a private TCPA claim makes sense as a matter of judicial discretion where original jurisdiction exists over an FDCPA claim arising out of the same conduct, telephone calls from a debt collector to a debtor."

Texas

Villarreal v. JP Morgan Chase Bank, Nat'l Ass'n, 2010 WL 2653484 (S.D. Tex. July 6, 2010). The creditor's motion to dismiss supplemental state claims was denied, since the FDCPA claims were "necessarily closely connected with [the consumer's] state law claims" and "because they arise out of the same allegedly harassing behavior."

Cushman v. GC Servs., L.P., 657 F. Supp. 2d 834 (S.D. Tex. 2009). Where the debt collector was a Texas corporation, opened plaintiff's account in Texas, and sent letters generated in Texas, the mere fact that plaintiff was not a Texas resident was not sufficient reason to deny her standing to bring a claim under the Texas Debt Collection Protection Act.

Prophet v. Myers, 2008 WL 1752137 (S.D. Tex. Apr. 14, 2008). Where the plaintiff alleged that defendant creditor retained the defendant debt collector knowing that the collector was engaged in illegal collection practices, the court had supplemental jurisdiction over the creditor regarding state law claims where there was federal jurisdiction based on the FDCPA claims against the co-defendant collector.

Virginia

Clements v. HSBC Auto Fin., Inc., 2010 WL 4281697 (S.D. W. Va. Oct. 19, 2010). Unanswered phone calls may constitute communications under a state counterpart to FDCPA. A state counterpart to FDCPA provides a "per violation" penalty, and not a single penalty.

Vaile v. Willick, 2008 WL 204477 (W.D. Va. Jan. 24, 2008). Claims state for intentional infliction of mental distress and defamation where lawyers seeking their attorney fees from a father arising out of a child support enforcement requested his dismissal from law school and sanction from the state bar for attempted kidnapping and nonsupport.

In re Gates, 2005 Bankr. LEXIS 2034 (Bankr. E.D. Va. May 10, 2005). Where the debt collector violated the bankruptcy discharge injunction by telephoning the consumer threatening arrest and withdrawing $50 from her checking account, the bankruptcy court found the collector, Rapid Recovery Credit & Collections, in contempt and awarded nominal actual damages, $500 punitive damages, attorney fees, an additional sanctions in the amounts of $50 per day for each day that the attorney fees remained unpaid, and a permanent injunction of further collection activities. The bankruptcy court lacked subject matter jurisdiction over the related FDCPA claims and the debtor failed to pursue a reference back of the FDCPA claims.

Washington

Leadbetter v. Comcast Cable Communications, Inc., 2005 WL 2030799 (W.D. Wash. Aug. 22, 2005). Collection lawyer's demand for money for copyright infringement arising from alleged music file sharing was not a "claim" as defined by the state debt collection statute. However, it was possible to state a claim under the state debt collection statute.

Hansen v. Ticket Track, Inc., 280 F. Supp. 2d 1196 (W.D. Wash. 2003). The imposition of a $25 violation fee by a collection agency for parking lots when customers failed to pay delinquent parking lot fees violated the state debt collection agency and UDAP statutes.

West Virginia

Stover v. Fingerhut Direct Mktg., Inc., 2010 WL 1507182 (S.D. W. Va. Mar. 19, 2010). The court refused to allow the debt collector to cite its FDCPA compliance efforts in defending a claim alleging a violation of the representation provision of the state Consumer Credit and Protection Act.

Chapman v. ACB Bus. Servs., 1997 U.S. Dist. LEXIS 23743 (S.D. W. Va. Feb. 13, 1997). Federal district court has supplemental jurisdiction under 28 U.S.C. § 1367 over state consumer act claim where jurisdiction over the FDCPA claim was based on § 1692k(d) and 28 U.S.C. § 1337.

Wisconsin

Tomas v. Bass & Moglowski, 1999 U.S. Dist. LEXIS 21533 (W.D. Wis. June 29, 1999). Federal district court has supplemental jurisdiction under 28 U.S.C. § 1367 over state consumer act claim where jurisdiction over the FDCPA claim was based on 28 U.S.C. § 1331 (federal question).

K.3.7.4 Long-Arm Jurisdiction and Venue

Bates v. C & S Adjusters, Inc., 980 F.2d 865 (2d Cir. 1992). Venue exists in the district in which the consumer resided and to which the debt collector's demand for payment was forwarded even though the envelope was not marked "do not forward." The 1990 amendment to 28 U.S.C. § 1391(b), which authorized venue in "(2) a judicial district in which a substantial part of the events or omissions giving rise to the claim occurred," was "at most a marginal expansion of the venue provision."

Michel v. Am. Capital Enters., Inc., 1989 U.S. App. LEXIS 20850

(9th Cir. Aug. 28, 1989) (citation limited except per Ninth Circuit Rule 36-3). Trial court had personal jurisdiction over out-of-state collectors where they contacted a company in the forum state to get the consumers' new address, sent one or two collection notices to the consumers in the forum state, and telephoned them in the forum state.

California

Butler v. Goldsmith & Hull, 2010 WL 3211702 (S.D. Cal. Aug. 11, 2010). Venue was proper in the consumer's home district where the defendants sent the allegedly offending collection letter.

Patterson v. Latimer Levay Jurasek L.L.C., 2009 WL 1862427 (S.D. Cal. June 29, 2009). Deference is given to a plaintiff's choice of forum, unless the defendant makes a strong showing of inconvenience that warrants upsetting plaintiff's choice of forum. A collection law firm sending a letter into the district has minimum contacts for the purposes of exercising personal jurisdiction over the firm. Venue is proper within the district where the collection letter was received.

Mason v. CreditAnswers, L.L.C., 2008 WL 4165155 (S.D. Cal. Sept. 5, 2008). Debt collector's motion to dismiss based on forum selection clause was denied because it would be unreasonable and unfair under federal law to require the financially distressed California plaintiff to pursue his FDCPA claims in Texas where the clause was not negotiated, not highlighted and ambiguous.

Connecticut

Korzeniowski v. NCO Fin. Sys., 2010 WL 466162 (D. Conn. Feb. 8, 2010). Claim against defendant's CEO, dismissed for lack of personal jurisdiction in that he did not participate in the alleged violations.

Musso v. Seiders, 194 F.R.D. 43 (D. Conn. 1999). If defendant raises lack of personal jurisdiction before discovery was conducted, the plaintiff can defeat motion to dismiss by a good faith allegation of jurisdiction in the complaint. If defendant raises lack of personal jurisdiction by motion for summary judgment, plaintiff has the burden of establishing jurisdiction by a preponderance of the evidence.

Gonsalves v. Nat'l Credit Sys., Inc., 1990 U.S. Dist. LEXIS 20944 (D. Conn. Aug. 13, 1990). An appropriate venue under 28 U.S.C. § 1391(b) for an FDCPA claim was the district where the injury occurred, or where the communication was received. Transfer to the venue of the collector would be inconvenient to the consumer and was denied.

District of Columbia

Bard v. W.J. Cohan, Ltd., 42 Antitrust & Trade Reg. Rep. (BNA) 695 (D.D.C. 1982). FDCPA venue was proper in D.C. where debtor received allegedly harassing telephone calls and letters from Nevada collector.

Florida

Gonzalez v. Asset Acceptance, L.L.C., 2008 WL 489557 (M.D. Fla. Feb. 20, 2008). Defendant's motion to dismiss *pro se* complaint was granted without prejudice to amend because the mere presence of a registered agent in the state was insufficient to grant personal jurisdiction over the corporation.

Ferguson v. Credit Mgmt. Control, Inc., 140 F. Supp. 2d 1293 (M.D. Fla. 2001). The court may decline to exercise a supplemental jurisdiction when all federal claims are dismissed or the state law claims raise a novel or complex issue of state law.

Griffin v. Collection Serv. Bureau, Inc., 1993 U.S. Dist. LEXIS 21385 (M.D. Fla. Feb. 10, 1993). Where the collector mailed letters from outside the state to an in-state consumer, the court may exercise jurisdiction under the state's long arm statute which allows extraterritorial service where a non-resident debt collector commits a tortious act by mailing letters into the state. Venue is proper in the district to which the out-of-state collector mailed its dunning letters because a substantial part of the events occurred where the consumer received the correspondence.

Texas Guaranteed Student Loan Corp. v. Ward, 696 So. 2d 930 (Fla. Dist. Ct. App. 1997). Dunning letters and phone calls to a Florida resident were insufficient to establish a general course of business in Florida necessary to invoke long arm jurisdiction under the Florida statute.

Georgia

Bailey v. Clegg, Brush & Assocs., Inc., 1991 U.S. Dist. LEXIS 21591 (N.D. Ga. June 14, 1991). Venue is proper where the claim arose; in an FDCPA case, the claim arose where collection letters were received. Although debt collector maintained no offices or employees in the state, attempting to collect debt owed a third party by mailing demand letters to at least one state resident constituted the transaction of business in the state covered by long-arm jurisdiction. Allegations of FDCPA violations are analogous to the commission of tortious act.

Gachette v. Tri-City Adjustment Bureau, 519 F. Supp. 311 (N.D. Ga. 1981). Venue proper where FDCPA claim could be said to have arisen in Georgia (where calls received and case filed) or Virginia (where calls placed and collector resided).

Long v. G.C. Servs. Corp., Clearinghouse No. 31,345 (S.D. Ga. 1979). Venue was proper since the collector was licensed statewide, the injury occurred in the district of the filing, and the collector's calls and letters to the district could be characterized as doing business in the district.

Hawaii

Maloon v. Schwartz, Zweban & Slingbaum, L.L.P., 399 F. Supp. 2d 1108 (D. Haw. 2005). Personal jurisdiction and venue proper in forum where plaintiff received collection letter. Florida debt collector purposely availed itself of the benefits of doing business in Hawaii.

Illinois

Hyman v. Hill & Assocs., 2006 WL 328260 (N.D. Ill. Feb. 9, 2006). Defendant's motion to dismiss for improper venue was denied because telephone calls were placed into the venue where the case was filed.

Scott v. Universal Fid. Corp., 1999 U.S. Dist. LEXIS 13425 (N.D. Ill. Aug. 30, 1999). Consumer alleged that collection agency used a false and misleading assumed name, Fidelity Financial Services, registered in Texas but not in Illinois, and was therefore liable under FDCPA. The Texas collection agency and its president sought to have the complaint dismissed for lack of personal jurisdiction in Illinois. The court found the company and its president subject to Illinois jurisdiction since they regularly collected for two Illinois creditors and sent collection letters into Illinois.

Brooks v. Holmes, Rich & Sigler, P.C., 1998 WL 704023 (N.D. Ill. Oct. 1, 1998). Where plaintiff's complaint alleged no action by the defendant directed to the district, the action would be transferred to the United States District Court where the alleged violation occurred.

Pope v. Vogel, 1998 WL 111576 (N.D. Ill. Mar. 5, 1998). Person who was the sole stockholder of out-of-state collection business as well as its sole officer, one of two employees and who directed the specific operations of the business that collected the debt in the forum state, had sufficient contacts with forum state for the court to exercise personal jurisdiction and was a "debt collector" by virtue of his indirect efforts to collect the debt.

Vlasak v. Rapid Collection Sys., Inc., 962 F. Supp. 1096 (N.D. Ill. 1997). Acts of mailing and telephoning consumer by out-of-state collection agency which were in violation of the FDCPA were sufficient to establish personal jurisdiction as "tortious acts" covered under the state's long-arm statute.

Brujis v. Shaw, 876 F. Supp. 975 (N.D. Ill. 1995). California corporate officers were subject to Illinois long-arm statute because they allegedly committed in the name of collection agency tortious acts against Illinois residents in violation of FDCPA. Fiduciary shield doctrine does not apply where employee has the power to decide what will be done and chose to commit acts that subjected him to long-arm jurisdiction.

Maryland

Fries v. Norstar Bank, 1988 WL 75773 (D. Md. Aug. 31, 1988). Sending letters and making phone calls from out of state are not contacts for long arm jurisdiction in the recipient's state). Denial of consumer's motion to amend the complaint to add class action allegations was not error where the proposed amended complaint was insufficient to satisfy the prerequisites of Rule 23(a).

Minnesota

Howard v. Judge Law Firm, 2010 WL 2985686 (D. Minn. July 26, 2010). Venue for a consumer's FDCPA claims is proper in the district where the consumer resides if that is where the consumer received the allegedly unlawful communications, as the events giving rise to the claims are the communications, rather than the underlying debt.

Krambeer v. Eisenberg, 923 F. Supp. 1170 (D. Minn. 1996). An out-of-state attorney who sent one dunning letter threatening to sue for a $16.96 book club debt to a Minnesota resident did not have sufficient contact to confer personal jurisdiction in Minnesota under the state's expansive long-arm statute.

Nevada

Karony v. Dollar Loan Ctr., L.L.C., 2010 WL 5186065 (D. Nev. Dec. 15, 2010). "Defendants complied with § 1692i by suing Karony in Las Vegas. . . ."

Paradise v. Robinson & Hoover, 883 F. Supp. 521 (D. Nev. 1995). In an FDCPA action the court had personal jurisdiction over a nonresident defendant where the defendant sent the collection letter into the local forum. Venue in an FDCPA action is proper in the district where the collection communication was received.

New Jersey

Sias v. Law Offices of Andreu, Palma, & Andreu, P.L., 2011 WL 345928 (D.N.J. Feb. 2, 2011). In granting a motion to transfer, the court noted that plaintiff had recently moved from Florida and all the operative facts occurred there, plaintiff had not indicated any difficulty in securing Florida counsel, and since this was a fee-shifting case under the FDCPA, she would bear only the additional costs (if any) of litigating this action in Florida if she did not succeed on the merits.

New Mexico

Russey v. Rankin, 837 F. Supp. 1103 (D.N.M. 1993). Whether the wrongful conduct is characterized as tortious or as the transaction of business, the cause of action arises where the consumer receives the violative dunning letter. Venue is proper if a substantial part of the events giving rise to the claim occurred in the forum district pursuant to 28 U.S.C. § 1391(a)(2).

New York

Tobey v. Nat'l Action Fin. Servs., Inc., 2009 WL 3734320 (E.D.N.Y. Nov. 4, 2009). Defendant debt collector's motion to transfer venue denied, and consumer's motion to transfer venue granted.

Cannon v. Kelly, 2009 WL 1158695 (W.D.N.Y. Apr. 28, 2009). In this FDCPA case the court exercised personal jurisdiction pursuant to the New York long arm statute over the lender.

Kucker v. Kaminsky & Rich, 2001 U.S. Dist. LEXIS 9877 (S.D.N.Y. July 12, 2001). Because "the receipt of a collection notice is a substantial part of the events giving rise to a claim under the FDCPA," quoting *Bates v. C&S Adjusters, Inc.*, 980 F.2d 865, 868 (2d Cir. 1992), the collector's motion to reassign the case from the division where the consumer received the dun to another division within the federal district was denied.

Fava v. RRI, Inc., 1997 WL 205336 (N.D.N.Y. Apr. 24, 1997). Collector's telephone and letter contacts in forum state to collect alleged debt from in-state resident created personal jurisdiction.

Sluys v. Hand, 831 F. Supp. 321 (S.D.N.Y. 1993). Suit may be brought where letters alleged to violate the FDCPA were received by the consumer.

Ohio

Vlach v. Yaple, 670 F. Supp. 2d 644 (N.D. Ohio 2009). The consumer's allegations that the out-of-state defendant attorney sent her two collection e-mails at her residence were sufficient to confer personal jurisdiction in the forum state.

Peacock v. Bayview Loan Servicing, 2005 WL 1277667 (N.D. Ohio May 26, 2005) (slip copy). Consumer failed to establish a basis for long-arm jurisdiction where collectors only responded to consumers calls and there was no showing that they were active in local endeavors.

Murphy v. Allen County Claims & Adjustments, Inc., 550 F. Supp. 128 (S.D. Ohio 1982). Venue was proper in the district where the consumer received a dunning letter even though the creditor's place of business was in another district and the letter was mailed from there. Defendant's request for a transfer of the case to its home district was denied where it failed to carry the burden of showing that a balancing of the interests weighed in favor of transferring the case.

Lachman v. Bank of La., 510 F. Supp. 753 (N.D. Ohio 1981). Long-arm jurisdiction and venue were proper in Ohio court presented with an FDCPA and Fair Credit Reporting Act complaint against VISA, two Louisiana banks and a VISA servicer. The banks were aware the consumer had moved to Ohio and billed the consumer in Ohio for Ohio purchases on the VISA credit card. The doctrine of agency by estoppel aids the finding of long-arm jurisdiction over VISA. Venue was proper since the tort-type cause of action arose in Ohio where the injury was suffered.

Oklahoma

Wensauer v. Martorella, 2008 WL 4131112 (W.D. Okla. Aug. 29, 2008). Defendant's motion to dismiss FDCPA claims for lack of personal jurisdiction and improper venue was denied because of the allegations that defendant was doing business within the state.

Oregon

Christopherson v. Gross & Siegel, 1991 U.S. Dist. LEXIS 21730 (D. Or. July 3, 1991). Court had personal jurisdiction over California attorneys whose letterhead was used to dun an Oregon consumer. While the attorneys clearly authorized the collector to use their letterhead to dun California residents, they did not instruct the collector not to send the letter to nonresidents. Therefore, the lawyers purposefully conducted business in Oregon.

Stone v. Talan & Ktsanes, 1991 WL 134364 (D. Or. July 2, 1991). Venue for FDCPA claim against out-of-state attorneys was proper in the district in which the consumer received the letter alleged to falsely represent the attorneys' intent to sue violating the FDCPA. The injury was allegedly suffered and the claim arose in that district. Transfer to Illinois where the attorneys resided and mailed their duns was also denied.

Texas

Bray v. Cadle Co., 2010 WL 4053794 (S.D. Tex. Oct. 14, 2010). The court found that the out of state debt collection employees took actions outside of Texas that were highly likely to result in serious harm within the state. The alleged acts were aimed at no other state but Texas, and were aimed at plaintiff specifically.

Utah

Bryner v. Mancini, Welch & Geiger L.L.P., 2010 WL 1418882 (D. Utah Apr. 7, 2010). The court lacked jurisdiction over Hawaii collectors who contacted the *pro se* consumer at his home in Utah to collect a medical debt incurred during a Hawaii vacation. The debt collectors' contacts, a few letters over a $200 medical bill, were not substantial and did not create a sufficient connection with Utah.

Wisconsin

Fried v. Surrey Vacation Resorts, Inc., 2009 WL 585964 (W.D. Wis. Mar. 6, 2009). FDCPA complaint alleging that the defendant unlawfully placed inaccurate information on the plaintiff's credit report with regard to a disputed timeshare debt dismissed for lack of personal jurisdiction since the plaintiff failed to meet the Wisconsin long arm statute requirement to show that "defendant carried out solicitation or service activities in the state;" in the alternative, there were insufficient minimum contacts to meet the requirements of due process since "[a]t most, defendant would send letters to plaintiff's Wisconsin address in order to collect timeshare maintenance fees only when plaintiff failed to pay on time."

K.3.7.5 Bankruptcy Court Issues

Simmons v. Roundup Funding, L.L.C., 622 F.2d 93 (2d Cir. Oct. 5, 2010). A proof of claim (even an inflated one) filed in bankruptcy court cannot form the basis for a claim under the FDCPA.

Smith v. Rockett, 522 F.3d 1080 (10th Cir. 2008). Chapter 13 filer had standing to bring an FDCPA claim in her own name.

Randolph v. IMBS, Inc., 368 F.3d 726 (7th Cir. 2004). Remanded to determine under FDCPA whether debt collectors knew debtors were represented by attorneys.

Goodrich v. Union Planters Mortgage, 196 Fed. Appx. 586 (9th Cir. Aug. 7, 2006). Creditor did not violate the automatic stay because it was without notice of the pending bankruptcy and thus its misconduct was not willful as required by the Bankruptcy Code; dismissal of the consumer's parallel FDCPA claim proper because the creditor "did not know of the bankruptcy proceeding at the time it foreclosed on Debtors' property. Furthermore, Debtors fail[ed] to prove that Creditor was not entitled to the adequate protection mortgage payments or that Creditor used 'litigation as a collective device,' as alleged."

Edwards v. OSI Collection Servs., Inc., 180 Fed. Appx. 642 (9th Cir. 2006). Any FDCPA claim against OSI was discharged in OSI's bankruptcy.

Yaghobi v. Robinson, 2005 WL 1800632 (2d Cir. Aug. 1, 2005). The Second Circuit concluded that because the bankruptcy court is the appropriate forum to determine whether a creditor has violated a discharge order, a plaintiff debtor who fails to secure such a determination lacks a colorable factual basis to plead an unfair debt collection practice based only on a 11 U.S.C. § 524 violation. The Second Circuit did not decide whether debtors in bankruptcy can ever maintain such claims based on violation of the Bankruptcy Code.

Randolph v. IMBS, Inc., 368 F.3d 726 (7th Cir. 2004). The FDCPA and the Bankruptcy Code do not conflict so long as the courts can enforce them both.

Hyman v. Tate, 362 F.3d 965 (7th Cir. 2004). A bona fide error defense was established by the debt collector which had in place reasonable procedures to avoid contacting debtors who had filed bankruptcy (1) by relying upon the creditor not to refer debtors who had filed bankruptcy and (2) by immediately ceasing collection activity upon learning of the bankruptcy filing.

Turner v. J.V.D.B. & Assocs., Inc., 330 F.3d 991 (7th Cir. 2003). Section 1692e generally prohibits "false, deceptive or misleading" collection activities without regard to intent. The collector's ignorance of the consumer's bankruptcy did not excuse its post-discharge violation of § 1692e in seeking collection of a discharged debt (reversing summary judgment in the debt collector's favor).

Arruda v. Sears, Roebuck & Co., 310 F.3d 13 (1st Cir. 2002). Sears' redemption agreements which did not impose personal liability on discharged debts did not form a claim for a violation of the bankruptcy discharge injunction. Defendant attorneys who sought only to replevy secured property post-bankruptcy were not attempting to collect a "debt," i.e., an obligation to pay money, and therefore were not subject to the FDCPA, even though the plaintiffs alleged that the replevin remedy was merely a pressure tactic to extract a cash settlement, since to rule otherwise would be contrary to the plain language of the definition. Unlike a reaffirmation agreement, there was no statutory requirement that a redemption agreement be approved by the bankruptcy court.

DuBois v. Ford Motor Credit Co., 276 F.3d 1019 (8th Cir. 2002). The consumer's payment of a discharged debt did not violate the reaffirmation and discharge protections of the Bankruptcy Code because the payment was initiated by the consumer and was voluntary and therefore did not violate the FDCPA. There was no coercion because the consumer could walk away from the new car lease transaction into which excess usage fees had been rolled from the discharged lease. The court did not rule on whether there was a private right of action to enforce the bankruptcy discharge injunction.

Walls v. Wells Fargo Bank, N.A., 276 F.3d 502 (9th Cir. 2002). There is neither an implied private action under the Bankruptcy Code nor an action under the FDCPA for a creditor's violation of the bankruptcy discharge prohibiting the continuation of debt collection efforts.

Siemer v. Nangle (In re Nangle), 274 F.3d 481 (8th Cir. 2001). A judgment for intentional infliction of mental distress that included punitive damages was nondischargeable in bankruptcy on the basis of collateral estoppel while an FDCPA claim would not have been.

Adair v. Sherman, 230 F.3d 890 (7th Cir. 2000). Collateral estoppel or issue preclusion prevented a former chapter 13 bankruptcy filer from using the FDCPA to attack a secured creditor's overvaluation of its collateral in the chapter 13 because the bankrupt failed to challenge the overvaluation in the bankruptcy.

In re Chaussee, 399 B.R. 225 (B.A.P. 9th Cir. 2008). FDCPA complaint based on filing a time-barred proof of claim in bankruptcy dismissed because the Bankruptcy Code (1) preempts debtor's state law CPA claim against debt collector and (2) precludes her FDCPA claim. Unlike in *Randolph*, where the debtor's claim against the creditor was based upon the creditor's actions taken after conclusion of the bankruptcy case, the purported FDCPA violation targets the act of filing a proof of claim in the pending

bankruptcy case. Court explains at length why the debt validation provisions required by FDCPA conflict with the claims processing procedures contemplated by the Bankruptcy Code and Rules. "Simply put, we find that the provisions of both statutes cannot compatibly operate." Concurring opinion notes, "Because of the . . . lack of any discussion in *Walls* of whether the Code impliedly repeals a competing federal statute, i.e., the FDCPA, I question whether the Ninth Circuit intended the holding of *Walls* to apply to any overlap between the two statutes or be limited to its facts: whether a violation of the discharge injunction of § 524 creates an FDCPA claim."

Alabama

In re Turner, 2010 WL 3211030 (M.D. Ala. Aug. 13, 2010). The bankruptcy court had jurisdiction over the consumer's FDCPA-based adversary proceeding.

In re Travis, 2009 WL 532363 (Bankr. M.D. Ala. Mar. 3, 2009). The court withdrew from the bankruptcy court the FDCPA claim pending as an adversary proceeding because 1) since the "claims arise out of nonbankruptcy federal law, the bankruptcy court has no special expertise in resolving the claims. Thus, it is not a more efficient use of judicial, and the parties', resources, to try these claims before the bankruptcy court," and 2) "the FDCPA claims are noncore; that is, they do not 'arise under' or 'arise in' Title 11. . . . At most, the bankruptcy court has non-core jurisdiction over the claims. The bankruptcy court's determinations, absent withdrawal, would therefore be subject to de novo review in this court, in any event."

In re Simpson, 2008 WL 4216317 (Bankr. N.D. Ala. Aug. 29, 2008). An FDCPA claim cannot be based on the filing of a time-barred proof of claim in bankruptcy, regardless of the ultimate validity of the underlying claim. The debtor's remedy in dealing with an objectionable claim is already set forth in the claims allowance process.

Shortsleeve v. Centurytel, L.L.C. (In re Shortsleeve), 349 B.R. 297 (Bankr. M.D. Ala. 2006). Withdrew its earlier referral of this FDCPA case to the bankruptcy court and ruled that it would also exercise jurisdiction over the consumer's adversary proceeding against the defendant debt collectors because the FDCPA claim is a non-core proceeding, and this ruling serves the interest of judicial economy since "the bankruptcy court has no special expertise in resolving the claims" and the FDCPA claim alleged violations of the discharge injunction.

In re Cambron, 2006 WL 1998662 (Bankr. M.D. Ala. June 30, 2006). In a chapter 7 bankruptcy if the trustee has abandoned the FDCPA claim, it is no longer property of the bankruptcy estate and has revested in the debtor. On the other hand, if the trustee has not abandoned the FDCPA claim, the claim remains property of the estate and must be maintained, if at all, by the real party in interest, the trustee, and not the debtor.

In re Lisenby, 2006 WL 802392 (Bankr. M.D. Ala. Feb. 22, 2006). Debt collector and its attorneys were held liable for violation of both the bankruptcy automatic stay and the FDCPA for continuing to withdraw funds from the consumer's bank account after they were notified of the bankruptcy filing, for which violations the court awarded the consumer actual damages of $287.50, $1000 punitive damages for violation of the automatic stay, $1000 additional FDCPA damages, plus fees and costs.

Arkansas

Marshall v. Deutsche Bank Nat'l Trust Co., 2011 WL 345988 (E.D. Ark. Feb. 1, 2011). Issue preclusion barred the § 1692g claims since prior adjudications had conclusively established the validity of the debt: "By overruling Plaintiff's objections to Wells Fargo's proof of claims in her second and third bankruptcies and confirming Plaintiff's Chapter 13 plan, the bankruptcy court validated Wells Fargo's claim, inherently finding that Wells Fargo had a right to collect the debt. . . . If confirmed plans do not have preclusive effect then debtors would be able to make bad faith claims to 'effectively prevent the collection of a debt, despite a court of competent jurisdiction having already adjudicated the dispute.' Thus Plaintiff's claim that Wells Fargo failed to provide § 1692g(a) notice, and violated § 1692g(b) by attempting to collect an unverified debt that it knew was disputed are also precluded because those claims depend on the underlying issue of the disputed mortgage debt."

Bagwell v. Portfolio Recovery Assocs., L.L.C., 2009 WL 1708227 (E.D. Ark. June 5, 2009). Motion to dismiss based on fifteen-year-old bankruptcy denied; here, the defendant debt buyer was not a party to the bankruptcy, was not listed as a creditor, and was not specifically enjoined by the bankruptcy court from collecting the debt. "Plaintiff is not attempting to hold Defendants in contempt for a violation of the bankruptcy discharge order but, rather, Plaintiff is attempting to establish FDCPA liability based on Defendants' pursuit of a debt which Plaintiff claims is not owed."

California

Goad v. MCT Group, 2010 WL 1407257 (S.D. Cal. Apr. 6, 2010). The complaint was dismissed under the Ninth Circuit's *Walls* doctrine since none of consumer's FDCPA claims were independent of defendants' alleged violation of the discharge injunction. The court noted that even where a debt is discharged, a debtor may pursue claims against a debt collector who harassed the debtor by making incessant telephone calls, threatened or intimidated the debtor, or lied about matters (other than whether the debt is owed), since these types of claims would not be precluded under *Walls*, but the consumer in this case did not make claims such as those.

Goad v. MCT Group, 2009 WL 4730905 (S.D. Cal. Dec. 7, 2009). Complaint alleging that the debt collectors continued collection after they knew that the debt had been discharged in bankruptcy was dismissed under the rationale of *Walls v. Wells Fargo Bank*, 276 F.3d 502 (9th Cir. 2002), since the complaint "seek[s] a remedy for Defendants' alleged violation of the discharge injunction" and therefore the consumer's sole redress is under the Bankruptcy Code.

Hapin v. Arrow Fin. Servs., 428 F. Supp. 2d 1057 (N.D. Cal. 2006). Court rejected argument that plaintiff had no standing because he had not listed the claim in his bankruptcy, on the basis that the schedules could be amended.

Wan v. Discover Fin. Servs., Inc., 324 B.R. 124 (N.D. Cal. 2005). The bankrupt's FDCPA claim based on the collector's communication to the consumer's attorney during bankruptcy was dismissed because bankruptcy law provided the exclusive remedy.

Foresberg v. Fidelity Nat'l Credit Servs., Ltd., 2004 WL 3510771 (S.D. Cal. Feb. 26, 2004). The consumer's allegation that the debt collector had pursued collection after the consumer had filed bankruptcy and then after the debt had been discharged was cognizable as an FDCPA violation notwithstanding the rule of *Walls v. Wells Fargo Bank*, since, unlike in *Walls*, the consumer here was not pursuing the creditor, which had been specifically enjoined under the Bankruptcy Code, but was only suing the third party debt collector, which had not been so enjoined, and, unlike in *Walls* where the aggrieved consumer sought both bankruptcy and FDCPA remedies in a putative class action, the consumer here was pursuing only FDCPA remedies in an individual case.

Molloy v. Primus Auto. Fin. Servs., 247 B.R. 804 (C.D. Cal. 2000). The court granted plaintiff's motion for referral of her claims regarding violation of the bankruptcy stay to the bankruptcy court but reserved jurisdiction over plaintiff's claims under RICO and the FDCPA for the collection of car lease payments that were discharged in the bankruptcy. The Bankruptcy Code did not preempt plaintiffs' FDCPA claim. The court rejected as hyperbole defendant's argument that plaintiffs failed to state an FDCPA claim because the debt had been discharged in bankruptcy.

Kibler v. WFS Fin., 2000 U.S. Dist. LEXIS 19131 (C.D. Cal. Sept. 12, 2000). Under the bankruptcy code, contempt was the exclusive remedy for dunning for a discharged debt and the Fair Debt Collection Practices Act did not provide a private remedy for that misconduct.

Ramirez v. GMAC, 273 B.R. 620 (Bankr. C.D. Cal. 2002), *aff'd on other grounds*, 280 B.R. 252 (C.D. Cal. 2002). Follows *Walls v. Wells Fargo Bank, N.A.*, 276 F.3d 502 (9th Cir. 2002) in holding that the sole remedy for violation of the Bankruptcy Code's discharge injunction was contempt pursuant to 11 U.S.C. § 105 (a).

Colorado

Christensen v. United Res. Sys., Inc., 2008 WL 2811749 (D. Colo. July 18, 2008). On the consumer's motion to reconsider the court's earlier dismissal of her FDCPA claim because she "was not the real party in interest . . . as a result of her Chapter 7 bankruptcy filing," the court granted the motion and vacated its dismissal upon the consumer's current showing that the bankruptcy trustee had now abandoned the claim.

In re King, 2010 WL 3851434 (Bankr. D. Colo. Sept. 24, 2010). The debtor's FDCPA claim, which was based on post-petition actions taken by the defendants, arose after the bankruptcy case was filed and was not property of the chapter 7 estate. Because the claim was not encompassed by the court's limited subject matter jurisdiction under 28 U.S.C. § 1334, it was dismissed.

Vogt v. Dynamic Recovery Servs., 257 B.R. 65 (Bankr. D. Colo. 2000). The FDCPA claim was for violating the bankruptcy discharge dismissed without prejudice as outside the bankruptcy court's jurisdiction five years after the discharge was granted. The court dismissed debtors' action against creditor for violation of discharge order entered five years earlier. Demand by creditor for payment, as a condition to dropping the debt from the debtor's credit report, was not an "act" to extract payment.

Miller v. Accelerated Bureau of Collections, Inc., 932 P.2d 824 (Colo. App. 1996). The court found that the debtors, discharged in bankruptcy, lacked standing to sue a collection agency for violating the FDCPA as the pre-petition rights of action against the agency remained property of the bankruptcy estate.

Connecticut

Jones v. Palisades Collection, L.L.C., 2008 WL 76212 (D. Conn. Mar. 19, 2008), *vacated in part*, 2008 WL 2468530 (D. Conn. May 7, 2008). Because the plaintiff's FDCPA claims "rest solely on allegations that the defendants' actions in attempting to collect her debt after it had been discharged constituted a violation of the Bankruptcy Code's discharge injunction," and "because the bankruptcy court is the appropriate forum" to make that determination, the court granted the defendants' motion to dismiss "without prejudice to refiling after an appropriate determination by the Bankruptcy Court."

Delaware

Sutton v. Law Offices of Alexander L. Lawrence, 1992 U.S. Dist. LEXIS 22761 (D. Del. June 17, 1992). Section 1692e was intended to penalize knowing and intentional misrepresentations by debt collectors, not a debt collector's failure to discover prior bankruptcy.

Hubbard v. Nat'l Bond & Collection Assocs., 126 B.R. 422, 427 (D. Del. 1991), *aff'd*, 947 F.2d 935 (3d Cir. 1991). Debt collector's attempt to collect a debt from a bankrupt did not violate FDCPA where collector was unaware of bankruptcy. Section 1692e was not intended to penalize debt collector for failure to discover prior bankruptcy, and debtor had responsibility to notify collector of facts which collector would not otherwise be aware, such as the existence of bankruptcy.

Florida

Bacelli v. MFP, Inc., 2010 WL 2985699 (M.D. Fla. July 28, 2010). Although there is some authority supporting the proposition that remedies under the Bankruptcy Code are the only recourse against post-bankruptcy debt-collection efforts, those authorities either do not address the arguments advanced in *Randolph* or do not involve FDCPA claims based on a violation of the stay or the discharge injunction.

Kuehn v. The Cadle Co., 2006 WL 845085 (M.D. Fla. Mar. 30, 2006). The debt collector's motion to transfer the FDCPA claim to the bankruptcy court which had the consumer's bankruptcy filing and substitute the trustee as plaintiff was denied as untimely after the expiration of the ninety-day time period in Bankruptcy Rule 9027. Plaintiff's could pursue her FDCPA claim listed in her bankruptcy schedules as the claim was abandoned by the trustee.

In re Wynne, 422 B.R. 763 (Bankr. M.D. Fla. 2010). The bankruptcy court lacked subject matter jurisdiction over the consumer's FDCPA claims to remedy the debt collector's alleged violations of the automatic stay and discharge injunction arising from its post petition reporting of misleading information to credit bureaus and its commencing and prosecuting a foreclosure action.

In re Pariseau, 395 B.R. 492 (Bankr. M.D. Fla. 2008). Only the Bankruptcy Act remedies, and not the FDCPA, are available to redress claims "that arise from the filing of a proof of claim during the pendency of a bankruptcy proceeding."

In re Williams, 392 B.R. 882 (Bankr. M.D. Fla. 2008). FDCPA claim filed in the bankruptcy proceedings to redress the creditor's filing of a proof of claim allegedly barred by the statute of limitations was dismissed since the consumer's only remedy for filing such a proof of claim, in contrast to "cases involving the applicability of the FDCPA to violations of the automatic stay and dischargeability issues," is under the Bankruptcy Code.

In re Walker, 336 B.R. 534 (Bankr. M.D. Fla. 2005). Bankruptcy debtor could not assert FDCPA claim but was limited to bankruptcy remedy. Moreover, the debt collector's response to the debtor's request for statement of account that included the § 1692e(11) FDCPA notice was merely a response to a request for information with no request for payment, and not an effort to collect a debt that would violate the automatic stay.

Georgia

Payne v. Bomar Credit Corp., Clearinghouse No. 46,786 (N.D. Ga. 1992). Debt collector's motion to dismiss claiming consumer lacked standing to sue due to pending bankruptcy was denied because collection letter was received five days after filing bankruptcy petition. Where consumer reopened his bankruptcy petition and claimed FDCPA cause of action as exempt, debt collector's motion to dismiss was denied.

In re McMillen, 2010 WL 5589096 (Bankr. N.D. Ga. Nov. 15, 2010). An FDCPA cause of action cannot be based on the filing of duplicate proofs of claim in a bankruptcy proceeding. Filing a bankruptcy proof of claim, by itself, is not a debt collection activity. Sending letters that violate the automatic stay are an attempt to collect a debt outside the bankruptcy system; filing a proof of claim is a permitted act in a bankruptcy case, and the debtor can protect his rights by filing a simple objection to the duplicate proof of claim.

In re Gilleland, 2004 WL 5846255 (Bankr. N.D. Ga. Dec. 16, 2004). The bankruptcy trustee's FDCPA claim was time barred even after adding the additional time permitted by 11 U.S.C. § 108(a).

Illinois

Greenfield v. Kluever & Platt, L.L.C., 2010 WL 604830 (N.D. Ill. Feb. 16, 2010). A *pro se* consumer who filed a bankruptcy petition on the same day as this FDCPA action without disclosing the FDCPA case nevertheless had standing since she voluntarily dismissed the bankruptcy action six weeks later.

Alexander v. Unlimited Progress Corp., 2004 WL 2384645 (N.D. Ill. Oct. 20, 2004). Where the debt collector did not maintain an effective procedure to inquire of the creditor whether the alleged debtor filed for bankruptcy, it could not establish a bona fide error defense.

Alexander v. Unlimited Progress Corp., 2003 WL 1562234 (N.D. Ill. Mar. 21, 2003). The Bankruptcy Code preempts claims that also would otherwise lie under the FDCPA only in those cases where preemption is necessary to safeguard the integrity of the bankruptcy process. Where the consumer's claimed violation of

§ 1692e(2)(a) arose from an attempt to collect a debt in violation of the automatic stay provision of the bankruptcy proceeding, the FDCPA claim was precluded by the Bankruptcy Code. Because the consumer's alleged violation of § 1692c(a)(2) did not arise from the bankruptcy proceedings, it was not precluded by the Bankruptcy Code.

Turner v. J.V.D.B. & Assocs., Inc., 211 F. Supp. 2d 1108 (N.D. Ill. 2002). Creditor's knowledge that the consumer had filed bankruptcy was not imputed under the FDCPA to the debt collector, which therefore was not liable for the resulting improper communication with the debtor.

Bolen v. Bass & Assocs., P.C., 2001 U.S. Dist. LEXIS 16964 (N.D. Ill. Oct. 17, 2001). Consumer may not proceed under the FDCPA for a violation of Bankruptcy Code § 524(c) because the only remedy was to seek contempt sanctions in the bankruptcy court.

Howell v. Ocwen Fed. Bank, F.S.B., 2001 U.S. Dist. LEXIS 15710 (N.D. Ill. Sept. 27, 2001). Since the alleged FDCPA violations occurred during the course of a bankruptcy, the court ruled that the matter should be dealt with by the bankruptcy court using the remedies allowed by the Bankruptcy Code rather than the FDCPA. The decision surveyed the case law regarding the FDCPA's interplay with bankruptcy.

Peeples v. Blatt, 2001 U.S. Dist. LEXIS 11869 (N.D. Ill. Aug. 14, 2001). Where the collection activities upon which the consumer's complaint was premised did not occur until after her bankruptcy, the Bankruptcy Code did not preclude an FDCPA action. The sole remedy for a violation of Bankruptcy Code § 524, however, was a contempt action brought in the bankruptcy court.

Gray-Mapp v. Sherman, 100 F. Supp. 2d 810 (N.D. Ill. 1999). Bankruptcy debtor's FDCPA claim based upon an allegedly inflated proof of claim filed during the bankruptcy proceeding must be litigated in the bankruptcy court because "[n]othing in either the Bankruptcy Code or the FDCPA suggests that a debtor should be permitted to bypass the procedural safeguards in the Code in favor of asserting potentially more lucrative claims under the FDCPA" and "nothing in the FDCPA suggests that it was intended as an overlay to the protections already in place in the bankruptcy proceedings."

Baldwin v. McCalla, Raymer, Padrick, Cobb, Nichols & Clark, 1999 WL 284788 (N.D. Ill. Apr. 26, 1999). Where, in a bankruptcy proceeding, the consumer debtor had an opportunity to raise post-confirmation objections to a proof of claim and failed to do so, the principles of res judicata barred his subsequent post-dismissal FDCPA challenge to the proof of claim.

Wilborn v. Dun & Bradstreet Corp., 180 F.R.D. 347 (N.D. Ill. 1998). Because defendant did not object to plaintiff's exemption of his FDCPA claim from the bankruptcy estate, this cause of action belonged to the plaintiff, not a bankruptcy trustee.

Kim v. Fayazi, 1998 WL 729753 (N.D. Ill. Oct. 14, 1998). Under local rule in Northern District of Illinois requiring that all cases under or relating to Title 11 be referred to the bankruptcy courts, judge dismissed bankruptcy claims with leave to refile in appropriate bankruptcy court. Motions to dismiss RICO claims were denied given that most details of the alleged scheme to trick plaintiff into repaying previously discharged credit card debts were within defendants' exclusive control and plaintiff's allegations

were sufficiently particular.

Perovich v. Humphrey, 1997 WL 674975 (N.D. Ill. Oct. 28, 1997). A claim for violation of the bankruptcy discharge should be initiated in the bankruptcy court under the local rules.

Indiana

Massa v. I.C. Sys., Inc., 2008 WL 504329 (S.D. Ind. Feb. 21, 2008). Collection letter to the consumer's attorney regarding payment of a debt discharged in bankruptcy was not actionable because the attorney of the consumer had filed for bankruptcy.

Kaiser v. Braje & Nelson, L.L.P., 2006 WL 1285143 (N.D. Ind. May 5, 2006). FDCPA claims are preempted by bankruptcy law.

Wehrheim v. Secrest, 2002 WL 31242783 (S.D. Ind. Aug. 16, 2002). The Bankruptcy Code precludes plaintiff's FDCPA claim based on defendant's attempt to collect a debt discharged in bankruptcy.

In re Davis, 158 B.R. 1000 (Bankr. N.D. Ind. 1993). Debtor's adversary proceeding alleging violations of the FDCPA was dismissed by the Bankruptcy Court since the FDCPA claim had neither been abandoned nor administered; therefore, only the trustee, not the debtors, had standing to bring the action. Sanctions were mandatory where the debtors failed to list the FDCPA cause of action on the schedules, filed an adversary proceeding for the FDCPA claim although lacking standing to do so, and failed to substitute the trustee as the real party in interest although the court had advised doing so; this resulted in the dismissal of the debtors adversary proceeding.

Iowa

In re Hromidko, 302 B.R. 629 (Bankr. N.D. Iowa 2003). Bankruptcy court held that collection agent was acting as an agent for the creditor when it sent a letter to the home address of the debtor's employer and telephoned the employer. Creditor's knowledge of the debtor's bankruptcy was imputed to the collection agent. The Bankruptcy court held that this conduct was willful pursuant to 11 U.S.C. § 362(h) violating the automatic stay provision, 11 U.S.C. § 362(a), and awarded $5000 in actual damages, $5000 in punitive damages, and $593.75 as attorney fees.

Louisiana

B-Real, L.L.C. v. Rogers, 405 B.R. 428 (M.D. La. 2009). The consumer's sole remedy against the collector for filing a proof of claim on a time-barred debt in the bankruptcy case was under the Bankruptcy Code, which precludes any remedy under the FDCPA.

In re Rogers, 391 B.R. 317 (Bankr. M.D. La. 2008). Following the reasoning of *Randolph v. IMBS, Inc.*, 368 F.3d 726 (7th Cir. 2004), the court held that debtors in bankruptcy may urge an FDCPA claim against debt collectors for alleged time-barred collection lawsuits.

Maine

In re Goldstein, 201 B.R. 1 (Bankr. D. Me. 1996). Bankruptcy court lacked jurisdiction over a chapter 7 debtor's post-petition FDCPA claims for violation of the bankruptcy stays as they did not arise under Title 11 since they were neither causes of action created by or determined by the Bankruptcy Code so any recovery would be the debtor's property.

Maryland

In re Pultz, 400 B.R. 185 (Bankr. D. Md. 2008). Communications by their lawyer's which included a notice required by RESPA did not violate the Act as the mortgage servicer had been granted relief from the automatic stay.

Massachusetts

In re Vienneau, 410 B.R. 329 (Bankr. D. Mass. 2009). In this comprehensive review of bankruptcy court jurisdiction to hear the pending FDCPA and other claims, the court held that it "cannot exercise supplemental jurisdiction" over those claims and concluded as follows: "Although the Court could stop at this juncture and simply dismiss counts III through VIII, the Court will follow the procedure espoused by other courts, namely granting the Plaintiffs an opportunity to have the district court withdraw the reference. *See, e.g., In re County Seat Stores, Inc.*, 2007 WL 4191946, *4 (Bankr. N.D. Tex. June 21, 2007). Should the district court then determine it has jurisdiction and chooses to withdraw the reference, the parties will still have a single forum in which to try this proceeding. Failing withdrawal of the reference, however, the Court will dismiss Counts III through VIII for lack of subject matter jurisdiction."

In re Curtis, 322 B.R. 470 (Bankr. D. Mass. 2005). The bankruptcy court denied the creditors' motion to reconsider the order which awarded compensatory damages of $15,000, attorney fees in the amount of $8220, and punitive damages of $30,000 for violations of the automatic stay, the post-discharge injunction, and the Fair Debt Collection Practices Act, 15 U.S.C. § 1692e(2)(A) and (5), by communicating directly with the debtor regarding the debt after knowledge that the debtor was represented by counsel in connection with the debt and by misrepresenting the status of the debt in its demands.

In re Maxwell, 281 B.R. 101 (Bankr. D. Mass. 2002). Collector purchased a defaulted home improvement note which had called for payment of 98% of the borrowers' monthly income. Even though the collector filed an affidavit of lost note, it was not able to substantiate its claims. Bankruptcy court found that the collector "in a shocking display of corporate irresponsibility, repeatedly fabricated the amount of the Debtor's obligation to it out of thin air. There was no other explanation for the wildly divergent figures it concocted in correspondence with the Debtor and her agents and in pleadings and documents filed with the bankruptcy court." FDCPA liability found.

Michigan

Tworek v. Asset Acceptance, L.L.C., 2010 WL 707365 (E.D. Mich. Feb. 23, 2010). The defendant's motion for summary judgment, asserting that the amount of its setoff of the debt allegedly exceeded the consumer's affirmative claims was denied: "First, Defendant has no right to setoff until the parties are mutually indebted, and there are no mutual debt obligations until the value of consumer's claims in this matter have been established. Second, '[t]he right to setoff does not operate as a denial of the consumer's claim but allows the defendant to set off the debt that the consumer

owes the defendant against the consumer's claim against the defendant.' "

Tworek v. Hudson & Keyse, L.L.C., 2009 WL 4946723 (E.D. Mich. Dec. 14, 2009). Consumer who failed to disclose her FDCPA claim in her bankruptcy papers lacked standing to now assert the claim.

Toma v. Gen. Revenue Corp., 2008 WL 302378 (E.D. Mich. Feb. 1, 2008). The plaintiff was judicially estopped from maintaining this FDCPA cause of action because the claim was not disclosed as an asset in her bankruptcy filing, thus creating the inconsistency to support judicial estoppel that no such claims existed.

Minnesota

Middlebrooks v. Interstate Credit Control, Inc., 2008 WL 2705496 (D. Minn. July 9, 2008). An FDCPA claim cannot be based on the filing of a time-barred proof of claim in bankruptcy, regardless of the ultimate validity of the underlying claim. The debtor's remedy in dealing with an objectionable claim is already set forth in the claims allowance process.

Drnavich v. Cavalry Portfolio Serv., L.L.C., 2005 WL 2406030 (D. Minn. Sept. 29, 2005). Relying upon *Randolph v. IMBS, Inc.*, 368 F.3d 726 (7th Cir. 2004), the court held that the Bankruptcy Code does not preclude plaintiff's FDCPA claims.

Mississippi

Buckingham v. Baptist Mem. Hosp., Inc., 283 B.R. 691 (N.D. Miss. 2002). Court denied motion to transfer FDCPA case to bankruptcy court, reasoning that (1) the cause of action was neither created nor determined by Bankruptcy Code provisions, (2) that the claims did not "arise in" the course of the bankruptcy case because they were not based upon rights that could not be pursued outside of the bankruptcy context, and (3) the claims were not "related to" the bankruptcy petition because they all dealt with post-petition conduct and any recovery would go to the plaintiff and would have no conceivable effect on the estate.

Missouri

Burkhalter v. Lindquist & Trudeau, 2005 WL 1983809 (E.D. Mo. Aug. 16, 2005). The district court denied the debt collector's motion to dismiss the claim that the collector had attempted to collect a debt discharged in bankruptcy and followed the decision in *Randolph v. IMBS, Inc.*, 368 F.3d 726 (7th Cir. 2004) that the consumer's FDCPA claim was not precluded by the Bankruptcy Code.

Nebraska

Clark v. Brumbaugh & Quandahl, P.C., L.L.O., 2010 WL 3190587 (D. Neb. Aug. 12, 2010). The court rejected *Walls* and followed *Randolph* to hold that the Bankruptcy Code does not bar an FDCPA claim in district court "for a violation allegedly arising from collection efforts initiated after the bankruptcy court entered the automatic stay and discharge injunction."

New York

Simmons v. Roundup Funding, L.L.C., 2009 WL 3049586 (S.D.N.Y. Sept. 23, 2009). FDCPA does not provide a remedy for allegations of wrongful proof of claim. Lawsuit based on the filing of a proof of claim in the plaintiffs' bankruptcy which allegedly exceeded their admitted debt "is a careless claim made without adequate allegations, and the complaint borders on frivolity."

Burchalewski v. Wolpoff & Abramson, L.L.P., 2008 WL 4238933 (W.D.N.Y. Sept. 8, 2008). Plaintiff does not have an independent cause of action under the FDCPA for the violation of a stay under the Bankruptcy Code.

Necci v. Universal Fid. Corp., 297 B.R. 376 (E.D.N.Y. 2003). Remedies under the Bankruptcy Code were the exclusive remedies available for the debt collector's misconduct that violated both the Bankruptcy Code and the FDCPA.

Degrosiellier v. Solomon & Solomon, P.C., 2001 U.S. Dist. LEXIS 15254 (N.D.N.Y. Sept. 27, 2001). Consumer was precluded from asserting any claims for money damages pursuant to the FDCPA that were premised on conduct otherwise remedied or governed by provisions of the Bankruptcy Code.

Diamante v. Solomon & Solomon, P.C., 2001 U.S. Dist. LEXIS 14818 (N.D.N.Y. Sept. 18, 2001). Bankruptcy law precluded claims under the FDCPA when those claims were based upon violations of the Bankruptcy Code.

Buffington v. Schuman & Schuman, P.C., 2001 U.S. Dist. LEXIS 2267 (N.D.N.Y. Feb. 21, 2001). Where the collection attorney knew of the debtor's bankruptcy but had not received notice that the debt had been discharged, its letter to the consumer requesting payment of the debt and subsequent deficiency claim in its foreclosure action did not violate the FDCPA.

Cronk v. Aid Assocs., Inc., 1991 WL 129804 (W.D.N.Y. July 11, 1991). FDCPA suit would not be dismissed for lack of standing where suit was filed while the consumer's bankruptcy petition was pending. The bankruptcy trustee's subsequent abandonment of the FDCPA claim related back to the time of the filing of the FDCPA action, mooting the standing issue.

Barletta v. Tedeschi, 121 B.R. 669 (N.D.N.Y. 1990). Consumer had standing to maintain an FDCPA claim brought during the consumer's bankruptcy since the claim was abandoned to the consumer upon the closing of the bankruptcy case.

In re Jacques, 416 B.R. 63 (Bankr. E.D.N.Y. 2009). Filing a proof of claim as authorized by the Bankruptcy Code is not wrongful conduct prohibited by the FDCPA.

Wegmans Food Mkts., Inc. v. Scrimpsher, 17 B.R. 999 (Bankr. N.D.N.Y. 1982). A bankruptcy court has jurisdiction over an FDCPA claim listed as an exempt asset.

Ohio

Kline v. Mortgage Elec. Sec. Sys., 2010 WL 1267805 (S.D. Ohio Feb. 8, 2010). The bankruptcy court is not the exclusive jurisdiction in which parties may pursue FDCPA claims that arose out of actions that occurred during a bankruptcy proceeding.

Kline v. Mortgage Elec. Sys., 659 F. Supp. 2d 940 (S.D. Ohio 2009). The Bankruptcy Code did not impliedly repeal the FDCPA in cases where the plaintiff's claim under the FDCPA arose out of actions that occurred during a bankruptcy proceeding, specifically, filing a proof of claim seeking attorney fees which were not

allowed. The FDCPA claim predicated upon the proof of claim filed in their bankruptcy case under chapter 13 was dismissed as barred by the statute of limitations, since the proof of claim was filed more than one year before this litigation was initiated. However, another claim was not barred, based on allegation that the defendants continued to seek illegal late fees and the like outside of bankruptcy.

Evans v. Midland Funding L.L.C., 574 F. Supp. 2d 808 (S.D. Ohio 2008). Court followed the Seventh Circuit (*Randolph*), ruling that FDCPA is not preempted "when the act alleged to transgress the FDCPA also violates the [Bankruptcy] Code."

Griffith v. Javitch, Block & Rathbone, L.L.P., 358 B.R. 338 (S.D. Ohio 2007), *reconsideration granted,* 241 F.R.D. 600 (S.D. Ohio 2007). In this non-certified, putative FDCPA class action where the named plaintiff subsequently filed bankruptcy and the trustee then negotiated an individual $4000 settlement on behalf of the bankruptcy estate over the objections of class counsel, the court approved the settlement but ordered that notice of the dismissal be sent to as many of the approximately 20,000 potential class members who could be identified.

Barany-Snyder v. Weiner, 2007 U.S. Dist. LEXIS 5137 (N.D. Ohio Jan. 24, 2007). The plaintiff who had filed bankruptcy had standing to assert, and the court had jurisdiction to entertain this FDCPA action because the claim was not the property of the bankruptcy estate since the trustee had abandoned any claim to the action, even though that abandonment occurred after the FDCPA case had been filed.

In re Gunter, 334 B.R. 900 (Bankr. S.D. Ohio 2005). Bankruptcy Code does not repeal FDCPA claims arising from the violation of the bankruptcy discharge.

Oregon

Whitworth v. Nat'l Enter. Sys., Inc., 2009 WL 2948529 (D. Or. Sept. 9, 2009). The consumer was not judicially estopped from seeking damages on his FDCPA claim in excess of the $1000 that he valued the claim in his bankruptcy petition.

Reed v. Am. Honda Fin. Corp., 2005 WL 1398214 (D. Or. June 10, 2005). The debtor's FDCPA claims accrued after the date when he filed bankruptcy and thus were the property of the debtor, not the bankruptcy estate.

In re Stoiber, 2008 WL 2473657 (Bankr. D. Or. June 18, 2008). Following *Walls v. Wells Fargo Bank,* 276 F.3d 502 (9th Cir.2002) the court held that Bankruptcy Code provides the exclusive remedy for violation of both automatic stay and discharge injunction of § 524, and a claim under the FDCPA based entirely on a violation of either of those provisions is barred.

Pennsylvania

Eastman v. Knight Adjustment Bureau, Inc., 2011 WL 382503 (E.D. Pa. Feb. 4, 2011). An FDCPA claim is a non-core proceeding in bankruptcy court that requires a jury trial. Accordingly, reference of the matter to the bankruptcy court was withdrawn.

Dougherty v. Wells Fargo Home Loans, Inc., 425 F. Supp. 2d 599 (E.D. Pa. 2006). The consumer's FDCPA claims were not precluded by the Bankruptcy Code.

Elsom v. Woodward & Lothrop, Inc., 1997 WL 476091 (E.D. Pa. Aug. 14, 1997). Where consumer's future FDCPA claim was speculative and not brought to the creditor's attention, it could be discharged in the creditor's bankruptcy with notice by publication. Personal notice was not required.

Crossley v. Lieberman, 90 B.R. 682 (E.D. Pa. 1988), *aff'd*, 868 F.2d 566 (3d Cir. 1989). FDCPA claim is an asset of the estate and is a non-core, related matter which may be heard by a bankruptcy court and finally determined on a *de novo* review of the record by the district court. FDCPA suit not excluded from bankruptcy court jurisdiction by the 11 U.S.C. § 157(b)(5) exclusion of personal injury actions.

In re Lambert, 2010 WL 3505140 (Bankr. M.D. Pa. Sept. 3, 2010). A bankruptcy court had jurisdiction to adjudicate violations of the automatic stay, but not the FDCPA claims.

In re Angulo, 2010 WL 1727999 (Bankr. E.D. Pa. Apr. 26, 2010). "[A]n FDCPA claim cannot be based on the filing of a proof of claim, regardless of the ultimate validity of the underlying claim."

In re Biege, 417 B.R. 697 (Bankr. M.D. Pa. 2009). Bankruptcy court dismissed FDCPA claim for lack of jurisdiction where it was not a core proceeding, did not involve the estate, and did not involve violation of a stay or discharge injunction.

In re Benson, 2009 WL 2957786 (Bankr. E.D. Pa. Sept. 10, 2009). In order for a debt to arise from a transaction within the meaning of the FDCPA, the obligation must be the result of a *pro tanto* exchange.

In re Keeler, 2009 WL 2902740 (Bankr. E.D. Pa. May 4, 2009). For purposes of this adversary proceeding, the FDCPA does not bar a creditor from filing a proof of claim, as permitted by § 501(a), where that claim is neither fraudulent nor improper.

In re Wingard, 382 B.R. 892 (Bankr. W.D. Pa. Mar. 6, 2008). Bona fide error defense of FDCPA is not available to the debt collector where relief is sought only under Bankruptcy Code for violation of the automatic stay.

In re Abramson, 313 B.R. 195 (Bankr. E.D. Pa. 2004). Once debtor is in Bankruptcy Court, the debtor's remedy to attack an allegedly inflated proof of claim is limited to that provided for in the Bankruptcy Code.

In re Csondor, 309 B.R. 124 (Bankr. E.D. Pa. 2004). Bankruptcy court has neither "core" nor "related to" jurisdiction over post-filing violations of FDCPA since the bankruptcy estate is not affected.

In re Belile, 209 B.R. 658 (Bankr. E.D. Pa. 1997). The alleged failure of the consumer to list her fair debt claims on her bankruptcy schedules could not be considered where the schedules were not offered into evidence.

Puerto Rico

In re Laboy, 2010 WL 427780 (Bankr. D. P.R. Feb. 2, 2010). In this bankruptcy adversarial action alleging violations of the FDCPA and the discharge injunction, the court denied the defendant's motion for summary judgment since the sale of the consumer's account in a discounted portfolio after receiving notice of the discharge constituted a deliberate act to collect the debt.

Texas

Vick v. NCO Fin. Sys. Inc., 2010 WL 1330637 (E.D. Tex. Mar. 15, 2010). The Bankruptcy Code does not preclude relief under the FDCPA.

In re Eastman, 419 B.R. 711 (Bankr. W.D. Tex. 2009). Defendants violated three sections of the § 1692e when they filed a claim to recover on a debt that was not recoverable due to a discharge in bankruptcy. The FDCPA is a strict liability statute; in contrast, the Bankruptcy Code requires intentional acts.

Virginia

Watson v. United Consumers, Inc., 2010 WL 2399682 (E.D. Va. June 15, 2010). The court granted summary judgment for the defendant where the consumer's settlement agreement with the collector's referring creditor covered the claims against the collector.

In re Meadows, 425 B.R. 806 (Bankr. W.D. Va. 2010). The court refused to enter a default judgment in this adversarial proceeding against debt collector and dismissed the complaint *sua sponte* without prejudice for failure to state a claim since the complaint is a mere "formulaic recitation of the elements of a cause of action" and contains only conclusions whereby "the Plaintiff paraphrased the language of [§§ 1629d, 1629f, 1629e, 1629e(5) and 1629e(10)] followed by words stating that the Defendant violated those portions of the statute."

In re Solt, 425 B.R. 263 (Bankr. W.D. Va. 2010). Only the bankruptcy trustee, and not the chapter 7 debtor, had standing to prosecute the scheduled FDCPA claim.

In re Varona, 388 B.R. 705 (Bankr. E.D. Va. 2008). An FDCPA claim cannot be based on the filing of a time-barred proof of claim in bankruptcy, regardless of the ultimate validity of the underlying claim. The debtor's remedy in dealing with an objectionable claim is already set forth in the claims allowance process.

West v. Costen, 558 F. Supp. 564 (W.D. Va. 1983). An FDCPA class action for statutory damages against, *inter alia*, the owner of a collection agency was transferred to a bankruptcy court upon the owner's filing for bankruptcy but transferred back to the original court in light of *Northern Pipeline Constr. Co. v. Marathon Pipe Line Co.*, 458 U.S. 50, 102 S. Ct. 2858, 73 L. Ed. 2d 598 (1982).

Washington

Kee v. Evergreen Prof'l Recoveries, Inc., 2009 WL 2578982 (W.D. Wash. Aug. 19, 2009). Plaintiff judicially estopped from proceeding with FDCPA claim not listed in bankruptcy.

Allers-Petrus v. Columbia Recovery Group, L.L.C., 2009 WL 799676 (W.D. Wash. Mar. 24, 2009). Dismissed plaintiff's FDCPA claim based on judicial estoppel where she had not listed the claim in her chapter 13 proceeding (despite pendency of her motion to amend in bankruptcy court).

In re Hodges, 342 B.R. 616 (Bankr. E.D. Wash. 2006). Debt collector violated § 1692f(1) by attempting to collect charges which were not authorized by the underlying fee agreement between the consumer and the attorney/creditor. Debt collector, acting on behalf of the debtor's former bankruptcy attorney, violated § 1692f(1) by attempting to collect the bankruptcy filing fee advance that was discharged by the debtors' bankruptcy, misconduct which also was a violation of the bankruptcy discharge injunction.

K.3.7.6 Other Jurisdictional Issues

Stark v. Sandberg, Phoenix & von Gontard, P.C., 381 F.3d 793 (8th Cir. 2004). Arbitrator's award which included $6 million punitive damages reinstated as the district court failed to give the required deference to the arbitrator's award. The homeowner's claims involved tort and FDCPA claims for debt collection harassment and wrongful foreclosure.

Long v. Shorebank Dev. Corp., 182 F.3d 548 (7th Cir. 1999). Tenant whose state court eviction was allegedly procured by fraud by a collector was not precluded by the *Rooker-Feldman* doctrine from pursuing FDCPA damages for the resulting loss of her job, loss of custody of her daughter, and six months of homelessness. Shorebank attorney allegedly agreed that Long did not owe rent, represented that Long would have time to work this out with the landlord, that the document she was signing was not a court document (it was a consent to eviction) and she could ignore the court proceedings. "The counts in Long's complaint alleging violations of the FDCPA are independent from the eviction, order and, therefore, *Rooker Feldman* does not apply to these claims." Long could not have raised the FDCPA claim in the state court action.

Anunciation v. West Capital Fin. Servs. Corp., 97 F.3d 1458 (9th Cir. 1996) (text at 1996 WL 534049). Plaintiff filed and properly served a complaint for violation of FDCPA, then filed an amended complaint with invasion of privacy claims but failed to serve a summons with it. The defendant defaulted. The court awarded statutory damages, actual damages, and attorney fees for obtaining the default judgment. On appeal the court held there was personal jurisdiction over defendant for all causes of action in the properly served initial complaint.

California

Partee v. United Recovery Group, 2010 WL 1816705 (C.D. Cal. May 3, 2010). Venue in FDCPA action is proper in the district where the consumer was located when she received the allegedly offending out-of-state collection calls on her cell phone. Although the court was unable to draw a reasonable inference that consumer received the phone calls in the judicial district from the mere allegation that she was a resident of this district at the time of the alleged telephone calls, it granted her leave to amend the complaint to address the pleading defects.

Palmer v. Stassinos, 348 F. Supp. 2d 1070 (N.D. Cal. 2004). Receiving communications that violate the terms of the FDCPA constituted sufficient injury to confer Article III standing.

Dale v. Johnson, 1997 WL 797913 (N.D. Cal. Dec. 12, 1997) (*pro se*). The court held that a § 1692i claim that the court action to enforce an arbitration award should have been instituted in another county should have been raised in the state court proceeding and not in federal court.

Connecticut

Bolden v. G.H. Perkins Assocs., Inc., Clearinghouse No. 31,470 (D. Conn. 1981). The court denied the collector's motion to dismiss which argued primary jurisdiction for an FDCPA action was in the FTC to which a complaint must be sent before an action could be filed.

G.E. Capital Mortgage Servs., Inc. v. Baker, 1999 Conn. Super. LEXIS 1791 (Conn. Super. Ct. July 2, 1999). Claims based upon alleged violations of the Fair Debt Collection Practices Act were not available as defenses to a foreclosure action.

Florida

Valencia v. Affiliated Group, Inc., 2008 WL 4372895 (S.D. Fla. Sept. 24, 2008). Defendant's rejected offer of judgment of $1001 plus reasonable attorney fees and costs did not moot the case and deprive the court of jurisdiction by satisfying the plaintiff's entire demand since the defendant did not offer declaratory and injunctive relief as sought in the complaint.

Illinois

Taylor v. United Collection Bureau, Inc., 2009 WL 1708762 (S.D. Ill. June 17, 2009). Rejected defendant's efforts to put its answer and counterclaim under seal lest it violate state privacy laws. State law privileges and protections do not control in federal question cases.

Maine

Shapiro v. Haenn, 176 F. Supp. 2d 42 (D. Me. 2002). The FTC's exemption of Maine from the FDCPA pursuant to § 1692o does not eliminate a consumer's private right of action or the federal court's jurisdiction pursuant to § 1692k.

Mississippi

Virgil v. Reorganized M.W. Co., 156 F. Supp. 2d 624 (S.D. Miss. 2001). The court remanded plaintiff's common law case to state court. Mention of defendants' collection practices did not warrant removal because the FDCPA's conflict preemption did not permit federal removal jurisdiction and no complete preemption exists. The court overruled its previous removal/preemption decision in *Thrasher v. Cardholder Servs.*, 74 F. Supp. 2d 691 (S.D. Miss. 1999).

Binion v. Franklin Collection Servs., Inc., 147 F. Supp. 2d 519 (S.D. Miss. 2001). The court remanded the consumer's common law case to state court. Mention of defendants' collection practices did not warrant removal because the FDCPA's conflict preemption did not permit federal removal jurisdiction and no complete preemption existed. The court rejected the since-overruled contrary decision in *Thrasher v. Cardholder Servs.*, 74 F. Supp. 2d 691 (S.D. Miss. 1999).

North Carolina

Meehan v. Cable, 489 S.E.2d 440 (N.C. Ct. App. 1997). North Carolina Superior Court $10,000 minimum amount in controversy requirement precludes jurisdiction for FDCPA claim for $1000 statutory damages.

Ohio

Vlach v. Yaple, 670 F. Supp. 2d 644 (N.D. Ohio 2009). Where the consumer alleged facts regarding the debt collector's contact with the jurisdiction which were disputed by the collector, the court denied the debt collector's Rule 12(b) motion to dismiss this FDCPA complaint for lack of personal jurisdiction.

Pennsylvania

Zhang v. Haven-Scott Assocs., 1996 WL 355344 (E.D. Pa. June 21, 1996). The arbitration clause in the underlying note did not require arbitration of the FDCPA claim because the FDCPA claim fell within an exception in the arbitration clause for a default on the note.

Itri v. Equibank, N.A., 464 A.2d 1336 (Pa. Super. Ct. 1983). Under § 1692k(d) a Pennsylvania Court of Common Pleas has subject matter jurisdiction over an FDCPA claim.

Tennessee

Vedder v. N. Am. Mortgage Co., 2004 WL 2731823 (Tenn. Ct. App. Nov. 30, 2004). The FDCPA confers concurrent jurisdiction in both federal and state courts.

K.3.7.7 *Rooker-Feldman* Issues

Kelley v. Med-1 Solutions, L.L.C., 548 F.3d 600 (7th Cir. 2008). Consumer's FDCPA federal suit claiming that the attorney fees that the collector sought and received in the underlying contested state court collection action were unlawful under state law was barred by the *Rooker-Feldman* doctrine since it was the collector's prevailing party status in state court that entitled it to fees under state law and thus the FDCPA claim was not independent of the state court judgment.

Todd v. Weltman, Weinberg & Reis Co., L.P.A., 434 F.3d 432 (6th Cir. 2006). *Rooker-Feldman* doctrine does not preclude jurisdiction over claim against collection attorneys who falsely misrepresented state of debtors' non-exempt assets in affidavits in support of state court garnishments.

Kafele v. Lerner, Sampson & Rothfuss, L.P.A., 2005 Fed. Appx. 1006N (6th Cir. Dec. 22, 2005). "The *Rooker-Feldman* doctrine does not preclude federal courts from reviewing claims alleging that the state court judgment was procured by fraud, deception, accident or mistake." *Pro se* claims against mortgagees barred but not those against their attorneys.

Harper v. Chase Manhattan Bank, 2005 WL 954331 (11th Cir. Apr. 25, 2005). *Pro se* plaintiff's FDCPA claim, the nature of which was not disclosed or otherwise discussed in this opinion, was held to be inextricably intertwined with underlying state court foreclosure proceeding and thus was barred by the *Rooker-Feldman* doctrine.

Epps v. Creditnet, Inc., 320 F.3d 756 (7th Cir. 2003). In this supplemental state law claim, the court held that *Rooker-Feldman* doctrine barred the state claim against a creditor for suing and receiving judgments in state small claims court for bad check fees in excess of that allegedly permitted by state law. The court applied the *Rooker-Feldman* doctrine because "the present case is not an FDCPA case, and it does not involve the representations made in filings in the Small Claims Court" before entry of judgment in violation of § 1692e but instead would require overturning the state court decision itself.

Johnson v. Riddle, 305 F.3d 1107 (10th Cir. 2002). *Rooker-Feldman* doctrine did not apply where the debt collector's earlier collection suit against the consumer was settled and dismissed with prejudice.

Kropelnicki v. Siegal, 290 F.3d 118 (2d Cir. 2002). Consumer's FDCPA claim regarding the misrepresentation by the collector to her attorney was barred by the *Rooker-Feldman* doctrine because it was inexplicably intertwined with the state court judgment in the underlying debt collection action where she had an opportunity to raise this claim on her motion to open the judgment in state court.

Ellis v. CAC Fin. Corp., 2001 U.S. App. LEXIS 4961 (10th Cir. Mar. 26, 2001). The *Rooker-Feldman* doctrine prevented FDCPA *pro se* claim based on the collector suing for fraud and perjury to obtain a state court judgment.

Bisbee v. McCarty, 2001 U.S. App. LEXIS 1512 (10th Cir. Feb. 2, 2001). Claim attacking a state court claim and judgment under the FDCPA as fraudulent was barred by the *Rooker-Feldman* doctrine.

Chambers v. Habitat Co., 2000 U.S. App. LEXIS 14703 (7th Cir. June 7, 2000). Following *Long v. Shorebank Dev. Co.,* 182 F.3d 548 (7th Cir. 1999), the court remanded a dismissal under the *Rooker-Feldman* doctrine because a tenant's counterclaims usually cannot be raised in an eviction proceeding taking them out of the doctrine.

California

Williams v. Cavalry Portfolios Servs., L.L.C., 2010 WL 2889656 (C.D. Cal. July 20, 2010). The court denied a claim alleging that by filing the state court action and never properly serving the complaint the defendant violated the FDCPA, since the *Rooker-Feldman* doctrine required a challenge to service of state court action and entry of default judgment to occur in state court.

Fleming v. Gordon & Wong Law Group, P.C., 2010 WL 2802157 (N.D. Cal. July 15, 2010). The *Rooker-Feldman* doctrine bars a district court from considering an FDCPA claim challenging the amount of an execution authorized by a state court judgment.

Reyes v. Kenosian & Miele, L.L.P., 619 F. Supp. 2d 796 (N.D. Cal. 2008). The *Rooker-Feldman* doctrine applies only when the federal plaintiff both asserts as her injury errors by the state court and seeks as her remedy relief from the state court judgment.

York Gee Au Chan v. North Am. Collectors, Inc., 2006 WL 778642 (N.D. Cal. Mar. 24, 2006). Pendency of state court collection case did not deprive the federal court of jurisdiction over the FDCPA and supplemental state collection abuse claims, since whether the plaintiff in the federal case will ultimately be found to owe the debt in the state court case is unrelated to the collection agency's alleged violations of state and federal debt collection laws.

Georgia

Farrell v. Poythress, 2010 WL 2411502 (N.D. Ga. May 11, 2010). The *pro se* tenant's case was remanded to state court pursuant to the *Rooker-Feldman* doctrine, since she sought federal review of a state eviction judgment.

Illinois

DeBenedictis v. Blitt & Gaines, 2010 WL 2836804 (N.D. Ill. July 19, 2010). Because the consumer's FDCPA claim that a collection law firm made misrepresentations to the state court regarding entitlement to attorney fees was "inextricably intertwined" with a state-court judgment, the *Rooker-Feldman* doctrine barred the court from exercising jurisdiction.

Buford v. Palisades Collection, L.L.C., 552 F. Supp. 2d 800 (N.D. Ill. 2008). FDCPA suit claiming that state suit on the underlying debt violated the FDCPA as it was time barred was not barred under *Rooker-Feldman* as the FDCPA violation occurred when the suit was filed and was complete before the judgment.

Martin v. Cavalry Portfolio Servs., L.L.C., 2008 WL 4372717 (N.D. Ill. Mar. 28, 2008). Denied motion to dismiss based on *Rooker-Feldman* and res judicata. As alleged in the complaint, plaintiffs' injury is distinct from the state court judgment itself. Plaintiffs do not target the state court's decisions, but defendants' alleged threatening, filing and collecting time-barred debts.

Byrd v. Homecomings Fin. Network, 407 F. Supp. 2d 937 (N.D. Ill. 2005). Consumer's allegations complaining of the "wrongful foreclosure actions" in the underlying state court proceedings established that the instant FDCPA claims were barred by the *Rooker-Feldman* doctrine and res judicata.

Clabault v. Shodeen Mgmt., 406 F. Supp. 2d 877 (N.D. Ill. 2005). The court granted the *pro se* plaintiff's motion to proceed in forma pauperis with regard to her FDCPA claim, but denied her motion with respect to her due process and FHA claims because they were barred by the *Rooker-Feldman* doctrine.

Cole v. Noonan & Lieberman, Ltd., 2005 WL 2848446 (N.D. Ill. Oct. 26, 2005). The claims that the *pro se* plaintiff had raised in a state court quiet title action were not within the jurisdiction of the federal court in view of *Rooker Feldman.*

Johnson v. CGR Servs., Inc., 2005 WL 991770 (N.D. Ill. Apr. 7, 2005). The court denied defendants' motion to dismiss the FDCPA claims on the basis of the *Rooker-Feldman* doctrine because the FDCPA claims occurred prior to this state court judgment; thus, rendering the doctrine inapplicable.

Weniger v. Arrow Fin. Servs., L.L.C., 2004 WL 2609192 (N.D. Ill. Nov. 17, 2004). *Rooker Feldman* did not divest the federal court of jurisdiction because the state court collection action had been dismissed. Even if judgment had entered in the state court action, the FDCPA violations were independent of the state court judgment, when defendants filed a time-barred lawsuit seeking unauthorized amounts in the wrong jurisdiction.

Hamid v. Blatt, Hasenmiller, Leibsker, Moore & Pellettieri, 2001 U.S. Dist. LEXIS 20012 (N.D. Ill. Nov. 30, 2001). Two FDCPA classes were certified regarding the collection of old Montgomery Ward accounts, but the subclasses relating to state court judgments were denied due to application of the *Rooker-Feldman* doctrine.

Indiana

Blanford v. St. Vincent Hosp. & Health Care Ctr., Inc., 2009 WL 500527 (S.D. Ind. Feb. 27, 2009). Defendant's motion under the *Rooker-Feldman* doctrine to dismiss the FDCPA claims accusing the plaintiff of unlawfully seeking attorney fees in the underlying state collection action was denied since the pleadings did not establish that the state court had in fact awarded fees, though the court opined, "The doctrine would apply if the state court had ordered [plaintiff] to pay attorney fees."

Stefanski v. McDermott, 2009 WL 418254 (N.D. Ind. Feb. 17, 2009). *Pro se* complaint dismissed under *Rooker-Feldman* as the claim attacked the judgment of the state court awarding the debt collector damages that included attorney fees.

Matthews v. Capital One Bank, 2008 WL 4724277 (S.D. Ind. Oct. 24, 2008). The *Rooker-Feldman* doctrine did not bar the current FDCPA claims since the allegations that the defendants made false representations in filings submitted in the underlying state court action were "independent of the state court's entry of judgment and subsequent orders."

Short v. Haith, 2004 WL 1798369 (S.D. Ind. July 12, 2004). *Rooker-Feldman* doctrine which precludes lower federal courts from applying appellate review to state court decisions precluded FDCPA action regarding state court's default judgment.

Bullock v. Credit Bureau of Greater Indianapolis, Inc., 272 F. Supp. 2d 780 (S.D. Ind. 2003). When a party attempts to apply the FDCPA to a facially valid state court judgment, the *Rooker-Feldman* doctrine may come into play as to bar jurisdiction in federal court.

Witt v. Westfield Acceptance Corp., 2002 U.S. Dist. LEXIS 7821 (S.D. Ind. Mar. 25, 2002). Court dismissed for lack of federal jurisdiction under the *Rooker-Feldman* doctrine the consumer's complaint asserting the alleged FDCPA violation of collecting a state court default judgment which contained a purportedly unlawful award of treble damages, explaining that in essence the consumer was complaining of "an injury inflicted on her by the state court judgment itself, and she could prevail on her claim only by showing that the state court judgment was erroneous."

Hill v. Priority Fin. Servs., Inc., 2001 U.S. Dist. LEXIS 16900 (S.D. Ind. Sept. 28, 2001). Although there had been a small claims court action to collect the debt, the *Rooker-Feldman* doctrine, res judicata, collateral estoppel, or issue preclusion did not bar all FDCPA claims. However, a challenge to court-awarded attorney fees must be addressed to the applicable trial court, not fashioned as an FDCPA claim, because such a challenge represents a collateral attack on the state court judgment.

Brooks v. Auto Sales & Servs. Inc., 2001 U.S. Dist. LEXIS 8059 (S.D. Ind. June 15, 2001). *Rooker-Feldman* doctrine did not preclude *pro se* consumer's claim that attorney sought excessive attorney fees in state court action which had gone to judgment, because the FDCPA claim arose before judgment was entered. Consumer was not estopped from litigating the issue because there was no showing that the validity of the fee amount was actually litigated in the state court action.

Clark v. Pollard, 2000 U.S. Dist. LEXIS 18934 (S.D. Ind. Dec. 28, 2000). Allegation that collection agency practiced law in state small claims court without a license in violation of § 1692e(5) was dismissed because the alleged actions were taken rather than threatened and the actions had not been attacked in state court where they were approved. The court's dismissal avoided *Rooker-Feldman* issues.

Kansas

McCammon v. Bibler, Newman & Reynolds, P.A., 515 F. Supp. 2d 1220 (D. Kan. 2007). *Rooker-Feldman* doctrine barred the plaintiff's claimed damages suffered as a result of the reporting to a credit bureau of the state court's entry of a default judgment allegedly fraudulently procured by the defendant collection attorneys but did not preclude the damages allegedly suffered as a result of the attorneys' unlawful practices of reporting the default judgment to the credit bureau without noting that the judgment had been paid.

Kentucky

Benjamin v. Citibank, 2008 WL 5192239 (W.D. Ky. Dec. 11, 2008). *Rooker-Feldman* did not prevent a claim alleging separate violation of the FDCPA in the course of state court collection action.

Maryland

Senftle v. Landau, 390 F. Supp. 2d 463 (D. Md. 2005). Defendant's alleged FDCPA violations were not barred by the *Rooker-Feldman* doctrine, since the violations pertain to the manner in which the defendant collected the consumer's debt and not to the validity of the underlying debt or of the state court judgment for the amount of the debt.

Michigan

Bond v. U.S. Bank Nat'l Ass'n, 2010 WL 1265852 (E.D. Mich. Mar. 29, 2010) (*pro se* consumer). Where the FDCPA cause of action arises out of the initiation of the state court action rather than its outcome, the *Rooker-Feldman* doctrine is not applicable.

Christian v. Wells Fargo Bank, 2009 WL 2876227 (E.D. Mich. Sept. 3, 2009). The court lacked subject matter jurisdiction as a result of the *Rooker-Feldman* doctrine to grant the *pro se* consumer's request for relief from a state court's eviction order.

Jones v. Heartland Home Fin., Inc., 2008 WL 4561693 (E.D. Mich. Oct. 10, 2008). Complaint was dismissed because plaintiffs' bare allegations did not allege any allege that the defendant was a debt collector or engaged in specific wrong doing in violation of the FDCPA in its foreclosure and eviction proceedings against the consumers. The FDCPA action was also barred by the *Rooker-Feldman* doctrine.

Stolicker v. Muller, Muller, Richmond, Harms, Myers, Sgroi, P.C., 2006 WL 3386546 (W.D. Mich. Nov. 22, 2006). *Rooker Feldman* prohibited recovery of actual damages in the amount of attorney fees awarded as part of a state court judgment.

Smith v. Provident Consumer Fin. Servs., 2006 WL 1999227 (E.D. Mich. July 17, 2006). Consumers who had litigated, appealed, and lost their state court case were barred by the *Rooker-Feldman* doctrine from bringing a subsequent federal FDCPA action alleg-

ing the same misconduct since "[g]ranting plaintiffs relief on their claims, now couched in terms of federal law, would necessarily imply that the [State] courts incorrectly decided plaintiffs' state-lawsuit."

Stolicker v. Muller, Muller, Richmond, Harms, Myers & Sgroi, P.C., 387 F. Supp. 2d 752 (W.D. Mich. 2005). Federal suit alleging that the defendant collection attorney's false affidavit submitted in support of the claim for attorney fees on default judgment in the underlying state court collection action violated the FDCPA was not barred by the *Rooker-Feldman* doctrine since the "alleged injury was independent of and complete prior to the state court taking any action."

Minnesota

Phillips v. Messerli & Kramer P.A., 2008 WL 5050127 (D. Minn. Nov. 20, 2008). Where the plaintiffs' FDCPA claims that the law firm had improperly levied upon their bank account were not "inextricably intertwined" with the state court judgment, the *Rooker-Feldman* doctrine did not apply.

Frisch v. Messerli & Kramer, P.A., 2008 WL 906183 (D. Minn. Mar. 31, 2008). Consumer's FDCPA claim alleging that the defendant collection attorneys filed a false affidavit in support of default judgment in the underlying state collection action was not barred by the *Rooker-Feldman* doctrine since the default judgment was never entered, the state case was ultimately dismissed, and thus "this[federal] Court is not being asked to review a [state] district court's order."

Wyles v. Excalibur I, L.L.C., 2006 WL 2583200 (D. Minn. Sept. 7, 2006). Suit challenging the debt collection practices used in obtaining state court judgment was not barred by *Rooker Feldman*. "Because an FDCPA plaintiff is not challenging the validity of the debt, but rather the collection practices of the creditor, a claim under the FDCPA is an 'independent claim' from a state court action to collect a debt, and federal courts have jurisdiction over the case."

Resler v. Messerli & Kramer, P.A., 2003 WL 193498 (D. Minn. Jan. 23, 2003). *Rooker-Feldman* barred a claim that a state court judgment had been procured by deceit either under state law or the FDCPA. FDCPA claim that the state court garnishment notice did not contain state required disclosure of exemptions did not affect the state judgment and was not barred.

Missouri

Smith v. Kramer & Frank, P.C., 2009 WL 4725285 (E.D. Mo. Dec. 2, 2009). *Rooker-Feldman* does not bar claims as to the deceptive methods used prior to entry of state court judgment. Failure to open the state court judgment based on deceptive methods in obtaining the judgment does not bar FDCPA claim; the claims against the defendant would continue even if the state court judgment were vacated.

Lavender v. Wolpoff & Abramson, L.L.P., 2008 WL 695399 (W.D. Mo. Mar. 12, 2008). The court dismissed on the basis of the *Rooker-Feldman* doctrine the plaintiffs' FDCPA claims that challenged the basis for and the merits of earlier arbitration awards since the FDCPA claims were inextricably intertwined with the arbitration awards and the state court judgments and thus this federal action was an indirect attempt to challenge the validity of the arbitration awards.

Nebraska

Jenkins v. General Collection Co., 538 F. Supp. 2d 1165 (D. Neb. 2008). The *Rooker-Feldman* doctrine did not prevent the FDCPA claims that the debt buyer brought time-barred and inflated claims in state court as the FDCPA claims were not inexplicably intertwined with the state court's default judgments because the latter did not involve the actual litigation of any issue underlying the consumer's FDCPA claims nor did the FDCPA claims require the rejection of any of the state court judgments.

New York

Schuh v. Druckman & Sinel, L.L.P., 602 F. Supp. 2d 454 (S.D.N.Y. 2009). Because the plaintiffs do not "complain of an injury caused by a state judgment," the *Rooker-Feldman* doctrine does not apply.

Mascoll v. Strumpf, 2006 WL 2795175 (E.D.N.Y. Sept. 25, 2006). The court held that the *Rooker-Feldman* doctrine did not bar this FDCPA case against the collection attorneys who allegedly wrongfully prosecuted the underlying state court collection case through default judgment and execution, since the FDCPA case does not constitute an appeal from the state court proceeding but instead "claims that Defendants misused judicial process by wrongly persisting in efforts to collect on a debt which they knew or, in the exercise of due diligence, should have known that [their clients] had no right to collect."

Ekinici v. GNOC Corp., 2002 WL 31956011 (E.D.N.Y. Dec. 31, 2002). Neither NJ's entire controversy rule for claim preclusion or *Rooker Feldman* prevented an FDCPA suit after a default judgment on the underlying gambling debt. The state and federal claims involved different facts and evidence and were not inextricably intertwined.

North Carolina

Brumby v. Deutsche Bank Nat'l Trust Co., 2010 WL 617368 (M.D.N.C. Feb. 17, 2010), *report and recommendation adopted*, 2010 WL 3219353 (M.D.N.C. Aug. 13, 2010). *Pro se* mortgagor's claims seeking damages and to enjoin the state court-ordered sale of the subject property were dismissed under the *Rooker-Feldman* doctrine.

Squirek v. Law Offices of Sessoms & Rogers, P.A., 2003 WL 21026580 (M.D.N.C. May 5, 2003), *aff'd per curiam*, 71 Fed. Appx. 268 (4th Cir. 2003). *Pro se* claim that defendant attorney had not proven existence of debt in state court action dismissed for lack of subject matter jurisdiction under *Rooker-Feldman* doctrine, since validity of debt had been adjudicated in state court action.

Ohio

Meyer v. Debt Recovery Solutions of Ohio, Inc., 2010 WL 3515663 (N.D. Ohio Sept. 2, 2010). The *Rooker-Feldman* doctrine does not bar a claim regarding a defendant's conduct in collecting on the debt where the plaintiff's injury does not arise from the state court judgment.

Roache v. Huron Valley Fin., 2010 WL 1882134 (N.D. Ohio May 11, 2010). The *pro se* consumers' motion to stay eviction challenged the state foreclosure decision and was barred by the *Rooker-Feldman* doctrine.

Whittiker v. Deutsche Bank Nat'l Trust Co., 605 F. Supp. 2d 914 (N.D. Ohio 2009). A federal plaintiff's allegations of fraud in connection with a state court proceeding did not constitute a complaint regarding the foreclosure decree itself, but concerned defendant's actions that preceded the decree, and therefore plaintiff's claim that the foreclosure decree was procured by fraud was not barred by the *Rooker-Feldman* doctrine.

Foster v. D.B.S. Collection Agency, 463 F. Supp. 2d 783 (S.D. Ohio 2006). Court rejected dismissal based on *Rooker Feldman* because plaintiffs were not attacking the judgments, but the allegedly illegal methods employed to get the judgments.

Kafele v. Shapiro & Felty, L.L.P., 2006 WL 783457 (S.D. Ohio Mar. 27, 2006). *Pro se*'s FDCPA claims based on purported defects in an underlying state foreclosure action were barred by *Rooker Feldman* since the "claims are inextricably intertwined with the state court's implicit determination that the foreclosure actions were valid . . . [and] have merit only to the extent the state court's judgment in this regard was wrong." FDCPA claims dismissed where *pro se* plaintiff failed to establish the consumer purpose for the underlying debt.

Lamb v. Javitch, Block & Rathbone, L.L.P., 2005 WL 4137786 (S.D. Ohio Jan. 24, 2005). The consumer stated a cause of action for violation of the FDCPA for the law firm's failure to set an oral hearing on its motion to confirm the arbitration award, and the court denied the law firm's motion to dismiss that was based in part on res judicata and *Rooker Feldman*. The claim that it was confusing—violating the FDCPA—to issue summons rather than the appropriate state process to confirm an arbitration in state court was dismissed because the summons was the court clerk's error, not the collection attorney's error, and because it was barred by *Rooker Feldman*.

Blevins v. Hudson & Keyse, Inc., 395 F. Supp. 2d 655 (S.D. Ohio 2004). The court held that the *Rooker-Feldman* doctrine, even if otherwise applicable, could not apply to deprive the federal court of jurisdiction over the consumer's FDCPA claims since no judgment or dispositive order had been entered in the underlying state court collection litigation.

Pennsylvania

Sherk v. Countrywide Home Loans, Inc., 2009 WL 2412750 (E.D. Pa. Aug. 5, 2009). To the extent that the consumers seek to challenge the state court's judgment in foreclosure by arguing that it was erroneously entered, their FDCPA claim was barred by the *Rooker-Feldman* doctrine.

Hawkins v. Apex Fin. Mgmt., L.L.C., 2006 WL 891169 (W.D. Pa. Mar. 30, 2006). Where a *pro se* plaintiff alleged that the collector's harassing conduct violated § 1692f and claimed damages of $4000 but failed to specify what special damages were incurred, the collector's motion to dismiss the complaint was granted unless the plaintiff filed an amended complaint within ten days.

Piotrowski v. Federman & Phelan, L.L.P., 2005 WL 3118031 (M.D. Pa. Nov. 22, 2005). The court lacked subject matter jurisdiction under the *Rooker-Feldman* doctrine following a successful state court foreclosure on the consumer's home where the basis for the federal FDCPA claim was that the mortgage assignment to the federal defendant was improper, since a finding in favor of the consumer on the FDCPA claim would "negate the state court's judgment."

O'Brien v. Valley Forge Specialized Educ. Servs., 2004 WL 2580773 (E.D. Pa. Nov. 10, 2004). *Rooker Feldman* barred plaintiffs' request to return amounts taken by allegedly wrongful executions, since the state court had rejected the claim that the executions were wrongful.

Tennessee

Livingston-Gross v. Bank of Am., 2009 WL 1471126 (M.D. Tenn. May 26, 2009). Where the *pro se* plaintiff requested that the amount of the state court judgment be determined to be incorrect, his FDCPA claims were barred by the *Rooker-Feldman* doctrine.

Texas

Naranjo v. Universal Sur. of Am., 679 F. Supp. 2d 787 (S.D. Tex. 2010). The consumer's federal action alleging that the debt collectors violated the FDCPA by obtaining a default judgment in the state court collection case when they knew that the debt was beyond the statute of limitations was not barred by the *Rooker-Feldman* doctrine since the consumer "is not asking this Court to review or reject the state default judgment itself [but] is complaining about Defendants' alleged practices of bringing time-barred collections actions."

Morris v. American Home Mortgage Serv., Inc., 2010 WL 3749399 (S.D. Tex. Sept. 22, 2010). The *pro se* consumer's FDCPA claims, accompanied by a request to enjoin state-court-ordered foreclosure, were barred by the *Rooker-Feldman* doctrine as they represented a challenge to the legality of the foreclosure that necessarily called upon the court to review state court determinations.

Gutierrez v. LVNV Funding, L.L.C., 2009 U.S. Dist. LEXIS 54479 (W.D. Tex. Mar. 16, 2009). Even though final judgments had been entered in the underlying state court proceedings, the *Rooker-Feldman* doctrine did not bar this class action alleging that the defendant debt buyer violated the FDCPA by filing its state court collection action complaints with an attached false "Affidavit of Account" since "the instant action does not seek damages for injuries caused by the state court judgments": "Here, Plaintiff and putative class members do not seek damages for injuries caused by state court judgments, nor do they invite the Court to review and reject those judgments. Rather, Plaintiff alleges that Defendants violated the FDCPA by filing state court petitions with false affidavits of account. The alleged violation, thus, was complete when Defendants filed the collection action in state court."

Gibson v. Grupo de Ariel, L.L.C., 2006 WL 42369 (N.D. Tex. Jan. 9, 2006). *Rooker Feldman* was not implicated when the alleged FDCPA violation was defendants' filing suit in the wrong venue.

Washington

Dexter v. Tran, 654 F. Supp. 2d 1253 (E.D. Wash. 2009). Where the consumer is seeking statutory damages pursuant to the FDCPA for the defendant's conduct in bringing the state court collection lawsuit and not asserting that the injury arose from legal errors by the state court, the *Rooker-Feldman* doctrine does not preclude the claims.

Kirk v. Gobel, 622 F. Supp. 2d 1039 (E.D. Wash. 2009). Neither the *Rooker-Feldman* doctrine nor res judicata applied since the underlying state collection case was on appeal and there was therefore no final state judgment.

Druther v. Hamilton, 75 Fed. R. Serv. 3d 316 (W.D. Wash. 2009). "The *Rooker-Feldman* doctrine does not prevent a district court from exercising subject matter jurisdiction simply because a party attempts to litigate in federal court a matter previously litigated in state court, as long as the federal plaintiff presents an independent claim even if that claim denies a legal conclusion reached by the state court. . . . Focusing on the relief that consumer is seeking in this current lawsuit, it is clear that the *Rooker-Feldman* doctrine does not bar this current action. The courts are clear that the FDCPA applies to the collection of the debt. It does not apply to the validity of the debt. Consumer is not seeking to overturn the money judgment on the debt that was entered against him in state court. Rather, he is seeking statutory and actual damages for Defendant's debt collection practices. He is not asserting as his injury legal errors by the state court and is not seeking relief from the state court judgment. Therefore, the *Rooker-Feldman* doctrine does not preclude consumer's claims."

Wisconsin

Derksen v. Rausch Strum Israel & Hornik, S.C., 2010 WL 3835097 (E.D. Wis. Sept. 29, 2010). The *pro se* plaintiffs' claims that the defendants violated federal and state debt collection laws by) attempting to enforce an illegal contract and to enforce a debt without sufficient evidence were precluded by the *Rooker-Feldman* doctrine, and, as a consequence, the court lacked subject-matter jurisdiction over those claims.

Schwoegler v. Am. Family Fin. Servs., 2006 WL 6021148 (W.D. Wis. May 16, 2006). Dismissed FDCPA complaint alleging wrongdoing in state foreclosure action based on *Rooker-Feldman*.

K.3.8 Pleadings and Motions Practice

Ruth v. Triumph P'ships, 577 F.3d 790 (7th Cir. 2009). The circuit court concluded that the district court had erred in granting the defendants summary judgment, as the letter and notice were sent in connection with a attempt to collect a debt and the plaintiff had failed to produce the extrinsic evidence to satisfy the "in connection with collection of a debt" element of her FDCPA claim.

Gorbaty v. Portfolio Recovery Assocs., L.L.C., 355 Fed. Appx. 580 (3d Cir. 2009) (unpublished). The mailing and receipt of a Cancellation of Debt notice (Form 1099-C) by itself, without any indication that the notice was used in connection with the collection of a debt, does not state a claim for a violation of the FDCPA.

Carter v. Daniels, 2004 WL 119886 (10th Cir. Jan. 27, 2004) (*pro se*). Complaint improperly dismissed as court relied on conduct outside the complaint. There is no requirement that consumer transaction must be pleaded with particularity. *Pro se* plaintiff stated a claim for relief based on the conclusory allegation that the defendant was a debt collector who failed to provide the required validation notice and that the defendant attorney was a debt collector who violated § 1692f by threatening to execute on the plaintiff's property without a present right of possession because the underlying judgment lien was not bonded as required under state law.

Kerr v. Dubowsky, 2003 WL 21751832 (9th Cir. July 24, 2003). *Pro se* FDCPA claims properly dismissed for failure to plead essential elements of the violations.

Nix v. Welch & White, P.A., 2003 WL 57936 (3d Cir. Jan. 8, 2003). Complaint failed to satisfy the minimal pleading requirements of Rule 8(a) because it merely alleged the collector's actions "embodied violations of the Act" and "violated the Act in other ways." These were conclusory allegations. The complaint failed to provide the "grounds upon which they rest." Furthermore, the remainder of the consumer's allegations failed to state a claim upon which relief can be granted. The district court noted, plaintiffs "fail to allege, however, any facts to support these allegations and provide no notice to defendants as to how the letters allegedly violated the FDCPA." As a result, plaintiffs did not provide notice to defendants as to how their actions allegedly violated the FDCPA. Court dismissing amended complaint abused its discretion by not including in its ruling leave for the consumer to amend.

Simpson v. Merchants Recovery Bureau, Inc., 171 F.3d 546 (7th Cir. 1999). In an action in which the consumer alleged that the collection agency improperly imposed a service charge, the court of appeals reversed district court's *sua sponte* grant of summary judgment in favor of the defendant collection agencies since the consumer was not given notice that the court was going to rule on summary judgment and was not given a chance to respond.

Arizona

Lams v. Accounts Receivable Mgmt., Inc., 2010 WL 3283517 (D. Ariz. Aug. 17, 2010). The court granted the consumer's motion in limine barring the defendant from commenting before the jury on the prevailing consumer's right to recover attorney fees.

Riordan v. Jaburg & Wilk, P.C., 2010 WL 3023292 (D. Ariz. July 30, 2010). Although the fact that the defendant subpoenaed the consumer's bank records after quashing three such subpoenas invites speculation that the defendant did not have the statutorily requisite reasonable belief that only nonexempt funds were in the account, the court could not conclude that such a theory was plausible without more facts.

Zavlunov v. Bursey & Assocs., P.C., 2009 WL 4730645 (D. Ariz. Dec. 3, 2009). The defendant's motion under Rules 19 and 20 to join the plaintiff's mother, the actual consumer who owed the debt that defendant was collecting, was denied: "[Mother/debtor] has claimed no interest in this action. Moreover, [mother] and [daughter's] potential claims are distinct and joinder of [mother] is not necessary in order to accord complete relief among existing parties."

Reichert v. Nat'l Credit Sys., 2005 U.S. Dist. LEXIS 5784 (D. Ariz. Mar. 31, 2005), *aff'd on other grounds*, 531 F.3d 1002 (9th Cir. 2008). The court granted the consumer's motion to strike materials regarding other FDCPA cases involving counsel because such material was "designed solely to impugn Plaintiff's counsel's professional reputation." The court granted sanctions in the amount of $250 against the debt collector for inclusion of scandalous material regarding the other FDCPA litigation.

Arkansas

Marshall v. Deutsche Bank Nat'l Trust Co., 2011 WL 345988 (E.D. Ark. Feb. 1, 2011). The complaint failed to state any facts to support the § 1692g claims showing that the subject communications were "in connection with the collection" of the debt or were initial communications, or that the consumer disputed the debt in writing within the thirty-day window.

California

Mitchell v. Kaiser Found. Health Plan, Inc., 2010 WL 5387712 (N.D. Cal. Dec. 22, 2010). A conclusory assertion that the defendants were debt collectors failed to state a claim absent some allegation of supporting facts regarding the nature of the defendants' businesses and whether the debt was in default when it was obtained. The court granted the motion to dismiss with leave to amend where the complaint did not include any additional facts in support of its FDCPA claim other than stating that by engaging in alleged RICO actions, the defendants also violated the FDCPA. The complaint recited the statutory elements of an FDCPA claim, but it did not contain any facts indicating that the statute was applicable in this case, since the billing statements at issue did not relate to any "debt" owed to the defendants, nor did it appear that the defendants could be considered debt collectors under the statute.

Lopez v. Rash Curtis & Assocs., 2010 WL 4968064 (E.D. Cal. Dec. 1, 2010). The plaintiff's complaint did not contain adequate factual allegations to state a claim for violation of § 1692(f),for threatening to add illegal attorney fees, or falsely threatening garnishment.

Christopher v. First Franklin Fin. Corp., 2010 WL 1780077 (S.D. Cal. Apr. 30, 2010). The court dismissed the complaint with leave to amend where consumer did not allege that any of the defendants were FDCPA debt collectors and did not specify which statutory provisions were allegedly violated.

Allen v. United Fin. Mortgage Corp., 2010 WL 1135787 (N.D. Cal. Mar. 22, 2010). Where amended complaint stated that a defendant acquired its interest in the subject transactions after the consumer defaulted on his obligations, the court inferred that the defendant acquired its interest in the loan or loans in order to foreclose on the consumer's property or to collect upon the consumer's debt. The court stated that the consumer thus "satisfied his low burden at the pleading stage" for establishing that CRC was a "debt collector."

Estrella v. G L Recovery Group, L.L.C., 2010 WL 679067 (C.D. Cal. Feb. 22, 2010). The consumer's allegation that the defendant violated § 1692b(2) by calling consumer's mother "on more than one occasion" and "communicating with consumer's mother and stating that consumer owes a debt" stated a claim for relief under the *Iqbal* standard without alleging any additional details.

Gonzalez v. HomeQ Servicing, 2010 WL 289303 (E.D. Cal. Jan. 15, 2010). The court granted the defendant's unopposed motion to dismiss where the plaintiff alleged only that the defendant instituted home foreclosure proceedings and thus failed to allege any facts suggesting either that the defendant engaged in unlawful debt collection practices or that the defendant qualified as an FDCPA debt collector.

Rogers v. Cal. State Mortgage Co. Inc., 2010 WL 144861 (E.D. Cal. Jan. 11, 2010). Consumers failed to state an FDCPA claim arising from the defendants' alleged foreclosure misconduct: "Foreclosing on a trust deed is distinct from the collection of the obligation to pay money."

Swain v. CACH, L.L.C., 699 F. Supp. 2d 1109 (N.D. Cal. 2009). The FDCPA claim was dismissed with leave to amend for insufficiently pleading only a legal conclusion by merely alleging, "Each of the defendants is a 'debt collector' within the meaning of 15 U.S.C. § 1692a(6)."

Allen v. United Fin. Mortgage Corp., 660 F. Supp. 2d 1089 (N.D. Cal. 2009). Dismissed without prejudice for failure to allege that any defendant is a debt collector or identify which provisions were violated.

Robinson v. Managed Accounts Receivables Corp., 654 F. Supp. 2d 1051 (C.D. Cal. 2009). Where the complaint specifically alleged the date and contents of several telephone calls made by defendants with specific alleged facts to show that the defendant knew that plaintiff's employer prohibited her from receiving collection calls at work, a claim was sufficiently stated for violation of § 1692d in order to survive the defendant's motion to dismiss.

Nool v. HomeQ Servicing, 653 F. Supp. 2d 1047 (E.D. Cal. 2009). FDCPA claim arising from the defendant's alleged misconduct in connection with its mortgage financing and foreclosure of the plaintiff's residence was dismissed for failure to allege that the defendant was a debt collector.

Escobedo v. Countrywide Home Loans, Inc., 2009 WL 4981618 (S.D. Cal. Dec. 15, 2009). The complaint stated claims for relief under state law that incorporates the FDCPA by sufficiently alleging FDCPA violations resulting from defendant's harassing phone calls, direct communications once informed that the plaintiff was represented by counsel, and unlawful calls to the plaintiff's employer.

Angulo v. Countrywide Home Loans, Inc., 2009 WL 3427179 (E.D. Cal. Oct. 26, 2009). Complaint dismissed for failure to state a claim since the defendant was an exempt lender collecting its own debt.

Ferrari v. U.S. Bank, 2009 WL 3353028 (N.D. Cal. Oct. 16, 2009). The FDCPA claim was dismissed because the complaint failed to allege facts that the defendant was a debt collector attempting to collect a debt covered by the FDCPA.

Crittenden v. HomeQ Servicing, 2009 WL 3162247 (E.D. Cal. Sept. 29, 2009). Court erroneously applied "fraud" pleading standard to FDCPA claim of deceptive or misleading tactics.

Ung v. GMAC Mortgage, L.L.C., 2009 WL 2902434 (C.D. Cal. Sept. 4, 2009). Section 1692f(6) claims arising from the defendants' alleged unlawful home foreclosure were dismissed for failure to plead "facts from which the Court could find Defendants had no enforceable, present right to the property."

Velazquez v. Arrow Fin. Servs., L.L.C., 2009 WL 2780372 (S.D. Cal. Aug. 31, 2009). Motion to dismiss granted citing *Iqbal,* with leave to amend, since "Plaintiff alleges that Defendant sought to collect a debt not actually owed, but fails to substantiate these allegations with something more than conclusory allegations not entitled to the assumption of truth."

Renteria v. Nationwide Credit, Inc., 2009 WL 2754988 (S.D. Cal. Aug. 27, 2009). The court disagreed that there were heightened pleading standards of Rule 9(b) as applied to FDCPA and Rosenthal state debt collection statutory claims, requiring a complaint to identify each communication violating the FDCPA in detail, as asserted by defendant, who cited *Townsend v. Chase Bank USA,* 2009 WL 426393 (N.D. Cal. Feb. 15, 2009), a *pro se* case. Thus, the court denied the debt collector's motion to dismiss.

Feliciano v. Wash. Mut. Bank, 2009 WL 2390842 (E.D. Cal. Aug. 3, 2009). Allegation in the complaint that the defendant in addition to being the servicer of the loan was also a "debt collector" was sufficient to survive the motion to dismiss the FDCPA claim.

Mendiola v. MTC Fin. Inc., 2009 U.S. Dist. LEXIS 45204 (S.D. Cal. May 29, 2009). FDCPA claim dismissed for failure to state a claim: "[T]he complaint is devoid of factual allegations that would give defendants notice of plaintiff's claims concerning unfair debt collection practices."

Walker v. Equity 1 Lenders Group, 2009 WL 1364430 (S.D. Cal. May 14, 2009). FDCPA claim dismissed against the defendant mortgage servicer because the complaint did not allege that this defendant was a "debt collector" and failed to allege any debt collection activity on its part, having alleged instead only that it had participated in the non-debt-collection activity of foreclosing on the plaintiff's property.

Hernandez v. Downey Sav. & Loan Ass'n, 2009 WL 667406 (N.D. Cal. Mar. 13, 2009). The consumers failed to state a claim for relief for the defendants' violation of § 1692g(b) since they did "not allege any facts demonstrating that Defendants continued their efforts to collect the debt following receipt of the [verification request]."

Hernandez v. Cal. Reconveyance Co., 2009 WL 464462 (E.D. Cal. Feb. 24, 2009). Where the complaint lacked allegations of violations of §§ 1692d, 1692e, and 1692f, defendant's Rule 12(b)(6) motion to dismiss was granted without prejudice. Because the complaint alleged "unsubstantiated, sweeping legal conclusions," it must be dismissed.

Townsend v. Chase Bank USA, 2009 WL 426393 (N.D. Cal. Feb. 15, 2009). "Courts have held that the date and contents of each alleged communication in violation of the FDCPA must be pled with particularity." Dismissed *pro se*'s third amended complaint.

Martinez v. Quality Loan Serv. Corp., 2009 WL 586725 (C.D. Cal. Feb. 10, 2009). Where consumer's complaint failed to allege sufficient facts to support claim that a loan servicing company was a "debt collector," defendant's motion to dismiss was granted.

Gutierrez v. Wells Fargo Bank, 2009 WL 322915 (N.D. Cal. Feb. 9, 2009). *Pro se* complaint dismissed with leave to amend where the failure to cease collecting after a request to validate the debt was not ascribed to a particular defendant.

Crowe v. Lynch, 2009 WL 250913 (S.D. Cal. Jan. 30, 2009). A plaintiff's obligation to provide the grounds of his entitlement to relief' requires more than labels and conclusions.

Arenas v. Countrywide Home Loans, Inc., 2009 WL 48231 (S.D. Cal. Jan. 7, 2009). Unopposed motion to dismiss granted since the plaintiff failed to allege in the complaint "any facts which, taken as true, would demonstrate a violation of the FDCPA."

Ramos v. Citimortgage, Inc., 2009 WL 86744 (E.D. Cal. Jan. 8, 2009). Because the complaint adequately pleaded a cause of action for violation of the FDCPA, defendant's motion to dismiss was denied.

Pineda v. GMAC Mortgage, L.L.C., 2008 WL 5432281 (C.D. Cal. Dec. 29, 2008). *Pro se* consumer's complaint, although "somewhat vague," stated a claim for defendants' violation of § 1692g by alleging that they failed to respond to his timely, written dispute but continued collection activity.

Chavez v. Recontrust Co., 2008 WL 5210893 (E.D. Cal. Dec. 11, 2008). Absent any alleged violations, unfair debt collection practices claim was dismissed as an unsubstantiated attempt to delay non-judicial foreclosure.

Ines v. Countrywide Home Loans, Inc., 2008 WL 4791863 (S.D. Cal. Nov. 3, 2008). Complaint dismissed with leave to amend where the FDCPA complaint failed to allege facts that the defendant was a debt collector and that the FDCPA had been violated.

Tina v. Countrywide Home Loans, Inc., 2008 WL 4790906 (S.D. Cal. Oct. 30, 2008). *Pro se* consumers' complaint was dismissed because it failed to allege any facts that the defendant was a debt collector pursuant to the FDCPA.

Catalfamo v. Countrywide Home Loan, 2008 WL 4158432 (E.D. Cal. Sept. 4, 2008). The court denied defendant's motion to dismiss complaint because on a motion to dismiss, court considers as true, the factual allegations in a complaint, particularly those of a *pro se* plaintiff.

Constable v. Hara, 2008 WL 2302599 (E.D. Cal. May 30, 2008), *report and recommendations adopted*, 2009 WL 465780 (E.D. Cal. Feb. 24, 2009). The complaint was dismissed as vague with leave to amend, where the *pro se* plaintiff failed to clearly identify the debt collector or provide proper information regarding the debt.

Navarro v. Eskanos & Adler, 2006 WL 3533039 (N.D. Cal. Dec. 7, 2006). Consumer granted leave to amend to assert collection lawyers who deceptively rubber stamped letters without legal review as the consumer promptly requested leave to amend after learning of this in depositions.

Yee v. Ventus Capital Servs., Inc., 2006 WL 1310463 (N.D. Cal. May 12, 2006). "Ventus has offered only somewhat cryptic notes presented by a custodian of records. While Ventus may be correct that the business records exception to the hearsay rule makes the notes themselves admissible, the custodian's attempt to explain and interpret what those notes mean is not competent evidence."

York Gee Au Chan v. North Am. Collectors, Inc., 2006 WL 778642 (N.D. Cal. Mar. 24, 2006). Plaintiff's conclusory allegations of FDCPA violations, including that the collector misstated the amount of the debt and added charges that were not permitted or authorized, stated a claim for relief notwithstanding the absence of detail.

Davilla v. Thinline Collections, L.L.C., 230 F.R.D. 601 (N.D. Cal. 2005). Pursuant to Rule 4(d) of the Federal Rules of Civil Proce-

dure the court awarded the consumer $170.28 in costs and $900 in attorney fees for the debt collector's failure to waive service of summons.

Abels v. JBC Legal Group, P.C., 229 F.R.D. 152 (N.D. Cal. 2005). Plaintiff permitted to add newly discovered purchaser of the debt, owned by defendant's president; there was no prejudice to defendant and the claims related back.

Palmer v. I.C. Sys., Inc., 2005 WL 3001877 (N.D. Cal. Nov. 8, 2005). Court refused to consider claim on motion for summary judgment that defendant pursued a time-barred debt because the complaint contained no allegations about such a claim and defendant was therefore denied an opportunity for discovery on that issue.

Gorman v. Wolpoff & Abramson, L.L.P., 370 F. Supp. 2d 1005 (N.D. Cal. May 4, 2005). Court granted the consumer leave to amend his complaint to provide detail to his insufficient conclusory allegations that the defendant violated the FDCPA.

Foresberg v. Fidelity Nat'l Credit Servs., Ltd., 2004 WL 3510771 (S.D. Cal. Feb. 26, 2004). The allegations that the debt collector misrepresented the number of prior contacts that it had made or attempted to make with the consumer and falsely threatened to report the debt to a credit bureau stated a claim for relief which could not be tested in a motion to dismiss.

Colorado

Vester v. Asset Acceptance, L.L.C., 2009 WL 2940218 (D. Colo. Sept. 9, 2009). Court denied the consumer's §§ 1692e and 1692f summary judgment motion since, contrary to the consumer's claim, the defendant's evidence showed that interest was added in accordance with the terms of the underlying written contract.

Webster v. Nations Recovery Ctr., Inc., 2009 WL 2982649 (D. Colo. Sept. 15, 2009). Court denied motion to strike allegation that defendant had been sued twenty-three times, since the information may be admissible under Fed. R. Evid. 404(b).

Allen v. P&B Capital Group, L.L.C., 2009 WL 2940206 (D. Colo. Sept. 9, 2009). Defendant's Rule 12(f) motion to strike allegations in the complaint that defendant "violates the FDCPA as part of its business practice" was denied because, *inter alia*, the allegations may be "relevant and admissible to show that the defendant has a history or plan of aggressive debt collecting" and thus the allegations may be admissible with regard to "claimed statutory damages as they relate to the 'frequency and persistence of the noncompliance by the debt collector, the nature of such noncompliance, and the extent to which such noncompliance was intentional.' "

Spektor v. Niagara Credit Solutions, Inc., 2008 WL 2782725 (D. Colo. July 7, 2008). Defendant collector's motion to set aside entry of default granted, where the defendant was merely inadvertent in not filing a timely answer, acted immediately to set aside the entry of default once on notice, and presented the meritorious defenses that generally denied the offending conduct occurred and asserted the bona fide error defense.

Zimmerman v. Arp, 2008 WL 793580 (D. Colo. Mar. 20, 2008). *Pro se* plaintiff's complaint conferred subject matter jurisdiction on the court by alleging that the defendants violated the FDCPA when they improperly filed a state court collection case wherein they falsely represented the character and legal status of the debt.

Cross v. Receivables Mgmt. Solutions, Inc., 2006 WL 446083 (D. Colo. Feb. 21, 2006). Court denied defendants' motion to dismiss, finding barebones allegations sufficient to survive.

Connecticut

Franke v. Global Credit & Collection Corp., 2010 WL 4449373 (D. Conn. Nov. 1, 2010). The court found that the plaintiff's complaint was bare of any specific facts that would support its claims, and permitted the plaintiff to file an amended complaint.

Korzeniowski v. NCO Fin. Sys., 2010 WL 466162 (D. Conn. Feb. 8, 2010). *Pro se* complaint dismissed because it was a laundry list of the elements of the statutory violations without any factual allegations that raised the right to relief to plausible. Plaintiff's complaint described as the epitome of a complaint that "tenders naked assertions devoid of further factual enhancement."

Zuppe v. Elite Recovery Servs, Inc., 2006 WL 47688 (D. Conn. Jan. 5, 2006). Defendant's motion was denied because motions for a more specific pleading pursuant to Rule 12(e) are disfavored due to their dilatory effect rather the preferred course is to encourage the use of discovery.

Musso v. Seiders, 194 F.R.D. 43 (D. Conn. 1999). If defendant raises lack of personal jurisdiction before discovery was conducted, the plaintiff can defeat motion to dismiss by a good faith allegation of jurisdiction. If defendant raises lack of personal jurisdiction by motion for summary judgment, plaintiff has the burden of establishing jurisdiction by a preponderance of the evidence.

Little v. World Fin. Network, Inc., 1990 U.S. Dist. LEXIS 20846 (D. Conn. July 15, 1990). An FDCPA pleading should state the facts forming the basis for each claim of an FDCPA violation.

Stewart v. Salzman, 1987 U.S. Dist. LEXIS 16865 (D. Conn. Nov. 2, 1987). A short plain statement showing the pleader is entitled to relief is all that Fed. R. Civ. P. 8 requires of FDCPA complaint.

SNET Info., Inc. v. Prime One/Prime Direct, Inc., 2009 WL 2784642 (Conn. Super. Ct. Aug. 7, 2009) (unpublished). Because the defendant-consumer failed to plead any facts to indicate that the underlying debt was incurred for personal, family, or household purposes or that the plaintiff was a debt collector, it failed to state a legally sufficient claim pursuant to the FDCPA and the motion to strike its special defense was granted.

Baker v. I.C. Sys., Inc., 2009 WL 1365002 (Conn. Super. Ct. May 11, 2009). A claim for contacting the consumer's friend despite having the consumer's location information was not well pleaded.

S. New England Tel. Co. v. Megos, 1996 WL 724103 (Conn. Super. Ct. Dec. 3, 1996). FDCPA raised as a defense was stricken on basis of consumer's failure to comply with local rules of pleading.

Bank of New Haven v. Liner, 1993 WL 107819 (Conn. Super. Ct. Apr. 1, 1993). FDCPA counterclaim raised against the bank's foreclosure action was dismissed because, *inter alia*, the alleged misconduct by the bank's employee did not arise from the same transaction.

District of Columbia

Antoine v. U.S. Bank Nat'l Ass'n, 547 F. Supp. 2d 30 (D.D.C. Apr. 22, 2008). In contrast to pleading a fraud claim, an FDCPA claim "does not require particularized pleading, [but] it does require, at a minimum, that the plaintiff identify the defendant individually, in the complaint, as a 'debt collector' . . ."

Florida

Clarke v. Weltman, Wienberg & Reis, Co., L.P.A., 2010 WL 2803975 (S.D. Fla. July 15, 2010). A complaint alleging that over a two and a half month period twenty-six messages were left on the consumer's cell phone was sufficient under *Twombly* and *Iqbal* to state a violation of § 1692d even if they also constituted a violation of the TCPA. "Each element of the particular statutory claim must be met, regardless of whether the same facts support multiple claims."

Dokumaci v. MAF Collection Servs., 2010 WL 1507014 (M.D. Fla. Apr. 14, 2010). The court dismissed the complaint with leave to amend for failure to plead sufficient facts under the *Iqbal* standard that the consumer was a consumer and the defendant was a debt collector.

Tucker v. Malcolm S. Gerald & Assocs., Inc., 2010 WL 1223912 (M.D. Fla. Mar. 24, 2010). Allegations that the defendant called the consumer's phone number without leaving any message, did not disclose that the call was from a debt collector, did not disclose its identity as a debt collector, and did not send the consumer a debt validation letter were dismissed by the court as formulaic rather than factual under *Iqbal*, and thus insufficient to support the FDCPA violations claimed.

Chalik v. Westport Recovery Corp., 677 F. Supp. 2d 1322 (S.D. Fla. 2009). "Consumer is only obligated to make minimal factual allegations demonstrating that there are legal grounds upon which a claim for relief may be based." Failure to specifically identify how defendants' conduct was unfair or unconscionable under § 1692f warranted dismissal of this claim.

Beeders v. Gulf Coast Collection Bureau, 632 F. Supp. 2d 1125 (M.D. Fla. 2009). Court refused to reconsider ruling that ordered eleven separate cases, each based on a separate phone call by the collector, to be consolidated, with $1000 per violation statutory damages in the consolidated action.

Lee v. Security Check, L.L.C., 2009 WL 3790455 (M.D. Fla. Nov. 9, 2009). Complaint failed to state a claim against the merchant to whom the subject dishonored check was written in the absence of any allegation that the merchant was an FDCPA debt collector.

Sullivan v. CTI Collection Servs., 2009 WL 2495950 (M.D. Fla. Aug. 11, 2009). The elements required for a cause of action under the FDCPA are: (1) Plaintiff is the object of a collection activity arising from consumer debt; (2) Defendant is a debt collector as defined by the FDCPA; and (3) Defendants have engaged in an act or omission prohibited by the FDCPA.

Sands v. Wagner & Hunt, P.A., 2009 WL 2730469 (S.D. Fla. Aug. 28, 2009). The court granted the consumer's motion to enforce the parties' settlement agreement that the defendant then refused to honor when the consumer would not agree to the additional term of a confidentiality clause.

Cavalier v. Weinstein & Riley, P.S., 2009 WL 2460740 (S.D. Fla. Aug. 7, 2009). Where the FDCPA complaint only alleged violation of "each and every provision of § 1692," defendant's motion for a more definite statement was granted.

Kuehn v. The Cadle Co., 2006 WL 845085 (M.D. Fla. Mar. 30, 2006). The requirements of Rule 15(c)(3) were satisfied where the claims set forth in the amended complaint arise from the same conduct set forth in the original complaint, and the plaintiff was allowed to substitute the correctly named defendant.

Agan v. Katzman & Korr, P.A., 328 F. Supp. 2d 1363 (S.D. Fla. 2004). The court denied collector's motion to strike pre-billing worksheets attached to the complaint, since they showed that law firm sought excessive fees in a state court action. The worksheets were in the nature of settlement documents in the state condominium assessment action, but contained otherwise discoverable evidence as to the federal FDCPA claim. Court rejected the argument that defendant's business would be adversely affected if they could not provide attorney fee substantiation to a debtor without fear that the debtor will turn around and sue: "any collection agency or collection lawyer must comply with the requirements of federal law in collecting on a debt. If that means the agency or attorney must scrutinize her attorney time records more carefully, that is a price that federal law requires."

Gottlieb v. Green Oil, Inc., 1998 WL 469849 (S.D. Fla. May 8, 1998). Magistrate judge recommended that motion to dismiss complaint be denied, based on letter attached to complaint which is the factual basis for the legal allegations. The court could not conclude that plaintiff could prove no set of facts in support of her claim.

Wright v. G.C. Fin. Corp., 1996 U.S. Dist. LEXIS 22664 (M.D. Fla. Oct. 22, 1996). The court denied the collector's motion to dismiss because the FDCPA complaint merely needed to plead violations that would meet the least sophisticated consumer standard.

Georgia

Vlahos v. Frederick J. Hanna & Assocs., P.C., 430 F. Supp. 2d 1375 (N.D. Ga. 2006). Service of process on associate attorney proper as Georgia law permits service on employees of suitable discretion.

Illinois

Kubert v. Aid Assocs., 2009 WL 1270351(N.D. Ill. May 7, 2009). After striking the plaintiff's survey evidence, the court entered summary judgment for the defendant since the only remaining evidence in support of the alleged deception was the plaintiff's own testimony, which was "insufficient to survive a motion for summary judgment."

Perry v. Capital One Bank, 2008 WL 4911474 (C.D. Ill. Oct. 24, 2008), *report and recommendations adopted*, 2008 WL 4911711 (C.D. Ill. Nov. 13, 2008). Motion to dismiss granted as to the *pro se* plaintiff's FDCPA claims against the debt collector's employees. There was no allegation that the employees had engaged in misconduct or were vicariously liable.

Clabault v. Shodeen Mgmt., 2006 WL 1371460 (N.D. Ill. May 15,

2006). Defendants' motion to dismiss *pro se* plaintiff's FDCPA claims was denied because plaintiff had adequately pleaded that defendants harassed, oppressed, or abused her in connection with the collection of the debt in violation of § 1692d and that defendants intentionally requested an incorrect debt amount in collection letters and thereby used false, deceptive, or misleading misrepresentations in connection with the collection of the debt in violation of § 1692e.

Clabault v. Shodeen Mgmt., 406 F. Supp. 2d 877 (N.D. Ill. 2005). The court granted the *pro se* plaintiff's motion to proceed in forma pauperis with regard to her FDCPA claim, but denied her motion with respect to her due process and FHA claims because they were barred by the *Rooker-Feldman* doctrine.

Hernandez v. Attention, L.L.C., 429 F. Supp. 2d 912 (N.D. Ill. Sept. 28, 2005). The consumer's attempt to show consumers' confusion through a consumer survey was flawed because the survey did not make use of a control group.

Patterson v. Asset Acceptance Corp., 2004 WL 1660838 (N.D. Ill. July 22, 2004). *Pro se* plaintiff stated a claim for violation of the FDCPA but not the FCRA.

Mikula v. Great Lakes Fin. Servs., Inc., 2004 WL 1656556 (N.D. Ill. July 22, 2004). Debt collector's motion to dismiss was premature when it sought to have the Court apply the unsophisticated consumer test and determine whether or not the evidence was such that the debt collector should succeed was a matter of law.

O'Chaney v. Shapiro & Kreisman, L.L.C., 2004 WL 635060 (N.D. Ill. Mar. 29, 2004). The allegation that a collector's statement to call the collector for further information, appearing at the end of its letter containing the § 1692g notice, was confusing and overshadowed the requirement to disclose that a verification request must be in writing stated a claim for relief for violating § 1692g in light of the Seventh Circuit's liberal rule of pleading but not for violating § 1692f.

Tucker v. Bank One, N.A., 265 F. Supp. 2d 923 (N.D. Ill. 2003). *Pro se* complaint dismissed for failure to state a claim where it failed to give any notice of what misconduct it accused the defendant of committing.

Durkin v. Equifax Check Servs., Inc., 2003 WL 22078331 (N.D. Ill. Sept. 8, 2003). Defendant's motion for judgment on the pleadings which would require the consideration of extrinsic evidence was improper. The debt collector was free to file a motion for summary judgment where extrinsic evidence of confusion would be considered.

Collins v. Sparacio, 2003 WL 21254256 (N.D. Ill. May 30, 2003). Consumer's unadorned allegations that the attorney debt collector from the underlying state court collection suit misrepresented in that suit the amount of the debt and attempted to collect sums not authorized by the contract or law sufficiently met the federal notice pleading requirements to state a claim for relief.

Bennett v. Arrow Fin. Servs. L.L.C., 2002 WL 31884941 (N.D. Ill. Dec. 26, 2002). *Pro se* plaintiff's complaint was dismissed for failure to state a claim with leave to amend within twenty-eight days.

Shula v. Lawent, 2002 WL 31870157 (N.D. Ill. Dec. 23, 2002). An amendment to an FDCPA complaint adding other FDCPA claims should relate back to the same "conduct, transaction, or occurrence" alleged in the initial pleading and would not be barred by the one-year statute of limitations.

Smith v. Continental Cmty. Bank & Trust Co., 2002 U.S. Dist. LEXIS 9025 (N.D. Ill. May 20, 2002). Banks' motion to dismiss was granted because the complaint did not allege that police officers were attempting to collect a consumer debt or were collecting for the bank using a false name.

Klco v. Elmhurst Dodge, 2002 U.S. Dist. LEXIS 1821 (N.D. Ill. Feb. 4, 2002). Consumer's motion to amend his complaint to add automobile dealership's corporate parent was denied where consumer failed to allege conduct which justified piercing the corporate veil and the motion was untimely.

White v. Fin. Credit Corp., 2001 U.S. Dist. LEXIS 21486 (N.D. Ill. Dec. 20, 2001). Court struck plaintiff's expert's testimony as failing to meet the Supreme Court's *Daubert* standard and then granted summary judgment dismissing claim that defendant's dun that stated that payment of the debt would "amend your credit report" was untrue and deceptive, holding that the issue was a question of fact and (without the expert testimony) the consumer produced no supporting evidence.

Miller v. Knepper & Moga, 1999 U.S. Dist. LEXIS 16362 (N.D. Ill. Oct. 21, 1999). A complaint need not cite any specific section of the statute in order to state a claim for relief for violating the FDCPA.

Keele v. Wexler, 1995 WL 549048 (N.D. Ill. Sept. 12, 1995). Appearance of attorney's name in letterhead was insufficient evidence to overcome affidavit that attorney was not a partner and was not involved in the sending of the letter which allegedly violated the FDCPA, and attorney was dismissed from the lawsuit.

Friedman v. HHL Fin. Servs., Inc., 1993 WL 367089 (N.D. Ill. Sept. 17, 1993). Alleged violations of the FDCPA not stated in the complaint could not be raised in responsive briefs and were dismissed without prejudice. Court recommended that each alleged violation of the FDCPA be plead in a separate count.

Kegley v. Miles Mgmt. Corp., 1992 WL 370251 (N.D. Ill. Dec. 3, 1992). Where affidavits and other evidentiary materials are submitted, the motion will be considered as one for summary judgment rather than a motion to dismiss.

Indiana

Hubbard v. Midland Credit Mgmt, Inc., 2009 WL 454989 (S.D. Ind. Feb. 23, 2009). The consumer's motion for approval of the proposed methodology and forms for an FDCPA survey was denied.

Reed v. AID Assocs., Inc., 573 F. Supp. 2d 1105 (S.D. Ind. 2008). A plaintiff must prove by a preponderance of the evidence that "the debt collector's communication would deceive or mislead an unsophisticated, but reasonable, consumer." No survey evidence is required, although that is one way to meet the burden. Plaintiffs' prior FDCPA lawsuits would be relevant only if they intended to use their own testimony as evidence of how an unsophisticated, but reasonable, consumer would have viewed the letter.

Miller v. Account Mgmt. Servs., 2008 WL 596011 (N.D. Ind. Feb.

29, 2008). Consumer's Rule 56(f) motion to obtain discovery in order to respond to summary judgment motion was granted.

Kansas

Burdett v. Harrah's Kansas Casino Corp., 260 F. Supp. 2d 1109 (D. Kan. 2003). Where events occurred both before and after the one year date prior to the filing of the FDCPA complaint, the court required the plaintiff to amend the complaint to identify each FDCPA violation, the party who committed the violation, and the date of the violation.

Burdett v. Harrah's Kansas Casino Corp., 2003 WL 124665 (D. Kan. Jan. 12, 2003). An extension of time was granted to conduct discovery to rebut debt collector's affidavit in support of summary judgment, but Fed. R. Civ. Pro. 56(g) sanctions against the collector denied for lack of substantiation that the collector's motion for summary judgment had been filed in bad faith.

Louisiana

Arrington v. Republic Credit Corp. I, 2002 WL 31844905 (E.D. La. Dec. 16, 2002). Consumer's bare allegation that the defendant violated the FDCPA by collecting on a void judgment stated a claim for relief, but court granted the defendant's motion for a more definite statement.

Maryland

Bradshaw v. Hilco Receivables, L.L.C., 2010 WL 2948181 (D. Md. July 27, 2010). The plausibility standard applies to affirmative defenses. The bona fide error defense was stricken absent compliance with Rule 9(b) including factual details as to the mistake.

Keller v. American Express Travel Related Servs., Co., 2009 WL 1473500 (D. Md. May 26, 2009). Motion to dismiss the FDCPA claims was denied because the complaint adequately stated a cause of action.

Nelson v. Diversified Collection Servs., Inc., 961 F. Supp. 863 (D. Md. 1997). Debtor's claim that defendant's garnishment of wages under the Higher Education Act was not in compliance with the FDCPA would not be addressed for the first time on appeal as the claim was not alleged in complaint.

Massachusetts

Krasnor v. Spaulding Law Office, 675 F. Supp. 2d 208 (D. Mass. 2009). Allegations tracking the statutory language survive motion to dismiss. "Consumer's complaint fits comfortably within a number of pre- and post-*Twombly* FDCPA decisions which, together, indicate that identifying the proper FDCPA subsections is typically sufficient for pleading purposes."

Michigan

Saltzman v. I.C. Sys., Inc., 2009 WL 3190359 (E.D. Mich. Sept. 30, 2009). Summary judgment for defendant on "kitchen sink" complaint raising several violations based on lack of credible evidence in the course of which court observed in dicta (erroneously) that same misconduct as alleged to support violation of one section of FDCPA cannot support violation of another section.

Jones v. Heartland Home Fin., Inc., 2008 WL 4561693 (E.D.

Mich. Oct. 10, 2008). Complaint was dismissed because plaintiffs' bare allegations did not allege that the defendant was a debt collector or engaged in specific wrongdoing in violation of the FDCPA in its foreclosure and eviction proceedings against the consumers. The FDCPA action was also barred by the *Rooker-Feldman* doctrine.

Kelly v. Bird, 2006 U.S. Dist. LEXIS 53457 (E.D. Mich. Aug. 2, 2006). Where the consumer settles and dismisses her suit, she should file the settlement with the court and request it reserve jurisdiction to enforce the settlement agreement. *See Kokkonen v. Guardian Life Ins. Co.,* 511 U.S. 375, 380–382 (1994).

Nelski v. Risk Mgmt. Alternatives, Inc., 2005 WL 1038788 (E.D. Mich. Apr. 21, 2005). The court granted the debt collector summary judgment where the consumer failed to substantiate with any evidence her claims of collector harassment.

Russell v. Standard Fed. Bank, 2002 U.S. Dist. LEXIS 12334 (E.D. Mich. June 19, 2002). FDCPA claim dismissed where plaintiff failed to provide the court with sufficient information as to whether defendant law firm collected debts regularly or how it violated the Act.

Minnesota

Burgi v. Messerli & Kramer PA, 2008 WL 4181732 (D. Minn. Sept. 5, 2008). Defendant's motion to dismiss *pro se* plaintiff's complaint was granted for failure to state a claim for violation of the FDCPA.

Fraenkel v. Messerli & Kramer, P.A., 2004 WL 1765309 (D. Minn. July 29, 2004). Undisputed documents attached to debt collector's answer did not require conversion of Rule 12(c) motion to motion for summary judgment, and consumer's FDCPA claim was dismissed as time barred.

Silbert v. Asset Res., Inc., 2000 U.S. Dist. LEXIS 6453 (D. Minn. Feb. 14, 2000). Upon a motion for judgment on the pleadings, the court declined to infer in the defendant's favor that a validation notice was sent solely because defendant alleged that it utilized a computerized collection system and that validation notices were routinely mailed the day that they are generated.

Mississippi

Hambrick v. Wells Fargo Bank, 2009 WL 1532676 (N.D. Miss. June 2, 2009). Complaint dismissed for failure to state a claim where the plaintiff did not allege that the defendant mortgage company, an exempt FDCPA creditor, was a debt collector; plaintiff's response that it needed to conduct discovery to determine whether the defendant obtained the debt after default so as to become a debt collector merely established that any claim based on the defendant's debt collector status "cannot meet the beyond-speculation standard" imposed by *Twombly.*

Valencia v. Miss. Baptist Med. Ctr., Inc., 363 F. Supp. 2d 867 (S.D. Miss. 2005). Consumer's motion for leave to file a second amended complaint to add FDCPA claims, filed three months after deadline for amendments, was denied as untimely.

Missouri

Eckert v. LVNV Funding L.L.C., 647 F. Supp. 2d 1096 (E.D. Mo.

2009). Plaintiff failed to plead facts that would show that the defendant was not entitled to prejudgment interest under state law.

Wells v. Southwestern Bell Tel. Co., 626 F. Supp. 2d 1001 (W.D. Mo. 2009). The complaint alleged sufficient facts from which violations within a year of filing the complaint could be inferred. Motion to dismiss denied.

Kramer & Frank, P.C. v. Wibbenmeyer, 2006 WL 1134479 (E.D. Mo. Apr. 26, 2006). The court misinterpreted defendants' counterclaim under FDCPA, FCRA, etc. for the arbitration misrepresentations as sounding in fraud and dismissed for failure to meet the heightened pleading standard.

Burkhalter v. Lindquist & Trudeau, 2005 WL 1983809 (E.D. Mo. Aug. 16, 2005). Consumer's short, concise pleading met the requirements for notice pleading.

Nebraska

Rios v. General Serv. Bureau, 2010 WL 323533 (D. Neb. Jan. 20, 2010). *Pro se* consumer's FDCPA complaint was dismissed in the absence of any alleged FDCPA violations; the complaint alleged only that the consumer disputed the debt with the defendant collector, that the defendant continued to report and verify the debt to the credit bureaus without contacting her, and that the debt remained on the consumer's credit reports, causing her " 'loss of self-esteem and peace of mind,' 'emotional distress,' and 'humiliation.' "

Kawa v. US Bank, 2009 WL 700593 (D. Neb. Mar. 13, 2009). The complaint sufficiently alleged a possible consumer purpose for the underlying debts to require the court to deny the defendants' motion to dismiss the FDCPA claim, since "at this point in the proceedings, the Court cannot definitively say that the extensions of credit were primarily commercial in nature."

Williamson v. Unifund CCR Partners, 2009 WL 187702 (D. Neb. Jan. 23, 2009). Denied motion to strike ten of many defenses. Defenses were precautionary, some were relevant, all gave plaintiff sufficient notice to allow discovery as to the issues raised.

Brown v. Jungers, 2009 WL 159700 (D. Neb. Jan. 22, 2009). Denied motion to strike seven of many defenses. Defenses were precautionary, some were relevant, all gave plaintiff sufficient notice to allow discovery as to the issues raised.

Clevenger v. Alltel Communications, Inc., 2007 U.S. Dist. LEXIS 2585 (D. Neb. Jan. 10, 2007). Rejecting the defendant's protest that it was an exempt creditor, the court denied its motion to dismiss, holding that the plaintiff's allegation that the defendant was a covered debt collector adequately met the notice pleading requirement for purposes of Rule 12(b)(6).

Nevada

Bernstein v. Noteworld, L.L.C., 2010 WL 3154518 (D. Nev. Aug. 9, 2010). The court dismissed the complaint with leave to amend so that the consumer could specify statutory subsections alleged to have been violated.

Kerr v. Wanderer & Wanderer, 211 F.R.D. 625 (D. Nev. 2002). A *pro se* complaint may be liberally construed but must allege facts that could prove the defendant to be a debt collector.

New Jersey

Siwulec v. Chase Home Fin., L.L.C., 2010 WL 5071353 (D.N.J. Dec. 7, 2010). Allegations that Chase is a "debt collector" by acquiring servicing rights after default were insufficient pleaded under the *Iqbal* and *Twombly*; consumer's complaint was dismissed without prejudice.

Kennedy v. United Collection Bureau, Inc., 2010 WL 445735 (D.N.J. Feb. 3, 2010). Dismissed hypothetical claims that creditor was not charged $214.18 by debt collector or that consumer may never have owed the principal to creditor as not sufficiently factual.

Nicholas v. CMRE Fin. Servs., Inc., 2009 WL 1652275 (D.N.J. June 11, 2009). Under *Twombly* and *Iqbal*, complaint dismissed where it "limit[ed] itself to the language of the statutes and fail[ed] to provide any facts specific to [plaintiff]." Plaintiff "must at least provide some relevant facts providing the context for her claim to remove vagueness and ambiguity."

Sakrani v. Koenig, 2006 WL 20514 (D.N.J. Jan. 3, 2006). FDCPA complaint was dismissed where plaintiff failed to allege any facts demonstrating that defendants were debt collectors.

New York

Ogbon v. Beneficial Credit Servs., Inc., 2011 WL 347222 (S.D.N.Y. Feb. 1, 2011). Complaint failed to state any facts to show that the defendants were debt collectors or that they engaged in collection activity.

Ehlrich v. Rapid Recovery Solutions, Inc., 680 F. Supp. 2d 443 (E.D.N.Y. 2010). Where consumer purchased two cellular telephones giving rise to the debt that the debt collector sought to collect, consumer adequately alleged that she incurred a consumer debt covered by the FDCPA thereby satisfying the *Twombly* standard and overcoming defendants' motion to dismiss.

Gargiulo v. Forster & Garbus Esqs., 651 F. Supp. 2d 188 (S.D.N.Y. 2009). Allegation that a "Non-Military Affirmation" affidavit submitted in the underlying collection suit was false failed to contain sufficient facts under the *Iqbal* standard to state a claim for relief.

Leone v. Ashwood Fin., Inc., 257 F.R.D. 343 (E.D.N.Y. 2009). The plaintiff need only establish one FDCPA violation to prevail.

Sembler v. Attention Funding Trust, 2009 WL 3055347 (E.D.N.Y. Sept. 24, 2009). Plaintiff's lawyer failed the *Iqbal* test. "Plaintiff is incorrect in asserting that the Court must, under any circumstances, read between the lines of his pleading, inserting where necessary any stray fact required to state a claim."

Sembler v. Advanta Bank Corp., 2008 WL 2965661 (E.D.N.Y. Aug. 1, 2008). Recommended ruling, going well beyond notice-pleading standards, that plaintiff's second amended complaint must set forth the following facts: each contact by the defendants, including the date and method of contact; the name of the individual who contacted plaintiff, if known; and what plaintiff specifically alleges defendants did that violated his rights under the FDCPA. The second amended complaint shall specifically state which cause of action is alleged against which defendant; it should plead facts that plausibly support the required elements of each cause of action; and it should not incorporate and re-allege prior causes of action unless the allegations apply to and are required to support a subsequent cause of action. The second amended complaint shall completely replace plaintiff's amended complaint filed on September 10, 2007. Plaintiff should attach to his second amended complaint any letters or notices he received from the defendants, any communications he made to the defendants, and any other documents that give notice of his claim. If he contacted the defendants by phone, plaintiff should state the dates and times of all calls to the best of his ability.

Schuh v. Druckman & Sinel, L.L.P., 2008 WL 542504 (S.D.N.Y. Feb. 29, 2008). FDCPA claim was dismissed with permission to amend because collection activities were outside the one-year statute of limitations and the complaint did not sufficiently alleged that HSBC was a debt collector.

Hall v. Salt City Recovery Sys., 2006 U.S. Dist. LEXIS 60472 (N.D.N.Y. Aug. 25, 2006). Plaintiff's tardy motion to amend to substitute the actual debt collector for the "John Doe" initially named did not relate back to the filing of the complaint since the defendant was not on notice and neither knew or should have known of the claim against him, and an amendment to add the defendant was futile since the claim was now time barred.

Reade-Alvarez v. Eltman, Eltman & Cooper, P.C., 369 F. Supp. 2d 353 (E.D.N.Y. 2005). FDCPA complaint was subject to no heightened pleading standard and must only comply with Rule 8's notice pleading requirements.

Colorado Capital v. Owens, 227 F.R.D. 181 (E.D.N.Y. 2005). *Pro se* plaintiff's FDCPA claim was barred by the one-year statute of limitations as it did not relate back to earlier pleadings because the consumer did not allege he was mistaken about the identity of the collector.

Redhead v. Winston & Winston, P.C., 2002 WL 31106934 (S.D.N.Y. Sept. 20, 2002). Debt collector's motion to dismiss was granted due to the failure to adequately state a claim for violation of the FDCPA in an amended complaint.

Jones v. Ocwen Fed. Bank, 147 F. Supp. 2d 219 (S.D.N.Y. 2001). The court dismissed *pro se* consumer's general allegations tracking the language of the FDCPA ("engaged in conduct, the natural consequences of which is to harass, oppress or abuse persons by use of language the natural consequence of which is to abuse plaintiff . . . caused telephone to ring, or engaged plaintiff or his family in telephone conversations repeatedly or continuously with the intent to harass or annoy . . . used false, deceptive, or misleading representation or means in connection with the collection of a debt") as insufficient because he failed to allege what the conduct consisted of, who specifically engaged in the conduct, and when the conduct took place.

Deutsche Bank Nat'l Trust Co. v. Gillio, 2009 WL 595560 (N.Y. Sup. Ct. Feb. 26, 2009) (unpublished). Where, in order to have his default judgment vacated, the homeowner claimed that the collector did not provide a timely validation notice pursuant to § 1692g(a), the court held that it did not constitute a valid defense to plaintiff's claim to collect the debt or foreclosure on the secured property.

Monogram Credit Card Bank v. Mata, 757 N.Y.S.2d 676 (N.Y. Civ. Ct. 2002). Alleged violation of the FDCPA by the attorney for the creditor/plaintiff in a state court collection action may state a claim against the attorney but is not a defense to the creditor's action to recover on the debt.

North Carolina

Adams v. Bank of Am., 2007 WL 2746871 (M.D.N.C. Sept. 19, 2007). The court dismissed for failure to state a claim the *pro se* consumer's complaint comprised of "thirty-three pages of indecipherable allegations" that amounted to "nothing more than bare conclusory statements that track the language of the statutory provisions," apparently part of "an attempt to avoid paying his credit card debt by employing a 'no-money-lent' argument" employed and rejected elsewhere around the country.

Ohio

Howard v. Huntington Nat'l Bank, 2010 WL 3743542 (S.D. Ohio Sept. 22, 2010). Because the *pro se* consumer's complaint did not mention by name the statute or any of the applicable code sections, and because it implied but did not contain any allegations that the defendant reported inaccurate credit information, the court found that the consumer lacked standing to assert a claim under the FDCPA.

Gionis v. Javitch, Block & Rathbone, 405 F. Supp. 2d 856 (S.D. Ohio 2005), *aff'd,* 238 Fed. Appx. 24 (6th Cir. 2007). The district court granted the law firm's motion for leave to take an interlocutory appeal of the court's ruling that the law firm's conduct violated § 1692e(5) and (10).

Canterbury v. Columbia Gas, 2001 WL 1681132 (S.D. Ohio Sept. 25, 2001). Violations of different provisions of the FDCPA added in a second amended complaint related back to the initial complaint and were not time barred as they related to the same events.

Lee v. Robins Preston Beckett Taylor & Gugle Co., 1999 U.S. Dist. LEXIS 12969 (S.D. Ohio July 9, 1999). Motion in limine granted precluding the defendant from raising the consumer plaintiff's eleven prior FDCPA cases or mentioning her past relationship with her attorney or the availability of attorney fees to the successful plaintiff.

Pennsylvania

In re Klein, 2010 WL 2680334 (Bankr. E.D. Pa. June 29, 2010). A bare allegation that the defendant contacted the consumer after knowledge of attorney representation, without specifics, was insufficient under *Twombly.* "The complaint is vague to the point of being wholly uninformative."

Kamara v. Columbia Home Loans, L.L.C., 654 F. Supp. 2d 259 (E.D. Pa. 2009). "These allegations are not supported by sufficient facts to withstand 12(b)(6) inquiry. The plaintiff does not describe in any detail what, if any, actual collection activities any of the defendants have undertaken. She does not identify a single communication between any of these defendants and the plaintiff, much less one that constituted an attempt to collect a debt. The complaint contains no allegations regarding specific collection methods used by these defendants, threats made by them, or illegal action taken by them. Nor does it allege that any collection or foreclosure action has been commenced by any of these defendants. In addition, with respect to [one defendant] in particular, the plaintiff does not state any actions whatsoever, other than that it

allegedly engaged in an unspecified 'assignment scheme.' The plaintiff has not shown that her FDCPA and FCEUA . . . claims go beyond mere 'the-defendant-unlawfully-harmed-me' accusations. *See Iqbal,* 129 S. Ct. at 1949. She thus fails to state a claim for violation of these statutes."

Donnelly v. Commonwealth Fin. Sys., Inc., 2008 WL 762085 (M.D. Pa. Mar. 20, 2008). The court denied the defendant debt buyer's motion to strike as "immaterial, impertinent, or scandalous" allegations in the complaint that it purchased the underlying debt at a "steeply discounted purchase price" for "pennies on the dollar" and that it contemptuously failed to produce any witness in the underlying state court collection case to prove the allegedly nonexistent debt, since the allegations were material to the claims presented.

Moyer v. Turnbrook Assocs., Inc., 2005 WL 2660353 (E.D. Pa. Oct. 17, 2005). Court would allow the pleadings to be amended to conform to the evidence that the defendant was not incorporated after the case had been arbitrated and attorney fees awarded to the consumer. The defendant would not be prejudiced where it had not denied it was incorporated and had defended the FDCPA suit.

Sullivan v. Equifax, Inc., 2002 U.S. Dist. LEXIS 7884 (E.D. Pa. Apr. 19, 2002). Absent a claim of fraud or mistake, an FDCPA complaint was subject only to the general pleading requirements of Rule 8 and not the heightened pleading requirements of Rule 9.

Skoczylas v. Atl. Credit & Fin., Inc., 2002 U.S. Dist. LEXIS 429 (E.D. Pa. Jan. 15, 2002). Collector's motion for summary judgment on consumer's complaint based upon consumer's failure to respond to request for admissions was denied, and consumer was granted permission to respond to request for admissions. Collector's motion for summary judgment on its counterclaim for the outstanding credit card debt was granted as to liability due to consumer's failure to reply to the counterclaim.

South Carolina

Scott v. TitleMax of Columbia, 2010 WL 2867336 (D.S.C. July 19, 2010). The court declined to dismiss the *pro se* complaint related to a delivery action for repossession and the sale of the consumer's automobile, since the question of whether the defendant met the FDCPA definition of "debt collector" involved a factual inquiry that was not well-suited for resolution through a motion to dismiss for pleading deficiency.

Clay v. Countrywide Home Loans, 2009 WL 223727 (D.S.C. Jan. 28, 2009). *Pro se* complaint failed to allege mortgage company was a debt collector.

Tennessee

Brown v. Hosto & Buchan, P.L.L.C., 2010 WL 4352932 (W.D. Tenn. Nov. 2, 2010). The court dismissed without prejudice the plaintiff's claim that the debt collector violated § 1692c(a)(2) where the complaint merely recited the statutory language almost word for word.

McKamey v. Financial Accounts Servs. Team, Inc., 2010 WL 3632192 (E.D. Tenn. Sept. 10, 2010). The court struck as redundant and unnecessary the defendant's attempts to restate the law in the recited defenses that FDCPA statutory damages are capped at

$1000 and that the defendant reserved the right to amend its answer.

Johnson v. Americredit Fin. Servs., Inc., 69 U.C.C. Rep. Serv. 2d 861 (M.D. Tenn. 2009). In this case, the consumer stopped payment on her down payment check because of alleged fraud by the car dealer and tried to cancel her car purchase with the seller shortly after the sale. The record was silent as to the precise time when the installment contract was assigned to its pre-arranged assignee. The assignee's motion for summary judgment, because it purportedly was an exempt creditor, was denied, since "a genuine issue of material fact exists as to whether the Plaintiff was in default when was assigned the loan."

Williamson v. Ocwen Loan Servicing, L.L.C., 2009 WL 5205405 (M.D. Tenn. Dec. 23, 2009). Consumer's FDCPA claim was sufficient to withstand defendant's motion to dismiss.

Texas

Bray v. Cadle Co., 2010 WL 4053794 (S.D. Tex. Oct. 14, 2010). The plaintiff alleged sufficient personal involvement by a debt buyer and his employee to raise a plausible inference that they were sufficiently involved in debt collection activities to constitute "debt collectors" under the FDCPA.

Johnson v. Vericrest Fin., Inc., 2010 WL 3464971 (N.D. Tex. Aug. 27, 2010). While a law firm had been retained by the defendant to send the plaintiff letters containing the notices of acceleration and foreclosure, it was not a defendant in the case, and therefore the court dismissed the FDCPA claim without prejudice.

McVey v. Bay Area Credit Serv., 2010 WL 2927388 (N.D. Tex. July 26, 2010). A complaint alleging that the defendant often called the consumer multiple times per week seeking payment of an alleged debt failed to state a claim for relief that was plausible on its face. "Consumer alleges no facts describing the types of conduct found by other courts to violate the FDCPA, nor does he allege conduct that would appear to have occurred 'repeatedly' or 'continuously.' "

Meroney v. Pharia, L.L.C., 688 F. Supp. 2d 550 (N.D. Tex. 2009). FDCPA complaint was dismissed for failure to state a claim where the court found that a least sophisticated consumer would not be misled by the state court collection complaint and affidavit.

Guajardo v. GC Servs., L.P., 2009 WL 3715603 (S.D. Tex. Nov. 3, 2009). Plaintiff's summary judgment motion denied where unpleasant comments were insufficient to show violation of FDCPA.

Prophet v. Myers, 645 F. Supp. 2d 614 (S.D. Tex. 2008). Whether the language of the debt collector's settlement offer is deceptive under the FDCPA cannot and should not be resolved on a motion to dismiss.

Hargrove v. WMC Mortgage, 2008 WL 4056292 (S.D. Tex. Aug. 29, 2008). *Pro se* plaintiff's global allegation that bad things "happen" did not state a cognizable FDCPA claim, and the complaint was dismissed.

Lozano v. Ocwen Fed. Bank, F.S.B., 489 F.3d 636 (S.D. Tex. 2005). The court reversed the lower court's decision to dismiss the consumers' FDCPA claim for failure to allege properly that the defendant qualified as a debt collector and whether there was an

actionable debt under the Act: "Based on our *de novo* review, we hold that the district court erred in dismissing the FDCPA claim *sua sponte* without notice."

Harding v. Regent, 347 F. Supp. 2d 334 (N.D. Tex. 2004). Collection lawyer's motion to dismiss was denied because factual issues existed as to the alleged violations of §§ 1692c(a)(2), 1692d, 1692e, and 1692f where the collector had repeatedly contacted the consumer after the consumer's lawyer had filed an answer to the collector's suit and faxed it to the collection lawyer.

Utah

Carvana v. MFG Fin., Inc., 2008 WL 2468539 (D. Utah June 17, 2008). Plaintiff given opportunity to amend where complaint did not sufficiently allege that individuals' own conduct, and not simply the company's, violated the FDCPA, and where the complaint did not specifically allege that the individuals materially participated in the debt collection activities.

Brumbelow v. Law Offices of Bennett & Deloney, P.C., 2005 WL 1566689 (D. Utah June 21, 2005). Defendant's motion for summary judgment denied. Issues of fact remained as to whether the telephone call within the statute of limitations involved misrepresentation of the amount of the fees owed.

Virginia

Watson v. United Consumers, Inc., 2010 WL 2399682 (E.D. Va. June 15, 2010). The court granted summary judgment for the defendant where the consumer's settlement agreement with the collector's referring creditor covered the claims against the collector.

Hill v. Select Group, Inc., 2009 WL 2225509 (E.D. Va. July 23, 2009). The court permitted the filing of an amended complaint to allege a class action to remedy the defendant's failure to provide compliant §§ 1692e(11) and 1692g notices; the defendant's opposition to the amendment based on futility, because the defendant purportedly was not a covered debt collector, was an issue that went to the merits of the claim that would not be considered in the case's current posture.

Hilgeford v. National Union Fire Ins. Co., 2009 WL 302161 (E.D. Va. Feb. 6, 2009), *aff'd without opinion*, 333 Fed. Appx. 784 (4th Cir. 2009). "It is settled law that the allegations of [a *pro se*] complaint, 'however inartfully pleaded' are held 'to less stringent standards than formal pleadings drafted by lawyers. . . .' *Hughes v. Rowe*, 449 U.S. 5, 9 (1980) (*quoting Haines v. Kerner*, 404 U.S. 519, 520 (1972))." Thus, "[a] document filed *pro se* is 'to be liberally construed. . . .' *Erickson v. Pardus*, 551 U.S. 89, 127 S. Ct. 2197, 2201 (2007) (*quoting Estelle v. Gamble*, 429 U.S. 97, 104–05 (1976))." Despite any liberal construction of *pro se* pleadings, "courts are not required to 'conjure up questions never squarely presented to them.' *Adkins v. Mathews, Nichols & Assocs., L.L.C.*, 2008 WL 565101, at *2 (W.D. Va. Feb. 29, 2008) (*quoting Beaudett v. City of Hampton*, 775 F.2d 1274, 1278 (4th Cir. 1985))." Moreover, *pro se* pleadings are not exempted from the federal rules and the case law interpreting them.

Neild v. Wolpoff & Abramson, L.L.P., 453 F. Supp. 2d 918 (E.D. Va. 2006). The heightened pleading requirements of Rule 9(b) do not apply to claims arising under the FDCPA.

Blevins v. West Vir. Fed. Credit Union, 2006 WL 1391441 (S.D. W. Va. May 18, 2006). Where *pro se* plaintiff filed a second supplementary amendment to complaint which minimally alleged federal jurisdiction pursuant to the FDCPA, the court declined to adopt the magistrate judge's proposed findings and recommendation to dismiss for failure to state a claim.

Washington

GMAC v. Gibbs, 2003 WL 314443 (Wash. Ct. App. Feb. 10, 2003). Creditor in state collection action is not subject to a counterclaim for the alleged FDCPA violations of its attorney in the pending action, nor do the alleged FDCPA violations affect the merits of the creditor's claim.

West Virginia

In re Meadows, 425 B.R. 806 (Bankr. W.D. Va. 2010). The court refused to enter a default judgment in this adversarial proceeding against Mann Bracken and dismissed the complaint *sua sponte* without prejudice for failure to state a claim. The court found that the complaint was a mere "formulaic recitation of the elements of a cause of action" and contains only conclusions whereby "the Consumer paraphrased the language of 15 U.S.C. §§ 1629d, f, e, e(5) and e(10) followed by words stating that the Defendant violated those portions of the statute."

Wisconsin

Mitchell v. CFC Fin. L.L.C., 230 F.R.D. 548 (E.D. Wis. 2005). Consumer's amendment of the complaint to name the successor entity which was formed from merger and acquisition of the defendant debt collector related back to the filing of the original complaint under the standards of Rule 15(c).

Hartman v. Meridian Fin. Servs., Inc., 191 F. Supp. 2d 1031 (W.D. Wis. 2002). Complaint that listed sections of the FDCPA that the collector was alleged to have violated but failed to list others did not waive the right to claim violations of the unlisted sections and instead stated a claim for violations of the unlisted sections under federal notice pleading requirements.

K.3.9 Discovery

Mangum v. Action Collection Serv., Inc., 575 F.3d 935 (9th Cir. 2009). The discovery rule is applied to the determination of the FDCPA statute of limitations.

Muha v. Encore Receivable Mgmt., Inc., 558 F.3d 623 (7th Cir. 2009). Consumer survey inadequate where questions were leading, drafted by lawyer, and there was no control group. A survey is not the only possible way to show that a collection letter is misleading. Recipients of an allegedly misleading dunning letter can testify that they were misled, and if they are shown to be representative unsophisticated (or, *a fortiori,* sophisticated) consumers, the trier of fact may be able to infer from their testimony that the letter is misleading.

Miller v. Wolpoff & Abramson, L.L.P., 321 F.3d 292 (2d Cir. 2003). It was an abuse of discretion to not postpone summary judgment until the consumer had an opportunity to depose the defendant

attorney affiants who stated in conclusory fashion that they had reviewed some parts of the consumer's credit card file before sending the consumer a collection letter on their letterhead. The consumer alleged that the lawyers had not engaged in a meaningful review of the high volume of accounts they received each month before sending a collection letter.

Chaudhry v. Gallerizzo, 174 F.3d 394 (4th Cir. 1999). Debtor sued lender's attorney under Fair Debt Collection Practices Act. Court distinguished general rule that attorney-client privilege did not apply to billing and expense records and held that entries that "reveal the motive of the client in seeking representation, litigation strategy, or the specific nature of the services provided, such as researching particular areas of the law, fall within the privilege."

Lewis v. ACB Bus. Servs., Inc., 135 F.3d 389 (6th Cir. 1998). Scope of discovery was within broad discretion of trial court. Order denying further discovery reviewed under abuse of discretion standard. Scope of examination permitted under discovery was broader than permitted at trial; test was where the line of interrogation was reasonably calculated to lead to discovery of admissible evidence. The Sixth Circuit held that the district court had properly denied (a) discovery of matter that was relevant only to defenses that have been stricken, or to events that occurred before applicable limitations, unless information sought was otherwise relevant to issues in the case, and (b) motion to compel debt collector to produce remainder of contract between debt collector and creditor, where claim was outside pleadings. Debtor not entitled to discovery of contract between creditor and debt collector where debtor did not dispute existence of debt and debt collector did not dispute that it had sent letter at issue, thus questions of whether letter was sent pursuant to contract or whether debt collector acted outside terms of contract was not relevant.

Wade v. Reg'l Credit Ass'n, 91 F.3d 158 (9th Cir. 1996) (text at 1996 WL 375037). The trial court's protective order was upheld, and the consumer's lawyer was forbidden to use a list of additional consumers, obtained during discovery from the collector, to solicit new clients. The consumer's lawyer lacked a legitimate business interest within the meaning of the disclosure exception of the Fair Credit Reporting Act to obtain the list of consumers, and the consumer's lawyer's offer of a separate settlement with the creditor—$3000 for the client, and $30,000 for agreeing not to use the list—which wrecked settlement negotiations, was a conflict of interest in violation of ethical rules.

California

Evon v. Law Offices of Sidney Mickell, 2010 WL 455476 (E.D. Cal. Feb. 3, 2010). Consumers entitled to copies of allegedly violative letters to other consumers prior to class certification. The debt collector was to not redact any discrete segments of its policy and procedure manuals that were relevant to the complaint. The cover pages of all FDCPA suits against the debt collector compelled if the violations were similar to those in this case. Evidence on net worth was compelled prior to certification, in part because it was volunteered. Compelled to state the number of its collection accounts and the number on which suit initiated. Collection law firm compelled to state the compensation formula for it in the case.

Nicander v. Hecker, 2009 WL 5084087 (N.D. Cal. Dec. 21, 2009). Debt collector was compelled to produce additional information regarding his financial condition and the net worth including his current tax return, his prepared financial statements, and further answer interrogatories.

del Campo v. American Corrective Counseling Servs., Inc., 2009 WL 3458298 (N.D. Cal. Oct. 23, 2009). Court ordered discovery into the individual defendants' personal net worth since the information was relevant to making the 1% class damages calculation and rejected defendants' request for bifurcation of liability and damages to allow an initial determination of liability before disclosing private financial information.

del Campo v. American Corrective Counseling Servs., Inc., 254 F.R.D. 585 (N.D. Cal. 2008). Plaintiffs' motion challenging the confidentiality designation of documents obtained through a public records request was granted.

Bretana v. Int'l Collection Corp., 2008 WL 4948446 (N.D. Cal. Nov. 12, 2008). Debt collector's motion to withdraw court ordered admissions was granted because plaintiff was unable to establish prejudice pursuant to Rule 36(b).

del Campo v. Kennedy, 2006 U.S. Dist. LEXIS 85462 (N.D. Cal. Nov. 17, 2006), *rev'd on other grounds sub nom. del Campo v. American Corrective Counseling Serv.,* 2007 WL 470262 (N.D. Cal. Feb. 8, 2007). The check collector's motion to compel production the consumers' bank records, to obtain possible evidence of repeated bad checks, was granted for the period of five years rather than the ten years requested.

Abels v. JBC Legal Group, P.C., 233 F.R.D. 645 (N.D. Cal. Mar. 9, 2006). Court denied class defendant's motion to compel production of the plaintiff's fee agreement since (1) the case had no yet proceeded to the fee stage where fee information might be relevant, and (2) the assertion that the fee agreement contained unethical provisions which would be relevant in determining the suitability of the plaintiff and counsel as class representatives was merely unsubstantiated hearsay from which the court could not conclude that production of the agreement was "reasonably calculated to lead to the discovery of admissible evidence." Federal Rule of Civil Procedure 26(b)(1). Though the court found it "not necessary" in reaching its conclusion, but in order to "put the issue to rest," the court accepted for filing class counsel's declaration stating that the fee agreement did not contain the alleged unethical provisions.

Renteria v. Collectcorp, 2005 WL 4019338 (N.D. Cal. Oct. 26, 2005). Plaintiff was not required to produce tapes of the conversation until after defendants' depositions, but was required to disclose before deposing any defendant, with respect to each telephone message: (1) the telephone number receiving the message, (2) the date and time received, (3) the caller (if identified or known to plaintiff), and (4) the length (in seconds) of the message.

Connecticut

Jones v. Midland Funding, L.L.C., 616 F. Supp. 2d 224 (D. Conn. 2009). Debt collector's FDCPA expert not allowed to testify as to legal liability.

Tzanetis v. Weinstein & Riley, P.S., 2009 WL 5128892 (D. Conn. Dec. 18, 2009). Debt collection firm was compelled to state the relationships among defendant, its principals, and others, the date and nature of all documents and information defendant received about the plaintiffs' account, all documents reflecting purchase or ownership of plaintiffs' account, all insurance documents, and all contracts and retainer agreements.

Salter v. I.C. Sys., Inc., 2005 WL 3941662 (D. Conn. May 3, 2005). Among several discovery orders, the court denied the defendant's request for a protective order regarding its policy and training manuals because of the inadequacy of its conclusory and unsupported claim that the information was confidential and proprietary.

Pullen v. Arrow Fin. Servs., L.L.C., 2002 WL 32864712 (D. Conn. Oct. 17, 2002). Consumer's motion to compel the identity of names on the collector's letter, the statutory or legal basis for the claimed fees, the collector's investigation and attempts to collect debt from the plaintiff, records received from the creditor, telephone records, and complaints and orders relating to the collector's acts and practices was granted.

Kimbro v. I.C. Sys., Inc., 2002 WL 1816820 (D. Conn. July 22, 2002). Collector's objections to routine FDCPA discovery requests, seeking, *inter alia,* itemization of the debt, a plain English translation of its collection/contact notes, details of the collector's reporting to credit bureaus, later changes made to the subject dun, copies of other complaints and judgments against the collector, and the arrangement and communication between the collector and the creditor, are all overruled, as each was found to meet the standards for discovery in federal court, with the court inviting the consumer to request an award of attorney fees for successfully prosecuting the discovery motion.

Boutvis v. Risk Mgmt. Alternative, Inc., 2002 U.S. Dist. LEXIS 8521 (D. Conn. May 3, 2002). The following information was deemed discoverable by the consumer in an FDCPA action: the amount of money the debt collector paid to purchase the debt, information regarding the legal relationship between the debt collector and the entity it purchased the debt from, manuals, written procedures, and protocols the collector used or employed in complying with the FDCPA and accessing and/or reporting to the credit bureaus, copies of judgments, court opinions, complaints, and orders concerning the collector's practices under the FDCPA and the FCRA for the relevant year, and all agreements the collector has with consumer reporting agencies.

Yancey v. Hooten, 180 F.R.D. 203 (D. Conn. 1998). Entirety of consumer's motion to compel granted, with all discovery requests found to be relevant and not privileged, including: (a) number of offending letters sent by the defendant, relevant to standard for statutory damages; (b) financial and business relationship among the collectors and the creditor, the process by which dunning letter was generated, attorney collector's in-state client list and annual advertisements, tax returns, and the job descriptions of all employees, relevant to the claim that the attorney collector was in fact not acting as an attorney but as an unlicensed collection agency; (c) the defendant's business and home address, refusing request for protective order on allegation that the plaintiff would use that information to harass the defendant and noting that any such abuse should be brought to the court's attention; (d) the number of cases in which the defendant filed suit in the state, relevant to whether threat of suit was intended; (e) creditor referral information, not subject to work product privilege in anticipation of litigation in absence of specific intent to litigate; and (f) attorney collector/client agreement, relevant and contains no privileged information.

Artese v. Acad. Collection Serv., Inc., 1997 WL 509404 (D. Conn. July 28, 1997). A motion to produce the collector's training and operations manuals was overbroad. If any of the manuals contained provisions dealing directly with the alleged violation, i.e., dealing with debtors who had retained counsel, the defendant should produce that portion of the manual. Production requests for "all judgments, court opinions and consent orders relating to this defendant and its acts or practices under the FDCPA" and communications with regulatory authorities concerning its collection practices since 1991 as well as documents relating to its licensing in Connecticut were far too broad. The collector was directed, however, to produce its current Connecticut license and the application. The consumer requested all form letters used by defendant to collect on this client's accounts. Defendant pointed out that it sent only one letter to the consumer. Plaintiff responded that the letter contained a settlement offer with a deadline. Other letters might give plaintiff a basis for amending the complaint and were discoverable. The collector was required to produce documents which focused upon the defendant's ability to determine that a debtor had other accounts which the collector was attempting to collect and that the consumer had counsel on some or all of those accounts. In addition, the collector should provide any documents that revealed its ability to obtain from its records the fact that it had earlier collections with the same debtor.

Bishop v. National Account Sys., Inc., 1991 WL 11675888 (D. Conn. Sept. Sept. 4, 1991). Rejected work product or privilege claims for advice of attorney where allegation was that defendant did not intend to take threatened action. "One would expect that a debt collector's attorneys would routinely obtain information regarding the remedies the debt collector might legitimately pursue. Once having enlisted an attorney to determine the remedies available, however, the debt collector may not turn around and claim that the information sought is protected as work product. To allow such a practice would be to prevent the consumer from obtaining discovery on this crucial issue." Overruled objection to interrogatory asking the defendant to state the reasons it contended that the plaintiff's debt is not a consumer debt. Interrogatories may properly seek the application of law to fact.

Florida

Martin v. Client Servs., Inc., 2010 WL 3702461 (M.D. Fla. Sept. 16, 2010). The court compelled the defendant to provide discovery regarding telephone calls made to the consumer, including the identity of the telephone service providers and its phone numbers involved in the collection of the debt in issue, and documentation that the collector received from and sent to the creditor regarding the debt.

Bianchi v. Bronson & Migliaccio, L.L.P., 2010 WL 940993 (S.D. Fla. Mar. 12, 2010). The court granted, in part, the consumer's motion to compel discovery. The law firm debt collector was required to ask its agent, who placed calls to consumer, for a copy of any written contract between them, and to file with the court and serve on consumer a supplemental verified response to the discovery request that: 1) provided consumer with a copy of the contract; 2) stated that it requested a copy of the contract from its agent but its agent would not provide it; or 3) stated that no written contract exists.

Drossin v. Nat'l Action Fin. Servs., Inc., 72 Fed. R. Serv. 3d 169 (S.D. Fla. 2008). Tapes of telephone conversations are previous statements subject to production on oral request, Rule 26(b)(3)(C), without formality of discovery. Defendant could not refuse to attend deposition until plaintiff produced the tapes, since the tapes were requested only forty-eight hours before the deposition.

Drossin v. Nat'l Action Fin. Servs., Inc., 2008 WL 5381815 (S.D. Fla. Dec. 19, 2008). The court compelled discovery, including requiring the defendant to identify potential class members in order to permit the plaintiff to establish numerosity, and to produce its written policies and procedures relating to the collection of debts.

Garcia v. Jefferson Capital Sys., L.L.C., 2006 U.S. Dist. LEXIS 56147 (M.D. Fla. Aug. 11, 2006). Consumer allowed to depose individuals who had some financial interest in the debt collector but was not entitled to obtain their personal financial documents at this early stage of the litigation.

Florida First Fin. Group, Inc. v. Castro, 815 So. 2d 789 (Fla. Dist. Ct. App. 2002). Neither privacy laws nor the FDCPA prevented the discovery of home addresses and phone numbers of debt collection employees or of correspondence of the creditor with other consumers.

Georgia

Stamps v. Encore Receivable Mgmt., Inc., 232 F.R.D. 419 (N.D. Ga. Mar. 11, 2005). Plaintiff's motion to compel initial disclosures was granted requiring a debt collector to provide the names, addresses, and telephone numbers of its employees using aliases and plaintiff's request for attorney fees and costs was also granted. Since the tape was to establish the FDCPA and tort violation rather than impeach the collector, the collector's motion to compel production of the audiotape of the telephone voice mail message prior to its deposition was granted without delaying it until the collector was deposed, but its request for attorney fees and costs were denied.

Young v. McDowell Servs., Inc., 1991 U.S. Dist. LEXIS 21814 (N.D. Ga. Apr. 30, 1991). Debt collector's motion to compel answers to interrogatories regarding FDCPA claims against others was denied. Debt collector's motion to compel answers to interrogatories regarding the underlying debt was granted. Debt collector's motion to compel answers to interrogatory regarding facts and circumstances leading to filing of the instant lawsuit was granted.

Whatley v. Universal Collection Bureau, Inc., Clearinghouse No. 31,818 (N.D. Ga. 1982). The collector's answer and pleadings were stricken due to the failure to respond to interrogatories with a jury trial set on the issue of damages alone.

Illinois

Hale v. AFNI, Inc., 2010 WL 380906 (N.D. Ill. Jan. 26, 2010). When FDCPA cases involve statements that are not plainly misleading but might mislead or deceive the unsophisticated consumer, the consumer must present extrinsic evidence—normally consumer surveys—to prove that unsophisticated consumers find the statements at issue confusing or misleading.

Heller v. Graf, 2004 WL 2057894 (N.D. Ill. Aug. 25, 2004). Motion to compel certain discovery related to the defendant attorney's practice of law was granted in part where the defendant denied that he qualified as a "debt collector" and the information sought was relevant to prove that issue.

Scott v. Universal Fid. Corp., 42 F. Supp. 2d 837 (N.D. Ill. 1999). Discovery of "net worth" of debt collector appropriate in FDCPA class action. Motion to compel granted.

Cusumano v. NRB, Inc., 1998 WL 673833 (N.D. Ill. Sept. 23, 1998). Based on "clear error" standard, the district judge affirmed magistrate judge's denial of plaintiff's attempt to discover litigation and administrative action against National Recovery Bureau as not pertinent to establish routine practice, intentional nature or frequency and persistence of noncompliance; and not helpful for impeachment or to counter the bona fide error defense. Plaintiff could use the defendant's training manual and collection guidelines for such purposes. While the defendant could not move to quash plaintiff's third party subpoena, it could seek a protective order that certain matters not be inquired into.

Holloway v. Pekay, 1996 WL 19580 (N.D. Ill. Jan. 18, 1996). Information regarding lender's attorney fees and costs charged to class members in collection actions was "reasonably calculated to lead to the discovery of admissible evidence"; and therefore, was discoverable pursuant to Rule 26(b)(2) in FDCPA action.

Indiana

Thomas v. Bowman Heintz Boscia & Vician, P.C., 2008 WL 5070471 (S.D. Ind. Nov. 26, 2008). Plaintiff was allowed discovery as to collection/fee agreements since they could relate to the bona fide error defenses.

Stavroff v. Midland Credit Mgmt. Inc., 2005 WL 6329149 (N.D. Ind. June 8, 2005). The court granted the collector's motion to "bifurcate discovery so that parties may conduct staged discovery regarding the merits of the case before conducting discovery on the issue of class certification."

Croteau v. Dearing, 2005 U.S. Dist. LEXIS 1948 (N.D. Ind. Feb. 8, 2005). Collection employees' Fed. R. Civ. P. 36 admission that they sent over 50 letters to collect a debt could not be denied by a later statement that the letters were sent by their employer and the employees were determined to be the debt collectors.

Lucas v. G.C. Servs., L.P., 226 F.R.D. 328 (N.D. Ind. 2004). The district court granted the consumer's renewed motion to compel responses to discovery mainly focused on factual issues related to certification of the class in an FDCPA suit and denied the collection agency's cross-motion to stay discovery. The court also imposed sanctions for discovery misconduct by the collection agency which included limiting the witnesses defendant could call, defendant paying attorney fees to plaintiffs, and deeming particular admissions admitted.

Kansas

Caputo v. Professional Recovery Servs., Inc., 2004 WL 1503953 (D. Kan. June 9, 2004). The court refused to order the defendant to disclose the hourly rate and total paid to its out-of-state attorney in its unsuccessful defense on the merits as the court determined

that the information would not be significant to determine the rate or total fees to be awarded the prevailing plaintiff for reasonable attorney fees.

Louisiana

Byes v. Credit Bureau Enters., Inc., 1995 WL 540235 (E.D. La. Sept. 11, 1995). Discovery regarding collector's policies and practices was relevant to the bona fide error defense.

Massachusetts

Argentieri v. Fisher Landscaping, Inc., 15 F. Supp. 2d 55 (D. Mass. 1998), *later op. at* 27 F. Supp. 2d 84 (D. Mass. 1998). Debtor not entitled to opportunity to discover evidence in support of debtor's claim that law firm collector was "debt collector" under FDCPA, given lack of any concrete basis in record for questioning firm's affidavit that no more than 0.4% of its practice was devoted to debt collection.

Montana

McCollough v. Johnson, Rodenberg & Lauinger, 2009 WL 44551 (D. Mont. Jan. 6, 2009). Collection law firm compelled to produce its retainer agreement with the debt buyer it had represented as the agreement was not protected by the lawyer client privilege. It is information preparatory to obtaining legal advice and not provided to obtain legal advice.

Nebraska

Harris v. D. Scott Carruthers & Assocs., 2010 WL 610978 (D. Neb. Feb. 18, 2010). The court granted in part and denied in part the consumers' motion to compel discovery responses involving the attorney-client privilege, holding that the privilege applied to certain areas but not to others that sought only non-privileged "business information."

Valderrama v. Nat'l Revenue Corp., 1981 U.S. Dist. LEXIS 18627 (D. Neb. Sept. 28, 1981). Discovery responses that would cost the poorly capitalized debt collector $9000 were not required.

New Mexico

Anchondo v. Anderson, Crenshaw & Assocs., L.L.C., 256 F.R.D. 661 (D.N.M. 2009). Collector who asserted the bona fide error of law defense (for its *Foti* violation) waived the attorney-client privilege as to the relevant legal research and opinions that it had received and the identity of the attorneys who performed the work. Discovery regarding, *inter alia*, putative class members identity, defendant's net worth, and the specific basis for the defendant's assertion of the bona fide error defense compelled as relevant.

Shelden v. J-K Collections, Inc., Clearinghouse No. 45,772 (D.N.M. 1990). The collector should have responded to the consumer's interrogatory requesting the number of other persons to whom had been sent the dunning form letter received by the consumer. Courts have held that the frequency and persistence of noncompliance with regard to all consumers is relevant to the amount of statutory damages awarded to a single consumer plaintiff. It would also be evidence of willfulness raised by a pendent state claim.

New York

Vagenos v. LDG Fin. Servs., L.L.C., 2010 WL 1608877 (E.D.N.Y. Apr. 15, 2010). Granted the consumer's motion in limine to preclude defendant from inquiring into or introducing evidence at trial regarding consumer's criminal history or prior debts.

Strom v. National Enter. Sys., Inc., 2010 WL 1533383 (W.D.N.Y. Apr. 15, 2010). The defendant was compelled to produce information regarding prior complaints filed against it by other consumers with the BBB and the state attorney general since the information could lead to "the discovery of admissible evidence in support of Plaintiff's claims or to enable Plaintiff to rebut Defendant's bona fide error defense."

Bank v. Pentagroup Fin., L.L.C., 2009 WL 1606420 (E.D.N.Y. June 9, 2009). Debt collector's fee discovery denied: "Since fees are available only if the plaintiff prevails, and the defendant contests liability, such procedures would be premature."

Barasch v. Estate Info. Serv., L.L.C., 2008 WL 782750 (E.D.N.Y. Mar. 21, 2008). Defendant was ordered to provide discovery regarding other consumers who received the form collection letter at issue as "[t]hat information clearly is relevant since plaintiff asserts claims on behalf of a nationwide class."

Bryant v. Allied Account Servs., Inc., 2006 WL 2620376 (E.D.N.Y. Sept. 13, 2006). The court denied the consumer's motion to compel inspection of the defendant collection agency's premises in order to "better understand the defendant debt collectors' actual collection dynamics, methods, and techniques as well as to help determine the degree of managerial oversight," explaining that a "deposition of one or more of defendant's employees will disclose the whereabouts of employees, the layout of the office, the degree of managerial oversight, and what they may have overheard" without the potential disruption to the agency's operations of an inspection. The court denied the consumer's motion to compel production of the collector's tax returns, explaining that while financial information is relevant in the assessment of punitive damages under state law, the information is readily available through deposition testimony and other discovery without the intrusion of producing actual tax returns.

Mailloux v. Arrow Fin. Servs., L.L.C., 2002 U.S. Dist. LEXIS 3314 (E.D.N.Y. Feb. 21, 2002). Plaintiff in class action was entitled to discover defendant's tax returns and other financial information relevant to statutory damage determination of the defendant's net worth, notwithstanding defendant's offer to provide an affidavit of net worth, since the plaintiff was entitled to examine the underlying data to test the defendant's calculations. Motion to compel granted.

Sokolski v. Trans Union Corp., 178 F.R.D. 393 (E.D.N.Y. 1998). Court entered protective order limiting the communication of trade secrets and proprietary data.

Read v. Amana Collection Servs., 1993 WL 286132 (W.D.N.Y. July 21, 1993). Collector's failure to produce documents and refusal to answer questions at court ordered post-judgment examination resulted in the imposition of sanctions pursuant to Fed. R. Civ. P. 37(b) including reasonable expenses and attorney fees.

Ohio

Davis v. Creditors Interchange Receivable Mgmt., L.L.C., 585 F. Supp. 2d 968 (N.D. Ohio 2008). The defendant collection agency was ordered in this discovery dispute "to provide the plaintiffs with a list of current and former employees, their last known contact information, and the position these employees held during the timer period relevant to this case" in order to allow the plaintiff to identify and contact the agency's current and former employees who were not represented by the agency's counsel.

Kelly v. Montgomery Lynch & Assocs., Inc., 2007 WL 4412572 (N.D. Ohio Dec. 13, 2007). Where the debt collector provided insufficient and unjustified responses to written discovery regarding the elements of FDCPA class certification, "[t]he Court . . . order[ed] the Defendant to produce materials relevant to" class certification.

Pennsylvania

Gregory v. Medical-Dental Bureau, 2010 WL 2926586 (M.D. Pa. July 26, 2010). In this FDCPA case, the consumer was ordered to respond to requests for admissions: "(1) You did not notify Defendant in writing within 30 days of receipt of the first correspondence from Defendant that you disputed the validity of the underlying debt Defendant was seeking to collect from you and (3) On at least one occasion since 1/15/09, you have disposed of one or more items received in the mail without opening or looking at the item(s)," but not "(4) Admit that of the 16 or more FDCPA cases filed by your attorney, only one has been tried and all others were dismissed."

Kiliszek v. Nelson, Watson & Assocs., L.L.C., 2006 WL 335788 (M.D. Pa. Feb. 14, 2006). Consumer's Rule 56(f) motion for further discovery was granted where information about form letters and mail collection policies to determine whether reproduced letter was a fabrication was sought.

Texas

Prophet v. Myers, 645 F. Supp. 2d 614 (S.D. Tex. 2008). Court refused to dismiss claims regarding involvement of attorney, truth of settlement offer; plaintiff was entitled to discovery on those issues.

Virginia

Padgett v. OneWest Bank, F.S.B., 2010 WL 3239350 (N.D. W. Va. Aug. 16, 2010). The court overruled the defendant's objection to answering discovery concerning the ownership of the underlying debt since the information was relevant to whether the defendant was an FDCPA debt collector.

Zhang v. GC Serv., L.P., 537 F. Supp. 2d 805 (E.D. Va. 2008). Court denied post-judgment request for defendants' time records. "Such production would be of marginal assistance to the Court, at best, while placing an undue burden on the defense."

Wisconsin

Muha v. Encore Receivable Mgmt., Inc., 236 F.R.D 429 (E.D. Wis. 2006). The court granted the consumer's motion to compel the defendant to provide information regarding the number of persons who were sent the collection letter and information regarding the collector's net worth as well as awarding plaintiff the reasonable expenses including attorney fees incurred in preparing the motion to compel.

Bode v. Encore Receivable Mgmt., Inc., 2006 WL 801017 (E.D. Wis. Mar. 29, 2006). The court granted the consumer's motion to compel the defendant to provide information regarding the number of individuals who may be members of the putative class and information regarding the collector's net worth as well as awarding plaintiff the reasonable expenses including attorneys fees incurred in preparing the motion to compel.

Blazek v. Capital Recovery Assoc., Inc., 222 F.R.D. 360 (E.D. Wis. 2004). For the purposes of discovery the court treated the defaulting debt collector as a non-party and required the plaintiff's attorney to travel to the defendant's location to take depositions.

K.3.10 Trials

Pope v. Man-Data, Inc., 209 F.3d 1161 (9th Cir. 2000). A new trial was improperly granted where the evidence showed a possibility of juror dishonesty on *voir dire* rather than the required demonstration of dishonesty. When asked about being involved in a prior significant dispute, the juror failed to mention three uncontested collection suits against her and her husband seven to ten years prior to the trial. The consumer was awarded $5000 actual and $100,000 punitive damages in the first trial but nothing in a second trial.

Morante v. Am. Gen. Fin. Ctr., 157 F.3d 1006 (5th Cir. 1998). After jury entered verdict for the plaintiffs, the magistrate judge entered judgment for the defendants. The Fifth Circuit vacated the judgment and directed that judgment for the plaintiffs under the FDCPA and Texas Debt Collection Act be reinstated.

Sibley v. Fulton Dekalb Collection Serv., 677 F.2d 830 (11th Cir. 1982). The consumer has a right to a jury trial under the Seventh Amendment in an FDCPA suit.

Connecticut

Jones v. Midland Funding, L.L.C., 616 F. Supp. 2d 224 (D. Conn. May 19, 2009). The testimony of the debt collector's expert witness "as to whether their collection letters were consistent with collection industry standards" was inadmissible on the issue of liability since "[the expert's] opinion regarding 'industry standards' is a thinly disguised legal opinion as to whether the defendants' letters violate the FDCPA" and thus "[the expert's] opinion contains legal conclusions that impermissibly invade the province of the court."

Delaware

Smith v. Law Offices of Mitchell N. Kay, 124 B.R. 182 (D. Del. 1991). A default judgment was entered against a law firm which failed to respond to an FDCPA complaint, and a jury trial on actual and statutory damages was ordered. Upon granting a new trial on the basis of an excessive jury verdict for actual damages, the court held that the issue of statutory damages should be retried since the two were not separate and distinct issues. Jury awarded $15,000 actual damages (remitted to $3000 later) and the maximum $1000 statutory damages, and the court awarded $1365 attorney fees after

a default judgment and uncontested trial on damages.

Smith v. Law Office of Mitchell N. Kay, Clearinghouse No. 45,914 (D. Del. 1990) (default judgment). Jury awarded $1000 statutory damages, $15,000 actual damages for emotional distress, and attorney fees of $1365.

Georgia

Whatley v. Universal Collection Bureau, Inc., Clearinghouse No. 31,818 (N.D. Ga. 1982). Since an action under the FDCPA sounds in tort, the consumer is entitled to a jury trial of FDCPA claims. The collector's answer and pleadings were stricken due to the failure to respond to interrogatories with a jury trial set on the issue of damages alone.

Illinois

Kubert v. Aid Assocs., 2009 WL 1270351 (N.D. Ill. May 7, 2009). The court disapproved and struck the survey evidence offered by the plaintiff as not meeting with the *Daubert* standard.

McCabe v. Crawford & Co., 272 F. Supp. 2d 736 (N.D. Ill. 2003). Finding it filled with legal conclusions and inappropriate opinions, the district court excluded the expert report of Manual H. Newburger but allowed him to testify at trial regarding the issue of practices and standards in the debt collection industry.

Holt v. Wexler, 2002 U.S. Dist. LEXIS 5244 (N.D. Ill. Mar. 27, 2002). Considering the *Daubert* factors, the court struck in part and retained in part expert's opinion regarding rehabilitation of credit by payment of a debt which was in default.

Indiana

Lucas v. U.S. Bank, N.A., 2010 WL 3159572 (Ind. Ct. App. Aug. 11, 2010). The consumers were entitled to a jury trial on their FDCPA claim.

Campbell v. Hall, 624 F. Supp. 2d 991 (N.D. Ind. 2009). The court withheld ruling on the defendant's bona fide error defense on the *Camacho* § 1692g(a)(3) violation to allow the defendant additional time to develop the factual record.

Hamilton v. Am. Corrective Counseling Servs., 2006 U.S. Dist. LEXIS 75588 (N.D. Ind. Oct. 4, 2006). Granted the defendant's motion to exclude the testimony of plaintiff's expert, Manuel Newburger, holding that his proffered testimony constituted inadmissible opinions of law presented on the following three topics: whether the defendants' conduct complies with the industry standards of debt collection; the nature and severity of the alleged violations; and whether the defendants are debt collectors within the meaning of the FDCPA.

Maryland

Keane v. Nat'l Bureau of Collections, Clearinghouse No. 35,923 (D. Md. 1983). There was ample evidence of deception and the jury verdict should not be overturned.

Michigan

Carrier v. LJ Ross & Assoc., 2008 WL 544550 (E.D. Mich. Feb. 26, 2008). The collector's motion in limine to preclude the consumer from introducing evidence of emotional distress was granted where the consumer failed to place the collector on notice of anything more than actual damages.

Minnesota

Venes v. Prof'l Serv. Bureau, Inc., 353 N.W.2d 671 (Minn. Ct. App. 1984). The consumer's attorney's closing argument was forceful and hard hitting but within the bounds of zealous representation.

Montana

McCollough v. Johnson, Rodenberg & Lauinger, 645 F. Supp. 2d 917 (D. Mont. 2009). Admission of evidence of the debt collector's approximately 2700 other lawsuits against other debtors pursuant to § 1692k(b)(1) did not cause a miscarriage of justice such that the debt collector was entitled to a new jury trial. Evidence of the debt buyers similar acts, such as filing time-barred or mistaken debts, directed at people other than the plaintiff was admissible to show reprehensibility to support the state law claim for punitive damages.

New York

Aslam v. Malen & Assocs., P.C., 669 F. Supp. 2d 275 (E.D.N.Y. 2009). "The proposed jury instructions submitted by the lawyer were lifted, almost verbatim, from Fair Debt Collection, a popular manual published by the National Consumer Law Center. The Court finds it difficult to accept that a relatively experienced consumer rights lawyer required more than thirteen hours to lift jury instructions from the most widely used manual in the field." Accordingly, the court reduced the time on the proposed jury instructions from 13.2 hours to 2 hours.

Vera v. Trans-Continental Credit & Collection Corp., 1999 U.S. Dist. LEXIS 6937 (S.D.N.Y. May 10, 1999). The court suggested that the collection agency allow it to enter $1000 statutory damages rather than mount a jury trial.

Beeman v. Lacy, Katzen, Ryen & Mittleman, 892 F. Supp. 405 (N.D.N.Y. 1995). The finder of fact must determine that the contradiction between the demand and the validation notice would induce the least sophisticated consumer to overlook the procedures contained in the validation notice.

Robinson v. Transworld Sys., Inc., 876 F. Supp. 385 (N.D.N.Y. 1995). Whether cumulative effect of language in letters violated §§ 1692g and 1692e(10) was a question for the jury.

Rabideau v. Mgmt. Adjustment Bureau, 805 F. Supp. 1086 (W.D.N.Y. 1992). At trial plaintiff utilized an expert in organizational communication to testify that the placement of the validation notice on the back of the collection letter, where writing from the front bled through, in smaller, dot matrix print discouraged reading of the validation notice; and although the language "SEE REVERSE SIDE FOR IMPORTANT INFORMATION" appeared on the front of the collector's letter, it would draw the recipient's attention to the larger type describing payment by credit card.

Ohio

Lee v. Javitch, Block & Rathbone, L.L.P., 2008 WL 1886178 (S.D. Ohio Apr. 25, 2008). Defendant's Rule 50 post-trial motion denied

where the evidence supported the jury's determinations: 1) that the defendant collection attorney's garnishment affidavit stating that "he had a 'reasonable basis' to believe that non-exempt funds 'may have' been in Plaintiff's bank account at the time he signed the affidavit' " which was not true; 2) that the defendant's policies and procedures were not "reasonably adapted to avoid" the violation, sustaining the jury's rejection of the defendant's bona fide error defense; and 3) that the plaintiff proved "the causal link between the lack of the 'reasonable basis' and Plaintiff's resulting damages" to sustain the jury's award of economic and non-economic damages. The court rejected the defendant's contention "that higher standards applicable to intentional infliction of emotional distress damages, or the standards imported from the common law claim for 'wrongful attachment' (requiring malice or something akin to it) should apply to FDCPA claims" and instead applied the rule applicable to other federal damage claims: "An injured person's testimony alone may suffice to establish damages for emotional distress provided that she reasonably and sufficiently explains the circumstances surrounding the injury and does not rely on mere conclusory statements."

Oklahoma

Bynum v. Cavalry Portfolio Servs., L.L.C., 2006 WL 897712 (N.D. Okla. Mar. 31, 2006). Consumer's motion limine to exclude "intimations as to plaintiff's character" was denied insofar as the consumer places such matters at issue by alleging damages for emotional distress. Consumer's motion in limine to exclude any reference to the attorneys' attempts to generate larger fees was granted and would be impermissible during trial.

Texas

Molinar v. Coleman, 2009 WL 435274 (N.D. Tex. Feb. 20, 2009). Plaintiff's motion for entry of judgment by default was entered for defendant's FDCPA violation with the court awarding no actual damages, $250 statutory damages, $2800 costs and attorney fees, and interest to run at 0.60% per annum.

K.3.11 Res Judicata

Lifeng Lee Hsu v. Great Seneca Fin. Corp., 2010 WL 1695638 (3d Cir. Apr. 28, 2010). All FDCPA claims were barred by the doctrine of res judicata because the state court had previously rejected them in the collection action.

Cross v. Arakaki, 284 Fed. Appx. 443 (9th Cir. 2008). The district court entered summary judgment in favor of the defendant and the plaintiff appealed. The Ninth Circuit affirmed the judgment on the basis that the claim was barred by Hawaii's robust res judicata rules which apply "when there is a final judgment on the merits in the original suit, the issues raised are the same, and both parties to the case are the same or were in privity with the parties in the original suit." And the plaintiff could have raised her FDCPA claim in her state court action as the issues in both the actions were related; the defendant in the present suit was in privity with the defendant in the previous suit and a claim under Haw. Rev. Stat. § 480-2 was common to both.

Whitaker v. Ameritech Corp., 129 F.3d 952 (7th Cir. 1997). While state principles of res judicata would bar a fraud and RICO claim against Ameritech once it obtained a default judgment against the consumer, an FDCPA claim would not be barred as it arose out of a different set of facts involving the collection of the debt.

Metzenbaum v. Huntington Nat'l Bank, 124 F.3d 198 (6th Cir. 1997) (unpublished) (text at 1997 WL 579155). Where the *pro se* consumer's claims had been raised in state court and dismissed, the federal courts could not review the state court decision.

Peterson v. United Accounts, Inc., 638 F.2d 1134 (8th Cir. 1981). An FDCPA claim was not a compulsory counterclaim to a state collection suit and could be filed in a federal court subsequent to the filing of the state court suit. It would be proper for the federal court to direct the consumer to file the FDCPA claim as a permissive counterclaim in the state proceedings and stay the federal proceedings unless the state court failed to address the FDCPA claim.

Alabama

Franklin v. Parnell, 2010 WL 5557044 (M.D. Ala. Dec. 17, 2010). The court found that the *pro se* consumer's claims were barred by res judicata since the same FDCPA claims against the same defendant had been litigated and dismissed in an earlier state court action.

Arkansas

Marshall v. Deutsche Bank Nat'l Trust Co., 2011 WL 345988 (E.D. Ark. Feb. 1, 2011). Issue preclusion barred the § 1692g claims since prior adjudications had conclusively established the validity of the debt: "By overruling Plaintiff's objections to Wells Fargo's proof of claims in her second and third bankruptcies and confirming Plaintiff's Chapter 13 plan, the bankruptcy court validated Wells Fargo's claim, inherently finding that Wells Fargo had a right to collect the debt. . . . If confirmed plans do not have preclusive effect then debtors would be able to make bad faith claims to 'effectively prevent the collection of a debt, despite a court of competent jurisdiction having already adjudicated the dispute.' Thus Plaintiff's claim that Wells Fargo failed to provide § 1692g(a) notice, and violated § 1692g(b) by attempting to collect an unverified debt that it knew was disputed are also precluded because those claims depend on the underlying issue of the disputed mortgage debt."

California

Swain v. CACH, L.L.C., 699 F. Supp. 2d 1117 (N.D. Cal. 2009). Although the consumer's FDCPA claim was generally related to the subject matter of the prior state collection action, consumer's claim arose out of a different set of facts related to the defendants' efforts to collect on that debt. Accordingly, the court found that Consumer's FDCPA claim was not a compulsory counterclaim that had to be raised in the prior state action.

Reyes v. Kenosian & Miele, L.L.P., 619 F. Supp. 2d 796 (N.D. Cal. 2008). No preclusion because law firm was not a party to the state court complaint and not in privity with a party.

Connecticut

Sundwall v. Reiner & Reiner, P.C., 1997 WL 117286 (D. Conn. Feb. 27, 1997), *aff'd*, 141 F.3d 1152 (2d Cir. 1998). Where debtor's

state action was dismissed "with prejudice" for failing to attend a deposition, a subsequent federal action alleging the same FDCPA violations, among other allegations, was barred under the doctrine of res judicata, and summary judgment for collectors was granted.

Colorado

O'Neil v. Wolpoff & Abramson, L.L.P., 210 P.3d 482 (Colo. Apr. 2, 2009). A triable issue of fact existed as to whether settlement of FDCPA claims arising from telephone calls precluded the consumer from later asserting TCPA claims against the same defendants.

Delaware

Lifeng Lee Hsu v. Great Seneca Fin. Corp., 2009 WL 29445 (D. Del. Jan. 5, 2009). *Pro se* consumer's instant FDCPA claims that were litigated and rejected in his counterclaim in the underlying state court collection case were barred by res judicata and collateral estoppel; however, the consumer's claim that the defendants violated § 1692g(b) by continuing to litigate that state court collection case after he disputed the debt was not part of the state court adjudication and thus survived.

Florida

Beeders v. Gulf Coast Collection Bureau, 632 F. Supp. 2d 1125 (M.D. Fla. 2009). Where the consumer filed multiple FDCPA lawsuits, one for each telephone message left, the lawsuits were joined into a single action with statutory damages limited up to $1000 pursuant to § 1692k.

Georgia

Brinson v. First Am. Bank, 409 S.E.2d 50 (Ga. Ct. App. 1991). Prior action in magistrate's court for recovery of money wrongfully garnished barred subsequent suit in state court as res judicata.

Christian v. M & R Collection Adjustment, Inc., 307 S.E.2d 523 (Ga. Ct. App. 1983). FDCPA claim should have been filed as compulsory counterclaim to debt action and was barred by res judicata in subsequent suit by debtor traversing garnishment after judgment.

Illinois

Buford v. Palisades Collection, L.L.C., 552 F. Supp. 2d 800 (N.D. Ill. 2008). State court default judgments did not bar, under state res judicata rules, an FDCPA suit claiming that the state suit on the underlying debt was time barred. The FDCPA claim was a separate transaction from the state court debt collection lawsuit, as the heart of the federal claims was that the agency and law firm injured debtors, whereas the heart of state claims arose out of their cellular telephone use.

Clabault v. Shodeen Mgmt., 2006 WL 87600 (N.D. Ill. Jan. 6, 2006). Consumer's current federal FDCPA claims were not barred by res judicata since the state court action to collect the debt and the FDCPA action for unlawful collection activity were different causes of action, contrary to the rule that res judicata requires that there two cases share "an identity of cause of action."

Gray-Mapp v. Sherman, 100 F. Supp. 2d 810 (N.D. Ill. 1999). Res judicata did not bar bankrupt debtor's FDCPA claim for allegedly inflated proof of claim where the issues were neither raised nor litigated in the bankruptcy court. However, the debtor's FDCPA claim could not be based upon a proof of claim filed during the bankruptcy proceeding because "[n]othing in either the Bankruptcy Code or the FDCPA suggests that a debtor should be permitted to bypass the procedural safeguards in the Code in favor of asserting potentially more lucrative claims under the FDCPA" and "nothing in the FDCPA suggests that it was intended as an overlay to the protections already in place in the bankruptcy proceedings."

Indiana

Matthews v. Capital One Bank, 2008 WL 4724277 (S.D. Ind. Oct. 24, 2008). The doctrine of claim preclusion barred one of the consumer's federal court FDCPA claim that the defendants falsified the attorney fees they presented in the underlying state court action because the FDCPA claim was a compulsory counterclaim under state law, "as a favorable judgment on this claim would nullify the state court's judgment awarding the attorneys' fees in the original action." The doctrine of claim preclusion did not bar the consumer's federal court FDCPA claim that the defendants made false representations in connection with a sheriff's sale in the underlying state court action since the state court refused to confirm the sale and thus a favorable judgment in the federal case could not undermine the validity of the state court's ruling.

Maryland

Miller v. Bank of Am., N.A., 2010 WL 1489990 (D. Md. Apr. 12, 2010). Res judicata from prior state court litigation barred the *pro se* consumer's FDCPA action.

Hawkins v. Citicorp Credit Servs., Inc, 665 F. Supp. 2d 518 (D. Md. 2009). The complaint alleging that the defendants collected an unlawful rate of interest and thus violated § 1692e(2)(A) was barred by res judicata where the consumer had litigated and lost the identical issue in the underlying state court collection case.

Massachusetts

Brady v. Nynex Info. Res. Co., 1997 WL 177605 (Mass. Super. Ct. Apr. 8, 1997). Consumers' claims for fraud in the inducement, UDAP, tortious debt collection, and FDCPA violations should have been raised as a counterclaim to Nynex's collection.

Michigan

Bond v. U.S. Bank Nat'l Ass'n, 2010 WL 1265852 (E.D. Mich. Mar. 29, 2010) (*pro se* consumer). Where the present FDCPA action involved the same parties and the same FDCPA issue as the state law case, claim preclusion applied under Michigan law, and the FDCPA claim was barred.

Bey v. Wells Fargo, 2009 WL 367963 (E.D. Mich. Feb. 10, 2009). Res judicata barred *pro se* FDCPA claims against eviction attorney as the FDCPA claims could have been raised against the mortgage servicer, which was in privity with its attorney.

Lintz v. Credit Adjustments, Inc., 2008 WL 880516 (E.D. Mich. Mar. 31, 2008). This FDCPA claim was barred by res judicata since the parties, in connection with the dismissal of the underlying

state court action, entered into a settlement agreement which did not purport to reserve the federal FDCPA claim and which the court construed in accordance with state law as a complete settlement of all claims.

Lintz v. Credit Adjustments, Inc., 2008 WL 835824 (E.D. Mich. Mar. 28, 2008). The court held that res judicata barred the instant federal court FDCPA claim against the defendants; the collector and its attorneys who filed the underlying state collection complaint that, together with the consumer's state law counterclaim, was dismissed with prejudice by stipulated order—since the collection court dismissal had such preclusive effect under applicable state law and "[f]ederal courts must give the same preclusive effect to state court judgments that they would have in a state court environment."

Minnesota

Seaworth v. Messerli, 2010 WL 3613821 (D. Minn. Sept. 7, 2010). The court concluded that the *pro se* plaintiff's claim was barred by collateral estoppel where she raised the FDCPA violation in a state court case and the attorney defendant in this case was in privity.

Phillips v. Messerli & Kramer P.A., 2008 WL 5050127 (D. Minn. Nov. 20, 2008). Res judicata did not bar the plaintiffs' FDCPA claim that the law firm had improperly levied upon their bank account.

Venes v. Prof'l Serv. Bureau, Inc., 353 N.W.2d 671 (Minn. Ct. App. 1984). The fact that FDCPA claim could have been raised as permissive counterclaim in prior action does not bar it from being raised in subsequent suit.

Nebraska

Jenkins v. General Collection Co., 538 F. Supp. 2d 1165 (D. Neb. 2008). Neither res judicata nor collateral estoppel barred the consumer's FDCPA lawsuit because the claim that the defendant brought time-barred claims in state court was not actually litigated in the state court collection action.

New Hampshire

Dillon v. Select Portfolio Servicing, Inc., 2009 WL 242912 (D.N.H. Feb. 2, 2009). Res judicata barred FDCPA claims against a mortgage servicer for imposing unauthorized fees where those fees were also a part of a prior successful state wrongful foreclosure action.

New Jersey

Jackson v. Midland Funding, L.L.C., 2010 WL 5036486 (D.N.J. Dec. 10, 2010). The plaintiff's FDCPA suit based on the debt collector's filing of a time-barred collection suit in state court was not barred by New Jersey's "entire controversy doctrine," which "requires whenever possible all phases of a legal dispute to be adjudicated in one action," since the two actions did not arise out of a common nucleus of operative facts.

New Mexico

Kolker v. Sanchez, 1991 WL 11691589 (D.N.M. Dec. 10, 1991). Settlement of the earlier FDCPA case with the current FDCPA attorney/defendant's collection agency client based on claims arising from the same underlying events was not res judicata because the attorney did not meet the requirements of the applicable joint tortfeasor test to show that the earlier settlement was intended to, and did in fact, cover the damages sought in the instant case.

New York

Schuh v. Druckman & Sinel, L.L.P., 602 F. Supp. 2d 454 (S.D.N.Y. 2009). FDCPA claim that a payout figure given two years after a foreclosure judgment was inflated was not barred by N.Y. res judicata or collateral estoppel as the issue could not have been decided in the judgment.

Grant v. Aurora Loan Servs., 2008 WL 4411323 (E.D.N.Y. Sept. 24, 2008). *Pro se* consumer's FDCPA claims against his mortgage holder were dismissed as barred by res judicata because the same claims were asserted as a counterclaim or affirmative defense and were rejected and litigated to final conclusion in the underlying state court foreclosure action.

Rosendale v. Citibank, 1996 WL 175089 (S.D.N.Y. Apr. 15, 1996) (*pro se*). An FDCPA claim was dismissed on grounds of res judicata because it had already been decided on the merits in a state action.

Cornett v. Bank of New York, 1992 WL 88197 (S.D.N.Y. Apr. 17, 1992). *Pro se* plaintiff's FDCPA and other claims, which had been previously litigated in small claims court, were dismissed on the basis of res judicata.

North Carolina

Vogler v. Countrywide Home Loans, Inc., 2010 WL 3394034 (M.D.N.C. Aug. 26, 2010). The prior state court adjudication collaterally estopped the *pro se* consumers from claiming an FDCPA violation based on the alleged invalidity of the underlying debt.

Ohio

Meyer v. Debt Recovery Solutions of Ohio, Inc., 2010 WL 3515663 (N.D. Ohio Sept. 2, 2010). Neither issue nor claim preclusion applies where the collection practices were not litigated in state court.

Whittiker v. Deutsche Bank Nat'l Trust Co., 605 F. Supp. 2d 914 (N.D. Ohio 2009). Court did not reach issues of preclusion, estoppel, or waiver on a motion to dismiss since they are affirmative defenses.

Todd v. Weltman Weinberg, Reis & Co., LPA, 2008 WL 419943 (S.D. Ohio Feb. 14, 2008). Where the consumers challenged the debt collector's a false garnishment affidavit, not the amounts that they owed to their creditors, the consumers' FDCPA claims were not precluded by res judicata.

Gasser v. Allen County Claims & Adjustment, Inc., 1983 U.S. Dist. LEXIS 20361 (N.D. Ohio Nov. 3, 1983). An FDCPA claim against a collection agency was not barred by res judicata after the consumer settled the claim on the underlying debt with the creditor. To permit the bar would frustrate the purposes of the FDCPA.

Pennsylvania

Zhang v. Haven-Scott Assocs., 1996 WL 355344 (E.D. Pa. June 21, 1996). Plaintiff's FDCPA claim was not barred by res judicata by a confessed judgment on the underlying debt. The FDCPA claim did not challenge the validity of the debt but rather attacked the methods by which the defendants attempted to collect the debt.

South Carolina

Johnson v. Sallie Mae Serv., L.P., 2006 WL 3541855 (D.S.C. Dec. 7, 2006). Defendant failed to show res judicata or collateral estoppel prevented relitigation of the student loan billing practices where the consumer alleged this was not a continuation of the practices previously litigated.

Texas

Naranjo v. Universal Sur. of Am., 679 F. Supp. 2d 787 (S.D. Tex. 2010). The consumer's federal action alleging that the debt collectors violated the FDCPA by obtaining a default judgment in the state court collection case when they knew that the debt was beyond the statute of limitations was not barred by claim preclusion since the consumer "is not asking this Court to review or reject the state default judgment itself [but] is complaining about Defendants' alleged practices of bringing time-barred collections actions."

Gutierrez v. LVNV Funding, L.L.C., 2009 U.S. Dist. LEXIS 54479 (W.D. Tex. Mar. 16, 2009). FDCPA action alleging that the defendant debt buyer violated the FDCPA by filing state court collection complaints with an attached false "Affidavit of Account" was not a compulsory counterclaim in the state collection action and therefore was not barred by res judicata.

Washington

Dexter v. Tran, 654 F. Supp. 2d 1253 (E.D. Wash. 2009). Where the consumer pleaded a violation of the FDCPA in his answer filed in the state court action and requested relief in the form of damages under the FDCPA and the state court did not grant such relief and entered judgment accordingly, the consumer's filing of the FDCPA claim in federal court was barred by claim and issue preclusion.

Kirk v. Gobel, 622 F. Supp. 2d 1039 (E.D. Wash. 2009). Neither the *Rooker-Feldman* doctrine nor res judicata applied since the underlying state collection case was on appeal and there was therefore no final state judgment.

Druther v. Hamilton, 75 Fed. R. Serv. 3d 316 (W.D. Wash. 2009). "The issues of whether Defendants' collection actions regarding service on the consumer were in violation of the FDCPA may have been involved in the state court collection proceeding, but it appears that these issues were not actually litigated. As the *Restatement (2d) Judgments*, § 28, comment e, notes: 'An issue is not actually litigated if the defendant might have interposed it as an affirmative defense but failed to do so. . . . In the case of a judgment entered by confession, consent, or default, none of the issues is actually litigated.' Neither does the concept of claim preclusion apply to bar the Plaintiff's actions in this case, because the causes of action raised in this proceeding are not the same as those raised in the state court collection proceeding."

K.3.12 Miscellaneous

Federal Trade Comm'n v. Check Enforcement, 502 F.3d 159 (3d Cir. 2007). The court entered summary judgment and awarded restitution of more than $10 million in this FTC enforcement action against the defendant check collectors for their serial violations of the FDCPA third party contact rules and multiple abusive, false, and unconscionable collection practices.

Greenwood Trust Co. v. Smith, 212 B.R. 599 (8th Cir. 1997). Same holding as *In re Montsko*, *infra*.

Connecticut

Saunders v. Stigers, 773 A.2d 971 (Conn. App. Ct. 2001). Since the home-foreclosure defendant's counterclaim for damages under the FDCPA would not affect the lienholder's right to foreclose, the lower court's granting of judgment of foreclosure while the FDCPA counterclaim remained pending was not an abuse of discretion.

Premier Capital, Inc. v. Grossman, 2000 Conn. Super. LEXIS 3137 (Conn. Super. Ct. Nov. 22, 2000), *aff'd in part, rev'd in part on other grounds*, 789 A.2d 565 (Conn. App. Ct. 2002). A violation of the FDCPA may establish a claim for damages but does not provide a defense regarding the validity of the underlying debt.

First Fed. Bank v. Craco, 1996 WL 176366 (Conn. Super. Ct. Apr. 2, 1996). The court set aside a default judgment against the consumer on a debt collection claim and allowed the consumer to file an answer raising a defense under the state UDAP statute based on an FDCPA violation. The court did not rule on the validity of the defense.

Connecticut Nat'l Bank v. Carbonella, 1993 WL 328803 (Conn. Super. Ct. Aug. 19, 1993). Claim that creditor's attorney violated the FDCPA did not prevent the creditor from pursuing its claim.

Porter v. Somers, 1993 WL 280118 (Conn. Super. Ct. July 12, 1993). The prohibition in § 1692f(1) on collecting an amount not permitted by law supported the claim under a state consumer protection act (UDAP) that such conduct was unfair.

Idaho

Shock v. CDI Affiliated Servs., Inc., 2010 WL 672148 (D. Idaho Feb. 20, 2010). The court rejected the *pro se* consumer's argument that Idaho is exempt from the FDCPA under 15 U.S.C. § 1692o.

Illinois

Greenfield v. Kluever & Platt, L.L.C., 2010 WL 604830 (N.D. Ill. Feb. 16, 2010). The federal court granted the *pro se* consumer's motion to appoint counsel since her complaint alleged "complex" issues involving the defendants' filing of a state court foreclosure action against although the underlying mortgage allegedly had not been assigned to them.

Chapman v. Ontra, Inc., 1997 WL 321681 (N.D. Ill. June 6, 1997). Violations of the FDCPA were not per se violations of the Illinois debt collection statute.

Indiana

Chester v. Purvis, 260 F. Supp. 2d 711 (S.D. Ind. 2003). Release

to debt collector, its affiliates and associates, does not extend to the debt collector's defense counsel. There is no immunity from suit under the FCRA, under the "litigation privilege" for a defense lawyer who wrongfully uses a credit report in an FDCPA case during the consumer's deposition.

Iowa

In re Montsko, 1997 WL 699817 (Bankr. S.D. Iowa Jan. 14, 1997). Noting similarity between state law and FDCPA, court held that creditor violated state law by sending to a represented debtor copies of correspondence addressing reaffirmation options sent to her attorney.

Louisiana

Lentini v. Northwest Louisiana Legal Servs., Inc., 841 So. 2d 1017 (La. Ct. App. 2003). SLAPP defamation complaint against legal services program that represented plaintiffs in an earlier case alleging violations of, *inter alia*, the FDCPA, stated a claim for relief.

New York

Arrey v. Beaux Arts II, L.L.C., 101 F. Supp. 2d 225 (S.D.N.Y. 2000). Tenant *pro se* removed eviction action to federal court because three-day eviction notice allegedly violated the FDCPA. Remanded: "[B]oth the removal and the contention that the alleged violation of the Act constitutes a defense to the nonpayment proceeding are utterly frivolous."

Conboy v. AT&T Corp., 84 F. Supp. 2d 492 (S.D.N.Y. 2000), *aff'd*, 241 F.3d 242 (2d Cir. 2001). A violation of the FDCPA does not automatically state a claim for intentional infliction of emotional distress. The issue is whether the conduct was so extreme or outrageous to give rise to liability for the tort. Court found that calling plaintiffs at unusual hours in an attempt to collect their adult daughter-in-law's debt did not rise to that level.

Sibersky v. Borah, Goldstein, Altschuler & Schwartz, P.C., 2000 U.S. Dist. LEXIS 14043 (S.D.N.Y. Sept. 22, 2000). Whether a state release as to the landlord and its agents also released federal FDCPA claims and applied to the landlord's attorneys was a question of federal law. Because of the parties' dispute as to their intent, it was a factual issue that could not be decided on a motion to dismiss.

Green Tree Fin. Servicing Corp. v. Lewis, 720 N.Y.S.2d 843 (N.Y. App. Div. 2001). The pendency of the state court foreclosure defendant's FDCPA action in federal court against the state court plaintiff was no basis to stay the state court proceedings.

In re Scheck, 574 N.Y.S.2d 372 (N.Y. App. Div. 1991). Allowing collection employees to act in a lawyer's name and violating the FDCPA were considered in a one-year suspension of a lawyer for violating the N.Y. Code of Professional Responsibility. Four charges of professional misconduct were upheld against an attorney who allowed a collection agency to use his name and letterhead without his supervision.

Dearie v. Hunter, 705 N.Y.S.2d 519 (N.Y. Sup. Ct. 2000). The trial court erred in dismissing the petition for back-rent on the grounds that the three-day rent demand by petitioner's attorney failed to comply with the FDCPA and was therefore ineffective as a jurisdictional predicate to the commencement of the landlord-tenant proceeding, since the FDCPA authorizes only a suit for damages against the debt collector as the remedy for any such violation.

Texas

Stewart v. Alonzo, 2009 WL 174938 (S.D. Tex. Jan. 26, 2009). To prevail on an FDCPA claim, the plaintiff must prove the following: (1) the plaintiff has been the object of collection activity arising from consumer debt; (2) the defendant is a debt collector defined by the FDCPA; and (3) the defendant has engaged in an act or omission prohibited by the FDCPA.

United States v. Cent. Adjustment Bureau, Inc., 667 F. Supp. 370 (N.D. Tex. 1986). Court's prior finding for purposes of determining the amount of administrative civil penalties, that the collector was not in bad faith and undertook efforts to comply with the FDCPA was withdrawn upon the showing at a second trial that the collector's FDCPA testing of collectors was a sham, collectors who were the worst offenders were not disciplined and sometimes promoted, and there was no effort to deal with consumer complaints. $150,000 civil penalty entered.

Villalon v. Bank One, 176 S.W.3d 66 (Tex. App. June 24, 2004). The court held that the mortgagee's alleged violation of the FDCPA in purportedly failing to provide requested § 1692g verification did not render the subsequent foreclosure wrongful and was not a defense in the instant forcible detainer action.

Debt Collection on the Web

Websites that may be useful to practitioners.

Trade Associations

ACA International: Trade association of collection agencies and others, formerly the American Collectors Association. ACAI has approximately 5300 members including third-party collection agencies, creditors, attorneys, and vendor affiliates.
www.acainternational.org

American Bankers Association: Trade association of banks that maintains a bookstore on banking.
www.aba.com

Association for Financial Professionals: The Association for Financial Professionals supports more than 14,000 corporate financial officers including member collection agencies. AFP provides continuing education, financial tools and publications, career development, certifications, research, representation to legislators and regulators, and the development of industry standards.
www.afponline.org

Commercial Law League of America: Organization primarily of collection and bankruptcy attorneys.
www.clla.org

National Association of Credit Management: Founded in 1896 to promote good laws for sound credit, protect businesses against fraudulent debtors, improve the interchange of credit information, develop better credit practices and methods, and establish a code of ethics.
www.nacm.org

National Association of Retail Collection Attorneys: Founded in 1993, the National Association of Retail Collection Attorneys is a 501(c)(6) organization dedicated to serving law firms engaged in the business of retail debt collection. To serve NARCA's members, the long-term objective is to continue to elevate the practice of retail collection law. NARCA's goals include networking, member education, outreach, and legislation.
www.narca.org

International Association of Commercial Collectors, Inc.: An international trade association comprised of more than 210 commercial collection specialists and 140 commercial attorneys. It is the largest organization of commercial collection specialists in the world.
www.commercialcollector.com

Debt Collection Vendors

Accelerated Data Systems: Retailer and developer of recovery management software known as "AdvantEdge," marketed as collection software created by bill collectors for bill collectors. Accelerated Data Systems provides training as well as other services to debt

collectors.
www.accelerateddata.com

Credit Worthy: Internet-based company, with roots in debt collection, providing information, products/services, and programs to the business credit community.
www.creditworthy.com

Debt Buyers' Association: Consultant that helps build markets for buying and selling delinquent receivables. Site provides links to debt buyers and sellers, collection companies.
www.debtmarketplace.com

Kaulkin Ginsberg: Debt collection consultants and merger advisors' site includes many useful links.
www.kaulkin.com

Fair Issacs: Consultant whose credit scoring model is widely used in making credit granting and marketing decisions.
www.fairisaac.com

Debt Collectors

ACA International: Has a directory of collection agencies and some collection attorneys.
www.acainternational.org

firstdetroit.com: Sells directory of debt collection agencies in the U.S.
www.firstdetroit.com

Collection Agency Report: Monthly newsletter on developments in the collection industry that also publishes a directory of more than 900 collection agencies worldwide.
www.firstdetroit.com

Creditworthy.com: Maintains an on-line directory of collection agencies and law firms.
www.creditworthy.com

The Ultimate Yellow Pages: Searches multiple on-line databases for street or e-mail addresses and phone numbers.
www.theultimates.com/yellow

Debt Collection Press

CFO.com Magazine: A new on-line resource center for corporate finance executives where one can research financial topics, including commercial debt collection.
www.cfo.com

insidearm.com: Provides on-line news and a searchable directory of products and services for the debt collection industry.
www.insidearm.com

Treasury and Risk Management: A publication for financial executives that provides perspective on forces already transforming the corporate world and uncovers trends i.e. what is new in debt recovery that will ultimately define the future of finance.
www.treasuryandrisk.com

Collections & Credit Risk: Monthly magazine for commercial and consumer credit professionals. Offers major industry news, commentary, and links to pertinent resources. Site provides current month's magazine and signup for e-mail advisories.
www.collectionsworld.com and
www.creditandcollectionsworld.com/pagedisplay.html?pagename=subscriptions

Collection Agency Report: Monthly newsletter on developments in the collection industry

including mergers, financial reports on the collection industry. It also publishes a directory of more than 900 collection agencies worldwide.
www.firstdetroit.com

Collector Magazine: One of scores of publications of the ACA International, The Association of Credit and Collection Professionals.
www.acainternational.org

Cards and Payments: Magazine focusing on all aspects of the credit card business including collections.
www.cardforum.com

Creditworthy News: Publishes a magazine on credit issues.
www.creditworthy.com

Recovery Advisor: Magazine targeting collection professionals. Website may be restricted.
www.recoveryadvisor.com[1]

Credit Reporting Agencies

Equifax: Large consumer credit reporting agency.
www.equifax.com

Experian: Large consumer credit reporting agency.
www.experian.com

Transunion: Large consumer credit reporting agency.
www.transunion.com

Website Archive

The Internet Archive: Digital library of Internet sites and other cultural artifacts in digital form; useful for investigating past practices and company history.
www.archive.org

Consumer Information

Federal Trade Commission: Information for consumers.
www.ftc.gov/os/statutes/fdcpajump.htm

www.budhibbs.com: Provides advice on dealing with debt and debt collectors.

Colorado Collection Agency Regulator: Information for consumers.
www.ago.state.co.us/CADC/CADCmain.cfm.html

California Dept. of Consumer Affairs: Information for consumers.
www.dca.ca.gov

Federal Citizen Information Center: Loads of useful information for consumers.
www.pueblo.gsa.gov and
www.consumeraction.gov

---

1 Use *www.archive.org* to see prior versions of this website.

Statute of Limitations[2]

www.cardreport.com/laws/statute-of-limitations.html

www.bcsalliance.com/y_debt_sol~ns4.html

Legal & Government Resources

Reporters Committee for Freedom of the Press: Analysis of state criminal laws on tape recording conversations without consent.
www.rcfp.org/taping/quick.html

Federal Trade Commission Fair Debt Collection:
www.ftc.gov/os/statutes/fdcpajump.htm

North American Collection Agency Regulatory Assoc.:
www.nacara.info

---

2 Statutes of limitations may require interpretation by a legal professional. These guides may be a starting point only. Another guide is National Association of Credit Management, Manual of Credit and Commercial Laws. *See www.nacm.org*.

| Appendix M | Finding Pleadings, Primary Sources on the Companion Website |

Fair Debt Collection includes free access to its companion website, which remains free with continued subscription to this treatise. The companion website includes all appendices found in *Fair Debt Collection* plus approximately 150 sample pleadings and over 1000 primary source documents—statutes, regulations, all FTC letters and interpretations, thousands of case summaries, and practice aids—all easily located with flexible, powerful search tools. Documents are in PDF format and the pleadings are also in Microsoft Word format.

This appendix describes the documents found on the companion website, how to access and print them, and how to download them onto your computer or copy-paste them into a word processing file.

M.1 Pleadings and Primary Sources Found on the Companion Website

The companion website to *Fair Debt Collection* contains the text of the Fair Debt Collection Practices Act, the FTC Official Staff Commentary, *all FTC staff opinion letters* with a subject-matter index, FTC Advisory Opinions, and the statute regarding federal standards for private tax collectors. The website also includes FDCPA case summaries and the full text of an FDCPA Supreme Court case.

Of special note are the thousands of FDCPA case summaries, all indexed and searchable, that can be printed or copied as desired. Also of note are approximately 150 sample pleadings, including case preparation checklists, demand letters and sample complaints, sample discovery requests, deposition transcripts of an FDCPA class representative and collection agency employees, voir dire questions, jury instructions and other jury trial documents. The website also includes other pleadings relating to expert testimony, class certification, summary judgment, appeals, and attorney fees and costs.

The website does *not* contain the full text of this treatise's chapters. See M.5, *infra*, about using Internet-based keyword searches to pinpoint page numbers in the treatise where topics are discussed.

M.2 How to Access the Website

One-time registration is required to access the companion website. Once registered, a user subsequently logging in will be granted immediate access to all the websites he or she is authorized to use. For example, one username and password allows a subscriber to four NCLC treatises to access all four companion websites.

To register for the first time, go to **www.consumerlaw.org/webaccess** and click on the "New users click here to register" link. Enter the Companion Website Registration Number found on the packing statement or invoice accompanying this publication. Then enter the requested information and click on "Login." An e-mail address may be used for the username or a different username may be chosen.

Subscribers do *not* need to register more than once. If subscribers purchase additional NCLC treatises later, they will automatically be given access to the corresponding companion websites. Registering a second time with the same registration number will override a prior username and password. (Note, however, that if users allow all their subscriptions to lapse and then subsequently purchase a manual, they will have to register again.)

Once registered, click on the log-in link at **www.consumerlaw.org/webaccess**, enter the username and password, and select the *Fair Debt Collection* website from the list of authorized websites.

An alternate log-in method may be particularly useful for libraries, legal aid offices, or law firms that subscribe to the entire set of NCLC treatises. Simply e-mail publications@nclc.org with a list or range of static IP addresses for which access should be permitted. Users from those addresses can then go to www.consumerlaw.org/ipaccess to be granted access *without* entering a username and password.

Once logged in, users can click the "My Account" link on the left toolbar to change their personal information. We also encourage users who find any mistakes to notify us using the "Report Errors" button, also on the left toolbar.

At minimum, **use of the companion websites with Internet Explorer requires Adobe Reader 7.0 or Adobe Acrobat 7.0 (or later versions of the software). Users of other browsers, or those experiencing problems with the websites, should download the latest version of the free Adobe Reader (currently 10) from Adobe's website at www.adobe.com.** A link to Adobe's site is provided on the NCLC companion website log-in page.

NATIONAL CONSUMER LAW CENTER

Consumer Law Manuals
Companion Web Sites

Login

Please take a moment to log in:

Username [   ]

Password [   ]

☐ Remember my credentials

[Login]

New Users Click Here Register.

Forgot Your Password and/or User Name?

Access Via IP Address

Important:
Internet Explorer users: This site requires Adobe Acrobat or Reader 7.0 or higher.
Firefox and Safari users: This site requires Adobe Acrobat or Reader 9.0 or higher.
Click Here to download the latest version of Adobe Reader
(Use of earlier Reader versions may result in documents showing as blank pages)

M.3 Locating Documents on the Website

The companion website provides three options to locate documents.

1. The search page (the home page) uses keyword searches to find documents—full text searches of all documents on the website or searches just on the documents' titles.

- Narrow the search to documents of a certain type (such as federal regulations or pleadings) by making a selection from the "Document Type" menu, and then perform a full text or document title search.
- To locate a specific appendix section, select the appendix section number (for example, "A.2.3") or a partial identifier (for example, "A") in the search page's "Appendix" drop-down fields.
- Click on the "Search Hints" link for a quick reference to special search operators, wildcards, shortcuts, and complex searches. Read this closely, as syntax and search operators may be slightly different from those of other websites.

2. The contents page (click on the "Contents" tab at the top of the page) is a traditional "branching" table of contents. Click a branch to expand it into a list of sub-branches or documents. Each document appears once on this contents tree.

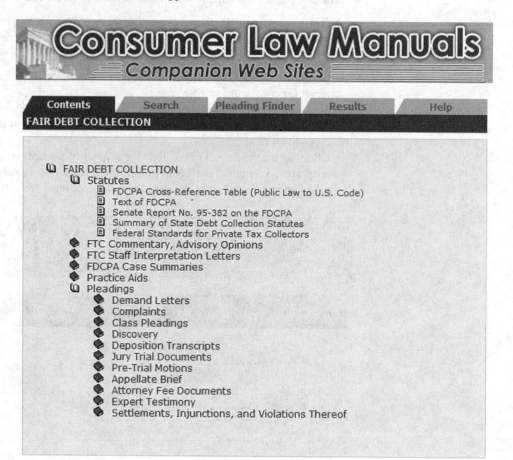

3. The pleading finder page (click on the "Pleading Finder" tab at the top of the page) allows pleadings to be located using one or more menus, such as "Type of Pleading—General" or "Subject." For many users, this will be the preferred method of finding a pleading. More than one item can be selected from a menu using the Ctrl key. For example, make one selection from "Type of Pleading—General," one from "Subject," and three from "Legal Claim" to locate all pleadings of that type and subject that contain one or more of the three legal claims selected. If this search produces insufficient results, deselect "Subject" and/or "Legal Claim" to find pleadings of that type in any subject area or based upon any legal claim.

Consumer Law Manuals
Companion Web Sites

| Contents | Search | Pleading Finder | Results | Help |

FAIR DEBT COLLECTION

Select one or more entries in the pleading categories below to find all pleadings matching your selection(s). Hold the Ctrl key while clicking to select multiple entries within a category. Though not required, you may also enter text in the Full Text Search or Search Document Titles fields to further narrow your search.

[Search Database]

Full Text Search [_____] [...]

Search Document Titles [_____] [...]

Type of Pleading - General

- Interrogatories
- Document Requests
- Requests for Admissions
- Request for Inspection
- Deposition Notice
- Deposition Transcript

Subject

- Debt Validation Notice
- Deception
- Disregard Attorney Represent
- Excessive Amount Sought
- Expert Qualifications
- Foreclosures

Pleading Type - Class

- Class Complaints
- Class Discovery
- Class Representative's Depo:
- Disclosures
- Re: Offer of Judgment
- Class Certification

Legal Claim

- FDCPA
- Fraud
- Fraudulent Conveyance
- Infliction of Emotional Distress
- Invasion of Privacy
- Servicemembers Civil Relief A

Type Pleading - Bankruptcy

- Complaint

[Search Database]

Click here to view the Basic Search Form.

M.4 How to Use the Documents, Find Microsoft Word Versions, and Locate Additional Features

All documents on the website are in Adobe Acrobat (PDF) format and can be printed, downloaded onto your computer, or cut and pasted into a word processing document. Pleadings and certain other documents also are available in Microsoft Word format, facilitating the opening of entire documents in a word processor. After opening the selected PDF file, click on the "Word Version, if available" link at the top of the page. If a Microsoft Word version is listed as available, click on the "DOC Download Document" link to save the Microsoft Word file to your computer.

Links on the left hand toolbar bring you to credit math software, search tips, other websites, tables of contents and indexes of all NCLC treatises, and other practice aids. Links to especially important new developments will be placed toward the bottom of the "Search" page.

M.5 Electronic Searches of This and Other NCLC Treatises' Chapters

Completely separate from the treatises' companion websites, NCLC offers a handy on-line utility to search the full text of this treatise's chapters and appendices. This free search utility is found at www.consumerlaw.org/keyword and requires no registration or log-in.

While the chapters' text is not available on-line, this web-based search engine will find a word or phrase that can then easily be located in the printed manual. Select this treatise, enter a search term or combination of search terms—such as a case name, a regulation citation, or other keywords—and the page numbers containing those terms are listed. Search results are shown in context, facilitating selection of the most relevant pages.

The full text of other NCLC treatises and supplements, *NCLC REPORTS*, and other publications can also be electronically searched to locate relevant topics at www.consumerlaw.org/keyword. Just select the desired treatise or search across all NCLC treatises.

Current tables of contents, indexes, and other information for all eighteen treatises in the NCLC consumer law series can be found at www.consumerlaw.org/shop. Click on the "Publications for Lawyers" link and scroll down to the book you want. The Adobe Acrobat PDF-format documents found there can be quickly searched for a word or phrase.

The Quick Reference at the back of this treatise allows you to pinpoint the correct NCLC treatise as well as the section within the treatise among over 1000 different subject areas. These subject areas are listed in alphabetical order and can also be electronically searched at www.consumerlaw.org/qr.

M.6 Finding Additional Pleadings

Pleadings specifically relating to this treatise are found in Adobe Acrobat PDF and Microsoft Word formats on the companion website. Over 2000 other pleadings are available at NCLC's *Consumer Law Pleadings* and can be found on the *Consumer Law Pleadings* companion website using the same search techniques discussed above. These 2000 pleadings can also be pinpointed using the *Consumer Law Pleadings* index guide, which organizes pleadings by type, subject area, legal claim, title, and other categories identical to those on the website.